THE SEVENTH INTERNATIONAL SYMPOSIUM ON ENVIRONMENTAL CONCERNS IN RIGHTS-OF-WAY MANAGEMENT

The Seventh International Symposium on Environmental Concerns in Rights-of-Way Management

**9-13 September 2000
Calgary, Alberta, Canada**

Edited by:
John W. Goodrich-Mahoney
Dean F. Mutrie
Colin A. Guild

Sponsored by:
TransCanada
TERA Environmental Consultants
Electric Power Research Institute

With Support from:
Alliance Pipeline
ATCO Electric
BC Hydro
Canadian Pacific Railway
ESG International
Gas Research Institute
Natural Resources Group, Inc.
PanCanadian
Westcoast Energy

Symposium Co-Chairmen
Colin A. Guild
Dean F. Mutrie

2002

ELSEVIER
AMSTERDAM – BOSTON – LONDON – NEW YORK – OXFORD – PARIS
TOKYO – SAN DIEGO – SAN FRANCISCO – SINGAPORE – SYDNEY

ELSEVIER SCIENCE Ltd
The Boulevard, Langford Lane
Kidlington, Oxford OX5 1GB, UK

© 2002 Elsevier Science Ltd. All rights reserved.

This work is protected under copyright by Elsevier Science, and the following terms and conditions apply to its use:

Photocopying
Single photocopies of single chapters may be made for personal use as allowed by national copyright laws. Permission of the Publisher and payment of a fee is required for all other photocopying, including multiple or systematic copying, copying for advertising or promotional purposes, resale, and all forms of document delivery. Special rates are available for educational institutions that wish to make photocopies for non-profit educational classroom use.

Permissions may be sought directly from Elsevier Science via their homepage (http://www.elsevier.com) by selecting 'Customer support' and then 'Permissions'. Alternatively you can send an e-mail to: permissions@elsevier.co.uk, or fax to: (+44) 1865 853333.

In the USA, users may clear permissions and make payments through the Copyright Clearance Center, Inc., 222 Rosewood Drive, Danvers, MA 01923, USA; phone: (+1) (978) 7508400, fax: (+1) (978) 7504744, and in the UK through the Copyright Licensing Agency Rapid Clearance Service (CLARCS), 90 Tottenham Court Road, London W1P 0LP, UK; phone: (+44) 207 631 5555; fax: (+44) 207 631 5500. Other countries may have a local reprographic rights agency for payments.

Derivative Works
Tables of contents may be reproduced for internal circulation, but permission of Elsevier Science is required for external resale or distribution of such material.
Permission of the Publisher is required for all other derivative works, including compilations and translations.

Electronic Storage or Usage
Permission of the Publisher is required to store or use electronically any material contained in this work, including any chapter or part of a chapter.

Except as outlined above, no part of this work may be reproduced, stored in a retrieval system or transmitted in any form or by any means, electronic, mechanical, photocopying, recording or otherwise, without prior written permission of the Publisher.
Address permissions requests to: Elsevier Science Global Rights Department, at the mail, fax and e-mail addresses noted above.

Notice
No responsibility is assumed by the Publisher for any injury and/or damage to persons or property as a matter of products liability, negligence or otherwise, or from any use or operation of any methods, products, instructions or ideas contained in the material herein. Because of rapid advances in the medical sciences, in particular, independent verification of diagnoses and drug dosages should be made.

First edition 2002

Library of Congress Cataloging in Publication Data
A catalog record from the Library of Congress has been applied for.

British Library Cataloguing in Publication Data
A catalogue record from the British Library has been applied for.

ISBN: 0-080-44117-3

⊚ The paper used in this publication meets the requirements of ANSI/NISO Z39.48-1992 (Permanence of Paper).
Printed in The Netherlands.

Preface

The Seventh International Symposium on Environmental Concerns in Rights-of-Way Management follows a series begun at Mississippi State University, Mississippi in 1976 and subsequently held at Ann Arbor, Michigan in 1979; San Diego, California in 1982; Indianapolis, Indiana in 1987; Montreal, Quebec, in 1993; and New Orleans, Louisiana in 1997. The Symposium was organized by a steering committee composed of representatives from industries, agencies and universities concerned with research and management of electric, pipeline, railroad, and highway rights-of-way.

The purpose of this Symposium was to achieve a better understanding of the current and emerging environmental issues related to rights-of-way management by sharing environmental research and practical experience throughout the world. The symposium attracted 460 registrants from 22 countries, giving it a truly international favor. The symposium consisted of two introductory addresses one by Chief Roy Whitney of the Tsuu T'ina people, a part of the Dene Nations and one by Dr. Dale Arner, Professor Emeritus at Mississippi State University and Honorary Chairman of this Symposium who started this series of symposia in 1976. Dr. Brain Bietz, Director of the Energy Counsel of Canada, gave a keynote address. Following Dr. Bietz's address a lively panel discussion was held on the "Corridor Concept Revisited: Multiple Rights-of-Way." Symposium sessions focused on Vegetation Management; Project Management; Cultural; Wildlife; Biodiversity; Geographic Information Systems; Wetlands; Soils; Aquatic Life; Public Participation; and Regulatory Compliance where 110 papers were given, of which 100 peer-reviewed papers appear in this proceedings.

The Eight International Symposium on Environmental Concerns in Rights-of-Way Management will be held in Saratoga Springs, New York, during September 12–16, 2004. See the Symposium web site at www.rights-of-way-env.com for updates and information on prior Symposia.

Acknowledgments

This Symposium could not have taken place without the dedicated efforts of many individuals. The editors would like to acknowledge the contributions of the steering committee whose tireless efforts again proved invaluable. The steering committee members are: Larry Abrahamson, Paul Anderson, Grete Bridgewater, Edward Colson, Allen Crabtree, James Crinklaw, G. Jean Doucet, James Evans, Kenneth Farrish, John Goodrich-Mahoney, Colin Guild, Harvey Holt, Stuard Lunn, Dean Mutrie, Wayne Marshall, Kevin McLoughlin, Peter Prier, Richard Revel, Jorge Roig Soles, Ian Scott, Glen Singleton, Richard Skarie, Gus Tillman, and James R. (Randy) Williams. We acknowledge the authors of the papers and posters for their efforts and the quality of their contributions, as well as the individuals who served as technical reviewers of the papers.

We acknowledge the main sponsors, TransCanada, Tera Environmental Consultants LTD, and the Electric Power Research Institute, and significant support from Alliance Pipeline, ATCO Electric, BC Hydro, Canadian Pacific Railway, ESG International, Gas Research Institute, National Resources Group, Inc., PanCanadian, and Westcoast Energy.

We also acknowledge the host organizing committee, Eric Mohun, Susan Austen and Michelle Richard whose efforts contributed significantly to the success of this Symposium. Finally, we appreciate the flawless efforts of the staff at the Calgary Westin Hotel.

Responsible Management through the Ages

The Calgary 2000 logo was designed specifically for this Symposium to convey the message that environmental management is a spatial and temporal responsibility. The indigenous theme suggests that environmental management has coincident with the evolution of man. We are the managers within a specific time and place. Overseeing two straight lines representing parallel rights-of-way, the top half of the logo signifies man as the steward of his environment. The images below represent the biophysical components, including tracks of the grizzly bear, an international icon for wildlife and wilderness and a key species of concern for right-of-way managers in the Province of Alberta.

Table of Contents

Preface v
Acknowledgments vii

Part I. Symposium Plenary Session

Plenary Session Opening Remarks and Presentations
  D. Mutrie and C. Guild 3

Corridor Concept Revisited: Multiple Rights-of-Way
  A.F. Crabtree III 11

Part II. Vegetation Management

Integrated Vegetation Management The Exploration of a Concept to Application
  K. McLoughlin 29

Integrated Vegetation Management on Electrical Transmission Rights-of-Way
  Using Herbicides: Treatment Effects Over Time
  B.D. Ballard, C.A. Nowak, L.P. Abrahamson, E.F. Neuhauser, and K.E. Finch 47

Versatile Plant for Multiple Use on Rights-of-Way
  D.H. Arner and J.C. Jones 57

Reducing Maintenance Costs using Integrated Vegetation Management on Electric
  Utility Transmission Lines in British Columbia
  T.C. Wells, K.D. Dalgarno, and R. Read 63

Tree, Shrub, and Herb Succession and Five Years of Management Following
  the Establishment of a New Electric Transmission Right-of-Way through
  a Mixed Woodland
  R.A. Johnstone, M.R. Haggie, and H.A. Allen, Jr. 73

Gray Birch Ecology on an Electric Powerline Right-of-Way in Upstate New York
  C.A. Nowak, B.D. Ballard, and E. O'Neill 83

Evaluating Native Shrub Plantings as a Control for Tall-Growing Woody Tree
  Species in Powerline Rights-of-Way
  M.H. Wolfe, N.S. Nicholas, A.K. Rose, P.A. Mays, T.A. Wojtalik, and K.D. Choate . . 89

Planting Shrubs for the Creation of Sustainable Power Line Rights-of-Way
  R.F. Young and E.J. Glover 97

Selecting Herbaceous Plant Covers to Control Tree Invasion in Rights-of-Way
  S. de Blois, J. Brisson, and A. Bouchard 103

Systematic Method for Forest Vegetation Management in the Rights-of-Way
  (ROW)
  *J. Arévalo-Camacho, J. Roig-Solés, L. González Cantalapiedra, C. Morla Juaristi,
  F. Gómez Manzaneque, E. Bermejo Bermejo, D. Galicia Herbada,
  and F. Martínez García* 111

Long-Term Vegetation Development on Bioengineered Rights-of-Way Sites
  D.F. Polster 121

Summary of the Mitigation Program for Rare Plant Populations along the
  Portland Natural Gas Transmission System (PNGTS) and PNGTS/Maritimes
  & Northeast Joint Facilities Projects
  J.R. Trettel, S.J. Lare, and B.M. Battaglia 127

Right-of-Way Disturbances and Revegetation in Alpine Tundra: An Evaluation
of Natural Revegetation on Plateau Mountain, Alberta
L.A. Van Ham and R.D. Revel 135

Managing the Green Heritage of Highways Rights-of-Way in Southern Quebec:
A New Ecological Landscape Approach
*Y. Bédard, D. Trottier, L. Bélanger, J.-P. Bourassa, N. Champagne, J. Gérin-Lajoie,
G. Lacroix, and E. Lévesque* 147

Roadside Vegetation Management on Québec's Highways: A Visual Landscape
Monitoring Research Project
P. Poullaouec-Gonidec, G. Domon, S. Paquette, and C. Montpetit 155

Natural Regeneration on a Pipeline Right-of-Way in the Boreal Forest
of West-Central Saskatchewan
E. Ealey and J. Virgl 165

Rare Plant Impact Mitigation for the Alliance Pipeline Project
G. Fryer, G. Dunn, and P. Anderson 171

Automating Monitoring and Management of Roadside Vegetation
N.P. Cain, K. McKague, L.A. Kingston, and S. Struger 179

Highway Rights-of-Way as Rare Plant Restoration Habitat in Coastal Virginia
P.M. Sheridan and N. Penick 185

Part III. Corridors

Co-Location of Linear Facilities: Realistic Opportunity or Unrealistic Expectation
D.F. Jenkins 195

Saturation Threshold in a Multi-Pipeline Corridor Expansion Project
J. Nixon, A. Jalbert, K. Etherington, T. Bossenberry, and D. Clark 201

Cumulative Effects Assessment and Linear Corridors:
The Representative Areas Approach
T. Antoniuk 209

Pipeline Projects and Cumulative Effects Assessment Issues
C.G. Finley and R.D. Revel 219

Innovative Co-Location of Telecommunications Facilities within
Existing Rights-of-Way
J.M. Rinebold, J.M. Donaldson, and M.F. Kohler 233

Practical Approach to Assessing Cumulative Effects for Pipelines
G. Hegmann, R. Eccles, and K. Strom 245

Managing Environmental Compliance on Linear Construction Projects:
Strategies for Success
J. Battey 255

Environmental Management System Challenge with Linear Facilities
P.G. Prier, D.S. Eusebi, and D.P. Wesenger 263

Planning and Performance of Wildlife Crossing Structures in a Major
Transportation Corridor
A.P. Clevenger, J. Wierzchowski, and N. Waltho 267

Part IV. Project Planning

CanCommit©: A Computerized Commitment Database for Pipeline
Construction and Operations
M. Pockar, P. Anderson, and T. Antoniuk 279

Right-of-Way Environmental Stewardship Bibliographic Database
S.M. Tikalsky and J.W. Goodrich-Mahoney 287

Part V. Cultural

Off Right-of-Way Mitigation of Archaeological Sites: A Pipeline Case
Study from Pennsylvania
J.D. Bloemker 293

Part VI. Wildlife

Rights-of-Way Management in Support of Biological Conservation
V. Schaefer 303

Wildlife Use of Riparian Vegetation Buffer Zones in High Voltage Powerline
Rights-of-Way in the Quebec Boreal Forest
F. Bélisle, G.J. Doucet, and Y. Garant 309

Endangered and Threatened Species and ROW Vegetation Management
K. McLoughlin 319

Evaluation of Wildlife Habitat Suitability in an Herbicide-Treated Utility
Right-of-Way
J.D. Lanham and J.E. Simmons III 327

Butterflies and Skippers in Utility Rights-of-Way in the Upper Piedmont
of South Carolina
J.D. Lanham and M.J. Nichols 337

Karner Blue Butterfly Habitat Restoration on Pipeline Right-of-Way in Wisconsin
F. Lowell and S. Lounsbury 345

Effects of Powerline Right-of-Way Vegetation Management on Avian Communities
J.S. Marshall, L.W. VanDruff, S. Shupe, and E. Neuhauser 355

Fragmentation Effects Caused by a Power Line Right-of-Way on a Mid-Elevation
Forest Bird Community in Central Colombia
L. Rosselli and S. De La Zerda 363

Management, Vegetative Structure and Shrubland Birds of Rights-of-Way
J.L. Confer 373

Deer Browse Monitoring in a Reconstructed 120 kV Powerline Right-of-Way
after an Ice Storm
G.J. Doucet and E.R. Thompson 383

Mitigating the Impacts of Electric Facilities to Birds
J.M. Bridges and T.R. Anderson 389

Mitigating Collision of Birds Against Transmission Lines in Wetland Areas
in Colombia, by Marking the Ground Wire with Bird Flight Diverters (BFD)
S. De La Zerda and L. Rosselli 395

Relationships Between Wing Morphology and Behavioral Responses to
Unmarked Power Transmission Lines
M.R. Crowder and O.E. Rhodes, Jr. 403

Developing a Species at Risk Conservation Plan:
The Thicksilver Pipeline Experience
A.J. Kennedy 411

Threatened and Endangered Species: A Case Study of the Maritimes
& Northeast Natural Gas Pipeline in Maine
M. Lychwala, M. Tyrrell, and G. McLachlan 421

Response of Bird Communities to Pipeline Rights-of-Way in the Boreal Forest
of Alberta
W. Fleming and F.K.A. Schmiegelow 431

Ground Squirrel Re-colonization of a Pipeline Right-of-Way in Southern Alberta
R.D. Lauzon, S.D. Grindal, and G.E. Hornbeck 439

Highway Improvements to Minimize Environmental Impacts within the
Canadian Rocky Mountain National Parks
T.M. McGuire and J.F. Morrall 447

Responses of Mountain Caribou to Linear Features in a West-Central
Alberta Landscape
P. Oberg, C. Rohner, and F.K.A. Schmiegelow 455

Recruitment of Gopher Tortoises (*Gopherus polyphemus*) to a Newly Constructed
Pipeline Corridor in Mississippi
D.P. Thomas 465

Effects of Brushmat/Corduroy Roads on Wetlands within Rights-of-Way
after Pipeline Construction
J.M. McMullen and S.D. Shupe 471

Designing Railroads, Highways and Canals in Protected Areas to Reduce
Man–Elephant Conflicts
A.P. Singh and S.M. Satheesan 483

Part VII. Biodiversity

Environmental Issues Associated with the Cuiabá Natural Gas Pipeline in Bolivia
B.D. Barnett 495

Direct Relevance to the Natural Gas Industry of the Habitat Fragmentation/
Biodiversity Issue Resulting from the Construction of New Pipelines
R. Hinkle, S. Albrecht, E. Nathanson, and J. Evans 509

Management of Native Prairie Fragments on Canadian Pacific Railway
Rights-of-Way
M. Bissonnette and S. Paradise 517

Part VIII. Geographic Information Systems

Using GIS Tools to Conduct Environmental and Asset Analyses Along
Rights-of-Way
E. Alkiewicz, J. Wingfield, D. Frazier, and L. Khitrik 527

Using GIS to Support Environmental Stewardship Objectives
in Maryland Rights-of-Way
M.T. Southerland, D.E. Strebel, A. Brindley, A.M. Perot, Jr., and S.S. Patty 537

Using GIS for Right-of-Way Vegetation Maintenance and Landowner Notification
C. Nyrose and T. MacNeill 547

GIS as a Tool to Address Environmental Issues in Rights-of-Way Planning
and Management: The Example of Rural Road Networks
C.F. Jaarsma and G.P.A. Willems 553

Innovative Airborne Inventory and Inspection Technology for Electric Power
Line Condition Assessments and Defect Reporting
M. Ostendorp 563

Part IX. Wetlands

Identifying Wetland Revegetation Goals in Pipeline Construction Rights-of-Way
B. Magdych 573

Effects of Soil Segregation Treatments on Revegetation of Wetlands Affected
by Pipeline Construction
S.A. Compton, D.J. Santillo, and P.G. Fellion 583

Rapid Approach to Required Post-Construction Wetland Vegetation Monitoring
after Pipeline Construction
J.R. Trettel and B.M. Battaglia 591

Evaluating the Effects of Muds on Wetlands from Horizontal Directional Drilling (HDD) Within Natural Gas Transmission Line Rights-of-Way
D. Cameron, C. Tammi, E. Steel, J. Schmidt, and J. Evans 599

A Comparative Assessment of Horizontal Directional Drilling and Traditional Construction Techniques for Wetland and Riparian Area Crossings in Natural Gas Pipeline Rights-of-Way
J. Hair, D. Cameron, C. Tammi, E. Steel, J. Schmidt, and J. Evans 609

Part X. Soils

Influences of Soil Acidity Levels on Vegetative Reclamation and Wildlife Habitat on Rights-of-Way Transecting Drastically-disturbed Lands
J.C. Jones 621

The Union Gas Crop Yield Monitoring Program: An Evaluation of Pipeline Construction Practices on Agricultural Lands
E.E. Mackintosh, E.J. Mozuraitis, and R.C. Rowland 629

Repairing Eroded Gas Lines
S.D. Shupe 637

Part XI. Pesticides

Human Health Risk Assessment for the Use of Herbicides on Electric Utility Rights-of-Way on the Allegheny National Forest, USA
L.A. Norris, F. Dost, and R. VanBossuyt Jr. 649

Chondrostereum purpureum: An Alternative to Chemical Herbicide Brush Control
P.Y. de la Bastide, H. Zhu, G. Shrimpton, S.F. Shamoun, and W.E. Hintz 665

Risk Analysis for Tree Growth Regulators (TGR) Used on Electric Utility Rights-of-Way
L.A. Norris, F. Dost, R. VanBossuyt Jr., and J. Jenkins 673

Groundline Decay Prevention without Toxic Materials
C. Roper, F. Pfaender, and J. Goodman 689

Part XII. Aquatic Life

A Performance Measurement Framework for Pipeline Water Crossing Construction
S. Reid, A. Jalbert, S. Metikosh, and M. Bender 697

Effects of Pipeline Rights-of-Way on Fish Habitat at Two Alberta Stream Crossings
C.M. Brown, R.D. Revel, and J.R. Post 705

Effects of Natural Gas Pipeline Water Crossing Replacement on the Benthic Invertebrate and Fish Communities of Big Darby Creek, Ohio
S. Reid, S. Stoklosar, S. Metikosh, J. Evans, and T. Huffman 717

Natural Resources that May Be Affected if Your Horizontal Directional Drill Fails: Open Cut Analysis of A Coastal Maine River
P.D. Martin and M. Tyrrell 725

Evaluation of Isolated Water Course Crossings during Winter Construction along the Alliance Pipeline in Northern Alberta
S. Reid and P.G. Anderson 735

Methods and Results of A Comprehensive Monitoring Program to Document Turbidity and Suspended Sediment Generated During Pipeline Construction
J.R. Trettel, S.A. Compton, and D.J. Santillo 743

Theoretical Modeling of Suspended Sediment, Turbidity Dynamics, and Fishery Impacts during Pipeline Construction across Streams
H.W. Harper and R. Trettel 753

An Investigation into the Influence of Marine Pipelines and Cables on Benthic Ecology and Biodiversity
R.G. Glaholt, M. Nunas, and S. Ong 765

Evaluation of Low Technology Large Woody Debris as a Technique to Augment
Fish Habitat in Streams Crossed by Transmission Corridors
G.C. Scarborough and T. Robertson 777

Part XIII. Public Participation

Right-of-Way Communication Strategies
T.L. Vierima and J.W. Goodrich-Mahoney 791

Infographic Simulations using Photographs as a Method to Gain Greater Social
Acceptance for Projected Lines and Substations
*J. Roig Solés, L. González Cantalapiedra, R. Arranz Cuesta,
and J. Arevalo Camacho* 797

Public-Private Cooperation in Electric Transmission Line Siting, The Dorchester
to Quincy Cable Project: A Case Study
F.P. Richards, F.S. Smith, J. Amodeo, and M. Mills 807

Part XIV. Regulatory Compliance

Recent Advances in Evaluating, Selecting, and Training Environmental Inspectors
L. Curthoys 819

Emergency Transmission Line Repair and Reinforcement Project: Environmental
Management Overview
F. Berry, L. Caldwell, C. Hiebert, and B. Poirier 825

Comparison of Canadian and US Regulatory Review Processes
for the Alliance Pipeline
H.R. Heffler 833

'Facts' Point to Reduced ROW Land Use Projections
S. Patty, A. Cressman, and D.L. Kowalczyk 843

FERC Regulated Third-Party Compliance Monitoring and Variance
Request Program — A Case Study during Construction of the Alliance
Pipeline Project
D.J. Lake and H. Heffler 853

Electronic Reporting as a Tool to Effectively Manage Compliance
During Pipeline Construction
D.J. Lake, E. Dolezal, and T. Antoniuk 861

The Value of a Third Party Inspection Program During the Construction
of Natural Gas Pipelines in Maine
L. Kokemuller 869

The Implementation of an Environmental Management System for Distribution
Pipeline Construction
M. Buszynski 875

Managing the Variance Process — Evaluation of Strategies Utilized
on Two Major Pipeline Projects
S. Craycroft, G. McLachlan, and M. Tyrrell 883

Electronic Reporting for Environmental Inspection
M. Pockar, P. Anderson, J. Myhre, and E. Dolezal 891

Operation and Maintenance Activities on Federal Lands: The Great Lakes/
Hiawatha National Forest Experience
J.W. Muehlhausen and F.J. Kott 901

The Iroquois Pipeline Operating Company Environmental Compliance Program
K.C. Owen and J.T. Barnes 907

Variability in Avoiding Impacts on Endangered Species:
The Sault Looping Project Experience
T.A. Mattson and F.J. Kott 911

Husky Moose Mountain Pipeline
    C.J. Engstrom and G.M. Goulet 919

Development of Pipeline Reclamation Criteria for Alberta
    A.W. Fedkenheuer, W.W. Pettapiece, J.D. Burke, and L.A. Leskiw 927

Symposium participants 933
Author index 951
Keyword index 953

Part I
Symposium Plenary Session

Plenary Session Opening Remarks and Presentations

Dean Mutrie and Colin Guild

THE FOLLOWING IS A TRANSCRIPT OF THE PLENARY SESSION OPENING REMARKS AND PRESENTATIONS

Good morning, everybody, my name is Dean Mutrie, and I am co-chairman of this symposium, along with Colin Guild, whom I'll introduce in a moment.

We are honored to be your host for this, the 7th in a series of leading edge symposia on environmental concerns on rights-of-way management. The purpose of this symposium is to achieve a better understanding of current and emerging environmental issues related to rights-of-way management by sharing environmental research and practical experience throughout the world.

We have assembled an excellent collection of papers from all around the globe. This symposium is the only forum where people from different utilities, countries and environmental disciplines meet to share information and ideas from their respective fields of expertise. We hope you come away with new ideas that you can apply to your own work back home, and that the social and business contacts that you make here will stand you in good stead the rest of your professional life.

As of this morning, I am pleased to announce that we have 460 registrants from 22 countries registered at the symposium. At this time I would like to take a few moments to thank our sponsors and acknowledge that their sponsorship of this is the only way that we could hold the symposium. It's taken a huge amount of work, which I have learned over the past months and particularly the last few days. There's past chairmen sitting in this audience and they will attest to the amount of work that it takes to pull one of these together. So with that, the following sponsors have provided both financial support and a lot of dedicated, talented people to help us pull this off. Our major sponsor is TransCanada, as well as the Electric Power Research Institute or EPRI, John Goodrich-Mahoney will be up later on. Our other sponsors, include TERA Environmental Consultants, BC Hydro, Alliance Pipeline, ATCO Electric, the Canadian Pacific Railway, ESG International, GRI, NRG, PanCanadian, and Westcoast Energy. We would like to thank our sponsors because they made this possible.

I would like to introduce my co-chairman Colin Guild from TransCanada.

Colin Guild
Thank you Dean. I would like to extend my welcome to everyone, and now I would like to introduce Brian McConaghy, vice president of TransCanada.

Brian McConaghy
Good morning, everyone. Welcome to Calgary and welcome to the symposium. I hope you're going to continue to be able to take in some of the sights in and around Calgary. We believe it's a beautiful setting, and we're quite proud of it. On behalf of TransCanada, I want to say that we are pleased to act as a major sponsor for the 7th in this series of quality symposiums.

The bringing together of experts like yourselves and the sharing of ideas, new procedures and new technologies will help us all meet the commitments that are expected in our communities, our companies and in the eyes of the general public as they view our industry. The oil and gas industry in North America and around the world has hundreds of thousands of kilometers of right-of-way, and for the most part, we just borrow the land from the landowners for our construction activities and ongoing operations.

We have the obligation to return the land to the landowner in such a condition as the owner can continue with past land management practices. This obligation has its challenges, but it's through your ideas that practices will continue to improve, and we, as an industry, can be proud of our efforts in caring for the environment. Thank you very much. Enjoy and learn. Thanks.

MR. DEAN MUTRIE INTRODUCES CHIEF ROY WHITNEY OF THE TSUU T'INA NATION

Chief Roy Whitney
Good morning. It's a pleasure to be here this morning with such a group of distinguished people that

really assist in determining how the next seven generations will endure or support the world environmental concerns. Thank you for that kind introduction and greetings from our elders, the Counsel and the citizens of the Tsuu T'ina First Nation.

Many of you may know that the Tsuu T'ina people are part of the Dene Nations of northern Canada. We settled in southern Alberta years ago as we followed the Dene migration trail from northern Canada as far into Mexico. Our Dene cousins, the Navajo and the Apache of the America southwest migrated there about the same time.

Tsuu T'ina lands are located very close to Calgary. In fact, if you cross 37th Street, South West, you will be standing on Tsuu T'ina lands, 69,000 acres south and southwest of the City of Calgary. Many of you will also know that we at Tsuu T'ina have been preparing for the past decade to take our place in the economy of this province. Through economic development, we believe our project plans will provide prosperity to our people and a level of financial independence unknown to us since the European settlement.

It is a pleasure to have an opportunity to address a gathering of this kind and to exchange ideas. We at Tsuu T'ina have some challenges ahead as we begin our negotiations with the City of Calgary and the Province of Alberta this fall regarding our largest project, a transportation corridor linking the southern extremity of Calgary with the northwest through Tsuu T'ina lands. We will have some major decisions to make regarding that project, particularly since there will be major environmental challenges.

We have already had questions raised by the citizens of Calgary regarding our plans for development along the corridor at off ramps and intersections with Calgary communities. Although the challenges are substantial, we have no doubt that we will be able to find a proper balance that will permit the kind of development we need while limiting the extent of intrusion to the neighboring communities. In addition, we will be searching for ways to create the least intrusion to the environment.

Since the transportation corridor will pass through areas of our land, which are a habitat of many species of wildlife, those of you have or will be involved in projects involving pipeline utility corridors and the likes should know and realize that when aboriginal lands and communities are involved, the perspective is very different. The considerations are not totally economic in nature, although there are economic considerations.

We in First Nations community have a strong relationship with the land that we occupy and live on. When our land is considered in a development context, consultations regarding our traditions and our direct participation are very important. First Nations community will always want to have an opportunity to participate in environmental screening and the work being done. It is critical from your point of view, as potential developers, to recognize that aboriginal environmental companies should be utilized particularly because of their special knowledge of the land others may not have. First Nations will want to make sure that something remains in their community of benefit from a project and, again, those are not simply economic in nature.

We at First Nations will also watch very carefully the reclamation of lands after a utility corridor or a pipeline is installed. It is important for you to know that First Nations' view of the standard of reclamation will not necessarily be the same as government standards. Because First Nations and the land itself are bound together in so many traditional ways, the standard may be dramatically higher. This is particularly so if the land has been used for traditional purposes at any time in the past. We, as aboriginal people, are acutely aware of our need to protect those things in nature that we value.

We believe that we have a duty to our future generations to use our land in a way that will not diminish their right to use the land later on. In our culture, all of our decisions are carefully measured because of the impact of the next seven generations. We take that duty very seriously. In fact, we at Tsuu T'ina have set aside 25,000 acres of our land as untouched wilderness for the use of future generations. I know that in the larger society there have been times when environmental concerns were given very little attention. Impacts on nearby villages, towns and communities were not always considered. We at Tsuu T'ina have watched as Calgary's development has appeared on our doorstep almost overnight.

Right now, we are becoming gradually surrounded by the suburbs of Calgary. Before the turn of the last century, one of our leaders had a dream. He dreamed one day that Tsuu T'ina people or Sarcee people, as we were then called, would be surrounded by boxes. Our people were puzzled about this and the dream was pondered many times.

Now, more than a century later, we know what the dream meant. As we watch Calgary grow, we note how little we have been consulted. We note that in many cases development improperly straddles the right-of-ways between our nation and Calgary. Regulatory agencies should be supervising this kind of development better. On that note, we have recently assured worried Calgarians that because of our sense of neighborliness, we will not be building a pig farm along the transportation corridor. We believe that human creativity and imagination is such that good solutions to development issues can be found. We know that it is important to consider others and to listen to others. Cooperation and consultation are all important in this process.

As I have mentioned, we as First Nations have much more than a passing interest in maintaining a proper balance between modern development and to meet our present needs while ensuring that the way of life that we value in nature remains very much a part of our lives and our enthusiasm to obtain those things that we need to live well in a modern society. We must take great care not to sacrifice what is most sacred of all things in any native community, the land, itself, and our nature.

We do not intend to depart from our commitment to nature. We will continue to protect the sensitive environmental areas located on our lands at the western end of the Glenmore reservoir. We intend to ensure that the natural habitat of the wildlife is disturbed as little as possible. We will consider designs for the transportation corridor that will give meaning to this approach. We have attempted to diminish the fears of those people who oppose us in our development plans by helping them to have a clear picture of who we are and what we hope to accomplish.

I was elected chief of the Tsuu T'ina nation 16 years ago. Back then the issues facing our people were very different from what we now face. But we continue to ask ourselves the same questions year after year; questions which are very fundamental to us; questions about who we are as a people and a nation; what direction do we want to move towards; how will our decisions affect our children or our grandchildren.

Are our goals right for our people? We believe that we must ask ourselves these questions again and again as we consider what development to allow and what the next steps are to take. We know that our value system is different from that of our partners in the transportation corridor project. Our partners, the City of Calgary and the Province of Alberta know that in doing project work with Tsuu T'ina, it must be the value system of our people which stays at the forefront.

It is realistic to assume that many Calgarians will move on to other communities in the future and in time. We at Tsuu T'ina have lived here for thousands of years. Our lands have been reduced to a small reserve with the making of Treaty No. 7 in 1877, and the establishment of our reserve in 1883. Our people will be here for centuries to come, that is why we must be very careful how we develop our lands. We will continue, however, to rely on the collective wisdom of our elders and our spiritual leaders within our community to guide us as we move ahead in this new developmental period.

We look forward to developing strong working relationships with the people of this city and southern Alberta. We ask our friends to pray for us as we seek the guidance of our creator to make good decisions, not only for our people, but as well for all Albertans. We at Tsuu T'ina continue to pray that each and every individual around the world will one day come to realize that all of the land which makes up this planet earth is as a precious living thing, a breathing thing, which deserves as much respect and protection as every pair of human hands can offer.

May I wish each and every one of you an excellent and wonderful symposium. Thank you very much for inviting me here.

DEAN MUTRIE INTRODUCES DR. DALE ARNER

Dean Mutrie
Dr. Arner is the department head and Professor Emeritus of the Department of Wildlife and Fisheries of Mississippi State University, and Dale is the fellow who founded the symposium series back in 1976. He also chaired the second one at Ann Arbor in 1979, and he's been on the steering committee for all subsequent symposia. At the 4th symposium in Indianapolis, Dr. Arner was presented with an award for foresight and dedication in fostering understanding of environmental concerns in rights-of-way management.

Dr. Arner has received many other awards during his illustrious 60-year career, including Wildlife Conservationist of the Year Award in 1970 from the Mississippi Wildlife Federation, and the Sears & Rowbuck Foundation; the CW Watson award in 1985 for significant contributions to fish and game conservation; and being nominated in 1973 by the School of Forest Resources for a listing in Outstanding Educators of America. Dr. Arner is still active in teaching wildlife management at MSU, and has written more than 70 peer reviewed or invited papers on wildlife and vegetation management with focus on black bear, beaver, wild turkey, ducks, bobwhite quail and the use of fire in vegetation management.

My personal favorite is a 1980 paper presented at the worldwide fur bearer conference at the University of Maryland entitled, "The Practicality of Reducing a Beaver Population Through the Release of Alligators." I don't know why we never thought of that in Alberta! Anyway, I could go on singing Dr. Arner's praises, but we'll just leave it! That the man is a pioneer in the application of environmental sciences to rights-of-way management, and we're lucky to have him with us today. Please join me in giving a warm Calgary welcome to our honorary chairman, Dr. Arner.

Dr. Dale Arner
I must say in defense of the beaver/alligator deal, that we found in Mississippi there were a lot more cotton mouths and a lot more other critters for the alligators than the beavers, so it wasn't too successful.

I appreciate the invitation to participate in the 7th International Symposium. It's been a very pleasant 24 years involved with the symposia. It started, as you mentioned Dean, back in 1976. And in case you might be wondering how that first symposium was started, many of us were concerned about the plethora of papers that were submitted in the mid 1960s and 70s concerning rights-of-way, and a lot of these papers were beginning to discuss the environment through the use of deer as an indicator of how old a particular treatment was in their rights-of-way maintenance program. If the deer ate it or just sniffed at it, they would call it a choice deer food plan. And we were concerned about all of the people that were trying herbicides, bulldozing and seeding, and their use of deer was an indicator of the success of these types of treatments on the environment.

I talked to a number of my colleagues back in the late 60s and 70s about their concerns with the papers being presented and their content. Dr. Eggler, you might know, was a big proponent of the U shaped right-of-way. You would use selective herbicide in developing low shrubs in the center of the right-of-way. This was beginning to be developed as the solution to right-of-way maintenance. I didn't quite see it that way, and Dr. Frank Egler didn't like what I saw, so he called me the smorgasbord man, somebody who was trying to develop a lot of high quality food for deer. That was unnecessary.

Anyway, this was the typical things that we were facing back in those days in all the papers that were being presented, and after talking to a number of people at the time we thought it would be good to start our own symposium, and have a question and answer session. We could talk to people who have different ideas than we had, and have a discussion of ideas. And it evolved, and in 1976 we held the first one at Mississippi State University, and there are several folks in the room here who participated in that first one, Kevin McLoughlin was one of the ones participating. Let me see, I might have some other names here. Gus Tillman, Ed Colson, and Allen Crabtree, those were the ones that participated in the first symposium. We had about 180 some people registered. We had 36 presented papers, and that covered 330 pages of the proceedings.

Now, we — I think we had a stroke of good luck with this thing because we were able to get some sponsors from the power and utility companies down there to host a happy hour, and then we found some other donors that would grant us all the bob white quail that we needed for the dinner. So we had all the quail you could eat and all the bourbon you could drink, and this was at $25 a head. So it went over so well that Gus Tillman, the next day at a critique, volunteered immediately to chair the next one in Ann Arbor. I think if we hadn't had this happy hour, we would have had very few volunteers, but as they were all anticipating another happy hour in Ann Arbor, the meeting was a success. We had some really good papers and we had some really good comments and arguments back and forth, and I think that's what it's all about to try to put our cards on the table and discuss the pros and cons of the different treatments that we are going to use and its impact on the environment.

I think one of the things that was lacking at that one, and the next one or two was we did not have papers about endangered plant species. Also, we did not talk very much about songbirds. It was mainly deer and a little bit about wild turkey. But I think those things are being considered now, and I feel very good about the rights-of-way symposia as they have been evolved.

I do have one concern that perhaps we are not getting enough input from people in the different state resource management groups, like the game and fish departments. At first we had more input from them and as the symposia went on, we seemed to have less and less input. And they are the people with the resources to all the different treatments, like fertilizer and lawn seed and so forth for any over seeding or any of other procedures, and I think we should make an effort to have them more a part of our symposia. I don't know how to do it or what it takes, but I think this is a challenge for us to try to influence them to attend and participate.

I believe that's it — I'll wind up my little discussion here. I just want to express my gratitude again for the invitation and the hospitality and kindness that has been shown to my wife and myself at this meeting and I hope I'll be able to attend the next one. I know darn well if Gus Tillman can make it, I can. I'm looking forward to that. Thank you.

Dean Mutrie
Thank you, Dr. Arner, that was great. It's good to know that you're part of a bigger movement and there's a history here.

Now I would like to introduce our keynote speaker this morning who is Dr. Brian Bietz. Dr. Bietz has been a member of the Alberta Energy and Utilities Board for close to 10 years. He has over 20 years of professional experience in environmental health and safety issues in the public and private sector, including Director of Environment and Technology for our Western Canadian Waste Management firm, and as an environmental consultant to government and industrial clients.

Dr. Bietz is a director of the Energy Counsel of Canada and serves on the Environmental Advisory Committee of the Calgary Airport Authority. He is also a member of the Public Advisory Committee for the Canadian Electricity Association's Environmental Commitment and Responsibility Program and is Registrar for the Alberta Society of Professional Biologists. Brian is also a home grown product. He is a rare commodity in these parts. He is actually a native of Calgary. From his perspective as a member of one of the most respected energy regulatory boards in the world, ruling on controversial pipeline, power line and energy projects, Brian will share his insights into the environmental and public issues associated with energy corridors. Please join me in welcoming Dr. Brian Bietz.

Dr. Brian Bietz

Thank you very much, Dean. That's going to be a difficult introduction to live up to.

Good morning, ladies and gentlemen. It's certainly an honor to be asked to address you at this prestigious conference. As a native Calgarian, I'm certainly proud of the Province of Alberta, and I hope that all of you that are visiting here will be able to find some time to also enjoy some of Alberta's natural beauty. And please don't be lured just by the siren call of the Rocky Mountains. Alberta has a vast number of special places that range from boreal forest, Aspen parkland through the wetlands, native prairie and all of these have a unique beauty and all are tremendous places to visit.

Now, the citizens of this province have long valued these wild areas and at the same time, the province has been blessed with these ecological treasures, Alberta has also been endowed with other natural resources. These include significant deposits of oil, gas, coal and oil sands. And in combination with the province's strong agricultural roots, both Alberta's economy and its population have been growing steadily over a number of decades. And of course, with this growth has come the age-old conflict in trying to balance the protection of one set of resources for the development of the other.

Now, the decisions and the ever growing economic resources perhaps make Alberta in many ways the perfect place for the 7th International Symposium on Environmental Concerns in Rights-of-Way Management. In Alberta there is an ongoing struggle to find the balance between environmental protection on the one hand and economic development on the other.

Clearly, though, Alberta has in no way a monopoly on sensitive natural environments with the now 400 plus delegates at this conference. With over 20 countries represented, every one of you has in this room in some fashion or another been directly involved, likely on an almost daily basis, in trying to find that balance between protection of a natural environment and enhancing the efficient and economic delivery of resources to the public, whether through pipelines, power lines, by road or by rail.

I also expect that every one of you has, at some time or another in your professional careers, struggled with the trade-offs that, on occasion, must be made to achieve that balance and to protect the public interest. And the fact is these aren't simple decisions. The value that the public may place on environmental protection versus economics is often anything but clear. And furthermore, just by following the rules can be less than satisfactory since the regulations themselves that we work under are often dated relative to current societal values. And finally, societal values themselves are not static but are evolving steadily over time. Even these values are subject to a number of both short and long-term pressures. A strong economy, an acute shortage of a resource can often lead to very different views on the relative value of environmental resources.

Now, the purpose of this conference is, of course, to consider the advances that have been made in addressing the environmental issues that are associated with the development and maintenance of rights-of-ways. And looking at the conference agenda, one cannot help but be struck by the level of sophistication that is now being brought to this subject. Sometimes, however, it is also important to take a step back from the details and to re-examine some of our most basic assumptions, and that is the goal of this, the first session of the conference.

The issue that we intend to address this morning, both in my opening remarks and later in the session that will be after the coffee break is the corridor concept. And corridors, for the purpose of this session, have been widely defined. They are rights-of-ways containing more than a single linear development. Therefore, they may include two similar systems such as two transmission lines of equal size, or alternatively several pipelines of different sizes carrying different materials. Finally, they could contain different forms of linear development.

Now, historically the development of corridors has been one of the most widely accepted approaches to addressing the environmental and social issues associated with rights-of-way. It is intuitively obvious that the use of corridors for linear developments is a potentially extremely useful tool for reducing environmental impacts. By focusing development within a single restricted area, it's clear that in turn other areas can be left unaffected. And if you happen to be one of those lucky species or people that lives in those other areas, then your needs have clearly been met.

But like any other form of conventional wisdom, it's also very important that these concepts on occasion be challenged. We need to do so, not only because we continue to gather more information about their performance, but also because sometimes we find that some of the basic truths underlying our earlier views have changed. Unfortunately this is not something that we, as a society, commonly do. Therefore, I find that it is particularly impressive that the organizers of this conference have made this the subject of the plenary session. I think it's fair to say that few disciplines are willing to make sure that the emperor really does have his clothes on. So my goal this morning is to introduce some of the issues that may cause us to begin to reconsider when and how the corridor concept should be applied.

As Dean said, I'm a board member with the Alberta Energy and Utilities Board, and although Dean said some nice things, in Alberta, all energy development is regulated by the EUB, or as we are often affectionately referred to by industry, "those bastards at the board." The latter comment is usually followed by a spitting noise.

Now, the EUB's regulatory authority is extensive and it includes approvals for all new oil and gas wells in Alberta, which this year will be approximately be 10,000 to 12,000 wells, and the associated pipelines, batteries, compressors and processing plants. It also includes approvals for new power plants and power lines. In Alberta, the board regulates a little more than 20,000 kilometers of transmission power lines and 275,000 kilometers of pipelines of which 170,000 kilometers are of four-inch diameter or greater. The EUB processes in the neighborhood of 25,000 applications a year.

Now, the EUB has a rather interesting structure. A virtual army of very dedicated and very professional staff handles these thousands of applications. Because they worked hard to develop a good, working relationship with the industry, and because the industry generally has an excellent understanding of Alberta's regulatory requirements, the vast majority of the applications they receive can be routinely processed and approved. However, for a very tiny minority of these applications, less than a hundred a year, routine approval is not possible. And for energy development applications in particular, the most common issue that prevents the EUB staff from processing the application is a concern raised by an affected landowner.

Now, in Alberta, any individual whose rights may be adversely affected by a decision of the EUB has the right to a public hearing, and I think it's a tribute to the excellent relationship between the industry and the public that there are, in fact, so few hearings a year. However, when a hearing is required, this is the point where my colleagues of the board and I come into the picture. Our mandate is set out in legislation. We are tasked with ensuring that the orderly and efficient development of the energy resources of Alberta takes place in the public interest. However, the legislation does not define that term in the public interest.

Now, the legislation does require that when we make our decisions, we take into account the environmental, social and economic impacts of the proposed project. Clearly, however, it is also expected the board can consider all of the relevant factors when determining whether proposed development is in the best interests of Albertans. The hearing process, while far from perfect, does provide the board with an excellent opportunity to better understand the concerns of the public. It also provides us with a unique opportunity to watch as those concerns change over time, and while many issues have remained the same, others appear to be changing, and some of those changes, I would suggest, may be particularly relevant to our consideration today of the corridor concept. And it is those changing conditions that I would like to just focus the remainder of my comments to you.

First of all, it is clear that the Alberta public still places significant importance on environmental protection. I think it would be fair to say that on public land in particular, and in Alberta, that is a significant amount of land, this continues to be one of the public's most important objectives; however, it is very noticeable that other issues begin to take on additional importance as the proposed development approaches privately owned lands. These issues quite naturally tend to revolve around the potential direct impacts of the development on the concerned individuals. What perhaps is most interesting, however, is how the public's view of some of these issues seems to be shifting, and I would like to address three of those.

I think one of the most interesting things that we have seen in recent years has been a negative reaction from the public regarding new development in areas where there has already been a long history of industrial activity. While objections to development in relatively undisturbed regions wouldn't be surprising, this recent rising concern from areas that already have significant development is somewhat unexpected.

Now, for example, and I think this is probably true across North America, but it's certainly true in Alberta, with the current restructuring of Alberta's energy industries, we are seeing a number of older fields and facilities, particularly gas plants being purchased, refurbished and often expanded by new and smaller and more aggressive companies. This has led in turn to increased drilling, plant upgrades and often-expansive new pipeline developments where there has already been previous development.

Now, the board has had a number of objections from landowners in these areas of expanded development, and this is what's — it's an interesting argument. What they argue is that they don't oppose energy development, and furthermore, they recognize the value that is brought to all Albertans. However, they also argue that they have directly borne the impacts of oil and gas activity for the last 20 years or more, and they are not prepared to do so for another 20.

Now, the first time I heard this argument, I must admit that I was just a little bit surprised. Again, conventional wisdom would seem to suggest that it should be easier to get public agreement to the expansion of energy development in an area where it was already common. But the landowners point out that they have always been led to believe that the fields and the region would decline usually over a 20 to 25-year period. However, just when they believed that the field, the associated facilities were approaching the end of their economic life, they suddenly find themselves being asked to agree to a significant life extension or even a major expansion. This, they argue, simply isn't fair. They shouldn't, as individuals, have to shoulder in perpetuity, all the impacts from developments that are designed to benefit the general public as a whole.

Now, one might have a little less sympathy for this argument if the landowners had moved into the area after the plant or the pipeline had been built. Often, though, the fact is that they were there first and, furthermore, hadn't been particularly happy with the development in the first place. And even if they had moved into the region after the development had started, most did so with the same information that they could expect activity to decline within two to three decades. In their minds, when the company told them that this new development would have a 20 to 25-year life span, this was a commitment, and in rural Alberta in particular, such commitments are expected to be honored.

Now, a second area that we are seeing of public concern appears to be arising around safety issues in general. Despite ongoing efforts by regulators and industry alike, public concern with the posed risk seems to be growing. Again, this is somewhat surprising since at the same time that same public seems to becoming much more knowledgeable about the actual relative risks of the various forms of energy development, including the risks of transporting that energy. The use of corridors is clearly one area where the directly affected public is raising safety concerns more frequently, and this is particularly true when it is proposed to transport new substances or commodities within the right-of-way. When this occurs, safety concerns often become a key issue that the public brings to the board for resolution. In Alberta, a common example is the addition of a sour gas pipeline with its potentially lethal hydrogen sulfide content into what was until then sweet gas rights-of-way.

Now, again, it is difficult for the board to easily dismiss these concerns. While it would seem unlikely that there would be anything greater than an additive increase in risks from such developments, the fact is that the database needed to confirm in this case is often not well established. For example, is the risk of failure in any one line increased or decreased? And if one line does fail, what are the new risks of sequential failure in another? Now, for a land owner living in proximity to a proposed rights-of-way to a proposed corridor, these are very serious questions, and it's a question I wouldn't mind leaving with this room because it's certainly one that in the future we believe has to be addressed in a more fulsome manner.

A third area of change in public attitudes is with the long-term economic impact of urban development. For example, the expansion of a right-of-way may raise significant economic questions. Again, this is particularly true when a change in the commodity being transported such as sour gas leads to a substantive increase in development setbacks.

Now, it's very rare anymore that an objection to development does not include a reference to likely negative effects on land values and our future development options. Again, this is a change from the past where many of your developments were primarily on agricultural land with little prospect in the future of being much more than agricultural land. In Alberta, certainly that scenario is changing.

Now, one could argue that economic impact should be irrelevant in protecting the broader public interest. For example, using corridors to reduce environmental or social impacts should outweigh any individual economic effects. And to a certain degree this is true, provided that society is prepared to offer fair compensation to the affected individual. However, since these public concerns lead to significant resistance to development, and we ultimately believe — that if we ultimately believe that corridors are environmentally and socially the best option in the region, we need to address the issue of appropriate compensation for affected individuals. But again, setting that fair economic value seems to also becoming increasingly difficult.

Now, what I would like to do is conclude very briefly and say that the benefits of right-of-way corridors to help manage environmental impacts are numerous. But it is important as you work towards that and examine that issue that we look for balance in the things that we do, and to remember that in serving the public interest, which ultimately is all of our goals, that many competing interests need to be addressed in arising at the best solution. I would like to invite your active participation in this morning's discussion after the coffee break because I think that will be a significant step in helping all of us to achieve that goal. Thank you very much.

MR. MUTRIE INTRODUCES MR. GOODRICH-MAHONEY

Dean Mutrie

Our next speaker is John Goodrich-Mahoney from the Electric Power Research Institute (EPRI). He is a program manager in EPRI's Environmental Department. He produced the proceedings from the sixth right-of-way sixth symposium in New Orleans, and we prevailed upon him to do it again. So he is our senior editor, and he is going to come up and make his editor's remarks.

Mr. Goodrich-Mahoney

Before I make a few comments about the editorial process for the proceedings, I would like to offer my congratulations to Dean and Colin. As many of you know, Randy Williams, from Entergy, and I co-chaired the last one, and I know intimately what it takes to do this. So a big hand to these fellows.

As Dean mentioned, EPRI will be funding the proceedings for this symposium, and I would just like to take a few minutes to comment about how this is going to happen. We have approximately 110 papers, and this is a tremendous turnout for this symposium. I would like to thank all the authors for their hard work, and also those individuals who developed posters, some of which will be submitted later as papers.

Your papers have been submitted for peer review, as we did for the first time after the New Orleans symposium. I will work with you to resolve any comments on your papers. After this process is completed the papers will be submitted to Elsevier Science Ltd. for publication. EPRI will mail a copy of the proceedings to everyone who attended this symposium.

Dean, I think that's pretty much what I wanted to cover. Enjoy the rest of the symposium and we look forward to seeing you at the next one. Thank you very much.

Corridor Concept Revisited: Multiple Rights-of-Way

Allen F. Crabtree III

A panel of five representatives from government, academia, private citizen groups, and landowners was assembled to discuss the pros and cons of the routing of multiple utilities in common rights-of-way corridors. The common wisdom for the last 30 years has been that "shared rights-of-way are good and green fields are bad." Many corridors, however, are now reaching saturation, carrying multiple utilities, transportation systems and other linear facilities. The question of "how much is enough" is a very germane topic for discussion. Routing has always been a balancing process, and there is not one easy solution. In the last 30 years, construction techniques and requirements have changed, societal values have changed, development has sprung up around corridors, and consequently developers of new lines will have to face significant environmental, engineering, safety, and land use issues. The panel discussion was an attempt to review the concept of how much is enough, when shared corridors are good and when they are not, when a green field corridor is preferable and when it is not.

Keywords: Common corridors, shared rights-of-way, utility corridors, transportation corridors

DISCUSSION

The traditional wisdom has been to route linear projects in corridors whenever possible, to consolidate impacts, to minimize land required for individual rights-of-way, and to better fit within regional and area planning efforts. Utility corridors have been established by Federal, state/provincial, and local governments in an effort to concentrate linear rights-of-way in common areas whenever possible. Regulatory agencies have issued policies and regulations that encourage the use of common rights-of-way.

This concept has proven itself in terms of reducing local impacts from construction, since shared rights-of-way allow for savings in the amount of required right-of-way. Over the years, the corridor approach has reduced the amount of new right-of-way acreage required, reduced impacts to wetlands, prime agricultural lands and wildlife habitat. However, too much of a good thing can be bad. When too many (and that is not defined) utilities are placed in common corridors, there are problems if maintenance must be done on one of these lines. The increasingly wide right-of-way affects wildlife use and travel. Landowners find that use of their property is constrained, and their ability to develop or sell is diminished. The potential for sympathetic explosions from gas and petroleum lines in common rights-of-way is increased, as is the potential for terrorism. When the number of shared lines expands beyond two or three together, questions have been raised about increased fragmentation of wildlife habitat, land use and property value impacts, potential safety issues, and aesthetic impacts. The base question is "how much corridor sharing is too much?"

A panel of experts in the field was assembled for a plenary session to discuss the pros and cons of linear facility corridors. They included the following:

- Dr. Brian F. Bietz, Board Member of the Alberta Energy and Utilities Board;
- Robert Arvedlund, Chief of the Environmental Review and Compliance Branch I for the Federal Energy Regulatory Commission (FERC) in Washington, DC;
- John Kobasa, Vice President of Engineering, Operations and Construction for CMS Energy Corporation's international gas pipeline unit, CMS Gas Transmission and Storage Company, in Detroit, Michigan;

- James Irving, a rancher and farmer with a lifetime involvement on the family grain and cattle farm near Regina, Saskatchewan;
- Dr. David S. Maehr, Assistant Professor at the Department of Forestry, University of Kentucky, in Lexington, Kentucky; and
- Michael Sawyer, landscape ecologist with the Citizen's Oil & Gas Commission in Alberta.

The panel discussed the range of potential impacts from locating utilities in common corridors, both positive and negative. Anecdotal examples were provided, including the areas where problems have been identified, solutions, species affected, etc. There were discussions in the following topical areas related to the corridor concept:
- Regulatory issues and policies;
- Construction, maintenance, engineering and safety issues;
- Wildlife impacts and habitat fragmentation issues;
- Land use, property values, and landowner concerns; and
- Impacts to natural resources and environmental concerns.

These questions were posed to the panel for discussion:
- What is a utility or transportation corridor, and what constitutes a shared right-of-way?
- When is a corridor too full?
- Can (or cannot) the maximum number of utilities in a corridor be determined?
- What is a compatible mix of utilities in a shared right-of-way?
- When is a green field corridor the best solution?
- What are the benefits of a third-party pipeline?
- What are the impacts on the future use of land from corridors?
- Do shared corridors have a greater impact on wildlife habitat fragmentation than green field corridors?
- How have the perceptions of people changed regarding shared corridors? and
- What is the trade-off of issues that should be dealt with in utility routing?

This is a many-faceted subject, and the panel concluded that there is no one simple solution. Clearly a balancing of resource values, environmental values, social and engineering values, all need to be considered in cases where multiple utility corridors are designated, and also when additional lines are proposed for addition in common with others in shared rights-of-way.

THE FOLLOWING IS AN EDITED TRANSCRIPT OF THE PANEL DISCUSSION

Mr. Allen Crabtree

I would like to welcome you all to the continuing plenary session. We will be having a panel session the rest of the morning on which we will be following up on the excellent introductory comments that Dr. Bietz provided in his keynote address. Sort of priming the pump as it were. If you anticipate walking away from this panel discussion with a lot of concrete answers and fast and hard rules, you probably ought to go back into the poster session.

One of the delightful things about us old hands having been around the right-of-way planning and the routing process for years is that there are no set rules. The business changes over the years. The variables change that we have to deal with, whether we are a regulator or a consultant or an applicant or any of the other individuals who are involved, particularly landowners. Brian brought out that many of us have had, for the last 30 years, the Animal Farm mantra that "shared rights-of-way are good, green fields are bad" doesn't work. It works sometimes and sometimes it doesn't work.

Since the 70s, the emphasis has really been on the co-location of utilities. And as Dr. Bietz pointed out, it's not just pipelines, it's not just electric transmission lines, it's all linear types of facilities, and sometimes they are by themselves and sometimes it's co-located with other types. Routing has always been a balancing process and we have all discovered that there isn't one easy solution. The construction techniques and requirements have changed, societal values have changed. Development has strung up around corridors and future lines have significant problems.

The toughest thing that all of us have to face, whether we're a regulator or a planner is when a land owner comes up and they say, I've got five pipelines on my property, how much is enough? You're proposing another pipeline, how much is enough?

What I would like to do with this group today is to throw around some of the concepts of how much is enough. When are shared corridors good; when are they not good; when is a green field corridor preferable; and when is it not preferable. We have some slides to illustrate some case studies that will help you get a feeling for some specific instances that the members of the panel have had to face, and we'll be throwing it open for questions to the audience toward the end of the session.

But let me first ask the panel, "What constitutes a shared right-of-way versus a single purpose one?"

Mr. Kobasa

In my mind, a shared corridor occurs once you have two companies in a corridor. I think to the extent that a pipeline company or overhead transmission power company puts an overhead transmission line, and they put a second one in there in my definition, I would say that's a shared corridor. I think it's called locating with your own facilities. So in my own definition, a shared corridor starts to occur when other companies come into that corridor.

Mr. Crabtree
When is a corridor too full then?

Mr. Kobasa
Let me first set out what I think is the basic premise for considering the routing of any utility. The preferred route eventually selected should have been based on a balance of its environmental impacts, constructibility, and operating and maintenance issues, and land owner and community impacts.

That said, I believe our topical question, "When is a corridor too full?" is best answered as follows: A corridor is certainly too full when an alternative green field routing exists which has fewer environmental impacts than would the corridor routing, and it also ameliorates, if not eliminates, any constructibility and operational and maintenance issues posed by the corridor. And while the green field route probably raises new land owner nimby (i.e., not in my back yard) issues, it certainly avoids affecting land owners who have previously been affected several times as a corridor was being developed over the years. The correct selection must be based on a carefully weighed balance of the issues identified.

And since generally all involved parties in these deliberations will have their own biases, it is vitally important that a proper and balanced perspective be taken so that the route finally selected has the best chance of getting by all the parties. Let me illustrate how I believe this — the issues I just raised would come into play in an example, which replicates the situation my company has been involved in.

In the recent route selection of a 130 mile long 36 inch pipeline through a Midwest region replete with pipelines, we, like all good pipe liners, looked at the routes of other pipelines in the area who are generally headed in the direction we need to go. In effect, fully embracing the corridor concept. As we went about our routing study, we saw opportunities to parallel other pipelines without any adverse consequences that couldn't be reasonably dealt with. However, we came into a segment of the route where paralleling other pipelines started to pose some very undesirable constructibility and operational and maintenance issues.

What we found is that existing corridor in this segment occupied by two different companies with as many as three to four pipelines of large diameter already in place, what requires some 16 crossovers, actually cross unders, because of the congested residential and commercial development that already encroached on the existing corridor. We were looking at diagonal crossings some 460 feet long by 250 feet across, and at least 12 feet deep.

With the construction related issues associated with working around multiple loaded pipelines in this way and concerns it raised for future safe operational and maintenance activities, we asked ourselves, is there a better alternative for routing our pipeline through this segment, and went looking. And what we found was a better alternative routing, some four to six miles to the west of the corridor. A green field routing which affirmatively addressed those issues I identified earlier as answering the question, "When is a corridor too full?"

This new routing affected less of the environment, since it is two and a half miles shorter than the corridor route affecting fewer overall lands. It affects fewer wetlands, 3200 feet versus 7800 feet crossed by the corridor route affects fewer forested areas, 13 acres versus 39 acres of the corridor, and the new route affects some 14 percent fewer landowners.

Mr. Crabtree
If an applicant came to you, Brian, with this logical process of going through the various variables and said, "this is what we recommend", what would your answer be or your challenge to it?

Dr. Bietz
I don't know that we would — I guess under our system, the first question that we would ask is, "Do you have the same sort of sign-off by those land owners?" That would be the key question from our perspective. If the design makes economic sense, economics would probably be the last question, but if it makes sense from a safety perspective and it makes sense from an environmental perspective, it meets the current rules and procedures, and then finally, the company had been able, through effective consultation, to get the land owner to buy into this, then from our perspective, we really wouldn't have a concern.

Mr. Arvedlund
I'm not going to comment on the specific project. It is obviously before FERC, a draft EIS has been put out, so I think staff's position is kind of well known. It was one — not the first time we were faced with this. We have a couple of others in-house that we're facing the same question of when is enough enough.

In the particular EIS that I'm speaking of, we did, in fact, embrace leaving the corridor for a variety of environmental and safety reasons. I don't know that we focused on the landowner issue for this particular one, but that's becoming more and more important.

It is obvious that if somebody comes in with a route that landowners have signed of on, that makes life a whole lot easier for everybody, and we probably would embrace it. But for this particular project, it just seemed to make sense to leave the corridor and go with a green field route. What you've got to kind of recognize is the minute that you do that you might actually be inventing another corridor, because once one comes in, then a lot more comes in, although, most companies don't want to admit that up front, but that is, in fact, a reality. So you do have to kind of keep that in mind. You're creating more than just one pipeline down the road.

To get most other federal agencies, particularly the land management agencies, to sign off on leaving a corridor could be one tough nut to crack. They don't normally embrace that very well, but — and it's rare that they do that, but in this particular instance, FERC is willing to embrace that particular end of the project, but it does make sense in this case.

Mr. Kobasa

And one issue I raised and one that Bob raised I think in our 140 miles, we do collocate with other utility corridors for about 40 miles. For instance, the forestry division in one of the States wanted us to parallel the pipeline through the forest, and we had to go a little bit out of our way to achieve that balance with them.

But one of the issues we did take a look at, Brian, was landowner acceptance. And we have a little bit of history because there was another project proposed several years earlier that perhaps was going to come through the same region, though it started from a different direction, the public record was replete with land owner concerns that went into the FERC that says, "Why me again?" And we saw a significant amount of land owner letters into the FERC with that earlier project and what we realized again that we may be bringing new land owners into play, it seemed like there could have been so much opposition to coming back in, especially trying to get through some of the congested areas that, coupled with the issues that seemed to favor going out of the quarter for that segment, unbalanced to us seemed like it made sense.

Mr. Crabtree

Well, let me ask Dave and Michael, what questions would you pose for John's company; or has he given an approach that would satisfy you?

Dr. Maehr

When I think of corridor concepts, it's totally opposite, in fact, 90 degrees different than what you all are talking about here.

My concept of corridor is a landscape system that provides movement of bioduct or ecological processes from one point to another. And more often than not, the types of corridors that we're discussing here are at 90 degrees to the processes, and they cause problems in terms of the movement of wildlife, the movement of water, the movement of fire, other natural processes, and it would be those kinds of concerns that I would raise, what's being done to mitigate or reduce or eliminate the problems that those utilities are going to cause. I guess my first question to that would be, do you really need it? Is it absolutely necessary to put this thing in?

Mr. Crabtree

Okay. Thank you. All right, John, you've had the resource agency staring you in the face asking you these hard questions.

Mr. Kobasa

Well, fortunately we didn't have difficult issues to face. I don't want to minimize the impacts to farmers on going through their agricultural lands, but virtually this entire 90-mile alternative section was through agricultural land. So it wasn't an issue of affecting perhaps some local ground life, I would guess, but it wasn't an issue of going through forested wood lots or going through endangered species territories. And on the basis that we had to do all the cultural resources investigations, and we do have some phase II digs that we have to do and follow through on. It becomes the balance that we talked about.

Mr. Crabtree

Michael, how about you? If you were representing landowners on either the corridor or on the green field, what are the hard questions you would be asking?

Mr. Sawyer

Well, obviously the selection of the route is a site specific case, and I'm not familiar with all of the details, but my concern would be that it appears just on the face of it that some of the routing issues here are primarily based on engineering questions.

And one of the questions that I would raise is notwithstanding the arguments that have been put forward about the lesser amount of force, the lesser amount of wetlands, it's still new wetlands, I would assume, that are being disturbed. So it would be with the specifics in the case, we would weigh up whether disturbing those new smaller amount of wetlands are actually better than keeping that development in an existing wetlands, and it depends on the site specific. But my concern would be that some of those considerations would be overwhelmed by the economic and engineering considerations that the pipeline component would be most focusing on.

Mr. Crabtree

Is there a maximum number of utilities that can be determined for a corridor? Is there a hard and fast number?

Mr. Iving

I'm here representing some of the concerns and issues that I have as a landowner. I'm going to start off trying to introduce the topic by giving just a brief history of our situation as landowners and how corridor development has affected us.

I grew up on a grain farm, a cattle farm in south central Saskatchewan about 40 miles west of Regina. Our farm was homesteaded in 1898. In the last 50 years we've experienced corridor development on our farm. And that's resulted in seven major oil pipelines occurring on our property in two distinct corridors. The inner section of these two corridors is roughly 240 m from our farmyard. The bulk of our property as a square, basically these corridors make a big X across our property.

So, what I want to get into first is kind of outline how these corridors were developed. In 1950, the first major pipeline goes through our land. It's a 20-inch line. Today that transports NGL, natural gas in liquid form, and light crude.

In 1954, the second line goes through, this is a 24-inch heavy crude. And also with that line, a tank farm is developed about a quarter of a mile from our property for storing heavy crude which is then transported by a branch line to a Moosejaw based asphalt company.

In 1967, a 34-inch, and this is still in the first corridor, a 34-inch pipeline is then put through. This is now transporting light and medium crude. In 1977, we see the development of the second corridor on our land, and the initial line there is a 12-inch ethylene/ethane propane line.

In 1994, in the initial corridor we have another 20-inch line going through, and this is refined products and heavy crude — or just refined products. In 1998, another line going through on the initial corridor, this is a 36-inch line. This is transporting heavy crude. In 1999, in the second corridor, we have a 36-inch line going through, and this is transporting natural gas. That's the latest line being developed.

So those are the two major corridors as far as pipelines goes. And along with that we have other smaller corridors and things like overhead power lines, underground power lines, fiber-optic cable lines and things like that. So, as you can see, we have a number of pipelines, a great variety of different ages, different sizes, volumes, products being carried, pumping pressures and critical locations, as I pointed out, the intersection of those two corridors.

So what does this mean to us as landowners? Well, as far as safety is concerned, we see more lines means an increase in safety risk to us and there is concern about the different ages of pipelines. Disruption of topsoil is an excellent example of how these corridors, in the last seven years, have affected us. There's construction, and reclamation, but really, the reclamation never gets to go into effect because by the time it's initiated, you're starting on another project.

Agriculture, is another area of concern. During the construction process, you have fragmentation of pastures, fields, again, soil degradation and disruption. Life-style, this is a major one for us. This is one — especially this summer, it just really hit home for us. Constant disturbances, it's basically like living in an industrial area or a construction area.

So where do we see a future as far as landowners? One of the major things I see is that there's a very high probability with these two corridors that there's going to be more lines, and again, that's going to affect us in a variety of negative ways with the natural gas exploration of the high Arctic, Northwest Territories and with the large demand for natural gas in the Chicago area in the US Midwest. We feel as landowners, these lines are here, but there's definitely going to be more. So that, again, is going to cause an accumulation of more negative stress on us.

So our attitude has changed, I guess, as a family as land owners from let's say from 1950 when my grandfather — when the first line went through, it was kind of a — he looked at it as acceptance, basically accepting the project of compliance. He felt like it was almost his patriotic duty in developing the west. And now it seems for us that we've just seen the impacts of it so many years after years, that, for us, we've kind of entered a stage of formal objection. We don't want any more lines. The carrying capacity of the land in relation to safety, environment, agricultural productivity, disturbance to life-style for further corridor development has been reach or exceeded. We, as landowners, believe it has. However, pipeline authorities and government regulating bodies do not. Thus, there is a definite gap between what we, as landowners, feel comfortable to live with, and what pipeline and government regulators see as feasible.

So here's the million dollar question: Is it possible to develop a system or guidelines to determine when enough is enough; and if so, how should this be accomplished?

Mr. Kobasa
May I ask a question? How many different companies are involved in those pipelines?

Mr. Irving
With the pipelines, we have three.

Mr. Sawyer
What's your sense, as a landowner, of the job that the regulator, which in this case would be the National Energy Board, has been doing?

Do you feel like they're representing the public interest, representing your interest in this case?

Mr. Irving
Definitely, from the experience we've had and especially in the last couple of years going to formal objections, I don't see the regulating body as an independent body. I don't see them as looking at both issues from a nonbiased point of view. It seems to me that when they regard the issues that we bring up, it seems like they only address the trivial. For instance, from our latest formal objection hearing, the only thing we really got out of it as a positive sign was a bit of dust

control, things like that. Things that are really trivial to us. I almost see the regulating body and the pipeline companies, like a buddy buddy system where they're working together and they don't really have perspective of the landowner's concern.

Mr. Sawyer
I want to follow up on that from our perspective, as an environmental group that deals with a lot of landowners. We often get the question raised about the issue of benefits and costs, and who's benefiting from this pipeline? Is it the private interest, particularly the pipeline owners or the shippers on that line? Is it the government or is it broader society? But then the question is, "Who is actually bearing the cost?" And our sense is, that as a rule of thumb, that these individual landowners who are burdened by these developments are bearing a disapportionate amount of the burden in terms of the broader public interest, but there isn't, in our view, a reasonable mechanism to compensate them. And then the other question is, even if compensation was addressed in a satisfactory way, some of those landowners simply don't want those activities to occur on their land.

Mr. Irving
Exactly.

Mr. Sawyer
And there's an imbalance here and that's what we have to address.

Mr. Irving
That's what I, as a land owner, find the most frustrating part is that while you're being compensated in monetary ways, but the reality of the situation for us is that, we don't want any more pipelines going through. If the question is, "Can we pay you more money if you put more lines in?", no, that's not addressing our concerns. We simply don't want any more pipelines. And I think it's almost unfair to say that you're being compensated for that. A lot of land owners realize that even once you get past the issue of this pipeline is going through anyway what else do we have left to restore some kind of value for this project going through? And I guess that's where we look at compensation.

Mr. Kobasa
I would like to make a comment. I think I'm always putting myself in regulator's shoes, I guess. The answer to your question of when should somebody say "enough is enough" probably establish a policy, I think goes to the point of saying, what is the alternative? You know, are we really not going to use the natural resources we have where we need them? So, again, it becomes a balance. It becomes an issue of what are the alternatives, and what's the impact of those alternatives.

Mr. Irving
Yes, I definitely see that. For obviously as far as costs go, developing more pipelines in the original right-of-way is probably the most cost efficient way of developing a pipeline. And then as far as developing a pipeline somewhere else, again, you're going to have to go through a whole different group of land owners, and it's going to be more trouble that way, too. So, again, I don't have the solution, but I do know that we have to establish some kind of limits to how many you can allow a landowner to have on his land. For us, I think that limit was six, maybe even less than that. Definitely not seven.

Mr. Crabtree
A lot of times when a company comes in with a pipeline, they will actually acquire a right-of-way for a second or third line as part of it, so when they come in with a future pipeline, they already have the easement secured. Is that the case here with any of these three companies?

Mr. Irving
In the initial pipeline, it was. In this last corridor, it was actually developed beside the initial right-of-way. There's two different companies involved with the second corridor, so it was developed beside that other company's right-of-way already in place. So now they don't have room for development of another line as we speak. But again, really, what does it matter? If they want to put another line through, if the government accepts that proposal, they'll build that right-of-way. They'll take that right-of-way. So, really, as far as their purchasing, you know, a tract of easement for two or three more pipelines, I don't think it really matters. Maybe it's just more paperwork when the time comes.

Mr. Crabtree
Brian, Bob, any comments on the situation that James has?

Dr. Bietz
I might make one. James, I understand what you're talking about in terms of our compensation system. When that first pipeline came through, there was a formula and it was based on, "we'll be disturbing your farmland one time," "it will be a certain amount of soil mixing and reclamation," and it was based on that. I really don't think our current system of compensation recognizes this ongoing and continuous impact on not only your livelihood, but also your quality of life. We're not supposed to deal with compensation when we address an issue, but you turn it on it's head in the sense that if somebody came to me and said, "Well, I'll give you $5,000 if you let me put an oil well on your front lawn in front of your bungalow in Calgary." I would say, "Forget it." But if they said, "I'll give you half a million dollars if you let me put an oil well on."

and I would say, "Well, put one in the backyard, too." I mean suddenly, you know, everything is relative.

Maybe what the companies need to have, and certainly it would make your decision-making a little more straightforward, is an economic formula that would allow them to make some of those decisions such that at some point in time, they own your farm. But maybe at the end of the day you don't mind because you've got enough money in the bank. You'll buy the next half dozen quarters to the west or to the east.

Mr. Irving
Yes, you see, that's definitely the point I agree on. The way the regulating bodies, the pipeline companies deal now is, it's property value, and the amounts of land in that easement that they are taking with the right-of-way. So I don't think the issue now is establishing compensation based on that. I think it's establishing compensation based on loss of rights. And I don't know how you put a dollar value on that, and when I say "loss of rights," I mean a loss of quiet enjoyment of our land. I don't know how you put a dollar value on that, but I know that that's what we feel is being taken by developing a right-of-way is our rights rather than our actual property, if that makes any sense.

Mr. Crabtree
At what point should the applicant or should the regulator back up and take a look at an alternate major corridor approach rather than going down the same old path?

Mr. Arvedlund
Well, I would say up to about a year or two ago, we never got to that point. I think the Federal Government, and particularly the land management agencies, absolutely made you stay in corridors. They didn't entertain ideas like leaving the corridor, or if they did, they definitely were going to put you through some hoops. You would not, for example, leave a corridor and probably get an environmental assessment. You would absolutely get environmental impact at the same time. So, leaving the corridor means a process of one or two years or maybe more instead of eight or nine months. It's an environmental decision, but it's also a very economic one to the company, because time is money. A gas pipeline, and I suspect with oil pipelines, the applicants are in a hurry. They want it now. And they can't afford a year's delay, so the route will be in the corridor one way or the other.

Now, particularly with landowners becoming more vocal, more aware and having more access to the government, I think, you better listening to them. We don't consider compensation in the formula of how we make decisions. Compensation is dealt with between landowner and an applicant or in the courts. You know sometimes I think certain regulatory people think that their landowner is using it to get a better price, and that's unfortunate. That's a crappy attitude to have, but people do have it, you know. I don't and my staff doesn't, but I can assure you in terms of routing, I can't think of a case where we thought about compensation being the answer. I'll leave it at that.

Dr. Maehr
I work as a consultant and as a scientist. I am a troubleshooter and have development issues, and it sure seems to me that we're doing our best here on the panel so far to skirt the issue of the environment. We are talking about economics. We are talking about legal issues and about quality of life issues, which I think are very important.

I would ask, how serious is the environment being considered by these big organizations? Is the environment truly a serious part of the process? How important is the environment? We find ourselves talking about these more practical human issues. Where does the environment fit in?

Mr. Kobasa
Well, I think the human species has taken the back seat to those environmental considerations regarding pipelines. I've been involved with two major corporations and started my construction activities on-shore and offshore back in 1968. Working for two major corporations and being an officer since 1980, I would say that, at least in my company, environmental considerations were always in the forefront of anything we did.

Mr. Sawyer
I would like to follow up on that and make a point that I think is relevant. If you look at the legislative and regulatory concepts of the United States versus Canada, there are some significant differences. For example, a lot of Americans make some assumptions about regulatory process. You know, you've got the Species Act, you've got the Clean Air and Water Act, and you've got others. In the Canadian context, there are no equivalents. When a person from an America company makes statements that those issues are forefront, it's probably because they have to be forefront because there is some specific legal requirements to address those issues.

In Canada, unless Brian significantly disagrees with me, I think it's a fair statement to say we don't have most of those laws and regulatory infrastructure. I think that's worth considering in the broad discussion of corridors in North America.

Dr. Bietz
Well, I think to some degree that Mike is correct. Specific laws are only as good as they are implemented, and the best law in the world doesn't necessarily accomplish things that you want to do if there are a ton of exemptions.

Just to get back to your question of the environmental issue, it is an interesting one. In my own particular position, my job is to not be an advocate for anything, which, if you know me very well, has always been a pretty uncomfortable position for me to be in, and I've learned to quell at least some of my impulses. But when I try to make these decisions, I am looking for others to argue those positions, so what tends to happen is, on public lands versus private lands you get into a different advocacy type of situation. When I'm dealing with an issue on public lands, I have a company coming forward with its position and it's got a bias, there's no question. I'm looking to the land managers to present that second position, and then quite often Mike and others present a position where, you know, that's quite a bit stronger with regards to environmental protection.

I'm actually limited in a sense. I can only address what I hear, and if those arguments aren't made in front of me in those cases, then I work with the evidence that I have. And it's an interesting process, and as a scientist I find very frustrating at times. The lawyers, however, will tell you it's the only way it can work. I guess the bottom line is, balance. If next to James, is 25 square miles of unbroken prairie, while James has half a dozen pipelines on his land, that's a really tough trade-off between green field corridor through native prairie and the existing corridor. I know personally that I would struggle with trying to find the balance.

Mr. Irving
Yes, I find that interesting, and John brought that up, too, about how the environment takes precedence or what seems to take precedence, over, I guess, human issues, land owner issues. I'll just give you a quick example with the latest pipeline that's gone through our property. One of our major concerns, is the intersection being so close to our farm yard, our house, things like that. And just down the way, the pipeline had actually been shifted in order to move around, I think it was peppered frogs, in a valley area.

And then when it came to our intersection, first of all, we didn't want the pipeline, and second of all, if it was going to go through, we wanted it farther away from where we live. And the kind of reaction we got out of it was, "Well, you'll move that pipeline for these frogs, but then for us, you know, you won't move it." So it is frustrating.

Mr. Crabtree
I can understand where you are. Let me ask, when is a green field corridor the best solution?

Mr. Sawyer
In the context of these proceedings we're talking about utility corridors, power lines, right-of-ways, highways, transportation infrastructure. But when I look at this question of green fields, I tend to fall on Dave's side of the equation. I look at it from a conservation/biologist's point of view. A corridor is a route that allows movement of individuals or species across the landscape. And there is a gap between those two things, and they're important to consider.

I want to propose a different definition of corridors from a utilitarian point of view — corridors are a linear tract of land used for human purposes that fragments natural landscapes and creates barriers to the movement of individuals or species across that landscape. Now, that may have different intensities depending on the context of any given project, but you know, I think that's true about all corridors, whether they are green field or not.

And the issue here is habitat fragmentation. The reason it's an issue is because we are entering into a significant period of extinction. To what extent do you consider that in making any individual decision?

It's reasonably well documented in the US, that there are over 750 species that are listed as threatened or endangered, and another three or 4000 that are potentially listed. Worldwide habitat fragmentation and habitat loss are the biggest single factor in putting the species at risk.

How do corridors affect landscapes and fragment lands?
I'm going to use an Alberta boreal forest example. The boreal forest occupies about 50% of the province, over 300,000 square km. This is a photograph taken from the late 1940s, an aerial photograph in the Swan Hills area of the boreal forest, and it shows a relatively pristine landscape without any linear features. This is what the same area looked like 12 years later. There was a significant oil pool discovered there. We have well sites. We have roads, pipelines, seismic lines and the landscape becomes more fractured. By the early 1980s, the forest industry had recognized that now that we have access to this landscape, we can actually go in and log. In addition, there's additional oil and gas development, and the landscape, in a very short period of time, is progressively becoming more and more fragmented.

Here's what the area looked like in the early 1990s. In a 40-year period, the area went from a pristine landscape to a landscape that is highly fractured and has really caused a lot of problem from a wildlife point of view. Now, some might suggest that this is just a nice little example for the sake of making a point. In fact, it's not that isolated an example. Let me show you some numbers.

In the boreal forest in Alberta, we have over 660,000 km of seismic lines since 1986 alone. Those seismic lines occupy a physical footprint of over 5000 square km. We've got over 100,000 wells with a physical footprint of over 2500 square km; 160,000 km of well access roads alone; with a 2400 km square footprint; 95,000 km of pipeline right-of-way, and an unknown amount of power line right-of-way, and these add up to over a 98 million km of linear disturbance or corridors which have a 12,000 square km physical footprint on that landscape. And that doesn't include the forest fragmentation from forest harvesting, agricultural conversion, utilities or other public transportation infrastructure.

When we look at this, we now have 74% of this landscape that has fragmented linear disturbance densities greater than one kilometer per kilometer square, that's about 74% of that landscape. Only 12% of that landscape remains roadless or uncorridored. Of course, these all have serious implications for wildlife species — wolves, grizzly bears, and others. The bottom line here is that, whether you call it the tragedy of small decisions or just simply call it the accumulative effects question, we have failed as a society to control the proliferation of corridors, for whatever purposes they are, and that, at the end of the day, is going to really exacerbate the extinction crisis and associated issues.

And I think what this screams out for, and I'm using an Alberta example here, but I'm sure we can find other examples where other people operate, what it says about corridors and neglected management in general is that we have to come up with scientifically and socially defensible thresholds that we determine in advance of any particular project. So that when a developer comes forward, he says, "this landscape is already full" or "it has some additional capacity," or "alternatively, I would have to free up some capacity by doing some restoration work in some way."

But in the absence of defined defensible scientifically and socially embedded thresholds, it's just going to be development, ad hoc development, every incremental proposal gets approved and we end up with landscapes that look like this, which are essentially void of any natural functioning. So I think the question, "When is it appropriate to have a green field versus an existing right-of-way?" I think it's a site specific, a landscape specific question. Obviously in a landscape like that, the corridor questions are irrelevant. It's already trashed and it doesn't really matter where you go.

If you have a relatively pristine landscape and you want to manage it, obviously it makes sense. Corridors make sense in other situations. At the end of the day, if we pay attention to managing the environmental aspects on a landscape scale, it really comes down to site-specific factors that decide between the two options.

Mr. Crabtree
When is a corridor too full?

Mr. Sawyer
Well, I think the solution to that is to work with the best available science to actually identify what the various biological thresholds that need to be applied and use that as the planning context to make the decisions about corridor routing and corridor proliferation.

Mr. Arvedlund
Yes, I don't think Brian would agree with you.

Mr. Sawyer
That wouldn't be a surprise.

Mr. Arvedlund
I feel the frustration of the landowners more so in the last couple of years than before. I just don't totally believe that there's an instant answer to, "When is enough enough?" because unless you can straighten somewhat by the width, you would just keep extending the width until you just physically ran out of room. So what might start out as a 200-foot corridor suddenly is a one-mile or two-mile corridor. And, if you're focusing on fragmentation issues, I don't think the average land owner could give a damn about that issue versus "I've got too much," you know, put it on somebody else's, let them go share the misery. Unfortunately, when you get to the new landowner, he or she feels the same way. You know, put it on Brian's land.

They're both legitimate comments, but I don't think the Federal Government has that answer. I don't have the answer, I know that.

Mr. Kobasa
Allen, I would like throw out an example, if I may. This situation might not apply because of site-specific things, but about 1967, I believe it was Shell Oil Company found the first Niagarin gas reef in the State of Michigan. This reef was defined several years later as running diagonally across the north central part of the State, from the Lake Huron coast line to the Lake Michigan coast line maybe some 300 miles overall. The State of Michigan, in concert with the producers, required one pipeline, one large gathering header that would carry both the condensates and natural gas that would be built along the trend, and then the producers would have to get transportation rights.

As the reefs were developed, there were over 200 reefs discovered, those then fed into that central header, so now you have each individual line, so to speak, coming in from the reservoirs. There was recognition back than what this pipe was going to look like overall in some master plan development, and eventually that master plan was pretty well followed.

Mr. Crabtree

You may also remember the Pigeon River saga. Here's a case where Shell and Amoco and some other developers as well wanted to develop the area. Pigeon River is state forest, and there was a lot of concern about fragmentation and what development is going to do to the elk habitat. It wasn't just the drilling of wells and the access roads. It was the treatment facilities and the gathering lines as well.

Ultimately, the field was developed, put under production and the elk herd has prospered, but that's kind of the exception rather than the rule. And it took an awful lot of work, and I'm not sure how applicable it is everywhere, but — Brian, you were shaking your head a moment ago.

Dr. Bietz

I was going to say, actually, I don't disagree with a thing that Mike is saying. I think he raises some very, very good points.

If I'm addressing a corridor in public lands, for example, and one of my major issues is environmental, then absolutely. If I have a threshold that I can measure that expansion, that corridor against, it makes my job infinitely easier. Mike is absolutely right. Then you look at the trade-offs between a new line versus expanding an existing corridor. If I can see evidence that says, well, look, I can make that corridor another 40 m wider, suddenly a whole group of species that normally was to go across 10 m, that won't go across 50 m, then my decisions become a little easier in terms of, well, maybe a green field corridor makes some sense.

I think the issue of compensation in terms of companies offering to do other things to balance off some of the new impacts, that's an area I don't think that has really been explored very well. I think some of the stuff that's been done so far is — it's not a lip service, but I don't think it's been all that practical. You know, I think as regulators, we've asked companies to do things, in my mind, they're much more effective types of compensation than we have asked for in the past. I find those are all very, very positive suggestions.

In terms of the coordination development, you're right, oil and gas companies are very difficult to get to coordinate. They're a competitive business by nature. The only real way in my mind that you do that is you tie future approvals to the success of the coordination, so that companies, when they go back to the boardrooms and they explain why they're now cooperating with what used to be their corporate enemy out there, they can go back and say again, "those bastards at the board" are making us do it. Future approvals are going to be tied to success. So there's a lot of opportunities out there for us to move forward with some new models.

Dr. Maehr

I think you're hinting at another issue and that is a development of what we want the future to look like, and environmental issues are very emotional ones in the US and I assume they're becoming increasingly so in Canada.

I think you can have more development as long as it's in keeping with some accepted vision by all parties. The compensation idea is something I'm involved in more and more in the consulting work I do in Florida. I encourage the developers and regulators to look at ways to compensate for losses of natural resources, wildlife species habitat in recreating it or promoting mitigation that actually makes things better once that development project is over with.

Mr. Crabtree

David, could you share with us what your corridors have on green field?

Dr. Maehr

In 1970, it was not even believed that the Florida panther still existed in the State of Florida, let alone in the southeast where it once raced around the southeast coastal plain. And over the course of 30 years, the panther became very popular with the public. School children designated it as the State mammal for the State of Florida and research on the panther continues today.

The Florida panther was a phoenix rising out of the ashes on its own accord as researchers studied where they were and what their problems were. And the basic problem was the panther does not have sufficient space. We can talk about genetics and problems associated with small populations, which are exacerbated by highways and utility corridors, but in fact, the problem is space. As an example, consider the movement of a single male panther moving away from its natural range, the place where it was born, in seeking a new home range for itself. And in this case the panther went from the big cypress swamp in south Florida and made it to within about four miles of the Epcot Centre in Orlando, a tremendous dispersal of over 200 km.

It was a very frustrated dispersal for him because he went to a place where there were no other panthers. There's highways, there's canals in here, there's all kinds of problems, but the animals are demonstrating the biological potential to commonize habitat. What we need to do is retrofit the landscaping in such a way that we could get females to move across these obstacles and barriers and filters that were created by humans.

One of the problems we have to overcome as the conservation biologist is not appearing too radical in our thinking. We can't move too quickly or we're shot down immediately. But one of the things that might sound strange to you is this whole idea of the park paradigm. I'm talking about the wonderful system of parks that now surface the globe, which started at the Yellowstone National Park. The Yellowstone, Yosemite, this idea of being able to capture by diversity and beautiful landscapes and postage stamp areas around the country, representatives of what we had, before our various countries were settled.

Conservation biologists now realize that parks in and of themselves were not enough. There is not a single national park in North America that in and of itself is capable of supporting all the native mammal species that were there originally. And so this begs the question of connecting or reconnecting those landscapes in such a way that regions can maintain those species that otherwise would be lost if all we had left were the parks.

Some of you may be aware of a great effort, you may hear about it later in the conference, the wild lands project would connect existing reserves with corridors and buffer zones in promoting large carnivores in recreating movement between these areas. And utility corridors, highways are a problem. They're still barriers. And from a strictly conservation/biologist's view, piggybacking as many of these corridors on top of each other, I think, is a benefit for diversity in minimizing the impacts of such a development on processes, such as, water flow, fire, parasitism, these sorts of things that are all natural processes that are interrupted by utility corridors, highways.

So I think my answer is pretty clear on new green field utility corridors. They are something to be avoided because they promote habitat fragmentation. It's being completely cold and mean to the other human issues that I think are also important. But strictly by a diversity concept, I think multiple utilities in a single corridor is the way to go.

I would challenge all of you in the room to think of ways that this process connection promotes that diversity. Are there other ways that landscapes can be retrofit by putting in new corridors? Can there be certain attributes in the landscape that can be restored and forests be planted in association with a new corridor? And I think as we see the wild lands project take off and become more accepted by the public, and this is an international effort now, we'll see it as possibilities increase.

Mr. Crabtree
Are there instances where a utility corridor can also function as a transportation corridor for wildlife?

Dr. Maehr
Where you create early successional habitats, you may encourage things like tortoises and sparrows and things that might otherwise be rare, as agriculture creates problems. You also invite exotic colonization; exotic species moving in, weedy species and you create edge effects that make it more difficult, more area sensitive than interior for species to survive.

But certainly I think it makes great sense to me to have power line corridors associated with highways, pipelines as well in those systems. You may have tremendous impacts in that particular corridor, but I think you're minimizing the overall sprawl of the various footprints of those types of utilities.

Mr. Crabtree
Do we have the right tools to answer the problem; or what tools do we need?

Mr. Arvedlund
Well, I don't think we have the right tools. I don't even think the Federal Government; the various agencies are talking among themselves about this problem. What needs to be fixed is recognizing the problem and even just sitting down and seeing if there's some common ground. I have a feeling there's not a common ground. You've got to go down to the local state agencies, and then how do you fit the landowner into the equation?

I think if you put all of those people in the same room, they would all walk out mad. So, I don't have the solution, and I didn't come here to try and say there was a solution. I certainly see the problem. I'm glad that this is one of the first conferences that I've come to that is at least openly airing to the subject. I think it's discussed behind closed doors or maybe, you know, on phone calls, but never quite open like this, so maybe this is a good start. In the Federal Government, I know there's a difference of opinion among the land agencies and the regulatory groups on this issue. I think, somewhere along the line we're just going to have to bring it out more and more. Maybe in future conferences like this we can get some of the land management agencies and maybe some state agencies as well, because I suspect they may even have more points than I have.

Dr. Maehr
In reference to tools, they're out there and available to us, to address potential problems.

This is a photograph of a wildlife underpass that was constructed when alligator alley was replaced with I-75, and it now connects Naples with the southern part of Florida. There were 30 of these things installed and it cost them about $800,000 apiece and they were heralded as a wonderful success. Panthers use them, at least six or seven out of 30, and so one could argue that indeed maybe they're not much of a success, but that all has to do more with landscaping configuration where the forest is than anything else.

The fact is, the underpass has reduced highway mortality on the Florida panther and other wildlife, and it may well be a very useful solution in some situations. The problem with having tools like this is I think it eases our guard — it allows us to lower our guard with some of the overall bigger arching —

overarching effects that new highway construction can bring.

Can we really solve the problems of fragmentation by putting in underpasses like this? I would say we can solve some of them, but we can't solve all of them. We might be able to fix problems with existing roads by retrofitting them with underpasses, but we need to be careful in avoiding looking at underpasses and overpasses as a panacea, but it definitely is one of the many tools that is out there.

Mr. Sawyer

I want to go back to the question of thresholds and I think until we, as a society, are able to step back and do some broad landscape scale planning so that we can decide on what that vision is and what the criteria to measure whether they were being successful or not. We always get bogged down in projects specific, get into the regulatory process, my sense is that that is, until we break out of this pattern, we are doomed to make small incremental decisions.

And even if a project is well planned and well implemented, there is always some incremental loss of habitat or fragmentation. And so the end result after years of ad hoc decisions, we end up with some serious problems. So I think we need a fundamental reshaping of how we think about resource development and what kind of planning context.

I wanted to raise one other point, which is fundamental, do we need these facilities? This is a broad topic. We could talk about this for a long time, but one of the things we don't talk about is demand for energy. And there's a lot of potential benefits from looking at how do we manage the demand for energy on the consumptive end, and does that trickle back up stream.

So, no, maybe we don't need that extra pipeline, and I imagine it can apply to transportation or any type of utility. And I think this needs to be considered in that big picture view that we need to adopt.

Mr. Arvedlund

It also applies, actually, to other resources as well. Do you build a new reservoir or do you have water conservation? We're focusing very hard on the regulated utilities, and yet, we have as many effects on wildlife habitat, on societal problems, on growth and development from what essentially are not federally and not provincially regulated type of problems, such as housing, for example, and some of the other items. So, I think we need to put this in the whole context.

Mr. Sawyer

And the approach that I would envision would capture those small decisions.

Mr. Kobasa

In the US, those of us in our industry have developed a good working relationship with our regulators as new issues have come up, and we've tried to sit down and tried to resolve them. But you know, in the US industry, the corridor concept was kind of no brainer up until about the mid 80s. We were regulated monopolies on the pipeline side and we all had our markets that we served, and nobody else went into those markets. You added capacity, you looped your existing systems and you stayed right along that corridor, so to speak, unless you had some other kind of deviation that was admissible.

The industry started to get deregulated with pipe to pipe competition in the late 80s. The pipes started going to other regions, connecting to different sources of supply, so this started to bring in new routing issues. Not every utility starts at the same place and goes to the same place, not even for incremental addition. So you have to say, "when can you use the corridor and when can't you use the corridor" and in the example I illustrated, there are areas where we are using corridors because it didn't pose any objectionable consequences that could be dealt with.

Mr. Irving

I think technology and a massive change of life-style into the future is going to provide the change, which is going to fix our situation. A change of life-style, where we have people trying to find other ways like solar power where you won't need a corridor with pipelines transporting natural gas to provide that energy. The answer is turning to other ways of providing that energy, and I think that will help the environment, too.

Mr. Crabtree

There are a lot of things, frankly, about corridors that we haven't talked about yet, and we could probably go on all day. There's a problem of putting two pipelines together. Are you reducing the risk of synergistic explosions? If one goes up, how far away does the other have to be? The problems of future maintenance in crossing over pipelines or working under a power line. The problems of different types of utilities running together.

Let open up the session for comments from the audience, and see if there's anything you would like to direct it to the panel as a whole or to any member of the panel.

Mr. Gartman

Well, let me give a comment as a recently retired environmental person from Columbia Energy or Columbia Gas Transmission. As far as compensation, this was addressed quite a bit, and the implication generally of eminent domain is sacrifices for the benefit of many, and maybe it's time we rethink that in terms of maybe some sacrifices of the people who are receiving this benefit for the benefit of the few that can be in terms of dollars, significant amounts, double trouble, whatever, but eminent domain has to be reconsidered.

Regarding technology, I don't know if directional drilling would have made a big difference for James's farm, but it certainly could have eliminated a lot of the surface disturbance, and so we've got methods now to go under the frog habitat and put the pipeline there if you didn't want it through your wheat field, and so those are things we can deal with. And one of the things also, all of this, the Swan Hills implications, habitat loss and such, of course, gets into the sticky issue which we won't get into, the growth in population. If you look at the population of North America when James's grandfather had his farm there, established the farm, compared to the population of North America today, I think you'll see that curve reflect just about all the problems that we're going to be talking about during this seminar. So that's my comment.

Mr. Crabtree
Would anybody on the panel like to comment?

Mr. Kobasa
Yes, I would be imposing a viewpoint on eminent domain in reconsidering eminent domain as related I think to gas pipelines. Non-regulated people like the oil companies certainly don't have federal protection, aren't under the Natural Gas Act, they can charge anything they want for their product. They have to go out and negotiate without the power of eminent domain as a rule.

I think as long as the gas pipeline industry has its rights regulated, there has to be a provision that allows us to say, what is fair and just compensation that I might have to pay for for my rights-of-way as I planned and execute projects? I can't go out and make a deal with a company to provide some service for them at some guaranteed rate without going into cases every year without having some basis for a fair pricing of the land I'm using relative to saying, I don't have the rights of eminent domain. Therefore, the last guy that wants to hold me up to keep my project from happening is the guy that's going to get the most money. There needs to be the balance that we talked about, and I think as long as our rates are regulated, I think we need the ability to have eminent domain as well as many other industries.

Mr. Crabtree
Anyone else on the panel want to comment?

Dr. Maehr
Well, look at the endangered species in the United States, and we, as citizens, voted for these types of legislation, and then we need to pay. If the landowner is losing some rights to develop his or her land, that person needs to be compensated from us, citizens of a country that voted for and supported that legislation.

So while I'm a proponent of saying I think eminent domain laws should be available to us in the gas industry, I'm just as firmly a proponent that land owners ought to be fairly compensated for what they're giving up as we build facilities across their land. I think we need imminent domain to be successful in the business. On the other hand, landowners should be fairly compensated for what they're giving up as a part of having that utility constructed. They're not mutually exclusive.

Mr. Crabtree
Another question, please?

Mr. Lind
My name is David Lind with the Land and Forest Service here in Alberta. I would to direct a comment to Brian.

One of the concerns we have as land managers is that there doesn't seem to be much of a concern, about the management of the right-of-way. No one has ever sat back and thought, well, what about when they committed that right-of-way we asked them to put in two pipelines of a certain size, one now being available for future use. When you move that right-of-way over five miles, now you've just created a problem down the road five miles over. If we could get some of the companies to work together and work on larger, Brian, are there any restraints right now, at least from the Alberta standpoint, in allowing that to happen?

Dr. Bietz
Yes, probably the fundamental restraint in terms of oil and gas development, and that's probably true for others, is your ability to predict into the future. I think it would be pretty hard to convince somebody to put parallel 36-inch pipeline into a corridor today on the anticipation of future gas, because that assumes that we will need to develop all those wells eventually to fill that pipeline. I think we really are starting to move to some degree in that direction in terms of asking companies to take these broader perspectives. How successful we're going to be is really yet to be seen.

Mr. Arvedlund
Well, that's the problem, you have to pay arbitrarily say twice the amount for another pipe and that's very hard to justify at a rate hearing. We have had some companies actually build larger diameter pipelines, which might be a little bit better answer than a wider corridor.

I like that idea, but you do have to convince not only regulators, but the people ultimately paying for the pipe that their costs are going to be higher today, but may be lower down the road. But I would rather see something like that in terms of bigger pipes, you know, that you can then expand later and maybe even higher pressure pipe so that you can expand later.

Mr. Sawyer

I just wanted to pick up on the comment from the gentleman from the Alberta Forest Service and point out the irony of the question, because we have Brian who is with the Alberta Energy Utility Board whose jurisdiction is to regulate energy projects, but they have no jurisdiction over the land. On the other hand, we have the forest service, which has the legislative jurisdiction to manage the land, but they have no jurisdiction over the activities.

It's that dysfunctional delegation of jurisdictions which results in those kinds of landscapes. So I thought it was kind of interesting, you know, that they don't talk. As a general rule they don't talk about how they're going to manage these things. So I wanted to point that out, it just struck me as an ironic situation.

But I also wanted to raise something particularly about costs and our — particularly in North America — our almost religious infatuation with this so-called market place and using the market as the determining factor. The problem with the marketplace is that it doesn't really exist and it doesn't really work, and there's all sorts of infractions with it. The point is, that when you get down to dealing with issues like quality of life, air issues, wildlife issues, fisheries issues, all these sort of things that the market doesn't capture.

So if we're using the marketplace as our decision-making of goal posts, but it doesn't consider most of the things that we want to consider, then clearly we have a problem. And I think that is one of the underlying root causes of many of our problems here is the over reliance on a marketplace that doesn't work.

Mr. Colson

I suggest that the marketplace did truly work, and perhaps it could in relation to another industry like the communications industry where they have to bid on building a particular project or a bid for an airway. What if the government was in a position to suggest that a particular developer wants to propose a pipeline project from point A to point B that it goes after a competitive bid. All these aspects will certainly arise, and then perhaps the issues would be deliberated with a greater forum. We would all wish that the best project would be built, not just one favored by a particular industry or a particular company.

Mr. Crabtree

And what would be the context for that? Would there be some type of new regulatory process?

Mr. Colson

It involves more government intervention, which is certainly something the capital, markets don't desire. Similar to what was going on in California with the Public Utility Commission. They decided what was in the best interest of Californians, and they sat and decided on who was going to build what route where.

Mr. Crabtree

And as I recall it was popular, too.

Mr. Colson

Yes, it was until they built too many projects.

Mr. Crabtree

Yes. Anyone have any comments to Ed's question? Interesting concept.

Mr. Bietz

It is, but in my mind it raises even a more fundamental question for me. I think that it goes back to the vision question. I don't think we even have a real good vision, what we believe is good environmental protection. But I suspect a grain farmer in Saskatchewan has quite a different vision than an oilman in Calgary or a forester in Grande Prairie in terms of what does the public really want in terms of environmental protection?

Some of you might know that we've got a real good berry crop this year and we've got a lot of grizzly bears coming down to the low country in Kananaskis. If you drive up there on the weekend, you're going to see a lot of yellow tape. It looks like somebody got murdered up there, but what it is is, they're just keeping you off the trails because they're trying to avoid conflict with the bears.

The interesting thing, there are two letters to the Herald, and let me add, we have had three maulings, no deaths, and interestingly, the people that were actually hurt, their reaction was, "well, we shouldn't have been there in the first place, it really isn't the bear's fault." When you read the newspaper articles there is a little bit of a dynamic. Well, the two letters were great, because they just show you how wide we are in this, and really still today. One letter said very clearly, "look, it's time the human beings stayed out of these areas, this is where bears live." The other letter was the exact opposite. "There's 10 to 15,000 bears in northern BC and Alaska, why in the world are we putting up with these wild savage animals when we're trying to enjoy our recreation?"

The problem that I have is, I don't know for sure just how widely those two positions really are held by the general public. And so that goes back to this whole vision question. I would like to think that we really put value on Florida panthers. I would love to believe that as a society. If there was a major gas shortage in the US, how long do you think it would be before we developed offshore fields in Florida? That's a question I'm not sure we really have the answers to in terms of our vision. I kind of digressed, but it sort of goes back to the economic model. Maybe we were prepared to pay for that, but I'm not sure as a society we really answered that. I'm not sure that I could ask a guy on the street, "How much are you prepared to really protect James's life-style?" and I don't know what answer I would get.

Dr. Maehr

Perhaps if I had more practicality or application if we controlled our own human population growth, I mean, that's the big wild card, and that's one thing we really can't address here.

Mr. McLoughlin

I used to be involved in routing transmission lines back in the 70s, and then in the early 80s, I was a project manager for a project entitled Environmental Externalities in New York State. I think that's what you've been talking about. Along with deregulation, energy conservation, demand side planing, environmental externalities have been cast aside in favor of direct market costs. I think what a lot of people are trying to get at here is the contingent valuation concept in economics, looking at those non-market values, willingness to pay, how much is something worth to us; willingness to be compensated for certain impacts. It's not a pure science. It's very subjective. As we said, the man on the street said, where do you go to get that information? It's a very subjective type of evaluation.

But looking back at all the impacts, in New York we're looking at natural gas as the fuel of choice. But you look back at the up stream costs of all the impacts that are occurring to get that natural gas to New York, this is where environmental externalities analysis can play a role, and unfortunately it is not conducted in New York.

Mr. Sawyer

I like what I hear there, and I would just like to point out one thing. This discussion that a lot of the energy use in the States is shifting to gas is because gas has been sold as a green fuel. If you look just at the burner tip, at the emissions and the cost, that's probably a true statement. But when you do a full cycle analysis and look at all of the upstream costs, both direct and externalities cost, that argument isn't as clear as it could be.

One of the things that I've been trying to get to are regulators, and people here in Alberta at the National Energy Board is to start considering the whole picture, and so far we haven't done that. The reality is, when we're talking about energy and energy management on a continental basis, if we actually start looking at full cycle costs and benefits we would be surprised at how inefficient we are using our resources. I think that doing a full cycle analysis would show us some real startling pictures, which would change how we treat energy in our society.

Mr. Goodrich-Mahoney

I would like to take a pessimistic viewpoint about what we're discussing today. I think one of the keys that I think Bob brought up earlier on that has not been discussed in full is fragmentation of the environment and its potential impact on the land and species.

But there also the continual disruption of the land by energy projects, which may be more important. I suspect that if James had those six pipelines put in at the same time, he would not have the same level of objection that he does today. He is faced with a continual process of development, which impedes his use and enjoyment of his land.

We need better metrics for assessing and analyzing costs and we need to integrate the public and regulatory process so that more individuals are talking to each other to reach a consensus on energy projects. I also think we need a longer term vision somewhat a kin to what Chief Whitney said about the next seven generations earlier today.

Mr. Crabtree

Anyone on the panel want to comment?

Mr. Kobasa

I don't know how we get a long-term vision. It certainly seems like something you can't be against, but how you get to that is a mind-boggling issue. It's hard enough to see a year down the road in the business with all the changes that are going on, let alone with somebody with the wisdom to say, "here is what we see 500 years up."

I mean, those are nice concepts. The reality is you're faced with it today, you're faced with it tomorrow and the next day, and to try to say "where are we." I've been through months of five-year planning programs, 10-year planning programs at corporations, and after the plan is reviewed and put to print, a month later it was almost useless.

Things are changing so fast in our society, but it's not that we shouldn't be thinking about those things. Certainly we need people thinking about, "where are we going in the future?" But we also have to say this has to be living and breathing thing and it's going to change, and we realize it's going to change. We should be thinking about the future, no question. But to think somehow we're going to predict 500 years from now or a hundred years from now or even 20 years from now is a major assumption, I think. We need to be thinking about the future, but we need to be making sure we're flexible enough in our plans to be able to direct them the right way, and the conditions change because change is inevitable.

Mr. Sawyer

Well, this may be a perverse sense of optimism. If we get into a hard winter this year, with our gas supply problems and lack of storage and the tying of electricity costs to gas now, we can expect to see dramatically increasing consumer costs for energy. That might take the North American population out of their assumption that they're being taken care of, everything is fine, and it might be that shift in public perception of energy that helps us move to this longer term vision.

So even though the energy — the looming winter energy crisis is maybe upon us any day, I think it's a good thing and it will help us move in the right direction.

Mr. Crabtree
Well, we're just about out of time, and I just want to thank, first of all, the panel for your comments and your insights, and I want to thank all of you who asked questions. And I have a charge for all of you. I started out by saying we didn't have the answers for you, and it's clear from listening to all of us talk up here that we sure don't have the answers. More over there isn't one answer that fits all situations.

I am optimistic, however, I've seen when we didn't have a lot of the knowledge and the tools that we have now. But, I'm also frustrated as a former of state and federal bureaucrat that a lot of times we don't have the tools, a lot of times we hamper ourselves with our own making, our own regulations, and certainly the communication is not as good as it could be. I would like to think we're making progress.

I would like to ask each of you to please send your comments in, because this is an area that deserves a closer look in the future. Your suggestions would be most welcome.

At that, I would like to thank all of you for spending time with us this morning.

Mr. Mutrie
I didn't quite know what to expect this morning. We wanted a lively debate and we got one, and I think that's great. So, anyway, on behalf of Colin, the steering committee, and myself I would really like to thank Allen and the entire panel for just a wonderful job. Thank you very much.

BIOGRAPHICAL SKETCH

Allen F. Crabtree
Navigant Consulting, Inc. 703 Bridgton, Sebago, ME 04029. Allen_crabtree@rminc.com. Phone: 207-787-2531
Allen Crabtree is a Principal with Navigant Consulting, Inc., an international management consulting firm, providing services to the power and water industries, among others. Mr. Crabtree was formerly Senior Vice President of the Environmental Division with Resource Management, Inc. until that firm was acquired by Navigant Consulting in 1997. He has been with RMI/Navigant since 1991. Prior to 1991, Mr. Crabtree was a private consultant with an environmental consulting firm in New Hampshire, Executive Director of the New Hampshire Fish and Game Department, Assistant Division Chief of the Geological Survey Division, Michigan Department of Natural Resources, several management positions with the Environmental Enforcement Division, Michigan DNR, the Michigan Public Service Commission, and worked at the Federal Power Commission in Washington, DC.

Part II
Vegetation Management

Integrated Vegetation Management
The Exploration of a Concept to Application

Kevin McLoughlin

With the seminal "Position Paper" issued (first released as an internal working paper format in the early 1990s) by the member utilities of the New York Power Pool entitled "Application of Integrated Pest Management to Electric Utility Right-of-Way Vegetation Management in New York State" the phrase Integrated Vegetation Management (IVM) was utilized, defined, and described in detail as being a more functional term. This IPM/IVM Position Paper described how many commonly accepted Integrated Pest Management (IPM) precepts (tactics and program elements) are incorporated into contemporary electric transmission right-of-way (ROW) vegetation management programs in New York State. As a result, the acronym IVM has since become synonymous with ROW vegetation management and is now used throughout the industry as an ambiguous descriptive term for virtually all ROW vegetation management activities. Unfortunately, the term IVM means different things to different people. The deployment of herbicides to achieve many of the goals and objectives of an authentic IVM program needs to be based upon the appropriate principles and practices of the much more rigorously established IPM body of knowledge. In order to gain scientific credibility and regulatory and public acceptance the entire concept of IVM (as a distinct subset of IPM) needs to be thoroughly "thought out" so that all it's various assumptions and premises are easily recognized and the benefits to be derived from the application of IVM are transparent to all. This paper will attempt to evaluate the original IPM/IVM Position Paper and focus on the rationale for the changes that have been made (and those that haven't) in the revised 2000 edition of this IPM/IVM Position Paper. The concepts espoused in this IPM/IVM Position Paper have now been subject to nearly 10 years of application experience and thus a more detailed understanding of how well the various ROW vegetation management practices qualify under the rubric of commonly accepted IPM (IVM) principles is needed.

Keywords: Rights-of-way, ROW, vegetation management, integrated pest management, IPM, integrated vegetation management, IVM, herbicides, pesticides

INTRODUCTION

The phrase Integrated Vegetation Management, IVM, has in a few short years become the expression of choice when referring to the management of right-of-way (ROW) vegetation, particularly when herbicides are the primary method of controlling the unwanted plant growth. More specifically, for the management of vegetation on electric transmission line ROW, the term IVM is now ubiquitous used and is virtually synonymous with these efforts. Practically every electric utility, contractor, chemical company, and consulting firm involved with ROW vegetation management espouse an adherence to all IVM principals and practices. This is especially true for those employing the various designated techniques commonly recognized in the industry as "best management practices" (BMPs), as determined by almost anything that is deemed appropriate and applicable within the burgeoning field of endeavor labeled IVM. This new moniker of IVM also allows one to embrace a generally well accepted concept that is recognized, by most, as a quite legitimate equivalent surrogate for the much more widely acknowledged pest control strategy, Integrated Pest Management (IPM). Moreover, the term IVM is actually more descriptive in respect to the field of ROW vegetation management than the much better known and historically well developed and mature term IPM. Let's face it, no one really likes to refer to a tree (well at least most trees) as a pest!

BACKGROUND

In the mid 1980s a major regulatory push for IPM occurred in New York State. Many of the definitions proposed during this period[1] by those desiring to discourage pesticide usage included such items as only using the least toxic alternatives and that pesticides should be used only as a last resort if nothing else will control the pest. At this point in time, if one were a pesticide user, a close acquaintance with the more commonly recognized basic tenets of IPM and how one's use of pesticides adhered to the more generally accepted scientific precepts of IPM was the latest, nearly obligatory, procedure to follow. The question being asked by state pesticide regulators was "how does your use of pesticides adhere to IPM dictates?"

Thus when explaining to various audiences during the mid 1980s how the NYS electric utility industry responsibly managed vegetation on ROW by using IPM, the many skeptics seeking ways to discredit this appeal would invariably clamor, "how can you legitimately call a tree a pest." During one such confrontational address before an environmental group, the snickers and chortles caused by this disclosure, (i.e., one of the "pests" being obliquely referring to was actually the NYS official Tree, the Sugar Maple) spoiled the entire message. Too often, this interspersion of the terms "tree" and "pest" while speaking to IPM concerns in regards to ROW vegetation management usurped the message the New York State electric utility industry was attempting to communicate. Hence, it was quite logical to conclude that if the word "pest" is the red flag utterance, lets simply move around it by inserting the more appropriate term "vegetation" and call the phenomena we are describing Integrated Vegetation Management. It was at this moment, in 1986, that the term IVM was born out of necessity to avoid the recurrence of this issue of calling one of the most beloved groups of plants, i.e., trees, a pest. Since many of the practitioners of the art and adherents of the science of ROW vegetation management are by academic training Professional Foresters this juxtaposing of terms was an easy path to follow and acceptance by professional Utility Arborists was akin to osmotic.

The first known use of the expression "Integrated Vegetation Management" as a descriptive term for ROW vegetation management along with it's derivation from IPM was in formal comments submitted by the eight electric utilities members of the New York Power Pool to the New York State Department of Environmental Conservation in regards to proposed new pesticide notification regulations in late 1987. This same document was then used again in a legal deposition in a successful court case as part of an Article 78 complaint by the New York electric utilities against the NYS Department of Environmental Conservation in regards to their issuance of new "arbitrary and capricious" rules for pesticide notification.

With this deposition as a starting point, the New York electric utilities began in 1992 to assemble an in-house working document that more suitably and thoroughly described how ROW vegetation management met the qualifications of a genuine IPM program. This in-house working paper evolved into a "IPM/IVM Position Paper" using the classical IPM tactics and IPM program elements as the framework for showcasing how ROW vegetation as practiced in New York State meets all applicable IPM standards. This IPM/IVM Position Paper was released for extensive industry review and comments were solicited from the regulatory community, academia and noted experts in the field of ROW vegetation management beginning in 1993. With the reception of approvals from over 50 reviewers and inclusion of comments where appropriate, the IPM/IVM Position Paper was finalized and finally approved by the Executive Committee of the eight member systems of the New York Power Pool for general distribution in 1995. This paper was then probably given its widest audience when it was also published in the proceedings of the Sixth International Symposium on Environmental Concerns in Rights-of-Way Management held in New Orleans in February of 1997. As a result of this relatively broad distribution for a regional electric industry "Position Paper" many new adherents to IVM and others involved with IPM took the opportunity to further express their views. With the acceptability of the IVM concept by the environmental regulatory personnel in New York State, the electrical utilities practicing IVM on their ROW were also subject to the increased scrutiny of the practical aspects of implementing the IVM concept and the various interpretations of what constituted an appropriate application of IVM.

With the movement to a deregulated electric utility industry and an unbundling of generation assets, the face of the NYS electric utility industry has changed dramatically. For instance, the New York Power Pool is now the NYS Independent System Operator, i.e., an ISO. With the demise of the NYPP, the handling of collective NYS environmental regulatory affairs by the state's electric utilities is now being arranged by the Environmental Energy Alliance of New York (EEANY). The former NYPP IPM/IVM Position Paper

---

1 Such efforts persist to this day.

is currently being updated and revised by the members of the Alliance to incorporate some of the latest terms and concepts in the ever changing field of IPM. This latest venture is attached as Appendix A. Over the eight-year existence of this IPM/IVM Position Paper numerous comments concerning the contents were received, mainly from entities outside of New York State, that questioned some of the substantive subject matter and points of view expressed. New information, updating of data, revised definitions, and experience in applying IVM have all contributed to the need for a fresh look at this IPM/IVM Position Paper that is approaching nearly a decade of existence. Thus, a reevaluation of some of these past comments and how best to understand and properly interpret the current rendition of this "IPM/IVM Position Paper" are in order. It is the purpose of this paper to provide some of the rationale behind these statements and explain the concerns that generated this IPM/IVM Position Paper in the first place. The following fourteen points provide a framework for discussion of most of the macro issues brought forth by various reviewers over the years since the NYS IPM/IVM Position Paper was first released.

IPM is generally misunderstood
Unfortunately, what is imprecisely grasped or even poorly comprehended by many well-meaning IVM practitioners and adherents is that not all "so called" BMPs are really all that good and some are quite noticeably better than others. Allowing and condoning virtually any and all ROW vegetation management activities, treatment procedures, application techniques, etc. as simply various commensurate IVM alternative methods to be prescribed on a site specific manner without reliable qualifiers and adequate safeguards can be an invitation to disaster and a golden opportunity for the antipesticide zealots to chip away at the Holy Grail of ROW vegetation management.

This fact was dramatized to the author by two distinct episodes in the mid 1990s that occurred while addressing utility audiences about this relatively new term, IVM, as embodied in the New York Power Pool seminal "Position Paper" entitled "Application of Integrated Pest Management to Electric Utility Rights-of-Way Vegetation Management in New York State." A couple of astute attendees brought home clearly this message; this reappraisal of current ROW vegetation management practices emphasizing, for the most part, the selective use of herbicides and announcing it as "IVM" is really just calling a rose by a different name. In other words, really nothing has changed in the ROW vegetation arena as a result of adopting this IVM nomenclature. What has actually occurred is only the insertion of a new phrase, "Integrated Vegetation Management" and it's acronym (IVM) has been brought on the scene and this new descriptive term has caught the fancy of the ROW vegetation management community and is now a highly popular expression. As more succinctly put by another seasoned and well-credentialed ROW observer, it was simply "adding a new term to a term rich field." These observations, although seemingly belittling the concept of IVM to some ROW Managers, are basically true. However, IVM is a more comprehensive descriptor than the formerly popular phrase "selective ROW vegetation management."

The second episode of concern was when a well meaning ROW Manager from the audience volunteered the observation "My company use's two kinds of IVM, ground broadcast and aerial applications and we let the contractor make the decision as to which technique to use." Other comparable comments along a similar vein (i.e., a very narrow assortment of available ROW vegetation management techniques) have been submitted over the years as an acceptable electric utility ROW IVM program. It seems that some ROW programs are still adhering to the "Silver Bullet" concept that "one size fits all" and are enamored by the possibility that one single technique or chemical (tank mix) combination will solve all their ROW vegetation management problems across the spectrum of vegetation conditions they find on their respective systems. Unfortunately, some chemical company advertising efforts seemingly promote this type of myopic viewpoint.

When taken collectively these two observations do not bode well for the long term health and well being of IVM on electric utility ROW. The proper application of IVM, as a direct offshoot of IPM, should usher into use a sophisticated system of decision making based upon all principals and tenets of applicable IPM science. This is the main thrust of the former and current NYS IPM/IVM Position Paper on this subject. In this IPM/IVM Position Paper we try to answer the question, in a point by point evaluation, of how contemporary ROW vegetation management as practiced by the NYS electric utility industry achieves or even exceeds all applicable IPM fundamental principles.

This somewhat strict adherence to the body of knowledge referred to as IPM may be due in some part to the unique regulatory nature of New York State. The NYS Department of Public Service may be the only regulatory body in the nation requiring the submission, review and eventual approval of System-Wide ROW Vegetation Management Plans under Part 84 of the Public Service Law. This set of regulations also requires annual updates of ROW vegetation work completed, as well as anticipated efforts for the forthcoming work season, which are then monitored through field inspections by the PSC staff. Closely coupled to this unique regulatory system is the complementary degree of involvement by the NYS Department of Environmental Conservation in the use of pesticides for the ROW Category under Part 325 of the Environmental Conservation Law. Personnel from both state agencies routinely inspect electric utility ROW vegetation management activities and are on call for any and all public complaints. The NYS IIPM/IVM Position Paper is thus used as by these regulators as yet another "yardstick" to measure the competence of the company ROW vegetation management programs. Consequently, due to these "checks and balances" the deployment of an IPM systematic approach to electric utility ROW vegetation management has become common place in New York State and thus some of the aforementioned concerns seemingly do not apply.

Thus, one of the most common errors or misinterpretations occurring by readers of the "IPM/IVM Position Paper" is a lack of understanding of IPM. Although, this concept (IPM) has been around in agriculture for about 50 years it is just emerging for many other sues of pesticides. Rudimentary IPM definitions and predecessor concepts were being generated back in the late 1940s. Literally hundreds of legitimate definitions of IPM have been created over the intervening five decades. As a relative upstart in the field of IPM application, we ROW Managers must, by necessity, borrow heavily from the body of literature and systematic approach that have been developed and so successfully applied by the agricultural sciences and industry. As IPM is now being applied to virtually all pesticide usage, the head start gained by agriculture is amply evident in the IPM literature and encountering solid information and examples outside the agricultural experience is a relatively recent event. In fact, when one thoroughly checks the IPM literature the ROW category for IPM is usually found under "Urban IPM" or another relatively new terminology of "Community IPM." Although we may think we are closer to the forestry type use of pesticides, the IPM literature has placed us as an extension of other manmade environments as in the "turf and ornamental" and "landscaping" pesticide use category.

IVM is a subset of ROW management

Another macro misinterpretation of IVM in general, is that this single concept is the all-inclusive phrase to cover all aspects of the broader field of endeavor that comes with the territory expressed by the term "ROW Management." Many activities performed on the ROW have little to do with IVM and among the foremost with an environmental orientation are some proactive wildlife management actions that do not directly have a bearing on the manipulation of the ROW vegetation. For instance, placement of blue bird boxes and the installation of raptor nesting platforms in towers are just two of many wildlife related actions taken in conjunction with ROW management that have little if any direct bearing on IVM. In fact the entire field of "avian interactions" as they relate to electric transmission support structures is not directly linked to the use of IVM on the ROW. Although mentioned peripherally in the New York IPM/IVM Position Paper, the building and maintaining of access roads, particularly across streams and through wetlands, is an important environmental aspect of ROW maintenance that is not directly linked to the IVM program. Certainly, better ROW access roads and routes will undoubtedly aid and abet the IVM program but it is not in the normal sense a direct part of it. In many northern States and Canada the opening of ROW to snowmobile use in winter with trail marking and grooming are popular activities that are in the ROW multiple use category not at all related to IVM. However, in those ROW programs that employ the use of herbicides to curtail the growth of trees, IVM is an appropriate and applicable moniker to describe this effort. However, if the ROW vegetation management program is completely mechanical, e.g., mowing, and/or manual, e.g., hand cutting, and no herbicides are used, then the term IVM would not technically apply and thus need not be used. Direct oversight and overt interest by environmental organizations and regulatory agencies[2] virtually disappears when pesticide use goes to zero and with it the need to use the term or even talk about IPM/IVM.

The utility IVM program could easily be subsumed under these broader more inclusive ROW undertakings be they entitled ROW Resource Management, Integrated Resource Management, Line Clearance Program, or ROW Environmental Management or whatever other descriptive title best fits the situation.

No herbicides, no IVM: Does IVM overemphasize herbicide use?

Another major complaint by some reviewers (usually not utility) was the emphasis on herbicide use in the original "NYPP IPM/IVM Position Paper" to achieve the benefits of IVM. This again was quite purposeful. When first developing the IPM/IVM Position Paper in the early 1990s, several IPM "Experts" were contacted for their ideas about the subject as it related to the control of ROW vegetation. One almost universal warning received from this bevy of IPM practitioners and specialists was that we (the electric utility industry) always have a quite viable non-chemical option available to us when the pest population reaches that predetermined threshold of economic harm. In other words, we (the utility industry) have the distinct advantage (unlike many other pesticide users) of being able to remove the pest threat from the ROW by exercising mechanical/manual/physical means to rid the system of the pest. For most other IPM practitioners, once the pest has reached a certain threshold level the action that must be taken is the application of a pesticide. In many agricultural situations, no other

---

2 This is not the case in New York State. The PSC looks at the costs, risks and total environmental compatibility of the ROW vegetation management program and thus encourages the judicious use of herbicides to create low growing relatively stable ROW plant communities requiring less long-term maintenance.

non-chemical approach is even possible. We, the electric utility industry, on the other hand always have a non-chemical option available to us that can be put to use right up to the last moment. Thus, to adequately address this real concern, the paper goes into repeated exacting detail about the myriad long-term advantages of employing herbicides in an ever more discreet and selective applications each treatment cycle resulting in less material being used over time.

Waiting (or not) for economic thresholds to be exceeded
An offshoot of the above discussion and another potential IPM problem for IVM is the timing of application based upon classical IPM dictates of waiting until one has reached the economic damage threshold of an intolerable pest level. It is inherently much more difficult to determine acceptable injury level for a ROW situation since the incremental damage done by growing trees is not easily computed. Complete adherence to this IPM prescription would have ROW Managers literally running around their system always "hot spotting" trees that are just ready to enter the wire security zone. This would actually be the antithesis of a proper IVM procedure that has as its concurrent goal the fostering of all the low growing desirable vegetation. Waiting until the trees on the ROW are so tall that they are encroaching on the wire security zone is foolish from an economic, system reliability and overall environmental viewpoint. With such tall trees allowed to remain on the ROW so long, the shading effects on the desirable vegetation would virtually eliminate these assets from the ROW. Since the promotion of all lower growing vegetation is touted as the equivalent of the well established IPM "biological control" tactic in the application of IVM to ROW vegetation management, this threshold concept if incorrectly applied as "just in time" maintenance could lead to serious long term problems, i.e., the reduction or even elimination of many low growing species, and is a complete misapplication of the IVM concept.

Preventive measures are not the same as treatment methods
One of the most common problems encountered with various well meaning reviewers and some IPM/IVM practitioners as well is understanding the differences between "preventive measures" on the one hand and the three classical IPM tactics of cultural, biological and chemical control methods on the other. Preventive measures in and of themselves are not a control tactic although they can sometimes be confused with the implementation of cultural control practices. Another ROW (albeit roadway) example might help. Expanding the road pavement out beyond the normal point of guardrails placement and then installing the guardrails through the pavement will eliminate the need for future under guardrail vegetation control. This procedure is customarily designated as an IPM preventive measure not as an IPM cultural pest control tactic. In other words, it is "changing the design of the facility to completely avoid the need for pest control." As for electric transmission line ROW, preventive measures usually are all those other "multiple uses" of the ROW that preclude the growth of trees. These range from parking lots to pastures.

One interesting preventive measure enhancement program recently instituted by a New York Sate transmission owner (and member of EEANY) is a cost sharing effort with the underlying ROW landowner. In ROW areas that are now "wildlands" and the ROW vegetation management is performed by the utility, if the underlying landowner has an opportunity to transform the ROW into a productive use, the company will cost share the work to be done (50/50) to convert the ROW to a landuse condition that will preclude the establishment of trees. So far, this effort has created pastures for sheep, cows, and horses. Deer food plots were a goal of another ROW landowner and grass cover to be mowed adjacent to a campground is another conversion project. The key to the success to date of this endeavor is the willingness of the landowner to match the monetary contribution of the electric utility so that the landowner has from the onset a vested interest in the success of the ROW land use conversion project.

Another quite unique ROW multiple use that has emerged recently is the use of the ROW in the production of raw materials for the increasingly popular rustic Adirondack stick and twig furniture. Large twigs (branches) and young sapling size boles of certain common tree species are the "feedstock" for this unique furniture form. Adirondack style furniture and other such rustic embellishments (e.g., picture and mirror frames) in the folk art tradition are becoming quite trendy for interior design and decoration in the mode of a "casual elegance." This means that such traditional tall growing target tree species as yellow birch, gray birch, white birch, pin cherry, black cherry, and hickory are now being purposefully grown on the ROW and carefully harvested (to prevent damage to the bark) in the sapling stage for eventual production of this unique, currently in vogue, primitive style furniture. The future of this stick and twig market for rustic furniture designs is being watched closely as any let up in harvesting of these tree saplings will leave the ROW in a situation requiring immediate attention.

IPM (IVM) control tactics: Cultural
The traditional "big three" IPM tactics of cultural, biological, and chemical were relatively easy to differentiate for IVM applications. Cultural tactics in an agricultural context stem from various "cultivating" practices like plowing the soil just prior to seeding to turn over the weeds and put under residues of last years crop. Both these outcomes, due to tillage, reduce the pest populations. Other classical agricultural

cultural tactics include strip cropping and crop rotation. These agricultural applications of cultural tactics involved various mechanical, physical, and manual methods and combinations of all three to produce the desired pest control effect. Thus, IVM cultural methods, considered in this context, could be regarded as *mechanical* tree removal by mowing or *manual* by hand-cutting with a chainsaw with either of them resulting in the *physical* removal of the tree(s) from the ROW environs.

IPM (IVM) control tactics: Biological

The biological controls in traditional IPM usage refer to the employment of other organisms that are usually a disease, predator or parasite to the target pest. These predators or natural enemies of the target pest are purposefully manipulated or applied as beneficial biological controls. For ROW IVM, the deliberate introduction of such tree pests to kill off such ecologically desirable and economically important plants is virtually impossible. Even giving members of the public the erroneous thought that this could occur would be cause for immediate serious concern. Nonetheless, currently under development is the first true biological control for application on ROW. A naturally occurring fungus is being commercially tested for application to the freshly cut stumps of red alder in the Pacific Northwest. It seems that this fungus will begin to infect the cut surface and spread far enough to thwart any forthcoming vegetative reproduction, i.e., stump sprouts, without infecting the healthy uncut trees just off the ROW. There are exceptions to every rule and this seems to be one of them, but it may become more prevalent as such biotechnology applications keep advancing.

Overall, the term biological control as used in an IVM context can also mean natural controls or ecological controls, which are also sometimes referred to in the IPM literature, and this is where the low growing desirable vegetation found on ROW fits so nicely into the picture. It is the wide assortment of lower growing species that are fostered and promoted by IVM practices and these become the assets (credits) of the ROW IVM program much as the tall growing target trees are the liabilities (debits). This "simple" objective of IVM is to increase the assets (percent vegetative cover occupied by desirable low growing vegetation) and simultaneously decrease the liabilities (the number of trees stems capable of eventually reaching the wire security zone). The ecological consequences of such tree removal actions and the fostering of all lower growing vegetation are well stated in the IPM/IVM Position Paper. The down-to-earth fact remains that two things, i.e., plants, cannot occupy the same space at the same time. All the IVM activities that degrade the presence of ROW trees and thus concurrently foster the establishment and growth of all the other low growing species will aid and abet this IPM biological control tactic.

IPM (IVM) control tactics: Chemical

The deployment of chemicals on ROW for IVM is not a last resort type of operation, but a very deliberate and focused approach to achieve a highly desirable endpoint. This message is the primary focus of the NY IPM/IVM Position Paper. We wanted to make it abundantly clear, to friend and foe alike, that without the judicious selective use of herbicides the relatively stable ROW plant community composed of an assortment of low growing shrubs, vines, herbs, grasses, sedges, reeds, ferns, etc. cannot be created let alone maintained. One of the basic IPM tenets repeatedly depicted in the literature is the statement that IPM is a system designed to provide long term management of pests, not temporary eradication of them. This is certainly the goal of IVM and by promoting the existence of all low growing plants on the ROW (by minimizing our treatment effects upon them) while focusing our efforts on the selective removal of target tree species, the long term maintenance of the ROW is always given a top priority.

IPM (IVM) control tactics: Physical

The newest official entry into the classical lists of IPM tactics is "physical." This forth IPM tactic was added to the latest EPA IPM definition back in 1994 (after the first drafting of the NYS IPM/IVM Position Paper) and is also the definition used by the NYS DEC in its latest set of pesticide regulations officially adopted this past January 2000. Thus both Federal EPA and State DEC definitions of IPM previously included only the three classical tactics; cultural, biological, chemical and now include physical as a forth. As a distinctly new set of pest control tactics encompassed by the addition of this new term, physical, the examples for IVM seemingly are overlain by the various cultural tactics of mechanical and manual that are also by nature physical. However, in the IPM literature physical means such things as the application of heat and steam as well as use of physical barriers and various other similar control methods such as hand picking, sticky traps and other trapping techniques. Hence in the latest version of the IPM/IVM Paper (Appendix A) the terms of cultural and physical are now purposefully used in an interrelated fashion. These other physical efforts (e.g., heat) are not addressed in the revised IPM/IVM Position Paper as they have yet to find a niche in the ROW manager's toolbox.

IPM (IVM) control tactics: Others

Other commonly used terms for multiple IPM tactics, otherwise referred to as methods of control, control measures or even tools, found in various IPM definitions also include such designations as legal, educational, pest resistance, sanitation, habitat modification, natural enemies, natural mortality, weather, and finally no action. None of these secondary IPM tactics are dealt with in the NYS IPM/IVM Position Paper.

Why isn't the popular term "brush control" used?

The long commonly used electric utility industry expression "brush control"[3] should now be considered almost an oxymoron when used in connection to IVM, since by the very definition of "brush" (actually the plural of bush or dense growth of bushes) meaning shrubby vegetation, i.e., shrubs, vines, and small trees, it gives an erroneous picture of what we are now trying to achieve with a balanced IVM approach to ROW vegetation management. A "balanced" IVM approach means that the eradication and subsequent decline of target tall growing trees on the ROW will be done in a manner that has the propensity to preserve, to the extent practical, all the existing desirable low growing plants (including many woody shrubs) that are compatible with the goals of long term ROW vegetation management. This is what is truly meant, in part, by the term "integrated" as used in the expression IVM. IVM is also an integration of techniques that will allow, nay, even promote and foster, the existence of one set of green plants while quite selectively discriminating against another set of green plants so that over time a conversion of the ROW plant community occurs resulting in a minimum maintenance situation. If a utility is constantly resorting to repeated indiscriminate broadcast applications (from the ground or air) of herbicides or is constantly mowing, this is not truly an IVM program but a ROW maintenance or "brush control" effort that will virtually never cease nor wane.

Isn't high volume foliar spraying the same as broadcast applications of herbicides?

In regards to the declaration in the IPM/IVM Position Paper that NYS electric utilities never use aerial spraying or indiscriminate ground broadcast applications of herbicides, the simple fact is that by definition and practice no utility has to resort to this type of ROW application anymore in New York State. However, many companies still routinely use high volume ground foliar applications albeit in a selective manner. In the conventional high volume foliar application of herbicides, each target tree species, i.e., the foliage and stem, is thoroughly wetted to the point of runoff. At the same time patches of desirable lower growing vegetation remain untreated. Whereas the definition of broadcast spraying requires a uniform coverage of an entire area with a predetermined rate of application, so that every square foot of surface receives a specified dosage. Although uniform high-density stands of trees selectively treated by the high volume technique will, admittedly, end up looking a lot like the same density of trees treated by a broadcast application under some circumstances, the general trend is noticeably different. Due to the inherent patchiness of ROW vegetation rarely is an entire span, let alone a sizable segment of ROW, so uniformly filled with a dense 100% coverage of target tree species. Another reason for emphasizing this difference is that the definition of the term and usage of "broadcast application" of herbicides has quite important legal meanings and connotations aside from those depicted on the pesticide labels directions (although the label is the law). A case in point, the state of Vermont has banned certain *ground broadcast applications* of herbicides. Another example, the new amended label for one herbicide allows the selective and spot applications of the product in active pasture situations while posing restrictions and other rate limitations on broadcast applications under the same circumstances.

Notwithstanding these nominal (so far) strictures on broadcast herbicide applications, some ROW situations elsewhere in the country (or world) may actually lend themselves to a broadcast treatment with certain qualifying factors. For example, tall high-density stands of trees can first be mowed to immediately gain control (reclamation) of the ROW and reduce the amount of aerial biomass needing treatment. Immediately following the mowing, a broadcast application with a radiarc type spray unit of a soil active residual herbicide (perhaps selective to dicots or legumes) can be performed that will leave some vegetation unharmed while effectively taking out all the woody vegetation prior to resprouting from the severed stem and untouched roots systems. Unfortunately, this type of control approach has been severely limited of late due to new label restrictions of the preferred selective herbicide for this application technique. Also, in remote regions with dense stands of trees occupying the ROW, the only feasible method to the control the growth of trees may be aerial application of herbicides.

Update and/or add new definitions of IPM

Many comments received over the years had to do with proposing new definitions for IPM and/or IVM that better fit the ROW circumstance. The IPM/IVM Position Paper used and still uses the most basic generic expressions found throughout the literature for describing IPM. There are literally hundreds of legitimate definitions of IPM found in the literature. One of these almost made it into the new IPM/IVM Position paper. This definition is probably the "best" existing definition of IPM found befitting the usage of IVM. This definition came into being in 1994 and J.R. Cate and M. K. Hinkle of the Audubon Society are credited for this unique succinct definition of IPM as follows.

---

[3] Another similarity that is drawn from the field of Forestry is the demise of the term "fire control" in preference for "fire management." Fire control was the popular term used to describe the entire fire program when it consisted only of fire prevention, detection and suppression. Now with the advent of allowing wild fires to burn if they meet predetermined conditions and the use of prescribed burning the term fire management is now the preferred term.

"Integrated Pest Management is the judicious use and integration of various pest control tactics in the context of the associated environment of the pest *in ways that complement and facilitate the biological and other natural controls* of pests to meet economic, public health, and environmental goals."

Point of comparison: No-till agriculture and IVM

Two items previously mentioned, i.e., the notable agricultural background for all things IPM and the fact that utilities always have a non-chemical option, brings us to another important point of comparison not mentioned in the IPM/IVM Position Paper or elsewhere. This comparison came while discussing IVM with some agricultural IPM practitioners. We may be able to draw some interesting similarities in the use of herbicides on ROW by the electric utility industry to achieve certain desirable environmental endpoints and the relatively new agricultural efforts to establish "no-till" farming practices to achieve the noble goal of sustainable agriculture.

The deployment of no-till agriculture is depicted as an environmental success story (and rightfully so) in progress. Its primary purpose is to minimize soil erosion (by water and wind) and the concurrent nutrient loss resulting in sedimentation and other water quality impairments by suspended solids and nutrient enrichment. By reducing soil and nutrient loss, less fertilizer is likewise needed as an added benefit. Long-term soil productivity is thus ensured. Improved soil moisture management is enhanced and reduced fuel costs are also results of no-till cropping systems. However, in order to control weeds and reduce the chance of pest buildups in the crop residuals a combination of increased chemical (herbicide) usage and cultural tactics must be used for this unique agricultural system to be successful. In a no-till cropping system, herbicides replace tillage for weed control. It is also important to rotate the crops in this system and avoid planting the same crop back into its own residue.

In many recent agricultural IPM scenarios, the no-till system is always mentioned as an anomaly, whereby herbicide usage in this instance is actually greater and more needed than previously with tillage. Without herbicides, the no-till system is a no-go. Without the judicious application of herbicides to selectively remove only the target tall growing tree species from the ROW while purposefully fostering all the desirable low growing species, the goals of IVM are likewise virtually impossible to achieve. We (both the electric utility industry and the agricultural industry) have individual success stories here to be proud of, but we must get our stories straight and strictly adhere to the basic tenets and principles of our respective sciences and not allow ourselves to be lulled into complacency with clever verbiage and adroit postulations. Unfortunately, there is simply no easy way to add this distinctive comparison into an already too lengthy NYS IPM/IVM Position Paper.

SUMMARY

Although not a lot has changed from the original IPM/IVM Position Paper first written as a New York Power Pool in-house document circa 1992–1993, released in 1995, widely published in 1997 and finally to the new slightly amended 2000–2001 version to be released under the Environmental Energy Alliance of New York banner. The many comments and suggestions, questions and inquires, interpretations and citations received over the years necessitated a hard new look at the original thesis in respect to both the changing times and all the new IPM/IVM information becoming available. The numerous well meaning observations and opinions proffered over the existence of this document demanded a public explanation as to why certain positions were taken and things said. Differences of opinion and emphasis will remain as to ascribing the low growing desirable ROW vegetation as a "biological" control or using the newer term, an "ecological" control or even "natural" controls. Moreover, some common IPM preventive measures as applied to the ROW situation may overlap with someone's perception of cultural control tactics. Irrespective of these minor semantic skirmishes, the overall message is now clear and the passage of time has now imbedded the term IVM firmly into the rubric of ROW vegetation management. So much so that now others are borrowing the same term (IVM) for their particular application of IPM to a solely vegetational situation, e.g., the control of alien invasive species in natural environments.

CONCLUDING REMARKS: IVM IN RESPECT TO HERBICIDE USAGE

It is still a long regulatory road ahead for all pesticide users, as the public perception (read social intolerance) of pesticide risk in general is still very high. Even though the herbicides in common IVM use on ROW today have very low toxicity, particularly as applied diluted in various carriers, and the mixing and delivery methods are substantially better than ever, the environmental and human health concerns over all pesticide usage are ever present. The fear and loathing still generated by the word "pesticide" by the vocal majority of Americans today may seem like an irrational response to those of us that have taken the time to thoroughly review the risks. However, it is these very same irrational and most often emotional fears that when taken collectively drive government policy, create the laws, and make the regulations that can jeopardize the continued use of pesticides. As an industry, as pesticide users, we must strive to continue to improve our performance, and use these valued tools in a manner consistent with the esteemed principles of IVM, which we all so highly tout and so emphatically espouse. Overuse, misuse or otherwise overtly harmful uses of these valuable materials must not be tolerated. We all have a lot to gain if these miracles of modern chemistry are allowed to do the job intended, we all have a lot to lose if these products are banished from our custodianship.

REFERENCES

Bramble, W.C. and W.R. Byrnes. 1996. Integrated vegetation management of an electric utility right-of-way ecosystem. Down to Earth, 51(2).

Cate, J.R. and M.J. Hinkle. 1994. Integrated pest management: The path of a paradigm. The National Audubon Society Special Report. 43 pp.

Committee on Pest Mangement. 1996. Ecologically Based Pest Management: New Solutions for a New Century. National Academy Press. 160 pp.

Daar, S. 1991. Vegetation management on rights-of-way: an ecological approach. The IPM Practitioner, XIII(2) February.

Dent, D. 1995. Integrated Pest Management. Chapman & Hall.

Harriman, J.A.E. 1999. Exploring Wildlife Habitat Management on Electric Transmission Rights-of-Way in the United States and Canada. Edison Electric Institute Natural Resource Committee Workshop, Williamsburg, Virginia.

Morse, S. and W. Buhle. 1997. Integrated Pest Management: Ideals and Realities in Developing Countries. Lynne Rienner Publishers.

Persley, G.J., ed. 1996. Biotechnology and Integrated Pest Management. Biotechnology in Agriculture Series, No 15. CABI Publishing, CAB International.

Zalom, F.G. and W.E. Fry. 1992. Food, Crops Pests, and the Environment: The Need and Potential for Biologically Intensive Integrated Pest Management. American Phytopathological Society.

BIOGRAPHICAL SKETCH

Kevin T. McLaughlin
New York Power Authority, PO Box 200, Gilboa, NY 12076. E-mail: kevin.mcloughlin@nypa.gov, Phone: 607-588-6061.

Currently (since 1998) System Forester for the New York Power Authority, and consultant to EPRI for the ROW Environmental Management Target. Formerly (20 years), Administrator for Land Use & Industrial Waste Programs for the New York Power Pool and concurrently Research Program Manager for the Empire State Electric Energy Research Corporation. Also worked for the US Forest Service in Idaho and Arizona. Education: BS(1971) in Natural Resource Management & MS (1975) in Environmental Management from State University of New York College of Environmental Science and Forestry at Syracuse University.

APPENDIX A

APPLICATIONS OF INTEGRATED PEST MANAGEMENT TO ELECTRIC UTILITY RIGHTS-OF-WAY VEGETATION MANAGEMENT IN NEW YORK STATE

Environmental Energy Alliance of New York Land Use Subcommittee Committee Position Paper

The Environmental Energy Alliance of New York is an association of electric and gas Transmission and Distribution (T&D) companies and electric generating companies that provide energy services in the State of New York. This position paper was prepared by the Land Use Subcommittee of the T&D Committee, which currently represents the following members: Central Hudson Gas & Electric Corporation, Consolidated Edison Company of New York, Long Island Power Authority, New York Power Authority, New York State Electric & Gas Corporation, Niagara Mohawk, Orange & Rockland Utilities, and Rochester Gas & Electric Corporation. For more information about this Position Paper please contact Kevin T. McLoughlin, the System Forester for the New York Power Authority at P.O. Box 200, Gilboa, New York 12076. Tel. (607) 588-6061 ext. 6903, Fax (607) 588-9826 or e-mail: Kevin.Mcloughlin@nypa.gov.

EXECUTIVE SUMMARY

As a matter of public safety and system reliability, electric utility rights-of-way (ROW) vegetation managers have a continuing need to preclude the establishment and subsequent growth of tree species that are capable of growing up into or even close to overhead electric lines. The members systems of the Environmental Energy Alliance of New York (EEANY) Transmission & Distribution (T&D) Committee employ the process of Integrated Pest Management (IPM) to ensure that tall growing trees do not interfere with these critically important electric power transmission facilities. IPM balances the use of cultural, biological, physical and chemical procedures for controlling undesirable tree species on utility ROW. These IPM procedures, as practiced by the New York State electric utility industry, can be more appropriately referred to as an Integrated Vegetation Management (IVM) strategy. One of the important components of the IPM/IVM process is the selective use of herbicides to curtail the growth of undesirable tall growing tree species while preserving, to the extent practical, the lower growing vegetation on the ROW to act as a biological deterrent to the future re-establishment of trees.

The EEANY Land Use Subcommittee members have been practicing IVM policies and programs for over two decades on those portions of the approximately ten thousand circuit miles of overhead transmission line ROW that require the vegetation to be managed.

IVM is an environmentally compatible activity that is cost effective and has all the elements of a conscientiously applied IPM strategy. This paper discusses the application of IPM to contemporary electric utility ROW vegetation management practices in New York State today.

Integrated Pest Management (IPM) is a process that balances the use of cultural, biological, physical and chemical procedures for reducing pest populations to tolerable levels. Rather than relying solely on chemicals (or eliminating chemicals completely) IPM seeks to produce a combination of pest control options that are compatible with the environment, economically feasible and socially tolerable. The control of vegetation, i.e., the contemporary management of vegetation, on electric utility line rights-of-way (ROW)[4] readily accommodates itself to an IPM process. This paper describes how the member electric systems of EEANY T&D Committee have been actually practicing an IPM strategy for about two decades. However, that strategy can be more appropriately referred to as an Integrated Vegetation Management (IVM) strategy.

BACKGROUND

In New York State after a forested landscape is cleared, or when a cultivated field is abandoned, the natural vegetation type that will ultimately re-occupy the site and dominate the area will be tall growing trees. When the cleared area is an electric utility ROW, these resurgent trees can grow too close to the overhead electric lines. When this occurs, there is the potential for an electrical discharge from the electric line through the air to the tree and then to the ground. This is known as a "line to ground fault" or "flash-over." The result of a line to ground fault is an instantaneous break in electric service and a potentially very dangerous situation on the ground in the immediate vicinity of the high voltage discharge. Therefore, as a matter of public safety and system reliability, utility ROW vegetation managers have a continuing need to preclude the establishment and subsequent growth of those tree species that are capable of growing into or even close to the electrical lines.[5] Utilities ensure that tall growing trees do not interfere with electric lines by committing to a long-term ROW vegetation management program.

---

[4] Electric utility ROW are strips of land, from 30 yards to over 300 yards in width, that are used by electric utilities as corridors for the transmission of electric energy.

[5] The electrical facilities being discussed herein are for the most part high voltage transmission lines and only those lower voltage distribution lines that have a discernible cleared ROW. There are more than 10,000 circuit miles of overhead transmission lines at or above 34.5 kV belonging to the member systems of EEANY. ROW vegetation management under these electric transmission facilities is quite distinct from roadside tree trimming around distribution lines and these street tree-pruning operations are not the subject of this paper.

INTEGRATED VEGETATION MANAGEMENT AS AN IPM STRATEGY

IPM has been described as a system of resource management that attempts to minimize the interaction between the pest and the management system through the integrated use of cultural, biological, physical and chemical controls. Implementation of an IVM program utilizing modern ROW vegetation management techniques meets this definition completely; IVM is a system of resource (vegetation) management that minimizes interaction between the pest (tall growing trees) and the management-system (safe and reliable electric service) through the integrated use of *cultural* (mechanical and manual methods that *physically* remove tree stems), *biological* (low growing plants and herbivory), and *chemical* (herbicides) controls.

Utilities use three general routine procedures for removing tall growing trees from the ROW: (1) mechanical methods such as mowing with large machines and hand cutting with chainsaws, (2) chemical treatments, i.e., the selective application of herbicides, and (3) combinations of both mechanical and chemical methods.

Mechanical methods of tree removal alone will clear the ROW of tree stems temporarily. However, employment of these mechanical methods allows trees to physiologically respond by regenerating quickly from the energy reserves contained in their undisturbed root systems. This tree regrowth occurs through such mechanisms as "stump sprouting" and/or in some species "root suckering." This regenerative capacity is characteristic of virtually all hardwoods,[6] e.g., maple, beech, birch, aspen, oak, ash, cherry, etc. and is particularly pronounced in the juvenile or sapling stage of tree maturation resulting in the eventual production of many more stems than were originally cut. By drawing upon the food reserves in their undisturbed root systems and through a series of complex compensatory physiological plant responses, the resurgent growth from the remaining portions of the tree (stump and/or roots) is actually enhanced when a tree stem is severed. It is through the production within the plant of naturally occurring stimulatory substances together with the loss of growth inhibitors (caused by the removal of the above ground growth centers) which then exert their influence on the remaining vegetative structure to promote excessive new tree growth. These new, more numerous stems, growing much faster than when left uncut, (e.g., five to ten feet or more the first year after cutting) makes subsequent tree removal from the ROW more frequent, laborious, hazardous and costly.

---

[6] Hardwood is a conventional term for all deciduous (broadleaved) trees belonging to the botanical class "Angiosperm." Softwoods, also commonly referred to as evergreens and conifers, belong to the botanical class "Gymnospermae" (and are practically confined to the order "Coniferae") do not posses this regenerative trait (with one lone partial exception in the northeast — young pitch pine), and once cut below the lowest whorl of live branches will not resprout.

The selective application of herbicides to only the tall growing target tree species can in most instances eliminate completely the resurgent tree growth problem because the herbicide when properly deposited on the target species translocates throughout the tree (including the root system) and arrests all future growth and development, i.e., killing the entire target plant not just temporarily removing the above ground portion. Selective herbicide application involves two general techniques:[7] a basal application to the lower stem of the tree and a foliar application to the leaves. Selective application of herbicides only to the target tree species allows retention of nearly all the desirable low growing vegetation on the ROW. The elimination of the tall growing trees from the ROW will also encourage the further growth and development of all the indigenous low growing woody shrubs, herbs (forbs and grasses), ferns, etc. by removing the trees that would otherwise begin to directly compete with and eventually "crowd out" the low growing species over time. With effective minimally disruptive tree removal, these lower growing desirable plant species will expand into the ROW areas formerly occupied by trees and produce a thick dense plant cover that will discourage the invasion of new tree seedlings and/or the future growth of any remaining tree seedlings. These desirable low growing plant communities act as the "biological controls" in this IPM/IVM scenario. The establishment and the preservation of these low growing plant communities on ROW serve to reduce over time the amount of work required and cost incurred by the utility to maintain the ROW each treatment cycle while coincidentally diminishing the amount of herbicide necessary for adequate coverage of the target species.

Mechanical and chemical controls are often used together with favorable synergistic results. For instance, a tree is manually cut with a chain saw and the resulting freshly severed stump is treated with a herbicide formulation to prevent resprouting. This procedure removes the immediate physical threat to the overhead electrical line as well as the future tree growth with little disruption to the surrounding desirable plant cover while requiring very limited use of herbicides in a highly efficacious spot application.

ESSENTIAL ELEMENTS OF AN IPM STRATEGY — ILLUSTRATIONS & EXAMPLES

Traditional IPM programs consist of five basic elements: (1) preventive measures, (2) biological controls, (3) monitoring, (4) assessment, and (5) control measures. These essential elements of a sound IPM/IVM program are illustrated in the following examples.

---

[7] Many variations of these two techniques exist.

Preventive measures

When the land use of a ROW is altered to preclude the establishment and growth of trees, the utility has little, if any, ROW vegetation management activities to perform. This advantageous situation occurs when a ROW fee owner or adjacent land owner productively uses the ROW in a manner compatible with the electrical facilities, and this use usurps the potential development of tall growing trees. The most common ROW multiple uses often involve various types of agricultural[8] activities, i.e., crop production, pastures for grazing livestock, and within certain height limitations even Christmas tree plantations and some types of orchards. Those agrarian activities, as well as many other types of allowable industrial, commercial and residential multiple uses, which effectively curtail the opportunity for any tall growing vegetation to become established can thus eliminate completely the burden for any ROW vegetation management by the utility. However, any use of the ROW that allows even one tree capable of growing up into the electrical lines, e.g., hedgerows between cultivated fields, requires due diligence by the utility to prevent an electrical discharge.

Biological controls

One of the principle goals of ROW vegetation management is to promote low growing relatively stable (long lived) plant communities, which consist of numerous species of woody shrubs, herbs (forbs and grasses), ferns, etc. on the ROW. These low growing plant communities are a very desirable ROW accessory in that they inhibit both tree establishment and their subsequent growth by directly competing with the tall growing species for the available site resources (sunlight, water, and nutrients). Thick low-growing plant communities, which hinder tree seed germination and the early development of the undesirable tree seedlings and small tree saplings, act as the biological control agents in this IPM/IVM strategy.

There may even be some indirect biochemical interactions, called allelopathy, occurring among various plants that result in a chemical competition of sorts between certain lower growing desirable ROW species and some of the tall growing tree species. Allelopathy has been defined as the influence of one plant on another via the production of natural growth inhibitors. Currently there exists only a limited understanding of this ability of plants to produce and release phytotoxic substances that can then be translocated to other plants and used to curtail certain critical physiological plant functions such as growth and reproduction.

---

[8] It should be noted that most agricultural pursuits require the use of significant amounts of various pesticides, e.g., insecticides, fungicides, herbicides, etc. on an annual basis. Thus, the total quantities of pesticide applications will often dramatically increase on those ROW areas converted to farmland as compared to the spot treatments of herbicides every four to seven years by the utility.

These naturally occurring "herbicides" offer yet another potential beneficial aspect of the biological controls in assisting the ROW vegetation manager to curb the spread of the undesirable tall growing trees.

In addition to their immediate benefits to the utility of reducing the undesirable tree population, these low growing plant communities offer an assemblage of plant species that provide diverse and productive habitat conditions for a wide variety of wildlife, e.g., birds and mammals. Managed ROW creates habitats that provide wildlife food and cover values that are remarkably different, and oftentimes surpassing, those of the neighboring forest. Also, this juxtaposition of two different, but complementary plant communities (one perpetually kept in a low growing condition and the other usually a forest) produces what is known as the "edge effect." This effect enhances wildlife profusion, i.e., abundance and diversity, in the boundary area transition zone (ecotone) between these two distinct habitat types. Some of the new and more numerous wildlife species attracted to these enhanced ROW created habitats provide yet another beneficial function of further reducing tree establishment and growth through their collective herbivory, e.g., browsing by deer and rabbits on young trees, girdling of tree seedlings by voles, and tree seed predation by mice.

Monitoring

As explicitly called for in an IPM program, monitoring of the pest population involves the following items:
– Regularly checking the area
– Early detection of pests
– Proper identification of pests
– Noting the effectiveness of biological controls.

The ROW vegetation managers of the EEANY member systems routinely carry out all of these monitoring activities as an integral part of their electric utility ROW vegetation management programs. Monitoring procedures have been integrated into the NYS Public Service Commission approved "Long Term ROW Management Plans" developed by each member system. Monitoring activities include an evaluation of the previous treatments to determine overall program effectiveness as well as the current condition of the ROW so as to ascertain when the next treatment should occur and by what means. All of these procedures are part of a sound IPM/IVM strategy. ROW throughout New York State are regularly inspected to determine the height and density of the tall growing target tree species as well as the condition of the lower growing vegetation. Inspection results help determine, to a large extent, the timing and type of ROW vegetation treatment that the utility implements.

These field inspections also serve another important function, i.e., the fulfillment of a quality assurance/quality control (QA/QC) program. This QA/QC component of the ROW vegetation management program provides feedback as to the conduct of the field crews regarding their adherence to the work specifications as well as to determine the longer-term efficacy of the treatments. In addition to the routine utility monitoring, the Department of Public Service staff annually inspects the results of the company ROW vegetation management programs to insure compliance with all applicable regulatory mandates.

Identifying the undesirable tree species is a critical component of an IPM/IVM program. With hundreds of species present on a ROW, all vegetation treatment personnel must be sufficiently knowledgeable of plant species to enable them to readily distinguish between target trees to be treated, and all non-target desirable low-growing species to be left as undisturbed as possible. Based upon field inspections, the type of vegetation treatment will also be determined in large part by the distribution and abundance of the lower growing species. For instance, when thickets of shrubs, such as viburnums or dogwoods, are present together with only a few target tree stems, the highly selective stem specific application of herbicides would produce the most acceptable results. The extensive use of mowing for example over such a ROW segment containing only a few target species would be quite disruptive to the existing desirable low growing vegetative cover. Such an ecological disturbance would unnecessarily leave the ROW in a much more open and vulnerable condition thereby actually enhancing the ROW site conditions for the eventual re-establishment of undesirable trees as well as significantly reduce its aesthetic and wildlife values.

Assessment

Assessment is the process of determining the potential for pest populations (target trees) to reach an intolerable level. For ROW vegetation managers, the most opportune time to eradicate target trees is well before they reach the height of the overhead electrical lines. From an assessment perspective, an effective IPM/IVM strategy needs to: (a) prevent any interruption of electrical service and avoid risk of injury to the public, (b) treat the target species at their optimum height range of five to ten feet or as they emerge from the lower growing plant cover (at this stage they can be conveniently treated with limited amounts of herbicide so as to achieve the highest degree of control possible), (c) cause the removal of the target tree species before they become tall and dense enough to begin to crowd out and adversely alter the composition, structure and density of the desirable lower growing vegetative cover, and (d) minimize any direct disruption by the treatments themselves to the existing desirable ROW plants so they continue to occupy the ROW and function as biological controls.

Control measures

IPM strategy dictates that once a pest population has reached the intolerable level action should be taken.

Typically, under an IPM program, chemical pesticides are used as a control measure when no other strategies will bring the pest population back under the economic threshold. In fact, the success of IPM often occurs by waiting until a pest population reaches this threshold and then often hinges on the availability of a pesticide to bring the pest population back under control quickly. For ROW vegetation management the pest population consists of only the target tree species that meet certain critical height[9] characteristics. Only those trees that have emerged from the lower growing plant "canopy" need to be selectively removed; thus many very small tree seedlings may remain untreated, submerged within the low-growing plant community on the ROW. Most of these small tree seedlings, left fully submerged within the dense low growing understory vegetation, will never fully develop into trees as they will succumb to the surrounding competitive pressures of the lower growing desirable vegetation and its associated biotic agents, e.g., animal herbivory. An additional positive attribute of this biological control feature occurs when those few remaining target trees that finally "escape" from the low growing plant communities only do so after a considerably longer time period than would normally happen under relatively (open) unencumbered circumstances. This helps to extend the duration between ROW vegetation treatments.

The choice of treatment technique as well as the explicit mode of application to ensure adequate control of the target tree species are also important aspects of selective ROW vegetation management that uniquely qualifies IVM as an IPM approach. As part of an IPM/IVM program, herbicides are used only to treat individual tree stems or groups of target trees, and no aerial or indiscriminate ground broadcast (blanket) applications (uniformly spraying the entire ROW) are used in New York State today. Herbicides that are used on ROW are matched to site-specific characteristics and target species, and the products are selected from dozens of commercially available materials based upon various attributes such as efficacy, toxicity, cost, etc. Furthermore, once a specific herbicide(s) is selected for application, its efficacy can be further enhanced (and its environmental impact minimized) by proper timing and selection of the most suitable method(s) of treatment (including integration with mechanical controls) together with choosing the most appropriate formulation and dosage rate.

The option of non-chemical mechanical clearing of the ROW; by hand cutting with chainsaws, mowing with large machines like a hydro-ax or even using massive earth moving equipment in a stump/soil shearing operation, is most always an available alternative. These physical methods of tree species removal are used for those ROW segments occupied by or located close to sensitive land uses or containing special resources that have been determined to be vulnerable to the application of herbicides. These designated ROW locations can be granted this extra protection through the judicious use of "no spray zones" or "set back distances" which are often referred to as "buffer zones" where herbicide use is not allowed. The determination not to use herbicides can be made by the ROW manager on a site-specific basis or through general company policy even when law, regulation, and label conditions allow such herbicide use. The discretion to employ buffer zones as well as the selection of the appropriate set back distances, must be made in a prudent manner since all the mechanical alternatives will inevitably cause an increase in the number and vigor of incompatible tree species on those portions of the ROW so treated. However, the opportunity to employ mechanical clearing of the ROW is an available option for the ROW manager on specifically chosen ROW segments with certain predetermined characteristics that warrant this treatment. Herbicide usage can be restricted in deference to specific notable ROW resources or as a consideration to particularly sensitive land use conditions while still maintaining the overall goals of a sound, long term, and effective IVM program when viewed from a system-wide perspective.

Even in certain ecologically sensitive areas, the selective use of herbicides may be apropos provided the appropriate precautions are taken. For instance, when treating vegetation in or adjacent to designated wetlands, a herbicide with the appropriate characteristics, e.g., an aquatic or wetland label could be selected. However, to assure that virtually no surface water contamination occurs (irrespective of any allowable label statements) buffer zones can be prescribed around streams, lakes, wetlands, and other sensitive water resources. Studies have shown that buffer zones of only 5–25 feet can effectively curtail the deposition of airborne spray particles and the movement of the herbicide by runoff into surface water resources. A dense stand of vegetation in the buffer zone will

---

9 This "critical tree height" is determined "electrically" by the distance between the tip of the tree and the overhead electric line with consideration for the voltage of the transmission facility, at any given point on the ROW. The higher the line voltage the more clearance that is necessary around the conductors which is often referred to as the wire security zone. For instance, a 765 kV line requires about 25 feet whereas a 345 kV line needs about a 15-foot wire security zone. Also, as the voltage of the transmission facility increases the minimum wire distance from the ground likewise increases. The minimum conductor sag at mid-span allowed for a 765 kV line is about 50 feet from the ground whereas a 345 kV line only requires a height of around 30 feet from the ground. Finally, the location of the tree on the ROW will determine the distance to the conductors and the resulting allowable maximum tree height that can be tolerated at that particular point. Trees located near the edge of the ROW or close to tall towers can be allowed to grow taller than their compatriots located in the center portions of the ROW near conductor mid-span which is within the area of maximum line sag, i.e., where the line is closest to the ground.

further reduce the linear distance of buffer zone necessary, as will very stem specific treatment techniques. Conversely, sparse vegetation in the buffer zone and high volume treatments will increase the distance of the buffer zone required to insure abatement of any herbicide movement. All established EEANY member system specifications for their buffer zones meet or exceed these threshold conditions.

ROW CONVERSION

One quite unique aspect of IPM, as applied to the management of ROW vegetation, is the relative long-term nature of the desired effects and the timeframe required to assess the consequences of actions taken. Although, mechanical removal of the tall growing trees will physically eliminate the immediate threat to electrical reliability and public safety, this method only serves to perpetuate the long-term tree problem and exacerbate future ROW maintenance requirements. Typically, mechanical tree removal will result in the need for more cutting as frequently as every two or at most about four years. After several mechanical treatments, i.e., over a number of ROW treatment cycles, the collection of tree stems requiring control can readily increase to over 20,000 stems per acre. Similarly, when a new ROW is cleared and all vegetation is allowed to grow back naturally, the target tree densities will likewise increase to very high levels in only a few years after the initial tree removal operations and prior to any herbicide application. In fact the term "ROW Reclamation" is customarily used to describe the extreme actions that must often occur to treat very high tree stem densities that are frequently found on a routinely mechanically treated ROW.

When herbicides are used over several treatment cycles, the period of time between treatments can usually be elongated from three or four to six or seven or even more years and concurrently the number of stems to treat each cycle becomes fewer. Herein lies the truly unique aspect of ROW vegetation management from an IPM/IVM perspective; the treatment of vegetation with herbicides must be viewed over the long term to fully grasp the significance of this system in reducing the target tree population that will also reduce the use of chemicals and concurrently increase the effectiveness of the biological controls, i.e., all the lower growing plants that volunteer to occupy the ROW. For example, when a new ROW (or an older ROW that has received only mechanical treatments) is first treated the amount of herbicide needed for proper coverage of the numerous target trees may be in the order of about two to four gallons of concentrate per acre. The following treatment, three to five years later, may require about half that amount because the number of target species has been reduced and the lower growing desirable vegetation is beginning to exert it's influence on the ROW vegetation dynamics. The next treatment, in four to six years, will continue this downward trend in herbicide usage until subsequent treatments produce "nearly" a tree-free ROW requiring a minimum of judiciously applied herbicide to produce the desired effect. At this stage the low growing vegetation is firmly established and offers a relatively stable condition that effectively inhibits the rapid resurgence of trees. However, in order to perpetuate this highly desirable minimum maintenance ROW condition, when new trees begin to emerge (as they most certainly will from the tree seed sources off the ROW) these target trees must still be controlled through the diligent efforts of the ROW vegetation manager to preclude their full development and ultimate dominance over their lower growing associates.

This process of "conversion" from a ROW that is literally filled with trees to one that is dominated by lower growing vegetation with only a few remaining tree stems capable of growing into the overhead electric lines is not a simple one step process, but requires an extended program commitment and adherence to a long range vegetation management plan. Each phase in the ROW conversion process can be quite complex depending in large part upon the target species mix coupled with tree height and density together with the abundance and distribution of the low growing vegetation as well as other site specific characteristics. As the stem density of the target species is reduced with each passing treatment cycle, the type of treatment chosen can then become more selective. Finally, after several treatment cycles when the ROW is occupied by a low density of target trees and the conversion process virtually completed some continuing herbicide use will still be required, but the focus at this stage shifts to selecting techniques which offer the minimum amount of disturbance to the desirable lower growing vegetation, i.e., the biological controls.

General considerations

The use of herbicides by the EEANY member systems is subject to regulation under the Federal Insecticide, Fungicide, and Rodenticide Act (FIFRA) administered by the US Environmental Protection Agency (EPA) and Article 33 of the New York Environmental Conservation Law (ECL) administered by the Department of Environmental Conservation (DEC). Pursuant to FIFRA regulations, no herbicide may be marketed, distributed, sold or advertised until the EPA registers it. After many years of product development, advanced toxicology studies and field testing, the pesticide manufacturers submit to EPA thousands of pages of research data that are compiled into a registration application. From this voluminous registration package, the manufacturer develops a proposed product label that identifies the pest or pests that the product will be effective in controlling and provides complete instructions for correct use, handling, and disposal of the product as well as other information required by FIFRA. In New York State, the DEC has the responsibility for establishing regulations and standards for the registration of pesticides, the certification of pesticides applicators, and all other matters pertaining to pesticide use as well as the responsibility for enforcement of all it's regulations and standards.

Other Federal, State and even local laws and their resulting regulations may impinge on the manner in which ROW vegetation management activities will occur. As mentioned previously, wetland protection requirements can have a pronounced effect on the types of vegetation management techniques chosen. Considerations for the protection of endangered or threatened species and their habitats can similarly become a dominant concern on some ROW. For instance, the nurturing of the endangered Karner blue butterfly and its requisite host plant, the blue lupine, has resulted in considerable evaluation of selected ROW herbicide use in the preservation and enhancement of the habitat conditions necessary for the survival of this endangered species of butterfly. Even the State requirements for management of river corridors under the Wild and Scenic Rivers Act provide definitions and requirements for IPM. Local ordinances, zoning mandates, as well as property owner concerns may sometimes play a critical role in the selection of ROW vegetation management techniques, e.g., the control of poisonous plants, invasive weeds, and allergy producing pollinators. In some instances voluntary compliance with provisions of the Federal Noxious Weed Act may require action on the part of utility ROW vegetation managers to prevent the spread of listed deleterious weeds and other alien invasive species. For example, the control of infestations of the introduced weed, purple loosestrife, which threatens the biological integrity of North American wetland ecosystems by displacing native vegetation is a goal shared by the electric utility industry with both state and federal environmental agencies.

Prevention of non-point sources of pollution & storm water discharge requirements

Another important regulatory program that can directly affect the choice of ROW vegetation management practices available under IPM/IVM is found within the authority of the Clean Water Act as amended by the Water Quality Act of 1987 and involves the control of non-point sources of water pollution along with some aspects of the permit requirements for stormwater discharges for point sources resulting from construction activities. These regulatory programs focus on water quality issues, i.e., the prevention and control of water pollution. In both programs, as they apply to the ROW maintenance situation, the focus is on using management practices to prevent, reduce, minimize or otherwise control the availability, release, or transport of substances that adversely affect surface and ground waters. They both act generally to diminish the generation of potential water pollution emanating from sources on the ROW.

The control of non-point sources of pollution is accomplished through the identification of "best management practices" (BMP's) and their implementation on a site-specific basis using best professional judgment and experience. The control of stormwater discharges which can be considered as point sources due to their collection of runoff into a single outlet, e.g., a culvert or ditch, are similarly treated by the requirement to prepare a "Stormwater Pollution Plan" under the auspices of a SPDES (State Pollutant Discharge Elimination System) General Permit. This plan essentially enumerates the BMP's that will be used to prevent and/or control polluted runoff from occurring. Neither of these programs imposes effluent limits for specific substances, rather they provide for an effective means of reducing or preventing the impact of pollution generated from land management activities. In addition to the ROW managers primary concern of minimizing pesticide related impacts within the context of an IPM strategy, these two somewhat interrelated regulatory programs broaden the environmental concerns arising from IVM to encompass other pollution control objectives. Thus, both of these clean water related programs could directly influence the decision-making process of the ROW vegetation manager and in some cases virtually dictate the menu of treatment choices available.

The most common potential source of pollution arising from a ROW is erosion and the resulting generation of sediment causing siltation in streams and other waterbodies. Sedimentation from all sources is a major water quality degradation issue in New York State. Also, the loss of soil nutrients and their entryway into surface watercourses or groundwater by excessive leaching or as attached to sediment particles is likewise an important water quality concern. Both of these major sources of water pollution can be generated from ROW if bare soils are present or insufficient plant cover occurs. Therefore, in choosing ROW vegetation management techniques, particularly on steep slopes or other areas of high erosive potential, e.g., riparian zones, the ROW vegetation manager must be concerned with their effects on the local hydrology. Vegetative disturbances resulting in bare surfaces or exposed soils and the degree to which vehicular traffic movement occurs causing rutting can become limiting factors in the selection of target tree control methods. For instance, mowing with a hydro-ax on a steep slope or along a streambank could cause erosion by vehicular rutting as well as through denuding the site by excessive removal of vegetation.

The imposition of these regulatory programs to prevent and/or control sources of potential degradation of water resources arising from ROW vegetation management activities results in the following two general precepts: (1) maintain as complete a vegetative cover as possible at all times, and (2) keep exposed soil and any soil disturbance/compaction operations to a minimum especially in critical areas. By keeping these two relatively simple fundamental principles a host of positive attributes can be ascribed to the ROW vegetation management program including: (1) dense low growing vegetation on the ROW will act as filter strips for the surrounding area thereby decreasing overland flow, increasing soil water percolation and removing pollutants, (2) complete vegetative cover on the ROW will stabilize soils and prevent erosion and sediment transfer, (3) minimizing soil compaction by restricting heavy vehicular traffic on the ROW decreases the amount of surface water generated on a given area and thus reduces the volume of stormwater runoff, and (4) avoidance of any soil disturbance on the ROW will reduce or eliminate the need for amelioration activities that would otherwise be required under these clean water programs to restore the disturbed area to its original slope, soil compaction, ground cover, and hydrologic condition.

ROW management research

IPM is never a finished or static process. As fresh data become accessible and new knowledge is obtained about the pests in question and the various control treatments available, the specifics and details of the currently acceptable IPM strategies will naturally be altered and thus subject to constant modification. IPM practitioners can aid and abet this dynamic adaptation and improvement process through conducting basic ecological research on the pests in question as well as applied research in new and promising control strategies. Also needed is the constant reappraisal of existing techniques in order to modify them to produce even more efficacious results. The member systems of the EEANY have individually conducted research into IPM related ROW management matters but even more so collectively, through the auspices of the former Empire State Electric Energy Research Corporation (ESEERCO),[10] have collaborated on numerous research projects over a 25 year span of time involving many diverse aspects of ROW vegetation management. These studies were conducted on a wide range of subjects and a host of issues important to utility ROW managers in their execution of ecologically sound and cost effective IPM/IVM programs.

Beginning with a literature review in 1973, this extended ESEERCO ROW management research program has included projects on ROW treatment cost comparisons, long term effectiveness, ROW treatment cycles, herbicide fate and mobility, allelopathy, ROW multiple uses, buffer zones, soil compaction and mitigation, repeated mechanical cutting effects on vegetation and costs and the effects of ROW treatments on wildlife. Two of the more recent multi-year studies have recently been published in the mid 1990s; *ROW Vegetation Dynamics* conducted by the Institute of Ecosystem Studies and *ROW Stability* by the State University of New York College of Environmental Science and Forestry. The final ROW research product to come out of ESEERCO program in 2000 involves a risk assessment and environmental evaluation of the use of tree growth regulators. These numerous and diverse research projects have greatly assisted the New York State electric utility industry to focus their ROW Vegetation Management Programs on the most cost effective and least disruptive techniques while also allowing them to tailor the research results to their own individual company circumstances. The latest ROW research efforts currently being undertaken by the electric utility industry are now found within the bailiwick of the Electric Power Research Institute (EPRI). EPRI has picked up where ESEERCO left off and has created a new research target, "ROW Environmental Management & Development" which is currently being subscribed to by 44 electric utilities across the nation.

SUMMARY

The overall goal of a utility ROW vegetation management program is to provide for the safe and reliable transmission of electric power in an economic and environmentally compatible manner. This lofty goal translates "on the ground" into the vegetative conversion of a strip of land, i.e., the ROW, often initially found filled with tree saplings to a ROW corridor that harbors mainly a profusion of lower growing species. This goal is currently being achieved in New York State by the implementation of sound IPM/IVM programs at each of the electric transmission and distribution systems of the EEANY members. To paraphrase applicable IPM terminology; ROW vegetation managers use multiple tactics to prevent pest (tree) buildups that could endanger electric system reliability and public safety by: monitoring pest (tree) populations, assessing the potential for damage (system reliability, public safety, preservation of the biological controls), and making professional management and control decisions, considering that all pesticides (herbicides) should be used judiciously. ROW management decisions depend in large part upon the mix of target species, the height and density of the dominate individual stems, and the abundance and distribution of the low growing desirable species. As the number of different target species is reduced and their stem density decreases with each passing treatment cycle, the type of vegetation treatment performed can become more selective with the attendant benefit of reducing

---

[10] ESEERCO ceased to exist in 1999 due to the increased economic pressures of a deregulated competitive electric market.

the amount of herbicide needed to maintain the ROW. Thus, after several treatment cycles, when the ROW is occupied by a greatly reduced number of target trees, some minimum herbicide use will still be required but the focus now shifts to selecting techniques with the least amount of disturbance to the lower growing vegetation.

It should be stressed in closing that these ideal ROW conditions of a "minimum maintenance" ROW (composed almost entirely of low growing plants) to be achieved through the attentive implementation of an IPM/IVM program, is simply just that, minimum not zero maintenance. Although the low growing plants will help immensely in precluding the growth of trees, due to the pressures of natural plant community succession that ultimately will occur, these voluntary biological controls can never be expected to fully exclude trees over long periods of time from invading the ROW and exploiting their well defined ecological niches. Even after many treatment cycles using herbicides, when the ideal ROW condition is seemingly achieved, if the ROW is left untreated or if mechanical methods are resorted to, the ROW will revert rather quickly to a tree dominated landscape and all the attendant benefits of a stable low growing mosaic of desirable ROW vegetation will be lost. These attendant benefits include species diversity in an aesthetically pleasing setting with increased wildlife abundance while protecting soil and water quality values.

REFERENCES

Abrahamson, L.P., PhD, Ch.A. Nowak, P.M. Charlton, Dr., and P. Snyder. 1992. Cost Effectiveness of Herbicide and Non-Herbicide Vegetation Management Methods for Electric Utility Rights-of-Way in the Northeast. Niagara Mohawk P Corporation Project JC28477AGP. Environmental Consultants, Inc., Southampton, PA and The Research Foundation of the State University of New Albany, NY. December.

Canham, Ch.D., A.R. Berkowitz, J.B. McAninch, M.J. McDonnell, and R. Ostfeld. 1993. Vegetation dynamics along utility rights-of-way: factors affecting the ability of shrub and herbaceous communities to resist invasion by trees. ESEERCO Research Report EP85-38. Institute of Ecosystem Studies, Millbrook, NY. December.

Cody, J.B. and J. Quimby. 1975. Vegetation management on utility rights-of-way an annotated bibliography. AFRI Research Report. State University of New York, College of Environmental Science and Forestry, Applied Forestry Research Institute. May.

Edwards, D., R. Jacoby, Dr., E. McKyes, Dr., M. Remington, S. Thew, and E. Thomas. 1990. Soil compaction: A comprehensive retrospective literature review. ESEERCO Research Report EP89-26. Atlantic Testing Laboratories, Limited. December.

Edwards, D., E. McKyes, Dr., M.B. Remington, S.F. Thew, and E.D. Thomas. 1996. Soil and crop response to power line construction traffic and shallow and deep tillage in New York state. ESEERCO Research Project EP89-26. Atlantic Testing Laboratories, Limited, March.

ESEERCO Research Project. 1977. Environmental and Economic Aspects of Contemporaneous Electric Transmission Line Right-of-Way Management Techniques, Volume 1, General Methods, Special Studies, Discussion of Trends, and Conclusions. Asplundh Environmental Services. Willow Grove, PA. June.

Hadlock, C.R. and D.E. Langseth. 1987. Herbicide residue and mobility study: existing and simulation model review, Volume I. ESEERCO Research Report EP84-8. prepared by Arthur D. Little, Inc., December.

Hadlock, C.R. and D.E. Langseth. 1987. Herbicide residue and mobility study: existing and simulation model review, Volume II. ESEERCO Research Report EP84-8. A.D. Little, Inc. December.

Johnston, P.A, W.C. Bramble, W.R. Byrnes, K.L. Carvell, D.E. White, and H.V. Wiant. 1985. Long-term right-of-way effectiveness. ESEERCO Research Report EP83-15. Environmental Consultants, Inc., Southampton, PA. October.

Johnston, P.A., W.C. Bramble, W.R. Byrnes, K.L. Carvell, D.E. White and H.V. Wiant. 1985. Right-of-Way Treatment Cycles. ESEERCO Research. Environmental Consultants, Inc., Southampton, PA.

Johnston, P.A., W.C. Bramble, W.R. Byrnes, K.L. Carvell, D.E. White, and H.V. Wiant. 1984. Cost comparison of right-of-way treatment methods. ESEERCO Research Report EP80-5. Environmental Consultants, Inc., Fort Washington, PA.

Kunzman, M.R. and C. Stevens. 1986 Right-of-way chemical treatments phase I — Site preparation. ESEERCO Research Project EP85-5. Tree Preservation Co., Inc. Briarcliff Manor, NY. October.

Leopold, D.J., J.R. Raynal, and G.S. Podniesinski. 1997. Vascular species richness and rarity in wetlands on electric power rights-of-way in New York State. ESEERCO Research Project EP91-6. SUNY College of Environmental Science and Forestry at Syracuse, NY.

Norris, L.A., PhD. 1991. Determination of the effectiveness of herbicide buffer zones in protecting water quality on new york state powerline rights-of-way. ESEERCO Research Report EP89-44. Environmental Consultants, Inc., Southampton, PA, August.

Schuler, M.D., P.A. Johnston and D.E. Holewinski. 1983. The effects of right-of-way vegetation management on wildlife habitat, gaps in the literature. ESEERCO Research Report EP82-13. Asplundh Environmental Services, Willow Grove, PA.

Wright, D.C., PhD. 1991. Development of natural growth inhibitors for overhead transmission rights-of-way in New York state, Phase I, Part A: Literature review/search/update. ESEERCO Research Report EP90-14. Brooklyn Botanic Garden, Brooklyn, NY, July.

Integrated Vegetation Management on Electrical Transmission Rights-of-Way Using Herbicides: Treatment Effects Over Time

Benjamin D. Ballard,[1] Christopher A. Nowak, Lawrence P. Abrahamson, Edward F. Neuhauser, and Kenneth E. Finch

The goal of vegetation management on electric transmission rights-of-way (ROWs) is to ensure safe, reliable transmission of power. A common, ecological approach to managing vegetation on ROWs — Integrated Vegetation Management (IVM) — is to promote desirable, stable, low-growing communities that will resist invasion by undesirable, tall-growing tree species. Vegetation management studies consistent with IVM took place on a 25-km section of Niagara Mohawk Power Corporation's Volney–Marcy 765 kV electric transmission ROW in upstate New York. Initial clearing treatments for establishment of the ROW occurred in 1983. Vegetation management treatments for the first and second conversion cycles were applied in 1984 and 1988, respectively. Selective and non-selective applications of stem-foliar and basal herbicide treatments were applied to replicated study areas during the second conversion cycle. Woody stem data from initial clearing to present (1999) were used to evaluate the effects of the herbicide treatments on stem densities of undesirable and desirable woody species over time. It was hypothesized that stem density of undesirable woody plants would continue to decrease over time and stem density of desirable species would increase or remain the same over time, thus, moving towards a more stable community of woody desirable species and a maintenance phase of management. Undesirable species densities were maintained and desirable densities increased over 11-years using an IVM approach. A stable community of woody desirable species (i.e., maintenance phase of management, as defined in this paper) has not been reached and may need another 10–20 years before it develops on the powerline. Shrub abundance needs to be increased to attain maintenance levels.

Keywords: Powerline corridor, shrub dynamics, stem-foliar herbicide, basal herbicide, herbicide, undesirable and desirable vegetation

INTRODUCTION

The goal of vegetation management on electric transmission rights-of-way (ROW) is to ensure safe, reliable transmission of power. A common, ecological approach to managing vegetation on ROW — Integrated Vegetation Management (IVM) — is to promote desirable, stable, low-growing communities that will resist invasion by undesirable, tall-growing tree species (McLoughlin, 1997). The impact that IVM has on both desirable and undesirable species dynamics over time is critical to its success. Establishing a stable, low-growing community is necessary to enter the maintenance phase of management (Nowak et al., 1992); therefore, an important purpose of this study is to determine whether the vegetation has reached the maintenance level. Research initiated during the establishment of a powerline corridor in New York State — the Volney–Marcy (V–M) powerline, established in 1983 — offers an opportunity to study the effects of nearly two decades of IVM and to determine how successfully low-growing communities have resisted tree invasion on the powerline corridor.

---

1 Corresponding Author: phone: 315-470-4821, fax: 315-470-6956, email: bballard@esf.edu.

Environmental Concerns in Rights-of-Way Management: Seventh International Symposium
J.W. Goodrich-Mahoney, D.F. Mutrie and C.A. Guild (editors)
© 2002 Elsevier Science Ltd. All rights reserved.

OBJECTIVE

The objective of the study was to describe the dynamics of woody vegetation over time on the V–M powerline corridor using selective and non-selective herbicide treatments with a focus on the establishment and ability of low-growing communities to resist tree invasion. The hypotheses to be tested were: (1) stem density of undesirable woody plants would continue to decrease over time and (2) stem density of desirable species would increase or remain the same over time.

MATERIALS AND METHODS

Study area description

The study took place on the 17-yr-old (1999 age) V–M powerline corridor, a 765 kV transmission line ROW in the Towns of Lee, Western, and Floyd in Oneida County, New York (43°21'N, 75°32'W–43°15'N, 75°17'W) (described previously by Nowak et al., 1992; paraphrased as follows). The corridor passes through the Interlobal Highland Region, between the Tug Hill Plateau and the Mohawk Valley; it is covered by northern hardwood forest with a predominance of red maple (*Acer rubrum* L.) and eastern hemlock (*Tsuga canadensis* [L.] Carr.), although there was a mixture of both abandoned and active agricultural and forest land on and surrounding the study area. The V–M ROW is 68.6 m wide. The study area is approximately 25-km in length, generally running east-west in direction. On the south side of the V–M powerline is the 28-yr-old (1999 age) New York Power Authority Fitzpatrick–Edic 345 kV transmission line; its ROW width is 45.7 m.

Soils of the study area are silt and sand loams, including a variety of Fragiaquepts, Eutrochrepts, and Haplaquepts of varied drainage; the dominant soil series encountered were Camroden, Pickney, Pyrities, Katurah, and Malone. Many of the soils have fragipans, which cause the sites to be wet with a perched water table. Most of the sites have mesic or hydric moisture regimes.

Experimental design and treatments

A randomized incomplete block factorial design (three to six replications, $n = 19$) was used to test second conversion cycle mode (non-selective and selective) and method (basal and stem-foliar) treatment effects on undesirable and desirable woody plant species density. Treatment plots ranged in size from 0.23 to 0.75 ha, extending from edge to edge of the ROW. Treatment plots were systematically assigned within randomly chosen areas located across the study site and treated in mid-summer 1988.

The four study treatments were composed of two basal and two stem-foliar herbicide treatments applied selectively and non-selectively at the beginning of the first conversion cycle (1984) and repeated at the beginning of the second conversion cycle (1988). The four treatments were applied during late July–August.

Selective basal
Treatment of undesirable vegetation (trees that can grow more than 6 m in height) during late July–August 1988 with a herbicide mixture consisting of 7.6 L of triclopyr at 0.480 kg ai ha^{-1} and 371 L of No. 2 fuel oil; it was targeted at the lower 0.3 to 0.6 m of individual stems, saturating the base of the stem and all exposed roots to the point of rundown and puddling around the root collar zone.

Nonselective basal
Treatment of all woody vegetation with a herbicide mixture and application method the same as that for the selective basal treatment. Herbaceous vegetation was not treated.

Selective stem-foliar
Treatment of undesirable vegetation with a herbicide consisting of a mixture of 1.4 L of triclopyr at 0.480 kg ai ha^{-1}, 1.9 L of a formulation of picloram at 0.060 kg ai ha^{-1} plus 2,4 D at 0.240 kg ai ha^{-1}, 0.95 L of adjuvant (crop oil concentrate) and 375 L of water, applied to leaves, branches and stems to a point of wetness.

Nonselective stem-foliar
Treatment of all woody vegetation with a herbicide mixture and application method the same as that for the selective stem-foliar treatment. Herbaceous vegetation was not treated.

Data collection

Vegetation was measured in 1999 using a series of systematic 1.8-m wide strip transects and 1.13-m radius regeneration plots located with a random starting point. Transects and regeneration plots started and ended at a minimum of 7.6 m from the plot edge. Transects and regeneration plots covered 6 to 16% and 1 to 2% of the treatment plot area, respectively.

Desirable and undesirable vegetation densities (number of stems per hectare as shoot sprouts, root sprouts, and seedlings) were measured by species and height in 1999. Stems 1.27 cm diameter at breast height (dbh; 1.37 m along stem above ground) or greater were tallied on strip transects, while stems less than 1.27 cm dbh were tallied on regeneration plots. Historic stem density data — 1987 and 1990 — for stems >0.9 m height were used from Nowak (1993) for comparisons through time.

Desirable woody plants were defined as those that attain maximum heights of less than 6.1 m, undesirable woody plants as those that can attain a maximum height growth greater than or equal to 6.1 m (Tables 1 and 2). Serviceberry was included with desirable species, but is also recognized as an undesirable species depending on specific site and transmission line conditions (Nowak, 1993).

Table 1. List of "undesirable" woody plant species[1] present on the Volney–Marcy study area

Common name	Scientific name
American basswood	*Tilia americana* L.
American beech	*Fagus grandifolia* Ehrh.
American hornbeam	*Carpinus caroliniana* Walt.
balsam fir	*Abies balsamea* (L.) Mill.
bigtooth aspen	*Populus grandindentata* Michx.
black cherry	*Prunus serotina* Ehrh.
butternut	*Juglans cinerea* L.
common chokecherry	*Prunus virginiana* L.
Eastern hemlock	*Tsuga canadensis* (L.) Carr.
Eastern hophornbeam	*Ostrya virginiana* (Miller) Koch
Eastern larch	*Larix laricina* (Duroi) Koch
Eastern white pine	*Pinus strobus* L.
elm	*Ulmus* spp. L.
gray birch	*Betula populifolia* Marsh.
hickory	*Carya* spp. Nutt.
pin cherry	*Prunus pensylvanica* L.f.
poplar	*Populus* spp. L.
quaking aspen	*Populus tremuloides* Michx.
red maple	*Acer rubrum* L.
red pine	*Pinus resinosa* Ait.
red spruce	*Picea rubens* Sarg.
scotch pine	*Pinus sylvestris* L.
striped maple	*Acer pensylvanicum* L.
sugar maple	*Acer saccharum* Marsh.
white ash	*Fraxinus americana* L.
white spruce	*Picae glauca* (Moench) Voss
yellow birch	*Betula alleghaniensis* Britt.

[1] Nomenclature follows Gleason and Cronquist (1991).

Herbaceous plants are considered desirable species. Percent cover of all species was tallied in 1999 using the 1.13-m radius regeneration plots (by height strata: <0.3, 0.3–0.9, 0.9–1.5, and >1.5 m). Relative percent of total cover by desirable and undesirable woody species and herbaceous (i.e., all non-woody) species was used in this study.

Data analysis and hypothesis testing

Paired t-tests were used for comparison of second conversion cycle changes in stem density for desirable and undesirable woody plant species between 1990 and 1999.

Analysis of variance and analysis of covariance were used to test treatment mode and method effects on undesirable and desirable woody plant density in 1999. An alpha level of 0.10 was used as the critical value for significance testing, though significance levels (P values) up to 0.20 were considered potentially meaningful.

Analysis of covariance was used to adjust for non-homogeneous pre-treatment stem densities, only if the correlation between the concomitant variable was greater than $r = 0.30$ (Cochran, 1957); the concomitant variable was pre-treatment (1987) stem densities for both desirable and undesirable woody plant density.

An unbalanced approach was taken to examine treatment mode and method effects on vegetation

Table 2. List of "desirable" woody plant species[1] present on the Volney–Marcy study area

Common name	Scientific name
alder	*Alnus* spp. Mill.
alternate-leaved dogwood	*Cornus alternifolia* L.f.
apple	*Malus* spp. P. Mill.
arrow-wood	*Viburnum dentatum* var. *lucidum* Aiton
black chokeberry	*Aronia melanocarpa* (Michx.) Ell.
common buckthorn	*Rhamnus cathartica* L.
common elderberry	*Sambucus canadensis* L.
common mountain holly	*Nemopanthus mucronatus* (L.) Loes.
dogwood	*Cornus* spp. L.
hawthorn	*Crataegus* spp. L.
hazel	*Corylus* spp. L.
highbush blueberry	*Vaccinium corymbosum* L.
holly	*Ilex* spp. L.
honeysuckle	*Lonicera* spp. L.
low sweet blueberry	*Vaccinium angustifolium* Ait.
meadowsweet	*Spiraea alba* Duroi.
nannyberry	*Viburnum lentago* L.
red elderberry	*Sambucus racemosa* L.
ribes	*Ribes* spp. L.
rose	*Rosa* spp. L.
serviceberry[2]	*Amelanchier* spp. Medik.
skunk currant	*Ribes glandulosum* Grauer
spicebush	*Lindera benzoin* (L.) Blume
steeple-bush	*Spiraea tomentosa* L.
sumac	*Rhus* spp. L.
wild black current	*Ribes americanum* Mill.
wild raisin	*Viburnum nudum* var. *cassinoides* (L.) T.G.
willow	*Salix* spp. L.
winterberry	*Ilex verticillata* var. *verticillata* (L.) A. Gray
witch hazel	*Hamamelis virginiana* L.
witch-hobble	*Viburnum alnifolium* Marsh.

[1] Nomenclature follows Gleason and Cronquist (1991).
[2] Serviceberry was included with desirable species, but is also recognized as an undesirable species depending on specific site and transmission line conditions.

because not all treatments were represented in all blocks; Type III hypotheses were tested (Milliken and Johnson, 1984).

Significant interaction effects were examined by graphing treatment means. Simple effects were analyzed when the slope of lines connecting means differed markedly, as interaction would affect interpretation of mode and method effects.

All statistical analyses were done using SAS computer software package (SAS Institute, 1998).

RESULTS AND DISCUSSION

Undesirable species

There was no significant difference in density of undesirable woody stems (0.9 m and above) in 1990–1999 ($P = 0.22$, paired t-test, $n = 19$). Density has not decreased over time as hypothesized; however, stem density of undesirables has been maintained with IVM even over a long treatment cycle (11 years; Fig. 1).

There was a significant mode x method interaction ($P = 0.15$) for 1999 density of undesirable stems over 0.9 m height (ANOVA with a covariate). Analysis of simple effects indicated that the selective treatment had higher densities than the non-selective mode for basal methods ($P = 0.06$), but not for stem-foliar methods ($P = 0.76$). The basal treatment had a higher undesirable stem density than the stem-foliar treatment method in the selective mode ($P = 0.05$), but not in non-selective mode ($P = 0.96$). It may be more difficult to successfully locate and treat undesirable stems in the selective mode for basal treatments than the other three treatments, resulting in more missed trees. Nowak (1992) found no difference by mode of treatment, but did find that basal methods had more undesirables than stem-foliar methods, which is not inconsistent with these findings.

In the study area there are 2.0 to 4.1 times more seedlings under 0.9 m than there are over (Table 3). There are large numbers of small undesirable seedlings below 0.9 m height in 1999 in all treatments (2913–7486 stems ha^{-1}), but the selective basal treatment had more than twice as many small seedlings than the other treatments (Table 3). These results may indicate a potentially problematic future for selective basal treatments, particularly when considering smaller seedlings. Trees less than 0.9 m will likely be hidden in the understory and missed during the next treatment cycle.

Large numbers of small seedlings with decreasing density for larger trees would be expected in hardwood forests. The same could be said for densities on powerline ROW. The high densities in the small height classes on the V–M may indicate that the desirable communities are not successfully resisting tree invasion; the density of desirable species required to effec-

Table 3. Undesirable woody stem density for treatments by height class in 1999

Treatment (mode/method)	Stem density (stems ha^{-1})		n	Ratio under/over
	Under 0.9 m height	Over 0.9 m height		
Non-selective/ stem-foliar	3230 (995)[1]	1215 (202)	6	2.7
Non-selective/ basal	3462 (1569)	843 (128)	3	4.1
Selective/ stem-foliar	2913 (1032)	1484 (623)	6	2.0
Selective/ basal	7486 (940)	2723 (586)	4	2.7

[1] Values in parentheses are standard errors.

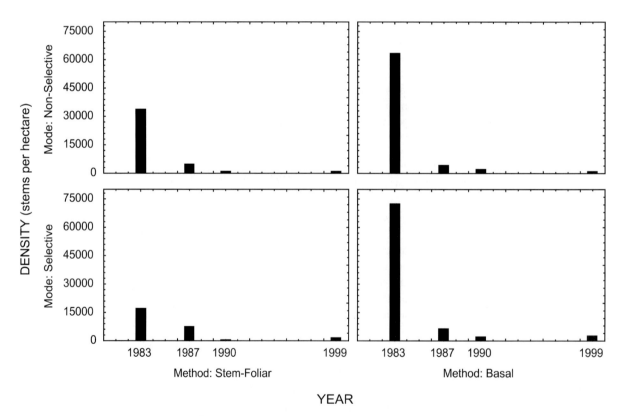

Fig. 1. Undesirable stem density since clearing[1] on the Volney–Marcy powerline for selective and non-selective modes of basal and stem–foliar herbicide treatment methods.

---

1 Initial clearing (1983), first treatment cycle (1984), second treatment cycle (1988).

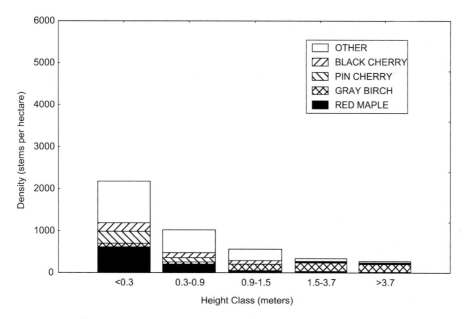

Fig. 2. Undesirable species[1] density distribution by species and size class for all treatments except selective basal in 1999.

1 Initial clearing (1983), first treatment cycle (1984), second treatment cycle (1988).

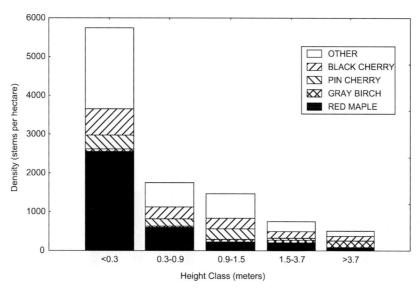

Fig. 3. Undesirable species density distribution by species and size class for the selective basal treatment in 1999.

tively resist tree invasion may not exist yet. Comparisons of shrub abundance (unpublished data) on the V–M and the Fitzpatrick–Edick powerline — the adjacent, older line — indicated that shrubs were less developed (lower abundance) on the V–M. It may take longer for the desirable communities to fully occupy the corridor and adequately resist tree invasion.

Small seedlings in the study area were dominated by red maple, black cherry, and pin cherry (Figs. 2 and 3), among a variety of other species (e.g., sugar maple, quaking aspen, white ash, and choke cherry; see Table 1 for scientific names). The larger trees in the study area had a much higher proportion of gray birch than the smaller classes. There appears to be a species shift through time from pioneer to later successional species. This shift is important because it indicates that the vegetation on the ROW is not yet stable.

Desirable species

There was a significantly higher density of desirable stems (0.9 m and above) in 1999 compared to 1990 ($P = 0.02$, paired t-test, $n = 19$; also see Fig. 4). Interpretation of this result must be tempered due to differences in methods for desirable woody plant inventories. Data collected in 1999 were more detailed than those collected previously; therefore, a more accurate accounting of stems by height classes might have falsely indicated an increase in desirable density. To minimize this possibility, only stems over 0.9 m height were used for comparison with 1990 data. The dominant desirable species included meadowsweet, steeple-bush, willow, and arrow-wood.

Analysis of 1999 data (ANOVA with a covariate) indicated that the selective modes had a marginally higher stem density than the non-selective modes ($P = 0.13$). There were no method-related differences ($P = 0.68$). These results are consistent with Nowak et al. (1992) for 1990 desirable densities.

Desirable woody species over 0.9 m height accounted for only a fraction of the total number of desirable stems present. It is important to consider the number of small stems (<0.9 m) that may indicate continued growth and proliferation of desirables. The smaller height class was 1.6 to 4.8 times larger than all desirable stems over 0.9 m (Table 4). Desirable woody species appear to be increasing in number in the study area and are more abundant than small undesirable species (13,769 compared to 4061 stems ha^{-1}; $P < 0.01$, paired t-test, $n = 19$). These results, collectively, give evidence to suggest that our hypothesis is true; desirable stem density is increasing over time with an IVM approach.

Woody desirable plants, with advantages of height and longevity, are not the only desirable species that are important in resisting tree invasion on powerline corridors [e.g., *Rubus*, ferns, goldenrod/asters; Bramble and Byrnes (1983), Bramble et al. (1990), Hill et al. (1995), Horsely (1993)]. Desirable woody species comprise only a fraction of the total relative cover on the powerline corridor (from <1 to 8%; Fig. 5). Herbaceous species (including *Rubus*) account for 73–91% of the total relative cover, and undesirable woody species account for 9–19% of the total relative cover. Clearly, woody desirable species can only tell a portion of the story; herbaceous communities will be an important factor in the future management of the ROW.

Table 4. **Desirable woody stem density for treatments by height class in 1999.**

Treatment (mode/method)	Stem Density (stems ha^{-1})		n	Ratio under/ over
	Under 0.9 m height	Over 0.9 m height		
Non-selective/ stem-foliar	12,762 (4616)[1]	3932 (1759)	6	3.2
Non-selective/ basal	10,380 (7834)	2186 (1142)	3	4.8
Selective/ stem-foliar	13,036 (5526)	6588 (2229)	6	2.0
Selective/ basal	18,923 (11,424)	11,986 (10,069)	4	1.6

[1] Values in parentheses are standard errors.

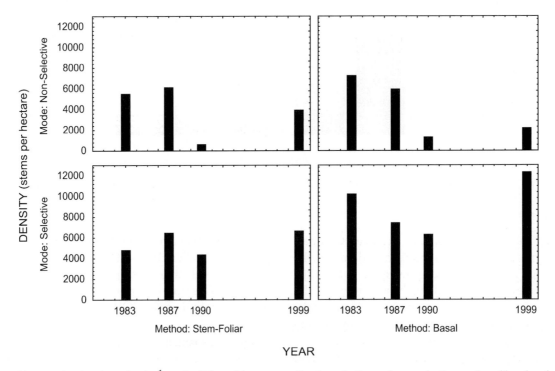

Fig. 4. Desirable stem density since clearing[1] on the Volney–Marcy powerline for selective and non-selective modes of basal and stem-foliar herbicide treatment methods.

1 Initial clearing (1983), first treatment cycle (1984), second treatment cycle (1988).

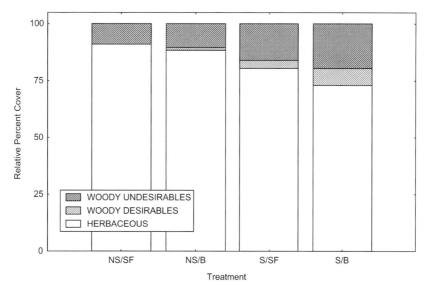

Fig. 5. Relative percent cover of undesirable and desirable woody plants and other herbaceous plants (including *Rubus*) by treatment[1] in 1999.

1 NS/SF — non-selective/stem-foliar, NS/B — non-selective/basal, S/SF — selective/stem-foliar, and S/B — selective/basal.

SUMMARY AND CONCLUSIONS

The 1999 treatment effect results are similar to those found by Nowak et al. (1992). The potentially important differences found here were that woody desirable species density has increased in abundance, while undesirable woody species density was maintained on the V–M ROW. The selective basal treatment had some potentially problematic symptoms. Not only were undesirable stem densities for the selective basal treatment high for all stems over 0.9 m in height, but more importantly, there were many stems in the smaller height classes (<0.9 m). All treatments had high densities of small seedlings, which indicate resistance to tree invasion can still be improved. Management of herbaceous communities may play a role here, but establishment of stable shrub communities will be crucial.

Interestingly, the species composition of the various height classes indicates a shift from gray birch in the taller (and older) classes to red maple and a variety of other species (e.g., cherries, sugar maple, white ash, quaking aspen) in the smaller height classes. The ability of these small seedlings to persist in the understory until the next treatment cycle poses another challenge to managers, as many of these trees will be misses and may escape from a predominantly herbaceous community.

There is sufficient evidence to suggest that the V–M ROW has not yet reached a maintenance phase of management due to the persistence of undesirable seedlings and increasing numbers of woody desirables. The dominant cover is herbaceous, and conversion to a stable, low-growing, woody community may require another 10 to 20 years.

ACKNOWLEDGEMENTS

Funding for this project was provided by the Niagara Mohawk Power Corporation. Thanks are extended to previous research on the Volney–Marcy line conducted by Craig Stevens, Tree Preservation Company, Inc., and Kurt Foreback and Dale Freed, Niagara Mohawk Power Corporation, and to the field crew for the 1999 work: Ted Andrejko, Lisa Casalmir, Marc Daly, Pablo Donoso, Katherine Johnson, and Erin O'Neill.

REFERENCES

Bramble, W.C. and W.R. Byrnes. 1983. Thirty years of research on development of plant cover on an electric transmission right-of-way. Journal of Arboriculture, 9(3): 67–74.

Bramble, W.C., W.R. Byrnes, and R.J. Hutnik. 1990. Resistance of plant cover types to tree seedling invasion on an electric transmission right-of-way. Journal of Arboriculture, 16: 130–135.

Cochran, W.G. 1957. Analysis of covariance: Its nature and uses. Biometrics, 3: 261–281.

Gleason, H.A. and A. Cronquist. 1991. Manual of vascular plants of the Northeastern United States and adjacent Canada. The New York Botanical Garden, Bronx, NY. 910 pp.

Hill, J.D., C.D. Canham, and D.M. Wood. 1995. Patterns and causes of resistance to tree invasion in rights-of-way. Ecological Applications, 5: 459–470.

Horsley, S.B. 1993. Mechanisms of interference between hay-scented fern and black cherry. Canadian Journal of Forest Research, 23: 2059–2069.

McLoughlin, K.T. 1997. Application of integrated pest management to electric utility rights-of-way vegetation management in New York State. In: Proceedings of the 6th International Symposium on Environmental Concerns in Rights-of-Way Management, February 24–26, 1997, New Orleans, LA. J.R. Williams, J.W. Goodrich-Mahoney, J.R. Wisniewski, and J. Wisniewski, eds. Elsevier Science Ltd, New York. pp. 118–126.

Milliken, G.A. and D.E. Johnson. 1984. Analysis of Messy Data. Vol 1: Designed experiments. Van Nostrand–Reinhold, New York.

Nowak, C.A. 1993. Effectiveness and other practical considerations of electric transmission line rights-of-way management in New York State. Ph.D. thesis. SUNY College of Environmental Science and Forestry, Syracuse, NY.

SAS Institute, Inc. 1998. SAS Campus Drive, Cary, NC 27513, USA.

Nowak, C.A., L.P. Abrahamson, E.F. Neuhauser, C.G. Foreback, H.D. Freed, S.B. Shaheen, and C.H. Stevens. 1992. Cost effective vegetation management on a recently cleared electric transmission right-of-way. Weed Technology, 6: 828–837.

BIOGRAPHICAL SKETCHES

Benjamin D. Ballard

218 Marshall Hall, State University of New York, College of Environmental Science and Forestry, 1 Forestry Drive, Syracuse, NY 13210, USA. Phone: 315-470-4821; email: bballard@esf.edu

Benjamin Ballard, Research Scientist at SUNY-College of Environmental Science and Forestry (SUNY-ESF), holds a BS and MS in Forest Resources Management from SUNY-ESF and an MS in Statistics from Syracuse University. He has been involved with research at SUNY-ESF for over 8 years, and is currently responsible for the day-to-day management of more than 15 studies associated with vegetation management on powerline corridors. Additionally, he is a PhD candidate working on issues related to integrated vegetation management on powerline corridors, focusing on the ecology and management of shrub communities.

Christopher A. Nowak

220 Marshall Hall, State University of New York College of Environmental Science and Forestry, 1 Forestry Drive, Syracuse, NY 13210, USA. Phone: 315-470-6575; email: canowak@esf.edu

Christopher A. Nowak, Associate Professor of Forestry at SUNY–College of Environmental Science and Forestry (SUNY–ESF), holds an AAS in Forest Technology and BS, MS, and PhD degrees in Forest Resources Management from SUNY–ESF. Prior to joining the Faculty at SUNY–ESF in 1998, he worked for 6 years as a Research Scientist for the Research Foundation of SUNY on issues related to nutrient cycling and acidic deposition, fast growing hardwoods, and vegetation management on powerline corridors, and 5 years as a Research Forester for the US Forest Service in northwestern Pennsylvania on ecology and silviculture of Allegheny hardwoods. He is currently responsible for teaching courses related to extensive and intensive silviculture and forest vegetation management. His contemporary research and service activities are related to integrated vegetation management on powerline corridors, phytoremediation of industrial waste sites, short-rotation intensive culture of willow and poplar, and silviculture in northern conifers and hardwoods.

Lawrence P. Abrahamson

126 Illick Hall, State University of New York College of Environmental Science and Forestry, 1 Forestry Drive, Syracuse, NY 13210, USA. Phone: 315-470-6777; email: labrahamson@esf.edu

Lawrence P. Abrahamson, Senior Research Associate, at SUNY–College of Environmental Science and Forestry (SUNY–ESF), holds a BS in Forest Management from Michigan Technological University, MS and PhD in Forest Entomology from University of Wisconsin–Madison. Prior to joining the Faculty at SUNY–ESF in 1977, he worked for 9 years as a Research Scientist/Pesticide Specialist for the USDA Forest Service in Stoneville, MS, Atlanta, GA and Ogden, UT. 1977–1979: He worked for 2 years with the Applied Forestry Research Institute, SUNY–ESF, Syracuse, New York on applied research in the fields of forest entomology and pathology as well as with herbicides in silvicultural use. For 4 years he was the Director of the Northeast Petroleum–Forest Resources Cooperative (NEP–FRC). Presently he has a joint appointment between the Faculty of Forestry and the Faculty of Environmental and Forest Biology SUNY–ESF, Syracuse, NY. He conducts applied research in the fields of forest entomology and pathology, and high-yield wood energy crops as they relate to problems in the State of New York. He is also presently engaged in research projects with Scleroderris canker (fungus disease) on conifers in New York; red pine scale studies in New York and Korea; evaluations of integrated pest management systems for gypsy moth and other forest insects; herbicide use on forest tree nurseries in the western plains and northeast; silvicultural management through use of herbicides and/or fire; pest management (vegetation, insects and diseases) in intensive culture of fast growing hardwoods (hybrid poplar and willow); vegetation management/plant dynamics on electric utility rights-of-way in New York; and the development of high-yield wood energy crops (willow dedicated feedstock supply system).

Kenneth E. Finch

Niagara Mohawk Power Corporation, 300 Erie Blvd West, C-1, Syracuse, NY 13202, USA

Kenneth E. Finch, Director, System Forestry, holds an AS from Paul Smith's College, and a BS in Resource Management from SUNY College of Environmental Science and Forestry. He is responsible for vegetation management programs on 72,000 acres of transmission right-of-way, and 36,000 miles of distribution lines. He is also responsible for environmental compliance issues for clearing and new construction projects, and serves as liaison for environmental compliance matters.

Edward F. Neuhauser, PhD
Niagara Mohawk Power Corporation, 300 Erie Blvd West, A-2, Syracuse, NY 13202, USA

Edward F. Neuhauser, Senior Research Specialist, holds a BS and PhD in Soil Biology from SUNY College of Environmental Science and Forestry. He is responsible for a variety of renewable and energy storage research programs, as well as environmental, water resource, hazardous material, remediation, and safety research adventures at Niagara Mohawk. He participates in task forces and review committees for the Electric Power Research Institute, Gas Research Institute, and Edison Electric Institute.

Versatile Plant for Multiple Use on Rights-of-Way

Dr. Dale H. Arner and Dr. Jeanne C. Jones

Today's rights-of-way (ROW) manager must be concerned more than ever before with multiple-use aspects of plant communities that resist invasion of woody plants, are aesthetically pleasing, provide food and cover for wildlife, and can be economically maintained. One plant species which has these and other desirable traits in the southeastern United States is partridge pea (*Chamaecrista fasciculata*). The purpose of this paper is to review field trial results of establishing partridge pea in different ecosystems by using different techniques, such as overseeding in herbicide treated, disked, and burned plots. The maintenance, as well as ecological aspects, of this plant in ROW management, are reviewed and discussed.

Keywords: Partridge pea, ROW, overseeding, herbicide, disking, burning, legume

INTRODUCTION

Today, right-of-way (ROW) managers must be concerned more than ever before with multiple use aspect of ROW management. Multiple use concerns necessitate the development of plant communities that resist invasion of woody plants, are aesthetically pleasing, provide food and/or cover for wildlife and can be economically established and maintained.

A plant species that exhibits these desirable traits is partridge pea (PP) (*Chamaecrista fasciculata*). This species is an annual legume native to the southeastern United States. PP is a noduled legume that is capable of nitrogen fixation (Allen and Allen, 1981). It generally grows in colony-like clusters and produces large yellow flowers from late summer into early fall (Radford et al., 1987). The profusion of blooms during this time of year is visually pleasing. Stoddard (1932) wrote "when the large flowering species (*Chamaecrista fasiculata*) blossom, areas miles in extent take on a bright yellow hue." The flowers produce nectar and pollen that are used by a variety of insect pollinators, including native bees and wasps, butterflies, and European honeybees (Martin et al., 1961). The use of the seed of PP by bobwhite quail (*Colinus virginianus*) for food is well documented. Stoddard (1931) reported that PP seeds are taken by bobwhite quail every month of the year with maximum consumption occurring during the winter months. He reported that nearly 80% of the quail crops examined during late winter contained PP. Rosene (1969) noted that PP seed was found in over 35% of the quail crop collected in Alabama. Brazil (1993) analyzed the contents of nearly 6,000 quail crops collected in Mississippi over a 2-year period. He reported that PP ranked 9th and 7th in importance. Seed of PP was utilized during winter months by northern bobwhite quail inhabiting upland disposal areas of the Tennessee Tombigbee Waterway in Mississippi. Warren and Hurst (1981) rated utilization of PP forage by white-tailed deer (*Odocoileus virginianus*) as high in the spring and moderate in summer.

Stoddard (1931) reported that PP developed dense stands of vegetation with very little herbaceous understory, creating conditions that are excellent for quail feeding and loafing. Although no pertinent references were found in a literature review it is believed that allelopathic properties of PP may be a major factor in the paucity of ground cover found growing beneath PP. The lack of understory vegetation creates conditions unfavorable for fire; this condition is an impediment to prescribed burning but is a desirable aspect for fire lane development.

PP has a tough impermeable seed coat that is capable of maintaining dormancy for extended periods of time. Rosene (1969) reported that PP seed can remain viable for 60 years or more. Dormancy is apparently broken by exposing the seed to sunlight

Environmental Concerns in Rights-of-Way Management: Seventh International Symposium
J.W. Goodrich-Mahoney, D.F. Mutrie and C.A. Guild (editors)
© 2002 Elsevier Science Ltd. All rights reserved.

or heat. Sunlight has been reported as an important catalyst in the germination of many herbaceous weed species (Duke 1944). Seed impermeability and long term viability of seed have management implications for the renovation of PP stands on ROW. If PP seed occur in the seedbank of a ROW, germination of PP could be stimulated by conducting soil disturbances, such as disking, fire, or the use of herbicide. This renovation of residual seedbanks into PP stands can produce valuable food and cover for wildlife and enhance soil quality due to plants' fixation of nitrogen-in root nodules.

The purpose of this paper is to report the results of field trials establishment and maintenance of PP in several different ecosystems of the southeastern United States.

ACKNOWLEDGMENTS

We sincerely thank The Mississippi Department of Wildlife, Fisheries, and Parks that provided the financial assistance for this study. Field assistance was essential and, when requested, was generously provided by Mississippi Agricultural and Forestry Experiment Station manager Frank Boykin at the Brooksville Experiment Farm and Donald Pogue at the Holly Springs Experiment Farm. Wildlife and Fisheries Department technician, Chris Bucciantini, provided invaluable assistance in the field.

FIELD TRIAL STUDIES

Farmland (temporarily out of cultivation)
Location
Mississippi Agricultural and Forestry Experiment Station (MAFES) Holly Springs, MS.

Soil type
Loess with good inherent fertility with a soil pH 6.0–6.5.

Dominant vegetation
Broom sedge (*Andropogon virginicus*).

Treatment
3 plots each (0.10 ha) in area were disked in late summer, two of the plots were sowed with ryegrass (*Lolium perenne*). One of the disked plots was unseeded. In January all 3 plots were overseeded with PP.

Results
Examination of the plots in late summer of the following year revealed little difference in PP coverage between the overseeded ryegrass plots and the fallow plot overseeded with PP. Examination during the following summer revealed an excellent stand of PP in all 3 plots; one year later examination in late summer showed invasion of native grasses and forbs, however PP was still common.

Renovation
The following August one of the ryegrass/PP plots was disked; the following August a dense stand of PP was evident while in the 2 remaining plots PP was declining.

Discussion
Utility ROW located on Loess soils have good inherent fertility quite sufficient for the development of good stands of PP without the additions of any soil amendments. Those ROW which have been maintained by herbicide will usually have a plant coverage dominated by grass frequently of the genus Andropogon. If these ROW are located in forested areas where deer, turkey, and/or quail are featured game species, annual ryegrass can be sowed one fall followed by overseeding of PP the 2nd fall, and disked after the 2nd year of establishment.

Location
Mississippi Agricultural and Forestry Experiment Station, Brooksville, MS.

Soil type
Brooksville Clay, developed from Selma Chalk. Soil is high in calcium and fertility (Pers. comm. Dr. David Pettry, Soil Scientist).

Dominant vegetation
Goldenrod (*Solidago altissima*).

Treatment
In early fall of 1993, three 4 m × 20 m plots were mowed in a field dominated by goldenrod (GR). In February, the mowed plots were sowed with PP at rates of 13.44 kg/ha.

Results
A good (>50% coverage) to excellent (>90% coverage) of PP developed beneath a moderate canopy of GR by the summer of 1994. By the summer of 1995, PP had declined to less than 50% coverage. By 1996, GR had spread through rhizome development and become dominant (>50% coverage) in all three plots. Although declines in PP occurred, the plant was still evident within the GR canopy.

Renovation
During the winter of 1996, an attempt was made to burn the GR/PP plots. Burning proved unsuccessful due to inadequate fuel in the understory. This paucity of understory plants may be due, in part, to allelopathy of both GR and PP to other plants found in abandoned agricultural fields. Bramble et al. (1990) reported that two species of GR were considered to be highly resistant to tree invasion. Duke (1985) reported that GR is one of the species that produces toxins which inhibit

black cherry (*Prunus serotina*) establishment. Field observation suggests that the scarcity of understory vegetation in fields dominated by PP may also be due to allelopathy.

To increase available fuel, hay was distributed on field trial plots. The increased fuel resulted in a fire sufficient for the regeneration of PP. The following summer PP was the dominant ground cover (>80% coverage) within plots and had spread to adjacent areas covering an estimated 0.5 ha. PP assumed dominance or codominance (90 to 45% percent coverage) within plots in 1997 and 1998. By the spring of 1999, GR canopy was increasing and in 1999, renovation of PP stands was undertaken. Within the 0.5 ha area, seven 3 m × 30 m plots were established to test renovation techniques. Three plots were disked with one pass of the disk over the plot to roughen the ground surface and expose GR rhizomes to the atmosphere while minimizing the severing and covering the rhizomes. Two plots received herbicide application with glyphosate at a rate of 3 pints per 40 gallons of water in late summer, 1999. Two plots received no treatment. By early summer of 2000, PP seedlings were evident in both herbicide and disking plots, but were scarce in control plots. In June, 2000, six hoops (51 cm in diameter) were randomly tossed and sampled for percent ground cover in each plot. Fifty-four percent of the disked plot hoops and 50% of the herbicide hoops exhibited PP seedlings. Brome grass (*Bromus japonicus*) was commonly found in herbicide plots, but was limited in disked plots. Brome grass has been reported to have chemical substances that depress growth of corn, wheat, and sorghum (Rice, 1974). Control plots where no renovation treatment had occurred exhibited less than 10% of hoops with PP seedlings. These plots were dominated by GR.

Dominant vegetation
Giant Ragweed (*Ambrosia trifida*), Brome grass, and Johnson grass (*Sorghum halapense*).

Treatment
In August 1998, six 4 m × 20 m plots were disked and sowed with hairy vetch (*Vicia villosa*). During winter 1999, frequent examination of vetch plots revealed limited germination of vetch. In late winter, 1999, PP was sowed at rate of 13 kg/ha over vetch plots with no soil preparation.

Results
Field examination of the plot in May and June, 2000 revealed very little PP germination and establishment. Poor germination of vetch and PP may have been due, in part, to inhibitive effects of the plants that dominated the site prior to disking. Root and top extract of brome grass have been shown to be inhibiting to all legumes except ladino clover (*Trifolium* sp.) (Rice, 1974). Duke (1985) listed giant ragweed as having alleged allelopathic activity in agroecosystems.

Location
Gasline ROW.

Soil Type
Impoverished soil — Boswell-Susquehanna. Texture — gravelly sandy loam complex. Soil low in calcium, phosphorous, and potash.

Dominant Vegetation
Broomsedge, Three-awned grass (*Aristida* spp.), Poor Joe (*Diodia teres*) was co-dominant.

Treatment
Four 20 m × 10 m plots were burned in mid-March and sowed with PP at the rate of 1.2 kg/ha. Two plots were fertilized at the rate of 11.2 kg/ha with nitrate of soda (16% N), 30 kg/ha of superphosphate (P_2O_2 18%), 9 kg/ha muriate potash (60% K_2O), and 224 kg/ha of lime.

Results
The two unfertilized plots had few PP seedlings the following summer, the fertilized plots moderate coverage of PP. During the second growing season, PP seedlings were common to plentiful in both fertilized and unfertilized plots; however, the PP in the unfertilized plots were spindly with a wilted appearance, while in the fertilized plots the PP were approximately twice the height of those in the unfertilized plots and were robust in appearance.

Discussion
Impoverished soils of the Lower Coastal Plain will require the use of soil amendment in order to develop a dominant or co-dominant stand of PP. It appears that once PP becomes established, no additional fertilizer is needed (Arner, 1959). Renovation by burning or disking appears to be all that is needed for rejuvenation of PP. PP stands established on some of the poor soil areas have been rejuvenated 10 years after establishment. Such areas revert to native grasses or forbs, but PP is easily rejuvenated by burning or disking. Burninig is more successful if sufficient understory herbaceous plant exist to provide adequate fuel for fire spread.

Location
DeSoto National Forest, Camp Shelby, MS. This south Mississippi land base is a training site for the Mississippi Army National Guard. Over 100,000 troops train annually for artillery, aircraft, tracked vehicle, and bivouacking preparedness. Located in the original range of the longleaf pine ecosystems, the indigenous plants and animals are adapted to fire. Military training results in high fire frequency in each year.

Soil type
Deep sands of Troup, Agala, and Eustis series with Susquehanna series intermixed. Soil pH levels ranged from 5.0 to 5.6 prior to soil amendment application.

Dominant vegetation
Bluestems (*Andropogon* spp.), Grease grass (*Tridens* spp.), three-awned grass, and genera of the family Asteraceae (*Solidago, Eupatorium, Erigeron* spp.).

Treatment
Eight, 20 m × 30 m plots were established within herbaceous plant communities on artillery firing points that surround the 2900-ha artillery impact area. Sites were prepared by disking to create a well-prepared seedbed. Lime was applied at a rate of 2200 kg/ha. Approximately 340 kg/ha of 0-14-14 fertilizer was applied to each plot. Scarified PP seed was planted at a rate of 17 kg/ha during March, 1991. Seed was not covered following seeding. Twenty, randomly established, 1 m^2 quadrats were surveyed in each plot during June–July, 1991 and 1992. Ocular estimate of percent coverages of PP and naturally colonizing plants was conducted in each quadrat using methods described by Hays et al. (1981).

Results
Coverage of PP ranged from 78% (SE = 8.0) to 100% in seven of the seeded plots during 1991. Grass and forb coverage within PP plots ranged from 4% (SE = 2.5) to 35% (SE = 10.5). A mean coverage of 45% (SE = 12.0) was observed in one plot which had been disrupted by tracked vehicle maneuvers. Coverage of PP did not differ in 1992 ($P > 0.10$) in seven of the eight plots. The plot that had been disturbed by tracked vehicle maneuvers in 1991 exhibited an increase in 1992, with percent coverage of PP averaging 67% (SE = 4.0) by 1992.

Renovation
Renovation was not conducted as part of this study; however, fire resulting from artillery ignitions occurred on all plots by 1992. Coverage of PP appeared to respond positively to fires, with coverages spreading outside of original plot perimeters on six of the eight experimental plots.

Discussion
Seeding of PP was judged successful due to observed coverages following seeding. Although sandy soils were droughty in nature and could be expected to limit PP growth during drought years, the years of 1991 and 1992 exhibited greater than normal rainfall (>8 cm/growing season). PP responded well to artillery-ignited fires. These fires generally occurred in late summer or fall during dry weather conditions. Spreading of PP was observed in the two years following the study although plots were not monitored through surveys. PP is considered an excellent native plant for establishment on the military reservations where fire and soil disturbance is eminent and upland game birds are featured wildlife species.

Location
Upland Disposal Sites of the Tennessee-Tombigbee Waterway, Tishomingo, Mississippi (TTW). This area is classified as a severely disturbed land base. Disposal area substrate is comprised of spoil material that was excavated from up to 54 m in depth. The spoil material contained acid overburden from the Eutaw and Cretaceous Layer Formations and therefore, exhibited high soil acidities (pH < 5.0) prior to reclamation (Jones et al., 1996, Ammons et al., 1983). Disposal areas were reclaimed through application of soil amendments and planting of agronomic grasses and legumes. Following reclamation, most disposal areas exhibited pH levels of 5.5 or greater in the upper 10 cm. Soil pH levels were more acidic in the >10 cm substrate depths reaching as low as 2.9 on site where acid overburden was within 35 cm of the soil surface (Jones et al., 1996). Sand content of spoil texture ranged from 47 to 90%, with most soils being classified as sandy to sandy loam (Jones, 1995).

Dominant vegetation
Experimental plantings were conducted in two vegetation cover types that were seeded for erosion control and reclamation: (1) sites exhibiting >60% coverage of sericea lespedeza *Lespedeza cuneata* and (2) sites exhibiting >60% seeded grasses [Kentucky 31 Fescue *Festuca elatior arundinacea*, common Bermudagrass *Cynodon dactylon*, and Weeping lovegrass *Eragrostis curvula*].

Treatment
Six disposal sites were selected through stratified sampling within the two cover types. All sites exhibited sandy substrates and pH levels ranging from 5.8 to 6.5 in the upper 10 cm of soil. Three 2 m^2 quadrats were sown with a mixture of kobe lespedeza (*Lespedeza striata*) and partridge pea at seeding rates of 22.4 kg/ha and 11.2 kg/ha, respectively. Inoculated, scarified seed were distributed over existing vegetation with no soil preparation during February, 1984. Percent coverage of PP within 2 m^2 quadrats was monitored during July, 1984 through 1988 using gridded ocular estimate methods described in Hayes et al. (1981). Percent coverage of PP was compared between the two cover types using the Ranked-sign Wilcoxon Test (Daniel, 1990).

Results
Coverage of PP averaged 90% (SE = 11.4) in quadrats that were dominated by seeded grass during the summer of 1984. Coverage of PP was significantly lower in quadrats located in the sericea lespedeza cover type ($P < 0.05$), averaging 15% (SE = 3.2). Coverage of PP increased in 1985 in both cover types, with coverage averaging 100% in the seeded grasses cover type and 33% (SE = 12.0) in the sericea lespedeza cover type. High rainfall during June through September of

1985 (>9 cm/4 months) was a probable reason for increases in coverage during this year. Percent coverage remained high on 2 of the grass cover type sites from 1986 through 1988, with mean ranging from 90% in 1987 to 100% in 1986 and 1987. A decline was detected on one of the grass cover type sites, with PP coverage dropping from 5% coverage in 1986 to less than 1% coverage by 1988. Colonization of this site by sericea lespedeza was recorded in 1986 through 1988 with percent coverage of this exceeding 60% in these years. Reduced PP coverage on this site was due, in part, to competition from this perennial lespedeza in drought conditions of these years (<4 cm rainfall/4 months). PP coverage in quadrats of sericea lespedeza cover types were averaged less than 1% coverage during 1986–1988.

Discussion

Seeding of partridge pea over existing grass cover types with no soil preparation was considered a success. Seeded grass cover types had at least 10% bare soil exposure which allowed seed contact with mineral soil. Seeding of PP over existing sericea lespedeza exhibited marginal success during the first two years; however, declines in PP coverage was observed during the last three study years. Competition from dense stands of sericea lespedeza, deep litter depths (>5.0 cm), and low rainfall are possible reasons for the observed declines. Renovation of dense stands of perennial agronomic cover may be necessary for retaining PP coverage over time. Disking, prescribed fire, or selective herbicide may be used to limit coverage of undesirable vegetation that may compete with PP. However, disking on drastically-disturbed sites that contain acid overburden, such as TTW disposal areas, may cause increased soil acidification and loss of all vegetation.

SUMMARY AND RECOMMENDATIONS

PP has been successfully established by overseeding or burned, mowed, disked, and herbicided old field plant communities. The native plant communities involved were goldenrod growing on prairie soils, broomsedge and annual ryegrass on loess soils, and three-awned grass and broomsedge on lower coastal plain gravely soils. Only the impoverished soil of the Lower Coastal Plain required fertilizer for establishment of PP. It is recommended that soil analysis be conducted before any management plans are developed. PP will grow in many different soil types even those of low fertility; however, application of lime will be required on soils with pH levels of 4.5 or less. ROW preparation for overseeding of PP may be accomplished as follows: disking in the late summer or early winter, treatment with a herbicide of low residual toxicity for legumes, ie glyphosate, in late summer, and mowing in late summer. Mowing and overseeding of PP was effective only in the GR and broomsedge communities; whereas, mowing was not effective in giant ragweed, brome grass, or Johnson grass communities. Mowing is not recommended for aggressive plants, such as tall fescue that spreads by underground stolons that may increase after mowing or grazing.

Burning is not applicable for renovation of PP communities where poor fuel conditions exist due to lack of understory herbaceous plants. This condition is often encountered in dense GR stands where ample fuel for fire does not exist beneath the GR cover. Adequate fuel loading is essential for successful burning that scarifies existing partridge pea seed and enhances PP stand development conditions.

PP is a noduled legume which improves impoverished soils, it provides both food and cover for quail and cottontail rabbits and appears allelopathic to many invading old field plant species. PP establishment should be given serious consideration in ROW management in the Southeastern United States.

REFERENCES

Ammons, J.T., P.A. Shelton, and G.G. Davis. 1983. A detailed study of five overburden cores and six disposal areas along the divide section of the Tennessee–Tombigbee Waterway. Final Rep. US Army Corps of Eng., Nashville, TN.

Arner, D.H. 1959. Experimental burning, fertilizing, and seeding on utility line rights of ways. Unpublished Ph.D. Thesis. Alabama Polytechnic Institute, Auburn, AL. 128 pp.

Allen, O.N. and E.K. Allen. 1981. The Leguminosae, A Source Book of Characteristics, Uses, and Nodulation. University of Wisconsin Press, Madison, WI. pp. 143–147.

Bramble, W., W. Byrnes, and R. Hutnick. 1990. Resistance of plant cover types to tree seedling invasion on an electric transmission right of way. Journal of Arborculture, 16(5): 130–135.

Brazil, C.D. 1993. Winter diet of hunter harvested northern bobwhite in Mississippi. Unpublished MS Thesis. 159 pp.

Daniel, W.W. 1990. Applied Nonparametric Statistics. PWS-KENT Publishing Company, Boston, MA. 635 pp.

Duke, S.O. 1985. Weed Physiology, Volume 1, Reproduction and Ecophysiology. CRC Press, Inc., Boca Raton, FL. pp. 137–148.

Hays, R.L., Summers, and C.W. Cietz. 1981. Estimating wildlife habitat variables. USDI Fish and Wildlife Service FWS/OBS-81147. 111 pp.

Jones, J.C. 1995. Vegetative succession, edaphic factors, and annelid densities on reclaimed disposal areas of the Tennessee–Tombigbee Waterway. PhD Dissertation. Mississippi State University, MS. 224 pp.

Jones, J.C., D.H. Arner, and C.H. Bucciantini. 1996. Soil sampling for the detection of acid overburden on small game management areas located on severely disturbed land bases. Proceedings of Annual Conference of Southeastern Association of Fish and Wildlife Agencies, 50: 583–591.

Radford, A.E., H.E. Ahles, and C.R. Bell. 1987. Manual of the Vascular Flora of the Carolinas. The University of North Carolina Press, Chapel Hill, NC. 1183 pp.

Rice, E.L. 1974. Allelopathy. Academic Press, New York, NY, 187pp.

Rosene, W. 1969. The Bobwhite Quail — It's Life and Management. Rutgers University Press. New Brunswick, NJ. 317 pp.

Stoddard, H.L. 1931. The Bobwhite Quail, Its Habits, Preservation, and Increase. Charles Scribner Sons, New York, NY. pp. 138–139.

Warren, R. and G. Hurst. 1981. Rating of plants in pine plantations as white-tailed deer food. Information Bulletin 18, Mississippi Agriculture and Forestry Experiment Station, Mississippi State, MS.

BIOGRAPHICAL SKETCHES

Dale Arner

Mississippi State University, Box 9690, Department of Wildlife and Fisheries, Forest and Wildlife Research Center, Mississippi State University, MS 39762, USA, Phone: 662-325-2617.

Dr. Arner is the department head and professor emeritus at the department of Wildlife and Fisheries at Mississippi State University. He obtained his BS and MS from Penn. State, and his PhD at Auburn University. Interest: applied wildlife habitat ecology. Research areas: Right-of-way and beaver pond ecology.

Jeanne C. Jones

Mississippi State University, Box 9690, Department of Wildlife and Fisheries, Forest and Wildlife Research Center, Mississippi State University, MS 39762, USA, e-mail: jjones@cfr.msstate.edu.

A native of Vicksburg, Mississippi, Jeanne is currently an associate professor in the Department of Wildlife and Fisheries at Mississippi State University. She teaches courses in wildlife and plant ecology, wildlife habitat management, and restoration ecology and received 7 outstanding teaching awards. She has authored and co-authored over 45 publications, technical reports, and book chapters on eco-tourism, native species diversity, reptile and amphibian conservation, and restoration ecology. Her primary research interests include restoration of degraded ecosystems and management strategies for conservation of sensitive plant, amphibian, bird, and reptile communities. Her hobbies include botanical and wildlife illustration, nature photography, organic gardening, horseback riding, backpacking and fly-fishing.

Reducing Maintenance Costs using Integrated Vegetation Management on Electric Utility Transmission Lines in British Columbia

Thomas C. Wells, Kevin D. Dalgarno, and Ray Read

BC Hydro maintains over 17,800 km of electric transmission lines in British Columbia spanning biogeoclimatic zones from desert grasslands to alpine tundra. The primary goals of the vegetation program are to maintain public safety and system reliability at reasonable cost while balancing environmental and social resources. These goals are accomplished within a process-based organization using Integrated Vegetation Management principles. LapMap, a mapping and database program, was developed to collect a wide array of data including civil, environmental, and social attributes. Vegetation inventories define the growth rates and stand densities of key target species, as well as identifying competitive ground cover, to determine action thresholds for treatment. Conductor-to-ground clearance models combined with target species growth rates permit treatment cycle optimization and identification of off-cycle problem areas. A prescriptive approach is taken to select the appropriate combination of manual, mechanical, chemical, and natural control methods to establish short and long-term site objectives. Results from transmission corridors in the Southern Interior and Vancouver Island indicate that selective approaches to right-of-way maintenance allow long-term site objectives to be met at reduced costs. This is achieved by optimizing treatment cycle lengths or reducing maintenance by clearing only what is necessary to establish compatible plant communities. With these programs, resources are used more efficiently while protecting key riparian and wildlife habitats as well as promoting opportunities for compatible use.

Keywords: Transmission, rights-of-way, balancing resources, inventories, prescriptive maintenance

INTRODUCTION

The primary objective of most rights-of-way vegetation maintenance programs is to ensure the safe and reliable transmission of power. There are many ways to achieve this objective. Historically most utilities, including BC Hydro, treated vegetation on their rights-of-way using non-selective methods of manual, mechanical, or chemical controls on a calendar cycle basis. After annual field patrols of rights-of-way, a list of areas requiring work were compiled along with cost estimates. When funding was confirmed, contracts were prepared using non-scaled mapping with little information being conveyed to contractors. Often the result was an uneven mix of different vegetation management cycles and treatments with frequently higher maintenance costs. This approach is giving way to site-specific maintenance based on Integrated Pest Management principles (Bramble and Byrnes, 1983; Finch and Shupe, 1997; McLoughlin, 1997). There are several drivers for this move at BC Hydro including public and regulatory expectations, the need for efficient use of financial and human resources, and the changing face of the electric industry across North America.

BC Hydro has adopted a triple bottom line approach to reflect the integration of environmental, social, and economic values in its business activities (BC Hydro, 1999). This has impacts across all business units including vegetation management. It is no longer sufficient merely to remove tall-growing vegetation under the

Environmental Concerns in Rights-of-Way Management: Seventh International Symposium
J.W. Goodrich-Mahoney, D.F. Mutrie and C.A. Guild (editors)
Crown Copyright © 2002 Elsevier Science Ltd. All rights reserved.

lines by whatever means necessary. Today, management practices are designed to minimize impacts on natural resources. This has led to significant changes in the way business is done. For example, Transmission and Distribution at BC Hydro is a process-based organization (Hammer, 1996) in part to focus on streamlining and standardizing maintenance practices. These changes have not occurred overnight but rather are a work in progress.

Vegetation maintenance at BC Hydro has evolved into a selective, prescriptive based approach to optimize treatment cycles and provide more diverse long-term benefits. The core strategy has been the implementation of Integrated Vegetation Management (IVM) which includes the following steps:
– Completion of inventories to assess current right-of-way conditions;
– Development of action thresholds to manage risk and determine optimum timing for work;
– Preparation of prescriptions and work plans using best practices to provide value added solutions and balancing of resources;
– Monitoring and evaluation of programs to create a cycle of continuous improvement.

The base model is rooted in Integrated Pest Management (IPM) principles but is increasingly incorporating Integrated Resource Management (IRM) aspects as well. To achieve this, a full spectrum of treatment options is employed including manual, mechanical, chemical, cultural, and biological controls to promote low growing, stable plant communities on rights-of-way (Morrow, 1997). This minimizes safety hazards and virtually eliminates line outages from tall growing species. Additional benefits are now incorporated, where feasible, into the regular maintenance program. The natural regeneration of selective plant communities results in an increase of available fish and wildlife habitat (Harriman, 1999). Compatible use opportunities include modifying rights-of-way as green spaces for public recreation or growing non-timber forest products to reduce the maintenance base, enhance social and economic value and contribute to the ongoing consent to operate the system. This paper outlines three examples of the application of IVM at BC Hydro. Changes to maintenance strategies will be discussed with emphasis on benefits that have been achieved and difficulties that have been encountered along the way.

METHODS

Three sites were chosen to implement IVM protocols on BC Hydro rights-of-way in the Southern Interior and Vancouver Island of British Columbia (Fig. 1). The sites chosen had detailed mapping available including as-built photogrammetric maps at 1:2500 scale and BC Terrain Resource Inventory Maps (TRIM) at 1:20,000 scale. The maps included the location of transmission

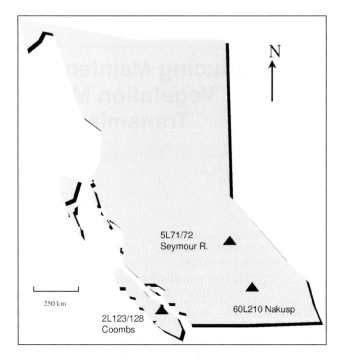

Fig. 1. Study sites on three BC Hydro transmission rights-of-way in British Columbia.

structures, conductor to ground clearance models displayed as isolines, riparian areas, access, topographic, and cadastral information. Data were entered into LapMap, a portable mapping and database system developed by BC Hydro that embodies many features of a Geographic Information System (GIS), but is not true GIS. Using LapMap, a variety of right-of-way data were documented from field surveys, including vegetation, wildlife, recreation, compatible use, and heritage attributes.

A number of parameters were used to describe right-of-way vegetation communities (Table 1) to define the type and scope of maintenance work required and to create a baseline for monitoring the efficacy of prescribed treatments. These data were entered into LapMap by creating work management area polygons on the map base. New boundaries were set when distinct changes in vegetation type or target species densities were noted or where changes in slope, riparian drainages or available access would dictate the use of different treatment options. Polygons were also defined on the basis of compatible right-of-way usage such as the presence of Christmas tree farms, agricultural land, or park boundaries.

Site descriptions and estimation of percentage cover abundance for deciduous and coniferous target species as well as competitive ground cover were based on standard methods (Mueller-Dombois and Ellenberg, 1974; Luttmerding et al., 1990). Conifer and deciduous target species densities were estimated in stems per hectare using a rapid plot method (Hide, 1974). Target and ground cover species recorded in LapMap are listed in Table 2. Within sample plots, growth rates for

Table 1. Vegetation site descriptors used in LapMap

Span information
   Circuit Name
   From Structure–To Structure
   Limit of Approach (automatically calculated based on voltage class)
   Minimum Conductor to Ground Clearance in polygon (m)
   Polygon Area (ha)

Site Description
   major topographic features, terrain, slope, aspect, target vegetation, and ground cover

Special Considerations
   hazards, special land use concerns

Target Species
   Deciduous/Coniferous Species
   Percent Cover of Deciduous/Coniferous Species
   Height of Deciduous/Coniferous Species (m)
   Age of Deciduous/Coniferous Species (years)
   Growth Rate (m yr^{-1})
   Alpha Deciduous/Coniferous Target Species — most problematical target species on site
   Alpha Deciduous/Coniferous Target Height (m)
   Alpha Deciduous/Coniferous Target Age (yr)
   Average Deciduous/Coniferous Density (stems ha^{-1})
   Percent Cover of Deciduous/Conifer Layer
   Control Cycle (calculated in years)
   Next Work Timing (estimated date of next work)
   Maximum Allowable Tree Height (m)

Ground Cover
   Species
   Cover Abundance
   Comments (on ground cover present)
   Competing Vegetation Complex

Prescription
   Last Treatment Year (date)
   Compatible ROW Use
   Biogeoclimatic Subzone
   Treatment Type: recommended methods to be used
   Treatment Targets: target vegetation to be treated
   Scheduled Treatment (date)
   Treatment Comments: detailed prescription for work site
   Work Completed (year)
   Evaluation Date
   Evaluation Comments

target species were determined by felling the tallest stem of an individual or coppice and measuring the stem length and recording its age by counting growth rings. Previous year's growth was also recorded by measuring the length between the end bud scars of the current and previous year.

Other data collected included determining the biogeoclimatic subzone for the site (Meidinger and Pojar, 1991) as well as the competing vegetation complexes present (Newton and Comeau, 1990). Treatment options based on field observations were also recorded. Estimates for the timing of work were automatically calculated in LapMap based on limits of approach or the maximum allowable tree height defined as acceptable for a section of circuit, and the height and growth rates of the target vegetation observed. The voltage class of the circuit determines limits of approach. This forms the action threshold by which work must be done although usually a further margin of safety is built in.

These data were then used to develop site specific prescriptions to meet both near-term and long-term maintenance objectives. Prescriptions formed the basis for creating work contracts. Lump sum contracts were employed for the majority of work with time and materials contracts used for clearing off-cycle problem areas. Contracts were based on open competition and awarded on price and contractor experience. After work was completed, the sites were reviewed to determine whether maintenance objectives had been met and to determine any necessary follow-up work. Before another work cycle commences, current site conditions are evaluated to refine the prescription. This is important to ensure a continuous cycle of improvement.

Cost analyses for these trials were based on calculating the cost per hectare of the various treatments employed or considered. These costs were derived from historical treatment records at the three sites as well as current contract pricing. Costs for collecting site information and prescription development were estimated from loaded staff time rates. All estimates were adjusted to 1999 present value costs using the Consumer Price Index Annual Averages (for all items), obtained from the BC Hydro accounting office.

RESULTS AND DISCUSSION

5L71/72 Seymour River to Celista Creek

This site is a 16 km long by 122 m wide section of dual 500 kV corridor approximately 184 ha in size situated in the Southern Interior (SI) from the Seymour River to Celista Creek. The area lies within the Thompson Moist Warm Interior Cedar–Hemlock (ICHmw3) biogeoclimatic variant and has cool, wet winters and warm, moderately dry summers (Lloyd et al., 1990). The ICH has the most suitable climate for tree growth in the Interior with climax stands of Western red-cedar and Western hemlock. Seral stands include Douglas-fir, lodgepole pine, trembling aspen, and birch. Growth rates of the deciduous target species on the right-of-way (typically birch, cottonwood, or aspen) ranged from 0.9–1.2 m yr^{-1} with conifers growing at 0.4–0.5 m yr^{-1}. Stem densities ranged from 2350 stems ha^{-1} to 103,460 stems ha^{-1} with an average of 26,487 stems ha^{-1}. Ranchers use sections of the right-of-way for grazing cattle.

Treatment history and costs were collected from archived files (Table 3). Most treatments involved manual slashing but the right-of-way was treated with Tordon 101 (picloram and 2,4-D) in 1978/79 and selected sections were mowed in 1992. The total cost for these treatments was calculated to be $241,965 CDN. Costs of vegetation maintenance over the next 20 years for this area are predicted to be even greater

Table 2. Target and cover species encountered at the study sites

Common name	Scientific name	Distribution in sites VI	SI
Deciduous Target Species			
vine maple	*Acer circinatum*	X	
Douglas maple	*Acer glabrum* ssp. *douglasii*		X
bigleaf maple	*Acer macrophyllum*	X	
Sitka alder	*Alnus crispa* ssp. *sinuata*		X
mountain alder	*Alnus incana* ssp. *tenuifolia*		X
red alder	*Alnus rubra*	X	
arbutus	*Arbutus menziesii*	X	
paper birch	*Betula papyrifera*	X	X
black cottonwood	*Populus balsamifera* ssp. *trichocarpa*	X	X
trembling aspen	*Populus tremuloides*		X
bitter cherry	*Prunus emarginata*	X	X
Coniferous Target Species			
grand fir	*Abies grandis*	X	
hybrid white spruce	*Picea glauca* x *engelmannii*		X
lodgepole pine	*Pinus contorta*	X	X
Western white pine	*Pinus monticola*	X	X
Douglas-fir	*Pseudotsuga menziesii*	X	X
Western red-cedar	*Thuja plicata*	X	X
Western hemlock	*Tsuga heterophylla*	X	X
Competitive Ground Cover			
Saskatoon	*Amelanchier alnifolia*	X	X
hairy manzanita	*Arctostaphylos columbiana*	X	
kinnikinnick	*Arctostaphylos uva-ursi*	X	X
snowbrush	*Ceanothus* spp.		X
red osier dogwood	*Cornus stolonifera*	X	X
beaked hazelnut	*Corylus cornuta*	X	X
broom	*Cytisus scoparius*	X	
common horsetail	*Equisetum arvense*	X	X
salal	*Gaultheria shallon*	X	
ocean spray	*Holodiscus discolor*	X	X
common juniper	*Juniperus communis*		X
Utah honeysuckle	*Lonicera utahensis*		X
black twinberry	*Lonicera involucrata*	X	X
Oregon-grape	*Mahonia* spp.	X	X
Indian plum	*Oemleria cerasiformis*	X	
falsebox	*Paxistima myrsinites*		X
reed canary grass	*Phalaris arundinacea*	X	X
ninebark	*Physocarpus* spp.	X	X
bracken fern	*Pteridium aquilinum*	X	X
currents	*Ribes* spp.	X	X
roses	*Rosa* spp.	X	X
Himalayan blackberry	*Rubus discolor*	X	
thimbleberry	*Rubus parviflorus*	X	X
salmonberry	*Rubus spectabilis*	X	
willows	*Salix* spp.	X	X
blue elderberry	*Sambucus caerulea*		X
red elderberry	*Sambucus racemosa*	X	X
soopolallie	*Shepherdia canadensis*		X
hardhack	*Spiraea douglasii*	X	X
common snowberry	*Symphoricarpos albus*	X	X
blueberries	*Vaccinium* spp.	X	X

because continual slashing of deciduous coppices has resulted in increased stem densities. This poses a problem for the use of the area by ranchers.

Inventory data collected in 1997 coupled with Lap-Map analysis of conductor to ground clearances for this circuit were used to develop selective treatment prescriptions. Areas of less than 14 m conductor to ground clearance can only sustain vegetation to a maximum height of 8 m before violating the 6 m limit of approach required on 500 kV circuits. However, these areas represent only 6.5% of the right-of-way (Table 4). The prescribed treatment for areas with less than 14 m conductor to ground clearance is to slash and spot herbicide treat all vegetation except shrubs

Table 3. Treatment history and costs for 5L71/72 structure 68/1-77/1 from 1978–1999

Year	Spans treated	Treatment type	Total treatment cost (1999 dollars CDN)
1978/1979	68/1-73/2	Chemical (Tordon 101)	89,858
1988	68/1-73/2	Slash	3,552
	73/2-77/1	Slash	31,412
1989	68/1-73/1	Slash	36,814
1992	68/1-72/1	Slash	28,152
	72/1-73/2	Mower head	28,676
	73/2-77/1	Slash	23,501
Total			241,965

Table 4. Total area in each treatment zone for 5L71/72 structure 68/1-77/1

Conductor to ground clearance	Number of hectares	Treatment area (%)
<11 m	2.5	1.4
11–14 m	9.4	5.1
14–20 m	58.4	31.8
20–33 m	102.1	55.5
>33 m	11.4	6.2
Total hectares	183.8	100.0

Table 5. Treatment techniques and the related costs per hectare for the Southern Interior in 1999

Treatment technique	Cost per ha ($CDN)
Hand Slashing	450
Treat with Herbicide (thin line)	600
Mechanical Mowing (track)	750
Mechanical Mowing (tire)	600
Cut and Treat with Herbicide	800

which at maturity would be less than 3 m tall. In areas with 14–33 m conductor to ground clearance, only target species capable of growing within the limits of approach would be removed. This allows Sitka alder and many willow species to be retained since they do not exceed 6 to 8 m in height at maturity. Areas with more than 33 m clearance would not have to be treated on a regular basis except for removal of danger trees that could fall within limits of approach. Such vegetation would only have to be treated on a 10–20 year cycle basis.

Past treatments on this circuit were not selective with periodic clearing of the entire right-of-way from edge to edge. The treatment cycles were quite variable and appeared to be the result of available budgets in certain fiscal years. The comparative costs for some common treatment methods used in the SI are listed in Table 5. To predict future costs, three scenarios were developed (Table 6) the use of repeated, non-selective slashing based on a six year cycle, selective slashing, and selective slashing with herbicide treatments of low line clearances less than 14 m. Conductor to ground clearance areas (Table 4) and treatment costs (Table 5) were used to develop budget estimates for the three treatment scenarios, with figures adjusted to 1999 dollars (Table 6). The estimates made are conservative but with the integrated management approach, cost savings were projected to be as much as $225,000 CDN over a twenty year period while maintaining line security and public safety. This does not take into account that selective approaches maintain biodiversity on the right-of-way and are favored by the public and regulatory agencies. Greater long-term savings are projected when spot herbicide treatments are used because target species densities are lowered further. Even with up front costs of $20,500 CDN to do the inventory and prescription for this section of corridor, the cost benefits of IVM are apparent.

60L210 Fauquier to Nakusp

This study site is a 46 km section of 69 kV transmission right-of-way running along the eastern side of the Arrow Lakes in southern British Columbia from the lake crossing 6 km north of Fauquier to the substation at Nakusp. The right-of-way is of varying width but in total encompasses approximately 150 ha. The southern end near Fauquier is predominantly Crown land and is situated on steep west facing slopes with poor accessibility. Toward Nakusp the right-of-way is situated on level or rolling terrain which is privately owned and often used for pasture. The area lies within the Dry Warm Interior Cedar–Hemlock (ICHdw) biogeoclimatic subzone and Columbia-Shuswap Moist Warm Interior Cedar–Hemlock (ICHmw2) variant (Braumandl and Curran, 1992). Western red-cedar and Western hemlock are climax species. On disturbed sites, birch dominates with mountain alder and cottonwood occurring on wet soils. Growth rates of birch ranged from 0.65–1.8 $m\,yr^{-1}$ with a median of 1.3 $m\,yr^{-1}$. Densities varied from 5000–108,000 stems ha^{-1} with a mean density of 45,550 stems ha^{-1}.

The circuit is important because it is a radial feed to Nakusp and New Denver and when it fails power goes out in the entire valley. Poor accessibility to the line owing to the rugged terrain renders the corridor difficult to maintain. Because of historical community resistance to herbicide treatments, the right-of-way had been repeatedly slashed on a four-year cycle from 1984 up to 1996. Near Nakusp, some sections on even ground were machine groomed and seeded and this achieved good control of target species. However, mechanical grooming is precluded on much of the corridor because of the steep terrain. In the hand-slashed sections, increasing stem densities from birch coppices made the right-of-way an impenetrable thicket. In addition, there was an accumulation of slash debris on the ground up to 2 m thick. This made it difficult for

Table 6. Predicted treatment cycle and costs in 1999 dollars CDN for three treatment options on 5L71/72 str. 68/1-77/1

Scenario 1				Scenario 2			Scenario 3		
Year	6 year cycle of non-selective slashing	ha	$000s	Using selective slashing only	ha	$000s	Selective with the use of herbicides	ha	$000s
1998	Slash all vegetation that can grow into limits of approach	172	77.6	Slash all vegetation in <11 m areas	70	31.6	Cut and use herbicides in <11 m areas	2.5	2
				Slash targets only in <14 and <20 m areas			Slash targets only in <14 m areas (use selective herbicides)	9	7.5
							Slash targets only in <20 m areas	58	26.3
2002							Control vegetation growth in <11 m areas	2.5	1.5
2003				Slash all vegetation in <11 m areas Slash targets only in <14 and 20–33 m areas	114	51.3			
2004	Slash all vegetation that can grow into limits of approach	172	77.6						
2006							Cut and use herbicides in <11 m areas	2.5	2
							Slash targets only in <14 m areas (use selective herbicides)	9	7.5
2008				Slash all vegetation in <11 m areas Slash targets only in <14 m areas	12	5.3			
2010	Slash all vegetation that can grow into limits of approach	172	77.6				Control vegetation growth in <11 m areas	2.5	1.5
2013				Slash all vegetation in <11 m areas Slash targets only in <14 and <20 m areas	70	31.6			
2014							Cut and use herbicides in <11 m areas	2.5	2
							Slash targets only in <14 m areas (use selective herbicides)	9	7.5
							Slash targets only in <20 m areas	58	26.3
2016	Slash all vegetation that can grow into limits of approach	172	77.6						
2018				Slash all vegetation in <11 m areas Slash targets only in <14 m areas	12	5.3	Control vegetation growth in <11 m areas	2.5	1.5
Total		688	310.4		278	125.1		158	85.6

workers to maneuver and created a potential fuel load threat. Coppices were so well established that they were growing at average rates of 1.5 ± 0.3 m relative to single stem seeded-in birch (1.1 ± 0.3 m). The faster growth rates of coppices necessitated more frequent clearing on a 2 to 3 year basis where there was low conductor to ground clearance. The combination of higher densities, growth rates and slash debris was making it increasingly difficult to maintain the right-of-way in a satisfactory condition. At the same time costs were escalating.

Clearly the status quo was not an option. In 1995, a thorough span by span inventory was developed for 60L210 with analysis of growth rates, stocking densities, terrain, accessibility, and line clearances. Based on the growth rates and line clearances it was determined that a majority of the circuit could be maintained on a six-year cycle. Areas of low clearance requiring more frequent treatment were identified and determined to be about 10% of the right-of-way. In the past, these low clearance sections were driving the entire treatment cycle. Public meetings were held in 1996 and options were discussed, including selective use of Garlon (triclopyr) basal, and Roundup (glyphosate) cut-stump treatments. The detailed data and prescriptive maintenance approach met with favorable public response. Approval was given to allow selective herbicide applications on Crown land portions of the right-of-way where the densities of birch were at their worst (60–100,000 stems ha^{-1}).

Contracts were developed for 1996–2000 to clear sections of the line using slashing and herbicide treatments to reduce target species densities. The results have been very promising. Stocking densities are falling and the corridor is now on a more manageable cycle of 6 years with spot clearing every 2–3 years in critical low clearance areas. Public response has been favorable and annual maintenance costs have been spread out. It is expected that over a 20-year period that costs for maintaining this line will be substantially reduced. Other benefits are becoming apparent as well. In areas where Garlon applications were made target vegetation densities have been dramatically reduced, opening up the right-of-way to establishment of low growing shrub cover. This is allowing old slash debris to rot down faster thereby reducing fuel loading, improving wildlife habitat and increasing accessibility to the line by workers.

2L123/128 Englishman River to Coombs

The Vancouver Island study site is located on a dual circuit 230 kV corridor between the Englishman River and Coombs, a relatively uniform and level area covering 42 ha. The corridor lies within the Eastern Very Dry Maritime Coastal Western Hemlock variant (CWHxm1) which occurs at lower elevations along the eastern side of Vancouver Island. This area is characterized by warm, dry summers and moist, mild winters with relatively little snowfall (Green and Klinka, 1994). Climax forests are dominated by Douglas-fir, Western hemlock, and Western red-cedar. Red alder, cottonwood, and bigleaf maple are common on seral sites.

In 1997, the corridor was thoroughly inventoried and short and long-term site objectives were developed. Past management of this area included mowing, hand slashing and girdling of the right-of-way every 4 years. Over time, this had resulted in high average densities of deciduous stems of 50,000 stems ha^{-1} with a range of 28,500 to 90,000 stems ha^{-1}. Over 85% of the targets were red alder that were growing at an average rate of 1.2 m yr^{-1} and were approaching 7 m in height (Fig. 2). Also present in smaller amounts were black cottonwood, arbutus, and willow. In contrast, conifer cover was typically low with densities of 5000 stems ha^{-1} or less. The majority of Douglas-fir and lodgepole pine individuals were 2.5 m tall with a few approaching 5 m tall. Minor amounts of Western red-cedar, and Western hemlock were also present. Ground cover was generally poorly developed (5–25% cover) over much of the treatment area with patches of bracken, grasses, salmonberry, thimbleberry, salal, and hairy manzanita present. The cost of $900 CDN per hectare to mow this right-of-way every four years was not sustainable. Therefore, this site was a good candidate for developing site specific treatments based on IVM principles.

Conductor to ground clearances dictated that tall growing target vegetation had to be removed in 1998 to maintain line security and public safety. An articulating excavator type mower was selected as the initial best management practice. This allowed for the selective removal of target vegetation while retaining any compatible ground cover present so that it could actively compete against target tree resprouts. The timing of this work was critical. The mowing was completed in late August when the target vegetation was under considerable stress and this resulted in a high level of natural mortality. In July 1999, the target vegetation that was mowed was followed up by a backpack foliar treatment using 2% Roundup (glyphosate) with the addition of Sylgard 309 (non-ionic silicone polyether surfactant). The results of the two step program were immediate. Selective mowing resulted in little disturbance to existing ground cover, the resprout of target vegetation was lessened because of the late summer mowing, and the spot herbicide treatment resulted in good mortality of surviving resprouts. The overall result was an excellent release of low-growing cover (Fig. 3).

This long-term, site specific management plan was instrumental in arguing for and getting sufficient project funds to do the work properly. Conducting a mandatory site preview of the work area resulted in contractor's expectations being clear which improved their bid prices and enhanced the quality of work performed. A more selective approach and use of best management practices has also improved relationships with regulatory agencies and with the public.

Fig. 2. Dense cover of mostly deciduous target species on 2L123/128 near the Englishman River prior to site treatments. Photo was taken in April 1998.

Fig. 3. 2L123/128 near the Englishman River after mowing in August 1998 with foliar application of glyphosate on target species resprouts in July 1999. A dense, compatible shrub layer has developed. Photo was taken in August 2000.

CONCLUSIONS

BC Hydro is beginning to accrue significant benefits from shifting to an Integrated Vegetation Management (IVM) approach. Using LapMap to create condition-based assessments of the right-of-way allows the development of site specific prescriptions with both short and long-term objectives to control problem vegetation. Different target species respond to manual, mechanical, and chemical treatments in different ways (BC Hydro, 1997). By assessing which species are causing problems, best practices solutions can be developed to reduce their densities. Having detailed information also allows for more accurate budget estimates and this helps to secure necessary funding to keep a smooth maintenance program running. It also allows for more meaningful consultation with the public and with regulatory agencies that gain confidence that rights-of-way are being properly managed. Integrated management also allows for the development of strategies to improve wildlife and recreational or even compatible business opportunities on rights-of-way.

The success of these trials has resulted in the approach being used more widely across the system on an operational basis. One benefit has been the standardization of work procedures (BC Hydro, 1997). The benefits have been so compelling that it has supported the development and implementation of a full scale Enterprise Geographic Information System at BC Hydro. This will eventually replace LapMap and allow for even more streamlined database, prescription and contracting functions.

The shift to IVM has also resulted in changes to contracting strategies. When contractors are given site-specific work, the initial reaction is to bid using the historical, non-selective cost of maintaining the right-of-way. But as contractors have become used to the selective approach, improvements in contractor prices have been seen. Contractors are now given more detailed work specifications that fully informs them of the amount of actual work, the target vegetation to be controlled, and clearer environmental guidelines to protect riparian and wildlife habitat. They are also able to benefit from the conductor to ground clearance models created for higher voltage circuits to identify potential low clearance hazards. Maintenance coordinators also use clearance isolines to ensure that tall growing vegetation in critical low clearance areas is not overlooked. This makes for a safer work environment.

Many contracts are now initiated with a mandatory on-site pre-tender meeting with contractors. This allows them to see exactly what they are bidding on which frequently results in better pricing. Contractors who do not attend are not allowed to tender blind and any such bids are rejected. Realistic pricing reduces the potential that a contractor who is awarded the work will walk away because they did not realize the full extent of the work required. Thus work is done in a more timely, organized manner.

The transition to full implementation of IVM takes some years to achieve. There is the need to obtain accurate mapping and inventories of the corridors upon which to base prescriptions and contracts. Follow up monitoring of work to determine whether site objectives are being met is also an ongoing endeavor. There are up front costs associated with these activities. But in the long run the benefits are worth it from an economic, environmental, and social point of view.

ACKNOWLEDGEMENTS

The authors wish to thank Edi Garrett, Rob Scagel, and Tania Perzoff for assistance in collecting and analyzing field data. Marv Everett and Les Westervelt in the Survey and Photogrammetry Department ably provided mapping and LapMap support. Willingness by field managers Nick Stevenson and Nelson Storry to try new approaches greatly aided progress in the work. Feedback and supportive efforts from Gwen Shrimpton, John Emery, Zig Hathorn, Glen Singleton, and Grant Baxter have helped to document and encourage the transition to Integrated Vegetation Management at BC Hydro.

REFERENCES

BC Hydro. 1997. Vegetation management manual for transmission and distribution rights-of-way. BC Hydro, Vancouver, Canada.

BC Hydro. 1999. Triple bottom line report. BC Hydro, Vancouver, Canada.

Bramble, W.C. and W.R. Byrnes. 1983. Thirty years of research on development of plant cover on an electric transmission right-of-way. Journal of Arboriculture, 9(3): 67–74.

Braumandl, T.F. and M.P. Curran. 1992. A field guide for site identification and interpretation for the Nelson Forest Region. Province of British Columbia, Ministry of Forests, Land Management Handbook Number 20, Victoria, Canada.

Finch, K.E. and S.D. Shupe. 1997. Nearly two decades of Integrated Vegetation Management on electric transmission rights-of-ways. In: The Sixth International Symposium on Environmental Concerns in Rights-of-Way Management. J.R. Williams, J.W. Goodrich-Mahoney, J.R. Wisniewski, and J. Wisniewski, eds. Elsevier Science, Oxford, England. pp. 67–75.

Green, R.N. and K. Klinka. 1994. A field guide to site identification and interpretation for the Vancouver Forest Region. Province of British Columbia, Ministry of Forests, Land Management Handbook Number 28, Victoria, Canada.

Hammer, M. 1996. Beyond Reengineering. Harper Collins Publishers, NY, USA.

Harriman, J. 1999. Exploring wildlife habitat management on electric utility transmission rights-of-way in the United States and Canada. In: Proceedings of the Natural Resources Conference Workshop, April 26, 1999. Edison Electric Institute, Williamsburg, VA.

Hide, R.H. 1974. "Curiouser and curiouser! Or the Germans have a word for it" *Das Stammabstandsverfahren*. Quarterly Journal of Forestry, 68(2): 126–140.

Lloyd, D., K. Angove, G. Hope, and C. Thompson. 1990. A guide to site identification and interpretation for the Kamloops Forest Region. Parts 1 and 2. Province of British Columbia, Ministry of Forests, Land Management Handbook Number 23, Victoria, Canada.

Luttmerding, H.A., D.A. Demarchi, E.C. Lea, D.V. Meidinger, and T. Vold. 1990. Describing Ecosystems in the Field, 2nd ed. Province of British Columbia, Ministry of Environment, Lands and Parks and Ministry of Forests, MOE Manual 11, Victoria, Canada.

McLoughlin, K.T. 1997. Application of Integrated Pest Management to electric utility rights-of-way vegetation management in New York State. In: The Sixth International Symposium on Environmental Concerns in Rights-of-Way Management. J.R. Williams, J.W. Goodrich-Mahoney, J.R. Wisniewski, and J. Wisniewski, eds. Elsevier Science, Oxford, England. pp. 118–126.

Meidinger, D. and J. Pojar. 1991. Ecosystems of British Columbia. Province of British Columbia, Research Branch, Ministry of Forests. Special Report Series #6, Victoria, Canada.

Morrow, S.D. 1997. Effective Integrated Vegetation Management. In: The Sixth International Symposium on Environmental Concerns in Rights-of-Way Management. J.R. Williams, J.W. Goodrich-Mahoney, J.R. Wisniewski, and J. Wisniewski, eds. Elsevier Science, Oxford, England, pp. 127–132.

Mueller-Dombois, D. and H. Ellenberg. 1974. Aims and Methods of Vegetation Ecology. Wiley, NY, USA.

Newton, M. and P.G. Comeau. 1990. Control of competing vegetation. In: Regenerating British Columbia's Forests. D.P. Lavender, R. Parish, C.M. Johnson, G. Montgomery, A. Vyse, R.A. Willis, and D. Winston, eds. UBC Press, Vancouver, Canada, pp. 256–265.

BIOGRAPHICAL SKETCHES

Thomas Wells (corresponding author)
Strategic Coordinator, Vegetation Maintenance, Transmission and Distribution, BC Hydro, 8475-128th Street, Surrey, BC Canada V3W 0G1, Phone: (604) 543-4151, Fax: (604) 543-1540, e-mail: thomas.wells@bchydro.com

Tom Wells is a Strategic Coordinator of vegetation maintenance in Transmission and Distribution at BC Hydro. He holds a BSc in Botany from the University of Guelph, a MSc in Plant Sciences from the University of Western Ontario, and a PhD in Botany from the University of British Columbia. Tom's research interest has focussed on the systematics and ecology of woody plants, particularly shrubs. He joined BC Hydro in 1994 as its only vegetation ecologist and presently coordinates the transmission rights-of-way vegetation maintenance program.

Kevin Dalgarno
Vegetation/Pest Biologist, Transmission and Distribution, BC Hydro, 1401 Kalamalka Lake Road, Vernon, BC Canada V1T 8S4, Phone: (250) 549-8549, Fax: (250) 549-8667, e-mail: kevin.dalgarno@bchydro.com

Kevin Dalgarno holds a BSc in Biology from the University of Victoria. He has worked as a Vegetation/Pest Biologist for BC Hydro since 1989. He has extensive expertise in pesticides. Kevin works to develop cost effective and environmentally sensitive work methods for maintaining vegetation on rights-of-way and in substations. In addition, he also provides support in regards to rodent control and remedial wood preservation of power poles. Interests away from work include water and snow skiing, mountain biking, boating, scuba diving, and flying.

Ray Read
Vegetation/Pest Biologist, Transmission and Distribution, BC Hydro, 400 Madsen Road, P.O. Drawer 1500, Nanaimo, BC Canada V9R 5M3, Phone: (250) 755-4741, Fax: (250) 755-4731, e-mail: ray.read@bchydro.com

Ray Read is a native of New Zealand where he was a Provincial Noxious Weeds Manager for nine years. He was responsible for planning and coordinating integrated pest/vegetation management programs to meet regulatory obligations. This involved raising public awareness of the use of pesticides, biological control agents, and alternative vegetation management techniques. Ray has been working for BC Hydro for the last eight years, based on Vancouver Island as a Vegetation/Pest Biologist in Transmission and Distribution. He provides multidisciplinary expertise and advice on vegetation management and natural resource management programs.

Tree, Shrub, and Herb Succession and Five Years of Management Following the Establishment of a New Electric Transmission Right-of-Way through a Mixed Woodland

Richard A. Johnstone, Michael R. Haggie, and Hubert A. Allen, Jr.

A five-year study on vegetation succession was undertaken following the construction of a new electric transmission right-of-way (ROW) in Delaware, USA, that utilized both clear and selective cutting methods. Integrated vegetation management (IVM) methods were used as secondary interventions and compared against control sites. Restrictions have been imposed by regulatory agencies declaring that only selective clearing of targeted incompatible tall-growing trees and retention of existing compatible low-growing trees and shrubs is permitted for new ROW construction. Permanent upland quadrants were established for this study that compared tree, shrub, and herb populations following clear-cut and select-cut tree removal, and integrated vegetation management and no treatment interventions. Baseline data were gathered prior to construction and changes were documented for species numbers, diversity, stem count, and relative density. The management of desirable species and their relative value to wildlife are considered. Results show that IVM interventions triggered vegetation succession from mature woodland trees to low shrub/herbaceous communities as successfully in the clear-cut as in the select-cut quadrants. Total species numbers remained relatively stable but reflect a substitution of trees for herbaceous species while shrub species numbers remained relatively constant. The environmental effects of electric transmission ROW establishment and various vegetation management techniques upon plant species succession are discussed.

Keywords: Relative dominance index (RDI), wildlife use index (WUI), upland, Delaware, clear-cut (CC), select-cut (SC), integrated vegetation management (IVM), selective treatment

INTRODUCTION

Several studies have shown vegetation changes in existing electric transmission rights-of-way (ROW) following a variety of treatments and management practices (e.g., Draxler et al., 1997; Finch and Shupe, 1997; Garant et al., 1997; and Haggie et al., 1997). This study documents 5 years of vegetation succession following the establishment of a new electric transmission line through a mixed oak-holly-pine (*Quercus-Ilex-Pinus*) upland and contrasts the use of clear-cutting (CC) and select-cutting (SC) of trees for initial ROW clearing, with subsequent integrated vegetation management (IVM) or no treatment controls.

Since 1983 Delmarva Power, now Conectiv Power Delivery (CPD), has gradually implemented IVM in their transmission ROW vegetation management. CPD has evolved an IVM system which includes hand-cutting, mechanical control, herbicide treatment, and biological control (Hallmark, 1996). Herbicide use is coupled with a high degree of field crew education concerning the identification of desirable and undesirable tree and shrub species. These methods have not only produced a significant cost savings of $3 million to the company (Johnstone, 1997, pers. comm.), but have also created more than 3642 ha of wildlife habitat along 9171 km of ROW in Maryland, Delaware, and Virginia (Wildlife Habitat Enhancement Council,

Environmental Concerns in Rights-of-Way
Management: Seventh International Symposium
J.W. Goodrich-Mahoney, D.F. Mutrie and C.A. Guild (editors)
© 2002 Elsevier Science Ltd. All rights reserved.

1992). Much of this habitat, ecologically termed old-field type, can have considerable value for certain wildlife species (Chasko and Gates, 1982 and Delorey, 1992). In this study undesirable species include all tall trees that are capable of growing to a sufficient height so as to interfere with overhead utility wires.

CPD, under whose auspices this research was initiated, has contracted with Chesapeake Wildlife Heritage to evaluate the effects of certain clearing methods, as well as herbicide and mechanical treatments, on plant succession in ROW sections on the Delmarva Peninsula.

GOALS AND OBJECTIVES

The research goal of this study was to document the vegetation changes that occurred following the establishment of a new ROW in a mid-Atlantic wooded upland area. The purpose was to address questions by federal and state regulatory agencies during the ROW construction permit process concerning the environmental effects of clear-cutting versus selective-cutting of trees. From an economic standpoint clear-cutting, the mechanical removal of all above ground vegetation, is preferred over selective cutting for ROW preparation and establishment. From an environmental standpoint selective-cutting has been suggested by the permitting agencies as the preferred method, since it retains the compatible low growing trees, shrubs, and herbaceous vegetation present at the time of initial ROW clearing.

Our research objective was to investigate whether a relatively stable shrub-herbaceous community could be established following a clear-cut, using judicious IVM interventions, that is as environmentally comparable as that perceptibly obtained with a selective-cut.

The utility company vegetation management objective is to cost-effectively foster relatively stable low-growing plant communities in order to minimize overhead transmission line interference and maintain access to facilities. This optimum situation can be most effectively achieved by using IVM with a gradual reduction of herbicides, ending with only periodic spot treatments (Bramble et al., 1987) and a reliance on natural allelopathy (Cain, 1997; Putnam, 1986; and Horsley, 1977).

This study explores the merits of clear-cutting versus selective-cutting in new ROW construction, accompanied by IVM interventions.

STUDY AREA AND SITE HISTORY

Located at Indian Mission off state Route 5 near Harbeson, Sussex County, DE, USA, the study area lies at coordinates 38°41'N and 75°14'W. New ROW construction commenced in the fall of 1992. This electric transmission line was initiated to facilitate power distribution from the generation point in Millsboro to Rehoboth Beach, Delaware (DP Circuit 13705 Indian River/Robinsonville). The 30 m wide construction line runs north to south through a 0.91 km tract of mixed timber, part of which was last logged in the 1950s. Age of the existing woodland was estimated based on tree size and ring count. Trees were of short to moderate size for the species norm due to the somewhat droughty underlying soil types, indicating an edatope. These were listed in the Soil Survey for Sussex County, Delaware as woodland classes 3o, 3s, and 2s (Ireland and Matthews, 1974). Trees consisted of primarily mixed oak-holly-pine woodland and the ROW is bisected west to east by Chapel Branch, a stream that drains into Rehoboth Bay via the Burton Prong of Herring Creek. The survey site was laid out along an upland ROW section to the south of the stream branch. The soils consist of loamy sand that is part of the Evesboro-Rumford association. These soils are moderately to excessively well drained having a highly permeable subsoil of sand to sandy loam. The upland study area lies on a 0–2% slope (Ireland and Matthews, 1974).

METHODS AND MATERIALS

A linear transect survey method suitable to following long-term vegetation succession was used (Smith, 1966). A 30 m wide by 100 m long centrally located section of ROW, with a 10 m central access route, was selected as representative of the upland woody vegetation. This block was subdivided into four 10 m × 50 m quadrants. The east side of the ROW was selectively treated (SS) in 1993 and 1997 with herbicide to control undesirable trees. The west side remained untreated (UT) as the control until 1997. ROW treatment history is summarized in Table 1.

Baseline data of tree, shrub, and herbaceous species were taken prior to new ROW construction in the fall (September to October) of 1992, and subsequently each fall from 1992 through 1997. Herbaceous data were also collected in the spring (May to June) from 1993 through 1997. A four letter code was assigned to each plant identified using the first two letters of the genus and species in the Latin name, e.g. *Vaccinium corymbosum* is VACO, or if only identified to genus, VASP.

Five 2 m × 10 m shrub plots, 10 m apart, were established north/south within each quadrant. Shrub survey lines were commenced 5 m from either end of each quadrant. One tree plot, 10 m × 50 m, was established within each quadrant. The end points of each transect line were marked with permanent stakes which allowed the same transect to be surveyed again in each subsequent year. See Fig. 1.

Table 1. Indian Mission Connective Power Delivery ROW construction and herbicide treatment history 1992–1997

Year/season	Treatment	Effected quads	Notes
1992 Fall	Clear-cut (CC)	NW, SE	CC = tree stumps & shrubs mown to ground level
	Select-cut (SC)	NE, SW	SC = undesirable trees and shrubs removed
1993 Fall	Initial herbicide Select-spray (SS)	NE, SE	Code 031[a], foliage/hydraulic broadcast NW, SW untreated (UT)
1994 Summer	Follow-up herbicide Select-spray	NE, SE	Same as 1993
1995	None	All	
1996	None	All	
1997 Summer	Follow-up herbicide Select-spray	All	Code 031G[b], foliage/hydraulic broadcast Code XG670[c]

Upland herbicide codes, mixtures, and rates

a-Code 031	1993	4.73L (1.25 US gal.) Accord* + 1.18dl (4 oz.) Arsenal + 1.89L (0.50 US gal.) Cleancut + 0.95L (0.25 US gal.) Weedar 64 + 1.18dl (4 oz.) 38F drift control in 378.5L (100 US gal.) water.
b-Code 031G	1997	4.73L (1.25 US gal.) Accord* + 0.95L (0.25 US gal.) Garlon 3A + 1.18dl (4 oz.) Arsenal + 1.89L (0.50 US gal.) Cleancut + 1.18dl (4 oz.) 38F drift controlin 378.5L (100 US gal.) water. *Glyphosate applied at a rate of 10.44 L/ha (4 qts/ac), 53.8% active ingredient (a.i.).
c-Code XG670	1997	4.73L (1.25 US gal.) Accord* + 4.14dl (14 oz.) Garlon 3A + 1.18dl (4 oz.) Arsenal + 56.78L (15 US gal.) Thinvert (total volume = 62.07L (16.4 US gal.)) in 378.5L (100 US gal.) water. Used in upland.

Trade names of herbicides used

Accord (common name: glyphosate isopropylamine), composition = 53% concentration of isopropylamine salt of N-[phosphono-methyl] glycine
Arsenal, (family name: imidazolinone), composition = isopropylamine salt of imazapyr (2-[4,5-dihydro-4-methyl-4-(1-methylethyl)-5-oxo-1H-imidazol-2-yl]-3-pyridine carboxylic acid)
Garlon 3A, (common name: Triclopyr), composition = 3,5,6-trichloro-2-pyridinyloxyacetic acid
Weedar (common name: 2,4-D), composition = dodecylamine + tetradecylamine salts of 2,4-D
(Meister and Sine, 1996)
Surfactants used were Cleancut, Thinvert and 38F used for drift control

Abbreviations for Tables 1 and 2

Species code	Common name	Latin name
ACRU	Red Maple	*Acer rubrum*
CLAL	Sweet Pepperbush	*Clethra alnifolia*
ILGL	Inkberry	*Ilex glabra*
ILOP	American Holly	*Ilex opaca*
LEUS	Fetterbush	*Leucothoe sp*
LYLI	Male Berry	*Lyonia ligustrina*
NYSY	Sour Gum	*Nyssa sylvatica*
PITA	Loblolly Pine	*Pinus taeda*
PIVI	Virginia Pine	*Pinus virginiana*
QUSP	Oak	*Quercus sp*
RHOV	Azalea	*Rhododendron sp*
RUBS	Bramble	*Rubus sp*
SAAL	White Sassafras	*Sassafras albidum*
SMRO	Greenbriar	*Smilax rotundifolia*
SPSH	Sprayed Shrub	*Sprayed shrub*
VACO	High bush Blueberry	*Vaccinium corymbosum*
VAGA	Low bush Blueberry/Huckleberry	*Vaccinium sp/Gaylussacia sp*

+ — new species since 1992 baseline, * — undesirable right-of-way species, CC — clear cut, SC — select cut, (X:X) = (U:D) ratio of undesirable to desirable ROW species. N.B. species are listed in order of dominance within each % group, % is rounded to the nearest whole number

Herbaceous plots 1 m square were laid out along the mid-line of the 2 m × 10 m shrub plots at 0, 5, and 10 m. These three points were permanently marked with wire flags. At either end of the transect a 5 m buffer was left to reduce the edge effect of shading from the adjacent woodland at the one end, and the wood debris effects within the access corridor at the other (Fig. 1). Herbaceous vegetation was stem counted by species and percent cover estimated following species identification. All specimens were identified to genus and, where practical, to species. A prefabricated meter square made from 12.5 mm PVC schedule 40 plastic water pipe was used along the survey line, within which the data were taken.

In the tree plots individuals were identified to species where possible, counted and measured at diameter breast height (DBH). Woody specimens ≥5 cm DBH were considered trees, and further subdivided into desirable and undesirable based on their potential to interfere with overhead wires. Woody specimens <5 cm DBH were considered shrubs and they were identified to genus or species and the number of stems counted. Only when these species reach a stage ≥5 cm DBH are they controlled by the utility company.

A relative dominance index (RDI) developed by Smith (1966) was applied in our studies (Haggie et al.,

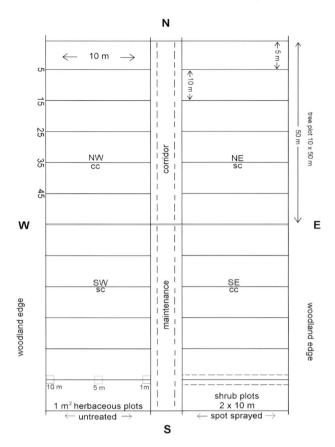

Fig. 1. Indian Mission Rights-of-Way Upland Research Plots. Quadrant NW is clear-cut (CC); removed trees and shrubs; left unsprayed for future maintenance. Quadrant NE is selective cut (SC); cleared trees and left shrubs; selective follow up. Quadrant SW is selective cut (SC); cleared trees and left shrubs; left unsprayed for future maintenance. Quadrant SE is clear-cut (CC); removed trees and shrubs; selective follow-up.

1997) and used to compare the various species groups to each other, between seasons and years.

Nomenclature used for herbaceous and woody species was taken from Brown and Brown (1972 and 1984), and for bryophytes, Shuttleworth and Zim (1967).

RESULTS AND DISCUSSION

The ROW through the woodland was clear-cut of trees and shrubs in the fall of 1992, the standard establishment procedure, except where the specific quadrant treatments were installed as in Fig. 1. Only in the access lane were the tree stumps ground down and the wood chips deposited. The vegetation changes that followed can be broken down into 6 groups for analysis.

General overview
Tall growing undesirable tree species ≥5 cm DBH were eliminated from the study site at baseline due to the primary intervention of clear-cutting (preferred utility method) and selective-cutting (permitting agency method) in the fall of 1992. They did not start to

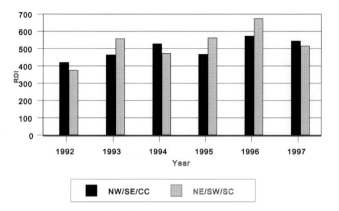

Fig. 2. Indian Mission Upland Shrub Relative Density Index (RDI) compares the close association of the desirable shrub densities in the CC and the SC. No significant difference was found between the plots (by ANOVA $p \leq 0.573128$).

reoccur in the select-cut until the fall of 1995 and in the clear-cut until 1996. The total number of shrub species remained relatively constant over the study period and even though their composition varied, their relative dominance as shown in Fig. 2 and total stem count increased over time. However herbaceous species increased dramatically after only 2 years from a baseline number of 5 to a maximum of 18 species in the fall of 1994. Thus from an aspect of plant diversity there was a shift from tree species to herbaceous species over the time of the survey once the tree competition that limited the herbaceous vegetation was removed.

Trees and shrubs (≥5 cm DBH)
The order of dominance in the baseline oak-holly-pine tree association consisted of three species of oak, (*Quercus alba* L., *Quercus rubra* L., *Quercus nigra* L.), American holly (*Ilex opaca* Ait.), loblolly pine (*Pinus taeda* L.) and red maple (*Acer rubrum* L.). This order was based on the total stem count of each species in all quadrants. Eleven total tree species were recorded in the 1992 baseline data.

In the select-cut quadrants the number of tree species dropped from a high of 10 [ratio 8 undesirable (U):2 desirable (D)] at baseline to 5 (4U:1D) at the end of the survey.

In the clear-cut quadrants species numbers were again 10 (8U:2D) at baseline to 3 (2U:1D) tree species at the end of the survey, two from sprouted stumps (red maple and American holly) and one from seed (loblolly pine).

In this type of woody association undesirable trees naturally dominate over the desirable species (ratio = 10U:2D at baseline). As the number of tree species reappeared in the SC following initial construction in 1992, there followed a significant annual increase in both the total stem count and RDI. These were composed of desirable species exclusively until 1995, since the undesirable species were either cut or selective

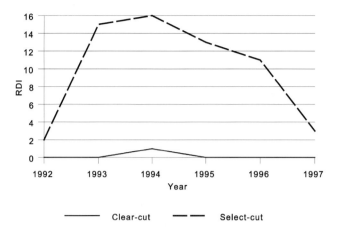

Fig. 3. Indian Mission Tree/Shrub for Flowering Dogwood compares the relative density (RDI) of Flowering Dogwood (*Cornus florida*) in the CC and the SC plots. The rapid increase in 1993 may be attributed to the release of the surrounding tree canopy. The drop in RDI after 1994 may be attributed to shrub competition and direct sunlight.

herbicide treated. The undesirable species started to attain tree dimension 3–5 years after construction but stem count remained low due to IVM interventions. No discernable difference was observed in numbers of desirable trees in the treated versus untreated plots, which indicated that the selective herbicide intervention in the year following construction was appropriately targeted by the field crews. (Field crew education is deemed an important aspect in achieving the stated goals.)

In the CC trees did not start to appear until 4–5 years after construction. The number of undesirable tree seedling species (<5 cm DBH) remained moderately constant each year (range 7–9) over the entire study period in both the CC and the SC, indicating that there was an ever-present natural cohort in this type of woodland ready for recruitment.

The desirable trees (<5 cm DBH) were differently affected, possibly due to their niche. These tended to be small, edge, or understory trees, such as hop-hornbeam (*Ostrya virginiana* (Mill.) K. Koch.) and flowering dogwood (*Cornus florida* L.) as shown in Fig. 3. The SC appeared to benefit these species after 2–3 years when their RDI peaked, but at the end of the five-year study their RDI was similar to the baseline. Competition from other plant species in the open ROW corridor diminished the initial benefit of their selective retention. The CC did not show an increase in RDI for these desirable species since they immediately had difficulty competing against other plant species after the initial clearing. The exception was American holly, the RDI of which peaked at the end of the study due to the sprouting of cut stems in the CC and possible allelopathic properties in the SC.

Shrubs, woody vines, and small trees (<5 cm DBH)
The total stem count of the shrub community remained quite constant over the five-year study. Range in total species numbers over time varied from 26 to 34 species with the peak occurring in 1995, 3 years post-treatment. At the commencement of the study 23 species of shrubs were identified in all quadrants and by the end there were 28 species. This represented a total gain of 5 species, with 3 (1U:2D) species being lost and 8 (1U:7D) gained. Twenty species persisted over the study period.

An analysis of the quadrants by CC and SC pairs evinces some useful comparisons in the similarities of shrub succession between the two construction methods as shown in Tables 2 and 3.

For taxonomic simplification, low-bush blueberry (*Vaccinium* (*vacillans*) Torr.) and huckleberry (*Gaylussacia sp.* H.B.K.) were combined into one botanical group (see VAGA, Tables 2 and 3). They were the dominant shrubs at baseline (CC = 68% and SC = 46%), but three years later demonstrated a reduction in stem count in both the CC (to 31%) and the SC (to 39%). The data in the two treatments following ROW construction correlate closely and eventually stabilize, despite there being an overall reduction of this species group by 46% in the CC (Table 3) and 10% in the SC (Table 2). This is partly explained by the higher baseline relative dominance in the CC and suggests that either this clearing method, type of competition and/or reduction in overstory does not benefit this species group. Statistically, however, no significant difference was found between the CC and SC quadrants (ANOVA $p \leq 0.573128$). Species that revealed an increase in the CC were sweet pepperbush (*Clethra alnifolia* L.), fetterbush (*Leucothoe racemosa* (L.) Gray), and blackberry (*Rubus sp.* L.), while fetterbush, blackberry, and inkberry (*Ilex glabra* (L.) Gray.) increased in the SC. Throughout the survey, irrespective of treatment, desirable shrub/trees, except for holly, appeared not to have good recuperative capabilities in this changed environment. Conversely undesirable species such as oaks, red maple, sour gum, and loblolly were found to persistently resprout and reseed.

Herbaceous vegetation, including succulent vines
From the baseline data herbaceous species increased from a total of 5 to 15 at the end of the study, with a peak of 18 species in the 3 middle seasons of 1994–1995. The drop in species numbers may be attributed to a maximum colonization at that time and subsequent interspecific competition from other herbs and shading from increased growth in the shrubs. This hypothesis is partly supported by the rapid increase in the herbaceous RDI over time (28.5–74.8) until the fourth year post-treatment (see Fig. 4).

Early dominant pioneering species of note were broom-sedge (*Andropogon virginicus* L.), panic grass (*Panicum* (*verrucosum*) Muhl. L.), sow-thistle (*Sonchus oleraceus* L.), greenbriar (*Smilax sp.*), sedges, (*Carex sp.* L.), and several mosses (bryophytes). After 2–3

Table 2. Indian mission upland shrub dominant species, selective cut

Year	1992	1993	1994	1995	1996	1997	%
							$\bar{x}$ # stems
							71–100
							61–70
	VAGA 46						51–60
		VAGA 42			VAGA 46	VAGA 43	41–50
			VAGA 36	VAGA 39			31–40
							21–30
	CLAL 16	CLAL 13	CLAL 14	LEUS 16	CLAL 12	CLAL 15	11–20
		ACRU* 12	LEUS 12	CLAL 17	LEUS 12	(SPSH) 11	
	RHOV 7	LEUS+ 8	VACO 9	VACO 6	ACRU* 5	VACO 7	5–10
	VACO 7	QUSP* 6	ACRU* 8	ACRU* 5	VACO 5	ACRU* 6	
	LYL 7				RUBS 5		
	QUSP* 4	VACO 4	ILOP 4	QUSP* 3	VACO 3	LEUS 4	>2–4
	ACRU* 3	NYSY* 3	QUSP* 3	SMRO 2	RHOV 3	SMRO 3	
	ILOP 3	ILOP 2	ILGL 3		PITA* 3	RUBS 2	
	PIVI* 2	ILGL+ 2	RHOV 3		QUSP* 2		
			SMRO 2		SMRO 2		
# sp < 2%	12 (6:6)	16 (5:11)	10 (5:5)	21 (7:14)	12 (5:7)	15 (7:8)	$\bar{x} = 14.3$
# sp ≥ 2%	9 (3:6)	9 (3:6)	11 (2:9)	7 (2:5)	11 (3:8)	8 (1:7)	$\bar{x} = 9.2$
# sp ≥ 5%	5 (0:5)	5 (1:4)	6 (1:5)	5 (1:4)	6 (0:6)	5 (1:4)	$\bar{x} = 5.3$
Total # sp	21 (9:12)	25 (8:17)	21 (7:14)	28 (9:19)	23 (8:15)	23 (8:15)	$\bar{x} = 23.5$
Total # stem	1882	2786	2364	2816	3368	2580	$\bar{x} = 2633$

Table 3. Indian mission upland shrub dominant species, clear cut

Year	1992	1993	1994	1995	1996	1997	%
							$\bar{x}$ # stems
							71–100
	VAGA 68						61–70
							51–60
		VAGA 42	VAGA 43				41–50
				VAGA 31	VAGA 36	VAGA 31	31–40
						(SPSH) 25	21–30
		CLAL 15	CLAL 13	LEUS 18	CLAL 18	CLAL 11	11–20
				CLAL 14	LEUS 13		
	VACO 7	ACRU* 8	LEUS 8	ILOP 7	VACO 6	ILOP 7	5–10
		LEUS+ 7	VACO 7	VACO 6	RUBS 5	VACO 5	
		VACO 6	ILOP 7			RUBS 5	
	ILOP 4	ILOP 4	QUSP* 4	ACRU* 4	ILOP 4	ILGL 4	>2–4
	CLAL 4	QUSP* 3	ACRU* 3	QUSP* 3	ACRU* 4	ACRU* 3	
	QUSP* 4	NYSY* 3	LYLI+ 3	NYSY* 2	LYLI 3	LEUS 2	
	LYLI 3	SAAL* 2		RUBS+ 2	ILGL 3		
					PITA* 3		
					QUSP* 2		
# sp < 2%	16 (8:8)	15 (4:11)	16 (6:10)	16 (4:12)	14 (7:7)	16 (8:8)	$\bar{x} = 15.5$
# sp ≥ 2%	6 (1:5)	9 (4:5)	9 (1:8)	10 (3:7)	12 (3:9)	9 (1:8)	$\bar{x} = 9.2$
# sp ≥ 5%	2 (0:5)	5 (1:4)	5 (0:5)	6 (0:6)	6 (0:6)	6 (0:6)	$\bar{x} = 5.0$
Total # sp	22 (9:13)	24 (8:16)	25 (8:17)	26 (7:19)	26 (10:16)	25 (9:16)	$\bar{x} = 24.7$
Total # stem	2105	2320	2637	2337	2861	2717	$\bar{x} = 2496.2$

years, several thoroughwort species, such as *Eupatorium sp.* L., started to appear in addition to deer-tongue grass (*Dichantelium clandestinum*) (L. Gould.) In the fourth year brambles (*Rubus sp.*) and lichens (*Lichenes sp.*) emerged. This living herbaceous group increased from 1% of the woodland floor at baseline to 48% at the end of the study, despite suppression from the 52% of non-living material (branches, logs, leaf litter) and associated shrub community. No differences were noticed between the CC and SC in the total living herbaceous RDI analysis, although there were species specific differences.

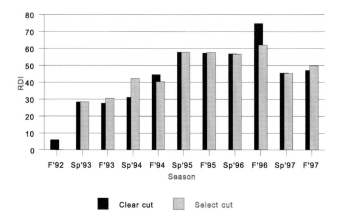

Fig. 4. Indian Mission Upland Herbaceous shows the very close comparison of herbaceous vegetation by relative density index (RDI) in the CC versus the SC plots. No significant difference was found between the plots in RDI but species variation was found.

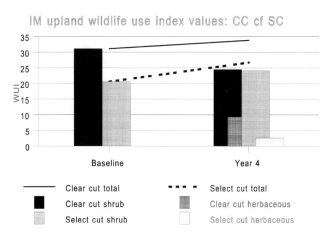

Fig. 5. Indian Mission Upland Wildlife Use Index Values: clear-cut compared with select-cut. An increase in total values in year 4 can be attributed to an increase in grasses with a high WUI, especially in the clear-cut.

Non-living material (NLM)

The herbaceous baseline data in the fall of 1992 consisted of a single dense layer of hardwood and softwood leaf litter that occupied the woodland floor (=99% NLM). In the fourth year following construction, prior to the final selective herbicide intervention, average NLM percent cover was 36.5% in the SC and 28.0% in the CC. This indicates a better rate of living plant colonization of ground cover in the CC, evidently due to shading by the remaining trees in the SC.

The RDI of the bare soil in the SC was 53.3 in the year after construction and 38.4 four years later while the CC was 47.6 after construction but 0 in the fourth year. The significantly greater SC bare soil RDI is only partly due to the shading and allelopathic effects of the remaining shrubs (Meilleur et al., 1994) and desirable trees (principally holly). This was unexpected and could have implications where clearing techniques are used in erosion-prone areas. This study suggests that long-term erosion control through increased plant cover of bare soil could possibly be better served with CC than SC. The authors however recommend further studies.

Wildlife implications

To determine a gauge of comparative wildlife use in the different ROW preparation methods, a Wildlife Use Index (WUI), adopted by the US Fish and Wildlife Service (USFWS), was adapted from Martin, Zim, and Nelson (1951). In order to make a valid comparison, trees (both desirable and undesirable) were excluded from the WUI evaluation. Trees such as oaks have a very high WUI, but only if allowed to grow to maturity, which is not possible within a ROW corridor. One limitation of the WUI is that not all species in the survey were evaluated by the USFWS. In such cases an assumed value of one was given.

A WUI was applied to the desirable dominant shrub and herbaceous species with an index ≥ 1 in order to assess comparative values for SC and CC. See Table 4. WUI values were also computed to compare baseline data with the final study year. At baseline, WUI of the CC quadrants was 31.1 (shrubs = 31.1, herbaceous = 0) and SC quadrants was 20.6 (shrubs = 20.6, herbaceous = 0). In the fourth year post-construction the CC was 33.8 (shrubs = 24.5, herb = 9.3) and the SC was 26.7 (shrubs = 24.1, herbs = 2.6) (see Fig. 5). The overall increase in the WUI can be attributed to an increase in shrubs and, particularly in the CC area, herbaceous species with a high wildlife value. These high WUI species include the panic grasses, *Panicum sps.*, deer-tongue grass, *Dichantelium sp.*, bramble, *Rubus sp.*, and sedges, *Carex sp.* (Table 4). The desirable trees do not have a high wildlife value, the exception being flowering dogwood. *Cornus florida* L., WUI = 58). Dogwood was retained in the SC area but its RDI declines over time in the open ROW corridor.

CONCLUSIONS AND RECOMMENDATIONS

The primary question of this investigation was whether adequate natural vegetation would colonize a clear-cut (CC) as opposed to a selectively cut (SC) newly constructed upland utility ROW. Data showed that early vegetation recovery (evaluated by % cover, total stem count, and RDI) in the CC quadrants was sufficient to reduce erosion as compared to the SC. In fact, shrub and herbaceous colonization of the CC areas was sufficient to achieve 100% living plant cover over the five-year study period, while the SC had more area of bare soil. This study suggests that the erosion control rationale for permitting agency restrictions on clear cutting and the preferences for selective cutting, may be misguided. This study showed that by solely evaluating the shrub and herbaceous colonization there can be equal or more potential cover and wildlife value after 5 years in a CC as opposed to a SC. Changes in

Table 4. Indian mission upland desirable vegetation wildlife use index values (WUI). From Martin, Zim, and Nelson, 1951*

Common name	Latin name	Species code	*WUI value
Bramble	*Rubus sp.*	RUBS	74
Deer-tongue grass	*Dichantelium sp.*	DISP	59
Panic grass	*Panicum sp.*	PASP	59
Flowering dogwood	*Cornus florida*	COFL	58
Sedge	*Carex sp.*	CASP	41
Low-bush blueberry	*Vaccinium sp.*	VASP	41
Greenbriar	*Smilax sp.*	SMIS	20
Azalea	*Rhododendron sp.*	RHOV	4
Huckleberry	*Gaylussacia sp.*	GAYS	2
Sweet pepperbush	*Clethra alnifolia*	CLAL	1
Fetterbush	*Leucothoe sp.*	LEUS	1

desirable shrub RDI and stem count all demonstrated comparable species occupation, species maintenance, species colonization, and extinction in both the CC and the SC. A general evaluation of the stem count and the RDI revealed that CC and SC do not significantly vary and colonized well two years after ROW construction and almost completely by the end of the study.

When select-cutting trees careful consideration should be given to the condition, growth stage and type of the tree selected. Tree density and tree height should be considered as well as the age of the woodland as a whole. Herbicide applicator education was found in this study to be of great importance in selecting the appropriate vegetation types to establish a viable desirable community. It is possible to make a general prediction of the eventual shrub/herbaceous composition following the clear-cutting of an eastern deciduous mixed upland forest with judicious follow-up selective application of herbicide to undesirable species. No replanting is needed to establish up to 100% ground cover. This can occur with either ROW method of establishment, clear-cut or select-cut, if a careful examination is made of the baseline shrub vegetation before ROW construction and knowledge has been acquired on the effects of cutting for different species. This study does not demonstrate that clear-cut is better than selective-cut. It simply shows that there are no major discernible differences between a clearcut and a selective-cut ROW in their vegetational composition 5 years post ROW clearing and preparation.

ACKNOWLEDGMENTS

Bob Molzhan, Environmental Affairs, Delmarva Power, for initial funding of the research project. Victor Williamson, Forestry Representative, Delmarva Power, for collaboration in ROW management. Deborah Collison, Chesapeake Wildlife Heritage, for proof reading text, editing and comments. Phil Shedaker, ROW Field Supervisor, Conectiv Power Delivery, for field crew collaboration. Wayne Longbottom, Anne Arundel Community College, for botanical identification. Henry Clifford and George Clifford for their field assistance. Roland Limpert, Power Plant Division, Maryland Dept. of Natural Resources, for study design and site layout.

REFERENCES

Bramble, W.C., W.R. Byrnes, and R.J. Hutnik. 1987. Development of plant cover diversity on an electric transmission right-of-way. In: Proc. of the Fourth International Symposium on Environmental Concerns in Rights-of-Way Management. W.R. Byrnes and H.A. Holt, eds. Indianapolis, IN. 595 pp.

Brown, M.L. and R.G. Brown. 1984. Herbaceous plants of Maryland. Port City Press, Baltimore, MD. 1127 pp.

Brown, R.G. and M.L. Brown. 1972. Woody plants of Maryland. Port City Press, Baltimore, MD. 347 pp.

Cain, N.P. 1997. Old field vegetation for low maintenance highway rights-of-way. In: Proc. of the Sixth International Symposium on Environmental Concerns in Rights-of-Way Management. J.R. Williams, et al., eds. New Orleans, LA. 511 pp.

Chasko, G.G. and J.E. Gates. 1982. Avian habitat suitability along a transmission-line corridor in an oak-hickory forest region. Wildlife Monograph, 82: 41.

Delorey, A. 1992. The power line ROW: An unexpected place to find many nesting birds. Birding, 24(6), 365–367.

Draxler, R., D. Uther, G. Praxl, and F. Hofbauer. 1997. New aspects of rights-of-way management for high-voltage power lines. In: Proc. of the Sixth International Symposium on Environmental Concerns in Rights-of-Way Management. J.R. Williams, et al., eds. New Orleans, LA. 511 pp.

Finch, K.E. and S.D. Shupe. 1997. Nearly two decades of integrated vegetation management on electric transmission rights-of-ways. In: Proc. of the Sixth International Symposium on Environmental Concerns in Rights-of-Way Management. J.R. Williams, et al., eds. New Orleans, LA. 511 pp.

Garant, Y., J. Domingue, and F. Gauthier. 1997. Effectiveness of three vegetation control methods in establishing compatible plant species in powerline ROW in northeastern Quebec. In: Proc. of the Sixth International Symposium on Environmental Concerns in Rights-of-Way Management. J.R. Williams, et al., eds. New Orleans, LA. 511 pp.

Haggie, M.R., R.A. Johnstone, and H.A. Allen. 1997. Vegetational succession following a broadcast treatment of glyphosate to a wild reed stand in a utility right-of-way. In: Proc. of the Sixth International Symposium on Environmental Concerns in Rights-of-Way Management. J.R. Williams, et al., eds. New Orleans, LA. 511 pp.

Hallmark, S. 1996. IVM: A competitive tool. Electric Perspectives. May–June, 16–28.

Horsley, S.B. 1977. Allelopathic inhibition of black cherry by fern, grass, goldenrod and aster. Canadian Journal of Forestry Research, 7: 205–215.

Ireland, W. and E.D. Matthews. 1974. Soil Survey of Sussex County, Delaware. US Government Printing Office, Washington, DC, 74 pp.

Johnstone, R.A. 1997. Personal communication. Supervisor of Forestry, Delmarva Power & Light Co., Salisbury, MD, 3 January.

Martin, A.C., H.S. Zim, and A.L Nelson. 1951. American Wildlife and Plants. A Guide to Wildlife Food Habits: the Use of Trees, Shrubs, Weeds and Herbs by Birds and Mammals of the United States. Dover Publications Inc., NY. 500 pp.

Meilleur, A., H. Veronneau, and A. Bouchard. 1994. Shrub communities as inhibitors of plant succession in Southern Quebec. Environmental Management, 18: 907–921.

Meister, R.T. and C. Sine, eds. 1996. Farm Chemicals Handbook. Meister Publishing Company, Willoughby, OH. C196 pp.

Putnam A.R. and Chung-Shih Teng. 1986. The Science of Allelopathy. John Wiley and Sons Inc., NY. 317 pp.

Shuttleworth, F.S. and H.S. Zim. 1967. Mushrooms and other non-flowering plants. Western Publishing Co., Inc., Racine, WI. 160 pp.

Smith, R.L. 1966. Ecology and Field Biology. Harper & Row, New York, NY. 686 pp.

Wildlife Habitat Enhancement Council. 1992. The economic benefits of wildlife habitat enhancement on corporate lands. Wildlife Habitat Enhancement Council, Silver Spring, Maryland. 61 pp.

BIOGRAPHICAL SKETCHES

Richard A. Johnstone

Conectiv Power Delivery, PO Box 9239, Newark, DE 19714-9239, USA, PH: 302/454-4841; FAX: 302/283-5828; E-mail: Richard.Johnstone@conectiv.com

Richard A. Johnstone is System Forester for Conectiv Power Delivery in Newark, DE. He serves on Edison Electric Institute's Vegetation Management Task Force and is the past President of the Utility Arborist Association. He received a BSc degree in Forest Resources Management from West Virginia University.

Michael R. Haggie

Chesapeake Wildlife Heritage, PO Box 1745, Easton, MD 21601, USA, PH: 410/822-5100; FAX: 410/822-4016; E-mail: info@cheswildlife.org

Michael R. Haggie is a Wildlife Ecologist with Chesapeake Wildlife Heritage in Easton, MD. His work focuses on wildlife ecology of utility rights-of-way and sustainable farming systems. He received a BSc degree in Agronomy from Cornell University, Ithaca, NY.

Hubert Allen

Hubert Allen & Associates, 720 Tramway Lane NW, #25, Albuquerque, NM 87122, USA, PH: 505/979-3520; FAX: 505/979-3521; E-mail: hubertaallen@compuserve.com

Hubert Allen, President of Hubert Allen & Associates, has a MSc in Biostatistics from The Johns Hopkins University, Baltimore, MD, and operates a consulting firm in Albuquerque, NM, specializing in "Statistics/Computing/Information Systems in Health and Environment."

Gray Birch Ecology on an Electric Powerline Right-of-Way in Upstate New York

Christopher A. Nowak, Benjamin D. Ballard, and Erin O'Neill

Gray birch (*Betula populifolia* Marsh.) is an important tree species on powerline rights-of-way (ROWs) in the north temperate zone of North America. It is a pioneer species that can proliferate in the early plant succession environment of powerline ROWs. While a short tree at maturity (10–15 m), it is commonly a danger for the transmission of electricity. On a 17-yr-old 765 kV ROW in New York, stem densities of the gray birch population (trees greater than 1 cm diameter at breast height and approximately 3 m height) averaged 350 ha^{-1}. The ROW had been last managed with herbicides 11 years previous using an Integrated Vegetation Management approach. Treatments were basal and stem-foliar herbicides applied using non-selective or selective modes as part of a long-term study. Fifty-four gray birch trees from across a 25 km section of ROW were examined for height-age development patterns. Population density and age structure were measured on 11 treatment plots. Tree heights ranged to over 11 m and trees ages from 4 to 13 years. Most of the trees were established within 3 years after treatment. Young powerline corridors that have mesic to hydric moisture regimes are well-suited to birch invasion, particularly with management-related disturbance. Minimizing site disturbance and promoting the development of a tall-shrub community should reduce birch presence in older powerlines.

Keywords: Electric transmission lines, integrated vegetation management, right-of-way management, life history, autecology

INTRODUCTION

Gray birch (*Betula populifolia* Marsh.) is a common species of northeastern North America, with a range that extends from southern Quebec and eastern Ontario in Canada, to Delaware, Maryland, and eastern Ohio in the United States. It can also be found far south in the mountains of north Georgia and north Alabama. Range of this species is apparently extending west, north, and east (Lavoie and Saint-Louis, 1999).

Gray birch is plentiful throughout New York and New England, where, as a pioneer or early plant succession species, it covers large areas on abandoned farms and recently disturbed sites following fire and windstorms. It can be an important species following clearcutting and other regeneration cuts associated with forestry (Liptzin and Ashton, 1999).

Environmental Concerns in Rights-of-Way Management: Seventh International Symposium
J.W. Goodrich-Mahoney, D.F. Mutrie and C.A. Guild (editors)
© 2002 Elsevier Science Ltd. All rights reserved.

Gray birch is an important species on powerline corridors in New York State (Environmental Consultants Inc., 1985; Nowak et al., 1995). It can grow tall enough to cause problems with the transmission of electricity. On some lines in upstate New York, gray birch is a recurrent problem, even with an integrated vegetation management approach aimed to control it (K. Finch, personal communication). One such problem line is the Volney–Marcy powerline in upstate New York. Birch has persisted for nearly two decades after initial clearing, surviving herbicide treatments in 1982, 1983, and 1988. Its persistence on this line seems inconsistent with life history characteristics and has befuddled both managers and scientists. In this paper, we investigate gray birch ecology on the Volney–Marcy line to: (1) determine how much gray birch is on the line and whether population densities and dynamics vary by mode and method of herbicide treatment, (2) determine why birch is on this right-of-way 17 years after initial clearing, and (3) predict the future presence of birch on this and like powerlines.

BACKGROUND: LIFE HISTORY CHARACTERISTICS OF GRAY BIRCH

Little has been written about the life history of gray birch, likely because it is not a commercially valuable species for most forestry objectives. The following literature, most of which pertains to other birch species, was used to extrapolate and compile information for gray birch: Marquis (1969), Brinkman (1974), Safford (1983), Perala and Alm (1990), and Hardin et al. (2000).

Reproduction of gray birch

Gray birch can regenerate both vegetatively and sexually. Vegative regrowth is by stump sprouting after the main stem has been severed. Birches are not prolific sprouters. In a study of 18 different powerline corridors in New York State, populations of gray birch stayed the same or were significantly decreased with handcutting or mowing treatments, indicating that many stems of birch can be killed with mechanical treatments (Environmental Consultants Inc., 1986). When birch does sprout, one to many stems are produced from each stump.

Birches, in general, are prolific seeders. They can produce large quantities of seed that may be dispersed long distances by the wind, particularly across crusts of snow. Birch seed is usually limited in dispersal to a distance of about two times the height of the producing tree. Bumper seed crops are infrequent, but moderate seed crops are common, with average annual production of up to 3–5 million seeds per hectare.

Sexual maturity and seed bearing seem to occur at an early age for gray birch. Gray birch generally begin producing seed at age 8, but has been observed producing seed as early as age 4 (Nowak and Ballard, personal observations). Seed matures in early fall and is dispersed from October to the early winter months.

As is common to most pioneer species, birch seed is small. Over 5,000,000 seeds are needed to total one kilogram. Small-seeded species are sensitive to environmental conditions at the time of germination. Condition of the seedbed and amount of exposure to direct sunlight affect germination and early survival. Best germination and early survival is where mineral soil has been exposed, and where there is shade. Moisture is critical. Soil organic horizons are often detrimental to germination of birch seeds because they have poor moisture holding capacity and regularly dry out in the summer. Scarification, the physical removal of the organic horizons or mixing with the mineral soil, is commonly used to promote birch regeneration, particularly on dry sites. On moist sites, it is not necessary to scarify the soil for seed germination. Good germination and survival occurs almost any place where soil moisture is high.

Growth of gray birch

Gray birch is shade intolerant and fast growing. Heights of 6–9 m are commonly attained by age 10 years, with a maximum height of 18 m.

Growth is affected by seedbed and light conditions. If the mineral soil is exposed, the loss of organic matter may create low nutrient levels or nutrient imbalances that lead to reduced growth. Birch requires highly illuminated environments to survive, but these environments can also reduce soil moisture. Best conditions for establishment and subsequent growth of birch is partially shaded conditions early, with full sunlight later. As young birch develop, increased light exposure leads directly to increased growth, particularly root growth. Root growth may be especially important where birch competes with other species.

Longevity of gray birch

Gray birch is recognized as being short-lived, but specifics on longevity are not published. Other short-lived birches such as paper birch (*Betula papyrifera* Marsh.) can live to 80 years. It is likely that gray birch may live to only half that age.

FIELD STUDY METHODS

Study site

The study took place on the 17-yr-old (1999 age) Volney-Marcy powerline corridor, a 765 kV transmission line ROW in the Towns of Lee, Western, and Floyd in Oneida County, New York (43°21′N, 75°32′W–43°15′N, 75°17′W) (described previously by Nowak et al., 1992; paraphrased as follows). The corridor passes through the Interlobal Highland Region, between the Tug Hill Plateau and the Mohawk Valley; it is covered by northern hardwood forest with a predominance of red maple (*Acer rubrum* L.) and eastern hemlock (*Tsuga canadensis* [L.] Carr.), although there was a mixture of both abandoned and active agricultural and forest land on and surrounding the study area, with sporadic inclusions of gray birch. The Volney–Marcy ROW is 68.6 m wide. The study area is approximately 25 km in length, generally running east–west in direction. On the south side of the Volney–Marcy powerline is the 28-yr-old (1999 age) New York Power Authority Fitzpatrick–Edic 345 kV transmission line; its ROW width is 45.7 m.

Soils of the study area are silt and sand loams, including a variety of Fragiaquepts, Eutrochrepts, and Haplaquepts of varied drainage; the dominant soil series encountered were Camroden, Pickney, Pyrities, Katurah, and Malone. Many of the soils have fragipans, which causes the sites to be wet with a perched water table. Most of the sites have mesic or hydric moisture regimes.

Experimental design

A completely randomized, unbalanced factorial design (two to three replications) was used to test second conversion cycle mode (nonselective and selective) and method (basal and stem-foliar) treatment effects on gray birch (see below). Treatment plots ranged in size from 0.23 to 0.75 ha, extending from edge to edge of the ROW. Treatment plots were systematically assigned within randomly chosen areas located across the study site and treated in mid-summer 1988. The original study had 19 treatment plots. Only 11 plots were used in this study.

Selective basal
Treatment of undesirable vegetation (trees that can grow more than 6 meters in height) during late July–August 1988 with a herbicide mixture consisting of 7.6 L of triclopyr at 0.480 kg ai ha^{-1} and 371 L of No. 2 fuel oil; it was targeted at the lower 0.3 to 0.6 m of individual stems, saturating the base of the stem and all exposed roots to the point of rundown and puddling around the root collar zone.

Nonselective basal
Treatment of all woody vegetation with a herbicide mixture and application method the same as that for the selective basal treatment. Herbaceous vegetation was not treated.

Selective stem-foliar
Treatment of undesirable vegetation with a herbicide consisting of a mixture of 1.4 L of triclopyr at 0.480 kg ai ha^{-1}, 1.9 L of a formulation of picloram at 0.060 kg ai ha^{-1} plus 2,4 D at 0.240 kg ai ha^{-1}, 0.95 L of adjuvant (crop oil concentrate) and 375 L of water, applied to leaves, branches and stems to a point of wetness.

Nonselective stem-foliar
Treatment of all woody vegetation with a herbicide mixture and application method the same as that for the selective stem-foliar treatment. Herbaceous vegetation was not treated.

Data collection

In summer of 1999, 11 years after treatment, gray birch population densities (only trees 2.5 cm diameter at breast height [1.37 m along stem above groundline] or greater) were measured using 1.8 m wide strip transects that covered 6 to 16 percent of the study plots. A 7.6 m wide buffer zone along the edge of a treatment plot was not sampled.

At the end of the 1999 growing season, five gray birch trees were felled from each study plot with a chainsaw. A large and a small tree were sampled at random, along with three moderate sized trees from along the edge of the study plot (away from permanent plant community measurement areas). Only four trees were used for stem analysis in one plot due to a sample transfer problem. One plot was not sampled due to an error in field work. A total of 54 trees were sampled. Diameter at breast height and total height of each tree was measured. Stem discs were cut at 1.2 m intervals, from the base of the tree to its tip. A total of 287 stem disc samples were collected.

Data analysis

Inspection of scatter plots of the data indicated that linear regressions would adequately describe height growth development patterns. Regressions equation slope coefficients were tested for homogeneity using analysis of variance. Regressions were fit to data from each treatment plot and the slope coefficients used as dependent variables. Regression intercept coefficients were held constant among treatments at a value of zero.

Analysis of variance was used to test treatment mode and method effects on gray birch population density. Age structure was determined by developing an age-dbh relationship: age $= 3.94x^{0.47351}$, $r^2 = 0.67$, $n = 54$; where x is dbh to the nearest centimeter). Age was predicted for all stems on the treatment plots using data from the strip transects. Age structure was used to determine the number of gray birch trees that were alive at time of treatment, but were not treated. Trees that were 12 years old or older were considered to be treatment misses.

An alpha-level of 0.10 was used as the critical value for significance testing, though p-values up to 0.20 were considered as indicative of potentially meaningful results.

HYPOTHESES, RESULTS, AND DISCUSSION

Height-age relationships
Hypothesis
Treatments with a high level of disturbance–the nonselective mode and stem-foliar method–would have larger slope coefficients in regressions of height vs. age. Greater disturbance would provide birch a less competitive environment, allowing it to grow faster.

Results and discussion
Height-age relations did not vary by treatment mode or method, hence, we reject the hypothesis. A single regression explained much of the variation in height growth as a function of age: height $= 0.70*$ age, where height is expressed in meters and age in years; $r^2 = 0.91$; $n = 287$. Height growth rates of over 0.7 m per year were defined by the slope coefficient, a low value compared to the 1-m rate observed by Environmental Consultants Inc. (1984). Lower values on the Volney–Marcy site may be due to lower site quality or older tree populations. Young trees usually grow faster in height than older trees. Trees sampled on the Volney–Marcy ranged in age to 13 years, extraordinarily old for

a powerline right-of-way. Usually, trees are removed before they reach 10 years age, else they grow into the conductors. Sample tree heights ranged from 2.4 to 11.6 m. The high clearance associated with a 765 kV line allowed for older, tall populations of trees to exist, yet still maintain a safe corridor.

Population densities

Hypothesis

Treatments with a high level of disturbance — the nonselective mode and the stem-foliar method — would have a larger number of birch trees and a greater proportion of gray birch trees than less disturbing treatments, such as the selective mode and basal treatment. Greater disturbance would provide birch more safe seedbeds, leading to greater number of trees established.

Results and discussion

No significant difference was observed among treatments in birch population density, which averaged 350 stems ha^{-1} (stems equal to or greater than 2.5 cm dbh) across all treatments. Total number of undesirable trees did differ among treatments, with the nonselective mode having less trees than the selective mode, 333–1255 stems ha^{-1}. Gray birch, as a percent of the total tree population, was marginally affected by treatment method ($p = 0.13$), with the basal treatments having relatively less birch than stem-foliar, 12–41%. It appears that stem-foliar treatments may have changed species composition by promoting the presence of birch, perhaps due to greater site disturbance. Hence, we tacitly accept the hypothesis that higher levels of disturbance increased the proportion of birch, but reject the hypothesis regarding total number.

Population age structure

Hypothesis

Age structure, i.e., the number of trees per age class, will show a progressive decrease with time. Most birch in forestry situations become established within the first 3 years after treatment (Safford, 1983). We hypothesized that most of the gray birch would be between 8 and 11 years old. Trees older than 11 years would be treatment misses.

Results and discussion

Sample tree ages ranged from 4 to 13 years. Sixty percent of the gray birch was established within the first 3 years after treatment, 34% between 4 and 8 years after treatment. Treatment misses accounted for 6% of the birch trees. This is consistent with our hypothesis. Most of the birch trees were established soon after treatment. However, a significant amount of birch continued to be established 4 years and more after treatment. We expected that the residual plant community would have fully reoccupied the site within a few years of treatment. Apparently, some areas must have remained relatively free of plants for the successful invasion of birch, or birch is more robust in its germination and establishment than described in the literature.

Percentage of trees that were missed from treatment was small and at a level consistent with other studies (Environmental Consultants Inc., 1984). We expect that the majority of missed trees were established just prior to treatment, and as such, were short and hidden by the herb and shrub community.

SUMMARY AND CONCLUSIONS

Young powerline corridors apparently can provide suitable environments for gray birch. Soils may be disturbed by heavy equipment during vegetation management treatments, particularly during initial clearing and early conversion treatments, providing adequate conditions for germination and early survival. Partial shade is provided by herbs and shrubs, but they do not effectively out-compete with birch for site resources because they themselves are also just becoming established. In the open environment of a young powerline corridor, birch can germinate in a cool, moist environment, develop for a few years, then have full sunlight after growing past the short desirable plant community.

Birch presence on the Volney–Marcy powerline corridor over the past decade can be attributed to the disturbance associated with the herbicide treatments, coupled with the generally wet soils across the study area.

Our expectation is that birch populations will be greatly curtailed with the next treatment, as long as site disturbance is minimized. This speculation is supported by Ballard et al. (this proceedings), as they observed that most of the advance regeneration of trees on the Volney–Marcy are maples and cherries. Birch will continue to be present on the Volney–Marcy into the future, primarily because of continued seed supply and moist seedbeds, but at much reduced amounts. Control of birch will be facilitated once a tall shrub community becomes established on the Volney–Marcy. But, as long as sites are disturbed and soil moisture is high, birch will be present.

ACKNOWLEDGEMENTS

Impetus for this project came from periodic discussions with and questions from Ken Finch, Niagara Mohawk Power Corporation, regarding gray birch on powerline corridors. Erin O'Neill, as an undergraduate college student in search of an independent study, expressed an interest in doing the field work and data management. This study was made possible with logistical and monetary support provided the Niagara Mohawk Power Corporation. Ed Neuhauser's support in these areas is acknowledged.

REFERENCES

Brinkman, K.A. 1974. *Betula* L. Birch. In: Seeds of Woody Plants in the United States. C.S. Schopmeyer, tech. coord. Agriculture Handbook No. 450. US Department of Agriculture Forest Service, Washington, DC. pp. 252–257.

Environmental Consultants, Inc. 1984. Cost comparison of right-of-way treatment methods. Research Report EP 80-5. Empire State Electric Energy Research Corporation, Schenectady, NY.

Environmental Consultants, Inc. 1985. Long-term right-of-way effectiveness. Research Report EP 83-15. Empire State Electric Energy Research Corporation, Schenectady, NY.

Environmental Consultants, Inc. 1986. Right-of-way treatment cycles. Research Report EP 84-26. Empire State Electric Energy Research Corporation, Schenectady, NY.

Hardin, J.W., D.J. Leopold, and F.M. White. 2000. Harlow and Harrar's Textbook of Dendrology. 9th ed. WCB/McGraw–Hill, Dubuque.

Lavoie, C. and A. Saint-Louis. 1999. The spread of gray birch (*Betula populifolia*) in eastern Quebec: landscape and historical considerations. Canadian Journal of Botany, 77: 859–868.

Liptzin, D. and P.M.S. Ashton. 1999. Early-successional dynamics of single-aged mixed hardwood stands in a southern New England forest, USA. Forest Ecology and Management, 116: 141–150.

Marquis, D.A. 1969. Silvical requirements for natural birch regeneration. In: Birch Symposium Proceedings. US Department of Agriculture Forest Service, Northeastern Forest Experiment State, Upper Darby, PA. pp. 40–49.

Nowak, C.A., L.P. Abrahamson, E.F. Neuhauser, C.G. Foreback, H.D. Freed, S.B. Shaheen, and C.H. Stevens. 1992. Cost effective vegetation management on a recently cleared electric transmission right-of-way. Weed Technology, 6: 828–837.

Nowak, C.A., L.P. Abrahamson, D.J. Raynal, and D.J. Leopold. 1995. Selective vegetation management on powerline corridors in New York State: Tree density and species composition changes 1975–1991. In: Proceedings of the 5th International Symposium on Environmental Concerns in Rights-of-Way Management, September 19–22, 1993, Montreal, Quebec. J.R. Williams, J.W. Goodrich-Mahoney, J.R. Wisniewski, and J. Wisniewski, eds. Hydo-Quebec, Montreal, Canada. pp. 153–158.

Perala, D.A. and A.A. Alm. 1990. Reproductive ecology of birch: A review. Forest Ecology and Management, 32: 1–38.

Safford, L.O. 1983. Silvicultural guide for paper birch in the northeast (revised). Northeastern Forest Experiment State Research Paper NE-535. US Department of Agriculture Forest Service.

BIOGRAPHICAL SKETCHES

Christopher A. Nowak (corresponding author)
220 Marshall Hall, State University of New York College of Environmental Science and Forestry, 1 Forestry Drive, Syracuse, NY 13210, USA. Phone: 315-470-6575; e-mail: canowak@esf.edu

Christopher A. Nowak, Associate Professor of Forestry at SUNY-College of Environmental Science and Forestry (SUNY-ESF), holds an AAS in Forest Technology and BS, MS, and PhD degrees in Forest Resources Management from SUNY-ESF. Prior to joining the Faculty at SUNY-ESF in 1998, he worked for 6 years as a Research Scientist for the Research Foundation of SUNY on issues related to nutrient cycling and acidic deposition, fast growing hardwoods, and vegetation management on powerline corridors, and 5 years as a Research Forester for the US Forest Service in northwestern Pennsylvania on ecology and silviculture of Allegheny hardwoods. He is currently responsible for teaching courses related to extensive and intensive silviculture and forest vegetation management. His contemporary research and service activities are related to integrated vegetation management on powerline corridors, phytoremediation of industrial waste sites, short-rotation intensive culture of willow and poplar, and silviculture in northern conifers and hardwoods.

Benjamin D. Ballard
218 Marshall Hall, State University of New York College of Environmental Science and Forestry, 1 Forestry Drive, Syracuse, NY 13210, USA. Phone: 315-470-4821; e-mail: bballard@esf.edu

Benjamin Ballard, Research Scientist at SUNY College of Environmental Science and Forestry (SUNY-ESF), holds a BS and MS in Forest Resources Management from SUNY-ESF and an MS in Statistics from Syracuse University. He has been involved with research at SUNY-ESF for over 8 years, and is currently responsible for the day-to-day management of more than 15 studies associated with vegetation management on powerline corridors. Additionally, he is a PhD candidate working on issues related to integrated vegetation management on powerline corridors, focusing on the ecology and management of shrub communities.

Erin O'Neill
Woodlands, Finch, Pruyn & Company, Inc., 1 Glen Street, Glens Falls, NY 12801, USA

Erin O'Neill earned a Dual BS in Environmental Forest Biology and Resource Management, completing all undergraduate course work at SUNY College of Environmental Science and Forestry in May 2000. She is currently employed as a District Forester at Finch, Pruyn & Company, Inc., in Glens Falls, NY.

Evaluating Native Shrub Plantings as a Control for Tall-Growing Woody Tree Species in Powerline Rights-of-Way

Mark H. Wolfe, N.S. Nicholas, A.K. Rose, P.A. Mays, T.A. Wojtalik, and K.D. Choate

The effectiveness of planted native shrubs as a method for suppressing undesirable tall-growing trees is being evaluated at six recently constructed powerline right-of-way locations in northern Georgia. Three of the sites were formerly forested, and three were a herbaceous/grass/wooded mixture prior to line construction. At each site two shrub spacing treatments (1 × 1 and 2 × 2 m) and a control shrub spacing (1.5 × 1.5 m) of native shrub seedlings were established in a Randomized Complete Block design after an initial site vegetation survey. Shrub plantings were established without the use of herbicides or mechanical site preparation. Survivorship of planted shrubs across all sites declined from 72% in the first growing season to 38% at the end of the third growing season. Results show that in the first growing season after shrub planting the competition from tall-growing woody stems increased dramatically from 4 to 10 fold. In the second growing season, tall-growing woody stem densities on the formerly forested sites (high pre-planting tall-woody stems density) increased an additional 20–40%. On sites with high grass/herbaceous coverage, tall-growing woody stem densities decreased by an average of 20% in the second growing season. Planted shrub spacing treatments so far have not significantly affected the numbers of tall-growing tree seedlings/sprouts after three growing seasons. The effectiveness of shrub plantings may have been further limited by early growing season drought effects on the growth and survival of the planted shrubs.

Keywords: Shrubs, planting, ROW, survivorship, riparian, herbicides, competition, woody stems, forest wetlands

INTRODUCTION

Vegetation control in powerline rights-of-way is a continual and costly effort for utility companies. Rights-of-way (ROW) vegetation control under electric transmission lines typically relies on mowing and or herbicide application to control unwanted vegetation, particularly tree species capable of growing into the danger zone of transmission lines. Environmental concerns, vegetation control costs, and aesthetic considerations are a few of the issues that are stimulating interest in methods of controlling vegetation that can reduce mechanical or herbicide use and lengthen rotation cycles.

One potential method of natural control that has received much attention stems from the ability of communities of shrubs to resist invasion by, or to suppress, tall-growing tree species beneath their canopies (Niering and Egler, 1955). Niering et al. (1986) report that a shrub community of *Viburnam lentago* remained highly resistance to tree invasion for more than 50 years. In southern Quebec, studies of shrub communities in ROW by Meilleur et al. (1994) have shown that a number of species of shrubs have inhibitory effects on tree establishment beneath their canopies. Research efforts to encourage shrub community development in ROWs have for the most part focused on selective herbicide applications to control tall-growing tree species while allowing native shrub species to develop relatively stable communities (Bramble and Byrnes, 1976; Niering and Goodwin, 1974). Less research, however, has been done to examine the effectiveness of establishing na-

---

Environmental Concerns in Rights-of-Way
Management: Seventh International Symposium
J.W. Goodrich-Mahoney, D.F. Mutrie and C.A. Guild (editors)
Elsevier Science Ltd.

tive shrub communities, a control for tall-growing tree species, particularly in riparian or wetland areas where herbicides use may be undesirable. Establishing and maintaining vegetation buffers in these areas using shrubs has the potential advantages of reducing maintenance activity to control tree species while providing cover to ameliorate water temperature effects and help maintain stable stream banks.

This study describes early results from direct plantings of native shrub species at three levels of spacing with respect to (1) the effectiveness of plantings to control re-sprout or seedling growth of tall-growing tree species, and (2) the survival rate of the planted shrub species. The plantings were made in forested riparian and forest wetland areas, transected by recently cleared powerline ROW. Study sites were mowed to facilitate planting but no further mechanical or herbicide control for competing vegetation was carried out during the three growing seasons of this study. A decision not to control existing vegetation was based on the objective to evaluate how effectively shrub plantings could be established in areas where the use of herbicides or extensive mechanical pre-planting preparation could be detrimental to the site environment or undesirable because of public concern.

METHODS

Study sites

Six sites were selected along powerline ROWs maintained by the Tennessee Valley Authority (TVA) in northwest Georgia (Fig. 1). The climate of the region is characterized by mild winters and warm humid summers with a mean annual precipitation of 136 cm evenly distributed through the year. The ROW at five of these sites were newly cleared within 1–2 years prior to initiation of the study in 1997, the Council Fire site had been cleared for 3 years. None of the six sites had experienced a vegetation maintenance cycle since line construction. The sites were selected based on the variety of soil conditions and vegetation type and abundance within and adjacent to the ROW. It was determined that this range of conditions would be representative of the conditions that could be encountered and would provide a realistic pilot test of the feasibility and effectiveness of shrub plantings within the ROW in this area.

Two of the sites, Calhoun and Swamp Creek, are classified as palustrian forested wetlands (PFO1A) by National Wetland Inventory (NWI) maps. The Bowater, Turner, Council Fire, and Peavine sites are forest riparian zone sites adjacent to second order streams in the study area. The Bowater, Calhoun, and Swamp Creek sites were 100% forested before ROW construction. The Council Fire, Turner, and Peavine sites had narrow (10–15 m) wooded zones along the stream bank sides of the plots with the remainder of the plots being covered by a mix of herbaceous and some tree species. The predominant forest type adjacent to all study sites is mixed-bottomland hardwoods with a component of upland species at the more well drained riparian sites. The forests adjacent to the Swamp Creek and Calhoun ROW sites are dominated by oaks (*Quercus sp.*), green ash (*Fraxinus pennsylvanica*), sweetgum (*Liquidambar styraciflua*), red maple (*Acer rubrum*), black willow (*Salix nigra*), and hickories (*Carya sp.*). The riparian sites were predominantly occupied by oaks (*Quercus sp.*), green ash (*Fraxinus pennsylvanica*), red maple (*Acer rubrum*), hickories (*Carya sp.*), elm (*Ulmus sp.*), and box-elder (*Acer negundo*).

Soils of each of the sites are formed in alluvial sediments and are acid to moderately acid with surface textures that range from silt loam to sandy loam. The riparian sites are well drained and do not exhibit redoximorphic features, however, the forested wetland sites at Calhoun and Swamp Creek are somewhat poorly drained and poorly drained, respectively. All sites are on nearly level ground with slopes of less than 3%.

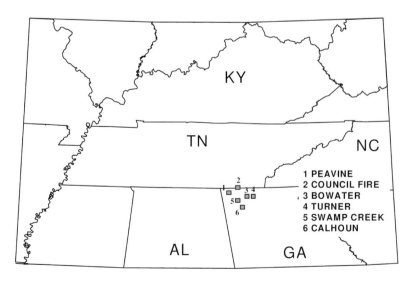

Fig. 1. Location of study sites in northwest Georgia.

Pre-planting vegetation measurements

Prior to the establishment of the plantings in the ROW existing herbaceous and non-shrub woody species within the 20 × 50 m plot areas were measured for stem density (stems/m^2) and species composition. Study plot boundaries were delineated and five randomly selected 5 × 10 m subplots within the plot area were used to visually estimate the percent cover of herbaceous species and to count and categorize woody stems by species and height classes of 0–0.5, 0.5–1.0, 1.0–1.5, 1.5–2.0, and >2.0 m. Herbaceous vegetation was identified to species when possible.

Experimental design

At each study site a single 20 × 50 m plot was established and oriented perpendicular to the ROW direction. At Swamp Creek and Peavine sites the ROW corridor was too narrow and plots were therefore oriented parallel to the ROW. The experimental design is a 3 × 4 randomized block with shrub seedling spacing of 2 × 2, 1.5 × 1.5, and 1 × 1 m, with each spacing randomly occurring once in each of the four blocks. This results in 12 treatment blocks, each with a dimension of 6.7 m × 12.5 m. A non-planted control was not used because under a mitigation or restoration scenario to maintain a buffer area, for riparian or wetland zones, some planting would likely be required. The 1.5 × 1.5 m spacing was thus considered a minimum planting density that would be used and thus served as the control for comparison with the 1 × 1 m and 2 × 2 m shrub spacing. Comparison of shrub spacing effects was within sites only. No statistical comparisons between sites were made.

Species selection

The species of native shrubs selected for planting by site are shown in Table 1. Shrub species chosen for use in this study were selected based on the following: commercial availability, native species, expected maximum height <15′, adaptability to soils and hydrology as indicated by published information, tolerant of moderate to full sun, moderate to fast rate of expected growth, and having potential as a food source and cover for wildlife. Planting of all study sites was carried out between late October 1997 and February 1998. Prior to planting each site, standing vegetation was mowed to facilitate plot layout and planting. No further chemical or mechanical vegetation controls were carried out through the three growing seasons of this study.

The number of shrub seedlings planted within each spacing x block combination at each plot was; 18, 32, and 72 for the 2 × 2, 1.5 × 1.5, and 1 × 1 m spacing, respectively. A total of 488 seedlings were planted at each site. Equal numbers of each of the four species selected for a site were planted in each of the spacing × block combinations. The bare-rooted 1–2 year shrub seedlings were planted using a 6″ power auger.

Vegetation and shrub survivorship measurements

During each growing season all study sites were re-measured for survivorship of planted shrub seedlings, herbaceous cover percent and the number and heights of tall-growing tree species (woody stem density). Shrub seedling survivorship was determined by counting each seedling in all treatment blocks and noting if seedlings were live or dead. Seedlings unaccounted for were added into the dead category. Survivorship of planted shrub seedlings was calculated as the percentage of the originally planted shrub species still alive. Herbaceous and woody stem density were measured in 3 replicate 1 m^2 quadrats randomly located in a 2 × 8 m area located in the center of each treatment block in order to avoid potential edge effects. All treatment blocks were measured at each study plot. Within each of the 1 m^2 quadrats a visual estimate of the percent cover of the five most abundant herbaceous

Table 1. Shrub species selected (•) for planting by site

Species	Site					
	Peavine	Calhoun	Turner	Bowater	Swamp Creek	Council Fire
Silky dogwood (*Cornus amomum*)			•	•		
American elderberry (*Sambucus canadensis*)	•	•	•	•	•	•
Winterberry holly (*Ilex verticillata*)			•	•		
Spicebush (*Lindera benzoin*)	•	•				•
Red chokeberry (*Aronia arbutifolia*)					•	
Gray dogwood (*Cornus racemosa*)	•	•			•	•
Nannyberry (*Viburnam lentago*)	•	•	•	•	•	•

species was made. Herbaceous plants were identified to the species level when possible but are reported here to family or genus level. Stems of all woody species within the 1 m² quadrats were counted by species and categorized into <0.5, 0.5–1, 1–1.5, 1.5–2, 2–2.5, 2.5–3, 3–5, and 5–7 m height classes. The mean woody stems density (stems/m²) was calculated by summing the number of woody stems of all height classes within each of the three replicate 1 m² quadrats of a treatment block and dividing by the number of replicates. The overall treatment mean of woody stems density was calculated from the average of the treatment block mean woody stems densities.

Data analysis of the mean woody stems density within a spacing treatment was analyzed using analysis of variance procedure (SAS Institute, 1989) with Duncan's mean separation test. Dunnett's t-test was also used to compare the mean woody stems density in the 1 × 1 and 2 × 2 m to the 1.5 × 1.5 m control spacing.

RESULTS AND DISCUSSION

Herbaceous and woody stems density

The herbaceous composition at the family and genus level of all study sites has shown little change in three years. The five most abundant herbaceous species observed at each of the six location in this study are shown in Table 2. The herbaceous composition at these sites generally breaks down between grass and non-grass dominated communities. The most dominant families/genuses at the Calhoun, Bowater, and Swamp Creek sites are non-grass species whereas grasses dominate at the Peavine, Turner, and Council Fire locations.

Generally speaking most herbaceous species are not considered a problem from a ROW management point of view as long as they pose no threat to powerline operation or are not exotics. Planting of many herbaceous species, most notably grasses and other forage species, are sometimes done to enhance wildlife use within ROWs. Some grass dominated ROW herbaceous communities can also be resistant to tree invasion as shown by Hill et al. (1995). Planting shrubs in direct competition with herbaceous vegetation can have an inhibiting effect on the growth and survival of the plantings. In contrast, however herbaceous cover can also be beneficial to the establishment of woody plantings. Clewell and Lea (1989), for example, note that early successional herbaceous species can provide cover and shade for the trees planted for restoration of bottomland hardwoods. Shrub species not tolerant of light may therefore benefit from the presence of some herbaceous cover. The most serious competition to developing a shrub community is the pre-existing tall-growing tree species (as stems or seedbank), or those species which might be recruited into the ROW.

The average stem density of all species of woody stems from 1997–2000 at each site is shown in Fig. 2. The initial woody stems densities in 1997 prior to shrub planting ranged from 0.08 stems/m² (Peavine) to 1.63 stems/m² (Bowater). Woody stem densities at the Peavine, Turner, and Council Fire sites, which where occupied by narrow riparian forests adjacent to pasture or old field before line construction, were 0.08, 0.14, and 0.31 stems/m², respectively. The previously forested sites at Bowater, Calhoun, and Swamp Creek had stem densities of 1.63, 0.94, and 0.47 stems/m² respectively. The numbers of stems at all sites are reflective of coppice regeneration and root sprouting particularly at previously forested sites. These sites

Table 2. Five most abundant herbaceous families/genus by site. Abundance ranked by number (1 = most abundant, 5 = least abundant)

Family/genus	Site					
	Peavine	Calhoun	Turner	Bowater	Swamp Creek	Council Fire
Poaceae	1	3	1	3		1
Asteraceae/Vernonia			4			
Asteraceae/Aster	2		3			2
Asteraceae/Solidago		5		5		4
Asteraceae/Eupatorium					5	
Asteraceae/Ambrosia	4					
Bignoniaceae/Campsis	3					
Fabaceae/Trifolium	5					
Cyperaceae/Carex		1			2	
Caprifoliaceae/Lonicera		2		4	1	
Rosaceae/Rubus		4		2	4	
Juncaceae/Juncus					3	
Polygonaceae/Polygonum			2			
Violaceae/Viola			5			
Anacardiaceae/Toxicodendron				1		
Convolvulaceae/Ipomea						3
Passifloraceae/Passiflora						5

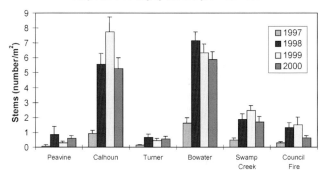

Fig. 2. Density of tall growing tree stems (number/m^2) for all study sites 1997–2000. Error bars represent standard error of the mean.

Table 3. Shrub seedling survivorship (percent of initial number planted) by study site for 1998 and 2000

Site	Species	Year	
		1998	2000
Peavine	Elderberry	96.7	42.7
	Gray dogwood	91.9	81.8
	Nannyberry	95.9	76.8
	Spicebush	45.1	5.0
Calhoun	Elderberry	55.7	24.4[a]
	Gray dogwood	84.3	67.0[a]
	Nannyberry	96.7	84.9[a]
	Spicebush	59.0	15.4[a]
Turner	Elderberry	69.1	61.8
	Silky dogwood	68.6	23.3
	Nannyberry	75.6	48.0
	Winterberry Holly	32.3	0
Bowater	Elderberry	78.5	11.7
	Silky dogwood	90.5	49.6
	Nannyberry	81.9	52.8
	Winterberry Holly	50.0	1.8
Swamp Creek	Elderberry	92.5	*
	Gray dogwood	76.2	*
	Nannyberry	96.7	*
	Spicebush	76.4	*
Council Fire	Elderberry	62.3	14.4[a]
	Gray dogwood	51.2	52.7[a]
	Nannyberry	63.6	43.3[a]
	Spicebush	56.2	4.4[a]

*Site damaged by mowing, re-planted early 1999.
[a] 3 subplots damaged by mowing, data from 9 of 12 subplots.

also face pressure from seedling recruitment from forests adjacent to the ROW.

Repeated cutting to control vegetation in these areas results in continual re-growth of woody species often in numbers greater than prior to cutting (Johnstone et al., 1984). This pattern can be seen at TVA sites in the large increases in the numbers of woody stems at all sites between 1997 and 1998 (Fig. 2). Woody stem densities in 1998 increased from 4 to 10 times the number in 1997. The greatest woody stem densities occur at Bowater and Calhoun sites with stem densities reaching 7.14 stem/m^2 in 1998 and 7.75 stems/m^2 in 1999, respectively. Overall stem densities from 1998 to 2000 remained high although a general trend of decreasing stem densities is occurring at each site (Fig. 2). A similar decline in overall stem density of woody species was observed by Brown, (1994) following clear-cutting for ROW near Toronto Ontario, Canada. Height growth of woody stems in this study has shifted from large numbers of small 0.5–1.0 m stems in 1998 to increasingly tall stems in 2000 (Fig. 3). Rapid height gain of competitive tall-growing tree seedlings can quickly and effectively shade out lower growing species.

Shrub survivorship

Survival rates of planted shrub species by site for 1998 and 2000 are shown in Table 3. Survivorship data for the Swamp Creek site in 2000 is not presented because initial 1998 planting at this site was accidentally mowed in the fall of 1998 and subsequently replanted in early 1999 so the current survival rate is not that of the original plantings. Not unexpectedly the survivorship of planted shrubs declined for all species across sites from the initial survivorship values in 1998. Large differences in survivorship are apparent between species across and within sites. The survival rate for silky and gray dogwood and nannyberry is greater than that of spicebush, winterberry holly and elderberry across almost every site. The somewhat lower survival rates of silky dogwood and nannyberry at the Turner site are largely due to herbivory by beaver and from early spring flooding, which washed out a number of seedlings in early 1999. The very poor overall survival rate of spicebush and winterberry holly are strongly reflective of the small size and low root-shoot ratio of the seedlings as planted.

Drought occurring in May 1998 and in July–September of 1999, while affecting all plantings, exacerbated the insufficiency of the small roots systems of these species to take up moisture. Planted elderberry seedlings while large, had coarse root systems lacking in fine (<2 mm) roots necessary for water uptake, which likely compounded the effects of drought thus reducing seedling survival of. Seedling size and adequate root-shoot ratio of the two dogwood species and nannyberry were factors contributing to their better overall survival across soil edaphic conditions and the competition from existing vegetation that are present across study sites. The variation of species survival across sites indicate the need to conduct trials on growth performance of native shrub species across a range of soil conditions and seedling parameters (i.e., seedling size, root/shoot ratio) to develop general recommendations for matching species with sites.

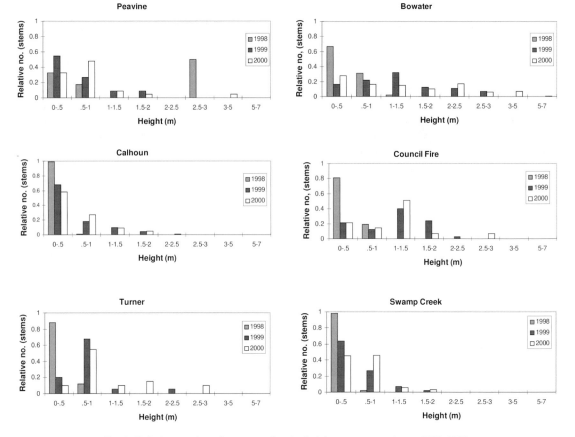

Fig. 3. Relative number of tree stems by site height category and year 1998–2000.

Shrub spacing effectiveness

Shrub spacing density had no effect on the numbers of tall-growing tree stems at any study site after three growing seasons (Table 4). Comparison of the 1 × 1 m and 2 × 2 m spacing to the control spacing 1.5 × 1.5 m using Dunnett's T test indicated no effect as well. The inability of planted shrubs in this study to control the seedling and re-sprout densities of tall-growing tree species after three growing seasons is not surprising considering the size of the seedlings when planted (0.5–1.5 m), low rate of planting survivorship and time necessary for establishment. Seedling survivorship and competition from herbaceous and other woody species are factors controlling the ability of any plantings to quickly develop into an effective control for tall-woody species. With the overall low level of shrub survival, the density of planted shrubs was not sufficient to be a controlling factor for tall-woody species in just three growing seasons. Additionally, the height of planted shrubs relative to competing vegetation particularly tree seedlings is another factor limiting the effectiveness of these plantings. Shrub seedlings planted in this study were 1–1.5 m tall with the exception of spicebush and winterberry holly (<0.5 m). Considering the time for plantings to become established, the seedlings could not develop enough height or spread to be competitive with existing vegetation particularly tall-growing woody species.

Table 4. Effect of shrub spacing on the density of tall growing tree stems by study site and year

Site	Shrub Spacing[1]	1998	1999	2000
Peavine	1 × 1	1.83a	0.42a	0.50a
	2 × 2	0.50a	0.33a	0.75a
	1.5 × 1.5	0.17a	0.25a	0.50a
Calhoun	1 × 1	4.58a	8.50a	4.67a
	2 × 2	7.17a	7.17a	5.00a
	1.5 × 1.5	5.00a	7.58a	6.17a
Turner	1 × 1	0.17a	0.33a	0.42a
	2 × 2	1.42a	0.87a	1.00a
	1.5 × 1.5	0.42a	0.08a	0.25a
Bowater	1 × 1	8.42a	5.41a	4.92a
	2 × 2	6.41a	6.67a	6.83a
	1.5 × 1.5	6.58a	7.00a	5.92a
Swamp Creek	1 × 1	1.17a	1.75a	1.42a
	2 × 2	2.60a	3.00a	1.79a
	1.5 × 1.5	1.92a	2.46a	1.92a
Council Fire	1 × 1	0.75a	1.38a	0.72a*
	2 × 2	2.50a	1.92a	1.00a*
	1.5 × 1.5	0.75a	1.50a	0.33a*

[1] Woody stems density values within year followed by the same letter are not significantly different (Duncans, $p = 0.05$).
*Only 3 of 4 treatment blocks measured.

Rapidly regenerating woody stems have the advantage in quick height growth over planted shrubs because of existing root structure and energy reserves. Some tall-growing woody species at Bowater for example, have increased in height from 0.5–1.0 m in 1998 to >3.0 m in 2000 (Fig. 3). This fact, coupled with the with low rates of survival and slow early growth of plantings, means that shrubs will not likely develop fast enough to compete with or control taller growing vegetation without measures to control competing vegetation and or increase the rate of spread and height growth of shrubs.

CONCLUSIONS

Spacing of planted shrubs showed no ability to control the numbers of tall-growing tree species after three growing seasons. The lack of effectiveness of plantings so far in this study are reflective of the short establishment time (three years), and the low overall rate of survival of the shrub species planted. The survivorship of the plantings was effected by both drought and competition from herbaceous and tall woody species within the ROW. Although gray dogwood and nannyberry had the highest survival rate across all sites, the need to better evaluate which species are suited for what conditions is indicated. While the principle of shrub community resistance to tree invasion is well established, the techniques for developing shrub communities where the shrub propagule pool may be sparse is not well established. For shrub plantings to develop into a control for trees species, methods which maximize the survival rate and competitiveness of shrub plantings must be developed. The survivorship and competitiveness of plantings for example, could be enhanced through planting of larger seedlings, periodic replanting to replace plants that die or planting very high densities of shrubs. Propagation methods like cutting back and layering could also be employed to increase growth and rate of spread of shrub species (Meilleur et. al., 1997). Controlling competing herbaceous and woody vegetation is likely the most important factor in how quickly shrub plantings become established and how effective they will become as a control for tall-growing tree species. Methods of controlling herbaceous and woody competition during the establishment phase of shrub plantings need to be developed. These methods, however, need to be compatible with the goals of the shrub plantings and any constraints which might limit how vegetation is controlled (i.e., herbicide use).

REFERENCES

Bramble, W.C. and W.R. Brynes. 1976. Development of a stable, low plant cover on a utility right-of-way. In: Proceedings of the First National Symposium on Environmental Concerns in Rights-of-Way Management. R. Tillman, ed. Mississippi State University, Starkville, MS, USA. pp. 167–176.

Brown, D. 1994. The development of woody vegetation in the first six years following clear-cutting of a hardwood forest for a utility right-of-way. Forest Ecology and Management, 65: 171–181.

Clewell, A.F. and R. Lea. 1989. Creation and restoration of forested wetland vegetation in the southeastern United States. In: Wetland Creation and Restoration: The Status of the Science, Volume 1: Regional Reviews. J.A. Kusler and M.E. Kentula, eds. EPA/600/3-89/038. pp. 199–237.

Hill, J.D., C.D. Canham, and D.M. Wood. 1995. Patterns and causes of resistance to tree invasion in rights-of-way. Ecological Applications, 5: 459–470.

Johnstone, P.A., W.C. Bramble, W.R. Byrnes, K.L. Carvell, D.E. White, and H.V. Wiant. 1984. Cost comparison of right-of-way treatment methods. ESEERCO Research Report EP80-5. Environmental Consultants, Inc., Fort Washington, PA.

Meilleur, A.H., Veronneau A., and A. Bouchard. 1997. Shrub propagation techniques for biological control of invading tree species. Environmental Management, 21: 433–442.

Meilleur, A.H., Veronneau A., and A. Bouchard. 1994. Shrub communities as inhibitors of plant succession in southern Quebec. Environmental Management, 18: 907–921.

Niering, W.A. and F.E. Egler. 1955. A shrub community of *Viburnam lentago*, stable for twenty-five years. Ecology, 36: 356–360.

Niering, W.A. and R.H. Goodwin. 1974. Creation of relatively stable shrublands with herbicides: arresting "succession" on rights of way and pastureland. Ecology 55: 784–795.

Niering, W.A., G.D. Dreyer, F.E. Egler, and J.P. Anderson, Jr. 1986. Stability of a *Viburnam lentago* community after 30 years. Bulletin of the Torrey Botanical Club, 113: 23–27.

SAS Institute. 1989. SAS/STAT Users Guide. Version 6, 4th ed., Vol. 1 and 2, Cary NC, USA: SAS Institute.

BIOGRAPHICAL SKETCHES

Mark H. Wolfe

Tennessee Valley Authority, Public Power Institute, P.O. Box 1649 Norris, TN 38282, USA

Mark H. Wolfe is an environmental scientist with the Tennessee Valley Authority's Public Power Institute in Norris Tennessee. He has been involved with various research projects ranging from the acid precipitation and ozone effects on plant growth to studies on the effects reduced soil moisture on tree root growth. He received his MS from the University of Tennessee in Plant and Soil Science.

N.S. Nicholas

Tennessee Valley Authority, Public Power Institute, P.O. Box 1649 Norris, TN 38282, USA

Niki Stephanie Nicholas is forest ecologist and manager of Environmental Impacts & Reductions Technologies with the Tennessee Valley Authority's Public Power Institute. Nicholas has a BA from Northwestern University in Biology, a MS in Ecology from the University of Tennessee and a PhD in Forestry from Virginia Polytechnic Institute and State University.

Anita K. Rose

Tennessee Valley Authority, Public Power Institute, P.O. Box 1649 Norris, TN 38282, USA

Anita Rose is an environmental scientist with the Tennessee Valley Authority's Public Power Institute. She has a BS in Biology and Botany from The University of Tennessee, and an MS in Ecology from The University of Tennessee.

Paul A. Mays
 Tennessee Valley Authority, Public Power Institute, P.O. Box 1649 Norris, TN 38282, USA
Paul Alan Mays is an environmental scientist with the Tennessee Valley Authority's Public Power Institute in Norris Tennessee. He has twenty years of experience in soil-plant-atmospheric interaction studies, soil classification, interpretation and sampling. He received his BS in Plant and Soil Science from the University of Tennessee.

Tom A. Wojtalik
 Tennessee Valley Authority
BS and MS Michigan State University — Limnology and Aquatic Science, post-graduate University of Minnesota. Mgr. Transmission Environmental Program and Mgr. Environmental Integration in Environmental Policy and Planning. Research-Aquatic Plant, US forest and ROW vegetation management, thermal impacts on aquatic life; transmission and generation impacts of all current applied generation types and transmission including 500-kv.

Kimberly D. Choate
 Tennessee Valley Authority
Kim has Bachelor and Master of Science Degrees in Civil Engineering from Tennessee Technological University. Upon graduation, she began her engineering career with Tennessee Valley Authority. She is a registered engineer. Kim is currently a projects manager with TVA's Public Power Institute. Her projects primarily focus on using innovative technologies and approaches to solve environmental related issues.

Planting Shrubs for the Creation of Sustainable Power Line Rights-of-Way

Robert F. Young and Edward J. Glover

Nova Scotia Power Inc. (NSPI) develops sustainable rights of way (ROW) to ensure safe, reliable delivery of electricity. To achieve sustainable ROWs, NSPI implements an Integrated Vegetation Management program to develop plant communities that are compatible with power lines. These communities are established via *selective management* to control the growth of incompatible species, and some *active planting* of compatible species. In 1994 NSPI planted 2000 speckled alder (*Alnus rugosa*) seedlings using typical forest industry methods on ROWs to determine the viability of growing native alders in a controlled environment and to determine the viability of using alder as a form of vegetation control. In 1996, 14,000 alders were planted with the intent to study impacts on wildlife. In 1998, NSPI adopted a new vegetation management strategy wherein planting compatibles is recognized as an integral part of the company's program to manage ROWs. Currently, the company estimates that 38% of transmission lines are sustainable through the development of stable compatible vegetation. NSPI plans to increase the sustainable area on transmission and distribution systems by 10 and 15%, respectively, within 5 years. To meet these targets the company is planning to plant hundreds of thousands of compatible species annually on rights of way, commencing in 2000. NSPI is developing partnerships and strategies with others who will gain from planting initiatives. Pilot projects with two provincial Government departments have been started: (1) The Nova Scotia Department of Natural Resources (NSDNR) non-timber Integrated Resource Management (IRM) objectives are being supported by planting ROWs which cross provincial Crown Lands, and (2) Projects with the Nova Scotia Department of Transportation and Public Works (TPW) which involve management of roadsides through shrub planting to eliminate the need for frequent maintenance and to compliment the aesthetics of the roadside are underway.

Keywords: Compatible vegetation, speckled alder, stable community, Nova Scotia Power Inc.

INTRODUCTION

There have been many documented accounts on the possible use of stable compatible plant communities on power line rights-of-way (ROW) as a viable method for controlling the establishment and growth of trees (Welch, 1984; Berkowitz and Canham, 1993; Brown, 1993; Bramble et al., 1996). Through the selective application of a variety of vegetation control techniques naturally occurring shrubs eventually predominate on ROW thereby creating a relatively stable community of vegetation (Bramble et al., 1991). A stable community, or an ecosystem in a steady state, is a climax condition that is self perpetuating. The climax community results when no other combination of species is successful in out-competing or replacing the stable community (Kormondy, 1984). Many utilities focus on a strategy of promoting dense, low growing vegetation on rights of way (Welch, 1991). Compatible vegetation competes well for light and nutrients and therefore offers early successional biological control of ROWs by slowing the rate of tree invasion through site occupancy. This strategy also enhances the value of the ROW for wildlife and aesthetically.

NSPI implemented an Integrated Vegetation Management (IVM) program on the transmission system in 1988 to accomplish objectives for sustainable ROW

Environmental Concerns in Rights-of-Way Management: Seventh International Symposium
J.W. Goodrich-Mahoney, D.F. Mutrie and C.A. Guild (editors)
© 2002 Elsevier Science Ltd. All rights reserved.

through selective management of stable plant communities. Through IVM, several progressive methods of controlling the growth of incompatible vegetation, with the use of herbicides (Tordon 101, and Garlon 4), were selectively applied to promote the growth of naturally occurring shrubs and establishment of a herbaceous layer. As a result, compatible vegetation, comprised mostly of herbaceous vegetation, has resisted tree invasion on ROWs to a certain extent through site occupancy. In 1993 the company directed efforts in developing, to a greater extent, a taller shrub layer of 2–4 meters to create a stable community for effective control on the establishment and growth of trees for longer periods. Although herbaceous communities are most often diverse, they are not considered stable and are eventually replaced by taller vegetation or shrubs and trees (Bramble and Byrnes, 1982). Not all shrubs resist tree invasion, however on poor sites where the soil is acidic and poorly drained, which are typical to parts of Nova Scotia (Browne and Davis, 1996) species with nitrogen fixing capabilities can occupy a site as a homogeneous community for up to fifty years (Kimmins, 1996). Species such as lambkill (*Kalmia angustifolia*), bayberry (*Myrica pensylvanica*), and Canada holly (*Ilex verticulata*) have also been found homogeneously on ROWs classified as poor sites in Nova Scotia.

Even though shrub communities can be considered stable, and provide for sustainable ROWs, there is a limited amount of published evidence of any utility company actively establishing shrubs for this purpose. The majority of planting projects on the ROW are directed toward improving aesthetics and wildlife values.

This paper traces the chronological history of NSPI's efforts of developing and implementing a formal program of planting shrubs as a viable alternative for the long term management of incompatible vegetation on power line ROWs. The vegetation management team at NSPI leveraged this option for more than vegetation control in developing a new strategy for the utility in 1998. The qualitative benefits associated with planting have gained a high degree of public acceptance as programs which rely solely on herbicides remains to be controversial. Planting projects were easily aligned with several community environmental projects as well.

SETTING THE STAGE FOR CHANGE

In 1993 Nova Scotia Power Inc. started to actively investigate growing speckled alder (*Alnus rugosa*) in mass quantities in a controlled environment by pursuing the idea with a local nursery interested in growing native shrubs from seed. Speckled alder (Fig. 1), referred to as alder hereafter, was identified as the preferred compatible plant due to its ubiquitous nature in Nova Scotia and the already present dense thickets along ROWs.

Fig. 1. Speckled alder established on a power line ROW.

Alder also have the following additional benefits:
– A maximum height of 5 m at maturity;
– Ability to vegetatively reproduce;
– Beneficial to wildlife by providing food and cover;
– Survives in dense thickets;
– Regenerates quickly after disturbance;
– Demonstrated ability to be self perpetuating;
– Not susceptible to disease;
– Commonly invades open areas;
– Abundant seed crop.

In 1994 Nova Scotia Power undertook an experimental trial in collaboration with a Federal Agency (National Community Tree Foundation), to establish an alder plantation on a power line right of way with the objective of creating a stable plant community. Two thousand seedlings were planted at a spacing of 2.2 m × 2.2 m along the edge of a 30 m wide corridor in this first project of its kind in Atlantic Canada. Pertinent information was gained in understanding: (1) the success of growing alder seedlings in a controlled environment, (2) the effectiveness of transplanting using methods typical of the forest industry and planting without any site preparation, and primarily, (3) the viability of using alder as a cost efficient form of vegetation control.

Observations of the planted site after six growing seasons indicate that: (1) alder is capable of occupying a variety of sites, (2) alder has proven to be a hardy

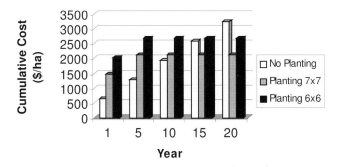

Fig. 2. Cumulative cost comparison of no planting versus a 6 ft. and 7 ft. plantation spacing.

species showing no signs of significant insect or disease damage, (3) alder has a high survivability rate as the percent mortality was recorded to be under 20%, and (4) alder exhibited a suitable growth rate. The 6-year-old plantation has achieved a height range of 1.4–2.5 m and an average crown width of 0.75 m.

Now that the planted stock are firmly established the company will determine if alder can sustain the site by restricting tree invasion in excess of ten years for the creation of a sustainable ROW. Key to the success of this project will be the ability of the plantation to provide crown closure before the next scheduled maintenance which is scheduled in 2004. The company expects that this will occur given the rate of crown expansion over the last two years which has averaged 20 cm/year. Annual monitoring of the plantation is very important in understanding the growth and development of this species as it has previously not been well documented.

If successful in establishing sustainable ROWs, Nova Scotia Power estimates that planting will provide cost savings when compared to the costs of traditional methods associated with IVM (Fig. 2).

IMPACT ON WILDLIFE

In 1997, 14,000 alder were used for another planting project implemented with funding from Habitat Canada, a national non-profit foundation, to gain insight on wildlife presence within ROWs characterized by predominantly alder cover versus existing vegetation conditions in relation to adjacent forest types. Ladino and Gates (1981) determined that certain small mammals crossed shrubby corridors 10 to 34 times as often as grassy corridors. Three study sites and three control sites were established adjacent to different forest types. Baseline tracking surveys were conducted in 1996. These surveys recorded red squirrel (*Tamiasciurus hudsonicus*), white tailed deer (*Odocoileus virginianus*), hare (*Lupes americanus*), and mice (*mice spp.*) as frequent users. There are no current results from this project as it is too early to report any change in wildlife use until the alder reach a significant size. NSPI intends to determine if there is a positive correlation between alder adjacent to specific forest stand types and the presence of wildlife on ROWs. These results will help direct future planting projects for habitat improvement.

Monitoring and the evaluation of this project is proposed to commence in 2002. It is expected that alder will have a significant impact on the use of ROWs by small mammals such as mice sp., and subsequently an increase in the number of red fox (*Vulpes vulpes*), bobcat (*Felis rufus*), and weasel (*Mustela erminea*) is expected. It is also hypothesized that a vegetation structure extending, both vertically and horizontally will increase the amount of wildlife movement across the right of way.

STRATEGIC APPROACH

In 1998, Nova Scotia Power Inc. undertook a review of its programs for vegetation management on transmission and distribution ROWs (Eddy and Young, 1998). As a result, the distribution system is now managed for the development of stable compatible plant communities by judicious use of herbicides and planting. Both systems are now managed under one strategy for creating sustainable ROWs. The company recognizes that the cost benefits of planting are long term and also that planting is a viable alternative to the use of herbicides.

Establishing compatible plant species is an integral part of the vegetation management program and, it is aligned with Nova Scotia Power's goal of continual improvement in environmental performance. Since 1995 the company has determined the percent of transmission line ROWs considered sustainable as a measure of environmental performance. Currently, the company estimates that 38% of transmission ROWs are sustainable (Fig. 3). Planting is now included in the management plans associated with all voltages of lines.

The strategic planting objectives are: (1) to actively establish compatible vegetation on 10% or 1650 ha of the transmission system, and (2) to actively establish compatible vegetation on 15% or 424 ha of the distribution system over the next 5 years. Since the adoption

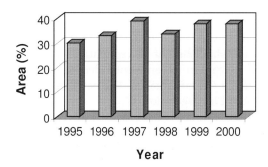

Fig. 3. Percent of transmission ROW not requiring vegetation control in a given year as a result of use of alternative vegetation management strategies.

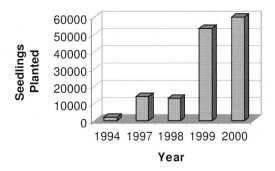

Fig. 4. Number of seedlings planted in Nova Scotia during the past 6 years.

of the new strategy, millions of shrubs will be planted as part of the regular maintenance program. Shrubs include: alder, red ozier dogwood, staghorn sumac, bayberry, and false mountain holly, high bush cranberry, etc. (Fig. 4).

To accommodate the effective implementation of a large planting initiative, three strategic changes were essential.

First, the distribution system was subdivided into four sub-programs which clearly defined the physical settings in which the system exists to more efficiently direct management: (1) rural wildland, (2) developing urban, (3) rural residential, and (4) mature urban. Rural wildland settings which comprise approximately 40% of the distribution system and the developing urban settings, are now managed under an IVM program of selective management which will promote the growth of naturally occurring compatible vegetation and include the active establishment of shrubs.

Second, the use of herbicides had to become an integral part of the selective management program on distribution, which prior to 1999 was not. The selective use of herbicides is required to control the growth of trees to promote the growth of naturally occurring compatible vegetation and protect the plantation from competing vegetation through site preparation and weeding applications. Nova Scotia Power recognizes that the use of herbicides may face some public controversy, however, the company is confident that the linkage with the goal of establishing compatible plant communities will effectively alleviate this concern and generate a greater public acceptance of this necessary component of an IVM approach.

Third, it was important that the costs associated with the establishment of compatible vegetation be viewed as capital expense intended to provide long term (15–20 yr.) advantages. The active establishment of compatible vegetation is now approached as an investment rather than a maintenance cost. In this context, the active establishment of compatible shrubs is viewed as a capital expense rather than an operating expense. Planting will result in an overall reduction in operating costs. Capitalizing this strategic initiative represents a significant contribution to the utility's funding efforts.

LEVERAGE TO CORPORATE COMMITMENTS

Within the Transmission and Distribution business unit, vegetation management on ROWs contributes significantly to the company's corporate commitments and strategies. Two general commitments being: "Safety as a First Priority" and "Continual Improvement in Environmental Performance;" Four corporate strategies being: Improvement in Customer Loyalty, Improvement in Employee Commitment, Managing Costs and Growing the Business.

Establishing compatible vegetation on ROWs contributes in some way to all of these areas of business focus.

- Increasing the amount of sustainable ROW will provide the public and the employees a much safer community in which to live and work.
- Planting creates environmental benefits through an eventual reduction in the use of herbicides and the creation of wildlife habitat.
- Planting is highly accepted by the public and is perceived as wise environmental stewardship.
- Planting contributes positively to "Customer Loyalty" by incorporating landowner's land use objectives and improving aesthetics.
- Increasing the amount of sustainable ROW will produce economic benefits — expected cost savings are $830.00/ha over a 20 year period.
- Employee Commitment is enhanced as employees may participate in the implementation of programs that contribute to the environmental and economic health of Nova Scotia communities.
- Planting projects provide opportunities for Nova Scotia Power to form positive partnerships with other stakeholders and government agencies.

SHARING STRATEGIES FOR SUCCESS

Two initiatives are currently underway to combine the expertise of external stakeholders and Nova Scotia Power for win-win outcomes. Nova Scotia Power, in developing new strategies is able to incorporate the objectives and strategies of others who use power line ROWs to conduct their business. The Nova Scotia Department of Natural Resources (DNR) and the Nova Scotia Department of Transportation and Public Works (TPW) are currently involved in projects that combine existing governmental expertise and planning resources for research with Nova Scotia Power's operational expertise and implementation budget.

Integrated Resource Management (IRM) Partnership

Nova Scotia Power Inc. strengthened working relations with the DNR in 1999. The company initiated a project to align its vegetation management program with a DNR objective of promoting areas of biodiversity, outdoor recreation, and wildlife habitat as part of a Provincial Integrated Resource Management (IRM) Strategy. The nature of this project provides many opportunities for publicising and promoting environmental stewardship.

A Memorandum of Understanding (MOU) was developed for the purpose of formalizing joint interests associated with the management of non-timber values on ROW. The specific objectives of the MOU are to facilitate both party's ability to:

1. Align NSPI's vegetation management on ROWs where they cross Crown lands, with the NSDNR's IRM objectives for areas of multiple land use, in particular the areas of wildlife habitat, outdoor recreation, and biodiversity;
2. Further develop and refine management planning and implementation techniques that will facilitate obtainment of IRM non-timber objectives within this context;
3. Develop a model that can be used to expand this form of management on powerline rights of way to private lands within Nova Scotia;
4. Further develop and refine a system of vegetation management on powerline ROWs that will reduce the long term requirement for repeated application of herbicides.

The first pilot project was established and designed early in 2000. As a first step, 2 hectares of ROW will be planted in August 2000 with a variety of compatible species, including; speckled alder (*Alnus rugosa*), wild raison (*Viburnum cassinoides*), and red ozier dogwood (*Cornus stolonifera*). In addition to habitat creation, the project is also designed to facilitate the evaluation of species selection, planting design and management. Comparisons will be made of species performance on a variety of sites and on sites that have and have not been treated with herbicides to remove competing vegetation before planting.

Roadside Partnership

Nova Scotia Power Inc. also outlined its new strategy and implementation plan to TPW personnel responsible for developing and implementing vegetation control programs on provincial roadways. The plan was well-aligned with the interests of the TPW for managing stable vegetative communities along roadsides. This presented the opportunity for a cost-sharing partnership between Nova Scotia Power Inc. and TPW on shared ROWs.

Nova Scotia Power made the necessary changes to it's implementation program to accommodate the needs of TPW and to establish a "roadside partnership." This common strategy for managing incompatible vegetation with an integrated vegetation management approach allows both parties to save on costs by sharing services that would otherwise be duplicated.

In addition, planting was completed as part of a pilot project with TPW in 1999. Through selective management, the entire right of way was managed for sustainability. The plants left to sustain the site differed across the ROW as only herbaceous growth was considered compatible at road side.

Roadside vegetation sustainability will reduce the frequency of regular vegetation control needed to provide appropriate sightlines and drainage. In addition, the aesthetics of the roadside are complimented through planting initiatives.

CONCLUSION

Creating sustainable power line ROWs using Integrated Vegetation Management is the essence of Nova Scotia Power's new vegetation management strategy for both the transmission and distribution systems. Actively establishing shrubs has been recognized as a viable long term method of controlling incompatible vegetation on ROWs through the creation of a stable compatible plant communities. Planting with compatible species will be implemented with target levels over the next five years.

Nova Scotia Power Inc. plans to carefully monitor the success of planting initiatives and discover ways of enhancing the effectiveness of planting compatible species.

Continual monitoring, tracking and studies are important for Nova Scotia Power Inc. to more fully understand and document how planting projects provide for economic, environmental and social benefits while maintaining ecological integrity.

Specifically, the possible use of alder as biomass needs to be investigated as alders can withstand repeated disturbance and continue to perpetuate as a dominant species. The possibility of planting alder as an option for the reduction of greenhouse gases through carbon sequestration is a possible area of evaluation.

Nova Scotia Power will continue to work with government conservation agencies and special interest groups with a mandate of environmental stewardship for implementing planting projects.

REFERENCES

Berkowitz, A.R. and C.D. Canham. 1993. Ecological perspectives on tree invasion in rights-of-way: Net competitive effects of intact vegetation. In: Proceedings of the Fifth International Symposium on Environmental Concerns in Rights-of-Way Management. Montreal, Quebec. pp. 54–58.

Bramble, W.C. and W.R. Byrnes. 1982. Development of wildlife food and cover on an electric transmission right-of-way maintained by herbicides: A 30-year report. Department of Forestry and Natural Resources. RB 974. October.

Bramble, W.C., W.R. Byrnes, R.J. Hutnik, and S.A. Liscinsky. 1991. Prediction of cover type on rights-of-way after maintenance treatments. Journal of Arboriculture, 17(2): 38–43.

Bramble, W.C., W.R. Byrnes, R.J. Hutnik, and S.A. Liscinsky. 1996. Interference factors responsible for resistance of forb-grass cover types to tree invasion on an electric utility right-of-way. Journal of Arboriculture, 22(2): 99–105.

Brown, D. 1993. The formation of stable rights-of-way vegetation with cover-crops — How do you choose which species to plant? In: Proceedings of the Fifth International Symposium on Environmental Concerns in Rights-of-Way Management. Montreal, Quebec. pp. 70–73.

Browne, S. and D.S. Davis, eds. 1996. The Natural History of Nova Scotia. V.1. Topics and Habitats. Nimbus, Nova Scotia, 180 pp.

Eddy A. and R.F. Young. 1998. Towards a new perspective. Nova Scotia Power Vegetation Management Strategy.

Kimmins, J.P. 1996. Forest Ecology, 2nd ed. Prentice-Hall Inc., Upper Saddle River, New Jersey. 415 pp.

Kormondy, E.J. 1984. Concepts of Ecology, 3rd ed. Prentice-Hall Inc., Englewood Cliffs, NJ. 215 pp.

Ladino, A.G. and J.E. Gates. 1981. Responses of animals to transmission-line corridor management practices. In: Proceedings of the Second Symposium on Environmental Concerns in Rights-of-Way Management. EPRI WS-78-141. pp. 53-1–53-10.

Welch, W.E. 1984. Control of unwanted vegetation on transmission line rights-of-way by compatible species. Canadian Electrical Research Report ST-173. January.

BIOGRAPHICAL SKETCHES

Robert F. Young, Bsc.F

Senior Forester, Nova Scotia Power Inc., P.O. Box 910, Halifax, NS, B3J 2W5 Canada, Fax: 902-428-7564, E-mail: robert.young@nspower.ca

Robert F. Young is a Senior Forester with Nova Scotia Power Inc. and holds a BSc in Forestry from the University of New Brunswick. He has been working in the field of vegetation management for over ten years with the majority being with Nova Scotia Power Inc. He is responsible for the development and effective implementation of vegetation management programs for transmission and distribution rights-of-way. He actively participates and serves on committees with organizations including; the Atlantic Vegetation Management Association, the International Society of Arboriculture and the Canadian Institute of Forestry.

Edward J. Glover, Bsc.F

Nova Scotia Power Inc., P.O. Box 910, Halifax, NS, B3J 2W5, Canada

Edward J. Glover holds a degree in Forestry from the University of New Brunswick. Previous work with the company involved the development of a methodology for the implementation of permanent sample plots on speckled alder sites. Mr. Glover is currently involved in research on compatible species to further benefit NSPI's initiative.

Selecting Herbaceous Plant Covers to Control Tree Invasion in Rights-of-Way

Sylvie de Blois, Jacques Brisson, and André Bouchard

Following construction of a right-of-way, environmental regulation often requires the rapid restoration of a herbaceous plant cover to control erosion and/or attenuate visual impact. Herbaceous species can be selected with the added long-term goal of inhibiting tree invasion. We present a review of empirical evidence that can guide species selection. This review is based on an extensive survey and critical evaluation of relevant North American studies published in scientific papers, technical reports, and conference proceedings. Vegetation managers and scientists were also consulted for up-to-date information on on-going experiments. Observational and experimental evidence of inhibition in both natural and managed communities confirm that the biological control approach has significant potential. However, scientific evaluation of the long-term inhibition capacity of seeding mixtures is still rare. Ecological mechanisms favoring competitive ability are not always well understood but involve the sequestration of available resources and the modification of environmental conditions. Two approaches characterized experimental inhibition studies in rights-of-way. The first aims to test the interference potential of commercially available species commonly used in restoration, while the second favors the establishment of wild communities. Both approaches have their advantages and limitations, but several studies show that the establishment phase is crucial. Knowledge is lacking especially for the establishment of wild species. This review allowed us to identify 66 herbaceous species based on a critical assessment of the evidence provided. Besides inhibition potential, factors such as species availability and possible nuisance should also be considered.

Keywords: Biological control, cover crop, inhibition potential, restoration, seeding, vegetation management

INTRODUCTION

There has been a great deal of interest in reducing both the costs and the environmental impact of vegetation management practices in utility rights-of-way. As ecological studies have demonstrated the ability of some herbaceous and shrub communities to inhibit tree invasion (Pound and Egler, 1953; White, 1965), vegetation managers have been encouraged to use highly selective herbicide applications or cutting practices that minimize disturbance to competitive cover when present (Niering and Goodwin, 1974; Bramble and Byrnes, 1983). But such cover could also be introduced right after construction, when environmental regulation requires the restoration of the site to control erosion and/or attenuate visual impact (Brown, 1995). This approach implies that species should be selected not only to satisfy immediate restoration concerns, but also for their potential to form, in the long-term, low-maintenance communities capable of inhibiting tree invasion. However, information on the inhibition potential of herbaceous species or on selection criteria for improving seeding mixtures is not readily available and, despite the obvious need for such information, there have been very few attempts to summarize current evidence from the literature (but see Brown, 1989). Apart from introducing competitive cover in rights-of-way, knowing which species have the potential to form stable communities could also help managers target more efficiently practices that will help maintain

Environmental Concerns in Rights-of-Way Management: Seventh International Symposium
J.W. Goodrich-Mahoney, D.F. Mutrie and C.A. Guild (editors)
© 2002 Elsevier Science Ltd. All rights reserved.

or spread them. As well, summarizing the currently available information on species potential to inhibit tree invasion is essential to orient future research needs on the integration of ecological principles in vegetation management strategies.

This study was prompted by the need expressed by vegetation managers working with Gas Metropolitain in Quebec (Canada) to improve restoration practices of newly constructed pipelines with the added goal of long-term vegetation control. Our objective was to assess the available empirical evidence on the use of herbaceous cover to control tree invasion in order to identify species that could be of interest in future vegetation management program. Although some shrub species have demonstrated strong inhibition potential, our study focuses on herbaceous species compatible with pipeline utilities. We report here our findings on observational and experimental studies of inhibition in both natural and managed communities and submit a list of the species whose capacity to inhibit tree invasion has been observed or tested.

METHODS

This review is based on an extensive survey and critical evaluation of relevant North American studies published in scientific papers, technical reports, and conference proceedings. Several vegetation managers and scientists were also consulted for up-to-date information on on-going experiments. Relevant scientific papers have been mainly accessed through searching different databases including AGRICOLA (U.S.D.A.), BIOLOGICAL ABSTRACTS, ICIST, and CURRENT CONTENT. The NTIS (National Technical Information Service) database was used to obtain information from US and Canadian government agencies and other sources from the private sectors in order to locate research reports often not available in other databases. All previous issues of the proceedings of the International Symposium on Environmental Concerns in Rights-of-Way Management were also searched for relevant information. Internet sites reporting information on research activities in universities, research institutes, federal or provincial agencies and ministries, and utility companies (e.g., Canadian Gas Association, Empire State Electric Energy Research Corporation, Gas Research Institute, Hydro-Québec, Ontario-Hydro, etc.) were consulted. Several of these sites identified people responsible for research activities, some of whom were contacted.

RESULTS

From more than 700 references uncovered in the literature search, 214 were found relevant and were retained for final analysis. Our review included a critical summary of ecological principles involved in inhibition studies that will be published separately. In order to identify species that presented a potential for the establishment of a stable cover in our area, we focused especially on information relevant to a north-eastern American context.

Evidence of inhibition comes from various sources including experimental evaluations in field or in greenhouse conditions of the inhibition potential of selected species, or field observation, in natural or managed environment, of relatively stable herbaceous communities. Ecological mechanisms favoring competitive ability are not always well understood but involve the sequestration of available resources and the modification of environmental conditions. Allelopathic effects, the emission by some species of substances capable of inhibiting germination or growth of neighboring species, are often cited as a possible competition mechanism (Horsley, 1977a,b; Tillman, 1982). Such processes remain controversial however (Byrnes et al., 1993), but the fact that complex competition mechanisms are not always well understood does not prevent using competitive effect to our advantage.

Summary of the available evidence allowed us to identify 66 herbaceous species whose potential to form stable populations or communities resistant to tree invasion has been observed or tested (Table 1). They include 25 grasses or sedges, 11 legumes, 25 herbaceous dicots, and 5 pteridophytes.

For each species, we provide a list of the scientific studies consulted (Table 1). Evidence comes from various sources. Because objectives and methodology widely differ from study to study, reliable comparisons and a definite assessment or ranking of the inhibition potential of a particular species are difficult to achieve. For example, a naturally occurring population of a species may have been investigated in the field for its capacity to form a stable cover, but such capacity may not have been demonstrated in experimental seeding. On the other hand, experimental seeding may have been conducted, but if the population failed to establish an efficient cover for different reasons (inadequate site preparation, unreliable seed sources, constraining environmental conditions, etc.), then it does not necessarily mean that the species has no potential for future use. Consequently, instead of trying to establish a definite ranking of the species that were uncovered in our literature search, we chose to report, for each species, the type of scientific evidence used to compile our list. Evidence was classified according to the following categories.

Experimental seeding in right-of-way

The 46 species in this category have all been planted in experimental plots in electrical, pipeline, or highway rights-of-way using a replicated design or, for two studies, as regular cover crop for restoration purposes that were later evaluated through observational design (Suffling, 1979; Sharp et al., 1980). A total of

Table 1. Herbaceous species whose capacity to inhibit tree invasion has been observed or tested

Species	Experimental seeding in rights-of-way	Field evaluation of inhibition potential	Greenhouse evaluation of inhibition potential	Observation of stable communities	Origin, uses or possible nuisance
		Reference number			
Grasses and sedges					
Agropyron repens[1]	21	32	20	4	Int-Inv
Agrostis alba	24-35-44-47-48-49		8-10	4	Ero-For-Int-Inv-Res
Agrostis canina			10		Int-Inv-Orn
Agrostis stolonifera		42			Int-Inv
Andropogon gerardii	35-43-48-49			37	Ero-For-Inv-Res
Bromus inermis[2]		31-42	2-10		Ero-For-Int-Inv
Carex sp.				51	
Carex crinita	47				
Dactylis glomerata[1]	11	18-39	8-9-10-40		For-Int-Inv-Orn
Danthonia spicata		5-14			
Elymus canadensis	43				For-Inv
Festuca arundinacea[1,2]	35-48-49	5-39-46	8-10		Ero-For-Int-Inv-Orn
Festuca ovina			10		Ero-Inv-Orn-Res
Festuca rubra[1]	11-21-24-30-35-44-48-49	12-19	8-9-10-20	33-37-41	Ero-Inv-Orn
Lolium perenne	21-35-48-49	12	20		Ero-For-Int-Inv-Orn
Panicum virgatum	35-48-49			37	Ero-For-Inv-Res
Phalaris arundinacae[2]	21-24-30-44-47	42	10		Ero-For-Inv-Orn
Phleum pratense	21-24-30-44-47	13-42	8-10	4-41	For-Int-Inv
Poa annua	44				Int-Inv
Poa compressa		42		4	Ero-Int-Inv-Orn
Poa pratensis	21-44-47	13-19	8-10-40	4	Ero-For-Inv Orn
Schizachyrium scoparium[1]	35-43-48-49	16-25		17	For-Inv
Scirpus pedicellatus	47				
Scirpus rubrotinctus	47				
Sorghastrum nutans	43				For-Res
Legumes					
Coronilla varia[1]	11-35-48-49	38-42	8-9-10		Ero-For-Int-Inv-Orn
Lathyrus sylvestris[1]	35-48-49			37	Int-Res
Lotus corniculatus	11-35-48-49	32-42	8-9-10		For-Int
Medicago sativa		1	9-10		Int
Melilotus alba		18-42	8-10		For-Int-Inv
Melilotus officinalis			8-10		For-Int-Inv
Trifolium hybridum	21				Ero-For-Int
Trifolium pratense	21				For-Int
Trifolium repens	24-30	12-42	8-10		For-Int-Inv
Vicia cracca	21		20		Int-Inv
Vicia sativa	44				Int-Inv
Dicots					
Achillea millefolium				4	Ero-Inv-Orn
Anaphalis margaritacea				4	Orn
Aster ericoides	15			3	Orn
Aster nova-angliae	15				Orn
Aster ontorianis	47				
Aster pilosus	15				
Aster ptarmicoides	15				
Aster puniceus	15				
Aster simplex	15				
Aster umbellatus	15				
Aster sp.	21-47			4-51	
Centaurea nigra[1]	21		20		Int-Inv
Desmodium canadense	43				
Epilobium angustifolium			9		Inv-Orn
Eupatorium maculatum	47				
Hypericum perforatum	21		20	4-41	Int-Inv
Hypericum repens			9		
Monarda fistulosa	43				Orn
Rudbeckia hirta	43				Orn
Solidago canadensis	15-47				Inv
Solidago gigantea	47				

Table 1. (continued)

Species	Experimental seeding in rights-of-way	Field evaluation of inhibition potential	Greenhouse evaluation of inhibition potential	Observation of stable communities	Origin, uses or possible nuisance
		Reference number			
Solidago graminifolia	15	5-14			
Solidago nemoralis	15				
Solidago rugosa		5-14			
Solidago sp	21-47			33-51	
Ferns					
Athyrium filix-femina			9		Orn
Dennstaedtia punctilobula[1]		5-14-25-29		36	Orn
Onoclea sensibilis			9	37	Orn
Pteridium aquilinum	47		9		Inv
Thelypteris noveboracensis		29		36	Orn

Numbers in the table refer to documents from the reference section.
Origin, uses or possible nuisance, according to USDA–NRCS (1999): Ero = erosion control; For = forage; Int = introduced; Inv = invasive; Orn = ornamental (lawn, etc.); Res = restoration.
[1] Best inhibition potential in field conditions.
[2] Best inhibition potential in lab conditions.

eleven studies, conducted in eastern United States and Canada, were included in this category. Their objective was generally to assess inhibition potential of one or several herbaceous covers seeded in the right-of-way or, at the very least, to determine the seeding conditions necessary for the establishment of a presumably low-maintenance herbaceous cover (U.D.A. Inc., 1996; Cain, 1997; Suffling, 1998). Monitoring of species establishment and competitive effect had been conducted for 1 year after seeding at the time of publication (Suffling, 1979; U.D.A. Inc., 1996) up to 10 or more years (U.S.D.A., 1981, 1983; Oyler and van der Grinten, 1984). Preselection of species to conduct experiments was based mostly on observed evidence of inhibition in natural or managed communities and/or, in a few cases, on greenhouse screening tests of inhibition potential (Brown, 1995; FRDF, 1993). Species traits such as rapid growth, vigorous vegetative reproduction, abundant seed production, dense underground, and/or aerial structures that are thought to correlate with competitive ability were often favored. Estimation of inhibition potential was done mostly through a statistical evaluation of the relationship between herbaceous cover and tree density in seeded and control plots. Failure of establishment of a cover dense enough to control tree invasion was occasionally invoked to explain a species relatively low performance in the field. There were, however, usually no thorough investigation of the factors that may have led to poor establishment. Inadequate site preparation and/or environmental constraints were generally suggested as possible causes.

Field evaluation of inhibition potential

This category comprises 16 studies that had as a main objective to provide a quantitative or semi-quantitative evaluation of inhibition of establishment or growth of tree species by a competitive herbaceous cover in field condition for forestry or horticultural purposes, or in natural environment. Inhibition, in these cases, is mostly seen as a non-beneficial effect. We have also included in this category studies that aimed to identify naturally occurring low-growing communities in rights-of-way and that provided a statistical evaluation of the potential of such communities to limit tree establishment under different abiotic conditions (Bramble and Byrnes, 1976; Byrnes et al., 1993; Canham et al., 1993; Hill et al., 1995). A total of 22 species were evaluated in these conditions, 13 of which were also included in the previous category (Table 1). Parameters used to evaluate inhibition potential in experimental plots compared to controls included survival, density, height, diameter, and biomass of tree species seeded, transplanted or naturally occurring in the parcels.

Greenhouse evaluation of inhibition potential

Six studies tested inhibition of establishment or growth of tree species by a total of 26 herbaceous species in greenhouse assays. Parameters used to evaluate inhibition potential included survival, density, height, and biomass of tree species grown in containers with herbaceous competitors. Experiments in controlled environment have generally been useful to rapidly screen species for inhibition potential for further field experiments (Brown, 1990, 1992, 1993; FRDF, 1993), but results in such conditions do not necessarily guarantee that the species will express the same potential in nature (FRDF, 1994).

Observation of stable low-growing communities

Included here are 8 studies reporting the observation of naturally established herbaceous communities that appeared to have been stable for several years in sites that were presumably capable of supporting trees, although there were no experimental evaluation or comparison of inhibition potential of the species involved. Twenty species were identified in this category. Several ecological studies on successional dynamics in old-fields or rights-of-way that greatly contributed to current interest in biological control approaches in vegetation management are included here (Bard, 1952; Pound and Egler, 1953; Beckwith, 1954; White, 1965; Stalter, 1978; Niering, 1987). Resistance to invasion by woody species was generally assumed to be the result of the highly competitive ability of the herbaceous cover, although other factors such as constraining abiotic conditions or low invasion pressure have not necessarily been ruled out.

Finally, the analysis of the evidence provided allowed us to identify a subset of 11 species for which experimental results demonstrated best potential in field and/or in lab conditions (Table 1). For example, *Dactylis glomerata* was tested in lab (Shribbs et al., 1986; Brown, 1990, 1992, 1993) and in right-of-way conditions for 5 years (Brown, 1995) where it was found to affect tree survival. As well, *Coronilla varia* and *Lathyrus sylvestris* have been the object of long-term monitoring that demonstrated their strong capacity to inhibit tree invasion (U.S.D.A., 1981, 1983; Oyler and van der Grinten, 1984). Information on best potential is given as an indication and readers are encouraged to consult available published data for detailed evaluation of a particular species.

DISCUSSION

In spite of the strong interest in enhancing ecological practices in right-of-way vegetation management, there are surprisingly few long-term experimental evaluations of inhibition potential of herbaceous cover in rights-of-way, or results of such evaluations are not readily available. Information from rigorous experimental settings in right-of-way conditions is extremely valuable and should be used whenever possible to determine species potential. Nevertheless, the majority of studies presented here suggest that low-growing species can be used to delay invasion of trees, and that some covers are better than others in doing so. However, information on a particular species inhibition potential is often hard to obtain. Because methodologies vary widely from study to study, it is not obvious, from a management point of view, how to select appropriate species. This, combined with a lack of critical synthesis of the available evidence, likely contributes to delay applications.

Apart from the evidence mentioned, other factors must be carefully considered especially when it comes to the introduction of species in rights-of-way. Among those, origin (indigenous, naturalized or exotic), ecology, use (erosion control, forage crop, ornamental, restoration), possible nuisance (e.g., invasive species, potential host to crop pests, toxicity to livestock), and availability of seeding mixtures are especially important. These factors must be carefully weighed against other possible benefits in terms of vegetation control before implanting a species. We are including, as an indication, information on origin and some potential uses and nuisance (Table 1). The latter point is especially important since species are selected for traits that can potentially make them aggressive in new habitats. Indeed, 31 of the species in our list have been reported as showing invasive behavior in some conditions or others (U.S.D.A.–N.R.C.S., 1999). It remains to be assessed locally how such behavior would limit applicability. A light-requiring species that has the potential to invade agricultural fields, for instance, may cause little problem in a forested context. It is therefore essential, if introduced in a new environment, that a species propensity to invade or modify adjacent habitats be closely monitored.

Two approaches broadly characterized inhibition studies in rights-of-way. The first aims to test the inhibition potential of regular cover crops generally widely used for erosion control and restoration purposes (e.g., Suffling, 1979; U.S.D.A., 1981, 1983; Brown, 1995), while the second favors the establishment of wild communities that have been shown to be relatively stable (e.g., U.D.A. Inc., 1996; Cain, 1997). Both approaches have advantages and limitations, and managers are faced with choices on the basis of available evidence. Indeed, some commercially available cover crops (e.g., *Dactylis glomerata*, *Coronilla varia*) have demonstrated their inhibition potential and such species could easily be integrated into a restoration program or could be used to fine-tune mixtures currently used. However, species in this category are usually of introduced origin, although most have long been naturalized in North America. As said before, the introduction of non-native organisms in a new environment should always be considered with extreme care. More data are needed, however, to determine inhibition potential of currently available cover crops, as relatively few studies have compared several crops for their long-term performance.

On the other hand, several vegetation management projects have promoted the use of wild species (e.g., Gouveia, 1987; Harper-Lore, 1996; Honig and Wieland, 1997; Suffling et al., 1998). This is especially true in the Prairies, where exotic species are seen as a threat to local diversity, or in highway rights-of-way, where local display of wild flowers often receive driver's as well as conservationist's approbation, while reducing maintenance cost. The establishment of communities of wild species known to form relatively stable communities in natural settings (e.g., *Solidago*, *Aster*) offers an interesting alternative for vegetation control in rights-of-way.

Such species are assumed to require little maintenance and contribute to enhance local biodiversity. Local species can be found for a wide range of environmental conditions. Moreover, the introduction of attractive communities of wildflowers, especially in areas where public acceptance and aesthetic appreciation is important, can facilitate right-of-way integration in the landscape. Often, commercially available non-native species are seeded with wild species to facilitate the establishment of the latter or to provide a ground cover prior to wild species establishment. Nevertheless the studies reviewed here show that several constraints still limit their use. There is still much to learn on how to establish wild communities and how to formulate seeding mixtures best adapted to local environmental conditions in rights-of-way. When experimental seeding fails, there is often no follow-up that would help correct problems and improve conditions for subsequent introductions. Getting a reliable local source of quality seeds may still be a problem in some areas, and quantities are often limited.

CONCLUSION

Ever since the studies of Pound and Egler (1953) and Niering and Goodwin (1974) on stable communities, there has been an interest in using low-growing species to interfere with tree establishment and/or growth for management purposes. The evidence presented in this paper is in support of this approach, but there are still several constraints that limit broad range applicability in rights-of-way, especially when it comes to species introduction. In particular, thorough investigation of the potential of species widely used in restoration programs to form relatively stable communities in the long-term is lacking, whereas the conditions of establishment of wild communities are often poorly known, at least in northeast Canada. Information from the studies that have been conducted is often not readily available, especially to the manager that has to make an efficient decision on which strategy and species to use to satisfy both immediate concerns with site restoration and long-term vegetation management objectives. Regarding the latter point, there is most certainly an advantage in coupling information on species ability to stabilize sites after construction with data on their long-term capacity to form stable communities that inhibit tree invasion, and this right form the early stages of restoration planning. By providing a synthesis on available evidence of inhibition for herbaceous species, we hope this review will facilitate further applications.

ACKNOWLEDGEMENTS

We are especially grateful to André Gougeon and Jean Trudelle from Gaz Metropolitain, and Urgel Delisle from U.D.A. Inc. for their support and collaboration. We would also like to thank all the managers and scientists from eastern Canada and the United States who gracefully shared their expertise with us.

REFERENCES

Bailey, A. 1972. Forage and woody sprout establishment on cleared unbroken land in central Alberta. Journal of Range Management, 25: 119–122. **(#1)**

Bailey, A. and R. Gupta. 1973. Grass-woody plant relationships. Canadian Journal of Plant Science, 53: 671–676. **(#2)**

Bard, G.E. 1952. Secondary succession on the piedmont of New Jersey. Ecological Monographs, 22: 195–215. **(#3)**

Beckwith, S.L. 1954. Ecological succession on abandoned farm lands and its relationship to wildlife management. Ecological Monographs, 24: 349–376. **(#4)**

Bramble, W.C. and W.R. Byrnes. 1976. Development of a stable, low plant cover on a utility right-of-way. In: Proc. of the 1st Symposium on Environmental Concerns in Rights-of-Way Management. Tillman, R., ed. Mississippi State Univ., MS. 6–8 Jan. pp. 167–176. **(#5)**

Bramble, W.C. and W.R. Byrnes. 1983. Thirty years of research on development of plant cover on an electric transmission right-of-way. Journal of Arboriculture, 9: 67–74. **(#6)**

Brown, D. 1989. Use of cover crops for the maintenance of rights-of-way vegetation: A survey of the literature on succession, cover crops, competition and trees. Report 89-275-K. Ontario Hydro Research Division. 46 pp. **(#7)**

Brown, D. 1990. The use of short term, controlled environment experiments for the selection of cover crops with high interference potentials 1. Identification of some parameters important to the experiment. Report 90-99-K. Ontario Hydro, Toronto. Res. Div. 20 pp. **(#8)**

Brown, D. 1992. A simple method to identify rights-of-way cover crops which can inhibit tree growth. Report 92-143-K. Ontario Hydro, Res. Div. Toronto, ON. 29 pp. **(#9)**

Brown, D. 1993. The selection of potential cover crops using a short term greenhouse assay. III. Evaluation of 14 grass and 6 legume candidates. Report 93-57-K. Ontario Hydro, Res. Div. Toronto, ON. 13 pp. **(#10)**

Brown, D. 1995. The impact of species introduced to control tree invasion on the vegetation of an electrical utility right-of-way. Canadian Journal of Botany, 73: 1217–1228. **(#11)**

Buckley, G.P. 1984. The uses of herbaceous companion species in the establishment of woody species from seed. Journal of Environmental Management, 13: 223–240. **(#12)**

Buckley, G.P., K.G. Chilton, and V.G. Devonald. 1981. The influence of sward control on the establishment and early growth of ash (*Fraxinus excelsior* L.) and Norway maple (*Acer platanoides* L.). Journal of Environmental Management, 13: 223–240. **(#13)**

Byrnes, W.R., W.C. Bramble, R.J. Hutnik, and S.A. Liscinsky. 1993. Right-of-way site factors responsible for resistance of certain plant cover types to tree invasion. In: Proc. of the 5th International Symposium on Environmental Concerns in Rights-of-Way Management. J. Doucet, C. Séguin, and M. Giguère, eds. Hydro-Québec, Montréal, Québec. Sept. 19–22. pp. 76–80. **(#14)**

Cain, N.P. 1997. Old field vegetation for low maintenance highway rights-of-way. In: Proc. of the 6th International Symposium on Environmental Concerns in Rights-of-Way Management. J.R. Williams, J.W. Goodrich-Mahoney, J.R. Wisniewski, and J. Wisniewski, eds. New Orleans, Louisiana. Elsevier Science. 24–26 Feb. pp. 47–54. **(#15)**

Canham, C.D., J.D. Hill, A.R. Berkowitz, and R.S. Ostfeld. 1993. Ecological perspectives on tree invasion in rights-of-way: Quantifying variation among communities in resistance to tree invasion. In: Proc. of the 5th International Symposium on Environmental

Concerns in Rights-of-Way Management. J. Doucet, C. Séguin, and M. Giguère, eds. Hydro-Québec, Montréal, Québec. Sept. 19–22. pp. 81–86. **(#16)**

Cody, J.B. 1975. Vegetation management on power line rights-of-way. A state of the knowledge report. Report 28. Applied Forestry Research Institute (AFRI). State Univ. of New York, College of Environmental Science and Forestry. Syracuse, NY. **(#17)**

Elliott, K. and A.S. White. 1987. Competitive effects of various grasses and forbs on Ponderosa pine seedlings. Forest Science, 33: 356–366. **(#18)**

Fales, S.L. and R.C. Wakefield. 1981. Effects of turfgrass on the establishment of woody plants. Agronomy Journal, 73: 605–610. **(#19)**

FRDF-Sauger Consortium. 1993. Contrôle biologique de la végétation incompatible sous les lignes de transport d'électricité d'Hydro-Québec. Essais en serre. Rapport final. Rapport HQ ENVI93 1229. Vice-Présidence Envir., Hydro-Québec. Montréal, Québec. 43 pp. **(#20)**

FRDF-Sauger, Consortium. 1994. Contrôle biologique de la végétation incompatible avec les lignes de transport d'électricité d'Hydro-Québec Phase II : Essais sur le terrain (1989–1994). Vol. 1 (rapport) et Vol. 2 (annexes techniques). Rapport HQ ENVI94 1311. Vice-Présidence Envir. Hydro-Québec. Montréal, Québec. 252 pp. **(#21)**

Gouveia, C.H. 1987. Native plants: cornerstone of low maintenance right-of-way management. In: Proc. of the 4th Symposium on Environmental Concerns in Rights-of-Way Management. R.W. Byrnes and H.A. Holt, eds. Purdue University. Department of Forestry and Natural Resources, West Lafayette, IN. Oct. 25–28. pp. 118–120. **(#22)**

Harper-Lore, B.L. 1996. Using native plants as problem-solvers. Environmental Management, 20: 827–830. **(#23)**

Heppell, M. 1988. Suivi d'efficacité de l'ensemencement aérien de graminées sous la ligne 1346, région La Grande. 2ième rapport de suivi. Hydro-Québec, Vice-présidence Envir. Montréal, Québec. **(#24)**

Hill, J.D., C.D. Canham, and D.M. Wood. 1995. Patterns and causes of resistance to tree invasion in rights-of-way. Ecological Applications, 5: 459–470. **(#25)**

Honig, R.A. and G.D. Wieland. 1997. The Houston region native grass seedbank: A natural partnership between right-of-way management and conservation. In: Proc. of the 6th International Symposium on Environmental Concerns in Rights-of-Way Management. J.R. Williams, J.W. Goodrich-Mahoney, J.R. Wisniewski, and J. Wisniewski, eds. New Orleans, LA. Elsevier Science. 24–26 Feb. pp. 83–89. **(#26)**

Horsley, S.B. 1977a. Allelopathic inhibition of black cherry by fern, grass, goldenrod and aster. Canadian Journal of Forest Research, 17: 205–216. **(#27)**

Horsley, S.B. 1977b. Allelopathic inhibition of black cherry. II. Inhibition by woodland grass, ferns, and club moss. Canadian Journal of Forest Research, 7: 515–519. **(#28)**

Horsley, S.B. 1981. Control of herbaceous weeds in Allegheny hardwood forests with herbicides. Weed Science, 29: 655–662. **(#29)**

Lacasse, J.M. 1987. Suivi d'efficacité de l'ensemencement aérien de graminées sous la ligne 1346, région La Grande. 1er rapport de suivi. Hydro-Québec, Direction Envir. 20pp. **(#30)**

Land, R.D. and A.L. McComb. 1948. Wilting and soil moisture depletion by tree seedlings and grasses. Journal of Forestry, 16: 344–349. **(#31)**

McLaughlin, R.A., P.E. Pope, and E.A. Hansen. 1985. Nitrogen fertilization and ground cover in a hybrid poplar plantation: Effects on nitrate leaching. Journal of Environmental Quality, 14: 241–245. **(#32)**

Niering, W.A. 1987. Vegetation dynamics (succession and climax) in relation to plant community management. Conservation Biology, 1: 287–295. **(#33)**

Niering, W.A. and R.H. Goodwin. 1974. Creation of relatively stable shrublands with herbicides: arresting "succession" on rights-of-way and pastureland. Ecology, 55: 784–795. **(#34)**

Oyler, J.A. and M. van der Grinten. 1984. Woody plant suppression on utility rights-of-way using herbaceous vegetation. Report. Big Flats Plant Material Center, U.S.D.A. Soil Conservation Service. Corning, NY. 15 pp. **(#35)**

Pound, C.E. and F. Egler, 1953. Brush control in southeastern New York: Fifteen years of stable tree-less communities. Ecology, 34: 63–73. **(#36)**

Richards, N.A. 1973. Oldfield vegetation as an inhibitor of tree vegetation. In: Powerlines and the Environment. R. Goodland, ed. Millbrook, NY. **(#37)**

Sharp, W.C., R.S. Ross, M.W. Testerman, and R. Williamson. 1980. Ability of crownvetch to suppress woody plant invasion. Journal of Soil and Water Conservation, May–June: 142–144. **(#38)**

Shribbs, J.M. and W.A. Skroch. 1986. Influence of 12 ground cover systems on young smoothee golden delicious apple trees. 1. Growth. Journal of the American Society of Horticultural Science, 111: 525–528. **(#39)**

Shribbs, J.M., W.A. Skroch, and T.J. Monaco. 1986. Interference between apple (*Malus domestica*) seedlings and four ground cover species under greenhouse conditions. Weed Science, 34: 533–537. **(#40)**

Stalter, R. 1978. Stable plant communities — Their development and maintenance. In: Proc. of the Northeastern Weed Science Society 32. pp. 71–83. **(#41)**

Suffling, R. 1979. Environmental aspects of cover crops on Ontario Hydro rights-of-way. Project no. 707-11. Univ. of Waterloo Research Institute. Ont. 207 pp. **(#42)**

Suffling, R., L. Lamb, and S. Murphy. 1998. Development of a native plant prescription for urban Hydro rights-of-way. Reclamation and restoration of settled landscapes. In: Proc. of the 23th Annual Meeting, Canadian Land Reclamation Association in Association with the Society for Ecological Restoration. Ont. Chapter. Markam, ON. **(#43)**

Tarte, D. 1999. Performance environnementale et efficacité de nouveaux modes de gestion de la végétation sous le réseau de distribution d'Hydro-Québec. Hydro-Québec, Direction Projets de distribution. Montréal, Québec. 101 pp. **(#44)**

Tillman, R.E. 1982. Potential role of allelopathy in row vegetation. In: Proc. of the 3rd International Symposium on Environmental Concerns in Rights-of-Way Management. A.F. Crabtree, ed. San Diego, CA. Feb. 15–18. pp. 416–420. **(#45)**

Todhunter, M.N. and W.F. Beineke. 1979. Effect of fescue on black walnut growth. Tree Planters' Notes, 30: 20–23. **(#46)**

U.D.A. Inc. 1996. Établissement de communautés végétales stables dans les emprises de pipelines au Québec. Report EN96-2/6. Ministère de l'Environnement et de la Faune. Québec. 114 pp. and annexes. **(#47)**

U.S.D.A. 1981. Annual Technical Report 1980–1981. Report 14814. Big Flats Plant Material Centre. Soil Conservation Service. Corning, NY. 81 pp. **(#48)**

U.S.D.A. 1983. Annual Technical Report. Report 14980. Big Flats Plant Material Centre. Soil Conservation Service. Corning, NY. 83 pp. **(#49)**

U.S.D.A., N.R.C.S. 1999. The PLANTS database (http://plants.usda.gov/plants). National Plant Data Center, Baton Rouge, LA 70874-4490, USA. **(#50)**

White, K.L. 1965. Shrubb-carr of Southeastern Wisconsin. Ecology, 46: 286–304. **(#51)**

BIOGRAPHICAL SKETCHES

Sylvie de Blois

Institut de recherche en biologie végétale, Université de Montréal, 4101 East Sherbrooke St., Montréal (Québec), Canada, H1X 2B2

Present address: Department of plant science, McGill University, Macdonald Campus 21, 111 Lakeshore Road,

Ste. Anne de Bellevue, (Québec) H9X 3V9, Canada; E-mail: Sylvie.deBlois@McGill.ca

Sylvie de Blois (MSc, PhD Univ. de Montréal) is an assistant professor of landscape and plant ecology at the plant science department and the school of environment of McGill University (QC, Canada). Her research interests include the ecology and management of linear vegetation units.

Jacques Brisson
Institut de recherche en biologie végétale, Université de Montréal, 4101 East Sherbrooke St., Montréal (Québec), Canada, H1X 2B2; E-mail: brissoj@magellan.umontreal.ca

Jacques Brisson (MSc Univ. de Montréal; PhD UC Davis/SDSU) is an assistant professor of plant ecology at the biology department of the Université de Montréal. His research centers mainly on plant competition and forest dynamics. Current research projects include vegetation analysis and management within utility rights-of-way.

André Bouchard
Institut de recherche en biologie végétale, Université de Montréal, 4101 East Sherbrooke St., Montréal (Québec), Canada, H1X 2B2; E-mail: Bouchaan@poste.umontreal.ca

André Bouchard (MSc McGill; PhD Cornell) is a professor of ecology at the biology department of the Université de Montréal (Québec, Canada). From 1975 to 1996, he was curator of the Montreal Botanical Garden. His research has centered on rare plants, vegetation, and land-use planning in Newfoundland and in southern Quebec. His current research projects focus on vegetation analysis and management within utility rights-of-way and landscape changes in southern Quebec during the 19th and 20th centuries.

Systematic Method for Forest Vegetation Management in the Rights-of-Way (ROW)

Javier Arévalo-Camacho, Jorge Roig-Solés, Leticia González Cantalapiedra, Carlos Morla Juaristi, Fernando Gómez Manzaneque, Elena Bermejo Bermejo, David Galicia Herbada, and Felipe Martínez García

---

The problems met in Spain when herbicides are used for management of the rights-of-way (ROW) for power transmission lines and the extensive current legislation that protects both vegetation and habitats, have made it necessary to search for and develop environmental-friendly methods to carry out the systematic removal of vegetation incompatible with the power line operation. To that end RED ELÉCTRICA has engaged a research project to draw up a manual that specifies the type of management applicable in each situation based on the existing type of vegetation. Due to the phytoclimatic variety in Spain it is impossible to define a sole procedure applicable to all the lines of the transmission grid. A systematic research plan has been carried out in ten stretches of different power transmission lines located throughout the country, requiring surveys of some 140 km of rights-of-way to identify the best-suited species for each type of forest or formation and find a customized method based on selective removal of species and proliferation of most suitable ones in order to preserve vegetation cover, to lower impacts, to increase time intervals between maintenance operations and to reduce costs of long-term management while keeping the existing safety ratios.

Keywords: Vegetation, forest management, rights-of-way (ROW), power lines

---

INTRODUCTION

This work describes the project RED ELÉCTRICA DE ESPAÑA has under way, in cooperation with the Botanics Unit of the Forest Engineering School of the Madrid Polytechnic University, to improve management of forest vegetation while maintenance work is carried out along the power transmission lines rights-of-way. The reliability of REE's environmental management policy, ISO 14001 certified, is fully matched by this work.

A research project has been carried out based on a systematic survey of the 18,000 km of 400 and 220 kV transmission lines that make up the Spanish Grid, in order to draw up a ROW management manual describing the applicable procedures and vegetation maintenance criteria. The manual will be helpful for maintenance personnel as a methodological guide that sets clear management criteria, identifies the existing "types" of vegetation and simplifies decision-making.

The target of this project is to supply scientific information about the existing vegetation in ROWs to transmission lines managers, and rationalize or improve their medium-long term maintenance operations spacing and even theoretically dispensing them, by changing the current vegetation cover to better suited one to the presence of the transmission line. In this way, a dual target can be met, besides the technical-financial issue through lowering maintenance costs and increasing safe periods for the transmission line also that of a rights-of-way best matched to the surrounding area.

The project was structured in three phases. During 1995–1996, the 445 forest species, trees, and shrubs, found in Spain were first studied to identify their "compatibility" with power lines based on an index or rating (ICL) according to their anatomical characteristics (Arévalo, Roig et al., 1997B).

Environmental Concerns in Rights-of-Way
Management: Seventh International Symposium
J.W. Goodrich-Mahoney, D.F. Mutrie and C.A. Guild (editors)
© 2002 Elsevier Science Ltd. All rights reserved.

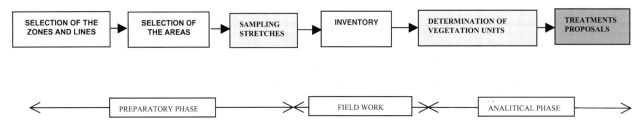

Fig. 1. Methodology.

During the second phase, carried out between 1996–1998, in three campaigns going from spring to fall, fieldwork was systematically performed to identify a number of forest type associations found in the ROWs. Management actions adequate to the current conditions were proposed for each of them to establish stable trees and shrub cover compatible with power lines and achieve long-term coexistence, removing or keeping from developing those species that might provoke problems to the lines while promoting the favorable ones.

At the present third phase we are drafting the respective manual and, in order to adjust further, we are carrying out surveys to determine the outcome of the proposed measures applied to predetermined plots and stretches.

Management actions have been proposed for each one of the identified vegetation types and defined in such a way that they can be applied to other stretches and power lines. Consequently from this project will issue a number of proposals or actions criteria that will allow managers to handle each identified vegetation formation in a similar way and help them to find solutions to problems that may arise when new ROWs management criteria are applied.

The effort is intended to develop a methodology that can rationalize the vegetation cover management along the high-voltage transmission lines. This management pretends, while meeting the required safety, to minimize negative impacts on vegetation and landscape, consequence of the erection and operation of such infrastructures.

Initially, time and money investment for implementing the proposed actions will be superior to that required by currently applied maintenance methods. In a large number of cases, their implementation can lead to results that show a clear improvement when compared to those achieved by the current management and, in general, lead to clear savings at a medium-long term. It has to be pointed out that these proposals have to be implemented in consensus with the owners of the affected areas or with those responsible for forestry management.

METHODOLOGY

First of all and considering the problems inherent to the development of the project we had to define a methodology in order to achieve the goals. The methodology that had to be designed meets the scheme shown in Fig. 1.

The works developed in each of the tasks that make up this methodology are described below.

SELECTION OF THE ZONES TO BE STUDIED

The selection of the zones to be studied was extremely relevant since the study was intended to determine a number of management proposals for the different vegetation communities in the power lines ROWs, susceptible to be applied along the power line or any other alignment where similar formations are found.

In order to study the most representative zones considering the vegetation formations crossed over by the lines, we first evaluated the existing Transmission Lines Grid throughout the country and its relation with the forest stands. We came to the conclusion that the territorial distribution is heterogeneous and power lines run through different phytoclimatic regions.

Other interesting features to make field work more cost effective, were: the concentration or proximity of several power lines, the protection status of natural areas crossed by the ROWs, the high diversity of forest stand and finally the need to have clear corridors in which maintenance work had not recently been performed so vegetation associations were most natural.

Accordingly ten zones crossed over by power lines were selected based on a geographic distribution whereby their biogeographic characteristics would be as different as possible. Four of them were located in the Atlantic zone; four in the Mediterranean zone, and two were intermediate zones where the botanical features of each zone and their transition could be observed.

The first four zones are located in the northwest of the peninsular, where and due to the abundant rainfall, Euro Siberian deciduous forests are found.

Typical Mediterranean brushwood and forests are located in the second four zones where holly oak and cork oak predominate as can be observed in the regions of Castile, Estremadura, and Andalusia.

Finally, the two intermediate zones are transition areas from the Euro Siberian to the Mediterranean

Table 1. List of the covered power lines

Surveyed areas	Power lines	Stretches	Length (km)	Sampling area
Lugo-Orense (96)	Belesar–Puebla de Trives	0–15		4
Barcelona (96)	Sentmenat–Begues	45–63		5
Cáceres (96)	Gillona–Almaraz	504–514		3
Cádiz (97)	D. Rodrigo–Pinar del Rey	220–254	15	
Cuenca (97)	Trillo–Olmedilla	154–185	14	
Toledo (97)	Aceca–Puertollano	119–145	13	
Orense-León (98)	Trives–La Lomba	85–110	12	
Barcelona (98)	Ascó–Sentmenat	322–337	9	
Asturias (98)	Lada–Velilla	54–88	15	
Guipuzkoa (98)	Arkale–Moguerre	32–47	7	

biogeographic regions. This is evidenced by the existing sclerophyllous formations that may reach a maximum in certain zones while an ocean deciduous forest would cover the balance. The Mediterranean element is predominant in the Catalonian area, mainly holly oak stands, although some sub Mediterranean species are also common. In addition and in this case, a significant stretch of the selected power line runs through an area protected by Law, the San Llorenç del Munt i Serra de l'Obac Natural Park.

Inside these overall surveyed areas, specific power lines, and spans between towers where the fieldwork would be carried out had to be selected.

This selection was carried out in a drafting room based on the study of the existing vegetation and power lines alignments maps and the careful viewing of available videos filmed from a helicopter. In this way, existing forest formations were identified beforehand to set them apart from crop and pasturelands, which were not worth surveying, and the stretches where the fieldwork had to be performed were determined.

Based on this selection, the fieldwork was targeted on some 120 km of power lines representing ten different line stretches. It should be kept in mind that the fieldwork has covered, approximately twenty-one kilometers, 8 stretches and 40 sampling areas, which were part of the above-mentioned lines and others located nearby. The covered ROWs are listed in Table 1.

Spain's bioclimatic zones and the selected areas for the study are shown in Fig. 2, location of the selected areas is shown in Fig. 3.

SAMPLING AREAS SELECTION

A sampling process including all the different vegetation formations was required due to the problems inherent to an exhaustive sampling of the selected stretches. In this way, only specific sampling locations would be surveyed based on the knowledge collected beforehand in the different zones of the stretch. Once the power lines and the respective stretches had been set aside, specific fieldwork zones or sampling areas were selected inside each stretch. An exhaustive inventory of the species had to be made that could be applied to the complete formation.

The selection was based on films of the power lines made by RED ELÉCTRICA. The films allowed identifying the sampling areas taking into account mainly the physiognomic or habit features of the vegetation representative of the diversified vegetation cover of the complete stretch. The size of the sampled areas was most often matched with the rights-of-way surface bounded by two successive pylons, a span. At times, the sampling area was larger, two spans or, in few occasions and due to variations in size of the existing vegetation units, smaller.

An inventory of the existing vegetation taxon was made for each sampled zone. A number of standard plots, about 20×20 m, were through the usual statistical methods identified to carry out an exhaustive field sampling of the existing woody vegetation and of the different ecological characteristics of the sampled plot, such as height, substrate, slope, in addition to a listing of the observed species and the relative quantity.

Although grasses were left out, all the brushwood, shrub, and trees were identified in the Mediterranean area, since these are the basic biological types most applicable in the rights-of-way management proposals.

FIELDWORK

The fieldwork was partly based on the information supplied by the power line design, specifically, the alignment, plan view, and profile elevation as well as the access sketches.

A card that shows all the information about the different items deemed relevant was drafted during the field data gathering process. In the species inventory, not only those identified in the ROW, including cover extent and average height of each specie, but also the ones found in the surrounding areas were noted. At the same time, a simple sketch or draft showing both a longitudinal section and a plan view was provided to see the vegetation structure and composition in these zones.

Fig. 2. Spain's bioclimatic zones (ALLUE).

1. Steppe zones and continental depressions (kermes oak, buckthorns, dogwood, Aleppo pine and juniper stands).
2. Typical Mediterranean zone. Sclerophylous formations (holly oaks and cork oaks stands, and Mediterranean pine forests).
3. Sub-humid Mediterranean zone. Wilting plants formations (mossy oaks, *quercus lusitánica* and pine forests).
4. Mountain Atlantic zone. Mountain deciduous trees formations (beech, oak, and birch stands).
5. Hilly Atlantic territory. Deciduous trees formations (oak stands) as well as holly oaks and laurel (bay) stands.
6. High mountains zone. Sub-alpine dwarf mountain pine stands, brushwood, scrub, alpine pasturelands.

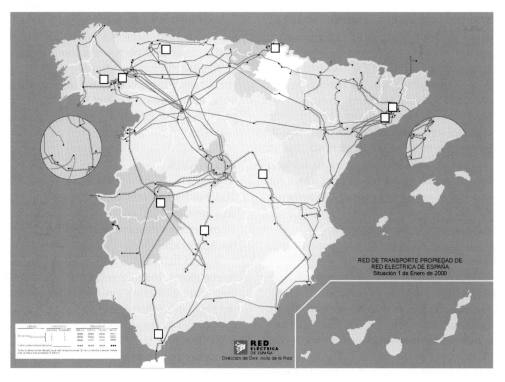

Fig. 3. The selected areas used.

BREAK DOWN LISTING OF THE VEGETATION COMMUNITIES

From the compiled data and the experience built up during the fieldwork and review of the videos, the different vegetation communities of each of the studied sections were broken down.

The term, *vegetation community*, has to be understood as that part of the ROW alignment that can be represented and holds a more or less, from a physiognomic and floristic point of view, homogeneous vegetation formation, showing boundaries that can clearly be distinguished from the adjacent areas inside the ROW itself.

Priority has been granted to the formal or physiognomical features to define the vegetation communities' typology and attention has been focused on the vegetation elements that can easily be seen due to their frequency and size, i.e., Quercus robur, Quercus ilex, Quercus suber, Fagus sylvatica, Pinus spp. On the other hand and due to the fact that it was going to be used by maintenance staff, the typology was planned to be synthetic, not broken down in excess, showing however the main characteristics or parameters, easy to understand, free of both, a too technical or specialized language and a highly complex nomenclature.

According to the mentioned principles, the following criteria was applied to define the identified units in the section under study:

1. *Heterogeneous composition*. It is mentioned only when a "mosaic" was found, i.e., unit consisting of a number of different intermingled formations of similar surface and, due to the small size, it was not possible to define them individually. Generally speaking, these units have been disturbed by human actions.
2. *Predominant structural type*. Five main types were found: forest; brushwood; grass, crop, and manmade pastureland.

    Due to its larger complexity and presence in all units, brushwood was divided into five subtypes based upon the RUIZ DE LA TORRE (1981) classification: shrub (3–7 m); high (1.5–3 m); medium (0.5–1.5 m); low (0.05–0.5 m), and creeping (0.05–0.5 m). The difference versus the preceding subgroup was only due to the habit or height.
3. *Vegetation Density*. The density of the vegetation formation was broken down in three classes: open, when trees were sufficiently spaced, over 2 or 3 meters between tops; thin when trees were close or adjacent, and; dense when trees structures were intertwined leaving no empty spaces between them.
4. *Floristic Composition: Predominant taxon (s)*. If one or two taxa were predominant, it has been stated as follows: "... are predominant."
5. *Modifiers*. If relevant taxa or formations were dispersed in stands or border strips of local significance only and, due to their size, could not be represented, they have to be shown preceded by the + sign.

It is deemed that, when combined, the mentioned different criteria can generate multiple types of vegetation communities, which are sufficient to clearly show the existing variability in the surveyed power lines.

The communities' characteristics were completed with two additional parameters, which are highly significant to recommend any possible action that would modify both their composition and structure: the traffic ability and the visual integration with the environment.

The traffic ability shows the level of difficulty to walk through the existing formation in the ROW. This characteristic has to be evaluated since a more or less thin vegetation cover in the rights-of-way is required to provide to individuals access to the facility, for technical inspection and maintenance operations. On the other hand, visual integration shows up to what point the rights-of-way vegetation blends in the natural environment under study.

PROPOSALS

The proposals for action were planned taking into account the following criteria:

1. The first and foremost requirement to be met by the proposals is the constitution of a vegetation cover in the ROW compatible with the power line management. The planned vegetation cover has to meet the established requirements for minimum vertical clearance from the vegetation cover to the power transmission cables; the current legal requirement is of 4.20 m for 400 kV, with an assured margin of a five years minimum. This is why the growth data and maximum height of all the plants in the intended vegetation cover are so significant.
2. The defined characteristics of the cover to be established have to meet the overall criterion of achieving the best and largest possible homogeneity with the environment, but always subject to line safety limits. This implies that just after safety comes the need to keep or restore ecological values by matching the territorial vegetation with the environmental conditions.
3. Generally, traffic ability under the power line will be negatively affected if a compatible vegetation cover is established. For this reason during the selection of the species and as far as possible, efforts have to be devoted by avoiding the selection of thorny vegetation and trying to achieve adequate densities to minimize that loss of traffic ability.
4. While designing the cover to be established we have to grant careful attention to the characteristics of the vegetation natural dynamics that arise from the territory where the power line is located. As far as the floristic structure and composition of the planned cover is more closely matched with the mentioned dynamics both implementation and

maintenance costs will be smaller. However seeding and planting operations will usually be required during initial stages of the project implementation, after which natural reproduction will do the work.

5. The new cover to be established shall also be designed to meet a criterion for optimal stability, taking into account the already mentioned characteristics of the regional vegetation dynamics. The review periods shown in a monitoring plan to be established for each stretch of the planned power line, have to be most expanded possible to reduce control works: pruning, propping, thinning, etc., that eventually might be performed. The ecological and biological characteristics of the species in question, as well as peculiar features of the regional climate will always determine those periods.

6. The starting conditions to plan the best possible alternative can obviously be rather different. The main one arises from whether it is a new or an existing power line where virtually and due to repeated cleaning and site clearing operations the soil is initially bare. To the contrary in the first case, that is to say that of a new line, the previously existing forest or shrub exception making of croplands, peripheral areas of a city and industrial zones, will usually be available, what implies a much better starting point. The initial conditions could also imply a type of vegetation, natural or man-made, not compatible with power line management. In this case, the initial tasks for implementing the vegetation cover will be more complex and costly.

Generally speaking, the proposals are intended to achieve either one or both of the following actions:

– *To remove some species*. The removal will be selective and manual, depending mainly on the compatibility and level of traffic ability in the unit. Therefore we will focus the tasks on removing or curbing those species that reach excessive heights and impair thus the compatibility, as well as thorny or intricately branched plants that generate more or less closed vegetation groups. These species are generally heliophilous and related to the pioneer stages of succession, having then a higher invasive capacity. The fastest growing species will also be candidates for removal.

– *To favor some species*. All species compatible with the power line in each unit have to be included. Both the species, which have to be left in the rights-of-way due to their good qualities as well as those to be promoted or restocked, are included in this chapter. The actions to keep and introduce other species will be intended to maximize the visual integration effect, taking into account the already mentioned considerations.

However, we have paid attention to traffic ability when drawing up a proposal. Consequently, in many instances, the role of those species considered to be adequate has to be to provide ecological conditions that discourage re-colonizing by the already mentioned invading species besides their contribution to increase environmental integration. The weight given to each criterion depends on the initial situation of the vegetation community, upon which we decide its priority.

Finally it has to be highlighted that the ecological integration criterion has been strictly met during the species selection. Native species found to be best suited to the edaphic and climatic conditions of the territory, have always been used to restock.

The intended integration with the environment will be even furthered, if these actions are implemented in a way that minimizes the negative impact that may arise if a too clear borderline is established at the boundary between the right-of-way and the surrounding area. Therefore, these actions have to be implemented making the difference from the center to the edges of the ROW and taking into account the composition and structure of the vegetation at surrounding area. It means that unless for maintenance reasons it is inconvenient, the removal of species has to be greater in the middle of the right-of-way than at the edges, while, for the retained or replanted species, this action will be more intensive at the edges than at the center.

The works to restore and establish the proposed vegetation cover have to promote natural regeneration as well as seeding and planting. It is necessary for such reestablishment that previous actions are properly performed to avoid increasing soil erosion.

Following the description of each proposed vegetation community; a table has been drafted with the most relevant species, in a positive or negative sense, for the development and maintenance of the proposed vegetation cover. In that table are mentioned besides the theoretical ICL (Compatibility Index of Lines, Arévalo et al., 1995), height, regeneration, and recommended rating found during the fieldwork.

RESULTS

Up to seventy different vegetation communities were identified during the project and proposals meeting the already mentioned criteria were submitted to define steps intended to lower the number of such units. Finally we got a total of nine different communities, this made possible a simplified, easier, and less costly long-term management.

The following units were defined:
1. Thin forest where oaks predominate
2. Thin forest where holly oaks predominate
3. Thin forest where cork oaks or *Quercus lusitanica* predominate
4. Thin forest where chestnuts predominate
5. Thin forest where beech trees predominate
6. Thin forest on riversides
7. Shrub-forest where trees species predominate (same as those found in the already mentioned forests)

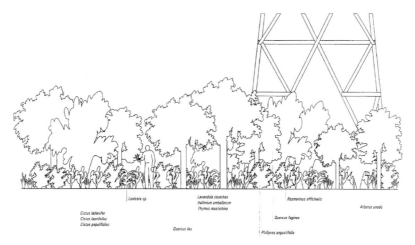

Dense shrub where *Quercus ilex* and *Arbutus unedo* predominate

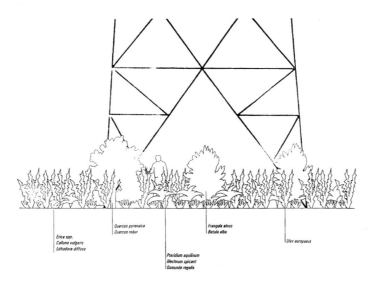

Dense shrub where *Erica spp* and *Ulex eropaeus* predominate

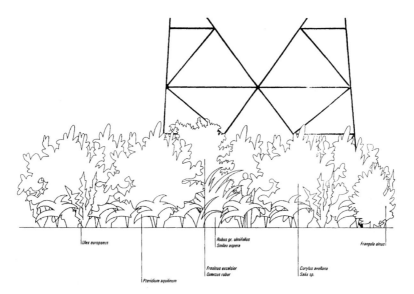

Dense shrub where *Corylus avellana* and *Pteridium aquilinum* predominate

Fig. 4. Examples of before treatment and after.

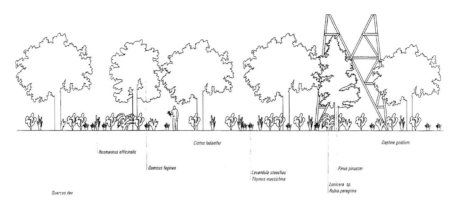

Thin forest where *Quercus ilex* predominate

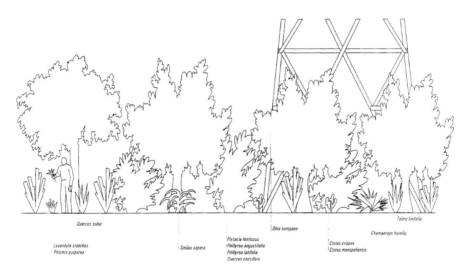

Thin forest where *Quercus suber* predominate

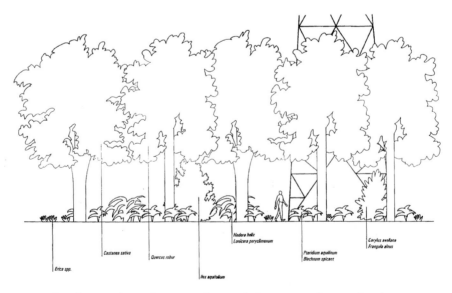

Thin forest where *Quercus robur* and *Castanea sativa* predominate

Fig. 4. (continued).

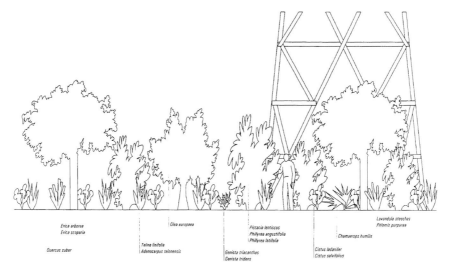

High thin shrub

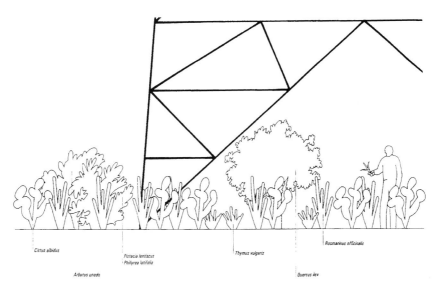

Medium thin shrub where *Rosmarinus officinalis* and *Cistus albidus* predominate

Fig. 4. (continued).

8. Medium thin shrub where soft stem species predominate
9. Medium thin shrub on degraded zones (broom and rock roses)

Management, always aiming at promoting a controlled speedup of natural evolution of the existing vegetation, has to be achieved in several steps.

– Removing selectively the thorny heliophylous shrub.
– Thinning out shrub vegetation to promote the natural regeneration of species with the best characteristics.
– Increasing the area covered by the higher vegetation, big and small trees, to control germination of the unwanted species.
– Establishing a high coverage and low-density stable trees stand with thinned undergrowth where one or several trees species of growth that can be easily controlled in height by pruning and/or topping are predominant.

In highly degraded zones, far from the most developed formations and where management will not improve the conditions, actions will be limited to some selective thinning, avoiding any increase of erosion processes, to improve traffic ability and boost the most favorable species. An example of before and after treatment is shown in Fig. 4.

ACKNOWLEDGEMENTS

We wish to thank the efforts of the Forest Botanical Department from the Escuela Superior de Ingenieros de Montes, Universidad Politécnica de Madrid, Ciudad Universitaria, Madrid, Spain, most specifically:

Jesús Maza Pecino, Susana Molinero Herranz, Leoncio Moreno Rivero, Elena Bermejo Bermejo, David Galicia Herbada, and Felipe Domínguez Lozano.

REFERENCES

Allue Andrade, J.L. 1990. Atlas Fitoclimático de España. I.N.I.A. Madrid. 223 pp.

Arevalo, J. and J. Roig. 1992. Métodos alternativos para el tratamiento de calles en el paso de líneas por masas arboladas 1as Jornadas Internacionales De Líneas Eléctricas y Medio Ambiente. Madrid, Mayo 1994. Libro de comunicaciones. pp. 127–143.

Arevalo, J., E. Bermejo, S. Camps, F. Dominguez, F. Gomez Manzaneque, J. Maza, S. Molinero, L. Moreno, C. Morla, and J. Roig. 1997A. Inventario de la flora vascular ibérica compatible con las líneas de alta tensión. 445 pp.

Arevalo, J., J. Roig, F. Gomez Manzaneque, C. Morla, F. Dominguez, D. Galicia, and L. Moreno. 1997B. Propuesta para la gestión de las líneas de Red Eléctrica de España. REE — Dpto de Silvopascicultura: Unidad de Botánica. E.T.S.I. de Montes Universidad Politécnica de Madrid. Inédito.

Aseginolaza, C., D. Gomez, X. Lizaur, G. Montserrat, G. Morante, M.R. Salaverria, and P.M. Uribe-Echebarrna. 1989. Vegetación de la Comunidad Autónoma del País Vasco. Servicio Central de Publicaciones del Gobierno Vasco. 361 pp.

Devesa, J.A. 1995. Vegetación y flora de Extremadura. Universitas editorial. 773 pp.

Dnaz Gonzalez T.E. and J.A. Fernandez Prieto. 1994. El Paisaje Vegetal de Asturias: Guía de la Excursión. Itinera Geobotánica, 8: 5–243.

Ferreras, C. and M.E. Arozena. 1987. Los bosques. Guía física de España. Alianza Editorial, S.A. 394 pp.

Folch, R. 1981. La vegetación dels Paisos Catalans. Ketres Editora. 513 pp.

Montoya, J.M. 1988. Los alcornocales (Revisión del estado de conocimiento en 1987). Ministerio de Agricultura, Pesca y Alimentación. Madrid. 267 pp.

Peinado, M. and S. Rivas Martínez, eds. 1987. La vegetación de España. Colección Aula Abierta. 544 pp.

Rivas Martínez, S. and cols. 1987. Memoria del mapa de las series de vegetación de España. Serie Técnica. I.C.O.N.A. Ministerio de Agricultura, Pesca y Alimentación. 268 pp.

Ruiz De La Torre, J. 1981. Vegetación natural y matorrales de España. En: Tratado del medio natural. Madrid.

Ruiz De La Torre, J. 1991. Mapa forestal de España. Escala 1:200.000. Ministerio de Agricultura, Pesca y Alimentación, I.C.O.N.A. Fundación General de la Universidad Politécnica de Madrid. E.T.S.I. de Montes.

BIOGRAPHICAL SKETCHES

Javier Arévalo
Red Eléctrica de España, S.A., P del Conde de los Gaitanes, 177, 28190 Alcobendas-Madrid, Spain — Is the company in charge of the national transmission grid management

Member of the Environmental Department, Red Eléctrica de España Javier is a Forest Engineer Specialist in Environmental Assessment. He has fourteen years experience in Environmental Impact Studies of power lines, in ten countries and a distance of around 4500 km. and four years in other infrastructure projects. He is Interested in vegetation control and management, landscape studies and environmental impacts of power lines in general.

Leticia González
Red Eléctrica de España, S.A., P del Conde de los Gaitanes, 177, 28190 Alcobendas-Madrid, Spain — Is the company in charge of the national transmission grid management

Member of the Environmental Department, Red Eléctrica de España, Leticia holds a degree in Biological Sciences from the Universidad Complutense de Madrid and a Diploma in Environmental Engineering and Management from the Escuela de Organización Industrial (Madrid).

Jorge Roig Solés
Red Eléctrica de España, S.A., P del Conde de los Gaitanes, 177, 28190 Alcobendas-Madrid, Spain — Is the company in charge of the national transmission grid management

Head of the Environmental Department, he is dealing with the environmental issues of Red Eléctrica de España since its constitution in 1985. He has over 20 years experience in environmental control in industry. Jorge is a Mining engineer from the Universidad Politécnica de Madrid and holds a Diploma in Environmental Engineering from the University of Strathclyde (Glasgow).

Carlos Morla Juaristi
Forest Botanical Department from the Forest Engineers Technical School, Polytechnic University of Madrid, Ciudad Universitaria, Madrid, Spain

Forest Doctor Engineer by the "Universidad Politécnica de Madrid," now Professor of Botany in the "Escuela Técnica Superior de Ingenieros de Montes" (Forestry School) of the "Universidad Politécnica de Madrid." He is specialist in paleophytogeography and geobotany, specially in the Mediterranean Basin. He has more than sixty published works on flora and woody vegetation analysis of the Iberian Peninsula.

Fernando Gómez Manzaneque
Forest Botanical Department from the Forest Engineers Technical School, Polytechnic University of Madrid, Ciudad Universitaria, Madrid, Spain

Doctor in biological sciences by the "Universidad Autónoma de Madrid," now assistant professor of Botany in the "Escuela Técnica Superior de Ingenieros de Montes" (Forestry School) of the "Universidad Politécnica de Madrid." He is expert in applied botany and mediterranean vegetation. He has more than forty published works on iberian flora and woody vegetation, with special interest on family Cupressaceae and genus Juniperus.

Long-Term Vegetation Development on Bioengineered Rights-of-Way Sites

David F. Polster

Soil bioengineering has been used for the treatment of steep and/or unstable rights-of-way sites for many years (Schiechtl, 1980). Although these techniques can provide initial stability, the question of long term stability of soil bioengineered sites has not been addressed. Pioneering plants such as willows are used for soil bioengineering. These provide an environment in which later successional species can invade. As this transition takes place the later successional species must take over the stabilizing function from the pioneering plants. Slope buttressing, soil arching and root reinforcement are the three principle means of slope support provided by these later successional species (Gray and Leiser, 1982). These must replace the structural support provided by the soil bioengineering structures to avoid collapse of the slope. This paper explores the transition from the initial support provided by soil bioengineering treatments to the long-term slope support provided by the later successional species. Right-of-way sites such as along a new railroad corridor, pipeline corridor and highway right-of-way where soil bioengineering was used to provide initial stability have been investigated to determine the nature of the transition from this initial stability to long term stability. Examples are drawn from British Columbian sites.

Keywords: Soil bioengineering, steep slopes, unstable slopes, plant succession, soil erosion

INTRODUCTION

Soil bioengineering is an effective tool for the revegetation of steep or otherwise unstable sites. Soil bioengineering uses living plant materials to construct structures that perform some "engineering" function. Steep slopes can be treated with wattle fences or modified brush layers to provide a stable surface on which vegetation can establish and grow. Seepage areas can be stabilized using live pole drains while riparian vegetation can be restored using various forms of live staking. Pioneering plant species, primarily willow, are used for soil bioengineering (Schiechtl and Stern, 1992). These short-lived initial species must give way to longer-lived later successional species in order for vegetation to be maintained on the treated site. This change in species must be accompanied by an equivalent change in roles performed by the species. For instance, where wattle fences are used to provide living retaining walls, the supporting function provided by the wattle fences must be retained by any subsequent vegetation or the vegetation cover will be lost. Similarly, where live pole drains have been used to provide drainage, the subsequent vegetation must also provide drainage. The function provided by the vegetation must be continuously provided even though both the species and the structure of the vegetation changes.

The study of the development of vegetation on reclaimed sites provides important information for the formulation of future reclamation programmes. Where soil bioengineering has been used to provide the initial stability needed to get vegetation started on a site, evaluation of the changes in both the species and the function performed by those species provides clues for solving future problem sites. Plant responses to external stresses (unstable slopes, seepage, etc.) are well known. The "harp" shaped trunks of trees develops in response to an unstable surface while "knees" and other structures develop in plants grown in anoxic seepage environments (Easu, 1960). Understanding the role played by the different species at each successional

Environmental Concerns in Rights-of-Way
Management: Seventh International Symposium
J.W. Goodrich-Mahoney, D.F. Mutrie and C.A. Guild (editors)
© 2002 Elsevier Science Ltd. All rights reserved.

stage can allow effective selection of species for subsequent reclamation projects. Successional reclamation (Polster, 1989) provides a model to emulate in the development of effective restoration programmes.

Successional reclamation has been used as a model for the treatment of a number of sites throughout western Canada. Although the early results of these reclamation programmes are promising, little attention has been directed at the long-term development of vegetation on sites where successional reclamation has been used. Initially, successional reclamation seeks to establish an erosion controlling cover of successionally appropriate vegetation on the disturbed sites. Typically agronomic grasses and legumes are used. This plant cover is supplemented with the establishment of pioneering woody vegetation, either directly through planting or by allowing native pioneering species to establish naturally. This vegetation cover provides conditions that assist in the establishment and growth of later successional species until eventually a cover of climax species is established on the disturbed site. The time required for this process to unfold on reclaimed sites dictates that the successional processes themselves be used as a surrogate for these later successional stages. Successional processes, primarily species replacement, provide an excellent tool for evaluating the potential long-term development of vegetation on disturbed sites.

This paper reviews those features of a successional reclamation programme that encourage the further development of vegetation on a site. Features of soil bioengineering that encourage natural successional processes are discussed. Key features of the early soil bioengineering work can have a profound influence on subsequent plant establishment and in turn on the establishment of later successional species. Successional stagnation (Kimmins, 1987) can develop on sites where inappropriate seed mixes have been used to establish the initial cover on a site. This can make it very difficult to establish later successional species and may prevent the establishment of woody species entirely. Keystone species (Mills et al., 1993) can play a critical role in the establishment of later successional species. The pioneering species used in soil bioengineering provide a key role in the development of plants on difficult sites. Conclusions regarding the development of effective reclamation programmes are presented.

SUCCESSIONAL RECLAMATION

Successional reclamation is the term applied to a reclamation model that seeks to enhance natural successional processes for the rehabilitation of drastically disturbed sites. The major aim of successional reclamation programmes is the re-integration of the disturbed sites with the natural successional processes. These processes operate in the local area to revegetate natural disturbances. The study of natural successional process on natural disturbances (Straker, 1996) can provide clues of the factors that can assist in the establishment of natural successional processes on sites disturbed by human activities. Polster (1991) lists five factors that limit natural vegetation growth on drastically disturbed sites. These are steep slopes; adverse texture; poor nutrient status; adverse chemical properties and soil temperature extremes. Amelioration of these adverse conditions is the first prerequisite in the development of a successional reclamation programme.

Steep slopes and unstable sites prevent vegetation establishment by having a continually moving surface. Soil bioengineering (Schiechtl, 1980) can be used to provide initial stability to sites where the surface movement is preventing natural plant growth. The use of soil bioengineering for treatment of unstable sites in British Columbia is becoming common (Polster, 1997 and 1999). By providing the initial stability, soil bioengineering allows other plants to establish and eventually provide the stability needed to maintain vegetation on the site. Soil bioengineering uses pioneering plants that quickly give way to later successional species. Once the later successional species are well established they can take over the support of the slope through buttressing as well as the root network that is formed (Gray and Leiser, 1982). The initial stability provided by the soil bioengineering thus solves the problem of unstable sites and initiates the successional processes that lead to stable ecosystems.

Adverse soil textures can prevent vegetation growth. The coarse rock that accumulates at the toe of free dumped waste rock dumps is very difficult to revegetate. Resloping waste rock dumps to cover this coarse material with fine textured materials that accumulate near the top of the dump slope is the major means of addressing this problem (Popowich, 1978). Natural talus slopes provide a similar condition and allow the study of natural means of overcoming the problems associated with coarse textured materials (Polster and Bell, 1980). Natural accumulations of organic matter in the crevices between the boulders at the base of talus slopes provide a substrate in which vegetation can become established. Pocket planting, where soil is placed in the interstitial spaces between the rocks mimics this natural process and can be used to establish pioneering vegetation in coarse rock areas. Modified brush layers are used to treat sliver fills composed of side cast blasted rock. Fine textured soils can also be problematic for plant establishment, although generally fine textured soil problems are associated with the stability of the soil. Soil bioengineering techniques such as live smiles and live staking can be used to treat fine textured soils.

Poor nutrient status can limit natural vegetation establishment on drastically disturbed sites. Typically drastically disturbed sites have very limited nutrient levels (SEAM, 1979). Fertilizer can be used to overcome this initial problem, however, in the long term, nutrients must be supplied by local nutrient cycling and the fixation of atmospheric nitrogen by legumes and other nitrogen fixing species. Use of a balanced seed mix that contains 30–40% legumes will assist in establishment of vegetation on low nutrient sites. The pioneering species used in soil bioengineering can survive on sites where nutrients are limited.

Adverse chemical properties such as acid rock drainage (ARD) or sodic spoils can present significant challenges for the establishment of vegetation (Morin and Hutt, 1997). Although there are some plants that can grow under extremes of pH, metals and other adverse chemical components, most plants are stressed under these conditions (Farmer et al., 1976). Treatment of these conditions is often very difficult and specific methods of treatment are used for specific sites.

Soil temperature extremes, either hot or cold, can slow or even prevent natural vegetation establishment and growth. Dark coloured substrates on south facing (Northern Hemisphere) slopes can become very hot under the summer sun. These hot temperatures can kill young plants by denaturing the proteins that make up the various constituents of the plants. Similarly, cold temperature such as occurs in arctic regions can severely limit or even preclude vegetation growth (Bliss and Wein, 1972). Modifications to the surface of the soil can be used to ameliorate adverse temperature conditions. Disking in an east-west direction will create small soil windrows with northern and southern exposures. With dark substrates that are prone to being too warm vegetation can be established on the northern exposures while in cold climates the southern exposures will provide slightly warmer micro-sites that will allow vegetation to establish. Dark substrates can be treated with heavy mulch applications that reduce the albedo of the surface and thus prevent overheating.

Other site features such as exposure to various environmental influences including prevailing winds, sunlight, salt spray and ice scouring can influence the patterns of vegetation establishment. Successional change in these communities may be primarily influenced by the site factors and therefore difficult to manage from a restoration perspective.

Once the vegetation limiting features of the site are addressed, pioneering vegetation can be established. The pioneering vegetation must provide a stable environment, space for invading native species and enhancement of the site relative to the species that will follow. One of the primary aims of the initial vegetation cover is to protect the site from excessive erosion. Invading vegetation can not become established on an actively eroding site. A cover of seeded grasses and legumes is typically used to control erosion, however, too dense a cover of seeded species will prevent invasion of later successional species by closing the space needed by the invading plants. Therefore an open cover of seeded species is needed. This cover should include a good balance of grasses and legumes to provide site improvements that enhance the ability of later successional species to establish and grow.

Establishment of the pioneering cover leads the way towards establishment of later successional species. Whereas the pioneering vegetation is typically herbaceous in nature in most parts of British Columbia woody species dominate the next phase of vegetation that establishes. The various alder species that occur in British Columbia act as pioneering woody species in many ecosystems. Other deciduous species such as cottonwood and aspen may act in this capacity in some ecosystems. These plants play a pivotal role as a bridge between the short-lived herbaceous cover and the longer lived conifers that dominate most forest ecosystems in the province. It is in this pioneering woody species cover that allows later successional conifers can establish. The role of these seral species is essential to the long-term health of forest ecosystems.

Replicating the essential features of natural successional patterns on drastically disturbed sites provides productive ecosystems. Each stage in the process is important, from the initial erosion controlling cover of grasses and legumes through the later successional woody species. Successional reclamation duplicates the vegetation patterns found in natural successional sequences.

MEASURES OF SUCCESS

The success of a soil bioengineering project can be measured by determining the stability of the treated site and by investigating the invasion of the reclaimed site by native species. Site manipulations that encourage establishment and growth of native species contribute to the long-term success of the reclamation efforts. The following case studies present examples of where soil bioengineering and successional reclamation have been used to reclaim drastically disturbed right-of-way and other sites.

Reclamation of landslides that arise from poorly constructed resource roads is undertaken to reduce erosion and lessen the impacts of the landslides on aquatic habitats. Reclamation treatments on two adjacent watersheds in Clayoquot Sound on the west coast of Vancouver Island were carried out in the mid 1990's. In one watershed, a successional approach, including soil bioengineering, was used and a balanced seed mix was applied resulting in the establishment of an open stand of vegetation. In the other watershed, the seed mix was not balanced and resulted in the establishment of a dense stand of seeded species. Assessments conducted in 1999 (Warttig and Wise, 1999) found that there were four times as many native pioneering species (primarily red alder) on the disturbed

Table 1. Plant[1] establishment on UBC slopes

Initially (1989/90) planted species	1999 established species	2001 established species
Agrostis gigantea	Agrostis gigantea	Agrostis gigantea
Dactylis glomerata	Alnus rubra	Alnus rubra
Festuca rubra	Cytisis scoparius	Cytisis scoparius
Medicago sativa	Dactylis glomerata	Dactylis glomerata
Phleum pratense	Festuca rubra	Festuca rubra
Poa compressa	Medicago sativa	Medicago sativa
Salix scouleriana	Phleum pratense	Phleum pratense
Salix lucida	Poa compressa	Poa compressa
Trifolium hybridum	Polystichum munitum	Polystichum munitum
	Pseudotsuga menziesii	Pseudotsuga menziesii
	Rubus spectabilis	Rubus spectabilis
	Salix scouleriana	Salix scouleriana
	Salix lucida	Salix lucida
	Trifolium hybridum	Sambucus racemosa
		Tolmiea menziesii
		Trifolium hybridum
		Tsuga heterophylla

[1] Nomenclature follows that given in Douglas et al., 1989–1994.

sites in the watershed where successional reclamation was used.

The CP Rail Roger's Pass Project was the first use of successional reclamation for a major project. Many soil bioengineering treatments were undertaken on difficult sites on the Roger's Pass Project. Reclamation work on this project was conducted from 1983 to 1989. The reclamation work conduced on this project was the subject of an intensive study that culminated in the production of a thesis in 1998 (Lamb, 1998). Conclusions from this study indicated that the agronomic species were persistent and native invasion was most rapid along the edges of the disturbed areas. Native species invasion on the reclaimed sites may be limited due to the planting of native pioneers on most sites. Later successional conifers such as spruce, hemlock and cedar have been found on the treated sites (Lamb, 1998). Soil bioengineering sites have performed well and have effectively stabilized the treated sites.

Soil bioengineering was used to treat actively eroding water control structures on the Vancouver Island Gas Pipeline adjacent to the Big Qualicum River near Qualicum Beach north of Nanaimo on Vancouver Island, BC, Live silt fences as well as live bank protection was used to control erosion on a constructed drainage ditch. Initially, the soil bioengineering provided immediate relief from the active erosion while over the long term the willows used in the bioengineering provided a pioneering cover that encouraged invasion of skunk cabbage, horsetail and other wetland species.

Although not on a right-of-way, reclamation of the sand cliffs surrounding the University of British Columbia in Vancouver, BC, undertaken from 1988 to 1990, provides an excellent example of how natural successional processes can be harnessed to lead to a stable long-term vegetation cover. Soil bioengineering and successional reclamation were used. This reclamation work resulted in the establishment and dominance of willow and agronomic grasses and legumes on the slopes during the early 1990s. An assessment of the species composition of the stand on the slope revealed that initial rapid invasion of the site by red alder lead to a dominance by alder by the late 1990s. In addition, Douglas fir, sword fern and salmonberry were found on the slopes in 1999. Table 1 presents a synopsis of the floristic changes that have occurred on this site since treatment.

CONCLUSIONS

The use of soil bioengineering and successional reclamation methods in the establishment of vegetation on drastically disturbed right-of-way sites can enhance the speed at which natural processes and native species establish on a site. Providing space for invasion by natives is essential. Space can be provided by avoiding the use of a sod forming seed mix for the initial cover. In addition, fertilizer should be applied carefully to avoid the establishment of a dense thatch that will restrict native species invasion and growth. Stability of the site is essential for the establishment of native species. Soil bioengineering can be an effective means of providing site stability. Additional study of the long-term development of vegetation on reclaimed sites is warranted. However, an initial evaluation of the progress of sites where soil bioengineering has been used indicates that the initial objectives of reclamation programmes, that of stability and revegetation, are being met.

REFERENCES

Bliss, L.C. and R.W. Wein, eds. 1972. Botanical studies of natural and man modified habitats in the Eastern Mackenzie Delta Region and the Arctic Islands. Indian and Northern Affairs. ALUR 71-72-14.

Douglas, G.W., G.B. Straley, and D. Meidinger. 1989–1994. Vascular Plants of British Columbia. Parts 1–4. Research Branch. Ministry of Forests. Province of British Columbia. Victoria, BC.

Farmer, E.E., B.Z. Richardson, and R.W. Brown. 1976. Revegetation of acid mine wastes in Central Idaho. Intermountain forest and range experimental station. Research Paper INT-178. US Department of Agriculture, Forest Service. Ogden, UT.

Gray, D.H. and A.T. Leiser. 1982. Biotechnical Slope Protection and Erosion Control. Van Nostrand Reinhold Company Inc. Scarborough, Ontario, 271 pp.

Kimmins, J.P. 1987. Forest Ecology. Macmillan Publishing Co. New York. 531 pp.

Lamb, T. 1998. A study of plant community structure and reclamation evaluation of disturbed subalpine sites in Glacier National Park, British Columbia. Unpublished MSc thesis. University of Alberta. Edmonton, Alberta.

Mills, L.S., M.E. Soule, and D.F. Doak. 1993. The keystone-species concept in ecology and conservation. BioScience, 43(4): 219–224.

Morin, Kevin A. and Nora M. Hutt. 1997. Environmental Geochemistry of Minesite Drainage: Practical Theory and Case Studies. MDAG Publishing, Vancouver, BC. 333 pp.

Polster, D.F. 1989. Successional reclamation in Western Canada: New light on an old subject. Paper presented at the Canadian Land Reclamation Association and American Society for Surface Mining and Reclamation Conference, Calgary, Alberta, August 27–31.

Polster, D.F. 1991. Natural vegetation succession and sustainable reclamation. Paper presented at the Canadian Land Reclamation Association/B.C. Technical and Research Committee on Reclamation symposium. Kamloops, BC. June 24–28.

Polster, D.F. 1997. Restoration of landslides and unstable slopes: Considerations for bioengineering in interior locations. Paper presented at the 21st Annual B.C. Mine Reclamation Symposium and the 22nd Annual Canadian Land Reclamation Association Meeting. Cranbrook, BC. September 22–25.

Polster, D.F. 1999. Introduction to soil bioengineering: soil bioengineering for forest land reclamation and slope stabilization. Course materials for training professional and technical staff. B.C. Ministry of Forests Resource Tenure and Engineering Branch. Polster Environmental Services, September.

Polster, D.F. and M.A.M. Bell. 1980. Vegetation of talus slopes on the Liard Plateau, British Columbia. Phytocoenologia, 8(1): 1–12.

Popowich, J. 1978. Spoil dump resloping at fording river operations. Paper presented at the Second Annual British Columbia Mine Reclamation Symposium. British Columbia Technical and Research Committee on Reclamation. Vernon, BC. March 1–3.

Schiechtl, H.M. (Trans. N.K. Horstmann) 1980. Bioengineering for Land Reclamation and Conservation. University of Alberta Press. Edmonton. Alberta. 404 pp.

Schiechtl, H.M. and R. Stern. 1996. Ground Bioengineering Techniques for Slope Protection and Erosion Control (trans. L. Jaklitsch). Blackwell Scientific. Oxford, UK. 146 pp.

SEAM. 1979. User Guide to Soils Mining and Reclamation in the West. Intermountain Forest and Range Experimental Station. General Technical Report INT-68. US Department of Agriculture, Forest Service. Ogden, UT.

Straker, J. 1996. Regeneration on Natural Landslides. Paper presented at the Coastal Forest Sites Rehabilitation Workshop. BC Forestry Continuing Studies Network. Nanaimo, BC. October 31–November 1.

Warttig, W. and M. Wise. 1999. Effectiveness Monitoring in Road Deactivation. Paper presented at the 1999 Coastal Forest Sites Rehabilitation Workshop. Nanaimo, BC.

BIOGRAPHICAL SKETCH

David F. Polster
Polster Environmental Services, 5953 Deuchars Drive, Duncan, BC, V9L 1L5, e-mail: gsingleton@seaside.net, Tel. (250) 746-8052, Fax. (250) 746-5307

David F. Polster, a plant ecologist with 23 years of experience in vegetation studies and reclamation graduated from the University of Victoria with an Honours Bachelor of Science degree in 1975 and a Master of Science degree in 1977. He has developed a wide variety of reclamation techniques for steep/unstable slopes as well as techniques for the re-establishment of riparian and aquatic habitats. He pioneered the concept of successional reclamation where the aim of the reclamation program is the re-integration of the disturbed site into the natural processes of vegetation succession. He has authored several papers on this topic.

Summary of the Mitigation Program for Rare Plant Populations along the Portland Natural Gas Transmission System (PNGTS) and PNGTS/Maritimes & Northeast Joint Facilities Projects

J. Roger Trettel, Sandra J. Lare, and Brett M. Battaglia

During 1998 and 1999, Portland Natural Gas Transmission System ("PNGTS") and Maritimes & Northeast Pipeline, L.L.C. ("Maritimes") (collectively the "Owners") constructed approximately 292-miles of 12-, 24-, and 30-inch outside diameter pipeline (the Projects) through portions of Massachusetts, New Hampshire, Maine, and Vermont. Prior to construction, background research and field surveys were performed identifying the rare, threatened, and endangered ("RTE") plant and animal species located along the project route. Field surveys identified a total of 25 different RTE plant species located in 57 discrete populations; no animal species were identified. All plant species identified were state-designated, and no Federally-designated Threatened or Endangered species were identified. Avoidance of RTE plant populations was the preferred form of mitigation considered, however avoidance was not always feasible. Where avoidance was not possible, alternative mitigation measures were developed in conjunction with the appropriate regulatory agencies. A key component of the mitigation program involved removal and temporary nursery storage of rare plants during construction, and subsequent replanting in their approximate original locations following the completion of construction. Other mitigation measures included topsoil segregation/replacement and use of timber mats to cover and protect the populations from heavy equipment traffic. Post construction monitoring after the first growing season revealed that all but one of the rare plant populations is viable and vigorous following the first growing season. Based on initial results, we conclude that the techniques implemented were successful. Proper transplanting during the appropriate season, special care and over-winter handling by a qualified nursery, and replanting in suitable habitat and during the appropriate time window, are critical factors in determining program success. Such techniques may be applicable to other pipeline projects.

Keywords: Rare plant populations, suitable habitat, mitigation, replanting, monitoring plan

INTRODUCTION

During 1998 and 1999, Portland Natural Gas Transmission System ("PNGTS") and PNGTS/Maritimes and Northeast Pipeline constructed approximately 292 miles of 12-, 24-, and 30-inch outside diameter pipeline through the states of Vermont, New Hampshire, Maine, and Massachusetts. As part of the environmental review and permitting process for the project, background research and field surveys were performed to identify the presence of state and/or Federal plant and animal rare, threatened, and endangered (RTE) species of concern. Results from this background research and field surveys identified a number of state-designated populations of various rare species of concern throughout the project area (see Table 1).

Environmental Concerns in Rights-of-Way Management: Seventh International Symposium
J.W. Goodrich-Mahoney, D.F. Mutrie and C.A. Guild (editors)
© 2002 Elsevier Science Ltd. All rights reserved.

Table 1. State designated species of concern-Portland Natural Gas Transmission System (PNGTS) and PNGTS/Maritimes and Northeast Joint Facilities projects

Common name	Scientific name	Town	Approximate MP	State status
New Hampshire				
Great Bur-reed	*Sparganium eurycarpum*	Newton	20.00–20.10	T/S2
		Greenland	39.13–39.15	
Atlantic White Cedar	*Chamaecyparis thyoides*	Newton	22.26–22.43	S1/S3
			24.04–24.34	
Swamp Azalea	*Rhododendron viscosum*	Newton	24.04–24.34	T/S3
Featherfoil	*Hottonia inflata*	E. Kingston	25.19–25.41	State Record
Small Whorled Pogonia	*Isotria medioloides*	E. Kingston	25.93–26.05	E/S2
Robust Knotweed	*Polygonum robustis*	Exeter	29.60–29.62	T/S2
Thin-leafed Alpine Pondweed	*Potamogeton alpinus*	Exeter	29.75–29.79	T/S2
Lined Bulrush	*Scirpus pendulus*	Stratham	37.08–37.09	T/S2
Bush's Sedge	*Carex bushii*	Greenland	39.15–39.18	E/S1
Hairy Hudsonia	*Hudsonia tomentosa*	Newington	45.11–45.30	T/S1
Northern Blazing Star	*Liatris scariosa*	Newington	45.11–45.30	?
Hidden Sedge	*Carex umbellata*	Shelburne	91.55–91.58	E
			91.58–91.63	
			92.90–93.10	
			93.45–93.49	
			93.73–93.84	
			94.12–94.28	
Maine				
Annual Salt Marsh Aster	*Aster sublatus*	Eliot	52.50–52.53	E/S1
Muhlenberg's Sedge	*Carex muhlenbergii*	Eliot	53.72–53.73	E/SH
Smooth Winterberry	*Ilex laevigata*	Eliot	53.98–54.14	SC/S2-S3
Small Reedgrass	*Calamagrostis cinnoides*	Eliot	54.00–54.05	E/S1
		S. Berwick	62.70–62.74	
		Wells	68.54–68.60	
			69.35–69.36	
			69.74–69.81	
			70.21–70.25	
			70.30–70.36	
		Kennebunk	77.76–77.93	
			78.03–78.11	
			78.16–78.24	
		Arundel	78.39–78.42	
			78.46–78.60	
White Wood Aster	*Aster divaricatus*	S. Berwick	55.88–55.91	T/S1
			56.03–56.06	
			56.39–56.51	
			56.54–56.58	
Pale Green Orchis	*Platanthera flava*	S. Berwick (Nowell Farm) N. Berwick	60.48–60.63	SC/S2
		Kennebunk	64.72–64.77	
			74.13–74.15	
Lined Bulrush	*Scirpus pendulus*	S. Berwick (Nowell Farm)	60.48–60.63	?
Swamp Saxifrage	*Saxifraga pensylvanica*	S. Berwick	60.48–60.63	T/S2
		S. Berwick (Nowell Farm)	60.63–60.67	
		N. Berwick	64.48–64.63	
			65.08–65.10	
			65.14–65.15	
Wiegand's Sedge	*Carex wiegandii*	Saco	85.53–85.61	S2
American Chestnut	*Castanea dentata*	Kennebunk	75.15–75.40	S2-S3
Northern Blazing Star	*Liatris scariosa*	Kennebunk	73.32–73.35	T/S1
White Topped Aster	*Aster paternus*	Kennebunk	73.32–73.35	T/S1
			73.55–73.66	
Water Starwort	*Callitriche heterophylla*	Gilead	98.69–98.79	E
Scarlet Oak	*Quercus coccinea*	S. Berwick	62.70–62.74	E/S1

E = State endangered species. S1 = State identified as critically imperiled because of extreme rarity (5 or fewer known occurrences). T = State threatened species. S2 = State identified as imperiled because of rarity (6–20 known occurrences). SH = State identified as historically known in one area. S3 = State identified as very rare or only found locally in a restricted range (21–100 known occurrences). SC = Specibel Concern.

Avoidance of RTE plant populations that were found along the project route was the first mitigation measure considered by the Owners. Avoidance measures included implementation of route changes and/or reduction of construction workspace in areas of rare plant occurrence. To further ensure that rare plant populations located adjacent to the work area would be protected during the construction phase, orange exclusion fencing was to be erected as a physical and visual barrier to equipment, and "Exclusion Zone" signs would be placed where they were visible to workers.

In approximately 57 cases, completely avoiding the species of concern locations was not feasible. This was due to constraints posed by existing land uses, other environmental resources, the large size of the populations, and engineering constraints. Where avoidance was not possible, the Owners developed alternative mitigation measures in conjunction with the appropriate species of concern agencies in each state. This report provides a summary of the mitigation program that the Owners implemented to minimize impacts to plant species of concern that were unable to be avoided.

STANDARD MITIGATION MODEL

As stated above, avoidance of species of concern population was the priority of both the Owners and the regulatory agencies in the development of the mitigation program. Where avoidance was not feasible, the initial mitigation model put forth by regulatory agency personnel was the concept of full right-of-way (ROW) sod salvage and storage of the segregated material adjacent to the workspace. Based on previous experience, this standard model seemed to present complications that would make the program difficult to implement and hamper its overall success. Such complications include the following:

- Full ROW sod salvage would require substantial extra workspace in the vicinity of the plant population, thus potentially impacting additional area of the population off-ROW and requiring acquisition of additional temporary workspace. Most often, the goal is to minimize workspace requirements, i.e., the project footprint, and consequent ground disturbance in such areas.
- In populated areas, this additional required workspace could be difficult to acquire and may adversely affect landowner relations.
- Segregated plant material stored on site is subject to accidental damage caused by construction equipment, as well as desiccation and risk of burial.
- Segregated plant material stored on site requires monitoring and maintenance throughout the construction period, including routine watering and exclusion fencing repair. Storage of material on site creates additional logistical issues to track.

ALTERNATIVE TO STANDARD MODEL

Based on the constraints identified above, the Owners coordinated with the regulatory agencies to develop an alternative set of procedures for implementing mitigation. The program that was developed, as presented below, consisted of a more tailored, less intensive set of techniques. The basic components of this program included:

1. Limited transplanting to adjacent sites of certain site sensitive species. In such cases, species with highly specific site requirements would likely only survive if moved to an adjacent site with very similar conditions (e.g., aquatic species such as featherfoil and water starwort).
2. For less sensitive species, transplanting of a significant percentage of the population and storage of plant material in a nursery. The percentage of the population transplanted would be based on the overall size and density of the original population. Following construction, the plants would be re-installed in their approximate original location on the ROW.
3. In a limited number of areas, the mitigation strategy would involve a combination of transplanting and nursery storage, combined with timber matting to protect the residual population.

SPECIFIC METHODS

Based on the basic model presented above, the following presents the specific procedures that were implemented relating to plant removal, handling, nursery storage, and replanting on the restored ROW.

Population exclusion and plant removal

Beginning in late May 1998, a qualified botanical field team initiated the mitigation program. The field team consisted of botanists from Northern Ecological Associates, Inc. (NEA), and representatives of a local qualified plant nursery.

In areas where the approved mitigation called for exclusion fencing to be erected, the field team installed orange flagging to indicate the locations for fence installation. Contractor environmental crews then installed orange exclusion fencing, and Environmental Inspectors posted "Exclusion Zone" signs to ensure these areas were avoided during construction.

The botanical team identified populations of individual species of concern and conveyed this information to the nursery staff. Nursery personnel used small hand spades and shovels to manually remove the plants. Care was taken to excavate the maximum amount of the root systems and to minimize damage to the plants. The size of the soil plugs removed was based on the root structure, density of the species, and size of the plants. For example, small reedgrass (*Calamagrostis cinnoides*) individuals were removed with large soil plugs due to the high density of the populations and braided root systems; whereas swamp saxifrage (*Saxifraga pensylvanica*) specimens were removed in individual plugs due to the low density of individuals and simple root systems. In areas where sod salvage was the approved mitigation/plant removal technique, large sections of the sod (approximately 50 × 50 cm) approximately 10–15 cm deep were removed in association with the individual identified plants.

The herbaceous portion of the plants were then "trimmed back" by clipping off the top of the plant at a height of 10–15 cm from the top of the soil. By reducing the aboveground portion of the plant, the root system can better endure the stress of removal, transport, and processing. The plants and sod sections were wrapped in moistened burlap, allowing the plants to receive oxygen and maintain moisture during transport to the nursery.

Nursery storage procedures

After delivery to the nursery, the plants were kept in a cool, dark, and damp holding area until they were processed. Processing generally was performed within a few hours of arrival at the nursery. Processing consisted of the division of plant material (except for woody RTE species) into manageable clumps to be potted into 1-gallon pots. Woody RTE species (e.g., American chestnut) were stored in a balled and burlaped condition and supported by a wire frame. Sod salvage sections were contained in the larger 50 × 50 cm portions. Once potted, the plants were lightly fertilized with *Osmocote Plus* (a widely used slow release nursery fertilizer) to help overcome the stress associated with transplanting and encourage regrowth. The plants were then inventoried and labeled for location in the nursery storage area for the remainder of the growing season.

Plants were stored in various outdoor locations at the nursery, based on the species' hydrologic requirements. For example, emergent herbaceous species were moved to a wetland/drainage swale area where natural moisture conditions would be available to the plants. Upland species were located in well drained, dry sites.

The plants received a second light application of fertilizer two to three months after processing, in preparation for the winter season. It is important to note that minimal fertilizer is used only to combat the stress of relocation to the nursery. The nursery attempted to best simulate normal habitat conditions by preventing the plants from becoming dependant on artificial fertilizers. Natural precipitation was the primary means of watering while the plants were stored in their outdoor locations. However, during dry periods and when the plants appeared stressed, the nursery provided supplemental watering to maintain the vigor of the plants.

During the winter dormancy season, the plants were moved to a common outdoor area near a large structure to minimize wind exposure. Three different layers of cover were used to protect the plants during the winter. First, a dark felt material was laid on top of the plants. Next, a foam pad ("microfoam") approximately 1 cm thick covered the felt. Finally, a special heavy-duty plastic material covered the foam. The purpose of the three layers was to minimize extreme temperature fluctuations during the cold season and to assist with maintaining a higher overall temperature, especially in the event of a severe cold spell or extended freeze period. When the winter dormancy storage season ended, the plants were returned to their respective areas at the nursery to simulate their hydrologic requirements until the time of replanting on the ROW.

Replanting procedures

The majority of sapling tree species were replanted in their approximate original location on the restored ROW during late autumn 1998, following leaf fall and establishment of winter dormancy. The timing of this planting served to minimize stress to the saplings, improving their chance for survival.

Based on weather conditions and consultation with the botanists and nursery representatives, all remaining RTE species were systematically replanted in their original locations in the spring of 1999. A light application of *Osmocote* fertilizer was used to minimize the stress of relocation and encourage regrowth. Watering occurred naturally, however during periods of low precipitation, the nursery compensated with supplemental watering until the plants were successfully re-established. Exclusion fencing and/or flagging surrounded the replanted sites in order to discourage disturbance until the populations reestablished themselves in their environment. Although it was acknowledged that this exclusion fencing/flagging could potentially draw attention to the species, the necessary protection from all terrain vehicle traffic offset this risk.

MONITORING

Permit conditions issued by the various regulatory agencies required that long-term monitoring be a component of the overall mitigation program. As required, the Owners sponsored post-construction monitoring of all rare plant sites affected by construction to assess the condition of the population and the success of mitigation efforts. Monitoring was performed by a qualified botanical team and was scheduled to maximize positive identification and accurate assessment of plant condition.

For RTE populations involving plug removal and replanting, the botanical team surveyed the sites once within the first 60 days of the first growing season (i.e., June–July, 1999). This first survey provided initial verification of the condition and survival of the transplants, and identified whether immediate remediation, such as watering, may be required.

Following this initial survival survey, the Owners initiated a systematic monitoring program required by permit condition for at least the first two growing seasons. The first growing season survey was to be performed at two different times during the first year: mid-season (July) and late-season (August–September), when plants are still vigorous and readily identifiable. The second year surveys will be conducted two separate times at similar intervals.

All locations were systematically surveyed to monitor the individual population. Randomly spaced 1-square meter quadrats were sampled as appropriate to provide a quantitative assessment of percent cover (portion of an area covered by the vertical projection of the plant to the ground surface) and density (number of individuals per unit area, e.g., # of stems/m^2). The number of quadrats sampled is dependent upon the relative size of the population within the area of suitable habitat (i.e., a wetland system), such that the area sampled will be approximately 10% of the total population area. Quadrats were sampled within the disturbed area and in adjacent undisturbed areas (where applicable) for comparison. Monitoring results were documented on data forms for each site. In addition, the results of this sampling were compared with records of preconstruction conditions to determine relative success.

During the first growing season surveys, detailed documentation concerning survival and relative vigor of the population was produced. This data indicated that the majority of the populations were viable and robust after the first growing season; therefore no consultation with appropriate state and federal agencies was necessary to consider the need to develop any necessary ameliorative actions.

REPORTING

Following completion of each year's monitoring program, permit conditions require the Owners to prepare a detailed report documenting the results of the surveys and the overall condition of the plant populations. Mitigation will be considered successful if the population has achieved 80% of its original cover or density within the disturbance area. If the 80% threshold has not been achieved after the second growing season, an assessment will be made in consultation with the New Hampshire Natural Heritage Inventory, Maine Natural Areas Program, or the Massachusetts Natural Heritage and Endangered Species Program regarding the need for continued monitoring and/or additional mitigation measures.

An additional component of the post construction monitoring report will be assessments of the relative success of different mitigation measures. The Owners will identify specific measures that have proven to be successful, as well as items that are ineffectual. Recommendations for improvement of the program will be presented as appropriate. This information will be useful in the development of future RTE plant mitigation programs for pipeline projects in the region.

OVERALL FIRST YEAR RESULTS

The objective of the RTE Mitigation Program was to ensure that the Project was in compliance with state and Federal permit conditions requiring the identification of RTE species prior to construction, that unavoidable impacts were effectively mitigated, and that post-construction monitoring of the mitigated species of concern was properly performed.

RTE species that had been removed from sites along the construction right-of-way prior to construction in 1998 were replanted between June and July of 1999 following construction, with the exception of sapling species, which were replanted on October 30, 1998. The status of these replanted populations was later monitored within a 60-day time period with one visit to each site. The monitoring occurred in late July and early August of 1999.

In general, the first year of monitoring indicated that the majority of the sites appeared to be in satisfactory condition. Many of the populations appeared vigorous and several plant populations had expanded in size, despite a growing season marked by unusually hot and dry conditions. Much of the initial success can be attributed to proper replanting and periodic watering/maintenance performed by the contracted nursery.

Marginal plant vigor was observed at five populations located in certain wetland emergent habitats. This appears to be due in most part to the quality of the topsoil segregation conducted at these wetland sites. In particular, topsoil and subsoil appear to have been mixed, thus leaving exposed and hardened clay at the surface. This clay layer appeared to reduce the amount of vertical water flow and penetration from rainfall. Surface and subsurface soil conditions were dry, although moisture was available in adjacent off right-of-way wetlands.

As would be expected, replanted RTE populations relocated at sites, which closely match original conditions of soil type, moisture content, and exposure appear to be most successful. Furthermore, grass and sedge species (particularly small reedgrass and hidden sedge) appear most likely to become thoroughly re-established. Continued monitoring in the year 2000 growing season will provide more conclusive data on these RTE mitigation efforts, especially on the response of these plants to the drought conditions of 1999 and to competitive exclusion by other species.

CONCLUSIONS

Implementation of the RTE monitoring program for this project has been shown to be initially successful in mitigating adverse impacts to plant species of concern. The concept of maximum avoidance coupled with transplantation and off-site storage is a workable methodology based on early monitoring results. Key to the success of this technique is working with an experienced and qualified plant nursery in the vicinity of the project area, that will ensure plant materials are properly monitored and cared for in appropriate soil and moisture conditions. Follow-up monitoring, maintenance, and watering during the first critical growing season also appears to be important.

Preliminary results appear promising, but are based on only one year of data. General survey results from this season's monitoring effort have identified some mortality due to competitive exclusion by aggressive pioneers on the newly revegetating right-of-way. Long-term monitoring will be required to assess the overall efficacy of the technique.

In economic terms, the overall cost of the Program was relatively low in comparison with the cost of rerouting of the pipeline and the potential added environmental impact of clearing new corridor. Because none of the species mitigated with this program had Federal legal protection under the Endangered Species Act, it was not necessary to employ particularly extreme measures or entertain the possibility of stopping the project. The Program that was implemented took into consideration the state-level status of each of the species, the relative abundance of the particular species, and the potential for success, and has been shown to be an effective means of mitigating impacts to rare plant populations under these circumstances.

ACKNOWLEDGMENTS

We gratefully acknowledge PNGTS Operating Company and Maritimes & Northeast Pipeline for supporting the use of data from their projects as a case study. We also acknowledge and thank the team that contributed to the development of the mitigation program and concepts presented in this manuscript, as well as the field crews for their careful replanting of the rare plant species and monitoring of the replanted populations.

REFERENCES

Portland Natural Gas Transmission System/Maritimes & Northeast L.L.C. April 1997. Rare, Threatened, and Endangered Species and Unique Natural Communities Survey Report for Joint Pipeline Project. Portland, ME.

Portland Natural Gas Transmission System/Maritimes & Northeast L.L.C. December 1997. Summary of Small Whorled Pogonia Surveys for the Joint Pipeline Project. Portland, ME.

Portland Natural Gas Transmission System/Maritimes & Northeast L.L.C. January 1998. Rare, Threatened, and Endangered Species Mitigation Report for Joint Pipeline Project. Portland, ME.

Portland Natural Gas Transmission System/Maritimes & Northeast L.L.C. May 1998. Post-Construction Monitoring Plan for Rare, Threatened, and Endangered Plant on the Joint Pipeline Project. Portland, ME.

BIOGRAPHICAL SKETCHES

J. Roger Trettel

Northern Ecological Associates, Inc., 451 Presumpscot Street, Portland, ME 04103, USA, Fax: (207) 879-9481, Email: rtrettel@neamaine.com

As a Principal of Northern Ecological Associates, Inc. (NEA) and a specialist in environmental impact assessment and restoration ecology, Mr. Trettel has over 19 years experience in the environmental field. Mr. Trettel's experience includes management of comprehensive environmental programs for the planning, assessment, permitting, construction, inspection, restoration, and monitoring of natural gas pipeline development projects. A certified Professional Wetland Scientist (PWS), Mr. Trettel has a master's degree in wetland ecology, and has extensive experience performing wetland, vegetation, and biological analyses and developing wetland and wildlife habitat mitigation and restoration plans. In addition, Mr. Trettel manages and prepares Environmental Impact Statements (EISs), Environmental Assessments (EAs), and Environmental Reports (ERs) for proposed development projects.

Sandra J. Lare

Northern Ecological Associates, Inc., 451 Presumpscot Street, Portland, ME 04103, USA, Fax: (207) 879-9481

Ms. Lare is a senior environmental planner with NEA with 11 years experience in managing and performing planning, assessment, permitting, construction inspection, and restoration of natural gas pipeline projects. Ms. Lare has extensive experience with the NEPA process and completing consultation and mitigation planning to address species of concern issues. Ms. Lare also has experience and training in ecological restoration and landscape design.

Brett M. Battaglia

Northern Ecological Associates, Inc., 451 Presumpscot Street, Portland, ME 04103, USA, Fax: (207) 879-9481

Mr. Battaglia is an environmental scientist with over nine years of experience with wetland investigation/delineation, qualitative and quantitative vegetation sampling, wetland mitigation planning, wetland restoration, development of rapid assessment wetland monitoring programs, and inventory of riparian areas. Mr. Battaglia's is a Certified Wetland Scientist (New Hampshire), and a member of the Maine Association of Wetland Scientists (MAWS) and the New Hampshire Association of Natural Resource Scientists (NHANRS). Mr. Battaglia also is experienced with rare, threatened and endangered plant and animal species and community surveys, habitat surveys and mapping, biological sampling and analysis, and environmental impact studies, assessments, and permitting. His background also includes marine science, fish identification/sampling, and wildlife species population studies.

Right-of-Way Disturbances and Revegetation in Alpine Tundra: An Evaluation of Natural Revegetation on Plateau Mountain, Alberta

Laura A. Van Ham and Richard D. Revel

Reclamation of abandoned rights-of-way at alpine and subalpine elevations as well as in arctic locations has long been a formidable task for industry. As a means to further explore reclamation options for high elevation and northern locations, the authors undertook an alpine revegetation research project on the summit of the Plateau Mountain Ecological Reserve (elevation 2348–2500 m asl), located near the south end of Kananaskis Country, Alberta, Canada (50°13′N, 114°31′W). Plateau Mountain is one of a limited number of southern Rocky Mountain permafrost sites, and as such, exhibits characteristics of alpine and arctic tundra soil, vegetation and climate. Plateau Mountain was developed for sour gas production in the early 1950s and several rights-of-way and well sites have since been abandoned but not formally reclaimed. This site provided an excellent opportunity to study natural revegetation processes operating in an alpine/arctic tundra environment. Two linear right-of-way (road, pipeline) and one point (well site/surface clearing) disturbance types were studied and four levels of disturbance recognized: *undisturbed, near disturbance, severe,* and *less severe*. Natural revegetation of disturbed sites was analyzed via an adapted transect and point frame sample plot vegetation inventory that included both disturbed and adjacent undisturbed terrain. Measured reclamation parameters (e.g., species presence, frequency of occurrence, species richness, and similarity to undisturbed vegetation (Is_S) are indicative of successful natural revegetation of disturbed sites. Portions of the field results are presented, including the species list and species presence in the four distinguishable terrain types (*undisturbed, near disturbance, severe disturbance, less severe disturbance*). Based on these and an extensive literature review of alpine and arctic tundra disturbances, considerations for reclamation of high elevation and arctic disturbances focussing on enhancement of natural revegetation processes are discussed.

Keywords: Natural revegetation, disturbance, reclamation, petroleum industry, right-of-way, alpine

INTRODUCTION

Alpine and arctic environments have long been subject to natural disturbance (e.g., landslide, frost heave) with differing levels of intensity and frequency depending on the site. Generally, these sites are left to recover naturally and in a relatively intact environment they will progress through patterns of vegetative succession from bare ground to vegetated alpine communities. Over the past century, and in some parts of the world even longer, incidences of human caused disturbance in alpine and arctic environments are increasing. Recovery of these disturbances varies in terms of success and timeframe depending largely on nature of the disturbance (i.e., size, intensity and frequency of the disturbance activity), site characteristics as well as the intentions of, and actions taken by, the disturber.

Plateau Mountain, the study site for this research project, is located near the south end of Kananaskis Country in the front ranges of the Rocky Mountains, Alberta, Canada (50°13′N, 114°31′W) (Fig. 1). Some-

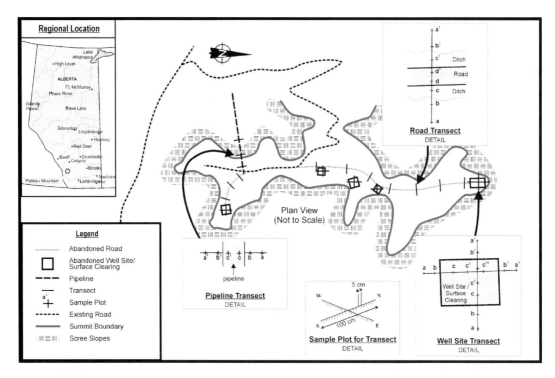

Fig. 1. Regional location of Plateau Mountain study area and vegetation inventory sampling design on disturbed sites.

Fig. 2. Looking west, area of micro-relief features and distinct patterned ground on the summit of Plateau Mountain. July, 1999.

what unique to the peaks in the vicinity, the summit of Plateau Mountain is an approximately 15 km² flat top. Elevations across the summit range from 2348 m above sea level (asl) near its northern extent to 2500 m asl near the south end. Treeline in the vicinity of Plateau Mountain is at approximately 2290 m (Woods, 1977), well below the summit's lowest elevations. The topography is generally flat with areas of very gently sloping terrain and micro-relief features (e.g., micro-hummocks) associated with patterned ground processes (Fig. 2). Plateau Mountain is located within the Savanna Creek gas field, where oil and gas exploration and production activity has been occurring since 1956.

Plateau Mountain is a relatively unique site in the southern Rocky Mountains in that large portions of the surface are covered by patterned ground features (Fig. 2) and it has a permafrost core. The summit of Plateau Mountain is believed to have been a

Fig. 3. Typical alpine tundra vegetation on the summit of Plateau Mountain. Note the well-camouflaged ptarmigan in the center of the photo. July, 1997.

"nunatak," meaning its surface was completely above the upper elevation limits of the late Pleistocene glaciation (Woods, 1977; Bird, 1990; Gadd, 1995). During this time, the glacier-free summit was exposed to a colder periglacial environment than surrounding glaciated areas, and experienced greater intensities of freeze-thaw activity (Woods, 1977). This periglacial environment has been documented as responsible for the mountain's relict permafrost core (Harris and Brown, 1982) as well as for initiation of many of the summit's patterned ground features (Woods, 1977).

Alpine areas in the front ranges of the Rocky Mountains are characterized by short, cool growing seasons, long, cold winters, high winds, effectively low precipitation, and intense radiation (Baig, 1972; Macyk, 1989; Walker, 1995; Millar, 1993). Soils on the summit of Plateau Mountain are classified as undeveloped or as orthic or cumulic regosols or turbic cryosols, indicating very poor profile development caused by unstable or perennially frozen conditions that inhibit horizon formation (Alberta Energy and Natural Resources, 1984). Vegetation on the summit is well adapted to the harsh growing conditions, with most plants being perennial and exhibiting short, clumped, or cushioned growth forms and both sexual and asexual reproductive capabilities. Large areas of the summit are described as fellfield tundra, with the stony, cryoturbated portions of the patterned ground features dominated by epipetric and terricolous lichens and the stable central portions by turf forming vegetation (Bryant, 1968;

Bryant and Schienberg, 1970; Griffiths, 1982). Wildlife inhabiting summit areas (e.g., marmot, pika, ptarmigan) are also well adapted to the alpine environment (Fig. 3).

The summit of Plateau Mountain and portions of its outlying areas were designated as an Ecological Reserve on December 12, 1991. Ecological Reserves are defined as "areas selected as representative or special natural landscapes and features of the province, which are protected as examples of functioning ecosystems, as gene pools for research, and for education and heritage appreciation purposes" (Alberta Environmental Protection, 1990). This designation limits the types of industrial activities and guides the types of research activities that are allowed within the ecological reserve boundaries.

Disturbance history

Mechanized access to the summit of Plateau Mountain was reached by 1956 with the construction of an oil and gas field road up the west slope and south across the middle portion of the summit to reach a sour gas well site (5-32-14-4 W5M). Further development activity occurred between 1956 and 1958 with the north-south extension of the summit road to access proposed drill sites near the north (3-17 and 7-5-15-4 W5M) and southeast (15-29-14-4 W5M) extents and in 1978 to reach a sour gas well site at the far southern extent (6-29-14-4 W5M). The Savanna Creek gathering system, constructed in about 1961, is located at the south end of Plateau Mountain. Construction activities for all phases of exploration and development have utilized native materials only (i.e., roads and well sites were prepared with materials present onsite).

The 5-32 and 6-29 well sites are currently in production and their access road is utilized daily by the Savanna Creek Gas Field operations staff. The 3-17 site was drilled in 1956 and abandoned in 1957. The 7-5 and 15-29 proposed drill sites were abandoned prior to drilling. In addition, between 1956 and 1958 a number of sites were prepared by surface clearing for an undocumented purpose and were likely abandoned immediately following preparation. The abandoned access roads, particularly to the 3-17 well site, were subject to regular vehicle traffic until a locked access gate was installed near treeline along the summit access road in 1980. From 1980 to 1989, vehicle travel on the abandoned summit roads was prohibited except with special permission from Alberta Environment. Since 1989, no vehicle traffic has been permitted on abandoned roads. Generally, sites were abandoned and no reclamation undertaken. At the time that the field work for this research project was conducted, most sites had been left to revegetate naturally for 37–40 years with one site for only 8 years.

Objectives

The objectives of this research project were as follows:
1. document the temporal and spatial characteristics of gas field related disturbances on Plateau Mountain;
2. document the natural revegetation of disturbed sites relative to disturbance severity in terms of species presence, frequency, frequency class, richness, and similarity to adjacent, undisturbed terrain;
3. evaluate the relative success of natural recovery of disturbed sites; and
4. develop recommendations for revegetation of disturbed sites within the Plateau Mountain Ecological Reserve and other similar alpine and arctic tundra sites.

METHODS

Two types of abandoned gas field surface disturbances were selected as sample sites for field investigation, linear right-of-way disturbance (road top, road ditch, pipeline) and point disturbance (well site/surface clearing).

Disturbed sites were classified at two levels according to Chambers (1995) and Chambers et al. (1990):
1. *severe* — which refers to disturbances that remove surface soil horizons and their seedbank and propagule pool (e.g., road ditch and well site/surface clearing); and,
2. *less severe* — which refers to disturbances that retain surface soil horizons and their seedbank and propagule pool in place (e.g., road top, and pipeline).

Adjacent, undisturbed terrain was also analyzed for comparison with disturbed terrain, and undisturbed sites were classified at two levels:
1. *undisturbed* — vegetation plots located 15 m from the disturbances and considered unaffected by the adjacent disturbed terrain; and,
2. *near disturbance* — vegetation plots located 5 m from disturbance and considered to be subject to influences from the adjacent disturbed terrain.

A transect based inventory system was established to cover vegetation sampling across the disturbed sites and in the adjacent undisturbed vegetation (Fig. 1). Transects were oriented perpendicular to the axis of linear disturbances (road top, road ditch, and pipeline) and marked at their approximate midpoint with a metal spike driven flush with the ground. Two transects were utilized to bisect point disturbances (well site/surface clearing). Transects started in undisturbed terrain 15 m from one side of the disturbance, extended across the disturbed areas and ended in undisturbed terrain 15 m from the opposite edge of the disturbance. Replicate (i.e., one on each side of the disturbance) sample plots were set-up along the transects in *undisturbed* (a, a') and *near disturbance* terrain (b, b') (Fig. 1). Along road right-of-way, disturbed terrain was sampled in replicate in the *severe* (road ditch, c and c') and *less severe* (road top, d and d') locations. *Less severe* disturbed terrain was also sampled along the pipeline right-of-way in replicate on either side of the right-of-way (c and c'). *Severe* disturbed terrain on well site/surface clearings was sampled in triplicate along each of the two bisecting transects (c, c', and c'').

A point frame sample plot was used to document vegetation along the transects (Fig. 1). Modeled after the standard 1 m^2 quadrat to sample herb cover (Krebs, 1989), the point frame is a 1 m by 1 m bisect with nails driven through the frame to mark sample points. Forty points in total were sampled, 20 along each axis spaced 5 cm apart. Terrain features were recorded where the forty sample points contacted the terrain surface. For the purpose of this study, a terrain feature refers to the following: (1) vascular plant genus and species, (2) moss, (3) terricolous lichen, (4) epipetric lichen, (5) unknown vegetation, (6) litter, (7) bare ground, (8) gravel/cobble/boulder, and (9) cryptogamic soil. In total, 168 sample plots were recorded including 43 in *undisturbed*, 45 in *near disturbance*, 52 in *severe disturbance*, and 28 in *less severe disturbance* terrain. Within each plot, terrain features were recorded at the 40 sample points for a total of 6720 sample points, including 1720 in *undisturbed*, 1800 in *near disturbance*, 2080 in *severe disturbance* and 1120 in *less severe disturbance*.

Data analyses for this research paper included: species presence, frequency (Krebs, 1989; Zar, 1984) and frequency class (Randall, 1978). Raw data from the 6720 sample points were recorded in a frequency table organized by sample plot. Frequencies were grouped by averaging the frequency values of similar sample plot locations (Krebs, 1989; Hurlbert, 1984). Frequency is the number of sample points terrain feature x is recorded out of a total of 1720 sample points for *undisturbed*, 1800 for *near disturbance*, 2080 for *severe disturbance*, and 1120 for *less severe disturbance*. Frequency classes (I to V) were also determined for similar sample plot locations (Raunkiaer, 1934 in Randall, 1978). Frequency class is obtained from the number of times terrain feature x appears in a sample plot location out of a total of 43 plots for *undisturbed*, 45 for *near disturbance*, 52 for *severe disturbance*, and 28 for *less severe disturbance*. This value is converted to a percent, and the frequency class obtained as follow: 0–20% = frequency class I, 21–40% = frequency class II, 41–60% = frequency class III, 61–80% = frequency class IV, and > 81% = frequency class V. Frequency class values were used in conjunction with the frequency data to evaluate the distribution and abundance of species and other terrain features on disturbed and adjacent undisturbed sites. A more detailed data analysis of the inventory results can be obtained from Van Ham (1998).

RESULTS

The results of the study are shown in Table 1. On the basis of the data gathered, the list of 79 species and other terrain features identified during the study is divisible into six general groups with subgroups. Group One includes nine species recorded only on undisturbed terrain (i.e., *undisturbed; near disturbance*). Group Two includes nine species recorded only on disturbed terrain (i.e., *severe; less severe; severe and less severe*). Groups Three and Four include 26 species recorded on both undisturbed (*undisturbed* and *near disturbance*) and disturbed (*severe, less severe*) terrain. Twelve species found on *near disturbance* and disturbed terrain (i.e., *near disturbance, severe; near disturbance, less severe; near disturbance, severe, less severe*) were separated from the other species into Group Three, as these species may reflect an influence of disturbed terrain colonizers on adjacent, *near disturbance* vegetation communities. Group Four includes 14 species recorded on *undisturbed, near disturbance* and disturbed terrain (i.e., *undisturbed, severe; undisturbed, near disturbance, severe; undisturbed, near disturbance, less severe; undisturbed, severe, less severe*). There were no species found in the *undisturbed, near disturbance, less severe* terrain combination. Group Five includes 30 species found on all terrain types (i.e., *undisturbed, near disturbance, severe*, and *less severe*). Group Six includes five non-vegetative/unknown vegetation terrain features that were recorded; each of these features was found in each of the terrain types (i.e., *undisturbed, near disturbance, severe, less severe*).

The total number of species recorded by terrain type was highest for *severe disturbance* terrain (57), followed by *near disturbance* terrain (56), *less severe disturbance* terrain (48) and *undisturbed* terrain (44). *Severe disturbance* terrain exhibited the highest number of unique colonizing species as well as the highest total number of colonizing species. A total of 56 plants were found in at least one undisturbed (*undisturbed, near disturbance*) and one disturbed (*severe, less severe*) terrain type. Thirty species were found in all four nondisturbance/disturbance types, nine species were found in undisturbed only and nine species in disturbed only.

The frequency and frequency class attributes for the vegetation and other terrain features are also included in Table 1. The top five frequency terrain features with a minimum frequency class of III (i.e., present in at least 41% of the plots sampled) for the four disturbance types are listed in Table 2.

DISCUSSION

Species abundance, distribution, and colonization patterns

In general, the vascular plants and other terrain features recorded during this inventory are typical of the study site's alpine location and environment. Where classification to species level was possible, plants recorded are all native, perennial species and most are described as alpine, subalpine, or mountain woodland species. Plant forms were invariably low growing, and many are characterized as cushion or sprawling plants. Shrubs and trees exhibited characteristic krummholz forms found in windy, alpine environments and were limited in distribution to wind protected slopes and depressions. Only nine species were limited to disturbed sites and nine species to undisturbed sites. Thirty species were found in all disturbance types and an additional 26 species were found in at least one undisturbed and one disturbed site. These findings reflect what Chambers (1993 and 1995) referred to as a limited number of viable life histories found in alpine/arctic tundra environments. Contrary to lower elevation and latitude areas, early seral plant species often persist into late seral communities in alpine and arctic areas. This reflects, in part, the low numbers of species with life-history traits adapted for survival and persistence in the extreme tundra environment.

All species found in either undisturbed (Group One) or disturbed (Group Two) terrain were found at relatively low frequency and frequency class indicating they are not abundant, nor are they widely distributed across the study area. Species found in Group One are not favorable for alpine revegetation efforts as they are naturally low in abundance and have not colonized the disturbed sites. However, while Group One species appear to be unfavorable for disturbance colonization from seed, they are potential

Table 1. Species presence, frequency and frequency class by disturbance type[1,2,3]

Species	UD		ND		S		LS	
	%F	FC	%F	FC	%F	FC	%F	FC
1. Species found on undisturbed sites only								
Agoseris glauca var. *dasycephala*	0.09	I						
Aster alpinus ssp. *vierhapperi*	0.25	I						
Carex maritime var. *incurviformi*	0.20	I						
Potentilla hyparctica	0.29	I						
Saxifraga oppositifolia	0.03	I						
Anemone lithophila			0.04	I				
Astragalus alpinus			0.50	I				
Phyllodoce glanduliflora			0.50	I				
Saxifraga lyallii			0.03	I				
2. Species found on disturbed sites only								
Pedicularis bracteosa					0.22	I		
Phacelia sericea					0.03	I		
Picea engelmanni					0.16	I		
Salix commutata					0.70	I		
Salix vestita					0.04	I		
Sibbaldia procumbens					0.39	I		
Campanula uniflora							0.05	I
Epilobium angustifolium					0.31	I	0.57	I
Saxifraga caespitosa ssp. *caespitosa*					0.21	I	0.38	I
3. Species found on disturbed and near disturbance sites only								
Achillea millefolium			0.50	I	0.20	I	0.14	I
Cassiope tetragona			0.25	I	0.04	I	0.05	I
Salix glauca L.			0.32	I	0.10	I	0.68	I
Stellaria longpipes var. *altocaulis*			0.06	I	0.05	I	0.26	I
Taraxacum ceratophorum			0.04	I	0.03	I	0.57	I
Trisetum spicatum			0.03	I	0.47	I	0.97	I
Oxytropis splendens			0.17	I	0.08	I		
Polygonum bistortoides			0.03	I	0.04	I		
Salix barrattiana			0.31	I	1.41	I		
Draba sp.			0.17	I			0.10	I
Poa sandbergii			0.25	I			0.33	I
Saxifraga cernua			0.33	I			0.14	I
4. Species found on disturbed and undisturbed sites, but not on all levels								
Oxytropis podocarpa	0.37	I			1.75	I		
Potentilla fruiticosa	1.33	I			0.08	I		
Arnica angustifolia ssp. *tomentosa*	1.07	I	0.08	I	0.03	I		
Carex obtusata	4.23	II	3.17	I	0.16	I		
Hedysarum sulphurescens	0.16	I	0.33	I	0.16	I		
Salix arctica	1.69	II	2.57	II	0.12	I		
Senecio Lugens	0.06	I	0.16	I	0.21	I		
Solidago multiradiata	0.25	I	0.96	I	0.12	I		
Cerastium beeringianum	0.04	I	0.17	I			1.17	I
Dodecatheon sp.	0.08	I	0.08	I			0.42	I
Haplopappus lyallii	0.58	I	0.24	I			0.42	I
Kobresia myosuroides	5.35	I	5.19	I			1.39	I
Erigeron compositus	0.08	I			1.24	I	1.75	I
Poa alpina	0.03	I			0.60	I	0.05	I
5. Species found on all levels of disturbed and undisturbed sites								
Agropyron violaceum	0.01	I	0.14	I	0.18	I	0.69	I
Androsace chamaejasme	1.33	II	0.32	I	0.31	I	0.24	I
Antennaria alpina	0.87	II	1.30	II	0.59	I	1.27	II
Carex albo-nigra	3.48	II	4.32	II	1.08	I	2.19	II
Carex phaeocephala	0.18	I	0.77	I	0.37	I	0.42	I
Deschampsia caespitosa ssp. *caespitosa*	0.67	I	0.87	I	0.08	I	1.44	I
Dryas octopetala ssp. *hookeriana*	13.02	III	14.23	III	1.44	II	2.57	I
Erigeron aureus	0.26	I	1.58	I	0.37	I	0.42	I
Festuca brachyphylla	0.23	I	0.63	I	2.32	II	2.34	II
lichen, epipetric	15.56	II	8.89	II	1.04	I	4.44	I
lichen, terricolous	6.72	IV	4.22	IV	0.52	I	2.27	II

Table 1. (continued)

Species	UD		ND		S		LS	
	%F	FC	%F	FC	%F	FC	%F	FC
Luzula spicata	0.17	I	1.27	I	1.41	II	0.42	I
Minuartia sp.	2.12	III	2.38	II	1.71	II	1.67	II
moss	4.65	IV	7.63	IV	10.73	IV	8.99	III
Myostis alpestris	0.03	I	0.33	I	0.03	I	0.33	I
Oxytropis sericea	0.66	I	0.17	I	0.86	I	0.28	I
Poa arctica	0.09	I	0.42	I	0.24	I	1.17	I
Poa pratensis	0.87	I	0.47	I	0.93	II	4.44	III
Poa sp.	0.03	I	0.28	I	0.03	I	4.67	I
Polygonum viviparum	0.79	II	1.63	II	0.71	I	0.28	I
Potentilla diversifolia	5.19	III	8.18	III	3.13	III	10.54	IV
Potentilla nivea	0.56	I	0.16	I	0.29	I	2.81	I
Rumex sp.	0.03	I	0.17	I	0.03	I	0.05	I
Saxifraga bronchialis	0.76	I	10.17	I	0.20	I	0.16	I
Saxifraga nivalis	0.12	I	0.35	I	0.11	I	0.28	I
Sedum lanceolatum	0.18	I	0.16	I	0.07	I	0.14	I
Silene acaulis	1.05	II	0.56	I	0.57	I	0.38	I
Smelowskia calycina	0.28	I	0.5	I	0.65	II	0.42	I
Stellaria monatha	0.45	I	0.76	II	0.34	I	1.39	II
Tolmachevia integrifolia	0.22	I	0.83	I	0.30	I	0.05	I
Total	44		56		57		48	
6. Non-vegetative and unknown vegetation								
unknown vegetation	0.18	I	0.08	I	0.44	I	0.42	I
litter	4.86	IV	7.42	IV	2.16	III	4.77	IV
bare ground	1.8	II	1.7	II	6.14	III	1.75	II
gravel/cobble/boulder	14.49	III	8.77	III	51.03	V	26.44	V
cryptogamic soil	1.72	II	0.85	I	0.72	I	0.42	I

[1] Disturbed and undisturbed sites were classified according to levels as follows: UD = undisturbed (15 m from edge of disturbation), ND = near disturbance (5 m from edge of disturbation), S = severe disturbance (removed surface soil/seed bank), LS = less severe disturbance (retained surface soil/seed bank).
[2] %F = frequency in percent, FC = frequency class. See methods section for explanation of frequency and frequency class.
[3] Species authorities sourced from Moss (1994), Hitchcock and Cronquist (1973), MacKinnon et al. (1992), Scotter and Flygare (1993), Gadd (1995) and Vitt et al. (1988).

Table 2. Top five frequency terrain features for disturbance types examined

Undisturbed	Near disturbance	Severe disturbance	Less severe disturbance
gravel/cobble/boulder (14.49%, III)	Dryas octopetala (14.23%, III)	gravel/cobble/boulder (51.03%, V)	gravel/cobble/boulder (26.44%, V)
Dryas octopetala (13.02%, III)	gravel/cobble/boulder (8.77%, III)	moss (10.73%, IV)	Potentilla diversifolia (10.54%, V)
terricolous lichen (6.72%, IV)	Potentilla diversifolia (8.18%, III)	bare ground (6.14%, III)	moss (8.99%, III)
Potentilla diversifolia (5.19%, III)	moss (7.63%, IV)	Potentilla diversifolia (3.13%, III)	litter (4.77%, IV)
litter (4.86%, IV)	litter (7.42%, IV)	litter (2.16%, III)	Poa pratensis (4.44%, III)

candidates for reclamation by transplanting if there is interest in increasing species richness and including later seral stage species in primary or secondary successional stage reclamation efforts. Species found in Group Two are also unfavorable for alpine revegetation efforts as they were not recorded in undisturbed (*undisturbed* and *near disturbance*) terrain (i.e., not typical to Plateau Mountain) and are also not abundant or widely dispersed in the disturbed terrain indicating only marginal colonization success.

Species recorded in disturbed terrain (*severe* and *less severe*) only (Group Two), likely colonized by one of several ways: seed rain from non-summit areas; seed rain from rare summit species; or, in *less severe disturbance* areas where the seed bank was retained, germination and propagation from the soil seedbank and propagule pool. Species dispersal from non-summit species is possible due to the extreme winds as well as transport by animals and vehicle traffic. Species dispersal to disturbed areas by rare summit species is also possible as early seral species in alpine environments are often present at lower abundance in later seral stages.

Species found only in the *less severe disturbance* areas are potentially recruited from their relatively intact seedbank and propagule pool that lie dormant until a disturbance instigates germination or propagation. Seedbank and propagule recruitment is quite likely happening in conjunction with seed rain colonization in *less severe disturbance* types on the summit of Plateau Mountain, however it does not dominate colonization. Only one species was found in *less severe disturbance* only (i.e., likely recruited from seed bank). From Group Five, it appears that colonization potential of several species is enhanced by seed bank recruitment. Twenty of the thirty species in Group Five have higher frequency in *less severe* than *severe disturbance* type. However, this difference may also be attributable to the more favorable site conditions found in *less severe disturbances*. The predominance of shrub species in the Group Two *severe disturbance* terrain reflects the nature of the disturbance. The majority of these shrubs were recorded in road ditch disturbance where the extra shelter has allowed shrubs to colonize more readily than in the other, more exposed undisturbed and disturbed terrain locations.

Species included in Groups Three and Four were also found at relatively low frequency and frequency class indicating they are not abundant, nor are they widely distributed across study area. Group Three represents species that were found in disturbed (*severe* and *less severe*) and only *near disturbance* terrain. This group was separated from those found in *undisturbed*, *near disturbance* and disturbed terrain as some of the species likely reflect invasion from disturbed to adjacent, *near disturbance* sites. Several of these species, 7 of 12, have higher frequencies in *disturbed* than *near disturbance* terrain. Species that are likely invading *near disturbance* areas include *Achillea millefolium*, *Taraxacum ceratophorum*, *Oxytropis splendens*, *Draba* sp., *Saxifraga cernua*, *Stellaria longpipes* var. *altocaulis*, and *Trisetum spicatum* which are typically found in disturbed sites, naturally disturbed sites (e.g., river banks, scree, rocky slopes) or dry, gravelly soils. Chambers (1993) has reported that despite lower vegetation cover and species numbers, severely disturbed borrow pits exhibit higher seed rain densities than undisturbed turf vegetation at the same site. Seed production and dispersal from disturbed sites to small-scale disturbances (e.g., cryoturbated soils, small mammal digging) in *near disturbance* areas may in part explain the inventory results.

Contrary to Group Three, Group Four species generally exhibit higher frequency and frequency class in undisturbed (*undisturbed*, *near disturbance*) than disturbed (*severe*, *less severe*) terrain. These data reflect movement of species from undisturbed to disturbed ground.

Group Five, representing species found across all disturbance types (*undisturbed*, *near disturbance*, *severe*, *less severe*) includes the greatest number of species and generally the highest frequency and frequency class values compared to all other groups. Species particularly worth noting include *Potentilla diversifolia* and moss in *severe* and *less severe* disturbances and epipetric lichen, terricolous lichen, *Poa pratensis* and *Poa* sp. in *less severe disturbance*. This pattern of most species occurring in all four disturbance types is to be expected as species found in high abundance (frequency) and widely distributed (frequency class) also appear to be the best natural colonizers of disturbed ground. This again reflects Chambers (1993) findings that early seral plant species often persist into late seral communities in alpine and arctic areas.

Also in Group Five, species frequency was higher in *less severe* than *severe disturbance*s for 20 of the 30 species and higher in *less severe* than all other disturbances (*less severe*, *undisturbed* and *near disturbance*) in 11 of the 30 species. This is indicative of more favorable site conditions in *less severe* vs. *severe disturbances* (see next section for discussion) propagation from the seedbank as well as species that are more prominent in early vs. later successional stages. A number of grass and sedge species reflect this early successional stage prominence. Similar tendencies have been previously noted by Rikhari et al. (1993) for alpine areas in other parts of the world where he found that grasses predominate early in secondary succession (*less severe disturbances*) of alpine Himalayan meadows, with sedges increasing thereafter.

Group Six highlights non-vegetative (and unknown vegetation) terrain features recorded during the inventory. As expected, bare ground and gravel/cobble/boulder dominate disturbed sites. However they are notably more predominant in *severe* over *less severe disturbance*, a difference that will be discussed in the following section. Bare ground and gravel/cobble/boulder are also quite prominent on undisturbed (*undisturbed* and *near disturbance*) terrain, a fact that must be considered in conjunction with the disturbed group results as alpine areas are typically rocky and small-scale disturbances are common. The gravel/cobble/boulder component of the *severe disturbance*s was generally small gravel and indicative of a poorly vegetated site, while this component of the *less severe disturbance*s was generally not indicative of poor vegetative cover or extensive gravel. Litter, most common in undisturbed areas (*undisturbed* and *near disturbance*), is also fairly common in disturbed areas particularly *less severe* disturbed areas. Litter is an important component of vegetation communities as its decomposition provides nutrients to existing and colonizing plants and its abundance increases as part of the natural revegetation process.

Severe vs. less severe disturbance

It is obvious from the results of this study, as well as literature reports, that reclamation success in alpine and arctic areas is greatly enhanced by sites that have retained their surface soil horizons (i.e., *less severe disturbances*). Vegetative ground cover, based on species frequency and observations of the researcher, is considerably higher in *less severe* than *severe disturbances*. This is expected as *less severe disturbances* retain soil nutrient content that is characteristically sparse in alpine environments and beneficial to species colonization as well as the seedbank and propagule pool. This allows for secondary successional processes.

However, the results of this study also indicate that in *severe disturbance* sites, a deficiency of available soil nutrients often favors colonization of nitrogen fixing species which in turn will ameliorate harsh disturbed site characteristics (Bishop and Chapin, 1989; Baig, 1992; Chambers, 1995; Smyth, 1997). Two of the three nitrogen fixing *Oxytropis* sp. (*O. podocarpa* and *O. splendens*) are found in *severe disturbances* only and *Oxytropis sericea* is found in both *severe* and *less severe*, but at a higher frequency in *severe*. This is characteristic of primary successional processes that necessitate a period of site amelioration to more favorable conditions for advanced stages of species colonization and maintenance.

Considerations for exploration, development, production, and interim reclamation

Developed in the 1950s, it is unlikely that gas field exploration, development, production and reclamation on Plateau Mountain underwent the level of environmental assessment that would be undertaken today. While certain measures were consciously taken to limit disturbance to the summit area, it is likely that more could have been incorporated into the planning stages of exploration and development. In addition, interim reclamation measures could have been taken prior to full gas field abandonment to enhance the success and shorten the timeframe of site recovery following abandonment. Several of the measures discussed below apply equally to arctic disturbances as conditions at high elevations, particularly areas of permafrost, tend to be similar to those experienced at high latitudes.

Measures for consideration during the exploration, development, and production and interim reclamation phases of alpine and arctic development include:

1. Limit areas of clearing and grading — Plateau Mountain is a flat, treeless summit that likely did not require the amount of grading that was conducted to construct rights-of-way and facilities. Well site, road, pipeline, and facility design should attempt to incorporate less traditional shapes and sizes to conform more readily with biophysical characteristics of the site while maintaining other technical and safety requirements. Initiate reclamation measures on unused portions of exploration and development disturbances by either allowing for/encouraging natural revegetation or undertaking formal reclamation.

2. Avoid removal of the vegetative and organic mat in areas of permafrost — Disturbance to vegetative and organic layers in areas of permafrost, particularly in arctic areas, has been shown to initiate permafrost degradation and terrain changes in both alpine and arctic areas (Hayhoe and Tarnocai, 1993; Nicholas and Hinkel, 1996; Swanson, 1996). Vegetation in alpine and arctic areas is generally limited to low-growing shrubs and herbs that generally will not interfere with standard construction activities. Where possible, the vegetation mat should be left in place, particularly for temporary disturbances (e.g., pipeline construction). For permanent or long-term disturbances, the vegetative and organic layers could be covered (e.g., geotextile mat, gravel or log cap) for removal post-abandonment.

3. Avoid permanent removal of soil — in areas of temporary disturbance, the soil horizons should be stockpiled and protected from erosion for replacement immediately following disturbance. Weed (i.e., non-native) species invasion on stockpiled soils is generally not an issue in alpine and arctic environments as weeds do not survive more than a few growing seasons. In areas of permanent or long-term disturbance the soil horizons could be left in place and rights-of-way and facilities constructed over top.

4. Avoid or limit disturbance to sensitive features — where possible, exploration and development activities should be planned to avoid sensitive features (e.g., patterned ground, rare plants, and plant communities). Loss of sensitive features may be impossible to mitigate, and as such, are permanent project losses. Under certain circumstances these losses may be considered as significant effects of the project on the environment.

5. Limit the introduction of non-native materials during facility construction — where possible, introduction of non-native materials for right-of-way and facility construction should be limited to minimize the cost of removal during final reclamation.

6. Modify our expectations for site reclamation to correspond with natural processes — natural revegetation in alpine and arctic environments is a slow process (Houle and Babeux, 1994) and the potential for full recovery of these landscapes following human disturbance is questioned by some researchers (Curtin, 1995). Climatic patterns (e.g., global warming) and other environmental conditions are continuously shifting and may no longer be commensurate with pre-disturbance characteristics of the site and existing alpine and arctic tundra vegetation may be in equilibrium with past not present climate (Curtin, 1995; Harper and Kershaw, 1996). Mimicking the natural revegetation processes on

disturbed sites will maximize the potential for site recovery to pre-disturbance or the "new equilibrium" of predisturbance condition. However, the timeframe for achieving pre-disturbance condition may not be synonymous with the time frame for reclamation approval from regulatory agencies.

CONCLUSION

The results from this research project indicate that natural revegetation of abandoned gas field disturbances on the summit of Plateau Mountain has been quite successful in terms of the sites following rather favorable natural successional process (i.e., species presence, expected patterns of primary and secondary succession on *severe* and *less severe disturbances*, overall frequency of vegetative ground cover). Where erosion is not an issue, which includes the majority of the abandoned disturbances, these processes should be allowed to continue without further disturbance. However, the following final reclamation measures could be incorporated into the abandonment plans for existing, used, or eroding abandoned disturbances on the summit of Plateau Mountain, as well as for other alpine and arctic areas:

1. Reclamation Goal — Prior to site reclamation, establish goals that reflect the nature of the disturbance, the needs of the surrounding area and the plans for post-disturbance land use. This should include consideration of erosion control and slope stability, aesthetics, wildlife habitat, recreation, and restoration to the sites original condition.
2. Site Preparation — Re-contour right-of-way and facility disturbances to predisturbance condition. On Plateau Mountain, this would include primarily the existing roadbeds where redistribution of the surface soil horizon across the disturbance (i.e., across ditches and roadbed) would facilitate site recovery. Re-contouring should be conducted to minimize disturbance to natural revegetation processes that are occurring on unused portions of existing right-of-way and facility disturbances (e.g., unused portions of well sites). Consider use of erosion control devices in areas where water erosion may be an issue. Wind erosion, particularly in alpine locations, is a very natural and common process and may be unmitigateable short of establishing a vegetative cover.
3. Surface Preparation — Utilize surface preparation techniques that will alleviate soil compaction, allow for moisture infiltration, reduce near surface wind speeds and provide sheltered micro-sites for seed and propagule entrapment (e.g., rough rip and harrow). However, attempt to find a balance that achieves surface preparation objectives while limiting the potential for wind erosion of the resulting soil texture. Additional measures could be taken to create small-scale surface manipulations that mimic natural conditions (e.g., create small depressions and elevations, use on-site boulder and rock material to provide micro-sites of wind protection, shade, and moisture collection). Addition of soil nutrients (e.g., fertilizer) is generally not recommended during surface preparation as this introduces an unnatural boost of nutrients into characteristically nutrient-starved alpine and arctic environments, potentially enhancing the establishment of non-native (i.e., weed) or invasive native species. However, in areas where topographical features increase the likelihood of water erosion, nutrient addition may be desirable to assist with quick (i.e., one season) establishment of a ground cover crop.
4. Revegetation — Select revegetation techniques carefully to coincide with desired results. As evidenced from this study, and several others in literature, harsh environmental characteristics of alpine and arctic areas limit the number of species that will survive and reproduce over the long-term. For long-term survival of vegetation and recovery to pre-disturbance condition, it is necessary to consider species adapted to alpine and arctic environments. For Plateau Mountain, where introduction of non-native material is prohibited from the Ecological Reserve, this may require onsite collection of seed for distribution to disturbed sites or allowing natural revegetation to take its course. For other alpine and arctic locations native seed, plugs, and seedlings are available from several distributors. In areas where wind and water erosion are an issue and the genetic source of the vegetation is not, revegetation using an aggressive cover crop to minimize erosion may be desirable. This technique limits erosion, adds organic content to the soil and allows for native seed entrapment during the first few seasons following reclamation. As previously discussed, weed species invasion on disturbed sites is generally not an issue in alpine and arctic environments, as weeds are unlikely to survive more than a few growing seasons.
5. Maintenance — Monitor the progression of revegetation, either assisted or natural, following site abandonment and reclamation. Monitoring should continue until goals specified in the reclamation plan are met. In alpine and arctic sites where environmental conditions are characteristically severe, the goal should be to achieve a desired combination of species presence (i.e., native species), progressive ground cover (i.e., increasing ground cover season to season) and levels of erosion comparable to adjacent, undisturbed sites (i.e., wind and water erosion is not counteracting revegetation success). More traditional goals such as soil structure and chemistry and vegetation density will likely not apply. Consultation with regulatory agencies should focus on establishing clear and agreed upon reclamation goals that are appropriate for the conditions of the site and the nature of the disturbance.

ACKNOWLEDGEMENTS

The authors wish to extend sincere gratitude to Husky Oil Operations Ltd. and the Faculty of Environmental Design at the University of Calgary for their interests that allowed this project to be initiated and their resources that assisted it through to completion.

REFERENCES

Alberta Energy and Natural Resources, Resource Evaluation and Planning Division. 1984. Ecological Land Classification and Evaluation: Kananaskis Country, Volume 1, Natural Resource Summary. Alberta Energy and Natural Resources, Edmonton, Alberta. 111 pp. + map.

Alberta Environmental Protection, Natural Resources Service. 1998. Plateau Mountain Ecological Reserve Draft Management Plan. January 18, 1998. 41 pp.

Baig, M.N. 1972. Ecology of Timberline Vegetation in the Rocky Mountains of Alberta. Doctorate of Philosophy Thesis. University of Calgary, Calgary, Alberta. 328 pp. + appendices.

Baig, M.N. 1992. Natural revegetation of coal mine spoils in the rocky mountains of Alberta and its significance for species selection in land restoration. Mountain Research and Development, 12(3), 285–300.

Bird, C.D. 1990. Alpine plants on Plateau Mountain. PICA, The Calgary Field Naturalists' Society. Volume 10, Number 2, Spring 1990, pp. 3–11.

Bishop, S.C. and F.S. Chapin III. 1989. Patterns of natural revegetation on abandoned gravel pads in arctic Alaska. Journal of Applied Ecology, 26: 1073–1081.

Bryant, J.P. 1968. Vegetation and Frost activity in an alpine fellfield on the summit of Plateau Mountain, Alberta. Masters of Science Thesis. Department of Biology, University of Calgary, Calgary, Alberta. 79 pp. + appendices.

Bryant, J.P. and E. Scheinberg. 1970. Vegetation and frost activity in an alpine fellfield on the summit of Plateau Mountain, Alberta. Canadian Journal of Botany, 48: 751–771.

Chambers, J.C. 1993. Seed and vegetation dynamics in an alpine herbfield: effects of disturbance type. Canadian Journal of Botany, 71: 471–485.

Chambers, J.C. 1995. Disturbance, life history strategies, and seed fates in alpine herbfield communities. American Journal of Botany, 82(3): 421–433.

Chambers, J.C., J.A. MacMahon, and R.W. Brown. 1990. Alpine seedling establishment: The influence of disturbance type. Ecology, 71(4): 1323–1341.

Curtin, C.G. 1995. Can montane landscapes recover from human disturbance? Long-term evidence from disturbed subalpine communities. Biological Conservation. Elsevier Science Limited, Vol. 74, pp. 49–55.

Gadd, B. 1995. Handbook of the Canadian Rockies, 2nd ed. Corax Press, Jasper, Alberta. 831 pp.

Griffiths, Dr. G.C.D. 1982. Vegetation Survey and Mapping of the Plateau Mountain Candidate Ecological Reserve. Alberta Energy and Natural Resources, Natural Areas Coordinator, Edmonton, Alberta. 46 pp. + appendices and map.

Harper, K.A. and G.P. Kershaw. 1996. Natural revegetation patterns on borrow pits and vehicle tracks in shrub tundra, 48 years following construction of the CANOL No. 1 pipeline, N.W.T., Canada. Arctic and Alpine Research, 28(2): 163–171.

Harris, S.A. and R.J.E. Brown. 1982. Permafrost distribution along the Rocky Mountains in Alberta. In: Proceedings of the Fourth Canadian Permafrost Conference, Calgary, Alberta, March 2–6, 1982. H.M. French, ed. National Research Council of Canada, Ottawa, Ontario. pp. 59–67.

Hayhoe, H. and C. Tarnocai. 1993. Effect of site disturbance on the soil thermal regime near Fort Simpson, Northwest Territories, Canada. Arctic and Alpine Research, 25(1): 37–44.

Hitchcock, C.L. and A. Cronquist. 1973. Flora of the Pacific Northwest. University of Washington Press.

Houle, G. and P. Babeux. 1994. Fertilizing and mulching influence on the performance of four native woody species suitable for revegetation in subarctic Quebec. Canadian Journal of Forestry Research, 24: 2342–2349.

Hurlbert, S.A. 1984. Pseudoreplication and the design of ecological field experiments. Ecological Monographs, 54(2): 187–211.

Krebs, C.J. 1989. Ecological Methodology. Harper Collins Publishers, New York, NY. 654 pp.

MacKinnon, A., J. Pojar and R. Coupe. 1992. Plants of Northern British Columbia. Lone Pine Publishing, Edmonton, Alberta. 345 pp.

Macyk, T.M., Z.W. Widtman, and V. Belts. 1989. Impact of climate on reclamation success in the foothills/mountains region of Alberta, Canada. In: Proceedings of the Conference, Reclamation: A Global Perspective, August 27–31, 1989, Calgary, Alberta (RRTAC). pp. 49–58.

Millar, B. 1993. The Rocky Mountains Alpine Ecosystem. Prepared for the Calgary Zoological Society. 28 pp. + appendices.

Moss, E.H. 1994. Flora of Alberta, 2nd ed. Revised by J.G. Packer. University of Toronto Press, Toronto, Ontario. 687 pp.

Nicholas, J.R.J. and K.M. Hinkel. 1996. Concurrent permafrost aggradation and degradation induced by forest clearing, central Alaska, USA. Arctic and Alpine Research, 28(3): 294–299.

Randall, R.E. 1978. Theory and Practice in Geography: Theories and Techniques in Vegetation Analysis. J.W. House, A.S Goudie, and J.H.C. Patten, eds. Oxford University Press. House, UK. 61 pp.

Rikhari, H.C., G.C.S. Negi, J. Ram, and S.P. Singh. 1993. Human-induced secondary succession in an alpine meadow of Central Himalaya, India. Arctic and Alpine Research, 25(1): 8–14.

Scotter, G.W. and H. Flygare. 1993. Wildflowers of the Canadian Rockies. Hurtig Publishers, Toronto, Ontario. 170 pp.

Smyth, C.R. 1997. Early succession patterns with a native species seed mix on amended and unamended coal mine spoils in the Rocky Mountains of southeastern British Columbia, Canada. Arctic and Alpine Research, 29(2): 184–195.

Raunkiaer, C. 1934. The life forms of plants and statistical plant geography (Clarendon).

Swanson, D.K. 1996. Susceptibility of permafrost soils to deep thaw after forest fires in interior Alaska, USA, and some ecological implications. Arctic and Alpine Research, 28(2): 217–227.

Van Ham, L.A. 1998. Natural Recovery of Human Induced Disturbance in an Alpine/Arctic Tundra Environment and Recommendations for Reclamation: Plateau Mountain Ecological Reserve. Master's of Environmental Design Thesis. Faculty of Environmental Design, University of Calgary, Calgary, AB. 153 pp. + appendices.

Vitt, D.H., J.E. Marsh, and R.B. Bovey. 1988. Mosses Lichens & Ferns of Northwest North America. Lone Pine Publishing, Edmonton, Alberta. 296 pp.

Walker, M.D. 1995. Patterns and causes of arctic plant community diversity. Ecological Studies, Vol. 113, Arctic and Alpine Biodiversity: Patterns, Causes and Ecosystem Consequences. Chapin, F.S III and C. Körner, eds. pp. 3–20.

Woods, Charles B. 1977. Distribution and Selected Characteristics of High Altitude Patterned Ground in the Summit Area of Plateau Mountain, Alberta. Masters of Science Thesis. Department of Geography, University of Calgary, Calgary, Alberta. 107 pp. + appendices.

Zar, J.H. 1984. Biostatistical Analysis, 2nd ed. Prentice–Hall, Englewood Cliffs, NJ. 718 pp.

BIOGRAPHICAL SKETCHES

Laura Van Ham
TERA Environmental Consultants (Alta.) Ltd., 205, 925-7th Avenue S.W., Calgary, Alberta, Canada T2P 1A5

Laura Van Ham, MEDes, is a terrestrial ecologist and an environmental planner. She has particular interest in alpine ecology and restoration of such areas where they have been affected by human activities. Laura has participated in several industrial projects at exploration, development and reclamation stages. She has also been involved in wildlife, wildlife habitat, aquatic and botanical studies.

Richard D. Revel
Faculty of Environmental Design, University of Calgary, 2500 University Drive N.W., Calgary, Alberta, Canada T2N 1N4

Richard D. Revel, PhD, professor of Environmental Science, is a plant ecologist by training but professes and practices in the area of applied ecology, resource management and integrated resource planning.

Managing the Green Heritage of Highways Rights-of-Way in Southern Quebec: A New Ecological Landscape Approach

Yves Bédard, Daniel Trottier, Luc Bélanger,
Jean-Pierre Bourassa, Nancy Champagne, José Gérin-Lajoie,
Gaston Lacroix, and Esther Lévesque

The Ministère des Transports du Québec maintains 2000 km of highway corridors scattered throughout southern Québec (Canada). Traditional methods of controlling vegetation along these highways result in a boring landscape, deteriorate the various wildlife habitats and impoverish wild plant life while generating high maintenance costs. Recently, it has been preferred to develop new maintenance methods that improve the safety of the highway system's users, satisfy neighboring residents, beautify the landscape and consider the plant life and wildlife present along the highways. The new approach eliminates systematic multiple annual mowing, except on the first two meters from the pavement, where maintenance will even be accentuated (four or five mowings per year) to ensure highway safety (visibility) and better control of ragweed (*Ambrosia artémisiifolia*), a noxious allergenic plant. Since 1998, three different highway sections have served as experimental sites for a three-year period to assess biodiversity benefits as well as road user's perceptions. These sites are located in three fragmented landscapes, one partially forested, another agricultural and the other suburban. The objective is to compare the experimental sites where the new approach is used with sections where the traditional way of management is maintained. The benefit on the plant and animal diversity, on the quality of the habitats of the new approach is evaluated herein after one year (1999). Preliminary results indicate that the plant diversity is minimal in the agriculturally intensive zone compared to the partially forested zone and the suburban zone. The roadside habitat near forests appears with the highest animal diversity (insects, small mammals, and birds) followed by suburban and agricultural sites. After this first year of monitoring, the results suggest, however, no differences have yet to appear in both animal and plant abundance and diversity between the new approach and the traditional way of managing roadside vegetation along highways in southern Québec.

Keywords: Vegetation, management, rights-of-way, landscape

INTRODUCTION

The Ministère des Transports du Québec (MTQ thereafter) maintains 2000 km of highway corridors scattered throughout southern Québec. Traditional methods of controlling vegetation along highways result in a less-than-exciting landscape, deteriorate the various wildlife habitats and impoverish wild plant life while generating high maintenance costs. The MTQ has thus preferred to develop according to information provided in recent literature related to landscape and road ecology (Drake and Kirchner, 1987; Noss, 1991; Bennet, 1991, 1992; Jaarsa and Langevelde, 1997; Farmar-Bowers, 1997), new maintenance methods that improve the safety of the highway system, satisfy neighbouring residents, beautify the landscape and enhance the plant life and wildlife present along the highways. Until now, the traditional method for the ecological management of highways has been multiple annual mowing, from the edge of the asphalt-covered pavement to the property line. In rural areas, two or three mowings per year were required, while in urban areas, three or four mowings were necessary each year, sometimes more.

The new approach eliminates systematic multi-annual mowing, except on the first two metres from the pavement, where the frequency will even be increased (four or five mowings per year) to ensure highway safety (visibility) and better control of ragweed, a noxious, allergenic plant. The new approach will consist of allowing the local plant life to flourish, thereby providing motorists with a more beautiful and diversified landscape. Only periodic cutting (in late autumn of each year or every two to three years, depending on the results of experimentation in progress; see below) will be used to control the growth of certain woody plants that can endanger the safety of highway users. Details regarding this method of management are presented in Table 1 and in Fig. 1.

This approach is based on experiences elsewhere, particularly in Ontario (Canada), in some US states, Netherlands, England, and in France (Way, 1977; Laursen, 1981; Warner, 1992; Camp and Best 1993a, 1993b; Bekker, 1995; Meunier et al., 1999a, 1999b, 2000). It also originated at the 5th *International Symposium on Environmental Concerns in Right-of-Way Management* held in Montréal in 1993, where the outcome of studies carried out in Southern France on the extensive management of roadside vegetation were presented. Some time later, some reference documents were drafted (Anonyme, 1994; Coumol and Chavaren, 1995). This information served as the foundation for developing the MTQ's project. A mission to France was then organized to find out how these new practices were implemented in this country and to learn about the major constraints encountered (Y. Bédard, MTQ, personal comm.).

The most important lesson drawn from this mission is that, even though ecologically and scientifically speaking, the benefits of this new management method appear obvious, its social approval is far from being won, and ignoring this aspect could be detrimental to the project. It is important, then, to understand from the outset that highway corridors benefit from a high degree of visibility and that they are part of many people's everyday reality. In addition, such people have their own viewpoint on plant maintenance that is not necessarily in keeping with that being proposed. Based on this observation, the MTQ has directed its approach as follows: (1) conduct public awareness campaigns, targeting the various sectors of the population, on the objectives and advantages of such new management methods, (2) conduct an experimental pilot project in different regions aiming to respond to public awareness, and (3) provide scientific documentation on the results of experimental sections of the highways. When these three stages have been accomplished, the MTQ should be able to develop the standards for maintaining vegetation, taking into account the following concerns: the surrounding landscape, wildlife habitats, biodiversity, wildlife hazards (Oxley et al., 1979) or other associated impacts (Reijnen and Foppen, 1994a, 1994b), highway safety (Bellis and Grave, 1971; Ferris, 1979), and economical factors.

The management standards shall be adaptable to the specific conditions of each region or landscape crossed in order to optimize the positive impacts. Savings generated by fewer mowings will be reinvested in part for new landscapings and their maintenance, as well as the planting of shrubs and trees along highway rights-of-way. In addition to having a positive impact on the landscape, tree planting will play a positive role in carbon dioxide fixation in order to reduce harmful effects of climate change. Objectives of this paper are to present the results of the first year of monitoring that aims at evaluating the overall biodiversity values of rights-of-way in southern Québec and comparing over the three-year period, the experimental sites where the new approach is being used with other sites still managed with the traditional method. The benefits of the new approach on plant and animal diversity and on the quality of the habitats will then be evaluated.

METHODS (EXPERIMENTAL DESIGN)

In 1998, three experimental stretches of roads varying in length from 3 to 7 km were established in different landscape settings, as follows: Partially forested (along highway A-40, Donnacona), Agricultural (along highway A-20, St-Hyacinthe), and Suburban (along highway A-573, Québec City). These stretches of roads were clearly identified by signs announcing the experimental project. Started in 1998 and originally slated for three years, the project was extended to five years, considering that the scientific monitoring was begun only in 1999 regarding the biological aspects and in 2000 for the visual impact (see Discussion).

Plant and animal communities are currently being monitored by specialists from the Université du Québec à Trois-Rivières and the Canadian Wildlife Service (Environment Canada). For flora, special attention will be given to the specific composition, the height and the proliferation of harmful species. For fauna, the specialists will be monitoring the bird population, small mammals, amphibians, reptiles and insects. Just like the plant species, special attention will be paid to any species that could be harmful to human and particularly to farmlands according to information provided by the existing literature (Bellis and Grave, 1971; Perris, 1979; Oxley et al., 1974). A follow-up on road kills will be carried out to assess the impact of the new method of managing roadside vegetation on the number of animal deaths.

RESULTS AND DISCUSSION

After the first summer (1999) of intensive plant and animal sampling, some interesting facts came to light.

Table 1. Summary of the new approach for using and managing roadside vegetation

Vegetation management	1 Middle ditch	2 Inner slope	3, 4 Green shoulder	5 Outer slope	6 Side ditch	7 Embankment
Existing situation	• Generally wet environment • High vegetation • Periodic mowing • Occasional digging	• Moderately drained environment • Low herbaceous vegetation • Periodic mowing	• Meadows • Annuals adapted to a dry, impoverished environment (e.g. ragweed) • Periodic mowing	• Moderately drained • Low herbaceous vegetation • Periodic mowing	• Wet environment • High vegetation (sometimes shrubby) • Cutting (variable) • Occasional digging	• Natural environment • Highly variable vegetation and maintenance
Proposals for managing green sections	• No maintenance (ditch shaded by shrubs) except for selective cutting every 10 years • Ditch cleaning using "lower third" method**	• Control of woody plants to maintain a high grassland (every 2 or 3 years) • Planting of shrubs to form hedges	• Mowing 4 times/yr (closer to soil)	• Control of woody plants to maintain high grassland (every 2 or 3 years)	• No cutting • Development of shrubby ground cover • Ditch cleaning using "lower third" method	• No maintenance • Development of fallow land • Planting • A certain control of vegetation to maintain visual openings
Impact of ecological management						
Ecological	• Creation of habitats for microfauna • Diversification of vegetation • Ecological filter	• Diversification of plant and animal species • Diversification of habitats	• Better control of ragweed	• Diversification of plant and animal species • Diversification of habitats • More valued fauna compared to zone 2	• Diversification of plant and animal species • Diversification of habitats • Protection of aquatic milieus • Ecological filter	• Defragmentation of riparian habitats • Development of an ecotone • Diversification of plant and animal species • Diversification of habitats
Landscape	• Integration in landscape	• Makes for a more interesting landscape according to different flowering times • Diversifies the landscape with local variation in plant species	• Transitional zone between road and zones 2 and 5 • Visual showcasing of meadow	• Ensures a visual continuity between zone 7 and the road • Makes for a more interesting landscape according to different flowering times • Diversifies the landscape with local variation in plant species	• Integration with the landscape	• Visual harmonization of the road with surrounding landscape • Structuring of the landscape as perceived by motorists
Economic	• Lower cleaning costs due to decrease in peat formation • Decrease in extent of excavation due to use of "lower third" method	• Lower cutting costs • Investment necessary for planting	• Higher costs compared to current frequency of mowing	• Lower cutting costs	• Lower cleaning costs due to decrease in peat formation • Decrease in extent of excavation due to use of "lower third" method	• Lower cutting costs • Decreased cost of maintaining fences when shaded by forest cover • Investment necessary for planting

Table 1. (continued)

Vegetation management	1 Middle ditch	2 Inner slope	3, 4 Green shoulder	5 Outer slope	6 Side ditch	7 Embankment
Safety	• Partial reduction in night glare for motorists	• Partial reduction in night glare for motorists • Snowtrap effect • Slowing of vehicles that lose control (skidding) • Increase motorists' attention	• Plainer view of guideposts and road signs	• Snowtrap effect • Slows skidding vehicles • Increase motorists' attention	• Snowtrap effect	• Snowtrap effect

*These sections are referred to in Fig. 1.
**Maintenance method not affecting vegetation alongside ditches.

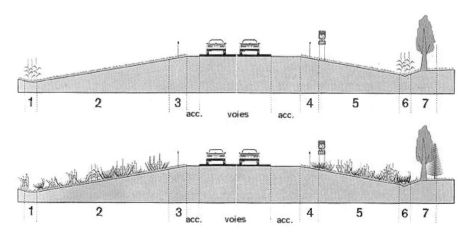

Fig. 1. Different highway areas regarding vegetation management, southern Québec.

Preliminary results of vegetation studies suggest that plant diversity is lower in the agriculturally intensive zone (187 species) compared to the partially forested zone (225 species) and the suburban zone (193 species) (Table 2). Such differences may reflect the influence of adjacent vegetation and the past mowing history of the site. For each zone, the sites with the highest frequency of mowing had the lowest plant diversity (Table 2). To evaluate the distribution and abundance of an aggressive species of reed-grass (*Phragmites communis*) a parallel study is being conducted. Water availability seems to play an important role on the height of these plants whereas adjacent habitats and the frequency of mowing seem to influence its distribution. The species is widespread in agricultural habitats and only scattered in the two other regions (Table 3). These patches will be monitored throughout the study to evaluate colonization rate.

The faunal composition of the three study sites has been evaluated. The results after the first year reveal a moderate diversity of insect groups, although a greater abundance within some of these groups such as Coleoptera, Collembola, and Hymenoptera (Fig. 2). The roadside habitats near forests appear to have the best insect diversity, followed by suburban and farming sites. Higher densities of insects were observed in late summer and that, for each study site (Fig. 3). Small mammals were also studied and findings show the highest diversity near forested habitats. Amphibians and reptiles seem to be rare in the agricultural landscape. The program of preservation of fragmented habitats will probably help creating corridor effects sustaining an animal life that is more diversified and less exposed to road influences.

Finally, observations of the bird community indicate that rights-of-way on farming sites were used by less species but by a greater number of individuals compared to other sites (Table 4). In the forested landscape, 51 different species were monitored compared to 25 species in the agricultural sites and 33 in the suburban one. In addition, there were fewer individuals and species observed in the highway corridor (all sites combined) than in the adjacent zone (51 species and 4271 individuals compared to 40 species

Table 2. General site characteristics and overall plant diversity based on 1999 vegetation sampling. Species were identified in permanent 1 m^2 quadrants ($n = 120$–150 per site) as well as in large scale surveys along 250 m stretch of the highway right-of-way located in southern Québec and totaling more than 2 km per site

	Agricultural	Partially forested	Suburban
Species richness	187	225	193
Number of plant families	47	52	41
Most frequent species	Festuca rubra	Vicia cracca	Agropyron repens
	Phragmites communis	Poa pratensis	Agrostis alba
	Poa pratensis	Taraxacum officinale	Taraxacum officinale
	Vicia cracca	Agropyron repens	Vicia cracca
	Taraxacum officinale	Agrostis alba	Poa pratensis

Table 3. Abundance, density and size of Phragmites communities in 1999 within the three experimental sites of the pilot project along highway rights-of-way in southern Québec

	Agricultural	Partially forested	Suburban
Number of colonies	Continuous	3	10
Size of colonies (m^2), $x \pm SE$	n/a	94 ± 33	32 ± 19
Linear proportion of right-of-way occupied by phragmites	66.7%	0.8%	1.3%
Density (shoot/m^2), $x \pm SE$	118 ± 8	94 ± 24	78 ± 19
Maximum height (m), $x \pm SE$	0.88 ± 0.08	1.98 ± 0.41	1.78 ± 0.18

and 1497 individuals, respectively). After the first year of monitoring, the results suggest no differences in the abundance and diversity of the bird community between the new approach and the traditional management method; the number of species varied from 34 to 49 whereas the total of number of individuals recorded ranged from 1160 to 1578 with no apparent relationship to mowing frequencies. Over the next two years, the quality of the habitats will probably increase in the three sites leading, in particular, to a greater diversity of plants and animals. In case of road-killed animals, sample size was too small to allow any statistical comparison.

The Chair of Landscaping and Environment at Université de Montréal received in 1999 the mandate to monitor the evolution and transformation of the landscape along the three experimental sections over the next three years. The follow-up will be performed using photographic surveys taken from different viewpoints and at different times of the year. The photographs will be used as a basis for the visual analysis. Interviews will also be carried out to find out how road users view the approach. The data from the flora monitoring and its changing situation will be used to predict the future changes in the landscape. No result are available on this aspect of the project.

CONCLUSION

Preliminary results of this study have shown that the value of rights-of-way along southern Québec's highways varied depending on the landscape type where they were located as observed by Meunier et al. (1999a,b, 2000). However, after one year of monitoring, there was no evidence yet of differences in plant and animal abundance or diversity between newly managed and traditionnaly managed studied rights-of-way. We believe, however, that over the next two years, the quality of the habitats will probably increase in the three sites leading, in particular, to a greater diversity of plants and animals as it has been noticed elsewhere in similar experiments (Oetting and Cassel, 1971; Page and Cassel, 1971; Way, 1977; Voorhees and Cassel, 1980; Laursen, 1981; Warner, 1992; Camp and Best, 1993a,b; Bekker, 1995). New way of ecologically managing roadside vegetation along southern Québec's highways should therefore help foster a greater biodiversity of wildlife habitats along roadsides and reduce their defragmentation, enhance the landscape, generate savings, boost highway safety, and in so doing contribute in a certain way to sustainable development. Influence on animal road-kills frequencies still have to be assessed to determine if newly managed areas could act as an ecological trap.

The final data from this monitoring study will be made available in 2002 as regards the biological aspects, and in 2003 for the visual landscaping aspects. We will then be in a position to illustrate the many advantages of this new approach to maintaining highway rights-of-way. Presently, preliminary results at least do not point out any particular drawbacks, only potential benefits. Regarding the landscape, the effect was remarkable right from the first year of implementation, when the wildflowers were left to bloom freely.

As to the communications aspect, much effort has been spent to reach the various groups of the population, mainly those affected by the pilot projects.

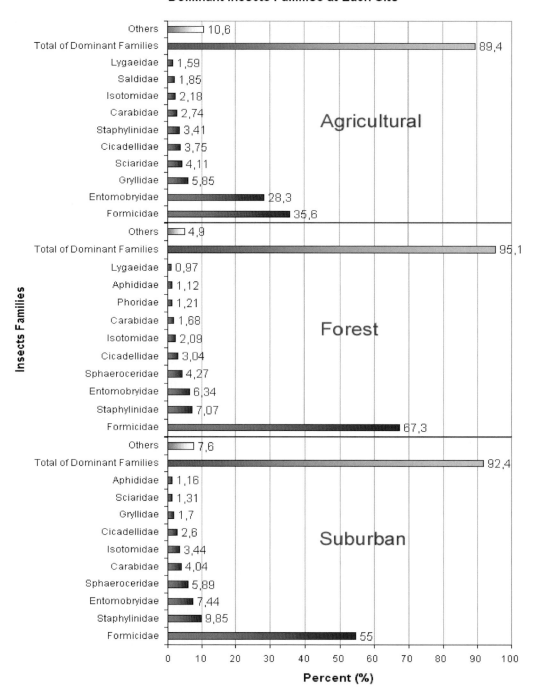

Fig. 2. Dominant insect families at each study site along highway rights-of-way, southern Québec.

Table 4. Overall bird abundance and diversity based on 1999 transect surveys along experimental stretches of highway rights-of-way, southern Québec

	Agricultural	Partially forested	Suburban
Species richness (total no. of species recorded)	25	51	33
Bird abundance (total no. of individuals recorded)	2828	1513	1473
Survey effort (total no. of bird surveys per study site)	9	9	9

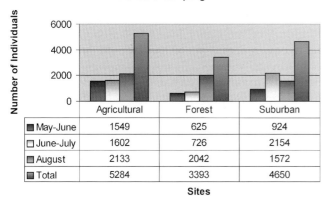

Fig. 3. Comparison of numbers of insects by study site and period of sampling, along highway rights-of-way, southern Québec.

People from the MTQ met with groups representing farmers, municipalities and various interest groups to inform them of the objectives sought by the pilot project. The employee groups of the MTQ were also informed, both as regards senior management and the maintenance teams in the various regions. Although overall the methods were met with approval, this new method has generated much apprehension; however, the pilot project should dispel these concerns. As regards the general public, several television and radio shows were produced, and a folder and many articles appeared in newspapers and magazines. A second wave of public awareness campaigns is expected to take place when the new method will be applied on a larger scale. To date, the bulk of public opinion has been very positive and often quite enthusiastic, to such an extent that many regions have been prompted by public pressure to manage certain stretches of highway in accordance with the new methods proposed.

REFERENCES

Anonyme. 1994. La gestion extensive des dépendances vertes routières. Ministère de l'Environnement de France, Direction de la nature et des paysages, et du Ministère de l'Équipement, des Transports et du Tourisme de France, Service d'études techniques des routes et autoroutes. 115 pp. + annexes.

Bekker, G.J. 1995. Fragmentation and roas-infrastructure in the Netherlands: From history to future. In: Environmental Concerns in Rights-of-Way Management. J.R. Williams, J.W. Goodrich-Mahoney, J.R. Wisniewski, and J. Wisniewski, eds. Elsevier science, pp. 359–365.

Bellis, E.D. and H.B. Graves. 1971. Deer mortality on a Pennsylvania interstate homa. University of Oklahoma Press.

Bennett, A.F. 1991. Roads, Roadsides and Wildlife Conservation: A Review. Nature Conservation 2: The Role of Corridors. D.A. Saunders and R.J. Hobbs, eds. Surrey Beatty and Sons. pp. 99–118.

Bennett, A.F. 1992. Restoring connectivity to fragmented landscapes: Does roadside vegetation have a role? Victorian Nat. Vol., 109(4): 105–111.

Camp, M. and L.B. Best. 1993a. Nest density and nesting success of birds in roadsides adjacent to rowcrop fields. Am. Midl. Nat., 131: 347–358.

Camp, M. and L.B. Best. 1993b. Bird abundance and species richness in roadsides adjacent to Iowa rowcrop fields. Wildl. Soc. Bull., 21: 315–325.

Coumoul, H. and P. Chavaren. 1995. Guide d'entretien des dépendances vertes. Autoroute du sud de la France. 66pp.

Drake, L. and B. Kirchner. 1987. Protecting remnant natural communities along rural roadsides. Natural Areas Journal, 7(2): 79–80.

Farmar-Bowes, Q. 1997. Implementing the national protocol system down-under: Coperative management device for biodiversity conservation on roasd corridors in Australia in Environmental Concerns in Rights-of-Way Management. J.R. Williams, J.W. Goodrich-Mahoney, J.R. Wisniewski, and J. Wisniewski, eds. Elsevier Science.

Ferris, C.R. 1979. Effects of Interstate 95 on breeding birds in northern Maine. Journal of Wildlife Management, 43: 421–427.

Jaarsma, C.F. and F.V. Langevelde. 1997. Right-of-way management and habitat fragmentation: an integral approach with the spatial concept of the traffic calmed rural areas. In: Environmental Concerns in Rights-of-Way Management. J.R. Williams, J.W. Goodrich-Mahoney, J.R. Wisniewski, and J. Wisniewski, eds. Elsevier Science.

Laursen, K. 1981. Birds of roadside verges and the effect of mowing on frequency and distribution. Biological Conservation, 20 (1981): 59–68.

Meuiner, F.D., C. Gauriat, C. Verheyden, and C. Jouventin. 1998. Végétation des dépendances vertes autoroutières: Influences d'un mode de gestion extensif et du milieu traversé. Rev. Ecol. Terre Vie, 53: 97–121.

Meunier, F.D., C. Verheyden, and P. Jouventin. 1999a. Bird communities of highway verges: Influence of adjacent habitat and roadside management. Acta Oecologia, 20: 1–13.

Meunier, F.D., J. Corbin, C. Verheyden, and C. Jouventin, 1999b. Effects of landscape type and extensive management on use of motorway roadsides by small mammals. Can. J. Zool., 77: 108–117.

Meunier, F.D., C. Verheyden, and C. Jouventin. 2000. Use of roadsides by diurnal raptors in agricultural landscapes. Biol. Conservation, 92: 291–298.

Noss, R.F. 1991. Landscape connectivity: Different functions at different scales. In: Landscape Linkages and Biodiversity. W.E. Hudson, ed. Island Press, Washington, DC 197 p., pp. 27–39.

Oetting, R.B. and J.F. Cassell. 1971. Waterfowl nesting on interstate highway right-of-way in North Dakota. J. Wildl. Manage, 35(4): 774–781.

Oxley, D.J., M.B. Fenton, and G.R. Carmody. 1974. The effect of roads on populations of small mammals. Journal of Applied Ecology, 11: 51–59.

Page, R.D. and J.F. Cassell. 1971. Waterfowl nesting on a railroad right-of-way in North Dakota. J. Wildl. Manage., 35(3): 544–549.

Reijnen, R. and R. Foppen. 1994a. The effects of car traffic on breeding bird populations in woodland, I. Evidence of reduced habitat quality for willow warblers (Phylloscopus trochilus) breeding close to a highway. Journal of Applied Ecology, 31: 85–94.

Reijnen, R. and R. Foppen. 1994b. The effects of car traffic on breeding bird populations in woodland. II. Breeding dispersal of male willow warblers (Phylloscopus trochilus) in relation to the proximity of a highway. Journal of Applied Ecology, 31: 95–101.

Voorhees, L.D. and J.F. Cassel. 1980. Highway right-of-way: moving versus succession as related to duck nesting. J. Wildl. Mange. 44(1): 155–163.

Warner, R.E. 1992. Nest ecology of grassland passerines on road rights-of-way in central Illinois. Biol. Conserv., 59: 1–7.

Way, J.M. 1977. Roadside verges and conservation in Britain: A review. Biol. Conserv., 12: 65–74.

BIOGRAPHICAL SKETCHES

Yves Bédard
Ministère des Transports du Québec, 475, boulevard de l'Atrium, 4e étage, Québec (Canada) G1H 7H9

Yves Bédard received his MSc in Biology from Laval University, Quebec City, and has worked for the Quebec Department of Transportation for 17 years. He has conducted numerous environmental studies for a variety of large-scale highway projects and led several research projects on the ecology of habitats in highway corridors. Plant life, wildlife and ecology have always been the focus of his concerns.

Daniel Trottier
Ministère des Transports du Québec, 475, boulevard de l'Atrium, 4e étage, Québec (Canada) G1H 7H9

Daniel Trottier has a degree from the School of Landscape Architecture at the University of Montreal. He has worked for the Quebec Department of Transportation since 1985. For more than 14 years, Mr. Trottier has collaborated on many highway corridor planning projects to ensure the harmonious integration of highways with their surrounding landscapes — projects in which he has always made trees the focal point. He has also actively participated in several research projects on the use and role of vegetation in highway corridors.

Luc Bélanger
Environnement Canada, Service canadien de la faune, 1141, de l'Église, P.O. Box 10100, Sainte-Foy (Canada) G1V 4H5

Luc Bélanger holds a PhD in Biology from Laval University, Quebec City. He is head of Evaluation, Research and Development, Habitat Division, at the Canadian Wildlife Service (Environment Canada, Quebec Region). He has worked at the Canadian Wildlife Service since 1989. His research program examines all aspects of the conservation and integrated management of wildlife habitats in southern Quebec agroecosystems.

Jean-Pierre Bourassa
Université du Québec à Trois-Rivières, Département de Chimie-biologie, C.P. 500, Trois-Rivières, Québec (Canada) G9A 5H7

Jean-Pierre Bourassa has a PhD in Entomology from the University Pierre and Marie Curie of Paris, France. He has been a professor in the Department of Chemistry and Biology at the University of Quebec at Trois Rivières for more than 30 years. His research in entomology led first to an interest in mosquitoes and his founding of the Biting Insect Research Group, while his work in recent years has focused on all aspects of biodiversity (especially insect, amphibian and small mammal) in natural habitats associated with agricultural land in southern Quebec.

Nancy Champagne
Université du Québec à Trois-Rivières, Département de Chimie-biologie, C.P. 500, Trois-Rivières, Québec (Canada) G9A 5H7

Nancy Champagne is enrolled in the Master's program in Environmental Science at the Department of Chemistry and Biology of the University of Quebec at Trois Rivières.

José Gérin-Lajoie
Université du Québec à Trois-Rivières, Département de Chimie-biologie, C.P. 500, Trois-Rivières, Québec (Canada) G9A 5H7

José Gérin-Lajoie is enrolled in the Master's program in Environmental Science at the Department of Chemistry and Biology of the University of Quebec at Trois Rivières.

Gaston Lacroix
Université du Québec à Trois-Rivières, Département de Chimie-biologie, C.P. 500, Trois-Rivières, Québec (Canada) G9A 5H7

Gaston Lacroix is enrolled in the Master's program in Environmental Science at the Department of Chemistry and Biology of the University of Quebec at Trois Rivières.

Esther Lévesque
Université du Québec à Trois-Rivières, Département de Chimie-biologie, C.P. 500, Trois-Rivières, Québec (Canada) G9A 5H7

Esther Lévesque received her Ph.D. in Plant Ecology from University of Toronto, Ontario. She has been a professor in the Department of Chemistry and Biology at the University of Quebec at Trois Rivières for several years. She is interested in all aspects of plant ecology in regions ranging from the tundra of Arctic Canada to southern Quebec, where the landscape is dominated by human activity.

Roadside Vegetation Management on Québec's Highways: A Visual Landscape Monitoring Research Project

Philippe Poullaouec-Gonidec, Gérald Domon, Sylvain Paquette, and Christiane Montpetit

Inspired by ecological, economical, landscape, and security concerns, the ministère des Transports du Québec recently initiated an alternative method to manage highway roadside vegetation. This method uses differential mowing to allow natural regeneration along three experimental corridors. As a part of an overall monitoring program, this landscape monitoring research attempts: (1) to characterize the landscapes generated by this new management in order to assess the changing visual experience and the users' perceptions; (2) to evaluate the achievement of the project's objectives (visual diversity, integration, etc.), and, finally, (3) to provide recommendations for improvement. This paper presents the original methodology developed to attain these goals. First, key viewpoints are selected using a two-step visual inventory. Using GIS, potential observation areas are identified based on typical situations derived from the highway layout, slope, viewshed and land use characteristics. These key viewpoints are then precisely located from a systematic visual analysis. Second, diverse mediums (panoramic photographs, videotapes) monitor the roadside vegetation changes (2000–2002) affecting visual experience. In addition to expert analysis, open-ended questions and *in visu* semantic scale tests produce a qualitative evaluation of highway users' attitudes. This evaluation explores overall landscape experiences, how roadside vegetation characteristics improve driving enjoyment and affect users' preferences.

Keywords: Aesthetic, landscape monitoring, Québec, roadside vegetation, user's perception

INTRODUCTION

This landscape monitoring research project is situated at the junction of two processes. On the one hand, the ministère des Transports du Québec (MTQ) recently initiated an alternative method to manage highway roadside vegetation reflecting ecological, economical, landscape, and security concerns. On three experimental highway corridors (Fig. 1), each representative of distinct highway contexts (forest, agriculture, and peri-urban areas), this method uses differential mowing to allow the natural regeneration of vegetation. From this perspective, the MTQ pursues landscape objectives (e.g., harmony, integration with surrounding context, etc.) for which landscape monitoring is necessary to characterize and assess vegetation changes that affect visual, aesthetic and sensory qualities. On the other hand, the Chaire en paysage et environnement de l'Université de Montréal (CPEUM) has already developed a general landscape monitoring framework in order to facilitate decision-making processes (Poullaouec-Gonidec and Domon, 1999). Within this context, the integrated roadside vegetation management project constitutes a unique opportunity to improve this framework and develop new tools for landscape management.

This visual landscape monitoring research pursues a three-fold objective. It attempts: (1) to characterize the landscape experience generated by the new vegetation management in order to assess the changes

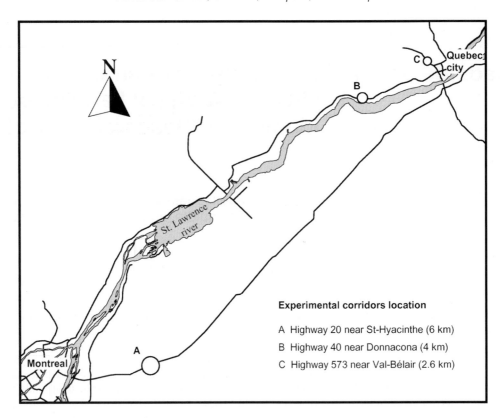

Fig. 1. Location of the three experimental highway roadside vegetation management projects in Québec (Canada).

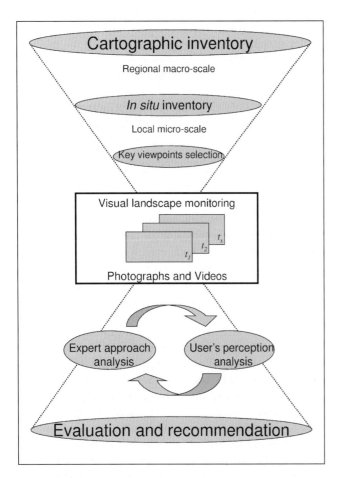

Fig. 2. Visual landscape monitoring research design.

in visual experience (expert approach) and the users' perceptions; (2) to evaluate the achievement of the experimental project's objectives (visual diversity, integration, etc.). Finally, this research endeavors to (3) develop a visual landscape monitoring system which includes the methodological strategy retained, recommendations for improvement and a didactic multimedia tool for results divulging and heightening public awareness. To successfully fulfil these objectives, it is imperative to develop innovative monitoring strategies adapted to the characteristics of the new vegetation management program.

In this way, the current paper gives particular attention to the original methodology developed that integrates the expert as well as the user's perception approaches (Fig. 2). Thus, it successively presents the key viewpoint selection strategy put forward and the landscape monitoring program conditions. It then gives an overview of the way visible landscape changes generated by the new roadside vegetation management are analyzed as well as the methodological design used to assess perceived landscape transformations from the highway users' perspectives.

METHODOLOGICAL FRAMEWORK

Landscape characterization and evaluation methodological approaches are numerous and diverse (Zube et al., 1982; Domon et al., 1997). Even if four groups of conceptual positions or paradigms can be distinguished (expert, cognitive, psychophysic, and experiential), the respective contribution of each of them is recognized and the combination of different approaches necessary (Smardon et al., 1986). However valuable, this combination of approaches is, in fact, rarely put into practice. By revealing and characterizing highway landscape on the basis of the visual landscape transformation (expert approach) and the user's perception, this research specifically aims to adopt such an integrated approach. In this manner, it constitutes a new and original methodological contribution.

Key viewpoints selection
Visual inventory methods generally help to provide a relatively exhaustive portrait of the visible landscape features. In the specific context of highway rights-of-way, landscapes scenes that could be monitored are nearly unlimited given that highway user are continuously in motion. Under such conditions, it is necessary to develop strategies capable of identifying and pointing out landscape situations that constitute a significant visual experience for the highway users. The cartographic inventory and the *in situ* visual inventory presented in the next sections attempts to precisely identify such significant key viewpoints.

Cartographic inventory
The contribution of cartographic and geographical information systems (GIS) for visual and landscape characterization studies is well recognized (Bishop and Hulse, 1994; Pâquet et al., 1994). Used at a preliminary stage of the visual inventory in this project, GIS tools provided a cartographic synthesis of the potential observation areas. Given this context, the cartographic inventory represents a determining methodological step considering that the MTQ intends to generalize the new roadside vegetation management to the whole of Québec's highway network.

Based on the highway visual experience described by many authors (Tunnard and Pushkarev, 1963; Appleyard et al., 1964), some visual effects appear to act more strongly on the driver's visual attention. Among these, horizontal curves, upgrade or downgrade slopes, lateral enclosures or visual openings are of special interest. Some of them appear to modify the driver's visual experience by bringing more roadside into view (e.g., horizontal curve, upgrade slope, etc.) while others seem to contribute to focus the highway user's visual attention on the surrounding landscape (downgrade slope, lateral openings, etc.).

In order to bring out these visual effects, the cartographic inventory attempts to institute a preliminary characterization of the experimental highway corridors on the basis of the highway layout, slope, land use, and viewshed (Fig. 3). Elevation, hydrographic, and highway network information provided from the

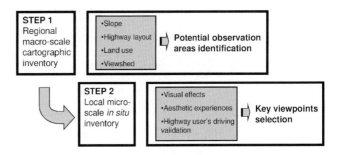

Fig. 3. Two step visual inventory.

1:20,000 scale cartographic database of the ministère des Ressources Naturelles du Québec is processed with Map Info (Version 4.1) and Vertical Mapper (Version 2.5) software. Land use is interpreted using 1:40,000 scale black and white aerial photographs (1994). The land use classification includes five categories: forest, open land, abandoned land, urban land, and hydrographic network. Based on the elevation data, potential views are spatially delimited for each experimental site using the Vertical Mapper (V.2.5) viewshed analysis tool. To do this, a multiple viewshed analysis is performed at an observation height of 1.2 m (corresponding to the car driver's vision) at points scattered along the highway corridor. As suggested by Pâquet et al. (1994), 500 m separates each point, a distance corresponding approximately to the foreground length. The resulting visibility frequency derives from a multiple viewshed area overlay. Thus, a cartographic synthesis resulting from topographic (Fig. 4), viewshed (Fig. 5), highway layout, and land use characteristics (Fig. 6) helps to identify potential observation areas. Ultimately, this cartographic inventory attempts to single out typical situations which appear to direct visual attention on the roadside vegetation or on the surrounding landscape. The following *in situ* visual inventory provides a more detailed examination of these situations.

In situ visual inventory
Before the selection of definitive key viewpoints, an *in situ* visual analysis is completed for each experimental highway corridor. While it contributes to the validation of visual effects identified at the cartographic inventory stage, this two-way inventory allows the identification of visually significant scenes (Fig. 3). A five step *en route* methodological strategy composes this analysis, with a multidisciplinary team of four experts participating in each of the stages. An overview of the visual experience perceived when driving through the highway experimental corridor is first obtained in order to formulate general impressions of the roadside as well as the surrounding area. Second, a low speed (10 km/h) tour allows to exhaustively describe all visual sequences (curves, visual corridors, lateral openings, etc.) and roadside elements (roadsigns, pylons, vegetation, buildings, etc.) which

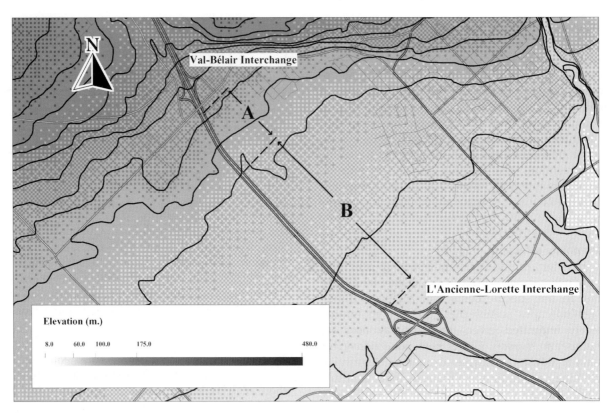

Fig. 4. Topographical situations along the Highway 573 experimental site (1:20,000). Highway section A corresponds to steeper slope (85–100 m) than section B (65–80 m).

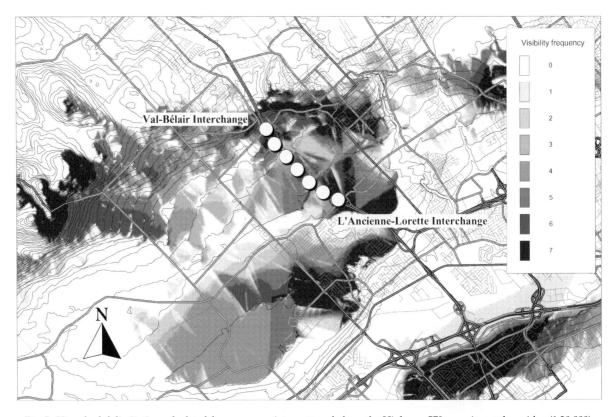

Fig. 5. Viewshed delimitation calculated from seven points scattered along the Highway 573 experimental corridor (1:20,000).

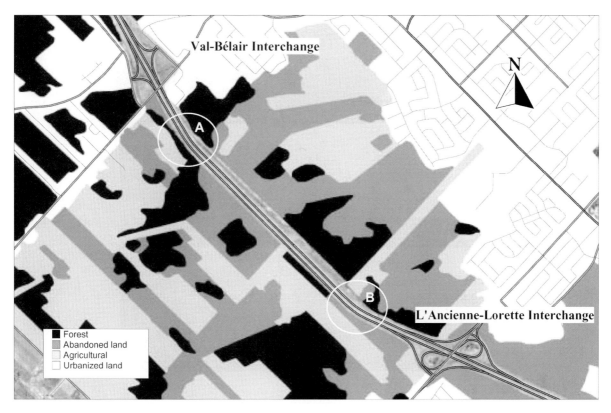

Fig. 6. Land use and highway layout of the Highway 573 experimental corridor (1:20,000). A and B sectors indicate anticipated curve effects.

capture the user's visual attention. At this stage, potential viewpoints are selected. A detailed visual analysis grid (characterization of the foreground, the middle ground and the background, landmark identification, rupture element, etc.) is completed to describe each viewpoint. A 100 km/h tour in the right lane of the experimental corridor that corresponds to a highway driving situation is then done to validate and, if necessary correct the key viewpoints selected. At this stage, a set of key viewpoints situated 60 cm into the highway's right shoulder as well as a set of complementary observation points (lateral angle views and contextual observation points) is identified (Fig. 7). For the purpose of this monitoring program, a total of 28 key viewpoints were selected. Finally, panoramic frontal view photographs and right lane frontal videos tracking (at 100 km/h) are used to document these key viewpoints and the highway experimental corridors in driving situations.

Landscape monitoring

Following examples of visual monitoring initiated particularly in France ("Observatoire photographique du paysage," ministère de l'Environnement, 1996), this visual landscape monitoring survey is based on a set of precise technical conditions which are strictly observed. The observation mediums and the technical monitoring conditions within these specifications are briefly described hereafter.

Documenting landscape changes over time

Color panoramic photographs (120–180°) obtained through QuickTime Software (Apple Computer Inc., 1997) constitutes the main observation medium upon which the monitoring project is founded. When integrated with QuickTime technology, the options given by these multiple shot panoramic photographs provide a visual field that is close to the *in situ* visual experience of the highway user. Moreover, considering the new possibilities resulting from multimedia systems, panoramic photographs provide more flexibility for analyses related either to the expert approach (visual monitoring) or to the user's perception data (e.g., preference tests).

For all monitoring projects, the initial conditions are of particular importance. These conditions must be strictly observed during the entire monitoring period in order to evaluate and analyze the observed phenomenon changes with the same accuracy. Thus, the photographic shot series (180°-view angle) for each of the key viewpoints selected and precisely identified on the shoulder's highway is taken with consistent optical height, lens format and orientation angle (Fig. 8). Particular photographic shooting conditions (weather, traffic conditions, etc) are also noted. As previously mentioned, scanned images are added using the QuickTime system. Panoramas created for each key viewpoint are used for further analysis (expert and user's perception approach). During the first monitoring year, photographic shots are taken every two

Fig. 7. Key viewpoint illustration of (a) a curve situation; (b) a lateral wooded screen situation; (c) a background predominance view, and (d) a wide-open view (Highway 20 near St-Hyacinthe).

weeks from May to October 2000 and once a month during the winter. If necessary, the photographic shot frequency for the second and the third monitoring years will be adjusted on the basis of the first year's (2000) roadside vegetation changes examination.

Unlike the panoramic photographs that capture fixed images, the frontal oriented video allows for movement, a condition that remains specific to the highway driving visual experience. Although video technology scans a relatively narrow visual field compared to standard driving conditions, it nevertheless provides more flexible manipulation possibilities in the context of recreating similar highway driving situation under laboratory conditions (Mertes et al., 1991). Moreover, many studies take advantage of the video technology at the user's perception level of evaluation (Craik, 1975; Evans and Woods, 1980; Feimer, 1984). From this perspective, video sequences are recognized for soliciting a wide range of individual interpretations (Bishop and Hulse, 1994) when compared to standard photographs. Thus, in addition to the photographic monitoring, frontal oriented video trackings

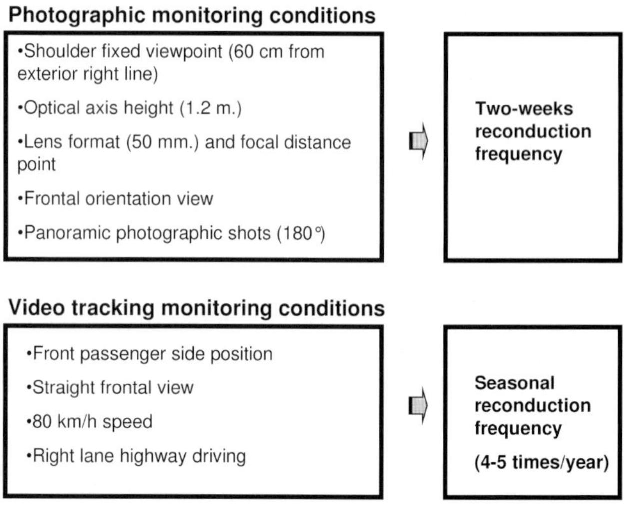

Fig. 8. Visual landscape monitoring conditions.

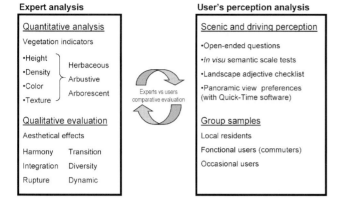

Fig. 9. Expert and user's perception analysis frameworks.

taken from the highway's right lane are seasonally documented in order to monitor the visual experience in movement (Fig. 8).

Analyzing landscape changes

As previously mentioned, landscape transformation analysis performed on the monitoring visual documentation collected is based on a combination of two distinct but complementary conceptual strategies: namely, the expert approach and the users' perceptions analysis.

Expert approach

From the expert perspective, three distinct image analyses are proposed (Fig. 9). A preliminary quantitative characterization of the roadside vegetation which affects the visual experience (height, density, color, texture related to each vegetation stage) is accomplished. Then, a qualitative reading of the visual changes bring out the aesthetic quality and the sensory nature of the changing landscapes. This qualitative evaluation is particularly useful to compare the expert approach evaluation with the aesthetic preferences observed from the user's perception analysis (see next section). On the basis of these complementary analyses, the achievement of the MTQ's landscape related objectives (visual diversity, integration, harmony, etc.) is assessed. The originally proposed landscape objective criteria are subjected to modifications or additions as the monitoring project advances and the user's perception results follow.

Furthermore, given the large amount of photographs resulting from the current monitoring project (more than 500 panoramic photographs per year), a semi-automatic image analysis system will be explored on an experimental basis. Such a system, derived from the development of content-based image retrieval systems (Nastar et al., 1998), would allow to classify and index, as well as perform multiple queries on the iconographic database (photographs and videos). This system would allow comparisons and contrasts based on quantitative as well as qualitative visual characteristics that contributed to the highway landscape's evolution.

Highway user's perception approach

The originality of this visual landscape monitoring research lies in its intent to integrate the expert approach as well as the user's landscape perception analysis. In this context, the landscape perception evaluation aims specifically: (1) to reveal dimensions (ecological, aesthetic, or functional) which appear to mark the users' overall experiences of the highway corridors under the new roadside vegetation management; (2) to show how roadside vegetation attributes improve driving enjoyment; and (3) how these attributes distinctly affect the highway user groups' preferences.

The proposed combination of qualitative analyses attempts more to acquire a comprehension of the predominant factors susceptible to influence user's aesthetic satisfaction and highway driving enjoyability than to validate or statistically generalized hypothesis. User group perception surveys are scheduled every year of the landscape monitoring project for a total of three survey sets. A brief description of the survey design including the population groups studied and the documentary sources used is presented in the following paragraphs.

User perception survey design

Three distinct highway user groups constitute the experimental sample population: (i) functional or commuting users (individuals using highway for work or business purposes); (ii) local residents familiar with the surrounding area; and (iii) occasional users taking the highway to touristic and recreational destinations, who would be more likely to focus their attention on landscapes attributes. Like the work of Brush et al. (2000), population subsamples are selected from a wide variety of local and regional associations: business, tourist, farmer, roadside resident, car driver, and regional planning professional. All subsamples are composed of ten individuals. A total of 30 subjects are then expected to participate during every year of the monitoring project (2000, 2001, and 2002). The size of these samples is sufficiently important to achieve objectives of the proposed qualitative survey.

The survey design is devised to assess perception in a progressive manner, starting with general impressions with regard to the highway landscape experience to specific aesthetic preferences. Each subject has to complete a questionnaire, which includes five distinct parts:

1. During video sequence viewing, subjects are first invited to express spontaneous impressions as well as to respond to open-ended questions. Answers and commentaries are recorded and transcribed. Then, a transcription content analysis helps to generate categories of discussion with regard to the overall representation of the experimental vegetation management project.

2. Second, from a selected set of panoramic photographs showing diverse roadside vegetation situations and successions, participants are asked to identify their preferred views. Full panoramas created with QuickTime technology allows each participant unrestricted horizontal movement. An open-ended questionnaire aims to identify elements which attract the participant's attention and whether they correspond to a pleasant or unpleasant aesthetical experience. The subjects are invited to justify their answers.
3. Third, attitude scale tests are completed by subjects from a set of selected views. Scales are constructed from a selection of binomial adjectives (e.g., diversified–monotonous; ordered–disordered) commonly used to describe landscape scenes (Craik, 1975; Evans and Wood, 1980; Feimer, 1984) as well as from preferences scales (e.g., favorable–unfavorable). Criteria underlying view selection are based on variables identified at the expert analysis stage which appear to influence visual experience (e.g., standard roadside vegetation management vs. experimental situations; year a vs. year b; spring vs. summer vegetation; flowers vs. scrubs).
4. In order to bring out factors which appear to act on expressed perceptions, information related to participants' sociodemographic status (age, occupation, sex, etc.) as well as to use and site familiarity (leisure activities, highway use frequency and motives; rural, suburban or urban place of birth, actual place of residence, etc.) are collected. A multivariate analysis will help to discern dominant tendencies with regard to the individual variability observed.
5. Finally, a set of questions focusing on the overall appreciation of the MTQ's roadside vegetation management experimental project and its further development is presented to every subject.

As mentioned above, in order to compare expert and non-expert points of view (Fig. 9), relationships existing between the user's perceptions and qualitative expert evaluations are systematically examined through multivariate analysis.

INTERESTS AND GOALS OF THE HIGHWAY ROADSIDE VEGETATION MONITORING

The interest in this monitoring project initiated by the MTQ and CPEUM is threefold. First, on landscape research level, this project allows the development of an original methodological strategy that combines expert and users' perception approaches as well as both quantitative analysis and qualitative aesthetic evaluation. Second, the highway landscape dynamics revealed during the three years monitoring project will enable to provide documented and informative recommendations for the improvement of the roadside vegetation management program. Third, the creation of a multimedia tool (available on CD-ROM or Internet) integrating multiple observation mediums (photographs, QuickTime panoramas, video sequences) will help to divulge monitoring results as well as to serve didactic and public awareness purposes from a user-friendly interface.

ACKNOWLEDGEMENTS

We gratefully acknowledge Tracey Hesse for editing. This research is made in collaboration with Daniel Trottier and Guy Bédard from the ministère des Transports du Québec.

REFERENCES

Appleyard, D., K. Lynch, and J.R. Myer. 1964. The View from the Road. MIT Press, Cambridge, MA. 64 p.

Apple Computer Inc. 1997. QuickTime VR Authoring Studio, Cupertino, CA.

Bishop, I.D. and D.W. Hulse. 1994. Prediction of the scenic beauty using mapped data and geographic information systems. Landscape and Urban Planning, 30: 59–70.

Brush, R., R.E. Chenoweth, and T. Barman. 2000. Group differences in the enjoyability of driving through rural landscapes. Landscape and Urban Planning, 47: 39–45.

Craik, K.H. 1975. Individual variations in Landscape description. In: Landscape Assessment: Values, Perceptions and Resources. E.H. Zube, R.O. Brush, and J.G. Fabos, eds. Dowden, Hutchinson & Ross, Inc., Stroudsburg, PA. pp. 130–150.

Domon, G., G. Beaudet, and O. Lacasse. 1997. Les méthodes de caractérisation des paysages: revue des approches visuelles, éco-géographiques et spatio-temporelles. Chaire en paysage et environnement, Université de Montréal.

Evans, G.W. and K.W. Wood. 1980. Assessment of environmental aesthetics in scenic highway corridors. Environment and Behavior, 12: 255–273.

Feimer, N.R. 1984. Environmental perception: the effects of media, evaluative context, and observer sample. Journal of Environmental Psychology, 4: 61–80.

Mertes, J.D., R.C. Smardon, and A.J. Miller. 1991. Applications of video technology in landscape architecture and environmental design. Design Methods and Theories, 25: 1353–1368.

Ministère de l'environnement, Direction de la nature et des paysages. 1996. L'Observatoire photographique du paysage. Mode d'emploi. Bureau du paysage, Paris.

Nastar, C., M. Mitschke, C. Meilhac, and N. Boujemaa. 1998. Surfimage: A flexible content-based image retrieval system. ACM-Multimedia 1998, Bristol, England.

Pâquet, J., L. Bélanger, and M.A. Liboiron. 1994. Aménagement de la qualité visuelle: Inventaire de la sensibilité des paysages, Ministère des Ressources Naturelles. Service de l'Aménagement Forestier.

Poullaouec-Gonidec, P. and G. Domon. 1999. Nature et contribution du suivi de l'évolution des paysages: le cas du SMVP (système de monitoring visuel des paysages). In: Actes du 4e colloque international des spécialistes francophones en évaluation d'impacts. Glasgow, Écosse, pp. 213–234.

Smardon, R.C., T. Costello, and H. Eggink. 1986. Urban visual description and analysis. In: Foundations for Visual Project Analysis. R.C. Smardon, J.F. Palmer, and J.P. Felleman, eds. John Wiley & Sons, New-York, pp. 115–135.

Tunnard, C. and B. Pushkarev. 1963. Man-Made America: Chaos or Control? Yale University Press, New Haven and London. 479 p.

Zube, E.H., J.L. Sell, and J.G. Taylor. 1982. Landscape perception, research, application and theory. Landscape Planning, 9: 1–35.

BIOGRAPHICAL SKETCHES

Philippe Poullaouec-Gonidec (corresponding author)

Chaire en paysage et environnement, Université de Montréal (CPEUM), C.P. 6128, succursale Centre-ville, Montréal (Québec) Canada, H3C 3J7, Phone: (514) 343-7500, Fax: (514) 343-6771, E-mail: philippe.poullaouec-gonidec@umontreal.ca

Philippe Poullaouec-Gonidec is a landscape architect, head of the Chaire en paysage et environnement (CPEUM) and a full professor at the École d'architecture de paysage de l'Université de Montréal. In 1991, he was guest professor at the École d'architecture de Paris-La-Villette. As a member of many juries, he participates in various national and international urban design competitions. He also conducts many innovative research projects, among which Québec's landscape characterization and landscape cultural invention and re-invention processes represent his major interests. He is the author of many theoretical papers on landscape projects in Québec.

Gérald Domon

Chaire en Paysage et Environnement (CPEUM), Université de Montréal, C.P. 6128, succursale Centre-ville, Montréal (Québec) Canada, H3C 3J7, Phone: (514) 343-6298, Fax: (514) 343-6771, E-mail: gerald.domon@umontreal.ca

Gérald Domon is an associate professor at the Faculté de l'aménagement de l'Université de Montréal where he teaches landscape ecology and rural landscape planning classes. He is regular researcher at the CPEUM, a member of the Groupe de recherche en écologie forestière interuniversitaire (GREFI) and co-director of a broad multidisciplinary research entitled "Haut-Saint-Laurent: Écologie et aménagement."

He has published more than a hundred articles on southern Québec's past and current rural landscape dynamics, landscape characterization tools elaboration as well as on the ecological management of protected areas.

Sylvain Paquette

Chaire en Paysage et Environnement (CPEUM), Université de Montréal, C.P. 6128, succursale Centre-ville, Montréal (Québec) Canada, H3C 3J7, Phone: (514) 343-6111 (ext.: 3899), Fax: (514) 343-6771, E-mail: sylvain.paquette@umontreal.ca

Sylvain Paquette is a PhD candidate at the Faculté de l'aménagement de l'Université de Montréal and a Doctoral Fellow of the Social Sciences and Humanities Research Council of Canada (SSHRC). In addition to his participation in the CPEUM's research projects, his own research manuscripts on southern Québec's landscape dynamics and rural community social recomposition processes have been recently published in *Journal of Rural Studies*, *Landscape and Urban Planning* and *Landscape Research*.

Christiane Montpetit

Chaire en Paysage et Environnement (CPEUM), Université de Montréal, C.P. 6128, succursale Centre-ville, Montréal (Québec) Canada, H3C 3J7, Phone: (514) 343-6111 (ext.: 2760), Fax: (514) 343-6771, E-mail: christiane.montpetit@umontreal.ca

Christiane Montpetit is an anthropologist (PhD, Université de Montréal) and a research agent with the CPEUM. Her noteworthy research activities include a collaboration with Hydro Québec on hydro-electric production and distribution landscape issues, a roadside vegetation visual landscape monitoring project for the ministère des Transport du Québec and a landscape concept definitions research for the ministère des Cultures et des Communications du Québec. She has developed an expertise related to landscape perceptions and environmental sensibilities expressed with regard to several project management implementation contexts.

Natural Regeneration on a Pipeline Right-of-Way in the Boreal Forest of West-Central Saskatchewan

M. Ealey and J. Virgl

Following pipeline construction activities, rights-of-way (ROW) that traverse previously undisturbed landscape units are typically seeded as part of the final reclamation program. Agronomic species are often used in these seed mixtures but there is growing awareness that these species may alter or influence the ecological integrity of the landscape unit disturbed by pipeline construction. We conducted a study on a pipeline ROW to assess the influence agronomic species have on natural secondary succession. The study was also completed to evaluate if there are any ecological impacts or benefits derived from not seeding the disturbance corridor at the end of a reclamation program and if there is significant differences in plant recovery among the three primary work lanes within a pipeline construction ROW. Results from the study indicated there was a significant variation in species richness between seeded and non-seeded areas, indicating that agronomic species pre-empt the reestablishment of a desired endemic community. However, there was not a significant variation between work lanes within the ROW, indicating that typical construction associated with each lane did not influence plant establishment and regeneration.

Keywords: Agronomic species, revegetation, species richness, succession, ecological integrity, vegetation management, species diversity

INTRODUCTION

Following pipeline construction activities, ROW that traverse landscapes units that were previously undisturbed (i.e., retain a native or endemic flora cover) are typically artificially seeded as part of the final reclamation program. The primary objective of this common revegetation practice is to accelerate the establishment of plant cover that in turn will mitigate soil erosion, promote terrain stability, and enhance aesthetics. Secondary goals include the reestablishment of forage cover, provide or assist in the regeneration of wildlife habitat, and, through resource competition, suppress plants that are deemed to be an invasive nuisance and noxious species or otherwise classified as undesirable on pipeline ROW (i.e., tall or large diameter woody species).

Historically in Saskatchewan and else where, seed mixtures used for revegetation programs on reclaimed pipeline ROW were largely comprised of agronomic or exotic/alien species with little regard to the ecological setting to which they were introduced. Usually, agronomic forage species were used due to their availability in commercial quantities, predictability in regards to viability and stand establishment, ease of handling (i.e., specialized equipment is not required for seeding), and most are relatively cheap to purchase. Furthermore, agronomic species have a good ability to withstand grazing, mowing, burning, mechanical, and chemical treatments (Romo and Lawrence, 1990), and there was more knowledge available on how to prepare seed beds, apply the seed, and manage stands of agronomic species in comparison to endemic species (Sims et al., 1984).

Though varieties of agronomic species were, and continue to be, widely used for revegetation programs, there is a growing volume of literature indicating that the introduction of these species to previously undisturbed landscapes can alter the function, structure, and ecological integrity of the natural biota (Simberloff, 1981; Vitousek et al., 1981; D'Antonio and Vitousek, 1992; McCanny et al., 1996). With this awareness, there is an increased desire to investigate and employ alternate ways of reclaiming natural habitats disturbed by pipeline construction and other developments. One growing and popular approach to minimize the use of agronomic mixtures is to utilize seed mixtures that are comprised of plant species that are endemic to the area that has being reclaimed. In addition to minimizing the introduction of exotic species to a natural landscape unit, it is anticipated that the use of native species in seed mixtures will circumvent or manipulate the temporal element associated with ecosystem succession. However, the wide scale use of native species has been compounded by inherent limitations that include: restricted availability in commercial quantities; high seed costs; erratic production of desired seeds; limited information on endemic species ecology and ecosystem processes; difficulties associated with storing and applying the seed; and, seeds are often unpredictable in regards to seed germination, viability, emergence, and survivability (Romo and Lawrence, 1990; Gerling et al. 1996; Pyke and Archer, 1991).

The objectives of this study were to: (1) evaluate natural regeneration or secondary succession of a plant community on a disturbed pipeline ROW, (2) assess if the use of an agronomic seed mixture used to revegetate segments of the ROW pre-empted native species succession, and (3) determine if plant recovery/growth varied among construction lanes (work side, trench area and storage/spoil side) within the ROW. The results of this study should contribute to the information necessary for making recommendations in regards to when it may or may not be necessary to use agronomic or native seed mixtures if the maintenance of ecological integrity is the prime objective of the revegetation program in similar areas. Furthermore, it will help determine if specific revegetation measures may be required for specific activity lanes within a typical pipeline construction ROW.

STUDY AREA AND METHODOLOGY

Study area

The study was conducted on a segment of the TransGas Ltd. (TGL) 20-m wide construction ROW used for the installation of a 500-mm O.D., high-pressure gas pipeline during the summer and autumn of 1995. During construction, all standing vegetation was cleared from the entire ROW, and topsoil/organic material was lifted and salvaged in storage windrows. During the reclamation stage, the ROW was re-contoured, salvaged topsoil/organic material was replaced, and residual slash was spread over the surface to mitigate erosion, provide a source of future organic material, and to create micro-sites (safesites) for germinating or recovering plants. Following completion of clean-up operations, ROW segments extending through natural habitats was aerial seeded with a seed mixture

Table 1. Seed mixture goodsoil to rosetown pipeline — North Spread TransGas

Species (scientific name)[1]	Variety	Percentage of seed mixture	Seeding rate (kg/ha)
Creeping Red Fescue (*Festuca rubra*)	Boreal	41.7	12.72
Timothy (*Phleum pratense*)	Climax	20.8	6.34
Slender Wheatgrass (*Agropyron trachycaulum*)	Revenue	9.2	2.80
Northern Wheatgrass (*Agropyron dasystachyum*)	Elbee	7.5	2.29
White Clover (*Trifolium repens*)	Common	20.8	6.34
Total		**100**	**30.5**

[1] Scientific names taken from Budd's Flora of the Canadian Prairie Provinces (Looman and Best, 1987).

comprised of agronomic species (Table 1). However, a 350-m section of the pipeline ROW within this area was intentionally not seeded. The rational behind this was to establish a plot that could later be used to assess the process of natural secondary succession on pipeline ROW through forested habitats and allow for a comparison analysis between artificially seeded and non-seeded portions of the disturbance corridor.

The ROW is located in the Bronson Upland landscape area of the Mid-boreal Upland Ecoregion of Saskatchewan (Acton et al., 1998). The area experiences a dry sub-humid continental climate characterized by warm summers and cold winters (Hart and Hunt, 1981) with mean daily temperatures ranging from a low of −18.1°C in January to a high of +16.5°C in July (Environment Canada, 1993). Average annual precipitation is approximately 424.2 mm, of which 74% falls as rain and 26% as snow (op.cit.). The terrain is generally characterized by a moderately sloping, hummocky glacial till plain with pockets of glaciofluvial deposits. The dominant soils are gray luvisolic soils that have formed in weakly to moderately calcareous, loamy glacial till (Saskatchewan Soil Survey, 1995). These soils are highly leached, resulting in low organic matter levels and have sandy loam to loam surface textures. The predominate vegetation community is a continuous canopy of trembling aspen (*Populus tremuloides*); however, mixedwood stands and small patches of white spruce (*Picea glauca*) and jack pine (*Pinus banksiana*) occur intermittently within the immediate study area.

METHODOLOGY

In 1997, five permanent transects were randomly placed perpendicular to the ROW alignment within a 300-m (length) non-seeded plot and repeated in an adjacent 300-m plot that was sown with the agronomic seed mixture. Within each plot, to compare plant establishment on each activity area or lane within the ROW, the disturbed corridor was divided into three strata; work side, trench area, and storage (spoil) side. In addition, a reference or control strata was located 10-m off ROW (undisturbed) on the west end of each transect.

At each strata location along the transect, a quadrat (1.0 × 1.0 m) was placed on the surface to delimit a data collection area. Data collected from each quadrate included species composition (type/diversity/richness), frequency (density) and percent cover. Data was collected in August 1997 and again in August 1999.

Though beyond the scope of this paper, common concerns associated with pipeline construction are the disturbance or modification of the soil profile (i.e., admixing, pulverization, displacement of organic material, compaction, etc.) which in turn can significantly influence reclamation and associated revegetation success. Nonetheless, during the field study, topsoil depths were measured along each transect and soil samples were collected and analyzed for macronutrients, pH, SAR, and organic content, as well, soil bulk density was measured at random locations within strata.

STATISTICAL METHODS

Statistical analysis

A three-way analysis of variance (ANOVA) was used to test the effect of location (seeded vs. non-seeded), site (control, spoil side, trench, work side), and year on species richness or species diversity. If a significant interaction was generated, the model was reduced to examine the effect of explanatory variables on species richness, independently. Subsequent to detecting a significant site or year effect, species richness between sites or years was deemed to differ significantly if 95% confidence intervals did not overlap. A $P > 0.05$ was judged to be not significant. Statistical analysis was performed using the SAS statistical package (Windows version) for microcomputers.

RESULTS

Analysis of variance generated a significant 3-way interaction between location, strata sites, and year ($F_{3,64} = 2.79, P = 0.05$). Although the number of species was lower on seeded transects than non-seeded transects, the effect was not similar across strata sites or between years (Fig. 1). Partitioning the analysis by location indicated that species richness was marginally different among strata sites on non-seeded transects ($F_{3,32} = 2.98, P = 0.05$), but varied strongly among sites on seeded transects ($F_{3,32} = 192.47, P < 0.01$). Most of

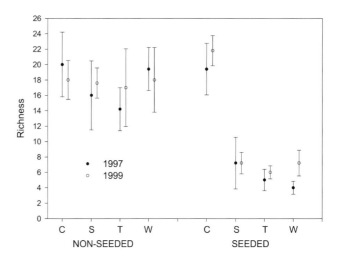

Fig. 1. Variation (mean ± 95% CI) in species richness among sites and between years on non-seeded and seeded areas (C, control; S, spoil; T, trench; W, work).

the variation on seeded transects was due to the difference between control and exposed sites. For seeded transects, species richness was 3–4 times greater on the control site than on exposed strata sites (Fig. 1). Examination of species richness by strata site indicated that control sites on seeded and non-seeded transects were not different. However, for the remaining sites, non-seeded transects contained significantly more species than seeded transects (Fig. 1, Tables 2 and 3). Finally, with the exception of the seeded work side, mean species richness was generally not different between years ($F_{1,64} = 3.14, P = 0.08$; Fig. 1).

CONCLUSION

In this case study, the results indicate through the variation in species richness that the practice of applying an agronomic seed mixture does hamper or pre-empt natural secondary succession processes on a reclaimed pipeline ROW. Romo and Krueger (1986), Wilson (1989), and D'Antonio and Vitousek (1992) and others also report a similar trend.

Considering that there was no significant variation between disturbance strata within the ROW, it appears that typical construction activities associated with each strata within the ROW did not hamper plant regeneration even though richness was marginally lower on the trench area. However, this also could be a function of employing construction techniques (i.e., removing and salvaging propagule laden topsoil and then replacing it during the reclamation stage) to ensure there is minimal soil loss and admixing, excessive compaction to the topsoil horizons, and minimal dilution of the seedbank.

If the goal of a revegetation or vegetation management program is to reestablish a native plant community in forest covered areas disturbed by linear

Table 2. Species richness — non-seeded vs. seeded goodsoil to rosetown pipeline – North Spread TransGas

Non-seeded plot				Seeded plot			
Transect[1]	Strata[2]	Species richness		Transect[1]	Strata[2]	Species richness	
		1997	1999			1997	1999
NS1	A	22	15	S1	A	22	23
NS2	A	14	18	S2	A	19	20
NS3	A	22	20	S3	A	18	21
NS4	A	22	17	S4	A	16	24
NS5	A	20	20	S5	A	22	21
NS1	B	19	18	S1	B	11	8
NS2	B	18	18	S2	B	9	8
NS3	B	18	16	S3	B	5	6
NS4	B	15	16	S4	B	5	8
NS5	B	10	20	S5	B	6	6
NS1	C	17	19	S1	C	5	7
NS2	C	16	20	S2	C	4	5
NS3	C	16	11	S3	C	4	6
NS4	C	12	15	S4	C	5	6
NS5	C	13	20	S5	C	7	6
NS1	D	20	17	S1	D	3	8
NS2	D	19	20	S2	D	4	9
NS3	D	19	15	S3	D	5	7
NS4	D	20	23	S4	D	4	6
NS5	D	16	15	S5	D	4	6

[1] Five permanent transects were placed across the right-of-way on the non-seeded and seeded plots (i.e., first transect on the non-seeded plot is NS1).
[2] On each transect, the right-of-way was divided into four strata; A = control (undisturbed), B = spoil side, C = trenchline, and D = workside.

Table 3. Species occurrence on the non-seeded (NS) and needed (S) plots goodsoil to rosetown pipeline — North Spread TransGas

Species[1]	Occurrence (1997 and 1999)[2]									
	NS		S		NS only		S only		NS and S	
	97	99	97	99	97	99	97	99	97	99
Achillea millefolium	x	x		x	x					x
Agrostis scabra	x	x			x	x				x
Agropyron trachycaulum	x	x	x						x	
Anemone canadensis		x				x				
Anemone cylindrica		x								
Antennaria spp.		x								
Aster ciliolatus	x	x	x			x			x	
Calamagrostis canadensis	x	x			x	x				
Campanula rotundifolia		x				x				
Carex sp.	x	x	x	x					x	x
Cirsium arvense	x	x			x	x				
Crepis tectorum	x				x					
Deschampsia caespitosa		x				x				
Eleocharis palustris	x				x					
Epilobium palustre	x	x			x	x				
Equisetum arvense	x	x			x	x				
Equisetum scirpoides	x	x								
Festuca rubra				x	x		x	x		
Fragaria virginiana	x	x	x	x					x	x
Galium boreale	x	x			x	x				
Galium triflorum	x	x							x	x
Gentiana amarella	x	x							x	x
Geranium bicknellii	x				x					
Geum aleppicum	x				x					
Geum macrophyllum		x		x						x
Hordeum jubatum		x				x				
Juncus bufonius	x				x					

Table 3. (continued)

Species[1]	Occurrence (1997 and 1999)[2]									
	NS		S		NS only		S only		NS and S	
	97	99	97	99	97	99	97	99	97	99
Juncus dudleyi	x				x					
Juncus spp.	x	x	x						x	
Lathyrus ochroleucus	x	x			x	x				
Lathyrus venosus		x				x				
Luzula spp.		x				x				
Maianthemum canadense	x	x	x			x			x	
Matricaria matricarioides	x				x					
Mentha arvensis		x				x				
Mertensia paniculata	x	x			x	x				
Mitella nuda	x	x			x	x				
Moehringia lateriflora	x				x					
Moss spp.	x	x	x	x					x	x
Oryzopsis asperifolia	x				x					
Petasites palmatus	x	x			x	x				
Phleum pratensis	x	x	x	x				x	x	
Picea mariana		x				x				
Plantago major	x	x	x	x					x	x
Poa palustris		x				x				
Poa pratensis	x	x	x			x			x	
Polygonum arenastrum	x				x					
Potentilla norvegica	x				x					
Ranunculus abortivus	x		x						x	
Ranunculus cymbalaria		x				x				
Ranunculus sp.		x				x				
Ribes lacustre	x				x					
Ribes oxyacanthoides	x	x			x	x				
Rosa acicularis	x	x	x			x			x	
Rubus idaeus	x	x	x			x			x	
Rubus pubescens	x	x			x	x				
Salix spp.	x	x			x	x				
Scirpus spp.	x				x					
Solidago canadensis		x				x				
Sonchus arvensis	x	x			x	x				
Stellaria longifolia	x	x			x	x				
Symphoricarpos albus	x	x			x	x				
Taraxacum officinale	x	x	x	x					x	x
Thalictrum venulosum	x				x					
Trifolium repens	x	x		x						
Urtica dioica	x		x						x	
Vicia americana	x	x	x						x	
Viola adunca	x	x			x	x				
Viola canadensis	x				x					
Viola renifolia	x				x					
Total	54	51	16	10	35	35	1	2	18	10

[1] Scientific names taken from Budd's Flora of the Canadian Prairie Provinces (Looman and Best, 1987).
[2] Excludes undisturbed control plot in adjacent forest.

developments, it appears that in some cases that it may be more beneficial to allow secondary succession to proceed in the absence of an artificial seeding program. This would be particularly applicable if soil erosion is not a concern and the revegetation program was considering the use agronomic or exotic species. Furthermore, in addition to cost saving associated with seed purchase and application, permitting secondary succession to proceed unimpeded will help maintain ecological integrity and promote biodiversity.

ACKNOWLEDGEMENTS

We wish to acknowledge TransGas Ltd. and Mr. Kerry Hanley (Supervisor Environmental Programs) for funding this project and for their continued commitment to evaluate their reclamation practices in order to identify measures or techniques that can be applied to future developments. The authors also wish to acknowledge the effort and plant identification skills of Ms. Beryl Wait and Ms. Crystal Stinson (Plant Ecologist's, Golder Associates) who assisted with the field work and data collection.

REFERENCES

Acton, D.F., G.A. Padbury, and C.T. Stushnoff. 1998. The ecoregions of Saskatchewan. Canadian Plains Research Centre, University of Regina and Saskatchewan Environment and Resource Management.

Environment Canada. 1993. Canadian Climate Normals 1961–1990, Prairie Provinces. Atmospheric Environment Service, Minister of Supply and Services Canada, Ottawa, ON.

D'Antonio C.M. and P.M. Vitousek. 1992. Biological Invasion by exotic grasses, the grass/fire cycle, and global change. Annu. Rev. Ecol. Syst., 23: 63–87.

Gerling, H.S., M.G. Willoughby, A. Schoepf, K.E. Tannas, and C.A. Tannas. 1996. A Guide to Using Native Plants on Disturbed Lands. Alberta Agriculture, Food and Rural Development and Alberta Environment Protection. ISBN 0-7732-6125-7. 247 pp.

Hart, R.T. and H.M. Hunt. 1981. Terrestrial wildlife habitat inventory of the St. Walburg (73-F) map area. Technical Report 81-14. Wildlife Branch, Dept. of Parks and Renewable Resources, Saskatoon, Sask.

Looman, J and K.F. Best. 1987. Budd's flora of the Canadian prairie provinces. Revised 1987. Research Branch Agriculture Canada. Publication 1662. 863 pp.

McCanny, S.J., P. Fargey, and S. Hohn. 1996. The effects of grazing and exotic grasses on the ecological integrity of upland prairie. Grasslands National Park. Annual Report, 1: 66–75.

Pyke, D.A. and S. Archer. 1991. Plant-plant interactions affecting plant establishment and persistence on revegetated rangeland. J. Range Mangement, 44: 550–557.

Romo, J. and W. Krueger. 1986. Vegetation management in national parks in the arid areas of the pacific northwest. Park Science: A Resource Management Bulletin, 6(4): 9–10.

Romo, J. and D. Lawrence. 1990. A review of vegetation management techniques applicable to Grasslands National Park. Canadian Parks Service Technical Report 90-1/GDS. Environment Canada. pp. 1–63.

Saskatchewan Soil Survey. 1995. The soils of the Loon Lake Rural Municipality No. 561 Saskatchewan. Saskatchewan Centre for Soil Research, University of Saskatchewan, Publication SM561.

Simberloff, D. 1981. Community effects of introduced species. In: Biotic Crises in Ecological and Evolutionary Time. T.H. Nitecki, ed. Academic Press, New York. pp. 53–81.

Sims, H.P., C.B. Powter, and J.A. Campbell. 1984. Land surface reclamation: A review of the international literature. Alberta Land Conservation and Reclamation Council Report No. RRTAC 84-1, 2 vols. 1549 pp.

Vitousek, P.M., L.L. Loope, and C.P. Stone. 1981. Introduced species in Hawaii: biological effects and opportunites for ecological research. Trends in Ecology and Evolution, 2: 224–227.

Wilson, S. D. 1989. The suppression of native prairie by alien species introduced for revegetation. Landscape and Urban Planning, 17: 113–119.

BIOGRAPHICAL SKETCHES

Mark Ealey BScAdv — Ecologist/Reclamation Specialist

Golder Associates Ltd., 209, 2121 Airport Drive, Saskatoon, SK S7L 6W5, Canada. Mark_ealey@golder.com. 306-665-7989

Mark has a BSc in Land Use and Environmental Studies from the University of Saskatchewan and has completed a portion of a MSc program with a thesis that focuses on reclaiming habitats disturbed by oil and gas activities. He joined Golder Associates in 1995 and currently functions as the senior terrestrial ecologist and reclamation specialist in the Saskatoon regional office. Mark has over ten years experience in the oil and gas sector and has worked on projects throughout western Canada, Russia, Yemen, Hungary, and Latin America. He has a special interest in the reclamation and restoration of disturbed habitats.

John Virgl PhD — Terrestrial Ecologist/Biometrician

Golder Associates Ltd., 209, 2121 Airport Drive, Saskatoon, SK S7L 6W5, Canada

Dr. Virgl joined Golder Associates in 1997 as one of the company's principal biometricians. He has eleven years experience in the design, statistical analysis, interpretation, and practical and theoretical application of ecological studies. He has published over a dozen research articles and contributed to more than twenty reports. His interests include understanding and maintaining the integrity of ecosystems, particularly as it relates to the potential cumulative effects of industry on the persistence and stability of wildlife populations and habitat.

Rare Plant Impact Mitigation for the Alliance Pipeline Project

Gina Fryer, Gordon Dunn, and Paul Anderson

Alliance Pipeline Limited Partnership (Alliance) has constructed approximately 2330 km of natural gas pipeline from northeast British Columbia, through Alberta to the Saskatchewan–North Dakota border. Vegetation assessment is a requirement of National Energy Board regulated pipeline projects. Rare plant surveys and vegetation community typing through nine distinct ecological regions were undertaken in the summers of 1996 through 1999, along the mainline and laterals in segments of native vegetation. Forty-seven species of rare plants, as well as a number of significant plant communities, were identified along the Alliance right-of-way. Mitigation to avoid or minimize impacts was developed for each rare plant site or significant community identified. Mitigation measures implemented during construction included re-routing or re-aligning the pipeline within the right-of-way, narrowing down the right-of-way, transplanting of individual plants, and seed collection for re-establishment after construction. Rare plant survey work is normally required for National Energy Board regulated pipeline projects that traverse native vegetation. Information regarding the effectiveness of the mitigation implemented for conservation of rare plants and sensitive plant communities would be of benefit for the planning of future projects. As part of Alliance's post-construction reclamation monitoring program, an assessment will be conducted to document the survival of rare plant populations disturbed during construction. Vegetation survey methodology, impact mitigation planning, and a preliminary assessment of the successes and difficulties of the mitigative measures implemented are discussed.

Keywords: Vegetation assessment, significant plant communities, rare plants, mitigation, survey methodology

INTRODUCTION

The Canadian portion of the Alliance pipeline includes the construction of approximately 2330 km of natural gas pipeline from northeast British Columbia, through Alberta to the Saskatchewan–North Dakota border. Clearing of the pipeline right-of-way began in February 1999. Mainline construction began in June 1999, and is now mechanically complete.

Rare vascular plant survey work is normally required along the segments of National Energy Board regulated pipeline projects that traverse native vegetation. Part VII of the Guidelines for Filing Requirements states (National Energy Board 1995):

"9 (2) *The assessment conducted pursuant to subsection (1) shall consider, but not be limited to, the following:*
   (e) *with respect to the biotic environment (all organic matter and living organisms and their interacting natural systems)*
      (iii) *for plant and forest communities of ecological, economic or human importance*
         (C) *rare or unique species or species assemblages, including plant species with federal, provincial, regional or local designated status (vulnerable, threatened, endangered or extirpated)."*

Since a large portion of the Alliance pipeline traverses native vegetation in forested areas, it was not feasible to conduct field surveys for rare plants along the entire route. Therefore, a vegetation assessment methodology had to be developed to prioritize areas along the route and identify vegetation community types with higher potential for the occurrence of rare plant species.

The objectives of the vegetation assessment undertaken by Alliance were:
1. to develop an effective method for identifying areas with high potential for rare plant occurrences;
2. to implement field surveys of the high potential areas for rare plant occurrences; and
3. to develop effective and feasible mitigative measures for the conservation of rare plant species found on the right-of-way.

Information regarding the effectiveness of the survey methods and of the mitigation implemented for conservation of rare plants and significant plant communities would be of benefit for the planning of future pipeline projects.

METHODS

Survey methodology

A literature review was conducted to obtain the most current information on known and potential rare plant species and significant plant communities occurring within the general project region. Primary sources included provincial Conservation Data Centres (CDC) and government agencies, plus various reports on rare plants (e.g. Argus and Pryer, 1990; Wallis, 1987; Wallis et al., 1987) and environmentally significant areas (e.g. Wallis and Knapik, 1990; Geowest Environmental Consultants Ltd., 1994, 1995).

The Alberta Natural Heritage Information Centre (ANHIC), British Columbia CDC and Saskatchewan CDC provided updated tracking lists of rare plant species known or expected to occur within the project region, plus element occurrence records of known rare plant locations in the vicinity of the proposed route (Alberta Natural Heritage Information Centre, 1996; British Columbia Conservation Data Centre, 1996; Committee on the Status of Endangered Wildlife in Canada, 1996; Saskatchewan Conservation Data Centre, 1996). Based on this information plus other relevant sources (e.g. Wallis et al., 1987; Argus and Pryer, 1990; Harms et al., 1992; Fernald, 1993; Saskatchewan Environment and Resource Management, 1996), a checklist of vascular plant species of concern in the vicinity of the proposed Alliance project by province was developed, to be used for field surveys.

Preliminary identification of native vegetation portions of the mainline route was undertaken during an aerial reconnaissance of the proposed route. Based on this assessment and on interpretation of aerial photographs, a selection process for the determination of priority sampling sites along the mainline was initiated.

In parkland and prairie areas, sampling segments were identified to include all large tracts of noncultivated land, river valleys, grazing reserves and other sites with expected high potential for the occurrence of rare plants (e.g. Environmentally Significant Areas). An attempt was made to sample all major vegetation community types in these areas subject to limitations imposed by accessibility, time constraints and weather conditions.

In the forest regions, areas of high potential, as determined from air photo interpretation of vegetation community types, were sampled. Sampling was conducted by teams of two botanists walking the proposed route. Rare plant surveys and vegetation community typing through nine distinct ecological regions were undertaken in the summers of 1996 through 1999, along the mainline and laterals in segments of native vegetation

Where rare plants were encountered, documentation using data sheets, airphoto mosaics, NTS maps and photographs was completed. An area up to a distance of 500 m away from the right-of-way in either direction was examined to determine if the species was distributed beyond the expected zone of disturbance. Rare plant sites were marked in the field with numbered stakes and GPS locations were recorded for each individual stake by the survey company responsible for right-of-way survey and staking. The GPS data of rare plant locations was then entered into the main survey data bank and survey sketches were produced showing the locations of rare plants in relation to the actual right-of-way boundaries.

Mitigation planning methodology

The survey sketches were used, along with other NTS topographic maps and aerial photography, to determine the most appropriate mitigative actions to be implemented. Factors commonly considered in selecting mitigation included but were not limited to: number of rare plant individuals at the site; rarity ranking of the species (i.e. S1, S2, SU); location of the individuals in relation to the right-of-way boundaries; and anticipated construction necessities (i.e. extra workspace requirements for grading hills or crossing watercourses, etc.).

Once a site was assessed in this way and the preferred mitigative measure selected, data sheets including the original survey notes from the field botanists, the survey sketches showing right-of-way boundaries and plant locations, and instructions for mitigation to protect the rare plant or community were provided to Alliance's Environmental Inspectors. The Environmental Inspectors were then responsible for supervising the implementation of mitigative measures during construction. Where unforeseen difficulties arose during construction, such as extra grading width requirements, the Environmental Inspectors were able to consult with a Vegetation Resource Specialist to adjust or change the pre-planned mitigation in order to best protect the plant species of concern.

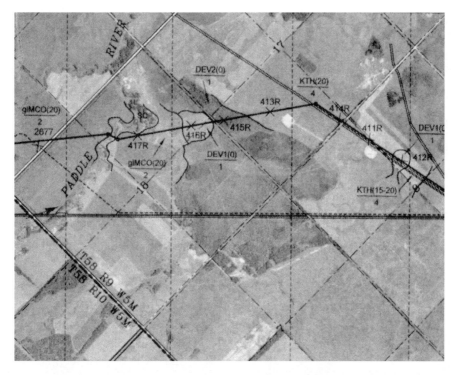

Fig. 1. Aerial photograph showing the re-route around the bog at KP 507 to avoid the *Malaxis paludosa*.

RESULTS AND DISCUSSION

Survey results

Forty-seven species of rare plants, as well as a number of significant plant communities, were identified along the Alliance construction right-of-way in Canada. Some of the rare plant species were downlisted, partially as a result of the number of areas these rare plant species were found in Alberta during the Alliance surveys (e.g. *Angelica genuflexa*, originally an S2 species at the start of the surveys was downlisted off the ANHIC watch list, in 1998 (Gould, 2000)).

Mitigation measure implementation

Mitigative measures implemented during construction for rare plants included re-routing or re-aligning the pipeline, narrowing down the right-of-way, transplanting of individual plants, topsoil seed bank salvage, and seed collection for re-establishment after construction. Mitigation measures utilized for rare plants are outlined below with brief descriptions and examples. Post-construction monitoring has been undertaken along segments of the pipeline constructed in 1999, and the success of some of the mitigative measures identified.

Re-routing

Re-routing the pipeline to avoid rare plants usually provides the most complete protection but is not always feasible or practical. Other considerations such as safety concerns, geotechnical constraints, engineering difficulties, or landowner routing preferences must also be considered before a re-route can be implemented. However, the Alliance pipeline was re-routed, when feasible, at a number of locations for the purpose of avoiding rare plant communities.

For example, the pipeline was re-routed around a bog where the bog adder's-mouth, *Malaxis paludosa* (S1) was found on the Alliance right-of way at KP 507 (Fig. 1).

Narrowing of right-of-way disturbance

Narrowing of the area of ground surface disturbance on the right-of-way as much as feasible within the constraints of safety and construction logistics will avoid the rare plant species and at least a portion of its habitat.

The right-of-way was narrowed down by 8 m on the workside to avoid the lance-leaved loosestrife, *Lysimachia lanceolata* (S1S2 in 1996, but no longer on the Tracking or Watch list for Alberta (Gould, 2000)) during construction over the summer of 1999 (Fig. 2). During post-construction monitoring in summer 2000, the plant was located (Fig. 2). This is in a low wet area surrounded by willow and aspen, within a cultivated field (KP 769.9–770.0). The landowner is planning to use the disturbed portion of the right-of-way for crop now, but the portion that was saved from disturbance remains native (Fig. 3).

Douglas hawthorn, *Crataegus douglasii* (S3W), was fenced and avoided during construction (KP 639.9). During post-construction monitoring in summer 2000, the Douglas hawthorn was thriving (Fig. 4).

Fig. 2. *Lysimachia lanceolata* at KP 769.9.

Fig. 4. *Crataegus douglasii* was fenced and avoided during construction.

Fig. 3. Photo showing the narrowing down of the right-of-way by 8 m at KP 769.9 (full right-of-way width shown in foreground).

Fig. 5. *Hedyotis longifolia* one year after the transplant, at KP 876.4.

Avoiding or minimizing extra workspace and grading requirements

Where extra workspace was necessary in areas of significant plant communities, a site-specific layout was developed and the area to be disturbed was minimized. Extra workspace and grading was minimized or avoided and the width of topsoil stripping restricted to reduce the extent of disturbance to native vegetation.

Salvage of plant species of concern

Species of concern that would have been affected by surface disturbance, were transplanted, using plugs, cutting collection or seed collection. Specific procedures for rare plant salvage were determined by the Resource Specialist based on factors such as species characteristics, location and timing of salvage, and construction operations. Salvaged plants or propagation materials were reestablished on the right-of-way or in nearby areas with appropriate habitat as directed by the Environmental Inspector or Resource Specialist.

Two clumps of long-leaved bluets, *Hedyotis longifolia* (S2), were transplanted to the immediate north of the right-of-way just prior to construction by hand (KP 876.4). The two clumps of long-leaved bluets were located again during post-construction monitoring in summer 2000 (Fig. 5). Goldthread, *Coptis trifolia* (S2 in 1996, S3W in 2000) was transplanted off the Windfall Compressor Station at KP 421 using a backhoe, in the spring of 1999, just prior to construction. It was transplanted to a similar habitat adjacent to the Compressor Station (Figs. 6–8). The goldthread survived the transplant and was located during post-construction monitoring in summer 2000 (Fig. 9).

In several instances involving rare annuals, seed was collected and stored for dispersal onto the right-of-way following construction. In these cases the plant species were also found in disturbed areas and therefore capable of surviving on the disturbed right-of-way.

In addition, for annual plants where transplanting was not practical and the seeds had already dispersed, the seeds in the topsoil or strippings were salvaged separately and re-distributed during clean-up. For example, topsoil at the linear-leaved plantain, *Plantago elongata* (S2S3) site were saved separately and replaced during clean-up (KP 943.3–943.4). The narrow-leaved plantain was noted during post-construction monitoring in summer 2000 (Figs. 10 and 11). Similarly, topsoil at the awned or mountain mousetail, *Myosurus aristatus* (S2) site was stored separately during construc-

Fig. 6. Vegetation left in an island surrounding the *Coptis trifolia*, on the Windfall Compressor station site, KP 421.

Fig. 7. Removal of *Coptis trifolia* and surrounding sod with a backhoe.

Fig. 8. Salvaged *Coptis trifolia* and sod being replaced in the cleared transplant site.

Fig. 9. *Coptis trifolia* one year after transplanting.

Fig. 10. *Plantago elongata* one year following construction.

Fig. 11. *Plantago elongata* habitat regenerating at KP 943.3.

tion (KP 1236.60–1236.64). Following construction, the slight depression in the right-of-way was recontoured and the strippings re-spread (Figs. 12 and 13). Although the awned or mountain mousetail was not seen during post-construction monitoring in the summer 2000, it may be found growing next year, once the vegetation has had a chance to fill in.

The awned umbrella sedge, *Cyperus aristatus* (S1) was located during a preconstruction vegetation survey (KP 1466.25). It was located on the Alliance right-of-way and an adjacent right-of-way. The Alliance right-of-way was narrowed down and 5 m of the adjacent right-of-way was used. Transplanting by hand with sod plugs was also conducted (Figs. 14 and 15). Monitoring will be conducted in 2001 to determine whether the transplanting was successful.

Fig. 12. Site where *Myosurus aristatus* was found. Strippings were removed separately and replaced following construction (KP 1236.60).

Fig. 14. *Cyperus aristatus* (wedding band on right for scale).

Fig. 13. Slight depression recontoured on the right-of-way following construction.

Fig. 15. Sod plugs of *Cyperus aristatus* prior to re-planting (KP 1466.25).

DISCUSSION

Alliance's vegetation survey methodology was highly successful in identifying and locating rare plant species that would be impacted during construction. As mentioned above, some species previously thought to be in peril were found in such abundance and widespread distribution that they were downgraded in rarity ranking on provincial species of concern lists. It is likely that some rare plants were overlooked in areas classified as low in priority and not field surveyed by Alliance. However, by concentrating on high priority areas, the limited resource of qualified botanists experienced in rare plant identification was best utilized.

Protection of rare plant communities that were located was most effective where pipeline re-routes were possible since both the rare species and the associated habitat were left undisturbed. Narrowing the right-of-way to avoid all or part of a rare plant community appears to be a good conservation method and was most often the method implemented because it presents fewer problems in coordinating with other considerations such as safety and engineering concerns.

Construction right-of-way avoidances may not be possible in areas that require extensive grading. Many of the areas of remnant native vegetation in Saskatchewan and eastern Alberta remain uncultivated due to adverse grade or drainage problems. As a result, these areas often require extensive right-of-way preparation making narrow downs difficult or impractical.

Disturbance of the rare plant and surrounding habitat was done when re-routing and narrowing down were not feasible. Salvaging rare plants, either by transplant, seed collection or topsoil seed bank salvage, appears to be initially successful in some of the locations where these methods were implemented by Alliance. However, Fahselt (1988) cautions that transplants of rare species often are initially successful but frequently die out or fail to reproduce a viable community in the longer term. Future monitoring of the sites along the Alliance right-of-way where rare plant salvage methods were implemented will hopefully provide some insight into the effectiveness of this as a conservation measure.

REFERENCES

Alberta Natural Heritage Information Centre. 1996. Draft for discussion — vascular plant tracking list.

Argus, G.W. and K.M. Pryer. 1990. Rare vascular plants in Canada. Canadian Museum of Nature, Ottawa.

British Columbia Conservation Data Centre. 1996. Rare vascular plant tracking lists for the Fort St. John Forest District (FD #48) and the Dawson Creek Forest District (FD #47).

Committee on the Status of Endangered Wildlife in Canada. 1996. Canadian endangered species and other wildlife at risk.

Fahselt, D. 1988. The dangers of transplantation as a conservation technique. Natural Areas Journal, 8(4): 238–244.

Fernald, M.L. 1993. Gray's Manual of Botany. Vol. 2. Diocorides Press. 1632 pp.

Geowest Environmental Consultants Ltd. 1994. Significant ecological features inventory of the Whitecourt-Swan Hills Integrated Resource Planning Area. Alberta Environmental Protection.

Geowest Environmental Consultants Ltd. 1995. Environmentally significant areas inventory of the Foothills Natural Region, Alberta. Land Information Division, Alberta Environmental Protection.

Gould, J. 2000. Alberta Natural Heritage Information Centre Plant Species of Special Concern, Alberta Environment, Edmonton, Alberta.

Harms, V.L., P. Ryan, and J.A. Haraldson. 1992. The rare and endangered native vascular plants of Saskatchewan. Development of the Saskatchewan rare plants database and summary sheets of the candidate rare species. Prepared for the Saskatchewan Natural History Society. The W.P. Fraser Herbarium, Department of Crop Science and Plant Ecology, University of Saskatchewan, Saskatoon, Saskatchewan.

National Energy Board. 1995. Guidelines for filing requirements.

Saskatchewan Conservation Data Centre. 1996. Vascular plant tracking list.

Saskatchewan Environment and Resource Management. 1996. Swift Current Region rare and sensitive vascular plant species.

Wallis, C. 1987. The rare vascular flora of Alberta: Volume 2. A summary of the taxa occurring in the Canadian Shield, Boreal Forest, Aspen Parkland and Grasslands natural regions. 9 pp.

Wallis, C. and L. Knapik. 1990. Environmentally significant areas of the County of Barrhead. County of Barrhead.

Wallis, C., C. Bradley, M. Fairbarns, and V. Loewen. 1987. The rare flora of Alberta. Vol. 3, Alberta forestry, lands and wildlife.

BIOGRAPHICAL SKETCHES

Gina Fryer

TERA Environmental Consultants (Alta.) Ltd., Suite 1100, 815-8th Avenue S.W., Calgary, AB T2P 3PZ, Canada

Ms. Fryer is a Senior Environmental Planner for TERA Environmental Consultants (Alta.) Ltd. She has a Bachelor of Science and a Master of Science Degree in Ecology from the University of Calgary. Ms. Fryer has 11 years experience in the field of environmental consulting.

Paul Anderson

Alliance Pipeline Limited Partnership, 600, 605-5th Avenue S.W., Calgary, AB T2P 3H5, Canada

Mr. Anderson is the Manager of Health, Safety and Environment of Alliance Pipeline. He has a Bachelor of Science degree in Biology from the University of Waterloo and a Master of Science degree in Watershed Ecosystems from Trent University. Mr. Anderson has extensive experience in water quality and fish habitat assessment.

Gord Dunn

TERA Environmental Consultants (Alta.) Ltd., Suite 1100, 815-8th Avenue S.W., Calgary, AB T2P 3PZ, Canada

Mr. Dunn is a Senior Environmental Planner for TERA Environmental Consultants (Alta.) Ltd. He has a Master of Science Degree in Agronomy from the University of Alberta. Mr. Dunn is an active member of the Alberta Institute of Agrologists and has 15 years of experience in reclamation, crop production, and problem soils remediation.

Automating Monitoring and Management of Roadside Vegetation

Nancy P. Cain, Kevin McKague, Laura A. Kingston, and Steven Struger

An integrated system was evaluated for monitoring of desirable roadside vegetation, weed locations and related features. The system incorporated a global positioning system (GPS) for locating the sites in the field and a geographic information system (GIS) for storing, managing, manipulating and displaying the data. Weed areas, desirable vegetation, water features, culverts and sensitive adjacent land use were recorded. Methods of recording each feature type, using polygon, linear or point data were explored using field collection tests. Two systems of collecting the information were compared — a polygon, field-based collection system and a linear, vehicle-based collection system. In a replicated field trial, the linear system provided an estimated one-third cost saving in field data collection, but only resulted in a 10% total time savings compared to the polygon system, due to the additional data post-processing required with the linear collection system. The data collected with these automated systems can be used for planning of operations, contract management, automating herbicide application, quality control and communication of vegetation features for planning, design and construction.

Keywords: Rights-of-way, integrated vegetation management, maintenance, GPS, GIS, weed control, brush control, selective maintenance

INTRODUCTION

One of the objectives of selective vegetation control, as part of integrated vegetation management (IVM) programs, is to leave desirable vegetation intact when applying chemical or mechanical brush and weed control. This desirable vegetation includes competitive vegetation that is resistant to invasion by weeds and brush, such as planted areas of crown vetch and bird's-foot trefoil, and naturally-occurring areas of raspberry, asters, goldenrods, dogbane, Canada blue-joint and other competitive species. Areas of competitive vegetation will expand if not stressed by herbicide applications or other maintenance activities. Over time, these areas can significantly reduce the amount of weed or brush control required on a ROW.

It is a time consuming task to identify areas of competitive vegetation on an extensive right-of-way (ROW) system, requiring specially-trained personnel.

Environmental Concerns in Rights-of-Way Management: Seventh International Symposium
J.W. Goodrich-Mahoney, D.F. Mutrie and C.A. Guild (editors)
© 2002 Elsevier Science Ltd. All rights reserved.

It is equally challenging to keep track of the locations of this vegetation and to communicate this information to in-house and contract staff.

Monitoring for IVM programs

A key component of IVM programs is to monitor for weed and brush species, as well as naturally occurring, competitive vegetation. Comprehensive monitoring can be done on a regular basis to evaluate where control is required and where natural vegetation is developing. The use of global positioning systems (GPS) and geographic information systems (GIS) provides a method of recording locational information in the field and storing it in a digital form on base maps. This information can then be updated on a regular basis or following ROW activities to evaluate the effectiveness of maintenance operations.

Integrating IVM with contract weed and brush control programs

The simplest approach for chemical weed and brush control programs is to apply one herbicide to all ROW areas in the target zone, in a continuous operation. A challenge of using selective weed control, as part of an IVM program, is to apply herbicides in a manner that will not damage stands of competitive vegetation. This involves using selective herbicides or physically selective applications. Since most of the herbicides used for weed and brush control on ROW will damage broad-leaved, competitive species, it necessary to use physically selective applications. Examples are spot applications such as basal-bark, cut-surface or targeted foliar applications; or turning broadcast sprayers off when an area of desirable vegetation is reached.

In order to accomplish this manually, applicators that are knowledgeable in identification of competitive species are required. Alternatively, maps or ROW markings identifying these sensitive areas are required to effectively guide the operations.

A second challenge is that contract operations are usually paid on the basis of area treated or amount of herbicide used. This is in direct conflict with the goal of not treating areas with competitive vegetation. A method is required to incorporate into tender documents the location of desirable, competitive vegetation, the location of target weed and brush vegetation, and to indicate exactly how much area requires herbicide application. Identification and recording of these areas can be done in–house or by a separate contractor. This information would allow preparation of more accurate tender information by property owners, submission of more realistic bids by contractors, and a method of monitoring the results of the weed and brush control operations.

If information on the location of desirable vegetation is available, then not disturbing desirable vegetation can be made a condition of a work contract. This would create a strong economic incentive for the contractor to not treat desirable vegetation, especially if there is a penalty.

Automated Vegetation Recording System
A system was evaluated using commercially available technology to monitor the location of desirable vegetation, weed locations and related features on highway ROW. The system evaluated incorporated a GPS for locating the sites in the field and a GIS for storing, managing, manipulating and displaying the data. An operational system was tested on two-lane and four-lane controlled access highways in southern Ontario. Different systems of collecting and organizing the data were compared for ease of operation and the time involved working in the field and on the computer.

METHODS

Software and hardware
For the field collection of vegetation and feature data for this project, a Trimble AgGPS model 132 Receiver was used, with an L-band satellite differential correction of the signal (provided by OmniSTAR Inc.). The GPS unit was used in a backpack frame or mounted on a vehicle, which required unscrewing the antenna from the backpack frame and placing it on the vehicle roof with a magnetic mount.

The GPS unit was connected to an Apple Newton Message Pad 130 computer used as either a hand-held unit in combination with the backpack or as a part of a truck-mounted system. The software used for the field data collection was Fieldworker Pro, Version 1.2.5. For GIS data processing and map production, ArcView GIS 3.0a software was used, on an Intel Pentium computer. ArcView was used for this project, since this software was being used for other GIS operations at the Ontario Ministry of Transportation (MTO). Fieldworker Connect was used to facilitate transfer of the data from the Newton Message Pad to the desktop computer.

Background mapping data
Ontario Base Map (OBM) digital data were used for the background map data. The OBM data was imported for the highway test areas in North American Datum 1927 (NAD 27). The OBM data was transformed from NAD 27 to NAD 83 using Geographic Translator software (Blue Marble Geographics). Only relevant data layers that provided useful background information for the mapping of vegetation data were used:
– transportation network,
– vegetation,
– fencelines,
– drainage network,
– water bodies,
– culverts,
– lot & concessions,
– gravel pits & piles,
– buildings not to scale,
– buildings to scale.

Field data collection
Two systems for field data collection were tested. In the first system, called the Polygon System, the locational data for each vegetation area of interest (for example, desirable or weed area) were collected by walking the boundaries of the polygon in the field and recording the location of these boundaries, resulting in polygon data. The limits of adjacent properties were recorded by walking along the fence line, resulting in linear data. Water courses such as rivers, drainage ditches and culverts were collected as lines or point features, whichever was most suitable. For this system, the GPS unit was mounted on the backpack and carried by one person; a second individual drove the vehicle along the road as required.

In the second system, called the Linear System, data was collected from the vehicle, driving on the shoulder of the road. This second system was developed, as a means of reducing the time in the field, with an eye to using only one person if possible. For this system, all features were recorded as point or line data, whichever was most suitable. For areas of vegetation and the limits of adjacent properties, the start and finish of each area was recorded, resulting in a line feature. Whether vegetation or weed areas were directly adjacent to the road or further back from the shoulder was recorded as attribute data.

For all data, appropriate attributes were recorded. Examples included weed identification and density, desirable vegetation identity, type of adjacent land use and type of water body.

For quality control of the GPS and mapping process, the locations of road intersection control points and structures, collected by GPS, were compared with the known locations of these points on the OBM base maps after conversion to NAD83.

Data management

The data were downloaded to a desktop computer in a comma-delimited format, and translated into an ArcView compatible format. The point, line and polygon data were imported as themes into ArcView, and saved and manipulated as shape files for mapping. The field data were manipulated to provide suitable visual representations on maps; for use in geoprocessing to determine the area of different operations; and for prescription map preparation for automated herbicide applications. These operations required that the weed areas to be treated and the sensitive areas to be avoided be represented by polygons in the GIS.

Linear data was offset (moved in one direction) a set distance and then buffered to create a polygon within the GIS. In this way, adjacent property qualities would be represented by polygons outside of the ROW. Likewise, point culverts would be represented by a 20 m diameter circle (10 m buffer), to indicate the desired spray buffer. With the linear data collection method, weed areas or desirable vegetation areas within the ROW would be represented by polygons, created by offsetting and buffering the original linear data. The polygons representing the weed areas were manually edited to reduce the length of the polygons to the original length of the collected line, so zones of herbicide application would not extend into sensitive zones.

Paper maps were prepared on 28 by 43 cm (11 by 17 in) sheets at 1:10,000 scale. For the map presentation, features from the OBM data were represented with colours and patterns that were consistent with the OBM source data. Colours and patterns were chosen for the collected features; sensitive vegetation, weeds, environmentally sensitive areas and sensitive adjacent land use; that were easy to distinguish and conveyed an appropriate message. The weed areas were portrayed in green, while the remaining areas were portrayed in patterns of red and yellow. Contour and spot height layers were not plotted on the maps, to reduce the amount of visual information, however these layers were processed since they could have potential application in the planning and design uses of the data.

Time trials to assess data acquisition costs

To help quantify operational costs of these data collection methods, time trials were completed for both data acquisition; and the data storage, management and mapping stage of the work. The time trial experiment undertaken compared the time required to use the Polygon Method of data collection versus the time required for the Linear Method. As indicated, the Linear Method was developed to reduce the field time needed to collect the necessary data. The trade-off with applying the Linear Method is the additional computer data post processing time required to offset and buffer zones of weeds, sensitive features or adjacent land uses and, in turn, produce polygons required for the identification of areas to spray. The objective of the time trials was to see if the extra computer time required for the Linear Method exceeded any savings in the time realized in the field data collection step.

The experiment compared field time (data collection and data preparation for input to a GIS) and computer data post processing time for vegetation mapping on two Ontario provincial highways, Highway 19 between Ingersoll and Tillsonburg and Highway 24 between Brantford and Cambridge. Both sites were located in rural agricultural areas and had weed infestations of thistle species, wild carrot and milkweed (noxious weeds in Ontario). Sensitive vegetation areas included prairie vegetation, sumac, crown vetch and other desirable species that would be sensitive to herbicides targeting broad-leafed weeds. The experiment was a randomized complete block design with 4 replicates. Each experimental unit was 4.2–4.9 km long and included both sides of the highway.

The unit costs used in the calculations were $58.10/hr plus $0.36/km for field data collection and $45.27/hr for computer data processing plus $1.12/km for paper costs. These cost estimates did not include overhead.

The data were analyzed for treatment main effects using SAS (SAS Institute Inc., 1992) GLM procedure for analysis of variance. The data were checked to ensure that they met normality and other ANOVA assumptions using the Shapiro–Wilk test statistic for normality and tests for homogeneity of variance (SAS, Univariate procedure).

RESULTS AND DISCUSSION

Results of time trial

The unit time, including field data collection and computer data post processing time per kilometer was significantly more for the Polygon Method of field data collection, 50 min/km, compared to 44 min/km for the Linear Method (treatment effect $P = 0.0077$, Table 1). This translated to about a 10% savings in time using the Linear Method. When converted to costs per hour,

Table 1. Comparison of time involved in field data collection and data post processing for the linear and polygon methods

Method of data collection	Time per length of highway (min/km)[1]		
	Field data collection	Data post processing	Total
Linear method	28.4	15.9	44.3
Polygon method	41.5	8.2	49.7

[1] Each mean represents 4 blocks.

Table 2. Estimated cost involved in field data collection and data post processing for the linear and polygon methods

Method of data collection	Estimated cost per length of highway ($/km)[1]		
	Field data collection	Data post processing	Total
Linear method	$27.51	$12.02	$39.53
Polygon method	$40.20	$6.21	$46.41

[1] Unit cost of $58.10/hr plus $0.36/km for field data collection and $45.27/hr for computer data processing plus $1.12/km for paper costs. Cost estimates do not include overhead.

using estimates of time and equipment (Table 2), there was a 15% cost saving with the Linear Method.

It took roughly 1.5 times as long to collect the field data using the Polygon Method (i.e., 42 min/km compared to 28 min/km). However, it only took one-half as long for the GIS operator to process the data following field data collection with the Polygon Method compared to the Linear Method (i.e., 8 min/km compared to 16 min/km).

The calculations above were based on using a two-person field crew. In an additional time trial, time measurements made on two blocks from the initial experiment indicated that one person could collect field data using the Linear Method in 29 min/km, compared to 28 min/km with two people. This one-person test can only give an indication of the actual time, since the operator had participated in the earlier field data collection. Since this would reduce the cost per hour to $37.45, the projected cost for a one-person linear data collection method would be $18.23 for field data collection and yield a total cost of $30.25. This translated into a one-third saving compared to the Polygon Method.

Factors such as the end purpose for the data being collected, staff availability, and roadside work safety issues would be significant in deciding which method might ultimately be used for a specific application. For example, in situations with a wide right-of-way, such as along a restricted access four-lane expressway, the more precise information possible with the Polygon Method could easily justify the extra cost associated with its use. Here, herbicide application could involve off-road equipment, compared to primarily truck-mounted application equipment on two lane highways with narrow ROW.

Use of GIS ROW vegetation data

Data on the location and attributes of desirable, competitive vegetation, weed or brush, sensitive zones such as water and sensitive adjacent land use, presented on a suitable background map, can be used for numerous applications relating to IVM and other operations that impact ROW vegetation. Examples of uses of this data relating to road ROW management are listed below.

Location and extent of weed or brush infestations
This information can be used to plan maintenance operations and to monitor the results of weed and brush control operations.

Area of herbicide application
With the data on weeds and brush, and sensitive zones such as desirable vegetation, water courses, and sensitive adjacent land use, GIS data processing can be used to determine the actual area or linear length of weeds or brush to be treated. This information can be used for planning of in-house operations or for preparation of tender and contract documents. Maps of the areas to be treated can be provided to staff or contractors to guide weed and brush control operations.

Automated herbicide application
The digital information indicating where herbicide applications are required can also be used to prepare a prescription map necessary to operate an automated herbicide sprayer. This herbicide application system uses the prescription map, a computer operated spray controller, and a GPS unit to apply the herbicide in the appropriate locations (Domingue and Turbide 1996).

Location of competitive vegetation
This information can be used to monitor the effects of maintenance on the development of desirable, competitive vegetation and to limit the effects of other maintenance that would have a negative impact on this vegetation, such as mowing.

Direction of vegetation maintenance activities

This type of system could be used to produce maps to guide other maintenance activities such as mowing for in-house staff or contractors. For example, maps could indicate where safety mowing is required, or where mowing is desired around landscape features and specialty plantings.

Planning, design, and construction

The location and identification of desirable vegetation and environmentally sensitive areas can be provided to staff or consultants involved in planning and design and contractors involved in construction. The retention of established, competitive vegetation wherever possible, will reduce revegetation costs and long term maintenance.

Use of GPS and GIS in an integrated system for selective vegetation management facilitates directed application of herbicides to target weeds and brush, while leaving desirable competitive vegetation intact. The data on vegetation and sensitive areas allows more effective preparation of vegetation management contracts and communication with both in-house and contract staff. Having an up-to-date record of the location and identity of desirable, competitive vegetation as well as weeds and brush, provides the tools to effectively monitor selective brush and weed control as part of IVM programs.

ACKNOWLEDGEMENTS

The authors gratefully acknowledge the technical assistance of D. Ryan, D. Hocking, and J. Bickle; GIS mapping provided by C. Gerstenkorn, Geo Grafix Inc.; equipment assistance provided by Halltech Environmental Inc.; and the input of Ministry of Transportation staff B. Gingerich, M. Purcell, and Wm. Snodgrass throughout this project.

REFERENCES

Domingue, J. and J. Turbide. 1996. GPS Guidance System for right-of-way aerial spraying of phytocides. Hydro-Quebec in conjunction with naturam environment. In: Proc. Sixth International Symposium on Environmental Concerns in ROW Management. J.R. Williams, J.W. Goodrich-Mahoney, J.R. Wisniewski, and J. Wisniewski, eds. Elsevier Science, Oxford, UK. pp. 417–420.

BIOGRAPHICAL SKETCHES

Nancy P. Cain

Cain Vegetation Inc., 5 Kingham Road, Acton, ON, Canada, L7J 1S3

Nancy Cain provides research and consultation services dealing with Integrated Vegetation Management approaches for right-of-way, industrial and landscape areas and the use of specialized technology to reduce maintenance costs. She has expertise in the use of naturally occurring vegetation for weed and brush control; and establishment and management of specialty vegetation such as wildflowers, prairie communities, and native plants. Nancy has a PhD in weed science from the University of Guelph and degrees in tree physiology and landscape horticulture. She worked previously for the Ministry of Transportation on roadside vegetation management research and at the University of Guelph on fruit and nursery crop weed control.

Kevin McKague

Environmental Management Specialist — Applied Research, Ontario Ministry of Agriculture, Food and Rural Affairs, 3rd Floor SE, 1 Stone Road W., Guelph, ON, Canada, N1G 4Y2

Kevin McKague is a registered professional engineer (Ontario) and Certified Professional in Erosion and Sedimentation Control. He obtained his BSc in Agricultural Engineering from the University of Guelph in 1984. Following graduation, he worked for the Grand River and Maitland Valley Conservation Authorities as part of a soil and water conservation extension team. In 1987, he joined Ecologistics Limited, where he undertook numerous projects addressing agro-environmental concerns related to pesticides, nutrients, and soil erosion. In 1999, Kevin joined the Ontario Ministry of Agriculture, Food and Rural Affairs (OMAFRA) as an Environmental Management Specialist. His focus in this applied research position is in the areas of nutrient management and the field-scale evaluation of related agricultural best management practices (BMPs) as tools to protect rural water quality.

Laura A. Kingston

Geomatics Office, Ontario Ministry of Transportation, 2nd floor, Garden City Tower, 301 St. Paul Street, St. Catharines, ON, Canada, L2N 7A7

Laura A. Kingston is the Land Information Coordinator in the Geomatics Office at the Ministry of Transportation Ontario (MTO). Her area of responsibility is maintaining the base spatial data used to produce the Official Road Map of Ontario, providing this base spatial data through Geographic Information System (GIS) and supporting the positioning and spatial referencing needs of MTO users. She received a BSc, in Surveying Science, in 1988, a MASc in 1991 and a PhD in 1995 from the University of Toronto. Her research interests include Geographic Information Systems, the Global Positioning System, the earth's gravity field, and the geoid.

Steven Struger
Roadside Vegetation Management Section, Ontario Ministry of Transportation, 301 St. Paul Street, St. Catharines, ON, Canada, L2N 7A7

Steve Struger has worked in the Roadside Vegetation Management unit of the Ministry of Transportation in St. Catharines, Ontario. He has been involved in the project since its inception as a member of the steering committee. Steve has worked at the Ministry for 11 years, providing operational expertise and direction in the area of vegetation management and landscaping. Prior to that he worked in the Departments of Zoology and Horticultural Science at the University of Guelph as a research technician. He holds a BSc in Agriculture from McGill University and a MSc from the University of Guelph.

Highway Rights-of-Way as Rare Plant Restoration Habitat in Coastal Virginia

Philip M. Sheridan and Nancy Penick

Significant loss of rare plants and their habitats have occurred on the coastal plain of Virginia through urbanization, drainage of wetlands, fire suppression, and land use changes. Existing conservation practices such as easements and preserves have been somewhat successful in preserving biodiversity but have neglected the role that highway rights-of-way could serve as restoration areas for rare plants and their ecosystems. We propagated a number of rare plant species, many only still surviving on powerline rights-of-way, and reintroduced them in appropriate habitat on mitigation projects and cloverleafs along Virginia Department of Transportation highway rights-of-way. Key elements of our program include: utilization of indigenous plant stocks from the local area, registry of reintroductions with state authorities, management of sites through mechanical or chemical means, and monitoring of the population biology of introduced plants. Highway rights-of-way represent a potentially underutilized area for rare plant conservation and could augment species preservation and recovery efforts.

Keywords: Biodiversity, bogs, pitcher plants, VDOT

INTRODUCTION

Rights-of-way have been studied and surveyed for their potential for harboring rare plant populations (Sheridan et al., 1997). Throughout the southeastern United States a unique assemblage of plants occurs in wetlands called pitcher plant bogs (Folkerts, 1982). These wetlands contain interesting species such as pitcher plants, sundews, bladderworts, and orchids. Pitcher plant bogs typically associate with xeric uplands dominated by longleaf pine, *Pinus palustris* Miller, to form an ecosystem, which is maintained in an early successional phase by natural, lightning-caused fires. After four centuries of European settlement in coastal Virginia, however, much of this original habitat has been destroyed or significantly altered through either urbanization, fire suppression, and agricultural and silvicultural practices (Frost, 1993; Sheridan, 1986).

Conventional approaches to conservation of pitcher plant bogs and longleaf pine habitats in Virginia have consisted of acquiring extant fragments of these rare habitats. However, this approach to biological conservation fails to mitigate for past losses in habitat and populations of rare species. In addition, conservation biologists in Virginia have typically tended to attempt to acquire large parcels of land and failed to acquire or protect smaller parcels, which although potentially threatened by future development trends, contain high biological diversity. As a result, a net loss of rare plant diversity occurs through extirpation of local populations.

What we have attempted to do over the past several years in Virginia is to demonstrate that highway rights-of-way, consisting of compensation, mitigation, and cloverleaf sites can serve as habitat and backup sites for potentially threatened indigenous rare plant populations. We use elements of the pitcher plant/longleaf pine ecosystem as models for rare plant conservation on highway rights-of-way and think that our methods may be successfully applied in other regions by conservation biologists and right-of-way managers. The use of highway rights-of-way as rare plant restoration habitat may prevent loss of rare plant biodiversity while at the same time providing an aesthetically pleasing alternative to the conventional suite of plants used in highway rights-of-way.

Environmental Concerns in Rights-of-Way
Management: Seventh International Symposium
J.W. Goodrich-Mahoney, D.F. Mutrie and C.A. Guild (editors)
© 2002 Elsevier Science Ltd. All rights reserved.

MATERIALS AND METHODS

Our study was confined to highway rights-of-way and mitigation sites on the coastal plain of Virginia. We developed a five-step process for rare plant conservation consisting of discovery, research, propagation, reintroduction, and education. Components of these methods follow.

Discovery
Rare bog plant propagules (seed or rhizome divisions) of *Drosera capillaris* Poiret, *Eriocaulon decangulare* L., *Helenium brevifolium* (Nutt.) Wood, *Platanthera blephariglottis* (Willd.) Lindl., *Sarracenia flava* L., and *S. purpurea* L., were located on power line rights-of-way as previously described (Sheridan et al., 1997) or were harvested from failing, fire suppressed sites. Plant rarity was determined by consulting Killeffer (1999). Longleaf pine seed was collected from one of the few natural stands left in Virginia on International Paper property (Sheridan et al., 1999a).

Propagation
Plants were raised (seed or rhizome divisions) in either above ground beds or pots at the Meadowview Biological Research Station in Woodford, Virginia following the methods of Sheridan (1997) and Sheridan and Karowe (2000).

Reintroduction
Field evaluations were performed to find appropriate sites for rare bog plant reintroduction. Since pitcher plant bogs are considered nutrient deficient, early successional communities (Juniper et al., 1989; Plummer, 1963) with a diagnostic suite of plant species (Folkerts, 1982) we selected sites for reintroduction based on presence of associate species. Typical associate species that we used to indicate appropriate hydrology, soils, and light availability were *Lycopodium appressum* (Chapman) Lloyd & Underwood, *Osmunda cinnamomea* L, *Magnolia virginiana* L, *Smilax laurifolia* L, and *Sphagnum* sp. Selection of sites for longleaf pine planting were based on site availability more than soils or hydrology since this species has a wider ecological tolerance than the bog species. Reintroduction procedures followed established protocols (Maryland Natural Heritage Program, 1999).

Four sites were located for rare plant reintroduction, three in Prince George and one in Greensville County, Virginia. An alphanumeric site code was assigned to each site as previously described (Sheridan et al., 1997) while specific site names utilized by the Virginia Department of Transportation (VDOT) were retained for ease of discussion and communication. Sites are as follows: Greensville County, Otterdam Swamp, VAGREE020; Prince George County, 35/95, VAPRIN004; Prince George County, 295/460, VAPRIN005; Prince George County, Fort Lee, VAPRIN006. Generally sites were not disturbed prior to planting with the following exception. VAPRIN004 had a canopy of red maple (*Acer rubrum* L.) which was mechanically removed in March 1998. Garlon herbicide was applied directly to cut stump bases as recommended by label directions for such treatment and woody debris removed from the site. Soil pH was measured for selected VDOT sites utilizing EM Science color pHast indicator strips in a 1 soil:1 distilled water solution or sent to the Virginia Cooperative Extension Service for analysis (natural sites). Soil pH was then compared to natural pitcher plant habitats in Georgia and Virginia.

Pitcher plant and associate wetland plant species reintroductions were done from April to September during 1998–2000 to assess the relative success rate of time of planting. Plantings consisted of either bare root or container stock and involved inserting plants in freshly opened holes in the ground followed by gentle soil closure around the crown of the plant. In previous pilot projects (Sheridan, 1996) we have found that hummocks, seepy (but not ponded or flooded) mineral soil, and toe slope seepage seem to be preferred habitats for pitcher plants and associate flora. Therefore we made an effort to select this habitat in our planting scheme for maximum success. Plants were then flagged and labeled. Longleaf pine seedlings were planted following the methods of Sheridan (2000) at the 295/460 site or were planted using a dibble bar at the Otterdam Swamp wetland mitigation site. We collected survival data for both longleaf pine and pitcher plants on an annual basis. Survival data was not collected on other bog plant introductions (e.g., *Drosera*, *Helenium*, etc.) due to logistic and time constraints. However, we think that longleaf pine and yellow pitcher plant survival data may provide a relative measure of the success of associate bog plant introductions.

A rare plant reintroduction form was then prepared listing the name of the site, map location, plants introduced, their quantity, and origin within the state. The rare plant reintroduction form was then provided to state regulatory authorities for tracking purposes.

Research
We utilized mitigation sites as virtual laboratories to perform large-scale experiments in plant ecology. Specifically, Otterdam Swamp is now being used to test *in situ* the long term fitness of progeny from our inbreeding/outbreeding experiments with *S. flava* (Sheridan and Karowe, 2000), to investigate the effects of nutrient inputs on pitcher plant seedlings, and to track local migration of rare plant species.

Education
We involved Potomac Elementary School (King George County, Virginia) in propagating, experimenting with, and introducing rare plants on the Otterdam Swamp wetland mitigation site (Sheridan et al., 2000a) via the

Toyota Tapestry Grant as a funding source. We wanted to determine whether young students could successfully complete a rare plant conservation program with a highway department while at the same time increase their awareness of environmental issues.

RESULTS

A total of 1126 yellow pitcher plant have been introduced on VDOT rights-of-way with survival averaging 66% (Fig. 1, Table 1). Somewhat surprisingly, the July pitcher plant introduction at Fort Lee had the highest survival rate. However, this must be tempered by our observation that clump size was greatly reduced by drought stress in comparison to plantings at other times of year. In addition, the lower success of the fall plantings at Fort Lee is largely due to a hurricane which dislodged and buried a number of pitcher plants. Soil pH at the introduced pitchers plant sites was 4.5 and fell within the expected pH 4–5 for natural pitcher plant bogs both in Virginia (Table 2) and Georgia (Plummer, 1963). Longleaf pine survival at the 295/460 site is 76% after two growing seasons (Sheridan, 2000) (Fig. 2).

The involvement of Potomac Elementary School in all phases of the rare plant reintroduction at Otterdam Swamp was successful (Fig. 3). Project objectives were met within the one year time frame of the Toyota Tapestry Grant. Students determined that pitcher plant seedlings benefit from a variety of fertilizers (Sheridan et al., 2000a). Students also gained new understanding of what rare plants occur in Virginia, where they are found, why they have become rare, and how they can prevent extinction of rare species through cooperative ventures with state agencies such as the Virginia Department of Transportation (Armstrong, 2000; Harris, 1999; Tennant, 2000).

DISCUSSION

To our knowledge, this is the first restoration effort to take indigenous rare plants and relocate them within their historic range on appropriate habitat on highway rights-of-way. Although rare plants are known to naturally occur on highway rights-of-way (Martz, 1987) their deliberate introduction into synthetic habitats on highway rights-of-way is new. Furthermore, the concept of using these habitats to maintain biodiversity in the face of continued urbanization and fragmentation of habitat expands the potential range of environments available to conservation biologists.

Highway rights-of-way are presently underutilized for rare plant conservation and have great potential for recovering losses in rare plant populations. As an example, there are now less than 100 clumps of native yellow pitcher plant (*Sarracenia flava*) left in the wild in Virginia. Our work with the Virginia Department of Transportation has increased the native population by seven times. Hence a significant increase in population

Fig. 1. Yellow pitcher plant, *Sarracenia flava* L., in bloom during their third successful year at Fort Lee wetland mitigation site.

Table 1. Month, year, quantity, and survival of *Sarracenia flava* planted at VDOT wetland mitigation sites

Site code	Site name	Mo./Yr.	Quantity	No. surviving	Surviving (%)
VAGREE020	Otterdam	4/2000	361	295	80
VAGREE020	Otterdam	5/2000	365	161	44
VAPRIN004	35/95	4/1998	36	28	78
VAPRIN006	Fort Lee	7/1998	45	45	100
VAPRIN006	Fort Lee	9/1999	319	215	67
Total			1126	744	66

Fig. 2. Longleaf pine, *Pinus palustris* Miller, grass stage seedling after two growing seasons at the 295/460 cloverleaf.

Table 2. Soil pH of native and introduced pitcher plant wetlands in Virginia

Site code	Site name	pH
Native		
VADINW001	Shands	4.0
VASUFF001	Kilby	4.4
VASUSS001	Sappony	4.8
Introduced		
VAGREE020	Otterdam	4.5
VAPRIN006	Fort Lee	4.5

Fig. 3. Jerry Pruyne, of Virginia Department of Transportation, helps Potomac Elementary School students plant yellow pitcher plant seedlings at Otterdam Swamp wetland mitigation site. Photo by Victor J. Griffin, Virginia Dept. of Transportation.

size of this rare species will have occurred due to use of appropriate habitat on highway rights-of-way for restoration purposes. In the case of longleaf pine (*Pinus palustris*), a keystone species in southeastern pineland ecosystems, highway right-of-way habitat is allowing a 11% increase in population size since only 4432 longleaf pine remain in Virginia (Sheridan, 1999b). Clearly these are significant contributions to rare plant species recovery.

Are there any regulatory consequences to planting rare plant species on highway rights-of-way? We designed our program to minimize or eliminate any potential conflicts. One of the more important components is providing state natural heritage personnel with a rare plant registry form with relevant data for tracking purposes. We were under no obligation to provide such information in Virginia, since we were not working with Federal or State endangered species, but felt that a cooperative effort with state authorities could only be beneficial. We also only used indigenous plant stocks from the local area to prevent any concerns about "genetic pollution" or importation of pests. We also selected species for reintroduction that were historically much more common but had been locally extirpated due to land use changes. Our choice of planting sites (wetland mitigation sites) also ensured that rare species plantings would not present a future problem since wetland mitigation sites are already tightly regulated and future road designs avoid impacting these habitats. In the case of our cloverleaf plantings, the choice of longleaf pine avoids potential conflict since this tree is a commercially utilized tree by the Virginia Department of Forestry and highly unlikely to be regulated by the Division of Natural

Fig. 4. Mark Mikolajczyk kneeling to the right of ten year old bald cypress, *Taxodium distichum* (L.) Richard, which has been stunted due to unusual soil chemistry at Otterdam Swamp wetland mitigation site.

Heritage. We think that innovative programs to maintain rare species, such as the safe harbor program with the red-cockaded woodpecker (Costa, 1999), will be one of the ways to minimize conflicts between regulators, private landowners, and other agencies while at the same time providing effective, cordial, conservation programs.

Highway rights-of-way are particularly good sites for rare plant refuges because they are monitored and maintained by local departments of transportation. Survival potential is high because the sites may be managed with either mechanical or chemical means. Given that many plant species have suffered significant habitat loss in coastal Virginia, and that appropriate habitat may be found on highway rights-of-way, a logical decision would be to use these areas as rare plant conservation habitat. Why insist that rare plants should only be allowed to persist in the few refugia that have escaped destruction or degradation? This extremely conservative approach needlessly handicaps rare plant conservation when alternative approaches to restoration are now available. Furthermore, state rare plant reintroduction guidelines now allow rare plants to be planted in areas where they may not have naturally occurred (Maryland Natural Heritage Program, 1999).

How do we evaluate the long-term success of our rare species plantings and what is the likelihood of their persistence? A key element to answering this question is the need to understand the ecology of the species that is being restored. In our case we have been working with pitcher plants and their wetland plant associates for over twenty years. Although we continually obtain new insights on the ecology of these species we are able to recognize habitat that offers the greatest likelihood of success and persistence.

Pitcher plants and associate species in the southeastern US are adapted to ecosystems that are considered nutrient deficient, early successional communities. Generally this early successional state, and suppression of woody competition, is naturally accomplished by frequent, lightning caused fires (Folkerts, 1982; Frost, 1993). However, in rare cases, persistent natural gaps can be found that apparently prohibit woody invasion by chemical means (Sheridan et al., 2000b). Two of the wetland mitigation sites we selected for our rare plant reintroduction (Fort Lee and Otterdam) contain pyritic soils which produce excessive acidity to the point that woody growth is either stunted or killed (Figs. 4 and 5). Prior to our restoration work these were considered problem sites because of failed plantings (Whittecar and Daniels, 1999). However, based on the presence of associate plant species suggesting appropriate pH, we were able to exploit this niche for the planting of rare species adapted to these conditions. Furthermore, the chemical inhibition of woody growth may ensure long-term persistence of our selected, herbaceous species. Monitoring of reproduction and spread of offspring will quantify this success.

ACKNOWLEDGEMENTS

Thanks to the staff of the Fredericksburg, Richmond, and Suffolk districts of the Virginia Department of Transportation. In particular we wish to thank Mark Denny, Nick Froelich, Robert Pickett, Larry Morris,

Fig. 5. Natural stunting of bald cypress has been recorded in western Florida peatlands where Keith Underwood and Guy Englin stand next to 300 year old cypress trees which only reach 2 m. Inhibition of woody growth provides refugia for rare wetland plant species such as pitcher plants.

Scott Nye, Jerry Pruyne, Steve Russell, Johnnie Wallin, and Brian Waymack. Additional thanks are due to Meadowview volunteers Jonathan Humphrey, Debbie Hunt, Cindy Ragan, and Chris Simon for their efforts to make this project a success. Toyota Motor Corporation provided a generous grant to Potomac Elementary school via the Toyota Tapestry Grant and played an invaluable role in facilitating the involvement of these students in rare plant conservation with us. We thank the staff of Potomac Elementary School including Deborah Bushrod, Scott Gilbert, Amy Keeton, Melissa Schmutte, and A.J. Rogers. Assistance was also provided by Master Gardener Susan Horman, Roger Horman, and numerous other volunteers with Potomac Elementary School. SPSA provided several free truckloads of mulch for our longleaf pine planting. Thank you all!

REFERENCES

Armstrong, Charles M. 2000. School children join in effort to propagate plants: Rare plants get new start in VDOT wetland. Bulletin, A VDOT Employee Newspaper, 66: 1.

Costa, R. 1999. Safe harbor, a private lands conservation strategy for longleaf pine habitat and red-cockaded woodpeckers. In: Longleaf Pine: A Forward Look, Proceedings of the Second Longleaf Alliance Conference. 1998 November 17–19; Charleston, SC. John S. Kush, ed. Longleaf Alliance Report No. 4. pp. 42–44.

Folkerts, G. 1982. The Gulf Coast pitcher plant bogs. American Scientist, 70: 260–267.

Frost, C.C. 1993. Four centuries of changing landscape patterns in the longleaf pine ecosystem. In: The Longleaf Pine Ecosystem: Ecology, Restoration and Management. S.H. Hermann, ed. Proceedings of the Tall Timbers Fire Ecology Conference, No. 18. Tall Timbers Research Station, Tallahassee, FL. pp. 17–43.

Harris, Carlla. 1999. Rebirth for "lost" longleaf pine. Independent-Messenger, 102: 1, 5.

Juniper, B.E., R.J. Robins, and D.M. Joel. 1989. The Carnivorous Plants. Academic Press, New York.

Killeffer, S.E. 1999. Natural heritage resources of Virginia: rare vascular plants. Natural Heritage Technical Report 99-11. Virginia Dept. of Conservation and Recreation, Division of Natural Heritage, Richmond, VA. Unpublished report. April. 35 pp. plus appendices.

Martz, C. 1987. Endangered plants along California highways: Considerations for right-of-way Management. In: Conservation and Management of Rare and Endangered Plants: Proceedings of a California Conference on the Conservation and Management of Rare and Endangered Plants. Thomas S. Elias, ed. California Native Plant Society. Sacramento, CA. November 5–8, pp. 79–84.

Maryland Natural Heritage Program. 1999. Guidelines for the reintroduction of rare plants in Maryland, report of the plant reintroduction task force. Maryland Dept. of Natural Resources, Annapolis, MD. 9 pp.

Plummer, G.L. 1963. Soils of the pitcher plant habitats in the Georgia coastal plain. Ecology, 44: 727–734.

Sheridan, P. 1986. The Sarraceniaceae of Virginia. The Virginia Journal of Science, 37: 83.

Sheridan, P. 1996. The use of native wetland plants in highway landscaping. Virginia Journal of Science, 47: 155.

Sheridan, P. 1997. Genetics of *Sarracenia* leaf and flower color. Carnivorous Plant Newsletter, 26: 51–64.

Sheridan, P. 2000. A method for planting longleaf pine, *Pinus palustris* Miller, on highway rights-of-way. Virginia Journal of Science, 51: 129.

Sheridan, P.M., S.L. Orzell, and E.L. Bridges. 1997. Powerline easements as refugia for state rare seepage and pineland plant taxa. In: The Sixth International Symposium on Environmental Concerns in Rights-Of-Way Management. J.R. Williams, J.W. Goodrich-Mahoney, J.R. Wisniewski, and J. Wisniewski, eds. Elsevier Science, Oxford, England. pp. 451–460.

Sheridan, P., N. Penick, A. Simpson, and P. Watkinson. 1999a. Collection, germination, and propagation of Virginia longleaf pine. In: Longleaf Pine: A Forward Look, Proceedings of the Second Longleaf Alliance Conference. John S. Kush, ed. 1998 November 17–19; Charleston, SC. Longleaf Alliance Report No. 4. pp. 151–153.

Sheridan, P., J. Scrivani, N. Penick, and A. Simpson. 1999b. A census of longleaf pine in Virginia. In: Longleaf Pine: A Forward Look, Proceedings of the Second Longleaf Alliance Conference. 1998 November 17–19; Charleston, SC. John S. Kush, ed. Longleaf Alliance Report No. 4. pp. 154–162.

Sheridan, P., R. Horman, S. Horman, S. Gilbert, A. Keeton, and M. Schmutte. 2000a. Rare plants in the classroom; Potomac Elementary School and the Toyota Tapestry Grant. Virginia Journal of Science, 51: 110, 130.

Sheridan, P., S. Langley, B. Sipple, K. Underwood, and J. Broersma-Cole. 2000b. Two new pitcher plant, *Sarracenia purpurea* L., wetlands on the western shore of Maryland. Association of Southeastern Biologists Bulletin, 47: 204.

Sheridan, P. and D. Karowe. 2000. Inbreeding, outbreeding, and heterosis in the yellow pitcher plant, *Sarracenia flava* (Sarraceniaceae), in Virginia. American Journal of Botany, 87: 1628–1633.

Tennant, Diane. 2000. A Bog's Life. *The Virginian-Pilot*. E1.
Whittecar, G.R. and W.L. Daniels. 1999. Use of hydrogeomorphic concepts to design created wetlands in southeastern Virginia. Geomorphology, 31: 355–371.

BIOGRAPHICAL SKETCHES

Philip M. Sheridan (corresponding author)
Meadowview Biological Research Station, 8390 Fredericksburg Turnpike, Woodford, VA 22580, USA; Blackwater Ecological Preserve, Dept. of Biological Sciences, Old Dominion University, Norfolk, VA 23529-0266, USA. meadowview@pitcherplant.org, Fax (804) 633-5056
Phil Sheridan is director of Meadowview Biological Research Station in Caroline County, Virginia and specializes in the study and conservation of rare plants. He is a graduate of Virginia Commonwealth University in Richmond, Virginia with both a Bachelor and Master of Science degree in Biology. He is currently enrolled in the PhD program in Ecological Sciences at Old Dominion University where he is an instructor of Botany and General Biology.

Nancy Penick
Meadowview Biological Research Station, 8390 Fredericksburg Turnpike, Woodford, VA 22580, USA
Nancy Penick has been a volunteer at Meadowview Biological Research Station since 1997 and is now a part-time staff biologist with that organization. She is a graduate of Mary Washington College in Fredericksburg, Virginia with a Bachelor of Science degree in Biology.

Part III
Corridors

Co-Location of Linear Facilities: Realistic Opportunity or Unrealistic Expectation

David F. Jenkins

Since the early 1970s, co-location of linear facilities (which includes the concepts of joint use of existing rights-of-way, paralleling of existing rights-of-way, multiple use [by various facilities] of existing rights-of-way, etc.) has been advocated as a means of reducing overall impacts associated with the construction of new linear facilities. Overall impacts may be reduced if a new linear facility is co-located with a well-sited existing linear facility. However, several factors affect the degree to which co-location offers benefits when siting linear facilities. Factors that affect the success of co-location include inconsistent siting criteria for different types of facilities (e.g., overhead facilities, such as electric transmission lines, versus underground facilities, such as pipelines) and reliability and safety issues for the co-located facilities. Additional effects of co-location on the landowners currently affected by an existing right-of-way must be considered in determining the advantages and viability of co-locating new facilities. Both utilities and regulatory agencies should consider not only the broad advantages of co-location, but also site-specific and landowner-related issues if co-location is to be used in the most advantageous manner.

Keywords: Co-location, joint use

INTRODUCTION

In 1970, the Federal Power Commission published guidelines for the siting of rights-of-way for electric transmission lines (Federal Power Commission, 1970). The first of 23 guidelines for the selection of routes for rights-of-way stated that "existing rights-of-way should be given priority as the locations for additions to existing transmission facilities, and the joint use of existing rights-of-way by different kinds of utility services should be considered." Since that time, the concept of co-location of linear facilities (including joint use of existing rights-of-way) has become doctrine for the siting and permitting of new linear facilities and co-location has become a standard part of permitting new facilities. Utilities planning new facilities propose co-location as a means of facilitating regulatory approval of their proposed facilities, and regulatory agencies advocate and require co-location as a well-intentioned effort to minimize overall impacts of new linear facilities. Thousands of miles of linear facilities have been co-located in rural and urban environments, wooded and agricultural areas, and on private and public lands. Experience over the last 30 years has shown that co-location can, in fact, minimize some impacts associated with new linear facilities. However, co-location of new linear facilities with existing linear facilities is not always the best approach to minimizing the overall impact of two (or more) linear facilities.

The concept and benefits of co-location have been discussed for years in professional publications and conferences, such as the Symposia on Environmental Concerns in Rights-of-Way Management. These discussions have ranged from the advantages of co-location with respect to regional planning goals, to the design, and construction factors that affect co-located facilities, and the compatibility of construction and operations parameters of co-located facilities (Howlett, 1976; Steinmaus, 1982; Jenkins, 1987). However, co-location of a new linear facility adjacent to an existing linear facility is not a universal means of mitigating the impacts of construction and operation of linear facilities and can exacerbate problems associated with the existing right-of-way.

This paper reviews factors that affect the benefit that can be realized by co-locating new linear facilities with existing linear facilities. The changing physical, regulatory, and social environments affect the applicability of co-location. Potentially conflicting criteria for the siting of different types of linear facilities (i.e., unlike linear facilities) may affect the viability and benefit of co-locating unlike linear facilities. Reliability and safety issues associated with co-located facilities and the effects of co-located facilities on landowners also influence the overall benefit of co-location in the "big picture" of linear facility siting. The discussion is directed to rights-of-way for electric transmission lines, pipelines, fiber optic facilities, and other facilities that typically allow secondary land uses.

THE CHANGING ENVIRONMENT

The physical, regulatory, social, and technological environments within which linear projects are being developed continue to change, affecting strategies in siting, permitting, and constructing new facilities on or adjacent to existing rights-of-way. The number of new rights-of-way continues to increase to meet the demands of growing population and the shifting of population centers. Simply put, more people need more of the services provided by linear projects.

However, development has affected the siting of linear facilities in different ways. Continued residential, commercial, and industrial development logically encourages co-location of utilities to minimize the construction of new rights-of-way and the associated impacts on existing land use patterns and new development. But, development can also reduce opportunities for co-location of new facilities. In many areas, development has occurred up to the existing rights-of-way, with not only developed properties abutting the right-of-way, but, in many cases, with the foundations of residential, commercial, and industrial structures adjacent to the edge of the right-of-way. This abutting development can eliminate or severely restrict the degree to which new linear facilities can be located on or adjacent to the existing right-of-way and also results in an increased number of potentially concerned landowners to participate in the permitting process.

Changing construction technologies have helped to eliminate the need for cleared rights-of-way in sensitive areas, thus eliminating the "existing right-of-way" and a primary advantage when applying the co-location concept. Notably, the horizontally controlled direction drill technology, so successfully used for pipeline and fiber optic construction, can allow (where appropriate subsurface conditions exist) these underground facilities to be installed under areas or features that should or must be avoided (e.g., waterbodies, wetlands, cultural resource sites, and other sensitive areas) without creating a cleared surface right-of-way. Horizontally controlled direction drill technology has been successfully employed to install segments of large-diameter pipeline of over a mile in length. As a result, the advantage of co-locating a new linear facility adjacent to an "existing" cleared right-of-way no longer exists along those route segments.

Advances in information technology have affected the social environment and the process for permitting new facilities, in general, including new linear facilities, whether co-located or not. Landowners, citizens, and special interest groups who take an active interest in the permitting of new facilities are using new communication technology to aggressively advance their particular objectives relative to new linear projects. In meeting their particular objectives (not infrequently, to oppose a proposed linear project), these groups are aggressively using the Internet to distribute information, organize support functions, etc. Few utilities have been able to use the Internet as effectively to meet their needs in developing new projects. Increased public scrutiny may, in fact, encourage the jurisdictional regulatory agencies and the utilities themselves to adopt co-location for certain segments of projects in the belief that the application of the co-location principle with the general benefits may reduce public opposition and delays in the regulatory process.

FACTORS INFLUENCING THE EFFECTIVENESS OF CO-LOCATION

Siting principles and co-location

Conceptually, co-location of a new linear facility with an existing linear facility can offer benefits by: (1) reducing the total width of required right-of-way and the associated clearing and construction impacts; (2) consolidating similar land uses; and (3) reducing fragmentation of wildlife habitat and other land use areas. However, a well-sited right-of-way for an electric transmission line or other aboveground linear facility is not necessarily a right-of-way also well suited for a pipeline or other underground facility.

When new linear facilities were sited in the past (those that now constitute the "existing rights-of-way"), little if any consideration was given to the shared or adjacent use of the right-of-way by new, subsequently constructed facilities. Occasionally, a company would purchase more right-of-way than needed at the time, construct the required facility on the needed right-of-way, and reserve the remaining (vacant) right-of-way for future expansion. However, planning was almost universally in terms of constructing a "like" facility on the additional right-of-way in the future. That is, an electric transmission company would purchase right-of-way not only to construct a new transmission line at that time, but also to ensure that (the additional) right-of-way would be available to upgrade the voltage of the existing electric transmission line or to construct an additional electric transmission line. Extra right-of-way was not typically purchased with the thought of that right-of-way being used for a different type of facility — not for the future construction of a pipeline.

The right-of-way requirements for unlike linear facilities are not necessarily consistent. Existing rights-of-way designed for one type of facility do not always present a logical location for a second, unlike facility. The construction and operations requirements of overhead versus underground facilities differ sufficiently that co-location of these unlike facilities may not only be unrealistic, but may actually result in more long-term impact than if the two facilities were sited on independent rights-of-way.

For example, the right-of-way for an electric transmission line could cross numerous non-forested wetlands. However, if the wetlands can be spanned, there may be little or no impact to the wetland resource. If the same right-of-way were used for co-location of a pipeline or other underground facility, the requirement for a continuous trench across the wetlands could result in significantly more impacts. Fewer overall impacts could result if the two different facilities were constructed on independent rights-of-way. Likewise, an underground facility, such as a pipeline or fiber optic facility, could be sited through or near a residential area with little or no visual impact. Co-location of an electric transmission line adjacent to that existing right-of-way could result in increased visual impacts. Clearly, the co-location of unlike linear facilities can result in additional site-specific impacts relative to independent sitings of the two facilities.

However, the conceptual benefits of co-location have lead several federal, state, and local land management agencies to apply the concept of co-location in the most generic of manners. Several agencies have established "utility corridors" across publicly owned or publicly managed lands in which all utilities (e.g., roadways, overhead electric transmission lines, pipelines, etc.) must be located if they are to cross that land. In many cases, these corridors have been sited only to avoid "sensitive areas." Even if appropriate siting criteria had been considered during the siting of the original corridor, differing construction and operations requirements for the unlike facilities (and associated impacts) that could potentially occupy the utility corridor could limit the effectiveness of the corridor. Consequently, the impacts from the construction of utilities in that single corridor without considering facility-specific characteristics may actually result in increased impacts within that corridor area.

In the zeal to co-locate a new linear facility on or adjacent to an existing right-of-way and to realize the conceptual benefits of co-location, the construction- and operations-related impacts of the new facility may not be adequately considered in the decision to co-locate the new facility. The site-specific, as well as the broad scale, impacts and benefits must be weighed in such a decision.

Facility reliability and safety

The affects of construction and operation of a new co-located linear facility on the existing facility, and vice versa, may also determine the feasibility of co-location and the benefits that may or may not be realized.

The reduction in right-of-way width requirements will be determined by how close the new facility can be located to the existing facility. Centerline separation between electric transmission lines, pipelines, and fiber optic facilities can be calculated on strict operational characteristics of each facility, based on such factors as electrical clearance between transmission line conductors, induced currents in pipelines located adjacent to electrical transmission lines and the need for cathodic protection for the pipeline, etc. However, other less technical factors may require increased centerline separation and affect whether co-location is acceptable.

The possible damage to the existing linear facility during the construction of the new co-located facility is a real concern, with numerous examples to justify that concern. In one case, the jurisdictional regulatory agency required co-location of a new natural gas pipeline adjacent to an existing electric transmission line right-of-way in a relatively undeveloped area in the northern United States. Damage to the transmission line from blast rock and other construction activities resulted in several outages on the transmission line during construction.

In another case, a pipeline company proposed the co-location of a proposed new natural gas pipeline with an existing high-voltage electric transmission line, with the right-of-way for the pipeline almost completely within the existing electric transmission right-of-way. However, the electric transmission line served a major metropolitan area and was considered by the state public utility commission to be a key link in the regional electric transmission grid. The state public utility commission opposed the co-location because of the possible damage to the electric transmission line during construction of the pipeline and the catastrophic results if the pipeline were to explode. An alternate route, suggested to avoid co-location with the electric transmission line, would have been co-located with existing roadways, but would have affected orders of magnitude more landowners.

Accidents involving conductor-to-equipment flashover and conductor-equipment contact during the construction of adjacent, co-located facilities have resulted in the death and injury of several construction workers. Damage to pipelines, fiber optic lines, and other underground facilities also occurs all too frequently during the construction of adjacent facilities. The resulting loss of service and damage (e.g., resulting from explosions of damaged natural gas pipelines) can be significant.

Although application of the co-location concept may be applied by the jurisdictional regulatory agency for valid reasons, the unanticipated secondary consequences of co-location can be negative. In cases such as these, increased centerline separation between the co-located facilities to reduce the possible risk of physical impact on the original facility during construction could have been a realistic consideration. More prescriptive conditions on permits and certificates to avoid the dangerous aspects of co-location should also be a consideration during permitting.

EFFECTS OF CO-LOCATION ON LANDOWNERS

The benefits of co-location are typically associated with broad land use planning principles or goals (e.g., consolidating land use types, reduced total clearing and land disturbance, reduced fragmentation of land use areas, etc.) and ecological benefits (e.g., reduced clearing, use of common access roads, reduced fragmentation of habitat, etc.). Although impacts may be consolidated and the number of new rights-of-way may be reduced, co-location of rights-of-way also consolidates, increases, and exacerbates the impacts on the underlying landowners.

Two types of "owners" can be affected by the co-location of new linear facilities on or adjacent to existing rights-of-way. The first is the underlying landowner of the right-of-way. This may be the utility company owning the linear facility (the facility landowner) if the right-of-way is owned in fee. Or, the underlying landowner may be a private party, in which case the utility company would own some form of easement on the property for the right-of-way. If the utility company owns an easement, it owns rights (through the easement) and the easement may also be affected by the co-location of a new facility.

The new co-located facility may also require additional new right-of-way adjacent the existing right-of-way, which could also involve additional owners.

Effects on the facility landowner

Utilities constructing a new linear facility adjacent to their own existing, like facility realize the greatest benefit of co-location. This is especially true if the utility company owns adjacent, vacant right-of-way. If the utility company had the foresight to purchase additional right-of-way or easement at the time the original facility was constructed, the loss of that right-of-way for the construction of unlike or unrelated facilities can have potentially significant affects. First, the utility company would lose the ability to develop a new facility if a second utility company used that vacant right-of-way for the development of a co-located facility.

Vacant right-of-way for future development can be of enormous value which protects against encroachment by future residential and commercial development that could make right-of-way acquisition and permitting much more difficult at a future time. However, under the co-location concept, this vacant right-of-way represents an ideal opportunity for siting a new linear facility. Even though the owning utility company may be compensated for the fair market value of the property by the second utility company, the value of having vacant right-of-way available for future development of a new facility will be lost.

If the facility landowner must, in fact, develop the new facility that was originally envisioned for the vacant right-of-way and the vacant right-of-way is no longer available, the owning utility company will now have to site the new facility on a new right-of-way with the attendant impacts. The additional costs to the facility landowner for permitting a new facility on a new right-of-way could be significant relative to the cost of using the previously available vacant right-of-way.

The requirement for co-location can necessitate special design, construction, and maintenance procedures for both the existing facility and the new, co-located facility. Insulating segments of conductors on electric transmission lines may be required to allow the safe operation of construction equipment next to the line for the installation of the co-located facility. Special blasting or horizontally controlled directional drill procedures may be required to avoid actual or potential damage to existing facilities adjacent to the new co-located facilities. Cathodic protection requirements may increase for a new pipeline if the centerline separation between the pipeline and the adjacent electric transmission line is decreased through the permitting process. Although the additional costs associated with these special design and construction considerations may be more than offset by the reduced impacts resulting from co-located facilities, they are still real costs associated with co-location that must be borne by the utilities.

Effects on the private landowner

Regardless of the circumstances under which a private landowner became an owner of a linear facility right-of-way, he/she is a prime candidate for the co-location of a second linear facility (or more) on his/her property. In many cases, the landowner does not realize that, regardless of the wording of the easement held by the utility company for the right-of-way across the property and regardless of commitments made by the utility company that only one facility would be constructed on the right-of-way, a second facility could, in fact, be constructed. Because of the simple fact that the landowner has an existing right-of-way on his/her property, they may be required to "sponsor" a second, co-located facility, and likely an expanded right-of-way, even if the original right-of-way was poorly sited and did not adhere to otherwise accepted siting principles.

Not only will the wider right-of-way result in restrictions on a much larger portion of the landowner's property, but the restrictions may also be multiple and different depending on the types of facilities. Co-located facilities (even of the same type) may have different inspection and maintenance schedules and requirements. Instead of having a single set of equipment and workers on the right-of-way over a given time interval, the different utilities may each be on their own inspection and maintenance schedule, resulting in more frequent activities on the rights-of-way.

Co-location of a new facility on or adjacent to an existing right-of-way can also limit a landowner's options with respect to negotiating payment for the new right-of-way or easement. If a new, non-co-located right-of-way or facility were to be negotiated with a landowner, some flexibility typically exists with respect to the exact location of the right-of-way on the property and (if the new right-of-way is not taken by eminent domain) in negotiating the price of the right-of-way or easement. If the jurisdictional regulatory agency dictates the co-location of a new facility, little if any flexibility remains for the landowner to negotiate since the location of the new co-located facility is dictated by the location of the existing facility. In addition, if the right of eminent domain is granted as part of the permit to allow the utility company to acquire additional right-of-way for a new co-located facility, the leverage that the landowner has available to negotiate price of the land or easement is typically defined by the state or local courts. As such, the application of co-location on a private property further limits a landowner's options.

Legitimate questions raised by various technical disciplines relative to Although the potential impact to each individual property will vary based on the configuration of the existing and co-located rights-of-way and based on restrictions on the secondary land uses on that existing right-of-way, the additional restrictions may be significant to the landowner.

CONSIDERATIONS AND RESPONSIBILITIES OF THE REGULATORY PROCESS

Regulatory agencies in general have come to embrace and adopt the concepts of co-location of linear facilities. The political and public scrutiny in the permitting of linear facilities has resulted in some land management agencies unrealistically embracing the co-location concept and in some jurisdictional regulatory agencies incorporating the requirement for joint use into permits, licenses, co-location of linear facilities and rights-of-way, but especially applicable to private landowners, are "How many adjacent co-located rights-of-way are too many? How wide is 'too wide' for adjacent co-located rights-of-way?" These questions have been raised relative to visual impact regarding the concept of "visual saturation" and the number of aboveground (electric transmission) facilities that can be co-located before "too many" have been located together. Ecologists and wildlife biologists, while embracing the use of co-location to minimize habitat fragmentation and right-of-way clearing, have also questioned the value of increasing widths of co-located rights-of-way when species of animals will no longer cross the open space of multiple cleared rights-of-way. The landowner can legitimately ask the same question regarding "How much is too much?" when the issue of new, additional rights-of-way on his/her property is again and again proposed in the name of "co-location." and certificates. The application of the joint use concept is becoming part of the rationale for the expedient justification for some regulatory agencies to approve needed utility projects. The burden of actually applying the concept is then left to the owners of the existing and proposed linear facilities.

The propensity for regulatory agencies to advocate and/or dictate co-location of new facilities is well understood by the utilities industry. In fact, some utilities will propose co-location of their proposed new facilities simply as a means to facilitate, and hopefully accelerate, the permitting process for the new facility. The utility company may not necessarily see the need for co-location of their proposed facility. However, even though co-location may not provide for the least impacting route or provide opportunities for the most economical or efficient design for the new facility, the additional cost associated with co-location is viewed by many utilities as the cost of getting the new facility permitted in the shortest amount of time.

It is the responsibility of the regulatory agencies to realistically evaluate proposals for new linear facilities and evaluate the overall impacts associated with co-located facilities versus independent facilities with new rights-of-way taking into account some of the factors discussed above.

CONCLUSION

Co-location of linear facilities and rights-of-way can reduce the overall impacts of construction and operation of new linear facilities. However, the benefits of co-location can be offset by negative aspects.

Co-location is not a panacea for the siting of new linear facilities. Both utilities and regulatory agencies should consider co-location as only one of many criteria in the planning and siting of new facilities and must weigh the broader advantages of co-location against site-specific and landowner-related issues and impacts. Co-location can compound and exacerbate impacts to the private landowner with the existing right-of-way on his/her property and to the utility with the existing facility on the right-of-way. While the siting, permitting, and construction processes for a new co-located linear facility are relatively short term, multiple linear facilities and the associated impacts on a private landowner will last for the operational lives of the co-located facilities. Co-location does represent an opportunity to reduce overall impacts from the construction and operation of linear facilities; however, the overall benefits of co-location may not live up to expectations.

REFERENCES

Federal Power Commission. Undated. Electric Power Transmission and the Environment.

Howlett, Bruce. 1976. Environmental selection of transmission route with maps and computers. In: Proceedings of the First National Symposium on Environmental Concerns in Rights-of-Way Management.

Jenkins, David F. 1987. Paralleling existing rights-of-way — Considerations frequently unconsidered. In: Proceedings of the Fourth International Symposium on Environmental Concerns in Rights-of-Way Management.

Steinmaus, J. Michael. 1982. Siting considerations: Multiple-use versus single-use rights-of-way. In: Proceedings of the Third International Symposium on Environmental Concerns in Rights-of-Way Management.

BIOGRAPHICAL SKETCH

David F. Jenkins
TRC Environmental Corporation, Boott Mills South, Foot of John Street, Lowell, MA 01852, USA, Telephone: 978/656-3501, Fax: 978/458-9140, e-mail: djenkins@trcsolutions.com

David F. Jenkins is Vice President of the National Linear Facilities Program at TRC Environmental Corporation and has over 30 years of experience in siting, impact assessment, and federal and state licensing of pipeline, electric transmission line, and other energy projects.

Saturation Threshold in a Multi-Pipeline Corridor Expansion Project

J. Nixon, A. Jalbert, K. Etherington, T. Bossenberry, and D. Clark

TransCanada PipeLine Ventures Ltd. Partnership, on behalf of NOVA Chemicals Corporation, constructed a 273.1-mm (10-inch) ethylene pipeline within an existing multi-pipeline corridor between two petrochemical plants in the Joffre area, east of Red Deer, Alberta. The ethylene pipeline was constructed within a 10-m (33-foot) wide area between two existing operating pipelines. The pipeline crossed in and out of the corridor seven (7) times between the two petrochemical plants. The objective of this paper will be to discuss thresholds and related saturation indicators arising from construction in a multi-pipeline corridor. The paper will evaluate the project-related communication with the regulatory agency, owner and contractor, the atypical planning required, and the specific use of certain construction equipment, such as Low Ground Pressure (LGP) dozers and backhoes to conserve topsoil, for safe construction of this pipeline within this multi-pipeline corridor. Environmental and safety concerns were met during construction by maintaining equivalent land capability and preserving the integrity of the operating pipelines within the corridor. The saturation point for the multi-pipeline corridor was based on stakeholder, environmental, and constructability thresholds. These thresholds may be useful in the assessment and planning of pipelines within other multi-pipeline corridors.

Keywords: Threshold, constructability, environmental assessment, management system, soils handling, stakeholder

INTRODUCTION

TransCanada PipeLines Limited ("TransCanada") operates approximately 38,000 km of natural gas pipelines across Canada. TransCanada has over 19,000 km of right-of-way in Canada, traversing many different environments ranging from Taiga Plains through to the Boreal Shield and Mixedwood Plains, and crossing some 21,150 properties. In managing this extensive linear system, TransCanada faces the challenges of corridor issues on an ongoing basis. One of the corridor issues to be addressed is the concept of the saturation level of a corridor based on the evaluation of thresholds.

TransCanada has developed working definitions for both threshold and saturation level which will be applied to the following discussion. A "threshold" is "the point at which an identified negative effect begins to be realized." An analogy would be a glass of water. At some point the glass becomes full (the threshold) and one more drop of water results in an overflowing cup (negative effect).

TransCanada sees three primary categories of thresholds in all its rights-of-way, each of which may consist of various other thresholds. Firstly, TransCanada has identified the need to manage the stakeholder thresholds. There can be numerous stakeholders interested in some or all of TransCanada's rights-of-way, and each brings to the table a unique view of the acceptable tolerance for development. Secondly, TransCanada recognizes the need for environmental thresholds to be addressed in its environmental assessment activities. The analysis of thresholds also forms an important component of a cumulative effects assessment. Thirdly, as a pipeline company, TransCanada must incorporate the concept of constructability thresholds into its planning activities. TransCanada must be able to construct and operate

Environmental Concerns in Rights-of-Way Management: Seventh International Symposium
J.W. Goodrich-Mahoney, D.F. Mutrie and C.A. Guild (editors)
© 2002 Elsevier Science Ltd. All rights reserved.

its pipelines in a safe manner and must therefore understand what construction and operation limitations exist. Each of these thresholds varies from location to location.

TransCanada submits that all thresholds must be taken into account when determining the saturation level for a particular corridor. The working definition of "saturation level" of the corridor is "the point at which mitigation of the effects of the proposed development on a given threshold is not attainable." For example, the space available for an additional pipeline in a corridor with four operating pipelines may exceed the threshold for constructability. That is, there may be too many pipelines within the corridor to safely construct another pipeline.

TransCanada manages its rights-of-way by seeking a balance of the multiple thresholds to be considered in all its work. By managing and working within the limits of each of these thresholds, the company is working towards the sustainable development of Canada's resources.

The focus of the following discussion is the management of multiple thresholds within a right-of-way, from a pipeline perspective. The 1999 Prentiss Ethylene Pipeline Project will be used in this paper to demonstrate how TransCanada applies its Health, Safety and Environment (HSE) Management system to address the challenges of working within an existing corridor that has multiple pipelines and thresholds.

Health, Safety, and Environment Management system

The primary tool that TransCanada uses to ensure consideration of the multiple thresholds is the Health, Safety, and Environment (HSE) Management system and its associated tools and processes. The basis of TransCanada's HSE Management system is to ensure: effective planning; implementation of the plan; monitoring of the plan implementation; and continuous improvement of the plans and processes. TransCanada has developed a set of environmental standards which outlines the company's policy approach to protection of natural resource integrity as well as the commitment to implementation of those protection measures (TransCanada PipeLines Limited, 1999). The standards are supported by "how to" procedures which align to meet or exceed all relevant legislative requirements. Through the management system, processes have been established to ensure communication of these standards and procedures to stakeholders for their comment and support.

Within the management system framework, TransCanada has developed an approach for managing thresholds that is applied consistently during the planning, implementation, and monitoring phases of a project. The steps of this approach include: identifying issues; understanding the thresholds; considering mitigation; and, developing a plan. Each of these steps is discussed below within the context of the Prentiss Ethylene Pipeline Project and the stakeholder, environmental, and constructability thresholds.

With the construction and installation of additional pipeline(s) within a multi-pipeline corridor, the need to manage activities within the limits of stakeholder, environmental, and constructability thresholds is critical. The limits of the various thresholds can be identified using the following measures:
– Stakeholder thresholds — stakeholder concerns are elevated into the political and socio-economic arena to the extent that communication, arbitration, or negotiation methods have not succeeded in modifying or changing attitudes and ideals to allow for additional development;
– Environmental thresholds — the environmental impacts associated with the development cannot be mitigated (e.g., where construction mitigation could only occur within a critical time of a species' life cycle, such as calving); and
– Constructability thresholds — construction of the pipeline would cause significant safety risks to individuals and adjacent pipelines.

Project

In 1999, TransCanada PipeLine Ventures Ltd. Partnership ("TransCanada Ventures") designed and constructed the Prentiss Ethylene Pipeline Project ("Prentiss Project") near Joffre, Alberta. TransCanada Ventures led the project on behalf of NOVA Chemicals Corporation ("NOVA Chemicals"). The Prentiss Ethylene Pipeline is NPS (Nominal Pipe Size) 10 and is 9.7 km in length. The pipeline is located northeast of Red Deer between the NOVA Chemicals' Joffre Petrochemical Plant and the Union Carbide Canada Ltd. Plant site.

The pipeline route was located in the Central Parkland natural subregion of Alberta. The pipeline route was dominated by clay loam till deposits that were the result of a compacted mixture of sand and clay transported by glaciers. Fluvial deposits occurred along existing and abandoned stream channels. Glacial till, and fluvial and glaciolacustrine veneers over glacial till made up 86, 9, and 3% of the route, respectively. Topsoil depths along the route ranged from 15 to 100 cm, with an average depth of 35 cm.

The area of the pipeline route is one of the most productive agricultural zones in Alberta with most native vegetation being replaced by barley, wheat, canola, and oat crops. The route also encountered pasture and hayland consisting of legume and grass species. The land use composition in the area was approximately: 7.3 km/66% cultivated; 1.9 km/17% hayland; 0.5 km/4% pasture; 0.4 km/3% native range; 0.05 km/0.5% wooded; 0.4 km/4.0% wetland; 0.5 km/4% industrial; and 0.3 km/2.4 stream/slough.

The project planning, construction, and operation had to consider that there were only 10 m of right-of-way available for pipeline installation within the

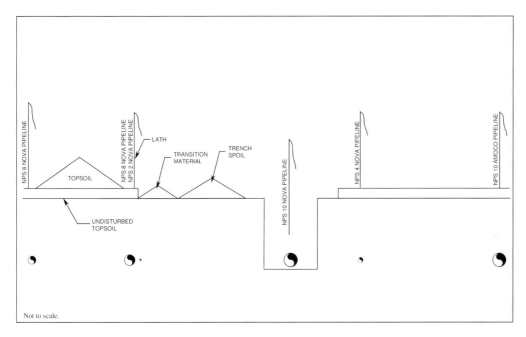

Fig. 1. Typical right-of-way configuration for the Prentiss Ethylene Pipeline Project.

existing multi-pipeline corridor. This 10-m space was bounded by an abandoned (nitrogen filled) NPS 4 pipeline and a dual pipe trench containing an NPS 8 and an NPS 2 pipeline. In addition, the corridor also contained two more pipelines, totalling five pipelines in a 48.3 m wide corridor (BOSS Environmental Consulting Ltd., 1999; TransCanada PipeLine Ventures Ltd. Partnership, 1999). The configuration of the corridor is shown in Figure 1.

The Prentiss Project was not only unusual by how it was constructed but also by how the various project activities were shared between NOVA Chemicals and TransCanada Ventures. For example, the landowner and public consultation process normally would have been undertaken by the main project team which, in this case, consisted mainly of TransCanada Ventures representatives. However on this project, NOVA Chemicals was the primary contact in discussing the pipeline expansion plans with landowners along the proposed right-of-way due to their long-term relationships to the Joffre and Red Deer communities. TransCanada Ventures supported the project by providing pipeline construction and operation expertise and by ensuring that the management framework integrated all issues that were identified during the public consultation process.

DISCUSSION

Although, each threshold had a different measure, the underlying issue on the Prentiss Project was the same for each threshold — soils handling. Soils handling became a concern due to past construction activities in the corridor that resulted in topsoil–subsoil mixing. Previous pipelines had been constructed under less rigorous regulatory requirements and construction techniques. As such, in many locations, the topsoil and subsoil were mixed to varying degrees.

The issue of soils handling manifested itself in a different way for each threshold category. The stakeholder threshold was identified as the existing width of a corridor (i.e., no more land could be taken for development). The environmental threshold was identified as soil quality, a surrogate in this case for equivalent land capability. The constructability threshold was the effective (i.e., safe) implementation of the construction plan, which included special requirements for soils handling in a narrowed right-of-way.

The resolution of the soils handling concern and the management of each of the thresholds was undertaken by working with the key stakeholders and "experts" for each of the thresholds when developing plans and monitoring implementation.

Stakeholder threshold
Identifying issues
Through stakeholder consultation, it was identified that soils handling was a key issue for landowners and regulatory personnel. As mentioned earlier, this area is one of the most productive agricultural areas in the province and it had already been affected by past construction activities (e.g., soil mixing). As a result of the soils handling practices undertaken in the past, many stakeholders did not want to see the corridor expanded any further.

Understanding thresholds
Many regulators receive numerous submissions from landowners identifying their concern that multiple pipeline rights-of-way can be a serious impediment

to use of their land. Landowners have questioned the need for each company to acquire a new right-of-way, thereby expanding the overall width of the corridor, when an existing right-of-way may contain only one pipeline.

For the Prentiss Project, the stakeholders (landowners) had reached their threshold limit and therefore, there was opposition to expanding the corridor. The stakeholders believed that further expansion of the corridor would result in decreased land capability resulting from soil mixing.

Considering mitigation
Once the thresholds are understood, the proponent can begin considering mitigation measures. Working with the concerned stakeholders, TransCanada Ventures and NOVA Chemicals agreed to mitigate the stakeholder threshold by working within the confines of the existing corridor. Further, a detailed soils handling plan outlining protection measures for the current construction, including how to address existing areas of soil admixing, was also developed. In many areas the right-of-way was actually returned to an improved condition following construction. For example, buried topsoil was recovered.

Developing plans
To address the stakeholder threshold, a plan was developed to include mitigation measures, ensure ongoing stakeholder communication, and to monitor the effectiveness of the implementation of the plan, including soils handling. The stakeholder threshold provided the boundaries for the design of the construction plan. To stay within the limits of the stakeholder threshold, the right-of-way had to be maintained within the existing corridor. This threshold strongly influenced the constructability of the pipeline.

Environmental threshold

Identifying issues
The evaluation and identification of environmental issues related to using the existing corridor was undertaken during the environmental assessment (EA) process. The EA evaluates the potential effects of the proposed project on natural resources such as: soils; vegetation; water; wildlife and fisheries, including the associated habitat; air; and historical and paleontological resources. TransCanada Ventures conducted the EA using standard guidelines and assessment procedures through which all projects are evaluated.

Although there were many issues along the right-of-way, the key environmental issue identified through the EA process was soils. In this case, the concern was related to soil quality, which can be used as a surrogate for land capability.

Understanding thresholds
The soil quality issue posed a concern for this project, as topsoil-subsoil mixing had occurred during past construction in the corridor, which potentially could not be mitigated using standard construction and mitigation practices. It is very difficult to separate soils that have been mixed and farmed for many years.

The collection of soil profiles along the proposed pipeline right-of-way was used to identify the soil quality. This information allowed for the planning of specific mitigation practices that addressed and alleviated concerns associated with previous construction practices that may have affected the equivalent capability of the soils. Within the context of the Prentiss Project this information ensured that the project team could address specific construction practices within the time frame of the project schedule and could incorporate innovative and practical approaches.

Considering mitigation
In the planning of appropriate mitigative measures, undertaking appropriate soils handling within the confines of the existing corridor was the key consideration. Technical constructability considerations to address soils handling included: space requirements for topsoil and spoil storage; extra temporary work space requirements for areas where congestion of existing oil and gas facilities would be encountered; and, constraints associated with watercourse, road, railway, and foreign pipeline crossings. These technical constraints were then evaluated in the context of potential mitigative measures that would assist in the alleviation of topsoil-subsoil mixing concerns.

Developing plans
The project team worked with regulatory personnel and affected landowners to address the soil mixing concern by implementing a stripping procedure for previously disturbed soil profiles. The objective of the procedure was to improve the soil condition by reducing and undoing some of the mixing that had occurred in the past.

To further address the environmental threshold of soil quality, TransCanada Ventures designed its reclamation plans and techniques to prevent topsoil loss from wind and water erosion in the short-term and establish compatible vegetation cover as soon as possible following construction. Seed mixes were developed with stakeholders to meet their needs and concerns while at the same time maintaining compatibility with the surrounding resources and land uses.

Also as part of the plan, TransCanada Ventures undertook environmental monitoring during construction to ensure the plan was implemented properly and that soil quality was protected, and improved where possible. TransCanada Ventures also undertook post-construction monitoring to assess the success of the mitigation measures and determine any outstanding issues.

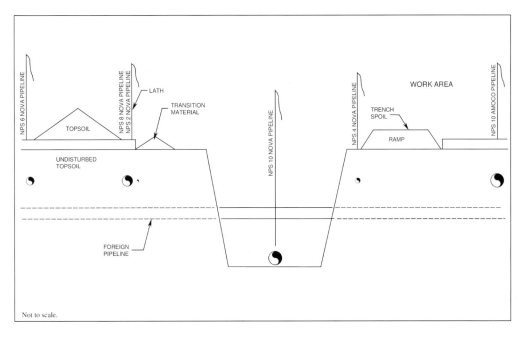

Fig. 2. Typical right-of-way configuration for a foreign line crossing for the Prentiss Ethylene Pipeline Project.

Constructability threshold

Identifying issues

During the planning phase of the project, the project team identified the need to address constructability concerns. One area of concern was a congested area located just north of the Joffre Plant site. Although there were many congested areas along the route, this one kilometre section was an area where the alignment:
- consecutively crossed two railway beds and a road crossing;
- was partially being used as a parking lot;
- crossed a major highway; and
- intersected four pipelines at the approach to the tie-in at the Joffre plant site (where there was a significant rise in elevation).

Understanding thresholds

As a result of managing the other thresholds through working within a confined right-of-way, the constructability threshold, measured by the level of safety, was close to its acceptable limit. The corridor contained multiple operating pipelines where standard construction techniques would need to be modified to address safety considerations of equipment and personnel to enable the effective implementation of the plan, including soils handling. Further, the congestion of oil and gas activities within the area and across the pipeline (i.e., foreign line crossings) increased the potential for the need to hand-expose pipelines and use of hydro-vac excavation equipment and associated containment equipment.

Considering mitigation

For the Prentiss Project, specific topsoil stripping equipment specifications were not outlined as part of the project scope. However, due to safety concerns associated with working between two operating pipelines, Low Ground Pressure (LGP) equipment was used to strip topsoil within the corridor. The LGP equipment ensured the safe construction of the pipeline even though the distance between the two operating pipelines was too narrow (10 m) for typical topsoil stripping procedures. Further, storage space requirements at road crossings for handling spoil material required modifications to handle spoil volume. The spoil was placed on the stripped work-side and was driven on due to right-of-way constraints (Fig. 2).

Another mitigation measure applied was the use of equipment with specialized clean-up buckets (i.e., no teeth on the bucket) that could scrape stockpiled topsoil off the 8 inch and 2 inch NOVA Chemicals operating lines in cultivated fields, hay land, and pasture lands. The clean-up buckets allowed for the removal of the stockpiled topsoil without damaging the vegetation that was left in place; this was key to the successful reclamation of the right-of-way.

Developing plans

TransCanada Ventures worked with construction personnel and applied its findings from the EA to determine site-specific construction plans for the Prentiss Project. TransCanada Ventures requested a specific grade plan from the Contractor prior to construction to address the construction constraints (i.e., congested areas) and to identify the potential for significant topsoil-subsoil mixing within this area if topsoil and spoil material were not handled properly. The identification of stakeholder and environmental thresholds allowed the project team the opportunity to refine the details of construction timing, further delineate the requirements for extra temporary workspace, as well as identifying alternative construction methods (i.e. constructing backwards to further reduce concerns about space limitations).

As with the other stakeholders, TransCanada Ventures ensured that monitoring of the construction was undertaken to ensure the proper implementation of the plan and to ensure worker safety. Post-construction discussions also took place to determine areas for improvement and to identify techniques that could be applied to other projects.

RECOMMENDATIONS AND CONCLUSIONS

In this paper, the authors have identified three categories of thresholds (stakeholder, environmental, and constructability) that could potentially impact construction within a multi-pipeline corridor. It is important to identify each threshold early to determine whether or not any thresholds are at their limit. If a threshold is at its limit and it cannot be mitigated, the corridor must be considered saturated. When the saturation point of the corridor is reached, the project team must assess other potential routing options.

The early identification of issues and thresholds was invaluable to the success of the Prentiss Project as it allowed for the development of a construction plan that all stakeholders (including regulators, landowners, and construction personnel) could agree to and implement. The other key to the success of the project was the implementation of the plan in the field. The plan allowed for all field personnel to understand the issues and goals of the project, which gave them a sense of ownership of the project and accomplishment with its successful outcome. The key to the implementation of the plan was open and clear communication between the project team, who developed the plan with key stakeholders, and individuals in the field who implemented the plan.

One other way to manage thresholds may be through the development of regional land use plans. Regional land use plans aid in decision making and provide a level playing field for operators and proponents in a given region. Regional land use plans can also help determine mitigation options by providing a measurable limit to development and surface disturbance.

In the absence of regional land use plans, all stakeholders, including industry, landowners, and government, need to work together to provide solutions for managing thresholds and saturation levels within existing and proposed new corridors.

ACKNOWLEDGEMENTS

The authors would like to acknowledge the following individuals who contributed support to this paper: Ernie Tromposch, Brian McConaghy, and Ilona Berbekar.

REFERENCES

TransCanada PipeLine Ventures Ltd. Partnership. 1999. Environmental Design Basis: Prentiss Ethylene Pipeline Project.

BOSS Environmental Consulting Ltd. 1999. Environmental Inspection Report: Ventures NPS 10 Prentiss Pipeline Project #16005240, Mainline Construction.

TransCanada PipeLines Limited. 1999. Conservation & Reclamation Standard.

BIOGRAPHICAL SKETCHES

Jeannette Nixon

Jeannette Nixon, Environmental & Inspections Services Ltd., 792 Shawnee Dr. S.W., Calgary, AB, T2Y 1V9, Canada

Jeannette Nixon is a professional biologist that has worked primarily in the oil and gas sector in Alberta over the past twenty-four years. She has a BSc (Zoology) from the University of Manitoba. Jeannette's professional expertise includes extensive experience in the assessment of gas pipelines relating to biophysical impacts of linear developments. She has comprehensive project management experience in the areas of environmental program planning, environmental impact assessment, mitigation and reclamation. Her interest lies in bringing collaborative problem solving and teamwork into the negotiation of environmental issues and project scope to addressing regulatory and stakeholder concerns and interests.

Andrea Jalbert

Andrea Jalbert, TransCanada PipeLines Limited, 450 1st Street S.W., Calgary, Alberta, T2P 5H1, Canada, fax: (403) 920-2330, e-mail: andrea_jalbert@transcanada.com

Andrea Jalbert is an environmental professional with 7 years of experience in the pipeline industry. Andrea is a biologist currently working for TransCanada PipeLines Limited as an Environmental Advisor with a focus on environmental planning and watercourse crossings. Andrea has a Bachelor of Science degree (Honours Biology — Cooperative Program) from the University of Waterloo.

Karen Etherington

Karen Etherington, TransCanada PipeLines Limited, 450 1st Street S.W., Calgary, Alberta, T2P 5H1, Canada

Karen Etherington is currently the Senior Environmental Leader in the Health, Safety & Environment Department at TransCanada PipeLines Limited. In this role, Karen provides technical leadership within HS&E, to other business divisions and to external interests. She also plays a key role in developing environmental strategies to manage policies and regulatory issues, ensuring high quality and compliant products. Karen has a Bachelor of Environmental Studies (Honours Geography — Cooperative Program) from the University of Waterloo. It was through this program that she was introduced to the company. Karen joined TransCanada in 1987, and has worked primarily on the Alberta system as a contributor to the environmental area. Over the past 14 years, Karen has progressed through several positions in support of the environmental planning, environmental management and reclamation activities. In leading these activities, Karen has had the opportunity to contribute to many external multi-stakeholder forums to progress pipeline environmental issues such as legislation and policy development through to pipeline abandonment.

Tim Bossenberry

Tim Bossenberry, BOSS Environmental Consulting Ltd., 171 Shawinigan Drive S.W., Calgary, AB, T2Y 2W1, Canada

Tim Bossenberry has been involved with environmental conservation and reclamation planning in the oil and gas industry for over 20 years. He worked for the Provincial Government from 1977 to 1989 as a resource planner, a regulator for pipelines, and a reclamation planner. Tim worked for a major pipeline company in Edmonton for four years, where he worked on developing construction procedures for new pipelines; operations and maintenance procedures; and remediation plans for crude oil and condensate leaks. For the past 8 years, Tim has worked as an environmental consultant in both Edmonton and Calgary, where his focus has been with pipelines and reclamation. He has authored and co-authored numerous guideline documents, procedures manuals, and working documents, mainly for pipelines.

Doug Clark

Doug Clark, Destiny Pipeline Consulting Ltd., Box 308, Warburg, AB, T0C 2T0, Canada

Doug Clark has over 30 years of pipeline experience holding positions in various capacities from Construction Superintendent, Construction Inspection, Chief Inspector. For the past 9 years, Doug has been an Environmental Inspector and Senior Environmental Construction Advisor.

Cumulative Effects Assessment and Linear Corridors: The Representative Areas Approach

Terry Antoniuk

Cumulative effects assessment differs from conventional project-specific impact assessment by considering larger geographic study areas, longer time frames, and unrelated projects or activities. Cumulative assessments of right-of-way proposals pose particular challenges for several reasons: (1) no prescribed or standard methods currently exist; (2) there are inherent, but frequently unrecognized, differences between project-specific cumulative effects assessments and those done for resource management or planning purposes; and (3) conventional approaches are more applicable to developments that are isolated in space rather than in long, linear corridors. The "representative areas" approach described here has been successfully used in recent federally and provincially regulated pipeline proposals in western Canada. With this approach, assessment of cumulative environmental effects is conducted for representative areas comprised of one or more 1:50,000 scale map sheets. These areas are selected to include multiple project facilities or activities and to reflect biophysical conditions and administrative boundaries. Impact analyses conducted for these representative areas consider indices of landscape conditions and compare these to established or derived thresholds for indicator species or groups. The relative merits and disadvantages of this approach are discussed from the perspective of proponents, regulators, environmental organizations, and practitioners. The use of representative areas and landscape indices is concluded to be a proven alternative for linear projects of all sizes.

Keywords: Cumulative effects, landscape indices, representative areas, thresholds, study area, impact assessment

INTRODUCTION

It is now recognized that the combined effects of unrelated individual projects or activities could result in aggregate effects that may be different in nature or extent from the effects of the individual activities (FEARO, 1994). Following passage of the *Canadian Environmental Assessment Act* in 1992 and subsequent passage of related federal, provincial, and territorial legislation, assessment of cumulative effects is now required for projects undergoing formal regulatory review (e.g., NEB, 1995). The regulatory objective of this review is to ensure that environmental effects within Canada are carefully considered and that unjustified significant adverse environmental effects do not occur. Since passage of this legislation, technical and legal developments have resulted in ongoing evolution of cumulative effects assessment (CEA) practice in Canada.

CEA differs from conventional project-specific impact assessment by considering larger geographic study areas, longer time frames, and unrelated projects or activities. In CEA, there is a requirement to draw discipline-specific information together to achieve an integrated appraisal at the larger regional or landscape scale at which most cumulative effects occur (CEARC, 1986; Sonntag et al., 1987; Cocklin et al., 1992a).

CEA of linear corridor proposals poses particular challenges for several reasons:
1. No prescribed or standard methods currently exist;
2. There are inherent, but frequently unrecognized, differences between project-specific assessments and those done for resource management or planning purposes; and

Environmental Concerns in Rights-of-Way Management: Seventh International Symposium
J.W. Goodrich-Mahoney, D.F. Mutrie and C.A. Guild (editors)
Crown Copyright © 2002 Elsevier Science Ltd. All rights reserved.

3. Conventional approaches are more applicable to developments that are isolated in space rather than in long, linear corridors.

Uncertain methods

CEA is affected by a variety of technical issues such as: lack of detailed monitoring information on past development activities and key environmental parameters; absence of defined resource use or ecological thresholds; availability of credible and defensible information on present and future development activities; and difficulty in predicting synergistic, discontinuous or unanticipated resource and system effects (CEARC, 1986; Sonntag et al., 1987).

Specific guidance for evaluation of cumulative effects in Canada is provided in federal documents (CEAA, 1996, 1999; Davies, 1996; Hegmann et al., 1999). There is general agreement that given the complexity of cumulative effects, no standard method is available. Instead, selection of appropriate approaches and methods depends on the objectives and issues (Cocklin et al., 1992b; Shoemaker, 1994; Hegmann and Yarranton, 1995; Smit and Spaling, 1995; CEQ, 1997; Hegmann et al., 1999; Alberta Environment, 2000). Several court decisions also provide inconsistent legal interpretations of acceptable methods.

Due to this technical and legal uncertainty, regulators, industry, stakeholders, and practitioners are unclear about how and when CEA should be conducted for proposed linear corridors.

Project-specific CEA versus regional CEA

The most common cause of misunderstanding stems from the difference between project-specific CEAs and those done for resource management or planning purposes. Regional resource management or planning studies generally consider the effects of all past, present, and possible disturbance sources (industrial, municipal, domestic, recreational) over a large geographic area and long time frames (10–100 years). Regional studies can gather information that is available, project trends into the future, and recommend effective management measures if appropriate (e.g., Banff-Bow Valley Study, 1996). For this reason, they are the responsibility of one or more government agencies and are most successful when all interested stakeholders are involved. Regional assessments should ideally be done for resource management or planning purposes before human activities begin.

In contrast, project-specific CEAs in Canada are clearly the responsibility of the proponent; these examine the proposed project in the context of other existing and likely disturbance sources. Potential combined effects are related to available management or environmental criteria so that the significance of potential cumulative effects can be assessed. Unfortunately, most linear projects are located in areas where explicit regional management plans are not available or existing plans are mutually incompatible because they were developed in isolation for different resources or sectors. For these reasons, public stakeholders participating in linear corridor proposal reviews frequently take one of two positions:

1. No rights-of-way should be allowed until an adequate regional assessment and resource management plan has been completed; or
2. The proponent should assume the government's role and complete a comprehensive regional assessment that exceeds normal project-specific requirements.

The multi-stakeholder processes required to generate regional resource management plans are generally unpredictable and protracted. This results in delays that have obvious financial and manpower implications for both project proponents and regulatory agencies.

While completion of a project-specific CEA may be viewed as a less desirable alternative by some, it ensures that regulatory requirements are met and provides regulators and stakeholders with information on potential cumulative effects that warrant mitigation and management.

Linear corridors and CEA

Unlike facilities that are isolated in space, a right-of-way footprint consists of a relatively long and narrow corridor that can cross numerous watershed, biophysical, and administrative units. Several approaches have been adopted for linear corridor CEAs since passage of the *Canadian Environmental Assessment Act*.

The most common approach, especially where formal project review was not required, has been to avoid CEA altogether because of its perceived complexity, uncertainty, and cost. A second approach has been to restrict evaluation of cumulative effects to a cursory or qualitative discussion of potential issues without any analysis or assessment. The pervasiveness of incomplete or inadequate CEAs has also been reported for the United States (CEQ, 1997).

A third approach has been to evaluate potential cumulative effects for a single indicator or biophysical unit (often referred to as a Valued Ecosystem Component or VEC). This approach provides an analysis of cumulative effects for a species or habitat type (e.g., grizzly bear or native prairie) of social, ecological, or economic importance that is potentially affected by the right-of-way.

For most linear corridors however, consideration of a suite of indicators is more appropriate because a single indicator is not capable of assessing the pertinent factors required by legislation (Noss, 1990; Cocklin et al., 1992a,b; Cairns et al., 1993; FEARO, 1994; Smit and Spaling, 1995; Hegmann et al., 1999). While this option may be the most appropriate, it has been the least common approach, likely because it expands the complexity, duration, and cost of CEA for proposed linear corridors.

Notwithstanding progress made over the last 20 years, proponents, regulators, stakeholders, and practitioners are still searching for the CEA Holy Grail: a legally and technically accepted method (or suite of methods) that can be consistently and economically applied to linear corridor proposals to understand, assess, and manage cumulative effects.

THE REPRESENTATIVE AREAS APPROACH

The "representative areas" approach described here is not the CEA Holy Grail, but it is a proven method applicable to linear corridor proposals of all sizes. This approach has been successfully applied in CEAs of recent federally- and provincially-regulated pipeline proposals in western Canada (Alliance, 1997; Salmo Consulting Inc., 1996, 1999a,b). It involves the following steps:

1. One or more map sheets (representative areas) crossed by the proposed linear corridor are selected for evaluation of potential cumulative effects.
2. Numerical measures of human-caused disturbances (landscape indices or metrics) with and without the project are calculated for these map sheets.
3. Calculated indices are compared to management criteria or thresholds for selected biophysical or socio-economic indicators to assess potential cumulative effects.

This approach provides meaningful information about disturbance levels with and without the proposed project that can be compared to established or derived ecological and social thresholds. These data supplement project-specific impact assessment and planning and allow potential incremental project effects and cumulative effects from all existing/planned activities to be evaluated. In contrast to many other CEA methods, it is relatively quick and inexpensive (less than US $7500 per map sheet) because it is based on Geographic Information System (GIS) analysis of readily available data.

Selecting representative areas

Potential environmental effects associated with pipeline and linear right-of-way projects are well understood and include: loss of rare and endangered species; loss of terrestrial habitat and habitat effectiveness; disturbance and mortality of wildlife; and loss of productive capacity of renewable resources. These may also contribute to cumulative effects at local, regional, and landscape scales.

Identification of appropriate study area boundaries is a critical component of CEA and impact assessment in general. Selection of a large study area increases the likelihood that an impact will be judged to be of no concern because it is relatively small in comparison. In contrast, selection of a small study area prevents consideration of incremental and cumulative effects that are best evaluated over large areas. Guidance documents recommend that spatial boundaries be based on the anticipated "zone-of-influence" for selected indicators (CEQ, 1997; Hegmann et al., 1999). This may lead to complex and costly analyses covering large study areas.

With the representative areas approach, a predefined study area is used for all indicators. In most analyses conducted to date, a 1:50,000 scale map sheet was used as the basic analysis unit. This unit was selected because it is one of the primary scales for both digital and hard copy data, which facilitates GIS spatial analyses. A 1:50,000 map sheet in western Canada includes an area of approximately 900 km^2. This is consistent with the study areas used for other CEAs in North America (e.g., Lee and Gosselink, 1988; CRC, 1996, 1999) and includes sufficient area to be meaningful for the ecological and resource use indicators (VECs) that are most commonly used.

Focus on representative areas is similar to the approach used for baseline or monitoring studies where specific sampling parameters, areas, and times are systematically or randomly selected to represent overall conditions. This widely accepted method is applied because it is impractical or impossible to measure everything and sampling representative sites or areas reduces effort and associated costs.

As with any sampling program design, the number and location of representative areas selected for evaluation is critical and should be based on the location, size, and nature of the proposed linear corridor as well as existing and potential cumulative effects. Selection of representative areas is based on following criteria as described more fully below:

– size and nature of the linear corridor and potential project effects;
– nature and location of past and future projects and activities;
– availability and utility of existing data and knowledge;
– inclusion of both common and uncommon biophysical conditions (i.e., vegetation, habitat, species);
– reflection of relevant ecological boundaries (i.e., Biogeoclimatic zone, Natural Region or Ecoregion, watershed, land use); and
– reflection of relevant administrative boundaries (i.e., provincial, municipal, regional).

One approach that has been used for small pipeline projects is to select all 1:50,000 map sheets intersected by the proposed route and associated facilities. Fig. 1 shows that for smaller projects less than about 30 km in length, this may restrict the analysis area to one map sheet. Nonetheless, this study area is large enough to allow cumulative effects to be considered in the context of existing disturbance such as roads, forest harvest,

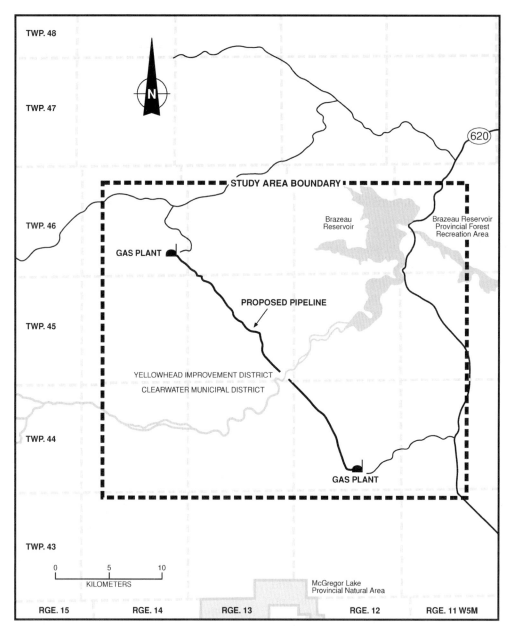

Fig. 1. CEA study area for a small pipeline project in west-central Alberta.

recreation, and urban areas (Salmo Consulting Inc., 1999a,b).

Additional map sheets can be added as needed for larger projects or those occurring in highly disturbed areas. This increases the analysis area and allows other biophysical or administrative units and existing or proposed activities to be considered.

As an example, fourteen map sheets were considered in the CEA conducted for the proposed Alliance Pipeline Project (Alliance, 1997). The Canadian portion of this project included a 1559 km long mainline, lateral pipelines totaling approximately 698 km, and associated compressors and facilities traversing three provinces and multiple ecological units. No CEA approach or method had been applied to a linear project of this scale, and conventional methods would have required evaluation of an expansive area of western Canada. For assessment purposes, the project was divided into six areas or "segments" with relatively consistent environmental, social, and project conditions. Potential cumulative effects were evaluated for a minimum of 2 1:50,000 scale map sheets for each segment. Fig. 2 shows the representative areas selected for the western half of this project. The combined evaluations for all six segments provided sufficient information to allow all cumulative effects to be evaluated (NEB, 1998).

For the Alliance Pipeline Project, comments were solicited from regulators, public stakeholders, and practitioners to evaluate the suitability of proposed representative areas. Although there was overall acceptance of the approach, a variety of concerns were expressed.

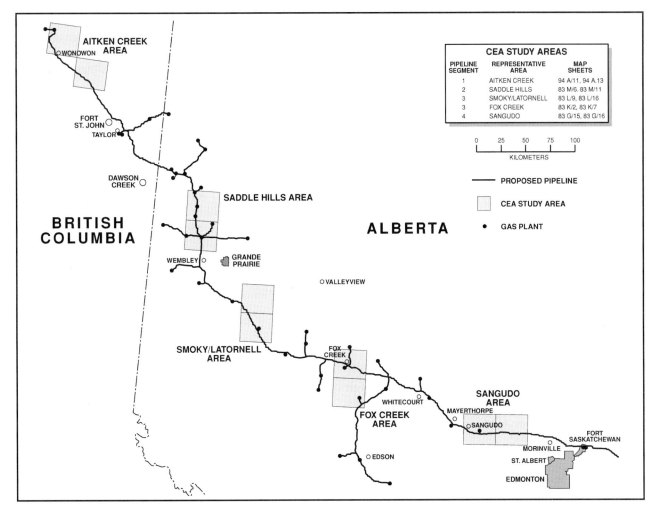

Fig. 2. Alliance Pipeline Project CEA representative areas west of Fort Saskatchewan, Alberta.

Some reviewers wondered how the analyses conducted for representative areas could be extrapolated to areas outside those selected for analysis. To address this concern, representative areas were selected to include a range of existing disturbance rates (relatively undisturbed to highly disturbed) in all major ecological units intersected by the route (boreal forest, parkland, grassland, agricultural). Others reviewers suggested that analyses should focus on areas with intensive existing development where cumulative effects were assumed to be more likely to occur. Although other activities were considered when selecting representative areas, the focus of this project-specific CEA was on activities associated with the Alliance Pipeline Project. As a result, representative areas were generally selected to include map sheets where multiple project-related activities such as mainline and gathering line construction were planned.

Calculating landscape indices

Once representative map sheets have been selected, numerical measures of human-caused disturbance (landscape indices) are calculated. Evaluation of indices is an accepted approach that provides meaningful information about existing disturbance levels and the incremental effect of the proposed linear corridor. Calculated metrics can also be compared to thresholds or management criteria to evaluate potential cumulative effects that could arise from existing, planned, and likely future activities (Beanlands and Duinker, 1983; Noss, 1990; Cocklin et al., 1992b; Noss et al., 1996).

Landscape indices used to date include access density (right-of-way $km\,km^{-2}$), stream crossing frequency (number of crossings per km of stream), total cleared area (ha), total edge area (area within a specified distance of a disturbance source), and total core area (area greater than a specified distance from a disturbance source).

Access density is used as a numerical index of habitat effectiveness and fragmentation associated with linear corridors. Research indicates that some animals avoid and are displaced by disturbances associated with roads. Relationships between access density and habitat effectiveness have been developed for some large mammals (e.g., Thomas et al., 1979, 1988; Lyon, 1984; Mace and Manley, 1993; Jalkotzy et al., 1997). Increased road density is also related to sediment transport to streams and has been correlated with declines in salmonid species including species of concern such as bull trout (USDA, 1996).

Total cleared or disturbed area is used as a numerical index of availability and fragmentation of the forest land base. Clearing, fire, and other forms of natural and man-made disturbance introduce changes into landscape patterns that affect the availability, distribution and juxtaposition of specific habitat types. Cleared or disturbed areas may also create barriers to movement of small animals (Wilcove et al., 1986) and affect stream flow and quality (e.g., Troendle and King, 1985; Nip, 1991).

Total edge and total core area are used as complementary landscape indices of terrestrial habitat suitability. Edge habitats are beneficial to many species, but excessive edge may lead to mortality or reduced populations of species such as grizzly bears and warblers that are dependent on forest interior (e.g., Reese and Ratti, 1988; Laurence and Yensen, 1991; Reijnen et al., 1995; Flather and Sauer, 1996; Gibeau et al., 1996; Reed et al., 1996a). The width of the edge zone varies with the species being considered, but in analyses completed to date, a 500-m zone of influence has been used as a representative figure applicable to a broad range of species. Minimum and maximum edge thresholds have been proposed (e.g., Thomas et al., 1979; With and Crist, 1995).

Theoretical models suggest that <40–60% core area represents an ecological threshold for interior species (Wilcove et al., 1986; Lee and Gosselink, 1988; Laurence and Yensen, 1991; With and Crist, 1995). Core area analysis is an accepted assessment technique for grizzly bear (CRC, 1996, 1999; Gibeau et al., 1996; Noss et al., 1996) and has also been applied in other physical and ecological evaluations (Laurence and Yensen, 1991; Reed et al., 1996b).

Stream crossing frequency is used as a numerical index of potential aquatic disturbance. Stream crossings represent points of access for subsistence and recreational fishermen as well as potential sources of sediment and in-stream and riparian habitat changes (e.g., Nip, 1991). A related measure, stream crossing density, is used in the British Columbia Interior Watershed Assessment Procedure (BCFS and BCE, 1995). Studies in western North America have shown that road and trail networks created for timber harvest and resource extraction can lead to direct effects on flow rates and patterns and sediment yield, and indirect effects on habitat, invertebrates and fisheries (e.g., Bosch and Hewlett, 1982; Cederholm et al., 1981; Furniss et al., 1991; McGurk and Fong, 1995).

With GIS programs, disturbance associated with the proposed linear corridor and other likely activities can be combined with existing disturbance sources to calculate cumulative impact indices at one or more points in the future. A tabular summary of indices calculated for existing and proposed disturbance in a representative area in boreal forest is provided in Table 1.

Figure 3 presents a map of landscape disturbance information for a portion of the same representative area so that access corridors, edge habitat (white areas), core habitat (gray areas), and stream crossings can be visualized.

Assessing cumulative effects

Landscape indices and maps like those shown in Table 1 and Figure 3 are then used to evaluate potential cumulative effects on selected physical, chemical, biological, and socio-economic indicators using conventional assessment methods. Selection of appropriate indicators and subsequent assessment methods has received extensive discussion in CEA guidance documents and literature (e.g., Beanlands and Duinker, 1983; Noss, 1990; Cairns et al., 1993; Smit and Spaling, 1995; Banff-Bow Valley Study, 1996; Hegmann et al., 1999).

As an example, existing access density values shown in Table 1 for the Fox Creek representative area exceed thresholds proposed for sensitive species such as grizzly bear and elk (Lyon, 1984; Mace and Manley, 1993). A new linear corridor and other likely activities will add to these existing disturbance levels and thereby increase the probability or magnitude of cumulative effects on sensitive ecological and land use indicators. This indicates that all technically and economically feasible mitigative measures should be implemented to avoid or reduce potential cumulative effects. It also suggests that explicit resource management objectives or criteria should be developed and implemented.

Merits and disadvantages

A successful CEA methodology must balance the sometimes-conflicting expectations of regulators, courts, proponents, environmental organizations, other public stakeholders, and practitioners. Regulators and courts must be satisfied that all environmental effects that could cause significant adverse effects or public concern have been addressed. Environmental organizations and other public stakeholders also seek assurance that appropriate management and mitigation measures have been identified and will be implemented to ensure long-term biological and resource use viability. Project proponents want to ensure that legislated CEA requirements are complied with efficiently, economically, and with minimal risk of delay. Finally, CEA practitioners prefer to utilize proven or standardized methods that are technically defensible in public hearings or legal proceedings.

The representative areas approach has generally been well received by stakeholders. It has been accepted by federal and provincial regulatory authorities and provided them with sufficient information to assess the significance of potential cumulative effects (EAO, 1996, 1999; NEB, 1998). General issues with this approach include the seemingly arbitrary way in

Table 1. Landscape indices calculated for a representative area in the Alliance Pipeline Project CEA (Alliance, 1997)

Boreal forest segment — Fox Creek representative area		Landscape index							
		Access density[1]	Seismic line density	Stream crossing frequency[2]	Total cleared area[3]	Core area[4]			
Area in map sheets 83 K/2 and 83 K/7	Activity	Mean (km/km^2)	Mean (km/km^2)	(#/km)	(ha, % of total)	Total area (ha, % of total)	Number	Mean (ha)	Range (ha)
Little Smoky R. Watershed (100,691 ha)	Existing	0.77	3.19	0.45	4605 (5%)	41,296 (41%)	87	475	<1–7614
	Proposed Alliance	0.03		0.02					
	Proposed other activities			?					
	Cumulative	0.80	3.19	0.47+	4605				
Athabasca River Watershed (80,557 ha)	Existing	0.72	3.32	0.31	3611 (4%)	37,953 (47%)	81	468	<1–8667
	Proposed Alliance	<0.01		0.02					
	Proposed other activities	?		?	850				
	Cumulative	0.72+	3.32	0.33+	4461 (6%)				
Total Area (181,248 ha)	Existing	0.72	3.25	0.53	8216 (5%)	81,649 (45%)	175	467	<1–8667
	Proposed Alliance	0.02		0.02	231	−1500			
	Proposed other activities	?		?	1040	−10,400			
	Cumulative	0.74+	3.25	0.55+	9487 (5%)	69,749 (38%)			

[1] Average total length of roads and utility corridors (pipelines, powerlines, rail lines) (km/km^2) in specified area.
[2] Stream crossing frequency represents number of road and utility corridor crossings (number/km) of stream in specified area.
[3] Total cleared area includes area cleared for roads, utility corridors, seismic lines and trails, well sites and facilities, and recreational sites in the specified area.
[4] Core Areas represent areas greater than 500 m from roads, utility corridors, well sites and facilities, and recreational sites in the specified area.

which representative area boundaries are selected and the value of landscape indices and thresholds for CEA and effects management.

A fundamental issue is whether it is appropriate to use a predefined CEA study area rather than ecologically based boundaries selected for each indicator or VEC. The ecological boundaries approach encourages a rigorous assessment of selected indicators. However, this traditional reductionist approach does not encourage an integrated assessment of all biophysical and socio-economic indicators, increases overall CEA costs, and is most applicable to large projects that are isolated in space. The complexity and cost of this approach is at least part of the reason that CEA has been qualitative or avoided altogether for most Canadian linear corridor projects.

Use of representative areas encourages an integrated assessment with consistent boundaries at lower cost. While these boundaries may appear to be arbitrary, as with any proper sampling program, the number and location of representative areas must be based on an evaluation of anticipated cumulative effects along with practical issues such as data availability. Experience has shown that when properly selected, these areas allow potential cumulative biophysical and socio-economic effects to be considered in an explicit, technically, and legally defensible way.

At present, most of the data on landscape indices and thresholds are from the United States, and the size and duration of the data sets are limited. This introduces another source of uncertainty into CEAs conducted for western Canadian linear corridor proposals and has caused some regulators and public stakeholders to question the value of landscape indices (and other accepted CEA methods). Research on the applicability of indices such as access density

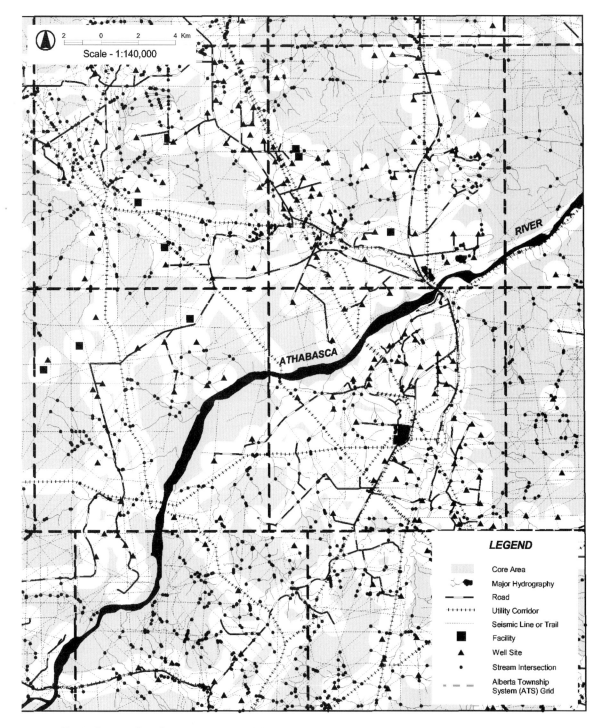

Fig. 3. Existing disturbance map generated for a representative area in the boreal forest of western Alberta.

and core area availability has begun in some areas of western Canada. Results of these studies will help refine these indices for CEA and effects management. In the meantime they provide a quantitative tool to help assess potential effects and identify the need for project-specific and regional mitigation and management measures.

Unlike other established methods, the representative areas approach can be efficiently applied to small linear projects that represent the majority of Canadian linear corridor proposals. Consistent with the intent of Canadian legislation, this will help ensure that regulators and stakeholders are provided with information on the significance of potential cumulative effects and over time will contribute to improved understanding of cumulative effects.

Use of representative areas and landscape indices is a proven and economical alternative that should be considered by practitioners and proponents for linear corridor proposals of all sizes.

ACKNOWLEDGEMENTS

The author wishes to acknowledge the support of Howard Heffler and Alliance Pipeline Ltd. in undertaking the Alliance CEA. Jim Bowen, GAIA Consultants Inc., helped turn GIS analysis concepts into reality and Donna Dowell completed the thankless tasks of locating and validating baseline data and editing dense text.

REFERENCES

Alberta Environment. 2000. Cumulative effects assessment in environmental impact assessment reports required under the Alberta Environmental Protection and Enhancement Act. Alberta Environment, Alberta Energy and Utilities Board, and Natural Resources Conservation Board. July. 6 pp.

Alliance (Alliance Pipeline Limited Partnership). 1997. Application to the National Energy Board for a certificate of public convenience and necessity. Volume IV Environmental and Socio-Economic Impact Assessment. Calgary, Alberta.

Beanlands, G.E. and P.N. Duinker. 1983. An ecological framework for environmental impact assessment in Canada. Institute for Resource and Environmental Studies, Dalhousie University, Halifax and the Federal Environmental Assessment and Review Office, Hull.

Banff-Bow Valley Study. 1996. Banff-Bow Valley: At the crossroads. Technical report of the Banff-Bow Valley Task Force. Prepared for the Hon. Sheila Copps, Minister of Canadian Heritage, Ottawa, ON.

BCFS and BCE (British Columbia Forest Service and British Columbia Environment). 1995. Interior Watershed Assessment Procedure Guidebook (IWAP) Level 1 Analysis. 82 pp.

Bosch, J.M. and J.D. Hewlett. 1982. A review of catchment experiments to determine the effect of vegetation changes on water yield and evapotranspiration. Journal of Hydrology, 55: 3–23.

Cairns, J. Jr., P.V. McCormick, and B.R. Niederlehner. 1993. A proposed framework for developing indicators of ecosystem health. Hydrobiologia, 263: 1–44.

CEAA (Canadian Environmental Assessment Agency). 1996. Guide to the preparation of a comprehensive study under the Canadian Environmental Assessment Act for proponents and responsible authorities (Draft 3: June 1996). Canadian Environmental Assessment Agency, Hull, Quebec. 31 pp. plus appendices.

CEAA (Canadian Environmental Assessment Agency). 1999. Operational policy statement: Addressing cumulative environmental effects under the Canadian Environmental Assessment Act. OPS-EPS/3-1999.

CEARC (Canadian Environmental Assessment Research Council). 1986. Cumulative environmental effects: A binational perspective. Canadian Environmental Assessment Research Council, Hull and US National Research Council.

Cederholm, C.J., L.M. Reid, and E.O. Salo. 1981. Cumulative effects of logging road sediment on salmonid populations in the Clearwater River, Jefferson County, Washington. In: Proceedings of the Conference on Salmon Spawning Gravel: A Renewable Resource in the Pacific Northwest. State of Washington Water Research Centre Report No. 39. Pullman, Wash. pp. 38–74.

CEQ (Council on Environmental Quality). 1997. Considering cumulative effects under the National Environmental Policy Act. Council on Environmental Quality. Washington, DC. 64 pp. + appendices.

Cocklin, C., S. Parker, and J. Hay. 1992a. Notes on cumulative environmental change II: A contribution to methodology. Journal of Environmental Management, 35: 51–67.

Cocklin, C., S. Parker, and J. Hay. 1992b. Notes on cumulative environmental change I: Concept and issues. Journal of Environmental Management, 35: 31–49.

CRC (Cardinal River Coals Ltd.). 1996. Cheviot Mine Project Application. Cardinal River Coals Ltd., Hinton, AB.

CRC (Cardinal River Coals Ltd.). 1999. Cheviot Mine Cumulative Effects Assessment November 1999. Cardinal River Coals Ltd., Hinton, AB.

Davies, K. 1996. DOE's CEAA Handbook: Appendix on Assessing Cumulative Environmental Effects and Socio-Economic Effects. Prepared for the Environmental Assessment Branch, Environment Canada. Ecosystems Consulting Inc., Orleans, Ontario. 31 pp.

EAO (British Columbia Environmental Assessment Office). 1996. Novagas Clearinghouse Ltd. Caribou Gas Processing Project: Report and recommendations of the Caribou Project Committee with respect to the issuance of a Project Approval Certificate. Environmental Assessment Office, Victoria, BC.

EAO (British Columbia Environmental Assessment Office). 1999. Paramount Resources Ltd. Maxhamish Pipeline Project: Report and recommendations of the Maxhamish Pipeline Project Committee with respect to the issuance of a Project Approval Certificate pursuant to the Environmental Assessment Act, R.S.B.C. 1996, c119 and partially fulfilling the requirements of a Screening Report pursuant to the Canadian Environmental Assessment Act, 1992 c.37. Environmental Assessment Office, Victoria, BC.

FEARO (Federal Environmental Assessment and Review Office). 1994. A reference guide for the Canadian Environmental Assessment Act: Addressing cumulative environmental effects. Federal Environmental Assessment and Review Office, Hull, Quebec. 23 pp.

Flather, C.H. and J.R. Sauer. 1996. Using landscape ecology to test hypotheses about large-scale abundance patterns in migratory birds. Ecological Society of America, 77(1): 28–35.

Furniss, M.J., T.D. Roelefs, and C.S. Yee. 1991. Road construction and maintenance. In: Influences of Forest and Rangeland Management on Salmonid Fishes and Their Habitats. W.R. Meehan, ed. American Fisheries Society Special Publication 19. 751 pp. pp. 297–324.

Gibeau, M.L., S. Herrerro, J.L. Kansas, and B. Benn. 1996. Grizzly bear population and habitat status in Banff National Park. University of Calgary, Calgary.

Hegmann, G. and T. Yarranton. 1995. Cumulative effects and the Energy Resources Conservation Board's review process. Working Paper #1, MacLeod Institute for Environmental Analysis, University of Calgary, Calgary.

Hegmann, G., C. Cocklin, R. Creasey, S. Dupuis, A. Kennedy, L. Kingsley, W. Ross, H. Spaling, and D. Stalker. 1999. Cumulative effects assessment practitioners guide. AXYS Environmental Consulting Ltd. and the CEA Working Group for the Canadian Environmental Assessment Agency, Hull, Quebec.

Jalkotzy, M.G., P.I. Ross, and M.D. Nasserden. 1997. The effects of linear developments on wildlife; a review of selected scientific literature. Prepared for Canadian Association of Petroleum Producers by Arc Wildlife Services Ltd.

Laurence, W.F. and E. Yensen. 1991. Predicting the impacts of edge effects in fragmented habitats. Biological Conservation, 55: 77–92.

Lee, L.C. and J.G. Gosselink. 1988. Cumulative impacts on wetlands: Linking scientific assessments and regulatory alternatives. Environmental Management, 12(5): 591–602.

Lyon, L.J. 1984. Field tests of elk/timber coordination guidelines. Intermountain Forest and Range Experiment Station Research Paper INT-325. US Department of Agriculture, Forest Service, Ogden, UT. 10 pp.

Mace, R.D. and T.L. Manley. 1993. South fork Flathead River grizzly bear project: Progress report for 1992. Montana Department of Fish, Wildlife and Parks. 34 pp.

McGurk, B.J. and D.R. Fong. 1995. Equivalent roaded area as a measure of cumulative effect of logging. Environmental Management, 19(4): 609–621.

NEB (National Energy Board). 1995. Guidelines for filing requirements. National Energy Board, Calgary, Alberta. 77 pp.

NEB (National Energy Board). 1998. Comprehensive study report in the matter of Alliance Pipeline Ltd. on behalf of the Alliance Pipeline Limited Partnership, GH-3-97. Calgary, Alberta. 178 pp.

Nip, A-K. 1991. The Tri-Creeks experimental watershed: Changes in hydrology and water quality following forest harvesting and their impact on salmonid fishes in the Tri-Creek basin. Alberta Forest Service, Forestry, Lands and Wildlife, Edmonton, Alberta. 66 pp.

Noss, R. 1990. Indicators for monitoring biodiversity: A hierarchical approach. Conservation Biology, 4(4): 355–364.

Noss, R.F., H.B. Quigley, M.G. Hornocker, T. Merrill, and P.C. Paquet. 1996. Conservation biology and carnivore conservation in the Rocky Mountains. Conservation Biology, 10(4): 949–963.

Reed, R.A., J. Johnson-Barnard, and W.L. Baker. 1996a. Contribution of roads to forest fragmentation in the Rocky Mountains. Conservation Biology, 10(4): 1098–1106.

Reed, R.A., J. Johnson-Barnard, and W.L. Baker. 1996b. Fragmentation of a forested Rocky Mountain landscape. Biological Conservation, 75: 267–277.

Reese, K.P. and J.T. Ratti. 1988. Edge effect: A concept under scrutiny. In: Transactions 53rd North American Wildlife & Natural Resource Conference. pp. 127–136.

Reijnen, R., R. Foppen, C. Ter Braak, and J. Thissen. 1995. The effects of car traffic on breeding bird populations in woodland. III. Reduction of density in relation to the proximity of main roads. Journal of Applied Ecology, 32: 187–202.

Salmo Consulting Inc. 1996. Application for a Project Approval Certificate: Novagas Clearinghouse Ltd. Caribou Gas Processing Project. Prepared for Novagas Clearinghouse Ltd., Calgary. Salmo Consulting Inc., Axys Environmental Consulting Ltd., BOVAR Environmental, Bower Damberger Rolseth Engineering Ltd., Diversified Environmental Services, Geo-Engineering (MST) Ltd., Heritage North Consulting Limited, Novagas Clearinghouse Ltd., and P.M. Ruby Consulting Inc.

Salmo Consulting Inc. 1999a. Application for a Project Approval Certificate: Maxhamish Project. Prepared for Paramount Resources Ltd., Calgary. Salmo Consulting Inc. in association with Diversified Environmental Services, E2 Environmental Alliance Inc., Fedirchuk, McCullough & Associates Ltd., Geo-Engineering (MST) Ltd., Golder Associates Ltd., Paramount Resources Ltd., Ramsay & Associates Consulting Services Ltd., and Wildlife & Company Ltd.

Salmo Consulting Inc. 1999b. Gulf Midstream Services Brazeau Pipeline Project cumulative effects evaluation. Unpublished report prepared for Gulf Midstream Services, Calgary. Salmo Consulting Inc., Calgary.

Shoemaker, D.J. 1994. Cumulative environmental assessment. University of Waterloo, Dept. of Geography. Publication Series No. 42. 129 pp.

Smit, S. and H. Spaling. 1995. Methods for cumulative effects assessment. Environmental Impact Assessment Review, 15: 81–106.

Sonntag, N.C., R.R. Everitt, L.P. Rattie, D.L. Colnett, C.P. Wolf, J.C. Truett, A.H.J. Dorcy, and C.S. Holling. 1987. Cumulative effects assessment: A context for further research and development. Prepared for the Canadian Environmental Assessment Research Council, Hull, Quebec. ESSA Environmental and Social Systems Analysts Ltd., Vancouver.

Thomas, J.W., H. Black Jr., R.J. Scherzinger, and R.J. Pedersen. 1979. Wildlife habitats in managed forests — the Blue Mountains of Oregon and Washington. USDA Forest Service, Agricultural Handbook, 553: 104–127.

Thomas, J.W., D.A. Leckenby, M. Henjum, R.J. Pedersen, and L.D. Bryant. 1988. Habitat-effectiveness index for elk on Blue Mountain winter ranges. General Technical Report. PNW-GTR-218. USDA Forest Service.

Troendle, C.A. and R.M. King. 1985. The effect of timber harvest on the Fool Creek watershed, 30 years later. Water Resources Research, 21(12): 1915–1922.

USDA (United States Department of Agriculture, Forest Service). 1996. Status of the interior Columbia Basin: Summary of scientific findings. Gen. Tech. Rep. PNW-GTR-385. Portland, Oregon. US Department of Agriculture, Forest Service, Pacific Northwest Research Station; US Department of the Interior, Bureau of Land Management. 144 pp.

Wilcove, D.S., C.H. McLellan, and A.P. Dobson. 1986. Habitat fragmentation in the temperate zone. In: Conservation Biology: The Science of Scarcity and Diversity. M.E. Sould, ed. Sinauer Associates, Inc. 584 pp. pp. 237–265.

With, K.A. and T.O. Crist. 1995. Critical thresholds in species responses to landscape structure. Ecology, 76(8): 2446–2459.

BIOGRAPHICAL SKETCH

Terry Antoniuk
Salmo Consulting Inc.

Mr. Antoniuk, the Principal of Salmo Consulting Inc., is a Professional Biologist registered in the provinces of Alberta and British Columbia. Mr. Antoniuk has more than twenty years experience in biological studies and research, environmental assessment and mitigation, and public involvement in federal, provincial, and territorial jurisdictions across Canada, and internationally. One of Terry's specialties is cumulative effects assessment; he also manages multi-disciplinary teams and designs and implements biophysical inventories, effects monitoring programs, and environmental protection programs.

Pipeline Projects and Cumulative Effects Assessment Issues

Chris G. Finley and Dr. Richard D. Revel

By virtue of their linear nature, pipelines provide interesting dilemmas that one must face when determining how best to address project-related cumulative environmental effects. Effects from pipeline construction and operation can act in combination with other projects and activities such as resource extraction, recreational use, and other land-use practices to cause significant adverse environmental effects. The challenge is to first determine the environmental effects of the project. Three main types of disturbances stem from pipeline construction and operation: those concentrated around or emanating from a point or local area (e.g., temporary work spaces), a linear area (e.g., right-of-way), or a regional area (e.g., emissions from compressor stations). Pipeline projects can also be separated into several phases including planning, construction, operation, decommissioning, and abandonment. Each of the project phases and associated activities has the potential to adversely affect environmental values. Pipelines, being linear, provide interesting cumulative effects issues. Key cumulative effects issues include habitat loss and fragmentation, access creation and management, upstream induced effects, and watercourse crossings. To effectively assess pipeline cumulative effects stakeholders should follow an established cumulative effects assessment (CEA) framework or approach. The Canadian Environmental Assessment Agency's Cumulative Effects Assessment Practitioners Guide provides an example of a CEA framework that provides a starting point to assist the determination of the significance of cumulative effects as a result of pipeline development. As part of project-specific environmental assessments, the potential cumulative environmental effects are often identified, evaluated, mitigative measures proposed and the significance of effects assessed. Proper implementation of mitigative measures in the field is critical to the management of project-related cumulative effects. This paper argues that an overall CEA approach or framework for a pipeline project should be developed in a manner that is similar to a CEA for a non-linear project or non-pipeline project although it also recognizes that pipelines have some effects that are unique. Cumulative effects from pipelines can be managed by applying standard environmental assessment principles, using guidelines as frameworks to assist the undertaking of CEAs, and by ensuring mitigation is effectively applied.

Keywords: Linear, cumulative environmental effects, framework, mitigative measures

INTRODUCTION

The objectives of this paper are to provide information to stakeholders, namely proponents, regulators, and citizens regarding the unique features of pipelines leading to cumulative effects, identify key pipeline cumulative effects and assessment issues, and discuss mitigation options. To consider potential cumulative effects of a pipeline proposal, stakeholders should have knowledge of how pipelines and associated activities can cause environmental effects. A knowledge of cumulative effects concepts and environmental assessment principles is also essential.

Pipeline construction and operation effects can act in combination with other projects and activities such as resource extraction, recreational use, and other land-use practices to cause significant adverse environmental effects. The challenge is determining those environmental values or valued ecosystem components

Environmental Concerns in Rights-of-Way Management: Seventh International Symposium
J.W. Goodrich-Mahoney, D.F. Mutrie and C.A. Guild (editors)
© 2002 Elsevier Science Ltd. All rights reserved.

(VECs) affected, how they will be affected, determining mitigation measures, and predicting significance of effects.

ENVIRONMENTAL EFFECTS OF PIPELINE PROJECTS

Pipelines serve as transportation mechanisms that connect production sources to end-point users. Pipeline projects normally consist of: the pipeline, right-of-way, compressor stations, mainline valve sites, electrical transmission lines, temporary and permanent access roads, pigging facilities, lateral pipelines, operating centres, temporary work spaces, storage areas, and borrow pits. Installing these project facilities could result in cumulative effects to VECs when combined with other projects and activities. Pipelines and their associated facilities create a disturbance to landscapes, aquatic systems, and the atmosphere. They may have wide ranging effects on ecosystems, resources, and human communities which may be either beneficial or detrimental, or in some cases both. There are three main types of disturbances as a result of pipeline construction and operation: those concentrated around or emanating from a point or local area (e.g., temporary work spaces), a linear area (e.g., right-of-way), or a regional area (e.g., emissions from compressor stations). Project facilities have different types of disturbances associated with them, depending on the phase of the project. For instance, a compressor station during operation causes both point and area effects due to its physical presence and related emissions, whereas after decommissioning, a station may cause a point disturbance from its physical presence (assuming it is not removed). Indirect activities associated with project facilities during construction or operation are also imminent. For example, during construction, the right-of-way requires human activity that includes the use of machinery that may create area effects due to noise disturbances. This would be an indirect area impact, compounded with the linear disturbance effects of the right-of-way.

Table 1 lists typical environmental effects of pipelines linked with the project phase, activity, and facility involved. The construction phase causes environmental effects most frequently (regardless of magnitude), while operation is a close second. The magnitude, permanence, probability, duration, and frequency of environmental effects may depend on the geographic or environmental setting, proper execution of environmental mitigation, technologies employed, and interactions with other activities.

Unique and challenging features

By virtue of their linear nature, pipelines create long narrow landscape disturbances and present unique and challenging issues as they affect a multitude of stakeholders, jurisdictions, ecological regions, and cultural features. The unique features associated with pipeline projects are substantial and warrant consideration to identify how they pose a challenge to stakeholders. These challenges and barriers can represent significant time, financial and human resource commitments. If we understand the issues, we can move forward to focusing on the pertinent issues and developing solutions that have benefits for stakeholders and the environment.

Unique and challenging features of pipeline projects are diverse and can be characterized as scientific, administrative, land use, and methodological issues. Emphasis is directed at scientific issues, as they constitute the greatest hurdle to stakeholders. Administrative and land use issues have a predictable nature, and organization and coordination of information are primary concerns. Methodological issues relate to common problems encountered by practitioners. Table 2 presents the unique scientific issues and provides example considerations for each issue relevant to the challenging features associated with pipeline projects.

Land can be considered a pattern or mosaic that is composed of patches, corridors, and matrices (Forman, 1995). A pipeline project is composed of structural features predominately of the corridor landscape element, that include disturbance corridors, such as roads, electrical transmission lines, and pipeline rights-of-way. Borrow pits, compressor stations, storage areas, temporary work spaces, and valve sites all have patch-like features.

Pipelines have both internal and external structure. Three components of internal corridor structure include: width characteristics, internal entities, and plant and animal community structures (Forman, 1995). A pipeline right-of-way constructed in a forested area creates a disturbance corridor with internal structural attributes. The width of the right-of-way often corresponds to the size of the pipe, and the depth of burial. Larger pipes and increased depths generally require more space to store soil and manoeuvre equipment (Alberta Environment, 1988). Narrower corridors may be dominated by edge species, while wider corridors may support a diverse group of species, depending on the types of internal entities (Jalkotzy et al., 1997). Pipeline right-of-way widths may vary greatly in different locations. Right-of-way widths may range from less than 25 m to over 100 m where looping is practiced. In a forested landscape, where right-of-way width is excessive, internal ecological features, such as grass and shrub communities or streams or rivers that cross the right-of-way, may be common. The right-of-way may also possess linear internal entities such as recreational trails, wildlife trails, or access roads. A right-of-way may be a component of a larger corridor that includes a road or a railway. The diversity of plant and animal species within a corridor are related

Table 1. Project phase, activity, and environmental attributes affected

Project phase	Activity	Component involved	Predominate environmental attributes affected	Examples of various types of effects
Planning/Surveying	(1) Aircraft overflights	Potential rights-of-way	Wildlife	Individual disruption
	(2) Pipeline Surveyors: (a) walking	Right-of-way	Wildlife	Social disruption
	(b) All-terrain vehicle usage	Right-of-way and vicinity	Wildlife, soils, vegetation, fisheries, aquatics	Habitat avoidance
	(c) Sporadic tree clearing; right-of-way marking; significant areas marked	Right-of-way	Wildlife, habitat	Habitat disruption/loss or enhancement
	(3) Environmental surveys: wildlife, soils, vegetation, fisheries, geotechnical, archaeological, historical	Right-of-way and vicinity	Wildlife, soils, vegetation, fisheries	Direct and indirect mortality
Construction	(1) Tree clearing; timber salvage (fencing and bridging may precede clearing activities)	Right-of-way (mainline and laterals), all areas where future facilities to be sited	Forestry, soils, fisheries, vegetation, wildlife, habitat, aesthetics	Population effects
	(2) Establishing access; building temporary water crossing structures	Permanent and temporary access roads	Wildlife, habitat, grazing, forestry, historical or archaeological resources, soils, vegetation, fisheries	Weed introduction
	(3) Soil removal, stockpile, and grading	Right-of-way, access roads, temporary work spaces	Wildlife, habitat, grazing, forestry, historical or archaeological resources, soils, vegetation, fisheries	Disturbance or loss of rare or endangered plants/plant communities
	(4) Excavate trench (may occur after (5) toreduce open-trench time)	Pipeline trench and right-of-way, access roads, temporary work spaces	Wildlife, habitat, grazing, forestry, historical or archaeological resources, soils, vegetation, fisheries	Disturbance or loss of critical wildlife habitat
				Loss of merchantable timber
	(5) Hauling, stringing, bending, welding, coating, and lowering-in	Pipeline (mainline and laterals), right-of-way, valve sites, meters, access roads, temporary work spaces	Wildlife	
	(6) Back fill trench	Pipeline (mainline and laterals), right-of-way	Wildlife, fisheries	Disruption of stream flow
				Barriers to fish migration
				Habitat alteration
	(7) Set-up ancillary facilities (top-soil removal and storage)	Compressor stations, electrical transmissionlines (where required), storage areas, valve sites and meters, access roads, pigging facilities	Wildlife, soils, fisheries, vegetation, historical, archaeological resources, livestock grazing	Sedimentation of stream bed
				In-stream blasting mortality
				Fish affected by new access
	(8) Testing	Pipeline (mainline and laterals), access roads	Wildlife, water bodies, aquatic habitat	
	(9) Clean-up and reclamation of right-of-way and disturbed areas	Right-of-way and vicinity, access roads	Vegetation, fisheries, soils, wildlife, habitat	
	(10) Water crossings	Pipeline (mainline and laterals), right-of-way	Terrestrial habitat, aquatics, fisheries	
Operation	(1) Compress hydrocarbon	Compressor Station	Habitat, climate, airshed	Emissions
				Climate change from greenhouse gas emissions

Table 1. (continued)

Project phase	Activity	Component involved	Predominate environmental attributes affected	Examples of various types of effects
	(2) Pipeline inspection and equipment maintenance	Pipeline (mainline and laterals), permanent (temporary) access roads, right-of-way, storage areas, valve sites, meters, pigging facilities	Wildlife	
	(3) Herbicide use for plant control over pipeline, maintaining right-of-way free of woody vegetation	Pipeline (mainline and laterals), access roads	Vegetation, fisheries, habitat, aquatics	Loss of soil structure
Decommissioning	(1) Pipe cleaning, flushing, and shutdown	Pipeline (mainline and laterals), compressor stations, pigging facilities	Vegetation, water bodies, aquatic habitat	
Abandonment (a combination of these activities is common)	(1) Pipeline left in ground	Pipeline (mainline and laterals)	None	
	(2) Removal of above ground facilities	Compressor stations, meters, valves, storage areas	Wildlife, pipe acts as a conduit for water	
	(3) Pipeline removed	Pipeline (mainline and laterals), right-of-way	Same as construction, all attributes	
	(4) Excavations to ensure cleaning quality, installations of plugs and caps	Pipeline (mainline and laterals)	Same as construction, all attributes	

to width, internal entities, and external structure, such as ecological zones.

External structure refers to the corridor's relationship to its surroundings or to the surrounding matrix. Stakeholders should not ignore external landscape elements and forget about other activities and natural features such as patches, corridors, and matrices that interact with the pipeline. Documenting the environmental setting is necessary for the environmental assessment and can also be used to aid the CEA.

Disturbance corridors, such as pipeline rights-of-way, roads, or electrical transmission lines, may provide habitat for wildlife (Jalkotzy et al., 1997). Rights-of-way can provide travel corridors for wildlife that reduce energy expenditures and provide food stuffs for wildlife. Small mammals, birds, and ungulates may utilize these corridors because of the richness of plant species and communities, and this in turn, encourages corridor use by carnivores such as coyotes (Jalkotzy et al., 1997). In fragmented habitats, vegetated corridors can facilitate plant and animal movement, effectively decreasing the fragmentation effect (Henein and Merriam, 1990).

Corridors that are created from pipeline projects (roads, rights-of-way, and possibly by electrical transmission lines) may facilitate wildlife movement and act as conduits (Jalkotzy et al., 1997). Black bear may use rights-of-way as travel routes to reduce energy expenditures or improve access to prey species (Eccles and Duncan, 1986 as cited in Jalkotzy et al., 1997). In addition, large mammals, such as elk and caribou may utilize backcountry roads and seismic lines during migration (Jalkotzy et al., 1997). However, people may also use these corridors to access previously remote or inaccessible areas causing a multitude of direct and indirect cumulative environmental effects (Eccles et al., 1994). Conduits may also act as connections between fragmented patches, and thereby decrease fragmentation effects for certain species. Species such as crested wheatgrass, once commonly used in pipeline reclamation on the prairies, have taken advantage of these corridors to extend their range to invade and outcompete many native plant species. Conduits have caused fragmentation effects in those instances.

Disturbance corridors may inhibit or effectively block any plant or animal movement. When no movement occurs, the corridor constitutes a functional barrier. Marten have displayed barrier effects from a pipeline right-of-way (Eccles et al., 1985 as cited in Jalkotzy et al., 1997; Eccles and Duncan, 1986 as cited in Jalkotzy et al., 1997). Excessive rights-of-way width, or the presence of certain internal entities, such as roads, may preclude species movement across a corridor. The result may be isolation of species, populations or communities, with the extreme result of local extirpation or inbreeding depression. Population effects are a major concern, although, they are difficult to determine and require an extended study period to confirm or deny any suspicion of significant adverse effects (Jalkotzy et al., 1997). Roadways and railways with larger traffic volumes may inhibit animal and plant dispersal

Table 2. Unique and challenging features of pipeline projects

Issue	Example considerations
(1) Structural attributes of pipeline corridors (including the right-of-way, access roads, electrical transmission lines)	Width Internal entities Plant and animal communities
(2) Functional attributes of pipeline corridors (including the right-of-way, access roads, electrical transmission lines)	Habitat creation Conduit Barrier: linear habitat fragmentation, filters, isolation of communities, width of corridor Source of habitat Sink for wildlife Uncertain effects
(3) Many environmental attributes affected	Soils, hydrology, wetlands, noise levels, air quality, fisheries, wildlife, plant species and communities, agricultural, recreational, paleontological, historical, and archaeological resources, conservation areas, forestry, hunting and trapping, access creation with many direct and indirect effects, ecosystems, watersheds, ecodistricts, aesthetics
(4) Contribution to cumulative effects	Soils, hydrology, wetlands, noise levels, air quality, fisheries, wildlife, plant species and communities, agricultural, recreational, paleontological, historical, and archaeological resources, conservation areas, forestry, hunting and trapping, access creation with many direct and indirect effects, ecosystems, watersheds, ecodistricts, aesthetics, climate change
(5) Interactions with other actions within the zone of influence of the pipeline	Policies, jurisdictions, programs, Integrated Resource Plans, management plans: urban growth or species protection, legislation, regulations, by-laws, guidelines Well sites Other pipelines Other linear facilities: roads, trails, seismic lines, railways, electrical transmission lines Hydro-dams Agriculture: ranching, cultivation, irrigation districts and canals Forestry operations Human settlement: townships, villages, cities Chemical plants Coal mines, mining Processing/Manufacturing plants
(6) Route selection	Avoiding sensitive areas Minimizing stream crossings Looping where possible How wide is too wide (width) Economic considerations
(7) Type of effect	Linear Point Area Environmental media affected: air, land, water Type of disturbance activity Effect on wildlife Cumulative effects attributes/pathways

very significantly directly and indirectly as compared to pipeline rights-of-way. (Jalkotzy et al., 1997).

Animals may have the ability to move long distances, but will not disperse due to behavioural responses that inhibit this action (Saunders et al., 1991). Some bird species may not cross distances greater than 100 m in agricultural fields, and therefore a functional barrier exists (Saunders and de Rebeira, 1991 as cited in Saunders et al., 1991). Fragmentation occurs when habitats and wildlife are functionally separated. These landscapes may possess some connectivity. However, it is quite poor and corresponds to poor exchange rates (Jalkotzy et al., 1997).

Habitat fragmentation is an important feature of pipelines. The geographic expanse of pipelines may fragment many types of habitats along the route including both forested and native prairie areas. For some bird species the width of an average pipeline right-of-way of 25 m has negative fragmentation effects, as cowbirds and other nest predators adversely influence adjacent interior forest habitat (Rich et al., 1994). Additionally, species and populations may become isolated. This may lead to reduced genetic variability, causing a reduction in the reproductive fitness of populations, and in the worse case, local species extirpation. Forest fragmentation can adversely affect insects by changing the abundance and richness of species (Didham et al., 1996). Some species are attracted to the right-of-way, and as a result may face death from hunters who have gained access to previously remote areas by using the pipeline corridor as a travel route. Of particular concern in Canada are those species that are designated with a special status, meaning that they are either vulnerable, threatened, at risk, or extirpated. The Committee on the Status of Endangered Wildlife in Canada (COSEWIC) and various provincial agencies maintain databases on the locations and status of many species of Canadian wildlife.

A disturbance corridor may benefit wildlife when the corridor becomes a source of habitat and provides links for wildlife to other landscape components. Edge species and habitat generalists may thrive in a disturbance corridor, using it as a conduit, and spreading out into the matrix (Jalkotzy et al., 1997). Corridors are beneficial for enhancing biotic movement and providing foraging areas and refuges (Saunders et al., 1991). In fragmented habitats, populations of species may be sustained when individuals use corridors that connect patches.

Disturbance corridors can also become sinks when animals from the surrounding matrix are drawn into the corridor, where they subsequently die. Corridors may be a direct or indirect sink. Roads and electrical transmission lines associated with pipelines may cause direct mortality through vehicle collisions and electrocutions, while indirect mortality can result from people not associated with the pipeline using the right-of-way corridor as a conduit to affect wildlife species. In remote areas, pipeline corridors may create new access and cause further wildlife mortality. Additionally, predators attracted to the corridor because of increased prey species often become the target of people through both legal and illegal means (Jalkotzy et al., 1997).

Fish and fish habitat can be adversely affected through habitat disruption and sedimentation of watercourses. Combined with other activities such as forestry operations, the effects to fish and fish habitat can be significant.

Practitioners and scientists generally have a poor understanding of natural and social systems and this leads to difficulties in undertaking CEAs (Ross in Kennedy, 1994). For instance, they lack specific information about how a disturbance corridor will affect certain environmental attributes (i.e., will the proposed corridor contribute to significant wildlife mortality, and will it act cumulatively?). For terrestrial attributes such as wildlife, we do not have many established thresholds to assist a determination of the significance of habitat loss and other effects on wildlife. Often, we are not able to prove that a threshold has been exceeded, and that significant effects have or will occur.

Best professional judgement normally must be used in the end.

Longer term environmental effects to populations may result because of the absence of solid data that identifies cause and effect relationships. For instance, practitioners often recognize information gaps regarding the identification of adverse population effects that could be attributed to a pipeline project. This has major implications for the CEA practitioner. As uncertainties unfold, they should be addressed through adaptive management, as identifying development or disturbance thresholds is not a trivial pursuit.

CUMULATIVE EFFECTS

Diverse views about cumulative effects exist, thus different ideas and definitions are common. To avoid excessive confusion on this issue the definition provided for the Canadian Environmental Assessment Agency (the Agency) by Hegmann et al. (1999) will be applied. Hegmann et al. (1999) apply a simple definition based on an important additional requirement of CEA as compared to environmental assessment: the specific consideration of effects due to other projects.

Cumulative effects generally refer to the effects of multiple human inputs to natural systems (Cocklin et al., 1992a). They develop from the incremental effect of the project or action when added to other past, present, or future actions regardless of who undertakes the activity (CEQ, 1996). These effects emerge over time and space to affect resources, ecosystems, and human populations (CEQ, 1996). Cumulative effects can have either a neutral, positive or negative effect depending on the recipient of those effects. These effects also have a duration (short, medium, long) and intensity (high, medium, low). Kalff (1995) captures the concepts of cumulative effects by identifying common elements. Three of the elements include: action, impact, and boundaries.

Actions as projects and activities are relevant to pipelines. A generic pipeline project includes five project phases, numerous facilities, and associated activities. The five phases of project development could create environmental effects, with some of them being residual and possibly acting as a source of cumulative effects. The test to determine if an effect is cumulative under the *Canadian Environmental Assessment Act* (CEAA), corresponds to examining interactions with other projects. Other actions that could interact with the pipeline to adversely affect the environment (i.e., affect a VEC) should be considered in a CEA. Cumulative effects may result from one pipeline project, several pipelines, interactions with existing projects, and interactions with past or future projects within overlapping spatial and temporal boundaries. Where reasonable and relevant, actions from the past, present and future should be examined for potential project interactions (FEARO, 1994; Hegmann, 1995; CEQ, 1996).

An environmental effect or impact occurs as a result of actions that change the status of the receiving environment. Cumulative effects can arise from either single or multiple projects. Activities in a region on their own may be individually insignificant, but when combined, cause significant cumulative effects to VECs. To illustrate this point, a wildlife population might be considered a VEC. A substantial increase in vehicular activity from an increasing number of projects in a region can effectively block migration corridors, feeding and breeding areas, and cause increased vehicle mortality. A single project in this area may cause minor effects, that would be insignificant on its own.

A boundary typically refers to the spatial (i.e., geographical) and temporal (i.e., time frame) area where environmental effects from a project or interactions with other projects can occur. For pipelines, the boundaries or zone of influence is variable and may be based on a consideration of the number of pipelines looped, local and regional environmental setting, and on any common connections or links that the pipeline possesses with other activities (e.g., when a grizzly bear home range crosses a pipeline corridor and forestry operations).

Key cumulative environmental effects

Through the identification of pipeline specific environmental effects, possible cumulative environmental effects can also be identified. Many possible types of cumulative effects exist, but only the key ones are highlighted here. Key cumulative environmental effects related to pipelines include terrestrial habitat loss and fragmentation, access creation and management, upstream induced effects, and aquatic habitat disruption through sedimentation at watercourse crossings (Finley, 1998). Each of these cumulative environmental effects has been identified as potential key issues when other developments act in combination. In areas where there may be excess pipeline capacity and where commodity prices are attractive for exploration, further development may be undertaken to meet the market demand. This would lead to an induced upstream effect that should be addressed.

To provide a basis for decision making, cumulative effects are normally evaluated to determine whether the effects are adverse, whether they are significant, and whether they are likely (FEARO, 1994). The next steps following the identification of cumulative environmental effects of pipelines is the assessment and management of those effects.

CUMULATIVE EFFECTS ASSESSMENT AND PIPELINES

CEA in simple terms means the identification, assessment, and determination of the likely significance of cumulative environmental change. Two types of approaches to CEA are commonly recognized; one scientific, and the other planning oriented (Spaling and Smit, 1993). The first type of CEA is "an information-gathering activity using principles of research and design and scientific analysis" (Smit and Spaling, 1995, p. 83). The second type of CEA utilizes "planning principles and procedures to determine an order of preference among a set of resource allocation choices" (Smit and Spaling, 1995, p. 83). These approaches, are distinctly different, in that the former applies a narrower analytical focus, whereas the latter approach applies a broader scope that includes normative evaluation and management (Smit and Spaling, 1995). These approaches, however, are not necessarily in opposition to one another, but may reflect a different scope of CEA (Smit and Spaling, 1995). The first approach has been stated as appropriate for assessing cumulative effects under the CEAA (Priddle et al., 1996). Analytical CEA approaches are normally used when the assessment is primarily focused on evaluating the effects of one project, in relation to other projects and activities. Recent CEAs have provided a further meshing of these approaches. CEAs for project-specific applications have considered land use designations, existing environmental effects monitoring programs, and acceptable use and thresholds.

Cumulative effects have largely been ignored in the past by traditional environmental assessment. Environmental assessment focuses on how the project affects the local area, and generally disregards other project interactions, and secondary activities derived from primary development (CEARC, 1988). Activities that are viewed as individually minor may have collectively significant effects, revealing the short-comings of traditional environmental assessment (Cocklin et al., 1992b), and pressing the need for the assessment of cumulative effects. CEA expands the scope of traditional environmental assessment to evaluate how multiple activities have caused cumulative effects at both local and regional scales. In general terms, it can be distinguished from environmental assessment in that it investigates a broader spatial and temporal scope of effects (Hegmann, 1995).

CEA FRAMEWORK FOR PIPELINES

The framework advocated by the Agency (Hegmann et al., 1999) for carrying out CEAs is used as a starting point for discussing generic pipeline CEAs. The framework involves the following tasks and sub-components: Scoping (Identify Regional Issues of Concern; Select Regional Valued Ecosystem Components; Identify Spatial and Temporal Boundaries; and Identify Other Actions), Analyze Effects (Collect Regional Baseline Data; and Assess Effects on Valued Ecosystem

Components), Identify Mitigation, Evaluate Significance, and Follow-up (Recommend Region-wide Monitoring) (Hegmann et al., 1999).

Based on the assessment of what a pipeline project normally entails (i.e., the physical aspects) and how it interacts with the environment through the phases of development the potential adverse environmental effects can be identified. In general, people look for a recipe list or a how-to guide that answers all CEA questions. In reality, however, CEA is complex, the process is wrought with uncertainty, and no generic guide can address all of the issues that develop in a "real world" pipeline CEA. Therefore, discussing generic pipeline CEAs can be hampered. Often, specific information is required before one can proceed to the next step. One goal in light of many uncertainties in CEA, is to address a broad range of issues and focus on the assessment process.

Scoping

Cumulative effects relevant to pipelines are diverse. This diversity challenges the practitioner to narrow the assessment to select appropriate issues and cumulative effects. In a generic sense, the impact that other actions cause on VECs are effectively the same as pipelines. However, they may occur through alternate pathways, and over different spatial and temporal scales. Several considerations are required to determine if cumulative effects are an issue:

1. Examine the potential environmental effects along the pipeline, and determine if interactions with other projects or activities are probable (e.g., use an impact checklist); and
2. Determine how the effects can be considered cumulative (i.e., examining what VECs could illustrate this interaction).

Scoping is one of the most important first steps in the assessment process. Scoping effectively reduces the number of variables that require study in a CEA by focusing on specific issues of importance (Ross, 1994 in Kennedy, 1994).

In order to examine and evaluate the potential cumulative effects of a pipeline project they must first be identified. The type, size, and location of a project are key issues with any environmental assessment, or any CEA. At the early planning stage, the type and size of a pipeline are normally known. However, the location, or the environmental setting is the main variable. No matter where pipelines are located they share common features such as their long linear nature. Therefore, we suggest that there are numerous generic cumulative effects for almost all pipelines and that certain effects could be highly relevant to a particular pipeline. Recognition that only a limited number of issues and other activities can realistically be addressed in a CEA is duly noted.

Identify issues of regional concern

The large geographic area that a pipeline encompasses and the linear nature of the project normally correspond to many more affected parties. Therefore, scoping appropriate issues takes on a new importance and challenges the practitioner to focus on non-trivial issues. Often the environmental assessment will provide clues to those issues of regional concern that should be addressed.

Select VECs

The purpose of selecting VECs for an environmental assessment or a CEA is to focus the assessment on pertinent areas of concern to the public or professionals (Beanlands and Duinker, 1983). VECs are the focus of the assessment because they integrate the effects of multiple projects (Hegmann et al., 1999).

VECs selected for a CEA may be the same as those selected for the environmental assessment (Hegmann et al., 1999). VECs that capture regional change however, may be added and required, to reflect change on a larger scale (Hegmann et al., 1999). For example, a CEA may use a watershed as a VEC, where an environmental assessment would use a fish species or fish habitat as a VEC and assess effects from watercourse crossings.

CEA study boundaries for a pipeline may be established with input from stakeholders and may require feedback from the regulating authorities. The selection of study boundaries should be based on the VECs that are being assessed. Each of the VECs can have a different relationship to the pipeline both spatially and temporally, and different project phases can affect VECs differently. Therefore, a pipeline CEA may have multiple study boundaries, with the boundaries being specific to VECs.

The study boundaries may be related to different project phases (Hegmann et al., 1999). The practitioner should disregard any boundaries when determining the other actions that could interact with the pipeline and consider anything that is a likely interaction. Other actions do not necessarily have to be in close proximity to the pipeline project. Using best professional judgement and consultation with stakeholders will aid the selection of possible project interactions. A significant criterion for selecting other actions that could interact with the pipeline is if the action causes similar effects (Hegmann et al., 1999).

Temporal boundaries

When establishing temporal boundaries, considering the type of VEC is essential. For instance, the recovery of a VEC to its original state differs greatly between VEC types. Soil can return to its productive state more rapidly than the return of vegetation to a mature forest. Thus, depending on the VECs used, time frames of assessment are quite variable.

Actions that occurred in the past in an assessment can often be incorporated into the existing background conditions. For project assessments stakeholders should be primarily concerned with assessing the incremental impact of the project in relation to other present and future activities.

Present activities to be included in an assessment can be addressed by advocating for the inclusion of those actions which cause similar effects to those resulting from pipeline development. In other words, actions that could significantly affect the VECs being studied in the assessment should be assessed.

If the temporal boundary projects too far into the future (i.e., where the uncertainty of predictions is excessive) then the boundary will not be useful for CEA predictions. Alternatively, if a fairly well known and predictable path of events is expected (e.g., vegetation succession of some communities) then extending the study boundary excessively into the future until a climax community is developing is also unnecessary.

In order to consider the inclusion of future actions, some aspects of the projects or activities must be known. The challenge is to determine what constitutes a future action that could be relevant to the pipeline project and should be considered in a CEA. Future actions must produce environmental effects that are similar in nature to the environmental effects that result from the pipeline development in order to be considered in a CEA. Under the CEAA, only those projects and activities that are relevant to the proposed project and "on the books" must be assessed in a CEA. The Agency notes three categories of future actions. These include: (1) certain actions, (2) reasonably foreseeable actions, and (3) hypothetical actions (Hegmann et al., 1999). These categories of future actions are on a continuum progressing from 1 to 3, where uncertainty increases with time and other factors. The practitioner must fulfil legal obligations and decide what one is professionally obligated to do (Hegmann et al., 1999). Future actions that are speculative should be addressed where they can not be assessed in a meaningful way because of the lack of specific data, such as a project size and location.

Spatial boundaries
When conducting a CEA for a pipeline a reasonable study boundary should be selected that addresses the zone of influence of a pipeline (which can be quite variable depending on the project). The spatial boundaries of a pipeline CEA are relevant to the types of VECs being assessed. For example, geographical patterns on the land, ecosystem type, the presence of wildlife and wildlife corridors or home ranges, watershed boundaries, and river networks among other factors should be considered. Study boundaries are also relevant to other actions that can be assessed in a CEA. For example, a VEC that is affected by the interaction of two actions (on it) may help define the size of the spatial boundary of assessment. The boundary would include the other action, and the geographical links or pathways between the action and the pipeline. In other words, the zone of influence of the pipeline assists the establishment of boundaries.

The challenge is to determine how much of the effects on the VEC is due to other actions, and how much is due to the incremental effect of the pipeline. Therefore, practitioners should be wary of choosing VECs that cause project effects to appear minimal in relation to other actions. For example, selecting an excessively wide, or large spatial boundary can cause any project related cumulative effects to appear negligible compared to other actions (Hegmann et al., 1999; Kingsley, 1997; CEQ, 1996). An excessively small boundary on the other hand may cause project related cumulative effects to appear very significant compared to other activities within the study boundary, and potentially important issues outside the established boundary may be overlooked (Hegmann et al., 1999; Kingsley, 1997; CEQ, 1996).

The scoping process in its entirety should identify other projects and activities requiring analysis. If interactions will occur between certain actions and pipelines, then a VEC should reveal the link. Determining which other actions are the most relevant to pipelines is difficult. Common actions that could combine with a pipeline to contribute to cumulative effects include: other pipelines; oil and gas development; other linear facilities (primary and secondary roads, trails, seismic lines, railways, electrical transmission lines); forestry practices; agricultural and rangeland practices; resource extraction; human settlement and community development (townships, villages, and cities); other industrial production; recreation; hydrodams; and irrigation districts (pipes and canals). Stakeholders should consider assessing projects and activities that will assist decision-makers by giving them the pertinent information on cumulative effects.

Analyze effects
Assessing the effects of multiple actions on VECs is a challenging aspect of CEA. There is no single right way to complete a CEA. Since the issues and VECs often vary from project to project, the methods used to assess the effects on VECs will also be different. In many cases, VECs determine the methods that will be used to assess the effects on them. Hegmann and Yarranton (1995) provide a comprehensive review of various approaches and methods of assessing cumulative effects.

Identify mitigation
After the CEA is completed the proposed mitigative measures must be carried into the field and properly implemented to manage potential cumulative effects. However, they must first be identified. Best management practices (BMP) implemented to mitigate project-specific effects, often also limit the potential cumulative environmental effects. For example, by selecting

an appropriate route for the pipeline, which avoids environmental constraints such as watercourses, the overall net potential for cumulative environmental effects is reduced. At watercourse crossings, effective measures that minimize project-specific sedimentation will reduce the potential for interaction with other projects or activities that cause sedimentation.

Identifying local mitigation strategies for pipelines can be quite different compared with mitigation for other projects. A pipeline also creates many local environmental effects that are variable between projects and that are relevant to a project phase or activity. These local effects can normally be successfully mitigated, and they represent the best opportunity for reducing cumulative effects (Hegmann et al., 1999). Operating guidelines and company policies form standard industry practices that provide general and site-specific techniques to ameliorate environmental effects. They may be directed at the planning phase, or other phases such as construction, or operation, given their importance as possible sources of cumulative effects. Mitigation may also be directed at an environmental attribute or a VEC. Site-specific mitigation can also be noted on environmental planning maps. Specific mitigation strategies applicable to most pipelines for reducing pipeline cumulative effects are listed in Table 3.

Normally, the goal of mitigation is to attempt to reduce adverse effects to acceptable or non-significant levels. More specifically, and where feasible, mitigation strategies are aimed at returning an environmental value to its former state before the incremental disturbance from project actions. Mitigation can consist of general guidelines with broad applications or they can be very specific in nature. The goal can be to reduce local project effects, regional project effects, and regional effects from multiple projects and activities. Approaches to the management of cumulative environmental effects can occur on many different spatial and temporal scales and also involve many different jurisdictions. Mitigative measures may be localized, project-specific and immediate, or longer-term regional approaches that involve many stakeholders. Municipal, provincial and federal agencies all have a stake in the proper management of cumulative environmental effects. Effective consultation and coordination among government agencies, the public, and industry may assist in developing management plans that identify thresholds for accepted levels and types of activities in a region.

When regional mitigation is a goal and multiple jurisdictions are involved, cooperation from regional stakeholders is required to achieve success (Hegmann et al., 1999). Where CEA issues are complex and affect large areas, regional initiatives are a necessity (Hegmann et al., 1999). When approaches to mitigation are unsuccessful, techniques such as compensatory measures can be applied. Given that mitigation will not reduce all cumulative effects below significant levels in every situation, actions such as donating or directing funds to a designated regional board for conservation purposes may be warranted as a last resort. The compensation should be relevant to projects that are aimed at reducing cumulative effects that are similar in kind to those of the proposed project.

Table 3. Mitigation strategies for pipeline CEAs

Phase where mitigation is applied	Example mitigation strategies
Planning/Surveying	Route selection (minimize watercourse crossings and choose the appropriate type and location; limit habitat fragmentation; select agricultural or less valuable land; avoid ESAs; looping or using existing disturbance corridors); fly over only when necessary; key avoidance areas flagged or fenced
Construction	Timing of construction; limit sediment and run-off; only build essential roads and coordinate with other resource sectors; avoidance; notification; re-contouring topography and drainage; appropriate type of river crossing technique; limiting size of right-of-way disturbance; specific mitigation for rare species; appropriate soil handling and storage techniques; reclamation; proper citing of facilities; treat and discharge water to stable vegetated land; use gates and shooflies; firearm sanctions; control vehicle speeds
Operation	Emission reduction technologies; minimize right-of-way use by personnel and others; gates; monitor; minimize overflights; minimize herbicide use by mowing and spot-spraying with non-residuals
Decommissioning	Treating discharge water and directing to stable vegetated land; preventing water from entering the pipe
Abandonment	Only removing pipe as required; preventing water from entering the pipe
Regional Issues or Compensation	Cooperate with regional stakeholders; develop boards that address issues such as access management; participate in regional studies; donating money to conservation organizations or other resources

Management plans or regional approaches that incorporate stakeholder needs applied in combination with project-specific BMPs are seen as key requirements to properly manage potential cumulative environmental effects from pipeline projects.

Evaluate significance and implement follow-up
Practitioners should be aware that seemingly insignificant environmental effects may result in collectively significant cumulative effects (Odum, 1982), and that other activities or projects from the past, present or foreseeable future within the zone of influence of the pipeline may be considered to determine any interactions.

The significance of environmental effects from pipelines is an issue that is key to the discussion. After applying mitigation techniques and industry standards, many of the effects can be reduced and are then considered non-residual. The challenge to the CEA practitioner is to determine if non-residual (non-significant in the environmental assessment sense) or residual effects can lead to cumulative effects. Because there are no significant environmental effects, there may still persist or develop significant cumulative effects (Kingsley, 1997).

Evaluating the significance of project cumulative effects is one of the most controversial aspects of CEA. Two practitioners can carry out an assessment of cumulative effects and arrive at the same result. Depending on how results are interpreted, however, the two practitioners could easily arrive at different conclusions about the significance of the effects. Therefore, establishing proper assessment criteria for evaluating significance is essential. This may be completed before a CEA is conducted as it brings credibility to the process and provides criteria for stakeholders to evaluate the significance of project effects.

Given that the interpretation of cumulative effects is so important, the Agency provides a list of useful factors that influence the interpretation of significance. These factors include: exceeding of a threshold, effectiveness of mitigation, size of study area, incremental contribution of cumulative effects, relative contribution of effects of other actions, relative rarity of species, significance of local effects, magnitude of change relative to natural background variability, and creation of induced actions (Hegmann et al., 1999). Additional factors include how the project effects and other actions compare to plans or policies for various VECs in different jurisdictions.

The factors listed above should be considered and then described in terms of significance attributes. These significance attributes or assessment criteria can be used to aid the assessment of significance. The assessment criteria could include the following: direction, geographical extent, duration, magnitude, frequency, probability of occurrence, level of confidence, and permanence. Each of these assessment criteria uses various classifications, such as low, medium, high, or short-term, medium-term, or long-term, to describe project effects. The effects on each VEC can be determined and then the assessment criteria applied to determine significance. The determination of significance may be based on different criteria depending on the VEC being studied. Under the CEAA, the Responsible Authority must decide if the effects of the project are adverse, and if they are adverse, whether they are significant, and whether they are likely (FEARO, 1994).

All of the assessment criteria and other factors that have been discussed regarding significance should be considered in a pipeline CEA. Follow-up and monitoring are a critical part of managing cumulative environmental effects. By conducting audits and inspections, failures of mitigative measures can be identified and corrected, and their effectiveness monitored and assessed.

CONCLUSION

By properly identifying project-related residual environmental effects, stakeholders can progress to the next step of identifying potential cumulative environmental effects. To move from project-related effects to identifying cumulative environmental effects, an assessment process or framework such as that identified in the Agency's Cumulative Effects Assessment Practitioners Guide (Hegmann et al., 1999) should be applied. A defined process gives credibility and provides additional certainty in CEAs.

The proper management of cumulative environmental effects will occur through applying the appropriate mitigative measure identified during the assessment process. By ensuring that the measures are implemented cumulative effects can be managed. This may occur through monitoring conditions of approval and by carrying routine environmental inspections and audits of facilities. Approaches to the management of cumulative environmental effects can occur on many different spatial and temporal scales. Mitigative measures may be localized, project-specific and immediate, or longer-term regional approaches that involve many stakeholders. Municipal, provincial and federal agencies all have a stake in the proper management of cumulative environmental effects. Management plans or regional approaches that incorporate stakeholder needs applied in combination with project-specific BMPs are seen as key requirements to properly manage potential cumulative environmental effects from pipeline projects. Even if stakeholders cannot measure the exact cumulative effect, we should be able to take a precautionary approach and ensure to the extent possible that all commitments specifically mitigative measures are monitored and implemented. Mitigation is the key and the bottom-line to effective management of cumulative effect issues from pipeline projects.

Stakeholders can do a better job of assessing and managing cumulative effects by following accepted environmental assessment practice. Assessment methods can be improved over time. Linking project-specific cumulative effects analysis to regional initiatives should be a goal of proponents, regulators, and citizens. To improve the overall consideration of and management of cumulative effects stakeholders should be involved in carrying out follow-up and monitoring of tangible cumulative effects issues.

REFERENCES

Alberta Environment. 1988. Environmental Handbook for Pipeline Construction. Regulated Operations Branch, Land Reclamation Division, Edmonton, Alberta.

Beanlands, G.E. and P.N. Duinker. 1983. An ecological framework for environmental assessment in Canada. Federal Environmental Assessment Review Office, Hull, Quebec.

Canadian Environmental Assessment Research Council. 1988. The assessment of cumulative effects: A research prospectus. Canadian Environmental Research Council, Hull, Quebec.

Cocklin, C., S. Parker, and J. Hay. 1992a. Notes on cumulative environmental change II: A contribution to methodology. Journal of Environmental Management, 35: 51–67.

Cocklin, C., S. Parker, and J. Hay. 1992b. Notes on cumulative environmental change I: Concepts and issues. Journal of Environmental Management, 35: 31–49.

Didham, R.K., J. Ghazoul, N.E. Stork, and A.J. Davis. 1996. Insects in fragmented forests: A functional approach. Tree, 11(6): 255–260.

Eccles, R. and J.A. Duncan. 1986. Wildlife Monitoring Studies Along the Norman Wells-Zama Oil Pipeline, April 1985–May 1986. 48 pp. as cited in Jalkotzy, M.G., P.I. Ross, and M.D. Nasserden. 1997. The Effects of Linear Developments on Wildlife: A Review of Selected Scientific Literature. Prepared for Canadian Association of Petroleum Producers. Arc Wildlife Services Ltd. Calgary, Alberta.

Eccles, R., J. Green, R. Morrison, and A. Kennedy. 1994. Approaches to cumulative effects assessment of petroleum development in Alberta. In: Cumulative Effects Assessment in Canada: From Concept to Practice. A.J. Kennedy, ed. Papers from the 15th Symposium held by the Alberta Society of Professional Biologists. Alberta Association of Professional Biologists.

Eccles, R., G. Searing, J. Duncan, and C. Thompson. 1985. Wildlife Monitoring Studies Along the Norman Wells-Zama Oil Pipeline, January to March 1985. 70 pp. as cited in Jalkotzy, M.G., P.I. Ross, and M.D. Nasserden. 1997. The Effects of Linear Developments on Wildlife: A Review of Selected Scientific Literature. Prepared for Canadian Association of Petroleum Producers. Arc Wildlife Services Ltd. Calgary, Alberta.

Federal Environmental Assessment and Review Office. 1994. A Reference Guide for the Canadian Environmental Assessment Act: Addressing Cumulative Environmental Effects. Federal Environmental Assessment and Review Office, Hull, Quebec.

Finley, C.G. 1998. Pipeline projects and cumulative effects assessment issues. A Master's Degree Project. Faculty of Environmental Design, University of Calgary, Calgary, Alberta.

Forman, R.T.T. 1995. Land Mosaics: The Ecology of Landscapes and Regions. Cambridge University Press, Cambridge, England.

Hegmann, G.L. 1995. Implementing cumulative effects assessments. A Master's Degree Project. Faculty of Environmental Design, University of Calgary, Calgary, Alberta.

Hegmann, G., C. Cocklin, R. Creasey, S. Dupuis, A. Kennedy, L. Kingsley, W. Ross, H. Spaling, and D. Stalker. 1999. Cumulative Effects Assessment Practitioners Guide. AXYS Environmental Consulting Ltd. and the CEA Working Group for the Canadian Environmental Assessment Agency, Hull, Quebec.

Hegmann, G.L. and G.A. Yarranton. 1995. Cumulative effects and the energy resources conservation board's review process. Working Paper #1 MacLeod Institute for Environmental Analysis, University of Calgary, Calgary, Alberta.

Henein, K. and G. Merriam. 1990. The elements of connectivity where corridor quality is variable. Landscape Ecology, 4: 157–170.

Jalkotzy, M.G., P.I. Ross, and M.D. Nasserden. 1997. The Effects of Linear Developments on Wildlife: A Review of Selected Scientific Literature. Prepared for Canadian Association of Petroleum Producers. Arc Wildlife Services Ltd. Calgary, Alberta.

Kalff, S.A. 1995. A proposed framework to assess cumulative environmental effects in Canadian national parks. Pks. Can.-Tech. Rep. Eco. Sci. No. 0001. 140 pp.

Kingsley, L. 1997. A Guide to Environmental Assessments: Assessing Cumulative Effects. Prepared for Parks Canada, Hull, Quebec.

Odum, W.E. 1982. Environmental degradation and the tyranny of small decisions. Bioscience, 32(9): 728–729.

Priddle, R., A. Cote-Verhaaf, R.D. Revel, and G.M. Lewis. 1996. Express Pipeline Project: Report of the Joint Panel. Prepared for the National Energy Board and Canadian Environmental Assessment Agency. National Energy Board, Calgary, Alberta.

Rich, A.C., D.S. Dobkin, and L.J. Niles. 1994. Defining forest fragmentation by corridor width: The influence of narrow forest-dividing corridors on forest-nesting birds in Southern New Jersey. Conservation Biology, 8(4): 1109–1121.

Ross, W. A. 1994. Assessing cumulative environmental effects: Both impossible and essential. In: Cumulative Effects Assessment in Canada: From Concept to Practice. A.J. Kennedy, ed. Papers from the 15th Symposium held by the Alberta Society of Professional Biologists. Alberta Association of Professional Biologists.

Saunders, D.A. and C.P. de Rebeira. 1991. Values of corridors to avian populations in a fragmented landscape. In: Nature Conservation the Role of Corridors. D.A. Saunders and R.J. Hobbs, eds. Surrey Beatty and Sons, Chipping Norton, Australia. pp. 221–244 as cited in Saunders, D.A., R.J. Hobbs, and C.R. Margules. 1991. Biological consequences of ecosystem fragmentation: A review. Conservation Biology, 5(1): 18–32.

Saunders, D.A., R.J. Hobbs, and C.R. Margules. 1991. Biological consequences of ecosystem fragmentation: A review. Conservation Biology, 5(1): 18–32.

Smit, B. and H. Spaling. 1995. Methods for cumulative effects assessment. Environmental Assessment Review, 15: 81–106.

Spaling, H. and B. Smit. 1993. Cumulative environmental change: Conceptual frameworks, evaluation approaches, and institutional perspectives. Environmental Management, 17(5): 587–600.

United States Council of Environmental Quality (CEQ). 1996. Considering Cumulative Effects Under the National Environmental Policy Act. Final Draft Interagency Review Version, September 24, 1996, Council of Environmental Quality.

BIOGRAPHICAL SKETCHES

Chris G. Finley

National Energy Board of Canada, 444 Seventh Avenue, SW, Calgary, AB T2P 0X8, Canada, Fax: 403-299-3110, E-mail: cfinley@neb-one.gc.ca

Chris Finley is an Environmental Specialist at the National Energy Board (the Board) in Calgary, Alberta,

Canada. Chris is primarily involved with environmental impact assessments of energy development proposals under the *Canadian Environmental Assessment Act* and the *National Energy Board Act*. He is also an Inspection Officer with the Board and routinely carries out environmental inspections of pipeline construction projects across Canada. Chris holds a Bachelor of Science Degree (Agriculture) specializing in Environmental Biology from the Nova Scotia Agricultural College and a Master of Environmental Design Degree specializing in Environmental Science from the University of Calgary, Alberta.

Dr. Richard D. Revel
Faculty of Environmental Design, University of Calgary, Calgary, AB T2N 1N4, Canada, E-mail: revel@ucalgary.ca

Dr. Revel is an ecologist and a Professor of Environmental Science in the Faculty of Environmental Design, University of Calgary. His interests lie in various areas of natural resource management and the relationship of humans to their environment. He has been involved in developing and evaluating environmental impacts of different projects related to the oil and gas industry and has experience in the regulation of these industries in both Canada and South America.

Innovative Co-Location of Telecommunications Facilities within Existing Rights-of-Way

Joel M. Rinebold, Julie M. Donaldson, and Mark F. Kohler

Customer demand for new wireless telecommunications service, including cellular telephone, personal communications services, specialized mobile radio, and other wireless telecommunications services, has manifested itself in the need to construct more than 100,000 new facilities in the United States alone by 2005, many of which will require tower structures. While the demand for service is a function of the market, the need for these new facilities is a function of the technology and the competitive nature of the industry, as guided by regulators. As a consequence of this new market and regulatory scheme for competitive services, new telecommunications towers will be developed in nearly all urban and suburban locations. Use of existing telecommunications towers, originally built to provide telecommunications services for other users, is possible in many locations, but planners will be forced to identify as many as six new sites per 10 km^2 area (4 mile^2) for the development of facilities as wireless service expands. The challenge to identify tower sites has resulted in opportunities to use existing towers, buildings and other tall structures, and to co-locate antennas within existing rights-of-way. Development of facilities within existing rights-of-way is now possible and practical by attaching antennas to existing electric transmission line support structures. This technical application yields a unique opportunity to provide wireless telecommunications services without the need to construct an entirely new support structure, thus avoiding additional costs, reducing potential public opposition for the construction of such facilities, and providing revenue to support ongoing maintenance and management activities within the right-of-way. This paper will explore and test new and innovative development of co-located telecommunications facilities on existing rights-of-way, using models to assess radiofrequency propagation and signal strength within a coverage area, analyze alternatives, assess environmental effects, assess use of existing structures, and examine contractual easements to provide legal rights to use the existing rights-of-way for telecommunications service. The results of this work is relevant to state and local planners, electric utilities, and telecommunications carriers as a method to assist in the guidance and planning of telecommunications services and the efficient use of existing rights-of-way.

Keywords: Electric transmission, wireless, siting, legal, regulation, telecommunications, co-location of telecommunications facilities

INTRODUCTION

The development of new towers for wireless telecommunications services for wireless telephone and data transfer has become a difficult task for local planners. These towers may exceed 200 feet in height and can become controversial for local planning and zoning commission regulators when opposed by members of the community as unsightly, unsafe due to the possibility of tower collapse, and harmful to human health due to the exposure of radiofrequency emissions.

Propagation from wireless facilities, that include cellular telephone, personal communications services, and specialized mobile radio, is limited by frequency and low-power output. These systems require the development of dense networks to provide seamless coverage that enable users to hand off from one facility to another without an interruption of service, reuse frequency to increase overall capacity, and meet coverage objectives without interfering with adjacent facilities. The result has been the need to develop numerous facilities and redundant networks in nearly every urban and suburban area. Wireless carriers are developing their networks at a density that ranges from facilities less than a mile apart in urban areas to facilities several miles apart in more rural areas. The need for this dense geographic distribution of facilities severely limits the ability of the wireless industry simply to co-locate on existing towers that were developed for public safety, radio and television broadcast, and microwave transmission, without developing numerous new facilities. Furthermore, physical space on existing towers, structural capability of the tower, and potential co-channel interference from transmitting equipment will also limit opportunities for co-location of wireless antennas on existing towers.

As shown on Fig. 1, the use of existing electric transmission line rights-of-way provides a technical opportunity for the placement of wireless antennas on existing electric transmission lines support structures. However, the placement of antennas within existing rights-of-way and on existing support structures must be carefully planned and legally executed. While the regulatory requirements and jurisdiction of each location may differ, the co-location of telecommunications facilities within existing rights-of-way has been accepted by the wireless industry, and can be achieved efficiently and without significant adverse environmental effect.

WIRELESS GROWTH

The number of wireless subscribers in the United States has grown from 91,000 in 1984 to 86,047,003 in 1999 (CTIA, 2000). The estimated number of the subscribers at the present time in the United States is over 93,780,200. It is further estimated that 45,924 new subscribers are added every day in the United States, and that approximately 238.7 million Americans have access to between three and seven wireless providers (CTIA, 2000). In the United States, much of this growth is the result of changes in federal law, including the Telecommunications Act of 1996. The purpose of this new legislation was to promote competition and reduce regulation in order to lower prices, improve quality, and encourage the rapid deployment of new telecommunications technology (Krattenmaker, 1996; Kearney and Merrill, 1998). Similar growth and market development has occurred or is expected to occur in Canada, Europe, and elsewhere, as the result of similar legislation and regulatory change with an estimated 1.26 billion persons to be wireless customers worldwide by 2005 (CTIA, 2000; Campbell, 1999; Kress, 1997; Ryan, 1993).

To support this increased use of wireless technology, wireless sites in the United States have grown from 346 in 1984 to 81,698 by December 1999 (CTIA, 2000). Wireless telecommunications service providers, bolstered by this rapidly growing market, are expected to continue to develop more new towers and facilities, including more than 100,000 towers and facilities within the United States alone by 2005 (Sweet, 1998).

POLICY

In the United States, electric utilities acquired property for the establishment of rights-of-way through the powers typically granted to franchised public utility monopolies. The rates of these utilities were historically regulated on a cost-of-service basis, where the utilities were allowed a reasonable rate-of-return in exchange for the provision of universal regulated service to all customers within the utilities' franchise service areas (Phillips, 1993; Strasser and Kohler, 1987). With a regulated rate-of-return, the utility owners of network infrastructure have little incentive to share or to provide access to the right-of-way. Consequently, each utility has both opportunity and regulatory incentive to develop separate parallel networks.

However, telecommunications providers, supported by regulatory policies encouraging competition, have sought to expand their services by developing additional facilities within the existing electric transmission infrastructure. Indeed, many jurisdictions have recognized the benefits of sharing this infrastructure, including the efficient use of scarce rights-of-way, orderly expansion, coordination with many users, competition for increased innovation, and lower cost of services for consumers.

Electric utilities have often developed internal telemetry systems on existing support structures and separate towers as part of their core business of electric supply and/or transmission. However, barriers to the development of common shared networks will develop if the owners of rights-of-way establish or assign legal rights that provide unfair advantage or deny access to other carriers. This can happen if an electric utility attempts to exploit its control over the ROW. For example, the discriminatory practice of preferential pricing or over-pricing will result in anti-competitive access and impede the development of common shared networks.[1] The development of commercial wireless telecommunications services by an electric utility on electric transmission support structures may further create a significant incentive to exploit the right-of-way resource in an anti-competitive,

---

1 Nonetheless, the owner of the right-of-way should not be deprived of an opportunity for reasonable compensation for owning, operating, and maintaining the right-of-way and its infrastructure. The price for shared access should be the subject of private negotiation, with the availability of a regulatory process for arbitration or rate-setting should negotiation fail.

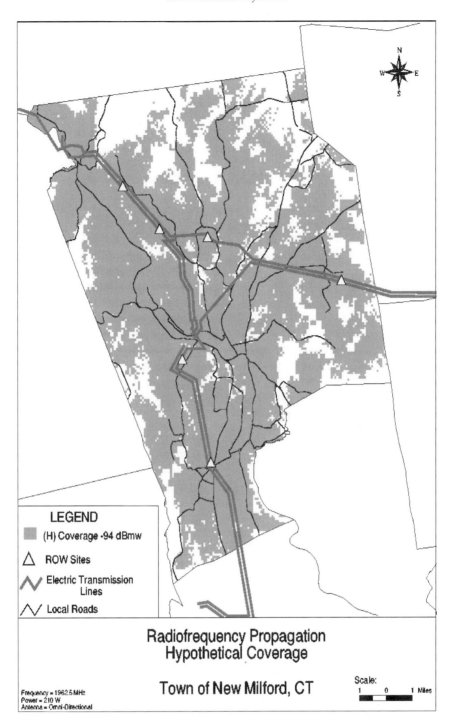

Fig. 1. Radiofrequency propagation, hypothetical ROW coverage, New Milford, Connecticut.

discriminatory fashion. Indeed, the consumer will benefit if the shared use of the right-of-way is subject to competitive pricing, nonexclusive access, proper maintenance, fair allocation of costs, reliable service, safe operations, and protection of the environment.

Physical access may be based on a first-come, first-serve basis. However, electric utilities may be faced with multiple (potentially) conflicting requests as more telecommunications carriers seek access to electric transmission lines. Any request for access or upgraded facilities should consider the needs of all existing and potential users. The resolution of these requests will likely require long-range planning with private negotiation and oversight by state or federal regulators. The right-of-way owners' denial of access should be restricted to competitively neutral grounds, including physical capacity, structural capacity, safety and reliability, radio-frequency interference, and damage to environmental resources.

Promoting the shared use of electric transmission rights-of-way does not require the elimination of the existing electric transmission monopoly held by most electric utilities. However, these rights-of-way should be considered a community resource as it may be technically unfeasible or cost prohibitive to duplicate a similar right-of-way for the development of a parallel network for telecommunications providers. The shift from potential multiple and redundant parallel networks to common infrastructure networks that serve as a platform for numerous competing carriers, sometimes referred to as lynchpin networks, will continue to gain favor as telecommunications carriers and rights-of-way owners establish master service agreements providing equal access on a non-discriminatory basis (Rosenberg, 1996). A natural symbiosis between the electric and telecommunications industries should be encouraged and could result in mutual benefit to both industries.

SITING CONSTRAINTS

All telecommunications siting must be carefully planned to provide the desired coverage within a selected service area without causing internal or external interference. System planners may test coverage using transmitting antennas located atop a crane to measure radio signal propagation, or use computer modeling to simulate coverage. Variables include frequency, power output, antenna type and gain, integration with adjacent cells, height of the support structures, and topography.

As shown on Fig. 1, placement of antennas on a transmission line support structure cannot change the physical laws which govern radio signal propagation; however, such placement can provide predictable and opportunistic locations to establish telecommunications sites. Furthermore, placement of antennas on existing support structures within maintained rights-of-way are more likely to be viewed as colocation of common infrastructure within an established utility corridor. Such established utility corridors may already be cleared of mature vegetation, served by roads, and segregated from sensitive community development. Thus, the incremental increased use of existing support structures for colocation of antennas will be less likely to affect ecological, scenic, and community resources than the development of separate towers to support such antennas. Consequently, these existing corridor locations are less likely to be publicly opposed and are more likely to be supported by regulators faced with the dilemma of telecommunications facility siting.

Access and utilities
Notwithstanding the legal issues associated with shared use of an existing right-of-way, to be discussed further herein, the use of an existing structure within an established right-of-way may preclude the need to develop a new facility. However, such shared use may require upgrades to the right-of-way to allow access to the telecommunications facility several times a month throughout the year. Such upgrades may include regrading, resurfacing, and drainage improvements. In general, the wireless industry will require permanent access to their facilities employing conventional four-wheel drive vehicles for facility maintenance and/or repair. Access for construction may require additional modification for delivery of equipment, structure members, and construction machinery; however, such construction access is temporary and may be limited to short-term modification to the site.

High capacity telephone connections and electric service from distribution lines may also be required for operation of a wireless facility. Such utilities may be installed either underground or overhead, at the preference of regulators and/or industry officials, but must comply with all electrical safety codes, including vertical and horizontal clearances for equipment within the right-of-way in proximity to high-voltage conductors. As a consequence of these codes, some equipment may be required to be located outside the right-of-way. In any event, the upgrade of an access road should be coordinated with the replacement of utilities and utility equipment during site construction.

Fencing, while generally not a requirement, may be preferred by some wireless providers for additional security of equipment. Such fencing must be in compliance with all vertical and horizontal separation distances and may require grounding to prevent induced static currents on metallic fence components.

Access onto the tower for maintenance and repair of antennas may be restricted. High-voltage electricity is inherently more dangerous than the lower voltage telecommunications facility, which would require telecommunications workers to have at least the same qualifications in terms of training as do electrical professionals. As a consequence of this safety issue, wireless carriers may seek to have their telecommunications technicians certified to access high-voltage structures, utility workers may seek to be certified to work on telecommunications equipment, or both industries may agree to use third-party professionals certified to work on both high-voltage electrical equipment and telecommunications equipment. Furthermore, access to antennas may be precluded unless high-voltage conductors are de-energized. Coordination between the wireless carrier and the electric utility is essential in order to de-energize conductors for scheduled maintenance and repair of antennas located in critical positions. However, it should be recognized that such coordination may be difficult during certain periods of high demand for electric dispatch, when conductors cannot be de-energized and access to antennas would be justifiably denied.

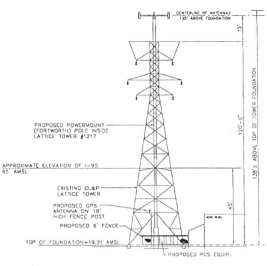

Connecticut Siting Council Petition No. 383 — Sprint PCS Compression Post Mount within a Connecticut Light & Power Company High-Voltage Electric Transmission Line Structure, Morehouse Drive, Fairfield, CT, December 18, 1997.

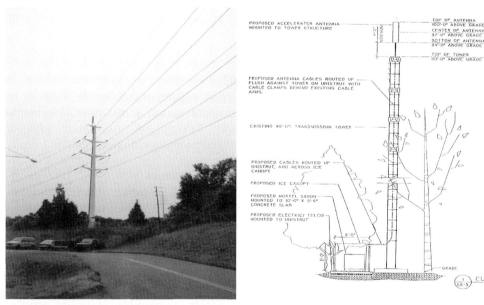

Connecticut Siting Council Petition No. 396 — Omnipoint Communications Direct Mast Mount on a Connecticut Light & Power Company High-Voltage Electric Transmission Line Structure, King Arthur Drive, East Lyme, CT, June 18, 1998.

Fig. 2. ROW structure modification.

Direct mast mounts

The potentially simplest method for placement of an antenna on an existing support structure is by use of a direct mast mount. In this application, as shown on Fig. 2, antennas are attached to a relatively short mast or pipe mount that in turn is attached directly to an existing support structure. Special mounting brackets, bands, and/or welding may be necessary to attach the mount to the support structure. Selection of the mounting technique is important to avoid over-stressing the structure or individual members of the structure, cutting or burning critical structure members, and compromising durability of the structure by impairing galvanization or by inducing electrolysis. Although this method may allow rapid development of the facility and deployment of service, the load carrying capacity of the support structure may limit the number and size of antennas to omni-directional whip or lower capacity installations using three or less flush mount or other panel antennas. These antennas may not necessarily limit the area of coverage, but may limit the number of simultaneous signals that can be transmitted from the site, thus limiting the capacity of the proposed antenna array.

The load carrying capacity of some structures can be increased with certain structural and foundation reinforcement; however this will increase the time, cost, and complexity for the installation. Consequently, it may be more cost effective to simply reduce the antenna loading to within the capability of the tower. Nonetheless, electric utilities and regulators may seek to over design certain tower structures at key locations, such as hilltops, when installing new structures to increase the opportunity and marketability for co-location of multiple full array antennas.

Structural compression post mounts

Compression posts mounted adjacent to or within existing support structures increase load bearing capacity for mounting larger antenna arrays. As shown in Fig. 2, the use of a compression post is more involved and requires a firm foundation, construction of the compression post within or against the existing structure, and securing the post to individual members of the existing structure. However, this method offers substantially increased load bearing capacity capable of holding large arrays of nine to twelve panel antennas on a structure platform. Some compression posts are capable of being shared by multiple carriers seeking to take advantage of common infrastructure such as electric and telephone utilities, and an access road to the structure. The time, cost, complexity of development will vary with this type of construction; however, this method will provide the structural latitude for wireless carriers to develop full-sectorized arrays.

Safety

Prior to any installation, a complete structural analysis is necessary with a full description of existing utility loads; assessment of the proposed telecommunications loads for all antennas, mounting brackets, and the load of the coaxial cables routed down through the support structure; and an assessment of the structure including all bracing, bolts, and connections. Loading criteria must, as appropriate, account for wind pressure, radial ice, uneven tension from broken shield wires and conductors, and an overload factor. In addition, a geotechnical analysis must be undertaken to confirm the capability of the existing foundation to support the loads of all electric conductors, protective gear, and telecommunications equipment.

Co-location of wireless antennas may be possible on any structure; however, the structures that offer the greater structural capacity and opportunity for co-location include:
- lattice structures built with integrated structural members on multiple foundation piers;
- guyed structures where steel cables provide additional lateral support to the tower;
- dead-end structures built to withstand the tension of electric conductors arranged in a static strain configuration; and
- angle structures built to withstand the tension of electric conductors at an angle location in a line.

All construction must meet local and regional code requirements for structural stability considering mechanical and wind loading. In the United States, the Telecommunications Industry Association/Electronic Industries Association has adopted "Structural Standards for Steel Antenna Towers and Antenna Supporting Structures" (TIA, 1996) to provide "minimum criteria for specifying and designing steel antenna towers and antenna supporting structures." These standards, which are periodically updated, may be adapted for international use; however, local meteorological wind and ice loading conditions must be applied. Equivalent international system of units are used and conversion factors are provided (TIA, 1996). The content of these standards include sections on materials, loading, stresses, foundations and anchors, guy loading, operation, grounding, maintenance and inspection, and analysis of existing structures. In addition, all electrical equipment, grounding, and connections must comply with local codes including electric safety codes (IEEE, 1997). However, these standards are not intended to replace or supercede applicable codes or to be used as instruction manuals, and are not a substitution for professional design and installation with verification by licensed professional engineers.

Schedule and cost

The schedule and cost of any proposed application will vary based on the existing conditions at the site, the existing structure, and the proposed installation. Variables may include the assessment and capability of the existing structure and foundation, assessment of the proposed loading by the antennas and coaxial cable connecting the antennas to a base station, site access, availability of utility service for distribution electric and telephone service, cooperation to de-energize conductors, access to the existing structure for analysis and construction, design and construction contracts, and the legal right to use the existing rights-of-way. Should the existing tower and foundation be incapable of supporting the additional load associated with the antennas, alternatives may include modifying the structure to increase its structural capability, reducing the loading of the proposed antennas, or selecting a different structure with increased structural capability to hold the proposed antennas. These activities and analysis of alternatives may increase pre-construction costs and lengthen the schedule, but may be necessary to balance the requirements of wireless antennas with the capability of existing structures on a right-of-way. The burden of costs for these activities will likely fall upon the telecommunications carrier, unless the electric utility has entered into an arrangement to accommodate certain antennas in exchange for a fee as part of a lease agreement which can range from 10,000 to $40,000 (US) per year.

Wireless carriers and utilities have the option to assess and design applications with in-house construction crews or to coordinate with independent specialty companies that design, develop, and maintain telecommunications towers and antennas. Indeed, some specialty companies can provide detailed information on loading conditions, analysis procedures, attachment designs, fabrication procedures, construction procedures, installation, and utility references. For example, FWT, Inc. has developed proprietary specialty products including PowerMount^{TM} compression posts for use at existing lattice structures and PowerArm^{TM} support devices to hold antennas on existing monopoles (Wrigley, 2000). FWT, Inc. reports that most PowerMount^{TM} sites are completed in two days, and can be operational in two to three days after construction begins, except for power and telephone connections which are affected by local issues. At one-half to two-thirds the cost of conventional network built-out, these facilities typically cost 30,000–$35,000 for a 85-foot to 110-foot unit including the costs of the foundation, standard grounding, PowerMount^{TM}, installation of the PowerMount^{TM}, and antenna/cable installation. PowerMount^{TM} maintains that stress analysis is completed within two weeks and the PowerMount^{TM} is shipped three weeks thereafter. To date, several hundred compression post PowerMount^{TM} structures have been developed, as shown in Fig. 2, and have become accepted by both the electric utility and wireless industries.

Electric transmission rights-of-way — Legal nature of the property right

Electric transmission rights-of-way can be publicly or privately owned.[2] For public rights-of-way, the legal issues regarding their shared use may be governed by existing access laws or policies. The telecommunications legislation adopted in many countries to open telecommunications to competition include provisions making public rights-of-way available on a nondiscriminatory basis to all telecommunications carriers, including wireless providers (Campbell, 1999; Ryan, 1993). These provisions may already extend to publicly owned electric transmission rights-of-way or could provide a model for a future regulatory framework.

In North America, however, electric transmission rights-of-way are predominately privately owned. Electric utility companies, either through private transactions or through the exercise of the government-delegated power of eminent domain (known in Canada and other countries as expropriation),[3] have obtained private rights-of-way over the land of others to place their transmission lines. Although it is possible for the utility to obtain fee ownership of such land, more typically the property right obtained is known as an easement.[4]

An easement is a nonpossessory interest in the land of another that grants the easement holder the right to use the land, usually for a defined purpose (Bruce and Ely, 1995, ¶1.01). The easement holder does not own the land nor does it have a right to possess it; rather, the easement holder may use the land in a manner that is consistent with the grant of the easement right. Because rights of the owner of the underlying property — known as the servient estate — are involved, consideration must be given to the scope of the easement granted in evaluating whether the right-of-way may be shared without first obtaining the agreement of the owner of the servient estate. These concerns can always be avoided if the servient estate's owner consents to the shared use. Such consent, not surprisingly, is not always forthcoming and at a minimum would likely require additional compensation to the owner. In the absence of obtaining consent or additional rights from the owner, two issues in particular must be addressed: (1) whether the existing easement rights can be apportioned — that is, can they be shared with another; and (2) whether the shared use by a wireless telecommunications provider is consistent with the easement holder's existing rights.

A determination of whether an easement can be assigned or apportioned must begin with the language of the easement document. In some instances an easement may expressly preclude assignment or apportionment of the rights and benefits granted. However, in the absence of such express language, United States courts generally view commercial easements such as electric transmission rights-of-way as divisible (Bruce and Ely, 1995, ¶¶2.01, 9.04). Further, in many cases, state statute may codify the public policy favoring

---

[2] An important caveat must be made at the outset. Property law is by its nature parochial and often varies from locale to locale not only in its details but sometimes in its broader outline. Generalizations are therefore difficult, and no effort is made to provide a complete codex of the legal rules for all jurisdictions. Instead, what is offered is a discussion of the nature of the issues that are posed, with a more focused discussion of the relevant legal principles of the United States, Canada and, to a lesser extent, other countries.

[3] Eminent domain or expropriation is the power of the government to take private property for a public purpose without the owner's consent. This governmental power has often been delegated to private entities, such as public utilities, because of the essential services that they provide and the land needed for the delivery of their services (Sackman, 1999, vol. 1A, §3.03[11]; Phillips, 1993, p. 120). Although most rights-of-way have been obtained through agreement rather than the recourse to eminent domain proceedings, the threat of such recourse often provides the leverage for achieving agreement of the landowner.

[4] This includes rights-of-way taken through the power of eminent domain or expropriation. The taking of property by an electric utility for transmission will generally result in an easement (Sackman, 1999, vol. 3, §11.08[20]; *Otter Tail Power v. Demchuk*, 1982).

assignment of public utility easements (Connecticut General Statutes §47-42).

Even if apportionable, the nature of the easement holder's rights must be evaluated to determine whether those rights could encompass use by a telecommunications provider. As a basic proposition of property law, an easement holder only has such rights as the grantor of the easement originally transferred to it. This would, at first blush, appear to pose an obstacle for the shared use by wireless providers given that it involves a recent technology that few could have envisioned at the time most electric transmission easements were granted. However, courts are reluctant to interpret easements in a way that preclude changes in use reflecting technological advances.

Historically, much of the existing electric transmission system was developed at the same time as the land line telephone system, resulting in a kind of symbiotic accumulation of easement rights. Electric and telephone companies, in seeking easements for their respective networks, typically also sought easement rights for the other's services. Thus, it is quite common for an electric transmission easement to include the right to use the land for telegraph and telephone as well as electric transmission lines. The question is whether such an easement can also be used for the placement of a wireless facility.

The resolution of such questions always begins with the language of the instrument creating the easement. The following is an example of the granting language in a typical electric transmission easement:

> Together with the right to enter upon said land and erect, inspect, operate, replace, repair and patrol and permanently maintain on said right of way, poles and towers, with necessary conductors, wires, cross arms, guy wires and other usual fixtures and appurtenances used or adapted for the transmission of electric current for light, heat, power or any other purpose, *and used or adapted for telephone purposes* (emphasis added).

The extent of the easement holder's right to use, and the corresponding right to apportion for the use of another, is determined by the language used in the grant of the easement (Bruce and Ely, 1995, ¶8.02[1]). However, the task of interpreting that language is not always simple. Courts have developed several basic rules for interpreting the language of an easement. Most fundamentally, the easement holder is entitled to reasonable use of its rights. The reasonableness of the use includes, among other things, consideration of changes in circumstances and technological developments (*Centel Cable TV v. Cook*, 1991; *Witteman v. Jack Barry Cable TV*, 1986; *Henley v. Cablevision*, 1985; *Minnkota Power Coop. v. Lake Shore Prop.*, 1980).[5] Moreover, the law presumes that advances in technology are contemplated in the grant of the easement (*Hash v. Sotinowski*, 1985). Therefore, it is not an obstacle that wireless facilities represent a new technology not specifically referenced or even imagined at the time of the grant of the easement.

Several United States and Canadian courts have evaluated the language of electric transmission easements in connection with the addition of new telecommunications technologies and have found the shared use consistent with the existing easement rights (*Stasium v. West Kootenay Power*, 1999; *Edgecombe v. Lower Valley Power & Light Co.*, 1996; *C/R TV, Inc. v. Shannondale, Inc.*, 1994; *Cousins v. Alabama Power Co.*, 1992). These courts concluded that the use of an existing electric transmission easement for new telecommunications technologies should be permitted if (a) the additional use is substantially consistent with the easement's original purpose, and (b) would not be substantially burdensome to the subservient estate. In each of these cases, the original grant of the easement was for electric transmission and telephone lines, and the proposed shared use involved the addition of fiber optic wires for a cable service provider. Even though not "telephone" service as the grantor might have recognized at the time of the original grant, the courts found cable television service to be a form of telecommunications substantially consistent with the easement's purpose and merely a natural extension of earlier technologies. The courts concluded the holder of the electric transmission easement had the right to permit the additional use without the consent of the servient estate owner.[6]

In principle, the same reasoning should pertain to wireless facilities. Wireless services are a technological advancement in telecommunications that should be considered within the scope of the reasonable use of an easement that includes telephone service as an intended purpose. However, the reasonableness of the additional burden on the servient estate must be evaluated on a case-by-case basis. As discussed above, different facilities and locations may require additional physical access or changes to the right-of-way that could rise to the level of a substantial burden on the servient estate. In most cases, the structures, equipment and activities involved will be consistent with the reasonable use associated with the existing easement rights.

Significant opportunities exist for the shared use of electric transmission rights-of-way by wireless providers. In light of the courts' approach to interpreting

---

5 The same rules apply in those instances in which an easement was obtained through the exercise of the power of eminent domain, except that the controlling instrument is the judgment issued by the court establishing the terms of the taking of the original easement. In all other respects, the easement holder has the same right to reasonable use including the right to take advantage of technological changes (Sackman, 1999, §11.08[2]; *Otter Tail Power Co. v. Demchuk*, 1982).

6 Similar conclusions have been reached regarding the shared use of electric transmission rights-of-way in litigation in Norway (Føyen, 2000).

easements as encompassing new telecommunications technologies, most existing electric transmission easements may already permit the addition of a wireless facility without securing additional rights or obtaining the consent of the servient estate owner.

Regulatory provisions and limitations to the promotion of shared use

The legal issues relating to shared use are not limited to the evaluation of property rights. Government regulatory policies must also be crafted to promote the shared use of electric transmission rights-of-way by wireless telecommunication providers.

Many countries have created or extended existing rules creating mandatory, nondiscriminatory access to public rights-of-way or other public properties for telecommunications providers as part of the regulatory shift to the competitive provision of telecommunications services (Campbell, 1999). Similarly, many have mandated access to existing facilities and structures of other telecommunications entities, often including the sharing of wireless facility structures (Campbell, 1999; Ryan, 1993). Less attention has been given to creating legal requirements with regard to electric transmission structures within rights-of way.

In some instances, existing laws regarding mandatory access may already be applicable to or could provide a model for mandating access to electric transmission rights-of-way. The US Pole Attachment Act provides an intriguing example. This legislation was originally enacted in 1978 as a mechanism to afford cable television providers access to the poles of electric and telephone companies. As part of the Telecommunications Act of 1996, these provisions of the Pole Attachment Act were amended to extend to telecommunications providers. Specifically, the amended legislation now requires that a "utility shall provide a cable television system or any telecommunications carrier with nondiscriminatory access to any pole, duct, conduit, or right-of-way owned or controlled by it" unless there is "insufficient capacity or reasons of safety, reliability and generally applicable engineering purposes" that justify the denial of access (47 U.S.C. §224(f)). It also gives authority to the Federal Communications Commission to establish just and reasonable rates for shared access (47 U.S.C. §224(b)–(c)).[7]

The Pole Attachment Act may have been crafted to provide access to public utility distribution structures. However, its scope is not necessarily so limited, and it could be a tool to promote the shared use of electric transmission rights-of-way. First, the Federal Communications Commission has clarified that the provisions of the Pole Attachment Act are available to wireless providers and not just wireline telecommunications carriers (FCC Report and Order, 1998, ¶¶36–42). The US Supreme Count recently upheld the FCC's rule extending mandatory access to wireless providers (National Cable v. Gulf Power, 2002). Second, by its terms the Pole Attachment Act's mandatory access requirements extend to all public utilities, including electric utilities, that own or control "rights-of-way used, in whole or in part, for any wire communications." (47 U.S.C. §224(a)(1)). If an electric transmission right-of-way is used for wire communications, a wireless provider should be able to invoke the nondiscriminatory access mandate.

Such laws may be a particularly effective mechanism for promoting shared use when an electric utility is pursuing the development of its own telecommunications business and has an inherent bias against providing access to its transmission rights-of-way to other telecommunications providers. For example, Svenska Kraftnät AB, the owner of most of the electric transmission network in Sweden, is developing a telecommunications network using its existing electric infrastructure. The Swedish Right of Way Act, as amended by the Telecommunications Act in 1993, is applicable to the development of this telecommunications infrastructure (Juhlen, 2000).

The ability of government to compel access to a private right-of-way, however, does have its limits. Under US constitutional law, for example, government-mandated access to private property such as that provided under the Pole Attachment Act is considered a taking of property (*FCC v. Florida Power Corp.*, 1987; *Loretto v. Teleprompter Manhattan CATV Corp.*, 1982). To satisfy the constitutional proscriptions against the taking of property, such access requirements must provide for the reasonable compensation of the property owner and a mechanism for judicial review of the compensation award (*Gulf Power Co. v. United States*, 1999; *Wisconsin Central Ltd. v. Public Service Comm'n*, 1996).

Interplay of public utility regulation and local land use

The proposed placement of a wireless facility in an electric transmission right-of-way may require approvals from several regulatory bodies. Particularly in a federal system, there may be multiple layers of legal regulation. For instance, in Canada, telecommunications are generally regulated at the federal level, while electric transmission rights of way are regulated at the provincial level. In the United States, the shared use of an electric transmission right-of-way may implicate federal, state and local regulation.

The US Telecommunications Act of 1996 purports to restrict state and local siting authority in several ways, including: (1) prohibiting state or local authorities from unreasonably discriminating among providers of functionally equivalent services; (2) barring state or local authorities from regulating the siting of wireless facilities in a manner that has the effect of prohibiting the provision of wireless services; and (3) preempting state

---

7 47 U.S.C. §224(b)–(c). The Commission has adopted rate formulas and complaint procedures that encourage resolution of rate issues by private negotiation. 47 C.F.R. §§1.1401–1.1418.

and local authorities from regulating radio frequency emissions in a manner that conflicts with federal regulations on such emissions (47 U.S.C. §332(c)(7)(B)). In most other respects, state and local authority over the siting of wireless facilities is expressly preserved (47 U.S.C. §332(c)(7)(A); Rosario and Kohler, 1996; Tuesley, 1999).

States differ, however, as to whether the regulation of wireless facility siting is within the jurisdiction of local land use agencies or of a specialized state agency. The decision of which level of government regulates siting is not in and of itself problematic for the promotion of shared use of rights-of-way. The potential for overlapping jurisdiction can arise, however, where local authorities have jurisdiction over wireless facilities. This potential exists because, in most states, the regulation of electric transmission lines is conducted at the state level, usually by either the public utilities commission or a state siting board (Williams, 1994). The rationale for state preemption of local land use control over electric transmission lines is that, given the nature of transmission and the need to cross multiple local jurisdictions, their regulation should not be the subject of conflicting municipal standards but rather a uniform state system of regulation (*East Greenwich v. O'Neil*, 1992; *Board of Supervisors v. Virginia Elec. & Power*, 1981; *Commonwealth Edison v. Warrenville*, 1997; *Preston v. Connecticut Siting Council*, 1990).

The same rationale does not necessarily extend to the siting of a wireless facility in an electric transmission right-of-way. Therefore, where local agencies regulate wireless facility siting, regulatory approvals may be necessary not only from the relevant local board but also a state agency having jurisdiction over the modification of transmission lines.

This dual, potentially conflicting or duplicative, regulatory authority does little to encourage the shared use of rights-of-way. Given the potential gains from such shared use, effort should be made to rationalize state and local siting authorities and to eliminate this otherwise unnecessary obstacle to the promotion of the use of existing rights-of-way.

SUMMARY

Electric transmission rights-of-way must be recognized as a resource with the potential to provide multiple services to customers. Although not a finite resource, these rights-of-way offer valuable options for strategic planning for both electric transmission service and wireless telecommunications providers. Government policy makers should recognize that the opportunity for sharing electric utility rights-of-way with telecommunications carriers exists, is both technically and legally possible, and is of great importance to the public. Emphasis should be placed on encouraging sharing without barriers, and discouraging opportunities for non-competitive discriminatory use. The result will be a shift from parallel networks providing discrete individual service to common shared networks acting as linear hubs deploying multiple services. Such relationships will generate revenues for the owners of the right-of-way and those who share the right-of-way; expand valuable essential services to customers; and increase siting efficiency using technological alternatives that provide better protection of environmental resources.

ACKNOWLEDGEMENTS

The authors wish to express their appreciation to the following persons for their gracious response to inquiries and helpful information relating to telecommunications relating in their respective countries: John Lowe and Willie Grieve, Canada; Anthony Sylvester, England; Anthony Burke, Ireland; Julian Ding, Malaysia; Patricia Osidach Igartua and Miguel B. De Erice Rodriguez, Mexico; Arve Føyen, Norway; Juan J. Montero, Spain; Eddie Juhlin, Sweden; Roderick S. Coy, United States.

The authors also wish to thank Donna S. Worroll for her accomplished and invaluable secretarial skills.

REFERENCES

Bruce, Jon W. and James W. Ely Jr. 1995. The Law of Easements and Licenses in Land. Warren, Gosham & Lamont, Boston.

Campbell, Dennis. 1999. International Telecommunications Law, BNA International, Inc., England.

Cellular Telecommunications Industry Association (CTIA). 2000. Semi-Annual Wireless Survey Results, Jan. 1985 to Dec. 1999. World of Wireless Communications Web Page: www.wow-com.com.

Institute of Electrical and Electronics Engineers, Inc. (IEEE). 1997. National Electrical Safety Code. IEEE, New York.

Juhlin, Eddie. 2000. Electronic correspondence with authors dated Mar. 27, 2000.

Kearney, Jospeh D. and Thomas W. Merrill. 1998. The Great Transformation of Regulated Industries Law. Columbia Law Review, 98: 1323–1409.

Krattenmaker, Thomas G. 1996. The Telecommunications Act of 1996. Connecticut Law Review, 29: 123–174.

Kress, Carl B. 1997. The 1996 Telekommunikationsgesetz and the Telecommunications Act of 1996: Toward more competitive markets in telecommunications in Germany and the United States. Federal Communications Law Journal, 49: 551–619.

Phillips Jr., Charles F. 1993. The Regulation of Public Utilities, 3d ed. Public Utilities Reports, Arlington, VA.

Rosario, Philip and Mark F. Kohler. 1996. The Telecommunications Act of 1996: A state perspective. Connecticut Law Review, 29: 331–351.

Rosenberg, Edwin A. and Stella Rubia. 1996. Rights-of-Way and Other Customer-Access Facilities: Issues, Policies, and Options for Regulators. National Regulatory Research Institute, Columbus, OH.

Ryan, Michael H. 1993. Canadian Telecommunications Law and Regulation. Carswell, Toronto.

Sackman, Julius L. 1999. Nichols on Eminent Domain, 3d ed. Matthews Bender & Co., New York.

Sweet, Greg. 1998. Build to Suit Success or Formula for Failure. RCA, 17(37): 31–32.

Telecommunications Industry Association (TIA). 1996. Structural Standards for Steel Antenna Towers and Antenna Supporting Structures, TIA/EIA-222-f. TIA, Arlington, VA.

Tuesley, Malcolm J. 1999. Not in my backyard: The siting of wireless communications facilities. Federal Communications Law Journal, 51: 887–911.

Williams, Jr., Sager A. 1994. Limiting local zoning regulation of electric utilities: A balanced approach in the public interest. University of Baltimore Law Review, 23: 565–617.

Wrigley, Mike. 2000. Personal Communication. Vice President of Sales, FWT, Inc., on July 11, 2000. www.fwtinc.com.

LEGAL REFERENCES

Board of Supervisors v. Virginia Elec. & Power, 222 Va. 870, 284 S.E.2d 615 (1981).
Centel Cable TV v. Cook, 58 Ohio St. 3d 8, 567 N.E.2d 1010 (1991).
Commonwealth Edison v. Warrenville, 288 Ill. App. 3d 373, 680 N.E.2d 465 (1997).
Cousins v. Alabama Power Co., 597 So.2d 683 (Ala. 1992).
C/R TV, Inc. v. Shannondale, Inc., 27 F.3d 104 (4th Cir 1994).
East Greenwich v. O'Neil, 617 A.2d 104 (R.I. 1992).
Edgecombe v. Lower Valley Power & Light Co., 922 P.2d 850 (Wyo. 1996).
FCC v. Florida Power Corp., 480 US 245 (1987).
FCC Report & Order, In re Implementation of Section 703(e) of the Telecommunications Act of 1996, CS Dkt. No. 97-151, at ¶¶36-42 (rel. Feb. 6, 1998).
Gulf Power Co. v. United States, 187 F.3d 1324 (11th Cir. 1999).
Hash v. Sotinowski, 338 Pa. Super. 451, 454, 487 A.2d 32 (1985).
Henley v. Cablevision, 692 S.W.2d 825 (Mo. App. 1985).
Loretto v. Teleprompter Manhattan CATV Corp., 458 US 419 (1982).
Minnkota Power Coop. v. Lake Shore Prop., 295 N.W.2d 122 (N.D. 1980).
National Cable+Telecommunications Association V. Gulf Power Co., 534 VS 327 (2002).
Otter Tail Power v. Demchuk, 314 N.W.2d 298 (N.D. 1982).
Preston v. Connecticut Siting Council, 20 Conn. App. 474, 568 A.2d 799, cert. denied, 214 Conn. 803, 573 A.2d 316 (1990).
Stasiuk v. West Kootenay Power, 87 A.C.W.S. 3d 826 (B.C. Sup. Ct. 1999).
Wisconsin Central Ltd. v. Public Service Comm'n, 95 F.3d 1359 (7th Cir. 1996).
Witteman v. Jack Barry Cable TV, 183 Cal. App. 3d 1001, 228 Cal. Rptr. 584 (1986), review dismissed, 742 P.2d 779, 240 Cal. Rptr. 449 (1987), cert. denied, 484 US 1043 (1988).

BIOGRAPHICAL SKETCHES

Joel M. Rinebold

Institute for Sustainable Energy, Eastern Connecticut State University, Forster Building, Willimantic, CT 06226, USA, Fax: 1-860-423-5096, E-mail: rineboldj@ casternct.edu

Joel M. Rinebold is the Executive Director of the Institute for Sustainable Energy at Eastern Connecticut State University where he focuses on sustainable use of energy. Prior to joining the Institute, Mr. Rinebold was Executive Director of the State of Connecticut Siting Council, and directed activities for the site regulation of energy, telecommunications, and waste management facilities with the Council since 1985. Prior to serving the Council, Mr. Rinebold worked as District Manager for the US Department of Agriculture Litchfield County Conservation District, and as a land use consultant. In addition, Mr. Rinebold served as adjunct faculty at Central Connecticut State University instructing senior and graduate level environmental planning classes.

Julie M. Donaldson

Hurwitz & Sagarin, LLC, 147 North Broad Street, Milford, CT, USA

Julie M. Donaldson is a partner in the law firm of Hurwitz & Sagarin, LLC and specializes in land use and all aspects of telecommunication law. She serves as counsel to several major telecommunications carriers and telecommunications tower companies in the negotiation, acquisition and implementation of wireless telecommunications facilities throughout southern New England. Ms. Donaldson has successfully obtained regulatory approval and negotiated agreements for the co-location of countless telecommunications facilities within existing electric transmission rights of way.

Mark F. Kohler, Esq.

State of Connecticut, Office of the Attorney General,[8] 55 Elm Street, Hartford, CT, USA

Mark F. Kohler is an Assistant Attorney General in the State of Connecticut Office of the Attorney General and has specialized in public utility and telecommunications siting law. He is also an adjunct faculty member at the University of Connecticut School of Law teaching regulated industries law.

---

[8] The opinions stated in this article are the authors' own and do not necessarily reflect the opinions of the Connecticut Siting Council, the Connecticut Office of the Attorney General, or any other official or agency of the State of Connecticut.

Practical Approach to Assessing Cumulative Effects for Pipelines

George Hegmann, Ross Eccles, and Kirk Strom

This paper describes a potential approach to the assessment of cumulative effects that may be adopted for larger federally regulated pipelines in Canada. The approach is based on a process originally developed for pipelines in the Rocky Mountain foothills of western Canada; therefore, the environmental components selected reflect some that are common for that region. The approach is based on the author's experiences in conducting cumulative effects assessments in Canada. Conditions or "triggers" are discussed under which cumulative effects need to be considered for a pipeline project, establishing an effects-based approach for assessing only those portions of the pipeline potentially contributing to cumulative effects. This establishes a focused approach that clearly identifies the scope of assessment. Specific pipeline effects that typically contribute to regional cumulative effects issues are identified, and approaches for assessing the significance of project contributions to such effects are broadly discussed.

Keywords: Cumulative effects, cumulative effects assessment, pipelines, triggers

ASSESSMENT FRAMEWORK

Cumulative effects are changes to the environment that are caused by an action (i.e., projects and activities) in combination with other past, present and future human actions. A cumulative effects assessment (CEA) is an assessment of those effects (Hegmann et al., 1999).

The proposed CEA approach for pipelines follows a four-step framework (see Fig. 1):
1. Describe the project components, environmental, and land use setting.
2. Identify key, project-related contributions to cumulative effects on selected resources of concern.
3. Assess the levels of cumulative effects on the selected resources, both with and without project effects.
4. Determine if the cumulative effects are significant.

The framework is based on the premise that, under Canadian legislation, a proponent will (or should) not be required to consider cumulative effects that are not of relevance to their project. In other words, only those effects resulting from the project need to be

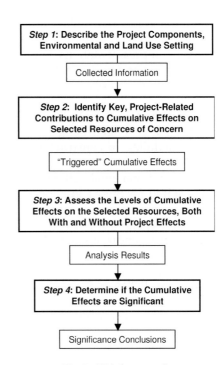

Fig. 1. CEA framework.

Environmental Concerns in Rights-of-Way Management: Seventh International Symposium
J.W. Goodrich-Mahoney, D.F. Mutrie and C.A. Guild (editors)
© 2002 Elsevier Science Ltd. All rights reserved.

considered from a CEA perspective, but they need not be significant to warrant their inclusion in the CEA. The other fundamental premise of the framework is that it is not necessary to include the entire length of the pipeline in a CEA unless justified by the nature of the project's effects. The framework instead first determines if only portions of the pipeline need to be assessed for possible contribution to cumulative effects, thereby avoiding unnecessary data collection over larger areas. Such an approach is in part a reflection of various unique attributes of pipelines in comparison to other types of projects; principally, the often considerable distance and variable land use settings traversed by the pipeline, and the limited footprint of disturbance created by such developments in any given area.

This approach is viewed as a practical and efficient application of assessment effort to meet the challenging task of assessing longer pipeline projects.

STEP 1: DESCRIBE THE PROJECT COMPONENTS, ENVIRONMENTAL AND LAND USE SETTING

In the first step, the components of the proposed project (both physical works and activities) and the project phases in which they would occur (e.g., construction, operation) are identified. Key project information requirements needed to help "scope out" important cumulative effect issues include:
- location and width of right-of-way (ROW), including laterals and access roads;
- location and dimensions of extra workspace (to the degree possible);
- location and dimensions of ancillary facilities;
- project-related emission sources and operating specifications (e.g., compressor stations, line heaters);
- location and nature of access requirements, during both the construction and operational phases of the project;
- specialized construction techniques to be used for the project (e.g., directional drilling of streams); and
- nature and scheduling of construction and operational activities.

The types of environmental setting and land use information required for Step 1 in support of a CEA generally include:
- native vegetation communities along the route;
- key wildlife habitat conditions along the route;
- streams crossed by the route, and their fisheries capability;
- opportunities for ROW and access sharing with existing operators in the area;
- other land use activities occurring in or proposed for the area;
- other industrial emission sources in the project area; and
- land use plans or resource management objectives for the area that may be relevant to the pipeline application.

STEP 2: IDENTIFY KEY, PROJECT-RELATED CONTRIBUTIONS TO CUMULATIVE EFFECTS ON SELECTED RESOURCES OF CONCERN

It is important that direct project effects with the potential of measurably contributing to regional cumulative effects issues be identified early in the scoping process. Such effects should be a subset of those identified and assessed for the projects environmental impact assessment (EIA).

Regional resource issues of concern can be identified during public and resource agency consultation sessions, and by the environmental specialists performing the assessment. Throughout much of western Canada, regional issues of concern generally include airshed quality, "at risk" vegetation and key wildlife resources, and fisheries resources. Direct pipeline effects on such resources that frequently persist after mitigation result from:
- air and noise emissions from ancillary facilities (e.g., compressor stations);
- alteration of fisheries habitat quantity and quality;
- alteration of native vegetation;
- alteration of wildlife habitat quantity and quality; and
- development of new access potential and associated increased recreational pressures on important resources.

Once important project effects have been identified, it is necessary to evaluate the potential for these effects to contribute to regional cumulative effects issues. Several basic questions need to be asked to assist in the identification of key project issues:
1. Are other land use activities in the project area having similar effects on the resource in question?
2. Do direct project effects have the potential to overlap with or incrementally add to those of other land use activities in a meaningful fashion?
3. Will project contributions to regional cumulative effects have the potential to measurably change the health or sustainability of the resource in question?

Step 2 is essential to ensure that assessment resources are not spent on irrelevant issues. For example, if a large portion of the proposed ROW will be predominantly sharing easement with or abutting to an existing road or utility corridor, that portion of the new pipeline will likely not be contributing in a meaningful manner to regional cumulative access potential; therefore, the issue of increased access need not be pursued. Conversely, where new ROW is to be developed for long stretches in a relatively remote area, then such an issue becomes more relevant.

Longer pipeline projects (e.g., 200 km) often encounter a variety of land use settings and jurisdictions, each with their own unique set of resource issues. For example, the implications of pipeline development through cleared, private agricultural land are very different from those for a pipeline in a remote forested

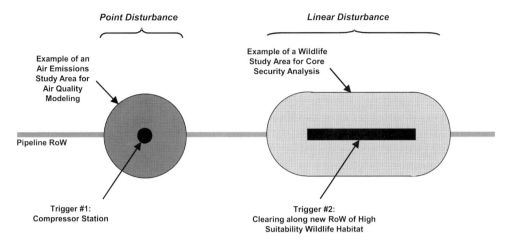

Fig. 2. Examples of use of triggers to establish location and size of study areas.

setting. Therefore, in developing an approach for a pipeline CEA, it should be recognized that different issues, study areas and assessment methods may have to be adopted for different portions of the route.

Each of the potential effects from the pipeline discussed above should be considered within the context of the various land use settings along the route. "Hotspots," where project contributions to cumulative effects are probable, should be identified. These "hotspots" serve as the geographic focus of assessment efforts, and are referred to here as CEA "triggers." Each hotspot will generally require its own unique assessment study area that reflects the nature of the project effect and the resource in question (see Fig. 2). Some discretion must be applied in the interpretation of what constitutes a study area in situations where the triggers or hotspots occur in succession for short distances but with short separations between them (i.e., triggers "on" and "off" over brief distances). In such cases, the separate study areas may be joined together to simplify the assessment.

STEP 3: ASSESS THE LEVELS OF CUMULATIVE EFFECTS ON THE SELECTED RESOURCES, BOTH WITH AND WITHOUT PROJECT EFFECTS

Methodological issues
For all resource issues, the assessment of cumulative effects requires identification of the following:
– timeframe for the assessment;
– spatial boundaries for the assessment;
– measurable parameters for the assessment; and
– inclusion list of "other activities" contributing to cumulative effects to be considered in the assessment.

Timeframe
Timeframe for the assessment refers to the periods or "slices of time" during the life of the project selected for the evaluation of cumulative effects. For a buried pipeline, timeframes could include baseline (i.e., pre-development), construction, operations, and abandonment. Selection of the appropriate assessment timeframe for pipelines is problematic as the peak effects of a pipeline can occur at different times for different resources. For example, effects on fisheries generally peak for a relatively brief period during and immediately after construction if open cut stream crossing procedures are employed, while effects on airshed parameters will likely peak at a relatively consistent level throughout the operational phase of the project (e.g., compressor station emissions). Therefore, it is suggested that the most appropriate timeframe for assessment purposes should be selected on a resource/issue specific basis and, at the very least, should address the period of worst-case project effects for the resource in question.

Spatial boundaries
To complete a credible CEA, the study area boundaries adopted for the assessment must be resource specific. In general the study area adopted for each resource issue should:
– reflect the nature and severity of the project's contribution to cumulative effects;
– represent a defensible regional unit for the resource in question (e.g., seasonal territory for wildlife species);
– encompass the effects of other land use activities acting in a cumulative fashion with the project; and
– allow for the collection and analysis of cumulative effects data at a reasonable cost.

As previously discussed, longer pipeline projects often encounter a variety of land use settings and jurisdictions, each with their own unique set of resource issues. Cumulative effects issues along one portion of the pipeline may not be relevant along other portions of the pipeline. Therefore, it should also be recognized that the CEA study area selected for resource issues may only cover a portion of the pipeline length.

Measurable parameters
Measurable parameters are the actual units to be used for quantifying cumulative effects for the resource issues in question. For example, if grizzly bear is a resource concern, possible measurable parameters for assessing project and cumulative effects could include human-related bear deaths (i.e., total number of bears killed from hunting, road kills, and removal of "nuisance" animals per year) or habitat availability. During the selection of appropriate parameters, the proponent should consider the availability of regional data for the parameter, and the ability to generate defensible regional data at a reasonable cost.

It is important to recognize that the parameters used for the CEA should reflect those used by the proponent to identify and assess project-specific effects in the EIA, although the scale of resolution may have to change for the broader regional CEA. For example, if project-related grizzly bear deaths are predicted in the EIA, then cumulative human-caused mortality predictions should also be pursued at the regional cumulative effects level to enable the effects contribution of the project to be evaluated within the context of regional pressures. Use of parameters not addressed in the EIA simply leads to reduced credibility for the CEA, and confusion for regulatory agencies responsible for project review and approval.

Inclusion list of other activities
The identification of other projects or activities whose effects could act in an additive fashion with those of the pipeline is a critical step in a CEA. Inclusion lists should be resource/issue specific, as different resources will be influenced by different land use activities.

Candidate projects and activities for consideration in CEAs (from nearest to most distant point in time) include: approved, approved and under construction, approval imminent, in approval process, project announced and application/construction anticipated during the life of the pipeline project. Generally, only projects that have a developed footprint or design specifications at the time of the CEA are considered for quantitative analysis. Effects of projects and activities more conceptual in design can only be dealt with in a qualitative fashion, and frequently add little value to the CEA. The inclusion/exclusion of such projects should be discussed with regulators early in the assessment process.

Resource-specific approaches
In the sections below, some broad approaches to CEA are discussed for several selected resources.

Air
Triggers. During normal operations, pipelines only contribute to cumulative airshed emissions in a meaningful way where gas fired compressor stations or pump stations are required as part of a project's design. Such point emission sources can be considered as triggers for emission-related CEAs. Many transmission pipelines link into gas plants or other processing facilities that were applied for and approved under different jurisdictions by different owners. In these situations, the pipeline proponent is not responsible for assessing the cumulative contributions of the processing plant unless project-specific emissions from the pipeline project have the potential to interact with those of the processing facility.

Timeframe. As discussed, airshed issues are generally only of relevance to pipeline projects if compressor stations, pump stations or other point emission sources form part of the principal project. Airshed issues associated with equipment emissions, dust, and noise during construction are generally of short duration and too transient to be considered in a CEA. Consequently, the point in time selected for assessing airshed-related cumulative effects is generally restricted to the operational phase of the project.

Study area. The study areas selected for the CEA are centered around project-related point emission sources, and their size is heavily influenced by the emission dispersion models used for the analysis. Study areas generally reflect the area over which measurable elevated levels of project emissions are predicted, and would include areas of plume overlap resulting from project and other unrelated facilities.

Measurable parameters and analysis. Airshed-related measurable parameters commonly selected for pipeline CEAs include SO_2, NO_x, VOCs, and noise levels. However, residents in close proximity to oil and gas infrastructures are becoming increasingly concerned that an assessment of cumulative emission levels alone does not provide the complete picture of airshed cumulative effects. They argue that, while atmospheric and terrain conditions may prevent emission plume overlaps and exceeding regulatory limits from multiple emission sources, their *exposure frequency* to noticeable odors, noise events, etc. nevertheless increases with increasing facility development. This "time crowding" cumulative effects issue therefore needs to be considered where residents are located in close proximity to an expanding development infrastructure.

Fisheries
Triggers. Pipeline projects primarily affect fisheries resources through two processes, which can be viewed as triggers for considering the need for CEA:
- alteration of habitat through instream activities, sediment introductions from approach slopes, and loss of riparian cover; and
- development of new access potential and associated increased fishing pressure.

If it is determined that the project has the potential to result in such effects, a second level of screening can be employed to focus on only those issues of real concern from a cumulative effects perspective. If instream habitat is to be adversely affected, the relative sensitivity of that habitat to stream productive capacity should be evaluated before initiating a CEA. For example, damage to fall spawning areas and overwintering eggs will have a much greater potential to contribute to cumulative effects than temporary disturbance to relatively common run habitat. Similarly, new ROW being constructed across a stream near an existing all-weather road and bridge has little potential of contributing to cumulative fishing pressures in a meaningful manner, relative to a new ROW accessing a stream in a remote unroaded portion of its watershed.

The degree to which these effects will contribute to regional cumulative pressures will be largely dependent on the construction and mitigation plans proposed for the project. For example, habitat alteration and fish mortalities can be eliminated or greatly reduced through directional drilling techniques or compliance with instream work windows and best available practices. Similarly, appropriate route selection, temporary run-off controls and reclamation initiatives can largely prevent sediment introductions from ROW approach slopes both during and after construction. Nevertheless, in some circumstances, residual effects will persist and may contribute towards cumulative pressures on fish.

Timeframe. Instream effects on fisheries are most prevalent during the construction phase, while the influence of new access potential on fishing pressure will persist throughout the operational phase of the project and beyond unless adequate access control measures along the ROW are implemented. Therefore, the timeframe for assessment may include construction as well as operations, depending on the final issues pursued at a cumulative effects level.

Study area. For instream habitat effects, separate study areas will generally be required for each affected stream, unless the pipeline crosses multiple tributaries and/or reaches of the same stream. The study area of focus will generally fall between and include the riparian areas on either side of the channel over some distance along its course. The length of channel selected for the CEA should:
- at the very least, encompass the extent of project effects; and
- be bounded by obvious habitat transition zones (e.g., confluence of two major streams, transition from pool/riffle mosaic to continuous high gradient run) or seasonal habitat boundaries for resident fish wherever possible.

Measurable parameters and analysis. If pipeline development is likely to cause the harmful alteration, disruption, or destruction of habitat (HADD), then the degree of harmful effects must be evaluated within the context of existing habitat availability and existing and future disturbance from other activities. This requires the following steps:
- classification and quantification of broad habitat types (e.g., run, riffle, pool) within the reach of stream(s) selected as the study area;
- the quantification of habitats that have been or will be adversely affected by other land use activities within the study area;
- the quantification of habitats that will be adversely affected by the project in question within the study area, both from trenching operations and downstream sediment deposition; and
- evaluation of the relative contribution to cumulative habitat alteration from the project.

The focus of the assessment is to determine if project contributions to cumulative effects will adversely affect important habitats that are restricted or underrepresented as a result of past, present, and future disturbance or natural conditions. For the purposes of CEA, the above information can typically be developed from air photos or aerial reconnaissance, and need not be prohibitive from a cost or timing perspective.

Recently, the number and density of linear corridor crossings of streams (e.g., number of crossings per km of stream) has been used as a measure of cumulative effects. It is generally assumed that such crossings contribute run-off and associated sediment into water channels, or provide access for anglers, influencing both fishing distribution and pressure. In many situations, this parameter is of questionable value for assessing cumulative effects for the following reasons:
- a large percentage of linear corridors do not contribute measurable amounts of run-off and sediment into streams because of natural terrain impediments, approach slope characteristics, and vegetative cover;
- similarly, a large number of linear corridors are not accessible to motorized travel because of terrain constraints or regrowth and hence do not contribute to fishing patterns; and
- there are no credible biophysical or resource use criteria for establishing acceptable density criteria.

In the absence of information to address the first two points, a crossing-density analysis tends to overstate the potential levels of cumulative effects in the area and, as a result, understates the potential contribution of the project effects to the cumulative effects.

The value of such a parameter as an assessment or decision-making tool should be discussed with project regulators and regional resource managers early in the planning process. If such a parameter is selected for CEA, additional supplemental information will be required for the linear corridors in the study area to make the analysis of value, including the terrain and vegetation conditions on the ROW and the potential for motorized access along the ROW.

Vegetation

Triggers. Pipeline projects primarily contribute to cumulative effects on vegetation through clearing related activities in native vegetation communities. Given the long, narrow configuration of pipelines, their contributions to cumulative vegetation alteration is generally of greatest concern where there is the potential to adversely effect native species or communities of restricted occurrences. Therefore, triggers for considering a vegetation-related CEA include:
- where project clearing will occur in native vegetation communities; and
- where there is a high probability for the project to encounter species or communities of restricted status or management concern.

Timeframe. Project development effects on vegetation resources are immediately and most acutely affected during the construction phase; however, effects also persist throughout the operational phase of the project and beyond. Therefore, the timeframe for assessment may include construction as well as operations, depending on the final issues pursued at a cumulative effects level.

Study area. Spatial boundaries should be broad enough to encompass direct project effects in addition to providing an ecological context for evaluation of the significance of localized project effects. In northern boreal and prairie landscapes, it is often difficult to utilize natural ecological boundaries (e.g., ecodistricts) to define appropriate study area boundaries. Therefore, arbitrary corridors centered on the ROW (e.g., 3 or 1.5 km on either side) have been adopted for use as CEA study area. Whatever the case, the selected corridor should be wide enough to:
- allow for quantification of direct effects on vegetation resources from project development, including new access roads and ancillary facilities; and
- provide a representative picture of the vegetation community structure along the route.

With a 3 km wide study area, the project footprint typically represents only 1% of the land base within the corridor, and the diversity and relative abundance of community types typical of the region are generally represented.

Measurable parameters and analysis. Although pipeline construction is designed to minimize loss of rare or under-represented vegetation communities and species, these effects are not entirely mitigable. The assessment of any residual effects focuses on changes in community and species representation in the study area intersected by the pipeline. Consideration of community representation entails application of an approach referred to as "gap analysis," which is defined as the process of protecting biodiversity by protecting a representative system of all vegetation or habitat types (Burley, 1988 in Wilson, 1988). Warranted, therefore, is an assessment of past, current and future changes to vegetation communities as an indicative measure of probable changes in regional terrestrial biodiversity. Such an assessment evaluates the extent of existing disturbance by identifying underrepresented communities within the study area, and the significance of incremental disturbance from the pipeline in the context of simulated pristine conditions and existing disturbed scenarios. In this process, assessment of project effects to vegetation and related biota are based on the distribution and abundance of communities along the entire length of the pipeline. Analysis of cumulative effects of underrepresented communities would be undertaken in areas intersected by the pipeline in which native communities are still intact. The process includes calculation of total project clearing (ha) for each community, and calculation of total community availability in the study area (as a percentage) to indicate relative significance of clearing.

Wildlife

Triggers. Pipeline projects primarily affect terrestrial wildlife resources through four processes, which can be viewed as triggers for considering the need for CEA:
- alteration of habitat availability, which is largely incurred during project construction;
- habitat fragmentation, a spatial outcome of alteration in habitat availability;
- direct wildlife mortalities (e.g., from vehicle-wildlife collisions); and
- development of new access potential and associated loss of habitat security.

If it is determined that the project has the potential to result in such effects, a second level of screening can be employed to focus on those issues of ecological importance from a cumulative effects perspective. For example, if forested habitat is to be adversely affected through clearing and construction, the relative sensitivity of that habitat to key indicator wildlife species should be evaluated before initiating a CEA. In the case of grizzly bear, for example, damage or loss of an important, localized fen habitat could have a much greater potential to contribute to cumulative effects on the population than disturbance to relatively common habitats. Similarly, new ROW being constructed adjacent to an existing all-weather road has little potential of contributing to measurable cumulative pressures on grizzly bear habitat availability and security compared to a new ROW accessing a previously remote unroaded portion of a watershed.

The degree to which these effects will contribute to regional cumulative pressures will be influenced by the construction and mitigation plans proposed for the project. As noted with regard to fisheries and vegetation resources, certain types of project effects are unmitigable and such residual effects will persist and contribute towards cumulative pressures on wildlife.

Timeframe. Risk of direct wildlife mortality is largely limited to construction and operational phases. Habitat related effects on wildlife (i.e., changes in habitat, availability, fragmentation, and security) first occur during the construction phase, and can occur through and persist beyond the project's operational phase. Specific timeframes for assessment will depend on the success of reclamation and on the realized effectiveness of access control during and following the life of the project. Hence, the timeframe for assessment can include construction, operations and post-operational phases.

Study area. Separate study areas will generally be required to account for the differing effects and ecological context of different wildlife species. To assess the effects of alterations in habitat availability on localized wildlife species, a relatively confined study area encompassing the project footprint would suffice. This is the case, for example, for the black-throated green warbler, an arboreal passerine species that is dependent upon mature coniferous forest and minimum patch sizes of 30 ha. With a commensurate minimum patch size diameter of 600 m, this species' spatial habitat requirements allow for assessment of effects on habitat availability and fragmentation (loss of minimum patch sizes) to be undertaken and based upon the Ecological Land Classification (ELC) data compiled within the 3 km wide study area.

For larger species, such as grizzly bear, that range widely and are particularly susceptible to the effects of access proliferation, associated loss of habitat security and increased vulnerability to hunting and poaching, appropriate study area boundaries are typically much larger that that described for the warbler. Where new access is developed in an area of high quality grizzly bear habitat, an appropriate spatial scale for analysis would extend from the project footprint to a distance approximating one diameter of an average female grizzly bear's home range ($\sim$100–300 km^2).

Measurable parameters and analysis. The following discusses two types of analysis and associated parameters: habitat availability and fragmentation analysis, and core security analysis.
– *Habitat Availability and Fragmentation.* Habitat availability is defined as a measure of an area's utility to a species following the effects of human disturbance. Fragmentation of habitat occurs from human alteration of habitat, and can affect species populations by impairing their ability to move between habitats, by creation of edge effects (related to habitat security), and by loss of minimum habitat size requirements to support individuals in a population. For habitat availability and fragmentation, assessment of cumulative effects are assessed only where key restricted habitats cannot be avoided or restored during construction. Habitat availability is normally calculated based on species-specific habitat requirements for communities within a given area. The association of habitat models to community mapping links the community representation analysis to the wildlife habitat availability impact component. Assessment of habitat availability will allow, through species-specific habitat and impact models, quantification of effects of clearing and associated areas of reduced habitat availability on species dependent on relatively rare or sensitive habitats in a given project region. The presence of such key habitat features would be identified once centreline surveys have been completed for the project.
– *Core Security Habitat.* One of the key issues that often arises for pipeline projects is the concern of access proliferation and associated impacts on certain vulnerable wildlife resources due to increased potential for hunting, poaching, trapping, and natural predation. The approach suggested here is to adopt a core security habitat analysis to assess the significance of project-related effects and cumulative regional effects on wildlife security based on accepted methodologies developed in other jurisdictions for assessment on grizzly bear (USFWS, 1993; IGBC, 1994). The grizzly bear is a far-ranging species that is vulnerable to access proliferation due to associated effects from hunting and poaching. Where the project leads to creation of new access in occupied grizzly bear range, a core security analysis is undertaken with the intent of estimating existing and future levels in access density with respect to known thresholds and goals. Core secure habitat for grizzly bears are those useable areas within the species' range minus human-affected habitats. Reduced security occurs within 500 m of linear or point sources of human disturbance, and with habitat blocks too small or fragmented to accommodate a minimum female grizzly feeding radius over a 24 h period ($\sim$4.5–10.1 km^2).

STEP 4: DETERMINE IF THE CUMULATIVE EFFECTS ARE SIGNIFICANT

Two questions need to be answered to establish significance: (1) On what basis is significance to be determined? and (2) What is the contribution of the pipeline being assessed to overall cumulative effects?

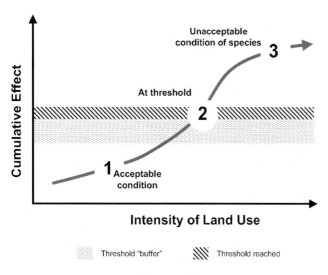

Fig. 3. Application of thresholds.

A basis for establishing significance

Significance ideally is determined based on a comparison of the effect to a threshold. A threshold is a point at which a resource undergoes an unacceptable change or reaches an unacceptable level. Thresholds may be based on ecological attributes (e.g., habitat availability, wildlife populations), physical-chemical attributes (e.g., air or water contaminant concentrations), land and resource use attributes (e.g., road densities, hunting harvest) or social attributes (e.g., acceptable perceived change). As land use pressures increase, the adverse effects on a resource also increase. At relatively undisturbed conditions, the condition of the resource may be acceptable (Point 1 in Fig. 3). Eventually, some condition is reached at which a threshold is met (Point 2), after which the threshold has been exceeded (Point 3) and the condition of the resource becomes unacceptable. A "buffer" can be used as an early-warning system for management purposes to reduce or halt the advancement of the effect towards the threshold.

If thresholds are not available, qualitative conclusions can be made that rely on professional judgement, on the evaluation of a suite of effect's attributes (e.g., magnitude, geographic extent, duration), on the recognition of the degree of existing disturbances and regional trends in development, and on the contribution of project-specific and possible regional mitigation measures in ameliorating effects.

In summary, the establishment of significance can be based on the following approach:

1. Compare the residual effect to a regulatory guideline, if such a guideline exists (e.g., air quality).
2. Compare the residual effect to a government policy, if such policy exists (e.g., land use).
3. Compare the residual effect to a state of adverse environmental condition, based on scientific and/or traditional information (e.g., ecological thresholds such as wildlife core security area).

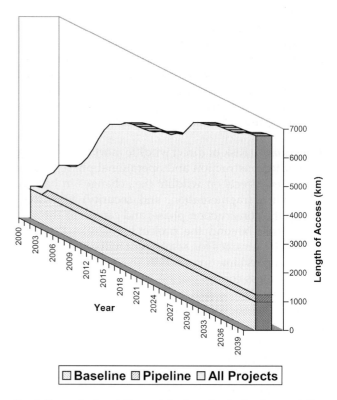

Fig. 4. Example of a relative contribution of a pipeline to cumulative effects.

4. Make a professional judgment based on personal experience, social concerns, and best available information, with all assumptions and uncertainties clearly stated.

Establishing the contribution of the pipeline

Regulators need to know both the potential contribution alone of the pipeline to cumulative effects and the cumulative effect of all projects. Fig. 4 illustrates, for example, a situation in which a pipeline over its operational life introduces some new but relatively incremental access in a region compared to the larger contributions from other projects (e.g., as is often evident in areas undergoing rapid resource development).

The following can be used as a guide to assist in this determination, starting from first principles:

1. The pipeline has a measurable effect on a resource (i.e., there is an effect).
2. The pipeline's effect acts in a cumulative fashion with the effects of other past, present, or future projects and activities (i.e., there is a cumulative effect).
3. The pipeline's effect, in combination with those other projects and activities, shifts the resource to an unacceptable state (i.e., there is a significant effect). "Unacceptable" is defined by whatever measure is applicable and appropriate for that resource.

If (3) is true, one of two conclusions can then be reached that clarify the contribution of the pipeline to those effects:

3.1 The pipeline's contribution to cumulative effects is responsible for causing that unacceptable shift to occur. If yes, then the pipeline's contribution to cumulative effects is significant.

3.2 Other project contributions are already responsible for the unacceptable state of the resource. In this case, the pipeline is contributing incrementally to already significant cumulative effects. Contributions by the pipeline therefore may or may *not* be significant, depending on the degree of change resulting from the pipeline and/or land use priorities for the region.

For many resources, significance criteria cannot be based solely on ecological parameters, but must also consider public policy and resource priorities. Project proponents are not resource or land use managers and, as a result, are not in the position to make decisions on resource priorities. As a result, they should not be expected to make subjective decisions on significance criteria for project-specific effects or cumulative effects. Clearly, the responsibility for the development of such criteria lies with provincial and federal resource management agencies and regulators, and such criteria should be clearly identified by the responsible review authorities for the proponent early in the project's assessment phase.

REFERENCES

Burley, F.W. 1988. Monitoring biological diversity for setting priorities in conservation. pp. 227–230. In: Biodiversity. E.O. Wilson and F.M. Peter, eds. National Academy Press. 521 pp.

Hegmann, G., C. Cocklin, R. Creasey, S. Dupuis, A. Kennedy, L. Kingsley, W. Ross, H. Spaling, and D. Stalker. 1999. Cumulative Effects Assessment Practitioners Guide. AXYS Environmental Consulting Ltd. and the CEA Working Group for the Canadian Environmental Assessment Agency, Hull, Quebec.

Interagency Grizzly Bear Committee (IGBC). 1994. Grizzly Bear/ Motorized Access Management. IGBC Task Force Report. np.

United States Fish and Wildlife Service (USFWS). 1993. Grizzly Bear Recovery Plan. Missoula, MT. 181 pp.

BIOGRAPHICAL SKETCHES

George Hegmann, MEDes, PEng
AXYS Environmental Consulting Ltd., Suite 600, 555 4th Ave SW, Calgary, AB, T2P 3E7 Canada, e-mail: ghegmann@axys.netfax: 403-269-5245

Mr. Hegmann is an Impact Assessment Specialist with AXYS Environmental Consulting Ltd. specialising in EIA and CEA process and implementation. He has been involved in numerous assessments under regulatory review (principally energy projects in Alberta), and has provided advice and recommendations to various agencies regarding their assessment approaches. Mr. Hegmann was the principal author of the *Cumulative Effects Assessment Practitioners Guide* for the Canadian Environmental Assessment Agency.

Ross Eccles, MSc, PBiol
AXYS Environmental Consulting Ltd., Suite 600, 555 4th Ave SW, Calgary, AB, T2P 3E7, Canada

Mr. Eccles is Vice President of Operations for AXYS Environmental Consulting Ltd. and Senior Environmental Advisor in the Calgary, Alberta office. Mr. Eccles has over 20 years of domestic and international environmental consulting for a variety of industrial and recreational developments.

Kirk Strom, MSc, PBiol
AXYS Environmental Consulting Ltd., Suite 600, 555 4th Ave SW, Calgary, Alberta, T2P 3E7, Canada

Mr. Strom, a senior biologist and grizzly bear expert with AXYS Environmental Consulting Ltd., has conducted or been a team member on many environmental planning programs, project assessments and cumulative effects assessments. These have included environmental assessments and the development of planning and management recommendations for various mountain resorts in Western Canada.

Managing Environmental Compliance on Linear Construction Projects: Strategies for Success

Jayne Battey

The cost of assessing, mitigating, and managing environmental issues on construction projects seems to rise with every passing year and, in some parts of the USA, has become a major issue in overall project scheduling and economics. This paper looks at the environmental compliance management experience of three long-distance, linear projects built in the United States between 1994 and 1999. Their stories provide valuable lessons in how to run effective environmental programs for utility construction projects. At the same time, a comparison of the projects shows that the real costs of these efforts, both financial and in terms of regulatory relationships, varied significantly.

Keywords: Inspection, regulatory, environmental compliance, environmental management programs, cost

INTRODUCTION

There is virtually no place in the United States today that you can build a long-distance utility project without facing significant regulatory and environmental hurdles. The cost of assessing, mitigating, and managing environmental issues on construction projects seems to rise with every passing year and, in some parts of the country, has become a major issue in overall project economics. The consequences of not effectively managing the environmental side of utility construction projects have also risen dramatically — projects can be delayed as permits are withheld, stopped for noncompliance actions during construction, and slowed by agency field monitors with extensive authority to impact construction progress and priorities on a daily basis.

This paper looks at the environmental compliance management experience of three utility projects built in the United States between 1994 and 1999. Although each project is a linear utility, each addresses different infrastructure needs: water, electric transmission, and natural gas. They include:

- **The Coastal Branch Phase II Project**: Owned and operated by the California Department of Water Resources (DWR) and the Central Coast Water Authority (CCWA) of Santa Barbara, California, this approximately 142-mile project was constructed between 1994 and 1997 to bring water to San Luis Obispo and Santa Barbara Counties.
- **The Alturas Intertie Project**: The Alturas Intertie Project consists of 164 miles of 345 kV electric transmission line between northern California and Reno, Nevada. The project was built in 1998 and is owned and operated by the Sierra Pacific Power Company (SPPCo).
- **The Maritimes and Northeast Phase II Pipeline Project**: The Maritimes Phase II Pipeline Project includes approximately 200 miles of 24- and 30-inch natural gas pipeline that stretches from Maine's northern border at Woodland to the southern terminus near Portland, Maine. The sponsor of the project was Maritimes and Northeast Pipeline Limited (Maritimes).

Each of these three projects faced significant regulatory hurdles, both prior to and during construction. The project proponents were all proactive, and designed and implemented extensive environmental compliance management programs to support their

Environmental Concerns in Rights-of-Way
Management: Seventh International Symposium
J.W. Goodrich-Mahoney, D.F. Mutrie and C.A. Guild (editors)
© 2002 Elsevier Science Ltd. All rights reserved.

construction efforts. Their stories are illustrative in terms of how to best design and implement effective environmental programs for new construction projects. At the same time, a comparison of the projects shows that the real costs of these efforts, both financial and in terms of regulatory relationships, varied significantly.

Shortest distance between two points is not always a straight line

The focus in this paper is primarily on environmental compliance management during construction. But in order to put these construction experiences into perspective, it is important to first understand where the projects began and how the regulatory process evolved.

Coastal Branch Phase II Project

The California drought that occurred between 1987 and 1992 had people in San Luis Obispo and Santa Barbara counties installing mandatory low-flow faucets and fined for irrigating landscaping. Bringing state water to California's central coast quickly became a priority.

But as has always been the history of water management in California, the battle lines were fairly well drawn between those who viewed imported water as an absolute necessity, and those who viewed it as yet another ploy to induce growth. This battle played out during the planning and permitting of the project, and continued to make headlines in the local press throughout the project's construction.

In addition to water politics, battles over the protection of natural resources in the region also made headlines on a regular basis. San Luis Obispo and Santa Barbara Counties are home to over 40 federal or state protected species of plants and animals. It is an area rich in California history, with Native American settlements dating back over 10,000 years. With over 125 miles of mostly unspoiled California coastline, the area provides what is truly one of the most spectacular natural environments in the United States.

The project alignment, design, and approval was, to say the least, controversial. Planning and regulatory approvals for the Coastal Branch Phase II Project were initiated in 1986, and after nearly seven years of alternatives analysis, public input, and regulatory negotiations, the project moved forward to construction in early 1994.[1]

Construction took nearly four years to complete, and the project was required to comply with approximately 1445 environmental conditions of approval. During the winter of 1996, when *El Nino* rains caused wide-spread property damage throughout northern and central California, the project experienced extensive erosion and soil failure. The winter of 1997 did not provide much relief, and while the project was essentially complete by that time, a significant amount of repair work was required to meet restoration requirements.

Alturas Intertie Project

The Alturas Intertie Project was first considered by the Sierra Pacific Power Company (SPPCo) in the late 1980s. The continuing growth of the Reno-Sparks area of Nevada brought with it the need for increased electric transmission service. There was little controversy over the need for greater system reliability, and in 1993 SPPCo received authorization from the Public Service Commission of Nevada to move forward with the project. The controversy, of course, was in the actual siting of the 735 above-ground towers that would be required to transport the energy across California and Nevada to where it was needed.

The project originated in northern California, where it tied in with the Bonneville Power Administration transmission grid, and crosses southeast across the high desert towards Reno, Nevada. This area of high desert scrub (elevation 3000–4500 feet) is relatively remote and unpopulated. While environmental concerns are limited, there are areas of federally- and state-protected plant and animal species. The California Department of Fish and Game (CDFG) has had a history of being particularly sensitive to the protection of biological and water resources in this landscape. On the Alturas Intertie Project, as well as other construction projects in the region,[2] CDFG has had a track record of tough mitigation standards and the strictest regulatory enforcement in the state.

The route crossed large tracts of privately owned land, including predominately grazing and ranch lands. More than half of the route (56%) crosses federal lands managed by the US Bureau of Land Management (BLM).

The Alturas Intertie Project was controversial from the start. Property owners were understandably concerned with the thought of 75-foot-high towers located on their property. In addition, federal and state agencies conducted an exhaustive environmental review and public input process that lasted over five years. After years of analysis, at a cost estimated at nearly $5 million, the US Forest Service continued to deny the project. In early 1996, with towers and cable already at the staging yards, and crews ready to start construction, the Humboldt Toiyabe National Forest (HTNF) issued a "no project" decision for eight miles of the project on forest service land.

---

1 A portion of the project constructed directly by the California Department of Water Resources actually started construction in the summer of 1993, but the CCWA portion was delayed until the following spring.

2 The Tuscarora Gas Transmission pipeline was built in a parallel corridor just three years prior to the Alturas Project.

It would take another two years to identify an acceptable reroute and to complete all required permits and mitigation plans. Construction originally planned for 1996 actually began in the spring of 1998. In all, SPPCo started construction with over a dozen permits from state and federal agencies and was required to comply with approximately 1400 environmental mitigation conditions. The project was further required to support full-time monitoring by the CDFG and the California Public Utilities Commission (CPUC).

Maritimes and Northeast Phase II Project
The original concept for the Maritimes and Northeast project dates back to the early 1990s, when a consortium of companies led by Duke Energy and all Maritimes & Northeast Pipeline Ltd (Maritimes) identified an opportunity to bring natural gas from Sable Island (off the northern coast of Nova Scotia, Canada) to the New England region. Sable Island is one of the largest gas reserves in the North America. As one newspaper article put it in 1999, "(Sable Island) promises more than a generation of abundant, clean-burning energy to eastern Canada and New England."

Planning and permitting efforts for the new pipeline began in earnest in late 1996. The route, which covers nearly 200 miles of privately owned land along the state of Maine's eastern shore, was shaped by customer locations, existing utility corridors, and adjustments for local "not-in-my-back-yard" (nimby) sentiments. But while some communities in Maine protested the project, others welcomed the new construction and economic boom it would bring to northern Maine's typically quiet economy.

The final pipeline route crossed over 1700 wetlands and 325 sensitive streams. While significant environmental challenges, including the protection of both historic and biological resources, were faced, the single biggest issue for the project was ensuring the protection of the state's highly valued salmon streams. Local residents and officials, as well as state and federal regulators, all expressed significant concern over the protection of waterways and water quality. By the time the permitting process was complete, the resulting authorizations specified 12 distinct methods of stream and wetland crossing procedures.

Maritimes understood from the outset that it faced significant environmental issues and a tough regulatory climate in New England, but agency and community scrutiny on the project reached new levels of intensity during the final permitting work in 1998. Regulators and residents in the state had seen other utility construction in action, and they weren't sure they liked what they saw. Fiber optic construction in the later part of the 1990s showed a less than stellar track-record for complying with requirements to protect the state's stream and wetland habitats. Even more relevant, the Portland Natural Gas Transmission System (PNGTS) construction of approximately 240 miles of 24- and 30-inch pipeline in New Hampshire and Maine during 1998 faced one of the wettest summers on record in the region. The pipeline project had a tough time complying with permit conditions.

As one Maritimes' manager put it, "[t]he timing couldn't have been worse." Final construction planning in 1998 included a multitude of conversations with state regulators who had little reason to believe in the project's ability to comply with environmental standards. Maritimes pushed forward, however, and participated in lengthy team-building and environmental training programs internally, as well as with regulators. Maritimes committed to an aggressive and exhaustive environmental program, with clearly defined environmental protection standards and methods. Between January and May 1999, the Maritimes team, including environmental specialists, contractors, and project managers, logged over 2000 person-hours in environmental (and safety) training and team-building.

Construction began in May 1999 and was completed on schedule in October of the same year. In addition to Maritimes' internal environmental inspection program, the project supported full-time field oversight by both the State of Maine Department of Environmental Protection and the Federal Energy Regulatory Commission (FERC). At the peak, it was estimated that nearly 30 environmental and/or safety inspectors were in the field monitoring construction. The project was required to comply with over 1440 environmental protection measures.

Seven steps to environmental compliance
It's clear that all three of these projects moved into construction with significant requirements to minimize and mitigate construction impacts on the environment. They also faced ongoing, relatively intense public scrutiny, as well as on-site regulatory oversight. In all cases, the project managers understood that meeting the environmental requirements of permit approvals was critical to getting the job built and operational.

Over the last decade, the utility industry has learned a lot about how to effectively manage environmental compliance for large-scale construction projects in the unoficial United States. In some cases, new environmental management methods have developed through painful experiences. In 1993, an advisory group to the United States Sentencing Commission provided some unoficial guidance on minimizing organizational exposure related to environmental violations. It suggested seven strategies to promote effective environmental management and reduce organizational risk. To varying degrees and in varying balance, each of the three projects discussed in this paper applied these strategies.

Table 1. Environmental program elements

	Coastal branch	Alturas	Maritimes
Program Design and Organization	Clearly Defined in *Environmental Quality Assurance Program (EQAP) and Environmental Monitoring Manual*	Clearly Defined in the *Interagency Implementation Plan*	Clearly Defined in the *Environmental Compliance Management Program Plan*
Unique Program Features	Incentive Program for Contractors Environmental Task Force	Monthly Interagency Meetings	Project Leadership Training Field Reference Cards for Environmental Specifications
Training	Comprehensive and Complete • Video • Handbook • Hardhat Decal • Resource Cards • Inspector Training Program • Segment Kick-off Meetings • Ongoing Tailgate Training	Comprehensive and Complete • Handbook • Hardhat Decal • Resource Cards • Inspector Training Program • Segment Kick-off Meetings • On-going Tailgate Training	Comprehensive and Complete • Video • Handbook • Hardhat Decal • Resource Cards • Field Reference Cards • Inspector Training Program • Segment Kick-off Meetings • On-going Tailgate Training
Inspection Staffing (at peak)	Environmental Field Supervisor, Planning Assistant, 12 Field Inspectors, and Resource Specialists	Environmental Field Supervisor, Planning Assistant, 8 Field Inspectors, and Resource Specialists	Environmental Field Supervisor, Planning Assistant, 19 Field Inspectors, and Resource Specialists
Reporting/Documentation • Daily Reports	Paper Reports from Field Input to Database Daily	Field Computers	Field Computers
• Variance Process		Clearly Defined and Tracked	Clearly Defined and Tracked
On-site Agency Presence	Intermittent by Two State agencies	Full-time by Two State Agencies and one Federal Agency	Full-Time by one State Agency and one Federal Agency
Quality Assurance Audits	Yes/Formal	Yes/Informal	Yes/Formal

1. **Make the Commitment**: As presented in Table 1, Environmental Program Elements, each of the projects presented in this paper demonstrated a significant management commitment to environmental compliance.

   All three companies supported the development of comprehensive environmental management programs, and defined clear procedures to manage the environmental effort throughout construction. Each company assigned key line managers with distinct responsibility for environmental oversight for the respective project.

2. **Make It Part of Everyone's Job Description**: All project participants, from managers to field crews, were well informed that environmental compliance was a part of everyone's job responsibilities. At the same time, however, the project-wide sense of environmental responsibility was not equal on all three projects. Based on interviews with project staff, it is clear that this sentiment was taken more seriously on some of the projects than on others. On the Maritimes Project, for example, there seemed to be a much stronger sense that the project would not succeed unless everyone contributed to management and implementation of the environmental mandates.

3. **Inspect and Document**: Each of the projects retained well-qualified, experienced environmental inspectors or monitors. The environmental field staff was tasked with the responsibility of overseeing environmental compliance on the project, documenting daily compliance, and coordinating on a daily basis with agency representatives in the field to resolve compliance issues and concerns. It should be noted, however, that the level of environmental staffing varied significantly. Maritimes had the most, with 19 environmental inspectors assigned to the field at the peak of construction.

4. **Train Everyone**: All three projects implemented comprehensive and complete environmental training programs. Every person on the projects, from managers to field crews, was trained in regulatory conditions and key resource protection requirements. A variety of tools, including videos, handbooks, and various handouts, were used to communicate the environmental message. Both the Coastal Branch project and the Maritimes project were particularly aggressive in using training as a tool to manage compliance. Training was held on an on going basis throughout construction — as both a preventative measure (e.g., in advance of work

Table 2. Environmental program indicators and results

	Coastal Branch	Alturas	Maritimes
Total Project Cost (Estimated)	$116,000,000	$155,300,000	$650,000,000
Estimated Environmental Costs	$7,600,000	$24,200,000	$11,200,000
Environmental Costs as a Percentage of Total Costs	6.5%	15.5%	1.7%
Number of Variances Required	No data available	437	204
Average Number of Variances Written per Project Mile	No available	2.65	1.02
Number of Internally Documented Non-compliances	82	524	144
Estimated Number of Field Inspection Hours	64,000	18,000	40,000
Ratio of Non-compliances written per 1000 inspection hours	1.3	29.1	3.6
Number of Regulatory Enforcement Actions	0*	0*	0*
Number of Work Shutdowns (due to environmental)	0	3	0
Total $ in Regulatory Fines	0	0	0

*All three projects each had one non-compliance action, documented and managed internally, that was observed by regulators and nearly became an enforcement action. In all cases, the non-compliance (and near violation) was related to protection of water resources.

commencing in sensitive areas) and on occasion as a punitive measure (e.g., requiring retraining after noncompliance occurrences).

5. **Reward Positive Behavior**: While each of the projects had both penalty and incentive programs to some degree, the Coastal Branch placed a significantly higher emphasis on rewarding positive behavior than either of the other two projects. Incentives were used at nearly every level of the organization — from relatively significant financial incentives for the contractor (e.g., for avoidance/preservation of certain flagged oak trees) to smaller tokens of appreciation (e.g., hot lunch delivered to the site; free sporting events tickets) to individual workers and work crews who demonstrated a commitment to environmental compliance. There is no question that this helped to generate a more positive attitude regarding environmental compliance.

6. **Be Clear About the Consequences of Non-compliance**: The consequences of non-compliance were well communicated in construction specifications and contracts, as well as project training, for all three projects. The message was clear: environmental non-compliance would not be tolerated. Of all the projects, however, this appears to have been most acutely perceived on the Maritimes project. It is interesting to note that two of the three projects dismissed or reassigned early in project construction company and contractor individuals who seemed to have a problem (attitudinal or operational) complying with the environmental requirements. This news traveled quickly, and sent a clear message to the entire project organization (as was the intent).

7. **Review Performance and Fix What You Find**: In addition to the project's dedicated field inspectors, each of the projects provided some level of additional oversight, or quality assurance (QA). The QA program was most formalized for the Coastal Branch project, where an independent consultant provided quarterly field reviews and reports to the project manager regarding the environmental effort. The review included an assessment of field activities, as well as documentation, training, and the implementation of incentive programs.

Did it work?

For the most part, the environmental management programs for each of the three projects were successful. All of the projects discussed in this paper were completed on or near schedule, and all are currently operational. As shown in Table 2, environmental program indicators and results, none of the projects were either charged with regulatory enforcement actions or subject to regulatory fines. While all three projects experienced "close calls" related to water quality issues, only one of the three projects (the Alturas Intertie Project) experienced an environmental-related regulatory mandated work shutdown.

Evaluating the environmental results of these projects is subject to broad interpretation. In addition to the obvious considerations discussed above, there are two important questions that should be answered:
1. What did it cost?
2. How are post-project relationships with the regulators?

What did it cost?

As shown in Table 2, the environmental programs[3] ranged in cost from $7.6 million for the Coastal Branch project to $24.2 million for the Alturas Intertie. As a percentage of total project costs, the range is staggering. Maritimes, with a project cost of $650 million, shows only 1.7% for environmental planning and management. Alturas, on the other hand, comes in with

---

3 These figures include direct environmental program dollars, including consultant fees for planning, permitting, and compliance management; environmental mitigation costs; agency inspection program costs; and environmental document development and production costs. They do not include contractor costs for implementing environmental mitigation.

15.5% for environmental. Aside from the obvious discrepancy in total project costs (or base), this range would be attributable to a number of factors. Based on the data available, the biggest variables appeared to be off-site mitigation costs (e.g., land purchases, mitigation payments) and payments for regulatory field inspection during construction. For example, in addition to its own environmental inspection program, Alturas paid an estimated $3.4 million for on-site inspectors representing various state agencies. In addition, Alturas paid a one-time fee of $3.1 million for wildlife land purchases and a $1.75 million fee for visual mitigation.

It is important to understand that the costs discussed above do not include the contractor cost of installing environmental structures and controls. Both Alturas and Maritimes report significant environmental-related construction costs, with Maritimes being significantly higher. On the Maritimes project, contractor payments for the installation of environmental structures (primarily at streams) are estimated at over $36 million. Maritimes also estimates it spent another $7.5 million on mats used to complete construction through wetlands.

How are post-project relationships with the regulators?
All three of the projects began construction with, at best, regulatory communities that were fairly skeptical of utility construction projects. There was not necessarily much confidence (or trust) that environmental compliance was a real priority for the project proponents. While all three projects had comprehensive environmental management programs, agency relationships on Coastal Branch and the Maritimes projects ended on a significantly more positive note than on the Alturas Intertie Project. The statistics provided in Fig. 2 help tell the story:
- The Alturas environmental inspection team documented 524 environmental non-compliances during construction. That's approximately four times the amount generated on either the Maritimes project or the Coastal Branch. While internally documented non-compliance is intended to be used as a tool to internally manage compliance, the level of activity on the Alturas Project was more indicative of an inherent conflict between project construction plans and regulatory expectations.
- Alturas wrote an estimated 437 variances for the project, or nearly 2.65 variances per mile. In effect, it became apparent within the first month of construction that it would be nearly impossible to build the project as originally described and according to the permit conditions written for construction. A variance team (including contractor, environmental, and construction management staff) was assigned to scout out ahead of construction, identify project modifications, and process variance requests from the agencies. The process left regulators and project staff in constant and often heated debate. While the day-to-day work environment improved as the project switched to construction using helicopters (thereby avoiding environmental impacts), relationships between the project team and regulators did not significantly recover.

CONCLUSIONS AND RECOMMENDATIONS

Managing the environmental efforts for large-scale utility projects is a difficult and complex undertaking. It is typically a lengthy process — that begins years before construction starts. While the guidelines for effective program management have a lot to tell us in terms of setting up an organization and program to assure environmental compliance during construction, there are other factors to consider.
- As a federal regulator once put it, "Remember who's driving the bus." The project's relationships with its regulators are nearly everything in project approvals and the negotiation of environmental conditions. Regulators are typically very patient people — and they have time on their side — so do all that you can to keep relationships positive and productive from the first meeting to the last.
- Be sure to have a plan that you can actually build. It will simply not work to be planning your project while you are also building it. Nor is it wise to agree to measures that are not workable or achievable. Almost every project has a few adjustments along the way, but nothing annoys regulators more (aside from non-disclosure) than constantly going back for modifications and additional authorizations.
- Complying with today's myriad of environmental requirements is challenging for any contractor. Make sure your company and the contractor understand that the environmental specifications are non-negotiable — that they are simply part of how the project will be built.
- Unfortunately, weather can play a huge role in the track-record of environmental compliance, particularly for projects with significant stream and wetland resources. If at all possible, time construction activities for the driest part of the year. If your climate is unpredictable, hope for the best — but you must be prepared for the worst.
- Remember that *people* ultimately build your project. It really comes down to human relationships — how well people work together, how they communicate, and what tone and energy they bring to the job. Don't underestimate the power of team chemistry. Reward positive behavior and productivity, and show little tolerance for anyone who fails to understand how the environmental aspect helps meet your project objectives.

– While you will need a construction team to build your project, make every effort to maintain some continuity from the planning to the construction phase. For large, complex projects subject to multiple regulatory jurisdictions, the permitting phase is typically correspondingly complex and difficult. There are often as many unwritten understandings with regulators as there are written requirements. The people who helped get the project to construction offer an invaluable sense of perspective and understanding that will help maintain positive regulatory relationships throughout construction.

REFERENCES

Essex Environmental. 1998. Final Construction Monitoring Report for Reaches A, B, C, 5A1/5A1.1, 5B and 6.

Essex Environmental. 1995. Central Coast Water Authority-Department of Water Resources California Aqueduct Expansion Environmental Monitor Manual.

Himelstein, L. and C. Yang. 1993. A warning shot to scare polluters straight. Legal Affairs, Newsweek, 60.

Maritimes & Northeast Pipeline. 1999. Environmental compliance Management Program Plan.

McManus, Greg. 1999. Blazing the Trail, Sable Island Gas Changing Economics of Energy in Maritimes, New England. Bangor Daily News Special Report, May 25.

Owens, John. 1998. Federal Energy Regulatory Commission Prepared Direct Testimony.

Personal communication. Gonzales, Maritimes and Northeast, L.L.C., ed. July 2000.

Personal communication. John Owens, Sierra Pacific Power Company, July 2000.

Personal communication. Dan Masnada, Central Coast Water Authority, July 2000.

Sierra Pacific Power Company. 1998. Alturas Intertie Project Environmental Requirements Database.

Sierra Pacific Power Company. 1998. Alturas Intertie Project Joint Inspector/Monitor Training Manual.

Sierra Pacific Power Company. 1998. Interagency Implementation Plan Alturas Intertie Environmental Monitoring and Mitigation Compliance & Reporting Program.

United States Sentencing Commission. 1993. Advisory Working Group on Environmental Offenses, General Application Principles.

BIOGRAPHICAL SKETCHES

Jayne Battey

Essex Environmental, Inc., 637 Main Street, Half Moon Bay, CA 94019, USA, Tel: (650) 726-8320, Fax: (650) 712-1190, E-mail: jbattey@essexenv.com

Ms. Battey is the co-founder and President of Essex Environmental, Inc. Ms. Battey has worked in the utility industry for over 15 years, focused primarily on environmental planning and compliance management for large-scale construction projects. She has particular expertise in training and regulatory relations, and has facilitated numerous workshops for major utilities throughout the United States. Ms. Battey holds a Masters degree in Urban, and Regional Studies from the London School of Economics and Political Science, and a Bachelor degree in English and Communication from Boston College.

Environmental Management System Challenge with Linear Facilities

Peter G. Prier, Daniel S. Eusebi, and David P. Wesenger

The implementation of an environmental management system based on the principles of ISO 14001 provides a unique challenge for linear facility organizations. Environmental Management Systems (EMS) have been established to control potential adverse environmental and socio-economic effects of corporate activities. A key component of an EMS is the communication framework and protocols. One of the unique features of a linear facility EMS is the need to consistently address varying external and internal stakeholder concerns across local, regional, and national regulatory jurisdictions. Linear facilities often correspond to extensive geographic areas, which may translate into cultural differences within the organization and, externally, among a greater number and diversity of stakeholders. This is less often the case with single site organizations. Internally, the management system must recognize and respond to the potential distrust by regional staff of a remote, centralized corporate headquarters, perceived to be out of touch with regional issues and management approaches. Geographic diversity may also demand mitigation and monitoring of a wider spectrum of potential environmental and socio-economic effects from facilities development and operations. To appreciate the unique interrelationships and geographic diversity of a linear facility requires a comprehensive and dynamic communication system to meet the numerous and possibly incompatible internal and external stakeholder demands. Thorough communication protocols and documentation are key to an effective linear facility EMS; stakeholder feedback on the procedures is also critical to ongoing improvement of the EMS particularly given the need for "continuous improvement within the EMS."

Keywords: Environmental management systems, communications, documentation, differences, stakeholders, linear facilities

INTRODUCTION

This paper documents the need for a more comprehensive communications framework within an Environmental Management System (EMS) for a linear facility organization. This is necessary in order to identify, respond to, and monitor the expectations of external and internal stakeholders along the length of the linear facility (NSC, 1996). Linear facilities encounter a large number and diversity of regulatory, cultural, and biophysical differences between their commencement and terminal points. The longer the linear facility is, the greater the differences are in regulatory requirements, cultural priorities, and environmental protection measures.

Stakeholders are defined as internal, within the linear facility organization, or, external to the organization. Internal communications between the various levels and functions within the organizations, and external communications for receiving, documenting, and responding to interests, need to be comprehensive and well documented. In a recent survey of the EMS status of 39, primarily manufacturing facilities, only 50–60% of the facilities had established communication protocols or procedures to receive and respond to communications from external stakeholders. For internal stakeholders (i.e., directors and employees), only 49% of the companies trained staff to be aware of the importance and operation of the EMS (Univer-

Environmental Concerns in Rights-of-Way Management: Seventh International Symposium
J.W. Goodrich-Mahoney, D.F. Mutrie and C.A. Guild (editors)
© 2002 Published by Elsevier Science Ltd. All rights reserved.

sity of North Carolina, 2000). Clearly, communication protocols, even on single site facilities, are often not well developed. Table 1 summarizes the survey results. Examples of regulatory, cultural, and biophysical differences along a linear facility are used in the following sections to support the need for a comprehensive communications system. The need for a comprehensive communication system is critical during the planning and construction of a linear facility due to the number of issues, concerns, and permit requirements that must be addressed prior to the operation phase. During operations, effective communication among stakeholders ensures mitigation promises are kept and facilitates feedback on the EMS process.

DEFINITIONS

A linear facility, for the purposes of this paper is defined as "infrastructure used to transport, transmit, or distribute goods and services from supply to demand points." The infrastructure types encompass: railways, roads, hydro-electronic transmission lines, pipelines (gas, oil, water, sewage), and telecommunication facilities. These facilities include a network of either rights-of-way or easements interconnected to operational nodes including transformer, pump, or compressor stations, interchanges, spurs, etc.

An external stakeholder is defined as a:
- member of the public with an interest in the facility, including residents and landowners, community organizations, and other interested groups or individuals;
- federal, provincial, or municipal government agencies with a legislative mandate for any aspect of the facility's planning; construction, or operations; and,
- non-government organization (NGO) with an interest in the goods and services transported or transmitted.

An internal stakeholder is defined as any director or employee of the linear facility organization whose activities have potential to cause an environmental effect.

An interest in the facility may be identified by comments from a person, group, association, or government agency that could be potentially affected, directly or indirectly, in a positive or negative manner during the planning, construction, operation, or decommissioning stages of the facility's life.

An environmental management system (EMS) is defined as a system to support corporate environmental policies through organizational structure, planning activities, practices, procedures, processes, and resources. These components are essential for developing, implementing, achieving, reviewing, and maintaining a formal management system to minimize the environmental effects of an organization's activities and resulting products/wastes.

A communication system within an EMS structures the organization's approach to:
- facilitate internal communications between the various levels and functions of the organization; and
- receive, document and respond to communications from external stakeholders.

The following sections document the rationale and need for a more comprehensive communications system within a linear facility organization.

REGULATORY DIFFERENCES

Regulatory requirements for the construction, operation, and decommissioning of linear facilities arise from essentially three levels or tiers of government, specifically, in North America: federal, provincial or state, and local/municipal. Furthermore, within any given regulatory or government agency, linear facilities often also cross regional or district government boundaries within the same government tier. Each of these jurisdictions and potentially districts, may require environmental permits or approvals for construction of new facilities, modifications to existing facilities and for routine construction, operation, or maintenance activities and ultimately decommissioning. The longer the linear facility, the greater the likelihood of a higher number of regulatory jurisdictions and associated approval requirements.

For the planning of a 72 km pipeline in Southwestern Ontario, five federal, twenty-nine provincial and forty-three municipal government agencies were contacted, requiring more than eighty permits (ESG International, 1998). For the Tuscarora pipeline that crosses portions of Oregon, northeastern California, and Nevada, more than ninety permits were required for a 366 km, pipeline (McCullough, J.A., 1997 p. 192). For pipelines crossing the US/Canadian international boundary between Alberta and Montana, approvals from fifteen federal agencies and thirteen provincial or state agencies could potentially be required to begin construction (Mutrie, D.F. and Gilmour, K.B., 1998).

Clearly, for the planning and construction of new facilities, external contacts for approval or permits are numerous and diverse. These onerous and extensive requirements are mirrored through the operation and decommissioning phases of a linear facility. In order to ensure compliance with regulatory requirements, a comprehensive communication and documentation system must be in place internally to ensure compliance with regulatory requirements.

CULTURAL DIFFERENCES

A linear facility that crosses nations, provinces or states, and local or municipal government jurisdictions also encompasses cultural environments, both

Table 1. How companies use EMSs

Category	Feature	Percent
Training	Trained employees to be aware of the importance and operation of the EMS	49
Communications	Established procedures for receiving communications from external interested parties	60
	Documented communications received from external interested parties	54
	Responded to relevant external communications from interested parties	51
	Had documents that described the core elements of their EMS	46

Percentages based on 39 facilities studied that have active environmental management systems.
Source: "National Database on Environmental Management Systems: The Effects of Environmental Management Systems on the Environmental and Economic Performance of Facilities," University of North Carolina at Chapel Hill and Environmental Law Institute, 2000.

internally and externally. These cultural differences are most distinguishable where the international boundary between Canada and the United States is crossed, and within Canada, between provinces with different languages. Cultural priorities such as the approach to stakeholder compensation and the importance of specific cultural features such as language differences (e.g., French, English, and Spanish) also require a comprehensive communications system that recognizes these differences.

Cultural differences also occur within the corporation that owns and operates the linear facility. Communication challenges sometimes result from decisions made in the Corporate "Head Office." Those decisions can be viewed with mistrust by regional staff (internal stakeholders), since they are directions from the "ivory tower", a culturally isolated division of the same organization that could be 2000 km or more away. Continuous and frequent communication within all layers of an organization is required to ensure that "grass-roots" buy-in is acquired before EMS initiatives are released. Frequent, two-way communication and documentation minimizes the "ivory tower" nature of directives and facilitates successful EMS implementation. Local employees must be involved with the development of the EMS and its' goals and objectives.

Aboriginal priorities also underline the importance of the communication system. Aboriginal lifestyles, cultural values, traditions, and economic, social, and political aspirations are recognized as distinct enough to warrant a corporate policy for aboriginal relationships and a steering committee of four Vice-Presidents within a major electrical utility (Tennyson et al., 1993). Aboriginal people have also been incorporated into alternate route evaluations for another linear facility organization (Mohun, 1993).

The number and diversity of cultural priorities, language differences, aboriginal groups, and a remote head office, dictate the need for frequent, well documented communications.

ENVIRONMENTAL DIFFERENCES

As the length of a linear facility increases, so does the number and type of environmental features. For example, there are approximately 17 biomes in continental North America (Smith, 1974). These are essentially life zones that encompass similar plant and animal species within different climates and/or physiographic zones. Each of these biomes and sub-zones within them, often require development of site specific protection measures during planning, construction, operation, and decommissioning of a linear facility.

Agricultural and urban environments also require different protection measures. Agricultural protection measures vary based on geographic location, soil and crop types, and regional management practices. Specific protection measures for urban areas are also needed to protect public interests. Measures specific to urban areas may include: noise measures around sensitive institutions, such as hospitals; aesthetically pleasing structures ancillary to the linear facility; and separation distances from residential or institutional land uses mandated by regulatory agencies.

As best management practices are more efficiently/effectively carried out for protection of different environmental features, it is essential that regional employees and corporate environmental specialists share information through established communication channels. A communication framework must be in place to ensure that best management practices are used and their success documented, to ensure the EMS principle of "continuous improvement" is fulfilled.

CONCLUSIONS AND RECOMMENDATIONS

With increasing length, linear facilities often encounter increasingly numerous, highly diverse regulatory regimes, cultural interests and environmental features. The concerns of the equally diverse external stakeholders must be identified, documented and responded to. Internal stakeholders must be actively involved in the development of the EMS and establishment of the appropriate communication framework or system. An effective communication system that facilitates information exchange among internal and external stakeholders is critically important within a linear

facility organization to ensure:
- regulatory compliance;
- the use of best management practices; and
- culturally appropriate development.

A comprehensive communication and documentation system will ensure "continuous improvement" of the EMS.

REFERENCES

ESG International Inc. 1998. Environmental and Socio-Economic Assessment, Millennium West Pipeline. pp. 21–22.

McCullough, John A. 1997. We, They, Us: A Case Study of Environmental Compliance. The Tuscarora Gas Transmission Project. In: Sixth International Symposium on Environmental Concerns in Rights-of-Way Management. J.R. Williams, J.W. Goodrich-Mahoney, J.R. Wisneiwski, and J. Wisniewski, eds. pp. 191–199.

Mohun, Eric and Doug Halverson. 1993. Reconciling aboriginal and industrial interests in right-of-way management. In: Fifth International Symposium on Environmental Concerns in Rights-of-Way Management. G. Jean Doucet, Colette Seguin, and Michel Giguere, eds. pp. 5–9.

Mutrie, Dean F. 1998. Environmental Comparison of Pipelines in Canada and the US. In: Sixth International Symposium on Environmental Concerns in Rights-of-Way Management. J.R. Williams, J.W. Goodrich-Mahoney, J.R. Wisneiwski, and J. Wisniewski, eds. pp. 191–199.

National Standard of Canada (NSC). 1996. Environmental Management Systems — Specification with Guidance for Use. ISO 14001:1996(E).

Smith, R.C. 1974. Ecology and Field Biology. pp. 555–557.

Tennyson, Jane, Chris A. Bancroft-Wilson, and John H. Peters. 1993. Aboriginal involvement in Ontario Hydro's transmission facilities planning. In: Fifth International Symposium on Environmental Concerns in Rights-of-Way Management. G. Jean Doucet, Colette Seguin, and Michel Giguere, eds. pp. 10–14.

University of North Carolina at Chapel Hill and Environmental Law Institute. 2000. National Database on Environmental Management Systems: The Effects of Environmental Management Systems on the Environmental and Economic Performance of Facilities.

BIOGRAPHICAL SKETCHES

Peter Prier (corresponding author)

ESG International Inc., 361 Southgate Drive, Guelph, ON, Canada, N1G 3M5, Phone: (519) 836-6050, Fax: (519) 836-2493, pprier@esg.net

Peter Prier is a principal of ESG International Inc., an environmental consulting firm with expertise in linear facility planning. His areas of interest are diverse and include policy development, public consultation, environmental assessment and environmental training.

David Wesenger

ESG International Inc., 361 Southgate Drive, Guelph, ON, Canada, N1G 3M5

David Wesenger has been a senior project manager at ESG International Inc. since 1990. He is responsible for the preparation and delivery of route selection and environmental assessment reports for ESG International's linear facility clients operating in Ontario. David has over 13 years of experience in providing environmental advise to the oil and gas industry in Ontario.

Daniel Eusebi

ESG International Inc., 361 Southgate Drive, Guelph, ON, Canada, N1G 3M5

Dan Eusebi is a senior project manager at ESG International Inc. He has been working in the environmental field for 14 years in a number of areas including environmental right-of-way management, site impact assessments, environmental and socio-economic impact assessments and planning and development. Dan is a lead ISO 14000 auditor and provides environmental expertise to linear facility clients who are developing their Environmental Management Systems.

Planning and Performance of Wildlife Crossing Structures in a Major Transportation Corridor

Anthony P. Clevenger,* Jack Wierzchowski, and Nigel Waltho

While there are few methodological approaches to determine the placement of mitigation passages along road corridors, the efficacy of these measures also is poorly known. We develop three black bear (Ursus americanus) habitat models in a GIS context to identify linkage areas across a major highway. We use an empirical model to measure the accuracy of two expert-based models and potential use in mitigation passage planning. Results showed the expert literature-based model most closely approximated the empirical model, both in the results of statistical tests and the description of the linkages. Our empirical and expert models represented useful tools for transportation planners determining the location of mitigation passages when baseline information is lacking and when time constraints are imposed. To determine the effectiveness of wildlife underpasses, we modeled species responses to 14 variables. We found that in the presence of human activity carnivores were less likely to use underpasses as compared to ungulates. Apart from human activity, carnivore performance indices were better correlated to landscape variables and ungulates performance indices were better correlated to structural variables. We suggest future underpasses designed around topography, habitat quality and location will be minimally successful if human activity is not managed.

Keywords: Banff National Park, mitigation, performance evaluation, planning, wildlife crossing structure

INTRODUCTION

Attempts to increase barrier permeability across road structures can be found in some road construction and upgrade projects. Until now few methodological approaches to determine the placement of mitigation passages along road corridors have been explored. Most have relied on techniques such as radiotelemetry or surveys along roads. But often baseline data have not been collected and time does not permit new studies to be initiated.

Modeling habitat linkages with a geographic information system (GIS) is another means of determining wildlife crossing structure placement. With increasing availability of digital biophysical and land-use data, GIS tools and applications are becoming more popular among land managers and transportation planners (Treweek and Veitch, 1996). A empirically-based model would be preferred to qualitative or conceptual models based on limited data. However, in many cases data necessary for empirical models are not available. As a substitute, expert information might be used to develop simple, predictive, habitat linkage models in a short period of time (Giles, 1998). Expert information may consist of models based on the opinion of experts or qualitative models based on information taken from the literature (Servheen and Sandstrom, 1993; Singleton and Lehmkuhl, 1999).

Aside from planning, a substantial amount of time and energy has been spent designing and building mitigation passages across roadways. Wildlife crossing structures (overpasses, underpasses, tunnels) were first constructed in the 1970s and are used as mitigation tools in many parts of the world today (Reed et al., 1975; Romin and Bissonette, 1996; Keller and Pfister, 1997). Surprisingly, few studies have assessed the efficacy of these measures (Romin and Bissonette, 1996)

---

* Corresponding author's address: 3-625 Fourth Street, Canmore, AB, T1W 2G7, Canada.

Environmental Concerns in Rights-of-Way Management: Seventh International Symposium
J.W. Goodrich-Mahoney, D.F. Mutrie and C.A. Guild (editors)
© 2002 Published by Elsevier Science Ltd. All rights reserved.

and most studies have focused on only one species (Reed et al., 1975; Singer and Doherty, 1985). Species do not function in isolation but are components of ecological systems, therefore, effective management strategies should be multi-species based (Fiedler and Kareiva, 1998).

The purpose of our study was twofold: (1) to develop three different habitat models (one empirical, two expert-based) to identify linkage areas across a major road corridor. We use the empirical model as a yardstick to measure the accuracy of the expert-based models and potential use in mitigation passage planning; and (2) to determine what underpass attributes influence passage by species, species groups, and the large mammal community.

METHODS

Study area

We collected data along the Trans-Canada highway (TCH) in Banff National Park (BNP), Alberta, Canada. The Trans-Canada highway in BNP runs along the floor of the Bow Valley (2–5 km wide), sharing the valley bottom with the Bow River, the township of Banff (population 9000), several high volume two-lane highways, numerous secondary roads, and the Canadian Pacific Railway. The TCH is the major transportation corridor through the park (length = 75 km) carrying an estimated 5 million visitors to the park per year, with an additional 5 million users en route between Calgary and Vancouver (Parks Canada Highway Services, unpubl. data). The first 45 km of the TCH from the eastern park boundary (phase 1, 2, and 3A) is four lanes and bordered on both sides by a 2.4 m high wildlife exclusion fence (phase 1 completed in 1986, phase 2 in 1988, and phase 3A late 1997). The remaining 30 km to the western park boundary (Alberta–British Columbia border, phase 3B) is two lanes and unfenced. Plans are to upgrade phase 3B to four lanes with fencing and passages within the next 5–10 years.

Planning of wildlife crossing structures

We selected black bears (*Ursus americanus*) to model habitat use and identify linkage areas across the TCH. Black bears were one of the few species we had sufficient empirical data to build a habitat model and data from crossings and mortality locations to test the model. Further, we assumed that mortality locations were crossing locations although we were unable to prove that the unsuccessful crossing locations were different from successful ones.

To develop the empirical habitat model we first determined the habitat characteristics of black bears in the study area. Location data were obtained from monitoring the movements of nine radio-collared bears between 1998 and 1999. Radiotelemetry was conducted from the ground using standard techniques (Kenward, 1987). Digital maps were in a raster format with a pixel size of 30 m × 30 m. More than 95% of all telemetry locations were <2 km from the TCH therefore we delineated the study area (16,170 ha) by buffering the road at that distance. A total of 580 radiolocations were used to determine habitat characteristics.

Nine biophysical variables were used in the analysis. *Elevation*, *slope*, and *aspect* were extracted from the 1:50,000 digital elevation model (DEM). *Terrain ruggedness (TR)* was calculated within a 250 m radius and within a 500 m radius using the formula:

$$\mathrm{TR} = \frac{[CDr] \times [AVr]}{[CDr] + [AVr]},$$

where CD is a density of contour lines within a given kernel, AV is a variability of eight cardinal aspects within a given kernel, r is a kernel size. A classified, validated habitat map did not exist for the study area, therefore we used a LANDSAT Thematic Mapper (TM) satellite image to develop a habitat map. The image was transformed into greenness and wetness bands by the tasseled cap transformation of the six TM bands designed to emphasize vegetation. Increasing values of *greenness* related to increasing amounts of deciduous, green vegetation. *Wetness* was designed to emphasize vegetation moisture content. From the hydrology theme of the digital 1:50,000 National Topographic database we obtained values for *distance to nearest drainage* (running water, i.e., streams, creeks, rivers), and *density of water bodies* (running water, ponds, lakes, reservoirs).

We used a probability function that ties the distribution of bear locations to the variables in the study area (Pereira and Itami, 1991). To account for the telemetry error, each location was buffered 175 m (the maximum average error recorded in our tests) and assigned a probability of occurrence (PO) value. We stratified the density maps into PO classes. We removed all density values less than 0.5 animals per kernel area (the null class), and calculated the 25th, 50th, and 75th percentile for each of the density distributions. These percentiles were used as the cut-out values in defining four PO categories: low (<25%), moderate (25–50%), high (50–75%), and very high (>75%). A stratified random sample of points ($n = 580$) was generated to compare with the biophysical variables in each of the PO categories. We identified explicitly directional trends in habitat selection across the full set of the PO categories, supported by the statistical analysis of the observed patterns.

To reveal the relative importance of the biophysical variables to habitat selection, we used a multivariate discriminant function analysis (DFA). We used the Mahalanobis distances criterion in the stepwise method for variables' entry and removal. Approximately 10% of the locations ($n = 68$) from the black bear telemetry database were excluded from the habitat selection analysis and reserved to test the validity of the model.

Both expert habitat models were developed as weighted linear combinations of each models' layers (biophysical variables) obtained by (a) expert opinion or (b) review of the literature on black bear habitat requirements. With a weighted linear combination approach, variables were combined by applying a weight to each followed by a summation of the results to yield a suitability map. This procedure is not uncommon in GIS and has a form similar to a regression equation (Eastman et al., 1995).

Although there are an assortment of techniques for the development of weights, one of the most promising appears to be that of pairwise comparisons developed by Saaty (1977) in the context of a decision-making process known as the Analytical Hierarchy Process (Eastman et al., 1995). In the procedure for multi-criteria evaluation using a weighted linear combination, it is necessary that the weights sum to 1. The comparisons concern the relative importance of the two criteria involved in determining suitability for the stated objective, in this study, black bear habitat Ratings were provided on a 9-point continuous scale, ranging from 1/9 (extremely less important) to 9 (extremely more important), and the midpoint 0 being equally important (Saaty, 1977). In developing the weights, a group of individuals (minimum of two) compares every possible pairing and enters the ratings into a pairwise comparison matrix.

The expert opinion-based model required the collaboration of experts in assessing the importance of variables influencing black bear habitat selection in the study area. We solicited the cooperation of five biologists with substantial experience in black bear habitat studies. Two experts committed to developing the weights for the pairwise comparison matrix. Both investigators had a combined 47 years of experience studying black bears and their habitat in the Bow River Valley. We provided the experts with a list of potential variables for the habitat model. Only variables having accompanying digital layers were considered. Initially we solicited input from the experts in regard to the variables selected for building the model and how the variables should be divided up for the pairwise comparion matrix. Once their input was received we carried out the weighting procedure using the pairwise comparison matrix.

We met with the experts to carry out the multi-criteria evaluation. The experts agreed on the variables selected and the within-variable categories to use in the model. However, they preferred to divide them into two seasons relevant to the biological needs of bears: pre-berry (den exit to 15 July) and berry (15 July to den entry). Scoring of the matrix was done within the variables and among the variables. Five habitat variables were used in the analysis: *elevation*, *slope*, *aspect*, *greenness* and *distance to nearest drainage*. Pixel and kernel sizes were kept constant throughout the analysis. The time required to perform the pairwise comparisons ($n = 12$) for both seasons was 90 min.

Literature-based expert models were developed in the same fashion as the expert opinion models. Instead of experts providing weights for the variables, the available literature on black bear habitat selection was used to assist us in weighting the variables and completing the pairwise comparison matrices. One of the authors (APC) and two other biologists carried out this part of the study. Two sources of information on black bear habitat use were selected for obtaining information for the model (Holroyd and VanTighem, 1983; Beak Associates Consulting, 1989). We used information from the study area and preferably within the same EcoProvince if possible. The same variables were scored in a pairwise comparison procedure as for the expert opinion model. All pairwise comparisons were carried out using the weight procedure in the Idrisi geographic analysis software (Eastman, 1997). The time required to conduct the 12 pairwise comparisons was 110 min. Once the comparisons were completed, criteria maps were developed by multiplying each factor map (i.e., each raster cell within each map) by its weight and then sum the results.

We based our linkage analysis model on the assumption that the probability of a bear crossing a highway increases in areas where the highway directly bisects high quality bear habitat and that the highest probability of crossings will occur in areas where a set of topographic and landscape features are conducive to lateral, cross-valley movements.

To facilitate statistical comparisons between the empirical and expert-based models, the latter being a habitat suitability index (HSI) type of model (US Fish and Wildlife Service, 1980), we reclassified the continuous empirical habitat quality surface into 20 habitat favorability (or probability) classes, indexed from low (0%) to high (100%). We then applied the same rule to the expert models. The reclassification process allowed us to express the best black bear habitat as a percentage of the maximum habitat favorability value, regardless of the unit of measurement. We defined prime black bear habitat as areas with habitat favorability values >70% for both model types.

We used the GIS environment to generate four classes of highway crossing/habitat linkage zones:
- *Class I* — Sections of TCH crossing prime black bear habitat extending up to 100 m on both sides of the highway.
- *Class II* — Sections of TCH crossing prime black bear habitat extending over 100 m on both sides of the highway.
- *Class III* — Sections of TCH, $\geq$250 m away from any permanent human development, nested within the Class II linkages, and within the areas conducive to cross-valley movement. This class was interactively mapped using the ortho-photographs and the DEM of the area.

– *Class IV* — Sections of TCH not directly crossing the prime black bear habitat but having the prime black bear habitat within no more than 700 m on both sides of the highway.

We tested each of the linkage models using a set of empirical black bear crossing and mortality points. Crossing locations were defined as the point on the TCH connecting a straight line between consecutive radiolocations on opposite sides of the road and obtained within 24 h. Mortality locations were obtained from the BNP wildlife mortality database (Banff National Park, Banff, Alberta). We tested whether black bear empirical crossing and mortality points were randomly distributed with respect to the distance to the linkage zones. To do this we generated a random set of highway crossings, equal in size to the empirical set, and calculated the distances from both sets of points to the Class III and IV linkage zones. We repeated these calculations for each of the habitat models. The kappa index of agreement was used to measure the similarity between models and linkage areas (p. 388–395, Campbell, 1996). The kappa index is a measure of association for two map layers having exactly the same number of categories. Indices range from 0.0 (no agreement) to 1.0 (spatially identical). Between map layers, values >0.75 indicate excellent agreement beyond chance; values between 0.4–0.75 demonstrate fair to good agreement; and values <0.4 indicate poor agreement (SPSS, 1998). We used SPSS version 8.0 statistical package for all analyses (SPSS, 1998). The software Idrisi was used to measure the kappa index of agreement (Eastman, 1997).

Performance of wildlife crossing structures

Along the fenced portion of the TCH, 22 wildlife underpasses and two wildlife overpasses were constructed. The effectiveness of such structures to facilitate large mammal movements, however, is unknown. Because no two structures are similar in all physical and ecological aspects we propose that species (i.e., large mammals) select passages that best correlate with their ecological needs and behavior. Attributes that best characterize high-use passages can then be integrated into new designs for an eventual phase 3B twinning process. We chose phase 1 and phase 2 underpasses for this study, because the recent completion of phase 3A mitigation structures did not permit sufficient time for wildlife habituation to occur at such landscape scales (first author, unpubl. data).

We chose 11 underpasses from phase 1 and 2 for this study: 9 of the 11 underpasses were cement open-span underpasses and 2 were metal culverts. We characterized each underpass with 14 variables encompassing structural, landscape, and human activity attributes (Table 1). Structural variables included underpass width, height, length (including median), openness = width × height/length; and noise level = mean of A-weighted decibel readings taken at the center point within the underpass and 5 m from each end. Landscape variables included distances to nearest forest cover, Canadian Pacific Railway, townsite, closest major drainage, and eastern-most park entrance (hereafter referred to as east gate). Human activity variables included types of human use in the underpasses characterized by counts of people on foot, bike, horseback, and a human use index calculated from the mean monthly counts of the three former variables combined.

We measured wildlife use of the underpasses using raked track pads (2 × 4 m) set at both ends of each underpass. At 3–4 day intervals each underpass was visited and species presence (wolves [*Canis lupus*], cougars [*Puma concolor*], black bears, grizzly bears [*Ursus arctos*], deer [*Odocoileus* spp.], elk [*Cervus elaphus*], and moose [*Alces alces*]), species abundance, and human activity counts were recorded. Track pads were then raked smooth in preparation for the next visit. Data were collected in this manner for two continuous monitoring periods 1 January 1995–31 March 1996 (15 months) and 1 November 1996–30 June 1998 (20 months).

We examined observed crossing frequencies in the context of expected crossing frequencies (i.e., performance indices). Expected crossing frequencies were obtained from independent data sets that included radiolocation data, relative abundance pellet transects, and habitat suitability indices. We defined our expected crossing frequencies as equal to the abundance data found at radii 1, 2, and 3 km from the center of each underpass. We used (1) radiolocation data for black bears ($n = 255$ locations), grizzly bears ($n = 221$ locations), wolves ($n = 2314$ locations) and elk ($n = 1434$ locations; Parks Canada, unpubl. data); (2) relative abundance pellet transects for deer ($n = 1579$ pellet sites), elk ($n = 26,614$ pellet sites), moose ($n = 43$ pellet sites) and wolves ($n = 30$ sites containing scat; Parks Canada, unpubl. data); and (3) habitat suitability indices for black bears, cougars, wolves, deer, elk, and moose (Holroyd and Van Tighem, 1983; Beak Associates Consulting, 1989). We derived species performance indices for each of the three data sets by dividing observed crossing frequencies by expected crossing frequencies. Performance indices were designed such that the higher the index the more effective the underpass appears to facilitate species crossings.

We used simple curvilinear and polynomial regression curves to optimize the fit between species performance indices and each underpass attribute (Jandel Scientific, 1994). For each species we ranked the regression models obtained according to the absolute value of each model's coefficient of determination. This three-step process allowed for the identification and ordering of underpass attributes (in order of importance) associated with each species performance

Table 1. Attributes of 11 wildlife underpasses used in analysis of factors influencing wildlife in Banff National Park, Alberta

Underpass attribute	Underpass										
	1	2	3	4	5	6	7	8	9	10	11
Structural											
Width (m)	9.8	13.4	4.2	9.8	9.5	14.9	10.0	9.8	10.3	9.0	7.0
Height (m)	2.8	2.5	3.5	2.9	2.9	3.2	3.0	2.7	2.8	2.9	4.0
Length (m)	63.0	83.2	96.1	40.0	39.7	38.0	27.1	27.2	25.6	40.1	56.0
Openness	0.43	0.4	0.15	0.71	0.69	1.25	1.1	0.97	1.12	0.65	0.5
Noise level	68.1	70.5	64.1	66.8	66.0	63.8	64.3	67.4	67.4	67.1	64.1
Landscape (distance to)											
East gate (km)	0.0	2.1	3.5	5.8	10.5	11.5	12.0	14.4	17.0	18.8	38.8
Forest cover (m)	22.3	63.3	11.9	15.2	47.3	16.1	35.9	23.3	27.5	23.9	35.4
Nearest drainage (km)	1.0	0.0	0.1	0.4	0.6	0.0	0.6	1.2	0.4	0.2	0.3
CPR[a] (km)	0.5	0.75	0.8	0.02	0.02	0.02	0.25	1.2	0.4	0.75	0.75
Nearest town (km)	1.6	3.5	5.5	6.0	1.5	0.5	0.2	1.7	5.2	7.2	0.8
Human activity											
Human use index	0.4	1.9	1.8	0.6	5.3	5.3	15.2	3.2	11.4	0.6	0.5
Bike	0	5	6	21	189	8	462	19	595	1	0
Horseback	6	3	6	5	42	138	186	12	58	10	10
Foot	7	45	14	20	34	77	129	80	241	10	29
Species passage											
Black bear	10	20	43	37	13	8	0	4	8	34	16
Grizzly bear	0	0	0	2	0	0	0	0	0	5	0
Cougar	5	29	3	30	7	0	4	4	20	15	0
Wolf	1	7	3	28	3	5	1	5	77	146	35
Deer	554	42	294	253	215	21	61	338	2882	291	54
Elk	825	201	331	1199	1062	467	1576	1522	821	683	272
Moose	1	0	1	0	0	0	0	0	0	0	0

[a] Canadian Pacific Railway track.

index, however, it failed to separate ecologically significant attributes from those that appeared significant but were statistical artifacts of the underpasses themselves. The process was repeated for each of the three scales of ecological resolution. We divided species into two groups, carnivores and ungulates.

RESULTS

Planning of wildlife crossing structures

Black bears selected for relatively gentle terrain at lower elevations, in the areas of high concentrations of and close proximity to water, and in the areas of reduced wetness index. The latter often corresponds with the valley bottom coniferous stands having the inclusions of the semi-open vegetation types. There was no selection for greenness. Bears preferred flat areas (0–3 degrees) with the southerly aspects ($X^2 = 3072.8$, d.f. = 32, $P < 0.0001$).

We generated the most parsimonious model by using eight variables, in order of importance: elevation, flat aspect, south-southeast aspect, south-southwest aspect, density of water bodies, distance to drainages, slope, and terrain ruggedness. The order of importance is that of a multivariate type and was based on the analysis of the standardized function coefficients.

Overall, the DFA produced a sound statistical model. The high canonical correlation coefficient (0.755) indicated that the DFA was strong and discriminated well between the groups. Also, the Wilk's Lambda was low (0.43) denoting a relatively high discriminating power of DFA. The overall cross-validated classification accuracy was 86.5%. The model correctly classified 78.6% of the set aside radiolocations into prime black bear habitat.

We tested each of the linkage models using a set of 37 empirical black bear crossing and mortality points. With respect to the distances to the Class IV linkages the analysis showed no statistical difference between the empirical crossings and random locations ($P > 0.05$). We interpreted this as an indication that Class IV linkages were a poor predictive tool for mapping cross-highway movement. The differences between the distance from the empirical points and random locations to the Class III linkages were significantly different. There was strong statistical evidence that the empirical bear crossing and mortality locations were much closer to Class III linkages than expected by chance for the empirical model ($P = 0.018$), the expert opinion-based berry season model ($P = 0.027$), and the expert literature-based model ($P = 0.005$). Distances from the empirical points to the Class III linkages for the expert opinion-based pre-berry season model were

Table 2. Descriptive statistics for the Class III linkages of empirical and expert linkage zone models. Measurements are in km

	n	Total length	Mean length	Minimum	Maximum
Empirical model	11	8.6	0.78	0.20	2.70
Expert opinion - *Pre-berry*	17	5.7	0.33	0.13	0.93
Expert opinion - *Berry*	18	4.7	0.26	0.08	0.72
Expert literature	9	6.3	0.70	0.30	1.90

Table 3. Comparison of kappa index of agreement of the empirical black bear habitat model with expert opinion-based models and expert literature-based model. See Methods for interpretation of kappa index.

Expert models	Empirical model		
	Class II	Class III	Class IV
Expert opinion - Berry	0.3679	0.3792	0.3618
Expert opinion - *Pre-berry*	0.3243	0.4411	0.0274
Expert literature	0.4271	0.5568	0.2529

not significantly different from the random locations ($P = 0.10$).

Of the Class III linkages, both seasonal expert opinion-based models had more linkage zones and were on average smaller in length compared to the empirical and expert literature-based model linkage zones (Table 2). When compared to the empirical model, there was a relatively strong correlation with the expert literature-based model (kappa index = 0.662). The expert opinion-based pre-berry season and berry season models were only fair (0.416) to moderate (0.569) in agreement with the empirical model.

The expert literature-based model most closely approximated the empirical model, both in the results of the statistical tests and the description of the Class III linkages. To further our understanding about the similarities and differences between the models, we compared them in terms of the level of juxtaposition of both the prime bear habitat maps and the Class II, III, and IV linkage zones (Table 3). The expert literature-based model was consistently more similar to the empirical model than either of the two expert opinion-based models. Class III linkages for all three expert models had the greatest similarity with the empirical model. Class IV associations were the weakest of all. Among the expert models, the literature-based model had the strongest correlation with the empirical model. Expert opinion-based models ranged in kappa index measures from 0.02 to 0.44, while expert literature-based models varied from 0.25 to 0.55.

Performance of wildlife crossing structures

We found that for each species the rank order of significant attributes was not significantly different between performance models (paired t test, all within-species comparisons not significant at $P > 0.05$). We therefore provide mean rank scores only. The rank order of significant attributes, however, does differ between species (paired t test, Bonferroni adjusted probability values; $P < 0.05$). For example, we found that underpass distance from east gate (positive correlation) was the most significant underpass attribute affecting black bear performance indices, whereas the underpass length (negative correlation) was the most significant attribute affecting elk performance indices (Table 4). For carnivores the most significant underpass attribute influencing the group's performance was distance to townsite (positively correlated); followed by human activities in the order of hiking (negatively correlated), human use index (negatively correlated), and horseback riding (negatively correlated). Landscape and structural variables were the least significant attributes influencing the group's performance index (i.e., distance to nearest drainage, negatively correlated; underpass openness, negatively correlated; Table 5). In contrast, we found that the most significant underpass attributes influencing ungulates were structural and landscape factors. Specifically we found the rank order to be: (1) underpass openness (negatively correlated); (2) noise level (positively correlated); (3) underpass width (negatively correlated), and 5 distance to nearest drainage. Human activity attributes, although significant, were ranked lower: (4) horseback riding (negatively correlated); and (6) hiking (negatively correlated). At the third scale of resolution, the large mammal community (i.e., all species together), we found that the most significant underpass attribute influencing the community's performance index was structural openness (negatively correlated; Table 5). Distance to townsites was the second most significant attribute (positive correlation), followed by human activity (human use index, horseback riding, hiking, and biking, all negatively correlated).

DISCUSSION

Planning of wildlife crossing structures

The most noteworthy result from the exercise was not the low performance of the expert opinion-based model, but the close proximity of the expert literature-based model to the empirical model. Our findings confirmed that the expert literature-based model was consistently more similar and conformed to the empirical model better than any of the expert opinion-based

Table 4. Species level rank ordering of mean coefficient of determinations and their slope for models explaining underpass interactions in Banff National Park, Alberta

Underpass attributes	Black bear	Grizzly bear	Cougar	Wolf	Deer	Elk	Moose
Width	8–				4–	3–	5–
Height			3–	3+		10+	
Length	7+					1–	4+
Openness	4–				5–	4+	1–
Noise level	12+		1+		3+	8+	
East gate	1–			2+			3–
Forest cover	11–	3–	4+		6–	11–	6–
Nearest drainage	9–			7–	2+	2+	
CPR[a]		4–		5+	8+		
Nearest town	3+	1+	2+	1+		12+	
Human activity index	6–	2–		6–		5–	8–
Bike	10–			4–		6–	7–
Horseback	5–				1–	7–	2–
Foot	2–		5–	8–	7–	9–	9–

[a]Canadian Pacific Railway track.

Table 5. Species group and large mammal community rank ordering of mean coefficient of determinations and their slope for models explaining underpass interactions at the level of species groups and large mammal community in Banff National Park, Alberta

Underpass attributes	Carnivore	Ungulate	Large mammal community
Width		3–	6–
Height			10–
Length		8+	11+
Openness	5–	1–	1–
Noise level	7+	2+	8+
Distance to east gate		10–	13+
Distance to forest cover		7–	12–
Distance to nearest drainage	6–	5+	
Distance to CPR[a]		12+	9+
Distance to nearest town	1+	13+	2+
Human activity index	3–	9–	3–
Bike	8–	11–	7–
Horseback	4–	4–	4–
Foot	2–	6–	5–

[a]Canadian Pacific Railway track.

models. These results were based on the test of distribution of the empirical points from actual crossing and mortality locations in relation to the linkages, the descriptive characteristics of the Class III linkages, the measure of agreement between models, and measure of agreement between model linkage zones.

The poor predictive power of the pre-berry expert opinion-based model may be explained by an overestimation of the importance of riparian habitat to the pre-berry habitat model, as compared to the opinions expressed in the literature. Another possible explanation for the difference between the two expert models is that the expert literature model is based on an analytical process (data have been collected, statistically analyzed and summarized), whereas the expert opinion model is based on information taken from how experts perceive attributes from memory and experience.

Further, the fact that only 35% of the empirical black bear crossing and mortality locations where those of the pre-berry season may also have influenced how well it predicted linkage areas.

There are several advantages to the expert-based techniques presented from this work. There are an assortment of GIS tools designed for model building purposes that are readily available today. GIS applications such as Idrisi (Clark University, Worcester, MA, USA), MapInfo Professional Software (MapInfo Corporation, Troy, NY, USA), and ArcView GIS (Environmental Systems Research Institute, Redlands, CA, USA) are relatively inexpensive and easy to use. Idrisi has decision support procedures as a program module built into the geographic analysis system. Remotely sensed data, digital land cover data and habitat suitability maps are increasingly accessible, frequently updated and refined for individual users or government agencies. Further, empirical data from field studies of most wildlife species, particularly game species, are obtainable in most developed countries where road mitigation practices are presently implemented. The use of the Saaty's pairwise comparison matrix requires little training and ensures consistency in developing relative weights in the development of the expert-based models. This procedure is readily available in the Idrisi software package.

Transportation planning for roads and highways has generally considered a one-dimensional, linear zone along the highway. Thus the engineering and design dimensions have been the primary concern for planners. However, the ecological effects of roads we know are many times wider than the road itself and can be immense and pervasive (Forman and Alexander, 1998). Because of the broad landscape context of road systems, it is essential to incorporate landscape patterns and processes in the planning and construction process. The results from our work should not be interpreted as a devaluation of the use of experts in developing resource management strategies. Identifying linkage areas across road corridors using both expert model types (opinion- and literature-based) we have presented can provide a useful tool for resource and transportation planners charged with determining the location of mitigation passages for wildlife when baseline information is lacking and when time constraints do not allow for pre-construction data collection. Regarding the latter, we spent approximately two months developing the four models. More than half of that time was dedicated to developing the more complex, data intensive empirical black bear habitat model. We do not advocate modeling linkage zones using exclusively expert information if empirical data are available. However, we do encourage others with empirical data for model building and testing to develop expert models concurrently so that their findings may be contrasted with ours.

Performance of wildlife crossing structures
Our results suggest that underpass attributes differentially influence species performance indices. However, depending on the scale investigated (i.e., species, species groups, large mammal community) different underpass attributes were perceived as dominant. One common thread at all resolutions was that human influence consistently ranked high as a significant factor affecting species performance indices. At the species level, for example, six of the seven species ranked at least one of these human attributes as the most or second most important attribute influencing the species performance index. At the group level carnivores showed a positive correlation between underpass performance indices and distance from town and a negative correlation to human activity. The inverse relation between the two human-related attributes occurs because the townsites serve as sources of human populations from which human use activity originates. The closer an underpass is to a townsite, the greater the human use activity observed (Mattson et al., 1987; Jalkotzy and Ross, 1993; but see Rodriguez et al., 1996).

Ungulates, however, failed to respond to human activity in the same manner. Although significant negative correlations in performance indices were observed the relative importance of human activity was ranked below that of structural attributes. Elk habituation to human presence close to town may, at least in part, have masked the performance indices of non-habituated elk further from town. At the community level, the most important attribute influencing species performance indices was structural openness. The second most important attribute, however, was distance to the townsites (positive correlation).

These results lend support to the BNP management plan that emphasizes stricter limits to human development be imposed and more effective methods of managing and limiting human use within the park be established (Parks Canada, 1997). The plan also recommends improving the effectiveness of phase 1 and 2 underpasses by "retrofitting." In this context we suggest that in such a multi-species system the most efficient approach to retrofitting is to manage human activity near each underpass. Specifically, we recommend that foot trails be relocated and human use of underpasses be restricted. Continued monitoring of wildlife passage frequencies at these structures will permit Parks Canada to evaluate how this management strategy may translate into greater permeability of the TCH and habitat connectivity for all wildlife populations in the Bow Valley.

Landscape variables other than distance to town may also be important attributes determining species performance indices. Carnivores had a greater tendency to use underpasses close to drainages, whereas ungulates tended to avoid them. Drainage are notorious travel routes for wildlife, particularly in narrow glacial valleys like Banff's Bow Valley. However, the inverse relationship between carnivores and ungulates with respect to drainages may be a result of predator-prey interactions rather than any direct effect of landscape attributes on underpass use per se. For example, deer are known to keep to the periphery of wolf territories (Mech, 1977) and reduce their feeding effort when exposed to odors of wolves and other predator species (Sullivan et al., 1985). There is some evidence that the presence of badgers [*Meles meles*] can disrupt their prey species (hedgehogs [*Erinaceus europaeus*]) use of tunnels under roads in England (C. Doncaster, unpubl. data).

The results from our analyses also suggest that structural attributes were significant in species performance indices, especially for ungulates. Ungulates preferred underpass structures with a low openness ratio, narrow width, and long tunnel dimensions. However, we doubt that such species prefer such constricted underpasses when compared to the availability of larger and more open underpasses. In a post-hoc regression analysis we found that openness was significantly correlated to length, noise, and distance to town (linear regression, $P < 0.05$). These post-hoc tests suggested that the importance of these structural attributes may be of more statistical artifacts than ecological significance.

It is possible that the overall weakness of structural attributes in explaining species performance indices could be due to species individual familiarization with the 12-year old underpasses. Individuals require time to adapt to underpass structures (Reed et al., 1975; first author, unpubl. data) and once this has occurred, the dynamics of human activity and landscape heterogeneity attributes may be more decisive in determining species performance indices than the structural attributes themselves.

The multi-scale approach we used demonstrates informational needs of a state transportation planner responsible for site-specific mitigation for deer (Reed et al., 1975; Romin and Bissonette, 1996) will likely be different from a land manager in BNP mandated to maintain ecosystem integrity of a 650,000 ha national park. However, independent of the ecological resolution used species performance indices were consistently negatively correlated to some measure of human activity. In the absence of human management the best designed and landscaped underpasses may be rendered ineffective and the barriers to habitat connectivity unmitigated.

ACKNOWLEDGEMENTS

We extend our appreciation to Parks Canada Highway Services Centre for providing funding for the project and Banff National Park for administrative and logistical support. This study was funded by Parks Canada and Public Works and Government Services Canada (under contract C8160-8-0010).

REFERENCES

Beak Associates Consulting Ltd. 1989. Ecological studies of the black bear in Banff National Park, Alberta, 1986–1988. Final report to Canadian Parks Service and Banff National Park Warden Service, Banff, Alberta.

Campbell, J. 1996. Introduction to Remote Sensing. Taylor and Francis Ltd., London.

Eastman, J.R. 1997. Idrisi for Windows, version 2.0. Clark University Laboratory, Clark University, Worcester, Pennsylvania.

Eastman, J.R., W. Jin, P.A.K. Kyem, and J. Toledano. 1995. Raster procedures for multi-criteria/multi-objective decisions. Photogrammetric Engineeering and Remote Sensing, 61: 539–547.

Fiedler, P. and P. Kareiva. 1998. Conservation Biology for the Coming Decade. Chapman and Hall, New York.

Forman, R.T.T. and L.E. Alexander. 1998. Roads and their major ecological effects. Annual Review of Ecology and Systematics, 29: 207–231.

Giles, R.H. Jr. 1998. Natural resource management tomorrow: Four currents. Wildlife Society Bulletin, 26: 51–55.

Holroyd, G.L. and K.J. Van Tighem. 1983. Ecological (biophysical) land classification of Banff and Jasper national parks. Volume 3. The wildlife inventory. Canadian Wildlife Service, Edmonton.

Jalkotzy, M. and I. Ross. 1993. Cougar responses to human activity at Sheep River, Alberta. Arc Wildlife Services, Calgary, AB.

Jandel Scientific. 1994. Tablecurve 2D Version 3 for Win32. Jandel Scientific, San Rafael, CA.

Keller, V. and H.P. Pfister. 1997. Wildlife passages as a means of mitigating effects of habitat fragmentation by roads and railway lines. In: Habitat fragmentation and infrastructure. K. Canters, ed. Ministry of Transportation, Public Works and Water Management, Delft, The Netherlands.

Kenward, R. 1987. Wildlife Radio Tagging: Equipment, Field Techniques, and Data Analysis. Academic Press, London.

Mattson, D.J., R.R. Knight, and B.M. Blanchard. 1987. The effects of developments and primary roads on grizzly bear habitat use in Yellowstone National Park, Wyoming. International Conference on Bear Research and Management, 7: 259–273.

Mech, L.D. 1977. Wolf-pack buffer zones as prey reservoirs. Science, 198: 320–321.

Parks Canada. 1997. Banff National Park management plan. Ministry of Canadian Heritage, Ottawa.

Pereira, J. and R. Itami. 1991. GIS-based habitat modeling using logistic multiple regression: A study of the Mt. Graham red squirrel. Photogrammetric Engineering and Remote Sensing, 57: 1475–1486.

Reed, D.F., T.N. Woodward, and T.M. Pojar. 1975. Behavioral response of mule deer to a highway underpass. Journal of Wildlife Management, 39: 361–367.

Rodriguez, A., G. Crema, and M. Delibes. 1996. Use of non-wildlife passages across a high speed railway by terrestrial vertebrates. Journal of Applied Ecology, 33: 1527–1540.

Romin, L.A. and J. Bissonette. 1996. Deer-vehicle collisions: status of state monitoring activities and mitigation efforts. Wildlife Society Bulletin, 24: 276–283.

Saaty, T.L. 1977. A scaling method for priorities I hierarchical structures. Journal of Mathematical Psychology, 15: 234–281.

Servheen, C. and P. Sandstrom. 1993. Ecosystem management and linkage zones for grizzly bears and other large carnivores in the northern Rocky Mountains in Montana and Idaho. Endangered Species Bulletin, 18: 1–23.

Singer, F.J. and J.L. Doherty. 1985. Managing mountain goats at a highway crossing. Wildlife Society Bulletin, 13: 469–477.

Singleton, P. and J. Lehmkuhl. 1999. Assessing wildlife habitat connectivity in the Interstate 90 Snoqualmie Pass corridor, Washington. In: Proceedings of the Third International Conference on Wildlife Ecology and Transportation. G. Evink, P. Garrett, and D. Zeigler, eds. Florida Department of Transportation, Tallahassee, FL.

Statistical Program for the Social Sciences (SPSS) 1998. SPSS version 8.0 for Windows. SPSS Inc., Chicago, IL.

Sullivan, T., L. Nordstrom, and D. Sullivan. 1985. Use of predator odors as repellents to reduce feeding damage by herbivores II. Black-tailed deer (*Odocoileus hemionus columbianus*). Journal of Chemical Ecology, 11: 921–935.

Treweek, J. and N. Veitch. 1996. The potential application of GIS and remotely sensed data to the ecological assessment of proposed new road schemes. Global Ecology and Biogeography Letters, 5: 249–257.

US Fish and Wildlife Service. 1980. Habitat evaluation procedures (HEP). Ecological Services Manual 102. US Department of Interior, Division of Ecological Services Government Printing Office, Washington, DC.

BIOGRAPHICAL SKETCHES

Anthony P. Clevenger

Faculty of Environmental Design, University of Calgary, Calgary, AB, T1N 2N4, Canada, Email: tony_clevenger@pch.gc.ca. Phone: (403) 760 1371; Fax: (403) 762 3240

Anthony P. Clevenger is a research ecologist currently contracted by Parks Canada to study road effects on wildlife in Banff National Park. He obtained a BS degree from the University of California, Berkeley, an MS from the University of Tennessee, Knoxville, and a PhD from the University of León, Spain. He has been an adjunct professor at the University of Tennessee since 1989 and the University of Calgary since 1998.

Jack Wierzchowski
Geomar, PO Box 1843, Grand Forks, British Columbia, V0H 1H0, Canada

Jack Wierzchowski is the principal researcher at Geomar Consulting Ltd. which specializes in computer modeling and its applications to environmental management. Jack's area of interest involves modeling of wildlife habitat and movement. He obtained his BS and MS degrees from the University of Warsaw, Poland, and a MED from the University of Calgary.

Nigel Waltho
Faculty of Environmental Studies, York University, North York, ON, M3J 1P3, Canada

Nigel Waltho is an assistant professor of environmental science at York University, Toronto, Canada (since 1996). He researches quantitative methods in the design and analysis of hierarch theory on coral reef fish, and highway crossing structures on large mammalian wildlife. He received his BS and PhD from McMaster University (1998 Hamilton, ON).

Part IV
Project Planning

CanCommit©: A Computerized Commitment Database for Pipeline Construction and Operations

Melissa Pockar, Paul Anderson, and Terry Antoniuk

Project managers must be aware of commitments made to regulators, landowners, communities, and other groups so that due-diligence can be properly implemented during linear facility construction and operation. In the past, commitments have been tracked by memory, or with lists and spreadsheets. These previous approaches may be insufficient where projects are large, complex, or involve large numbers of non-standard commitments. This manuscript describes CanCommit©, a computerized environmental database developed for the Canadian portion of the Alliance pipeline system. The concepts introduced and structure of CanCommit© are readily transferable to a variety of projects. CanCommit© was developed in Microsoft Access© and was designed to enable project managers and construction staff to document and track generic and location-specific environmental commitments. The documentation process, combined with the database searching and reporting capabilities, allowed conflicting conditions and commitments to be readily identified. More than 6000 records were entered into the database over a three-month period. These included commitments made by Alliance during the regulatory applications, submissions and negotiations phases of the project. Tracking of status and compliance was facilitated through user-friendly database fields, drop-down lists, and help messages. Keyword searches of commitment text and summary reports could be generated by commitment topics, source documents, responsible parties, due dates or geographic locations. The status of individual commitments were tracked and updated by Alliance during the course of construction and reported back to management and field inspectors.

Keywords: Due-diligence, environment, commitment tracking, linear construction

INTRODUCTION

The Alliance Pipeline Limited (Alliance) system extends from northeastern British Columbia, Canada, to Chicago, Illinois, USA (Fig. 1). The Canadian portion of the project includes:
- 1559 km of mainline and related facilities from a point near Gordondale, Alberta, to a point on the Canada/United States border near Elmore, Saskatchewan; and
- 698 km of lateral pipelines and related facilities in British Columbia and Alberta.

On July 3, 1997, Alliance applied to the National Energy Board (NEB) for a Certificate of Public Convenience and Necessity to construct the Canadian portion of its natural gas pipeline system. Public hearings were initiated in February 1998, followed by the release of the NEB Comprehensive Study Report (CSR) (National Energy Board, 1998a) in September 1998 that satisfied the requirements of the *Canadian Environmental Assessment Act*. The CSR incorporated the results of public participation, including advice from the NEB, Fisheries and Oceans Canada (DFO), the Prairie Farm Rehabilitation Association (PFRA), Environment Canada (EC), various government agencies from the Provinces of Alberta, Saskatchewan and British Columbia, affected landowners and other stakeholder groups. The NEB Reasons for Decision (RFD) issued in November 1998 concluded that the project

Environmental Concerns in Rights-of-Way Management: Seventh International Symposium
J.W. Goodrich-Mahoney, D.F. Mutrie and C.A. Guild (editors)
© 2002 Elsevier Science Ltd. All rights reserved.

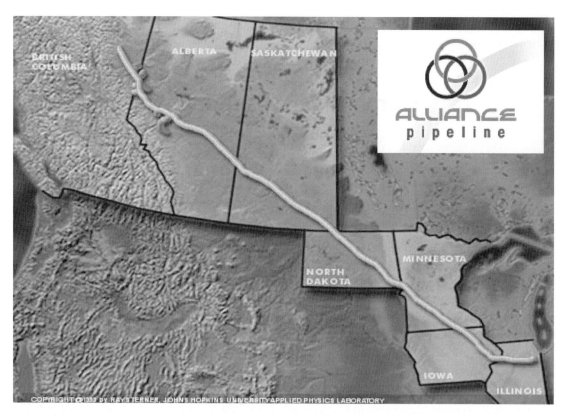

Fig. 1. Alliance Pipeline Ltd. system map.

was in the public interest (National Energy Board, 1998b). The project was subsequently approved by the Governor in Council and the Certificate of Public Convenience and Necessity (Certificate GC-98) from the NEB was issued on December 3, 1998 (National Energy Board, 1998c) (Fig. 1).

Through the consultation, negotiation, hearing and regulatory approval phases, Alliance made thousands of environmental commitments to the public and to regulators. Traditionally, these types of commitments have been tracked by memory, or with lists or spreadsheets. However, due to the size of the Alliance Project and the volume of non-standard environmental commitments, Alliance developed an electronic database tool to assist project managers and construction staff in tracking commitment implementation and status. The principal design objective was to provide identification of all environmental commitments made during the regulatory and approval processes and to document their implementation and resolution during the construction and operation of the pipeline system.

CanCommit© was designed to store and manage both non-standard and generic commitments that were gleaned from over two hundred individual documents, including the NEB application and approval documents, hearing transcripts, supporting resource assessment documents (wildlife, archaeology, soils, vegetation, aquatics, air quality, noise), regulatory correspondence, authorizations and permit conditions. CanCommit© was designed to supplement but not replace standard environmental planning documents such as the Environmental Alignment Sheets (Alliance, 1997a) and the Environmental Plans — Volume V (Alliance, 1997b) document.

The commitment information incorporated into CanCommit© included the Conditions and View of the Board as specified in the NEB RFD and Conclusions and Recommendations specified in the CSR. Also included were any proposed mitigation or commitments for issues as identified on the Environmental Issues List (Alliance, 1997c) filed with the NEB (such as sensitive watercourse crossings, land use conflicts, problem soils, unstable slopes, wildlife habitat, rare or significant plant communities, heritage, archaeological, and palaeontological sites, and traditional aboriginal use areas). Mitigative measures specified in federal, provincial, and local approvals, permits, and licenses issued during the initial regulatory phase were incorporated into CanCommit©, as were special mitigation procedures for rare plants, alternative soil handling techniques, and watercourse crossings shown on Construction and Environmental Alignment Sheets and Designed Watercourse Crossing drawings (Alliance, 1998). Proposed mitigation or commitments for unusual issues or those issues which required special attention or consideration by Alliance, environmental inspectors, contractors, or regulators were also included.

Standard (i.e., not site specific) environmental protection procedures and mitigative measures identified

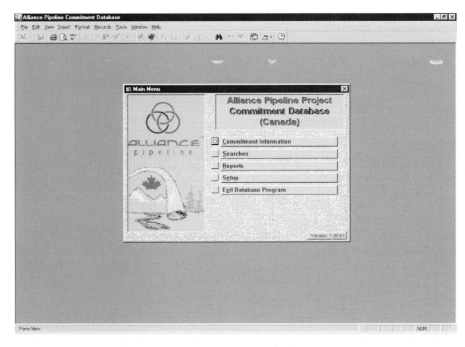

Fig. 2. CanCommit© user interface.

on Construction and Environmental Alignment Sheets, or within the Environmental Plans (Volume V) were not included in the CanCommit© database.

Design criteria methodology

Through consultation between the database programmers and Alliance environmental personnel, the scope of the database and the desired data inputs and outputs for the program were determined. Meetings were conducted with the Alliance Environmental Manager and the Supervisor of Environmental Inspection to incorporate the practical attributes from a management point of view, as well as from a field-level implementation (environmental inspector) perspective.

It was necessary to capture non-standard environmental information in a consistent format that would support keyword queries by environmental inspectors, technical specialists and project managers. Documentation of the source of the data and specific reference for each commitment was also important for additional follow-up work if required. The design of the database was to allow for conflict identification and resolution among commitments and to ultimately provide a permanent record for due-diligence purposes.

It was also necessary to track the status of these commitments in a consistent format. This capability allows outstanding and upcoming items to be identified on a regular basis for planning and compliance assurance purposes. Documentation regarding the date and specific reference for each completed commitment was also required information.

CanCommit© was programmed in Microsoft Access© through the collaborative efforts of Salmo Consulting Inc, E2 Environmental Alliance Inc., TERA Environmental Consulting (Alta.) Ltd., and Alliance (here-after referred to as the "Design Team"). In order for CanCommit© to be readily updated, it was divided into two components: a "front-end" which includes the database program, reports, and forms, and a "back-end," which includes the commitment records and tables. Data (back-end) updates were forwarded to users via e-mail or disk to ensure the most current information available from the database was utilized. When required, program changes were provided to users through "front-end" updates.

The program was designed to be user-friendly with as many drop-down menus and help messages incorporated as possible (Fig. 2). The breakdown of data into required and non-required fields ensured a base level of essential information was included for the purposes of systematic database queries and representative search results. Required fields also ensured that pertinent source and reference information were recorded for due-diligence in tracking the status of a commitment. The relevant data fields that were accessible under the "Commitment Information" tab (Fig. 2) are illustrated in the Commitment Data Form (Fig. 3). This form was for data entry or revision, and was not accessible for changes in the read-only state; only the Database (DB) Manager had the authority (and the responsibility) to maintain this information via the Commitment Data Form. A brief description of the meaning and contents in each field follows. Required fields are denoted in bold font.

Each commitment entered into the system was automatically assigned a unique number or "commitment code." The primary category for commitment data classification was "topic," which referred to a

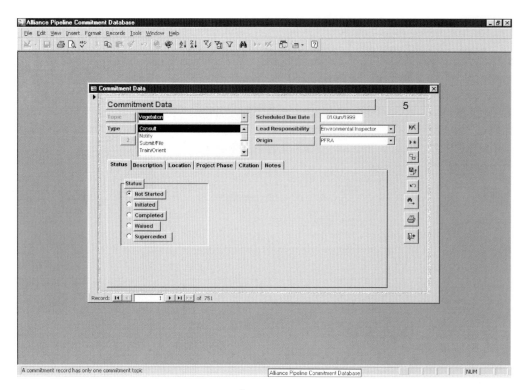

Fig. 3. CanCommit© "Commitment Data Form."

discipline or resource that required protection (such as vegetation, wildlife, heritage sites), that related to contingency measures for emergencies, or health and safety, or was associated with the handling of wastes and other hazardous materials. The "topic" was selected from a drop-down list and a record could not be saved until a topic was selected. "All" was selected if a commitment was general in nature and pertained to all topics, or "Other" if the topic was not one specified in the drop-down menu.

The commitment "type" field allowed multiple entries from the drop-down menu. The "type" of commitment indicated to the user the nature of the commitment such as notification or consultation with external groups, preparation or submission of applications or reports, and monitoring, sampling or mitigation. The number under the "type" box (Fig. 3) indicated how many "types" had been selected.

The dates entered into the "scheduled due date" field were dates that were pre-assigned to various phases of construction (for example, Winter 1999/2000 construction program, Commissioning, In-service). In many cases, one commitment would apply to various phases of construction. In these instances, the earliest possible due date was selected.

The "lead responsibility" drop-down menu consisted of various Alliance departments (for example, Alliance Environment, Alliance Land, Alliance Engineering), as well as consultants and construction personnel. The Environmental Inspector was the default selection in the "lead responsibility" field as these individuals represented Alliance's environmental presence at the construction level.

"Origin" of the commitment identified the group or regulatory agency that identified the commitment (for example, NEB, other regulators, landowners, or resource users). Alliance was the default selection in the "origin" field as most commitments were the result of promises made to regulatory agencies, specifications for environmental protection measures, or commitments made by senior Alliance representatives at the public hearings or open houses.

The status of implementation of a commitment was identified under the "Status" tab (Fig. 3). The default selection was "not started." The selection of any other "status" (for example, initiated or waived) required the input of a reference citation, which was entered into the fields located under the "citation" tab. This information included the source document reference, date, and page numbers.

The "description" tab contained the verbatim commitment text taken from the original source document. Any additional comments relevant to the commitment (such as other related commitments or other desired information to assist in database queries) was entered under the "notes" tab.

The "location" to which a commitment applied was referenced in various ways with respect to the level of detail required. For example, a commitment that referred to a specific location was identified by a Kilometer Post and pipeline segment, whereas broader commitments could be applicable to all locations within one or several provinces. Facility types and/or names as well as land features and geographic names were also used to identify the location of a specific commitment.

Multiple selections from the "project phase" field were allowed as various commitments could pertain to different phases of construction. The "activity" field allowed for multiple choices of project activities from a drop-down menu (for example, clearing, erosion control, facility construction). The default selection was "all," meaning that the commitment pertains to all construction activities.

Data-entry processes
Quality assurance
A data-entry protocol was developed for the identification and review of environmental commitments for the initial data input into CanCommit©. Commitments were initially identified and marked in source documents. This marked source document, along with any pertinent references or notes were maintained as original records in a central location.

In the initial data-entry phase, the required database fields (as denoted by bold text above) were entered and saved prior to the entry of any additional information. A commitment number was assigned by the program and was written in the source document margin. A report was then generated for each commitment, including the assigned commitment number, commitment text, source document, and topic. Data-entry forms containing location data and other non-required database fields were appended to the report, and a reviewer verified the information against the source documents.

The designated reviewer then identified the appropriate selections for each of the non-required fields on the data-entry forms. These forms were then checked by a secondary reviewer to confirm the appropriate information was identified. A note (N/A) was made where a field was deliberately left blank. The information contained on the data entry forms was then entered under the respective commitment in the database. Ideally, all fields were entered to support queries, even where not required by CanCommit© program design.

Quality control
A data-entry quality control report including all fields was printed out for independent review. Commitment summary reports were then provided to a secondary reviewer to confirm the appropriate information was identified and all required revisions were made. Final record approval for CanCommit© was designated once all required revisions from the secondary record review were completed.

Data management — Roles and responsibilities
The Database (DB) Manager was responsible for maintaining, updating, revising, and backing-up CanCommit© in the Alliance Calgary office. Sources of revisions were reports or submissions prepared by the environmental inspectors, resource specialists, or Alliance personnel, or information resulting from ongoing consultation and correspondence with regulators and stakeholders. The DB Manager was responsible for maintaining the database and forwarding updated copies of the CanCommit© back-end to the program users on a regular basis via computer disks, CDs or e-mail transmissions.

Users maintained a read-only copy of CanCommit© on their computers for reference and querying purposes. The program users were responsible to ensure that their database was current with the most recent version of the back-end and/or front-end information forwarded by the DB Manager. Typically, the users of the database were also the personnel implementing the commitments at the field level. These users (environmental inspectors, consultants, etc.) were responsible for communicating any changes in status of a commitment for which they were the "lead responsibility" to the DB Manager for incorporation into the master database. The Canadian Environmental Inspection Reporting System (CanEIRS©) included a data field for reference to a specific CanCommit© commitment code and the documentation of any pertinent information related to the status of that commitment (Fig. 4). These activity inspection reports were submitted daily to the DB Manager.

Training
A training program was implemented by the Design Team for Alliance environmental staff on the use and maintenance of CanCommit©. The Environmental Manager and Supervisor of Environmental Inspection were trained on the utilization of database searching and reporting capabilities and guided on how to implement the tool into the Environmental Inspection Program. The DB Manager was trained on the structure of the database, how to maintain the data, and how to provide technical assistance and data to the program users.

Training sessions were also conducted for approximately 22 environmental inspectors on the CanCommit© applications that related to their responsibilities at the field level. CanCommit© User Guides (Salmo et al., 1999) were provided for additional reference and trouble shooting in the field. Follow-up questionnaires were circulated to the environmental inspectors to procure their thoughts on the commitment database and its functionality at the implementation level. This survey was distributed towards the end of the construction period.

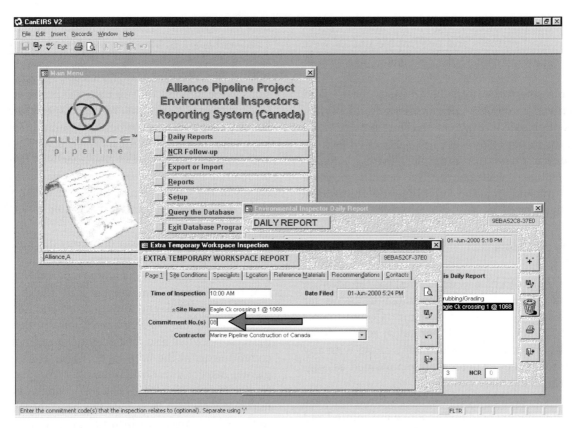

Fig. 4. CanEIRS© data entry field for communication of CanCommit© status data to database manager.

Results

The initial data entry and quality assurance/quality control (QA/QC) processes for the construction of the CanCommit© database was ongoing over a three-month period. Approximately 6000 unique records were identified and entered into CanCommit©. The back-end of the database was downsized from the master database to a working database that contained commitment information related to the Alliance environment department, the environmental inspectors, construction personnel and resource specialist consultants. This database downsize eliminated over 1500 commitments and reduced searching and reporting time.

All non-standard commitment information from the regulatory and approval process period was centrally located with searching and reporting capabilities. However, the majority of the commitments made subsequent to the initial regulatory period (i.e., during construction) were not incorporated into the database as was originally expected. The manhours required for the upkeep and maintenance of CanCommit© as a current reference tool were underestimated. As a result, the database became a compliance tool that was referenced mostly at the outset of a construction spread or phase and again as that construction phase neared its completion. The original objective of continual communication of current commitment information to and from the DB Manager and the environmental inspectors, consultants, resource specialists and construction personnel was not fully achieved due to timing constraints of all parties. The database was therefore not used as an up-to-date referenced tool.

The database was an effective searching and reporting tool for commitment information; however, searching and reporting activities often took long periods of time (at times in excess of an hour to generate a report) due to the size of the database. Reports generated from the database could be in excess of standard printer capacities. A strong understanding of the searching techniques and capabilities was required for consistent commitment results. These skills were generally acquired through practice or from prior database knowledge or familiarity. CanCommit© was found to be most useful to the environmental inspectors as they were introduced to their respective construction spreads, particularly during training periods when support was readily available. The environmental inspector feedback through the de-briefing questionnaire identified that the tool was too cumbersome and time consuming for utilization on a regular basis in the field.

CanCommit© provided an assurance level to management that the Environmental Compliance Management Program was functioning properly as commitments were being followed-up. CanCommit© provided a central and permanent record for due-diligence purposes.

DISCUSSION

The original design objectives for CanCommit© to be utilized on a regular basis by environmental inspectors and other users and maintained with current information were not fully obtained for various reasons. The underestimation of the time requirement for the upkeep of information in the database was one reason why this objective was not completely met. As many of the commitments applied to various stages of construction, the status was constantly changing. Additionally, the objective to continue with the entry of commitment data into the construction and post-construction phases was not achieved. In part, this was reflective of the type of commitment information generated during construction. These commitments were more efficiently tracked by traditional methods (such as lists or spreadsheets) as they were typically standard industry practices or special measures implemented over relatively short time frames. Also, those persons responsible for implementing the commitments at the field level were the same individuals conducting the consultation with local regulatory agencies and other stakeholders. This situation varied from the initial regulatory and approval phases that were completed prior to the involvement of any field-level personnel who would eventually be responsible for the implementation of the commitments.

A more thorough understanding of the searching and reporting capabilities of the database was attainable through practice or through general familiarity with database programs. Another reason all of the design objectives were not met was an overestimation of the computer skill levels of the environmental inspectors, and the underestimation of available field time to practice conducting database searches and becoming more familiar with the software. Basic computer skill set levels of the users should be clearly defined from the project outset and all those participating in the training of the software should have a base level of computer knowledge. The success of the program could have been enhanced by the provision of ongoing training in the field and software and hardware support.

CanCommit© was designed to complement the environmental inspection reporting system (CanEIRS©), although this objective was not sufficiently communicated and reinforced during the training and reporting phases. The transfer of commitment status information was intended to be provided to the CanCommit© database (DB Manager) via the CanEIRS© reporting window illustrated in Fig. 4. This communication of information was not consistent amongst the inspectors. Paper copies of commitment reports were distributed from the central database to the lead environmental inspectors on each spread, who in turn communicated back any relevant status information on the report sheets. This method successfully achieved the end results, although the means of information transfer were not those outlined in the objectives of the software program.

The "down-sizing" of the database to a working copy proved to benefit the management applications, but was too late into the project to benefit the environmental inspectors. Opinions were already formed regarding the utility of the database on a regular basis at the field level. The search times and the report generation times were expedited following the omission of commitments irrelevant to the Alliance Environmental department, as well as those commitments that had been waived or superceded in status.

The main objectives and the impetus behind the software development were to create a tool that would allow for the tracking of non-standard commitments, provide a permanent record of commitment implementation and identify commitments made by planning and management staff to the field level. These objectives were clearly met with CanCommit©. Although not updated and used regularly during the construction phase of the project, the database served as an assurance tool that commitments made in pre-construction phases of the project were being implemented in the field and tracked in a central location.

Future alternatives to the provision of the electronic database tool to the environmental inspectors may be to transfer pertinent site-specific commitment information into a more traditional tool (such as environmental alignment sheets). These sheets may be easily referenced on a daily basis at the field level and the changes in status may be communicated via the inspection reporting system. The database could be provided to the lead environmental inspector who would be designated as responsible to communicate the status of the commitments that are more globally related to the spread, or to the project in general.

CONCLUSION

The development of CanCommit© was a worthwhile endeavor, however, the tool was found to be more effective for use by management than by those who were implementing the commitments at the field level. These results varied from the objectives identified during the program design period; however, the desired objectives were still achieved through modified means.

The main objective of the design of the electronic tool was to provide a means of assurance that all commitments made during the regulatory and approval processes were properly implemented during the linear facility construction and operation. The design of CanCommit© certainly achieved these objectives and will continue to serve as a due-diligence tool through the construction phase and into the operations phase of the Alliance Pipeline project. It provided a sense of assurance to project managers that commitments were being consistently tracked and followed-up, which indicated the functionality of the overall Environmental Compliance Management Program. CanCommit© served well as both a planning and cross-referencing exercise, and will serve as a permanent record for Alliance.

With the implementation of modifications based on lessons learned during the original trial use of CanCommit©, the system has many applications that would be relevant to a variety of projects. Sufficient software training to individuals with a specified base level knowledge of computer systems is essential. Clear communication of expectations and protocols during the training period to those who will be using the system and implementing the commitments would enhance the utility of the database at all levels.

ACKNOWLEDGEMENTS

The authors wish to acknowledge Dr. Brian Zelt of E2 Environmental Alliance Inc. for his technical expertise and doses of originality in the CanCommit© program design. Appreciation is extended to the many members of TERA Environmental Consultants (Alta.) Ltd., in particular Jon Stuart-Smith, for the endless hours dedicated to the data entry process to transform an idea into a functional tool.

REFERENCES

Alliance Pipeline Limited Partnership. 1997a. Environmental Alignment Sheets. June 1997. Volume VI-A.

Alliance Pipeline Limited Partnership. 1997b. Environmental Plans. Volume V. NEB Facilities Application.

Alliance Pipeline Limited Partnership. 1997c. Environmental and Socio-Economic Impact Assessment. Volume IV. NEB Facilities Application.

Alliance Pipeline Limited Partnership. 1998. Designed Watercourse Crossings (Mainline and Laterals) Plans. Response to Direction of the NEB (T1871).

National Energy Board. 1998a. Comprehensive Study Report in the Matter of Alliance Pipeline Ltd. on behalf of the Alliance Pipeline Limited Partnership. GH-3-97.

National Energy Board. 1998b. Reasons for Decision. Alliance Pipeline Ltd. on behalf of the Alliance Pipeline Limited Partnership. GH-3-97.

National Energy Board. 1998c. Certificate of Public Convenience and Necessity GC-98. Governor in Council Approval. December 3 1998 by Order in Council P.C. 1998-2176.

Salmo Consulting Inc., E2 Environmental Alliance Inc. and TERA Environmental Consultants (Alta.) Ltd. 1999. Alliance Pipeline Limited Partnership Canadian Environmental Commitments Database User Guide.

BIOGRAPHICAL SKETCHES

Melissa Pockar, PBiol

Environmental Analyst, Alliance Pipeline Ltd., 400, 605-5 Avenue S.W., Calgary, AB T2P 3H5, Canada

Melissa Pockar graduated with a Bachelor of Science degree in Environmental Systems from the University of Lethbridge and joined Alliance Pipeline Ltd. in 1999. One of Ms. Pockar's responsibilities includes the "Database Manager" role for the CanCommit© system. Ms. Pockar has had previous experience in environmental and reclamation planning in the coal mining industry, and has related experience in the agricultural research sector.

Paul Anderson, MSc, PBiol

Manager, Health, Safety & Environment, Alliance Pipeline Ltd., 400, 605-5 Avenue S.W., Calgary, AB T2P 3H5, Canada

Paul Anderson, is the Manager of Health, Safety & Environment at Alliance Pipeline Ltd. and is responsible for managing health, safety and environmental affairs in both the US and the Canadian portions of the pipeline project. Paul has a Bachelor of Science degree in Biology from the University of Waterloo and a Master of Science degree in Watershed Ecosystems from Trent University.

Terry Antoniuk, PBiol., RPBiol

Principal, Salmo Consulting Inc., 230, 323-10 Avenue S.W., Calgary, AB T2R 0A5, Canada

Terry Antoniuk, the Principal of Salmo Consulting Inc., is a Professional Biologist registered in the provinces of Alberta and British Columbia. Mr. Antoniuk has more than twenty-two years experience in biological studies and research, environmental assessment and mitigation, and public involvement in federal, provincial, and territorial jurisdictions across Canada, and internationally. One of Terry's specialties is cumulative effects assessment; he also manages interdisciplinary teams and designs and implements biophysical inventories, effects monitoring programs, and environmental protection plans.

Right-of-Way Environmental Stewardship Bibliographic Database

Susan M. Tikalsky and John W. Goodrich-Mahoney

There is now a significant body of research on environmentally sensitive approaches to right-of-way (ROW) management. Utility ROW managers would find a great use for a comprehensive reference that will compile and organize relevant ecological ROW information from a wide variety of sources. Such a reference can serve as a basis for complex technical decisions and can help prepare managers for public and regulatory information requests. Comprehensive, organized, and accessible information can assist ROW professionals in their efforts to manage environmental concerns before these concerns unduly complicate, delay, or halt ROW development. This effort will produce a comprehensive bibliographic database pertaining to environmental stewardship on ROWs. Beyond keyword searches for title and author, unique search capabilities of this database feature an ability to search the entire abstract and to search for specific subject matter by selecting among the nearly 100 ROW-specific coded fields. Each of the approximately 800 entries is coded for subjects of interest to ROW siting and maintenance professionals. Because of this extensive coding, users can refine their searches to review the available literature in a very specific area of interest. This user-friendly, searchable, and sortable database will be produced on CD-ROM.

Keywords: Bibliography, database, environment, right-of-way, stewardship

INTRODUCTION

Reliability concerns, together with an accelerating demand for energy and increasing difficulty in siting and maintaining utility rights-of-way (ROW), bring increased importance to sensitive land-management practices. Utility managers are faced with the difficult choice of siting facilities away from population centers and exerting increased pressure on natural areas, publicly-owned lands, and open space. When this occurs, the siting of a utility ROW is brought into the public arena for debate over the environmental consequences of corridor development and management. It is critical that ROW managers have the best scientific information available — to serve as a basis for their technical decisions on ROW performance and for communications with the public, company executives, and in regulatory proceedings.

METHODOLOGY

The primary sources of entries for this database are the Biological Abstracts© and Dialog© databases. The reference sections and bibliographic listings in many of the documents located through the database searches also were reviewed and additional entries identified. Following each search, the abstracts were examined to assess relevancy, and whenever possible, the full text of the selected articles was examined to produce a comprehensively coded entry.

Typically the abstract is presented as it appears with the article. When entries did not include abstracts, a brief summary was written or excerpted from the full article.

The coding hierarchy was established after review and comment by energy industry ROW professionals.

SCOPE OF THE BIBLIOGRAPHIC DATABASE

The entries for this EPRI bibliographic database encompass a vast array of studies, strategies, and ap-

Environmental Concerns in Rights-of-Way Management: Seventh International Symposium
J.W. Goodrich-Mahoney, D.F. Mutrie and C.A. Guild (editors)
© 2002 Elsevier Science Ltd. All rights reserved.

proaches to the numerous issues facing those responsible for the environmental management of utility ROWs. All entries in this database address some facet of utility corridor design, siting, construction, or management with regard to environmental concerns. (Human biological or cultural impacts are not included.) Because so many topics are relevant to utility corridors and their impacts, this database contains over 800 entries. Since the needs of individual users will vary greatly, the database was made as inclusive as practicable. The extensive search capabilities of the database are designed to help users sift through entries and to assemble an individualized bibliography to meet specific needs.

Entries were limited to those references accessible to the user through the public domain. A great many of the database entries reflect work done in the past 10 years; however, age was not a filtering factor, and many important early studies and historically interesting articles are included. Most entries are from journal articles, but some relevant books, proceedings, and technical reports identified in the search process are included in the database.

SEARCH FEATURES

Users can search the database with keywords or can filter on coded fields. Each article presented as a result of a database search contains numerous identifying characteristics. In addition to having the entire abstract and title keyword-searchable, each entry in the database has been extensively coded to produce specific results from a hierarchical search request. The information displayed falls into two groupings: *Standard Citation Information* and *ROW Environmental Elements*.

The *Standard Citation Information* (see Table 1) includes the identifying information necessary to complete a reference: title, author(s), abstract, name of publication, date of publication, volume/issue, and page numbers. In addition, this grouping contains an indication of whether or not the article holds peer-reviewed status.

The second grouping, *ROW Environmental Elements*, (see Table 2) contains identifying information from the coding scheme developed specifically for the specialized needs of ROW professionals. The coding scheme

Table 1. Standard citation information

Category	
Author(s)	Searchable by last name
Title	Searchable in keyword search
Abstract	Searchable in keyword search
Date of publication	Searchable by year
Peer reviewed status	Searchable by status — yes, no, unknown
Name of publication	Included in output, but not searchable
Volume/issue, page numbers	Included in output, but not searchable

Table 2. ROW environmental elements — database fields (categories, subcategories, and characteristics)

Category	Subcategory	Characteristics
Environmental Subject	Wildlife	Mammals
		Birds
		Fish/aquatics
		Reptiles/amphibians
		Insects/arthropods
		Land invertebrates
		Threatened/endangered species
	Collisions and electrocutions	Yes/no
	Vegetation	Plant succession
		Invasive species
		Native/non-native species
		Threatened/endangered species
		Community composition
		Habitat (forage/cover)
		Species-specific study
		Agriculture
		Other*
	Water	Water quality — ground
		Water quality — surface
		Flow/permeation — ground
		Flow/permeation — surface
	Soil	Physical condition (compaction, density, temperature)
		Chemistry
		Disturbance/erosion
	Biodiversity	Fragmentation
		Edge effect
		Corridors as habitats
		Corridors as travel routes
Habitat		Wetland
		Forest (all woodlands)
		Riparian area/stream
		Desert (arid and semi-arid)
		Agricultural
		Tundra/permafrost
		Urban/residential
		Grassland (includes all types of prairie)
		Shrubland
		General
	Other*	
Geographic Regions		Twenty seven world-wide geographic regions, and one code for unknown/not applicable
Techniques and Impacts	Management Technique	Revegetation
		Fire
		Chemical treatment
		Mechanical treatment
		Multiple use
		Other*
	Siting/Management Issues	Cost
		Siting/design
		Public relations

Table 2. (continued)

Category	Subcategory	Characteristics
		Regulatory/legal
		Construction
		O&M/monitoring/training
Focus of Study		Quantitative
		Qualitative
		Process/Methodology
		Overview/Perspective

*"Other" fields are not searchable, but will appear in the output, including the text that was written in for other.

contains five primary code *categories*, which are further divided into eight searchable *subcategories*. Selecting on one or more of the 79 searchable characteristics can further refine subcategory information requests. A description of each of the primary code *categories* and *subcategories* is presented below.

CODES

A guiding principle of the coding process was to avoid inferences and allow the user to explore the implications of a study's findings. For example, the construction of any ROW is likely to disturb soil, but unless a study directly explored the nature or consequence of that disturbance, the article was not assigned the "soil disturbance" characteristic. An abstract accompanies each entry, but as originally written some were not informative enough to provide a full understanding of the article's contents. All articles that offered insubstantial abstracts, as well as most of the other database entries, have been coded following an examination of the complete document.

The following describes each of the five primary coded categories, and their subcategories. Each subcategory description identifies the number of characteristics associated with it. For further information on the characteristics, see Table 2.

Environmental study subject

All features of the ROW or study-site environment that are detailed in each article have been coded in this section of the database. An entry has been given a code for each topic it covered. For articles specific to ROWs, all coding relates to a ROW's impact or potential impact on the flora, fauna, and physical characteristics of the area.
- *Wildlife* — Six of the database's seven wildlife *characteristic* codes refer to the specific type of animal discussed. The remaining *characteristic* includes references to specific wildlife management issues for endangered/threatened species.
- *Collisions and electrocutions* — Each article was reviewed for information on bird or mammal collisions and/or electrocutions identified in the study.
- *Vegetation* — Nine *characteristic* codes were established for studies relating to floristic characteristics ranging from invasive species to wildlife habitat.
- *Water* — Studies relating to water were coded into four *characteristics* as relevant to surface water or ground water and with respect to their water quality or to flow/permeation.
- *Soil* — Entries that included soil studies were coded into three *characteristics*: physical condition, soil chemistry, or disturbance/erosion.
- *Biodiversity* — This subcategory allows the user to explore four *characteristics* of biodiversity issues that are known to significantly affect the ecology of an area. Articles coded with these *characteristics* focus on the role of ROW corridors in promoting or inhibiting biodiversity of both flora and fauna in terms of habitat (preference and avoidance behavior), movement (disease transmission and exchange of genetic material), producing edge effects, and increasing fragmentation.

Habitat

Each entry has been assigned to at least one of ten habitat *characteristics*. Because the habitat type of the ROW itself is typically that of early successional herbaceous or shrubby vegetation, it is the habitat surrounding the ROW that is coded. For non-ROW entries, the habitat type is that in which the study took place. Obviously, habitats are rarely discrete entities; to the extent that the article indicates overlap, it has been coded for all habitats mentioned.

Geographic region

Entries were assigned one of 28 geographic codes. Code numbers 1–27 correspond to geopolitical boundaries shown on the map that is built into the database. An article was assigned to the "0" category if a geographic area wasn't specified or if it discusses a concept rather than a location, voices an opinion, or presents a methodology. Occasionally, entries report the results of literature searches. In such cases, numerous locations often are only touched upon; thus, the entry is coded "0." However, if a few substantive case studies are included, the relevant geographic codes have been applied.

Techniques and impacts

Practitioners use many techniques — mechanical and chemical — to obtain the desired management goals. Additionally, ROWs are used occasionally for secondary purposes (snow storage). The following subcategories indicate the extent of the literature available on these practices.
- *Management Technique* — When an article describes an approach to managing the vegetation of a study area or ROW (hypothetical or actual), it has been assigned to this *subcategory*. The five *characteristic* fields allow the user to become more specific in the search with regard to using revegetation, fire, chemical or mechanical treatments, and multiple uses.

– *Siting/Management Issues* — Entries coded under this heading specifically address six *characteristics* that include basic areas of concern in the siting and operations of utility ROWs: cost, siting/design, O&M/monitoring/training, public relations, regulatory/legal, and construction.

Focus of study

Most entries in this database have a quantitative component. Many others offer a different approach to presenting information. To assist users who wish to isolate a particular approach, the articles have characteristics coded as quantitative, qualitative, process/methodology, and overview/perspective.

CONCLUSION

This EPRI project will produce a tool that will enable ROW environmental managers to search a wide range of scientific literature in a very efficient manner. This information will increase the credibility and effectiveness of ROW environmental stewardship efforts.

NOTE

Subsequent to this presentation, the final product for this project has been produced (EPRI, 2001).

REFERENCE

EPRI. 2001. Right-of-Way Bibliographic Database, Version 1.0. Product #1006380.

BIOGRAPHICAL SKETCHES

Susan M. Tikalsky
Resource Strategies, Inc., 22 N. Carroll St., Suite 300, Madison, WI 53703, USA, phone 608-251-5904, e-mail tikalsky@rs-inc.com

Ms. Tikalsky has spent over twenty years as an environmental scientist, manager and communicator in the energy industry. She has held positions as a state regulator and has served as corporate spokesperson and director of environmental, research and development, and corporate communications departments in an energy company. Ms. Tikalsky presently serves the energy industry as a management consultant. The strength of her work lies in the identification, organization, management, and resolution of complex or controversial issues. Ms. Tikalsky holds two MS degrees from the University of Wisconsin-Madison.

John W. Goodrich-Mahoney
EPRI, 3412 Hillview Avenue, Palo Alto, CA 94304, USA, phone 202-293-7516, e-mail jmahoney@epri.com

Mr. Goodrich-Mahoney is a Program Manager in EPRI's Environment Department, and manages the Department's right-of-way and water quality research programs. He is responsible for the development and management of research to help reduce surface water, vegetation and other regulatory compliance costs for the energy industry, and to help promote beneficial uses of rights-of-way. Mr. Goodrich-Mahoney holds a BS in chemistry and geology from St. Lawrence University and a MSc in geochemistry from Brown University.

Part V
Cultural

Off Right-of-Way Mitigation of Archaeological Sites: A Pipeline Case Study from Pennsylvania

James D. Bloemker

Mitigation of archaeological sites can be a costly endeavor in a pipeline company's effort to comply with environmental regulations. Avoiding a site is often impractical and excavating it may appear to be the only solution. Unfortunately, these traditional mitigation measures are too often the only solutions considered when dealing with archaeological sites. This paper discusses traditional mitigation measures and presents an alternative strategy to archaeological site treatment. Off-site, or off right-of-way, mitigation is a creative mitigation alternative that can be applied to some sites if conditions and circumstances permit. Within the body of this paper, an example of an alternative mitigation measure utilized by Williams Gas Pipeline–Transco on the construction of a recent gas pipeline across Pine Breeze Island in Pennsylvania is discussed.

Keywords: Section 106 compliance, creative mitigation, Clemson Island prehistoric culture

INTRODUCTION

Section 106 of the National Historic Preservation Act (NHPA) requires that federal undertakings, projects that involve a federal agency's licensing, permitting or funding, must be evaluated for their effects on significant cultural resources and take those effects into consideration when planning and constructing projects. According to the NHPA, a significant cultural resource is one that is listed on or eligible for listing on the National Register of Historic Places. Cultural resources are identified by conducting surveys, commonly called Phase I investigations, using subsurface site discovery techniques or visual observations where the ground is free of vegetative cover. Located archaeological resources are evaluated for their significance by excavating test units (Phase II investigations) and any project effects to cultural resources determined to be eligible for the National Register must be mitigated (Phase III investigations).

Thirty-four years after the NHPA was enacted, compliance with Section 106 has become routine for federal government agencies and businesses which get licenses, permits or funds from them; so too have the methods for mitigating significant cultural resources. Standard forms of mitigation for architectural resources are Historic American Building Survey/Historic American Engineering Record (HABS/HAER) documentation. For archaeological resources, mitigation routinely involves either avoidance or excavations conducted according to National Park Service regulations. Too often the decision on mitigation options is left up to agency regulators, however, they represent only a part of the Section 106 compliance process (Crisler et al., 1999).

Sometimes the standard treatment measures for mitigating cultural resources are not the best measures for the situation at hand. For example, HABS/HAER documentation often results in expensive over-documentation of historic resources. National Park Service guidelines for architectural documentation emphasize reserving this measure for resources of national significance (Barrett, 1999). In some cases neither avoidance nor excavation of an archaeological site is the right mitigation option. A better solution may be what is referred to as "mitigation banking" or "off-site mitigation." Off-site mitigation involves excavating an ar-

*Environmental Concerns in Rights-of-Way
Management: Seventh International Symposium*
J.W. Goodrich-Mahoney, D.F. Mutrie and C.A. Guild (editors)
© 2002 Elsevier Science Ltd. All rights reserved.

chaeological site, or site portion, in place of the site (portion) affected by a federal undertaking; essentially one site is traded for another. Underlying precepts of this mitigation strategy are that the sites have comparable research values and that they are located in close proximity to one another (Bloemker, 1994).

Nonstandard solutions such as that described above have become known as "creative mitigation alternatives" or "innovative mitigation measures." The Section 106 process is meant to be flexible and allow for creative mitigation solutions. This policy was explicitly stated in the 1986 regulations implementing Section 106 [at 36 CFR 800.3(b)] and is implicitly implied in the recently revised version. In fact, Tom King (1999), the guru of Section 106, says that when complying with Section 106 almost anything is permitted beyond what is legally prohibited. What 106 participants can agree to for mitigation solutions is limited only by their imagination (King, 1999).

The following discussion examines the development of a creative mitigation alternative that was proposed by Williams Gas Pipeline–Transco (WGP–Transco) to mitigate an archaeological site affected by the construction of a buried natural gas pipeline on its Leidy Line System in Pennsylvania. The Leidy Line consists of 310.60 km of pipeline connecting the Leidy Storage Field in Clinton County, Pennsylvania to the New York City market area. The Leidy Line currently consists of three parallel pipelines: Line "A" a 60.96 cm (24-inch) diameter pipeline built in 1959; Line "B" a 60.96 cm (24-inch) diameter pipeline built in 1971; and Line "C" a 76.20 cm (30-inch) diameter pipeline built in 1991. Lines "A" and "B" were built prior to the need to comply with the NHPA and a cultural resources survey for Line "C" failed to locate site 36 Ly 263 within the right-of-way. The site was located during the cultural resources investigations required prior to the installation of Line "D." Avoidance of the archaeological site by horizontal directional drilling was not possible because of the sharp drill angles caused by the steep mountain slopes on either side of the island.

WGP–Transco proposes to increase capacity on the Leidy Line System by adding 25.75 km of 106.68 cm (42-inch) diameter pipeline in the summer of 2001 and that will be parallel to three existing pipelines on the right-of-way. The 25.75 km section of proposed construction crosses undulating terrain with average elevation peaks of 774.19 m above mean sea level (msl) and valley lows of 170.69 m msl. Pine Breeze Island, on which archaeological site 36 Ly 263 is located, lies in one such valley. Before specifics on the project are provided, a review of the background natural and cultural history of the region and the island is necessary.

THE RESOURCE BASE

Natural history

Pine Breeze Island is a long, narrow island located in Pine Creek approximately 8.05 km north of the confluence with the West Branch of the Susquehanna River in central Pennsylvania's Lycoming County. Harrisburg, the state capitol of Pennsylvania, is located 104.61 km south of the island. Pine Breeze Island is roughly 1.61 km long and 304.80 m in maximum width (Fig. 1). Archaeological site 36 Ly 263, a Late Woodland Clemson Island occupation, is located at the northern portion of the island.

Pine Breeze Island is located in an east–west trending escarpment known as the Allegheny Front. The island lies between the Ridge and Valley physiographic province to the east and the Appalachian Plateau to the west. Bedrock in the region ranges from the Lower Ordovician (oldest) to the Lower Pennsylvanian (youngest). The project area is at the southern terminus of the Wisconsin glacial advance.

The geomorphology of Pine Breeze Island (Fig. 2) was determined by mapping and profiling the sediments found in 7–6 m long trenches excavated to a depth of three meters. Examination of the sedimentological and pedological features of the main strata produced a provisional stratigraphy that indicated several cycles of alluviation, soil development and erosion that were critical to the archaeological site's interpretation.

From most recent to oldest, four layers of stratigraphic sequences were established:

– Unit I, dating from 2000 BP to the present, is found in the upper 100 cm on the west side of the island and to 50 cm on the east side. Sediments of this unit include a sod/humus horizon overlying compacted silts and fine soils. Soils of this unit have been classified by the United States Department of Agriculture (USDA) as loamy Udifluvents.
– Unit IA soils date from 2000 BP to 3000 BP. They contain the first buried surface which is between 50 and 70 cm thick with slightly thicker depths to the north. This unit contains well bedded silts and sands and thin discontinuous bands of lamellae. Lamellae are laterally thin red bands of oxidized and clay enriched soil particles that formed as episodic flood events of Pine Creek ceased.
– Unit II soils contain the second buried surface and date from 3300 BP to 5000 BP. This unit is between 1.25 and 1.75 m thick and consists of Cambic soils with impermeable gleyed clay at its base.
– The deepest soil sediments of Unit III date to 5000 BP and older. This soil consists of medium to medium coarse sands that directly overlay the basal gravels that form the base of the island (Doershuk, 1991).

Given that the top of soil sequence Units IA and II preserve an A horizon, it has been determined that the island's soils became stable around 4200 BP and 2100 BP which corresponds to the Late/Terminal Archaic and Early Woodland cultural periods of Pennsylvania prehistory.

Palynological studies are the basis for describing the paleoenvironment of the project area. Between 8000 and 6500 BC a transition from a Pleistocene to

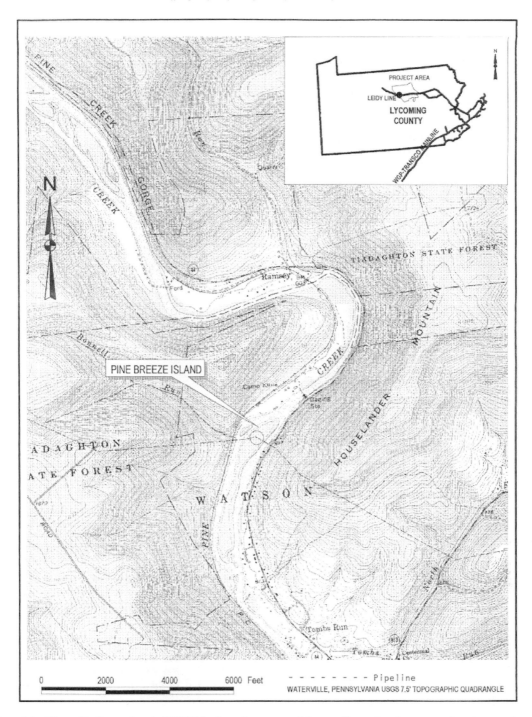

Fig. 1. Portion of the Waterville, Pennsylvania USGS 7.5 min series topographic map illustrating the proposed project area location (adapted from Doershuk, 1991).

a Holocene climate occurred. The transition resulted in the reduction of open grasslands to the expansion of boreal forests consisting of spruce and pine trees with some oaks. A warming trend called the Atlantic climatic episode occurred around 6500 to 3100 BC. Changes included an increase in precipitation and a spread of mesic forests. Mesic forests consisted of hemlock and oak trees with oak dominant by 5000 BC. The Sub-boreal climatic episode of between 3100 and 800 BC brought a warm, dry period to the region. The environment consisted of hickory forests with an expansion of grasslands. Around 810 BC to AD 1000 the region of Pine Breeze Island experienced an increase in moisture and cooler temperatures. This climatic period was known as the Sub-Atlantic episode. It more closely resembled the environmental conditions found in central Pennsylvania today. The modern climate of the project area can be described as humid continental. The project area has an average summer temperature of 21.66°C and an average winter temperature of 1.66°C. Annual precipitation in the project area averages 104.14 cm.

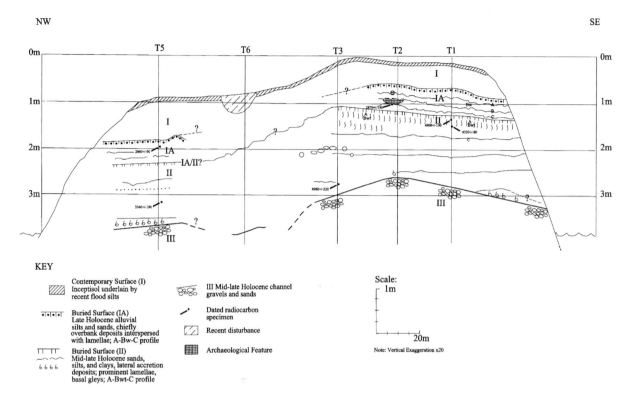

Fig. 2. Geomorphological reconstruction of sedimentary deposits of Pine Breeze Island based on data obtained from seven trenches excavated across the island (Doershuk, 1991).

Cultural history

The cultural history of central Pennsylvania follows a general pattern identified for most of the Middle Atlantic region of the United States. The earliest period of prehistory is known as the Paleoindian and dates from 14,000 BC to 8000 BC. Archaic period cultures superceded the Paleoindian around 8000 BC and lasted until around 2100 BC. A period of Transition (2100–900 BC) exists between the Archaic and Woodland periods. Like the Archaic before it, the Woodland period (900 BC–AD 1000), is subdivided into the Early, Middle and Late periods. The Late Woodland is the final period of prehistory in Pennsylvania before the arrival of Europeans into the region. It lasted from 1000 to 1600 AD and includes the Clemson Island culture whose archeological remains have been located on Pine Breeze Island.

Clemson Island cultures were composed of agriculturalists who occupied major portions of the Susquehanna River valley from approximately AD 800 to AD 1200. In addition to cultivating domesticated plants, Clemson Island people exploited resources in a manner similar to preceding cultures. Clemson Island sites are known to be present in an 18-county "core area" of central Pennsylvania and which is defined in the State Historic Preservation Office's (SHPO) management plan for this prehistoric period (Hay, 1987).

Recognized Clemson Island site types include hamlets associated with burial mounds, hamlets with no mound association, temporary camps and special purpose camps. Clemson Island hamlets are believed to be clustered according to kinship ties and associated with a single, mound-related hamlet. Later Clemson Island sites show a shift from hamlet settlements to villages at which time the use of burial mounds ceases. The Clemson Island cultural period is defined by archaeologists primarily from the excavations of village sites. The Pine Breeze Island site is unique in that it is located between the large village sites to the south and the smaller hamlet sites in the uplands to the north (Bergman, personal communication).

Toolkits used by Clemson Island folk were similar to those used by other Late Woodland cultures of the Middle Atlantic region. Artifact assemblages include broad triangular projectile points, net sinkers and fish hooks and seed grinding equipment. Pottery, however, distinguishes the Clemson Island culture from other Late Woodland period sites. The definitive pottery includes a variety of punctated ceramics with cord-marked or fabric-impressed motifs on the outer surface of the vessel (Fig. 3) (Stewart, 1988).

PROJECT SPECIFICS

The Clemson Island site was found through the initiation of Phase I investigations for WGP–Transco's proposed Leidy Line "D" expansion. Subsurface testing techniques included the excavation of 90 shovel test pits (STPs) at 15 m intervals, the placement of 14 auger probes and 7 backhoe trenches and the digging of 107 m^2 of hand dug units. The Phase I survey was

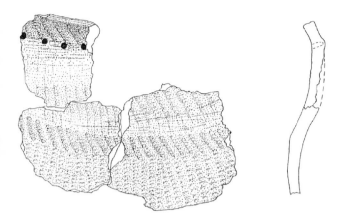

Fig. 3. Pottery is the distinguishing artifact that separates Clemson Island sites from other neighboring Late Woodland sites. Definitive Clemson Island pottery includes a variety of punctated ceramics with cord-marked or fabric-impressed motifs. An example is illustrated here (Hay, 1987).

spread over a 60.96 m wide by 198.12 m long corridor south of the existing "C" pipeline and a 60.96 m by 99.06 m work space area located at the east half of the island north of the existing "A" pipeline. The total area of Phase I survey coverage equaled 1.74 ha for a 198.12 m long by 22.86 m wide construction corridor. The corridor width was narrowed to 15.24 m after the Phase I survey results were revealed.

Survey results yielded 741 artifacts of which only one diagnostic artifact, the remnants of a Levanna projectile point, was located in the proposed pipeline trench. Additionally, only one feature was encountered and it was found to be 45.72 m south of the proposed pipeline. An additional piece of data that proved to be important in the planning of future archaeological investigations on the island was the fact that 89% of the artifacts found during the Phase I survey were located in the upper 50 cm of Unit IA soils (Doershuk, 1991). Based on the Phase I survey results that documented the site as a Clemson Island occupation, the SHPO recommended testing of the site to determine its National Register eligibility.

A plan for conducting Phase II excavations was presented to the SHPO in March 1994. The proposal had three objectives: (1) verify the low density of artifacts observed during Phase I investigations in the area southeast of the proposed pipeline by excavating 4 — 1 m × 2 m blocks within the 15 m construction right-of-way south of proposed "D" line on the eastern half of the island and east of Phase I trench 3; (2) verify the probable disturbance resulting from previous construction of pipeline "C" by excavating 3 — 1 m × 1 m test units within a 7.5 m right-of-way north of proposed line "D" between Phase I trenches 5 and 3 and (3) excavate 15 — 2 m × 2 m blocks and 15 — 1 m × 1 m test units interspersed equally between Phase I trenches 5 and 3. This field strategy was modified slightly, with SHPO permission, based on early field results and a request by WGP–Transco engineers for a slightly wider construction right-of-way of 16.76 m.

Phase II testing resulted in the recovery of 157 pieces of lithic debitage, 9 lithic tools and 670 ceramic sherds. Predominate were ceramic types related to the Clemson Island phase of occupation with Owasco and Shenk's Ferry components, neighboring Late Woodland cultures, identified less often in the ceramic assemblage. Aside from the unique setting and nature of the site, another item which made 36 Ly 263 unusual in the eyes of the SHPO was that it occupied a zone at the northern periphery of the Clemson Island culture and the southern periphery of the Owasco culture (Bergman, personal communication). Levanna points were the only diagnostic lithic artifact recovered from the excavations. Seven features were identified during Phase II testing. The features tended to be shallow and void of large artifact concentrations which was most likely due to flood water scouring that truncated the pit bottoms. Positive and negative test unit results of the Phase II excavations reinforced the Phase I survey investigations that showed the more significant portions of the site to be located south of WGP–Transco's right-of-way (Bergman et al., 1997).

Except in a small area at the southwest end, the results of the archaeological investigations in the existing pipeline and proposed construction right-of-way were disappointing from a research perspective. Testing at these locations confirmed Company representative suspicions that the site was disturbed by previous construction activity related to the installation of the three other pipelines or that the right-of-way was void of cultural material. Using data from the Phase I investigations (Doershuk, 1991) the artifact densities in the areas to be affected by the pipeline construction show reasons for the suspicions. A total of 15 — 3 m by 3 m units were dug across the island of which 7 were located in project affected areas. Artifacts from 8 of the units outside the affected areas numbered 588, whereas artifacts from the 7 units inside the affected areas equaled only 72. The numbers spoke loudly for attention to this revealing statistic.

A Phase III data recovery strategy that was based on the results of the Phase I and II investigations was developed in consultation with the SHPO in September 1997. The strategy involves excavating a single 50 m^2 block to be placed where Phase II artifacts were concentrated between coordinates N450 E460 and N465 E475 on the western side of the island (Fig. 4) (Bergman, 1997). Another key component of the data recovery plan involves donating Pine Breeze Island to a government agency of the Commonwealth of Pennsylvania for their use as an archaeological/nature preserve. WGP–Transco acquired 17 of the island's 17.4 ha (0.4 ha with three summer cabins was not purchased) specifically with the mitigation on Pine Breeze Island in mind. The donation of the island will protect the archaeological site from future development. A clause in the deed transferring the island allows for expansion

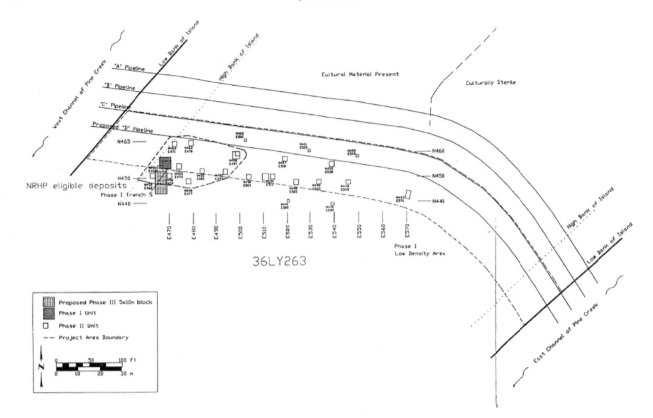

Fig. 4. The distribution of Phase I, II, and III excavation units across the construction right-of-way of Pine Breeze Island (Bergman, 1997).

of additional pipelines on the north side of the right-of-way where archaeological investigations demonstrated that little or no effects to the site would occur.

Company representatives were convinced that the better portions of the site were located to the south of the right-of-way and that any mitigation excavations to be done by the Company should be conducted there. When the island was purchased WGP–Transco was able to offer what, through Phase I and II investigations, appeared to be the better portions of the site in exchange for less excavations in the construction right-of-way. The strategy proved to be acceptable to the SHPO and the Federal Energy Regulatory Commission, the federal agency WGP–Transco must obtain a license or certificate from to build the pipeline, since a legal document (Memorandum of Agreement) was signed authorizing the strategy to be implemented.

CONCLUDING REMARKS

Circumstances for WGP–Transco at Pine Breeze Island were ideal for the employment of a creative mitigation alternative involving off right-of-way mitigation. The proposed 106.68 cm (42-inch) "D" Line crossing of the island by horizontal directional drill in order to avoid archaeological site 36 Ly 263 was not possible because of the sharp drill angles caused by the steep mountain slopes on either side of the island. The results of Phase I and II investigations demonstrated that the greater portions of the archaeological site were south of WGP–Transco's right-of-way. By offering Pine Breeze Island (the cost of the island is about third of what it will cost to excavate the 50 m^2 block) and the archaeological site it contains to the Commonwealth of Pennsylvania, WGP–Transco will be able to avoid more extensive and costly excavations in the right-of-way in exchange for the SHPO's opportunity to conduct research on a significant archaeological site at a more leisurely pace than compliance archaeology permits. It appears that this mitigation solution is a win-win situation for both the SHPO and WGP–Transco.

ACKNOWLEDGMENT

Dr. Chris Bergman of BHE Environmental, formerly 3D/Environmental, was instrumental in providing the background data on Pine Breeze Island. I would also like to thank him for taking the time to critique this paper.

REFERENCES

Barrett, Brenda. 1999. A framework for creative mitigation. Cultural Resource Management, 22: 27–30.

Bergman, C.A. November 1997. Phase III Mitigation Plan of the Pine Breeze Island Site (36 Ly 263) for TGPL's Market Link Project in Lycoming County, Pennsylvania. Unpublished report prepared by 3D/Environmental, Cincinnati, OH.

Bergman, C.A., K. Russell, M. Purtill, Phillip LaPorta, R. Moeller, and J. Herbstritt. 1997. Phase II Testing of the Pine Breeze Island Site (36 Ly 263). Unpublished report prepared by Kemron Environmental Services, Cincinnati, OH.

Bloemker, James D. 1994. Mitigation alternatives for some sites in the Delaware Valley. Christopher Bergman and John Doershuk, eds. Journal of Middle Atlantic Archaeology, 10: 181–188.

Crisler, J.K. Mitchell and C. Gluchman. 1999. Working together for better solutions. Cultural Resource Management, 22: 3–5.

Doershuk, J. 1991. Phase I Cultural Resources Report on Transcontinental Gas Pipe Line Corporation's Pine Breeze Island Portion of the 6.7 Mile Leidy Storage Line "D" in Lycoming County, Pennsylvania. Unpublished report prepared by 3D/Environmental, Cincinnati, OH.

Hay, C. 1987. A Management Plan for Clemson Island Archaeological Resources in the Commonwealth of Pennsylvania. Pennsylvania Historical and Museum Commission, Bureau of Historic Preservation. Harrisburg, PA.

King, T.F. 1998. Cultural Resource Laws and Practice: An Introductory Guide. AltaMira Press, Walnut Creek, CA.

Stewart, M. 1988. Clemson's Island Cultures in the West Branch Valley: Phase II and III Archaeological Investigations of 36 Un 11. Unpublished report prepared by The Cultural Resource Group, Louis Berger and Associates, East Orange, NJ.

BIOGRAPHICAL SKETCH

James Bloemker
Williams Gas Pipeline–Transco, PO Box 1396, Houston, TX 77251, USA

James Bloemker is a Senior Environmental Scientist specializing in archaeology and employed by Williams Gas Pipeline–Transco, a position he has held since 1991. Prior to 1991 he was a Staff Archaeologist at the West Virginia State Historic Preservation Office. Mr. Bloemker is a Registered Professional Archaeologist.

Part VI
Wildlife

Rights-of-Way Management in Support of Biological Conservation

Valentin Schaefer

Rights-of-way provide greenway linkages between fragments of natural areas. Within an urban context, rights-of-way provide connectivity between parks and other protected areas, creating larger breeding populations, better gene flow, larger food webs and greater opportunities for plants and animals to help each other reproduce. Managing rights-of-way to increase biodiversity produces a more effective natural network. The Green Links Project, started in 1995, focuses on strengthening ecological connectivity within Greater Vancouver. This urban area is on the Fraser River Estuary and delta, a major stopover point along the Pacific Flyway for migratory birds. The Fraser River itself is home to the world's largest salmon run. Biological conservation here is of international importance. BC Hydro and BC Gas have worked in partnership on the Green Links Project to take a regional approach to biological conservation through plantings of native vegetation and putting up bird and bat boxes with student and community participation in utility corridors, backyards, and balconies. Issues and problems that had to be addressed included ownership of lands, trees under power lines, and city maintenance crews cutting new plantings.

Keywords: Greenway, biodiversity, urban, connectivity, fragmentation

INTRODUCTION

Rights-of-way play an important role in connecting ecosystem fragments. Within British Columbia there are 71,000 km of rights-of-way, much of which can be incorporated into strategies for biological conservation. They can be used to join small areas of habitat and enable them to function as larger, more viable ecosystems.

Connectivity in biological conservation is especially important in urban areas. Cities often develop in unique and valuable natural ecosystems such as estuaries and floodplains because of their strategic importance or suitability for agriculture. In British Columbia, Canada, examples are the Fraser River estuary in Vancouver and the Garry Oak Woodland in Victoria. The location of the ecosystem fragments in cities can make them far more important than their limited size and disturbed plant life might initially suggest (Schaefer, 1994).

The loss of natural habitat due to urbanization is considerable. In the United States from 1959 to 1982, 22 million acres (8.7 million hectares), of land were converted to urban and other developed land uses, an increase of 45% (Heimlich and Anderson, 1987). In the Lower Mainland of British Columbia, about 70–80% of the original wetland habitat has been lost because of dyking in support of urban and agricultural development (Fraser River Estuary Study Steering Committee, 1978). Land that has been converted to agriculture or other similarly cultivated landscapes has only 50% of the average net primary productivity of original forested ecosystems and urban landscapes have only 13% (Healey, 1997).

Within cities the remaining natural areas exist as fragments of habitat. With fragmentation, wildlife population sizes decrease, local extinctions increase, and isolation interferes with recolonization by native species (MacArthur and Wilson, 1967; Opdam, 1991; Wilcox and Murphy, 1985).

Connectivity is one approach to solving the problem of habitat fragmentation. Connecting islands of habitat enhances species richness of breeding birds (MacClintock et al., 1977), increases seed dispersal of climax trees by wildlife (Levenson, 1981), and maximizes the

Environmental Concerns in Rights-of-Way Management: Seventh International Symposium
J.W. Goodrich-Mahoney, D.F. Mutrie and C.A. Guild (editors)
© 2002 Elsevier Science Ltd. All rights reserved.

biological diversity of fragmented habitats by promoting critical breeding densities and an increased gene pool in populations (Harris, 1984). Rights-of-way can therefore provide for larger breeding populations, better gene flow, more complex food webs and symbiotic relationships. Any degree of connectivity adds value to ecosystem fragments, with the benefits increasing with the increased degree of connection (Rudis and Ek, 1981).

The strength of network connectivity is determined by the number of networks in a region, the links within the networks and the number and sizes of the nodes of habitat fragments (Linehan et al., 1995). Utility rights-of-way can be used to form a significant part of this network. It is clear from metapopulation theory that the greater the number of patches and the closer they are, the better the colonization (Hanski and Gilpin, 1993). Seed dispersal and wildlife movements are key processes in determining the survival of metapopulations. Such movements are directly related to the connectivity of the landscape (Schippers et al., 1996). Increasing biodiversity within the connecting corridors to more closely match that of the fragments they connect increases their usefulness.

The value of connectivity in forestry conservation is generally accepted (Harris, 1984), even though it is difficult to predict if a link will function as expected (Simberloff and Cox, 1987). Wildlife movement through corridors between habitats has been demonstrated for small and large mammals (e.g., Wegner and Merriam, 1979) and for birds (e.g., Dmowski and Kozakiewicz, 1990).

In wilderness forest ecosystems, connectivity is established by deliberately leaving connections of unlogged stands between nodes. In urban systems, links usually need to be created from disturbed habitat. This can be accomplished through community stewardship and through the planning efforts of landscape architects to increase the structural complexity of vegetation. Having a corridor of adequate dimensions may in itself be insufficient (Henein and Merriam, 1990). The best wildlife corridors have good vegetation layering, a diversity of plant life and a minimum of invasive alien species (Thorne, 1993).

Greenways

Landscape architects and city planners usually refer to corridors of green space as greenways. The value of greenways to ecosystem function has been actively cultivated and several case studies have been described such as the southwestern Wisconsin environmental corridors and the Boulder greenways (Smith and Hellmund, 1993). A greenway that also serves to biologically connect two ecosystem fragments is classified as a third generation greenway (Searns, 1995).

Rights-of-way typically are used as first and second generation greenways by providing people corridors with multiuse pathways and beautifying the community. With some sensitivity to the use of native annuals, perennials, and shrubs they can act as third generation greenways, contributing significantly to the conservation of biodiversity. In urban areas the plantings can be done as a stewardship activity with the local communities and can be expanded to include backyard habitat and balconies in adjacent residential neighborhoods.

The Green Links Project

Green Links is a project of the Douglas College Centre for Environmental Studies and Urban Ecology. It was started in 1995 to establish and maintain ecological corridors in urban areas throughout Greater Vancouver. Its primary objective is to increase the ecological value and biodiversity of urban wildlife habitats and green spaces. There are two secondary objectives: to increase the value of green spaces to the community, and; to reduce ongoing maintenance, thereby decreasing monetary costs in terms of vegetation management in rights-of-way or environmental costs involving the demand for pesticides and potable water associated with managing home gardens.

Fragmentation of urban wildlife habitats is becoming a particular problem for Greater Vancouver. Over the past 10 years the region has grown to 2 million people, with the population expected to reach 3 million people by the year 2025 (GVRD, 1995). This population growth will exacerbate the already advanced state of fragmentation in the Lower Mainland's wildlife habitats.

Links are created by plantings of native vegetation (primarily shrubs and perennials). The plantings are done in partnership with schools, service clubs (e.g., Optimists, Rotary), youth groups (e.g., scouts, guides), municipal and regional governments (e.g., City of Burnaby, Greater Vancouver Regional District) and nongovernmental environmental organizations (e.g., Vancouver Natural History Society, Burns Bog Conservation Society).

METHODS

The first step in Green Links was to create a composite map of Environmentally Sensitive Areas (ESAs) in the municipalities of Greater Vancouver. The result — a regional perspective. Maps of ESAs were produced by individual municipalities without any attempt to standardize the process or the criteria. Thus, coming up with a regional map was the first step in the defragmenting process.

Three initial Green Links demonstration projects were immediately apparent from the composite map. Each offered opportunities to connect several fragments at once. In particular, rights-of-way were examined for their potential to connect several important islands of habitat with each other and the "continent," which in this case is the surrounding wilderness on the urban outskirts.

Measuring biodiversity

A baseline measure of biodiversity was established for comparison in 10 years. The 10 years seemed appropriate to provide time for the plantings to establish themselves as communities and to allow time for the wildlife populations to respond.

Two measures of biodiversity are being used to evaluate the effectiveness of Green Links. One is the Simpson's Index (D) of biodiversity where:

$$D = 1 / \sum p_i^2.$$

In this formula, p represents the proportion of species i in the total sample of individuals. The arbitrary target is to use Green Links to raise the average biodiversity Simpson's index for birds (used as an indicator of overall biodiversity) by 30% over the 10-year horizon.

A second measure is the presence of indicator species. The assumption is that encouraging such species with more sensitive habitat requirements encourages more numerous species with less sensitive requirements. Examples of such indicator species may be Dark-eyed Junco (*Junco hyemalis*) for ground cover, Rufous-sided Towhee (*Pipilo erythrophthalmus*) for shrub layer, Rufous Hummingbird (*Selasphorus rufus*) for nectar-producing flowers, and Yellow Warbler (*Dendroica petechia*) for tree canopy habitat.

Increasing connectivity

The following activities are being used to increase connectivity:
1. Restore native plant species, depending on the conditions and requirements of each specific site. Various planting programs possible are:
   - *butterfly and hummingbird gardens* (herbaceous, low-growing, plants)
   - *multiple species habitats* (incorporating shrubs such as native beaked hazelnut for Steller's Jay and squirrels)
   - *green space maintenance* (ground cover and shrubs to out compete nuisance species)
2. Remove invasive species such as Scotch broom
3. Construct multiuse pathways
4. Cleanup refuse
5. Create interpretive sites
6. Conduct community workshops and erecting bird and bat boxes

Green Links is working on three demonstration sites — two are rights-of-way (Coquitlam and Surrey) and one is through a matrix of residential development (Burnaby). The Coquitlam right-of-way (Fig. 1), is the prototype and is the one being reported on here.

The Coquitlam right-of-way approximately 5 km long and 100 m wide and 128 ha in area. The land is primarily owned by the City. We work with BC Hydro to ensure plantings meet required height and species requirements for the utility. Green Links increases connectivity between five ecosystem fragments in this area:

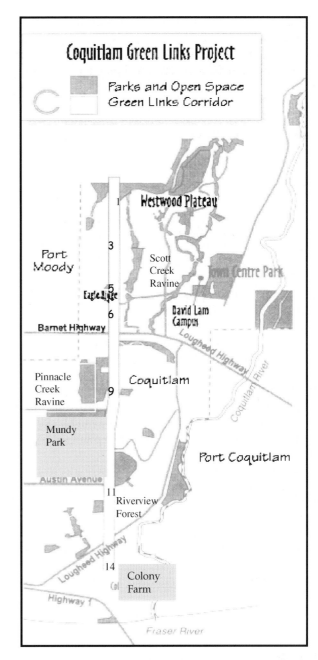

Fig. 1. The right-of-way in Coquitlam, British Columbia, used as the first Green Link Project demonstration site. The patches of green space it connects are shown in dark grey. The corridor links Scott Creek Ravine, Pinnacle Creek Ravine, Mundy Park, the Riverview Forest and Colony Farm. Sites 1, 3, 5, 6, 9, 11, and 14 are indicated as reference for the biodiversity index.

- *Colony Farm* (65 ha), a habitat of field and marsh adjacent to the Coquitlam River, was recently made into a Greater Vancouver Regional District Park in recognition of its natural value.
- *Riverview Lands* (31 ha), possesses an ecologically unique arboretum stewarded by the Riverview Horticultural Society and contains every tree species known to grow in British Columbia.
- *Mundy Park* (192 ha), a large municipal park containing a remnant forest and small lake with bog habitat, is on the top of a moraine marking the boundary

between the Burrard Inlet and Fraser River watersheds.
- *Pinnacle Creek ravine* (59 ha), part of the Chine Heights escarpment running between Coquitlam and Port Moody.
- *Scott Creek ravine* (8.5 ha), part of the Westwood Plateau and an important urban salmon stream of the Coquitlam River watershed.

RESULTS

Baseline biophysical inventories were completed for 14 sites along the right-of-way in 1996 (Schaefer and Sulek, 1997). The utility corridor supports 121 species of plants and 51 species of birds. The Simpson's biodiversity index for birds from the 14 sampling sites along the 8 km corridor (Fig. 2) ranges from 7.4–16.74, with an average of 10.7. The biodiversity index of 13.0 found at a site second closest to the wilderness fringe of the corridor was set as the 10-year target.

Implementation activities in 1996/1997 in the Coquitlam corridor included planting native vegetation at 7 locations with about 3000 plants covering approximately 6 ha, water channeling (1 location), removal of invasive species (Scotch broom, Himalayan blackberry, purple loosestrife) at 3 locations, and a plant salvage of 500 trees at 1 location.

A community survey of 2300 households resulted in 327 respondents, the majority of which appreciated the green spaces in their community and supported habitat enhancement work.

In 1996/1997, the Green Links Project as a whole, encompassing all three corridors, resulted in the planting of about 6000 plants covering about 10 ha, presentations to 2500 school children, construction of 350 bird and bat boxes, community workshops attended by about 250 people, 70 newspaper and magazine articles, a symposium attended by 120 people representing over 30 organizations, 100,000 seeds of perennials mailed to households, over 1000 plants salvaged and the implementation of a native plant propagation program in 4 schools. About 600 people attended 12 public speaking engagements, and a Green Links Display was present at over 20 public events.

As of the year 2000, five years into the Green Links Project, 25,000 plants have been planted with the involvement of 3700 school children and community members.

Problems

The Green Links plantings were done in consultation with BC Hydro and City of Coquitlam. Unfortunately there was little or no communication with the maintenance staff who actually cut the vegetation on the sites with brush cutters or flail mowers. Such communication also proved difficult to establish because of staff changes in the mowing crews. A number of plantings were cut before we implemented a procedure to protect the perimeters of the plantings with logs. Signs are also used but are somewhat impractical because of vandalism.

DISCUSSION

Wildlife corridors are most effective if the plant species in the corridor approximate those in the green spaces they connect. Although rights-of-way are frequently "green" and perhaps even lush with vegetation, their biodiversity is typically low. The disturbance created in constructing the right-of-way favors the establishment of a few pioneer plant species. These can perpetuate themselves because the periodic cutting of the site to control the pioneers keeps the system perpetually in an early successional stage.

Planting more native species will encourage more use of the rights-of-way as a corridor by more species. In this way Green Links allows for the greater use, movement, dispersal, and interaction of plants and animals between more fragments of urban wildlife habitat. The stronger the connection, the greater the ecological value of the habitat. This should result in an increase of biodiversity to higher levels.

It will be difficult to scientifically prove a cause-and-effect relationship between the enhancement of rights-of-way and increased biodiversity. There are no controlled conditions in this natural experiment. Habitat is being destroyed, or enhanced, in other places used by the wildlife, perhaps even in wintering areas found in other countries. Conversely, positive changes may be due to conservation measures taken elsewhere. These changes may override the impacts of the Green Links project in ways which are unknown

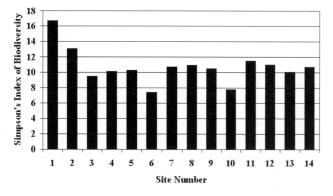

Fig. 2. Simpson's Index of biodiversity calculated for 14 sampling sites along the Coquitlam corridor. Site 1 is the farthest north next to the wilderness fringe. The five patches of green space (environmentally sensitive areas) joined by the utility corridor are represented by Sites 4, 5, and 6 adjacent to Scott Creek Ravine, Sites 7 and 8 adjacent to Pinnacle Creek Ravine, Site 10 adjacent to Mundy Park, Site 11 adjacent to the Riverview Lands, and Site 14 in Colony Farm Regional Park.

or cannot be measured Nevertheless, the relationship between increased biodiversity in corridors and its significance in connectivity is well established and should not be ignored.

ACKNOWLEDGEMENTS

The Green Links Project was established through the efforts of Gary Holisko of BC Hydro and Sharon McCarthy of BC Gas. Mart Sulek of Douglas College played an important role in building community partnerships. The Coquitlam Link is being created in partnership with Rick Daykin, David Palidwor and Mike Nihls of the City of Coquitlam Parks Department. Many thanks to the community members and participants of youth employment programs who made Green Links possible.

REFERENCES

Dmowski, K. and M. Kozakiewicz. 1990. Influence of a shrub corridor on movements of passerine birds to a lake littoral zone. Landscape Ecology, 4: 99–108.

Fraser River Estuary Study Steering Committee. 1978. Fraser River Estuary Study: Habitat, Vol. 4. Victoria, BC.

Government of Canada and Province of British Columbia. Greater Vancouver Regional District. 1995. Livable Region Strategic Plan. Burnaby, BC.

Hanski, I. and M. Gilpin. 1991. Metapopulation dynamics: Brief history and conceptual domain. Biological Journal of the Linnean Society, 42: 3–16.

Harris, L. 1984. The Fragmented Forest. University of Chicago Press, Chicago.

Healey, M.C. 1997. Prospects for Sustainability: Integrative Approaches to Sustaining the Ecosystem Function of the Lower Fraser Basin. Westwater Research Centre and the Sustainable Development Research Institute of the University of British Columbia, Vancouver, BC.

Heimlich, R.E. and W.D. Anderson. 1987. Dynamics of land use change in urbanizing areas: Experience in the Economic Research Service. In: Sustaining Agriculture Near Cities. Soil and Water Conservation Society, Ankeny, IA.

Henein, K. and G. Merriam. 1990. The elements of connectivity where corridor quality is variable. Landscape Ecology, 4: 157–170.

Levenson, J.B. 1981. The southern mesic forest of southwestern Wisconsin: Species composition and community structure. Milwaukee: Contributions to Biology and Geology, Milwaukee Co. Public Museum.

Linehan, J., M. Gross, and J. Finn. 1995. Greenway planning: Developing a landscape ecological network approach. Landscape and Urban Planning, 33: 179–193.

MacArthur, R.H. and E.O. Wilson. 1967. The Theory of Island Biogeography. Princeton University Press, Princeton.

MacClintock, L., R. Whitcomb, and B. Whitcomb. 1977. Evidence fore value of corridors and minimization of isolation in preservation of biotic diversity. American Birds, 31: 6–16.

Opdam, P. 1991. Metapopulation theory and habitat fragmentation. Landscape Ecology, 5: 93–106.

Rudis, V.A. and A.R. Ek. 1981. Optimization of forest island spatial patterns: Methodology for analysis of landscape pattern. In: Forest Island Dynamics in Man-Dominated Landscapes. R.L. Burgess and D.M. Sharp, eds. New York: Springer-Verlag.

Schaefer, V.H. and M. Sulek. 1997. Green Links: Connecting Ecosystem Fragments in the City. Volume 1: Coquitlam Demonstration Project. Douglas College, New Westminster, BC.

Schaefer, V.H. 1994. Urban Biodiversity. In: Biodiversity in British Columbia. L. Harding and E. McCullum, eds. Environment Canada. pp. 307–318.

Schippers, P., J. Verboom, J.P. Knaapen, and R.C. van Apeldoorn. 1996. Dispersal and habitat connectivity in complex heterogeneous landscapes: an analysis with a GIS-based random walk model. Ecography, 19: 97–106.

Searns, R.M. 1995. The evolution of greenways as an adaptive urban landscape form. Landscape and Urban Planning, 33: 65–80.

Simberloff, D. and J. Cox. 1987. Consequences and costs of conservation corridors. Conservation Biology, 63–71.

Smith, D. and P.C. Hellmund. 1993. Ecology of Greenways: Design and Function of Linear Conservation Areas. University of Minnesota Press, Minneapolis.

Thorne, J.T. 1993. Landscape ecology. In: Ecology of Greenways: Design and Function of Linear Conservation Areas. D. Smith and P.C. Hellmund, eds. University of Minnesota Press, Minneapolis.

Wegner, J.F. and G. Merriam. 1979. Movements of birds and mammals between wood and adjoining farmland habitat. Journal of Applied Ecology, 16: 349–357.

Wilcox, B.A. and D.D. Murphy. 1985. Conservation strategy: The effects of fragmentation on extinction. American. Naturalist, 125: 879–887.

BIOGRAPHICAL SKETCH

Valentin Schaefer
Executive Director, Douglas College Centre for Environmental Studies and Urban Ecology, P.O. Box 2503, New Westminster, BC V3L 5B2, Canada

Valentin Schaefer has researched urban biodiversity for 15 years. He has been using utility rights-of-way to establish connectivity in Greater Vancouver since 1996. He received his BSc from McGill University in Montreal, MSc from the University of Toronto and PhD from Simon Fraser University in Burnaby, BC. His awards include the BC Minister of Environment Award for Environmental Education and BC Society of Landscape Architects Award for Community Service.

Wildlife Use of Riparian Vegetation Buffer Zones in High Voltage Powerline Rights-of-Way in the Quebec Boreal Forest

Francis Bélisle, G. Jean Doucet, and Yves Garant

TransÉnergie operates a network of 33,000 km of high voltage powerlines. Approximately 6000 riparian vegetation buffer zones are located in these rights-of-way (ROWs), mostly to protect stream habitat. A field study was conducted in 1998 and 1999 to compare spring and summer wildlife activity in riparian vegetation buffers in rights-of-way to that in riparian habitat in adjacent forest. Vegetation structure in buffers consisted of a low stratum with a high herbaceous cover and high stem density of small DBH. Riparian vegetation in adjacent forest was characterized by higher vegetation, and a lower stem density with a higher mean DBH. A total of 49 buffer zones were sampled for vegetation, mammals, and anurans. We captured 1436 individuals from 11 species of small mammals during 10,080 trap-nights over two years. Results show a similar abundance of small mammals in buffers and adjacent forest but there were differences in species composition and species diversity. Pigmy shrew and rock vole, two uncommon species in this region, were captured in both habitats. The presence of black bear, snowshoe hare, ruffed grouse, and porcupine was detected inside vegetation buffers. Anuran and bird vocal activity was similar in buffers and adjacent forest.

Keywords: Buffer zones, small mammals, anurans, birds, biodiversity

INTRODUCTION

TransÉnergie operates a network of 33,000 km of high voltage powerlines and approximately 6000 vegetation buffer zones are located in these rights-of-way, mostly to protect stream habitat. These riparian buffers are made up of woody vegetation strips about 10 m wide, and span the width of the rights-of-way. The majority of these buffer zones were left in place when the ROWs were originally cleared. It was assumed that such buffer zones would protect streams from erosion and siltation while maintaining physical attributes of both aquatic and riparian habitats. The role of these buffer zones for terrestrial wildlife was never evaluated (Deshaye et al., 1996). In recent years, it has been postulated that forested buffer zones in ROWs in the dry boreal forest were a hazard for conductors, often resulting in outages when a forest fire ran underneath the conductors. Rights-of-way have also been suspected of presenting barriers to some species of small mammals (Schreiber and Graves, 1977). Consequently, there was some pressure to remove trees and convert forested buffer zones into permanent shrubby areas. The objective of the study was to compare wildlife activity in riparian vegetation buffers in ROWs to that in riparian habitat in the adjacent forest. Our study focused mainly on the activity and abundance of passerines, anurans, and small mammals.

STUDY AREA

Field work was carried out during two consecutive summers (1998, 1999) in the southern limit of the boreal forest, north of Baie Comeau and Forestville, Quebec (49°20'N, 68°80'W). The study area was about 10,000 km^2. It was located in the Grenville geologic province, which is dominated by igneous rocks, and where deposits are limited, thin, and more important

Environmental Concerns in Rights-of-Way Management: Seventh International Symposium
J.W. Goodrich-Mahoney, D.F. Mutrie and C.A. Guild (editors)
© 2002 Elsevier Science Ltd. All rights reserved.

in valleys. The study area is made up mainly of an uneven plateau broken by the deep valleys of the Manicouagan, Outardes and Bersimis rivers. The altitude varies between 50 and 500 m ASL. The forest vegetation is composed mainly of balsam fir (*Abies balsamea*), black spruce (*Picea mariana*), white birch (*Betula papyrifera*) and, to a lesser extent, trembling aspen (*Populus tremuloides*). Large clear-cuts and burnt areas are also common features of the landscape. Streamside vegetation was characterized mainly by alder (*Alnus* spp.), willows (*Salix* spp.) and other shrubs. Buffer zones were selected from 17 different powerlines of 315 kV (60–90 m wide) and 735 kV (120–150 m wide) based on the vegetation structure in the buffer zones and access from existing roads. A total of 2423 spans were examined to select about 50 suitable buffers contiguous to similar control sites.

METHODS

Study design

We defined buffer zones as the strip of riparian vegetation (about 10 m wide) located on each side of a stream crossing a high voltage powerline ROW (Fig. 1). In order to compare wildlife activity or abundance, each buffer was paired to a control represented by a riparian habitat of the same size located along the same stream in the adjacent and relatively undisturbed forest. Buffer zones spanned the entire width of the ROW. Controls were set at least 150 m from the buffers.

A first group of 10 sites were located north of Baie-Comeau and a second group of 39 sites were located north of Forestville. In these 49 sites, five groups were sampled: vegetation, small mammals, birds, anurans, and mid-size mammals. Sampling took place in August 1998 and 1999 for vegetation, small mammals, and mid-size mammals. Vocal activity of birds and anurans was sampled only during spring of 1999.

Vegetation structure

Vegetation structure was evaluated in 49 sites at 2 sampling stations in both buffer and control zones, using 4 variables. Circular sampling stations (40 m^2) were established on each side of riparian habitat, along small mammal trapping transects. Low vegetation composition (<0.5 m high) was measured using a modified point intercept method (Jonasson, 1988). Using this method, vegetation classes (deciduous shrubs, coniferous shrubs, herbs, bare ground, mosses, and woody debris) were identified at all intersection points within a table grid (50 × 50 cm) containing 36 intersection points. High vegetation composition (>0.5 m high) was determined by measuring diameter at breast height (DBH) of each tree in the sampling station, for 3 diameter classes (0.5–3.0; 3.1–7.0, and >7.0 cm) and 3 vegetation classes (deciduous, coniferous, and snags). Lateral vegetation density was measured using a vegetation profile board (Nudds, 1977) 2 m high by 0.3 m wide divided in 4 rectangles of 0.5 m in height. The percentage of lateral visual obstruction was estimated by an observer standing 15 m north and south of the board. Percentage of obstruction was noted by classes of 20% (0–20; 21–40; 41–60; 61–80; 81–100%) for each rectangle.

Small mammals

Small mammals were trapped in 49 sites using Museum Special traps, Victor Mouse traps (Ecko Canada), and pitfalls (2L plastic containers), distributed along linear transects, parallel to the stream, in the middle of the riparian habitat. Sampling stations were set 10 m apart in such manner as to cover the entire width of the right-of-way. In both buffer and control zones, 16 trapping stations were positioned (8 on each side of the stream) along the transects. One Museum Special trap and one Victor Mouse trap were set side-by-side at each station. One pitfall trap was also set beside

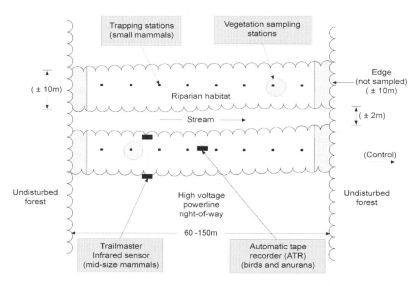

Fig. 1. Study design.

snap traps at each station in 8 sites in 1999. Traps were baited with peanut butter and oatmeal, left in place for 3 consecutive nights, and visited daily. Pitfalls were half filled with water and set with the opening at ground level. Each extremity of the buffer zone between the right-of-way and the surrounding forest was not sampled to minimize edge effect. Small mammals were identified to species level (Banfield, 1977) and total body mass (± 1 g) was determined for each specimen captured. Small shrews were kept to double check identification using dental structure analysis according to Van Zyll de Jong (1983).

Birds and anurans

Vocal calls of birds and anurans were recorded at 8 sites in 1999 using automatic tape recorders (ATR) coupled to a programmable timer. An ATR was set in both buffer and control zones and left in place for 3 consecutive nights. Vocal calls were recorded synchronously in both zones during 3-minute periods distributed between 2 recording sessions, for a total of 15 minutes of listening per day. Field tests conducted in 1998 revealed that ATR registered calls only in short range so that buffer and control can be considered independent. A first recording session occurred in the morning (4h00 and 5h00) and a second one in the evening (20h00, 21h00, and 22h00). Birds and anurans were subsequently identified with their respective vocal calls using reference calls (tapes, CD).

Mid-size mammals

The presence of mid-size mammals in buffer and control zones was assessed in 2 sites in 1998 and 8 sites in 1999 using Trailmaster® infrared sensors (model TM 1500) coupled to a photographic camera (model TM-35). Infrared sensors were left in place for 4 consecutive nights and were installed on one side of riparian habitats, perpendicular to the stream, on an axis covering the entire width of the vegetation buffer zone (10 m). The infrared sensor was placed just above the ground in such a manner as to register each animal passing. A flash slave was used for better quality photography. A bait (peanut butter and oatmeal) was placed on the ground at the half way point (5 m) of the transect during sampling. Infrared sensors were visited daily and data were logged relative to passage counts and pictures taken (number of events, date, and hour).

Data analysis

Comparison analysis between buffer and control zones considered those 2 habitats to be within a complete random block. Data collected in 10 sites in 1998 were first statistically treated to adjust sampling methods and effort for sampling period of 1999. Almost all data from 1998 and 1999 were subsequently pooled and statistically treated.

Data on low vegetation structure were expressed as percent cover by vegetation classes. Data on high vegetation structure were expressed as the number of woody stems/40 m^2 for each vegetation classes and each DBH. Data on lateral visual obstruction were expressed as mean percentage (%) by height levels for north and south sides and for total height of the board using ANOVA. Data on vegetation height were compared using ANOVA (SAS Institute, 1997). Relative abundance of small mammals (captures/100 trap-nights) and total body mass of specimens captured were compared using ANOVA. The Shannon index (Zar, 1984) was used to compare vegetation and small mammal species diversity between buffer and control zones and was calculated as follow:

$$H = \frac{n \log n - \sum fi \log fi}{n},$$

where H is the Shannon index, n is the number of small mammals captured in one stratum, and f is the number of small mammals captured/species in the same stratum.

Bird and anuran calls were computed as number of 3-minute periods with at least 1 call heard for one species. This procedure was established to minimize the bias of counting a high number of individuals for a given species without knowing if calls were emitted by one or many individuals. Vocal activity was expressed as occurrence probability (% of chance for a given species to be heard during a 3-minute period). Data were analyzed for dominant species to compare vocal activity between buffer and control zones using a LOGIT model (McCullagh and Nelder, 1989). Data for mid-size mammals were limited and no statistical analysis was performed. Results are nevertheless presented and discussed on a descriptive basis.

RESULTS AND DISCUSSION

Vegetation structure

The goal of the vegetation sampling done in this study was to establish vegetation variables, relevant to rights-of-way and robust enough to support the discussion of the wildlife sampling results. Vegetation in buffers consisted of a low stratum with a high density of small woody stems and herbaceous cover (Table 1). The vegetation in the adjacent control was characterized by a high stratum with a low stem density and a high mean DBH. In the vegetation stratum >50 cm above ground, there were significantly more small trees and more deciduous cover in the buffer zones than in the forested control. There were more large snags (DBH > 7.0 cm) in the control areas than in the buffer zones. Species richness (woody species) was higher in the control zones. Vegetation ≤1 m in height was denser in the buffer than in the control zones. Overall, the vegetation available to wildlife as cover or food under 1m in height was greater in the buffer zones than in the adjacent forest.

Table 1. Comparison of vegetation structure measured in 1998–1999 (mean ± SD) between buffer and control zones; underlined values are significantly higher (ANOVA, $P < 0.01$, $n = 49$ sites). DBH = diameter at breast height.

	Buffer zones	Control	P value
Low vegetation stratum (<0.5 m high)			
(% of ground cover)			
Coniferous shrubs	1.08 ± 0.83	4.08 ± 0.83	0.0136
Deciduous shrubs	21.86 ± 3.38	20.20 ± 3.38	0.7294
Herbs	<u>55.74 ± 2.97</u>	31.79 ± 2.96	<0.0001
Mosses	7.34 ± 1.72	13.38 ± 1.72	0.0166
Bare ground	7.55 ± 1.99	14.78 ± 1.98	0.0130
Woody debris	6.44 ± 1.70	<u>15.77 ± 1.70</u>	0.0003
High vegetation stratum (>0.5 m high)			
(stems/40m^2)			
All species and DBH	<u>35.29 ± 2.95</u>	23.66 ± 2.95	0.0076
(0.5–3 cm DBH; all species)	<u>32.81 ± 2.93</u>	19.49 ± 2.93	0.0023
(3.1–7 cm DBH; all species)	2.24 ± 0.45	2.51 ± 0.45	0.6778
(>7 cm DBH; all species)	0.23 ± 0.14	<u>1.65 ± 0.14</u>	<0.0001
Coniferous cover (all DBH)	1.05 ± 0.27	<u>2.73 ± 0.27</u>	<0.0001
Coniferous cover (0.5–3 cm DBH)	0.64 ± 0.18	1.17 ± 0.18	0.0386
Coniferous cover (3.1–7 cm DBH)	0.24 ± 0.10	<u>0.74 ± 0.10</u>	0.0008
Coniferous cover (>7 cm DBH)	0.17 ± 0.12	<u>0.82 ± 0.12</u>	<0.0001
Deciduous cover (all DBH)	<u>33.42 ± 3.05</u>	19.53 ± 3.05	0.0023
Deciduous cover (0.5–3 cm DBH)	<u>31.45 ± 2.94</u>	17.62 ± 2.94	0.0017
Deciduous cover (3.1–7 cm DBH)	1.91 ± 0.46	1.35 ± 0.46	0.3819
Deciduous cover (>7 cm DBH)	0.06 ± 0.09	<u>0.56 ± 0.09</u>	0.0003
Snags (all DBH)	0.81 ± 0.18	1.40 ± 0.18	0.0205
Snags (0.5–3 cm DBH)	0.71 ± 0.15	0.70 ± 0.15	0.9608
Snags (3.1–7 cm DBH)	0.09 ± 0.06	<u>0.43 ± 0.06</u>	0.0003
Snags (>7 cm DBH)	0.00 ± 0.04	<u>0.28 ± 0.04</u>	<0.0001
Specific richness			
(Index)			
Shannon	0.60 ± 0.06	<u>1.01 ± 0.06</u>	<0.0001
Vegetation height (m)			
Visual mean height of vegetation in habitat	3.42 ± 0.64	<u>10.31 ± 0.64</u>	<0.0001
Horizontal visual obstruction			
(% of visual obstruction)			
From ground up to 2 m high	71.06 ± 2.48	74.13 ± 2.48	0.3876
Ground to 0.5 m high	<u>56.28 ± 2.74</u>	37.30 ± 2.74	<0.0001
From 0.5 to 1.0 m high	<u>47.44 ± 2.74</u>	36.66 ± 2.74	0.0058
From 1.0 to 1.5 m high	31.66 ± 2.74	30.64 ± 2.74	0.7909
From 1.5 to 2.0 m high	21.40 ± 2.74	23.58 ± 2.74	0.5959

Small mammals

During the summers of 1998 and 1999, we captured 1436 small mammals belonging to 11 species, for a trapping effort of 10,080 trap-nights (all trap types, Table 2). Red-backed vole, woodland jumping mouse, and deer mouse were the 3 most abundant species and accounted for 55% of the total number of small mammals captured. Red-backed vole and deer mouse are relatively abundant species in this region but the high abundance of woodland jumping mouse was unexpected since this species was relatively rare in the same area a few years ago (Bélisle, 1997).

Overall mean relative abundance of 14.36 and 14.02 small mammals/100 trap-nights were similar between buffer and control zones, respectively (ANOVA, $P =$ 0.8121). The similarity of overall relative abundance was unexpected because of the clear difference in vegetation structure between the 2 zones. O'Connell and Miller (1994) have demonstrated that the overall relative abundance of small mammals can remain high in mechanically disturbed sites where some vegetation was left in place, resembling buffer zones in our study.

A species habitat segregation seems to have occurred between the 2 zones. Buffer zones were dominated by woodland jumping mouse (2.83 captures/100 trap-nights), meadow jumping mouse (2.58 captures/100 trap-nights) and meadow vole (2.41 captures/100 trap-nights). The latter 2 species and short-tailed shrew were significantly more abundant in buffers (ANOVA,

Table 2. Comparison of small mammals relative abundance (captures/100 trap-nights) measured in 1998–1999 (mean ± SD) between buffer and control zones; underlined values are significantly higher (ANOVA, $P < 0.01$, $n = 49$ sites).

Species	Buffer zones	Control	P value
Red-backed vole (*Clethrionomys gapperi*)	1.89 ± 0.85	4.97 ± 0.85	0.0003
Meadow vole (*Microtus pennsylvanicus*)	2.41 ± 0.45	0.88 ± 0.45	0.0066
Rock vole (*Microtus chrotorrhinus*)	0.06 ± 0.03	0.02 ± 0.03	0.1679
Deer mouse (*Peromyscus maniculatus*)	1.36 ± 0.38	2.59 ± 0.38	0.0050
Meadow jumping mouse (*Zapus hudsonicus*)	2.58 ± 0.29	0.40 ± 0.29	<0.0001
Woodland jumping mouse (*Napaeozapus insignis*)	2.83 ± 0.56	2.37 ± 0.56	0.4443
Masked shrew (*Sorex cinereus*)	2.00 ± 0.40	2.39 ± 0.40	0.3178
Pygmy shrew (*Microsorex hoyi*)	0.06 ± 0.03	0.03 ± 0.03	0.1594
Water shrew (*Sorex palustris*)	0.09 ± 0.03	0.00 ± 0.03	0.0264
Short-tailed shrew (*Blarina brevicauda*)	1.01 ± 0.13	0.24 ± 0.13	<0.0001
Eastern chipmunk (*Tamias striatus*)	0.08 ± 0.04	0.12 ± 0.04	0.4517
All species	14.36 ± 1.28	14.02 ± 1.28	0.8121

$P < 0.01$). Adjacent control zones were dominated by red-backed vole (4.97 captures/100 trap-nights), deer mouse (2.59 captures/100 trap-nights), masked shrew (2.39 captures/100 trap-nights) and woodland jumping mouse (2.37 captures/100 trap-nights). The abundance of red-backed vole and deer mouse was significantly higher in control areas (ANOVA, $P < 0.01$).

Meadow voles are known to be relatively abundant in habitats such as grassland, herbaceous, and generally disturbed habitats (Grant, 1975, 1971; Alder and Wilson, 1989). According to our results, meadow vole and short-tailed shrew were more abundant in buffers, which contained more herbs than controls. Their relative abundance in this type of disturbed habitat was, respectively, 2.5 and 4 times higher than in a forested habitat. The presence of the short-tailed shrew has been documented in several types of habitat and can be considered a generalist species, often associated to riparian habitat (Banfield, 1977; DeGraaf and Yamasaki, 1999).

Red-backed vole and deer mouse have been associated with more woodland habitat structure (Grant, 1975; Maisonneuve and Rioux, 1998) while some authors have classified them as habitat generalists (Maisonneuve et al., 1996). Our results show that these two species were more abundant in woodland habitat like control zones when compared to a more shrubby and herbaceous habitat like buffer zones in rights-of-way. Consequently, differences in small mammal composition between buffer and control zones could be explained by differences in vegetation structure along the same riparian habitat. These results stress the importance of considering the vegetation structure when explaining species habitat segregation (Jules et al., 1999).

Three relatively rare species were captured in the buffer and control zones. Four specimens of rock vole, one of the rarest small mammals in Quebec and Canada (Banfield, 1977; Beaudin and Quintin, 1991), were captured in both habitats. Five specimens of pygmy shrew, also a very rare species in the area and sometimes mistaken for masked shrew (Banfield, 1977), were also identified in both habitats in 1999. Five specimens of the water shrew, a third relatively rare species in the area, were captured in buffers only, in 1998 and 1999. These results suggest that for rare small mammals species, composition in the buffers is similar to the one in the adjacent forested habitat.

Comparison of mean body mass of the 6 most abundant species revealed no significant difference between buffers and controls (ANOVA, $P > 0.01$). Nevertheless, a tendency can be seen for at least 2 species of voles; red-backed vole and meadow vole, for which mean body mass was higher in buffers. Red-backed vole mean body mass averaged 23.11 vs. 20.04 g in buffers and forested habitats (control) respectively. Meadow vole mean body mass was 25.86 g in buffers compared to 20.18 g in controls (Table 3). Mean body mass values of the more abundant species were similar to those found in the literature for Canada and Quebec (Banfield, 1977; Beaudin and Quintin, 1991). The higher mean body mass found in buffer zones for these 2 species could be associated to a denser herbaceous and generally low stratum vegetation, offering food source and cover for microtines (Birney et al., 1976).

Species diversity of small mammals was significantly higher in buffer than in control habitat (Table 4, ANOVA, $P = 0.002$). The Shannon index is a function of the number of species in a given habitat and the distribution of abundance between those species in the same habitat. Since overall abundance and number of species are similar between the 2 habitats, it appears that the difference is due to the distribution of abundance between species in each habitat. In control zones, 88% of the overall abundance can be explained mainly with values from 4 species while in the buffer zones, relative abundance of 6 species are required to explain the same level of abundance. From this point of view, buffer zones could be considered to have more small mammal diversity than the surrounding forest.

Table 3. Comparison of mean body mass (g) of the more abundant small mammals species captured in 1998–1999 between buffer zones and control (ANOVA, $P < 0.01$, $n = 49$ sites).

Species	Buffer zones	Control	P value
Red-backed vole (*Clethrionomys gapperi*)	23.11 ± 1.35	20.04 ± 0.71	0.0567
Meadow vole (*Microtus pennsylvanicus*)	25.86 ± 1.04	20.18 ± 1.88	0.0178
Deer mouse (*Peromyscus maniculatus*)	17.64 ± 0.61	17.66 ± 0.49	0.9771
Meadow jumping mouse (*Zapus hudsonicus*)	16.03 ± 0.61	14.86 ± 1.22	0.4220
Woodland jumping mouse (*Napaeozapus insignis*)	22.00 ± 0.54	22.39 ± 0.70	0.6712
Masked shrew (*Sorex cinereus*)	3.82 ± 0.39	4.12 ± 0.34	0.5766

Table 4. Comparison of small mammals specific richness (Shannon index) measured in 1998–1999 between buffer and control zones; underlined values are significantly higher (ANOVA, $P < 0.01$, $n = 49$ sites).

	Buffer zones	Control	P value
Specific richness	<u>1.32</u>	1.09	0.0021

Table 5. Comparison of vocal activity (number of 3-minute periods with at least 1 vocal call heard for one given species) for all birds and amphibians heard between buffer and control zones ($n = 10$ sites).

Species	Buffer	Control
Birds		
White-throated sparrow (*Zonotrichia albicolis*)	57	55
Swainson's thrush (*Catharus ustulatus*)	25	31
Common yellowthroat (*Geothlypis trichas*)	30	21
American robin (*Turdus migratorius*)	30	13
Alder flycatcher (*Empidonax alnorum*)	29	4
Magnolia warbler (*Dendroica magnolia*)	18	10
Nashville warbler (*Vermivora ruficapilla*)	17	8
Northern waterthrush (*Seiurus noveboracensis*)	13	11
Red-eyed vireo (*Vireo olivaceus*)	11	8
Winter wren (*Troglodytes troglodytes*)	8	7
Chestnut-sided warbler (*Dendroica pensylvanica*)	5	9
Veery (*Catharus fuscescens*)	5	8
Hermit thrush (*Catharus guttatus*)	5	6
Ruby-crowned kinglet (*Regulus calendula*)	1	7
Yellow-rumped warbler (*Dendroica coronata*)	2	4
Ovenbird (*Seiurus aurocapillus*)	6	0
Lincoln's sparrow (*Melospiza lincolnii*)	4	0
Common nighthhawk (*Chordeleis minor*)	2	1
Least flycatcher (*Empidonax minimus*)	2	1
Solitary vireo (*Vireo solitarius*)	3	0
Black-throated green warbler (*Dendroica virens*)	0	2
Hairy woodpecker (*Picoides villosus*)	1	1
Northern flicker (*Colaptes auratus*)	1	0
Common raven (*Corvus corvax*)	0	1
Dark-eyed junco (*Junco hyemalis*)	0	1
White-winged crossbill (*Loxia leucoptera*)	0	1
Northern parula (*Parula americana*)	1	0
Black-capped chickadee (*Parus atricapilus*)	0	1
American redstart (*Setophaga ruticilla*)	1	0
Anurans		
Spring peeper (*Hyla crucifer*)	38	17
Wood frog (*Rana sylvatica*)	9	1
American toad (*Bufo americanus*)	2	3

Birds

Twenty-four and 23 species of birds were identified, respectively, in the buffer and control zones based on their vocal activity recorded by ATR (Table 5). Eighteen of these species were common to both zones. White-throated sparrow, Swainson's trush, and American robin were the most frequently recorded in both zones. Approximately 60% of birds were recorded 5 or more times in a given habitat (buffer or control). Most birdcalls (70%) were recorded at sunrise. Six species were found only in buffer zones: ovenbird, Lincoln sparrow, solitary vireo, northern flicker, American redstart, and northern parula. The vocal activity of the latter 3 species however was recorded in 1 period only and their presence in buffer zones was considered anecdotal. The Lincoln sparrow, an open habitat species, was detected in 4 periods in buffer zones but never in control zones (Table 6). Occurrence probability of the alder flycatcher, another early-successional habitat species, was almost 3 times greater in the buffer areas but the difference was not statistically significant (Table 6, LOGIT model, $P = 0.097$). In a northern mixed forest landscape, Morneau et al. (1999) measured significantly higher abundance of alder flycatcher in powerline rights-of-way.

If we exclude species that were detected only once, the black-throated green warbler was the only species found only in the control zones. This species is often associated with closed canopy of deciduous or coniferous stands (Thompson and Capen, 1988). The black-throated green warbler was not detected in a powerline ROW of a mixed landscape, but breeding pairs were observed in the edge and interior forest (Morneau et al., 1999).

Among the 8 most common species, the white-throated sparrow, common yellowthroat, magnolia warbler and Nashville warbler form a seral association linked with early succession (regeneration and pole stand) habitats (Thompson and Capen, 1988). Swainson's thrush is generally associated with coniferous stands but it is also observed in dense understory of younger habitat where it often breeds (Gauthier and Aubry, 1995).

The vegetation profile in the buffer zones was characterized by a dense deciduous cover made of poles and saplings. This structure should theoretically provide good breeding and feeding habitat for edge and open habitat species such as the Nashville and

Table 6. Comparison of occurrence probability (percent chance to be heard per 3-minute periods) of the more abundant birds and anurans species identified between buffer and control zones (LOGIT model, $P < 0.01$, $n = 8$ sites).

Species	Buffer	Control	P value
Birds			
White-throated sparrow (*Zonotrichia albicolis*)	42.7 ± 8.5	40.1 ± 8.5	0.7516
Swainson's thrush (*Catharus ustulatus*)	20.1 ± 7.0	26.7 ± 11.1	0.5819
Common yellowthroat (*Geothlypis trichas*)	21.8 ± 8.9	10.3 ± 5.4	0.2433
American robin (*Turdus migratorius*)	23.6 ± 5.8	10.4 ± 3.6	0.0967
Alder flycatcher (*Empidonax alnorum*)	24.5 ± 8.8	8.8 ± 4.2	0.1170
Magnolia warbler (*Dendroica magnolia*)	6.8 ± 5.4	3.1 ± 2.9	0.3515
Nashville warbler (*Vermivora ruficapilla*)	12.7 ± 4.1	9.3 ± 3.2	0.4311
Northern waterthrush (*Seiurus noveboracensis*)	6.4 ± 3.9	3.8 ± 2.8	0.5339
Amphibians			
Spring peeper (*Hyla crucifer*)	45.0 ± 8.3	29.1 ± 7.5	0.2363

magnolia warblers. Darveau et al. (1995) observed that 20 m wide forested strips were more favorable to ubiquitous species than to forest dwelling species. We did not measure the number of breeding pairs at each site and our study does not provide precise bird abundance in each type of habitat. However, if we assume that breeding birds have a similar level of vocal activity, no matter which type of habitat they occupy, our results would then suggest that bird abundance in streamside habitat in powerline ROWs could be comparable to abundance in the adjacent control areas. In landscapes where forest harvesting is dominant, bird abundance in streamside zones can be correlated with streamside zone width (Darveau et al., 1995; Dickson et al., 1995). In our study area, the landscape was largely dominated by forest and the impact of 60–150 m wide powerline ROWs is most likely different than the impact of a large clear-cut.

Anurans

Spring peeper was the most active anuran species with respectively 38 and 17 3-minute periods with at least 1 call in the buffer and control zones (Table 5). The occurrence probability however was not statistically different (LOGIT model, $P = 0.236$, Table 6). The wood frog and the American toad were also detected in both zones: but their vocal activity was less frequent with respectively 10 and 5 periods. Vocal activity of anurans was greatest during the night recording sessions (82.9% of all periods). The American toad and the wood frog are common inhabitants of the boreal biome (Cook, 1984). Based on their specific life history information such as habitat and food requirements, mobility and reproductive strategies, these species are considered among the least vulnerable to transmission corridors and facilities (Kamstra et al., 1995). Even though our sampling effort (8 sites) was not as extensive as the effort (49 sites) for small mammals, our results suggest that anuran activity in buffer zones is comparable to the activity in the adjacent undisturbed riparian zone. We found the same species in those two habitats with a higher, although not significant, occurrence probability in the rights-of-way. A higher number of replicates would be necessary to detect any significant differences, between the 2 zones.

In the past decade, anurans and more generally, amphibians, have been the focus of increasing concern because of many reported population declines (Semlitsch, 2000). Forest fragmentation can impede juvenile dispersal and has been identified as one of the many possible causes of the decline. Vegetation in both the understory and overstory layers contributes to closure of forest canopy and are important structural elements of forest anuran habitat (deMaynadier and Hunter, 1999). Buffer zones in powerline ROWs had a different vegetation profile than control areas (Table 1). Large snags, trees (DBH > 7.0 cm), and woody debris were significantly less abundant in buffer zones. Overall stem density, herbaceous and lateral cover (height <1 m) however were highest in buffers and could possibly compensate, at least partially, for the lack of an overstory canopy. This would have to be tested in future research.

Mid-size mammals

In this study, our effort was oriented more towards testing the use of remote cameras to detect presence and activity levels of larger animals in buffer zones. We only operated 4 camera locations at a time. The data on large and mid-size mammals and grouse are presented in Table 7. Overall, black bear and snowshoe hare were most often recorded. Photographic data indicate presence (at least passage) of black bear, snowshoe hare, beaver, and ruffed grouse in buffer zones. No porcupine was photographed in buffer zones, but there was activity nearby. Porcupines likely cross rights-of-way using buffer zones but the general absence of large trees in most buffer zones make them unattractive to porcupines.

Sampling limitations

Buffer zones were sampled with the objective of assessing their use by wildlife represented by small

Table 7. Comparison of mid-size mammals species and grouse observed (pictures) between buffer and control zones in 1998–1999 ($n = 10$ sites).

Species	Buffer	Control	Total
Black bear (Ursus americanus)	1	2	3
Snowshoe hare (Lepus americanus)	2	3	5
American Beaver (Castor canadensis)	1	0	1
Ruffed grouse (Bonasa umbellus)*	1	0	1
American porcupine (Erethizon dorsatum)	0	1	1
All species	5	6	11

*Species not identified with other sampling method in this study.

mammals, birds, anurans, and mid-size mammals. Two sampling limitations were encountered during our study. First, a large number of sampling sites is needed to provide useful data for several taxa in order to test specific hypotheses related to birds. The second limitation was related to the relatively small size of buffer zones in rights-of-way and the difficulty of sampling for some wildlife species. In such small areas, the presence of people and/or trapping equipment could interfere with wildlife activity.

Small mammals were sampled using simple and inexpensive methods with snap traps and pitfalls that provided a great amount of data in a short time. The ATR technique used offers some advantages to researchers over other sampling techniques for birds and anurans. It is affordable and gives satisfactory results with limited manpower, for comparison between 2 sites as in this study. It does not however give any information on the abundance of anuran populations at a given site.

Infrared sensors were also used as a quick sampling method to assess mid-size mammal activity in riparian buffer zones. Infrared sensors are more expensive than the other sampling gear used but are easy to use and provided reliable data on species presence when coupled with a photographic camera. While the technique would be practical to obtain data in a given buffer zone, to sample a series of them simultaneously would require a large number of cameras, increasing costs and manpower.

CONCLUSIONS AND MANAGEMENT IMPLICATIONS

Overall, our results indicated that wildlife activity (small mammals, birds, and anurans) is somewhat similar in buffer zones and adjacent forest in wide powerline rights-of-way in the southern boreal forest. We recorded relatively high species richness and we even observed rare small mammals in right-of-way buffer zones. Differences in species richness and abundance are attributed to differences in vegetation structure in the 2 habitats. Most buffer zones in our study presented dense herbaceous cover, thick shrubby layer and absence of forested overstory canopy and were comparable to early succession habitat. Open habitat species such as the meadow vole and Lincoln sparrow were sampled more frequently in buffer zones. Right-of-way vegetation management has been shown to be favorable to the maintenance of biodversity in Sweden (Kyläkorpy and Gardenäs, 1997) and Doucet and Bider (1984) reported high small mammal, bird and amphibian activity in a narrow (20 m) experimental right-of-way. We can only speculate that buffer zones will contribute to biodiversity in rights-of-way; certainly the ecological trap issue must be considered in this context.

In 2000, amphibian populations appear to be cause for concern on a worldwide basis. In this context, perhaps rights-of-way can bring a modest contribution to the problem. Vegetation in overstory and understory layers contribute to provide cover and are important structural elements of forest amphibian habitat and the maintenance of natural vegetation buffer along streams increases the probability of amphibian persistence (Semlitsch, 2000). If powerline rights-of-way can maintain natural habitat attributes needed by amphibians along streams and wetlands (connectivity to breeding pools, woody debris, cover), we hypothesize that potential negative effects on anurans could be minimized.

Although our study did not test specifically the necessity of maintaining buffer zones in rights-of-way for wildlife in the boreal forest, data indicate that species richness was high, some rare species were present and amphibians were well represented. Therefore, we hypothesize that potential negative effects on the groups of species studied, especially amphibians, could be minimized by adopting a prudent management approach in the maintenance of vegetation buffer zones in transmission rights-of way. The average height of the vegetation in buffer zones was 3.42 m high and included some woody plants. Although our results do not permit conclusive statement on the importance of larger trees, we would advocate that buffers with a minimum of woody and herbaceous components be maintained at least in the low stratum. The structure of such buffers should include poles and saplings, along with shrubs and herbaceous species. In addition, it is only logical to recommend that the tallest tolerable arborescent vegetation should be maintained in ravines and deep narrow valleys.

ACKNOWLEDGEMENTS

Financial support was provided by Hydro-Québec. The authors thank S. Blais, S. Bois, L. Gagnon, G. Tremblay, and F. Tremblay for technical field work. The authors also thank G. Daigle, from Université Laval, who did all statistical analyses.

REFERENCES

Alder, G.H. and M.L. Wilson. 1989. Demography of the meadow vole along a simple habitat gradient. Canadian Journal of Zoology, 67: 772–774.

Banfield, A.W.F. 1977. Les mammifères du Canada. Musée national des sciences, Musées nationaux du Canada. Les Presses de l'Université Laval, Québec.

Beaudin, L. and M. Quintin. 1991. Mammifères terrestres du Québec, de l'Ontario et des Maritimes. Éditions Michel Quintin.

Bélisle, F. 1997. Impact à court terme de l'épandage des boues de papetières en milieu forestier boréal perturbé sur la microfaune mammalienne. MSc Thesis. Université du Québec à Rimouski.

Birney, E.C., W.E. Grant, and D.D. Baird. 1976. Importance of vegetative cover to cycles of *Microtus* populations. Ecology, 57: 1043–1051.

Cook, F. 1984. Introduction aux amphibiens et reptiles du Canada. Musées nationaux du Canada.

Darveau, M., P. Beauchesne, L. Bélanger, J. Huot, and P. Larue. 1995. Riparian forest strips as habitat for breeding birds in boreal forest. Journal of Wildlife Management, 59: 67–78.

DeGraaf, R.M. and M. Yamasaki. 1999. Bird and mammal habitat in riparian areas. Chapter 8. In: Riparian Management in Forests of the Continental Eastern United States. Elon S. Verry, James W. Hornbeck, and C. Andrew Dollof, eds. Lewis Publishers.

deMaynadier, P.G. and M.L. Hunter. 1999. Forest canopy closure and juvenile emigration of pool-breeding amphibians in Maine. Journal of Wildlife Management, 63: 441–450.

Deshaye, J., J. Brunelle and F. Morneau. 1996. Étude de la biodiversité des emprises de lignes de transport d'énergie électrique en forêt mixte. Vice-présidence Environnement et Collectivités, Hydro-Québec, Qc.

Dickson, J.G., J.H. Williamson, R.N. Conner, and B. Ortego. 1995. Streamside zones and breeding birds in eastern Texas. Wildlife Society Bulletin, 23: 750–755.

Doucet, G.J. and J.R. Bider. 1984. Changes in animal activity immediately following the experimental clearing of a forested right-of-way. In: Proceedings 3rd Symposium Environmental Concerns in Rights-of-Way Management. pp. 592–601.

Gauthier, J. and Y. Aubry, eds. 1995. Les oiseaux nicheurs du Québec : Atlas des oiseaux nicheurs du Québec méridional. Association québécoise des groupes d'ornithologues, Société québécoise de protection des oiseaux, Service canadien de la faune, Environnement Canada, région du Québec. Montréal.

Grant, P.R. 1971. The habitat preference of *Microtus pennsylvanicus*, and its relevance to the distribution of this species on islands. Journal of Mammalogy, 52: 351–361.

Grant, P.R. 1975. Population performance of *Microtus pennsylvanicus* confined to woodland habitat, and a model of habitat occupancy. Canadian Journal of Zoology, 53: 1447–1465.

Jonasson, S. 1988. Evaluation of the point intercept method for the estimation of plant biomes. Oikos, 52: 101–106.

Jules, E.S., E.J. Frost, L.S. Mills, and D.A. Tallmon. 1999. Ecological consequences of forest fragmentation in the Klamath region. Natural Areas Journal, 19: 368–378.

Kamstra, J., S. Hounsell, and W. Weller. 1995. Vulnerability of reptiles and amphibians to transmission corridors and facilities. In: Proceeding of the Fifth International Symposium on Environmental Concerns in Rights-of-way Management. G.J. Doucet, M. Giguère, and C. Seguin, eds. Montreal. pp. 300–304.

Kyläkorpy, L. and S. Gardenäs. 1997. Effects of the transmission system on biodiversity in Sweden. In: Proceedings of the Sixth International Symposium on Environmental Concerns in Rights-of-Way Management. J.R. Williams, J.W. Goodrich-Mahoney, J.R. Wisniewski, and J. Wisniewski, eds. Elsevier Science Ltd. Oxford. pp. 393–397.

Maisonneuve, C., A. Desrosiers, R. McNicoll, and M. Lepage. 1996. Évaluation de la diversité faunique des plaines inondables du sud du Québec : avifaune et micromammifères. Ministère de l'Environnement et de la Faune du Québec, Direction de la faune et des habitats, Québec.

Maisonneuve, C. and C. Rioux. 1998. Influence de l'étagement de la végétation dans les bandes riveraines en milieu agricole sur leur utilisation par les micromammifères et l'herpétofaune. Ministère de l'Environnement et de la Faune du Québec, Direction de la faune et des habitats.

McCullagh, P. and J.A. Nelder. 1989. Generalized Linear Models, 2nd ed. Monographs on Statistics and Applied Probability 37. Chapman and Hall, London.

Morneau, F., G.J. Doucet, M. Giguère, and M. Laperle. 1999. Breeding bird species richness associated with a powerline right-of-way in a northern mixed forest landscape. Canadian Field-Naturalist, 113: 598–604.

Nudds, T.D., 1977. Quantifying the vegetation structure of wildlife cover. Wildlife Society Bulletin, 5: 113–117.

O'Connell, W. and K.V. Miller. 1994. Site preparation influences on vegetative composition and avian and small mammal communities in the South Carolina upper coastal plain. Proc. Annu. Conf. Southeast Assoc. Fish and Wildlife Agencies, 48: 321–330.

SAS Institute Inc. 1997. User's Guide. Version 6.12; Statistics. SAS Institute Inc. Cary, NC.

Schreiber, R.K. and J.A. Graves. 1977. Powerline corridors as possible barriers to the movements of small mammals. American Midland Naturalist, 97: 504–508.

Semlitsch, R.D. 2000. Principles for management of aquatic breeding amphibians. Journal of Wildlife Management, 64: 615–631.

Thompson, F.R. and D.E. Capen. 1988. Avian assemblages in seral stages of a Vermont forest. Journal of Wildlife Management, 52: 771–777.

Van Zyll de Jong. 1983. Les marsupiaux et les insectivores. Traité des mammifères du Canada. Volume 1. Musée national des Sciences naturelles, Musées nationaux du Canada, Ottawa.

Zar, J.H. 1984. Biostatistical Analysis. Prentice-Hall, Englewood Cliffs, NJ.

BIOGRAPHICAL SKETCHES

Francis Bélisle (corresponding author)

Naturam Environment Inc., 31 Marquette, Baie-Comeau, Québec, Canada, G4Z 1K4, e-mail: belisle.francis@hydro.qc.ca

Francis Bélisle holds a MSc degree in Wildlife and Habitat Management from Université du Québec at Rimouski (UQAR). He has been working as an environmental consultant for 5 years. He has conducted studies on small mammals and riparian habitat on the North Shore region of the St-Lawrence River, Québec.

G. Jean Doucet

TransÉnergie, 800 De Maisonneuve, E. Montréal, Québec, Canada, H2L 4M8

Jean Doucet holds a PhD in wildlife ecology from McGill University and has been a member of the environmental unit at TransÉnergie for 4 years. He is currently managing a research program on interactions between wildlife and energy transmission activities and equipment. Issues under study include biodiversity, habitat fragmentation, habitat management and avian interactions with structures.

Yves Garant
 Kruger Inc., Scierie Parent, 3300 Bellefeuille, Trois-Rivières, Québec, Canada, G9A 3Z3

Yves Garant is a wildlife biologist and holds a MSc degree in Renewable Resources from McGill University. As a consultant from 1986 to 1998, he has conducted many projects on furbearers and ungulate management, environmental impact assessment, and vegetation control in rights-of-way. He currently works as a sustainable forest management coordinator for Kruger inc. Scierie Parent and is in charge of the environmental management system.

Endangered and Threatened Species and ROW Vegetation Management

Kevin McLoughlin

The electric utility industry concern for those species listed as endangered or threatened found to reside within our transmission and distribution line rights-of-way (ROW) is twofold; first we often welcome the fact that our ROW vegetation management practices have created these unique and valuable habitats that have allowed such "species of concern" to become a resident of the ROW environs. The basic objective of ROW vegetation management is to virtually eliminate, to the practical extent feasible and necessary, all the tall growing trees that could cause electrical disruptions from the ROW and conversely to facilitate the development of various low growing plant assemblages. This process, often referred to as Integrated Vegetation Management (IVM), then may provide opportunities (new ecological niches) for colonization by various endangered, threatened, rare, unique or other species of interest or concern within the confines of the limits of the ROW and/or its area of ecological influence, i.e., along the immediate ROW edge. The second concern is that due to these highly developed ROW vegetation management strategies that have promoted the floristic evolvement of the low growing shrubs, herbs, grasses, ferns, etc., the electric industry is now in some instances being "penalized" for having achieved these milestones in biodiversity in that costly studies, inventories, and surveys, are often requested/mandated when these listed endangered/threatened species (or even prospective ones) are "found" or even thought to occur on or close to our ROW. In addition, when these endangered/threatened species are actually physically detected on a ROW segment the resultant instantaneous reaction following their discovery by some members of the environmentally informed public and even some staff of environmental regulatory agencies is to immediately request a halt to all ongoing utility ROW vegetation management practices in the near vicinity of the newly discovered species of concern. This drastic "rescue" action is believed required to provide the species of concern needed "protection" and thus "preserve" it's ROW habitat from any further undue meddling by the electric utility. This paper explores the possible ramifications of the Endangered Species Act in regards to ROW vegetation management as well as some of the resulting potential consequences of regulatory programs designed to enhance the recovery of listed, proposed and even candidate species.

Keywords: Endangered species, threatened species, biodiversity, rights-of-way (ROW), vegetation management

IMPLICATIONS OF THE ENDANGERED SPECIES ACT IN REGARDS TO ROW VEGETATION MANAGEMENT

The Endangered Species Act (the Act) provides significant legal protection for those species that are listed by the Secretary of the Interior under one of two protected categories; either as an endangered or as a threatened species (E&T). An endangered species is one that is in danger of extinction throughout all or a significant portion of its range. A threatened species is one that is likely to become endangered in the foreseeable future. Both the lists for endangered species as well as threatened species stipulate the geographic range over which the species of concern is considered threatened or endangered. In addition, in some special instances, it will also specify any "critical habitat" within such a

---

Environmental Concerns in Rights-of-Way Management: Seventh International Symposium
J.W. Goodrich-Mahoney, D.F. Mutrie and C.A. Guild (editors)
© 2002 Elsevier Science Ltd. All rights reserved.

range that is also protected under a distinctly different regulatory criterion.

An interesting side note is that the Act prohibitions against the taking of listed fish and wildlife species apply only to endangered species and is not explicitly stated to cover those species listed as threatened. The protective language in the statute for those species to be listed as threatened is located within section 4(d) which specifies that the Secretary of the Interior is to issue regulations "as he deems necessary and advisable to provide for the conservation of such species." However, the Secretary has issued the regulations via the Fish and Wildlife Service (FWS) that apply the same section 9 prohibitions of the Act to both endangered and threatened species. Thus, from a practical application and management viewpoint, these two terms; endangered and threatened (E&T), once so legally distinct in the Act itself, are now virtually interchangeable in as far as their consequences regarding regulatory "rulemaking" restrictions apply.

One other relatively minor point to mention (at least for most ROW vegetation management scenarios) so as to insure adequate coverage of the macro issues surrounding the Endangered Species Act and its applicable regulatory requirements is that the FWS executes all the provisions of the Act, except for those provisions relating to ocean going fish, anadromous fish and marine mammals. All such provisions of the Endangered Species Act relating to maritime species are implemented by the National Marine Fisheries Service, of the National Oceanic and Atmospheric Administration (NOAA), which is located in the Department of Commerce. Interestingly, the National Marine Fisheries Service (NMFS) has not seen fit to adopt regulations that extend the same protections to threatened species as are provided to endangered species by the Interior's FWS (Jointly referred to as the "Services" in regulatory jargon.)

These listed E&T species are protected through two sections of the Act; section 7 which provides for a review and limitation of all Federal actions that may harm these listed endangered and threatened species; and section 9, which prohibits the taking of protected fish and wildlife anywhere, and forbids the destruction of protected plants on federal lands.

Section 7

Section 7 of the Act only applies to prospective Federal actions and the direct management of Federal lands. For most electric utilities, the provisions of section 7 would only be invoked by ROW vegetation management activities if a proposed federal agency action were involved. For example, the granting of a federal permit, such as a Federal Energy Regulatory Commission (FERC) license, is such a Federal action subject to section 7 review. In situations where ROW vegetation management activities are an integral part of or are by design encompassed within a pending FERC license an informal consultation with the Secretary of the Interior in concert with FERC would minimally be required. This informal contact begins when the agency or the applicant contacts the appropriate local FWS office to determine if any listed species are known to occur or possibly may occur in the project area vicinity. If the FWS provides a negative response, no further consultation is required.

However, when the applicant or Agency has reason to believe that a listed E&T species may be an occupant of the area affected by the proposed project then the Agency and the FWS must determine if the action will affect these species of concern. A "may effect determination" includes those actions not likely to adversely affect as well as those likely to adversely affect a listed E&T species. If the Agency and the FWS agree that the proposed action is not likely to adversely effect listed species (the effects are beneficial, insignificant, or discountable) no further consultation is needed.

However, when it is determined that implementation of such action will likely affect this species of concern, then the consultation process becomes formalized with specific timeframes coming into play. This request to initiate formal consultation is made by the Agency to the FWS in writing and is accompanied by a complete initiation package. With the initiation of a formal consultation process with the applicant and Agency (nominally a 90-day period) the FWS must then prepare and submit a biological opinion (within 45 days). The biological opinion is the document that states the opinion of the FWS as to whether or not the action is likely to "jeopardize" the continued existence of listed species or result in the destruction or "adverse modification" of critical habitat. If the biological opinion reaches a jeopardy or adverse modification of critical habitat conclusion, reasonable and prudent "alternatives" may be proposed for project implementation that would avoid or minimize impact to the species. Even if the FWS recognizes that a project will not jeopardize the species or adversely modify critical habitat it still may require additional reasonable and prudent "measures" be taken to minimize the impact of any potential for incidental take. If after all this, it is determined by the FWS that some unavoidable "take" will still occur then an incidental take statement must be developed to exempt such take from the section 9 prohibitions.

All Federal Agencies have a continuing obligation to contribute to the conservation of E&T species under section 7(a) (1) of the Act. The list of Federal land management actions that may activate the consultation process could conceivably entail even ordinary ROW vegetation management activities of a Federal utility such as the Bonneville Power Administration (BPA) or the Tennessee Valley Authority (TVA). In fact, any such ROW activity expected to occur in the near vicinity of E&T species by such a federal entity could, as a minimum, trigger the informal review/consultation procedures by the FWS. The potential reiterating of the informal review/consultation process activated by the annual implementation of routine ROW vegetation management actions of a Federal utility could become an incessant recurring affair to these entities as new species are added to the listings, new information emerges or fresh concern over the welfare of certain listed species appears within the FWS. It is a fact of life for such Federal Agencies; that of a reinitiating the consultation process with a constant reexamination of previous mitigation measures as well as a fresh look at all ongoing ROW vegetation management activities in regards to listed and even proposed new species listings. However, for the great majority of electric utilities contemplating vegetation management along their transmission line ROW, in the absence of any federal action, Section 7 would have very limited applicability.[1]

Section 9
Section 9 of the Act prohibits the *taking* by any *person* of any fish or wildlife species listed as endangered under the provisions of the Act. The term "person" used above refers to virtually anybody, i.e., individual, corporation, partnership, private entity, or government (federal, state, municipal or other political subdivision) employee or agent or any other entity subject to the jurisdiction of the United States. The acts that comprise a "taking" include such activities as harassing, harming, pursuing, hunting, shooting, wounding, killing, trapping, capturing, or collecting of an endangered (read threatened also) species or the attempt to engage in such conduct. Harm has also been interpreted to mean significant habitat modification or degradation where it actually kills or injures wildlife by significantly impairing essential behavioral patterns, including breeding, feeding, or sheltering.[2] Thus, significant adverse habitat modification on privately owned land can become a regulated undertaking within the purview of the Endangered Species Act if the action contemplated amounts to a taking of a listed E&T species as broadly defined above.

While listed fish and wildlife species secure ample protection under the Act (and subsequent regulations), section 9 applies a distinctly different and lesser level of protection to plants listed as endangered (including threatened[3]). Section 9(a) (2) makes it illegal to remove or damage plants endangered (or threatened) from federal lands, or from any property if it is done in knowing violation of any state law or regulation including state criminal trespass law. This prohibition is much more constrained than that provided to protect fish and wildlife species, as it only applies directly to federal lands and to those acts in contravention of state law.

Section 6
Section 6 of the Act provides a framework for the development of federal and state cooperative agreements. The Secretary of the Interior may enter into a cooperative agreement with any state, which establishes and maintains an adequate and active program for the conservation of endangered and threatened species. In order for a state program to be considered "adequate," it must be demonstrated that it is consistent with the Endangered Species Act and include all resident species of fish, wildlife and plants that are federally listed as endangered or threatened under the provisions of the Act. This arrangement for Federal and state cooperative agreements was adopted because delegation of the authority to the States was viewed as the most effective way to fulfill the provisions of the Act.[4] However, in practice executed cooperative agreements only establish a system of joint implementation and enforcement between the FWS and the reciprocating state environmental/natural resource agency.

For instance, New York State has entered into two separate cooperative agreements with the Interior's FWS, one for E&T fish and wildlife (1976) and another for E&T plants species (1983). While the primary purpose of the cooperative agreements is to provide a mechanism by which the federal government can fund a portion of the state's species conservation efforts, they also provide for the cooperation between the state's environmental/natural resource agency and the FWS in enforcing the Act and related state laws. In regards to the taking issue for E&T species, state law is specifically allowed to be more restrictive than federal law, but it is prohibited from being less restrictive.

Interim discussion
Electric utilities either own their ROW outright in fee or hold permanent easements that grant an ownership interest in the perpetuity of facility maintenance and the condition of the ROW to insure the safe and reliable transmission of electric energy. ROW vegetation management activities that involves the physical removal of incompatible vegetation or the treatment of target tree species by the judicious application of herbicides occurs either on property owned or essentially under the ownership of the utility. In New York, the state prohibitions against damaging protected plants can be waived by the landowner. Thus, the utility owner status nullifies the prohibition against damaging listed plants species at the federal level and under New York

---
1 For example, the consultation process for a Habitat Conservation Plan required to secure a section 10 permit is derived from section 7.
2 Babbit v. Sweet Home Chapter for a greater Oregon 1995.
3 By regulation, threatened species are afforded the same protection as endangered.

4 Senate Committee on Commerce Report on Endangered Species Act, S. Doc. No. 93-307 93rd Cong., 1st Sess. (1973).

State law, at the state level as well.[5] Therefore, in regards to all E&T plant species a violation of the Federal Endangered Species Act by the utility cannot occur in New York unless a protected plant is damaged on federal land because it is not in violation of state law.

Regarding the protection of fish and wildlife, unless essential habitat will be significantly modified to the extent that essential behavior patterns are impaired and actual species death and or injury occur, ROW vegetation management practices should not directly result in the harming or taking of any protected fish or wildlife. However, this determination is subject to a species-specific site by site resolution and assumes the vegetation management events at issue do not include the direct taking (e.g., wounding killing, trapping) of any protected fish and wildlife species. However, if a ROW segment is identified to overlap or encircle the essential habitat of E&T species of fish or wildlife, severe alteration of that habitat could be considered a taking, if essential behavioral patterns are jeopardized and actual species death or injury occurs.

Section 10
If it is determined that a taking will occur due to the ROW vegetation management operations, it is then necessary to first obtain a section 10 permit. Section 10 of the Endangered Species Act allows for the incidental taking of protected species in projects which otherwise have no Federal involvement. Section 10 permits will only be granted if a conservation plan is submitted and approved which details the incidental takings impact mitigation and offsetting strategies to be implemented. In practice, these conservation plans are referred to as Habitat Conservation Plans (HCPs) and typically require extensive involvement on the part of federal and state wildlife agencies before they are approved and the section 10 permit is granted.

Of all the various protective provisions of the Act provided to species listed as E&T, the ban against "taking" is one of the most essential. However, until 1982 there was simply no mechanism available under the Act to allow for the "take" of listed species that might occur inadvertently during the normal progression of events associated with various operations performed by private landowners. In 1982 Congress provided for such "taking" actions by amending Section 10(a)(1)(B) of the Act to allow for the issuance of "Incidental Take Permits" (ITP). An ITP authorizes the "take" of listed E&T species that is incidental to, and not the purpose of, the carrying out of an otherwise lawful activity. Thus, anyone who believes that his or her otherwise lawful activities will result in the "incidental take" of a listed E&T species requires a permit. Private parties wishing to conduct activities on their own lands that might result in the incidental take of a listed species cannot simply walk up to the FWS and ask for and receive an ITP. A HCP must be prepared and accompany an application for an ITP and then be approved by the FWS before a permit can be issued.

Habitat Conservation Plans and Incidental Take Permits
A HCP must include among other things, what the effects of the "taking" on the species will be and how those effects will be mitigated. HCP defines the "conserved habitat areas" which are areas explicitly designated for habitat restoration, acquisition, protection or other conservation purposes. The eventual settlement of the many issues in large HCPs can be a daunting exercise, requiring in some cases years of preparatory work. Once the HCP is completed, processing the permit application can likewise be complex and difficult undertaking requiring copious amounts of time. Publication in the Federal Register and a mandatory public comment period as was well as NEPA compliance and the possible generation of an Environmental Assessment (EA) or even a full Environmental Impact Statement (EIS) as well as other review requirements of the Endangered Species Act itself are all part of the process. While processing the application the FWS will prepare an intra-Service biological opinion under Section 7 of the Act and the ITP, and finalize any NEPA documents required. Consequently, ITPs have a number of associated documents besides the HCP.

No surprises assurances
Once completed, the HCP approach allows private development to proceed while at the same time ensuring the conservation of the species listed as E&T. As an extra incentive for landowners to go through such an arduous process, additional promises are provided by the government through what was known as the "No Surprises" assurances that provides more certainty in regards to future E&T regulatory activities. Basically, private landowners are assured that if unforeseen circumstances arise, any adjustments or modifications by the FWS will not require the commitment of additional land, water or financial compensation or additional restrictions on the use of land, water or other natural resources otherwise available for development beyond the level otherwise agreed to in the HCP with out the consent of the permittee. As noted above, there are no Federal prohibitions under the Act for the take of listed plants on non-Federal land, unless taking of those plants is in violation of State law. However, before the FWS issues an IT permit, the effects of the permit on listed plants must likewise be analyzed because section 7 of the Act requires that the approval of a HCP and issuance of an ITP must not jeopardize any listed species, including plants. Moreover, currently unlisted species can also be named on the HCP permit.

---

5   Since each state can pass laws and set it's own E&T species rules to be more restrictive then the federal requirements one must check the respective state laws and their subsequent rule makings in regards to the state-specific body of law.

Case studies

Two examples are available of HCPs that may have some bearing on the application of this unique partnership to electric utility ROW vegetation management programs. The Karner blue butterfly is a listed species on both the Federal and on the state level in New York. Some of the most productive Karner blue habitat is found on electric transmission line ROW that has the prerequisite host species for the butterfly larvae, the blue lupine, growing in abundance. The blue lupine is an open growing and sunloving, relatively shade intolerant species that is one of the many potential low growing species that may occupy ROW that have had the tall growing trees and shrubs selectively removed by stem specific/spot applications of herbicide. When the presence on the ROW of copious patches of blue lupine flowers was initially discovered along with the Karner blue butterfly, the clamor by environmentally organizations for eliminating the use of herbicides by the local electric utility to insure the survival of this critical host plant was tantamount to the gospel of how best to preserve this existing habitat condition. Within a few years the hand cutting of surrounding trees, particularly of black locust (a prolific stump and root suckering species) proved this advice quite shortsighted. After thorough study, selective herbicide use is now back in place on the ROW and the blue lupine plants are flourishing once again.

In Wisconsin, a state wide HCP for the protection of the Karner blue butterfly with 28 partners including utilities is in the final development stages. The HCP alleviates the need for processing multiple site-specific individual permits while allowing the Karner blue butterfly and its habitat to be conserved while it is simultaneously used and managed. This Wisconsin effort may prove to be a suitable model for other ROW habitats that engender the growth of such sun loving ROW induced E&T species.

Another HCP situation that may have applicability to electric utility ROW vegetation management from a system-wide perspective is the Potlatch Corporation approach to the HCP process. This timber products company was concerned about the impact its timber management activities had on the endangered red-cockaded woodpecker. The company believed that its current forest management programs actually benefit the woodpecker population on its landholdings and complied with the law. However, Potlatch desired some certainty in regards to their future timber harvesting plans proceeding without being hampered by the presence of the listed woodpecker. The approved HCP provides the company with flexible management options while ensuring that the red cockaded woodpeckers on the company's lands will be maintained and protected. It is anticipated that the woodpecker population will actually expand because of the forest management regime used by the company. Thus this HCP protects Potlatch's long-term investment in it timberlands and provides incentives to actively conserve the endangered woodpecker. Again, such a HCP may have applicability to an utilities system wide approach to vegetation management that demonstrates that the various Integrated Vegetation Management (IVM) techniques actually provides the needed habitat for various species of concern including those listed as E&T.

Safe Harbor Agreements

In a related effort by the Services to provide additional incentives for private property owners to restore, enhance, or maintain habitats, for listed species is the "Safe Harbor Policy." This collaborative stewardship approach to the proactive management of listed E&T species provides participating private landowners with technical assistance to develop "Safe Harbor Agreements" that manage habitat for listed species, and provide assurances that additional land, water, and/or natural resources use restrictions will not be imposed as a result of their voluntary conservation actions to benefit covered species. In addition, when the landowner meets all the terms of the agreement, the Services will authorize incidental taking of the covered species. Although this Policy sounds like a duplicative procedure for the HCP's "No Surprises" described above without having to go through the elaborate HCP process there is another interesting twist. Instead of being triggered by potentially negative "unforeseen circumstances" as in the "No Surprises," this voluntary "Safe Harbor" agreement provides its benefits if, as a result of the conservation measures implemented by the landowner, the covered species becomes even more numerous. Private property owners that implement conservation practices for certain listed species covered under a "Safe Harbor Agreement" will receive assurances from the Services that additional conservation measures will not be required and additional land, water or natural resource use restrictions will not be imposed should the covered species become more numerous as a result of the property owners actions.

Candidate species

As noted above for HCPs, the species covered by the conservation plans could include not only listed E&T species but also, unlisted species. Although technically unlisted, some species may be very close to being listed and are referred to as candidate species. Candidate species are plants and animals for which the FWS has sufficient information on their biological status and threats to propose them as endangered or threatened. NMFS defines candidate species even more broadly to include species whose status is of concern but more information is needed before they can be subject to the listing process. From the list of candidate species, those with the highest priority actually become "proposed" for listing. For instance, as of late 1999, there were 258 candidate species and another 56 species were proposed for listing. In additional there is still another slate of species that are potential future nominees that are considered "likely" to become candidates. None of these three quasi-official species rosters, i.e., proposed, candidates or those likely to become candidates receives any statutory protection under the Act.

However, the Services encourage the formation of partnerships to conserve these species since they are by definition species of concern that may warrant future protection under the Act. These partnerships are termed "Candidate Conservation Agreements" (CCA) and are formal arrangements between the Services and one or more parties to address the conservation needs of proposed, candidate and species likely to become candidates before they actually are listed. The participants, usually Federal, state, and local agencies and conservation groups, voluntarily commit to implementing certain actions that will remove or reduce threats to these species. These CCA have been expanded to private landowners with assurances that their conservation efforts will not result in future regulatory obligations in excess of those that they have agreed to at the time they entered into the agreement. In other words, the Services will provide assurances to private property owners that, in the event a species covered in the CCA is subsequently listed as endangered or threatened, the Services will not request added restrictions or require supplemental actions above those the property owner voluntarily committed to in the CCA. In return for participating in this voluntary proactive management, at the time the parties enter into the CCA, the Services would also issue a permit under section 10(a)(1)(A) authorizing the property owner to take individuals or modify habitat as specified by the terms and conditions in the agreement and consistent with the overall goal of precluding the need to list. The effective date on the permit would be set to the date any covered species becomes listed. The overall goal of the CCA is to remove enough threats to the covered species to eliminate the need for listing under the Act.

Critical habitat

Habitat considerations and concerns are an integral part of practically every procedure called for in the Act. For most listed species, the threats to their habitat are the most important consideration when determining if a species meets the requirements for protection under the Act. The FWS describes in great detail the habitat needs of these selected species, and all threats to its habitat, in all their promulgated listing rules. Habitat considerations are an essential key element in all recovery plans,[6] and recovery plans include maps and descriptions of the habitat needed to recover the species. The section 7 consultation process likewise deals with the dynamic characteristics and seasonal cycles of the habitat requirements for all listed E&T species.

When a candidate species is proposed for formal listing as either endangered or threatened under the Act, the additional consideration of whether there are specific areas of habitat that are essential to the species conservation so that these areas may also be formally proposed for designation as "Critical Habitat" must be made. Critical Habitat as used in the Act refers to specific geographic areas that are essential for the conservation of listed species, which may require special management considerations. These areas do not necessarily have to be currently occupied by the species at the time of their designation. Unlike the listing of a species, the designation of critical habitat requires that the economic impact must be taken into account when specifying any particular area as critical habitat. Setting specific boundaries is also required. Critical habitat, *if prudent and determinable*, must be proposed and designated by regulation at the time of listing and thus required to be codified in the Code of Federal Regulations. However, the FWS has long believed that, in most circumstances, the designation of "official" critical habitat is of little additional value for most listed species.

Due to these requirements, the designation of critical habitat is one of the most controversial and confusing aspects of the Act. This situation is only enhanced by the fact that all listed species and their associated habitats are already protected by the Act whether or not they are in an area officially designated as critical habitat. Thus for most listed species the designation of critical habitat is felt to be by the FWS a redundant and unnecessary procedure. The costly and time consuming process of designation of critical habitat by the FWS is a constant problem and a major drain on their limited resources (staff and funding) that the Service is still struggling with to find acceptable solutions. Seemingly, the only benefit of designating critical habitat is that of protecting suitable or even prime potential habitat in areas where the species of concern is physically not located at present in the expectation that future colonization will occur in these areas.

In recent years the FWS has been challenged on many of their "not prudent" critical habitat determinations and as a result has been inundated with citizen lawsuits for their perceived failure to complete the of Critical Habitat designation process. Many environmental groups view critical habitat as providing additional regulatory protection, thus provoking the growing number of lawsuits to prompt critical habitat designations. The consequence of all this critical habitat litigation activity is often the hasty designation of significant land areas of critical habitat (often unoccupied by the listed E&T species) resulting in a

---

[6] A document drafted by the Service or other knowledgeable individual or group, that serves as a guide for activities to be undertaken by Federal, State, or private entities in helping to recover and conserve endangered or threatened species.

new additional regulatory layer that has the potential to significantly impede proposed projects under section 7(a)(2). Under this section all Federal agencies must, in consultation with the Service, insure that all actions they authorize, fund, or carry out are not likely to result in the destruction or adverse modification of critical habitat.

Pesticides and the Endangered Species Act
Finally, one of the last areas that the implementation of the Endangered Species Act may encroach directly upon the ROW vegetation management activities of electric utilities is the Environmental Protection Agency's (EPA) Endangered Species Protection Program (ESPP). Although the EPA Office of Pesticide Programs has included endangered species considerations in its risk assessments for many years, the Endangered Species Protection Program (ESPP), as an entity, started in 1988. It is largely voluntary now and relies on cooperation between the FWS, EPA Regions, States, and pesticide users. ESPP has its goals to simultaneously protect E&T species from harmful pesticide usage and to minimize the impact of the program on pesticide users. In order to protect listed species from detrimental effects from the use of pesticides, the EPA does the following:
1. Use's sound science to assess the risk of pesticide use to listed species.
2. Attempts to find methods to avoid concerns for listed species.
3. When the EPA cannot avoid concerns it then consults with the scientists at the FWS.
4. The FWS issues a biological opinion on the potential for adverse effects on particular species and the EPA implements pesticide use limitations that are either specified in the opinions or developed from those opinions.
5. This implementation is done by:
   – adding a generic label statement;
   – developing county bulletins that contain maps of species locations and pesticide use limitations;
   – distributing the bulletins and other materials by a wide variety of methods; and
   – providing a toll-free telephone number to assist users in determining whether they need a bulletin and where to obtain one.

The EPA encourages individual States to develop their own plans by whatever approach they determine is best for them as long as that approach meets the goals of protecting E&T species while minimizing the impact on pesticide users. States are also a part of the county bulletin review process, along with other agencies, and are encouraged to include State agencies oriented toward agriculture and those aligned with fish and wildlife as well as pesticide users and environmental groups in their review process. EPA fully realizes that it cannot adequately protect endangered species without having some impact on pesticide users. In order to minimize the impact, EPA tries to assist pesticide users in dealing with the impacts of the program. Some of the activities EPA is undertaking to do in relation to pesticide usage and protecting E&T species are:
– utilizing the minimum limitations that will protect the listed E&T species;
– recommending that States provide EPA with alternative, but protective, pesticide use limitations that are appropriate for their location and situation;
– recommending alternative pesticides;
– working with USDA to inform users about wetlands reserve and conservation reserve programs to offset impacts by offering compensation for land taken out of production; and
– occasionally the FWS will provide reimbursement for crops not harvested when the crops are important to a species.

These EPA initiated limitations on pesticide use are not law at this time, but are being provided now for application by pesticide users in voluntarily protecting E&T species from harm due to pesticide use. The EPA encourages all pesticide users to utilize this information. Once the EPA's Endangered Species Protection Program is in effect, these voluntary recommendations will undoubtedly become requirements of the program. EPA is currently soliciting comments regarding the information presented in their voluntary ESPP. The EPA particularly wants to know if the information they are disseminating about the protection of E&T species and pesticide usage is clear and correct as well as to what extent their recommended measures would affect typical pesticide use or productivity.

Potential negative consequences?
Ironically, there is now an ongoing legal case that has the potential to thwart many of the aforementioned attempts to abate the negative regulatory aspects of dealing with endangered and threatened species on ROW. An upstate New York electric utility is currently being "sued" by an underlying fee owner for having engendered a listed species to inhabit the ROW. The utility constructed a line years ago on an easement through an old field habitat that has naturally reforested on either side of the ROW. The utilities dutiful implementation of integrated vegetation management practices and over the intervening years has, as a byproduct, fostered an early succession endangered species within its transmission line ROW easement. This legal case involves a segment of ROW that through the selective removal of tall growing trees by herbicide application over the years has caused the area to become inhabited by many lower growing sun loving species. One of these lower growing species that is flourishing particularly well within the ROW is the blue lupine that is the sole host plant for an endangered insect, the Karner blue butterfly. The ROW area in question is zoned as an industrial park and the utility transmission line ROW easement cuts through a portion of this

commercial property. The landowner alleges that due to the presence of the endangered species (only on the ROW) the remainder of the property cannot be accessed for development, and thus has lost a significant amount of potential commercial development. Because the endangered species host plant cannot tolerate the shaded forest area off ROW, it grows only in patches within the ROW, and thus the ROW itself cannot be developed. The utility contends that there are practical ways to accommodate the landowner's proposed development plans. Due to the presence of the endangered species (only on the ROW) the landowner can not access the remainder of the property and thus has lost a significant amount of potential commercial development. The lawsuit alleges that Federal and state laws restrict development on endangered species habitat, so the utility's actions have limited the marketing and development potential and thus lowered the value of this parcel of land zoned for industrial development! As further espoused by the plaintiff, "It is an expensive, protracted and expensive proposition to get relieve from the Endangered Species Act."

For years after finding the presence of this endangered species on its ROW this utility has had significant environmental regulatory oversight and consultation. This has resulted in site-specific studies to determine the best course of action to follow in regards to future ROW vegetation management treatments to ensure compliance with competing environmental and public service obligations. Alleging that the local utility has fostered the presence of this species through its vegetation management activities, has initiated studies and brought out experts from academia, environmental agencies and environmental groups for purposes of field research, technical advice and the use of portion of the ROW to conduct IVM research, the landowner has asserted a variety of claims including trespass.

Although, the claimants in this legal action assert this case is not about endangered species per se but is simply a trespass case, a negative court decision could have impact on other similar situations whereby an electric utility comes into possession of ROW inhabited by E&T species assisted by its vegetation management actions and then attempts to comply with the letter and spirit of the Endangered Species Act and promote and foster the welfare and recovery of these listed species. Upon seemingly complying with all applicable laws, appropriate rules and relevant guidelines in regards to the protection of listed E&T species, the utility may ultimately find itself with a disgruntled underlying fee owner, or even adjacent ROW landowner, that now claims economic loss resulting from the presence of these ROW biological assets and will resort to a lawsuit to seek redress.

REFERENCES

Barnes, B.V., et al. 1998. Forest Ecology, 4th ed. John Wiley & Sons Inc., New York. 774 pp.

Bond, W.J. 1993. Keystone species. In: Ecosystem Function and Biodiversity. E.D. Schulze and H.A. Mooney, eds. Springer-Verlag, New York.

Callicott, J.B. and K. Mumford. 1997. Ecological sustainability as a conservation concept. Conserv. Biol., 11: 32–40.

Endagered Species Act of 1973, as amended, 16 U.S.C. 1531 et seg.

Noss, R.F., E.T. LaRoe III, and J.M. Scott. 1995. Endangered ecosystems of the United States: a preliminary assessment of loss and degradation. USDI, Nat. Biol. Serv., Biol. Report 28. Washington DC. 58 pp.

National Research Council. 1995. Science and the Endangered Species Act. National Academy Press. Washington, DC. 271 pp.

Slidle, J.G. 1987. Critical habitat designation: Is it prudent? Environmental Management, 11(4): 429–437.

BIOGRAPHICAL SKETCH

Kevin T. McLaughlin

New York Power Authority, PO Box 200, Gilboa, NY 12076, USA. E-mail: kevin.mcloughlin@nypa.gov, Phone: 607-588-6061

Currently (since 1998) System Forester for the New York Power Authority, and consultant to EPRI for the ROW Environmental Management Target. Formerly (20 years), Administrator for Land Use & Industrial Waste Programs for the New York Power Pool and concurrently Research Program Manager for the Empire State Electric Energy Research Corporation. Also worked for the US Forest Service in Idaho and Arizona. Education: BS (1971) in Natural Resource Management and MS (1975) in Environmental Management from State University of New York College of Environmental Science and Forestry at Syracuse University.

Evaluation of Wildlife Habitat Suitability in an Herbicide-Treated Utility Right-of-Way

J. Drew Lanham and James E. Simmons III

We investigated the effects of 8 low-volume herbicide treatments (Imazapyr, Imazapyr/Glyphosate, Imazapyr/Metsulfuron, Imazapyr/Fosamine, Imazapyr/Triclopyr, Imazapyr/Picloram, Glyphosate, and Triclopyr/Picloram) on plant species composition and wildlife habitat in a power line ROW in the lower coastal plain of South Carolina from 1996–1998. Mechanically mowed and untreated control plots were also included for comparisons. Trends in vegetative response showed increases in forb and grass groups in most herbicide-treated plots. Decreasing or stable trends were observed in soft mast, vine and woody species among most chemical treatments. Ratings from Habitat Suitability Index models using life-requisite components (Suitability Indices) for white-tailed deer (*Odocoileus virginianus*), eastern bobwhite quail (*Colinus virginianus*), wild turkey (*Meleagris gallopavo*), bobcat (*Felis rufus*), and eastern cottontail (*Sylvilagus floridanus*) showed that one year after treatment, ROW habitats were least suitable for northern bobwhite and wild turkey and most suitable for white-tailed deer, bobcat, and eastern cottontail. We suggest that herbicides may be successfully used to manage ROW habitats for some wildlife species in the Southeast. Habitat Suitability Index Models provide valuable tools for evaluating ROW wildlife management efforts.

Keywords: Habitat-Suitability Index Models, rights-of-way, wildlife

INTRODUCTION

Rights-of-way (ROW) have long been recognized as potentially valuable wildlife habitats (Egler, 1952; Bramble and Byrnes, 1972, 1974). Accordingly, the effects of different vegetation management techniques on the quality and quantity of wildlife habitat offered by utility ROW has also been a topic of interest (Arner, 1977; Mayer, 1976; Hartley et al., 1984; Huntley and Arner, 1984).

Woody vegetation that may eventually grow into electric lines and/or limit accessibility for maintenance has traditionally been controlled with rotary mowing, hand cutting or selective herbicide treatments (Johnston, 1982; Arner, 1977). However the increasing value being placed on management for multiple uses has generated interest in the efficacy of low-volume herbicide treatments for controlling woody vegetation while enhancing the value of the ROW for wildlife with a minimal effect on soil and water resources.

With increased public concerns about the way that natural resources are used, management of ROW for wildlife habitat enhancement has become a powerful public relations tool for utility companies. Many cooperative opportunities for ROW wildlife management exist among private landowners, corporate entities (including the utilities), conservation organizations and state/federal natural resource agencies. Just as importantly, these cooperative opportunities exist across a wide range of physiographic regions and habitats in the southeastern United States.

Various methods have been used to evaluate the wildlife value of ROW vegetation. These include observational data that summarize wildlife use (Mayer, 1976) as well as evaluation of vegetative structure and composition as indicators of potential wildlife use (Bramble and Byrnes, 1979). Although more emphasis is being placed upon the importance of managing ROW for wildlife, we believe that there are few if any standardized methods or consistent efforts to do so. Moreover, few efforts at evaluating ROW wildlife habitat have been conducted in the United States southeastern coastal plain. In an attempt to efficiently evaluate wildlife habitat in ROW we used Habitat Suitability Index Models (HSI) developed by the US Fish and Wildlife Service (USFWS) to rank the relative value (0.0 = low to 1.0 = optimal) of herbicide and mechanically-treated ROW vegetation for selected early-successional wildlife species including white-tailed deer (*Odocoileus virginianus*), bobcat (*Felis rufus*), eastern cottontail (*Sylvilagus floridanus*), northern bobwhite quail (*Colinus virginianus*), and eastern wild turkey (*Meleagris gallopavo*). These models are comprised of individual Suitability Indices (SI) representing habitat characteristics that also have values on a continuous scale from 0.0 to 1.0. SI values are calculated from Suitability Index Variables (SIV) that comprise the various SI's. Although HSI models are often criticized because of a lack of validation by empirical data (Cole and Smith, 1983), the habitat information contained in these models offers a coarse estimator of potential habitat value which might offer an effective means for evaluating ROW wildlife habitat.

STUDY AREA

The site for this project was 0.6 km of Santee Cooper Electric 115 kV electric line and the associated 45 m wide easement located on the Mount Holly Plantation, in Berkeley County, South Carolina USA. Elevation on the study area ranges from 5.1 to 13.8 m above sea level. Xeric plots in the area were predominately poorly drained Meggett loam (thermic Typic Albaqualf) and moderately permeable Duplin, Lenoir, or Lynchburg fine sandy loam soils (Long, 1980). Major habitat types on the property included natural stands of longleaf pine (*Pinus palustris*), loblolly pine (*Pinus taeda*) plantations, second-growth bottomland hardwoods and hardwood-cypress bays along with grassy fields, ROW and wildlife food plots.

METHODS

Vegetation sampling
Thirty 30 m × 19.2 m experimental units (EU) totaling 576 m^2 were established in August of 1996. Each of the 30 EU systematically received one of eight herbicide mixtures (Imazapyr, Imazapyr/Glyphosate, Imazapyr/Metsulfuron, Imazapyr/Fosamine, Imazapyr/Triclopyr, Imazapyr/Picloram, Glyphosate, Triclopyr/Picloram). Mechanically mowed and untreated control plots were also included for comparisons. Pre-treatment vegetation sampling was conducted during August and September of 1996. Pre-treatment sampling included obtaining plant species composition and species coverage. Composition of plant groups included woody species, vine/bramble species, grass/grass-like species and forbs. Wildlife food plant groups (as determined from Radford et al., 1964 and Martin et al., 1951) included soft mast producers, blackberries (*Rubus spp.*), desirable legumes, desirable vines, and desirable forbs. We included blackberries as a separate group because of their dual importance as both a food and cover resource. Because mechanically treated plots were mowed in June 1996 during normal ROW maintenance rotations, pre-treatment data was not available for these plots. Estimates of species composition and coverage were obtained from five randomly located 2.25 m^2 samples per EU that were delineated using a 3-sided PVC plot. Percent cover was estimated for each class and species within a class to the nearest 5% by an ocular estimate of vertical projection of ground cover before and after treatments. These data were recorded during late August and early September of 1997. Mowed plots were sampled during this period to allow for comparisons of vegetation among treatments.

Herbicide application
Herbicide treatments were applied on in late September 1996 to take advantage of hardwood nutrient translocation to roots for more efficient root kill of woody stems. Herbicides were applied using a Hy-Pro, low-volume spray gun. A $\frac{1}{4}$% non-ionic surfactant was added to all treatments to increase application effectiveness. Herbicide treatments and rates of application (l/ha) were as follows: Imazapyr (1.18); Imazapyr + Glyphosate (1.18 + 9.5); Imazapyr + Metsulfuron (1.18 + 0.15); Imazapyr + Fosamine (1.18 + 10.93); Imazapyr + Triclopyr (1.18 + 4.75); Imazapyr + Picloram (1.18 + 4.75); Glyphosate (23.75); Triclopyr + Picloram (7.13 + 4.75).

Rating wildlife habitat suitability
To evaluate the quality of wildlife habitat present on treated plots after one growing season, habitat variables related to the nature of ROW vegetation were extracted from HSI models for selected species. Habitat variables that were not affected by ROW management techniques were not used in the analysis in order to develop generalized conclusions about the value of ROW vegetation without regard for surrounding habitats (see Bramble and Byrnes, 1979).

Vegetation was evaluated according to SI variables in HSI models for bobcat (Boyle and Fendley, 1987), northern bobwhite (Schroeder, 1985b), eastern wild turkey (Schroeder, 1985a), eastern cottontail (Allen, 1984), and white-tailed deer (Short, 1986). Data corresponding to these variables were recorded from three 0.004 ha (0.01 acre) samples taken in each Experimental Unit (EU) or extracted from species composition/coverage data (Tables 1 and 2). When variables concerned percent cover, ocular estimates of these variables were used. Data for summer SI variables was collected in August and September 1997, one full growing

Table 1. Percent coverage (ocular estimation) of special plant groups on treatment plots

Treatment	Plant group	Pre-treatment		Post-treatment	
		Mean	SD	Mean	SD
Imazapyr	Soft mast species	25.0	9.2	36.7	13.9a
	Blackberry species	21.3	6.5	35.3	15.6a
	Desirable legumes	4.3	5.8	3.3	2.3b
	Desirable vines	28.0	13.0	45.3	18.8a
	Desirable forbs	17.7	10.0	24.7	20.2
Imazapyr/Glyphosate	Soft mast species	30.7	18.0	3.7	4.2c
	Blackberry species	25.0	17.8	12.3	5.5c
	Desirable legumes	3.0	1.4	3.7	1.5b
	Desirable vines	31.7	19.0	20.3	6.1bc
	Desirable forbs	26.3	9.3	21.7	12.5
Imazapyr/Metsulfuron	Soft mast species	26.7	12.1	10.7	3.2c
	Blackberry species	25.0	14.1	6.7	5.0c
	Desirable legumes	10.5	9.2	5.0	—b
	Desirable vines	27.3	1.0	13.0	4.4c
	Desirable forbs	28.3	6.8	18.7	20.2
Imazapyr/Fosamine	Soft mast species	23.3	18.8	10.7	3.2c
	Blackberry species	22.3	19.6	9.7	8.1c
	Desirable legumes	1.5	0.7	1.3	0.6c
	Desirable vines	24.0	18.2	16.3	7.4bc
	Desirable forbs	16.7	4.9	32.0	28.9
Imazapyr/Triclopyr	Soft mast species	44.7	27.4	20.3	16.4bc
	Blackberry species	41.3	29.4	15.3	18.0bc
	Desirable legumes	1.0	—	2.0	—b
	Desirable vines	44.3	25.9	22.3	15.9bc
	Desirable forbs	15.3	7.4	29.0	23.5
Imazapyr/Picloram	Soft mast species	35.3	9.6	13.3	2.3c
	Blackberry species	31.7	13.1	9.0	3.5c
	Desirable legumes	8.0	8.5	2.0	—b
	Desirable vines	36.0	10.5	15.0	3.0bc
	Desirable forbs	22.7	8.5	33.0	24.6
Glyphosate	Soft mast species	42.3	24.2	11.0	3.0c
	Blackberry species	42.0	23.8	9.3	4.5c
	Desirable legumes	3.0	2.0	4.0	1.0b
	Desirable vines	48.7	30.7	25.0	18.2bc
	Desirable forbs	17.7	7.2	27.0	11.8
Triclopyr/Picloram	Soft mast species	37.0	14.1	29.7	4.0ab
	Blackberry species	31.7	12.7	28.0	4.0ab
	Desirable legumes	4.3	3.2	2.3	1.2b
	Desirable vines	39.3	18.5	32.3	0.6ab
	Desirable forbs	13.0	6.0	14.0	7.5
Mowed	Soft mast species	—	—	17.7	6.4bc
	Blackberry species	—	—	13.7	3.8bc
	Desirable legumes	—	—	8.3	1.2a
	Desirable vines	—	—	20.0	8.7bc
	Desirable forbs	—	—	27.7	5.0
Untreated Control	Soft mast species	49.7	18.0	39.3	7.6a
	Blackberry species	42.0	23.1	32.3	7.6a
	Desirable legumes	9.5	6.4	3.0	1.0b
	Desirable vines	52.0	18.1	45.0	5.3a
	Desirable forbs	31.3	17.4	20.3	8.7

a, b, c — Categories with the same letter are not significantly different at the $P \leq 0.05$ level.

Table 2. Treatment scores for suitability index (SI) variables of bobcat, northern bobwhite, eastern wild turkey and eastern cottontail rabbit in an herbicide-treated South Carolina coastal plain ROW

Variable	I	I/G	I/M	I/F	I/T	I/P	G	T/P	M	U/C
Bobcat										
SIV 1–% area in grass/forb/shrub veg.	0.9	0.9	0.9	0.9	0.9	0.9	0.9	0.9	0.9	0.9
SIV 2–% grass/forb/shrub in grass/forb veg.	0.9	0.9	0.9	0.9	0.9	0.9	0.9	0.9	0.9	0.9
FSI–Food ≥ 4 ha	0.9	0.9	0.9	0.9	0.9	0.9	0.9	0.9	0.9	0.9
FSI–Food < 4 ha	0.6	0.6	0.6	0.6	0.6	0.6	0.6	0.6	0.6	0.6
Northern Bobwhite										
SIV 1–% cover preferred herbaceous foods	0.5	0.5	0.5	0.2	0.5	0.2	0.5	0.5	0.9	0.5
SIV 2–% ground bare or w/light litter	0.5	0.2	0.2	0.2	0.2	0.5	0.2	0.2	0.2	0.2
WFSI–Winter food	0.16	0.06	0.06	0.03	0.06	0.06	0.03	0.06	0.12	0.06
SIV 6–% cover woody veg. < 2.0 m (cover)	0.5	0.2	0.5	0.5	0.2	0.5	0.2	0.2	0.2	0.5
SIV 7–% herbaceous cover	0.9	0.9	0.9	0.9	0.9	0.9	0.9	0.9	0.5	0.5
SIV 8–Avg. height of herbaceous canopy	0.9	0.2	0.2	0.5	0.0	0.2	0.2	0.2	0.9	0.0
SIV 9–% herbaceous cover in grasses	0.5	0.9	0.9	0.9	0.9	0.9	0.5	0.5	0.9	0.5
NSI–Nesting (moist soil)	0.3	0.2	0.2	0.3	0.0	0.2	0.2	0.2	0.3	0.0
Eastern Wild Turkey										
SIV 1–% herbaceous cover	0.9	0.9	0.9	0.9	0.9	0.9	0.9	0.9	0.9	0.2
SIV 2–Avg. height of herbaceous canopy	0.9	0.2	0.2	0.5	0.0	0.2	0.2	0.2	0.9	0.0
FBSI 1–Summer food/brood	0.9	0.4	0.4	0.7	0.0	0.4	0.4	0.4	0.9	0.0
FBSI 2–Summer food/brood distance to cover	0.8	0.4	0.4	0.6	0.0	0.4	0.4	0.4	0.8	0.0
SIV 6–% shrub crown cover (food)	0.9	0.9	0.9	0.9	0.9	0.9	0.5	0.9	0.9	0.9
SIV 7–% shrub crown cover (behavior)	0.9	0.9	0.9	0.9	0.9	0.9	0.9	0.9	0.9	0.2
SIV 8–% shrub cover in soft mast producers	0.9	0.9	0.5	0.5	0.9	0.9	0.9	0.9	0.9	0.9
FWSSI 2–Fall/Winter/Spring food	0.3	0.3	0.2	0.2	0.3	0.3	0.2	0.3	0.3	0.07
Eastern Cottontail										
SIV 1–% shrub closure	0.9	0.5	0.9	0.9	0.5	0.9	0.2	0.2	0.2	0.9
SIV 2–% tree canopy	0.0	0.0	0.0	0.0	0.0	0.0	0.0	0.0	0.0	0.0
SIV 3–% cover persistent herbaceous veg.	0.5	0.5	0.5	0.5	0.5	0.5	0.5	0.5	0.5	0.5
WCFI–Winter cover/food	1.0	0.9	1.0	1.0	0.9	1.0	0.7	0.7	0.7	1.0

season after application of herbicide treatments. Values for winter SI variables were collected in January 1998. For ranking purposes, the continuous scale data from 0.0 to 1.0 were converted into discrete classes following methodology established by Wakeley (1988). Resulting levels included zero (SI = 0), low (0 < SI < 0.33), medium (0.33, SI < 0.67), and high (SI, 0.67) classes that represented relative habitat values for variables (Wakeley, 1988). Actual values of the variables measured related to these various levels is shown in Table 2. These classes facilitated habitat evaluation with less sampling effort and provided HSI scores very similar to the original models (Wakeley, 1988). For purposes of calculating HSI scores and scores for various life requisite components, values of 0, 0.2, 0.5, and 0.9 corresponded to low, medium, or high levels of these variables (Wakeley, 1988).

The primary SI variables in the bobcat HSI model (SIV 1 = the percent of the area covered in grass/forb/shrub vegetation; SIV 2 = the percent of the grass/forb/shrub portion of the area covered by grass/forb vegetation) were vegetative characteristics related to food availability. These two factors were used to determine the Food Suitability Index (FSI) that was then weighted by an area factor (Boyle and Fendley, 1987).

Variables examined for the northern bobwhite HSI (Schroeder, 1985b) included a Winter Food Suitability Index (WFSI 1 = 2/3 [SIV 1 × SIV 2], where SIV 1 = percent canopy cover of preferred herbaceous foods calculated from species composition data; SIV 2 = percent of bare ground or light litter cover). The percent canopy cover of woody vegetation <2.0 m (SIV 6) was used as an indicator of cover available. Other variables examined included the percent of herbaceous canopy cover (SIV 7), the average height of the herbaceous canopy in summer (SIV 8), and the proportion of the herbaceous canopy cover in grass (SIV 9) and soil moisture (SIV 10) as parts of the Nesting Suitability Index (NSI = [SIV 7 × SIV 8 × SIV 9]$^{1/2}$ × SIV 10). NSI was determined for all three moisture levels indicated in the model with wet/saturated soils representing low values (0.2), moist for medium values (0.5) and relatively dry for high values (0.9). Variables that were not examined concerned crop management and over story vegetation as well as interspersion of these different components.

Life requisite components extracted from the HSI for the eastern wild turkey included portions of the Summer Food/Brood habitat (FBSI 1 and 2) and Fall/Winter/Spring Food Suitability indices (FWSSI 2) (Schroeder, 1985a). FBSI 1 was composed of the percent herbaceous canopy closure in the summer (SIV 1) and the average height of the summer herbaceous canopy (SIV 2). This relationship was expressed as FBSI 1 =

(SIV 1 × SIV 2)$^{1/2}$. FBSI 2 (=FBSI 1 × SIV 3) incorporated the distance to forest or tree cover (SIV 3) into this relationship and was used to rank food/brood resources in ROW. For our study, SIV 3 was deemed to be high (0.9) since the lower limit of this ranking is not reached within the ROW corridor. FWSSI 2 (=SIV 6 × SIV 8)/2 × SIV 7 × SIV 3) was the Fall/Winter/Spring Food suitability index in shrub cover types where SIV 6 = percent shrub crown cover affecting food availability, SIV 7 = percent shrub crown cover affecting behavior; SIV8 = the percentage of the shrub crown cover in soft mast producers and SIV 3 = distance to forest cover.

Variables chosen from the eastern cottontail HSI model (Allen, 1984) composed the Winter Cover/Food Index; WCFI = 4 (SIV 1) + (SIV 2)/5, where SIV 1 = percent shrub crown closure; SIV 2 = percent tree canopy closure; SIV 3 = percent cover of persistent herbaceous vegetation left standing after the growing season. This relationship was equal to the maximum value between WCFI and 1.0. We chose Model IV of the white-tailed deer HSI model as a simple predictor of presence or absence of deer on a habitat block (Short, 1986). This model only considered the presence or absence of four major forage classes (leafy browse, edible fungi, cool season grasses and forbs, mast producers) as indicators of potential deer use. Suitability was conferred to habitats where one of the four major forage classes is present on 1/3 of the samples. Due to the lack of edible fungi and the presence of only soft mast producers on the study site, only leafy browse and cool season grass/forb categories were used. Cover offered to white-tailed deer was not quantified since adequate cover is usually available in coastal habitats and there is little need for thermal cover in the warm climate of coastal South Carolina (Short, 1986).

Vegetation data analysis
Percent cover estimates for both plant groupings were averaged for all five samples within each EU. ANOVA (*proc glm*; SAS Institute, 1996) was used to determine differences in coverage between EU = s for each year. Differences in coverage between sampling periods were compared using a Student's T-test. Significance levels for all tests were set at $\alpha = 0.05$.

RESULTS

Vegetative composition
Few statistically significant differences were found in coverage data by plant group or special plant group in pre-treatment or post-treatment samples (Tables 1 and 3). However, several notable patterns (pre treatment to post treatment) were observed. Forb coverage increased in all treatments except Imazapyr/Metsulfuron and untreated control plots. Grass/grass like species increased in all but Imazapyr, Imazapyr/Fosamine and Imazapyr/Triclopyr plots. In post-treatment samples, untreated controls and Imazapyr plots were the only treatments to show positive responses in vine coverage. Woody coverage decreased for all treatments except for mowed and control plots.

Differences between treatments for the coverage of special plant groups also showed limited statistical significance. Again, however we observed several patterns in response that were noteworthy. Imazapyr plots were the only treatment to show positive responses for soft mast producers like blackberry, an important food and cover resource for many wildlife species. Desirable legume responses were generally negative with only Imazapyr/Glyphosate, Imazapyr/Triclpyr, and Glyphosate showing slight positive responses. Although we had no pre-treatment data for comparison, mowed plots had the highest coverage of legume species during post treatment measurements. As in the broader vine group, the special vine class only showed positive responses in Imazapyr treated plots. Desirable forb (e.g., ragweed *Ambrosia spp*.) response was positive in Imazapyr, Imazapyr/Fosamine, Imazapyr/Triclopyr, Imazapyr/Picloram, Glyphosate, and Triclopyr/Picloram plots. The lowest desirable forb coverage was found in mowed plots.

Wildlife habitat suitabilities
Bobcat
Values contributing to the Food Suitability Index for bobcats occurred at high levels (0.9) for all treatments. When these values were used to calculate the FSI for areas of different size according to model specifications, there would be changes in quality between different sized areas, but not between treatments. For areas ≥ 4 ha the FSI was 0.9 for all treatments, which indicated a high value of foraging habitat. For areas <4 ha the FSI was calculated to be 0.6 for all treatments, which was at the upper end of the medium quality rating (Table 2).

Northern Bobwhite
There was limited variability among the rankings for the various components of the northern bobwhite HSI that were examined. The Winter Food Suitability Index (WFSI 1) was ranked low (0.06–0.12) for all treatments. The cover component relating to the amount of woody cover <2.0 m in height was low for most treatments with the exception of Imazapyr, Imazapyr/Metsulfuron, and Imazapyr/Fosamine which were calculated to have medium suitability, as well as the untreated control plot which had high levels of woody cover. For the nesting component (NSI) of the model, values were calculated across the three moisture gradients indicated (saturated/wet, moist, and dry). For saturated/wet and moist levels, all treatments were ranked as low quality (0.04–0.006) nesting

Table 3. Mean coverage on treatment plots by plant group (% cover by ocular estimation)

Treatment	Plant group	Pre-treatment		Post-treatment	
		Mean	SD	Mean	SD
Imazapyr	Forbs	26.7	16.7	41.3	15.9
	Grass/Grass-like	28.7	12.7	12.0	6.0
	Vine/Bramble	35.7	19.0	47.0	18.5ab
	Woody	31.7	6.7	10.3	3.8
Imazapyr/Glyphosate	Forbs	33.0	10.8	48.0	25.1
	Grass/Grass-like	18.7	13.5	31.3	23.6
	Vine/Bramble	40.0	22.1	24.0	7.2c
	Woody	37.0	9.5	20.5	19.1
Imazapyr/Metsulfuron	Forbs	39.0	5.6	36.3	21.2
	Grass/Grass-like	31.3	25.3	37.3	15.8
	Vine/Bramble	37.0	14.7	18.0	10.0c
	Woody	29.3	7.6	14.3	10.7
Imazapyr/Fosamine	Forbs	28.7	8.1	54.7	20.9
	Grass/Grass-like	30.0	21.4	26.0	16.5
	Vine/Bramble	39.7	37.2	21.0	8.7c
	Woody	28.7	8.1	31.5	13.4
Imazapyr/Triclopyr	Forbs	28.0	19.3	46.0	20.0
	Grass/Grass-like	33.0	1.4	26.0	16.5
	Vine/Bramble	56.0	36.4	27.7	18.4bc
	Woody	18.0	4.4	12.7	14.2
Imazapyr/Picloram	Forbs	31.3	7.8	51.0	21.0
	Grass/Grass-like	23.3	9.5	25.3	6.0
	Vine/Bramble	51.0	17.3	18.7	2.1c
	Woody	38.0	8.5	15.3	13.3
Glyphosate	Forbs	30.0	6.6	53.3	11.6
	Grass/Grass-like	20.0	14.9	25.3	12.5
	Vine/Bramble	57.7	37.2	30.3	19.3bc
	Woody	31.3	13.1	4.0	1.4
Triclopyr/Picloram	Forbs	27.0	3.6	34.3	9.0
	Grass/Grass-like	20.3	10.7	28.0	4.4
	Vine/Bramble	53.0	13.5	38.3	4.0bc
	Woody	27.7	14.0	5.0	2.0
Mowed	Forbs	—	—	43.0	1.0
	Grass/Grass-like	—	—	50.0	17.1
	Vine/Bramble	—	—	24.0	8.9c
	Woody	—	—	13.3	10.5
Untreated Control	Forbs	36.0	18.4	29.0	18.2
	Grass/Grass-like	9.3	4.0	12.0	4.4
	Vine/Bramble	71.0	19.1	60.7	17.0a
	Woody	18.3	5.5	29.7	15.3

a, b, c — Categories with the same letter are not significantly different at $P \leq 0.05$ level.

habitat except Imazapyr/Triclopyr and untreated control treatments which were ranked to have zero (0.0) suitability for nesting.

If this same vegetative structure had occurred on dry sites, the ranking would have increased to medium (0.4–0.6) for all treatments with low rankings in other categories. EU ranked as zero retained this ranking for dry soils. For plots within this study area, rankings relating to saturated/wet or moist soils were the most accurate representations of conditions in the field (Table 2).

Eastern Wild Turkey

There was also variability in values assigned to the various components of the eastern wild turkey HSI examined in this study. The Food/Brood Summer Index 1 (FBSI 1) was calculated as medium (0.4) for most treatments with some exceptions. High (0.7–0.9) levels of FBSI 1 were present on EU treated with Imazapyr, Imazapyr/Fosamine, and mowing. EU treated with Imazapyr/Triclopyr and controls had zero (0.0) value for summer foods. These rankings were consistent with the Food/Brood Summer Index 2, which took into account the distance from forest cover, with the exception of Imazapyr/Fosamine treatments which dropped from a high rating to a medium rating when this variable was included (0.7 to 0.6). When examining the value of ROW vegetation to the Fall/Winter/Spring food index (FWSSI 2) for shrubland habitats, all treatments were calculated to have low (0.07–0.3) values for this measure due to dense vegetation (Table 2).

Eastern Cottontail Rabbit
The variables measured for the eastern cottontail HSI were related to the Winter Cover/Food Index (WCFI). Values of this index were calculated to be high (0.7–1.0) for all treatments (Table 2).

White-tailed Deer
For model IV in the white-tailed deer HSI, habitat was determined to be adequate for use by deer if cool season grasses and forbs or leafy browse were present on $\frac{1}{3}$ of the samples taken. Cool season grasses and forbs as well as leafy browse were present on all samples taken for every treatment. These components also comprised approximately $\frac{1}{3}$ cover in all samples taken for all treatments (27% minimum). Habitat was ranked as adequate for white-tailed deer for all treatments (Table 2).

DISCUSSION

Differences in the amount of Vine/Bramble coverage on treatment EU during the post-treatment period was most likely attributable to treatment effects and environmental conditions. Greater coverage of this category on Imazapyr plots was due to an abundance of blackberry cover on these plots as compared with other treatments. Imazapyr is noted to have a minimal negative impact on blackberry species (American Cyanamid Tech. Bulletin, 1996). This was also responsible for the higher coverage of Blackberry species, Desirable Vines, and Soft Mast producing species found on Imazapyr treated plots. The presence of high Vine/Bramble coverage on untreated controls was clearly a result of these areas remaining undisturbed and the abundance of vigorous blackberry growth on these plots. Higher Vine/Bramble coverage on Triclopyr/Picloram and Glyphosate treated plots was more likely a result of proliferate growth of honeysuckle and other vine species, rather than blackberries.

High levels of Desirable Legume coverage on mowed plots was due to the low-growing cover on mechanically treated sites. Legumes present on these plots were interspersed with low-growing grass and forb cover and their presence was most likely due to the absence of dead vegetation shading the ground in the early growing season. The removal of woody and herbaceous biomass from the mowed plots allowed for greater solar penetration and most likely favored germination and establishment of a greater diversity of species on these plots. Higher levels of legumes on Imazapyr/Metsulfuron and Glyphosate treated plots were more likely a result of differential chemical coverage at the time of treatment, as well as differences in the seed bank, soil moisture and other microsite factors affecting species composition. We feel that important differences between the abundance of other plant groups in chemically treated plots will become evident in subsequent growing seasons as vegetative communities become established along the ROW. Sampling after two or three growing seasons should be more representative of conditions present during normal management rotations and will be more useful in the interpretation of differences among treatments. Additionally, we expect mowed plots to develop a denser woody component from sprouts than chemically treated areas. In addition to complicating future efforts to maintain this area with mechanical means, woody cover will likely shade forb and grass communities and prove less suitable for some valuable wildlife food plants.

Wildlife habitat suitability
The assumption that prey availability is the limiting factor concerning the quality of habitat for bobcats in the southeast (Boyle and Fendley, 1987) was the basis for using the Food Suitability Index (FSI) as an indicator of the quality of foraging habitat offered by ROW vegetation. The dense nature of native vegetation on the ROW within this study area provided the grass/forb/shrub habitat that is considered highly productive prey habitat for bobcats (Boyle and Fendley, 1987).

While all treatments were rated to have high values of the FSI for areas ≥ 4 ha and medium values for area <4 ha, we believe that the quality of foraging habitat was higher on chemically treated plots and controls than on mowed areas. Boyle and Fendley (1987) note that newly created early successional areas with qualifying levels of variables may not be as productive as older, intact areas. Chemically treated areas may provide a more consistent prey base since the structure of vegetation was not altered as drastically as on mowed areas. On chemically treated areas, there was a dense layer of residual cover from standing grasses, forbs, vines and brambles providing cover for prey species which was not present on mowed areas. ROW vegetation on an area could provide foraging habitat for bobcats even when other portions of a home range would provide unsuitable conditions for foraging. In addition, chemical treatments that lengthen or eliminate the need for traditional mowing rotations might increase the value of habitat for bobcats through time.

Habitat offered for the northern bobwhite was relatively poor for all treatments according to the factors measured in this study. Low levels of the Winter Food Suitability Index occurred due to the low to medium levels of preferred bobwhite foods on most treatments as well as the limited occurrence of bare ground. In addition to providing limited food resources, ground cover within the ROW was too dense to allow bobwhite foraging, especially for young chicks. Mowed treatments did provide high levels of preferred bobwhite foods, but due to the dense nature of the vegetation on these plots, the overall WFSI 1 was still rated as low. Treatments ranked as having a medium quality (Imazapyr, Imazapyr/Metsulfuron, and Imazapyr/Fosamine), or high quality (untreated control) cover component may have some value as escape cover for the northern bobwhite. These higher levels of woody cover, however, could conflict with the ultimate line maintenance goal of ROW managers. Woody cover on low-rated treatments would increase in subsequent years, but treatment rotations that would remove this woody cover would limit their value to quail populations. Woody cover on the chemically treated plots was mostly attributable to residual cover from low-growing, shrubby species (e.g., wax myrtle *Myrica cerifera*) that would not threaten the transmission of power, but would provide important cover for northern bobwhite and other wildlife. Low or zero values for the nesting component (NSI) for all treatments with saturated/wet or moist soils could be expected to decrease even further as the height of the herbaceous canopy continues to increase in future growing seasons after treatment. Therefore, NSI can be considered zero when considering the long-term value of ROW under these treatment regimes. Increases in the NSI under a dry moisture regime should not be viewed optimistically considering that changes in soil moisture would also lead to changes in vegetative structure.

Due to the limited presence of preferred foods, the lack of bare ground, the loss of woody cover, and moist soils in this study area, ROW treated with herbicide or mowing treatments can be considered little more than supplemental escape cover in areas already supporting northern bobwhite populations. While it has been suggested that prescribed fire could mitigate low food resources and the lack of bare ground (Arner, 1977), this is not an option that is often available to utilities considering the extensive area needing management and the liabilities associated with private landholdings and service interruption.

Habitat potential for the eastern wild turkey was also limited on ROW under most of the treatment methods examined in this study, even though high or medium rankings were given to all treatments except the control for the Food/Brood Suitability Index (FBSI) in the first year after treatment. These values are likely to decrease rapidly with successive growing seasons when the height of the herbaceous canopy would easily exceed 1 m that produces an overall HSI of zero (Schroeder, 1985a).

Low values were assigned to all treatments for the Fall/Winter/Spring Food Suitability Index (FWSSI) due to the dense layers of blackberry which would limit wild turkey visibility and limit use of these areas. These values could also be expected to approach zero as blackberry coverage becomes denser in subsequent growing seasons after treatment due to release from woody competition. According to the value determined from the HSI model, ROW under these management regimes could be expected to be of limited value for wild turkeys during the first 1–2 years after treatment.

Winter cover and food are considered to be the limiting factors determining the value of habitat for eastern cottontail rabbits (Allen, 1984). This was the basis for using the Winter Cover and Food suitability Index (WCFI) to evaluate the value of habitat offered by ROW vegetation. According to the ranking system used in this study, all treatments offered high quality habitat for use by eastern cottontails. The complete absence of a tree canopy (SIV 2) did not have a negative influence on this ranking because of the dense cover offered by blackberries, residual woody cover, and dense layers of standing herbaceous matter. Once again we suspected that chemically treated areas would provide a more stable habitat through time since mowing treatments remove almost all standing and cover for some portion of the year. The absence of this cover often coincides with the winter season when it is most needed by this species. The model predictions of optimal habitat were reinforced by frequent observations of cottontails and rabbit pellets within the study site.

Model IV of the white-tailed deer HSI did not lend itself to the ranking system used for other species. Since this model was intended to evaluate the potential presence or absence of deer on a habitat block, treatments were simply ranked as adequate or inadequate for use by white-tailed deer. Leafy browse and cool season grasses and forbs were present in all samples for all treatments within the study area. Therefore, all treatments were ranked as adequate for use by white-tailed deer. Our observations of abundant trails, pellets, beds and sightings throughout all treatment units indicated that these areas were highly suitable for white-tailed deer.

CONCLUSIONS AND MANAGEMENT IMPLICATIONS

The primary goal of ROW managers is to ensure the distribution of power and allow access for line maintenance while meeting as many secondary objectives for use of the ROW as possible. An ideal scenario for control of ROW vegetation may develop from a combination of chemical and mechanical management practices. For example, if mowing treatments were followed at the end of the following growing season with a broadcast or selective herbicide treatment, reduction in the vegetation height from mowing would increase effectiveness of chemical coverage and chemical treatments would provide some control of prolific root and sucker sprouting that consistently trouble ROW managers. At the same time such treatments would probably promote increases in many desirable wildlife plants. Alternatively, where structural diversification is the desired objective, selective application by backpack units (basal application) might encourage patchy growths of vegetation that add vertical heterogeneity within the ROW and increase wildlife habitat value.

From the model factors examined in this study, the dense vegetation occurring in our lower coastal plain ROW provides few long-term benefits to wild turkeys and bobwhite quail. However, results from this study cannot be extrapolated to evaluate ROW traversing other habitat types and environmental conditions. Habitats within this study area were most suitable for bobcats, white-tailed deer and cottontail rabbits. This is not surprising considering the abundance of food and cover offered for these species within the ROW. Hartley et al. (1984) also observed higher use of ROW by rabbits and deer in areas with more structure as opposed to less heterogeneous open grass areas. Other researchers have also found quality deer habitat on chemically treated ROW (Bramble and Byrnes, 1972, 1974).

Our study showed that no single ROW management technique served as a management panacea for all wildlife habitats in our ROW. Implementing management practices so that they are adaptive will allow managers to determine the best scenario for maintaining service and providing viable habitat in southeastern ROW. We believe that HSI models and their various components offer a valuable tool for meeting wildlife management and service goals in ROW.

REFERENCES

Allen, A.W. 1984. Habitat suitability index models: Eastern cottontail. US Fish Wildl. Serv. Biol. Rep., 82(10.66): 23.

American Cyanamid Company. 1996. Arsenal herbicide for industrial uses. Tech. Bulletin PE-11283. 18 pp.

Arner, D.H. 1977. Transmission line rights-of-way management. US Fish and Wildlife Service FWS/OBS-76/20.2. 12 pp.

Boyle, K.A. and T.T. Fendley. 1987. Habitat suitability index models: Bobcat. US Fish Wildl. Serv. Biol. Rep., 82(10.147): 16.

Bramble, W.C. and W.R. Byrnes. 1972. A long-term ecological study of game food and cover on a sprayed utility right-of-way. Research Bulletin No. 885. Feb. 1972. Purdue University Ag. Exp. Station. Lafayette, IN. 20 pp.

Bramble, W.C. and W.R. Byrnes. 1974. Impact of herbicides upon game food and cover on a utility right-of-way. Research Bulletin No. 918. Dec. 1974. Purdue University Ag Exp. Station. Lafayette, IN. 16 pp.

Bramble, W.C. and W.R. Byrnes. 1979. Evaluation of the wildlife habitat values of rights-of-way. Journal of Wildlife Management, 43(3): 642–649.

Cole, C.A. and R.L. Smith. 1983. Habitat suitability indices for monitoring wildlife populations — An evaluation. Proceedings North American Wildlife Conference, 48: 367–375.

Egler, F.E. 1952. Transmission lines as wildlife habitat. The Land, 11(1): 149–152.

Hartley, D.H., D.H. Arner, and J.W. Lipe. 1984. A comparison of right-of-way maintenance treatments and use by wildlife. In: Proc. Third International Symp. on Environmental Concerns in Rights-of-Way Management. San Diego CA. pp. 623–629.

Huntley, J.C. and D.H. Arner. 1984. Right-of-way maintenance to reduce costs and increase vegetative diversity and wildlife habitat — A demonstration. In: Proc. Third International Symp. on Environmental Concerns in Rights-of-Way Management. San Diego, CA. pp. 342–351.

Johnston, P.A. 1982. Cost comparison of right-of-way treatment methods. In: Proc. of the Third International Symposium on Environmental concerns in Rights-of-Way Management. San Diego, CA. pp. 320–323.

Long, B.M. 1980. Soil survey of Berkeley County, SC. National Co-op Soil Survey; USDA, SCS, SC Land Resources Conserv. Comm., SC Ag. Exp. Station.

Martin, A.H., H.S. Zimm, and A.J. Nelson. 1951. American Wildlife and Plants. A Guide to Wildlife Food Habits. New York, McGraw-Hill, Inc.

Mayer, T.D. 1976. An evaluation of chemically sprayed electric transmission line rights-of-way for actual and potential wildlife use. In: Proc. First National Symp. on Environmental Concerns in Rights-of-Way Management. Mississippi State University. pp. 288–294.

Radford A.E., H.E. Ahles, and C.R. Bell. 1964. Manual of the Vascular Flora of the Carolinas. The University of North Carolina Press. Chapel Hill, NC. 1183 pp.

SAS Institute. 1996. The SAS System for Windows. Release 6.11. Cary, NC.

Schroeder, R.L. 1985a. Habitat suitability index models: Eastern wild turkey. US Fish Wildl. Serv. Biol. Rep., 82(10.106): 33.

Schroeder, R.L. 1985b. Habitat suitability index models: Northern bobwhite. US Fish Wildl. Serv. Biol. Rep., 82(10.104): 32.

Short, H.L. 1986. Habitat suitability index models: white-tailed deer in the Gulf of Mexico and South Atlantic coastal plains. US Fish Wildl. Serv. Biol. Rep., 82(10.123): 36.

Wakeley, J.S. 1988. A method to create simplified versions of existing habitat suitability index (HSI) models. Environmental Management, 12(1): 79–83.

BIOGRAPHICAL SKETCHES

J. Drew Lanham, Associate Professor

Clemson University Department of Forest Resources, 261 Lehotsky Hall, Clemson, SC 29634-0331, USA; lanhamj@clemson.edu

Drew Lanham is an Associate Professor and Certified Wildlife Biologist in the Department of Forest Resources at Clemson University in Clemson, South Carolina. His research program focuses on the effects of forest management on nongame species with emphasis on songbird and herpetofauna. He has been a member of the Forest Resources faculty at Clemson since 1995.

James E. Simmons III, MS
Georgia Department of Natural Resources, 22814 Highway 144, Richmond Hill, GA 31331, USA
Jim Simmons completed the research in this paper as a portion of his Master's of Science (MS) degree in Forest Resources at Clemson University. He is currently a Wildlife Biologist with the Georgia Department of Natural Resources.

Butterflies and Skippers in Utility Rights-of-Way in the Upper Piedmont of South Carolina

J. Drew Lanham and Maria J. Nichols

Rights-of-way (ROW) are increasingly being recognized for their value to early-successional wildlife species. However, little or no information exists about diurnal Lepidopteran (butterflies and skippers) diversity in these areas. In the spring, summer, and fall of 1997 we conducted daily butterfly and skipper surveys on 6, 0.6 km transects of ROW in Greenville and Oconee counties in the Upper Piedmont of South Carolina. A total of 101 butterfly and skipper species (24,057 individuals: 14,727 butterflies and 9330 skippers) were recorded across all seasons. Overall diversity, evenness, and richness did not differ among the 6 study sites for butterflies. However, abundances of butterflies and skippers and skipper richness did differ among the six ROW. Vegetative composition assessed in the spring, summer, and fall of 1997 revealed no differences in vegetative structure among the ROW for any season. We believe that ROW may provide vital habitats for Lepidoptera in many southeastern landscapes.

Keywords: Butterflies, skippers, rights-of-way, southeastern US

INTRODUCTION

Utility rights-of-way (ROW) are ubiquitous landscape features across the United States. Although the primary function of ROW is the distribution of service (e.g., electrical, gas, communication), these areas are increasingly being enhanced for wildlife. Such actions are important since they may provide some of the only areas of early-successional habitat in human-developed or mature forest environments.

While our understanding of the importance of ROW to some vertebrate species has increased significantly, we know of no published studies that have systematically assessed the suitability of habitats for butterflies and skippers in the southeastern United States. This lack of attention is critical given the important roles Lepidoptera play as pollinators and prey in many ecosystems. Moreover, because of the declines documented for a number of butterfly and skipper species, it is important to increase our understanding of how Lepidopteran communities and species are distributed in various habitats. To address the lack of information in this area, we initiated a study to determine the species composition of butterfly and skipper fauna found on selected ROW in the Upper Piedmont of South Carolina and relate plant species structure and composition within ROW to the butterfly and skipper fauna present.

STUDY AREA AND METHODS

Study area

Six, 0.6 km transects were located on selected Duke Energy transmission rights-of-way (ROW) in the Upper Piedmont region of South Carolina. Three sites were located on the 7287 ha Clemson Experimental Forest in the Lower Foothills of Oconee County, South Carolina. Three additional sites were located in the Interior Plateau Region of Greenville County, South Carolina. Site elevations ranged from 150 to 330 m and were comprised primarily of second growth oak-hickory and mixed hardwood-pine forests growing in a transitional zone from sloping and rugged terrain to gently rolling hills (Myers et al., 1986).

Vegetation sampling and habitat evaluation

Important habitat requisites for Lepidoptera include the presence of warm, open areas, escape/protective cover, bare ground for puddling and basking, flowering plants for nectar feeding, and a diverse herbaceous component for larval target-host plants. In order to quantify these requisites, spring, summer, and fall vegetation were sampled on each ROW in 75-1 m^2 circular plots. In each plot, vegetation was placed into 1 of 6 general categories: trees >2 m, shrubs and saplings 1–2 m, herbs and forbs, woody, vines, and grasses. Percent cover estimates for the vegetation categories were measured for each plot and assigned a rank (e.g., 0 = no cover, 5 = abundant cover of 20–25%, 10 = 100% cover) following the Domin Scale (Kershaw, 1973). Nectar producing flowering plants and larval target host plants were identified to species where possible (Appendices 1 and 2). We used 2-factor analysis of variance procedures (PROC ANOVA; SAS Institute, 1996) to determine if vegetation in each of the 6 classes differed among ROW and by season. Tukey's W procedure (SAS Institute, 1996) was used to separate response means. Significance was determined at $P \leq 0.05$.

Lepidopteran censuses

Using the Pollard Transect Method (Pyle, 1992) to census diurnal Lepidoptera in our 6 study sites, we established a single 0.6 km transect through the longitudinal center of each ROW. Transect widths were equivalent to the width of the 6 ROW (40–80 m). Within each transect, all butterflies seen were identified to species and counted. Butterflies and skippers not positively identified in the field were either collected or photographed for later identification (Moore, 1975; Thomas, 1983a; Pollard, 1977; Pyle, 1992). Each ROW was censused 18 times with 1 survey conducted each week for each ROW. Surveys were run from 1 May to 31 October 1997. Again, 2-factor ANOVA was used to compare estimates of overall richness, butterfly and skipper richness, butterfly and skipper abundance and Shannon–Weiner Diversity (H') and Evenness (J') (Shannon and Weaver, 1949) by ROW and by season. Tukey's W Procedure was used to determine differences among means with significance determined at $P \leq 0.05$. Sorenson's Quotient of Similarity (QS; Sorenson, 1948) was also used to quantify the similarities in Lepidopteran communities among ROW.

RESULTS

ROW vegetation

All of the habitat requisites necessary for butterflies and skippers were present on all 6 ROW. This included an abundance of open habitat, bare ground and moist puddling areas. Vegetative cover was also abundant in the form of trees, shrubs, and dense areas of vines, herbs, and forbs. Eighty-two flowering nectar sources (Appendix 1) and 102 larval-target host plants (Appendix 2) were identified in the 6 ROW. Herbs and forbs dominated both nectar sources and larval target-host species. ANOVA revealed no statistically significant differences in vegetation among ROW or by season. Therefore we pooled vegetation class data (e.g., trees >2 m, shrubs, grasses, etc.) for the 6 ROW to assess seasonal differences within vegetation classes. Although, grass, herb/forb and bare ground classes had the highest numerical coverage percentages across all seasons and all ROW, ANOVA showed no statistically significant differences within vegetation classes across seasons ($P \leq 0.05$) (Table 1).

Table 1. Seasonal comparisons* of vegetative percent cover occurring on 6 rights-of-way in SC, May–Oct. 1997

Vegetation class	Spring	Summer	Fall
Trees >2 m	8.00 A	9.00 A	9.00 A
Shrubs 1–2 m	10.0 A	10.0 A	9.00 A
Grasses	18.0 B	22.0 B	24.0 B
Vines	13.0 A	14.0 A	13.0 A
Herbs and forbs	23.0 B	22.0 B	25.0 B
Other woody vegetation	5.00 C	6.00 C	6.00 C
Bare ground	23.0 B	17.0 B	14.0 B

*Values across rows with the same letter are not significantly different ($P < 0.05$).

Lepidopteran communities

One hundred and one (101) species (59 butterflies and 42 skippers) were recorded in censuses conducted across all seasons for all 6 ROW (Appendix 3). A total of 24,057 individuals (14,727 butterflies and 9330 skippers) were recorded. The five most frequently recorded species included the Eastern Tailed Blue (*Everes comyntas*), Monarch (*Danaus plexippus*), Pearly Crescentspot (*Phyciodes tharos*), Painted Lady (*Vanessa cardui*), and European Cabbage Butterfly (*Artogeia rapae*).

No statistically significant differences were reported for diversity (H'), evenness (J'), and butterfly richness (S') among ROW. However, ANOVA did reveal some significant differences for butterfly species abundance ($F = 6.24$, $P = 0.001$, $R^2 = 0.55$), skipper abundance ($F = 5.25$, $P = 0.003$, $R^2 = 0.36$), and skipper richness ($F = 6.09$, $P = 0.001$, $R^2 = 0.44$) among some ROW (Table 2). Sorenson's index, a function that reflects the similarities in species composition between two samples, was also used to compare Lepidopteran communities among ROW.

Sorenson's index is defined as:

$$QS = \frac{2c}{(a+b)};$$

where c is the number of species common to samples 1 and 2, and a and b represents the species richness of samples 1 and 2, respectively. Estimates of QS range from 0 (no common species between samples) to 1 (identical species composition). Sorenson's estimates showed that the butterfly and skipper communities

Table 2. Lepidopteran community comparisons[a,b] on 6 rights-of-way in SC, May–Oct. 1997

ROW	H′	J′	S	Butterfly richness	Butterfly abundance	Skipper richness	Skipper abundance
1	1.50 A	0.827 A	66 A	34.0 A	360 A	16.8 B	164 B
2	1.60 A	0.866 A	71 A	34.2 A	777 B	22.0 A B	181 B
3	1.56 A	0.832 A	76 A	34.6 A	771 B	21.6 A B	211 B
4	1.57 A	0.891 A	72 A	34.2 A	346 A	17.8 A B	526 A
5	1.64 A	0.877 A	74 A	34.2 A	343 A	20.4 A B	548 A
6	1.60 A	0.856 A	74 A	35.2 A	348 A	22.8 A	233 B

[a] H′ = Shannon–Weiner diversity, J′ = Shannon–Weiner evenness, S = richness.
[b] Values in a column followed by the same letter are not significantly different ($P < 0.05$).

Table 3. Lepidopteran community comparisons[a] on 6 SC rights-of-way, May–Oct. 1997

Sites	1	2	3	4	5	6
1						
2	0.77					
3	0.77	0.82				
4	0.78	0.75	0.81			
5	0.77	0.80	0.80	0.75		
6	0.81	0.81	0.81	0.82	0.85	

[a] Comparisons reflect Sorenson's Indices ($QS = 2c/(a + b)$; where c is the number of species common to samples 1 and 2, and a and b represents the species richness of samples 1 and 2, respectively).

were more similar than dissimilar among the ROW as values for all of the pairwise comparisons ranged between 0.75 and 0.85 (Table 3).

DISCUSSION

The ROW censused in this study were botanically diverse, structurally heterogeneous, early-successional habitats. We found all of the habitat requisites for butterflies and skippers available on the utility rights-of-way that were censused. This is a result of the floristically diverse habitat found in these areas. We suggest that these areas might be critical in landscapes where quality early-successional habitats are limited and can be managed with minimal effort to provide optimal habitats for many butterflies and skippers. Given the vital role Lepidoptera play, the popularity of butterfly gardening and watching, and the increasing attention being given to ROW as wildlife habitat, one would expect that more studies would be published regarding the Lepidopteran communities in ROW. However, we found no published information regarding butterfly and skipper communities in southeastern ROW. Thus, our study provides important baseline data for further investigation of Lepidopteran habitat relationships in ROW and other habitat types.

The continuation of research investigating lepidopteran communities in ROW is critical since they play such vital roles as primary consumers, pollinators and prey in most terrestrial ecosystems. Aside from the intrinsic value of understanding the habitat relationships of Lepidoptera in ROW and other early-successional habitats, new information gained about the abundance and distribution of butterflies and skippers may ultimately increase our understanding of how other species like insectivorous passerines or native, insect-pollinated flora might respond to management that affects pollinators or prey.

Although a number of factors are associated with declines in butterflies and skippers including specimen collection, prolonged bouts of inclement weather and habitat destruction (Thomas, 1984b), habitat alteration is frequently cited as a factor in the declines observed among many Lepidopteran species (Thomas, 1984b). Efforts to recover species such as the federally endangered Karner Blue Butterfly (*Lycaeides melissa*) and the Kirtland's Warbler (*Dendroica kirtlandii*) have focused more attention on the need to manage early-successional habitats and the species dependent upon them. While the convention in conservation biology has typically been the minimization of anthropogenic disturbance, many species like the Karner Blue butterfly and other Lepidoptera may derive benefits from some anthropogenic disturbances (Swengal, 1993; Criswell, 1995). Otherwise, if the habitats on which these species depend decreases or changes in quality, then populations may continue to decline or become extinct (New, 1991).

Early-successional habitats that are important to a wide array of species may be lost or altered by urbanization, changes in agriculture, and changes in forest management practices. In urban, suburban, and rural landscapes, early-successional habitats may be altered or otherwise limited by a number of factors. Activities such as frequent, persistent mowing in urban and suburban areas and "clean-farming" in rural areas may inhibit herbaceous plant development, remove nectar-producing flowers from the stalks of grasses or other "weedy" plants and decrease the structural heterogeneity of an area. In largely forested landscapes, changes in forest management practices dictating smaller areas of disturbance or cessation of forest regeneration practices may also contribute to declines in some early-successional species (New, 1991; Pyle, 1992; Pollard and Yates, 1993).

Controversy surrounding forest management practices like clearcutting may conflict with efforts to manage some early-successional species. Additionally, the proliferation of "clean-farms" and manicured gardens and parks where desirable "weeds" and other vegetation are suppressed is unlikely to decrease as human development and demand spread. As a result, "new" means of managing for disturbance-dependent species must be investigated. Since this study and a number of other previous studies indicate that utility ROW may provide adequate early-successional habitat for a number of species, ROW may offer a legitimate management/conservation strategy for some disturbance-dependent species in some landscapes. Since the uninterrupted delivery of service to customers will continue to be priority of utility companies, ROW will continue to be managed on a consistent basis. As such these areas will become increasingly important to species dependent upon disturbed habitats in landscapes that otherwise would not support them. Current ROW wildlife habitat improvement initiatives by state, private, and industrial agencies are illustrative of the increasing desire to gain added value from ROW. However, the majority of these efforts focus almost exclusively on vertebrates. Unfortunately, while the enthusiasm for managing ROW for wildlife is increasing, our knowledge of how to do it most effectively has not. The entities responsible for managing vegetation on ROW (e.g., utility companies) should be cognizant of the potential effects that different management regimes have on *all* species. The ROW we censused had not received any treatments beyond the scheduled 2–3 year mowing. Unlike many vertebrate species that may require a great deal of time, effort, and financial input above and beyond traditional ROW maintenance, we suggest that utility companies, management agencies, and private landowners in the Southeast can, with minimal additional effort, provide important habitats for diverse Lepidopteran communities.

REFERENCES

Arner, D.H. 1977. Transmission line rights-of-way management. US Fish and Wildlife Service. FWS/OBS-76/20.2. 12 pp.

Bramble, W.C. and W.R. Byrnes. 1972. A long-term ecological study of game food and cover on a sprayed utility right-of-way. Research Bulletin No. 885. February. 1972. Purdue University Agricultural Experiment Station. Lafayette, IN. 20 pp.

Bramble, W.C. and W.R. Byrnes. 1974. Impact of herbicides upon game food and cover on a utility right-of-way. Research Bulletin No. 918. December 1974. Purdue University. Agricultural Experiment Station Lafayette, IN. 16 pp.

Bramble, W.C. and W.R. Byrnes. 1979. Evaluation of the wildlife habitat values of rights-of-way. Journal of Wildlife Management, 43(3): 642–649.

Bramble, W.C. and W.R. Byrnes. 1985. Effects of a special technique for right-of-way maintenance on deer habitat. Journal of Arboriculture, 11(9): 278–284.

Bramble, W.C., W.R. Byrnes, and R.J. Hutnik. 1990. Resistance of plant cover types to tree seedling invasion on an electric transmission right-of-way. Journal of Arboriculture, 16(5): 21–25.

Bramble, W.C., W.R. Byrnes, R.J. Hutnik, and S.A. Liscinsky. 1991. Prediction of cover types on rights-of-way after maintenance treatments. Journal of Arboriculture, 17(2): 38–43.

Cavanagh, J.B., D.P. Olson, and S.N. Macrigeanis. 1976. Wildlife use and management of power line rights-of-way in New Hampshire. In: Proceedings of the 1st National Symposium on Environmental Concerns in Rights-of-Way Management. R. Tillman, ed. Mississippi State University, Starkville, MS. pp. 276–285.

Criswell, R. 1995. Regal Lady. Pennsylvania Wildlife, XVI(5): 17–20.

Kershaw, K.A. 1973. Quantitative and Dynamic Plant Ecology. 2nd ed. England: Edward Arnold. 297 pp.

Moore, N.W. 1975. Butterfly transects in a linear habitat 1964–1973. Entomologist's Gazette, 26: 71–78.

Myers, R.K., R. Zahner, and S.M. Jones. 1986. Forest Habitat Regions of South Carolina from Landsat Imagery. Clemson University. 31 pp.

New, T.R. 1991. Butterfly Conservation. New York. Oxford University Press. 224 pp.

Pollard, E. 1977. A method for assessing changes in the abundance of butterflies. Biological Conservation, 12: 115–134.

Pollard, E. and T.J. Yates. 1993. Monitoring Butterflies for Ecology and Conservation. Chapman & Hall, New York. 274 pp.

Pyle, R.M. 1992. Handbook for Butterfly Watchers. Houghton Mifflin Company, New York. 280 pp.

SAS Institute. 1996. The SAS system for Windows. Release 6.11. Cary, NC.

Shannon, C.E. 1949. The Mathematical Theory of Communication. University of Illinois Press, Urbana, IL. 117 pp.

Sorenson, T.A. 1948. A method of establishing groups of equal amplitude in plant sociology based on similarity of species content, and its application to analyses of the vegetation on Danish commons. Kongekige Danske Videnskabernes Selskab Biologiske Skrifter, 56: 1–34.

Swengal, A. and S. R. Swengal. 1993. Observations of Karner Blues and the barrens community in Wisconsin. Unpublished report. Wisconsin Field Office. 39 pp.

Thomas, J.A. 1983a. A quick method for estimating butterfly numbers during surveys. Biological Conservation, 12: 195–211.

Thomas, J.A. 1984b. The conservation of butterflies in temperate countries: Past efforts and lessons for the future. 11th Symposium of the Royal Entomological Society of London, Imperial College, London, MS. pp. 333–353.

BIOGRAPHICAL SKETCHES

J. Drew Lanham, Associate Professor
Clemson University Department of Forest Resources, 261 Lehotsky Hall, Clemson, SC 29634-0331, USA; lanhamj@clemson.edu

Drew Lanham is an Associate Professor and Certified Wildlife Biologist in the Department of Forest Resources at Clemson University in Clemson, South Carolina. His research program focuses on the effects of forest management on nongame species with emphasis on songbird and herpetofauna species. He has been a member of the Forest Resources faculty at Clemson since 1995.

Maria J. Nichols, MFR
Fatima717@aol.com

Maria J. Nichols completed this research as a portion of a Master's of Forest Resources (MFR) at Clemson University. She has worked as a wildlife control officer in Greenville, South Carolina for the past 5 years.

APPENDIX 1. NECTARING PLANTS RECORDED ON 6 SOUTH CAROLINA ROW, MAY–OCTOBER 1997

Common Name	Scientific Name	Common Name	Scientific Name
Yarrow	*Achillea millefolium*	Common Morning Glory	*Ipomoea purpurea*
Wingstem	*Actinomeris alternifolia*	Crape-myrtle (white)	*Lagerstroemia indica*
Field Garlic	*Allium vineale*	Motherwort	*Leonurus cardiaca*
Pigweed	*Amaranthus spp.*	Wild Peppergrass	*Lepidium virginicum*
False Indigo	*Amorpha canescens*	Creeping Bush Clover	*Lespedeza repens*
Mayweed	*Anthemis cotula*	White Campion	*Lychnis alba*
Dogbane	*Apocynum spp.*	Lance-leaved Loosestrife	*Lysimachia lanceolata*
Swamp Milkweed	*Asclepias incarnata*	Whorled Loosestrife	*Lysimachia quadrifolia*
Common Milkweed	*Asclepias syriaca*	Monkey Flower	*Mimulus spp.*
Butterfly Weed	*Asclepias tuberosa*	Prickly Pear	*Opuntia humifusa*
Saint Andrew's Cross	*Ascyrum hypericoides*	Yellow Wood Sorrel	*Oxalis europaea*
Aster	*Aster spp.*	Sourwood	*Oxydendrum arboreum*
Trumpet Creeper	*Campsis radicans*	Carolina Phlox	*Phlox carolina*
Wild Sensitive Plant	*Cassia nictitans*	Garden Phlox	*Phlox panicalata*
Spurred Butterfly Pea	*Centrosema virginianum*	Phlox	*Phlox spp.*
Button Bush	*Cephalanthus occidentalis*	Clammy Ground Cherry	*Physalis heterophylla*
Bull Thistle	*Cirsium vulgare*	Pokeweed	*Phytolacca americana*
Butterfly Pea	*Clitoria mariana*	Smartweed	*Polygonum spp.*
Greater Coreopsis	*Coreopsis major*	Cinquefoil	*Potentilla spp.*
Tickseed Sunflower	*Coreopsis spp.*	Hoary Mountain Mint	*Pycnanthemum incanum*
Crown Vetch	*Coronilla varia*	Winged Sumac	*Rhus copallina*
Queen Anne's Lace	*Daucus carota*	Smooth Sumac	*Rhus glabra*
Rocket Lackspar	*Delphinium ajacis*	Rose species	*Rosa spp.*
Rocket Lackspar	*Delphinium ajacis*	Common Blackberry	*Rubus alleghieniensis*
Indian Strawberry	*Duchesnia indica*	Black-eyed Susan	*Rudbeckia hirta*
Daisy Fleabane (pink)	*Erigeron annuus*	Short-styled Snakeroot	*Sanicula canadensis*
Daisy Fleabane (white)	*Erigeron annuus*	Skullcap	*Scutellaria spp.*
Horseweed	*Erigeron canadensis*	Balsam Ragwort	*Senecio pauperculus*
Sweet Everlasting	*Gnaphalium obtusifolium*	Sensitive Brier	*Shrankia microphylla*
Fine-leaved Sneezeweed	*Helenium amanum*	Common Nightshade	*Solanum americanum*
Woodland Sunflower	*Helianthus divaricatus*	Horse Nettle	*Solanum carolinense*
Sunflower species	*Helianthus spp.*	Goldenrod species	*Solidago spp.*
Jerusalem Artichoke	*Helianthus tuberosus*	Spiny-lvd. Sow Thistle	*Sonchus arvensis*
Yellow Hawkweed	*Hieracium pratense*	Venus Looking-glass	*Specularia perfoliate*
Hawkweed species	*Hieracium spp.*	Goat's Rue	*Tephrosia virginiana*
Long-leaved Houstonia	*Houstonia longifolia*	Cranefly Orchid	*Tipularia discolor*
Saint Johnswort	*Hypericum spp.*	Goat's-Beard	*Tragopogon spp.*
Yellow Star Grass	*Hypoxis hirsuta*	White Clover	*Trifoinum repens*
		Red Clover	*Trifolium pratense*
		Blue Vervain	*Verbena hastata*
		Zinnia	*Zinnia elegans*

APPENDIX 2. LARVAL TARGET-HOST PLANTS ON 6 SOUTH CAROLINA ROW, MAY–OCTOBER 1997

Trees
Common Name	Scientific Name	Common Name	Scientific Name
River Birch	*Betula nigra*	Virginia Pine	*Pinus virginiana*
Pignut Hickory	*Carya glabra*	American Sycamore	*Platanus occidentalis*
Mockernut Hickory	*Carya tomentosa*	Chickasaw Plum	*Prunus angustifolia*
Hawthorn	*Crataegus spp.*	Black Cherry	*Prunus serotina*
American Beech	*Fagus grandifolia*	White Oak	*Quercus alba*
White Ash	*Fraxinus americana*	Southern Red Oak	*Quercus falcata*
Honey Locust	*Gleditsia triacanthos*	Water Oak	*Quercus nigra*
American Holly	*Ilex opaca*	Northern Red Oak	*Quercus rubra*
Eastern Red-cedar	*Juniperus virginiana*	Post Oak	*Quercus stellata*
Sweet Gum	*Liquiddambar styreciflua*	Black Oak	*Quercus velutina*
Yellow-Poplar	*Liriodendron tulipifera*	Black Locust	*Robinia pseudoacacia*
Shortleaf Pine	*Pinus echinata*	Black Willow	*Salix nigra*
Loblolly Pine	*Pinus taeda*	Sassafras	*Sassafras albidum*

Shrubs/Vines
Common Name	Scientific Name	Common Name	Scientific Name
New Jersey Tea	*Ceanothus americanus*	Lowbush Blueberry	*Vaccinium vacillans*
Strawberry Bush	*Euonvmus americanus*	Trumpet Creeper	*Campsis radicans*
Spicebush	*Lindera benzoin*	Japanese Honeysuckle	*Lonicera japonica*
Winged Sumac	*Rhus copallina*	Common Blackberry	*Rubus spp.*
Smooth Sumac	*Rhus glabra*	Fox Grape	*Vitaceae labrusca*
Sparkleberry	*Vaccinium arboruum*	Muscadine	*Vitis rotundifolia*
Deerberry	*Vaccinium stamineum*		

Herbs/Forbs
Common Name	Scientific Name	Common Name	Scientific Name
Wingstem	*Actinomeris alternifolia*	Jerusalem Artichoke	*Helianthus tuberosus*
Pigweed	*Amaranthus spp.*	Wild Lettuce	*Lactuca candensis*
False Indigo	*Amorpha canescens*	Prickly Lettuce	*Lanctuca scariola*
Hog Peanut	*Amphicarpa bracteata*	Wood Nettle	*Laportea canadensis*
Pearly Everlasting	*Anaphalis margaritacea*	Motherwort	*Leonurus cardiaca*
Plantain-leaved Pussytoes	*Antennaria plantaginifolium*	Sericea	*Lespedeza cuneata*
Virginia Snakeroot	*Aristolochia serpentaria*	Partridgeberry	*Mitchella repens*
Swamp Milkweed	*Asclepias incarnata*	Prickly Pear	*Opuntia humifusa*
Milkweed spp.	*Asclepias spp.*	Panic grass	*Panicum spp.*
Aster spp.	*Aster spp.*	Passion Flower	*Passiflora incarnata*
Wild Indigo	*Baptisia tinctoria*	Clammy Ground Cherry	*Physalis heterophylla*
Beggars Tick spp.	*Bidens spp.*	English Plantain	*Plantago lanceolata*
Wild Sensitive Plant	*Cassia nictitans*	Common Plantain	*Plantago major*
Spurred Butterfly Pea	*Centrosema virginianum*	Mayapple	*Podophyllum peltatum*
Black Cohosh	*Cimicifuga racemosa*	Cinquefoil	*Potentilla spp.*
Bull Thistle	*Cirsium vulgare*	White Lettuce	*Prenanthes alba*
Butterfly Pea	*Clitoria mariana*	Short-styled Snakeroot	*Sanicula canadensis*
Coreopsis spp.	*Coreopsis spp.*	Common Nightshade	*Solanum americanum*
Tickseed Sunflower	*Coreopsis spp.*	Horse Nettle	*Solanum carolinense*
Whorled Coreopsis	*Coreopsis verticillata*	Goldenrod spp.	*Solidago spp.*
Crown Vetch	*Coronilla varia*	Spiny-lvd. Sow Thistle	*Sonchus aspen*
Queen Anne Lace	*Daucus carota*	Goat's Rue	*Tephrosia virginiana*
Wild Pea Vine	*Desmodium nudiflorum*	Goat's-Beard	*Tragopogon spp.*
Dutchman's Breeches	*Dicentra cucullaria*	Rabbit Foot Clover	*Trifolium arvense*
Horseweed	*Erigeron canadensis*	Red Clover	*Trifolium pratense*
Spurge spp.	*Euphorbia spp.*	White Clover	*Trifolium repens*
Grasses	*Poaceae*	Stinging Nettle	*Urtica dioica*
Sweet Everlasting	*Gnaphalium obtusifolium*	Blue Vervain	*Verbena hastata*
Rabbit Tobacco	*Gnaphalium spp.*	Narrow-leaved Vetch	*Vicia angustifolia*
Woodland Sunflower	*Helianthus strumosus*	Viola spp.	*Viola spp.*

APPENDIX 3. BUTTERFLIES AND SKIPPERS CENSUSED ON 6 SOUTH CAROLINA ROW, MAY–OCTOBER 1997

Sleepy Orange Sulphur	*Abaeis nicippe*	Carolina Satyr	*Hermeuptychia sosybius*
Hoary Edge	*Achalarus lyciades*	Cobweb Skipper	*Hesperia leonardus*
Sickle-winged Skipper	*Achylodes thraso*	Fiery Skipper	*Hesperia metea*
Gulf Fritillary	*Agraulis vanillae*	Brown Elfin	*Hylephila phyleus*
Lace-wing. Roadside Skipper	*Amblyscirtes aesculapius*	Eastern Pine Elfin	*Incisalia augustinus*
Bell's Roadside Skipper	*Amblyscirtes belli*	Buckeye	*Incisalia niphon*
Carolina Roadside Skipper	*Amblyscirtes carolina*	Clouded Skipper	*Junonia coenia*
Pepper and Salt Skipper	*Amblyscirtes hegon*	Eufala Skipper	*Lerema accius*
Reverse Roadside Skipper	*Amblyscirtes reversa*	Snout Butterfly	*Lerodea eufala*
Roadside Skipper	*Amblyscirtes vialis*	Northern Blue	*Libytheana bachmanii*
Least Skipperling	*Ancylophora numitor*	American Copper	*Lycaeides argyrognomon*
European Cabbage White	*Artogeia rapae*	Little Wood Satyr	*Lycaena phleas*
West Virginia White	*Artogeia virginiensis*	Olive Hairstreak	*Megisto cymela*
Great Southern White	*Ascia monuste*	Mourning Cloak	*Mitoura gryneus*
Tawny Emperor	*Asterocampa clyton*	White 'M' Hairstreak	*Nymphalis antiopa*
Sachem	*Atalopedes campestris*	Long-winged Skipper	*Panhasius m-album*
Great Blue Hairstreak	*Atlides halesus*	East. Black Swallowtail	*Panoquina ocola*
Logan Skipper	*Atrytone logan*	Spicebush Swallowtail	*Papilio polyxenes*
Dusted Skipper	*Atrytonopis hianna*	Cloudless Sulphur	*Papilio troilus*
Golden-banded Skipper	*Autochton cellus*	Common Sootywing	*Phoebis sennae*
Viceroy	*Basilarchia archippus*	Pearly Crescentspot	*Pholisora catullus*
Red-Spotted Purple	*Basilarchia astyanax*	Saffron Skipper	*Phyciodes tharos*
Pipevine Swallowtail	*Battus philenor*	Hobomok Skipper	*Poanes aaroni*
Red-Banded Hairstreak	*Calycopis cerops*	Broad-winged Skipper	*Poanes hobomok*
Spring Azure	*Celastrina ladon*	Yehl Skipper	*Poanes viator*
Large Wood Satyr	*Cercyonis pegala*	Zabulon Skipper	*Poanes yehl*
Gorgone Crescentspot	*Charidryas gorgone*	Crossline Skipper	*Poanes zabulon*
Silvery Crescentspot	*Charidryas nycteis*	Tawny-edge Skipper	*Polites origenes*
Orange Sulphur	*Colias eurytheme*	Whirlabout Skipper	*Polites themistocles*
Common Sulphur	*Colias philodice*	Comma	*Polites vibex*
Gemmed Satyr	*Cyllopsis gemma*	Question Mark	*Polygonia comma*
Monarch Butterfly	*Danaus plexippus*	Little Glassywing	*Polygonia interrogationis*
Nothern Pearly Eye	*Enodia anthedon*	Bunch-grass Skipper	*Pompeius verna*
Creole Pearly-Eye Satyr	*Enodia creola*	Tiger Swallowtail:	*Problema byssus*
Pearly-Eye Satyr	*Enodia portlandia*	Comm. Checkered Skipper	*Pterourus glaucus*
Silver-spotted Skipper	*Epargyreus clarus*	Little Yellow Sulphur	*Pyrgus communis*
Wild Indigo Duskywing	*Erynnis baptisiae*	Banded Hairstreak	*Pyrtsita lisa*
Horace's Dustywing	*Erynnis horatius*	Striped Hairstreak	*Satyrium calanus*
Dreamy Duskywing	*Erynnis icelus*	Appalachian Brown	*Satyrium liparops*
Mottled Dustywing	*Erynnis martialis*	Great Spangled Fritillary	*Satyrodes appalachia*
Sedge Skipper	*Euphyes dion*	Gray Hairstreak	*Speyeria cybele*
Dun Skipper	*Euphyes vestris*	Southern Cloudywing	*Strymon melinus*
Variegated Fritillary	*Euptoieta claudia*	Northern Cloudywing	*Thorybes bathyllus*
Fairy Yellow Sulphur	*Eurema daria*	Red Admiral	*Thorybes pylades*
Northern Hairstreak	*Euristrymon ontario*	Painted Lady	*Vanessa atalanta*
Eastern Tailed Blue	*Everes comyntas*	American Painted Lady	*Vanessa cardui*
Harvester Butterfly	*Feniseca tarquinius*	Northern Broken Dash	*Vanessa virginiensis*
Silvery Blue	*Glaucopsyche lygdamus*	Broken Dash	*Wallengrenia egremet*
Coral Hairstreak	*Harkenclenus titus*	Dogface Sulphur	*Wallengrenia otho*
Giant Swallowtail	*Heraclides cresphontes*	Leonardus Skipper	*Zerene cesonia*
Hermes Satyr	*Hermeuptychia hermes*		

Karner Blue Butterfly Habitat Restoration on Pipeline Right-of-Way in Wisconsin

Fran Lowell and Scott Lounsbury

The Lakehead Pipe Line Company (Lakehead) SEP-II project, constructed in 1997 and 1998, includes ten miles of pipeline right-of-way in Wood and Adams Counties, Wisconsin where the federally endangered Karner blue butterfly (KBB) is known to occur. Authorization for incidental take of KBBs was granted with US Fish and Wildlife Service Terms and Conditions intended to restore and enhance disturbed KBB habitat. In compliance with these conditions, KBB-occupied right-of-way was reseeded with a combination of native grasses, lupine, and other KBB nectar species in fall 1998. Lakehead is required to monitor the right-of-way for three years to determine the success of this restoration effort. Monitoring includes assessment of frequency and density of lupine and nectar plants, as well as KBB surveys, which consist of a modified presence/absence survey during the first year and formal counts in the subsequent two years. First-year monitoring was conducted in July 1999 during the peak of the KBB second flight. KBBs were observed at 86% of the sample sites, which was consistent with second-flight results of pre-construction surveys. Planted nectar species were present on 60–98% of the reseeded property tracts depending on the species, reflecting good diversity. Frequency within sample plots varied greatly by species, ranging from zero to 100%. First-year density data reflect the small size of the seedlings, but seedling coverage was generally good, with some variation between sites due to soil conditions and amount of disturbance unrelated to the project. Preliminary results suggest that restoration efforts will, at a minimum, replace disturbed habitat, and will likely enhance KBB habitat in the long term.

Keywords: Butterfly, lupine, mitigation, endangered species, reseed

INTRODUCTION

Lakehead Pipe Line Company (Lakehead or the Company) constructed its System Expansion Project-Phase II (SEP-II project) in 1997 and 1998. The SEP-II project involved construction of approximately 450-miles of 24-inch-diameter liquid petroleum pipeline in Wisconsin and Illinois. The pipeline in Wisconsin was constructed adjacent and parallel to an existing pipeline on a maintained right-of-way along a route that crossed portions of the known range of the federally listed endangered Karner blue butterfly (*Lycaeides melissa samuelis*) (KBB). To obtain necessary permits to construct the SEP-II project, Lakehead participated in an interagency consultation process that resulted in authorization to take KBB provided that several mitigation measures would be implemented to minimize take and restore habitat. Permit conditions also included a three-year monitoring program to determine the success of the restoration effort. This paper describes the regulatory process that was required by the federal agencies for compliance with the Endangered Species Act of 1973 (ESA) as amended, discusses the restoration measures implemented in compliance with regulatory requirements, and summarizes the results of the first-year post-construction monitoring, conducted in 1999.

OBJECTIVES

Within the context of regulatory requirements, the specific objectives of the SEP-II project were to construct the project in a manner that would minimize adverse impacts on the KBB, restore disturbed habitat and, if possible, enhance habitat for a net benefit to the KBB. Mitigation measures and restoration and monitoring plans were developed in accordance with permit requirements and based on guidelines provided by the US Fish and Wildlife Service (USFWS). These activities were designed and implemented primarily for regulatory compliance rather than as a controlled research project.

KARNER BLUE BUTTERFLY STATUS, HABITAT, AND LIFE CYCLE

The KBB was listed as an endangered species by the USFWS in 1992. Factors contributing to its endangered status include a reduction in the butterfly's range and population numbers due to habitat loss, degradation, and fragmentation; collection pressure; and lack of habitat protection (WDNR, 1999). The endangered listing was driven primarily by KBB losses in eastern portions of its range. The largest and most extensive remaining populations occur in Wisconsin, Michigan, and northern Indiana (Lane, 1997).

KBB populations are thought to have originally occurred as shifting clusters across vast landscapes altered by periodic fires. While fires resulted in localized elimination of the species, vegetational succession following the fires promoted colonization and rapid population increases. Periodic disturbance, such as that caused by fires, is necessary to maintain open areas in which wild lupine (*Lupinus perennis*), the only known larval food source for the KBB, can thrive (Lowe et al., 1990).

Habitat for the KBB is characterized by the presence of wild lupine. In addition, availability of nectaring species is an important component that strongly affects the suitability of KBB habitat (Trick, 1997). KBB habitat in the midwestern US includes oak savanna, jack pine areas, and dune/sandplain communities (Lowe et al., 1990 and WDNR Karner Blue Technical Team, 1997). In Wisconsin, KBB populations occur in areas with sandy soils mainly across the central counties, with some populations occurring in northwestern Wisconsin. Known habitat in Wisconsin includes old agricultural fields reverting to sand prairie, actively managed brush prairie, semi-closed or closed oak/jack pine forest with scattered clearings, mowed utility and road rights-of-way, managed forest lands, and military training areas (Bleser, 1994 and WDNR, 1999).

The KBB usually has two broods per year. The first generation hatches in April from eggs that have overwintered from the previous year. The larvae feed on wild lupine leaves, and pupate around mid-May. Adults emerge in late May or early June. During the first flight, which takes place in June, adult females lay eggs on or near lupine plants. These eggs hatch after about a week, and larvae feed on lupine for about three weeks before pupating. Second brood adults emerge in mid-July and, from July through early August, females lay eggs on lupine or on plant litter or grass near the base of the lupine plants. These eggs overwinter to hatch the following spring (Lowe, et al. 1990 and US Department of the Interior, undated).

REGULATORY REVIEW PROCESS

Consultations with the USFWS in 1996 identified the KBB as a federally protected species that could potentially be affected by the SEP-II pipeline project. At the suggestion of the USFWS, lupine surveys were conducted that year along approximately 80 miles of the route that were identified by the Wisconsin Department of Natural Resources (WDNR) as having high potential for lupine growth. Where lupine was present, KBB surveys were also conducted. Through this process, fourteen segments of the pipeline route were determined to contain KBB-occupied habitat. These fourteen segments became the focus of subsequent regulatory review.

To "take" a protected species, as defined by the ESA, is to harass, harm, pursue, hunt, shoot, wound, kill, trap, capture, or collect the species, or to attempt to engage in any such conduct. The term "incidental take" refers to a take that is incidental to, and not the purpose of, the carrying out of an otherwise lawful activity. Because the SEP-II project would result in the destruction of lupine in KBB-occupied areas, the USFWS determined that incidental taking of KBB eggs and larvae would occur during construction activities (e.g., clearing, excavation) and future maintenance activities. Under Section 9 of the ESA, taking of the KBB during the pipeline construction project would have been prohibited unless authorization for incidental take was obtained. Such authorization would typically be sought either through an interagency consultation under section 7 of the ESA (if other permits or authorizations were required from a federal agency), or by applying directly to the USFWS for a permit under Section 10 of the ESA. In an unusual coincidence of timing, however, both processes were ongoing on parallel tracks as discussed below.

Statewide Incidental Take Permit

During the planning of the SEP-II project, a separate effort was underway by the WDNR to obtain, under section 10 of the ESA, a statewide Incidental Take Permit (ITP) that would authorize the incidental take of KBBs on non-federal lands in Wisconsin pursuant to a Statewide Habitat Conservation Plan (HCP). Parties to the permit would ultimately include a partnership of 27 public and private entities, including Lakehead (WDNR, 1999). The WDNR, in cooperation with the partnership, was in the process of developing the HCP that would outline conservation strategies for the KBB. In addition, each member of the partnership would develop individual Conservation Agreements describing lands and activities included in the KBB conservation effort and related activities that the partner agreed to conduct such as public outreach, monitoring, and reporting. If the WDNR were successful in obtaining an ITP, and if the ITP were issued prior to construction of the SEP-II project, it would have been possible for project-related take of the KBB to be authorized under the ITP provided that the project was implemented in accordance with the HCP and Lakehead's individual Conservation Agreement. However, when the KBB issue was being considered for the SEP-II project, it was not known when the statewide incidental take application process would be completed or when the ITP might be issued. Therefore, Lakehead elected to pursue project-specific authorization for incidental take of KBB through the interagency consultation process described below. The ITP was eventually issued in September 1999 (well after construction of the SEP-II project was complete).

Interagency consultation under Section 7 of the Endangered Species Act

Because the SEP-II project crossed waters of the United States, authorization was required from the US Army Corps of Engineers (Corps) under Section 404 of the Clean Water Act. Under Section 7(a)(2) of the ESA, any federal agency that permits, licenses, funds, or otherwise authorizes an activity must ensure that its actions will not jeopardize the continued existence of a federally listed species.

When informal consultation determined that the pipeline project was likely to adversely affect the KBB, the Corps requested a formal consultation with the USFWS in accordance with Section 7 of the ESA. The Company subsequently prepared a Biological Assessment that described the proposed activity, quantified the estimated take, described measures that would be implemented to minimize take, and proposed measures to mitigate for unavoidable take. After reviewing the Biological Assessment and conducting its analysis, the USFWS issued to the Corps a Biological Opinion that concluded that the proposed action would not jeopardize the continued existence of the KBB or result in the destruction or modification of critical habitat. The Biological Opinion described reasonable and prudent measures to minimize take and specified Terms and Conditions required in order for the project to be exempt from the prohibitions of Section 9 of the ESA. The Terms and Conditions of the Biological Opinion were incorporated as conditions of the Corps authorization. The Terms and Conditions included measures to minimize take and requirements for site restoration, three years of post-construction monitoring, and ongoing management of the KBB-occupied portions of the right-of-way. The Biological Opinion concluded that, with implementation of the specified measures, no more than 0.05 ha (0.13 acre) of existing lupine habitat would be incidentally taken during construction, and that a small number of eggs would be taken during the course of habitat management activities.

The statewide HCP effort was ongoing throughout this interagency consultation period, and a draft of the conservation plan was well underway. Protocols for mitigation, management of KBB habitat, and monitoring for the long-term effectiveness of the HCP had been developed by the WDNR and were being refined. These protocols were considered by Lakehead in developing its Biological Assessment, and by the USFWS in developing its Terms and Conditions and evaluating the proposed compliance plans. Therefore, the following sections refer to some of the protocols developed for the HCP.

KBB-OCCUPIED SITES

Through lupine and KBB surveys conducted in 1996, fourteen segments of right-of-way in Wood and Adams Counties, Wisconsin were identified as being occupied by the KBB (Fig. 1). For the purposes of this work, "segments" are lengths of right-of-way separated from adjacent stretches of right-of-way by features such as streams or roads. The KBB-occupied segments are

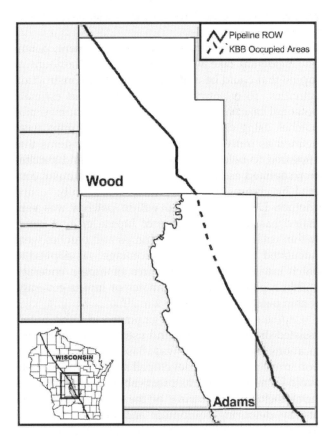

Fig. 1. Locations of Karner blue butterfly-occupied pipeline segments in Wood and Adams counties, Wisconsin.

numbered consecutively, from north to south, and are referred to herein as Segments 1–14. Each segment may include one or more property tracts. The KBB-occupied segments are not all contiguous and, although a given segment may have been identified as KBB-occupied, in several instances lupine was present only in a portion of the segment and not continuous throughout the length of the segment. The 14 segments cumulatively comprise approximately 15.5 km (9.7 miles) of right-of-way.

The right-of-way in the KBB-occupied areas is generally characterized by dry, sandy soils with little organic matter. Vegetation surrounding the right-of-way generally comprises red or jack pine plantation or mixed red oak, bur oak, and jack pine scrub or woods. Several prairie grasses and forbs are present in these areas, and dominant species observed in association with lupine include sedge (*Carex pensylvanica*) and little bluestem grass (*Schizachyrium scoparium*). The majority of the lupine was located along the east side of the existing maintained right-of-way. In many cases, lupine appeared to be present because of periodic right-of-way maintenance that controlled growth of woody vegetation and provided an open area in which lupine could thrive. At some locations, the lupine extended beyond the right-of-way into adjacent mixed woods or pine plantations.

ESTIMATED TAKE AND MEASURES TO MINIMIZE TAKE

For the purposes of the Biological Assessment, potential incidental take was estimated as the amount of lupine that could be affected by pipeline construction activities. To quantify lupine coverage and estimate potential take, lupine was delineated in clumps and patches using civil survey techniques. Clumps were defined as individual stems or groups of stems that appeared to belong to one root system, and patches were defined as areas more or less continuously covered by clumps in relatively close proximity to one another. Density of lupine within patches was estimated based on percentage of lupine ground cover within each patch. Areas of clumps and patches were calculated, and the density percentage was applied to patch areas to estimate the area of lupine coverage within a patch. Density estimates of lupine coverage within patches ranged from 2 to 30%.

Lupine survey data were imported to a computer-assisted drafting program and used to map the lupine locations on the right-of-way. Based on this information, project engineers developed site-specific plans to avoid as much lupine as practicable. Avoidance measures included narrowing of the construction right-of-way, detouring equipment and personnel around lupine areas within the right-of-way, and strategic placement of spoil piles. Lupine to be avoided was protected by orange safety fencing to prevent access by equipment and personnel. Lupine that could not or might not be avoided was included in the estimated take. Through this process, it was determined that the total lupine coverage on the 14 KBB-occupied segments was approximately 1446 m^2 (15,563 ft^2), and that ~520 m^2 (5595 ft^2), or ~36%, might be taken during construction.

Lakehead worked with the pipeline contractor prior to construction to identify avoidance measures and emphasize the importance of compliance. Environmental inspectors helped manage implementation during construction. With the cooperation of all parties, avoidance measures were implemented in close accordance with the site-specific plans that had been developed in advance.

RESTORATION METHODS

Post-construction restoration and monitoring methods were developed based on guidelines provided by the USFWS and in compliance with the Biological Opinion. Reseeding and monitoring plans had to be approved by the USFWS prior to implementation.

The Terms and Conditions of the Biological Opinion required that disturbed areas on property tracts where lupine-occupied habitat occurred prior to construction were to be reseeded with a mixture of lupine, native forbs and grasses using seed obtained from local sources. The total amount of area seeded to lupine was required to be a minimum of one acre. The native forbs were to be selected from a list of known KBB nectar species, including at least four species each of those used in spring and summer flight.

Based on a list of KBB nectar species developed by the WDNR, a "KBB seed mix" was developed that met the required criteria. Table 1 describes the species included in the KBB seed mix. A local nursery with extensive experience in prairie restoration provided seed and installation services. Seed for most species was obtained from sources within a 80 km (50 mile) radius of the project area.

Although the Biological Opinion addressed reseeding only on property tracts that contained lupine prior to construction, the Company elected to extend the use of the KBB seed mix (minus lupine in some instances, as described below) throughout the full length of each segment. This decision was made after consideration of lupine distribution along the right-of-way, seed and installation costs, logistics of two separate reseeding operations within a limited area (i.e., application of KBB seed mix by prairie restoration contractor and application of standard project seed mix by construction contractor), ongoing management implications, and the opportunity presented by this situation to enhance KBB habitat. Unless the landowner requested otherwise, the KBB mix that included lupine seed was applied to property tracts that had contained lupine prior

Table 1. USFWS-approved seed mix for KBB-occupied right-of-way segments

Latin name	Common name	Percent of mix by weight (excluding nurse crop)	Percent of mix by number of seeds (excluding nurse crop)	KBB flight period[a]
Forbs				
Asclepias syriaca	Common milkweed	4.5	1.1	2
Asclepias tuberosa	Butterflyweed	1.2	0.3	2
Coreopsis lanceolata	Lanceleaf Coreopsis	13.7	10.8	1 and 2
Euphorbia corollata	Flowering spurge	6.9	4.3	1 and 2
Liatris aspera	Rough blazingstar	1.8	1.5	2
Lupinus perennis[b]	Wild lupine	9.7	0.6	1 and 2
Monarda punctata	Horsemint	1.8	10.5	2
Potentilla arguta	Cinquefoil	0.7	10.1	1[c]
Rudbeckia hirta	Black-eyed Susan	2.8	17.6	2
Solidago rigida	Stiff Goldenrod	4.2	12.1	2[c]
Subtotal		**47.2**	**68.9**	
Grasses				
Andropogon gerardi	Big bluestem	7.6	3.9	N/A
Panicum virgatum	Switchgrass	3.8	4.3	N/A
Schizachyrium Scoparium	Little bluestem	41.3	22.8	N/A
Subtotal		**52.8**	**31.1**	**N/A**
Total		**100.0**	**100.0**	**N/A**
Nurse crop				
Lolium multiflorum	Annual ryegrass			N/A

[a] List provided by Wisconsin Department of Natural Resources (WDNR).
[b] Lupine included in mix only for property tracts identified as containing lupine prior to construction.
[c] WDNR list indicates that the KBB uses various species within this genus.

to construction. To avoid possible concerns about encumbering new landowners with a protected species, lupine was omitted from the seed mix on property tracts within the KBB-occupied segments that had not contained lupine prior to construction. While omitting lupine would preclude creation of new habitat for KBB larvae on these properties, seeding of nectaring species is beneficial for KBB adults, which may travel distances up to 3.2 km (two miles) (Smith, 1998). Further, presence of nectaring species between lupine sites might encourage movement between habitat areas, which is important for genetic interchange and long-term population viability. In total, the 14 segments included 49 property tracts, of which 18 were to be reseeded with the full KBB seed mix (including lupine), and 24 tracts were to be reseeded with the nectar species/native grass (mix without lupine). Some overlap occurred during the reseeding process resulting in lupine inadvertently being seeded at a few locations where it should have been omitted. Seven landowners refused either seed mix, and two landowners outside of the KBB-occupied segments requested the KBB seed mix.

The width of the SEP-II construction right-of-way was generally 29 m (95 ft) wide, including 24.4 m (80 ft) of permanent right-of-way and 4.6 m (15 ft) of temporary workspace. Because much of the lupine on the occupied segments occurred along the east edge of the right-of-way, the width of the construction right-of-way on these KBB-occupied segments was narrowed at many locations to avoid lupine. In total, approximately 20 ha (50 acres) were seeded with the full KBB-seed mix (including lupine), greatly exceeding the required one-acre area, and about 8.5 ha (21 acres) were seeded with the nectar species/native grass mix (without lupine).

Seed was applied at a rate of about 11.2 kg/ha (10 lbs/acre) using an eight-foot wide Brillion drop seeder specially adapted for native seed mixtures. A nurse crop of annual ryegrass was seeded at 5.6 kg/ha (5 lbs/acre). Seeding occurred in late October and early November, 1998 to avoid fall germination. Mulch was applied in areas with steep slopes to minimize the potential for erosion and loss of seed.

Monitoring methods

To determine the success of restoration efforts, the Biological Opinion required that quantitative data on density and frequency of lupine and nectar plants be collected on representative samples of restored areas. The Company worked with the USFWS to determine a reasonable level of sampling to achieve compliance with this requirement in a cost-effective manner.

Monitoring was conducted in July 1999 to coincide with the peak of the KBB second flight in accordance with WDNR protocols. Because this timing was also conducive to plant identification, vegetation sampling and butterfly monitoring were conducted during the same time period.

Vegetation monitoring

Quantitative sampling was conducted on property tracts that contained lupine prior to construction and

had been reseeded with the KBB seed mix including lupine. A linear transect was walked along the center of the construction right-of-way. Sampling was conducted on one m^2 (11 ft^2) sample plots located at 75-m (248 ft) intervals along the transect. Plots were located at a random distance and direction from each transect point. To document species diversity, species within each sample plot were identified. Density was assessed by estimating percent coverage. Because seedlings were in their first year of growth, they were generally too small to make meaningful estimates of coverage by individual species. Therefore, coverage was estimated for each of the following categories:
- native forbs and grasses,
- woody native species (e.g., shrubs),
- perennial weeds,
- annual/biennial weeds, and
- bare ground.

Qualitative monitoring was conducted on property tracts that were on the KBB-occupied segments where lupine was not present prior to construction. These tracts had been reseeded with the nectar species/native grass mix but without lupine. The monitoring team walked generally linear transects along the construction right-of-way and recorded the occurrence of the nectar species that were included in the seed mix. Because this information was recorded on the basis of a single walk-through, the absence of a species on the checklist does not necessarily mean that the species was not present.

KBB monitoring

Because KBB habitat was not anticipated to be fully re-established during the first year (1999) of monitoring, a modified presence/absence assessment of adult KBBs was conducted during the peak of the second flight period. In subsequent monitoring years, KBB abundance will be assessed using the more extensive monitoring protocols developed by the WDNR for a statewide effectiveness monitoring program under the HCP. A WDNR-trained monitor walked the length of each segment one time and recorded whether KBBs were observed. Formal counts were not required, but informal tallies were taken and, where possible, the sex of butterflies was recorded.

Under the WDNR-defined protocols, KBB surveys should be conducted on warm, sunny days. In most cases, the KBB monitoring was conducted when weather conditions were within acceptable WDNR guidelines. If conditions were not favorable and no KBBs were observed, a second site visit was made when weather conditions had improved.

Although the ITP was not yet in place at the time this work was conducted, the WDNR had already begun statewide KBB effectiveness monitoring efforts. Sites for statewide monitoring were selected from a pool of partner-managed lands, including KBB-occupied portions of Lakehead's right-of-way. In 1999, four of the Lakehead right-of-way sites, which coincided with SEP-II study segments, were selected for monitoring under the statewide monitoring program. Where statewide monitoring was conducted on SEP-II study sites, those findings are included in this paper.

RESULTS AND DISCUSSION

Vegetation
Tracts with lupine prior to construction
Sampling was conducted on a total of 104 sample plots for the 14 segments. The number of sample plots on any given segment ranged from 2 to 24. The results of vegetation sampling were used to make a preliminary determination regarding the success of the reseeding effort. The information collected was not analyzed statistically as this work was not designed as a research study and, other than the area of lupine present prior to construction, no baseline data are available for comparative purposes. Further, although sampling information has been condensed to segments in the tables below to summarize preliminary results, extrapolation of quantitative data to entire property tracts or segments should be avoided because of the early stage of development of the perennial seedlings during this first year, high variability among samples, and the dynamic state of the study area. Nonetheless, the data collected provide a good picture of overall reseeding success. The results of second-year sampling will be used to determine quantitatively whether the amount of lupine affected by construction has been replaced. Tables 2 and 3 provide summary results of frequency and density monitoring, respectively.

Some key observations based on sampling of tracts on which lupine was present prior to construction are provided below:
- Lupine was observed on all reseeded segments and was present in 41% of the sample plots.
- All reseeded segments contained native grasses, which were observed in 93 of the sample plots (89%).
- Four of the segments contained all ten of the native forbs planted, and five segments contained nine species. Remaining segments contained from five to eight of the forbs, including species that were observed on three segments where they were not captured in sample plots.
- The most frequently occurring forbs were black-eyed Susan (present in 86% of the sample plots) and lanceleaf coreopsis (present in 74% of the sample plots). The least frequently occurring forbs were rough blazingstar (present in 14% of the sample plots) and common milkweed (present in 18% of the sample plots). These species, as well as butterflyweed and cinquefoil, appear to be slower to develop than some of the other species, and it is anticipated that they will be observed with greater frequency during subsequent monitoring.

Table 2. Species frequency summary by segment for property tracts seeded with KBB seed mix including lupine

Seg. No.	Approx. total length of tracts (m)	No. sample plots	Common milkweed	Butterfly-weed	Lanceleaf coreopsis	Flowering spurge	Rough blazingstar	Wild lupine	Horsemint (Dotted mint)	Cinquefoil	Black-eyed Susan	Stiff Goldenrod	Native grasses
1	305	4	0	2	3	3	1	1	4	1	3	3	4
2	1106	15	0	4	11	9	3	5	12	6	15	14	15
3	183	3	1	0	3	2	0	1	3	2	3	0	3
4[a]	430	5	0	0	2	0	0	1	2	0	2	0	4
6	N/A[e]												
5	1758	24	8	8	22	21	4	7	17	8	21	14	23
7	626	9	3	3	8	7	2	6	9	4	8	3	9
8[b]	866	6	0	2	5	4	2	3	4	3	6	1	6
9	333	5	1	2	4	2	1	2	3	0	4	1	4
10	529	7	2	2	6	4	1	4	5	3	6	3	5
11	381	4	2	2	3	4	0	4	1	2	4	4	2
12	1296	15	1	5	8	10	1	9	5	3	13	5	12
13[c]	349	5	1	0	2	1	0	0	1	2	4	1	4
14[d]	100	2	0	0	0	1	0	0	0	0	0	1	2

[a]On Segment 4, butterflyweed was observed in the right-of-way but not in sample plots.
[b]On Segment 8, one property tract (426 m) had been tilled and reseeded by landowner to clover and bluegrass.
[c]On Segment 13, lupine was observed in the right-of-way but not in sample plots.
[d]On Segment 14, lanceleaf coreopsis, wild lupine, horsemint, and black-eyed Susan were observed on the right-of-way but not in sample plots.
[e]Segment is single property tract for which landowner refused KBB seed mix.

Table 3. Density summary by segment for property tracts seeded with KBB mix including lupine

Seg. No.	Approx. total length of tracts seeded with *lupine* (m)	No. of sample plots	Percent native forbs and grasses	Percent woody native species	Percent perennial weeds and non-natives	Percent annual or biennial weeds and non-natives	Percent bare ground	Percent other (e.g., trees)
1	305	4	9.3		<1	29.8	60.8	
2	1107	15	8.1		7.6	44.3	39.8	
3	183	3	33.3		11.7	13.3	41.7	
4	430	5	45		0.4	14.0	38.6	
5	1760	24	26.5	3.2	12.0	18.4	39.9	
6	N/A[b]							
7	626	9	38.3	0.6	10.1	21.1	29.9	
8[a]	867	6	33.3	0.8	6.7	10.8	48.3	
9	333	5	12.2		14.0	32.0	41.8	
10	530	7	36.4	5.9	1.4	21.6	34.7	
11	381	4	37.5	1.3	5.3	9.0	47.0	
12	1297	15	20.7	16.5	7.3	9.0	38.5	8.0
13	350	5	11.4	17.4	10.0	14.4	46.8	
14	100	2	3.0		2.5	15.0	79.0	0.5

[a]On Segment 8, one property tract (426 m) had been tilled and reseeded by landowner to clover and bluegrass.
[b]Segment is single property tract for which landowner refused KBB seed mix.

- Percentage of bare ground was relatively high, with averages on segments ranging from about 30% to 79%. Three factors may contribute to the high percentage of bare ground: (a) the very sandy soil conditions in this area, which generally support sparser natural vegetation; (b) the small size of the seedlings; and (c) the occurrence of bare spots on the right-of-way due to landowner activities, traffic by private vehicles (e.g., snowmobiles and all-terrain vehicles), and erosion.
- Native species coverage, which ranged from zero to 90% across all sample plots, varied considerably within and between property tracts. This variability may be due to in part to post-seeding disturbance, as described above, and in part to differences in soil moisture among segments. These factors, in

combination with the natural slow development of these perennial species, may result in different germination and growth rates.

Non-lupine tracts

Qualitative sampling was conducted on property tracts that did not contain lupine prior to construction. Diversity was generally good on non-lupine property tracts comprising about 8.5 ha (~21 acres) of disturbed right-of-way, which were reseeded with the nectar species/native grass seed mix without lupine. Four segments contained only property tracts that were reseeded with lupine, and applicable landowners on four segments refused the nectar species/native grass mix; key observations are summarized below for the remaining six segments:

- Native grasses were observed on all segments.
- Of the nine nectaring forbs planted, all nine were observed on five of the segments and eight were observed on the remaining segment.
- The most infrequently observed species were common milkweed and cinquefoil, which were observed on the fewest number of non-lupine property tracts. These species are among those that appear to be slower to develop, and were generally more difficult to see while walking over the right-of-way. Therefore, the actual occurrence of these species may be higher than observed.
- Lupine was observed on five property tracts on which it was to have been omitted from the seed mix. It appears that the lupine on these tracts was a result of inadvertent overlap during seeding.

Butterflies

KBBs were observed at 12 of the 14 right-of-way segments (Fig. 2). No butterflies were observed at Segments 2 and 6, both of which had relatively low butterfly counts during the 1996 pre-construction survey. Although the 1999 monitoring protocol did not call for butterfly counts, an informal tally was maintained by the monitoring team. Numbers of butterflies observed on a given segment during the 1999 SEP-II monitoring effort ranged from zero to 10.

Butterfly monitoring results are provided in Table 4. The table includes HCP effectiveness monitoring results for those sites that coincided with the SEP-II study sites as well as second-flight counts from the 1996 KBB survey (pre-construction). Because of variations in methodologies, direct comparisons among the sampling events may not be appropriate, but some observations can be made.

Where the HCP statewide effectiveness monitoring sites coincided with the SEP-II sites, numbers of butterflies observed during the HCP effectiveness monitoring were considerably higher. The difference may be due to the more formal survey protocol used during the effectiveness monitoring (including more than one visit), and to weather conditions, which were

Fig. 2. Karner blue butterfly on SEP-II right-of-way.

especially favorable during HCP effectiveness monitoring. At all four of the sites where HCP effectiveness monitoring was conducted, the number of butterflies observed exceeded the second-flight counts in the 1996 pre-construction survey.

CONCLUSIONS

KBB-occupied lupine along the SEP-II pipeline right-of-way was identified and quantified in advance of construction. Where possible, avoidance measures were designed, implemented and enforced, and where avoidance was not possible, mitigation measures were implemented to restore habitat. Although success of restoration could not be conclusively determined after one year due to the small size of seedlings and various rates of growth of different species, first-year monitoring results were encouraging. Results suggest that post-construction reseeding with lupine, nectar species, and native grasses has been generally successful and will likely exceed USFWS requirements.

Seedling native grass and forb species included in the KBB seed mix were common at most of the study sites, diversity on most segments was good, and plants generally appeared to be in good health. Seedlings were in an early stage of development during first-year monitoring, and it is not uncommon for perennial species to delay germination until the second (or subsequent) growing seasons. Therefore, while 1999 data provide a positive snapshot of restoration success, frequency and density of nectar species are expected to be higher during subsequent monitoring.

Results of butterfly monitoring exceeded expectations and indicate that the majority of the areas that were KBB-occupied prior to construction were again occupied in 1999. Although habitat on the right-of-way was not yet fully re-established, KBBs were present on

Table 4. 1999 KBB monitoring results

Segment No.	Total KBB observed during 1999 SEP-II monitoring[a]	Total KBB observed during 1999 HCP effectiveness monitoring[b]	KBB observed during second flight in 1996 surveys (pre-construction)
1	4	11	10
2	0	N/A	3
3	1	2	1
4	1	N/A	1
5	2	N/A	7
6	0	N/A	0
7	9	N/A	0
8	2	17	5
9	1	N/A	11
10	10	N/A	19
11	3	18	11
12	2	N/A	19
13	2	N/A	2
14	1	N/A	20
Total	38		109

Total in 1999 based on maximum observed at each site: 76.
[a] Formal counts were not conducted. Numbers provided are based on informal tallies and reflect the highest number of KBBs observed at a site on a single day.
[b] Numbers reflect the total number of KBBs observed at each site during three second-flight surveys.

most segments and in relatively high numbers compared to those recorded prior to construction. The KBBs were observed both in areas that were fenced off during construction to protect existing lupine, and on disturbed portions of the right-of-way that were reseeded with the KBB seed mix. Where HCP statewide effectiveness monitoring (which was conducted in better weather conditions and using more formal protocols) occurred on the SEP-II study sites, results were higher than those obtained during this work, suggesting that informal counts conducted on other sites may have underestimated the number of KBBs present.

Annual and biennial weeds were common on most segments; perennial weeds were present but less abundant. However, weeds did not generally appear to be outcompeting native species, perhaps due to the sandy soil conditions, which are not conducive to dense weed growth. Further, it is common for weeds to be present following native prairie seeding, with the slower-growing native species eventually gaining dominance as they become established. The need for special weed-control measures will be re-evaluated during 2000 monitoring.

In summary, the preliminary results of post-construction monitoring on the Lakehead SEP-II project right-of-way suggest that with proper mitigation, short-term, temporary disturbance of KBB habitat will not necessarily result in long-term adverse impacts on the KBB. This experience also suggests that with landowner cooperation, such mitigation can be reasonably incorporated into a pipeline construction project and may offer the opportunity to enhance KBB habitat without significantly higher restoration costs.

When considering implementation of measures to enhance KBB habitat, it is recommended that implications for future operation, maintenance, and expansion activities on restored rights-of-way be carefully considered. To the extent possible, requirements for future management and expansion activities should be discussed during the regulatory process in which the initial take is authorized and specified in the authorization. Where the take is authorized through an ITP, measures to be implemented during ongoing maintenance activities should be included in the Habitat Conservation Plan required under Section 10 of the ESA. Where authorization is provided in a Biological Opinion as a result of interagency consultation under Section 7 of the ESA, the applicant should seek to have requirements pertaining to future activities included in the Terms and Conditions of the Biological Opinion.

ADDENDUM — PRELIMINARY 2000 RESULTS

Second-year vegetation and butterfly monitoring was completed in late July 2000. Due to production schedules, those results cannot be incorporated into this paper. A few observations from 2000 monitoring are worth noting and are provided below: The total percentage of bare ground in vegetation samples has decreased by more than 10 percent as the native species included in the KBB mix have become larger and slower-growing species have begun to grow.

The relative percentage of weeds, particularly annual and biennial weeds, is substantially lower than in 1999.

Total second-flight butterfly counts for 2000 exceed the second-flight totals from the 1996 pre-construction KBB surveys.

ACKNOWLEDGEMENT

The authors would like to thank Joel Trick of the US-FWS Green Bay, Wisconsin Field Office for his support and guidance in developing Karner blue butterfly mitigation plans and navigating the regulatory process.

REFERENCES

Bleser, Catherine A. 1994. Karner blue butterfly survey, management and monitoring activities in Wisconsin: 1990–Spring 1992. In: Karner Blue Butterfly: A Symbol of a Vanishing Landscape. Andow, D.A., R.J. Baker, and C.P. Lane, eds. Minnesota Agricultural Experiment Station, St. Paul.

Lane, Cynthia. 1997. Forestry management guidelines: Developing management plans compatible with karner blue butterfly persistence. Unpublished report for the Wisconsin Department of Natural Resources (Madison, WI) and the US Fish and Wildlife Service (Fort Snelling, MN).

Lowe, David W., John R. Matthews, and Charles J. Moseley, eds. 1990. The Official World Wildlife Fund Guide to Endangered Species of North America. Beacham Publishers, Washington DC.

Smith, Janet. 1998. Written communication (Biological Opinion) on March 25, 1998, between J. Smith (US Fish and Wildlife Service) and B. Wopat (US Army Corps of Engineers).

Trick, Joel. 1997. Telephone communication on August 21, between F. Lowell (Natural Resource Group, Inc.) and J. Trick (USFWS, Green Bay, WI).

US Department of the Interior, Fish and Wildlife Service. Undated. Endangered Species Facts: Karner Blue Butterfly.

Wisconsin DNR Karner Blue Technical Team. 1997. Wildlife Management Guidelines for the Karner Blue Butterfly.

Wisconsin Department of Natural Resources. 1999. Wisconsin Statewide Karner Blue Butterfly Habitat Conservation Plan and Environmental Impact Statement, Madison, WI.

BIOGRAPHICAL SKETCHES

Fran Lowell
Senior Scientist, Natural Resource Group, Inc., 1000 IDS Center, 80 South Eighth Street, Minneapolis, MN 55402, USA

Ms. Lowell is a scientist and project manager with Natural Resource Group, Inc. in Minneapolis, Minnesota. Ms. Lowell manages environmental permitting and compliance activities for pipeline construction projects. She has conducted numerous protected species consultations and has assisted project sponsors in working with federal, state, and local natural resource agencies to identify potential environmental impacts and develop appropriate mitigation plans. Ms. Lowell received a MA in Public Affairs from the University of Minnesota Humphrey Institute and a BS in Biology from Dowling College in New York. Prior to her current position, Ms. Lowell was employed by the Minnesota Department of Public Service as an analyst with the Energy Planning and Intervention Division.

Scott Lounsbury
Supervisor, Environment Department, Enbridge (US), 21 West Superior Street, Duluth, MN 55802, USA

Mr. Lounsbury supervises the Environment Department of Enbridge (US), which operates Lakehead Pipe Line Company, L.P. Mr. Lounsbury oversees and conducts operational, corporate and compliance-related environmental matters for Lakehead Pipe Line and other entities. He has been involved in several large pipeline construction projects, coordinating and managing environmental review, permitting and environmental inspection. Mr. Lounsbury received a MS in Environmental Health from the University of Minnesota and a BA in Biology from the University of Minnesota-Duluth. Prior to joining Enbridge (US), Mr. Lounsbury worked for the US Environmental Protection Agency's Office of Air Quality Planning and Standards, and prior to that with the Minnesota Pollution Control Agency.

Effects of Powerline Right-of-Way Vegetation Management on Avian Communities

James S. Marshall, Larry W. VanDruff, Scott Shupe, and Edward Neuhauser

Shrub-dominated habitats and the birds that nest in them are declining in the Northeast. Rights-of-way can provide productive avian habitat with appropriate vegetation management. This study evaluated the avian productivity of two right-of-way vegetation management options. We measured avian density and nesting success on two adjacent power lines near Rome, NY. The mowed line had more nesting birds than the herbicide-treated line. The mowed line had more shrub cover, and birds had more territories and nests in areas with more shrub cover. Mowing may create better short-term habitat for birds, but selective herbicide treatments may create a more stable long-term shrub layer. Since neither treatment provided more productive habitat, whichever treatment produces more abundant stable habitat would be more beneficial for birds.

Keywords: Right-of-way, birds, shrubs, selective herbicide

INTRODUCTION

Researchers have recently implicated power line rights-of-way as a source of forest fragmentation negatively affecting nesting birds of forest interiors (Askins, 1994). Given the increasing demand for electricity and therefore rights-of-way to transmit electricity, whatever problems rights-of-way cause are likely to continue for the foreseeable future. Despite the negative impacts, do rights-of-way provide any benefits to avian communities?

Rights-of-way may be beneficial if considered as habitat instead of a disruption of habitat. Forest bird species are not the only birds experiencing declines. Birds of early successional habitats are also in decline (Askins, 1994). Agricultural land use in the Northeast has declined in the last few decades, and much abandoned farmland has become secondary forest (Porter and Hill, 1998). The decrease in adequate nesting habitat has led to declines in shrub-nesting bird species like the golden-winged warbler (*Vermivora chrysoptera*). Many other species in early successional habitats exhibit a preference for nest sites with relatively heavy shrub cover (Knopf and Sedgewick, 1992; Burhans and Thompson, 1999). Managing right-of-way habitat for shrubs potentially makes a necessary narrow corridor into beneficial bird habitat for at least some species.

Mowing, selective herbicide treatments, or a combination of the two could provide suitable nesting habitat for shrubland birds. Studies have shown that both treatments provide nesting habitat with relatively high fledging rates (Chasko and Gates, 1982; Bramble et al., 1994). Bird densities were highly positively correlated with shrub cover (Chasko and Gates, 1982; de Waal Malefyt, 1987). Densities declined after mowing, but remained constant or increased after selective herbicide treatments. The treatment producing a more stable, denser shrub layer should therefore provide birds with the best nesting habitat.

The purpose of this study was to investigate the relationship between birds and shrub cover in power line rights-of-way. Although bird density has often been correlated with shrub cover (Bramble et al., 1992), few studies have explicitly considered nest density and shrub cover (Chasko and Gates, 1982), and none have provided a sufficient comparison of nest success between mowing and herbicide treatments. Because density may not accurately reflect nest success (Vickery et al., 1992), such considerations are especially important. If mowing or selective treatment with herbicides does promote increased nest densities with

Environmental Concerns in Rights-of-Way Management: Seventh International Symposium
J.W. Goodrich-Mahoney, D.F. Mutrie and C.A. Guild (editors)
© 2002 Elsevier Science Ltd. All rights reserved.

high nest success, then these treatments will produce viable habitat for threatened shrub-nesting species.

The objectives of this study were to: (1) compare vegetation between the two treatments, (2) compare territory and nest density between the two treatments, (3) determine if bird density is related to vegetation, and (4) compare nest success between the two treatments.

STUDY AREA

The two power lines we studied run through a common right-of-way centered north of Rome, New York. The Volney–Marcy line, operated by the Niagara Mohawk Power Corporation, was cleared in 1982 and has since been managed using Niagara Mohawk's Integrated Vegetation Management strategy (Finch and Shupe, 1997). The adjacent Fitzpatrick–Edic line, operated by the New York Power Authority, was cleared in 1971, and through 1985, received selective herbicide treatments. From 1985 to 1999, the vegetation management switched to mechanical treatments that included mowing. NYPA managers have since resumed selective herbicide treatments.

The right-of-way cuts through a landscape that is a mix of eastern deciduous forest and agricultural land. Agricultural activities on the right-of-way are usually limited to cattle pastures. The right-of-way is otherwise a shrub community or various types of wetlands. Beaver (*Castor canadensis*) ponds and many other areas are flooded and dominated by emergents like cattails (*Typha* spp.). Drier areas on the Volney–Marcy line are dominated by herbaceous species, especially goldenrods (*Solidago* spp.). Shrub cover, when present, is usually northern arrowwood (*Viburnum recognitum*), nannyberry (*Viburnum lentago*), and various *Spirea* species. Shrub cover was noticeably denser on the Fitzpatrick–Edic line, but usually included the same species, with occasional patches dominated by willow (*Salix* spp.) or honeysuckle (*Lonicera* spp.).

We chose six sites along a twenty-five mile stretch of the right-of-way. The closest sites were within two miles of one another, but most sites were separated by five or more miles. Each site was surrounded by forest, relatively free of running or standing water, and free of agricultural activity. We established two adjacent 300 m plots at each site, one under each power line. The Volney–Marcy plot received a consistent herbicide treatment across the full 300 m. Our information suggests that the Fitzpatrick–Edic plot was mechanically treated with at least some mowing.

METHODS

Vegetation in the two treatments

To compare the general vegetation present in the two treatments, we measured vegetation in three systematically established subplots within each plot. The plots were under the center power line — one in the middle of the plot, and the other two each 50 m into the plot. We established a 5-m radius circle at each of these points. We counted all stems above 50 cm within that circle and estimated the percent cover of herbaceous plants, ferns, and shrubs.

Bird density and nest success

To quantitatively survey avian community composition, we used spot-mapping as outlined in the International Bird Census Committee (1970) guidelines. We used color-coded PVC pipe to establish a grid in each plot. The poles were under the center line of each power line and down the line dividing the two plots at each site. Poles were spaced at 50 m intervals. We recorded bird contacts on a map of this grid.

We intensively searched for and monitored nests on two plots every morning from May 17 through the end of July. We monitored a few nests through early September. We marked discovered nests with a small piece of flagging about five to ten meters from the nest and then monitored each nest every three to four days until failure or fledging of the nestlings. A nest was considered active once an egg appeared and fledged if nestlings disappeared at an appropriate time for that species.

DATA ANALYSIS

Vegetation differences between the two treatments

Vegetation on the two lines was noticeably different from visual inspection. We used the general vegetation subplots to analyze the differences. We categorized each plant species as herbaceous plant, fern, *Rubus*, shrub, or tree. Shrubs referred to all woody species that when mature grow as multiple stems from approximately the same place. Trees included all species that typically occurred as single-stem plants once mature. Although *Rubus* species are generally considered shrubs and were considered as shrubs in percent cover analyses, we separated them from shrubs for stem count analyses. *Rubus* stems usually equaled or exceeded all other shrub stems combined, making them a disproportionately important group in the right-of-way; and *Rubus* grows as dense stands of thorny stems. We pooled all plots on a line to compare against all plots on the other line using a two-sample t-test. We ran these tests on the three cover categories and the five stem count categories.

Territory and nest differences between the two treatments

We used paired t-tests to test for differences in individual species territory density between mowed and herbicide treatments. We first standardized density by dividing the number of territories on each plot by the area of the plot in hectares since most plots differed

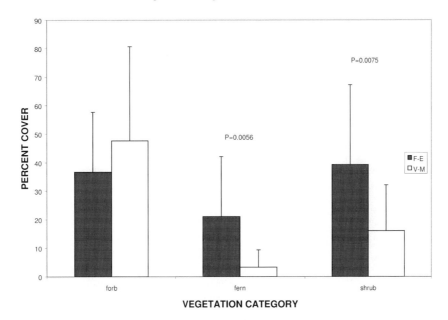

Fig. 1. Average percent vegetation cover on Fitzpatrick–Edic (F–E; $n = 18$) general vegetation plots and on Volney–Marcy (V–M; $n = 17$) general vegetation plots, New York, summer 1999. Error bars represent standard error, and p-values are from two-tailed, pooled-variance t-tests comparing average percent cover on Fitzpatrick–Edic general vegetation plots and average percent cover on Volney–Marcy general vegetation plots.

in size. We did not attempt to correct for small areas within plots that birds may have been less likely to use. We then used the number of territories per hectare on a plot as one observation and compared the number of territories per hectare in one treatment to the number of territories per hectare in the other treatment. Finally, we also pooled all species in a plot for a total territory comparison between the two treatments.

We also compared the number of nests between the two treatments. As with territories, we summed across all nests of each species in each plot and standardized by dividing by plot area. We used two-sample t-tests to compare the number of nests per hectare of each species between the two treatments. We also pooled the nests of all species and compared total nests per hectare between the treatments.

Relationship between bird density and vegetation

To evaluate the relationship between bird density and vegetation, we ran a set of regressions of stem counts on number of territories and number of nests per hectare. We used the stem count data from the non-nest plot surveys. We pooled all species for the average number of territories and nests per hectare for each plot. We first ran a simple linear regression of total stem count per plot on territories and nests per hectare. We then used a backwards stepwise procedure to choose the vegetation categories that had the most influence on the numbers of territories and nests in each plot. The vegetation categories were the five above-listed stem count classes. Variables were entered and removed from the model at an alpha level of 0.15. Evaluation of the residuals showed that although the errors were not normally distributed, they were independent with constant variance. Normality is a minor concern in regression unless conducting hypothesis tests or constructing confidence intervals (Moore and McCabe, 1999).

Nest success

We estimated daily survival probabilities for nests of each species using Mayfield's (1975) method. We also calculated standard errors for these estimates (Johnson, 1979). We then used the program CONTRAST (Sauer and Williams, 1989) to compare daily survival estimates of each species between the two treatments.

For all tests, the significant alpha level was 0.10. We report p-values, however, because some relationships were much more significant than others, and because any alpha level is an arbitrary measure of significance (Johnson, 1999).

RESULTS

Differences in vegetation between the lines

Vegetation subplots on the mowed Fitzpatrick–Edic line had more shrub (df = 31, $t = 2.864$, $p = 0.0075$) and fern cover (df = 31, $t = 2.974$, $p = 0.0056$) than vegetation subplots on the herbicide-treated Volney–Marcy line, but the herbaceous cover was not significantly different ($P > 0.10$) (Fig. 1). In contrasts of stem counts between the two treatments, non-nest vegetation plots on the mowed Fitzpatrick–Edic had more ferns (df = 33, $t = 2.689$, $p = 0.011$) and shrubs (df = 33, $t = 2.471$, $p = 0.019$) than non-nest plots on the Volney–Marcy (Fig. 2).

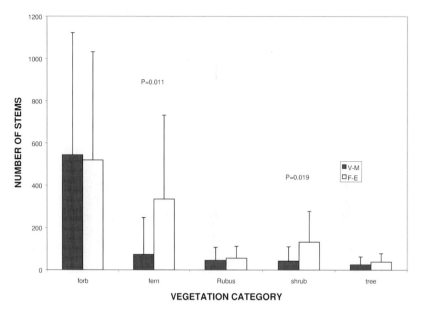

Fig. 2. Average stem counts from general right-of-way vegetation plots ($n = 35$) on the Volney–Marcy (V–M) line and the Fitzpatrick–Edic (F–E) lines, New York, summer 1999. Error bars represent standard error, and the p-values are from two-tailed, pooled-variance t-tests comparing the stem counts between the two treatments.

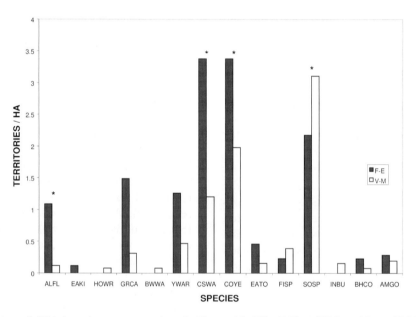

Fig. 3. Territories per hectare of all bird species spot-mapped on the Fitzpatrick–Edic (F–E) and Volney–Marcy (V–M) lines. Asterisks indicate significant differences at an alpha of 0.10.

Densities of territories and nests

Fourteen species had detectable territories from spot-mapping, eleven on the Fitzpatrick–Edic plots and thirteen on the Volney–Marcy plots (Fig. 3). Only song sparrows and common yellowthroats (*Geothlypis trichas*) had mappable territories on all twelve plots.

Most species were not more abundant on one of the two treatments. Two species, alder flycatcher (*Empidonax alnorum*) and common yellowthroat, exhibited significantly different densities between the treatments (ALFL: df = 5, $t = 4.366$, $p = 0.0073$; COYE: df = 5, $t = 3.501$, $p = 0.017$). They were far more abundant on the mowed Fitzpatrick–Edic line. Chestnut-sided warblers had a weakly significant tendency to be on the Fitzpatrick–Edic line (df = 5, $t = 2.017$, $p = 0.10$). The song sparrow was the only species with a weakly significant preference for the herbicide-treated Volney–Marcy line (df = 5, $t = 2.0579$, $p = 0.095$) (Fig. 3).

We found a total of 134 nests of fourteen species (Fig. 4). Eighty-nine (66%) of those nests were on the mowed Fitzpatrick–Edic line. Although most species did not nest more frequently on one or the other power line, alder flycatchers and chestnut-sided warblers both nested far more commonly on the Fitzpatrick–Edic line (ALFL: df = 10, $t = 2.689$, $p = 0.023$; CSWA: df = 10, $t = 2.66$, $p = 0.024$), and the American gold-

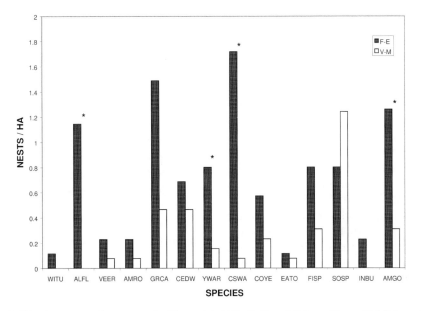

Fig. 4. Nests per hectare of all bird species with nests on the Fitzpatrick–Edic (F–E) and Volney–Marcy (V–M) lines, New York, summer 1999. Asterisks indicate significant differences at an alpha of 0.10.

finch and yellow warbler nested somewhat more often on that line (AMGO: df = 10, $t = 1.948$, $p = 0.080$; YWAR: df = 10, $t = 2.111$, $p = 0.061$) (Fig. 4).

Relationship between bird density and vegetation

Total stem count per plot was not correlated with the number of territories or the number of nests in a plot ($r^2 < 0.01$). In the stepwise territory regression, however, the average number of shrubs was significantly positively related to the number of territories ($F = 19.702$, df = 1, $p = 0.002$; $r^2 = 0.687$). Shrubs were also positively related to the number of nests ($F = 10.321$, df = 1, $p = 0.012$; $r^2 = 0.631$).

Nest success

Overall percent nesting success for 120 nests of all species was 55.8% with 55.1% success in 78 Fitzpatrick–Edic nests and 57.1% success with 42 Volney–Marcy nests. CONTRAST comparisons of Mayfield daily survival probabilities for nests of each species between the two treatments showed only one moderately significant difference for yellow warblers which were more successful on the herbicide-treated Volney–Marcy line (df = 1, $\chi^2 = 4.212$, $p = 0.040$). The overall daily survival probabilities for all species combined did not differ between the treatments.

We observed only one nest predation event — an eastern chipmunk (*Tamias striatus*) feeding on eggs in a song sparrow nest. Exploratory artificial nest studies using clay eggs in other areas of the right-of-way indicated that eastern chipmunks and mice (*Peromyscus* spp.) were the most common visitors to nests. Other potential predators observed in the right-of-way included blue jay (*Cyanocitta cristata*), American crow (*Corvus brachyrhynchos*), common raven (*Corvus corax*), common grackle (*Quiscalus quiscala*), weasel (*Mustela* sp.), striped skunk (*Mephitis mephitis*), gray fox (*Urocyon cinereoargenteus*), coyote (*Canis latrans*), domestic cat (*Felis catus*), and eastern garter snake (*Thamnophis sirtalis*).

DISCUSSION

The mowed Fitzpatrick–Edic line had higher densities of both shrubs and ferns. Territory and nest densities were also greater on the Fitzpatrick–Edic line. Shrubs, but not ferns, were highly correlated with bird density. In general, species nested with equal success between the two treatments. As a result, even though success was equal between the treatments, the differences in abundance suggests that the mowed line produces more young per hectare than the herbicide-treated line.

Bird density

Past research has used abundance as the measure of habitat quality without spending the enormous amounts of time necessary to gather nest success data. Territory density, which we mostly determine by singing males, may be a misleading indicator of habitat quality (Vickery et al., 1992). Many inexperienced males unable to secure territories in better habitat may congregate in suboptimal habitat. Such a concentration of birds rarely results in high productivity. In this study, however, nest success data did not contradict density data. Birds nested with equal, relatively high success on either line, regardless of density. Wherever birds could find suitable nesting habitat, they seemed to nest successfully.

Treatment implications

Based on the literature, we expected the Volney–Marcy line to have a more substantial shrub layer than the

Fitzpatrick–Edic line. We found the opposite to be true. Two factors may explain this vegetation profile. Mowing promotes shrub growth. A tree's root system usually has as much biomass as its aboveground stems and leaves. When the stems are cut, food stored in the roots supports vigorous sprouting from the stump. The single cut stump often sprouts ten to fifteen new stems, compounding a vegetation manager's work. Many woody species of open habitats also sprout stems whenever roots reach near the surface, a process called "root-suckering" (Johnstone, 1990). The mowing on the Fitzpatrick–Edic line should encourage stump-sprouting which could easily result in a dense shrub layer. In addition to mowing concerns, the Fitzpatrick–Edic line is ten years older. That extra time may have allowed shrubs to invade more fully. Several patches of shrubs have invaded the Volney–Marcy line, but most of the line is still dominated by herbaceous cover. We cannot separate time since initial clearing from treatment effects with our study design, but we suspect that both factors have influenced the current vegetation profile. Given another ten years, the Volney–Marcy line vegetation may resemble the vegetation of its neighbor.

Nesting success

Birds need productive nesting habitat, regardless of how it came into existence. Both lines provided such habitat. Overall nesting success was over fifty percent, which agrees with other right-of-way studies (Bramble et al., 1994) but is higher than average for open-cup nesters (Martin, 1993). Nesting success did not differ between the two lines except for the yellow warbler. In that case, the only nesting on the Volney–Marcy line was two successful nests. Given a larger sample, we would not expect a difference. The fact that both lines were equally productive indicates that either vegetation treatment can provide suitable nesting habitat. The only difference between the lines is the quantity of nesting habitat available.

The quantity of available nesting habitat was related to shrub cover. From a management perspective, whatever treatments provide the densest shrub cover for nesting birds should be the recommended treatments. Our results suggest that mowing is the best option. Some caveats must, however, be considered. This study occurred several years post-treatment. After several years of regrowth, the mowed Fitzpatrick–Edic line has a dense shrub layer, but immediately after mowing that shrub layer will disappear. The diminished shrub cover may not regenerate for one or even two years (Bramble et al., 1992), and the high undesirable stem density currently characterizing the mowed plots will eventually necessitate treatments every two to four years (McLoughlin, 1997). Most songbirds have a reproductive life of only one to two years (Ehrlich et al., 1988). Mowing will therefore produce habitat that is unsuitable for maintaining a viable breeding bird population. Such instability would certainly limit the long-term productivity of right-of-way habitat.

Selective herbicide treatments may take longer to develop dense shrub layers. Once in place, however, these shrub layers will change only moderately with further treatments. Viewed from a long-term perspective, the stable shrub layer of selective herbicides may be more beneficial to birds than the variable shrub layer produced by mowing. Chasko and Gates (1982) reported a correlation between birds and shrubs, and bird density was higher on sites treated with selective herbicides.

Other limitations of the study leave the conclusions open to further scrutiny. All of the conclusions were based on a one-year study. Central New York experienced a severe drought in 1999. That drought could have altered the usual ecology of the right-of-way. Many of the conclusions were also based not on individual species, but on all of the species pooled. This pooling brings together species with very different nesting ecologies and may obscure significant differences. Unfortunately, small sample sizes precluded individual analysis in most cases. In species that were individually analyzed, samples were small and pooled across sites with often drastically different landscape and habitat characteristics. Such sources of variation may also obscure important differences. The six sites were relatively small and spread over twenty-five miles of right-of-way. Large portions of the right-of-way are either wetland habitat or agricultural lands. Conclusions drawn from such a small portion of the right-of-way may not translate well up to the whole right-of-way. Finally, we used only one right-of-way for each treatment. Without replication, conclusions drawn about treatments are applicable to this right-of-way but should be applied far more cautiously to other rights-of-way.

With these limitations in mind, our results still provide useful information on birds in rights-of-way. The bird community significantly preferred the mowed Fitzpatrick–Edic line. That line had much denser shrub cover than the Volney–Marcy line. Bird density was highly correlated with shrub density. Given that preference, the presence of more birds on the line with more shrubs was not surprising. Time since right-of-way clearing and vegetation treatment may both contribute to the dense shrub layer, but which is most important is not clear from this study. Regardless of how the shrubs became established, birds of early successional habitats do successfully nest in the right-of-way. If maintaining these populations is an important goal, then right-of-way managers should encourage shrub growth. Further study of immediate post-treatment effects, however, is necessary to evaluate which vegetation management methods would most benefit bird populations.

ABBREVIATIONS USED IN FIGURES

WITU: Wild Turkey
ALFL: Alder Flycatcher
EAKI: Eastern Kingbird
HOWR: House Wren
VEER: Veery
AMRO: American Robin
GRCA: Gray Catbird
CEDW: Cedar Waxwing
BWWA: Blue-winged Warbler
YWAR: Yellow Warbler
CSWA: Chestnut-sided Warbler
COYE: Common Yellowthroat
EATO: Eastern Towhee
FISP: Field Sparrow
SOSP: Song Sparrow
INBU: Indigo Bunting
BHCO: Brown-headed Cowbird
AMGO: American Goldfinch

ACKNOWLEDGMENTS

Thanks to the Niagara Mohawk Power Corporation for providing the bulk of the project funding. The Edna Bailey Sussman Fellowship also provided funding. The New York Power Authority allowed us access to their power line. T.M. Donovan, H.B. Underwood, and C.A. Nowak provided valuable assistance on the project and earlier drafts of the paper. None of this would have been possible without the hours of work put in by P. Glover and T. Schlegel.

REFERENCES

Askins, R.A. 1994. Open corridors in a heavily forested landscape: impacts on shrubland and forest-interior species. Wildlife Society Bulletin, 22: 339–347.

Bramble, W.C., R.H. Yahner, and W.R. Byrnes. 1992. Breeding-bird population changes following right-of-way maintenance treatments. Journal of Arboriculture, 18: 23–32.

Bramble, W.C., R.H. Yahner, and W.R. Byrnes. 1994. Nesting of breeding birds on an electric utility right-of-way. Journal of Arboriculture, 20: 124–129.

Burhans, D.E. and F.R. Thompson. 1999. Habitat patch size and nesting success of yellow-breasted chats. Wilson Bulletin, 111: 210–215.

Chasko, G.G. and J.E. Gates. 1982. Avian habitat suitability along a transmission-line corridor in an oak-hickory forest region. Wildlife Monographs, 82: 1–41.

de Waal Malefyt, J. 1987. Effects of herbicide spraying on breeding songbird habitat along electric transmission rights-of-way. In: Proceedings of the 4th Symposium on environmental concerns in rights-of-way management. W.R. Byrnes and H.A. Holt, eds. pp. 28–37.

Ehrlich, P.R., D.S. Dobkins, and D. Wheye. 1988. The Birder's Handbook. Simon and Schuster, New York, NY, USA.

Finch, K.E. and S.D. Shupe. 1997. Nearly two decades of integrated vegetation management on electric transmission rights-of-ways. In: Proceedings of the 6th International Symposium on Environmental Concerns in Rights-of-Way Managment. Elsevier Science, Oxford, UK. J.R. Williams, J.W. Goodrick-Mahoney, J.R. Wisniewski, and J. Wisniewski, eds. pp. 67–75.

International Bird Census Committee. 1970. Recommendations for an international standard for a mapping method in bird census work. Audubon Field Notes, 24: 723–726.

Johnson, D.H. 1979. Estimating nest success: The Mayfield method and an alternative. Auk, 96: 651–661.

Johnson, D.H. 1999. The insignificance of statistical significance testing. Journal of Wildlife Management, 63: 763–772.

Johnstone, R.A. 1990. Vegetation management: Mowing to spraying. Journal of Arboriculture: 186–189.

Knopf, F.L. and J.A. Sedgewick. 1992. An experimental study of nest-site selection by yellow warblers. Condor, 94: 734–742.

Martin, T.E. 1993. Nest predation among vegetation layers and habitat types: revising the dogmas. American Naturalist, 141: 897–913.

Mayfield, H.F. 1975. Suggestions for calculating nest success. Wilson Bulletin, 87: 456–466.

McLoughlin, K.T. 1997. Application of integrated pest management to electric utility rights-of-way vegetation management in New York State. In: Proceedings of the 6th International Symposium on Environmental Concerns in Rights-of-Way Management. J.R. Williams, J.W. Goodrich-Mahoney, J.R. Wisniewski, and J. Wisniewski, eds. pp. 118–126.

Moore, D.S. and G.P. McCabe. 1999. Introduction to the Practice of Statistics. W.H. Freeman, New York, NY, USA.

Porter, W.F. and J.A. Hill. 1998. Regional trends of biological resources — Northeast. In: Status and Trends of the Nation's Biological Resources. Volume 1. US Department of the Interior, US Geological Survey, Reston, VA, USA. pp. 181–218.

Sauer, J.R. and B.K. Williams. 1989. Generalized procedures for testing hypotheses about survival or recovery rates. Journal of Wildlife Management, 53: 137–142.

Vickery, P.D., M.L. Hunter, and J.V. Wells. 1992. Is density an indicator of breeding success? Auk, 109: 706–710.

BIOGRAPHICAL SKETCHES

James S. Marshall (Corresponding author)

State University of New York, College of Environmental Science and Forestry, Environmental and Forest Biology Currently, Ohio State University, Dept. Evolution, Ecology, and Organismal Biology, 1735 Neil Ave., Columbus, OH 43210, USA, (614) 292-0691, e-mail: marshall.298@osu.edu

James S. Marshall, currently enrolled at the Ohio State University for a PhD in Evolution, Ecology, and Organismal Biology, holds a BS in environmental science from Texas Christian University and an MS in Environmental and Forest Biology from the SUNY College of Environmental Science and Forestry. His primary interest is the relationships between birds and their habitats.

Larry W. VanDruff

State University of New York, College of Environmental Science and Forestry Environmental and Forest Biology, 1 Forestry Dr., Syracuse, NY 13210, USA, (315)470-6803, e-mail: lwvandru@syr.edu

Larry W. VanDruff is an emeritus professor on the faculty of Environmental and Forest Biology at the SUNY College of Environmental Science and Forestry.

He received his PhD from Cornell University. His primary research interests have been urban wildlife ecology, especially gray squirrel, raccoon, and mallard population ecology.

Scott D. Shupe

Niagara Mohawk Power Corporation, 300 Erie Blvd. West, Syracuse, NY 13202, USA, 315-428-6616, e-mail: shupes@NiagaraMohawk.com

Scott D. Shupe, Environmental Analyst at Niagara Mohawk, holds a BS in Biology and a MS in Water Resource Mgt. from SUNY College of Environmental Science and Forestry, and a MS in Science Mgt. from the University of Alaska-Anchorage. His career has spanned the planning-construction-operations spectrum, including powerline construction, small hydropower and navigation planning, hydroelectric relicensing, gas pipeline licensing and operations, and is currently involved with other regulatory issues associated with utility ROW management.

Edward F. Neuhauser

Niagara Mohawk Power Corporation, 300 Erie Blvd. West, Syracuse, NY 13202, USA, 315-428-3355, e-mail: neuhausere@NiagaraMohawk.com

Edward F. Neuhauser, Senior Research Specialist at Niagara Mohawk, holds a BS and PhD in Soil Biology from the SUNY College of Environmental Science and Forestry. He is responsible for a variety of renewable and energy storage research programs as well as environmental, water resource, hazardous material, remediation, and safety research activities at Niagara Mohawk.

Fragmentation Effects Caused by a Power Line Right-of-Way on a Mid-Elevation Forest Bird Community in Central Colombia

Loreta Rosselli and Susana De La Zerda

In this first Neotropical study of its kind, we evaluated the effect of the segmentation caused by a right-of-way corridor on the avian community of a central Colombian forest. There were no differences in species richness or composition between the two forest fragments created by the opening of the ROW. Forest interior bird species were almost absent from the corridor and less abundant close to it, open-area species were common in the corridor and up to 20 m inside the forest although there was a significant difference between the portion of the ROW with second growth and the portion that is kept clean of vegetation. The movement of forest-restricted birds across the ROW was noted in the second-growth portion, which served as a bridge and prevented the ROW from isolating populations on either side It is concluded that the ROW reduces original habitat and creates a double edge that affects the distribution of forest as well as open-area bird species. On the other hand, vegetation regrowth in the ROW is extremely important in mitigating the fragmentation effect, reducing the entrance of open-area species and permitting the movement of forest species between remnant forest patches. These findings will help to provide guidelines for the management of the extensive ROW areas in the Neotropics.

Keywords: Neotropics, forest fragmentation, conservation, edge effect, sensitive species

INTRODUCTION

The construction and operation of high-voltage transmission lines has generated considerable concern for the environment in recent decades (Rosselli and De La Zerda, 1996). Several international studies have shown that high-tension lines may cause high bird mortality due to collisions with the conductors or the ground wire, and fragmentation of forest habitats by clearing of the right-of-way for the construction and maintenance of the lines. Since 1995, Interconexión Eléctrica S.A. (ISA), the Colombian state company in charge of energy transmission, and the Colombian Ministry of the Environment have sponsored a series of pioneer studies on the effects of transmission lines on Neotropical wildlife. These included an extensive literature review and a pilot field project (Rosselli and De la Zerda, 1996; De La Zerda and Rosselli, 1997; Rosselli and De la Zerda, 1999), as well as the present study.

Both in the tropics and in the temperate zone the vegetation that develops in the Rights of Way (ROWs) that cross forested areas consists of second growth, different from that of the surrounding forest, that permits the entrance of plant and animal species associated with open vegetation (Chasko and Gates, 1982; Luken et al., 1992). In the Neotropics the particular type of fragmentation caused by linear projects, called internal fragmentation or segmentation, has been little studied (Goosem, 1997; Malizia et al., 1998) although it may interrupt or delay the movement of individuals across the ROWs thereby dividing populations. The presence of highly specialized endemic groups or "sensitive species" such as the antbirds (Formicariidae), the woodcreepers (Dendrocolaptidae), ovenbirds (Furnariidae) and tapaculos (Rhinocryptidae) that are restricted to the lower levels of mature forest, probably results in more severe effects in the American tropics. According to our preliminary observations and Bierregaard and Stouffer's

Environmental Concerns in Rights-of-Way
Management: Seventh International Symposium
J.W. Goodrich-Mahoney, D.F. Mutrie and C.A. Guild (editors)
© 2002 Elsevier Science Ltd. All rights reserved.

(1997) studies in the Amazon, if secondary vegetation reaches a certain height in cleared areas, bird species sensitive to fragmentation cross more easily without their populations becoming divided.

Our objective was to analyze the effect of a ROW corridor on the presence and distribution of forest restricted species sensitive to fragmentation, documenting the occupation of the ROW by open area species and their penetration into the surrounding forest, also the extent of any edge effect into the forest. We also compared the impact of different types of vegetation in the ROW on the fragmentation caused by this type of opening and evaluated the extent to which the corridor acted as a barrier to movement of individuals across the ROW.

METHODS

The eastern portion of Antioquia Department in the Central Andes of Colombia is important for its hydroelectric plants. In this area, forest patches of a few hundred hectares are common and frequently crossed by the transmission lines. Our study site is on the western extreme of a 141.5 ha protected patch of forest (6°20'N, 75°W), 56 km east of Medellín, between 1010 and 1200 m elevation: mean annual temperature is between 17°C and 23°C and mean annual rainfall is 4200 mm (Empresas Públicas de Medellín, 1995). The forest is highly disturbed, has a canopy about 20 m high with abundant ferns, Melastomataceae, Rubiaceae and Piperaceae on the understory; palms (*Euterpe*), and trees of Myristicaceae, Clusiaceae, and Moraceae are common in the canopy. ISA's 230 kV Guatapé-San Carlos transmission line, constructed in 1985, crosses the forest over ca. 400 m between towers No. 11 and 12, dividing it into two fragments of approximately 120 and 20 ha (Fig. 1). The width of the ROW is 32 m, however regrowth has been permitted on the lower 290 m of the corridor next to Río Guatapé and there is currently a secondary forest 5–10 m high with pioneer trees such as *Ochroma, Cecropia, Heliocarpus* and *Vismia*. The upper 110 m, adjacent to tower 11, is regularly maintained and vegetation is cut down to the ground: during our study this portion of the ROW was covered by herbaceous vegetation up to 80 cm tall, dominated by sedges.

During a preliminary visit on 9–22 December 1997, we prepared the area for sampling, cutting trails parallel to the ROW corridor at distances of 5, 20, 60, and 100 m from it in both the large (G) and small (P) fragments as well as one (0 m) down the center of the corridor. Trails were named according to the fragment they were in and the distance to the ROW. In the 0 and P5 and G5 trails, the portions in or adjacent to second growth were named M (0M, P5M, G5M). We were careful to leave at least 50 m from any large clearing in the area different from the ROW corridor (Fig. 2). During

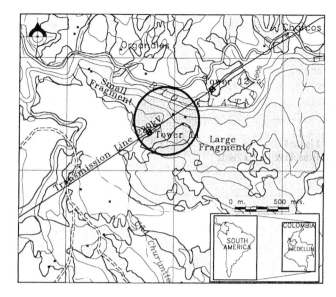

Fig. 1. Location of study area.

this visit mist nets were also set to capture and band as many birds as possible.

Most data were obtained during three two-week sampling periods in January, April, and July 1998. During the first 5 days of each period we conducted visual and auditory censuses to detect and quantify bird species at different distances from the ROW corridor. During the remaining 9–10 days we captured birds with mist nets to complement data on the presence of bird species at different distances from the ROW and to obtain information on movements of individuals within the study area.

During each sampling period, between 9 and 11 censuses were conducted on each trail. Censuses were conducted by pairs of trained biologists who walked slowly (0.33 km/h) along the trails between 06:00 and 10:30 and 15:00 and 18:00. Each bird detected was identified and its exact location in the area noted. A tape recorder was also used to try to attract birds for identification and to record unseen birds for later identification by an expert. Census schedules were planned so that each trail was visited at all times of day. Groups of observers were as far as possible from each other and censuses on the same trail were separated in time to minimize disturbance. Observations were standardized according to the kilometers walked (65.7 during the whole study). A total of 78–88 censuses were conducted during each sampling period.

We set twelve-meter black nylon mist nets (30 mm mesh) on all trails except P100 and G100. Nets were installed in two groups and opened from 05:30 to 10:30 and from 14:30 to 17:30, depending on time of dawn and dusk and rains. We banded most birds with unique color combinations of Hughes plastic bands; boreal migrants and hummingbirds were marked with spots of nontoxic paint on the back and by clipping different combinations of tail feathers. Capture locations of all birds were carefully mapped. Each bird

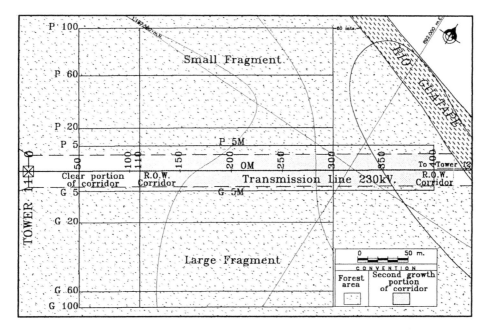

Fig. 2. Scheme of study area.

captured was also checked for signs of reproduction, molt and immaturity. The sampling unit was a mist net hour (mnh) equal to one 12 m mist net open for an hour. We accumulated approximately 800–900 mnh per sampling period, and 3481.7 mnh over the entire study (including December 1997). Total mnh per trail varied between 114 on P5 and 602 in 0M. Due to local topography, we accumulated more mnh in the small fragment (1564.7) than in the large one (1153.0). This difference is even greater for several analyses in which we considered birds caught by A.M. Umaña in her thesis research, part of this project (Umaña, 1998) since she concentrated her capture efforts in the small fragment. Adding in her mist net hours yields a grand total of 2555.8 in the small fragment and 1223.4 in the large one.

For analysis, prior to calculations, birds were grouped in several categories according to their habitat preferences, based upon information in the literature, our own observations and advice from a Neotropical ornithology expert. The categories were:

1. Forest restricted species (Forest°) — species that live inside mature forest and rarely go to borders or other types of vegetation.
2. Forest non-restricted species (Forest*) — birds that mainly inhabit forests, but frequently range out to forest edge and into other types of vegetation.
3. Mixed habitat species (Mixed) — birds that live in different types of semiopen habitats such as second-growth woodland and scrub, showing no marked preferences.
4. Open area species (Open) — birds that inhabit areas with mostly low vegetation like pastures, although they may also occur in scrub or along forest edges.

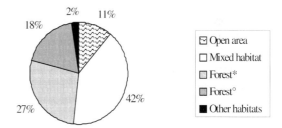

Fig. 3. Composition of species detected in the study area in San Rafael (1997–1998) according to habitat category.

5. Non terrestrial species — species not particularly associated with any terrestrial habitat such as vultures and water birds.

RESULTS

A total of 125 bird species belonging to 31 families was recorded in study area. The tanager family (Thraupidae) had the largest number of species, followed by flycatchers (Tyrannidae) and antbirds (Formicariidae) (Appendix 1). Almost half of the species are forest species followed by mixed-habitat species, with only a small proportion of open-area species (Fig. 3). Even considering the large number of forest species found, including good populations of important endemics such as the Sooty Ant-Tanager (*Habia gutturalis*) and White-mantled Barbet (*Capito hypoleucus*), the degree of human disturbance in the site is evident through the absence of very sensitive species such as guans, curassows, large parrots, and raptors.

Mist nets

We obtained a total of 755 captures of 69 species and 524 individuals in the entire study. Due to the higher sampling effort in the small fragment, we made more captures there (446 vs. 209 in the large fragment), but capture rates were very similar (0.175 captures/mnh in the small fragment vs. 0.171 in the large one). The most frequently captured species included the Striped Manakin *Machaeropterus regulus* (65 captures), Orange-billed Sparrow *Arremon aurantiirostris* (44), Swainson's Thrush *Catharus ustulatus* (44), White-breasted Wood-Wren *Henicorhina leucosticta* (43) and Sooty-headed Wren *Thryothorus spadix* (39). Fifteen species were captured only once, 17 were captured between 2 and 4 times, 16 between 5 and 9, 8 between 10 and 20, and 14 more than 20.

Most species captured less than 5 times are open-area species, present only sporadically in the area, or are species with habits (e.g., canopy specialists) or sizes (larger than ca. 50 g) than make them hard to catch with the nets used.

Recapture rates varied considerably among species; 99 individuals were captured at least in two different sampling periods. Species with greatest numbers of recaptured individuals include Striped Manakin (10), Sooty-headed Wren, White-breasted Wood-Wren, Sooty Ant-Tanager, and Orange-billed Sparrow with 7 each. These 5 forest species were recorded during all visits to the field, and also are among those with most individual captures, which indicates that they are abundant and resident in the area. Sixteen species had between 2 and 5 recaptured individuals, 15 one and 34, none. Among the recaptured individuals, 69 were netted in two sampling periods, 18 in 3, 6 in 4 (including the preliminary visit), and 3 individuals were caught in all of these as well as by A.M. Umaña. The individuals with most recaptures (6, excluding captures made in the same sampling period) were an Orange-billed Sparrow and a Sooty-headed Wren. Several hummingbirds and North American migrants with many captures had low recapture rates, probably due in part to the fact that the marking methods used were less reliable. This undoubtedly resulted in less reliable identification of recaptured individuals, which in turn inflated the presumed number of individuals captured, especially among the hummingbirds. Low recapture rates for migrants doubtless also reflected their transitory use of the area, especially in the case of the two notably abundant thrushes (Swainson's and Gray-cheeked).

Censuses

One hundred and six species were detected in censuses, 35% more than in mist net captures. Excluding birds not identified to species and repeated observations of marked individuals, 1963 visual and auditory detections were made during the whole study. In most cases (1357) it could not be seen if the birds were banded; 531 observations were made of definitely unbanded birds and only on 75 occasions were individuals positively identified by their band combinations.

Table 1. Comparison between capture and detection rates, and species composition according to habitat categories in both fragments caused by the ROW corridor between 1997 and 1998 in San Rafael, Antioquia

	Large fragment	Small fragment
Detection rate	838/28.43 km = 29.5	773/27.03 km = 28.6
Capture rate	209 captures/1223.41 mistnet-hours = 0.171	446 captures/2555.79 mistnet-hours = 0.175
Forest°	18	18
Forest*	30	27
Mixed habitats	37	40
Open areas	9	6
Total	94	91

°Forest restricted species.
*Forest non-restricted species.
Mixed: Mixed habitat species.
Open: Open area species.

Most detected species included the White-breasted Wood-Wren (104 records) and the Sooty Ant-Tanager with 101, followed by the Sooty-headed Wren (87), Yellow-browed Shrike-Vireo (76), and Striped Manakin with 69. Twenty-three species were observed only once and 56 more than 5 times. We must bear in mind that these detections include auditory and visual data and the most vocal and conspicuous species tend to be detected more frequently. Censuses detected several species rarely or never captured in nets due to their size (raptors like the Roadside Hawk, Laughing Falcon, and Turkey Vulture) or habits (e.g., forest canopy specialists like the Shrike-Vireo). By contrast, a few inconspicuous, scarce or secretive species like the White-whiskered Puffbird, Wedge-billed Woodcreeper, and Checker-throated and Sooty Antwrens, hard to detect either visually or by voice, were found only through mist nets.

Comparison between fragments

The bird communities of the two fragments were very similar. Both capture and detection rates were alike (Table 1) as well as the species composition. Ninety-six species were found in the large fragment and 93 in the small one. The proportions of forest, mixed habitat and open area species were very similar (Table 1, $\chi^2 = 0.83$, $p > 0.75$, 3 df). Twenty-one species were exclusive to the large fragment and 18 to the small one but they shared 75 giving a Similarity Index = 79%. Exclusive species correspond to observations or captures of species not regularly found in the study area such as the White-whiskered Puffbird, American Redstart, and Blue-black Grassquit in the large fragment and Black-throated Trogon, Blackburnian Warbler and Pale-breasted Spinetail in the small one.

Species distributions and individual movements relative to the ROW corridor

Considering data from both censuses and mist nets, we found positive correlations between the proportion of

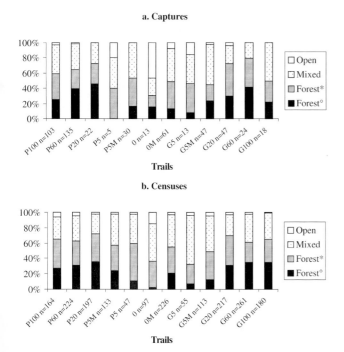

Fig. 4. (a) Species proportion according to habitat category in mist-net captures. Recaptures excluded. (b) Species proportion according to habitat category in census detections. Repeated observations of ringed individuals excluded.

Table 2. Non parametric correlation coefficients (r_s) between proportions of forest restricted species, forest non-restricted species, mixed habitat species and open area species versus distance to the ROW corridor

	MIST Nets	Censuses
Distance vs. Forest°	0.517[c]	0.631*
Distance vs. Forest**	0.324	0.323
Distance vs. Mixed habitat	0.291	0.230
Distance vs. Open area	−0.390	−0.05

*Significant, $p < 0.05$, in all cases the number of pairs is 12.
[c] Almost significant, $0.10 > p > 0.05$.
°Forest restricted species.
**Forest non-restricted species.
Mixed: Mixed habitat species. Birds that live in different types of semiopen habitats such as second growth vegetation and scrub and do not show a marked preference for any of them.
Open: Open area species.

Table 3. Number of individuals caught in the ROW corridor or in both fragments in 1997 and 1998 in San Rafael (Antioquia). Species with more than 4 individuals recaptured in two or more sampling periods are included.

Species	Category	No. Individuals	
		That did not use the corridor	That used or crossed the corridor
Henicorhina leucosticta	Forest°	3	4
Habia gutturalis	Forest°	4	2
Arremon aurantiirostris	Forest°	5	2
Machaeropterus regulus	Forest°	8	2
Mionectes oleaginea	Forest*	2	2
Thryothorus spadix	Forest*	2	5
Saltator maximus	Mixed	2	2
Manacus manacus	Mixed	1	4
Coereba flaveola	Mixed	0	4

°Forest restricted species.
*Forest non-restricted species.
Mixed: Mixed habitat species. Birds that live in different types of semiopen habitats such as second growth vegetation and scrub and do not show a marked preference for any of them.
Open: Open area species.

forest-restricted species and distance from the ROW corridor (Fig. 4). For censuses, this correlation ($r = 0.631$) was the only one that was statistically significant (Table 2). The only negative correlations (although non significant) were between the proportions of open area species and distance from the corridor. The proportions of mixed-habitat and non-restricted forest species were not correlated with distance from the ROW (Table 2, Fig. 4). For forest-restricted species, the corridor definitely appears to reduce available habitat while facilitating penetration of open-area species 20 m or more into the forest.

Analyzing the capture-recapture locations of the 9 most frequently captured species, we found that even in those belonging to the forest-restricted habitat category, there were individuals that were caught in the ROW corridor and in most there were individuals caught in both fragments — i.e., they had crossed the corridor (Fig. 5, Table 3). In all forest-restricted species except the White-breasted Wood-Wren, most individuals were caught in only one fragment (even those with high numbers of recaptures), but in most non-restricted forest and mixed habitat species, the number of individuals caught in the corridor or in both fragments was equal to or greater than the number that were caught in only one fragment and by this criterion did not cross the ROW (Table 3, Fig. 5A). The proportion of non-restricted forest and mixed-habitat species found to use or cross the ROW corridor was significantly higher than for forest-restricted species (Fig. 5B, $\chi^2 = 6.08$, 1 df, $0.01 < p < 0.025$).

Effect of regrowth in the ROW corridor

A significantly higher proportion of open-area species were captured in the clearcut portion of the ROW corridor and its adjoining edges than in that part of the corridor with tall second growth (Fig. 6a, $\chi^2 = 19.61$, $p = 0.0002$, 3 df). The census data also show a significant difference between the composition of birds belonging to different habitat categories in the areas close to the second growth vs. clearcut portions of the corridor (Fig. 6b, $\chi^2 = 28.69$, $p < 0.0001$, 3 df) although in this case the main difference is due to the higher proportion of forest-restricted species in the former.

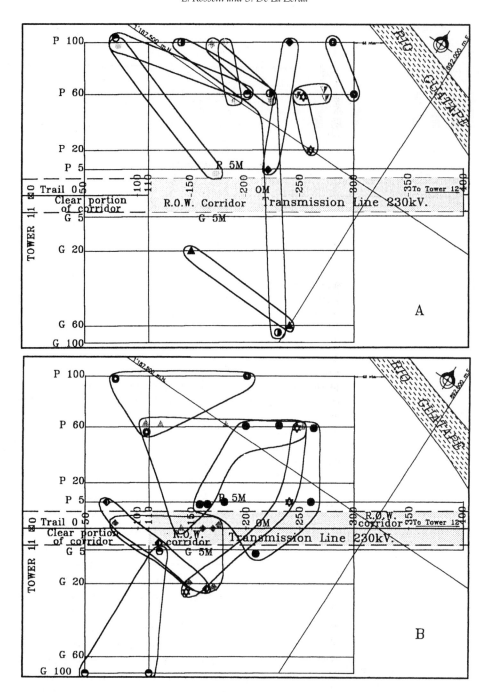

Fig. 5. (A) Spatial localization of Stripe Manakin (Forest restricted species) individuals recaptured in more than one sample period between December 1997 and July 1998 in San Rafael. Each symbol represents an individual. (B) Spatial localization of Sooty-headed Wren (Forest non restricted species) individuals recaptured in more than one sample period between December 1997 and July 1998 in San Rafael. Each symbol represents an individual.

Looking at the individual trails in the corridor and adjoining borders, in most cases the proportion of open-area species is higher in the clearcut part of the corridor (trails 0, P5, G5) and the proportion of forest restricted species is higher in the second growth part (trails 0M, P5M, G5M) (Fig. 4).

DISCUSSION

In interpreting our results, one must bear in mind that the San Rafael reserve had already suffered considerable human disturbance prior to the construction of the ROW corridor in the form of fragmentation (the entire reserve qualifies as a medium-sized fragment according to Kattan and Alvarez-Lopez, 1996), hunting (indicated by the lack of large raptors, tinamous, and cracids) and disturbance to the vegetation. According to Kattan and Alvarez-Lopez (1996) a fragment of Andean forest of this size should hold around 140 species of forest birds, and we found only 60 (36 non-restricted, 24 restricted). At lower elevations the total number of bird species in similar humid forests

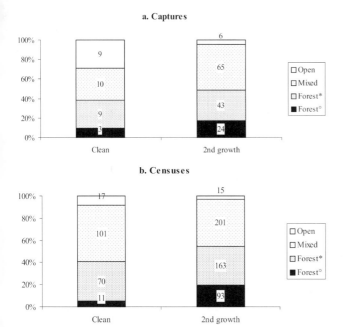

Fig. 6. (a) Comparison of mist net captures according to habitat category in the second growth and clean cut portions of the ROW corridor and bordering trails (P5 and G5) (recaptures not included). (b) Comparison of census detections according to habitat category in the second growth and clean cut portions of the ROW corridor and bordering trails (P5 and G5) (repeated observations of banded individuals not included).

should exceed 300 (Blake et al., 1990; Karr, 1990; Robinson and Terborgh, 1990; see also Stiles and Bohórquez, 2000). However, in spite of its impoverished nature, the avifauna still contains a variety of species with diverse habitat requirements, including enough species restricted to the interior of closed forest, to provide quantitative answers to the questions raised at the outset. Given that this study is the first of its kind to deal with a rich Neotropical avifauna, however impoverished, our results should provide valuable guidelines for future work on the effects of lineal clearings such as those caused by Right-of Way corridors of high-tension lines. Our results are especially relevant to conservation of Andean birds, bearing in mind that the Andean forests represent an already highly fragmented ecosystem which in Colombia has been reduced to a small fraction of its former area: conservation efforts in many areas are perforce restricted to these type of fragments that hold a fair amount of diversity (Bierregaard et al. 1997; Guindon, 1996; Schelhas and Greenberg, 1996).

We feel that the combination of methods used was effective for the type of study we conducted. Considerably more species were detected in the censuses than with mist nets, showing once again that for short inventories, visual, and auditory observations are more efficient even though they have the disadvantage of depending a good deal on the experience of the observers (Stiles and Rosselli, 1998). The use of tape recorders was important in supplementing the observations and in helping the observers to acquire experience with auditory identifications (cf. Parker, 1991). The use of mist nets was critical in detecting movements of marked individuals because it proved very difficult to see and identify band combinations in the dense vegetation. We emphasize, however, that use of mist nets as the sole method for evaluating bird communities is not recommended, especially in Neotropical forests, due to the limited coverage and many biases in capture data (Remsen and Good, 1996; Stiles and Rosselli, 1998).

We found virtually no differences in bird community richness and composition between the small and large fragments created by the ROW corridor. There are several possible explanations for this:

1. The small fragment is large enough to hold an avifauna similar to that of the large. We doubt that this is the case because the difference in sizes is too great and the proportion of area affected by edge effect is larger in the small fragment. The 20 ha small fragment fits in the "small" category of Kattan and Alvarez-López (1996); the large one belongs to their medium size category (100–600 Ha), and expected species richness in the former is much less than what we observed.

2. The ROW corridor in this place does not act as a barrier or fragmentation agent. This explanation is at best partially correct. Part of our data and Umaña's (1998) thesis indicate that the clearcut portion of the corridor was not crossed by sensitive species and that individuals of forest-restricted species tended to remain on one side of the corridor in this area. Furthermore, studies done in the Amazon have found that cleared belts of similar widths have had fragmentation effects on mature forests (Stouffer and Bierregaard, 1995; Bierregaard and Stouffer, 1995, 1997).

3. The second-growth portion of the corridor acts as a bridge that permits the passage of individuals of forest birds between the two fragments. We think this is what is happening, based upon capture data and direct observations in both portions of the corridor. Moreover, the translocation experiments of Umaña (1998) showed that forest-restricted birds transported across the corridor returned to their territories via the second-growth portion, avoiding the clearcut section. This bridge, in combination with the minor differences in habitat between fragments found by Montes (1998), allows similar avifaunas in the two fragments. A similar effect of second-growth reducing the isolation of forest fragments was found on a larger scale in the Amazon by Bierregaard and Stouffer (1997). An additional effect of the regrowth in the ROW is that it ameliorates the double edge effect facilitating penetration of open-area birds, thereby permitting more forest species next to the corridor.

We feel strongly that in future studies of this type in the Neotropics, especially those involving monitoring, attention should be focused on a limited number of indicator species sensitive to the type of disturbance in question; this is especially important given the limited resources available for environmental studies in Colombia (and other Latin American countries). In the present study, we attempted to identify forest-restricted species that rarely use edges or more open habitats, as the species most likely to be affected by the ROW. We had initially suspected that the suboscine passerines, especially the antbirds (Formicariidae), ovenbirds (Furnariidae), woodcreepers (Dendrocolaptidae), and tapaculos (Rhinocryptidae) would provide most such indicator species (see also Stiles and Bohórquez, 2000), an expectation only partially fulfilled due to the fact that many sensitive species of these families expected on the basis of distributions, were absent from the study area, doubtless due to the degree of fragmentation and disturbance antedating the ROW construction. Nevertheless, the 24 forest-restricted species identified (from a variety of families) were effective indicators in that as a group they definitely responded to the ROW corridor and the vegetation therein. We emphasize that attention should be focused on the individual species, according to their observed ecological attributes, and not on the presence or absence of certain families: virtually all of the larger Neotropical families include species with very diverse habitat requirements.

We conclude that for forest restricted species a clean cut corridor may be a barrier and that there is an edge effect that affects the presence and distribution of forest and open area species. The presence of secondary vegetation is very important in diminishing isolation of specialist bird populations and edge effect in the forest.

We recommend that Power Companies should permit the regrowth of vegetation in ROW corridors when possible, taking advantage of topographic features such as valleys and ravines without risking the line's safety and function.

ACKNOWLEDGEMENTS

We thank Beatriz Arjona, Amelia Moncada and all personnel in the Interconexión Eléctrica S.A. Environmetal Department for important and enthusiastic help. Miguel Jaramillo and collaborators in "Balneario el Castillo" kindly offered their assistance in the field in San Rafael. F. Gary Stiles carefully checked and commented all stages of the study. Peter Feinsinger made valuable suggestions on the proposal. We are especially grateful to the field biologists Juan David Amaya, Alejandro Camero, Sergio Córdoba, María Isabel Moreno, and Juan Carlos Verhelst and the students that did their thesis research associated with this project (Ana María Umaña and Jairo Andrés Montes) for their unconditional collaboration and careful work under difficult conditions. Our attendance of the 7th International Symposium on Environmental Concerns in Rights-of-Way Management was made possible by the organizers and Dean Murtrie.

APPENDIX 1

Bird species detected in censuses and mist-nets in the San Rafael (Antioquia, Colombia) forest. December 1997–July 1998

Family	Species	Habitat category	Family	Species	Habitat category
Tinamidae	Crytpurellus soui	Mixed		Pteroglossus torquatus	Mixed
Cathartidae	Corapyps atratus	Non terr.	Picidae	Veniliornis kirkii	Forest*
Accipitridae	Buteo magnirostris	Mixed		Picumnus olivaceus	Mixed
	Herpetotheres cachinnans	Open		Dryocopus lineatus	Mixed
Cracidae	Ortalis motmot	Mixed	Dendrocolaptidae	Dendrocincla fuliginosa	Forest°
Phasianidae	Odontophorus erythrops	Forest°		Sittasomus griseicapillus	Forest°
Charadriidae	Vanellus chilensis	Open		Glyphorhynchus spirurus	Forest°
Psittacidae	Forpus conspicillatus	Mixed		Lepidocolaptes souleyetii	Mixed
Cuculidae	Piaya cayana	Forest*		Xiphorhynchus picus	Mixed
	Tapera naevia	Open		Campylorhamphus trochilirostris	Forest*
	Crotophaga ani	Open	Furnariidae	Automolus ochrolaemus	Forest°
Trochilidae	Glaucis hirsuta	Mixed		Automolus rubiginosus	Forest°
	Threnetes ruckeri	Forest*		Xenops minutus	Forest*
	Phaethornis longuemareus	Mixed	Formicariidae	Thamnophilus punctatus	Forest°
	Androdon aequatorialis	Forest*		Thamnophilus multistriatus	Mixed
	Thalurania colombica	Forest*		Thamnophilus doliatus	Mixed
	Anthracothorax nigricollis	Mixed		Cercomacra tyrannina	Forest*
	Heliothryx barroti	Forest*		Cercomacra nigricans	Mixed
	Amazilia tzacatl	Mixed		Myrmeciza immaculata	Forest°
	Amazilia amabilis	Forest*		Myrmotherula schisticolor	Forest°
Trogonidae	Trogon rufus	Forest°		Myrmotherula fulviventris	Forest°
	Trogon violaceus	Mixed		Dysithamnus mentalis	Forest°
Momotidae	Baryphthengus ruficapillus	Forest°	Pipridae	Manacus manacus	Mixed
Bucconidae	Malacoptila panamensis	Forest°		Machaeropterus regulus	Forest°
Capitonidae	Capito hypoleucus	Forest*	Cotingidae	Pachyramphus cinnamomeus	Mixed

(continued)

Family	Species	Habitat category	Family	Species	Habitat category
	Cotinga nattererii	Forest°		Wilsonia canadensis	Forest*
Tyrannidae	Zimmereus viridiflavus	Mixed		Basileuterus fulvicauda	Non terr.
	Leptopogon superciliaris	Mixed		Basileuterus rufifrons	Mixed
	Elaenia frantzii	Mixed	Coerebidae	Coereba flaveola	Mixed
	Contopus fumigatus	Mixed	Tersinidae	Tersina viridis	Mixed
	Contopus borealis	Mixed	Thraupidae	Euphonia xanthogastra	Forest*
	Mionectes olivaceus	Forest°		Euphonia trinitatis	Mixed
	Mionectes oleagineus	Forest*		Euphonia laniirostris	Mixed
	Myiornis ecaudatus	Forest*		Euphonia musica	Mixed
	Oncostoma olivaceum	Mixed		Tangara guttata	Forest*
	Platyrhynchus sp.	Forest°		Tangara gyrola	Forest*
	Empidonax virescens	Forest*		Tangara larvata	Mixed
	Myiarchus tuberculifer	Forest*		Tangara inornata	Mixed
Tyrannidae	Pitangus sulphuratus	Open	Thraupidae	Tangara cyanicollis	Mixed
	Myiozetetes cayanensis	Open		Thraupis episcopus	Mixed
	Myiodynastes maculatus	Mixed		Thraupis palmarum	Mixed
	Legatus leucophaius	Open		Ramphocelus dimidiatus	Mixed
	Tyrannus savana	Open		Piranga rubra	Mixed
	Tyrannus melancholicus	Open		Habia gutturalis	Forest°
Hirundinidae	Stelgidopteryx ruficollis	Non terr.		Tachyphonus luctuosus	Forest*
Troglodytidae	Thryothorus spadix	Forest*		Tachyphonus delattrii	Forest°
	Thryothorus nigricapillus	Forest*		Hemithraupis flavicollis	Forest*
	Henicorhina leucosticta	Forest°		Chlorospingus flavigularis	Mixed
	Microcerculus marginatus	Forest°		Chlorophanes spiza	Forest*
Turdidae	Turdus ignobilis	Mixed		Dacnis cayana	Forest*
	Catharus ustulatus	Mixed		Dacnis lineata	Mixed
	Catharus minimus	Forest*	Emberizidae	Pytilus grossus	Forest*
Vireonidae	Vireolanius eximius	Forest*		Atlapetes atricapillus	Forest*
	Vireo olivaceus	Forest*		Saltator maximus	Mixed
	Hylophilus semibrunneus	Forest*		Saltator albicollis	Mixed
	Hylophilus flavipes	Mixed		Saltator caerulescens	Mixed
Corvidae	Cyanocorax affinis	Mixed		Arremon aurantiirostris	Forest°
	Amblycercus holoseriseus	Forest*		Oryzoborus angolensis	Open
	Psarocolius decumanus	Mixed		Oryzoborus. crassirostris	Open
Parulidae	Dendroica fusca	Forest*		Sporophila intermedia	Open
	Dendroica castanea	Mixed		Sporophila nigricollis	Open
	Setophaga ruticilla	Forest*		Sporophila schistacea	Open
	Oporornis philadelphia	Mixed			

°Forest restricted species. Species that live inside mature forests and rarely go to borders or other types of vegetation.
*Forest non-restricted species. Birds that mainly inhabit forests, but frecuently go out to borders and other types of vegetation.
Mixed: Mixed habitat species. Birds that live in different types of semiopen habitats such as second growth vegetation and scrub and do not show a marked preference for any of them.
Open: Open area species. Birds that live mainly in open areas with low vegetation such as meadows with isolated trees although sometimes enter scrub and forest borders.
Non terr: Non terrestrial species. Birds not particularly related to any terrestrial habitat such as vultures and acuatic species.

REFERENCES

Bierregaard, R.O. Jr. and P.C. Stouffer. 1995. Use of Amazonian forest fragments by understory insectivorous birds. Ecology, 76: 2429–2445.

Bierregaard, R.O. Jr. and P.C. Stouffer. 1997. Understory birds and dynamic habitat mosaics in Amazonian Rainforest. In: Tropical Forest Remnants: Ecology, Management and Conservation of Fragmented Communities. W.F. Laurance and R.O. Bierregaard Jr., eds. University of Chicago Press, Chicago. pp. 138–155.

Bierregaard, R.O., W.F. Laurance, J.W. Sites, A.J. Lynam, R.K. Didham, M. Andersen, C. Gascon, M.D. Tocher, A.P. Smith, V.M. Viana, T.E. Lovejoy, K.E. Sieving, E.A. Kramer, C. Restrepo, and C. Moritz. 1997. Key priorities for the study of fragmented tropical ecosystems. In: Tropical Forest Remnants: Ecology, Management and Conservation of Fragmented Communities. W.F. Laurance and R.O. Bierregaard Jr., eds. University of Chicago Press, Chicago. pp. 515–525.

Blake, J.G., F.G. Stiles, and B.A. Loiselle. 1990. Birds of La Selva Biological Station: Habitat use, trophic composition, and migrants. In: Four Neotropical Rainforests. A.H. Gentry, ed. Yale University Press, New Haven. pp. 161–182.

Chasko, G.G. and J.E. Gates. 1982. Avian habitat suitability along a transmission-line corridor in an oak-hickory forest region. Wildlife Monographs, 82: 1–41.

De La Zerda, S. and L. Rosselli. 1997. Efectos de las líneas de transmisión sobre la fauna colombiana. Interconexión Eléctrica S.A., Informe Final. Medellín, Colombia. 156 pp.

Empresas Públicas de Medellín, 1995. Diagnóstico preliminar sobre el estado de conservación de dos bosques nativos en los municipios de San Rafael y Carolina del Príncipe. Empresas Públicas de Medellín, Medellín, Colombia.

Goosem, M. 1997. Internal fragmentation: The effects of roads, highways, and powerlines clearings on movements and mortality of rainforest vertebrates. In: Tropical Forest Remnants: Ecology, Management, and Conservation of Fragmented Communities. W.F. Laurance and R.O. Bierregaard, Jr., eds. University of Chicago Press, Chicago. pp. 241–255.

Guindon, C.F. 1996. The importance of forest fragments to the maintenance of regional biodiversity in Costa Rica. In: Forest Patches in Tropical Landscapes. J. Schelhas and R. Greenberg, eds. Island Press, Washington D.C. pp. 168–186.

Kattan, G.H. and H. Alvarez-López. 1996. Preservation and management of biodiversity in fragmented landscapes in the Colombian Andes. In: Forest Patches in Tropical Landscapes. J. Schelhas and R. Greenberg, eds. Island Press, Washington D.C. pp. 3–18.

Karr, J.R. 1990. The avifauna of Barro Colorado Island and the Pipeline Road, Panama. In: Four Neotropical Rainforests. A.H. Gentry, ed. Yale University Press, New Haven. pp. 183–198.

Luken, J.O., A.C. Hinton, and D.G. Baker. 1992. Response of the woody plants community in power-line corridors to frequent antropogenic disturbances. Ecological Applications, 2: 356–362.

Malizia, L.R., R. Aragón, N.P. Chacoff, and A.C. Monmany. 1998. Son las rutas una barrera para el desplazamiento de las aves? El caso de la Reserva Provincial La Florida (Tucumán, Argentina). Hornero, 15: 10–16.

Montes, J.A. 1998. Caracterización de la estructura de un bosque fragmentado por el corredor de servidumbre de una línea de transmisión eléctrica utilizando medidas de hábitat relacionadas con aves. Tesis, Universidad de los Andes, Contrato ABO-ISA, Bogotá.

Parker, T.A., III. 1991. On the use of tape recorders in avifaunal surveys. Auk, 108: 443–444.

Remsen, J.V. and D.A. Good. 1996. Misuse of data form mist net captures to assess relative abundance in bird populations. Auk, 113: 381–398.

Robinson, S.K. and J. Terborgh. 1990. Bird communities of the Cocha Cashu biological station in Amazonian Peru. In: Four Neotropical Rainforests. A.H. Gentry, ed. Yale University Press, New Haven. pp. 119–216.

Rosselli, L. and S. De La Zerda. 1996. Avifauna colombiana y líneas de transmisión. Vulnerabilidad, amenazas, recomendaciones y revisión de literatura pertinente. Ministerio del Medio Ambiente, Dirección Ambiental Sectorial, Bogotá, Colombia. 150 pp.

Rosselli, L. and S. De La Zerda. 1999. Avifauna Colombiana y líneas de transmisión Fase III, Informe final. Interconexión Eléctrica S.A. — Asociación Bogotana de Ornitología, Medellín, Colombia. 202 pp.

Schelhas, J. and R. Greenberg. 1996. Introduction. The value of forest patches. In: Forest Patches in Tropical Landscapes. J. Schelhas and R. Greenberg, eds. Island Press, Washington D.C. pp. xv–xxxvi.

Stiles, F.G. and C.I. Bohórquez. 2000. Evaluando el estado de la biodiversidad: el caso de la avifauna de la Serranía de las Quinchas, Boyacá, Colombia. Caldasia, 22: 61–92.

Stiles, F.G. and L. Rosselli. 1998. Inventario de las aves de un bosque altoandino: Comparación de dos métodos. Caldasia, 20: 29–43.

Stouffer, P.C. and R.O. Bierregaard, Jr. 1995. Effects of forest fragmentation on understory hummingbirds in Amazonian Brazil. Conservation Biology, 9: 1040–1085.

Umaña, A.M. 1998. Efecto de barrera causado por el corredor de servidumbre de una línea de transmisión eléctrica de alta tensión, sobre algunas especies de aves del sotobosque, Thesis. Universidad de los Andes, Contrato ABO-ISA, Bogotá, Colombia.

BIOGRAPHICAL SKETCHES

Loreta Rosselli

Interconexión Eléctrica S.A., Asociación Bogotana de Ornitología. Current address Dg. 109 No. 26-10, Bogotá, Colombia, lrosselli@yahoo.com, Fax 57-1-285-4550

Loreta Rosselli, born in Bogotá, Colombia, obtained her biologist degree from the Universidad de Los Andes in 1982 and her Master's degree from the Universidad de Costa Rica in 1989. She is a University Professor in ornithology and has participated in several research projects in various Latin American countries. Besides the effect of transmission lines on Colombian birds other research interests include frugivory, bird behavior and conservation. She is cofounder and active member of the Bogotás Ornithological Society. She translated to Spanish the Guide of Birds of Costa Rica and is co-author of the Birds of the Sabana de Bogotá.

Susana De La Zerda (corresponding author)

Interconexión Eléctrica S.A., Asociación Bogotana de Ornitología AA 3751, Bogotá, Colombia, sdelazerda@yahoo.com

Susana De La Zerda is a Colombian biologist with graduate studies in Ecology at the Hebrew University of Jerusalem in Israel and Master's degree in Wildlife Science from Virginia Tech. Since 1995 she has been working on the effect of transmission lines on birds on a series of projects sponsored by the Colombian Ministry of the Environment and ISA, the State Company in charge of energy transmission. She has attended several international courses in conservation biology and tropical ecology. She is founder and active member of the Bogotá Ornithological Society and co-author of books on Colombian National Parks and birds.

Management, Vegetative Structure and Shrubland Birds of Rights-of-Way

John L. Confer

During 1998–1999, 287 point counts of birds were taken in rights-of-way (ROW) in northeastern US, primarily in Massachusetts, Rhode Island and New York with a few counts in New Hampshire. Bird density was high with a mean of 14.8 individuals and 12.2 species per point count for birds nesting or foraging in the ROW. Federal surveys show that shrubland birds are declining throughout northeastern US. Thus, ROW support an abundance of shrubland birds that are declining elsewhere probably because of the succession of shrublands into forests throughout most of northeastern US. The effect of management by fire, selective herbicide application and cutting on the avian community was compared. Management by fire, although generally impractical, supported the greatest density and diversity of birds. Management by selective herbicide sustained more individuals and species than cutting. Most shurbland species showed a habitat preference for about 50% shrub cover. However, some rare and rapidly declining species occurred in greatest density in areas with only 5–20% shrub cover. ROW would support the greatest diversity of shrubland birds if management created some areas dominated by herbs and other areas dominated by shrubs. The density of Brown-headed Cowbirds might be reduced if shrub height is low.

Keywords: Herbicide application, habitat management, shrubland guild, avian diversity, habitat preference

INTRODUCTION

This report describes the avian communities in shrublands managed by three different procedures: selective herbicide application, mechanical cutting and burning. The effect of selective herbicide application was assessed in three locations: in the rights-of-way (ROW) of Orange and Rockland Utilities in Sterling Forest State Park, New York, in ROW of New England Electric System companies in Massachusetts and in ROW of Eastern Utilities Associates in Rhode Island. Mechanical cutting was assessed in ROW of the New York Power Authority within the Huyck Preserve near Albany, NY. Management of shrublands by fire was assessed in Finger Lakes National Forest, New York.

These studies were stimulated by a dramatic decline in the abundance of most shrubland birds. The federal North American Breeding Bird Survey (BBS) (Sauer et al., 1999) shows that 65% of the shrubland species of northeastern United States are declining. A major cause of this decline is a loss of habitat as abandoned farmland undergoes natural succession from shrubland into forest. As the trend for forest regeneration continues, management for shrublands will become increasingly important (Askins, 1998).

Only power utilities manage large areas of shrubland in the northeastern US. For example, within New York the shrubland managers include: New York State Department of Environmental Conservation, which administers but does little management on 27,000 acres of shrubland, The Nature Conservancy, which manages 3000 acres of shrubland, and the US National Forest Service, which manages 1300 acres of shrubland. Shrubland management by electric power utilities dwarfs the effort of all other managers collectively. In New York, there are well in excess of 10,000 miles of high voltage transmission line ROW. Approximately half that length with an area of about 125,000 acres is managed as shrubland. In addition, many miles of low

Environmental Concerns in Rights-of-Way
Management: Seventh International Symposium
J.W. Goodrich-Mahoney, D.F. Mutrie and C.A. Guild (editors)
© 2002 Elsevier Science Ltd. All rights reserved.

voltage distribution lines are also managed as shrubland. This report provides data-based guidelines that will enhance the density of birds and the diversity of bird species on managed shrublands.

POINT COUNTS: METHODS

The extreme heterogeneity of habitat along ROW influenced the experimental design for these studies. A few miles of ROW commonly present steep slopes with shallow soils or even rock outcrops, flatlands with fertile soil, ravines and wetlands. In addition, many ROW plants have a very patchy distribution of vegetation partially due to clonal growth or allelopathic effects. Further, supposedly uniform management along a segment of ROW actually varies, e.g., around the base of supporting poles and near water bodies. Consequently, ROW provide a highly variable habitat. Detection of statistically significant effect on the avian community due to management techniques requires a large number of replicate counts that produces a small standard error despite the large variance.

Point counts, a standard avian census method, were used throughout this study. During a point count all birds detected by sight or sound within a prescribed area in a measured time are recorded. Our point counts were compiled by a field crew of 2–4 individuals with the most experienced individual designated as the primary observer and one observer designated as recorder. Field assistants were rigorously trained and tested before they were allowed to work independently as primary observers.

Identification began with sufficient light to recognize subtle differences in plumage, i.e., 0530–0600 h. Counting ended daily by 1100 h before May 20, by 1030 h between May 20 and May 31 and by 1000 h between May 31 and June 15. Point counts were not taken when wind kept small twigs in constant motion, nor when temperature was below 32 F or above 80 F, nor during any precipitation, nor after 30 June.

All birds detected within 100 m up and down the length of the ROW were counted. At the Finger Lakes National Forest, birds were counted within a radius of 100 m. Experience has shown that the low height of the plants, as is common in managed shrublands, allows aural and visual detection of many birds at 100 m. The censused width of the ROW extended to the trunks of trees lining the ROW. Thus, birds in branches that extended from such trees towards the ROW were counted, but birds that remained on the far side of trees lining the ROW were not counted.

Point counts were spaced at least 250 m apart along the ROW as measured with a laser range finder. When possible, each count center was located on a promontory located 250–350 m from the preceding count center. All count centers were located more than 100 m from roads that transected a ROW. Thus, if a road crossed a ROW and truncated the 200 m diameter of a potential count area, then the next count center was advanced more than 100 m past the far side of that road. Count centers were located so that the vegetation was fairly uniform within each of four quadrants, front left, front right, back right and back left. For example, if the vegetation in front of a potential count center consisted of 50 m of shrub followed by a large expanse of mowed grass, then the count center was advanced to that transition so that the front quadrants consisted of all mowed vegetation and the back quadrants consisted of all shrubby vegetation. All ROW surveyed in this study were surrounded by largely forested areas.

Special attention was given to both the Golden-winged Warbler (*Vermivora chrysoptera*) and the Blue-winged Warbler (*V. pinus*) in the ROW of Orange and Rockland Utilities. Both species have declined so severely in parts of their range that they are under status assessment by the US Fish and Wildlife Service to determine if they should be listed for protection under the Endangered Species Act. Further, these two species and their hybrids have been the focus of my studies for 20 years and are central to my conservation interests. During each 10-min point count, a tape with 2.5-min of recordings of the songs of each species was played. This lured into view almost 100% of the males of both species. Visual observation is necessary for identification within this hybridizing group because hybrid song is indistinguishable from parental song.

POINT COUNTS: RESULTS

Point count reliability

The validity of our standard point count procedure was tested by comparing point counts taken in the same locations during 1998 and 1999 in the FLNF (Table 1), the only site from which we obtained a moderate sample size of replicate counts during consecutive years. The number of individuals in 1998 vs. 1999 and number of species for 1998 vs. 1999 per point count were statistically indistinguishable. The probability (P) that observed differences could occur due to random variation exceeded 80% (t-test for number of individuals, $t = 0.242$, $P = 0.81$; t-test for number of species, $t = 0.212$, $P = 0.83$). The repeatability of results from year to year suggests our point counts are a reliable measure of avian density and diversity.

Table 1. Replicate point counts. Counts were taken in the same sites in consecutive years in fire-managed shrublands in the Finger Lakes National Forest

	1998		1999	
	Mean (n)	SE	Mean (n)	SE
Species	13.29 (17)	0.95	13.95 (21)	0.92
Individuals	15.24 (17)	1.17	15.82 (21)	0.93

Table 2. Abundance and population trends for species in ROW in northeastern US: Rhode Island, eastern Massachusetts, southern New Hampshire and central and southern New York. Listed species occurred on at least 25% of the point counts taken in May–June of 1998–1999. Values represent the mean number of individuals from 287 point counts, the ratio of the mean number per point count in ROW to the mean number per point count for the North American Breeding Bird Survey from 1966 to 1996 for the northeastern US, and the population trend for northeastern US, according to BBS data for the same time period. Declining populations are underlined

Species	No./point count	Ratio point count/BBS	Population trend northeastern US
Eastern Towhee	1.34	7.87	−4.20
Common Yellowthroat	1.26	4.06	−0.20
Gray Catbird	1.09	4.81	−0.10
Brown-headed Cowbird	1.02	7.35	−1.20
Prairie Warbler	0.98	20.56	−0.90
American Goldfinch	0.66	2.89	−2.30
Field Sparrow	0.64	6.19	−4.00
Song Sparrow	0.62	1.48	−1.30
Chestnut-sided Warbler	0.60	5.07	−0.40
Yellow Warbler	0.57	2.91	0.90
American Robin	0.50	0.50	−0.40
Common Grackle	0.42	0.56	−1.90
Mourning Dove	0.40	1.01	2.10
Red-winged Blackbird	0.39	0.55	−2.80
Blue-winged Warbler	0.37	10.11	−2.80
Blue Jay	0.27	1.31	−1.20
Black-capped Chickadee	0.26	1.19	1.80
Cedar Waxwing	0.25	1.48	0.90

Point count locations

During 1998–1999 we compiled 287 point counts in ROW using the standardized procedure. Most counts were taken in areas dominated by shrubs maintained by selective herbicide application. We obtained 141 counts in eastern Massachusetts, 24 in southern New Hampshire, and 63 throughout Rhode Island using ROW maintained by New England Electric System and Eastern Utilities Associates. In 1999 we obtained 21 point counts in central New York on ROW maintained by the New York Power Authority. Eleven of these point counts were in areas maintained by mechanical cutting in fall 1998 and one site was sprayed. The remaining 9 point counts were taken on a ROW, which has not been managed since its installation 20 years ago. Although this is not typical of ROW management, these counts are included because they contribute unique data on avian habitat selection in an older stage of succession on ROW. We obtained 38 standardized point counts in southern NY in ROW maintained by Orange and Rockland Utilities. In addition, we obtained 31 counts in shrubland managed by fire in FLNF during 1998–1999. In the following we compare our point count results on ROW to point count results for the federal BBS. We counted for 10 min for a limited distance while BBS point counts last for only 3 min but include birds from an unlimited distance. These differences somewhat cancel each other and comparisons indicate the relative abundance of each species detected by the two variations in point count procedures.

The avian community in ROW of northeastern US

A total of 93 species were identified within a count area during a point count. This diversity makes ROW an appealing place for watching birds. The density of shrubland birds in ROW throughout the northeast is quite high. We observed an average of 14.84 individual birds and 12.24 species per standardized point count. Birds included in this tally used the ROW during the count period for foraging and the great majority appeared to have nesting territories. Shrubland birds are much more abundant in ROW than in the general northeast. Fourteen of 18 species that nest in ROW and which were detected on at least 25% of the point counts are more abundant in ROW in the northeast in general as indicated by BBS (Table 2). It is particularly significant that 15 of these species have negative population trends throughout the northeast, but maintain high abundance on ROW. Thus, ROW support a high density of birds by providing habitat of high quality and significant area even as other shrubland habitats decline.

Management by selective herbicide application

Surveys were conducted in 1998–1999 in Sterling Forest State Park in ROW managed by Orange and Rockland Utilities within the Hudson Highlands of southern NY. The Hudson Highlands is a rugged, extensively forested area. It includes several state parks supervised by the Palisades Interstate Park Commission plus areas of protected watershed and lands of

Table 3. Abundance and population trends for species in ROW of Orange and Rockland Utilities within Sterling Forest State Park in southern New York. Listed species utilized the ROW as part or all of their nesting territory and occurred on at least 25% of 38 point counts taken in May–June of 1998–1999. Values represent the mean number of individuals per point count, the ratio of the mean number for point counts in ROW managed by a mixture of selective herbicide application and mechanical cutting compared to the number per point count for the North American Breeding Bird Survey from 1966 to 1996 for New York, and the population trend for New York according to BBS data for the same time period. Declining populations are underlined

Species	No./point count O&R ROW in SFSP	Point count ratio SFSP/BBS	Population trends New York
Prairie Warbler	1.38	127.71	6.80
Gray Catbird	1.28	5.67	0.10
Eastern Towhee	0.97	23.10	−6.30
Yellow Warbler	0.97	3.21	0.50
Common Yellowthroat	0.93	2.59	0.00
Golden-winged Warbler	0.62	155.17	−5.00
Field Sparrow	0.62	10.59	−4.10
Blue-winged Warbler	0.59	20.08	2.50
Black-and-white Warbler	0.52	18.74	−1.50
Northern Oriole	0.48	4.23	−0.70
Chestnut-sided Warbler	0.48	4.29	−0.90
American Goldfinch	0.45	1.36	0.20
Indigo Bunting	0.41	3.78	0.30
Brown-headed Cowbird	0.38	2.63	−2.40
Rose-breasted Grosbeak	0.28	4.46	−0.70

West Point Military Academy. This large, wild area has many important ecological assets, including, especially, the coexistence of stable populations of Golden-winged and Blue-winged Warblers (Frech and Confer, 1987; Confer et al., 1998). The Hudson Highlands is the only known portion of their entire range where these similar, hybridizing species coexist in stable abundance. Maintenance of appropriate shrubland habitat for these species within this region is extremely important to their survival. Sterling Forest State Park and the ROW of Orange and Rockland Utilities provide an unexcelled opportunity to determine what habitat conditions support continued coexistence of these species.

The ROW in Sterling Forest State Park have attained a nearly stable community of herbs and shrubs maintained for several decades by selective herbicide applied by Orange and Rockland Utilities. The abundance of shrubland birds nesting in these ROW are exceptionally high in comparison to the statewide abundance estimated by BBS data (Table 3). For these specific ROW, slightly more than half of the species with a high abundance have negative population trends for all of New York. These ROW enhance the local avian diversity by providing the only known breeding habitat for Prairie Warblers within Sterling Forest State Park. Further, computer-based, GIS maps show that ROW provide most of the habitat for Golden-winged and Blue-winged Warblers within Sterling Forest State Park (Confer, 1999).

Management by mechanical cutting

Surveys were conducted in central New York in the 2000-acre Edmund Niles Huyck Preserve in 1999 in ROW managed by New York Power Authority. Vegetation on the Preserve is primarily second-growth forest plus small areas of old field succession and old-growth forest. Partridge Run Wildlife Management Area, which is adjacent to the Huyck Preserve, has similar vegetation cover. Farms and rural homes occur throughout the region but occupy less than half the landscape. Our point counts were conducted on the Blenheim-Gilboa ROW of the New York Power Authority. Point counts were determined on this ROW as it passes through the continuous forest of the Huyck Preserve and as it passes through adjacent private property owned by V. Husik, which is primarily forested.

Mechanical cutting in fall of 1997 removed the clumps of shrubs such as dogwood (*Cornus* spp.), viburnum (*Viburnum* spp.), and staghorn sumac (*Rhus typhina*). Before cutting, the herbaceous growth under the dense clumps of shrubs was quite scanty. By mid-May of 1999, when most migrant birds return and establish their breeding territories, the cut areas provided very little vegetative cover. Many ecological studies show a strong correlation between the structural diversity of the plants and the diversity of the animals living there. Consequently, a reduction in the avian community on the ROW for at least the first year after cutting would be expected. Results of this survey (Table 4) are assessed subsequently.

Management by fire

The managed shrublands in FLNF near Seneca Lake in central New York are on abandoned farmland and have extensive growth of herbs with moderate growth

Table 4. Abundance and population trends for species in ROW of the New York Power Authority within the Edmund Niles Huyck Preserve and adjacent Husic property. Listed species occurred on at least 25% of 11 standardized point counts taken in June, 1999 in cut areas. Values represent the mean number of individuals per point count for species that included the ROW in their nesting territory, the ratio of the mean number for point counts in ROW managed by mechanical cutting compared to the number per point count for the North American Breeding Bird Survey from 1966 to 1996 for New York, and the population trend for New York according to BBS data for the same time period. Declining populations are underlined

Species	No./point count Huyck Preserve	Point count ratio Huyck/BBS	Population trends New York
Common Yellowthroat	1.55	4.30	0
Chestnut-sided Warbler	1.55	13.73	−0.9
Song Sparrow	1.09	1.82	−1.1
American Robin	1.00	0.83	−0.5
Alder Flycatcher	0.82	22.73	4.1
Field Sparrow	0.55	9.31	−4.1
Blue Jay	0.27	1.41	−0.5
Indigo Bunting	0.27	2.49	0.3
White-throated Sparrow	0.27	1.66	−1.3

Table 5. Abundance and population trends for species in managed shrublands of the Finger Lakes National Forest in New York. Listed species occurred on at least 25% of 31 standardized point counts taken in May–June of 1998–1999. Values represent the mean number of individuals per point count, the ratio of the mean number for point counts in FLNF to the mean number detected per point count for the North American Breeding Bird Survey from 1966 to 1996 for New York, and the population trend for New York according to BBS data for the same time period. Declining populations are underlined

Species	No./point count finger lakes national forest	Ratio point counts FLNF/BBS-NY	Population trends New York
Song Sparrow	2.08	3.48	−1.10
Common Yellowthroat	2.00	5.57	0.00
Eastern Towhee	1.42	34.00	−6.30
Yellow Warbler	0.97	3.23	0.50
Blue-winged Warbler	0.92	31.54	2.50
American Goldfinch	0.92	2.79	−2.00
Field Sparrow	0.89	15.27	−4.10
Chestnut-sided Warbler	0.71	6.31	−0.90
American Robin	0.66	0.55	−0.50
Gray Catbird	0.58	2.57	0.10
Cedar Waxwing	0.50	2.35	0.10
Ovenbird	0.47	1.99	2.60
Brown-headed Cowbird	0.39	2.73	−2.40
Black-capped Chickadee	0.37	1.71	2.20
Indigo Bunting	0.32	2.88	0.30
Alder Flycatcher	0.29	8.06	4.10
Veery	0.26	2.34	−1.30

of shrubs and some trees in clusters and along old fence lines. Managed ground fires are started on cool March mornings. They rarely kill trees and burn only a short distance into clumps of shrubs, including *C. racemosa*, *C. stolonifera*, *V. lentago*, and *V. recognitum*. Vegetation recovers quickly and many birds nest in the burn areas the spring of a fire. This management by fire retards, but does not prevent, succession leading to an increase in woody vegetation. This kind of management produces shrublands with clusters of herbs, clusters of shrubs and clusters of trees. This provides great structural variation, which suggests support for a high diversity of bird.

Comparison of the effects of management on avian community

The two-year survey in FLNF showed that 17 species occurred on at least 25% of the point counts (Table 5). Management by fire supported about 30% more species per point count than herbicide application and about 70% more species than mechanical cutting (Table 6). The high number of species in point counts

Table 6. Avian abundance in shrublands managed by fire, selective herbicide application, and mechanical cutting. Surveys were conducted in shrublands in the Finger Lakes National Forest managed by fire, and in ROW of Orange and Rockland Utilities in Sterling Forest State Park managed by selective herbicide application, and in ROW of the New York Power Authority in the Edmund Niles Huyck Preserve managed by mechanical cutting. Data are the means for the number of species of birds and the number of individual birds per point count for all birds which used the census area as part of their nesting territory. Statistical analyses used a t-test comparing data from ROW in the Huyck Preserve to data from ROW of Orange and Rockland Utilities and then comparing data from the ROW of Orange and Rockland Utilities to data from the Finger Lakes National Forest. Results have not adjusted for multiple comparisons nor for differences in ROW width and are still under evaluation

	Number of individuals				Number of species			
	Mean	P	(n)	SE	Mean	P	(n)	SE
FLNF	15.12		(26)	0.88	13.11		(26)	0.74
P from t-test =		0.014				0.003		
SFSP	12.07		(29)	0.82	10.31		(29)	0.55
P from t-test =		0.036				0.018		
Huyck Preserve	8.82		(11)	1.10	7.64		(11)	1.00

in the area managed by fire is partially due to the clumps of trees and the presence of forest-adapted species, i.e., Veery (*Catharus fuscescens*), Black-capped Chickadee (*Poecile atricapillus*), and Ovenbird (*Seiurus aurocapillus*). When forest species are omitted from consideration, then the ROW of Orange and Rockland Utilities that were managed by selective herbicide application supported the highest number of shrubland species. Fire management cannot be used in many circumstances. Furthermore, burning alone cannot maintain shrubland permanently since fire only slows the rate at which trees become dominant in management areas.

It appears that management by selective herbicide application supports more birds than management by mechanical cutting. We compiled only 11 point counts in a ROW that was cut. In the middle of this surveyed portion of the cut ROW, we acquired one point count in an area that was sprayed. The point count in this sprayed portion of the ROW had a higher number of individuals and species of birds than any of the 11 point counts in the adjacent portions of the ROW that were cut. The ratio of the number of individual birds and number of species for sprayed ROW in Sterling Forest State Park compared to cut ROW in the Huyck Preserve was 1.37 and 1.35, respectively. However, the width of ROW in Sterling Forest State Park is 30% larger than in the Huyck Preserve, 66–50 m, respectively. Because of the greater width, each point count in ROW within Sterling Forest State Park encompassed a greater area, which would partially account for the difference in number of individual birds. Although the greater width may be a partial cause of the enhanced avian community in ROW in Sterling Forest State Park, the management by selective herbicide probably also contributes to the enhancement. The structural diversity of the vegetation in the Huyck Preserve was greatly simplified by cutting. In contrast, selective spraying leads to a structural diversity of patches of shrubs and patches of herbs, which should support a greater diversity of avian species. Further, many species did not increase in abundance with increasing ROW width as seen in our study (see Multi-factor, logistic regression). Some species used the edge on one side or the other of the ROW and their abundance was independent of width. Other species expanded their territory to fill the width of the ROW and their abundance would be largely independent of width. Multifactor analyses described subsequently, show that the number of species per point count does not increase in proportion to width. Our results suggest that a larger sample size will substantiate a reduction in bird density related to mechanical cutting.

HABITAT SELECTION: METHODS

The habitat within a point circle often varied greatly. To more accurately associate the presence of a species with its nesting habitat, each count was visually partitioned into quadrants, i.e., front left, front right, back right, back left, for a total of 1148 quadrants from 287 point counts along utility ROW. Each bird was assigned to the quadrant the bird used most frequently during the count, which provide a precise indicator of the habitat preference for that bird.

The percent cover by herbs, shrubs or trees was visually assessed. We assigned the percent cover to the following categories: 0–5%, 6–33%, 34–66%, or 67–100%. After two days of practice, all members of a field crew made identical estimates at trial sites. Our visual estimate provides a rapid method to assess environmental conditions. With this procedure, field crews conducted as many as 15 point counts along 3 miles of ROW in a day. This rapid inspection allowed us to obtain a large sample size, which reduced standard error and enabled us to detect statistically significant differences in bird distribution despite a high variance in habitat conditions.

Vegetation under a ROW is managed to produce a cover of herbs or shrubs in order to prevent tree growth that might ground the current. The ratio of cover by herbs or shrubs can be altered considerably by management while other environmental conditions, such as streams and wetlands, are little influenced by management. Because the proportion of cover by herbs and shrubs is largely under the control of management, we focused our analyses of habitat selection on these two types of vegetative cover.

Results from all standard point counts in 1998–1999 were pooled to increase the reliability of the statistical inference and to test if there were detectable habitat preferences that applied throughout much of northeastern US. Habitat preference was determined for species detected on at least 25% of the point counts on ROW and which we thought were in their nesting territories when counted. This eliminates consideration of several species that foraged in the ROW but nested in adjacent forests, such as the Black-capped Chickadee. This also eliminated Cedar Waxwing (*Bombycilla cedrorum*), a late nesting species that was just starting to nest by the time we finished our surveys, and Common Grackle (*Quiscalus quiscula*), an early nesting species that appeared in post-breeding flocks on the ROW during our counts.

Habitat selection is described with the aid of two kinds of statistical analyses. We used Chi-square, univariate analyses to determine if the frequency of occurrence of a species varied among the different density categories for herbs or shrubs. However, single-factor analyses such as Chi-square do not provide statistical control for correlation among samples and the possible influence of one factor on another.

We also used repeated-measures logistic regression to evaluate the effect of each habitat characteristic, while simultaneously controlling for additional factors that might influence the presence/absence of a species. Variables used in these statistical analyses are:
– Density of herb cover
– Density of shrub cover
– Height of shrub
– Width of rights-of-way
– Observer
– Time of day
– Julian date (i.e., days since 1 January with a mean of 160 days)

Observer, time of day and Julian date affects our ability to detect birds that are there, but do not affect the probability of a bird being there. These "nuisance" factors can alter the efficiency of point counts taken at different times and were included in the initial statistical analyses for all species. *Julian date* adjusts for the decline in singing and the related decline in easy with which a bird may be detected. *Time of day* accounts for the peak of singing in the early morning. *Observer* adjusts for differences in skill between Confer and the other recorders. The width of the ROW was measured with a laser range finder. Average shrub height was estimated. The logistic regression incorporates the density of herbs, the density of shrubs and observer as categorical variables. All other factors were used as continuous variables. The results were adjusted for correlation among conditions for the simultaneously recorded quadrants at each point count.

The initial, full analysis for each species was run with all variables including the nuisance variables. ROW width and shrub height were measured only for the last 75% of the point counts so that the initial statistical analyses, which tested for an effect of all variables, omitted 25% of the counts with this information missing. The following steps were used to reduce the complexity of the initial, full analysis. If either the ROW width or shrub height had p-values >0.1, they were dropped and the analysis was repeated to take advantage of the larger sample size. Nuisance variables in the full statistical formulation for each species were dropped if the p-values were >0.1. Vegetation variables with p-values >0.2 were similarly eliminated and the analysis was repeated. Vegetation variables in the initial statistical formulation that were close to $p = 0.2$, were retained in the reduced model in order to confirm that they explained insignificant amounts of variation in species presence.

HABITAT SELECTION: RESULTS

Chi-square analyses

The Chi-square analyses show that 9 of 12 nesting species detected on at least 25% of our point counts have a statistically significant preference among the categories for the density of herbs and/or shrubs (Figs. 1 and 2). For instance, Blue-winged Warblers occurred in highest density in habitat with at least 67% herbaceous growth and less than 6% shrub growth. These results show that many species have very specific preference or avoidance for specific cover categories. These results enable managers to tailor management practices for particularly rare species.

Analyses of all 93 detected species showed that significantly more species occurred in quadrants with higher densities of shrubs (Chi-square contingency test, $p < 0.01$). Management for about 50% shrub cover would support the greatest number of species per

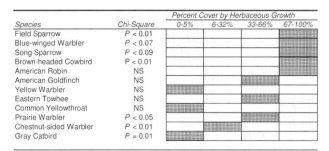

Fig. 1. Selection by common shrubland birds for herb cover. Results based on 284 point counts. Chi-square analyses were based on the presence or absence of each species by quadrant.

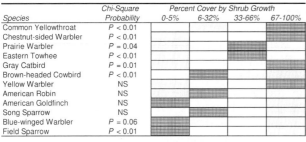

Fig. 2. Selection for shrub cover by common ROW birds. Results based on 284 point counts. Chi-square analyses were based on the presence or absence of each species by quadrant.

quadrant. However, some species, such as the Blue-winged Warbler and the Field Sparrow, occurred in maximum density in habitat dominated by herbs. A long segment of a ROW that provides a varied habitat, some segments with dense shrubs and some with extensive herbs would support the largest number of species. In some regions a particular species may be in severe jeopardy, such as the Golden-winged Warbler in ROW of Orange and Rockland Utilities. In this instance, management should be designed to produce a high density of herbaceous cover for this very rare species even if this lowers the overall avian diversity.

Multi-factor, logistic analyses

Chi-square analyses, although easy to display and interpret, do not assess the potential for more than one factor to influence the probability of a bird's presence and do not consider the potential for the preference for one condition to be altered by changes in other conditions. The following multi-factor, logistic regression analyses adjust for these kinds of factor interactions for each species.

Eleven of the 12 common species showed a significant correlation with one or more environmental variable, excluding only the American Robin (*Turdus migratorius*). The multi-factor analyses, as anticipated, show that habitat preference is influenced by a variety of factors, sometimes involving non-linear responses. Breeding density for five species was highest at moderate to high shrub densities. Five species preferred high densities of herbs, including the nest parasite, the Brown-headed Cowbird (*Molothrus ater*). Cowbird abundance can be reduced by keeping shrubs at a low height, although this would be disadvantageous for the three other species that prefer taller shrubs. Six species increased in number per point count as ROW width increased. Only two species increased in proportion to the width. For four of these species, the rate of increase in abundance was less than the rate of increase in width, which infers these species have a higher concentration on the edge. Most species, including the American Robin, showed either a small response or no response to the width of ROW that we sampled.

– Common Yellowthroat (*Geothlypis trichas*) Highest breeding density obtained with high density of shrubs abundance increased slightly by an increase in ROW width.
– Yellow Warbler (*Dendroica petechia*) Highest breeding density obtained with high density of shrubs; abundance nearly in proportion to ROW width.
– Gray Catbird (*Dumatella carolinensis*) Highest breeding density obtained with a high density of taller shrubs.
– Prairie Warbler (*Dendroica discolor*) Highest breeding density obtained with taller shrubs.
– American Goldfinch (*Carduelis tristis*) Highest breeding density obtained with taller shrubs; abundance increased slightly with an increase in ROW width.
– Eastern Towhee (*Pipilo erythrophthalmus*) Highest breeding density obtained with moderate density of shrubs.
– Chestnut-sided Warbler (*Dendroica pensylvanica*) Highest breeding density obtained with moderate density of herbs and slight density of low shrubs; abundance increased slightly by an increase in ROW width.
– Blue-winged Warbler (*Vermivora pinus*) Highest density obtained at high density of herbs.
– Song Sparrow (*Melospiza melodia*) Highest densities obtained at high density of herbs; abundance nearly in proportion to ROW width.
– Field Sparrow (*Spizella pusilla*) Highest densities obtained at high density of herbs; abundance only slightly increased by an increase in ROW width.
– Brown-headed Cowbird (*Molothrus ater*) Density reduced by decreasing shrub height and/or by decreasing density of herbs.

SUMMARY

Results show that shrubland birds are abundant on ROW throughout the northeastern US. Notably, ROW support high densities of species which are declining throughout the northeast outside of the ROW. As forest regeneration continues throughout the Northeast, managed ROW will become increasingly significant for shrubland species. Both the Golden-winged and Blue-winged Warblers are declining very rapidly in part of their ranges. The ROW in Sterling Forest State Park, managed by herbicide application, provide a nationally significant habitat where both species have co-occurred for nearly a century.

Three techniques for managing shrublands were compared in this study. Management by fire supported the greatest density and diversity of species, including some forest species. However, fire management is impractical in most locations. Selective herbicide application supported a high diversity and density of birds and the highest density of shrubland species. Maintenance by cutting appeared to support the lowest diversity of birds. However, this trend requires further statistical evaluation.

We observed 93 species during the point counts on ROW. The univariate Chi-square analyses show that the greatest number of species occurred at higher shrub densities. The multi-factor analyses show that half of the 12 most common species prefer at least 50% shrub cover and half prefer at least 50% herb cover. The abundance of 8 of the 12 most common species was related to two or more factors. Cowbirds prefer extensive herb cover and their impact on other species can be minimized by managing for low shrubs. Because of the species-specific differences in habitat preference, the greatest avian density can be obtained by managing for habitat diversity along ROW. Areas of extensive herbs alternating with areas of extensive shrubs, each at least 200 m in length, would support the highest diversity of breeding birds.

ACKNOWLEDGMENTS

New England Electric System companies funded part of these studies while System Forester Tom Sullivan coordinated surveys of the effect of selective herbicide application in their ROW. Eastern Utilities Associates provided support while System Forester Peter Simpson assisted with the design of surveys and Todd McLeish assisted with fieldwork.

Orange and Rockland Utilities supported this work while Steve Grandinali, Superintendent of Electrical Operations, assisted surveys in their ROW. This work was conducted within Sterling Forest State Park, a unit of the Palisades Interstate Park Commission. Ken Kreiser, Deputy Director of PIPC, Tom Lyons, Director Environmental Management Bureau of NYS Office of Parks, Recreation and Historic Preservation, and Jack Focht, Museum Director for PIPC, provided administrative assistance. Jim Gell, Park Manager, and Bill Ledwitz, Director of Education assisted studies within Sterling Forest State Park. John Gebhardts, Director of the Sterling Forest Coalition, provided particular help with this work.

Kevin McLoughlin assisted surveys of the effect of cutting in the Blenheim-Gilboa ROW maintained by New York Power Authority. Part of this survey was conducted in and supported by the Edmund Miles Huyck Preserve in Rensselaerville, NY, Inc. and assisted by Dr. Rick Wyman, Director, and Carolyn Barker. Surveys on the Blenheim-Gilboa ROW extended into the contiguous property of Vern Husik with his gracious permission.

Finger Lakes National Forest, Hector, NY also provided support. Clayton Grove, Wildlife Biologist for the U.S.N.F., provided considerable guidance.

These studies were also supported by a grant from the National Fish and Wildlife Federation. The Electric Power Research Institute supported the compilation of these surveys, as coordinated by John Goodrich-Mahoney.

Statistical direction was provided by Peter Wrege.

Field assistants, who provided extremely dedicated and competent work, were Carrie Cloutier, Christopher Dougherty, Mark Erickson, Wilmur Faux, Gerard Phillips, Shelagh Tupper and Alison Wright.

REFERENCES

Askins, R.A. 1998. Restoring forest disturbances to sustain populations of shrubland birds. Restoration and Management Notes, 16: 166–173.

Confer, J.L. 1999. Right of way refuge for declining shrubland birds. Edison Electric Institute Natural Resources Workshop, Williamsburg, VA.

Confer, J.L., J. Gebhards, and J. Yrizarry. 1998. Golden-winged and Blue-winged Warblers at Sterling Forest: A unique circumstance. Kingbird, 39: 50–55.

Frech, M. and J.L. Confer. 1987. The Golden-winged Warbler: competition with the Blue-winged Warbler and habitat selection in portions of southern, central and northern New York. Kingbird, 37: 65–71.

Sauer, J.R., J.E. Hines, I. Thomas, J. Fallon, and G. Gough. 1999. The North American Breeding Bird Survey, Results and Analysis 1966–1998. Version 98.1, USGS Patuxent Wildlife Research Center, Laurel, MD.

BIOGRAPHICAL SKETCH

John L. Confer

Biology Department, Ithaca College, Ithaca, NY 14850, USA

Mr. Confer teaches at Ithaca College and has worked with Partners in Flight and Cornell's Laboratory of Ornithology. For 20 years, his research has centered on shrubland birds. During this time, shrubland habitat has declined in northeastern US as forest regeneration progressed. Not surprisingly, the relative change in habitat abundance has led to the current decline in shrubland birds and increase in woodland birds. Because utilities manage far more shrubland than the sum of all other habitat managers in eastern US, he has been pleased to work with EPRI, New England Electric Systems, National Grid USA, Central Maine Power, and Orange and Rockland Utilities to assess the effect of management options on the density of nesting birds and their nesting success. He would like to develop plans for habitat management that maximize avian reproduction on utility ROW. His recent studies document that shrubland rights-of-way support a high density of shrubland birds which generally sustain a high reproductive success and that utility ROW in forested landscapes do not have a major impact on the nesting success of birds in the adjacent forest, and suggest that small patches of shrubs are poor nesting sites.

Deer Browse Monitoring in a Reconstructed 120 kV Powerline Right-of-Way after an Ice Storm

G. Jean Doucet and Eric R. Thompson

The Rigaud white-tailed deer (*Odocoileus virginianus*) winter yard is located approximately 100 km west of Montreal, QC. The forest stands attractive for deer in the yard are those provided by white cedars (*Thuja occidentalis*), an excellent cover for wintering deer in the northeast. Two powerline rights-of-way (120 and 735 kV) bisect cedar stands in the southwest section of the yard. In January 1998 the 120 kV powerline collapsed due to a major ice storm, which deposited more than 50 mm of ice on the structures. The line was rebuilt in the summer and fall of 1998. During and after the reconstruction period we monitored the fate of winter browse in the right-of-way. The objectives of the paper are to discuss the implications of the reconstruction of the 120 kV powerline for deer browse production and to present the 1999 and 2000 browse survey results. In the spring 1999 it was obvious that no food was yet available to deer in the right-of-way. The 2000 spring survey established the available browse at 16,644 stems/ha and 35,196 twigs/ha. The rate of browsing by deer was 81.0%, which is similar to that of previous winters in that right-of-way.

Keywords: Deer browse, monitoring, ice storm, reconstruction, right-of-way

INTRODUCTION

The clearing and subsequent vegetation control in rights-of-way located in white-tailed deer (*Odocoileus virginianus*) winter yards in Eastern Canada and the Northeast United States remain significant environmental issues (Evans, 1982; Dominske, 1997; Doucet and Garant, 1997; Jackson and Hecklau, 1995). Over the years, Hydro-Québec has carried out a major research program on deer and rights-of-way (Doucet et al., 1997). This paper addresses a relatively new issue in right-of-way habitat management, that of access and activities into sensitive habitats under emergency situations, including reconstruction of powerlines. Two transmission powerlines are located in the Rigaud deeryard, a 120 kV built in 1972 and a 735 kV built in 1976. The presence of these large structures in the yard creates an excellent opportunity to study deer and right-of-way interactions in winter (Fig. 1). Studies on deer/right-of-way interactions have been conducted in the yard since 1974 (Doucet et al., 1981; Doucet et al., 1983; Brown and Doucet, 1991), thus a good database already existed for the rights-of-way in the deeryard.

In early January 1998 the entire 120 kV line, between the Rigaud and St-Polycarpe substations (22 km) collapsed due to a major ice storm which lasted 5 days and deposited between 50 and 75 mm of ice on the

Fig. 1. Deer crossing the 120 kV right-of-way in winter 1997.

Environmental Concerns in Rights-of-Way Management: Seventh International Symposium
J.W. Goodrich-Mahoney, D.F. Mutrie and C.A. Guild (editors)
© 2002 Elsevier Science Ltd. All rights reserved.

Fig. 2. Collapsed 120 kV powerline in January 1998.

structures (Fig. 2). Fallen materials such as poles, wires, insulators and other hardware were cleared during the 1998 winter and the line was rebuilt in the summer and fall of 1998. The corporate and public attitude dictating the construction was spirited by a sense of urgency related to still having fresh in mind the effects of the so-called "ice storm of the century." Under these conditions, no specific plan was elaborated to protect deer habitat during the rebuilding of the 120 kV line in the Rigaud yard. The collapse and reconstruction of the 120 kV line created a unique situation to monitor what happens when a sensitive area must be accessed and submitted to heavy construction activities in an emergency situation. The objective of the study was to monitor the state and response of deer browse in the right-of-way during and after the reconstruction of the powerline. The objectives of this paper are twofold: (1) to discuss the implications of the reconstruction of the 120 kV powerline for deer, and (2) to present browse survey results from monitoring 2 years after construction.

STUDY AREA

The deeryard under study is located on the Rigaud mountain approximately 100 km west of Montreal, QC, and covers an area of approximately 25 km^2. In 1978 the population was estimated at approximately 285 animals (Parent 1978). Although no recent population surveys have been conducted, biologists responsible for the management of the Rigaud yard estimate the present population between 100 and 150 animals. The forest habitat near the right-of-way is characterized by deciduous or mixed stands interspersed with small islands of hemlock (*Tsuga canadensis*) and Balsam fir (*Abies balsamea*). Other species included hawthorn (*Crataegus* spp.), sumac (*Rhus typhina*), red-osier dogwood (*Cornus stolonifera*), trembling aspen (*Populus tremuloides*), Eastern cottonwood (*Populus deltoides*), balsam poplar (*Populus balsamifera*), American elm (*Ulmus americana*), ashes (*Fraxinus* spp.), choke-cherry (*Prunus virginiana*), black cherry (*Prunus serotina*), sugar maple (*Acer saccharum*), red maple (*Acer rubrum*), and willows (*Salix* spp.). The forest stands attractive for deer in the Rigaud yard are those provided by white cedars (*Thuja occidentalis*), an excellent cover for wintering deer in the northeast. The two powerline rights-of-way (120 and 735 kV) intersect each other and bisect cedar stands in the southwest section of the deeryard. Each right-of-way is approximately 30 m wide and the 735 kV right-of-way was only cleared under the conductors; a condition to route through the yard. The section of the 120 kV right-of-way studied was approximately 1 km long, located on a gentle south-facing slope.

METHOD

The approach to collect data was simple and consisted of three parts. The first part consisted in taking a series of photographs at various project steps as preconstruction and construction activities progressed in winter, summer and fall 1998. This enabled to record how deer browse was being reduced by the access road, traffic of various types of vehicles, stock piling of materials and digging and filling in the right-of-way. We also kept a field logbook in which we recorded numerous descriptive notes related to the encroachment of construction activities on browse. After construction we continued taking photographs over time to maintain a pictorial record.

The second part was carried out during the winters 1998, 1999, and 2000. Observations were made on deer activity in the right-of-way. More specifically we were interested if deer crossed the right-of-way and/or if they fed in the right-of-way. This was achieved by making direct observations from vantage points along the right-of-way.

The third part was to conduct browse counts in the right-of-way in the spring after snowmelt. A visit to the site on 5 May 1999 indicated that practically no twigs were available 50 cm above ground. Thus no browse had been available to deer during the 1999 winter and it was decided not to conduct a browse count that spring. In May 2000, a total of 202 5 m^2 plots were sampled to determine browse availability and use in the right-of-way 2 years following the reconstruction of the line. All woody twigs between 50 and 200 cm in height were identified and counted to enable comparison with previous data.

RESULTS AND DISCUSSION

As far as we could determine from visual observations, the ice storm of January 1998 by itself did not damage the available browse in the 120 kV powerline right-of-way in the Rigaud yard. Small stems bent over but did

Fig. 3. Deer browse in the right-of-way before mowing and construction in June 1998.

Fig. 4. Construction of the 120 kV powerline in August 1998.

not seem to have broken under the ice load (Fig. 3). Several deer were observed feeding in the right-of-way on 15 January 1998, just a few days after the storm. Emergency access to the right-of-way in winter 1998 when deer were in the yard was not a major issue, since only minor activities related to clean up and pick up of hardware were involved. A small crew required only a few days to complete the job. Surveying was done in the spring 1998 but the bulk of the reconstruction was done in summer 1998, when deer were absent from the yard except for a few individuals that, based on track observations, remained in the right-of-way area during the summer.

Shortly after the ice storm, clean-up crews cleared a winter access road on the frozen ground on the west side of the entire length of the right-of-way. This was a 3 m wide access road in which the snow was pushed to the side, creating a small snow bank that did not impede deer movement. In winter 1998, preparation work only involved clearing the hardware and debris after the collapse of the line. All fallen 8 twin wooden structures, insulators and wires were carried away from the study area. On 30 July 1998, as part of the regular vegetation control program, a motorized mower was used to mow the entire surface of the right-of-way. In August 1998, construction activities started in the section under study. This involved improvement of the access road, transportation of materials, including gravel and fine materials to compact the foundation of the towers. In the section studied, 2 steel towers and 8 twin poles (2 more supports than before the collapse) were erected during August and conductors were strung (Fig. 4). Movement by heavy machinery, digging for the 2 steel towers and storage of gravel; in addition to the mowing operation appeared to severely reduce deer browse. As spring and summer 1998 progressed, it became apparent that deer browse was being cumulatively reduced by various activities related to the pre-construction and construction phases. Traffic of heavy and light vehicles in the access road eventually made it deep rutted and characterized by puddles and bare soil. The stockpiling of materials such as steel, wood poles, gravel, and sand, along with digging and stockpiling of earth for poles and towers, made areas around pole sites totally devoid of vegetation.

Deer appeared to be disturbed very little by the changes over the 3 winters of the study. Deer were observed crossing the right-of-way just a few days after the storm and track patterns indicated that deer crossed the right-of-way throughout the 1998 winter, sometimes between conductors at ground level. In 1999, direct observations and track patterns also indicated that deer were crossing the right-of-way in great numbers, but that very little time was spent browsing in the right-of-way. During the 2000 winter deer spent more time browsing in the right-of-way than the previous winter. On a few occasions, we observed deer feeding for more than 10 min in the right-of-way at dusk. Doucet et al. (1987) reported deer spending as much as 14 min browsing in the same right-of-way.

The browse available in spring 1998 was not surveyed since we already have a good database on browse production and use in the Rigaud yard rights-of-way from several previous years. We planned to conduct a browse count in the spring 1999 but cursory visual observations at the site in May 1999 quickly indicated that browse above 50 cm from the ground was almost non existent (Fig. 5). This was mainly the result of the 1998 mowing operation in the entire right-of-way, since long sections of the east side of the right-of-way were spared any construction traffic and stockpiling. In summer 1999 however, it was easy to observe that several stems were going to provide some browse above the 50 cm snow line during the following (2000) winter (Fig. 6).

The browse survey conducted in May 2000 indicated that the total stem density in the right-of-way was 16,644 stems/ha, while the twig density was 35,196 twigs/ha (Table 1).

Red-osier dogwood and willows represented over 60% of the twigs browsed. These data reflect that all stems were small and the majority each provided only one twig to the browse count. For example, red-osier

Table 1. Browse available and used by deer in the Rigaud right-of-way in winter 2000

Latin names	Common names*	Stems available # (ha)	Stems available (%)	Twigs available # (ha)	Twigs available (%)	Twigs browsed # (ha)	Twigs unbrowsed # (ha)	Rate of browsing (%)	Importance in the diet (%)
Acer saccharum	Sugar Maple	200	1.2	270	0.8	270	0	100.0	0.9
Betula papyrifera	Paper Birch	1538	9.2	3816	10.8	2837	979	74.3	9.9
Betula populifolia	Grey Birch	80	0.5	150	0.4	80	70	53.3	0.3
Carya cordiformis	Bitternut hickory	90	0.5	150	0.4	140	10	93.3	0.5
Cornus stolonifera	Red-Osier Dogwood	5884	35.4	9990	28.4	9550	440	95.6	33.5
Crataegus spp.	Hawthorn	99	0.6	300	0.9	160	140	53.3	0.6
Fraxinus americana	White Ash	1249	7.5	2018	5.7	1259	759	62.4	4.4
Fraxinus nigra	Black Ash	310	1.9	588	1.7	208	380	35.4	0.7
Larix laricina	Larch	10	0.1	80	0.2	40	40	50.0	0.1
Populus balsamifera	Balsam Poplar	70	0.4	150	0.4	120	30	80.0	0.4
Populus tremuloides	Trembling Aspen	190	1.1	370	1.1	260	110	70.3	0.9
Prunus serotina	Black Cherry	40	0.2	180	0.5	140	40	77.8	0.5
Prunus virginiana	Choke Cherry	30	0.2	110	0.3	90	20	81.8	0.3
Rhamnus alnifolius	Buckthorn	160	1.0	450	1.3	290	160	64.4	1.0
Rhus typhina	Sumac	30	0.2	30	0.1	30	0	100.0	0.1
Salix spp.	Willow	4316	25.9	11,378	32.3	9500	1878	83.5	33.3
Sambucus spp.	Elderberry	20	0.1	20	0.1	20	0	100.0	0.1
Spirea latifolia	Meadow Sweet	1039	6.2	1459	4.1	110	1349	7.5	0.4
Thuja occidentalis	Eastern Cedar	430	2.6	2278	6.5	2278	0	100.0	8.0
Tilia americana	Basswood	569	3.4	889	2.5	859	30	96.6	3.0
Ulmus americana	White Elm	270	1.6	500	1.4	270	230	54.0	0.9
Viburnum cassinoides	Nanny Berry	20	0.1	20	0.1	10	10	50.0	0.0
Totals		16,644	100.0	35,196	100.0	28,521	6675	81.0	100.0

*Trees in Canada.

Fig. 5. Absence of deer browse in the right-of-way in the winter 1999.

Fig. 6. Deer browse in the right-of-way in the winter 2000.

dogwood contributed 5884 stems/ha for a total of 9990 twigs/ha, indicating that each plant contributed on average 2 twigs to deer browse in the right-of-way. Red-osier dogwood is a privileged species from a right-of-way management perspective as it can be heavily browsed by deer in winter and never becomes a problem with conductor clearance. Deer browsed 81.0% of available twigs in the right-of-way in winter 2000 (Table 1). This rate is similar to that reported over the years (Doucet and Brown, 1983; Garant, 1989). In general, browse production results are consistent with those observed in past studies in relation to the vegetation control cycle in the right-of-way. Doucet and Brown (1983) reported 15,730 stems/ha and 47,970 twigs/ha 2 years after a cut and herbicide treatment; while Garant (1989) reported 16,240 stems/ha and 67,360 twigs/ha, 2 growing seasons after a manual cut of the vegetation in the Rigaud right-of-way. The dominant species in 1989 were *Cornus stolonifera*, *Fraxinus* and *Salix* but *Fraxinus* represented a greater proportion of the browse than that in 2000 (Garant, 1989).

The browse density of 35,196 twigs/ha observed in the present study is well short of the 100,000 twigs/ha recommended in the Québec deeryard management guide (Germain et al., 1986) for food patches in deeryards. The main reasons for this are the following: (1) all stems were very small, (2) the micro-drainage in the right-of-way has been modified in the lower slope, and (3) species such as purple loosestrife (*Lythrum Salicaria*), cat-tails (*Typha* spp.), and reed-grass (*Phragmites communis*) seemed to be more aggressive in the right-of-way. In addition, Rigaud's browse production has seldom exceeded 70,000 twigs/ha mainly due to the short cycle of vegetation control and severe browsing by deer in winter. It remains somewhat difficult to predict gains in browse production in the next 2 years due to changes in species composition and soil and drainage disturbance in the right-of-way. Observations during a site visit in September 2000 lead us to speculate based on a visual estimate that it could take 2 more years for the browse to approach 70,000 twigs/ha. It appears that only aggressive management could lead to browse availability approaching 100,000 twigs/ha in that right-of-way.

CONCLUSIONS

The elimination of browse in the right-of-way was a cumulative process. The removal of snow for the access road in winter 1998 did not affect browse availability very much, although it did damage some shrubs. The intense use of this road in the summer 1998 during construction eliminated the browse and eventually the road surface became bare soil. The vegetation control with a mower in July 1998 and the subsequent construction activities completely eliminated the browse from the right-of-way. The ground disturbance near all new towers left patches of bare soil extending the width of the right-of-way, and where no browse was recorded even in the spring 2000 survey. Had the mower not been used, considerable browse would have been available, at least in mid-span sections on the east side (side opposite the road) of the right-of-way.

Deer did not seem to be disturbed by the fallen lines and clean-up activities in the right-of-way in the winter 1998. Despite lack of planning for browse protection specific to reconstruction, the browse available in 2000 was relatively close to that recorded 2 years after regular vegetation control. We speculate that with minimal planning, at no extra cost, and without mowing, the site could have produced close to 70,000 twigs/ha in winter 2000. Despite its shortcomings, we believe this case presents evidence that, with some planning, it would be possible to access some sensitive habitats under emergency conditions; and comply with established environmental requirements.

REFERENCES

Brown, T.D. and G.J. Doucet. 1991. Temporal changes in winter diet selection by white-tailed deer in a northern deeryard. Journal of Wildlife Management, 55: 361–376.

Dominske, K.R. 1997. Effects of the introduction of a pipeline right-of-way with planted travel corridors to a deer wintering area in northern New York. In: Proceedings Sixth National Symposium on Environmental Concerns in Rights-of-Way Management. New-Orleans, LA. pp. 285–290.

Doucet, G.J., R.W. Stewart, and K.A. Morrison. 1981. The effect of a utility right-of-way on white-tailed deer in a northern deeryard. In: Proceedings Second Symposium on Environmental Concerns in Rights-of-Way Management. EPRI WS-78-141, 59: 1–9.

Doucet, G.J. and D.T. Brown. 1983. Étude sur le cerf de Virginie dans l'emprise à 120 kV traversant le ravage de Rigaud. Rapport final, Service Écologie biophysique, vice-présidence Environnement, Hydro-Québec. (Contract: Office of industrial research, McGill University). 120 pp.

Doucet, G.J., D.T. Brown, and P. Lamothe. 1983. White-tailed deer response to conifer plantation as a mitigation measure in a powerline right-of-way located in a Quebec deeryard. In: Proceedings Northeast Wildlife Conference 40, pp. 150–156.

Doucet, G.J., D.T. Brown, and P. Lamothe. 1987. Deer behaviour in a powerline right-of-way located in a northern wintering yard. In: Proceedings Fourth National Symposium on Environmental Concerns in Rights-of-Way Management. Indianapolis, IN. pp. 7–12.

Doucet, G.J., Y. Garant, M. Giguère, and G. Philip de Laborie. 1997. Emprises de lignes et ravages de cerfs de Virginie — Synthèse et bilan des études. TransÉnergie, Hydro-Québec, Montréal, QC. 132 pp.

Evans, R.R. 1982. The effects of crossing wintering habitat with transmission facilities — a literature review. Ontario Hydro, Land Use and Environmental Planning. Report no. 82528. 90 pp.

Garant, Y. 1989. Les emprises de lignes dans les ravages de cerfs de Virginie. Production de nourriture et utilisation par les cerfs. Ravages de Bedford, Rigaud, Hill Head, Kingsey Falls, Rawdon, lac David, Notre-Dame-du-Laus, lac Témiscouata et lac Trente-et-Un-Milles. Pour le Service Recherches en Environnement et Santé publique, Vice-présidence Environnement, Hydro-Québec. 74 pp.

Germain, G., C. Pichette, and F. Potvin. 1986. Guide d'aménagement des ravages de cerfs de Virginie. Ministère du Loisir, de la Chasse et de la Pêche, Direction Générale de la Faune. 70 pp.

Jackson, L.W. and J. Hecklau. 1995. Construction effects of a 345 kV electric corridor on New York deer. In: Proceedings Fifth International Symposium on Environmental Concerns in Rights-of-Way Management. Montreal, QC. pp. 290–299.

Parent, R. 1978. Population et habitat du ravage de cerf de Virginie du Mont-Rigaud, hiver 1977–1978. Ministère du Tourisme, Chasse et Pêche, Serv. Faune, Québec, Rapp. Tech. 28 pp.

BIOGRAPHICAL SKETCHES

G. Jean Doucet (corresponding author)
TransÉnergie, 800 De Maisonneuve, E. Montreal, QC, Canada H2L 4M8

Jean Doucet holds a PhD in wildlife ecology from McGill University and has been a member of the environmental unit at TransÉnergie for 4 years. He is currently managing a research program on interactions between wildlife and energy transmission activities and equipment. Issues under study include biodiversity, habitat fragmentation, habitat management and avian interactions with structures.

Eric R. Thompson
E.R. Thompson and Associates Inc., 15-101 Don Quichotte, Suite 302, Île Perrot, QC, Canada J7V 7X4

Eric Thompson holds a MSc degree in wildlife ecology from McGill University. He has participated in the environmental assessment and monitoring of many linear projects over the past 25 years. He is currently an environmental consultant specializing in integrated natural resources inventories, assessment and management.

Mitigating the Impacts of Electric Facilities to Birds

John M. Bridges and Theodore R. Anderson

There is a great deal of pressure on the electric utility industry to solve all of its problems with collisions, electrocutions and other bird interactions. Resource management agencies and utility managers are looking for a quick fix to make the problem go away. However, in many cases the need for speed results in solutions that are poorly thought out, and may cause more problems than they solve. The purpose of this paper will be to discuss the mitigative measures found in the literature and provide a brief evaluation of their effectiveness and some of the problems the may create. The evaluation will be based on Western's experience, existing literature and personal experience. For example, collisions with man-made structures are one of the major impacts to avifauna associated with transmission and distribution lines. Raptor silhouettes, different color marker balls, and various "bird diverters" all work to some degree. However, marking with the wrong color or wrong type of device may not be effective, could be a maintenance problem or may even cause lines to go down. Eliminating a perch site to solve an electrocution problem may create an electrocution problem that was not there in the first place, relocate the problem or become a maintenance nightmare. Providing nesting platforms may adversely affect non-target sensitive species, or not be used at all. The overall objective of the paper will be to suggest reasonableness in the mitigative measures and provoke thought prior to implementation.

Keywords: Birds, collisions, electrocutions, nesting, impacts, mitigation, outages, perch

INTRODUCTION

The US Department of Energy's Western Area Power Administration (Western) has approximately 17,000 miles of transmission lines in 15 western states. The ecosystems encountered range from subalpine to low desert, from tall grass prairie to live oak savannah. Since 1977, when it was legislated into existence, Western has dealt with bird collisions, electrocutions, and nests in and on its facilities.

It is generally acknowledged that the construction of electric transmission and distribution lines results in the direct impact of habitat alteration due to right-of-way clearing. Unless a particularly sensitive species is present, this is not a long-term impact and is not usually considered significant. Once a line is up and operational, the problem of bird collisions and electrocutions is a long-term impact, and for certain species could be significant.

METHODS

The identification of bird interactions generally comes from Incident or Outage Reports submitted to the National Electric Reliability Council, maintenance surveys, or citizen reports. The methods used to minimize the impacts is based on the authors' personal experience and published literature.

ELECTROCUTIONS

The electric utility industry, both here and abroad, find wildlife electrocutions to be significant environmental and economical issues. Environmental issues tend to get "fixed" following the completion of other more electrical needs. However, according to Western incident reports, from June 1, 1999 to June 1, 2000, Western bird-caused outages totaled 62½ Megawatt-hours

(MW-h). For Western, these are just the "reported outages" known to be caused by birds. Nearly 1200 MW-h were lost due to "wildlife or unknown causes" during this same timeframe. Dedon and Colson (1987) reported that Pacific Gas and Electric lost an average of $354,129 per year during 1983–1986. There are additional outages and possibly electrocutions that go unreported on most of Western's system, due to automatic reclosures (these are devices that sense when an electricity has stopped flowing through a circuit and seek out where the circuit is not complete and try to reconnect it). There is an increase in the published and unpublished information (Chris van Rooyen, Eskom, personal communication, 2000; Burnham, 1995; and Blume, 1982) indicating some of the reported, "unknown outages" may be the result of "bird streamers." These are the long stringy defecation of raptors and other large birds across electrical equipment causing outages and possible avian mortality. What all this means is, in the de-regulating electric utility industry many of these outages, which for the most part are preventable, are an economic as well as an environmental issue.

Birds will use transmission and distribution structures for perching and nesting. Young birds, which are not yet efficient at hunting on the wing, will hunt from utility structures. Mature birds will also occasionally hunt from these structures. This is especially true in open habitats without natural perches (Stahlecker, 1978). The end result of this use is occasionally an electrocution. Dedon and Colson (1987) found that birds caused about 5% of outages on their system, and 57% of those were electrocutions. In South Africa, Kruger (1999) reported that in 32 months, 147 raptors, representing 19 species were electrocuted on the Eskom distribution system.

APLIC (1996) has thoroughly described the cause and effect of large bird electrocutions. There are three basic measures for minimizing bird electrocutions. The first is to stop the bird from perching on the equipment. A number of deterrents are available, including different types of triangles, single dowels, multiple points and anti-perching irons. Some of these, such as the triangles, are very effective for large to medium sized raptors, but placement is important. Harness (2000) has found that raptors can use the triangles as a perch, which sometimes can put the bird at greater risk. The long, sharp-pointed devices could injure some larger birds, while smaller birds, such as rock doves (*Columba livia*), will pile nest material on the projections until they are no longer effective. Keep in mind the perch location initially attracted the bird for a reason, and unless that reason is no longer present, a bird will want to use the perch.

The second is to provide a safe, alternative perch site. Chervick (1999) developed a multi-perch for Harris hawks (*Parabuteo unicinctus*). Harris hawks are unique in North America in that they tend to hunt and perch in family groups and when they perch on distribution lines they tend to get electrocuted in groups. The perch was designed to accommodate several individuals at one time, and get them up and away from the energized lines. Bridges and Lopez (1995) added single perches to distribution line poles to minimize raptor electrocutions.

The third is to prevent a phase to phase or phase to ground contact by the bird. There are covering devices manufactured for wires, conductors, insulators and bushings, which will minimize the potential for electrocutions. Information on these coverings is provided in APLIC (1996). It is important to note, especially to maintenance crews, that these coverings are not insulation designed to protect humans, meaning that handling energized wires with this covering may still cause a severe trauma. Also, Roig and Navazo (1997) noted that anti-electrocution measures used in Spain did not prove equally effective for all species.

Whether the fix is to deter perching, provide safe perches or cover the equipment, it is important to be aware of the species involved, and why, as well as how, they are using the equipment. Roig and Navazo (1997) found that insulating measures were more effective in preventing electrocutions than perch deterrents. Perch deterrents sometimes put a bird in even more jeopardy than would occur if you did nothing to the facility (Bridges and Lopez, 1995; Harness, 2000; Harness and Garret, 1999). Always follow up on the measures you have used to ensure they are working.

NESTING PLATFORMS

A large number of bird species use transmission and distribution structures for nesting (Gilmer and Wiehe, 1977 and Stahlecker and Griese, 1979). There are two reasons for providing artificial nesting facilities. First is the need to relocate a nest away from energized equipment, either out of concern for the bird, or for reliability reasons. Second, is to enhance nesting habitat (Hamerstrom et al., 1973; Grub, 1980; Howard, 1980; Base and Sievert, 1987, and Hunter et al., 1997). If the decision is made to use artificial nesting facilities for either reason, the target species must be identified and the nesting substrate must be preferred by that species. Howard used platforms to enhance nesting habitat for ferruginous hawks (*Buteo regalis*) and found that they preferred a platform without a shading device. Bridges and McConnon (1987) reported on the success of three different types of platforms in North Dakota. While all three types of platforms were used, great horned owls (*Bubo virginianus*) seemed to prefer the platforms with a shading device and ferruginous hawks seemed to prefer the platforms without a shading device.

Follow-up studies on the use of the platform and whether the target species is being accommodated are important. Occasionally, platforms will adversely affect prey species, especially where their populations have dwindled. In the southwestern deserts, ravens (*Corvus corax*) will use nesting platforms and prey on juvenile desert tortoises (*Gopherus agassizii*), which are listed as a threatened species. A growing problem in the Western US is the use of platforms by non-target species. In Montana, for example, hundreds of platforms have been put up for ospreys (*Pandion haliaetus*), to keep them out of utility structures and provide alternate nesting habitat. Other species have moved in, and in one area, thirteen platforms are being used, but only six are used by ospreys. The others according to Milodragvich (2000) are occupied by Canada geese (*Branta canadensis*) and one by a great blue heron (*Ardea herodias*). The result has been ospreys are moving back onto the transmission line structures.

COLLISIONS

Bird collisions with overhead wires have been noted as a cause of mortality in the US at least since 1876 (Coues, 1876). Avery (1978) summarized the collision issue dealing with transmission lines for the US Fish and Wildlife Service. The problem is not restricted to North America (see also Alanso et al., 1993; Telfer et al., 1987; Ledger et al., 1993; Bevanger, 1993; Roig and Navazo, 1997). Hess (1999) reports the problem to be quite widespread in Tasmania as well as the rest of Australia.

Birds collide with transmission lines because they can't see the line, either due to weather conditions or because they are occupied by something else such as courtship, hunting, or escape. Bird collisions typically occur with the overhead ground wire when the bird veers up to avoid the conductors. Panic flushes, particularly of flocking birds (e.g., waterfowl, wading birds, or shorebirds) have been documented by Krapu (1974) and Schroeder (1977). Spring mating season often leads to collisions, as does the late summer and fall when young of the year are learning the intricate maneuvers of flight (Hugie et al., 1993).

The Avian Power Line Interaction Committee has summarized the methods used to reduce collisions (APLIC, 1994). These include careful location of the line when originally routed. If the line is already in place, a two-year, four-season, study is recommended to determine the aerial extent of the collision problem and the species involved. Based on the results of the study, the problem can be minimized by removing the overhead ground wire when appropriate, and/or marking it with some type of device to draw the bird's attention to it. Marking devices include aviation marker balls, spiral vibration dampers, air flow spoilers, bird flight diverters of various design and dimension, and several swinging devices such as swinging plates, or flappers.

Beaulaurier et al. (1984) found that removing the overhead groundwire, or shield wire was very effective in the Pacific Northwest. Meyer (1978) found marking the groundwire works with varying degrees of success. Brown and Drewien (1995) studied the effectiveness of two different marking devices (i.e., swinging plates and spiral vibration dampers) and found that they both reduced collisions, but the effectiveness varied by season and species. Roig and Navazo (1997) found that "white spirals" spaced every 10 m on the overhead ground wire were effective. Where overhead ground wires were not present, they attached a 35 cm long, black, neoprene strip to the conductor and that worked almost as well. Koops and de Jong (1981) studied the effectiveness of "bird flight diverters" in Denmark and found that, depending on the spacing of the diverters on the wires, they reduced bird collisions by 57–89%. Telfer (1999) found that bird flight diverters had little effect on shearwater (*Puffinus* sp.) collisions but yellow, aviation marker balls with 8-inch black dots worked quite well. Beaulaurier et al. (1984) also used orange aviation marker balls, fishing floats and yellow streamers, all with some success. Bird flappers, a device that attaches to either the groundwire or conductor, have been suggested by Miller (1993) and Ledger (1993) and placed on lines in South Africa (van Rooyen, 2000). Janss et al. (1999) studied the use of static raptor models (i.e., golden eagles and accipiters) mounted on transmission line structures, to reduce collisions. They found that the models had no effect on collisions or the potential for collisions.

With all of these techniques, it is important to remember that the purpose of the facility is the reliable transmission of electricity. The amount of lightning activity has to be considered before removing the overhead groundwire. Ice- and wind-loading potential needs to be evaluated before attaching anything to either the conductors or the groundwires. The attached device, aviation marker ball or flapper may also wear on the wire it is attached to resulting in failure of the wire. And finally, whatever mitigation is applied, needs to be reviewed periodically to ascertain its effectiveness.

CONCLUSIONS

There is a great deal of pressure on the electric utility industry to solve all of its problems with collisions, electrocutions and other bird interactions. Resource management agencies, including game and fish departments, and environmental organizations are pressuring utility managers for a quick fix. They, in turn, just want to make the problem go away. However, in many cases the need for speed results in solutions that are poorly thought out, and may result in more problems than they solve. Marking lines to prevent collisions may not be effective or may cause lines to go down. Eliminating a perch site may create an electrocution problem that was not there in the first place or just relocate the problem. Providing nesting platforms may adversely affect non-target, sensitive species, or not be used at all. Site specific and species specific solutions should be adopted.

REFERENCES

Alanso, J.C., J.A. Alanso, R. Munoz-Pulido, J. Roig, V. Navazo, and J. Arevalo. 1993. Senalizacion de lineosdealta tension para la proteccion de la avifauna. Red Electrica de Espana, S.A. 58 pp.

Avery, M.T., ed. 1978. Impacts of transmission lines on birds in flight. USDI Fish and Wildlife Service. FWS/OBS-78/48. 151 pp.

Avian Power Line Intreraction Committee (APLIC). 1994. Mitigating Bird Collisons with Power Lines: The State of the Art in 1994. Edison Electric Institute, Washington, DC. 103 pp.

Avian Power Line Intreraction Committee (APLIC). 1996. Suggested Practices for Raptor Protection on Power Lines: The State of the Art in 1996. Raptor Research Foundation and Edison Electric Institute, Washington, DC. 148 pp.

Base, D.L. and G.A. Sievert. 1987. Experimental use of artificial nesting structures for grassland raptors in the Oklahoma Panhandle. EYAS, 10: 30–31.

Beaulaurier, Diane L., B.W. James, P.A. Jackson, J.R. Myers, and J.M. Lee, Jr. 1984. Mitigating the incidence of bird collisions with transmission lines. P539–550. In: Proceedings of the Third International Symposium on Environmental Concerns in Rights-of-Way Management. A.F. Crabtree, ed. Mississippi State Univ., MS. 689 pp.

Bevanger, K. 1993. Hunting mortality versus wire-strike mortality of willow grouse (*Lagopus lagopus*) in an upland area of southern Norway. P11-1–11-10. In: APLIC. Proceeding: Avian Interactions with Utility Structures International Workshop. EPRI, TR-103268 (Project 3041), Palo Alto, CA.

Blume, S.A. 1982. 345-kV line outage study. Sierra Pacific Power Company, Reno NV. 164 pp.

Bridges, J.M. and R. Lopez. 1995. Reducing large bird electrocutions on a 12.5-kV distribution line originally designed to minimize electrocutions. P263–265. In: Proceedings: Fifth International Symposium on Environmental Concerns in Rights-of-Way Management. G.J. Doucet, C. Seguin, and M. Giguere, eds. Hydro Quebec, Montreal, QC, Canada. 558 pp.

Bridges, J.M. and D. McConnon. 1987. Use of raptor nesting platforms in a central North Dakota high voltage transmission line. P46–49. In: Proceedings of the Fourth International Symposium on Environmental Concerns in Rights-of-Way Management. W.R. Byrnes and H.S. Holt, eds. Purdue Univ., West LayFayette, IN. 595 pp.

Brown, Wendy M. and R.C. Drewien. 1995. Evaluation of two power line markers to reduce crane and waterfowl collision mortality. Wildlife Society Bulletin, 23: 217–227.

Burnham, J.T. 1995. Bird streamer flashovers on FPL transmission lines. IEEE transactions on Power Delivery, 10(2): 970–977.

Chervick, T. 1999. Swift Creek Consulting, Vernal, UT. Personal Communication.

Coues, E. 1876. The destruction of birds by telegraph wire. American Naturalist, 10(12): 734–736.

Dedon, M.F. and E.W. Colson. 1987. Investigation of bird caused outages in the Pacific Gas and Electric Company service area. P34–45. In: Proceedings of the Fourth International Symposium on Environmental Concerns in Rights-of-Way Management. W.R. Byrnes and H.S. Holt, eds. Purdue Univ., West LayFayette, IN. 595 pp.

Gilmer, D.S. and J.M. Wiehe, 1977. Nesting by ferruginous hawks and other raptors on high voltage power line structures. Prairie Naturalist, 9: 1–10.

Grub, T.G. 1980. An artificial bald eagle nest structure. Research Note RM-383. USDA Forest Service, Ft. Collins, CO.

Hamerstrom, Frances, F.N. Hamerstrom and J. Hart. 1973. Nest boxes: An effective management tool for kestresl. Journal of Wildlife Management, 37: 400–403.

Harness, R.E. 2000. Effective line retrofitting — Moon Lake Electric Association. Raptor Electrocution and Collision Prevention Workshop, April 13–14. Seward, AK. EDM International, Inc., Ft. Collins, CO.

Harness, R.E. and M. Garret. 1999. Effectivenss of perch guards to prevent raptor electocutions. Journal of the Colorado Field Ornithologists, 33: 215–220.

Hess, Jo. 1999. Tasmania Hydro. Personal communication.

Howard, R.P. 1980. Artificial nest structures and grassland raptors. P117–123. In: Proceedings of a workshop on raptors and energy developments. R.P. Howard and J.F. Gore, eds. Idaho Chapter Wildlife Socity, Boise, ID.

Hugie, R.D., J.M. Bridges, B.S. Chanson, and M. Skougard. 1993. Results of a post-construction bird monitoring study on the Great Falls-Conrad 230-kV transmission line. P16-1–16-21. In: APLIC. Proceedings: Avian Interactions with Utility Structures International Workshop. EPRI, TR-103268 (Project 3041), Palo Alto, CA.

Hunter, P., N.A. Mahony, P.J. Ewins, D. Baird, and M. Field. 1997. Artificial nesting platforms for bald eagles in southern Ontario, Canada. Journal of Raptor Research, 31: 321–326.

Janss, G.F.E., A. Sazo, and M. Ferrer. 1999. Use of raptor models to reduce avian collisions with powerlines. Journal of Raptor Research, 33: 154–159.

Koops, F.B.J. and J. de Jong. 1981. Vermindering van draadslachtoffers door markering van hoogspanningsleidengen in de omgeving van heereven. Overdruk uit:lektrotechniek, 60: 641–646. (Translation provided by Dulmison, Inc., Lawrenceville, GA).

Krapu, G., 1974. Avian mortality from collisions with overhead lines in North Dakota. Prairie Naturalist, 6(1): 1–6.

Kruger, R. 1999. Towards solving rator electrocutions in Eskom distribution structures in South Africa. MS Thesis, Univ. Orange Free State , Blomfontein, South Africa. 104 pp.

Ledger, J.S., J.C.A. Hobbs, and T.V. Smith. 1993. Avian Interactions with utility structures: South African experience. P4-1–4-11. In: APLIC. Proceedings: Avian Interactions with Utility Structures International Workshop. EPRI, TR-103268 (Project 3041), Palo Alto, CA.

Meyer, J.R. 1978. Effects of transmission lines on bird flight behavior and collision mortality. USDOE Bonneville Power Admin. 200 pp.

Miller, A.D. 1993. The engineering perspective of power line marking systems to reduce avian collisions. P13-1–13-14. In: APLIC. Proceedings: Avian Interactions with Utility Structures International Workshop. EPRI, TR-103268 (Project 3041), Palo Alto, CA.

Milodragovich, S. 2000. Montana Power Company, Butte, MT. Personal communication.

Roig, J. and V. Navazo, 1997. A five-year Spanish research project on bird electrocutions and collision with electric lines. P317–325. In: The Sixth International Symposium on Environmental Concerns in Rights-of-Way Management. J.R. Williams, J.W. Goodrich-Mahoney, Jan R. Wisniewski, and J. Wisniewski, eds. Elsevier Science, Ltd. Oxford, UK. 511 pp.

Schroeder, C. 1977. Geese hit power transmission line. North Dakota Outdoors, 40: 1.

Stahlecker, D.W. 1978. Effect of a new transmission line on wintering prairie raptors. Condor, 80: 444–446.

Stahlecker, D.W. and H.J. Griese. 1979. Raptor use of nest boxes and platforms on transmission towers. Wildlife Society Bulletin, 7: 59–62.

Telfer, T.C. 2000. Hawaii Department of Forestry and Wildlife. Personal communication.

Telfer, T.C., J.L. Sincock, G.V. Byrd, and J.R. Reed. 1987. Attractions of Hawaiian birds to lights: conservation efforts and effects of moon phase. Wildlife Society Bulletin, 15: 406–413.

Van Rooyen, C. 2000. Eskom, South Africa. Personal communication.

BIOGRAPHICAL SKETCHES

John M. Bridges
Western Area Power Administration, 12155 W. Alameda Parkway, Lakewood, CO 80228, USA, bridges@wapa.gov
John Bridges has been a consultant to the energy industry for 15 years and a terrestrial biologist for the US Department of Energy, Western Area Power Administration (Western) for eleven years. His areas of expertise include the biological impacts of construction, operation and maintenance of electrical facilities. In his current position, he conducts Endangered Species Consultations with the US Fish and Wildlife Service and maintains the Avian Protection Program for Western.

Theodore R. Anderson
Western Area Power Administration, 2900 4th Street, Billings, MT 59101, USA, tanderso@wapa.gov
Ted Anderson has worked with the US Government for 25 years over 10 years of which has been with the Western Area Power Administration. He is responsible for implementing the National Environmental Policy Act and coordinating cultural resource and natural resource consultations for all the projects in Western's Upper Great Plains Region. This includes all or a portion of the states of Iowa, Minnesota, Montana, Nebraska, North and South Dakota, and Wyoming.

Mitigating Collision of Birds Against Transmission Lines in Wetland Areas in Colombia, by Marking the Ground Wire with Bird Flight Diverters (BFD)

Susana De La Zerda and Loreta Rosselli

Collision of birds against the ground wire and conductors of high tension lines can be a serious problem in some habitats and for some bird species. Data on collision were gathered in a wetland locality crossed by a 2 circuit 500 kV line in northern Colombia. After 2 years of study, mitigation devices (yellow plastic spirals) were installed on one circuit and observations were carried on after the installation in order to evaluate the effectiveness of the spirals. The bird flight diverters proved to reduce mortality of birds as shown by fewer birds reacting close to the line, fewer birds flying at the height of the conductors and lower collision rates with the marked line.

Keywords: High tension lines, ground wire marking, bird flight diverters, collision rates, neotropics

INTRODUCTION

Birds can be affected by electric transmission lines mainly in two ways: Collision with the ground wire and conductors and fragmentation of their habitats (especially forest) when ROWS are opened up (Rosselli and De La Zerda, 1996). In two field studies contracted by Interconexión Eléctrica S.A., the first carried on in Colombia (De La Zerda and Rosselli, 1997; Rosselli and De La Zerda, 1999), we found that collision was high mainly in a wetland study area located in the north part of the country. We found high collision rates for species like the Purple Gallinule (*Porphyrula martinica*), Blue-winged Teal (*Anas discors*), Whistling Ducks (*Dendrocygna* spp.) and the Black-crowned Night-Heron (*Nycticorax nycticorax*) among others. According to Palacios (1998) the populations of these species might be affected by the loss of individuals against the lines. Based on the studies mentioned (De La Zerda and Rosselli, 1997; Rosselli and De La Zerda, 1999) the objective of this phase of the study was to evaluate the efficiency of marking the ground wire with bird flight diverters (BFD) to mitigate the collision of birds in the area.

Most of the research on this topic has focused on the mortality, the species affected and the environmental and technical factors that can affect these. Some papers report results of mitigation studies (Alonso and Alonso, 1999; Alonso et al., 1994; Archibald, 1987; Beaulaurier, 1981; Brown, 1993; Brown and Drewien, 1995; Brown et al., 1987; Heijins, 1980; Janss and Ferrer, 1998; Koops and de Jong, 1982; Morkill and Anderson, 1991a,b, 1993; Raevel and Tombal, 1991; Savereno et al., 1996). The most studied and effective method registered in the literature is plastic spirals installed on the ground wire. Therefore, this type of mitigation device was chosen for this study.

STUDY AREA

The study site is located near the Caribbean coast of Colombia at 7m above sea level. This is an important wetland area that hosts large numbers of birds vulnerable to collision like herons, ducks, ibises, rails, etc. (Rosselli and De La Zerda, 1996). The area is also located on the main migratory routes for aquatic birds

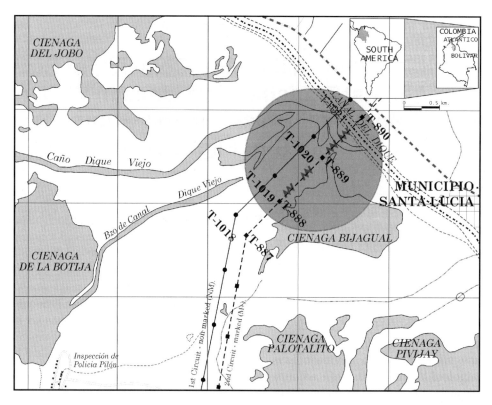

Fig. 1. Study area in Santa Lucía, Colombia.

like the Blue-Winged Teal (*Anas discors*), the most common migratory duck in Colombia (Hilty and Brown, 1986). Observations were made on the 888–889 and 889–890 spans of the 2nd Circuit (I.S.A. 500 kV Line Chinú–Sabanalarga) and 1019–1020, and 1020–1021 spans of the 1st Circuit that runs parallel to the 2nd (Fig. 1). These spans cross a wide area of wetlands mainly between the Ciénagas del Jobo and Pivijay, Palotal and Palotalito, as well as the Canal del Dique with its old sloughs and branches (Fig. 1). This situation of the 2 parallel circuits between two large bodies of water provides an excellent opportunity to study collisions because many accidents occur against the lines (De La Zerda and Rosselli, 1997 and papers cited therein). The lines usually interfere with the movements of the birds between feeding and roosting sites. In the area, there is a dry season from December through March and a rainy season between May and October, with a less rainy period from June through August. The mean annual precipitation is 962.4 mm and mean annual temperature is 28.4°C.

METHODOLOGY FOR COLLISION STUDIES

Sampling was carried on following the methodology used by De La Zerda and Rosselli (1997), based on work done by Meyer (1978), James and Haak (1979) and Beaulaurier (1981). The studies concentrate in 3 main aspects.

Observation of diurnal and nocturnal flights across the lines

Flights of the birds across the lines were recorded by 2 observers. Each span was sampled for 5–6 continuous hours, obtaining 2 complete days for each (05:30–18:30). Data on species, flock size, reactions to the line, height of flight were recorded. For the nocturnal flights, a Moonlight® Night Vision COMPACT™ Scope NV-100 with illuminator was used. These observations were carried out during 2 nights (one for each circuit). Observations were done a few minutes during each hour of the night and only on a small portion of the span.

Search for corpses

Since it is almost impossible to see and count the collisions by direct observations (Anderson, 1978; Beaulaurier, 1981; Bevanger, 1995; Dedon et al., 1989; James and Haak, 1979; McNeil et al., 1985; Meyer, 1978, Rusz et al., 1986), searches of bodies under the line must be carried out. Two people searched up to 50m from the center of the line to each side, looking for and identifying corpses of birds that presumably collided with the lines.

Bias studies

The search for bodies can be biased by several factors that have to be taken into account when calculating the collision rates:

Search bias: Each searcher looked for bodies of quail planted by someone else on the field. An error for each searcher can be calculated as the percentage of birds not found.

Removal bias: 20 quail bodies were planted on the study area and their fate followed daily. The bias was calculated as the number of birds that disappeared in the first 24 hours.

Habitat bias: Proportion of the area where the search for bodies is not possible.

Crippling bias: Calculates the number of birds that collide against the line but do not fall inside the study area. It is calculated by direct observation of the collisions.

Calculations

The total number of collisions is calculated adding the results of the bias studies to the total of fresh bodies found as follows (Meyer, 1978; James and Haak, 1979; Beaulaurier, 1981):

Search bias

$$SB = \frac{TDBF}{PBF} - TDBF$$

SB is a search bias, TDBF is a total fresh dead birds and feather spots found, PBF is a proportion of planted birds found during the plant/found recovery study.

Removal bias

$$RB = \frac{TDBF + SB}{PNR} - (TDBF + SB)$$

RB is a removal bias, PNR is a proportion of planted birds not removed by scavengers.

Habitat bias

$$HB = \frac{TDBF + SB + RB}{PS} - (TDBF + SB + RB)$$

HB is a habitat bias, PS is a proportion of the area that is searchable.

Crippling bias

$$CB = \frac{TDBF + SB + RB + HB}{PBK} - (TDBF + SB + RB + HB)$$

CB is a crippling bias, PBK is a the proportion of observed collisions falling within the search area. Estimate of total collisions:

$$(ETC) = TDBF + SB + RB + HB + CB.$$

Collision rate estimate

$$(CRE) = (ETC/TF) * 100$$

TF is a total number of flights in 24 h (calculated as the mean of the 2 day observations for each span plus night observations). More details on methodology and calculations are found in De La Zerda and Rosselli (1997, 2000) and Rosselli and De La Zerda (1999).

Methodology for the study of the BFD effectiveness

To study the effectiveness of the mitigation devices, 2 kinds of methodology can be used:

1. compare mortality or collision rates before and after installation of the mitigation devices in one study site (Janss and Ferrer, 1998; Koops and De Jong, 1982; Beaulaurier, 1981);
2. carry on simultaneous sampling periods where marked spans or portions of the line are compared to nonmarked ones (Brown and Drewien, 1995; Savereno et al., 1996; Morkill and Anderson, 1991).

Since we had previous studies on the line, we used the first method, comparing before and after installation of the BFD. We also left one circuit unmarked to be able to compare the marked and unmarked circuits. With this methodology we were able to compare all the premarking samples with all the postmarking samples, pairs of data sets taken at the same time of the year but in different years (one by one). Since we carried out sampling immediately before and immediately after marking, we could compare these two sets of data. We also were able to make all these comparisons between the marked (M+) and non marked (NM) circuits.

BFD installation

The BFD installed were yellow polypropylene spirals of 25 cm diameter and 80 cm length approximately. They were installed every 10 m on each ground wire of the 888–889 and 889–890 spans of the 2nd circuit, in an alternate fashion on each ground wire so that the general view is as if they were located at 5 m distances and therefore are more easily seen by the birds (Fig. 2).

RESULTS

Flights

The mean number of daily flights across the line varied widely through the study with extreme values 87.5 and 837.2. There was no significant difference between circuits in these numbers (mean number of flights: NM before: 324.27, NM after: 650.61, M+ before: 254.13, M+ after: 551.67; Wilcoxon Test, $p = 0.5286$). The group that flew more across the line was the Heron family (Ardeidae) and the most abundant species was the Cattle Egret (*Bubulcus ibis*) with more than 90% of the total number flights across the line. Other abundant families were Cormorants (Phalacrocoracidae),

Fig. 2. Alternate installation of BFD in the ground wire (seen from above) of the 500 kV Line Chinú–Sabanalarga, Colombia.

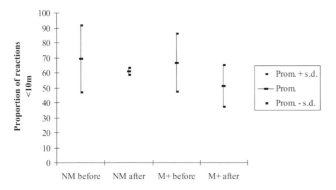

Fig. 3. Mean ± s.d. of the percentage of reactions that occurred at less than 10 m from the line in M+ and NM before and after the BFD were installed ($n = 4$ sampling periods before marking for NM and M+, $n = 3$ sampling periods after marking in NM and M+). Santa Lucía, Atlántico, Colombia.

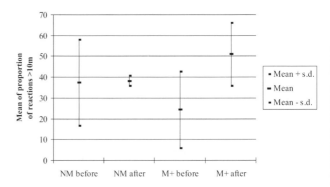

Fig. 4. Mean ± s.d. of the percentage of reactions at more than 10 m from the line and at heights of flight 3 and 4 before and after marking the line ($n = 4$ sampling periods before marking for NM and M+, $n = 3$ sampling periods after marking in NM and M+). Santa Lucía, Atlántico, Colombia.

Ibises (Threskiornithidae), Ducks (Anatidae), American Vultures (Cathartidae), Doves (Columbidae), Parrots (Psittacidae), and Swallows (Hirundinidae). Other common species were the Olivaceus Cormorant (*Phalacrocorax olivaceus*), Great Egret (*Casmerodius albus*), Snowy Egret (*Egretta thula*), Little Blue Heron (*Egretta caerulea*), Whispering Ibis (*Phimosus infuscatus*), White-faced, and Black-bellied Whistling Ducks (*Dendrocygna viduata, D. autumnalis*), Blue-winged Teal, Jacanas (*Jacana jacana*), Pale-vented Pigeon (*Columba cayennensis*), Brown-throated Parakeet (*Aratinga pertinax*), and Shiny Cowbirds (*Molothrus bonariensis*).

Lists of species present in the area and species flying across the line are available upon request to the authors.

Reactions

After marking the line, all sampling periods considered, there was a decrease in the mean number of birds reacting closer to the line (10 m) but the difference was not significant for either circuit (Mann–Whitney, $p = 0.40$ for NM and M+) (Fig. 3). This might indicate that the birds are detecting the line at a greater distance and can react on time. Analyzing the proportion of reactions of flights at heights III (between conductors and the ground wire) and IV (up to 50 m above the ground wire; these two are the most dangerous heights) and farther than 10 m from the line, before and after marking M+ we found that for NM the percentage was almost the same while for M+ it increased after marking the line (Fig. 4) even though the tendency is not significant (Mann–Whitney, $p = 0.4$ for NM and 0.22 for M+). Comparing the samples just before and just after marking we found that in M+ the rate of reaction doubled after marking (6.5–13.0%) while in NM it decreased (14.7–13.2%). In M+ the proportion of reactions farther than 10 m from the line increased from 65 to 95% ($\chi^2 = 460.2, p < 0.001$, 1 d.f.) while in NM this proportion increased from slightly less than 50% before marking to just over 50% after marking ($\chi^2 = 46.6, p < 0.001$, 1 d.f.) (Fig. 5).

Height of flight

The percentage of flights at the most dangerous height (III: between conductors and the ground wire) decreased in both circuits, but significantly in M+ (Mann–Whitney, $p = 0.0238$ for M+ and $p = 0.5714$ for NM) after marking the line (Fig. 6). This may indicate that the birds were detecting the line sooner and then changing the height of flight to a less dangerous one. The decrease in NM may be due to the fact that since the two circuits run parallel and very close one to the other, it can happen that a bird changes its altitude to cross M+ and stays at that height when crossing NM.

Corpses

During the study we gathered a total of 812 bird corpses belonging to 47 species under the lines. The number of corpses per sampling period varied between 24 in June 1998 and 138 in March 2000. The most common victims were members of the Heron (Ardeidae), Duck (Anatidae) and Rail (Rallidae) families with similar proportions (29, 25, 21%, respectively) these families included 75% of the corpses. The most commonly killed species were the Purple Gallinule, Black-crowned Night-Heron and Blue-winged Teal. A list of the victims is available upon request to the authors.

Before marking the line there was no significant difference in the mean number of corpses/ha between M+ and NM (10.3 vs. 6.2 corpses in M+ and NM, respectively; $n_1 = n_2 = 5$, $U = 9$, $p = 0.274$) while after marking the difference was significant (5.3 corpses in M+ vs. 13.6 in NM; $n_1 = n_2 = 3$, $U = 0$, $p = 0.05$) (Fig. 7).

Collision rates

Collision rates varied between 0.14% in January 2000 in M+ and 7.32% in January 1997 also in M+ (Table 1). In general the lowest rates of collision were registered after marking and the highest before the marking of M+ but values before marking were highly variable in both circuits. The high variability found in these results

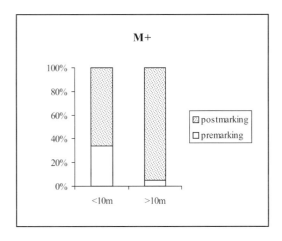
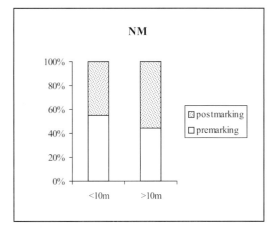

Fig. 5. Proportion of reactions that occurred at distance 1 (less than 10 m from the line) and at distance 2 (more than 10 m from the line) before and after marking the line. Santa Lucía, Atlántico, Colombia.

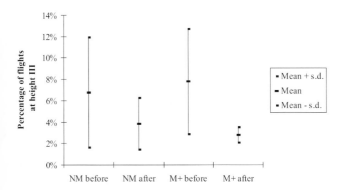

Fig. 6. Mean ± s.d. of the percentage of flights that occurred between the conductors and the ground wire in each sampling period before and after marking the line ($n = 5$ sampling periods before marking in NM, $n = 6$ sampling periods before marking in M+, $n = 3$ sampling periods after marking in NM and M+). Santa Lucía, Atlántico, Colombia.

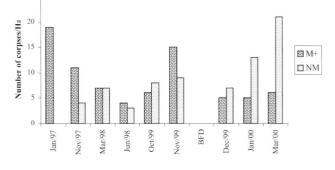

Fig. 7. Corpses per hectare found under the line in each sampling period. Santa Lucía, Atlántico, Colombia.

reflects changes in the factors taken into account in the calculations of the rates (# fresh corpses, # flights across the line, % searchable area, etc.); for example in January 2000 the combination of a very high number of flights with few fresh corpses gave low collision rates in both circuits.

1. Comparing immediately before and immediately after marking the line (November–December 1999).[1]
2. Comparing sampling periods one by one, to eliminate other sources of variation by involving more or less same type of birds, reproduction times and same weather conditions:
   – January 1997 vs. January 2000: The collision rate decreased dramatically after marking M+ (Table 1).
   – Even though the sampling periods were not carried on at exactly the same month, November 1997 and November 1999 can be compared to December 1999 and once again there is a decrease in the collision rates in M+ (60 and 50%), while in NM it increased as compared to November 1997 (29%) and had a small decrease as compared to November 1999 (10%) (Table 1).
   – For March 2000 rates for both circuits showed a small increase as compared to March 1998 (Table 1).
3. Mean collision rates. The mean of collision rates decreased in both circuits after marking the line and although it is not significant in either of them (Mann–Whitney, $p = 0.167$ for M+, $p = 0.57$ for NM), the difference is larger in M+ (Fig. 8).

For the calculations of the collision rates we used a 0.35% crippling bias obtained from 24 collisions observed during the different phases of this study.

CONCLUSIONS

The BFD installed in the 2nd circuit of the 500 kV line Chinú–Sabanalarga had a positive effect for the birds as shown by some of the results. It is evident that birds detected the line at a greater distance after the installation of the BFD. This is shown by the higher proportion of reactions farther from the line, the

---

[1] The collision rate right after marking the line decreased by half in M+ while in NM it decreased very slightly (Table 1).

Table 1. Collision rates for the 1st (1019-1020-1021, not marked NM) and 2nd (888-889-890, marked, M+) circuits in all sampling periods in Santa Lucía, Atlántico, Colombia

	Jan97	Nov97	Mar98	Jun98	Oct99	Nov99	BFD Dec99	Jan00	Mar00
M+	7.32%	0.82%	0.47%	0.18%	1.16%	0.70%	0.34%	0.14%	0.48%
NM	No data	0.48%	0.27%	0.29%	4.28%	0.74%	0.67%	0.16%	0.30%

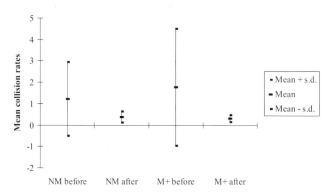

Fig. 8. Mean ± s.d. of collision rates registered before and after marking the line ($n = 5$ sampling periods before marking for NM, $n = 6$ sampling periods before marking for M+, $n = 3$ sampling periods after marking in both NM and M+). Santa Lucía, Atlántico, Colombia.

decrease in the number of flights at the most dangerous height and the increase in the rate of reactions in the marked circuit M+ right after the installation of the BFD. The number of corpses per hectare decreased significantly in M+ while it increased in NM; the collision rate decreased by half in M+ immediately after installing the BFD while in NM the decrease was very slight. In 2 out of 3 cases when comparing samples of the same time of the year before and after marking the line (one by one), the collision rate decreased strongly in M+ but not in NM.

After almost 4 years of study, a valuable contribution of the study is the development and adaptation of a methodology. There are some differences between studies carried on in the temperate zone and ours, such as the smaller number of flights, the greater number of corpses and therefore higher collision rates and the very high rate of removal of corpses under the line in the our study area. It was not previously suspected that a high proportion of the colliding birds are crepuscular or nocturnal. In the temperate zone seasonal variations are expected but it was a surprise to find such a high degree of seasonality in Colombia, and this emphasizes the need for long term studies even in "stable" environments. This study had other important aspects. It provided information for a region which previously had none; it was long enough so that different times of the year and different seasons of the bird life were covered, it covered all the different aspects (day and night flight counts, search of bodies and bias studies) recommended for studies of this type by Bevanger (1999). Also we were able to evaluate the effectiveness of the BFD by comparing data from before and after installation, and between marked and non marked circuits, and to identify the most vulnerable species in the area; these species are in general conspicuous and can be used as bio-indicators of highly dangerous places.

RECOMMENDATIONS

– When planning the lines, avoid vulnerable places with high concentrations of birds (wetlands, roosting-resting and feeding areas) (APLIC, 1994).
– Before installation of the lines, conduct studies to locate critical areas, type and number, movements and height of flight of the birds present.
– Identify the presence and abundance of bio-indicator species, vulnerable to collision according to the results of this study and the vulnerability list (Rosselli and De La Zerda, 1999).
– Given the potential of collision to have a major impact on some local bird populations, we think BFD's should be installed in every portion of every line located in critical areas. Prior to the installation, evaluation observations along long spans (since the flight routes are highly variable) of the line should be carried out. It is important to keep monitoring the collision rates in all cases.
– Even though the BFD used in this study were effective, the research that has been carried on in this field is very limited and therefore it is important to continue to evaluate other ways of marking the lines that may be more effective or less expensive.
– Wetlands have been identified as one of the most critical habitats for collision of birds but they are not the only one. It is important to keep studying the problem in other habitats (mountain ridges, local and latitudinal migratory routes and in general areas with high concentrations of birds) (APLIC, 1994).
– If the problem remains, mainly in areas were species of concern are present (endemic, endangered, etc.) there is a need to compensate by restoring or conserving nearby areas with similar habitat, ensuring that the losses of the populations maybe replaced.

ACKNOWLEDGEMENTS

We would like to thank Interconexión Eléctrica S.A. and specially the Environmental Department Team for their support and for giving us the opportunity to carry out these important series of studies. We thank all the biologists that worked in the field and Gary Stiles our general consultant. Thank you to Dean Mutrie and the 7th International Symposium on Environmental Concerns in Rights-of-Way Management for helping us to be able to attend the meeting and to the editors of the proceedings for their reviews and comments on the paper.

REFERENCES

Alonso, J.C., J.A. Alonso, and R. Muñoz-Pulido. 1994. Mitigation of bird collisions with transmission lines through groundwire marking. Biological Conservation, 77: 79–86.

Alonso, J.A. and J.C. Alonso. 1999. Mitigation of bird collisions with transmission lines through ground wire marking. In: Birds and Power Lines. M. Ferrer and G.F. Janss, eds. Quercus, Madrid, España. pp. 113–124.

Anderson, W.L. 1978. Waterfowl collisions with power lines at a coal-fired power plant. Wildlife Society Bulletin, 6: 77–83.

Avian Power Line Interaction Committee (APLIC). 1994. Mitigating bird collisions with power lines: The state of the art in 1994. Edison Electric Institute. Washington, DC.

Archibald, K. 1987. The conservation and status of the breeding of the Red Crowned Crane in Hokkaido, Japan. In: Proceedings of the 1983 International Crane Workshop. Bharatpur, India. pp. 63–86.

Beaulaurier, D.L. 1981. Mitigation of bird collisions with transmission lines. Prepared for Bonneville Power Administration, US Dept. of Energy, Portland, Oregon. 83 pp.

Bevanger, K. 1995. Tetraonid mortality caused by collisions with power lines in boreal forest habitats in central Norway. Fauna Norv. Ser. C, Cincus, 18: 41–51.

Bevanger, K.J. 1999. Estimating bird mortality caused by collision and electrocution with power lines; A review of methodology. pp. 29–56 in M.

Brown, W.M. and R.C. Drewien. 1995. Evaluation of two power line markers to reduce crane and waterfowl collision mortality. Wildlife Society Bulletin, 23: 217–227.

Brown, W.M., R.C. Drewien, and G. Bizeau. 1987. Mortality of cranes and waterfowl from power line collisions in the San Luis Valley, Colorado. In: Proceedings of the 4th Crane Workshop, 1985. Plate River Whooping Crane Habitat Maintenance Trust. pp. 128–135.

De La Zerda, S. and L. Rosselli. 1997. Efectos de las líneas de transmisión sobre la fauna colombiana. Interconexión Eléctrica S.A. Final Report. Medellín, Colombia. 156 pp.

De La Zerda, S. and L. Rosselli. 2000. Mitigación del efecto de colisión causado por líneas de alta tensión sobre aves de humedales. Interconexión Eléctrica S.A. Avifauna Ltda. Final Report. Medellín, Colombia. 51 pp.

Dedon, M., S. Byrne, J. Aycrigg, and P. Hartman. 1989. Bird mortality in relation to the Mare Island 115 kV transmission line: Progress report 1988/1989.

Ferrer and G.F. Janss, eds. Birds and Power Lines. Quercus, Madrid, Spain.

Brown, W.M. 1993. Marking power lines to reduce avian collision mortality in the San Luis Valley, Colorado. In: Proceedings of the International Workshops on Avian Interactions with Utility Structures, Miami.

Heijins, R. 1980. Bird mortality from collision with conductors for maximun tension. Ökologie der Vögel, 2: 111–129.

Hilty, S.L. and W.L. Brown. 1986. A Guide to the Birds of Colombia. Princeton University Press. 836 pp.

James, B.W. and A. Haak. 1979. Factors affecting avian flight behavior and collision mortality at transmission lines. BPA report, Portland, Oregon. pp. 1–108.

Janss, G.F.E. and M. Ferrer. 1998. Rate of bird collision with power lines: Effects of conductor-marking and static wire marking. Journal of Field Ornithology, 69: 8–17.

Koops, F.B.J. and J. De Jong. 1982. Verminderin van draadslachtoffers door markering van hoogspanningsleidingen in de omgeving van Heerenveen. Electrotechniek, 60: 641–646.

McNeil, R., J.R. Rodríguez, and H. Ouellet. 1985. Bird mortality at a power transmission line in northeastern Venezuela. Biological Conservation, 31: 153–165.

Meyer, J.R. 1978. Effects of transmission lines on bird flight behavior and collision mortality. BPA Report, Portland, OR. pp. 1–200.

Morkill, A.E. and S.H. Anderson. 1991a. Aviation marker balls deter Sandhill Cranes from collisions with a transmission line on the Platte River, Nebraska. Prairie Naturalist, 23: 177–178.

Morkill, A.E. and S.H. Anderson. 1991b. Effectiveness of marking powerlines to reduce Sandhill Crane collisions. Wildlife Society Bulletin, 19: 442–449.

Morkill, A.E. and S.H. Anderson. 1993. Effectiveness of yellow aviation balls in reducing Sandhill Crane collisions with powerlines. In: Proceedings of the International Workshops on Avian Interactions with Utility Structures, Miami.

Palacios, S. 1998. Estimación de la densidad de cinco especies de aves (*Nycticorax nycticorax*, Dendrocygna spp. (*D. bicolor, D. viduata, D. autumnalis*), *Porphyrula martinica*) vulnerables a colisión con líneas de transmisión eléctrica en la zona cenagosa del bajo Magdalena en la Costa Caribe Colombiana. Tesis. Universidad de los Andes. Bogotá. Contrato ABO-ISA.

Raevel, P. and J.C. Tombal. 1991. Impact des Lignes Haute-Tension sur l'avifaune. Les Cahiers de L'A.M.B.E., Francia.

Rosselli, L. and S. De La Zerda. 1996. Avifauna colombiana y líneas de transmisión. Vulnerabilidad, amenazas, recomendaciones y revisión de literatura pertinente. Ministerio del Medio Ambiente, Dirección Ambiental Sectorial. Bogotá, Colombia. 150 pp.

Rosselli, L. and S. De La Zerda. 1999. Avifauna Colombiana y Líneas de Transmisión, Fase III. Interconexión Eléctrica S.A., Asociación Bogotana de Ornitología, Final Report. Medellín, Colombia. 202 pp.

Rusz, P.J., H.H. Prince, R.D. Rusz, and G.A. Dawson. 1986. Bird collisions with transmission lines near a power plant cooling pond. Wildlife Society Bulletin, 14: 441–444.

Savereno, A.J., L.A. Savereno, R. Boettcher, and S.M. Haig. 1996. Avian behavior and mortality at power lines in coastal South Carolina. Wildlife Society Bulletin, 2.

BIOGRAPHICAL SKETCHES

Susana De La Zerda (corresponding author)

Avifauna Ltda., Interconexión Eléctrica S.A. A.A.3751, Bogotá, Colombia, S.A., Fax: 571-285-4550, E-mail: sdelazerda@yahoo.com

Susana De La Zerda is a Colombian biologist with graduate studies in Ecology at the Hebrew University of Jerusalem in Israel and Master's degree in Wildlife Science from Virginia Tech. Since 1995 she has been working on the effect of transmission lines on birds on a series of projects sponsored by the Colombian Ministry of the Environment and ISA, the State Company in charge of energy transmission. She has attended several international courses in conservation biology and tropical ecology. She is a cofounder and active member of the Bogotá Ornithological Society and co-author of books on Colombian National Parks and Birds of the Sabana de Bogota.

Loreta Rosselli
Avifauna Ltda., Interconexión Eléctrica S.A., Dg. 109 No. 26-10, Bogotá, Colombia, S.A., E-mail: lrosselli @yahoo.com

Loreta Rosselli, born in Bogotá, Colombia, obtained her biologist degree from the Universidad de Los Andes in 1982 and her Master's degree from the Universidad de Costa Rica in 1989. She is a University professor in ornithology and has participated in several research projects in various Latin American countries. Besides the effect of transmission lines on Colombian birds other research interests include frugivory, bird behavior and conservation. She is a cofounder and active member of the Bogotá Ornithological Society. She translated to Spanish the Guide of Birds of Costa Rica and is co-author of the Birds of the Sabana de Bogotá.

Relationships Between Wing Morphology and Behavioral Responses to Unmarked Power Transmission Lines

Michael R. Crowder and Olin E. Rhodes, Jr.

Ground wires associated with high voltage power transmission lines have been identified as a source of mortality for numerous avian species. This research was conducted at the Cinergy-PSI Gibson County Power Generating Station in Gibson County, IN, USA. This site is characterized by a high density of power transmission lines with a 1214-ha cooling lake and numerous small wetlands in close proximity. Large numbers of waterfowl and other wetland-associated avian species utilize this area in the fall and winter. Bird flight observations were conducted along with corresponding ground searches to determine the species specific reactions of birds to the power lines. The birds most likely to react to power lines were those that approached the lines at a height between the conductor and ground wires. No relationship between flock size and the proportion of birds reacting to the lines was found; however, a significant difference was found in the reaction distances between flocks >10 birds and single birds. Species were grouped into four categories according to wing morphology, and it was determined that species at the greatest risk for collisions were those that showed high wing loading and low wing aspect ratio.

Keywords: Birds, collisions, ground wires, observations, power lines

INTRODUCTION

Avian mortality associated with power line strikes has been well documented with numerous studies on the effects of power line related mortality on avian species (Willard et al., 1977; Anderson, 1978; Meyer, 1978; James and Haak, 1979; Faanes, 1987; Bevanger, 1995). In addition, numerous power line ground wire marking studies have been conducted to test the effectiveness of marking devices in reducing avian collisions (Alonso et al., 1994; Brown and Drewien, 1995; Savereno et al., 1996; Janss and Ferrer, 1998). Utility companies are concerned about this issue for two major reasons: (1) collisions kill thousands of birds each year that are protected by the Migratory Bird Treaty Act and related treaties, and (2) reliability of service to their customers can be compromised by bird strikes.

Environmental Concerns in Rights-of-Way
Management: Seventh International Symposium
J.W. Goodrich-Mahoney, D.F. Mutrie and C.A. Guild (editors)
© 2002 Elsevier Science Ltd. All rights reserved.

Due to a more competitive deregulated market system, power utilities companies are anxious to alleviate problems that could create poor public relations or compromise service to their customers. Utilities that do not correct collision hazards promptly could at worst face large fines and/or imprisonment of company employees, or at least face bad publicity in the local media. For example, the Moon Lake Electric Association was required to pay $100,000 in penalties, to retrofit poles to make them bird friendly, and to serve 3 years probation for the electrocution of 170 raptors, mostly Golden Eagles (*Aquila chrysaetos*; Williams, 2000). Research on bird reactions to power lines could help design future power grids that reduce collision probabilities; this will better serve the customer by a reduced risk of interruptions, and better serve the company through lower risks of negative publicity.

Previous research has shown that characteristics such as normal flight altitude and flock size can influence the frequency of power line strikes by birds. The size of a bird and its wing shape and morphology also can play an important role in determining the susceptibility of avian species to power line strikes. Rayner

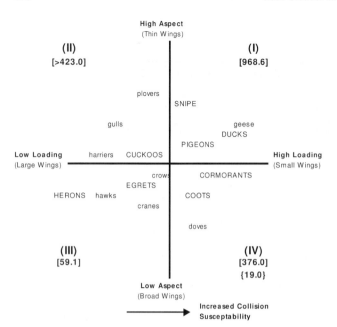

Fig. 1. Groups of birds that interacted with power lines on our study site arranged according to wing morphology expressed in principal component form where statistically independent measures of size and wing proportions are derived (modified from Bevanger 1998, after Rayner 1988).

(1988) used principal component analysis (PCA) applied to wing morphology to derive statistically independent measures of wing size and wing proportions. Variables based on wing loading (i.e., ratio of body weight to wing area), wing aspect ratio (i.e., ratio of wing span^2 to wing area), and body weights of avian species were used in PCA. A scatterplot was then constructed of the size independent components of wing aspect and wing loading for a large number of avian species (Fig. 1, after Bevanger, 1998 from Rayner, 1988).

Using the information generated by Rayner (1988), Bevanger (1994, 1998) compared known "collision species" from 16 previous studies on avian power line collisions (Scott et al., 1972; McKenna and Allard, 1976; Anderson, 1978; Meyer, 1978; Gylstorff, 1979; Christensen, 1980; Grosse, et al., 1980; Heijnis, 1980; Willdan, Associates, 1982; Longridge, 1986; Rusz et al., 1986; Bevanger, 1988; Thingstad, 1989; Hartman et al., 1992; Bevanger, 1993; Bevanger and Sandaker, 1993) to species categorized as having high wing loading and found an interesting relationship. In general, as the wing loading of a bird increases, so does its susceptibility to collisions with power lines. Alternatively, as a bird's wing aspect ratio decreases, so does its susceptibility to collisions.

In theory, birds that are most susceptible to wire strikes are those with high wing loading (e.g., small wings for its body size) and low wing aspect ratio (e.g., broad wings; Fig. 1, Quadrant IV). This group includes Rayner's (1988) "poor" fliers, which contains many birds in the orders of Galliformes (e.g., grouse and quail) and Gruiformes (e.g., rails and cranes). Rayner (1988) points out that birds in Quadrant IV (Fig. 1) have few favorable aspects of flight performance and have probably never faced serious pressure to improve sustained flight performance. Many of these species are ground dwelling birds that use flight only for rapid escape.

Our objectives in this research were to: (1) document collision mortality through direct observation and ground searches, (2) describe the relationship between wing morphology (after Bevanger 1998) and collision mortality, and (3) determine whether the frequency at which birds reacted to power lines or the distances at which they reacted are influenced by flock size or wing morphology.

METHODS

Study area

This research was conducted on unmarked power transmission lines during the fall and early winter of 1999–2000. The study site was the Cinergy-PSI Gibson County Power Generating Station which sits on the edge of the Wabash River in southwest Indiana. This area attracts numerous avian species because of its close proximity to the river and the 1214-ha Gibson Lake and associated wetlands. Gibson Lake is a manmade, elevated lake that is the source of the cooling water for the Gibson plant site. The lake stays warm and open all year. Large numbers of waterfowl and other wetland-related species are attracted to this area in the fall and winter during migration south, especially at times when other lakes and wetlands in the area are frozen. At one point in the study, 27 January 2000, nearly 41,000 birds were counted on the lake and associated wetlands, with the vast majority of the birds being waterfowl (Anseriformes) species. This area serves as a good model for study of bird reactions to power lines, not only because of the large numbers of birds present, but also due to the presence of several transmission lines situated over the wetland complex. Three specific locations were used for behavioral observations and dead bird searches near the power plant, these lines were named the Gibson Line, the High Line, and the Flooded Timber Line.

Field observations

To examine the relationship between wing morphology and behavioral responses to unmarked power lines, observational data were collected a minimum of once per week from 27 September 1999 to 13 December 1999. Behavior response data included the physical reactions (if any) of birds to the power lines (for categories see Appendix 1) and the relative distances at which birds reacted to the power lines. As suggested by the Avian Power Line Interaction Committee (APLIC 1994), additional data collected for each power line over-flight included flock size, species, flight direction, and altitude during approach, crossing, and departure from the lines. Data also were collected on human activity at the study site along with wind speed, wind direction, temperature, light intensity, cloud cover, precipitation, visibility, and line corona noise (in 0.5 h intervals; Appendix 1).

Bird flight observational periods lasted a minimum of 2.5 h. Observational data were collected with the aid of 7 × 50 light gathering binoculars from the cover of a ground blind strategically placed to have clear sight of all lines being recorded. When observing lines that had no ground blind in place, researchers observed from existing ground cover so as not to disturb passing birds. Power line spans were chosen for observation on the basis of location (transmission lines ran over water commonly used by waterfowl and other wetland related species) and degree of bird activity in the area. The specific line selected for flight observation was chosen daily so as to achieve the greatest flight intensities in the allotted time period. Because of difficulties in identification of many Passerines, they were grouped into 1 category with the exception of the American Crow (*Corvus brachyrhynchos*).

Dead bird searches

Following each behavioral observation period from 27 September 1999 to 13 December 1999, two of the three focal transmission lines were searched for dead birds or feather piles regardless of the focal line observed that day. Ground searches were also conducted from 22 December 1999 to 1 April 2000, but were not included in over-flight/kill data. The Flooded Timber Line was not searched for dead birds due to underlying water. Areas under lines that were not submerged were searched in a slow zigzag fashion so as to maximize coverage of the search zones. Search zones were minimally the width of the right-of-way, but if water conditions permitted, as during the fall and winter of 1999–2000, most areas were searched up to 50 m beyond the outer edge of the lines. All birds and feather piles found were removed or clearly marked to avoid duplicate counting. Unknown birds were marked and bagged for later identification. It was assumed that all crippled or dead birds and feather piles found under the lines were collision mortalities. There was no hunting allowed in this area and admittance was restricted to researchers and plant personnel.

Using the results of PCA based on wing morphology (Rayner 1988), we classified birds into four quadrants, based on size adjusted variables representing wing loading and wing aspect (Fig. 1). Using data from power line observations and ground searches, we calculated the number of over-flights/kill for each species and compared these data among quadrants. This was accomplished by dividing the total number of over-flights in each quadrant by the number of dead birds found in each quadrant after the initial dead bird searches were conducted.

No statistical analyses were performed to compare numbers of over-flights/kill among quadrants. This decision was made on the basis that two potential biases might exist in the dead bird search data set. First, the dead bird searches may be biased if searches resulted in the detection of a higher percentage of larger birds than of smaller birds. Larger birds are easier to find and collect than smaller ones, and previous removal bias studies indicate that smaller birds are often removed faster by predators than larger ones (Raevel and Tombal, 1991; Brown and Drewien, 1995). Thus, weekly dead bird searches might incorrectly lead to the conclusion that larger bird species strike the power lines relatively more frequently than actually is the case. Our second potential bias in the calculation of numbers of over-flights/kill is related to the fact that the over-flight data and the dead bird searches are not precisely matched. The fact that the Flooded Timber Line could be observed but not searched as well as the fact that only one line could be observed at a time, means that the observational data may not always reflect the intensity of over-flights that produced the observed mortalities.

Behavioral responses

Only data from non-Passerine species approaching the power lines at 10m above the ground wires or below were included in analyses of behavioral responses. Variables were defined for analysis in the following manner. We defined the distance at which birds reacted to the lines (if a reaction was recorded) in a continuous manner [i.e., reaction distance: (1) 0–5 m, (2) 6–10 m, (3) 11–25 m, (4) 26–45 m, and (5) >45 m]. We defined all recorded bird reactions to the lines in a bivariate manner such that the birds were classified as either having reacted to the line (i.e., collision, near collision, flare, altitude change, abort, direction change, flutter, or landed) or no reaction was recorded (Reaction; Yes or No). We recorded flock sizes of birds that reacted to the lines as a discrete variable [i.e., flock size: (1) 1 bird, (2) 2–5 birds, (3) 6–10 birds, and (4) >10 birds]. We classified birds into 4 groups, with differing expected susceptibilities to power line strikes, based on a plot of principle component scores for wing aspect and loading (Quadrant: I, II, III, or IV, after Rayner 1988, Fig. 1). We defined the altitude at which birds approached the power lines as a discrete variable with three classes [Approach: (1) ground to conductor height, (2) conductor to ground wire, and (3) <10 meters above ground wires].

Data analyses were performed using subroutines in the Statistical Analysis System (SAS; 1989) and all statistical tests were considered significant at a probability value of 0.05 (unless corrected for multiple comparisons). We used Contingency Chi Squared statistics to test the hypothesis that birds approaching the power lines at different altitudes (Approach) did not differ in the frequency with which they reacted (Reaction) to the line. We also used Contingency Chi Squared statistics to test the hypotheses that the frequency at which birds reacted to the lines was independent of Flock Size and Quadrant. We used general linear models to test the hypotheses that the mean distances (Reaction Distance) at which birds reacted to the power line did not differ in regard to either Flock Size or Quadrant. If the main effect of Flock Size or Quadrant was found to account for a significant proportion of the total variance, a means separation test corrected for multiple comparisons using the Dunn-Sidak correction was used to test for differences among mean values of Reaction Distance.

RESULTS

Collisions

During the course of this investigation, we observed and recorded a minimum of 33 species of birds interacting with three transmission lines on the Gibson County Power Generating Station study site with a total of 36,327 over-flights including Passerine species, and a total of 7993 over-flights of non-Passerine species. During a total of 47.5 hours of observation, there were three instances in which bird collisions with conductors or overhead ground wires were observed.

A total of five collisions were observed during bird flight observations in three separate instances. These collisions involved four Mallards (*Anas platyrhynchos*) and one Double-crested Cormorant (*Phalacrocorax auritus*). The first instance involved a single Double-crested Cormorant flying north at an altitude between the conductor and ground wires of the Gibson Line at 0755 h on 9 September 1999. The bird reacted to the line less that 5 m from the edge of the conductors, flared away from the lines, and struck the ground wire in the process. It fell down to the water and swam over to a nearby group of three other cormorants. The bird was observed for over 30 min before it flew away, exhibiting no ill effects from the collision. The wind was calm at the time of the collision (10.1 km/h) with good visibility.

On 10 November 1999, at approximately 1730 h, a flock of three Mallards were flying north at an altitude between the conductor and ground wires when 1 hen struck the ground wire of the Gibson Line and flew off apparently unharmed. The light intensity was low (23 lux) with a wind speed of 7.5 km/h. Finally, on 13 December 1999, at 0930 h, a group of approximately 400 Mallards were feeding in the water under the Flooded Timber Line when a truck moving up the levee of Gibson Lake, which is adjacent to this area, flushed the birds. In the confusion, two birds struck the ground wires and one struck the conductor itself. All three birds flew off, apparently unharmed.

Dead bird searches

A total of 48 crippled birds, dead birds, or feather piles, representing 14 species, were found under the power lines during ground searches. Of these, 20 birds were found and identified on the initial power line searches and 13 birds were found after bird flight observations were stopped, leaving only 15 birds that were included in the calculation of over-flights/kill (Table 1). Over-flights/kill ranged from 423/0 in Quadrant II to 59.1/1 in Quadrant III (Fig. 1).

Behavioral responses

Our analysis indicated that the proportions of birds that reacted to the power lines were not independent of the altitude at which they approached the power line ($\chi^2 = 253$, 2 df, $P < 0.001$, $N = 725$). Birds approaching the power lines at an altitude between the conductor and ground wires were much more likely to react (66.5% reacting) than were birds below the conductor height (13.5% reacting) or <10 m above the ground wires (4% reacting, Table 2). In addition, our analysis indicated that the proportions of birds reacting to the power lines were not independent of the structural wing morphology (Quadrant) of the bird species represented on our study area ($\chi^2 = 14$, 3 df, $P < 0.002$, $N = 734$). Birds with high wing loading (Quadrants I and IV; 25.5% and 28% reacting, respectively) were about twice as likely to react to the power lines as birds with low wing loading (Quadrants II and III; 15% and 14% reacting, respectively; Table 2) regardless of wing aspect. We detected no relationship between flock size and the proportions of birds reacting to the power lines ($\chi^2 = 0.47$, 3 df, $P < 0.93$, $N = 731$; Table 2).

Our analysis of the relationship between reaction distance and flock size indicated that there were significant differences in mean reaction distances of birds traveling in different sized groups ($F = 2.7$, 3 df, $P = 0.048$, $N = 146$). Further analysis of differences among mean values indicated that birds traveling in groups of >10 individuals reacted to the power lines at a greater distance ($\bar{x} = 3.08$; ~11.2 m away from outer ground wire) than did birds traveling alone ($\bar{x} = 2.24$; ~6.96 m away from outer ground wire; Table 3). Our analysis of the relationship between reaction distance and structural wing morphology (Quadrant) indicated that there were significant differences in mean reaction distances of birds with differing wing loading and aspect characteristics ($F = 4.84$, 3 df, $P = 0.0031$, $N = 147$). Further analysis of differences among mean values indicated that birds with the highest aspect and highest wing loading factors (Quadrant I) reacted to the power lines at a greater distance ($\bar{x} = 2.59$; ~8.36 m away from outer ground wire) than did birds with the lowest aspect and highest wing loading factors (Quadrant IV; $\bar{x} = 1.71$, ~3.55 m away from ground wire; Table 3).

Table 1. Totals for dead bird searches and over-flight data for the Gibson County Power Generation Station study site for 1999–2000

Species	Scientific name	Total number of birds found	Number of dead birds included[a]	Number of over flights[b]	Quadrant[c]
American Bittern	*Bothaurus lentiginosus*			7	3
American Black Duck	*Anas rubripes*	3	2	15	1
American Coot	*Fulica americana*	3	1	1	4
American Crow	*Corvus brachyrhynchos*			98	3
American Wigeon	*Anas americana*			12	1
American Woodcock	*Scolopax minor*			1	1
Black-crowned Night-Heron	*Nycticorax nycticorax*	1	1	0	3
Blue-winged Teal	*Anas discors*			12	1
Canada Goose	*Branta canadensis*			117	1
Common Goldeneye	*Bucephala clangula*			3	1
Common Snipe	*Gallinago gallinago*	1		3	1
Double-crested Cormorant	*Phalacrocorax auritus*	4		18	4
Gadwall	*Anas strepera*	2	2	107	1
Great Blue Heron	*Ardea herodias*	7	5	194	3
Great Egret	*Ardea alba*	10	1	112	3
Green-winged Teal	*Anas crecca*			19	1
Hooded Merganser	*Lophodytes cucullatus*			181	1
Killdeer	*Charadrius vociferus*			62	2
Lesser Scaup	*Aythya affinis*			1	1
Mallard	*Anas platyrhynchos*	6	1	5918	1
Mourning Dove	*Zenaida macroura*			357	4
Northern Harrier	*Circus cyaneus*			3	2
Northern Pintail	*Anas acuta*			30	1
Northern Shoveler	*Anas clypeata*	2	1	20	1
Red-winged Blackbird	*Agelaius phoeniceus*	3			
Ring-billed Gull	*Larus delawarensis*			300	2
Rock Dove	*Columba livia*	1	1	3	1
Sandhill Crane	*Grus canadensis*			1	3
Snow Goose	*Chen caerulescens*			29	1
Wood Duck	*Aix sponsa*	1		309	1
Yellow-billed Cuckoo	*Coccyzus americanus*	2		0	2
Raptorial spp.				2	3
Shorebird spp.				58	2
Unknown		2			
Totals		48	15	7993	

[a] Total number of dead birds found minus the birds found on initial searches, and birds found after bird flight observations had stopped.
[b] The total number of over-flights did not include Passeriformes species.
[c] From Fig. 1.

DISCUSSION

Avian collisions with power lines are relatively rare events, with the majority of strikes occurring during low light conditions or inclement weather. Anderson (1978), in a study of avian interactions with power lines in central Illinois, estimated that one collision occurred for every 250,000 over-flights and stated that waterfowl almost never collide with power lines during daylight hours when visibility is good. Our data indicate that the total rate of collision for non-Passerine species on the Gibson County Power Generating Plant site in southern Indiana is much higher than would be predicted from Anderson's work. In fact, our observation of five collisions with power lines in only 7993 over-flights is among the higher reported collision rates. However, it should be noted that three of the strikes we observed were a result of non-researcher human disturbance.

Bevanger (1998) predicted that the birds that were most susceptible to collisions with power transmission lines were "high risk" species with high wing loading and low wing aspect characteristics (Quadrant IV), and that the birds that were least susceptible to collisions were those with low wing loading and high wing aspect characteristics (Quadrant II; Fig. 1). Our estimates of the number of over-flights/kill for these quadrants fit this prediction well, although the lowest number of over-flights per kill was actually observed in Quadrant III. However, if Mourning Doves (*Zenaida macroura*), with strong flying abilities compared to other Quadrant IV species, are omitted from the calculations in Quadrant IV, the average number of over-flights/kill drops to 19.0, by far the lowest observed. Alternatively, there were 423 over-flights in Quadrant II with no dead birds found, indicating, as expected, that this quadrant experiences little collision mortality. In general, our data on number of

Table 2. The number and proportion of birds that reacted to power lines by approach altitude class [(1) below conductor height; (2) between conductor and ground wires; (3) <10 m above the ground wires], flock size group, and quadrant (quadrants based on wing morphology from Fig. 1)

	Altitude class		
	1	2	3
Yes	37	101	12
%	13.45	66.45	4.03
No	238	51	286
%	86.55	33.55	95.97

	Flock size			
	1	2–5	6–10	>10
Yes	77	49	10	13
%	19.74	20.68	20.41	23.64
No	313	188	39	42
%	80.26	79.32	79.59	76.36

	Quadrant			
	I	II	III	IV
Yes	85	99	251	50
%	24.45	15.15	14.34	28.00
No	249	84	215	36
%	74.55	84.85	85.66	72.00

Table 3. Mean values for bird reaction distance from the power lines for each flock size group and quadrant (quadrants based on wing morphology from Fig. 1)

	Flock size			
	1	2–5	6–10	>10
$\bar{x}$	2.24	2.25	2.40	3.08
SE	0.11	0.15	0.31	0.38
n	76	48	10	13

	Quadrant			
	I	II	III	IV
$\bar{x}$	2.59	2.07	2.08	1.71
SE	0.11	0.23	0.16	0.27
N	83	15	36	14

over-flights per kill indicate that as wing aspect decreases (e.g., become broader) collision mortality increases.

Our data on distances at which birds react to power lines support the general trends observed in the over-flight per kill data, specifically for those birds in Quadrants representing high wing loading. Of birds that have high wing loading values (i.e., species found in Quadrants I and IV) average reaction distances are significantly smaller for those species showing low wing aspect (Quadrant IV) as opposed to species showing high wing aspect (Quadrant I). This finding strengthens the conclusion that birds with low wing aspect and high wing loading are "poor" fliers relative to species with other wing morphologies and may have a higher probability of experiencing collision mortality than most other species. Additionally, the data on how frequently birds with differing wing morphologies react to power lines suggests that regardless of wing aspect, birds with high wing loading values may be almost twice as likely to react to power lines as those with low wing loading values.

Flock size has long been recognized as a factor influencing the probability of avian interactions with power lines and has been cited as a factor that can lead to collisions due to reduced visibility of trailing birds in a flock (Scott et al., 1972; James and Haak, 1979). Our data show no statistical relationship between flock size and the proportion of birds that reacted to the power lines. Thus, the frequency at which single birds reacted to the power lines was not different from the frequency of reaction by larger groups of birds. However, for those birds that did react to the power lines, we found that the mean distance at which flocks of >10 birds reacted to the power line ($\bar{x} = 3.08$; ~11.2 m away from outer ground wire), was significantly greater than the distance at which solitary birds reacted to the lines ($\bar{x} = 2.24$; ~6.96 m away from outer ground wire). While this finding seems logical, in that the more eyes there are in a flock scanning for obstacles the faster a flock could react to power lines or other objects that are in their way, it does not rule out the possibility that the trailing birds in large flocks may have a higher risk of power line collision than would single birds. Unfortunately, our data are insufficient to test that particular hypothesis.

CONCLUSION

We recorded a total of 7993 power line over-flights representing over 33 non-Passerine avian species during 47.5 h of power line observations at the Gibson County Power Generating Station. Fifteen birds were found during ground searches under the focal power lines after bird flight observation periods. Five avian collisions were observed during observational periods involving four Mallards and one Double-crested Cormorant. The number of crossings per collision observed during this study was much lower than those reported by other researchers, suggesting that there is a potential problem with strike mortality at this site.

Birds most likely to react to power lines are those that approach power lines between the conductor and ground wires, as opposed to under the conductor or <10 m above the ground wires. This would indicate that birds approaching power lines near the height of the wire are likely to perceive the lines and react to avoid them. There was no relationship found between flock size and the proportion of birds reacting to the lines; however, birds in flocks >10 reacted to power lines at greater distances that did solitary birds.

Our data suggest that the avian species that are at the greatest risk for collision mortality are those with high wing loading and low wing aspect. In addition, species with high wing loading were nearly twice as likely to react to power lines than were birds with lower wing loading characteristics, although species with high wing loading and high wing aspect react to the lines at greater distances than do species with high wing loading and low wing aspect.

ACKNOWLEDGEMENTS

We would like to acknowledge and thank Cinergy-PSI and Purdue University for funding of this project. We also thank Cinergy-PSI for access to their property to conduct this research, they were helpful in every way possible. We especially thank Mr. Tim Hayes of Cinergy-PSI for all his help in locating and gaining access to study sites. We acknowledge W. McCoy and R. Dodd of the Patoka River National Wildlife Refuge for help in waterfowl surveys. Thanks also go out to R.E. Gregg, R.N. Williams, E.K. Latch, and J.B. Dunning, Jr. for assistance with the literature search and reviews of the manuscript.

APPENDIX 1 — KEY OF TERMS

Wind Speed = The speed of the wind in the survey area, given in km/h.

Temperature = Temperature of the survey area at the start of the survey given in °C.

Cloud Cover = The estimated percent cloud cover at the start of the survey period.
- Clear = C = Less than 10% cloud cover.
- Scattered = S = Cloud cover from 10–50%.
- Broken = B = Cloud cover from 5–90%.
- Overcast = O = Cloud cover >90%.

Light Intensity = The intensity of the light on the study area, given in lumens.

Wind Direction = The direction from which the wind is coming.
- North = N
- South-West = SW
- Etc.

Precipitation = Type of precipitation on the survey area (if any).

Visibility = Visibility in the area in relation to distances due to fog or precipitation.
- Class 1 = Visibility > one km.
- Class 2 = Visibility between 1/2 and one km.
- Class 3 = Visibility between 1/4 and 1/2 km.
- Class 4 = Visibility < 1/4 km.

Line Noise = The amount of corona noise due to the power lines. Given as:
- Quiet
- Light
- Moderate
- Loud

Flight Direction = Flight direction of birds given as:
- North = N
- South = S
- Etc.

Altitude Classes (Approach, Crossing, and Departure) = The height of the birds being surveyed in relation to the power lines. Given as:
- Class 1 = Area between the ground and the conductor.
- Class 2 = Area between the conductor and the ground wire.
- Class 3 = Area between the ground wire and 10 m above the ground wire.
- Class 4 = Area between 10 and 50 m above the ground wire.
- Class 5 = Area above 50 m above the ground wire.

Reaction of Birds to Line = The reaction of birds to lines as they near them. Given as:
- Collisions = C = Collisions of birds with power lines and ground wires.
- Near-Collisions = NC = Birds narrowly missing the power lines and ground wires.
- Flares = F = A severe flight reaction as a bird or flock nears a power line and ground wires.
- Aborts = A = Birds turning 180° in response to power lines and ground wires.
- Altitude Change = AC = The change in altitude by a bird or flock in response to power lines and ground wires.
- Direction Change = DC = The change in direction by a bird or flock in response to power lines and ground wires.
- Flutters = FLT = A flight reaction of birds to the power lines or ground wires less severe than a flare.
- Landing on Power Lines = L = Birds landing on power lines or ground wires.

Reaction Zone = The distance in which the bird reacted to the power line and ground wire. Given as:
- Class 1 = Area between the wires and 5 m away from the wires.
- Class 2 = Area between 6 and 10 m away from the wires.
- Class 3 = Area between 10 and 25 m away from the wires.
- Class 4 = Area between 25 and 45 m away from the wires.
- Class 5 = Area greater than 45 meters away from the wires.

REFERENCES

Alonso, J.C., J.A. Alonso, and R. Munoz-Pulido. 1994. Mitigation of bird collisions with transmission lines through ground wire marking. Biological Conservation, 67: 129–134.

Anderson, W.L. 1978. Waterfowl collisions with power lines at a coal-fired power plant. Wildlife Society Bulletin, 6(2): 77–83.

Avian Power Line Interaction Committee (APLIC). 1994. Mitigating bird collisions with power lines: The state of the art in 1994. Edison Electric Institute. Washington, DC.

Bevanger, K. 1988. Transmission line wire strikes of capercaillie and Black Grouse in Central Norwegian coniferous forest. Økoforsk Rapport, 9: 1–53.

Bevanger, K. 1993. Bird collisions with a 220 kV transmission line in Polmak, Finnmark. NINA Forskningsrapport, 40: 1–26.

Bevanger, K. and O. Sandaker. 1993. Power lines as a mortality factor for willow grouse in Hemsedal. NINA Oppdragsmelding, 193: 1–25.

Bevanger, K. 1994. Bird interactions with utility structures: Collision and electrocution, causes and mitigation measures. Ibis, 136: 412–425.

Bevanger, K. 1995. Estimates and population consequences of tetraonid mortality caused by collisions with high tension power lines in Norway. Journal of Applied Ecology, 32: 745–753.

Bevanger, K. 1998. Biological and conservation aspects of bird mortality caused by electricity power lines: A review. Biological Conservation, 86: 67–76.

Brown, W.M. and R.C. Drewien. 1995. Evaluation of two power line markers to reduce crane and waterfowl collision mortality. Wildlife Society Bulletin, 23(2): 217–227.

Christensen, H. 1980. Undersøgelser over fuglekollisioner mod højspÅœndingsledninger gennem det naturvidenskabelige reservat Vejlerne-efteråret 1979. Report to The Museum of Natural History, Arhus. pp. 1–25.

Faanes, C.A. 1987. Bird behavior and mortality in relation to power lines in prairie habitats. US Fish and Wildlife Service General Technical Report 7. pp. 1–24.

Grosse, H., W. Sykora, and R. Steinbach. 1980. Eine 220-kV-Hochspannungstrasse im Über-spannungsgebiet der Talsperre Windischleuba war Vogelfalle. Falke, 27: 247–248.

Gylstorff, N.H. 1979. Fugles kollisioner med elledninger. MS thesis, University of Arhus.

Hartman, P.A., S. Byrne, and M.F. Dedon. 1992. Bird mortality in relation to the Mare Island 115-kV transmission line: Final report 1988–1991. Department of Navy, Western Division, California PG and E Report 443-91.3.

Heijnis, R. 1980. Vogeltod durch Drahtanflüge bei Hochspannungs-leitungen. Ökologie der Vögel. Sonderheft, 2: 111–129.

James, B.W. and B.A. Haak. 1979. Factors affecting avian flight behavior and collision mortality at transmission lines. Bonneville Power Administration, US Department of Energy, Portland, OR. pp. 1–109.

Janss, G.F.E. and M. Ferrer. 1998. Rate of bird collision with power lines: Effects of conductor-marking and static wire-marking. Journal of Field Ornithology, 69(1): 8–17.

Longridge, M.W. 1986. The impacts of transmission lines on bird flight behavior, with reference to collision mortality and systems reliability. Bird Research Community, ESCOM, Johannesburg. pp. 1–279.

McKenna, M.G. and G.E. Allard. 1976. Avian mortality from wire collision. North Dakota Outdoors, 39(5): 16–18.

Meyer, J.R. 1978. Effects of transmission lines on bird flight behavior and collision mortality. Prepared for Bonneville Power Administration, US Department of Energy, Portland, OR. pp. 1–200.

Raevel, P. and J.C. Tombal. 1991. Impact des lignes haute-tension sur l'avi faune. Les Cahiers de L'A.M.B.E. et Environnement, Vol. 2. pp. 1–31.

Rayner, J.M.V. 1988. Form and Function in Avian Flight. In: Current Ornithology, Vol. 5. R.F. Johnston, ed. Plenum, New York. pp. 1–66.

Rusz, P.J., H.H. Prince, R.D. Rusz, and G.A. Dawson. 1986. Bird collisions with transmission lines near a power plant cooling pond. Wildlife Society Bulletin, 14: 441–444.

SAS Institute Inc. 1989. SAS/STAT User's Guide, Version 6, 4th ed. Cary NC: SAS Institute Inc. pp. 1–943.

Savereno, A.J., L.A. Savereno, R. Boettcher, and S.M. Haig. 1996. Avian behavior and mortality at power lines in coastal South Carolina. Wildlife Society Bulletin, 24(4): 636–648.

Scott, R.E., L.J. Roberts, and C.J. Cadbury. 1972. Bird deaths from power lines at Dungeness. British Birds, 65: 273–286.

Thingstad, P.G. 1989. Kraftledning/fugl-problematikk i Grunnfjorden naturreservat, Øksnes kommune, Nordland. Universitetet i Trondheim, Vitenskapsmuseet. Zoologisk avdeling. Notat, 2: 1–26.

Willard, D.E., J.T. Harris, and M.J. Jaeger. 1977. The impacts of a proposed 500 kV transmission route on waterfowl and other birds, A Report for the Public Utility Commissioner of the State of Oregon. Salem, OR. pp. 1–89.

Willdan Associates. 1982. Impacts of the Ashe-Slatt 500 kV transmission line on birds at Crow Butte Island: Postconstruction study final report. Prepared for the Bonneville Power Administration Report, US Department of Energy, Portland, OR. pp. 1–155.

Williams, T. 2000. Zapped. Audubon, Jan.–Feb.: 32–44.

BIOGRAPHICAL SKETCHES

Michael Crowder

The Barker Ranch Ltd., 85305 Snively Road, West Richland, WA 99353. 509-967-3023. gdbarker@gte.net (at the time the paper was presented) Purdue University, Department of Forestry and Natural Resources, 1159 Forestry Building, West Lafayette, IN 47907

Michael Crowder was a graduate research assistant in the Department of Forestry and Natural Resources at Purdue University working under Dr. Olin E. Rhodes, Jr. He completed his MS degree in Wildlife Science during the fall of 2000, and was the field researcher on this project. Michael received an AS degree from Vincennes University during the spring of 1996 in Natural Resources and Environmental Science and went on to complete a BS degree in Natural Resources and Environmental Science at Purdue University in the spring of 1998. He has worked on previous research projects for Vincennes University, Purdue University, Cinergy-PSI, Eli Lilly Corp, and the Delta Waterfowl Research Foundation.

Dr. Olin E. Rhodes, Jr.

Purdue University, Department of Forestry and Natural Resources, 1159 Forestry Building, West Lafayette, IN 47907

Dr. Rhodes is an Associate Professor of wildlife ecology in the Department of Forestry and Natural Resources at Purdue University. He received his BS in Biology from Furman University in 1983, his MS in wildlife biology from Clemson University in 1986, and his PhD in wildlife ecology from Texas Tech University in 1991. Dr. Rhodes has active research programs in wildlife genetics, genotoxicology, and wildlife ecology, and has published over 50 articles in the scientific literature.

Developing a Species at Risk Conservation Plan: The Thicksilver Pipeline Experience

Alan J. Kennedy

The development of the recent Canadian Species at Risk Act, as well as Alberta government initiatives to protect sensitive plant and animal species, has accentuated the need for special treatment of these species in pipeline developments. Accordingly, the Thicksilver pipeline implemented a species at risk conservation program within its application for regulatory approval. During the development of the program it became clear that there are several regulatory issues regarding species at risk. For example, regulatory requirements lack clarity and are not transparent to the proponent. Furthermore, there are significant jurisdictional inconsistencies and overlaps between federal and provincial concerns. The species at risk conservation program presented here includes the following chronological steps. An information review, including all pertinent federal and provincial regulations and guidelines. A species screening step which includes an initial full listing of potential species from literature and unpublished surveys, and a systematic process to focus on the most likely species at risk involved. Detailed field surveys that are based on knowledge of the natural history and biology of the species concerned are then conducted to provide explicit documentation on the particular species at risk. Species assessment, including a professional opinion on the potential impact of the activity on the livelihood of the species at risk, is required next. A species at risk mitigation plan is then provided to mitigate the predicted impacts. Finally, a follow up plan is put into place to ensure that mitigation has been effective.

Keywords: Endangered species, rare plants, conservation biology

INTRODUCTION

This paper deals with the requirements to manage species at risk in pipeline planning and construction. Plants and/or animals are considered at risk when their continued existence as a viable population is threatened. Consideration of species at risk is currently required in Canada by several pieces of legislation including the Canadian Wildlife Act and Migratory Bird Act and Regulations, and in Alberta, the Environmental Protection and Enhancement Act and Regulations and the Wildlife Act.

Despite these existing regulatory requirements for protection of species at risk a number of issues have risen regarding the implementation of a species at risk program. In 1995 the federal government determined that the existing legislation was not clear enough or sufficiently robust to adequately protect species at risk. A draft Act, termed the Endangered Species Act was introduced for review in 1996. This draft Act resembled the United States Endangered Species Act. However, following nearly five years of review this draft Act was withdrawn and in 2000 a newly proposed Act entitled the Canadian Species at Risk Act (Environment Canada, 1998; Environment Canada, 1999) was introduced. This disclosure has presented considerable confusion to practitioners charged with developing species at risk programs. In fact, there now seems to be confusion even if species at risk need to be included in pipeline approvals. For example, a review of three pipeline proposals (AEC, 1997; Suncor, 1997; Suncor, 1997a) very similar in scope and route to the Thicksilver pipeline, found no species at risk programs had been contemplated. Additionally, a major international pipeline did not include a species at risk program until

Environmental Concerns in Rights-of-Way Management: Seventh International Symposium
J.W. Goodrich-Mahoney, D.F. Mutrie and C.A. Guild (editors)
© 2002 Elsevier Science Ltd. All rights reserved.

Table 1. Canadian species at risk classification system (COSEWIC, 1999)

Category	Description
Extinct	Species no longer exists
Extirpated	Species no longer exists in the wild in Canada, but may occur elsewhere
Endangered	Species facing imminent extirpation or extinction
Threatened	Species likely to become endangered if limiting factors are not reversed
Vulnerable	Species of special concern due to characteristics that make it particularly sensitive to human activities
Not at risk	Species that have been evaluated and found not to be at risk

the issue was raised in public hearings (National Energy Board, 1996). Clearly, there is a lack of clarity for species at risk pipeline regulatory requirements in Alberta.

An additional confounding issue relates to the paucity in the regulations and the general literature in Canada on methods and protocols to develop a species at risk conservation program. Existing programs seem to be ad hoc and rely on unpublished guidelines. A common method to devising species at risk program would be beneficial to practitioners working on pipeline development plans. To this end, this paper intends to fill this gap in pipeline environmental management literature.

The paper is presented in the following manner. A review of existing regulatory literature on species at risk is given as a framework. The Thicksilver project is then described as a background to the requirements the species at risk program. The details of species at risk program are then discussed. Finally, I will present a succinct review of the key components of a species at risk conservation plan.

REGULATORY REVIEW

Species at risk legislation

Plants and/or animals are considered at risk when their continued existence as a viable population is threatened. The principal cause for species to become at risk is the loss of habitat from human activity (Environment Canada, 1994). However over-exploitation, the use of persistent toxic chemicals, reduction in prey can also contributed to a decline in some populations. Species at risk can be well known wildlife species (e.g., grizzly bear {*Ursus arctos*}) or lesser known plants (e.g., western blue flag {*Iris missouriensis*}) and animals (e.g., dwarf wedge mussel {*Alasmidonia heterodon*}) known only to scientists with specific interest in those organisms. The Committee on the Status of Endangered Wildlife in Canada (COSEWIC) has listed 339 species as being in difficulty across Canada (COSEWIC, 1999). Forty-six of these species are from western Canada.

Some Canadian species at risk have a very high international profile, especially in Europe, and have been used as a lobby tool by environmental groups seeking trade sanctions and restrictions. The species at risk issue has also been gaining increasing prominence within Canada as the public is requesting more action to protect threatened organisms and habitats. Concerns regarding the adequacy of Canadian legislation have been raised as being piecemeal, jumbled and cosmetic (Singleton, 1977). One author suggests that Canadian conservation legislation allows the modern tragedy of species to continue unabated (Versteeg, 1984).

These concerns have spurred initiatives on species at risk by the federal government. For example, Canada has joined the international convention on biological diversity and currently plans to enact legislation to protect vulnerable species. A new Act termed the Species at Risk Act has been introduced to Parliament in 2000. The federal government has also stepped up public consultation on species at risk and has initiated a federal–provincial accord on the subject.

The federal initiatives for protection of species at risk centers on the COESEWIC listing activity. The Committee has developed a risk status for most native fish, amphibians, reptiles, plants, birds, and mammals in Canada. The risk categories are defined in Table 1.

The Canadian species at risk strategy uses the COESIWIC listing as its base. Once the list has been approved by the federal government two key features of the species at risk strategy come into effect. The first is automatic prohibitions on destroying threatened and endangered species or their habitat. This is an important step for pipeline developments as the federal list supercedes all other lists (i.e., provincial status reports). It is the responsibility of the pipeline proponent to determine the status of any species at risk that may be encountered within the pipeline project plans. The second feature includes recovery planning that requires the federal government to develop an approach to include all stakeholder concerns (e.g., landowners, ranchers, farmers, industry representatives, and environmental groups). The federal government is evidently hoping that voluntary actions from these stakeholders will create a stewardship climate that encourages species at risk protection.

In Alberta, species at risk are managed through the provincial Wildlife Act and the Status of Alberta Wildlife initiative. The Wildlife Act lists twelve species that are protected by penalties of fines or other punitive actions. However, the remaining species, which

Table 2. Alberta species at risk classification system (Alberta Environment, 1996)

Category	Description
Red	Species at risk. Populations have declined to nonviable levels, or show a rate of decrease indicating that they are at immediate risk of declining to non-viable levels in Alberta. These species may be candidates or may have received formal designation as Endangered or Threatened species in Alberta
Blue	These species may be at risk. This list includes species particularly vulnerable because of non-cyclical declines in population or habitat, or reductions in provincial distribution
Yellow	Sensitive species that are currently not at risk. However, these species may require special management to address concerns related to naturally low populations, limited provincial distributions, or life history features that make them vulnerable to human-related changes to the environment. The yellow list has been divided into two categories. Yellow A are species for which concern has been expressed over long term declines in numbers. These species merit extra attention as they may be in trouble. Yellow B species are species that are naturally rare but are not in decline. They may have clumped distributions or deteriorating habitat elements
Green	These species are not considered at risk. Their populations are stable and their key habitats are generally secure
Not Determined	Species not known to be at risk but for which insufficient information is available to determine an accurate status

Table 3. Alberta rare plant classification (ANPC, 1997)

Rank[1]	Classification
G1/S1	Less than 5 occurrences or only a few remaining individuals
G2/S2	6–20 occurrences or with many individuals in few occurrences
G3/S3	21–100 occurrences may be rare and local through out its range, or in a restricted range
G4/S4	Apparently secure under the present conditions, typically greater than 100 occurrences but may be fewer with many large populations. May be rare in parts of its range
G5/S5	Demonstrated to be secure under present conditions. Greater than 100 may be rare in parts of its range especially peripherally
GU/SU	Status uncertain due to lack of information
GH/SH	Historically known, may be relocated in the future

[1]G = global, S = Alberta.

is the majority of wildlife in Alberta, are dealt with within the Status of Alberta Wildlife document.

The wildlife status evaluation system in Alberta follows the five categories as shown in Table 2.

An additional intricacy occurs in Alberta in dealing with rare plants. The Alberta Natural Heritage Information Center (ANHIC) has developed a list of rare plants species for Alberta [Alberta Native Plant Council (ANPC), 1997]. The list incorporates both the rare tracking list for Alberta, and the national list produced by the COSEWIC. The ANHIC's tracking system denotes seven ranks of rarity for vascular plants where the plants are evaluated and ranked on their status globally and provincially. Ranking is based on the number of occurrences of the species. Information on population size and trends, life history, reproductive strategy and recent threats are also used when available. Table 3 describes the ANHIC rare plant ranking classification.

Although there are a number of classification systems available, the actual determination of a species at risk remains capricious. For example, different endangered species occur on different endangered species lists. The white pelican (*Pelecanus erythrorhynchos*) is considered in Alberta to be a Red list species but it is not even a COSEWIC threatened species. Additionally, the required remedial action for the species in question is not consistent between lists. COSEWIC may require a recovery plan, but Alberta only requires survey and listing. Perhaps the most significant issue in the vulgarities of the species at risk listing process involves rare plants. In Alberta there is an elaborate set of criteria (Table 3) to determine rare plants, however, plant species are not included in the Alberta status report, only wildlife. Furthermore, COSEWIC includes plant species in their list but has no clear classification strategy or survey method. Due to these irregularities the entire species at risk listing process has been considered by some to be confusing (Bryson, 1995).

Pipeline regulatory process

In Alberta pipelines require regulatory review and approval prior to being constructed. There are basically two forms of approvals required. An Energy and Utilities Board (EUB) Permit and an environmental Approval under the Alberta Environmental Protection and Enhancement Act (EPEA). The EUB permit requires an application including an environmental assessment plan. However, this plan may, or may not, include species at risk. It is most likely that if species at risk is not a major public issue there will not be a requirement to include species at risk in the EUB

Application. The EPEA approval requirement relates to the size of the pipeline. Two classes of pipelines have been established by EPEA (Alberta Environment, 1994) that define class I (large) and class II (smaller). Class II pipelines do not require and environmental Approval. However, a class I pipeline must comply with the terms and conditions of an EPEA Approval as well as EPEA environmental protection guidelines. They are subject to environmental protection orders and must meet the criteria for reclamation certification. Pipelines within class I in Alberta must therefore complete a Conservation and Reclamation Application. However, the Application only requires an environmental protection plan. This plan includes a strategy to avoid adverse effects that encompasses all physical biological and cultural aspects of the project. Other than wildlife habitat documentation and "timing requirements" there are no explicit requirements related to species at risk.

To further complicate Alberta species at risk approval matters, a pipeline may be considered either a federally regulated pipeline or a provincially regulated pipeline. The distinction is made based on the material the pipeline is carrying, the length of the pipeline and if it crosses provincial boundaries or connects to pipelines that may be trans-boundary. Federally regulated pipelines trigger the Canadian Environmental Assessment Act and must have a Regulatory Agency (usually the National Energy Board {NEB}) review the project.

Federally regulated pipelines have explicit requirements for species at risk. For example, the NEB Guidelines for Filing Requirements (National Energy Board, 1995) state that environmental assessments for pipeline applications require identification of any rare species, or species with federal, provincial, regional or local designated status (e.g., vulnerable, threatened, endangered, or extirpated).

The conundrum is therefore if a pipeline is designated as federal in Alberta the species at risk requirements are distinctly mandated and articulated in Guidelines. However, if the pipeline is considered within the Alberta jurisdiction the requirements are not necessarily documented in regulatory instruments. The Thicksilver pipeline as proposed crosses a large portion of Alberta but falls within this indistinctive category for species at risk.

THICKSILVER PIPELINE PROJECT

The pipeline project actually proposes two pipelines, one pipeline of 914 mm (36 inch) to carry bitumen and one 324 mm (12 inch) pipeline that is to be used to transport lighter hydrocarbon liquids used in the heavy oil production process. The first pipeline is required to ship heavy oil production from the Imperial Oil facilities at Cold Lake to Hardisty and then further on to markets in the east and the south, via an existing pipeline system. The second pipeline would ship natural gas liquids from Hardisty back to Cold Lake to blend with the bitumen to make the bitumen suitable for shipment by pipeline.

The two pipelines are to be laid in a common trench, approximately 2 m wide with an average of 1.2 m of cover. A twenty-five meter wide permanent right-of-way will be required with a 5-m temporary work area taken over the entire main line right of way to ensure that soil conservation standards are met.

The proposed pipeline route is shown in Figure 1. The 250-km route parallels existing pipeline rights-of-way whenever possible. The route goes from Cold Lake to Lindberg and from Lindberg by Vermillion to end in Hardisty.

The most notable aspect of the Thicksilver pipeline project from a species at risk perspective is its total length and capability to impact a large range of habitat and species. The pipeline right-of-way will disturb 250 km of land, cross 52 watercourses and pass through two recognized environmentally sensitive areas.

DEVELOPING A SPECIES AT RISK PLAN

As mentioned previously, the requirements for wildlife species at risk are quite distinct from that of rare plants. It is therefore recommended that these groups be handled separately. The following section describes an appropriate methodology to develop a species at risk plan, first for wildlife, and then for rare plants. Examples from the Thicksilver case are given throughout to elucidate key requisites.

WILDLIFE

Information review

Because wildlife species at risk lists can be exhaustive (Appendix 1) and there are contradictions between federal and provincial lists it is strongly recommended to do an initial review of all information sources. The initial review should include the following constituents:
– the pipeline construction design and schedule;
– habitat overview and seasonal limitations;
– regulatory requirements.

Information on pipeline construction details includes a thorough understanding of the final route selection, a compilation of detailed pipeline alignment sheets and construction schedule particulars. Without this critical information is not possible to determine potential key species at risk.

Using the pipeline alignment sheets it is possible to go to aerial photography and map, in a general

Proposed ThickSilver Pipeline Route

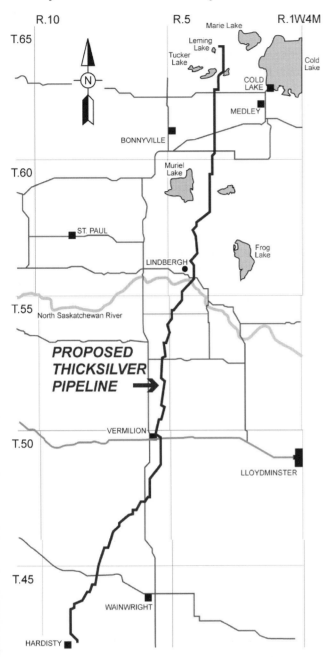

Fig. 1. The Thicksilver pipeline route.

fashion, the habitat along the right-of-way. Thicksilver habitat maps were useful in determining that there were several locations at the north end of the right-of-way (mainly boreal forest) that had a distinct potential for finding wildlife species at risk. The maps also showed that no critical habitat occurred in the central portion of the pipeline route (mainly parkland). However, critical habitat appeared on the southern area (native grassland) that may be important to certain species at risk.

The habitat information was then augmented with known species abundance surveys completed near the pipeline right-of-way. This specific task is labor intensive as most of the information is found in unpublished reports such as government wildlife population surveys, as well as baseline data from earlier pipeline applications. However, by completing this task an initial wildlife species at risk list is possible. The Thicksilver initial list is shown in Appendix 1. The initial list suggests that there are potentially a large number of species, however, the list can be trimmed using a logical screening process.

Species screening

Screening of the initial species at risk list is completed using pipeline construction data, timing information and wildlife habitat mitigation plans. The first task is to review the potential species against the construction and habitat data. Then the screened list is discussed with federal and provincial biologists for accuracy and completeness. At this point it is also important to determine the regulators interpretation of their species at risk lists. The provincial species at risk list is especially important to review, as there may be difficulty distinguishing between the categories of wildlife species at risk.

For Thicksilver, the wildlife species selected were those listed by COSEWIC, and those listed as either red or blue in Alberta, as confirmed by Alberta Fish and Wildlife. The proposed winter timing of the Thicksilver construction in the northern portion, pipeline route selection and the commitment to rapid reclamation of the habitat, greatly reduced the number of species from this section.

Avian species focussed on those inhabiting southern native grasslands, which included: burrowing owl, loggerhead shrike, sharp-tailed grouse, short-eared owl, and Sprague's pipit. Sharp-tailed grouse were included in the species at risk plan under advisement from the Alberta Fish ad Wildlife. While sharp-tailed grouse are only listed as Yellow A by the Alberta Status of Wildlife Report (1996) the breeding grounds are quite sensitive. The Thicksilver pipeline will potentially pass near suspected sharp-tailed grouse breeding areas. Sharp-tailed grouse males display communally at traditional dancing grounds (termed leks) in order to attract females. Females approach the lek, choose a mate from the displaying group, and leave to nest and rear the young alone (Erhlich et al., 1988). Leks are used repeatedly year to year, and disturbance to leks could have a significant impact on the species.

Bay-breasted warblers, black-throated green warblers and Cape May warblers were all listed in the initial species at risk list, but were not included in field surveys. These species are found in the northern-forested area of the right-of-way where winter construction will be utilized. As these species migrate from the area they will not be affected by winter construction. Additionally, field surveys were not conducted for peregrine falcons or piping plovers. These species did not have sufficient habitat along the proposed right-of-way to warrant detailed investigation.

Canadian toads were included on the initial list of species at risk. However, mitigation plans included in the conservation and reclamation plan for the right-of-way included routing the pipeline around the various wet lands and riparian areas where possible. Therefore the amount of Canadian toad habitat disturbed was minimal.

Northern long-eared bats, the Alberta Blue rated mammal on the initial list, was screened from further investigation as it does not inhabit the right-of-way during the construction phase.

Field surveys

The wildlife field surveys for the Thicksilver were conducted in two phases. An early phase for sharp tailed grouse leks was conducted in early May. The timing of this survey was selected to coincide with the period when grouse would most likely be using the leks. A second phase was conducted for burrowing owls, loggerhead shrikes, short-eared owls, and Sprague's pipits later in June to correspond to these species life histories. While the grouse survey focussed on areas with historical lekking records, all the other surveys were habitat based. This consisted of investigations of native pasture, improved pasture, and hayland. Surveys were conducted during light conditions to allow good visibility and ceased under inclement conditions when the possibility of detection was reduced.

It is important to understand and integrate the life history of the species at risk in the design of the survey. For example, where there was potential for burrowing owl nests, call-playback tapes were used. From a distance of approximately 200–300 in from the potential nesting area, a tape containing burrowing owl calls was played for 1–2 min. This was followed by a 5 min listening period where observers watched and listened for evidence of burrowing owls. Male burrowing owls are highly territorial and will immediately respond to the calls by flying into the area. As breeding owls typically do not stray more than 1 km from their burrow site, call playback tapes were expected to elicit responses from adults in active nesting areas.

Loggerhead shrikes are mainly found in lightly wooded river valleys and coulees. Nests usually occur in trees or shrubs, 1–10 cm above ground. Loggerhead shrikes eat mainly small birds and large insects such as grasshoppers, crickets, and beetles. Shrikes often impale their food for storage and to anchor prey for consumption. Such caches may be observed along barbwire fence lines or on the thorns or branches of various shrubs or trees. Observers looked for all visual sign of loggerhead shrikes in potential shrike habitat.

For sharp-tailed grouse, potential lek locations were visited in the early morning, approximately one-half hour before sunrise to approximately 10:00 a.m. The potential lek sites were also visited the night prior to the survey to determine access. Grouse may be active in the early evening, as well, and observations at any time of the day were recorded. Lekking grouse can be heard as far as 1 km away, under calm or low wind conditions. Thus, observers carefully approached all areas, listening and watching for signs prior to entering an area. Observers stayed a minimum of 200 in from active leks, in order to avoid disturbing dancing males.

Species assessment

No species from the screened list of species at risk were identified from the detailed field surveys conducted for the Thicksilver pipeline right-of-way.

Mitigation and follow up plans

Areas of native pasture or native grassland that could be disturbed due to construction will be reclaimed to native vegetation to provide habitat for species at risk. Mitigation measures will also include the introduction of native plant species from adjacent land. With these mitigation techniques it is expected that the areas will return to suitable habitat for species at risk. The time frame for the reclamation is three years with a follow up species at risk survey planned to occur at that time.

RARE PLANTS

Information review

Using the ANPC (1997) definition of rare plants, 43 vascular plants were found to have a potential to occur on the proposed Thicksilver pipeline alignment (Appendix 2).

Species screening

Twenty-one occurrences were found on the ANHIC tracking list. To refine the initial rare plant list the ANHIC were contacted to determine if there were site specific plant records within the ANPC tracking list. Ten species had been recorded by the ANHIC within the vicinity of the Thicksilver pipeline alignment (Table 4).

Table 4. Rare plants documented within the Thicksilver region by ANPC (1997)

Botanical name	Common name	Status
Carex retrorsa	turned sedge	S2/S3/G5
Carex vulpinoidea	fox sedge	S2/G5
Coptis trifolia	goldthread	S2/G5
Houstonia longifolia	long-leaved bluets	S2/G4/G5
Juncus confusus	few-flowered rush	S2/G5
Lomatogonium	marsh felwort	S2/G5
Lysimachia lanceolata	lance-leaved loosestrife	Sl/S2/G5
Oenothera serrulata	shrubby evening	S2G5
Polygala paucifiblia	fringed milkwort	SIG5
Spergularia marina	salt-marsh sand spurry	S2/G5

Field surveys

Using the list of potential rare species and the list of recorded rare species botanists began field studies. Two rare plant field surveys were conducted on the Thicksilver alignment and a 200-m adjacent buffer zone. One survey was conducted in mid June and one survey in late July to ensure both early and late flowering phenologies were recorded. Surveys were floristic in nature and covered the area thoroughly in an attempt to identify every plant species in the survey area to a level at which it's rarity can be determined (ANPC, 1997).

It became readily apparent early in the survey process that in order to make the survey representative habitat type classification was required. The plant habitats were classified using the scale:
- 0, no potential;
- 1, low potential;
- 2, low to moderate potential;
- 3, low to moderate potential;
- 4, moderate to high potential.

Field searches concentrated on the most likely habitats while still sampling each plant community type. Transects were used for the survey (Nelson, 1986). Spacing of transects depended on the density of vegetation cover, visibility and plant size.

Species assessment

Of the rare plant species with a potential to be near the right-of-way the Manitoba maple (S2/G5) and the sand millet (S1/G5) were found in the vicinity of the Thicksilver pipeline alignment. No rare plants were found on the right-of-way itself.

Mitigation and follow up plan

Although there were no rare plants found on the right-of-way the following mitigation measures were adopted for the project as a means of protecting species at risk:
- the boundaries of the pipeline right-of-way will be clearly staked to ensure construction equipment stays on track;
- control of all equipment on the pipeline alignment;
- reclamation of disturbed area to native seed mixes. On site salvaged vegetative material will be used to promote reestablishment of conditions suitable for rare plant colonization over time;
- workforce education on rare plants;
- construction scheduling in wetlands and organic soils in winter months to reduce impacts;
- follow-up field surveys are scheduled.

CONCLUSION

In Alberta there is currently a regulatory gap in planning for species at risk for pipeline developments. If a pipeline project is not regulated by the federal government the requirements for species at risk may be vague. Therefore a major pipeline proposal like Thicksilver requires a transparent planning tool to properly consider species at risk. As a guide for practitioners completing species at risk plans I offer the following six key steps:

1. Information review; including all pertinent federal and provincial regulations and guidelines.
2. Species screening; which includes an initial full listing of potential species at risk from literature and unpublished surveys, and a systematic process to focus on the most likely species.
3. Detailed field surveys; based on knowledge of the natural history and biology of the species field work is conducted to provide detailed species documentation.
4. Species assessment; includes a professional opinion on the potential impact of the pipeline on the livelihood of the species at risk.
5. Species at risk mitigation plan; is a plan to mitigate the predicted impacts.
6. Follow up management plan; is put in place to follow up to ensure that the mitigation plan is effective.

ACKNOWLEDGEMENTS

The author would like to thank Golder and Associates for their contribution to the species at risk field program. Greg Sutor and Kelly Gurski contributed to the development of the rare plant plan. Marylyn Collard worked on the wildlife plan. David Kerr and Evan Baker were responsible for the Golder review of the plans.

APPENDIX 1

Potential wildlife species at risk affected by the Thicksilver pipeline[1]

SPECIES	NATIONAL STATUS	PROVENCIAL STATUS
Avian		
American avocet	–[2]	Sensitive species in decline
American bittern	–	Sensitive species in decline
American white pelican	Not at risk	Species at risk
Bald eagle	Not at risk	Sensitive species not in decline
Bay-breasted warbler	–	Species may be at risk
Black-and-white warbler	–	Sensitive species not in decline
Black-crowned night heron	–	Sensitive species not in decline
Black tern	Not at risk	Sensitive species in decline
Black-throated green warbler	–	Species may be at risk
Broad-winged hawk	–	Sensitive species not in decline
Brown creeper	–	Sensitive species not in decline
Burrowing owl	Endangered species	Species at risk
Cape May warbler	–	Species may be at risk
Cooper's hawk	Not at risk	Sensitive species not in decline
Double-crested warbler	Not at risk	Sensitive species not in decline
Forster's tern	–	Sensitive species not in decline
Golden eagle	–	Sensitive species not in decline
Great species may be at risk heron	–	Sensitive species not in decline
Great gray owl	Not at risk	Sensitive species not in decline
Herring gull	–	Sensitive species not in decline
Homed grebe	–	Sensitive species in decline
Lesser yellowlegs	–	Sensitive species in decline
Loggerhead shrike	Threatened	Sensitive species in decline
Marsh wren	–	Sensitive species not in decline
Mourning warbler	–	Sensitive species not in decline
Northern goshawk	Not at risk	Sensitive species not in decline
Northern harrier	–	Sensitive species in decline
Osprey	–	Sensitive species not in decline
Peregrine falcon	Endangered species	Species at risk
Pied-billed grebe	–	Sensitive species in decline
Pileated woodpecker	–	Sensitive species not in decline
Piping plover	Endangered species	Species at risk
Species at risk-necked grebe	Not at risk	Sensitive species in decline
Ring-necked pheasant	–	Sensitive species not in decline
Sedge wren	Not at risk	Sensitive species not in decline
Sharp-tailed grouse	–	Sensitive species in decline
Short-eared owl	Vulnerable	Species may be at risk
Sprague's pipit	–	Species may be at risk
Swainson's hawk	–	Sensitive species in decline
Turkey vulture	–	Sensitive species not in decline
Upland sandpiper	–	Sensitive species in decline
Western tanager	–	Sensitive species not in decline
Mammals		
American badger	Not at risk	Sensitive species in decline
Canada lynx	Not at risk	Sensitive species not in decline
Hoary bat	–	Status undetermined
Northern flying squirrel	–	Sensitive species not in decline
Northern long-eared bat	–	Species may be at risk
Prairie shrew	–	Status undetermined
Prairie vole	–	Status undetermined
Amphibians and reptiles		
Canadian toad	–	Species at risk
Species at risk — sided garter snake	–	Sensitive species in decline
Plains garter snake	–	Sensitive species in decline

[1] Only common names are given in Appendix 1. Nomenclature follows Godfrey (1966), Banfield (1976), and Porter (1972).
[2] Not ranked.

APPENDIX 2

Potential rare flora for the Thicksilver pipeline

BOTANICAL NAME	COMMON NAME	RANK	HABITAT
Trees			
Acer negundo	Manitoba maple	S2G5	stream banks
Forbs			
Aster pauciflorus	few-flowered aster	SI S2G4	alkaline flats
Aster umbellatus	flat-topped white aster	S2G5	moist woodland
Astragalus bodinii	Bodin's milk vetch	SIG4	gravel banks sand
Botrychium multifidum	leather grape fern	SIS2G5	moist sandy areas
Botrychium simplex	dwarf grape fern	SIG5	meadows/shores
Dryopteris cristata	crested shield fern	SIG5	woods/marshes
Geranium carolinanum	Carolina wild geranium	S2G5	clearings
Houstonia longifolia	long-leaved bluets	S2G4G5	open sand/dunes
Lomatogonium rotatum	marsh felwort	S2G5	meadows/saline
Lysimachia lanceolata	lance-leaved loosestrife	SIS2G5	meadows/shores
Oenothera brevifolia	evening primrose	SIG5	clay flats
Oenothera serr-ulata	shrubby evening-primrose	S2G5	sandy and dunes
Osmorhiza longistylis	smooth sweet cicely	S2G5	moist woods
Plantago maritima	sea-side plantain	SIG5	saline marshes
Polanisia dodecantha	clammyweed	SIG5	gravelly or sand
Polygala paucifolia	fringed milkwort	SIG5	coniferous woods
Potamogeton obtusifolius	blunt-leaved pondweed	S2G5	boreal water
Potamogeton strictifoliu	linear-leaved pondweed	SIS2G5	water
Potentilla finitinia	sandhills cinquefoil	SIG?	sandy and dunes
Potentilla plattensis	low cinquefoil	S2G4	grassland, coulees,
Rorippa curvipes		S2G5	moist ground
Ruppia maritima	widgeon grass	S2G5	saline water
Spergularia marina	salt-marsh sand spurry	S2G5	tufa dune
Viola maclosteyi	Macloskey violet	SIS2G5	moist woods
Viola pedantifida	crowfoot violet	SlS2G5	grassland
Graminoids			
Bromus altissimus	Canada brome	SIG5	moist banks
Carex pseudocyperus	cyperus-like sedge	S2G5	swamp/marsh
Carex retrorsa	turned sedge	S2S3G5	swamp/meadow
Carex tincta	tinged sedge	SIG4G5	meadows
Carew vulpinoidea	fox sedge	S2G5	swampy ground
Coptis trifolia	goldthread	S2G5	damp mossy woods
Danthonia spicata	poverty oat grass	SIS2G5	woodlands
Dichanthelium leibergii	Leiberg's millet	SRG5	prairies woods
Dichanthelium ofigosanthes	sand millet	SIG5	dry open areas
Juncus confusus	few-flowered rush	S2G5	low grassland
Muhlenbergia racemosa	marsh muhly grass	SIG5	sand-hills/slopes
Munroa squarrosa	false buffalo grass	SIG5	plains, slopes
Oryzopsis canadensis	Canadian rice grass	SIG5	open woods
Rhynchospora capillacea	slender beak-rush	SIG5	calcareous bogs
Scirpuis fluviatilis	river bulrush	SIG5	margins of lakes
Scirpuis pallidus	pale bulrush	SIG5	marshy areas
Scirpuis pumilus	dwarf bulrush	S2G	calcareous bogs
Spartina pectinata	prairie cord grass	SIG5	shores and marshes

REFERENCES

AEC Pipelines. 1997. Lakeland Pipeline Project. Alberta Energy and Utilities Board Application. EUB, Calgary, Alta. Canada.

Alberta Environment. 1994. Environmental protection guidelines for pipelines. Conservation and reclamation information letter. Alberta Environment, Edmonton, Alberta.

Alberta Environment. 1996. The status of wildlife in Alberta. Edmonton, Alberta.

Alberta Native Plant Council (ANPC). 1997. Information bulletin: ANPC guidelines for rare plant surveys in Alberta. Alberta Native Plant Council, Edmonton, Alberta.

Banfield, F. 1976. The mammals of Canada. National Museum of Canada, Ottawa.

Bryson, C. 1995. What's an endangered species? Environment Views, 18(1).

COSEWIC. 1999. Canadian species at risk. 1999. Committee on the Status of Endangered Wildlife in Canada.

Environment Canada. 1994. Endangered species legislation in Canada: A discussion paper. Canadian Wildlife Service.

Environment Canada. 1998. Environment Canada workshop on essential elements for federal endangered species legislation, workshop proceedings. October 22–23, 1999. Hull Quebec.

Environment Canada. 1999. Canada's plan for protecting species at risk: an update. Canadian Wildlife Service. Ottawa.

Erhlich, P.R., D.S. Dobkin, and D. Wheye. 1988. The birders handbook: A field guide to the natural history of North American birds. Simon & Schuster Inc. New York.

Godfrey, F. 1966. The birds of Canada. National Museum of Canada. Ottawa.

National Energy Board. 1995. Guidelines for filing requirements. NEB, Calgary, Alta.

National Energy Board. 1996. Express pipeline Ltd. Reasons for decision (OH-1-95) NEB, Calgary, Alta. Canada.

Nelson, J.R. 1986. Rare plant surveys. techniques for impact assessment. Natural Areas Journal, 5(3): 18–30.

Porter, K. 1972. Herpetology. W.B. Saunders Co. Toronto.

Singleton, M. 1977. Endangered species legislation in Canada. In: Proceedings of the symposium on Canada's threatened species and habitats. M. Mosquin et al., eds. Canadian Nature Federation.

Suncor Inc. 1997. Athabasca Pipeline Project. Alberta Energy and Utilities Board Application. EUB, Calgary, Alta. Canada.

Suncor Inc. 1997. Wildrose Pipeline Project. Alberta Energy and Utilities Board Application. EUB, Calgary, Alta. Canada.

Versteeg, H. 1984. The protection of endangered species: A Canadian perspective. Ecology Law Quarterly, Vol. II, No. 3.

BIOGRAPHICAL SKETCH

Alan Kennedy, Environmental Scientist
Imperial Oil Resources, 237-4 Ave. S.W., Calgary, AB, Canada T2P 3M9

Alan Kennedy received a PhD Environmental Science from the University of Calgary. Dr. Kennedy has worked as an environmental professional for the past 20 years. During this time he has held positions in a wide variety of energy sectors. Alan is currently working on an environmental assessment for the Mackenzie Delta Gas Project and is also acting as an advisor on the Sable Offshore Energy Project Environmental Effects Monitoring Program.

Threatened and Endangered Species: A Case Study of the Maritimes & Northeast Natural Gas Pipeline in Maine

Michael Lychwala, Michael Tyrrell, and George McLachlan

From 1995 to 1999, Maritimes & Northeast Pipeline acquired permits and constructed approximately 200 miles of 24″ natural gas pipeline in Maine. Over the course of the multi-year permitting and construction process, the project encountered a number of challenges concerning rare, threatened, and endangered species. Target species were identified and survey methodologies developed based on available databases and numerous agency consultations. Local expertise from academia and consulting firms were used as necessary. Vascular plants, several species of freshwater mussels, the Tomah mayfly, two species of turtles, two species of dragonflies, and bald eagles were identified for field surveys. Over 25 professional botanists and biologists performed numerous field surveys and report input to provide the data required for the permitting process. Several challenges were overcome in dealing with time restrictions, data gathering, and the expansive, and sometimes remote, project range. Results for the final mainline route included identification of 13 species of state listed vascular plants at 17 locations, two bald eagle essential habitats within $\frac{1}{4}$ mile of the pipeline route, and three streams with state listed freshwater mussels. Many additional sites were identified for a number of species, however were avoided by route changes. Survey results were submitted to the appropriate agencies and methodologies were developed for construction mitigation where avoidance was not possible. Mitigation work was performed while corresponding with the rigorous construction schedule. Mitigation results were compiled and additional monitoring will continue for specific sites.

Keywords: Permitting, wildlife, vegetation, mitigation, monitoring

INTRODUCTION

Maritimes & Northeast Pipeline, L.L.C. (Maritimes), in conjunction with Maritimes Pipeline Limited Partnership, obtained the required permits and constructed a natural gas pipeline that connects natural gas customers in New England with the Sable Offshore Energy Project off the coast of Nova Scotia, Canada (the Maritimes Phase II Pipeline Project). The constructed Phase II facilities consists of 24″ and 30″ diameter natural gas pipeline that extends approximately 200 miles from the US–Canada border at Baileyville, Maine to Westbrook, Maine (see Fig. 1). The original project scope also included several proposed lateral lines that accounted for an additional 150 miles of various diameter pipeline but were not constructed as part of the overall project. However, with the laterals included in the initial scope of work, over 350 miles of proposed pipeline corridor within the State of Maine was evaluated for the presence of threatened and endangered (T&E) species.

MAINE

During the permitting and construction phases of the project, several tasks were developed to address the issues concerning T&E species. Items such as project range, time constraints, permitting requirements, survey methodologies, and pre and post-construction issues were addressed as the project developed and progressed. A number of federal and state agency personnel were involved throughout the process. As a

Environmental Concerns in Rights-of-Way
Management: Seventh International Symposium
J.W. Goodrich-Mahoney, D.F. Mutrie and C.A. Guild (editors)
© 2002 Elsevier Science Ltd. All rights reserved.

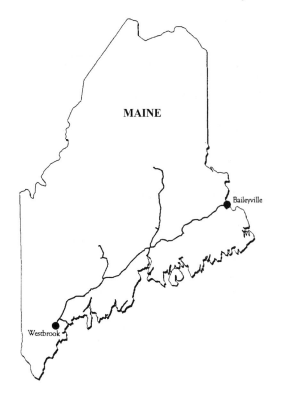

Fig. 1. Project Locus Map.

result of the large project size and aggressive time frame, several challenges were overcome to effectively evaluate the project corridor for the presence of T&E species and to develop effective mitigation.

This paper is based on information gathered for the required Maritimes' permits obtained throughout the regulatory process. Numerous biologists, ecologists, and consultants provided invaluable resources to gathering scientific information and preparing information on T&E species throughout this permitting process.

OBJECTIVES

Given the complexity, aggressive timeframe, and wide range of the project, several objectives were developed to successfully complete the permitting and construction goals in reference to T&E species:

– identify possible T&E species habitat along the proposed corridor based on existing information and agency consultation;
– develop survey objectives with project biologists and federal and state agency personnel;
– develop and agree upon survey methodologies that cover the required range, meet the survey objectives, and satisfy the project timeframe and permitting requirements simultaneously;
– identify and coordinate the qualified personnel to effectively survey the 100-ft to 200-ft wide project study corridor;
– develop and evaluate the survey results with project managers and federal and state agencies;
– utilize the survey results to adjust or modify the project for T&E avoidance or to identify possible areas for T&E mitigation;
– work with federal and state agencies to design T&E mitigation and monitoring for the construction phase of the project;
– coordinate T&E mitigation and monitoring to ensure minimization of impacts to identified T&E species along the route.

METHODS

Site description

The Maritimes Phase II Pipeline Project corridor extended for approximately 350 miles with the mainline extending southwest from Bailyville to Westbrook Maine roughly paralleling the coast. The route location crossed three biophysical regions of Maine (McMahon, 1991): the Eastern Interior, Central Interior, and Southwest Interior. Within these ranges, ten major habitat types were identified along the route based on the Maine Natural Heritage Program Ecosystem Classification system (MNHP, 1991). These habitat types included spruce-fir forest, northern hardwood forest, white pine-mixed hardwood forest, early successional and clearcut, agricultural, forested wetland, scrub-shrub wetland, emergent wetland, riparian wetlands, estuarine wetlands, and aquatic habitats. This project setting presented a number of challenges as it relates to the identification of T&E species.

Existing resources/agency consultation

The initial effort in identifying T&E species involved multiple federal and state agency contacts as well as review of existing database information. This was the first step in developing an overall list of potential T&E species that may have been in the project area. During this effort, contacts were made with the US Fish and Wildlife Service (USFWS), National Marine Fisheries Service, Maine Natural Areas Program (MNAP), Maine Department of Inland Fisheries and Wildlife (MDIFW), Maine Land Use Regulation Commission, and the Maine Department of Marine Fisheries.

This preliminary research developed the first initial T&E search parameters for the project. Several species known to occur within the project range were identified. The initial T&E species list included the federally endangered shortnose sturgeon (*Acipenser brevirostrum*) and threatened bald eagle (*Haliaeetus leucocephalus*). Also, targeted by federal and state agencies were the black tern (*Chlidonias niger*), New England cottontail (*Sylvilagus transitionalis*), Blanding's turtle (*Emydoidea blandingii*), brook floater (*Alasmidonta varicosa*), yellow lampmussel (*Lampsilis cariosa*), tidewater mucket (*Leptodea ochracea*), pygmy snaketail dragonfly (*Ophiogomphus howei*), irregular snaketail dragonfly (*Ophiogomphus anomalus*) and the Tomah mayfly (*Siphlonisca aerodromia*). In addition to the identified wildlife species, the entire route was evaluated for the presence of T&E vascular plant species.

Target species

As a result of additional habitat identification from field surveys and continued agency consultation through 1996 and 1997, a final list of T&E species requiring survey work was developed and the majority of the surveys were scheduled for the field season of 1998. This list include the bald eagle, brook floater, yellow lampmussel, tidewater mucket pygmy snaketail, irregular snaketail, Tomah mayfly, blanding's turtle, and spotted turtle. In addition to the T&E wildlife species identified, T&E vascular plant surveys continued to address the primary route, route modifications, access roads, and additional temporary workspace.

Survey methodologies

Once the target species were identified the appropriate survey methodologies were developed using existing data, collected habitat information, professional biologists, local knowledge and expertise, and agency input. One of the major challenges in developing these survey methodologies involved meeting the survey requirements in line with the project timeframe. Traditional surveys for specific species are often tailored to identify far more detail than whether the species is simply present or not. With a project range of over 350 miles, the initial scope of the surveys was limited to determine if the project location would directly impact an identified target species. Another challenge in developing survey methodologies involved the multiple species targeted, and the vast range that they covered. Each species had a separate survey window and procedural survey protocol.

Vascular plants — Survey methodology

Prior to field searches, and to some degree (based on field experience as the searches progressed) concurrent with them, an analysis of the project layout was undertaken utilizing existing data on the distribution of T&E species. The analysis also included a review of land use from recent (April 1997) aerial photographs, and habitats from USGS topographical maps, National Wetlands Inventory maps, surficial and bedrock geology maps and other available information.

Except for known locations of rare species, further review of existing information indicated that much of the project area had a low potential for such species. Regionally, rare species are primarily concentrated in southern Maine (i.e., south of the current project area), in northern and eastern Aroostook County (remote from the project area), along the coast and in alpine zones (both also remote from the project area), and along large rivers. Of these, the project as proposed involved only major river corridors as areas of high potential for rare species. It is well-known, for example, that much of interior eastern Maine has not been well-botanized (Campbell et al., 1995), and furthermore, the distribution and ecology of many of Maine's rare plants are not well known (Eastman and Gawler, 1985). Therefore no area was, a priori, excluded from field review.

From these reviews and considerations, field work was planned with highest priority given to searching areas near known populations and the proposed river crossings. Field searches were undertaken on foot to review such areas. Special attention was given to areas where the study corridor was wider, e.g., at stream crossings and major road crossings. Habitats were judged in the field according to the searcher's expertise as to whether in-depth or cursory searches were appropriate, and as to whether additional areas other than those originally identified should be searched. Special attention was paid to such habitats as rivershores, streams, small ponds, rock outcrops, sloping deciduous forest habitats, seeps, northern white cedar swamps, natural openings, borrow pits and other areas of disturbed soils, areas of calcareous bedrock, etc. Common habitat types such as cut-over second or third-growth forest, mixed forest on uplands, farm fields, pastures, abandoned land, etc. were generally considered to have little potential and were not searched as thoroughly.

Blanding's and spotted turtles — Survey methodology

The goal of this study was to identify and document the occurrence of two listed turtle species on or within the immediate vicinity of the proposed Phase II pipeline corridor. This goal was accomplished through a two-phased approach: (1) the identification of areas having species occurrence or potential occurrence (landscape analysis); and (2) on-site field surveys documenting the occurrence of the species.

- *Landscape analysis* — Based on pre-survey planning, aerial photo and NWI map interpretation, and previously conducted wetland surveys, critical habitats along the pipeline route were identified. Based on preliminary analysis, the emergent and shrub wetlands located along approximately 50 miles were targeted as the most likely areas to harbor the two species.
- *On-site field surveys* — Since the turtles (especially the spotted turtle) could have occurred in several wetland areas traversed by the pipeline project, on-site surveys to determine the actual presence or absence of the species was necessary. Areas of known occurrence or potentially suitable areas within the targeted areas were surveyed by qualified biologists in the spring of 1998. The biologist searched potential turtle habitats visually for basking turtles in the early spring shortly after emergence from hibernation and growth of vegetation. In additional, information was used from other previous 1997 field surveys associated with wetland delineation, and rare plants which did not yield any sightings of these turtles.

Tomah mayfly — Survey methodology
A literature review was conducted to collect information on the life history and habitat requirements of this species. Information reviewed included entomological journals, Master's theses, and literature on the natural history of the region. Dr. K. Elizabeth Gibbs, who re-discovered the Tomah mayfly in Maine in 1978 was recruited to participate in developing the survey methodology as well participating in oversight of the survey process. Dr. Gibbs provided expertise and played a crucial role in the survey design process for the Tomah mayfly.

- *Landscape analysis* — A landscape analysis was conducted to identify potential survey sites for the Tomah mayfly. The targeted survey sites consisted floodplain marsh habitat that provided standing water in the spring. A variety of information was reviewed during the analysis, including USGS topographic maps and Maritimes pipeline alignment sheets, which included $1'' = 200'$ aerial photographs of the proposed pipeline corridor and information collected during the wetland delineation efforts in 1997. In addition, alignment sheets showing delineated wetland areas were examined and wetland field data forms were reviewed. Wetland data forms provided information on the wetland community and plant species composition at the wetland crossings, and on the stream width and substrate characteristics at stream crossings. However, data collected for wetland or stream crossings was not always detailed enough to complete the analysis. It is often difficult to collect general wetland information associated with delineation activities that can provide information for any particular wildlife species. Therefore, a site visit was performed for those streams where additional data was required to determine if the location contained sufficient habitat and was an acceptable survey location.

  The list of potential survey sites was then cross-referenced with work completed by the MDIFW and Dr. Gibbs to identify sites that had been previously surveyed. The sites were then prioritized for surveys based on habitat characteristics and the recommendations of Dr. Gibbs. Those crossings which exhibited potentially acceptable habitat were identified and selected for survey. These sites were reviewed with the USFWS and MDIFW prior to performing the 1998 field surveys.

- *Final survey design* — Six locations were initially identified for Tomah mayfly surveys during the last week of May, 1998, just prior to the emergence of adults. Additional sites were subsequently added to cover route modifications. The field surveys for Tomah mayflies were designed to be largely qualitative, although measures of relative abundance was obtained and compared to surveys conducted by Dr. Gibbs in Maine, New York, and New Brunswick (Gibbs and Siebenmann, 1994). Two training events were hosted by Dr. Gibbs, one in a classroom setting and the one in the field at a known Tomah mayfly site. The training ensured adequate knowledge of the potential habitats and survey methods. Investigators were able to develop a search image for this species.

Searches were designed to use 1 m D-frame aquatic net sweeps through submerged vegetation. Contents of net sweeps were placed in white enamel sorting trays and the number of Tomah mayfly nymphs were recorded. Relative abundance was determined based on the number of nymphs observed in the pans. At any site where Tomah mayfly nymphs were found, reference specimens were collected and identification was verified in the laboratory. Maine Natural Areas Program Data sheets were also completed and photographs were taken.

Pygmy and irregular snaketail dragonflies — Survey methodology
A literature review was conducted to collect information on the life history and habitat requirements of each of the dragonfly species. Information reviewed included entomological journals, Master's theses, and literature on the natural history of the region. Dr. K. Elizabeth Gibbs, also played a critical role for the dragonfly surveys as well. Dr. Gibbs participated in developing the survey methodology and provided specific training to biologists that conducted the surveys.

- *Landscape analysis* — As with the Tomah mayfly, a similar type landscape analysis was conducted to identify potential survey sites for the dragonfly species.

- *Field surveys, Fall 1997 field visits* — Several survey sites requiring additional characterization were visited in the fall of 1997 to confirm habitat conditions and to determine suitability for inclusion in the 1998 field survey. These site visits were undertaken when the existing site information was inadequate to establish the need to conduct a detailed survey at a particular location.

- *Final survey design* — Field surveys for snaketail dragonflies were conducted during the last week of May and the first week of June, 1998, when adults were emerging from riverine habitats. A training session for field personnel was hosted by Dr. Gibbs in a classroom setting on April 15, 1998. The training ensured adequate knowledge of the target species, potential habitats and survey methods.

Since the emergence of the two focus species begins approximately one week apart (Bradeen, 1996), each site was visited once during each week. As the spring season progressed, low rain fall levels and warm temperatures required monitoring of the potential advancement of the hatch period. Based on consultation with Dr. Gibbs and MDIFW, surveys were conducted approximately two weeks earlier than previously scheduled. To ensure that the timing of the surveys was correct, several regional sites that were likely to contain these species in the vicinity of the Phase II pipeline route were investigated. These sites were not located on the Phase II pipeline route, and were chosen based on consultation with MDIFW. One regional site did not produce the target species during this initial survey. However, when the pipeline route was surveyed in that region, over 700 irregular snaketail exuviae were collected, thus confirming that the survey fell within the appropriate time window.

During each site visit, all dragonfly exuviae were collected along three 30-m transects located parallel to the shoreline. Where applicable, all three transects were located within the proposed corridor, with two located on one shoreline and one on the other. Where access was difficult or restricted, the three transects were located on one stream bank, located centrally over the proposed location of the pipeline. Water temperatures were recorded at each site during each visit. Exuviae were then identified to species according to Carle (1992) and Walker (1933) and those of pygmy and irregular snaketails were counted by transect and by site.

Bald eagle — Survey methodology

The primary goal of this study was to identify the location of documented bald eagle nests as well as any additional nests within the immediate vicinity of the pipeline corridor. This goal was accomplished through two stages: (1) the use of the most up to date MDIFW database in determining known eagle nest locations, as well as correspondence with the appropriate regional biologists, and (2) fly-over of the corridor in areas where additional, unmapped nests may be located.

- *Use of up-to-date MDIFW database* — Based on existing information provided by the MDIFW, such as the 1997 endangered species database and specific correspondence with the various regional biologists, known bald eagle nests and essential habitats were identified. Known eagle nests along the pipeline corridor were updated by information through a MDIFW database. A total of 17 bald eagle nests were initially documented to occur within one mile of the pipeline route.
- *Corridor fly-over* — Since bald eagle nests could have occurred in several areas not previously documented or surveyed by the MDIFW, a helicopter fly-over of targeted segments of the pipeline was planned. As recommended by MDIFW, specific areas targeted for this survey included the northeast section of the route and areas near major river crossings. This survey was conducted by staff scientists of the MDIFW and Maritimes in April, 1998 during leaf-off conditions.

A survey corridor of approximately one-mile in width, centered on the proposed center-line, was investigated by both DIFW and Maritimes biologists.

The DIFW recommended survey procedure entailed three passes over a swath (i.e., centerline and two outer edges) at a flight height of approximately 300 feet and a typical airspeed of less than 75 knots. Off-sets from the survey corridor were conducted to cover other potential nesting areas such as lake and stream shorelines. Surveys were conducted from April 14 through April 22, 1998 and corresponded to the period typically used by MDIFW for surveying Maine nesting pairs. Conditions conducive to the survey included clear or cloudy skies (i.e., one-mile visibility), and winds less than 15 mph. Any new nests or other pertinent information was recorded by the supervising MDIFW biologist.

Freshwater mussels — Survey methodology

The following describes the protocol for surveying freshwater mussels in the vicinity of selected streams crossed by the Martimes Pipeline project. This protocol was developed based on an August 28, 1997 meeting with staff of the MDIFW, Endangered Species Unit. At the time of the project, five species of mussels were listed as state threatened or of special concern. The yellow lampmussel (*Lampsilis cariosa*) and tidewater mucket (*Leptodea ochracea*) are State Threatened, and three species are of special concern; the brook floater (*Alasmidonta varicosa*), squawfoot (*Strophitus undulatus*), and triangle floater (*Alasmidonta undulata*). The target species for these surveys are the three mussels considered to be the rarest in the State of Maine; the yellow lampmussel, tidewater mucket, and brook floater.

Based on the analysis of existing agency data on known T&E mussel locations within one mile of the pipeline route, and the inclusion of waterbodies with potential habitat conditions for target mussel species, a list of waterbody crossings targeted for survey was developed. This list was based on a minimum stream width of 25 feet as measured at the pipeline crossing either directly in the field or using aerial photographs.

The general procedure for the mussel surveys consisted of three levels of intensity. The actual stream crossing ROW was intensively searched for the target species. The entire ROW was searched, making a complete count of each target species found. The width of the ROW was generally 75 feet but depended on site specific conditions, which varied for each stream. An estimate of the count for all other species found within this ROW was grouped as <50, 50–100, and >100. A cursory search was made in the area five meters upstream of the ROW and an estimate of abundance noted for each species.

An area 50 m downstream of the ROW was searched at a less intensive level. Approximately 1 m wide transects parallel to the stream bank were searched. A count of each target species and an estimate of all other species found were recorded. Two transects were searched in streams less than 50 feet wide, and four transects were searched across streams greater than 50 feet. The third level of effort consisted of a timed search that was conducted in an area 50–150 m downstream from the ROW. The amount of time varied depending on the stream size and conditions but commonly ran one half to one hour each for a two person team. A count was recorded for each target species as well as a note of general abundance of other species (rare, common, and abundant).

Mussel searches were done through a combination of visual assessment in shoreline areas and snorkeling. At larger crossings, divers were used to search for mussels in deeper waters where access was not limited by safety concerns.

RESULTS

Vascular plants — survey results

The T&E vascular plant surveys identified over 25 separate T&E vascular plant sites, with over 15 different species. Due to numerous route modifications and adjustments, only nine sites comprised of six species along the route were directly within the pipeline corridor. The site locations were spread across the entire 200 miles of the mainline. These species are included in the Table 1.

Blanding's and spotted turtles — Survey results
Maritimes completed the required surveys for the two turtle species, Blanding's turtle and the spotted turtle in the early spring 1998. The two target species were not found during the surveys. However, based on these 1998 field surveys, the participating biologists identified 18 areas of quality habitat that may support these species. These areas were targeted for pre-construction surveys using the same methodology as the previous surveys. Pre-construction surveys were completed in these locations just prior to the initiation of clearing activities. No observations of the target species were made during the entire construction phase of the project.

Tomah mayfly — Survey results
A total of 10 streams and their associated floodplains were selected for the Tomah mayfly survey. The Tomah mayfly was found within the construction ROW at only 1 of the sites: the Passadumkeag River.

As the spring season progressed, low rain fall levels and warm temperatures required monitoring of the potential advancement of the hatch period. As a result of the climate and river flow conditions, surveys occurred approximately 2 weeks earlier than normal.

The majority of the floodplain areas were dry at the time of survey, leaving few areas of potential habitat for the Tomah mayfly. It is not known if the dry conditions are typical of these areas at that time of year, or the result of the lower, regional spring flood levels during the survey effort.

Pygmy and irregular snaketail dragonflies — Survey results
A total of 36 streams were surveyed for the pygmy and irregular snaketail dragonflies across the project range. A total of 7796 dragonfly exuviae were collected during this survey effort. Of this total, 3317 of the exuviae were identified to be within the *Ophiogomphus* family, and 1771 were identified to be from the irregular snaketail. None of the exuviae collected were from the pygmy snaketail. The irregular snaketail was found within the construction ROW at four of the survey sites. However, due to adjustments to the final route alignment, and removal of the proposed laterals, none of the streams identified to have the target species were affected.

Bald eagle — Survey results
Based on the database review and consultation with the MDIFW, two designated bald eagle Essential Habitats were identified within the pipeline corridor. During the 1998 fly-over surveys, no new nest sites were identified. In addition to the 1998 fly-over survey, an additional survey was performed prior to the mainline construction in 1999. As with the earlier fly-over, no new nest sites were identified during the 1999 survey.

Freshwater mussels — Survey results
Target species were generally found in low numbers and at only nine crossing locations. The tidewater mucket was found at only one site, the Passadumkeag River crossing of the Millinocket Lateral. The yellow lampmussel was found at only three sites, the Passadumkeag River, Millinocket Stream, and the West Branch of the Penobscot River, all on the Millinocket Lateral. The third target species, the brook floater, was found in low numbers at six stream crossing locations. Live specimens were found within the study area at five locations: Marsh Stream, Machias River, West Branch Sheepscot River at the mainline and Skowhegan Lateral crossing locations, and the Carrabasset Stream. Only two relic shells were found at the Penobscot River crossing on the Millinocket Lateral. Due to route modifications prior to construction, the pipeline corridor crossed only three streams with identified target species. These included Marsh stream, the West Branch Sheepscot, and the Machias River.

Table 1. Rare, threatened and endangered species within constructed pipeline ROW

Common name	Scientific name
Velvet sedge	*Carex vestita*
Slender blue-eyed grass (multiple sites)	*Sisyrinchium mucronatum*
Broad beech fern	*Phegopteris hexagonoptera*
Wiegand's sedge	*Carex wiegandii*
Alga-like Pondweed	*Potamogeton confervoided*
Vasey's rush	*Juncus vaseyi*

MITIGATION APPROACH

Several approaches to mitigation were considered during the design of the pipeline and the development of the construction procedures. The mitigation measures were consistent with the federal and state agency regulatory policies and guidelines. These mitigation measures were developed and utilized for the target turtle species, the bald eagle, the target freshwater mussels species, and the T&E vascular plant sites within the project corridor. A significant degree of agency consultation was initiated to assist in the development of effective mitigation. Maritimes first considered avoidance as the primary mitigation measure.

As a result of the extensive agency consultation, numerous route modifications, and removal of the proposed laterals, a number of T&E sites were avoided by construction. This reduced T&E impacts as well as mitigation efforts that may have been used for construction. The following are some examples of identified T&E sites that were avoided by construction:
- six streams and rivers with target freshwater mussel species were avoided;
- over 15 species of T&E vascular plants located at over 25 separate stations were avoided;
- four stream and river crossings identified to contain irregular snaketail dragonflies were avoided because of the removal of the proposed laterals.

Vascular plants — Mitigation approach

For the nine T&E vascular plant sites identified within the pipeline construction corridor, specific mitigation was developed for each site. Maritimes' representatives met with the MNAP on April 16, 1998, to discuss the status of the 1997 surveys and to review the surveys required in 1998. The MNAP described some recommended mitigation measures for the species identified during the 1997 and 1998 surveys. During the April 16, 1998, meeting, Maritimes also discussed mitigation measures recommended by the MNAP.

As a result of consultation with the MNAP, Maritimes developed a mitigation approach for each population of protected plants along the project route that was incorporated into the project alignment sheets and construction specifications (see Table 2). These plans were developed by the consultants working together with the project owners, project engineers and appropriate state and federal agencies. All plant mitigation efforts will be monitored for three years after construction. The basic mitigation techniques that were utilized included the following:
- Sod salvage — Sod salvage included the transplantation of entire, intact sods, rather than individual plants, for use where a population consisted primarily of interconnected plants or large clones, or where it was beneficial to move large sods with small plants, rather than excavating individual plants as plugs. In this instance, sods were dug either by track-hoes or by hand immediately prior to construction.

The sod salvage technique was utilized primarily for the slender blue-eyed grass and velvet sedge sites. The plants were removed in sod sections approximately 1.5-ft by 2.5-ft in size that contained anywhere from five to 25 individuals and stored at a plant nursery throughout the construction phase. The plants were cared for during the summer months and maintained in excellent condition. Most of these plants were placed back on the original construction ROW after construction. In some instances, where the ROW restoration was not completed during the growing season, the plants were held at the nursery for an additional year. Based on the first year observation of the sites restored after construction, the sod salvage technique has been very successful. One concern observed while using this technique occurred during the slender blue-eyed grass mitigation effort. Slender blue-eyed grass can easily be out-competed by other species of upland grasses, and survives well where conditions prevent thick dense herbaceous cover. Under the conditions of the nursery, sods received scheduled watering and small amounts of fertilizer. Many plants in the sods responded better than the slender blue-eyed grass and began to overgrow the sod sections. Careful monitoring, trimming, and fertilizer restrictions were needed to keep the plants in check and maintain the slender blue-eyed grass population.
- Plant plugs — Plant plugs were used where a population consisted primarily of separate individuals. In some cases, this technique was used in addition to sod salvage. Where individual plants were scattered, and sod sections were not practical, individual plant plugs were taken by hand. As with sod salvage, the plants were held at a nursery for care through the construction phase, and replanted on the corridor in their original locations after construction. In the case of the Vasey's rush, individuals were removed and planted in a corner of an additional temporary workspace nearby and replanted at their original location after construction.

This mitigation technique was also used for the aquatic alga-like pondweed. For this instance, the plants were removed by hand and placed upstream within the same habitat immediately prior to construction These plants were left in place after construction was completed. It is anticipated that the transplants will re-colonizing the construction ROW.

The plant plug technique proved highly successful for the broad beech fern. A large stand of broad beech fern (probably a single large clone) was removed from the construction ROW and stored at a plant nursey during construction. Over two hundred individual ferns were potted and maintained at the nursery. After construction, these individuals were planted within the shaded tree-line adjacent to

Table 2. Rare, threatened and endangered vascular plant species — mitigation techniques

Common name	Scientific name	Mitigation technique
Velvet sedge	Carex vestita	Sod salvage, plant plugs
Slender blue-eyed grass (multiple sites)	Sisyrinchium mucronatum	Sod salvage, plant plugs, topsoil segregation
Broad beech fern	Phegopteris hexagonoptera	Plant plugs
Wiegand's sedge	Carex wiegandii	Avoidance
Alga-like Pondweed	Potamogeton confervoided	Plant plugs
Vasey's rush	Juncus vaseyi	Plant plugs

the ROW. These plants were inspected this spring and were determined to be in excellent health.

- *Topsoil segregation* — Soil segregation was a technique that was used where continued presence of a particular species may depend more on maintaining a seedbank than on salvaging mature individuals. In these areas, the top eight inches of topsoil was stripped from the project area and stored nearby during construction, then replaced to the same depth and grade as prior to construction. This technique was utilized, in addition to sod salvage and plant plugs, for the slender blue-eyed grass sites. Slender blue-eyed grass responds to disturbance and is an early colonizer on exposed soil. It is anticipated that these plants will colonize on newly disturbed sections of the ROW from the seedbank held within the topsoil.

Blanding's and spotted turtles — Mitigation approach
Although no target species of turtles were identified during the survey effort, Maritimes conducted pre-construction surveys in identified quality habitat prior to the initiation of clearing activities. Any turtles observed on the ROW during the survey were to be captured and relocated to an adjacent area of similar habitat. A temporary silt fence would have been installed along both sides of the ROW in the vicinity of the capture, in order to prevent the relocated individual from returning to the construction site. However, no sightings were recorded throughout the entire construction phase of the project.

Bald eagle — Mitigation approach
Two Essential Habitat areas for bald eagle nest sites were located along the project corridor. Both of these nest sites were along the Penobscot River and within close proximity to each other. This river was crossed using horizontal directional drill (HDD) technology. The HDD activity was considered by MDIFW as an alteration of the Essential Habitats because of the noise and human activity associated with construction. Therefore, measures to mitigate disturbance were required at these sites. These measures included the following:
- *Timing restriction* — The critical nesting season for bald eagles in Maine generally runs from February 1 through August 31 but can vary from coastal to northern, interior regions. Thus, as required by MDIFW, any construction activity within the Essential Habitat area, such as clearing, directional drilling, trenching and pipe placement, had to be conducted outside of this nesting window (i.e., fall and early winter).

Construction activity around the identified bald eagle nests was restricted during February, March, April, and May. However, MDIFW monitored for bald eagle activity at the two nest sites. No activity was observed during the late winter and spring months. Once the MDIFW biologist were confident that the nest was not going to be used that year, construction activities were allowed to proceed in June instead of waiting for the full timing restriction to end in August. With the nests uninhabited as late as June, it was highly unlikely that a nesting pair could have come in and successfully bred that season.

Freshwater mussels — Mitigation approach
Maritimes consulted with the MDIFW on possible mussel mitigation methods. Maritimes also researched mussel relocation studies and other mitigation measures used on natural gas pipeline and other stream construction projects. The research revealed that mussel tagging and relocation studies were sometimes conducted when substantial numbers of mussels occur within the construction impact area. Relocation efforts with rare mussels have had mixed results in part due to the difficulty in relocating individual tagged and relocated mussels.

At the three streams designated for open cut or dry crossing methods and for which at least six live specimens of any target species have been found within the study corridor, Maritimes committed to re-surveying the impact zone shortly before construction. This pre-construction survey effort also involved removing all target mussels found and transporting them to an upstream location where suitable habitat was available. No state threatened species were found during these pre-construction surveys, however, three state Species of Concern were found. A total of 26 brook floaters, one squawfoot, and 44 triangle floaters were re-located during this effort.

CONCLUSION

The T&E survey program and mitigation effort initiated by Maritimes proved to be a successful endeavor. The success of the program was the result of Maritimes' environmental commitment to the overall project and the continued cooperation of the federal and state regulatory agencies involved in the review of the mitigation plans and during construction. Each of the objectives of the T&E effort were realized over the approximately four year development and implementation schedule of the project.

ACKNOWLEDGEMENTS

Information used for this paper was the result of the dedicated effort put forth by a large number of professionals during the development of the Maritimes Phase II Pipeline Project. We thank and gratefully acknowledge the support from Maritimes throughout the project. Special thanks goes to Earth Tech, Duke Engineering & Services, Woodlot Alternatives, Normandeau, W.D. Countryman (in particular Arthur Gilman), S.W. Cole, Paul Corey, and to all of the biologists/ecologists who participated during the project and provided the technical expertise needed to make the project a success.

REFERENCES

Bradeen, B.J. 1996. Life Histories of Sympatric Ophiogomphus spp. (Odonata: Gomphidae) in the Aroostook River, Maine. Master's Thesis. University of Maine. Orono, ME.

Campbell, C.S., H.P. Adams, P. Adams, A.C. Dibble, L.M. Eastman, S.C. Gawler, L.L. Gregory, B.A. Grunden, A.D. Haines, K. Jonson, S.C. Rooney, T.F. Vining, J.E. Weber, and W.A. Wright. 1995. Check-list of the vascular plants of Maine, 3rd rev. Josselyn Botanical Society Bull., 13: 1–100.

Carle, F.L. 1992. Ophiogomphus (Ophionurus) australis spec. nov. from the gulf coast of Louisiana, with larval and adult keys to American Ophiogomphus (Anisoptera: Gomphidae). Odonatologica, 21(2): 141–152.

Eastman, L.M. 1978. Rare and Endangered Vascular Plants of Maine. The New England Botanical Club in cooperation with the US Fish and Wildlife Service.

Eastman, L.M. and S.C. Gawler. 1985. Rare Vascular Plants of Maine, revised. State Planning Office. Augusta.

Gibbs, K.E. and M. Siebenmann. 1994. 1994 Studies on Siphlonisca aerodromia. Final Report to the Endangered and Nongame Wildlife Program, MDIFW, Bangor, ME.

Maine Natural Heritage Program. 1991. Natural Landscapes of Maine: A Classification of Ecosystems and Natural Communities. MNHP, Office of Comprehensive Planning. Augusta, ME. 77 pp.

McMahon, J.S. 1991. Benchmarks in a Changing Landscape. Ecological Reserves: a Missing Link in Maine's Conservation Agenda. Habitat, 8: 16–21.

Walker, E.M. 1933. The nymphs of the Canadian species of Ophiogomphus Odonata, Gomphidae. Canadian Entomologist, 65(10): 217–229.

BIOGRAPHICAL SKETCHES

Michael Lychwala

TRC Environmental Corporation, Lowell, MA 01852, USA, Phone (978) 970-5600

Michael Lychwala is an environmental biologist with TRC Environmental Corporation responsible for environmental permit/document coordination and preparation and scientific data gathering and analysis. Mr. Lychwala's areas of interest include wetland ecology, wildlife biology, soils, and hydrology. Mr. Lychwala is responsible for environmental permitting work including preparation and coordination of Federal Energy Regulatory Commission (FERC) Environmental Reports, Army Corps of Engineers Section 404/10 Individual Permits and 401 Water Quality Certifications, Coastal Zone Management Consistency Statements, Massachusetts Environmental Policy Act (MEPA), Environmental Notification Forms and Impact Reports, and Biological Assessments. Mr. Lychwala has a Bachelor of Science and Master of Science in wildlife biology from the University of Massachusetts.

Michael Tyrrell

TRC Environmental Corporation, Lowell, MA 01852, USA, Phone (978) 970-5600

Michael Tyrrell is a Senior Pipeline Program Manager and Professional Wetland Scientist with TRC Environmental Corporation. Mr. Tyrrell has over 12 years of consulting experience, primarily on natural gas pipeline projects and other energy related development projects. He has been involved in the licensing and permitting of more than 1000 miles of natural gas pipelines throughout the Unites States and has been involved in the permitting of numerous power plants. As a Senior Pipeline Program Manager, he is responsible for developing and managing linear projects in the Northeast and throughout the country. He has direct experience with both onshore and offshore pipeline projects. Mr. Tyrrell has participated in project scoping meetings with the FERC, regulatory/resource agency interface and coordination, corridor/route selection, environmental inventory and assessment and EIR/EIS preparation, mitigation planning, public participation, expert witness testimony and preparing federal, state and local permit/license applications. He has a Bachelor of Science degree in Natural Resources/Wildlife Biology from the University of Rhode Island.

George A. McLachlan

Maritimes & Northeast Pipeline, 5 Batchelder Road, Seabrook, NH 03874, USA, Phone (603) 474-8188

George A. McLachlan has been with Duke Energy for over 10 years in the environmental field. For 5 years he has been environmental manager for Maritimes & Northeast Pipeline, L.L.C. responsible for all environmental aspects for the company. Mr. McLachlan has managed all FERC, federal, state, and local environmental permit filings for the various Maritimes projects over the past several years. In addition, he has been responsible for the environmental inspection and compliance programs during construction. Mr. McLachlan has a Bachelor of Science Degree in Natural Resources Conservation from the University of Connecticut.

Response of Bird Communities to Pipeline Rights-of-Way in the Boreal Forest of Alberta

Warren Fleming and Fiona K.A. Schmiegelow

There is considerable concern over the effects of habitat loss and fragmentation on forest birds, particularly neotropical migrants. Resource development in forested regions may reduce the available habitat for forest-dependent species both directly, by removing forest, and indirectly, by creating edges and introducing novel habitat. These factors can further affect the structure of animal communities by influencing species that compete with, or prey upon, forest-dependent species. Linear developments, such as roads, seismic exploration lines, powerline rights-of-way (ROW) and pipeline ROW, may contribute significantly to forest fragmentation. We studied the local response of birds to pipeline ROW in the boreal forest of northwestern Alberta by comparing community structure, predation rates on artificial nests, and willingness to cross ROW in response to playbacks, at varying ROW widths, and between forest adjacent to and away from ROW. Total species richness was not affected by the presence or width of ROW, however overall bird abundance was highest adjacent to narrow ROW. Differences in the abundance of individual species adjacent to ROW, and across ROW widths indicated that these features did influence bird community structure. Nest predation was greater adjacent to wider ROW, but did not differ with distance from edge across width classes. Tests for willingness to cross ROW were generally inconclusive, due to low sample sizes. We conclude that local effects of pipeline ROW might be mitigated by minimizing ROW width. However, regional planning requires more careful consideration of the landscape-level implications of creating a greater number of linear disturbances for an equivalent level of pipeline development, as well as the cumulative effects of various industrial activities.

Keywords: Linear development, right-of-way management, forest songbirds, edge effects, boreal mixedwood forest

INTRODUCTION

Forested landscapes throughout the world are subjected to many types of human activities. In cases where such activities cause habitat loss or fragmentation, wildlife species dependent on forests may suffer population declines, reductions in range, or even local extinction. Historically, much of this disturbance has been attributed to agricultural development and forest harvesting. However, there is an increasing awareness of the potential impact of various linear developments on wildlife. Such linear developments include roads, hydro-electric corridors, seismic lines and pipeline rights-of-way (ROW) associated with oil and gas exploration and development.

The boreal mixedwood natural region of Canada (Achuff, 1994) has recently come under intense pressure from logging interests, due to the increased value of deciduous tree species for pulpwood (Marchak, 1995; AEP, 1998). Concomitant with these activities, the oil and gas industry continues to expand throughout the region (AEP, 1998). Habitat loss and fragmentation have become important concerns for land managers. Research is required to determine how these disturbances are affecting wildlife, and to identify management practices that mitigate negative effects. Our study was initiated in 1997 to evaluate the effect of linear developments, specifically pipeline rights-of-way (ROW), on the structure and dynamics of bird communities in Alberta's boreal mixedwood forest. We focused our research on pipeline ROW due to the prevalence of these features in the boreal forest region of Alberta, and the projected increase in pipeline construction in the near future. Alberta's boreal forest has an overall density of pipeline ROW equivalent to 0.21 km/km² as of 1996 (AEP, 1998). In the dry mixedwood sub-region, where this research took place, the density is 0.41 km of pipeline per km². Numbers for the Grande Prairie region specifically are not available, however it is one of the most active regions in the province for oil and gas exploration and development (AEP, 1998).

Edges created by anthropogenic disturbances may contribute to declines in forest-dependent species, through edge avoidance, changes in habitat at edges, and increased competition with species attracted to edges or the adjacent habitat (e.g., Kroodsma, 1982; Small and Hunter, 1989). Such edges also may cause changes in predator communities (Wilcove, 1985; Nour et al., 1993), which affect rates of predation on forest nesting songbirds. Large gaps in forest cover may also affect the movement and dispersal of some bird species (Matthysen and Currie, 1996).

Pipeline ROW vary in width, depending on the number of lines they support, and associated construction and maintenance requirements. As the transportation network for oil and gas expands, it is important to know whether, from an ecological perspective, it is less detrimental to widen existing ROW for additional pipelines, or to develop a greater number of narrow ROW. We examined the local effects of pipeline ROW of various widths on bird community structure, nest predation and movement in a 2-year field study in west-central Alberta. We predicted that the diversity and abundance of forest-dependent species would be lower, and nest predation higher, in areas adjacent to ROW, when compared to similar areas in contiguous forest. We further expected these effects to increase with ROW width. We also predicted that the willingness of birds to cross ROW would decrease with width. Here, we present preliminary results from these studies.

METHODS

Study area
This study was conducted in the dry boreal mixedwood forest, ~40 km south of Grande Prairie, AB, Canada (Fig. 1), during the summers of 1998 and 1999. This area was chosen on the basis of existing and projected pipeline developments, and because we were able to identify replicates of established ROW, within four width classes, located in consistent forest cover. The forest in the area is dominated by trembling aspen (*Populus tremuloides*), with varying amounts of white spruce (*Picea glauca*) located primarily in the understory. All study sites were in forest between 80 and 120 years of age.

Fig. 1. Location of the study area, 40 km south of Grande Prairie, AB, Canada.

Three sites were located at each of four ROW width classes: 15–16 m, 22–24 m, 32–34 m, and >50 m (width classes 1 through 4, respectively), for a total of 12 sites. At each site, we established two sampling grids: one immediately adjacent to the ROW, and a control grid located a minimum of 500 m from the ROW edge and any other disturbances.

Bird community data
Standardized, 5-min points (Ralph et al., 1995) were conducted during the breeding seasons of 1998/1999. All birds seen and heard within a 100-m sampling radius of each station were recorded. Three point count stations were located in the forest adjacent to each ROW (Fig. 2), and within each control grid. Point counts were carried out in fair weather, between dawn and 10:00 a.m., between May 27 and July 5 of both years. In total, each site was sampled five times: three times in 1998 and twice in 1999.

Nest predation data
We used artificial nests and plasticine eggs as a measure of predation pressure (e.g., Haskell, 1995; Major and Kendal, 1996). At each site, nests were placed along transects running parallel to the ROW, in each of four locations: within 5 m of the edge, 50 m from the edge, 100 m from the edge and within the control grid, 500 m from the edge. On each transect, 20 nests were placed at 25 m spacing, alternating between ground scrapes and shrub nests (10 cm diameter, commercially available canary nests). Two plasticine eggs, resembling the eggs of typical passerine species (~1.5 × 1.2 cm oval), were placed in each nest. The plasticine eggs permitted predator identification, based on markings left behind by teeth or bills. The nests were placed at four sites simultaneously (one in each width class of ROW), in each of three time periods (late spring, early summer, mid-summer) in 1999. They were checked for predator activity after five days, and at 10 days, when

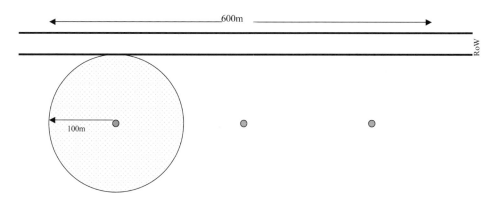

Fig. 2. Diagram of point count stations (small circles) and a sample census area (large circle) in relation to the right-of-way (dark lines). Equivalent control stations (not shown) are located 500 m from ROW edge.

they were removed. Predator species were placed into five groups; small mammals (mice, voles), intermediate mammals (squirrels, chipmunks), large mammals (large weasels, bears), avian (jays, crows, etc.), and unknown.

Gap crossing data

Data on willingness to cross forest gaps were collected using playbacks of Black-capped Chickadee (*Poecile atricapillus*) mobbing calls. This method has been used successfully to elicit responses from a variety of species (Desrochers and Hannon, 1997). At each site, two sample points were established on the edges of the ROW, 400 m apart. Playbacks were conducted during two time intervals: 08:00–12:00 and 18:00–22:00, between July 23 and August 9, 1999. At this point in the breeding season, most juveniles have fledged and are moving around, and most adults are no longer territorial. The playbacks were conducted using a portable cassette player with 5 W amplified speakers, set in the forest within 2–3 m of the ROW edge. At one of the sample points during each visit, volume was controlled (70 dB far side of ROW; digital sound meter), to test whether choice to respond was influenced by the perceived distance from the source.

During the 10-min playback interval, two observers were stationed approximately 20 m on either side of the sound source along the edge of the ROW, and watched for birds arriving at or near the speakers. All birds responding to the calls were recorded to species, and classified as to their origin, i.e., whether they crossed the ROW, or came from the forest adjacent to the sound source. Birds observed or heard responding from the opposite side of the ROW, but not crossing, were also recorded. Each site was visited four times: twice in the morning and twice in the evening, and each point was sampled twice with controlled volume and twice with uncontrolled volume.

Data analysis

All data were tested for normality prior to analysis, and non-parametric tests were used where appropriate. To reduce the probability of committing Type II errors, we use $\alpha = 0.10$ for all tests (see Schmiegelow et al., 1997). We used Bonferroni corrections for multiple comparisons when testing for pairwise differences.

Most passerine species, and the Yellow-bellied Sapsucker (*Sphyrapicus various*) were included in analyses, but we excluded all corvids, raptors, grouse, waterbirds, and all other woodpeckers, as these species are not adequately sampled using point counts. Differences in bird community structure (species richness and total abundance), between adjacent and control stations, were examined using paired-samples tests, with measures paired by site. Differences in the total number of records for individual species with 10 or more detections were tested using the same method. The effect of ROW width was examined using only counts from adjacent locations at each site.

Overall nest predation rates for each of the four transect types (varying distance from edge), and between width classes for each transect type, were examined using Mann-Whitney U tests.

RESULTS

Bird community

Neither the number of species ($p = 0.250$), nor total abundance of birds ($p = 0.402$), differed between sampling areas adjacent to pipeline ROW and control areas in large forests removed from human created edges ($n = 12$ in both cases). There was also no significant difference in the number of species detected at adjacent locations between the four width classes of ROW ($p = 0.720$; $n = 3$ for each width class). The total number of bird detections, however, did differ with ROW width ($p = 0.096$), with more individuals recorded adjacent to the narrowest ROW (15–16 m) than any of the wider ROW (Fig. 3).

Species trends

Detection frequency was sufficient (10 or more) for 24 species. Differences in frequency of detection between locations adjacent to ROW and control areas

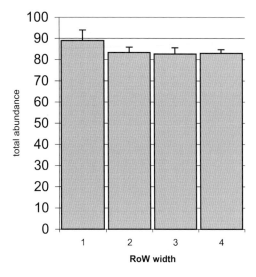

Fig. 3. Number of bird records at point count locations adjacent to ROW of different width classes (increasing from class 1 to 4). Boreal forest in Northwest Alberta, 1998 and 1999 ($p = 0.096$).

Table 1. Mean number of detections at adjacent vs. control counts for seven species. Only significant results shown

Species	Mean number of detections		Z	P
	adjacent	control		
Black-capped Chickadee (*Poecile atricapillus*)	1.42	0.833	−1.725	0.084
Golden-crowned Kinglet (*Regulus satrapa*)	1.00	1.58	−1.841	0.066
Least Flycatcher (*Empidonax minimus*)	6.83	4.00	−1.942	0.052
Lincoln's Sparrow (*Melospiza lincolnii*)	0.583	0.167	−1.667	0.096
Magnolia Warbler (*Dendroica magnolia*)	0.833	0.083	−2.060	0.039
Mourning Warbler (*Oporornis philadelphia*)	0.583	1.33	−1.897	0.058
Red-eyed Vireo (*Vireo olivaceus*)	6.50	4.42	−1.976	0.048

were found for seven species. Five species showed significant increases in forests adjacent to ROW, including Black-capped Chickadee, Least Flycatcher (*Empidonax minimus*), Lincoln's Sparrow (*Melospiza lincolnii*), Magnolia Warbler (*Dendroica magnolia*), and Red-eyed Vireo (*Vireo olivaceus*). Only two showed significant decreases adjacent to ROW; Golden-crowned Kinglet (*Regulus satrapa*) and Mourning Warbler (*Oporornis philadelphia*) (Table 1). Two species exhibited significant differences in detection across ROW width classes (Fig. 4). Detections of the Black-capped Chickadee declined with increasing ROW width ($p = 0.039$) and detections of the Yellow Warbler (*Dendroica petechia*) were greatest at intermediate widths ($p = 0.068$).

Nest predation

In total, 255 of the 960 artificial nests showed evidence of predator activity over the 10 day period that each

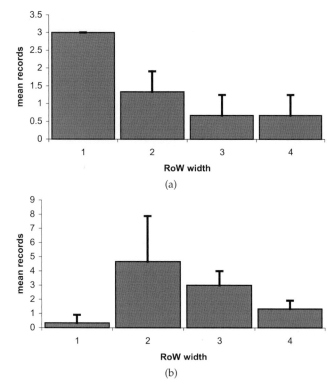

Fig. 4. Records of (a) Black-capped Chickadee ($p = 0.039$) and (b) Yellow Warbler ($p = 0.068$) at point count locations adjacent to ROW of different width classes (increasing from class 1 to 4). Boreal forest in Northwest Alberta, 1998 and 1999.

was monitored (total predation rate = 26.6%). There were no significant differences in predation rate between transect types (nests placed at varying distances from the ROW edge), across all width classes ($p = 0.700$). However, differences were apparent between width classes, for transects immediately adjacent to the ROW ($p = 0.029$), and for nests placed along transects 50 m from the edge ($p = 0.097$) (Table 2). Pairwise tests, adjusted for multiple comparisons, were significant only for adjacent transects, between the narrowest (15–16 m) and 2 widest width classes ($p = 0.056$; $p = 0.079$, 32–34 m and >50 m, respectively).

Over half of the predators that attacked the artificial nests were not identifiable, as, in many cases eggs, or entire nests were removed. Small mammals (mice, voles) were the most abundant identifiable predator type, with small numbers of predators classified as the other two mammalian size classes, or as avian predators (Table 3).

Willingness to cross gaps

The mobbing calls were effective in attracting a variety of species, including chickadees, sparrows, warblers, vireos, thrushes and hummingbirds. However, the overall response rate to our playbacks was very low (6.5 birds/site, over 4 visits), and differences in crossing rate (crossed/responded but did not cross) were not apparent among width classes (Fig. 5). Interpretation of this data awaits more careful analysis.

Table 2. Predation rate on artificial nests along transects (a) immediately adjacent to, and (b) 50 m into the forest from the edge, of ROW of varying width. Data were collected in 1999, near Grande Prairie, Alberta, in the boreal mixedwood forest. Superscript indicates homogeneous groups where detectable

(a) Transects within five meters of forest edge			(b) Transects 50 meters from forest edge		
ROW width (m)	# predated	%	ROW width (m)	# predated	%
15–16[1]	5	8.3	15–16	5	8.3
22–24[1,2]	18	30.0	22–24	13	21.7
32–34[2]	20	33.3	32–34	22	36.7
>50[2]	19	31.7	>50	15	25.0
	62	25.8		55	22.9

Table 3. Frequencies and percentages of each of the five predator groupings over all transects. Data collected adjacent to ROW of different widths in boreal forest south of Grande Prairie, Alberta, 1999

Predator type	Frequency	Percent
Unknown	131	51.4
Small mammal	73	28.6
Intermediate mammal	23	9.0
Large mammal	12	4.7
Avian	16	6.3
Totals	255	100.0

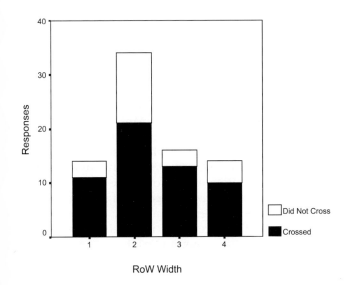

Fig. 5. Frequency of responses (crossed and did not cross) for all species at edges of four width classes of ROW. Boreal forest near Grande Prairie, Alberta, July and August, 1999.

DISCUSSION

Narrow, forest dividing corridors, such as pipeline ROW, have not generally been perceived as a large threat to wildlife, or to forest habitat. However, the visible loss of habitat that results from a road or pipeline, may represent only a small part of the picture when considering the effects of these ROW on forest wildlife, due to associated edge effects (Reed et al., 1994; Rich et al., 1996). The density of linear disturbances is becoming very high in areas where resource extraction and development are prevalent, and the potential problems they present for wildlife are often difficult to assess. Subtle changes in reproductive success along edges, or in the ability of animals to disperse, may have far reaching effects on long term viability of populations of some animals, particularly in the case of species that are naturally rare, or have limited dispersal ability.

We present evidence that some effects of pipeline ROW do extend into the adjacent forest habitat. Overall species richness was not influenced by either proximity to ROW or ROW width, however the total abundance of birds was highest adjacent to the narrowest ROW. At the level of individual species, more species occurred with significantly higher frequency adjacent to ROW, than with reduced frequency (5 vs. 2 species), but our power to detect differences was generally low. These results are somewhat contrary to our predictions, although in the analyses presented here we have not differentiated forest-dependent from more generalist bird species. Such distinctions, by habitat, foraging and nesting guilds, will be made in future analyses of species diversity, species turnover and patterns in abundance. This is important because changes in community composition or the abundances of certain groups of birds may represent the addition of species that directly affect productivity, such as nest predators or parasites (Ambuel and Temple, 1983; Schieck et al., 1995).

Introducing a novel habitat type into a forest will change the overall species composition of the area. ROW are typically planted with commercial grass seed mixes, which facilitates colonization by certain species, such as some species of mice, and birds associated with open areas. Our data indicate that some bird species may be benefiting from the increases in forest edges that border the grass dominated areas within the ROW (see Table 1). The forest along the ROW edges had increased abundance of several species, although actual use of the grass dominated habitat in the ROW themselves was limited to Lincoln's sparrows and White-throated Sparrows (*Zonotrichia albicollis*). White-throated sparrows are the most abundant bird species, and occur in almost all habitat types throughout the study area. Lincoln's sparrows are not typically associated with interior forest, and are likely becoming much more abundant in the areas where our study sites were located, as a result of the ROW themselves. This result is consistent with findings by Morneau et al. (1999), who found that Lincoln's sparrows only occurred within ROW in their study sites in mixed forest in Quebec. Our concern lies with forest dependent species that may be affected by the changes in bird community, either by edge avoidance or decreased productivity. This change in the abundance of potential predators and competitors may have a large effect on forest birds nesting near ROW. Other studies have emphasized the importance of the predator species community in influencing nest predation rates (e.g., Nour et al., 1993; Haskell, 1995).

These factors may lead to a decrease in productivity for birds that nest in forests near the ROW. If birds do not perceive forests adjacent to ROW as being unsuitable habitat, these may become population sinks: areas where recruitment into the population is lower than the death rate (Gates and Gysel, 1978). Over long time periods, such habitat sinks may have effects on regional populations of species. Existing pipeline ROW are usually maintained in perpetuity, while new ones are continuously added. When this is considered, along with the existence and development of roads, powerlines, seismic lines and openings created by the forest industry, bird species that reproduce poorly in areas near edges, may be hard pressed to find productive breeding territories.

With respect to the ability of birds to cross ROW, our results are inconclusive, although several species did show unwillingness to cross even the narrowest gaps. Other studies have shown that forest birds are reluctant to cross gaps in forest cover. Desrochers and Hannon (1997) found that gaps less than 30 m in width had little effect on bird movements, but wider gaps constrained movement significantly for some species. They also found that wooded areas strongly facilitated movements, by providing forested detours around gaps; a situation which, at present, does not exist on pipeline ROW in the study area. St. Clair et al. (1997) also found that birds used forested detours in winter, when they were available. If birds do experience difficulty in crossing gaps caused by ROW, due to the unbroken nature of most pipelines, a ROW may effectively divide habitat, and therefore, populations of wildlife. The dispersal of juvenile birds after fledging could also be affected, compromising their ability to locate potential breeding sites for the following year (Matheson and Currie, 1996).

MANAGEMENT IMPLICATIONS AND FUTURE RESEARCH

Given the rate and extent of linear disturbances in Alberta's boreal forest, determining the effects of these developments, and identifying potential mitigating strategies, is an important management issue. With respect to pipeline ROW, width is an obvious consideration. While creating several narrow ROW, in place of a single, wide ROW, may result in the same amount of absolute habitat loss for an equivalent level of pipeline development (actual amount of forest removed), associated edge effects and barriers to movement might be reduced.

We found that bird community structure was affected by the presence of ROW, and that nests adjacent to narrow ROW experienced lower predation rates than those adjacent to wider ROW. This latter result suggests that wider ROW may contribute to greater effective habitat loss, through reductions in reproductive potential in adjacent forests. However, the changes we observed in the abundance of some bird species in forests adjacent to pipeline ROW of all sizes suggest that even narrow linear disturbances may influence community structure and dynamics. Rich et al. (1994) documented strong effects of narrow forest-dividing corridors, in a different forest type. The decision on whether it is better as a conservation strategy to construct single wide vs. several narrower pipeline ROW cannot be resolved by considering only local-level effects. The continued addition of ROW of all types to the boreal forest decreases the total available forest area, as well as fragmenting the remaining forest, and regional patterns of development must be included in the planning process, in order to ensure that some undisturbed areas remain. As well, regional assessment of cumulative effects requires knowledge of other resource development activities, particularly those associated with forest harvesting. Many species of birds considered most at risk from human-caused habitat alteration are those that nest in relatively large tracts of older forest. For instance, in the boreal forest region, Schmiegelow and Hannon (1999) have documented strong fragmentation effects for Black-throated Green Warbler (*Dendroica virens*), a species of special concern in the province of Alberta.

Much additional research is required on the response of wildlife communities to linear developments. We have yet to fully assess our data with respect to changes in community composition, responses of guilds, colonization of the ROW (novel habitat in forested landscapes), and analysis of vegetation data. However, these data will not directly address issues of source/sink dynamics and barriers to dispersal, which influence the regional persistence of populations. Future studies should focus on the specific effects of changes in competitor and predator communities on forest bird productivity in areas adjacent to ROW, the penetration distances of such effects, and the willingness of birds to cross ROW of varying widths during breeding, juvenile dispersal, and non-breeding periods. Existing and planned wide ROW, containing multiple pipelines, extend over long distances, and if these developments represent movement barriers, then construction of habitat corridors may be necessary to prevent population division.

ACKNOWLEDGEMENTS

We thank TransCanada pipelines and NSERC for financial support for this research. We also thank Canadian Forest Products, Petro-Canada and Rio Alto Exploration for their cooperation in the study area, and Sarah Weber, Pat Marklevitz, Lance Engley, and Katherine Reid for their assistance in the field. We also thank one anonymous reviewer for helpful comments on this manuscript.

REFERENCES

Achuff, P.L. 1994. Natural Regions, Subregions and Natural History Themes of Alberta. A Classification for Protected Areas Management. Protected Areas Report No. 2. Prepared for Parks Services, Alberta Environmental Protection, Edmonton, AB, 72 pp.

Alberta Environmental Protection (AEP). 1998. The Boreal Forest Natural Region of Alberta.

Ambuel, B. and S.A. Temple. 1983. Area-dependent changes in the bird communities and vegetation of southern Wisconsin forests. Ecology, 64(5): 1057–1068.

Cassady St. Clair, C., M. Belisle, A. Desrochers, and S. Hannon. 1998. Winter responses of forest birds to habitat corridors and gaps. Conservation Ecology [online], 2(2): 13.

Desrochers, A. and S.J. Hannon. 1997. Gap crossing decisions by forest songbirds during the post-fledging period. Conservation Biology, 11(5): 1204–1210.

Gates, J.E. and L.W. Gysel. 1978. Avian nest dispersion and fledging success in field-forest ecotones. Ecology, 59(5): 871–883.

Haskell, D.G. 1995. A reevaluation of the effects of forest fragmentation on rates of bird-nest predation. Conservation Biology, 9(5): 1316–1318.

Kroodsma, R.L. 1982. Edge effect on breeding forest birds along a power-line corridor. Journal of Applied Ecology, 19: 361–370.

Major, R.E. and C.E. Kendal. 1996. The contribution of artificial nest experiments to understanding avian reproductive success: A review of methods and conclusions. Ibis, 138: 298–307.

Marchak, M.P. 1995. Logging the Globe. McGill-Queen's University Press. Montreal and Kingston, PQ and ON. 404 pp.

Matthyson, E. and D. Currie. 1996. Habitat fragmentation reduces disperser success in juvenile nuthatches *Sitta europaea*: Evidence from patterns of territory establishment. Ecography, 19: 67–72.

Morneau, F., G.J. Doucet, M. Giguère, and M. Laperle. 1999. Breeding bird species richness associated with a powerline right-of-way in a northern mixed forest landscape. The Canadian Field Naturalist, 113(4): 598–604.

Nour, N., E. Matthysen, and A.A. Dhondt. 1993. Artificial nest predation and habitat fragmentation: different trends in bird and mammal predators. Ecography, 16: 111–116.

Ralph, C.J., J.R. Sauer, and S. Droege, ed. 1995. Monitoring Bird Populations by Point Counts. Gen. Tech. Rep. PSW-GTR-149. Albany, CA: Pacific Southwest Research Station, Forest Service, US Department of Agriculture. 187 pp.

Reed, R.A., J. Johnson-Bernard, and W.L. Baker. 1996. Contribution of roads to forest fragmentation in the Rocky Mountains. Conservation Biology, 10(4): 1098–1106.

Rich, A.C., D.S. Dobkin, and L.J. Lawrence. 1994. Defining forest fragmentation by corridor width: the influence of narrow forest-dividing corridors on forest-nesting birds in southern New Jersey. Conservation Biology, 8(4): 1109–1121.

Schieck, J., K. Lertzman, B. Nyberg, and R. Page. 1995. Effects of patch size on birds in old-growth montane forests. Conservation Biology, 9(5): 1072–1084.

Schmiegelow, F.K.A. and S.J. Hannon. 1999. Forest-level effects of management on boreal songbirds: the Calling Lake fragmentation studies. In: Forest Fragmentation Wildlife and Management Implications. J.A. Rochelle, L.A. Lehmann, and J. Wisniewski, eds. Koninklijke Brill NV, Leiden, The Netherlands. 301 pp.

Schmiegelow, F.K.A., C.S. Machtans, and S.J. Hannon. 1997. Are boreal birds resilient to forest fragmentation? An experimental study of short-term community responses. Ecology, 78(6): 1914–1932.

Small, M.F. and M.L. Hunter Jr. 1989. Responses of Passerines to abrupt forest-river and forest-powerline edges in Maine. Wilson Bulletin, 101(1): 77–83.

Wilcove, D.S. 1985. Nest predation in forest tracts and the decline of migratory songbirds. Ecology, 66(4): 1211–1214.

BIOGRAPHICAL SKETCHES

Warren Fleming

Department of Renewable Resources, University of Alberta, 751 General Services Building, Edmonton, AB, T6G 2H1, Phone (780) 492 9084, e-mail: wdf@ualberta.ca

Warren Fleming is an MSc student of Ecology and Wildlife Management in the Department of Renewable Resources at the University of Alberta. His research interests involve the study of boreal forest wildlife in the context of promoting sound management techniques for industry. His recent work has been on bird communities and the effects of removal and fragmentation of forest habitat.

Fiona K.A. Schmiegelow (corresponding author)

Department of Renewable Resources, University of Alberta, 751 General Services Building, Edmonton, AB, T6G 2H1

Fiona Schmiegelow is an Assistant Professor of Conservation Biology in the Department of Renewable Resources at the University of Alberta. Her research focuses on the broad-scale effects of land-use policies and practices on wildlife, with an emphasis on northern forests. Using a variety of both field-based and modelling approaches, she seeks to better understand the interactions between human activities and natural diversity, in order to evaluate existing, and explore potential, land management strategies.

Ground Squirrel Re-colonization of a Pipeline Right-of-Way in Southern Alberta

Richard D. Lauzon, Scott D. Grindal, and Garry E. Hornbeck

Ground squirrels are important in the prairie ecosystem as a prey base for carnivores, as well as providing potential burrows for other species (e.g., burrowing owls). However, little is known about the response of ground squirrels to pipeline construction, and any resulting impacts on the prairie ecosystem. We investigated the effects of a recently constructed pipeline on the density and distribution of Richardson's ground squirrel (*Spermophilus richardsoni*) burrows in the dry mixedgrass ecoregion of southeastern Alberta. We predicted that ground squirrels would be attracted to the ditchline (excavated area) of a pipeline right-of-way (ROW) because of the reduced soil density, but would avoid the workspace (area of vehicle traffic) of the ROW because of soil compaction. Burrow densities, vegetation cover (%), and vascular plant height were estimated along a recently constructed (1997) pipeline ROW in the late summers of 1998 and 1999. Fifty sample plots (4 m × 100 m) were established in each of three treatment groups: (1) native prairie, adjacent to the ROW; (2) ROW workspace; and (3) ROW ditchline. Burrow densities increased during the first ($\bar{x} = 0.54$/plot) and second ($\bar{x} = 1.3$/plot) years after pipeline construction in the ditchline, but remained consistently low in the workspace ($\bar{x} = 0.48$ and 0.38/plot). These values were approximately 14–47% of expected densities of burrows in adjacent prairie control sites ($\bar{x} = 2.76$ and 2.78/plot). After reclamation, vegetation cover was similar for all three treatment areas ($\bar{x} = 51.2$–66.1%), but vascular plant height tended to be greatest on both the ditchline and workspace of the disturbed ROW ($\bar{x} = 41.4$ and 37.2 cm, respectively) than in the undisturbed native prairie ($\bar{x} = 18.2$ cm). Our results suggested that ground squirrels re-colonized the pipeline ROW shortly after construction, but areas of compacted (workspace) soil are less suitable than excavated (ditchline) areas after two years. However, disturbed areas in general associated with the pipeline ROW were used less than undisturbed native prairie. This preference for undisturbed sites may be related to differences in both soil compaction and vegetation cover and height. Although soil compaction may be difficult to mitigate, successful reclamation of pipeline ROWs for ground squirrels may be increased by careful management of vegetation, such that it approximates more closely to native prairie ground cover.

Keywords: Richardson's ground squirrel, Spermophilus richardsoni, pipeline construction, impacts

INTRODUCTION

The Richardson's ground squirrel (*Spermophilus richardsoni*) is found in the northern Great Plains from Alberta to Manitoba and south to northern Colorado and they are an important species to the prairie ecosystem (Banfield, 1977; Burt and Grossenheider, 1976). For example, this species is important prey for a number of mammalian, avian, and reptilian predators such as the ferruginous hawk, Swainson's hawk, prairie falcon, badger, coyote, red fox, western rattlesnake, and bull snake (Banfield, 1977; Hunt, 1993; Michener, 1979; Michener, 1995; Pattie and Hoffmann, 1992; Schmutz, 1993; Schmutz et al., 1980). The burrows constructed by the Richardson's ground squirrel provide essential nesting, cover, and hibernating habitat for burrowing owls, snakes, and amphibians (Banfield, 1977; Konrad and Gilmer, 1984; Pendlebury, 1977; Russell and Bauer, 1993; Wellicome and Haug, 1995). Therefore,

Environmental Concerns in Rights-of-Way Management: Seventh International Symposium
J.W. Goodrich-Mahoney, D.F. Mutrie and C.A. Guild (editors)
© 2002 Elsevier Science Ltd. All rights reserved.

disturbances that affect the abundance and distribution of Richardson's ground squirrels would also affect a number of other species on the prairies.

Resource extraction on the Canadian Prairies is prominent landuse activity and pipelines constructed to transport oil and gas are an environmental concern because of the short and long-term affects these developments may have on the prairie ecosystem. There development effects may include disturbance to soil profiles and compaction, and impacts to vegetation composition and structure.

The Express pipeline is a 434 km large diameter pipeline that extends from Hardisty to Wildhorse, AB. This pipeline was constructed during fall 1996 with reclamation activities continuing through summer 1997 (Express Pipeline, 1997). Initial wildlife surveys were conducted in 1995 and 1996, prior to construction (AXYS Environmental Consulting Ltd., 1995, 1996).

Express Pipeline committed to studying the effects of pipeline construction on the abundance of the Richardson's ground squirrel on the reclaimed right-of-way (ROW) and initiated a five-year monitoring program to determine these effects. In this paper, we discuss the results of the first three years of this monitoring program. We predicted that ground squirrels would be attracted to the ditchline (excavated area) of a pipeline ROW because of the reduced soil density, but would avoid the workspace (area of vehicle traffic) of the ROW because of soil compaction. The vegetation growing on the ROW may have an affect on the recolonization of the ROW by ground squirrels. We predicted that the taller vegetation growing on the ROW would inhibit recolonization by ground squirrels.

STUDY AREA

This study was conducted in southeastern Alberta, northwest of Medicine Hat (Fig. 1). The Dry Mixedgrass Subregion is the warmest and driest area in Alberta. It has a continental climate with cold winters, warm summers and low precipitation. Two-thirds of the annual precipitation occurs as rain, primarily in June. Warm summer temperatures, low precipitation, and strong winds produce high potential evapotranspiration deficits. Dry summer conditions, coupled with low winter temperatures and shallow snow cover severely limits plant growth (Achuff, 1994). The resulting vegetation is a mixture of short and mid height grasses in the uplands, shrubs on protected north faces or in seepage areas, and trees along streambanks and river floodplains (Strong, 1992).

METHODS

Preliminary sampling plots
To establish sub-sample areas along the 434 km length of pipeline, preliminary sampling was conducted prior to construction in 1996. A ground squirrel burrow survey was conducted along the entire length of the Express Pipeline for each quarter section of native prairie within a 2 m wide corridor along the centerline of the pipeline. The results of this survey indicated that ground squirrels within the ROW were patchy in occurrence and variable in density where they occurred.

Data from the 1996 burrow counts was highly variable (mean burrow density 15.12 burrows/4000 m^2 ± 10.16). Based on this information, it was possible to predict that within high density ground squirrel habitat, a sample plot of 4 m by 100 m (400 m^2) would encounter at least 1.5 burrows, and the standard deviation of the estimate would be approximately 1.3.

With this information, and an *a priori* level of acceptable error that was selected to estimate burrow density within 20% of the mean, the target number of sample plots was determined to be approximately 54:

	Confidence level			
	80%	90%	95%	99%
Required sample size	33	54	77	133

Long-term monitoring plots
The long-term monitoring program was implemented in three localized areas of the Express Pipeline based on the 1996 preliminary sampling (Fig. 1). These three areas had similar vegetation and soils characteristics and had sufficient ground squirrel burrow densities to conduct this study. The sampling plots for the long-term monitoring program were initially established during late August 1997.

The size of individual sample plots was constrained by the dimensions of the ditchline, which was a relatively narrow strip of unconsolidated soil, about 2–3 m wide. At the same time, sample plots needed to be sufficiently large in total area to encompass the low density of burrows on the landscape. However, very large narrow sample plots can be expected to yield imprecise counts (i.e., plot locations tend not to be reproducible annually, which introduces large boundary errors), while very small sample plots can be expected to yield a large number of zero burrow counts, which are problematic for statistical analysis.

Fifty sample plots centered on ditchline were located at alternating 100 m intervals (200 m between beginning of each sample plot), with the other treatment plots being established in parallel positions on adjacent workspace and undisturbed prairie (Fig. 2). Irregularities in topography required that the intervals between some plots varied from 100 m (range 50–500 m).

In order to accurately locate sample plots each year, the three treatment plots (ditchline, workspace, and

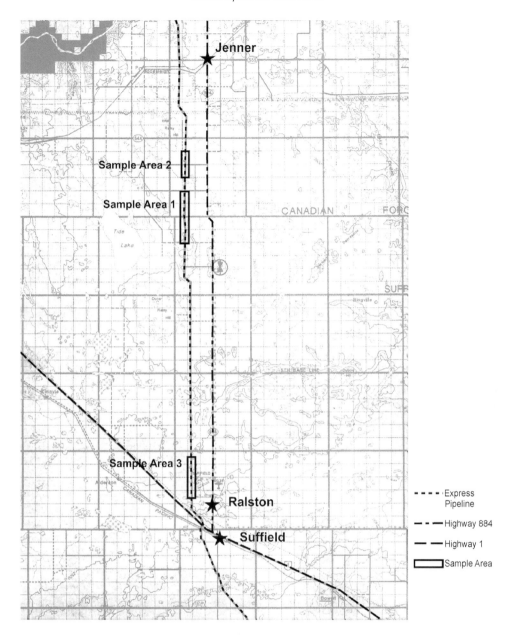

Fig. 1. Location of the study area showing the three ground squirrel monitoring sample areas.

prairie) were marked with a single wooden 1″ by 4″ stake at the southwest corner of each plot and a single stake at the northwest corner of the Ditchline plot (Fig. 2). Plot stakes were pounded into the ground to near ground level to prevent damage by cattle or vehicles. Each stake was painted fluorescent orange and a metal numbered tag was attached to the prairie stake to identify individual sample locations. At each sample location, workspace and prairie treatment plot stakes were laid using the ditchline sample plot stake as a reference point. The ditchline sample plot stake was pounded into the ROW about 1 m inside (east of) the west boundary of the area stripped of topsoil over ditchline. The distance to the workspace and prairie plot stakes varied among individual sample locations depending upon changes in ROW stripping methods (e.g., blade width vs. full width stripping).

Burrow counts

All burrows present within the sampling plots of each treatment were filled during initial establishment of plots in 1997 with soil or duff from areas adjacent to the burrow so that only new burrows would be counted the following year. Burrows were filled during subsequent years to ensure that only new burrows were counted during each year of sampling. Burrow counts were conducted at all plots during late August/early September in 1998 and 1999.

Vegetation sampling

At the 25 and 75 m mark of each treatment plot, vegetation parameters were collected with a 0.5 m by 0.5 m frame, 1 m from the west edge of the plot. Parameters collected included the percent of vascular

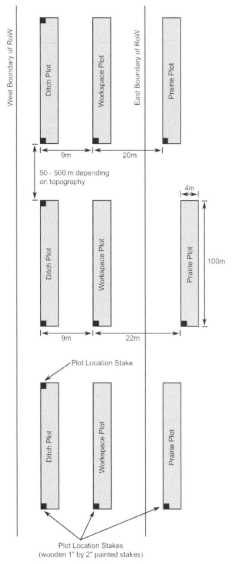

Ditchline plot is 1 m east of the edge of the stripping along the west boundary of the ROW. Workspace and Prairie plots are measured eastward from the Ditchline plot stake. The distance to Workspace and Prairie stakes at each sample location varries according to the width of ROW stripping. The stakes are 1″ by 2″ wooden stakes pounded in to leave about 2″ to 3″ above ground and painted florescent orange. This shallow height above ground helps prevent breakage by cattle and vehicles. Each series of plots is identified by a metal numbered tag affixed to the Prairie plot stake.

Fig. 2. Configuration of ditchline, workspace, and prairie sample plots.

plant cover, the percent of bare ground and the average height of vegetation within the frame.

Statistical analysis

Since reclamation, the final phase of construction, was completed during summer 1997, data from this year was not included in the analysis. Two-way Analyses of Variance (ANOVA; Zar, 1984) tests were used to examine the effect of year (i.e., time since pipeline construction) and sample type (ROW ditchline, ROW workspace, undisturbed prairie) on the abundance of

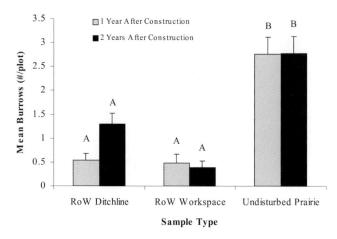

Fig. 3. Mean (+1 SE) burrow density for ground squirrels after the first (1998) and second (1999) years of pipeline ROW construction in southeast Alberta. Means with the same letters are not significantly different ($p > 0.05$).

ground squirrel burrows and vegetation characteristics (% vegetation cover, % bare ground, vegetation height). We conducted Tukey's multiple comparisons when main effects were significant.

Pearson correlations were used to test relationships between the abundance of ground squirrel burrows and vegetation characteristics (% vegetation cover, % bare ground, vegetation height). We used Statistica® (Statsoft, 1997) for all statistical analyses, employing an α level of 0.05.

RESULTS

Burrow densities differed significantly between sample types ($F = 48.9$; df = 294,2; $p < 0.001$), but not between years ($F = 1.2$; df = 294,1; $p = 0.27$; Fig. 3). Burrow densities tended to increase during the first ($\bar{x} = 0.54$/plot) and second ($\bar{x} = 1.3$/plot) years after pipeline construction in the ditchline (although not significantly), but remained consistently low in the workspace ($\bar{x} = 0.48$ and 0.38/plot). These burrow densities in the pipeline ROW were significantly less (14–47%) than expected in adjacent prairie control sites ($\bar{x} = 2.76$ and 2.78/plot; Fig. 3).

The abundance of ground squirrel burrows was positively correlated with percent vegetation cover ($r = 0.16$, $p = 0.007$), and negatively correlated with percent bare ground ($r = -0.34$, $p < 0.001$) and vegetation height ($r = -0.21$, $p < 0.001$).

Both vegetation cover and height differed significantly between sample types (cover: $F = 15.2$; df = 294,2; $p < 0.001$; height: $F = 46.9$; df = 294,2; $p < 0.001$) and between years (cover: $F = 19.9$; df = 294,1; $p = 0.27$; height: $F = 38.6$; df = 294,1; $p = 0.27$; Figs. 4 and 5). A marginally insignificant interaction existed between year and sample type ($F = 2.7$; df = 294,2; $p = 0.071$) for vegetation height. Vegetation cover on the pipeline ROW ($\bar{x} = 39.9$–58.5%) was similar to that of

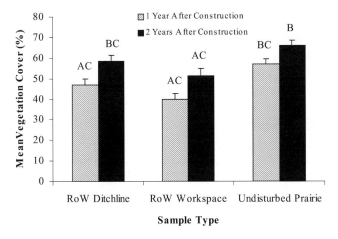

Fig. 4. Mean (+1 SE) vascular vegetation cover after the first (1998) and second (1999) years of pipeline ROW construction in southeast Alberta. Means with the same letters are not significantly different ($p > 0.05$).

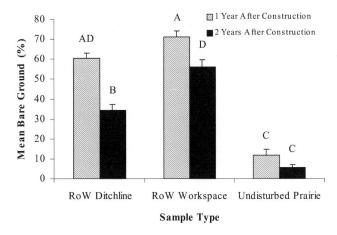

Fig. 6. Mean (+1 SE) bare ground after the first (1998) and second (1999) years of pipeline ROW construction in southeast Alberta. Means with the same letters are not significantly different ($p > 0.05$).

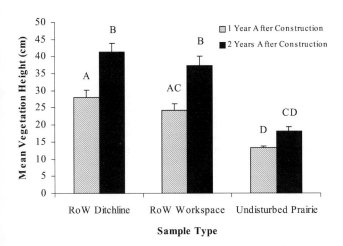

Fig. 5. Mean (+1 SE) vascular vegetation height after the first (1998) and second (1999) years of pipeline ROW construction in southeast Alberta. Means with the same letters are not significantly different ($p > 0.05$).

the native prairie ($\bar{x} = 57.1$–66.1%) in both years 1 and 2 following construction (Fig. 4). However, vegetation height was significantly greater in both the ditchline and workspace of the disturbed ROW, than in the undisturbed native prairie for both years (Fig. 5). Vegetation height also increased significantly from year 1 to year 2 after pipeline construction in the ROW, but not in the native prairie (Fig. 5).

The amount of bare ground differed significantly between sample types ($F = 195.7$; df $= 294,2$; $p < 0.001$) and between years ($F = 46.6$; df $= 294,1$; $p \leq 0.001$; Fig. 6). There was also a significant interaction between year and sample type ($F = 6.1$; df $= 294,2$; $p < 0.005$). Similar to vegetation height, the amount of bare ground was significantly greater in the ditchline and workspace of the pipeline ROW than in the native prairie. Correspondingly, the amount of bare ground decreased significantly on the ROW (Fig. 6) with the increase in vegetation cover (Fig. 4) between years.

DISCUSSION

Although soil density measurements were not collected in the workspace and ditchline plots, we assume that the soil in the excavated ditchline plots will be uncompacted and the soil in the workspace will be compacted due to the large volume of traffic during construction.

Our data suggests that there was an insignificant difference between the burrow densities in ditchline plots and workspace plots. Ground squirrels are substrate burrowers and therefore, we anticipated that ground squirrels would prefer areas with uncompacted soil (ditchline plots) rather than areas with compacted soil (workspace plots) because it would require less effort to construct burrows. Although our data currently shows no significant difference between ditchline and workspace plots, we suspect that these results may be confounded by the tall vegetation growing on the ROW.

Growth characteristics of the vegetation on the ROW may inhibit the recolonization by ground squirrels. Typically, the vegetation on the ROW consisted of weedy species such as kochia (*Kochia scoparia*) and Russian thistle (*Salsola kali*) as well as tall grass species such as slender wheatgrass (*Agropyron trachycaulum*). Native plant species, typical of the area were seeded and were present as well but at the time of this study they occurred at lower densities. Two years after reclamation, the height of vegetation was significantly higher than that of the adjacent native prairie.

The Richardson's ground squirrel is a grassland species with a habitat preference influenced by vegetation height. This species prefers grasslands with low vegetation providing an adequate view of the surrounding habitat so that predators can easily be detected (Pattie and Hoffmann, 1992). Tall vegetation is avoided because predators can hide amongst the vegetation and aerial predators such as hawks can easily see prey.

A study to evaluate the re-introduction of Richardson's ground squirrels at a sight near Picture Butte, Alberta, showed that vegetation height was a key component of ground squirrel habitat (Michener, 1995). During this study, it was found that predators used tall cover to ambush ground squirrels and it was not until grazing was introduced that the population grew and expanded into adjacent areas. Recommendations for successful re-introductions included maintenance of short vegetation by burning, mowing, or grazing (Michener, 1995).

Ground squirrels are expected to use this ROW more frequently once native species become dominant and the height of vegetative cover is reduced. Weedy pioneer species as well as species seeded specifically to provide immediate cover on the ROW will dominate the vegetative cover of a newly reclaimed ROW for a period of at least two years. Eventually, the native species are expected to become more dominant and weedy species and species like slender wheatgrass will become less prevalent.

RECOMMENDATIONS

After pipeline construction is complete, the ROW must be reclaimed to as near existing conditions as possible. Reclamation procedures balance numerous environmental concerns such as wind and water erosion, preservation of native prairie, preservation of rare plant and wildlife resources, replacement of wildlife habitat, and landowner concerns. To promote the recolonization of the ROW by ground squirrels, a number of mitigative options are available including adjusting seed mixes, mowing, or grazing.

Seed mixes used to reclaim a pipeline ROW incorporate seeds of species native to that area as well as species that will colonize the ROW quickly to provide cover, preventing water and wind erosion. Slender wheatgrass, a species used as a cover species, provides tall cover that is not suitable for ground squirrels. The seed mix could be revised by reducing the seeding rate of slender wheatgrass and other tall plant species in the seed mix thereby reducing the height of cover on the ROW.

Weeds are pioneer species that quickly colonize disturbed areas such as pipeline ROWs. Regardless of the seed mix used, weeds will dominate the ROW for at least a few years, reducing the habitat capability for ground squirrels. Mowing and/or grazing may reduce the height of cover on the ROW so that it more closely resembles the native prairie condition.

ACKNOWLEDGEMENTS

Express Pipelines Ltd. provided funding for this project with additional funding from AXYS Environmental Consulting Ltd. Peter Balagus, Dave Scobie, Liz Parkin, Harry Blanchert, Garry Hornbeck, and Richard Lauzon conducted the fieldwork. Marilyn Neville provided expertise on reclamation recommendations. Lyn Turnbull provided the graphics expertise.

REFERENCES

Achuff, P. 1994. Natural Regions, Subregions and Natural History Themes of Alberta. Prepared for Alberta Environmental Protection, Parks Service.

AXYS Environmental Consulting Ltd. 1995. Wildlife surveys for the proposed Express pipeline project. Prepared for Express Pipelines Ltd., a division of Alberta Energy Company Ltd. and TransCanada Pipelines Ltd. Calgary, AB.

AXYS Environmental Consulting Ltd. 1996. 1996 wildlife surveys for the proposed Express pipeline project. Prepared for Express Pipelines Ltd., a division of Alberta Energy Company Ltd. and TransCanada Pipelines Ltd. Calgary, AB.

Banfield, A.W.F. 1977. The mammals of Canada. University of Toronto Press. Toronto, ON, Canada. 438 pp.

Burt, W.H. and R.P. Grossenheider. 1976. A field guide to the mammals. Houghton Mifflin Company Boston, MA. 289 pp.

Express Pipeline. 1997. Environmental As-Built, Spread 'B' – Vol. 2. Express Pipelines Ltd. Calgary, AB.

Hunt, L.E. 1993. Food habits of nesting Prairie Falcons in southern Alberta, Canada. Pg. 143. In: Proceedings of the third prairie conservation and endangered species workshop. G.L. Holroyd, H.L. Dickson, M. Regnier, and H.C. Smith, eds. Prov. Mus. Alberta Nat. Hist. Occ. Paper No. 19, Edmonton, AB. 384 pp.

Konrad, P.M. and D.S. Gilmer. 1984. Observations on the nesting ecology of burrowing owls in central North Dakota. Prairie Nat., 16: 129–130.

Michener, G.R. 1979. Yearly variations in the population dynamics of Richardson's ground squirrels. Can. Field-Nat., 93(4): 363–370.

Michener, G.R. 1995. Establishment of a colony of Richardson's ground squirrels in southern Alberta. Pp. 303–308. In: Proceedings of the fourth prairie conservation and endangered species workshop. W.D. Willms and J.F. Dormaar, eds. Prov. Mus. Alberta Nat. Hist. Occ. Paper No. 23, Edmonton, AB. 337 pp.

Pattie, D.L. and R.S. Hoffman. 1992. Mammals of North American parks and prairies. Copies available from: Donald L. Pattie, Edmonton, AB. 579 pp.

Pendlebury, G.B. 1977. Distribution and abundance of the prairie rattlesnake, Crotalus viridis viridis, in Canada. Canadian Field Naturalist, 92(2): 122–129.

Russell, A.P. and A.M. Bauer. 1993. The Amphibians and Reptiles of Alberta. University of Calgary Press. 264 pp.

Schmutz, J.K. 1993. Grassland Requirements by Ferruginous Hawks. Pp. 37–38. In: Proceedings of the third prairie conservation and endangered species workshop. G.L. Holroyd, H.L. Dickson, M. Regnier, and H.C. Smith, eds. Prov. Mus. Alberta Nat. Hist. Occ. Paper No. 19, Edmonton, AB. 384 pp.

Schmutz, J.K., S.M. Schmutz, and D.A. Boag. 1980. Coexistence of three species of hawks (Buteo spp.) in the prairie-parkland ecotone. Canadian Journal of Zoology, 58: 1075–1089.

Strong, W.L. 1992. Ecoregions and Ecodistricts of Alberta. Vol. 1. Prepared for Alberta Forestry, Lands and Wildlife. Edmonton, AB.

Wellicome, T.I. and E.A. Haug. 1995. Second update of status report on the Burrowing Owl, Speotyto cunicularia, in Canada. Committee on the Status of Endangered Wildlife in Canada. 32 pp.

Zar, J.H. 1984. Biostatistical analysis. Prentice Hall Inc., Englewood Cliffs, NJ.

BIOGRAPHICAL SKETCHES

Richard Lauzon
AXYS Environmental Consulting Ltd. Suite 600, 555 Fourth Avenue S.W., Calgary, AB, Canada, T2P 3E7 (fax: 403-269-5245, email: rlauzon@axys.net)
Richard Lauzon is a wildlife biologist who has worked for AXYS Environmental Consulting Ltd. since 1991. He has been responsible for conducting Environmental Impact Assessments throughout western Canada for the oil and gas industry, tourism, waste management, forestry and mining. He is also responsible for co-ordinating and conducting many of the field surveys required for these projects.

Scott Grindal
AXYS Environmental Consulting Ltd. Suite 600, 555 Fourth Avenue S.W., Calgary, AB, Canada, T2P 3E7
Scott Grindal specializes in wildlife ecology, with experience across Canada and overseas. His range of experience involves the design, management, implementation, and statistical analyses of projects dealing with wildlife habitat use and impact assessments.

Garry E. Hornbeck
Wildlife & Company Ltd., #312 Cedarille Crescent, S.W., Calgary, AB, Canada, T2W 2H7
Garry E. Hornbeck is principal of Wildlife & Company Ltd., a consulting company incorporated in Calgary, AB, in 1996. He holds a BSc (Botany & Zoology) from Brandon University, Manitoba (1975) and an MSc degree in Wildlife Ecology from Colorado State University, Fort Collins (1979). His research interests include ungulate behavior and ecology and environmental impact assessment. He is currently working on effects of linear pipeline corridors on migratory songbirds. He has been a member of The Wildlife Society since 1979, and is past-president (2001–2002) of the Alberta Society of Professional Biologists (ASPB).

Highway Improvements to Minimize Environmental Impacts within the Canadian Rocky Mountain National Parks

T.M. McGuire and J.F. Morrall

This paper describes two highway engineering techniques that have been developed or adopted to mitigate the unique environmental impact highways and roads have within Canadian Rocky Mountain National Parks, which are also World Heritage Sites. The first is the development of the passing lane system on the Trans Canada Highway in the Rocky Mountain Parks to defer four-laning (twinning). The second example is the twinning of 18.6 km of the Trans Canada Highway within Banff National Park. Twinning represents a logical next step following the passing lane phase. The paper describes how highway improvements were developed to address and mitigate numerous potential twinning impacts identified during environmental assessment. Included within the environmental mitigation were a series of measures, such as fencing and animal crossing structures, to address wildlife movement, biodiversity, and mortality as well as stream, terrain, and vegetation disturbance minimization techniques. Research has found that the mitigation measures have been effective in reducing wildlife/vehicle collisions by 97% for some species.

Keywords: Highways, national park, environment, mitigations

INTRODUCTION

Parks Canada is responsible for the maintenance and repair of approximately 1200 lane km of highways and roads within the Canadian Rocky Mountain National Parks of Banff, Yoho, Kootenay, Jasper, Glacier, and Mount Revelstoke National Parks within the provinces of Alberta and British Columbia. Of this total, approximately 500 lane km are major through highways that are part of provincial highway systems including the Trans Canada Highway (TCH).

The TCH and other major highways passing through national parks are part of a national transportation system that responds to transportation objectives and demands that are not always compatible with national park objectives. Major transportation corridors can have a number of damaging impacts on park environments. They act as barriers to natural animal movement and are a source of mortality. Exhaust emissions contribute to declining air quality, particularly in valley bottoms. Routine winter maintenance requires gravel and salt. Extracting gravel from park land damages habitat and alters the natural landscape. Spills of hazardous materials can occur accidentally in transportation corridors. Previous road construction has resulted in changes to alluvial fans, natural water channels, and seasonal processes such as flooding. In turn, this affects aquatic habitat, nutrient and productivity levels, seasonal fish movement, erosion rates, and water quality.

Development within National Parks

Any proposed development in the Canadian National Parks, including highways, is subject to the most rigorous environmental assessment procedures in Canada as outlined within the 1992 Canadian Environmental Assessment Act (CEAA). This, along with the National Parks Act (NPA), 1930, subsequent amendments and 1994 policy statement stressing the ecological role of

Environmental Concerns in Rights-of-Way Management: Seventh International Symposium
J.W. Goodrich-Mahoney, D.F. Mutrie and C.A. Guild (editors)
© 2002 Elsevier Science Ltd. All rights reserved.

national parks, provide the basic guidelines for highway improvements. The Canadian National Parks Act states that "The Parks are dedicated to the people of Canada for their benefit, education, and enjoyment... such parks shall be maintained and made use of so as to leave them unimpaired for the enjoyment of future generations." The Act further stresses that ecological integrity through the protection of natural resources shall be the first priority in the consideration of visitor use.

PASSING LANE SYSTEM ON THE TRANS CANADA HIGHWAY

The Trans Canada Highway (TCH) is the major route that transverses the Canadian Rocky Mountain Parks of Banff, Yoho, Glacier, and Mount Revelstoke and provides access via the Icefields Parkway to Jasper National Park and the Yellowhead Highway and to Kootenay National Park via Highway 93 South within the provinces of Alberta and British Columbia. The TCH was officially opened in 1962 and at 7900 km in length is the longest paved highway in the world stretching from Pacific to Atlantic Oceans. The TCH was constructed as a two-way, two-lane highway, with 3.65 m lanes and 3.0 m paved shoulders. The design speed is 113 km/h and the nominal posted speed is 90 km/h, although posted speeds vary between 60 and 90 km/h. The highway passes through level, rolling and mountainous terrain.

Traffic volumes on this section of the TCH vary from a high Annual Average Daily Traffic (AADT) of 14,870 in 1997 at the Banff East Gate to a low of 4400 in Yoho. Summer Average Daily Traffic (SADT) in 1997 at both locations were 21,580 and 8380 in Banff and Yoho, respectively. Historical traffic data indicate a long term linear growth trend of 2–2.5% per annum (Parks Canada, 1999).

Traffic composition varies widely depending on season and time of day. Recreational vehicles can account for up to 25% of the traffic stream during daylight hours in summer months. Heavy trucks (semi-tractor trailers and combination units such as B-trains) can account for up to 50% of the traffic stream at night during winter months on the TCH in Glacier National Park.

Passing/climbing lane system

It is recognized that four laning (twinning) of the TCH, through the Rocky Mountain Parks may be inevitable in the very long term. The overall strategy adopted by Parks Canada is to extend the design life of the TCH as long as possible as a two-lane facility subject to maintaining safety and an acceptable level of service. This has been accomplished by constructing a passing lane and climbing lane system and intersection improvements. The passing lane program will be followed by sequential twinning and grade separation of critical intersections.

Parks Canada pioneered the concept of a system of passing/climbing lanes in the early 1980s (Morrall and Blight, 1985). This was a departure from previous highway engineering practice, which considered only isolated climbing lanes on long steep upgrades. During the early days of the passing lane project, conventional highway engineering studies continually rejected passing lanes in favor of twinning. Analysis procedures of the day, such as the 1965 Highway Capacity Manual (HCM) (Highway Research Board, 1965), had served for two decades as the primary guide for determining the level of service on two-lane highways. The level of service analysis procedures in the 1965 HCM manual did not account for the effect of passing lanes on level-of-service. Therefore, it is not surprising that previous studies of the TCH (Transport Canada, 1985) rejected passing lanes in favor of twinning. Although the then just released 1985 Highway Capacity Manual (Transportation Research Board, 1985) included a number of refinements, such as the introduction of percent time delayed, average speed instead of operating speed, and the effect of directional split, in determining the capacity and level of service on a two-lane highway, the procedures still did not account for the effect of passing lanes on level of service.

In order to determine the need for passing lanes, and their effect on the level of service, a traffic simulation model of the TCH was utilized (Morrall, 1987). The simulation model used was the TRARR (Traffic on Rural Roads) model developed by the Australian Road Research Board (Hoban et al., 1985). The overall objective of the level of service analysis was to determine if the TCH, with low-cost operational improvements such as passing lanes and intersection improvements, could provide an acceptable level of service until the twinning was required (Morrall and Thompson, 1990).

The need and location of passing lanes on the TCH was based on a criteria of 60% time spent following, which corresponds to level of service C in the 1985 Highway Capacity Manual (Transportation Research Board, 1985). In Glacier National Park, identification of potential passing lane locations was also based on the need to increase traffic storage capacity to hold vehicles safely during avalanche stabilization as well as the aforementioned level of service criteria (Morrall, 1991).

The passing/climbing lane system on the TCH in the four Mountain Parks consists of 29 auxiliary lanes, as summarized in Table 1, providing an average spacing of 8.3 km, and 9.1 km between assured passing opportunities eastbound and westbound, respectively. While passing lanes and climbing lanes are classified as auxiliary lanes, they have two distinct functions. A climbing lane is an auxiliary lane provided for the diversion of slow vehicles from the through lane

Table 1. Passing and climbing lane system on the Trans-Canada Highway in the Mountain National Parks

Mountain National Park	Number of passing and climbing lanes	Length of system (km)	Total highway length in park (%)
Banff[a]			
Eastbound Direction	1	2.24	10.2
Westbound Direction	3	4.50	18.0
Yoho			
Eastbound Direction	6	17.30	37.7
Westbound Direction	5	9.01	19.6
Glacier			
Eastbound Direction	7	13.83	31.4
Westbound Direction	5	9.63	21.8
Mount Revelstoke			
Eastbound Direction	1	1.97	15.4
Westbound Direction	1	0.93	7.3
Total number	29		

[a]Phase IIIA TCH twinning has replaced 2 passing lanes in Banff reducing the passing lane system from 6 to 4.

and hence the passing of slow vehicles on upgrades. A passing lane is an auxiliary lane to improve passing opportunities that are restricted due to roadway geometry, downhill grades, or lack of adequate gaps for passing in the oncoming traffic stream. A passing/climbing lane system consisting of 12 auxiliary lanes has been constructed on the Kootenay Parkway, and passing/climbing lane systems are under development for the Icefields Parkway and Yellowhead Highway in Jasper National Park.

The effect of the passing lane system has resulted in a 6–7% reduction in percent time spent following in the 500–700 veh/h range, thereby keeping the overall percent time spent following less than 60% and hence by definition, level of service C. A more important impact of the passing lane system is a 20–25% increase in the number of overtakings in the 500–700 veh/h range (Morrall and Thompson, 1990). An unique aspect of the passing lane system on the TCH are two downgrade passing lanes located on long downgrades in Glacier and Yoho National Parks.

Construction of the passing lanes involved shifting the highway centerline by approximately 1.75 m and constructing pavement widening on one or both sides depending on terrain, environmental constraints and existing shoulder width. Shoulder widths were reduced to 1.2 m in the passing zone to minimize environmental impacts and costs. Costs were approximately $90,000/km Cdn for widening on one side and about $125,000 Cdn for widening on both sides, excluding final full width overlay. Full width overlay of highway once widened, added another $150,000/km Cdn. Depending upon the selected option, costs range between one tenth and one quarter the cost of twinning (excluding environmental mitigations).

HIGHWAY TWINNING

Project description

The need for twinning is based on maintaining an acceptable level of service and highway safety. The passing lane system on the TCH helped extend the design life of the highway as a two lane facility by approximately 15 years. However, steadily increasing commercial, private, and tourist traffic have ultimately led to the need to commence twinning the TCH in Banff in phases over the past decade (Parks Canada, 1995). The latest 18.6 km stretch between Sunshine and Castle Mountain Interchanges, and known as Phase IIIA, was completed in 1998.

This section of the TCH prior to twinning comprised two lanes with passing lanes added in the early 1980s utilizing existing shoulders to enhance the level of service as part of the strategy to extend the design life of the TCH. Accident rates were higher than the average Canadian two-lane highway, and double that on the adjacent four-lane divided section. A level of service (LOS) analysis determined that for 2000 h of the year the highway was operating at LOS D and E which affected 1.6 million vehicles or 54% of the yearly volume of 3 million vehicles. Thus this section of the TCH was operating well below the design LOS C. During summer months, daily volumes between 18,000 and 20,000 veh/day were recorded on a regular basis. In addition, this section had a high wildlife collision mortality, affecting the safety of the driving population as well as the animal population (Parks Canada, 1995).

The phase IIIA twinning project involved the construction of 18.6 km of rural divided freeway with a design speed of 110 km (posted at 90 km/h). The cross-section for each carriageway consists of two 3.7 m lanes, a 3 m outside shoulder, 2 m inside shoulder, and variable median widths averaging 14 m. Grades do not exceed 3% and the alignment was carefully fitted into the existing topography while making use of the existing two-lane highway. The east and west carriageways are separated by a grass median for a length of 14.1 km, by a treed median for a length of 3 km, and by a concrete barrier median for a length of 1.5 km. Constructed at a cost of $31 Cdn million, approximately 30% or $9.2 million was for environmental assessment and mitigation measures.

Environmental challenges and mitigation measures

The design and implementation of such a large scale project in an environmentally sensitive and high profile setting as Banff National Park created a wide variety of challenges. The importance of addressing these challenges is reinforced by Parks Canada's legislated requirement to give the maintenance of ecological integrity and biological diversity the highest priority in management and administration of the parks. An extensive environmental assessment and public review process, lasting over two years, was undertaken prior to project approval. The main areas of environmental concern related to the project included potential effects on wildlife, vegetation, and aquatics, measuring success of any measures introduced to minimize effects as well as employing sustainable construction practices reflective of a national park setting.

Wildlife

The highway follows along the bottom of the Bow River Valley, through a relatively rare montane ecosystem. The project area provides valuable habitat for a wide variety of wildlife species, including elk, deer, moose, wolf, black and grizzly bear, cougar, lynx, coyote, wolverine, and a number of small mammals, birds, reptiles, and amphibians. The primary concern resulting from the interaction between the highway and wildlife is the potential for vehicle/wildlife collisions, with resulting wildlife mortality, as well as human injury or fatality. Although ungulates represent the highest proportion of animals killed, population impacts are thought to be most severe for rare or uncommon species with low reproductive rates, such as wolf, bear, and cougar.

The problem of wildlife mortality resulting from vehicle collisions was addressed through the installation of 2.4 m high wildlife exclusion fencing along the right-of-way. The fence height has proven adequate to prevent most species from jumping or climbing the fence. The fence is located as close to the highway as allowed by traffic safety clear zone requirements and logistical constraints, except in a few areas with high aesthetic values. The fence fabric has a reduced mesh size varying from 150 mm square to 50 mm × 150 mm at the bottom to reduce intrusion by smaller animals. A variety of wildlife species have been known to penetrate the exclusion fencing on previous projects by pulling up or digging beneath the fence. To reduce this potential problem, a 1.5 m chain link fencing apron was attached to the fence and buried at a 45° angle. Total cost of exclusion fencing was approximately $1.9 million Cdn with the buried apron representing 15% of this cost.

Fig. 1. Animal overpass.

The use of fencing creates a barrier to movement for many species that require different, widely separated habitats during different seasons and phases of their life cycles. Due to concern over the effects of this habitat fragmentation on such rare or uncommon species, it was decided to try a particularly innovative approach to increasing the opportunities for wildlife to safely cross the Trans-Canada Highway. Two wildlife overpasses, each 50 m in width, and costing $1.75 million each, were constructed at locations determined by research and wildlife/vehicle accident data to be wildlife movement corridors (shown in Fig. 1). The structures were built of pre-cast concrete arches off site to allow rapid construction with minimal site and traffic disruption. Figure 2 provides cross-sectional dimensions for these structures. The concrete head walls at the ends of the structures were cast-in-place using coloured concrete to match the large native boulders salvaged from the project site which were used to retain earth fill between, above, and on approaches to the arches. Fill salvaged from the project was used to create gentle approaches to the structures as well as 2 m high berms along the outside of the structures to reduce traffic noise and visual disturbance. Approaches were shaped to retain maximum amounts of existing vegetation. Native trees and shrubs indigenous to Banff National Park were planted on and around the

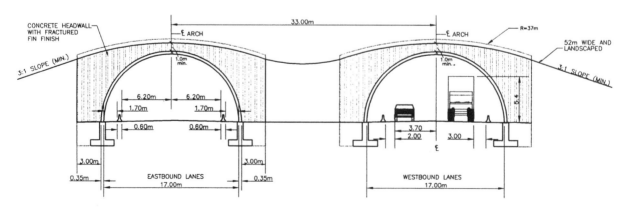

Fig. 2. Cross sectional dimensions of animal overpass structure.

overpasses to provide wildlife cover and reduce aesthetic impacts.

In addition to the two overpasses, 14 underpass structures of varying size provide additional crossing opportunities for a range of wildlife within this 18.6 km stretch of highway. These underpasses include two walkways in association with major creek crossing structures, three 4 by 7 m elliptical steel culverts, and four 3 by 2.4 m concrete box structures. Most underpass approaches have been designed and landscaped to provide maximum vegetative cover and have earth berms protecting the approaches from traffic noise and visual disturbance.

Vegetation and aquatics

The project had the potential to negatively impact both rare vegetation and aquatic resources through direct habitat loss and the introduction of potentially harmful surface run-off including winter road maintenance salt into sensitive vegetated wetland areas, streams, and the Bow River. The alienation of valuable existing montane that comprises only 4% of Banff National Park's 6640 km^2 but where the majority of flora and fauna occur was also of prime concern.

Reduction in right-of-way width and avoidance of wetlands were achieved through careful alignment design, strict clearing limits, varying cut/fill slopes to lie between 2 to 1 and 3 to 1, and use of steep rock fills. These allowed the potential impacts to be minimized. Colonies of rare plants were marked and brought to the attention of equipment operators to avoid disturbance.

The National Parks Act precludes the introduction of non-native species into park lands. Hence seeds and cuttings were collected from native shrubs and trees along the road right of way and were used to start 49,000 seedlings within greenhouses that were subsequently planted to help rehabilitate disturbed slopes affected by construction. Disturbed areas were seeded with native grass mixture specially formulated from commercially available species but which were reflective of the native grasses found in the project area.

Through much of the project area, the highway is in close proximity to the Bow River, as well as numerous sensitive wetlands. The Bow River system provides habitat for a variety of species, including endangered populations of native bull trout and west slope cutthroat trout. Associated wetlands provide habitat for waterfowl, semi-aquatic mammals, and amphibians.

The highway was designed to avoid encroachment on the Bow River and to minimize disturbance to streams and wetlands in areas adjacent to the project. This was primarily accomplished through the use of steep fills of coarse rock or pre-cast, colored and textured concrete reinforced earth retaining walls to match nearby rock. In the few cases where encroachment on wetlands could not be avoided, a no net loss objective was applied. A wetland habitat area, equivalent to wetland areas disturbed during construction, was built at a site near the new highway. It is expected to provide habitat for amphibians, waterfowl, and small mammals.

A variety of measures were undertaken to reduce potential negative effects during the installation of culverts and stream crossings by timing work to avoid critical fish life phases and fully spanning the wetted perimeter of stream banks. To reduce both short and long term construction effects on water quality and aquatic resources, drainage was designed to flow into vegetated areas rather than into water bodies. Where this was not possible, settling basins or ditch blocks were built to allow settlement of suspended materials from road surface runoff, and to contain hazardous material spilled during accidents. To reduce potential siltation caused by construction activities from entering streams and the rivers, settling ponds, ditch blocks, straw bales, and geotextiles were installed as required to slow and filter water through disturbed areas. Culverts carrying water year round were installed at gradients compatible with fish passage, and culvert bottoms and outlets were lined with rock to reduce erosion and eliminate drops that could prevent fish passage.

Sustainable construction practices

The physical beauty of the project area and surrounding landscapes is a primary reason for Banff National Park's popularity and status. Maintaining the aesthetic integrity of the project site and views were an important consideration during project design and construction as was maintaining a minimum level of service C traffic flow through the construction area. The project traverses a variety of terrain types, including steep earth and rock slopes. Opportunities to avoid difficult terrain were limited by the proximity of the Bow River on one side of the highway, steep side slopes on the other, and a requirement to minimize the areal extent of disturbance and resultant habitat loss.

Tree clearing limits were designed to reduce disturbance while avoiding long straight edges, particularly in dense, uniform pine stands. Clearing edges were modulated to follow natural landforms. Tree limbs, stumps and non-merchantable debris were chipped and stockpiled for composting and use in future parks projects thus avoiding traditional burning of grubbing and the resulting air pollution. Smaller diameter timber was bucked into firewood for use within park campgrounds or sold to contractors for use in furniture or log cabin rails. Merchantable timber was sold for lumber or posts and rails with the proceeds applied against the cost of the project.

The new highway was designed to minimize its footprint by utilizing existing alignment and varying median width including centerline concrete safety shape barrier sections to avoid wetlands and reduce the amount of terrain and habitat disturbance. Steep rock fills/cuts, downhill retaining walls, and the use of salvaged rock to improve stability of steep fill slopes helped achieve this goal. Cut slopes were shaped and modulated to avoid unnatural, uniform appearance. Natural gullies and ridges were continued from the undisturbed surrounding areas through the disturbed slopes wherever possible. Rock outcroppings were incorporated into slopes to create visible relief and contrast. To minimize off site disturbance to landform, cuts and fills were balanced, and most rock and aggregate materials were obtained from within the highway right-of-way.

Erosion potential was reduced through the creation of benches on larger cut slopes, and rapid revegetation through hydro seeding and tree planting. In particularly steep areas, and areas adjacent to sensitive wetland habitats, a special tackifier and mulch was used. Siltation fences and other temporary measures were introduced to control erosion.

Maintaining traffic through the construction area was of paramount concern. Hourly traffic volumes were analyzed and blasting was scheduled to coincide with low volume periods when the highway was shut down for no more than one half hour to allow blasting and clean up to occur. Blasts, therefore, had to be sized accordingly. A 1-800 number was advertised on radio and in newspapers for motorists to get daily information on blast/closure schedules. To reduce congestion through the construction zones, contractors were permitted to haul on the existing highway only at night. Animal overpass structures were designed with no false work, and detours were implemented only during daylight hours for the seven days required to erect the pre-cast arches for each overpass.

The major environment mitigation measures used during design and construction are summarized in Table 2.

Environmental monitoring

Environmental and design committees consisting of engineers, biologists, technicians, and administrators were established and met independently and jointly to review and solve environmental issues and concerns related to the project. A full time environmental surveillance officer responsible for ensuring the proper environmental protection measures and the committee's recommendations were implemented was hired. All workers on the project were given an environmental briefing outlining environmental rules, concerns, and expectations prior to the commencement of work. Regular meetings with contractors were held to assess performance related to environmental protection measures. Non quantifiable items such as silt fencing and other erosion control measures were paid on a time and material basis to ensure prompt attention to these matters.

While physical construction of the subject section of highway is complete, the project will not officially be complete for several years. At the time of project approval, a commitment was made to carry out detailed monitoring program to ascertain the effectiveness of mitigations. An intensive four year research program to determine the effectiveness of the TCH wildlife protection measures is underway. Ungulates, coyotes, cougars, and black bears have discovered and utilize all the crossing structures quite readily while wolves and grizzly bears seem to be taking a longer familiarization period. Table 3 provides a record of total through passages by various species at the major animal overpasses and underpasses in the project area as of September, 1999 (Clevenger, 1999). Study results, while monitoring effectiveness of structures, also provides highway designers the opportunity to compare cost effectiveness of various structure types for future highway mitigation measures.

While the usage results are encouraging, the overpasses remain subject to high public and media attention. Most people are satisfied that $31 million was a reasonable expense for 18.6 km of highway to achieve the needed twinning and to protect Canada's flagship park, with 30% of that budget expended on environmental protection measures. Some specialized interest groups criticize that the highway continues to be a significant barrier to some species movement and further mitigations including elevating the roadway for significant distances need to be undertaken. Only time and the environment will ultimately judge the success of the mitigations and hence the project.

SUMMARY

The corridor recapitalization plan for the Trans-Canada Highway through the Mountain National Parks of Banff, Yoho, Glacier, and Mount Revelstoke will extend the design life of the existing facility into the next century. A system of passing lanes and climbing lanes will allow an acceptable level of service to be maintained for the design life. The passing and climbing lane system was constructed at a cost of approximately 10% the cost of twinning. However, as twinning is inevitable towards the end of the design life, all work proposed is compatible with that long term objective.

The passing lane system in Banff National Park has extended the design life of the TCH between Sunshine and Castle Junction interchanges as a two-lane facility by approximately 15 years. Twinning represents a logical next step in a program of sequential twinning following the passing lane phase. The TCH twinning program, which began in 1979, now totals 47 km and is considered a leading Canadian example of a balance between highway development and environmental protection and mitigation.

Table 2. Major environmental mitigation measures

Design
- Highway footprint designed to minimize alienating land from park
- Highway designed to minimize landform impacts and be aesthetically pleasing
- Utilize steep rockfills to avoid wetlands and river
- Minimize traffic disruptions

Construction
- Chipping/composting all grubbed and limbed material
- All merchantable timber sold for lumber or post/rails (>125 mm dia)
- Smaller timber bucked up for park campground firewood
- All old steel W-beam guiderail salvaged from highway recycled
- All old creosoted posts recycled or disposed of in properly designated landfill
- All surplus native topsoil stockpiled for future use
- No falsework in streams. Work near streams restricted to late fall to early May
- Cut/fill balanced to reduce off right of way impacts
- Majority of granular material (260,500 t) obtained, processed and stockpiled on new right of way
- All back slopes shaped and contoured to provide natural appearance
- Angle of back slopes kept as steep as possible
- Asphalt plant equipped with state of the art bag house to reduce emissions
- All old asphalt pavement milled and re-used in road structure
- Wetlands/fish habitat reconstructed to replace affected areas (no net loss)
- Existing culvert grades adjusted in potential fish spawning streams to permit fish passage again
- Retention ponds/"Stormscepter" catch basins built to reduce siltation/fuel spills into nearby watercourses
- Temporary erosion control silt fences and straw ditch blocks installed to minimize siltation during construction
- Total of 16 animal highway crossing opportunities built (approx. one every km)of varying size including 2–50 m overpasses; 3 elliptical CSP underpasses (4 m × 7 m), 4 concrete box culverts (2.4 m × 3 m)
- Special openings in concrete guiderail every 50 m to permit small mammals/waterfowl to cross
- Entire length 18.5 km of highway fenced on both sides with 2.4 m high variable size mesh game fence c/w buried chain link apron
- 45 ha of road right of way and borrow areas mechanically seeded using special indigenous seed mix specially grown by/for Parks Canada
- Old borrow pit used as storage and staging area partially rehabilitated for ungulate grassing use
- 25 ha of special hydro seeding mix with tackifier plus special bonded fibre matrix to reduce erosion and encourage growth on steep slopes and near wetlands and watercourses.
- 39,000 lodge pole pine and white spruce seedlings grown from seeds collected within the park and planted
- 9700 native shrubs grown from seeds collected along right of way and planted
- 1500 plantation grown trees (1–3 m) and 2800 nursery grown indigenous shrubs planted
- Full time environmental surveillance officer on project keeping log
- Full time environmental mitigation evaluation team employed after construction
- Environmental briefings conducted with all contractor staff at commencement of contract

Table 3. Wildlife passage frequency by crossing structure type TCH Twinning Sunshine to Castle Mountain Interchanges Banff National Park (December 1997–September 1999)

Number and structure type	Number of total crossings (%)	Average number of crossings/structure	Average construction cost of structure ($/m)
4 – 2.4 m × 3 m concrete box culvert	416 (18%)	104	$2800.00
3 – 4 m × 7 m elliptical CSP culverts	517 (22%)	172	$5400.00
2 – Creek pathways within open span CSP culverts	268 (11%)	134	$560.00
2 – 52 m overpasses	1147 (49%)	574	$33,650.00

A wide range of environmental protection measures have been developed and advanced along this stretch of road, including extensive wire fencing in combination with animal crossing structures. Research has found that this mitigation method has been effective in reducing wildlife/vehicle collisions by 97% for some species. Some species, such as ungulates, have adapted more quickly to using animal crossing structures than others such as wolves and grizzly bears. Monitoring of animal behavior and usage continues to better understand how structural and landscape characteristics influence their effectiveness.

In summary, the highway investment strategy adopted by Parks Canada conforms to the environmental policy and code of ethics approved by the Transportation Association of Canada (1992). In particular, Parks Canada has been vigilant in the protection of surface and ground water, conservation of land resources, ensuring the protection and enhancement of natural habitats for the long-term survival of plants, animals and aquatic life, and the preservation of historical and archaeological resources. Environmental considerations are integrated into Parks Canada's day to day activities and long-term decision making within the framework of an open communications policy with the general public and all stakeholders.

REFERENCES

Clevenger, A.P. 1999. Trans Canada Highway Research Project. Publication and Summary Data, October, 1999, Banff, AB.

Highway Research Board. 1965. Highway Capacity Manual. Highway Research Board, Special Report 67, Washington, DC.

Hoban, C.J., Fawcett, G.J., and Robinson, G.K. 1985. A Model for Simulating Traffic on Rural Roads: User Guide and Manual for TRARR version 3.0. Australian Road Research Board, Technical Manual, STM No.10A. Vermont South, Australia.

Morrall, J.F. and Blight, L. 1985. Evaluation of Test Passing Lanes on the Trans-Canada Highway in Banff National Park. Transportation Forum, 2(3): 5–12.

Morrall, J.F. 1987. Preliminary Location of Passing Lanes Using a Simulation Model. In: 12th Annual Meeting of the Institute of Transportation Engineers. Hamilton, ON, 5.2–5.22.

Morrall, J.F. 1991. Cross-section Elements to Accommodate Passing Lanes and Vehicle Storage During Avalanche Control for the Trans-Canada Highway in Rogers Pass, Canadian Journal of Civil Engineering, 18(2): 191–200.

Morrall, J. and Thompson, W. 1990. Planning and Design of Passing Lanes for the Trans-Canada Highway in Yoho National Park. Canadian Journal of Civil Engineering, 17(1): 79–86.

Parks Canada 1995 Initial Assessment of Proposed Improvements to the Trans-Canada Highway in Banff National Park. Phase IIIA Sunshine Interchange to Castle Mountain Interchange Final Report March 1995. Parks Canada, Calgary, AB.

Parks Canada. 1999. Highway Traffic Count Summary Report. Calgary, AB.

Transport Canada. 1985. Western Trans-Mountain Parks Highway Study — Phase II. Transport Canada. Ottawa, ON.

Transportation Association of Canada. 1992. Environmental Policy and Code of Ethics. Ottawa, ON.

Transportation Research Board. 1985. Highway Capacity Manual, Transportation Research Board, Special Report 209. Washington, DC.

BIOGRAPHICAL SKETCHES

T.M. McGuire

Highway Service Center, Parks Canada Agency 220 4 Ave S.E., Room 530 Calgary, AB, Canada, T2P 3H8, Telephone: (403) 292-4707, Fax: (403) 292-4886, E-mail: terry_mcguire@pch.gc.ca

Terry McGuire is Director of highway operations, maintenance and reconstruction within the Canadian Rocky Mountain National Parks. He is a professional engineer and mitigation of impacts highways have on ecological integrity within these national parks is of prime concern to him.

J.F. Morrall

Department of Civil Engineering, University of Calgary, 2500 University Drive N.W., Calgary, AB, Canada, T2N 1N4, Telephone: (403) 220-5836, Fax: (403) 282-7026, E-mail: morrall@ucalgary.ca

Dr. John Morrall is a Professor of civil engineering specializing in transportation at the University of Calgary. He has developed a number of modeling techniques for identifying and predicting effectiveness of passing lanes on existing two lane highways.

Responses of Mountain Caribou to Linear Features in a West-Central Alberta Landscape

Paula Oberg, Christoph Rohner, and Fiona K.A. Schmiegelow

Resource expansion into previously undeveloped areas requires increases in access, which may have detrimental effects for some wildlife species. We studied the response of migratory mountain caribou to linear landscape features, including streams, roads, and seismic exploration lines, in the foothills along the eastern slopes of the Canadian Rocky Mountains. Data from GPS telemetry collars during the two winters 1998–2000 were compared to a base map of linear features in a GIS, using distance buffers and compositional analysis. Caribou locations were distributed non-randomly around streams and roads, with preference increasing with distance from these linear features. This pattern of avoidance was also significant at a fine-scale, including only caribou that were in the vicinity of 0.5 km of linear features. We did not detect a significant avoidance or preference by caribou for seismic lines in either winter. This study adds evidence that caribou avoid linear landscape features in forests. The exact mechanism is not known, but may relate to the presence of natural predators or human disturbance on these corridors. We did not detect a significant effect of seismic lines in our area, possibly due to differences in ecology from other regions, low statistical power in our design, or success in measures to reduce impacts. We emphasise three approaches to reduce effects of linear features as prescribed by current operating guidelines for industrial activity on caribou ranges.

Keywords: Rangifer tarandus caribou, linear landscape features, resource development, wildlife telemetry, compositional analysis

INTRODUCTION

Populations of woodland caribou (*Rangifer tarandus caribou*) in Alberta have declined substantially in recent decades (Edmonds, 1988). Concurrently, resource-based industries associated with the forestry and energy sectors have expanded dramatically (Edmonds, 1988). Whereas the natural forested landscape was intersected primarily by rivers and creeks, this expansion has resulted in an increased network of rights-of-way (ROWs) for seismic exploration, pipelines, and roads. Human activities resulting in such linear landscape features, and the associated increases in access, have been implicated as possible causes for caribou declines (James, 1999).

Linear features may enhance an area for wildlife by providing a variety of browse, and by acting as travel corridors (Hurst, 1997; Revel et al., 1984). Predators, wolves in particular, are attracted to linear features as easy travel corridors (Eccles et al., 1985; Seip, 1992). They use frozen rivers as travel routes to search for prey (Huggard, 1993), and may exploit linear developments caused by human activities in a similar fashion. Prey species, such as moose and elk, are attracted to the early successional browse found near natural linear features, such as streams (Seip, 1992), as well as that found near anthropogenic linear features (Revel et al., 1984).

There are concerns that landscape changes associated with resource development in the Alberta foothills may affect the predator-prey dynamics to the detriment of caribou (Edmonds, 1988). Bergerud et al. (1984) suggested that caribou selection of low productivity wintering habitat created a spatial separation from other prey species (commonly moose), as an anti-predator strategy against wolves. Linear features have been hypothesized to erode the effectiveness of these habitat refuges for caribou by providing access routes for both alternative prey and predators, and increased search efficiency by predators in caribou ranges (Jalkotzy et al., 1997; James, 1999).

Woodland caribou in Alberta have been classified into two ecotypes, based principally on habitat use (Edmonds, 1991). The boreal ecotype inhabits fens, muskegs and jack pine or lodgepole pine habitats of the boreal forest, and herds are non-migratory. The mountain ecotype inhabits mountainous terrain for spring calving and during the summer, then migrates down into the lower elevation forested habitats to winter. Management of these woodland caribou ecotypes may vary, as well as the impacts of industrial development on their habitat (Edmonds, 1991).

Little is known about the effects of linear features on the woodland caribou mountain ecotype, which migrates from calving grounds in the mountains to winter ranges in the resource-rich foothills of west-central Alberta. Most research on pipelines and roads has focused on barren-ground caribou (e.g., Cameron et al., 1992; Curatolo and Murphy, 1986), and only recently, woodland caribou distributions have been examined in relation to linear development features in northeastern Alberta (e.g., Dyer, 1999; James, 1999). James (1999) found that woodland caribou showed a strong selection for habitat different from moose and wolves. Caribou tended to occur further from linear developments, while wolves and their kill sites were closer than random to linear developments (James, 1999; Stuart-Smith et al., 1997). Wolves were also found to travel faster on linear developments than in the surrounding forest (James, 1999), which may improve their predation efficiency. Dyer (1999) found that the density of caribou locations was significantly lower in areas closer to roads and seismic lines than expected, and that caribou crossed roads less frequently than expected from random movement. Such avoidance patterns may reduce the useable habitat for caribou considerably, and linear development structures may form movement barriers for woodland caribou (Dyer, 1999). It is not clear whether these results from the boreal, non-migratory ecotype also apply to migratory mountain caribou in Alberta and woodland caribou in other regions.

In order to sustain industrial activity on caribou ranges, while ensuring the integrity and supply of caribou habitat, regionally specific operating guidelines have been developed. The "Operating Guidelines for Industry Activity In Caribou Ranges in West Central Alberta" became effective September 1, 1996. Access development and management, habitat supply, and timing of activities are the primary mitigation strategies targeted within the caribou range operating guidelines (WCACSC, 1996). The guidelines will receive periodic review and modification based on experience in implementation, new research information, and/or efficiency in conserving caribou populations and habitats (WCACSC, 1996).

The objective of this study was to determine the distribution of mountain caribou in relation to natural linear features (streams) and anthropogenic linear features of varying type (seismic lines, roads, pipelines, powerlines), in order to test for avoidance patterns. We determined caribou distributions by overlaying Global Positioning System (GPS) caribou locations onto accurate base map coverages of linear features within a Geographical Information System (GIS). Avoidance effects were determined using compositional analysis (Aebischer et al., 1993). We predicted that the density of caribou locations would increase as the distance from linear features increased, and that caribou would avoid roads at greater distances than seismic lines. We also predicted that streams, as natural linear features and documented predator travel corridors, would also be avoided by caribou.

Here, we present preliminary results from our analyses, and discuss their implications for industrial operating guidelines in west-central Alberta.

STUDY AREA

The study area is part of the eastern slopes and foothills of the Canadian Rocky Mountains in west-central Alberta, adjacent to Jasper National Park (54°N, 119°W), and covers the winter ranges of the Redrock/Prairie Creek mountain caribou herds. These caribou calve in June above treeline in the alpine areas of Willmore Wilderness Area and adjacent mountains in British Columbia. Alpine rutting grounds are used in September and October, and with increasing snowfall the caribou migrate to forests in lower elevation forests in November and December (Edmonds, 1988). The core of the winter ranges of the Redrock/Prairie Creek herds is located on either side of the Kakwa River, west of Highway 40 (Brown and Hobson, 1998).

Our study area covered the caribou management zone, which reflects previously recorded winter distribution of the caribou herds, and an added 5 km buffer to this zone. Adjacent areas, occurring within Willmore Wilderness Area, were not included, as no development is planned in wilderness parks. The study area encompassed a total area of 4202 km^2.

Elevation ranges from 1100 m to 1800 m (amsl) (Kansas and Brown, 1996), with portions of the Subalpine and the Upper Foothills natural subregions (Beckingham and Archibald, 1996). The area is bisected by the Kakwa River flowing in a northeast direction. The topography is dominated by this river and its numerous tributaries, with undulating terrain and moderate to steep slopes and ridges (Edmonds and Bloomfield, 1984). The climate is subarctic, characterized by short, cool, wet summers and long, cold, dry winters (Bjorge, 1984). The Foothills region is well forested and has been described in detail by Edmonds (1988). Dry sites support primarily pure lodgepole pine (*Pinus contorta*) or lodgepole pine/black spruce (*Picea mariana*) forests. At higher elevations, mixed fir (*Abies lasiocarpa*), spruce (*Picea* spp.) and lodgepole pine forest predominates. Willow (*Salix* spp.) and birch (*Betula glandulosa*) meadows, interspersed with dry grassy benches, are found along the drainages.

Primary land uses in the study area include timber harvesting, oil and gas exploration and development, coal mining, non-motorized outdoor recreation (hiking, horse travel, camping, fishing), off-road vehicle use (snowmobile, all-terrain vehicles), recreational hunting, and commercial trapping (Brown and Hobson, 1998). Access occurs in the form of all-weather and dry-weather resource roads, and rights-of-way for pipelines, powerlines, and seismic lines for petroleum exploration (Smith et al., 2000).

METHODS

Caribou location data

Wintering female caribou from the Redrock/Prairie Creek herds were fitted with GPS transmitters. GPS wildlife telemetry data (non-differentially corrected) were collected for five female caribou during the 1998/1999 winter, and differentially corrected data were obtained for eight females during the winter of 1999/2000. The accuracy of GPS transmitters is within 100 m, 95% of the time, using non-differentially corrected data (Lotek Engineering Inc., 2000) and within <5 m for differentially corrected data (Rempel and Rodgers, 1996). GPS caribou locations from winter 1999/2000 were differentially corrected using N-4 Version 1.1895 software (Lotek Engineering Inc., 2000). All locations were imported into ArcView Version 3.1 (Environmental Systems Research Institute Inc., 1993).

The following criteria were applied to select caribou location data for this study:

1. Only winter location data, collected between early December and late April, were considered. (At the time of analysis 1999/2000 GPS transmitter location data had only been downloaded to March 24, 2000 for all but 2 animals.)
2. Only locations within forested caribou winter ranges were included for analysis. As both winters of study were mild, several caribou returned to alpine ranges when only little snow cover was left on the winter range. As caribou may behave differently in or at the edge of open alpine areas, locations occurring at or above treeline, in the Alpine and higher Subalpine regions (elevation >1800 m), were removed.
3. To maintain consistency between variable data collection schedules of the transmitters, and to maintain reasonable independence between subsequent locations, only one location per animal per day was used in the analysis (at, or closest available to, 12:00 pm).

As caribou on the winter ranges did not have stable home ranges, but showed nomadic movements on a portion of the study area, we applied a buffer technique to determine the availability of linear features to each individual. Instead of delineating a home range using a minimum convex polygon approach (Aebischer et al., 1993), we buffered caribou locations by the distance travelled in a day, and used these combined buffers as a more realistic representation of what portion of the landscape was available to each caribou (Fig. 1). As an estimate of daily travel distances, we calculated the 90th percentile of subsequent daily locations (Arthur et al., 1996). This distance was then

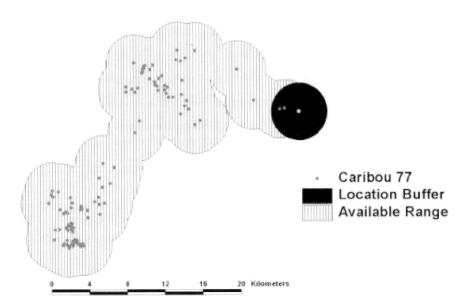

Fig. 1. Example of how available winter range was determined for individual caribou. GPS locations from early December to late April were buffered by a radius equal to the maximum distance traveled per day (90th percentile of data, range of 1.4–4.1 km for individual caribou, Table 1). All point buffers for each individual caribou were then joined for analysis to form the available range.

Table 1. GPS data were collected from 13 female wintering caribou in the Redrock/Prairie Creek herd ranges, winters 1998–2000. Total available area for each caribou was determined by buffering locations by a radius equal to the 90th percentile for maximum daily travel distance. Buffers of 250 m around wellsites and cutblocks were excluded from the total available areas to avoid confounding effects on the analysis of responses to linear features

Caribou ID	Data winter	N location days	Daily travel distance (90th percentile) (km)	Excluded area (km^2)	Total available area (km^2)
4c	1998–1999	117	2.7	3.0	354.9
51	1998–1999	117	1.6	11.1	112.1
52	1998–1999	100	2.5	0.0	141.0
5a	1998–1999	144	3.6	47.0	618.1
5b	1998–1999	140	1.9	0.0	191.7
72	1999–2000	50	1.4	7.4	41.5
73	1999–2000	87	3.7	0.3	335.6
77	1999–2000	144	2.9	7.5	347.0
78	1999–2000	141	3.6	22.3	543.7
79	1999–2000	94	4.1	8.9	411.8
7a	1999–2000	111	2.4	0.0	223.4
7b	1999–2000	110	3.0	0.0	331.7

Table 2. Density of linear features occurring within the study area. Total study area was 4202 km^2

Linear Feature	Total length (km)	Density (km/km^2)
Streams	1500.1	0.36
Roads	1345.7	0.32
Seismic Lines	2803.7	0.67

Table 3. Linear features were buffered at specified distances. Each distance buffer acted as a "habitat category", to which to compare caribou use in the compositional analysis

Buffer	Distance to stream (m)	Distance to road (m)	Distance to seismic line (m)
1	<100	<100	<100
2	101–250	101–250	101–250
3	251–500	251–500	251–500
4	501–1000	501–1000	501–1000
5	1001–2000	1001–2000	>1001
6	>2000	>2000	–

used to define the buffer radius for the locations for each animal using ArcView 3.1 (Fig. 1). Buffers were merged, overlaps dissolved, and a final available area calculated for each animal (Table 1).

Linear feature map coverages

Accurate base map coverages of linear features (roads, seismic lines, pipeline ROWs, and powerline ROWs), as well as cutblocks and wellsites were obtained by digitizing 1998 Indian Resource Satellite (IRS) imagery (5 m × 5 m pixels, rectified, UTM Nad 27) using ArcView GIS. A stream coverage was obtained from the Resource Data Division of Alberta Environment. Rivers and streams which occurred perennially throughout the study area were used in the analysis. Table 2 summarizes the density of each linear feature in the study area.

To remove wellsites and cutblocks as potential confounding variables to caribou distributions around linear features, buffered areas around each of these landscape features were excluded from analysis. We chose a buffer width of 250 m as there is evidence for this avoidance distance from a study in northeast Alberta (Dyer, 1999), and a similar distance may apply to cutblocks in our area (Rohner and Szkorupa, 1999). The total of these excluded buffer areas are summarized for each caribou in Table 1. Any caribou locations occurring in these areas were also removed. One caribou (71), collared during the 1999/2000 winter, was removed from the analysis due to a dysfunctional collar and insufficient locations.

Linear features were buffered by 100, 250, 500, 1000, 2000, and >2000 m distances (Table 3), consistent with Dyer (1999), thus permitting comparisons between caribou ecotypes. Buffer categories were pooled where necessary to ensure that all available distance classes were wide enough to contain at least 0.5% of expected caribou locations. No caribou had sufficient pipeline and powerline buffer areas, so these linear landscape features were removed from the analysis.

Statistical analysis

We used standard techniques of comparing use and availability to test for preference or avoidance of linear structures by caribou. For a descriptive and graphic illustration of preferences we used a common index of preference (Manly's alpha, calculated according to Krebs, 1989). Such indices, however, can be biased when data points are not entirely independent. Therefore, for statistical testing, we performed compositional analyses of habitat use as described by Aebischer et al. (1993). For this method, each distance buffer acted as a "habitat category," to which to compare caribou use. The area within each caribou's winter range defined "available habitat." The number of locations occurring in each buffer distance defined "habitat use."

Percent available was defined as the proportional area of each distance buffer within the caribou's winter range area. Percent use was defined as the proportional number of caribou locations occurring in each buffer distance of the total number of caribou locations. If there was no use of a buffer distance, but the buffer distance was available, the 0% use was replaced by 0.01%, an order of magnitude less than the smallest recorded nonzero percentage (Aebischer et al., 1993). See Appendix I for percent available and percent use mean values for each of the linear feature distance buffers.

Habitat selection or avoidance occurs when a particular type of habitat is used more or less often than expected at random (Johnson, 1980). All distance buffers were examined simultaneously, testing the hypothesis that the log-ratio of used habitat (y) equalled the log-ratio of available habitat (y_0) (H_0: $d = y - y_0 = 0$). The residual matrix of raw sums of squares (R_2) and the matrix of mean-corrected sums of squares and cross-products (R_1) were calculated from d (Zar, 1984) and used to generate a chi-squared value:

$$\Lambda = |R_1|/|R_2|,$$

$$X^2_{(\alpha=0.05:\ df=no.\ buffers-1)} = (-N)\ln\Lambda,$$

where N is the number of caribou used in the analysis.

The null hypothesis of random use was rejected at $\alpha \leq 0.05$.

If caribou use of distance buffers was significantly non-random, the distance buffers were ranked by order of use and any significant selections were identified. Ranking was achieved by determining the pairwise differences (t-tests) between distance buffer use and availability log-ratios using the equation:

$$\ln(\chi_{U_2}/\chi_{U_1}) - \ln(\chi_{A_2}/\chi_{A_1}).$$

If the pairwise difference was less than zero, then use of habitat "1" was assumed greater than habitat "2" and vice versa when the pairwise difference was greater than zero. A matrix containing all pairwise differences was created (Appendix II), and the number of positive pairwise differences was tallied. The total for each distance buffer determined its ranking for caribou selection.

The outlying buffers (5th for seismic lines and 6th for roads and streams) were used to determine preference or avoidance. If a distance buffer was used significantly less than the outer buffer, we conclude it was avoided by caribou.

RESULTS

Caribou locations showed a highly significant deviation from a random distribution in relation to streams ($\chi^2 = 16.71$, df = 5, $p < 0.005$). As illustrated in Fig. 2, there was a clear trend for increased preference of those portions in the landscape that were further away

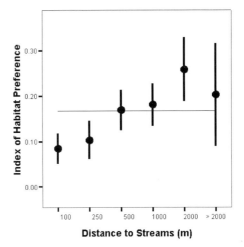

Fig. 2. Preference indices for 12 female caribou from distances to streams during winters 1998–1999 and 1999–2000. Index of habitat preference for each distance buffer is the mean of Manly's alpha. Manly's alpha ranges from 0 to 1. A random distribution over the landscape would produce a neutral value of 0.17, higher values indicate preference and smaller values indicate avoidance.

from streams (Fig. 2). This trend was consistent for coarse and fine scale (<0.5 km) analyses. However, an inconsistency occurred at the coarse scale, as the >2 km buffer did not follow this trend (Table 4; Appendix II for details). Individual comparisons of buffer preferences confirmed that avoidance of streams occurred (Table 4). Areas <100 m from streams were used significantly less than distances 0.25–2 km from streams. The 100–250 m buffer was also used significantly less than both the 0.5–1.0 km and 1.0–2.0 km buffers. In summary, these results allow a clear rejection of the hypothesis that caribou moved independently of streams: there was significant fine-scale avoidance of streams for caribou within 2 km of these linear features, and an unexplained but not significant drop in preference for areas that occurred at distances >2 km.

Caribou use of roads paralleled their distribution around streams, with more locations than expected as distance from roads increased ($\chi^2 = 17.11$, df = 5, $p < 0.004$; Table 4). The ranking of distance buffers was consistent, from least preference close to roads to highest preference at distances >2 km from roads (Table 4, also reflected in the values of the preference index in Fig. 3). Significant contrasts between buffers were found from the outermost buffer (>2 km), to all buffers closer to roads, except to the adjacent buffer of 1–2 km distance (Table 4, details in Appendix II). However, because roads in the study area generally occur along the northern and eastern extent of historical caribou ranges, some caribou included in this analysis had only small proportions of roads available to them along the fringes of their range. In fact, five caribou did not occur at all within 500 m of roads. To examine whether the statistical significance of results was based on these caribou occurring far away from roads,

Table 4. Caribou selection and ranking of distance buffers during winters 1998–2000, as determined from compositional analysis. If non-random selection of distances from linear features occurred, then ranking matrices were used to rank distance buffers according to their preference by caribou. Significant contrasts between ranks displayed by the symbol '≫' in the last column, with comparisons starting from the outermost buffer looking successively inward

Linear feature	Caribou selection	Chi-square	df	P	Distance buffer ranking	Significant ranks
Streams	Non-random	16.7	5	<0.005	5 > 4 > 3 > 6 > 2 > 1	6 ≫ 1
						5 ≫ 1, 2, 3
						4 ≫ 1, 2
						3 ≫ 1, 2
Streams (<500 m)	Non-random	7.4	2	<0.02	3 > 2 > 1	3 ≫ 1, 2
Roads	Non-random	17.1	5	<0.004	6 > 5 > 4 > 2 > 3 > 1	6 ≫ 1, 2, 3, 4
						5 ≫ 1
Roads (<500 m)	Non-random	10.0	2	<0.005	3 > 2 > 1	3 ≫ 1
Seismic	Random	8.2	4	>0.12	N/A	N/A
Seismic (<500 m)	Random	0.4	2	>0.25	N/A	N/A

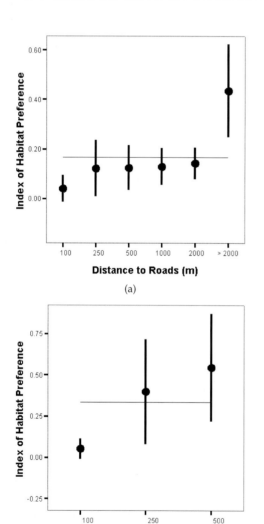

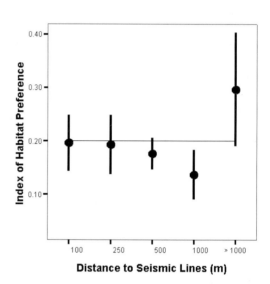

Fig. 3. Preference of 12 female caribou for distances from roads during winters 1998–1999 and 1999–2000. Index of habitat preference for each distance buffer is the mean of Manly's alpha. (a) Coarse-scale selection for winters 1998–2000. A random distribution over the landscape would produce a neutral value of 0.17, higher values indicate preference and smaller values indicate avoidance. (b) Fine scale selection for winters 1998–2000. A random distribution over the landscape would produce a neutral value of 0.33, higher values indicate preference and smaller values indicate avoidance.

Fig. 4. Preference indices for 12 female caribou from distances to seismic lines during winter 1998–1999 and winter 1999–2000. Index of habitat preference for each distance buffer is the mean of Manly's alpha. Manly's alpha ranges from 0 to 1. A random distribution over the landscape would produce a neutral value of 0.20, higher values indicate preference and smaller values indicate avoidance.

which may have used a different part of the study area due to unrelated factors, we conducted an additional fine-scale analysis. For this analysis, only caribou with individual locations occurring within 500 m of roads were analyzed. The results also revealed a significant response to roads by these caribou ($\chi^2 = 10.02$, df = 5, $p < 0.005$, Table 4). The ranking remained consistent, showing a clear trend for increased selection of areas further away from roads (Fig. 2). The closest buffer to roads (within 100 m) was preferred significantly less than areas at distances from 251 to 500 m from roads (see Appendix II for details). Caribou locations in relation to seismic lines did not differ from random over the two winters studied ($\chi^2 = 8.19$, df = 4, $p > 0.12$). No trends in preferences for distance buffers from seismic lines were found (Fig. 4). Since the overall χ^2 value was not significant, we did not rank distance buffers (Aebischer et al., 1993).

DISCUSSION

Our results show that caribou avoided perennial streams, which are a natural linear feature in our study area. Consistent with our prediction, caribou also avoided linear landscape structures of anthropogenic origin: roads were significantly avoided, while no consistent trend was apparent for seismic exploration lines in our study area. This is the second study investigating the response of caribou to linear development in forested areas that has found an effect of human infrastructure.

There are several explanations for the avoidance of streams by mountain caribou in our area. The winter distribution of caribou could be indirectly affected by rivers and creeks, for example by habitat variables that are associated with topography. Caribou in our area have been reported to prefer pine stands with a rich supply of terrestrial lichens, which tend to grow along well drained landforms such as topographical ridges (Edmonds and Bloomfield, 1984; Bjorge, 1984; Edmonds and Smith, 1991). Therefore, one potential explanation for avoidance of streams could be the lack of preferred habitat in the vicinity of these landscape features. If edges along slopes to stream valleys are preferred, then a drop in preference further away from streams on higher plateaus as observed in Figure 2 might be expected. On the other hand, there may be direct effects that are being perceived negatively by wintering caribou. With concentrations of other ungulate species such as moose and elk, which prefer habitats with ample supply of shrubs and grasses along rivers, and wolves moving on frozen rivers that connect these habitats, caribou may attempt to alleviate predation pressures through spatial separation. The two explanations are not mutually exclusive and could both apply. Further work into habitat relationships is needed to test these hypotheses.

Our study adds evidence to findings in northeast Alberta that caribou may avoid roads in forested areas (Dyer, 1999). We found a pronounced preference for areas far away from roads, with a significantly reduced preference by caribou up to 1000 m. We consider our results on exact avoidance distance as preliminary, because our study area was heterogeneous and we are only learning about other potentially confounding factors that may also affect caribou distribution. However, there was also a fine-scale effect by caribou that were in the vicinity of 500 m of roads, corroborating our results of an avoidance pattern. The exact mechanism for such avoidance is currently not known. A behavioural avoidance could have similar causes as postulated for streams: caribou may perceive roads as travel corridors for predators or avoid other ungulates associated with these areas. In addition, caribou may avoid roads due to increased human activity associated with these developments. Potential consequences on caribou populations are twofold. It is possible that roads, as easy travel routes, could lead to an increase in caribou/wolf encounters, and lead to higher caribou mortality near lines (Stuart-Smith et al., 1997; James, 1999). Another consequence may consist in habitat loss because otherwise suitable habitat is avoided. At present, an avoidance of 100 m from roads would translate into an area of reduced use of 253 km^2 or 6% of available habitat for caribou in our study area. Depending on intensity of effects on caribou and level of development, this area of reduced use could grow to 40% of the available habitat (Dyer, 1999).

We did not detect a significant response by caribou to seismic lines. This result is in contrast to Dyer (1999), who found that caribou in northeast Alberta avoided both roads and seismic lines. This difference may be explained by several factors. First, the differences found from Dyer (1999) may be attributed to regional differences, either in habitat and level of development of the study area, or in variation among woodland caribou ecotypes due to differing life history characteristics. Our study area in the foothills of the Rocky Mountains consists of an undulating topography, with greater variation in topography than the boreal forest in northeastern Alberta. Many seismic lines in our area were of older origin and showed various stages of re-forestation. As well, the density of seismic lines in west-central Alberta is much lower at 0.67 km/km^2 than in northeastern Alberta, where Dyer (1999) reported that caribou had an average of 1.15 km/km^2 of seismic lines in their home ranges. Higher variability and lower density of lines may explain a lower influence of seismic lines in our study area. In contrast to the migratory and nomadic ecotype, woodland caribou in northeastern Alberta are also yearly residents in their home ranges. For these animals, which showed avoidance up to 100 m from seismic lines (Dyer, 1999), there may be higher selective pressure to avoid anthropogenic linear features in the landscape.

Perhaps more importantly, our sample sizes were small, and assuming that potential distance effect is smaller for seismic lines than for roads, the statistical power of our design was very limited. Our current results have to be considered preliminary, and further study is necessary. Our results certainly lack the statistical power to allow a firm conclusion that caribou are not affected by seismic lines in our study area. Besides continued monitoring of caribou to increase sample size, an understanding of habitat relationships may help to reduce variance in understanding caribou distributions in relation to linear human developments.

MANAGEMENT IMPLICATIONS

If caribou avoid roads and potentially other linear features, it will become increasingly important for managers to minimize road access into caribou range, if the goal of sustaining both caribou and industrial development is to be attained. This could be achieved in several ways. First, new linear features can be reduced by using existing access, shared/common access, and by limiting access. Temporary access structures can be removed, reclaimed and reforested. The current operating guidelines for the area (WCACSC, 1996) include such access-reducing strategies.

Second, public access on roads can be controlled and temporarily restricted to reduce disturbance or mortality on caribou winter ranges, for example by gates, signs, education, temporary rollback, or manned access control. Managing access is difficult, and can be expensive. A pressing challenge will be to engage members of the public who typically resent restrictions on their use of crown land. Frequently, signs, gates, and other management measures are ignored, particularly if strong public support for the restrictions cannot be demonstrated (BCRC, 1998). As a result, bans on existing roads may not be feasible (Cumming, 1996). What is possible, however, is the prevention of new access into important caribou habitat and controlling access on existing linear developments (Cumming, 1996).

Third, the structure of new lines can be designed to minimize potential impacts. Since the introduction of operating guidelines in west-central Alberta, several measures have been implemented to reduce the potential effects of seismic lines on caribou. Low Impact Seismic (LIS) is a desirable target for exploration work. LIS are exploration lines cut with a narrow line width (<4.5 m) as compared to conventional seismic lines (8 m), and in a continuously meandering path to reduce line of sight. Heli-portable and hand-cut lines further reduce any potential effects on vegetation changes, new travel corridors for wolves, or increased disturbance by human recreational users. In addition, winter operations have taken an "early in, early out" philosophy, so that activity occurs prior to caribou arrival on winter ranges. The fact that we did not detect caribou responses to seismic lines may also reflect the success of these measures and the importance of maintaining the current operating guidelines.

ACKNOWLEDGEMENTS

This study received funding, logistic support, and expert advice from the West Central Alberta Caribou Standing Committee (WCACSC), a cooperative board consisting of members from industry and the provincial government of Alberta. In particular, we acknowledge the contributions of Dave Hervieux, Kirby Smith, Luigi Morgantini, Al Kennedy, Arlen Todd, Rick Bonar, Lorne Greenhorn, Jeff Kneteman, Adam James, George Mercer, Jan Ficht, and Dave Hobson. Also, we thank Susan Shirkoff and Tara Szkorupa for their help preparing GPS data, and Rick Pelletier from the Spatial Information Systems (SIS) lab at the University of Alberta, for his GIS advise. The Alberta Government, Resource Data Division, kindly provided the digital hydrography coverage for streams. Additional financial support for P. Oberg was provided by the Natural Sciences and Engineering Research Council of Canada and the Alberta Sport, Recreation, Parks and Wildlife Foundation.

APPENDIX I

Distribution of caribou locations in buffers of increasing distance to each type of linear feature in the study area. The data are given as percentage (mean and standard error), both for use and availability. The analysis was performed on the complete set of distance buffers (all), and within close range (<500 m) of these linear features (fine-scale)

		Distance buffers											
		1 used	1 avail.	2 used	2 avail.	3 used	3 avail.	4 used	4 avail.	5 used	5 avail.	6 used	6 avail.
Streams (all)	Mean	2.55	5.93	4.50	8.03	10.79	12.43	20.41	22.59	39.80	31.74	21.95	19.29
	SE	0.47	0.36	1.02	0.48	1.70	0.74	2.70	1.26	4.41	0.99	6.90	3.17
Streams (fine-scale)	Mean	14.82	22.45	24.30	30.42	60.88	47.12	–	–	–	–	–	–
	SE	2.77	0.24	3.80	0.16	3.95	0.38	–	–	–	–	–	–
Roads (all)	Mean	0.53	3.20	1.84	1.99	2.99	3.11	5.98	5.86	8.71	11.18	79.96	74.67
	SE	0.34	1.78	0.80	0.78	1.24	1.08	2.65	1.57	3.27	2.66	8.03	7.54
Roads (fine-scale)	Mean	4.66	32.69	34.34	25.50	61.06	41.81	–	–	–	–	–	–
	SE	2.60	5.96	12.79	1.93	13.05	4.08	–	–	–	–	–	–
Seismic Lines (fine-scale)	Mean	12.84	12.67	15.60	15.63	17.79	19.97	17.37	27.15	36.40	24.58	–	–
	SE	2.32	0.92	2.57	1.11	2.03	1.20	2.97	3.35	6.42	3.37	–	–
Seismic Lines (all)	Mean	27.23	26.16	32.31	32.32	40.46	41.52	–	–	–	–	–	–
	SE	2.09	0.30	3.17	0.17	3.08	0.30	–	–	–	–	–	–

APPENDIX II

Ranking matrices identifying selection of linear feature distance buffers by mountain caribou, winters 1998–1999 and 1999–2000. Reported are t-test statistics for multiple comparisons of buffers, count of positive differences, and resulting ranks. Bold values indicate significant differences in selection ($p < 0.05$)

Streams winters 1998–2000, df = 11

	1	2	3	4	5	6	No. Positives	Ranking
1	—	−1.3	−8.6	−21.7	−9.1	−5.4	0	6
2	+	—	−5.6	−2.8	−6.9	−1.5	1	5
3	+	+	—	−0.4	−4.4	+0.38	3	3
4	+	+	+	—	−1.8	+0.8	4	2
5	+	+	+	+	—	+1.4	5	1
6	+	+	−	−	−	—	2	4

Streams within 500 m, winters 1998–2000, df = 11

	1	2	3	No. Positives	Ranking
1	—	−1.3	−2.2	0	3
2	+	—	−2.5	1	2
3	+	+	—	2	1

Roads winters 1998–2000, df = 11

	1	2	3	4	5	6	No. Positives	Ranking
1	—	−2.1	−2.1	−2.0	−2.8	−5.5	0	6
2	+	—	−0.2	−0.5	−1.1	−3.1	1	5
3	+	+	—	−0.4	−1.0	−3.0	2	4
4	+	+	+	—	−0.6	−2.7	3	3
5	+	+	+	+	—	−2.1	4	2
6	+	+	+	+	+	—	5	1

Roads within 500 m, winters 1998–2000, df = 6

	1	2	3	No. Positives	Ranking
1	—	−1.5	−2.8	0	3
2	+	—	−1.2	1	2
3	+	+	—	2	1

REFERENCES

Aebischer, N.J., P.A. Robertson, and R.E. Kenward. 1993. Compositional analysis of habitat use from animal radio-tracking data. Ecology, 74(5): 1313–1325.

Arthur, S.M., B.F.J. Manly, L.L. McDonald, and G.W. Garner. 1996. Assessing habitat selection when availability changes. Ecology, 77(1): 215–227.

Beckingham, J.D. and J.H. Archibald. 1996. Field Guide to the Ecosites of West-central Alberta. Canadian Forest Service, Northwest Region, Northern Forestry Centre, Edmonton, AB. 509 pp.

Bergerud, A.T., Jakimchuk, R.D., and D.R. Carruthers. 1984. The buffalo of the north: Caribou (*Rangifer tarandus*) and human developments. Arctic, 37(1): 7–22.

Bjorge, R.R. 1984. Winter habitat use by woodland caribou in west-central Alberta, with implications for management. In: Fish and Wildlife Relationships in Old-growth Forests. Proceedings of a Symposium Held in Juneau, Alaska, 1982. W.R. Meehan, T.R. Merrel, and T.A. Hanley, eds. American Institute of Fisheries Research Biology, Morehead City, NC. pp. 335–342.

Boreal Caribou Research Committee (BCRC). 1998. Boreal caribou research program: Research summary progress report 1998. BCRC, Edmonton, AB. 32 pp.

Brown, W.K. and D.P. Hobson. 1998. Caribou in west-central Alberta — information review and synthesis. Prep. for: The Research Subcommittee of the West-central Alberta Caribou Standing Committee, Grande Prairie, AB. 74 pp.

Cameron, R.D., D.J. Reed, J.R. Dav, and W.T. Smith. 1992. Redistribution of calving caribou in response to oil field development on the arctic slope of Alaska. Arctic, 45(4): 338–342.

Cumming, H.G. 1996. Managing for caribou survival in a partitioned habitat. Rangifer Special Issue, No. 9: 171–180.

Curatolo, J.A. and S.M. Murphy. 1986. The effects of pipelines, roads, and traffic on the movements of Caribou. Canadian Field Naturalist, 100(2): 214–218.

Dyer, S. 1999. Movement and distribution of woodland caribou (*Rangifer tarandus caribou*) in response to industrial development in northeastern Alberta. MSc. Thesis, Department of Biological Sciences, University of AB, Edmonton, AB, Canada. 106 pp.

Eccles, T.R., G. Searing, J. Duncan, and C. Thompson. 1985. Wildlife monitoring studies along the Norman Wells–Zama Oil Pipeline, January–March 1985. LGL Ltd., Environmental Research Associates, Calgary, AB. 96 pp.

Edmonds, J.E. 1988. Population status, distribution, and movements of woodland caribou in west-central Alberta. Canadian Journal of Zoology, 66: 817–826.

Edmonds, J.E. 1991. Status of woodland caribou in western North America. Rangifer Special Issue, No. 7: 91–107.

Edmonds, J.E. and M. Bloomfield. 1984. A study of woodland caribou (*Rangifer tarandus caribou*) in west-central Alberta, 1979–1983. Alberta Energy and Natural Resources, Fish and Wildlife Division, Edmonton, AB. 150 pp.

Edmonds, J.E. and K. Smith. 1991. Mountain caribou calf production and survival, and calving and summer habitat use in west-central

Alberta. Wildlife Research Series Number 4. Alberta Forestry Lands and Wildlife, Edmonton, AB. 17 pp.

Environmental Systems Research Institute, Inc. 1993. ArcView Software, Version 3.1. 380. New York Street, Redlands, CA.

Huggard, D.J. 1993. Effect of snow depth on predation and scavenging by gray wolves. Journal of Wildlife Management, 52(2): 382–388.

Hurst, G. 1997. Project habitat: ROW management to enhance wildlife habitat and utility image. In: Proceedings from The Sixth International Symposium on Environmental Concerns in Rights-of-Way Management, New Orleans, Louisiana, 24–26 February 1997. J.R. Williams, J.W. Goodrich-Mahoney, J.R. Wisniewski, and J. Wisniewski, eds. Elsevier Science Ltd. pp. 311–314.

Jalkotzy, M.G., P.I. Ross, and M.D. Nasserden. 1997. The effects of linear developments on wildlife: A review of selected scientific literature. Prep. For: Canadian Association of Petroleum Producers (CAPP). Prep. By: Arc Wildlife Services Ltd. Calgary, AB. 115 pp.

James, A. 1999. Wolf use of linear corridors in caribou habitat as revealed by global positioning system collars. Ph.D. Thesis, Department of Biological Sciences, University of Alberta, Edmonton, AB, Canada. 70 pp.

Johnson, D.H. 1980. The comparison of usage and availability measurements for evaluating resource preference. Ecology, 61: 65–71.

Kansas, J.L. and W.K. Brown. 1996. Ecologically integrated caribou habitat mapping in the Prairie Creek winter range: Assessment of map accuracy and product utility. Prepared for Weyerhaeuser Canada Ltd., Grande Prairie, AB. 46 pp.

Krebs, C.J. 1989. Ecological Methodology. Harper & Row, NY. 654 pp.

Lotek Engineering Inc. 2000. N4 Version V1. 1895. Differential post-processing software. Newmarket, ON.

Rempel, R.S. and A.R. Rodgers. 1996. Effects of differential correction on accuracy of a GPS animal location system. Journal of Wildlife Management, 61(2): 525–530.

Revel, R.D., T.D. Dougherty, and D.J. Downing. 1984. Forest Growth and Revegetation along Seismic Lines. University of Calgary Press, Calgary, AB. pp. 228.

Rohner, C. and T. Szkorupa. 1999. Fine-scale avoidance of cutblocks by two GPS-collared caribou in the Redrock-Prairie Creek Area. WCACSC Research News Issue 1. University of Alberta, Edmonton, AB. 4 pp.

Seip, D.R. 1992. Factors limiting woodland caribou populations and their inter-relationships with wolves and moose in southeastern British Columbia. Canadian Journal of Zoology, 70: 1494–1503.

Smith, K.G., E.J. Ficht, D. Hobson, T.C. Sorensen, and D. Hervieux. 2000. Winter distribution of woodland caribou in relation to clear-cut logging in west-central Alberta. Canadian Journal of Zoology, 78: 1433–1440.

Stuart-Smith, K., C. Bradshaw, S. Boutin, D. Hebert, and A. Rippin. 1997. Woodland caribou relative to landscape patterns in northeastern Alberta. Journal of Wildlife Management, 61(3): 622–633.

West-central Alberta Caribou Standing Committee (WCACSC). 1996. Operating guidelines for industry activity in caribou ranges in west-central Alberta, WCACSC, Grande Prairie, AB. 13 pp.

Zar, J.H. 1984. Biostatistical Analysis, 2nd Edition. Prentice-Hall Inc., NJ. pp. 718.

BIOGRAPHICAL SKETCHES

Paula Oberg

MSc Candidate, Department of Renewable Resources, 7-51 General Services Building, University of Alberta, AB, Canada T6G 2H1.

Paula Oberg, BSc, is a MSc Candidate within the Department of Renewable Resources at the University of Alberta (supervisors Dr. F. Schmiegelow and Dr. C. Rohner). Paula's research focuses on the distribution of mountain caribou in relation to linear features (including type, width, and activity attributes), in west-central Alberta. Paula has a background in environmental regulations pertaining to the oil/gas industry.

Dr. Christoph Rohner

Department of Renewable Resources, 7-51 General Services Building, University of Alberta, AB, Canada T6G 2H1

Christoph Rohner is a Research Associate at the Department of Renewable Resources at the University of Alberta. His research interest is linking individual behaviour and population processes to the conservation and management of endangered species and ecosystems. He is currently directing a cooperative research project on integrating caribou conservation and resource development along the eastern slopes of the Canadian Rocky Mountains. Previous research addressed population processes in relation to habitat fragmentation in agricultural landscapes, ecology of predators in the northern boreal forest, and conservation of ungulate-vegetation dynamics in arid ecosystems.

Dr. Fiona K.A. Schmiegelow (corresponding author)

Department of Renewable Resources, 7-51 General Services Building, University of Alberta, AB, Canada T6G 2H1. Email: Fiona@Schmiegelow@ualberta.ca

Fiona Schmiegelow is an Assistant Professor of Conservation Biology in the Department of Renewable Resources at the University of Alberta. Her research focuses on the broad-scale effects of land-use policies and practices on wildlife, with an emphasis on northern forests. Using a variety of both field-based and modelling approaches, she seeks to better understand the interactions between human activities and natural diversity, in order to evaluate existing, and explore potential, land management strategies.

Recruitment of Gopher Tortoises (*Gopherus polyphemus*) to a Newly Constructed Pipeline Corridor in Mississippi

David P. Thomas

In 1998, thirty-nine gopher tortoises (*Gopherus polyphemus*) were located in seventy-five active/inactive burrows along a proposed natural gas pipeline corridor in southeastern Mississippi. Thirty-four tortoises were temporarily displaced from these burrows, and were prevented from returning to the corridor while the pipeline was being constructed. Upon completion of pipeline construction and restoration of the pipeline corridor, barricades were removed, and the tortoises were again given access to the new pipeline corridor. One year after completion of the pipeline, the corridor was resurveyed. Nine tortoises were identified from twenty-two newly-dug burrows on the pipeline corridor. The actual number of tortoises from these burrows may be as high as seventeen, as conclusive occupancy could not be determined for some burrows. In addition to the new burrows located on the pipeline corridor, there were forty-two new burrows observed in the adjacent habitat, possibly indicating that additional gopher tortoises were taking advantage of the maintained right-of-way for foraging, basking, and as a travel corridor.

Keywords: Gopher tortoise, corridor, protected species, natural gas pipeline, ruderal habitat

INTRODUCTION

The Destin Pipeline (Destin) is a large diameter natural gas pipeline constructed in 1998. It originates from an offshore gathering platform in the Gulf of Mexico and makes landfall near Pascagoula, Mississippi. The pipeline continues northward for about 120 miles through Jackson, George, Greene, Wayne, and Clarke counties, and terminates at a compressor station near Enterprise, Mississippi (Fig. 1).

A major portion of the pipeline route is in the range of the federally protected western population of the gopher tortoise, *Gopherus polyphemus* (Auffenberg and Franz, 1982), and a segment of it (~4.41 mi.) traverses the Chickasawhay District of the DeSoto National Forest. Destin typically required a 75-foot wide corridor to be cleared for construction of the pipeline, and in most areas will maintain a 50-foot wide corridor in a herbaceous vegetative state.

Pipeline construction can have serious implications to gopher tortoise survival. While preliminary evidence indicates that tortoises are able to excavate themselves from burrows collapsed by machinery (Wester, 2000), tortoises away from their burrows are at risk of being crushed by moving vehicles. In addition to the threat to individual tortoises from heavy equipment, populations may be adversely affected if burrows and nests are destroyed. Tortoises also are at risk of falling into open construction trenches and becoming heat-stressed or entombed. Drowning is a danger if the trenches contain water. Indirectly, adverse impacts of pipeline construction may include disruption of essential behaviors such as mating, feeding, and dispersal (USFWS, 1997).

In recognition of the danger posed to gopher tortoises by pipeline construction activities, environmental surveys for protected species documented the locations of gopher tortoise burrows within the proposed Destin construction corridor (ENSR, 1998a). Since avoidance is a primary option for tortoise mitigation, re-routes of the project corridor were made, where possible, to avoid larger concentrations of tortoises. In some areas, however, impacts were unavoidable.

Environmental Concerns in Rights-of-Way
Management: Seventh International Symposium
J.W. Goodrich-Mahoney, D.F. Mutrie and C.A. Guild (editors)
© 2002 Elsevier Science Ltd. All rights reserved.

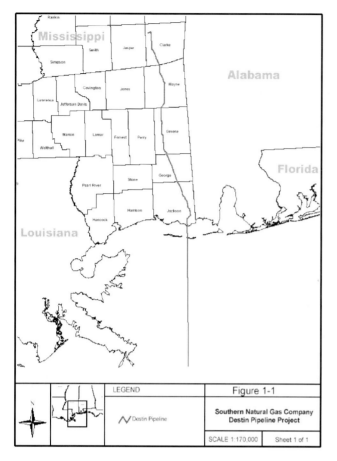

Fig. 1. Southern Natural Gas Company Destin Pipeline Project.

In coordination with the United States Fish and Wildlife Service (USFWS) and the Federal Energy Regulatory Commission (FERC), Destin prepared a Sensitive Species Mitigation Plan (ENSR, 1998) that provided for the temporary removal of gopher tortoises from the pipeline construction areas. In accordance with this plan, tortoises were trapped or excavated from their burrows and removed from the Destin construction corridor. The US Forest Service required that an additional 25-foot buffer zone on both sides of the corridor be cleared of tortoises in the DeSoto National Forest. Captured tortoises were translocated short distances to unused burrows adjacent to the corridor. Silt fence barriers were erected to prevent the tortoises from returning to the right-of-way until construction of the pipeline was complete. Upon completion of construction and re-vegetation of the corridor the fences were removed, allowing the tortoises to return to the right-of-way (ENSR, 1998a).

In accordance with the terms of the Biological Opinion issued for the Destin Project (USFWS, 1997) and the Destin Pipeline Project Sensitive Species Mitigation Plan (ENSR, 1998), Destin agreed to re-survey its right-of-way for the presence of gopher tortoises within one year of completion. Construction of the Destin Pipeline was completed in November 1998, and in compliance with this regulation, a post-construction survey was conducted in September 1999.

METHODS

Tortoises were removed from the pipeline corridor between April and September 1998. Prior to construction of the Destin Pipeline, multiple biological surveys were conducted of the proposed corridor and adjacent habitat. Burrows found during these surveys were photographed, flagged and numbered. Activity status of the burrows was made by direct observation and recorded as active/inactive or old (abandoned) (Auffenberg and Franz, 1982; Estes and Mann, 1996). All adult burrow aprons were inspected for the presence of eggs prior to disturbance. Any eggs found were carefully excavated, carried without rotation, and re-buried away from the construction area, where they could be monitored. Occupancy was then determined by the use of an infra-red video system.

Burrows that were occupied by a tortoise were fitted with pitfall or wire traps. If after two weeks of trapping the efforts were unsuccessful, the burrows were excavated. Excavations were done primarily by hand, but on some occasions were done with a backhoe. On rare occasions, tortoises were captured by hand outside their burrows. Burrows from which gopher tortoises were removed were re-inspected to ensure that no additional tortoises or vertebrate commensals were present. These burrows were then collapsed. Burrows that were too small to examine with the video system, and burrows for which conclusive occupancy determinations could not be made, were excavated. Burrows that were not occupied by a gopher tortoise or vertebrate commensal were collapsed.

All tortoises captured were measured (carapace length, plastron length, total length, bridge width, and height) weighed, sexed (if mature), aged, photographed, and marked with a standard carapace marking scheme before release (ENSR, 1998). A blood sample was also taken when possible to determine exposure to *Mycoplasma agassizii*, the organism linked to Upper Respiratory Tract Disease (URTD) in gopher tortoises (Jacobson, 1992). Twenty-six samples were tested by an enzyme-linked immunosorbent assay (ELISA) specific for *M. agassizii* at the Department of Pathobiology of the College of Veterinary Medicine at the University of Florida. All tortoises were released into unused burrows away from the construction corridor, but usually in close proximity to the original burrow. The right-of-way was barricaded with silt fence to prevent the tortoises from returning during construction. All burrow cameras, traps, and equipment used to excavate burrows were disinfected after each use with a dilute chlorine bleach solution to prevent possible disease transmission. After completion of the pipeline construction, the corridor was restored to its original contours and re-seeded with grass mixtures recommended by local offices of the Natural Resources Conservation Service (NRCS). The

Table 1. Gopher tortoise burrows on the Destin pipeline

County	1998 (pre-construction)			1999 (post-construction)		
	Active/inactive burrows	Number tortoises	Percent occupancy	Active/inactive burrows	Number tortoises	Percent occupancy*
Jackson	1	1	100	5	1	50
George	3	0	0	1	0	0
Greene	20	15	70	4	3	100
Wayne	51	24	47	12	5	63
Total	75	39	52	22	9	64

*Percent occupancy calculated by using only those burrows of known occupancy.

silt fence barriers were then removed, allowing displaced tortoises access to the right-of-way.

Post-construction surveys were conducted between September 14 and 29, 1999. Historically, no documentation exists of tortoises from Clarke County, Mississippi (Auffenberg and Franz, 1982; Estes and Mann, 1996), and no evidence of gopher tortoises was documented in Clarke County on the pipeline corridor during any of Destin's pre-construction surveys (ENSR, 1998; ENSR, 1998a). Therefore, post-construction surveys began immediately north of the Wayne County line west of the town of Shubutta (T10N-R8W, S11).

The entire 75-foot wide Destin construction corridor and adjacent buffer area in Desoto National Forest was surveyed for gopher tortoise burrows. These surveys consisted of a 4-person team walking contiguous transects south to State Highway 614 in Jackson County, Mississippi (T5S-R6W, S1). Total distance surveyed was approximately 90 miles. Suitable gopher tortoise habitat exists in disjunct areas in southern Mississippi from northern Jones and Wayne counties to the coastal flatwoods region of the Gulf Coast (Estes and Mann, 1996; ENSR, 1998a). By using previous survey records, topographical maps, and on-site inspections, it was determined that suitable gopher tortoise habitat did not exist south of Highway 614 along the Destin Pipeline, and the survey was terminated at that location.

All burrows documented on the restored pipeline corridor would have been newly excavated since the completion of the pipeline. An initial status determination was made of each burrow based on appearance (Auffenberg and Franz, 1982; Estes and Mann, 1996; Mann, 1995) using the same criteria as the 1998 surveys. General information was recorded regarding soils and vegetation around the burrow, measurements were taken at the burrow opening, and each was photographed. All adult burrows were then inspected with the video system to determine occupancy. Burrow locations were estimated with reference to the pipe centerline, and exact locations were recorded by Global Positioning System (GPS). Burrows within 100 yards of two or more active tortoise burrows were considered part of a colony.

RESULTS

Prior to construction of the Destin Pipeline in 1998, a total of 75 active/inactive burrows were located within the proposed 75-foot wide construction corridor and adjacent buffer in the DeSoto National Forest. Of these burrows, a total of 39 (52%) were occupied by tortoises (Table 1). Thirty-four tortoises were displaced prior to construction (others either moved of their own accord prior to construction, or were located in an area where they were able to remain in their burrows while construction worked around them). One tortoise was fatally injured during construction activities.

Pre-construction population density along the pipeline corridor was approximately 0.43 tortoises/mile. Occupied burrows were found in Jackson, Greene, and Wayne counties. Four of the burrows (5%) recorded were juvenile burrows. All were in Wayne County. One of the juvenile burrows and one adult burrow in Wayne County had two tortoises in it. The adult sex ratio was weighted towards females (17 F, 13 M).

All tortoises from the captured group tested negative for exposure to *M. agassizii*. Only one tortoise captured showed any evidence of the clinical signs of URTD (watery eyes, nasal exudate), but it also tested negative and was released. This tortoise was recaptured during the same season and showed none of the symptoms previously exhibited. The test results indicated a suspect level of antibodies in another tortoise, which showed no clinical signs of the disease. It was re-tested during the same season with negative results.

During the 1999 survey, a total of 22 new burrows were found on the restored corridor of the Destin Pipeline and the adjacent buffer area in the DeSoto National Forest (Table 1). Tortoise burrows were found on the right-of-way in Jackson, George, Greene, and Wayne counties. The most northerly burrow noted during the survey was an active one beyond the edge of the right-of-way corridor at milepost (MP) 180.5 (T9N-R7W, S30) in Wayne County. The most southerly burrow was a very old burrow outside of the corridor at MP 105.5 (T4S-R6W, S15) in Jackson County. No inquiline species were seen in any of the burrows examined.

Of the recently dug burrows, it was determined that 9 were occupied, 5 were unoccupied, and 8 were of unknown occupancy. Tortoise colonies were noted at four separate locations. Two of the burrows recorded (9%) were juvenile burrows. Occupancy could not be determined for some burrows because the camera could not be maneuvered to the bottom of the burrow, or because the burrow had been dug by a juvenile tortoise, making it too small for the camera to enter. None of the burrows was excavated. Occupancy rates for the new burrows potentially could range from 41 to 77% (9–17 tortoises). All burrows within the right-of-way, whether occupied or not, showed signs of recent use. Tortoise density on the new pipeline corridor is presently estimated at 0.1–0.19 tortoises/mile.

DISCUSSION

Distribution of gopher tortoises throughout their range is uneven (Mount, 1986), and this is especially true in the western population area of Louisiana, Mississippi, and Alabama (Auffenberg and Franz, 1982). In areas where native gopher tortoise habitat has been severely degraded by silvicultural and agricultural practices, gopher tortoises frequently make use of ruderal habitats, such as is found along powerlines, natural gas transmission lines, and road rights-of-way. If grasses and forbs are sufficient, they may occur in higher densities in these ruderal habitats than in their natural habitat (Auffenberg and Franz, 1982). Throughout much of southern Mississippi, native longleaf pine (*Pinus palustris*) and turkey oak (*Quercus laevis*) habitats, preferred by gopher tortoises, have been supplanted with economically profitable fast growing loblolly (*Pinus taeda*) and slash pines (*Pinus elliotti*). Rapid habitat destruction in suitable gopher tortoise areas has been attributed to current tree harvesting and reforestation methods, as well as to pasture improvement practices (Lohoefener and Loheimer, 1981; Auffenberg and Franz, 1982).

In general, habitat quality for gopher tortoises along the Destin pipeline corridor can be considered poor, and environmental surveys of the Destin route found that throughout its entire length tortoise distribution was patchy and sparse. Pine plantations are a predominant land use along much of the Destin route (FERC, 1997). These areas provide little forage for gopher tortoises and the density in which they are planted can restrict tortoise movements. The habitat clumping produced by these pine monocultures may also contribute to reduced gene flow between populations and increased competition for food (Lohoefener and Lohmeier, 1981). Many areas, although having an open canopy, are too mesic to support gopher tortoises. Areas having priority gopher tortoise soils had the highest numbers of tortoises, followed by areas having suitable soils (Estes and Mann, 1996). Priority soils are defined as having sand texture to a depth of 40 inches or more, a drainage class better than well drained, have rapid or very rapid permeability rate, no water tables within 8 feet, and are not subject to flooding (Wester and Haas, 1995).

Where suitable habitat was found, the area generally had tortoises. The route of the Destin Pipeline traverses mainly rural areas, and a significant portion of it (47%) parallels existing powerline or pipeline rights-of-way. Gopher tortoise numbers were higher along the open areas associated with parallel rights-of-way, especially in the DeSoto National Forest, although isolated burrows and remnant populations were found elsewhere (ENSR, 1998, 1998a). The higher numbers of tortoises found on the Destin corridor in DeSoto can probably be attributed to the availability of open space, as well as the protection afforded by the National Forest designation, since habitat quality can only be considered fair, and no priority soils exist within the areas traversed.

The construction of the Destin Pipeline is a unique opportunity to monitor the progress of gopher tortoise populations in southeastern Mississippi. The data gathered for this project may be used as a benchmark with which to compare future investigations. A baseline having been established, habitat improvement associated with the construction and maintenance of the pipeline corridor and gopher tortoise population response can be evaluated over time. Because so much of the Destin route was cut through pine plantations, the construction of an open corridor can be expected to attract gopher tortoises. The corridor was re-graded to its original contours and seeded with fast growing annual grasses upon completion to maintain erosion control, but none of the grasses planted are typically associated with gopher tortoise forage (Lohoefener and Lohmeier, 1981). The succession of perennial native grasses and forbs more typical of gopher tortoise forage in subsequent growing seasons will undoubtedly increase its attractiveness to tortoises.

One year after its completion, post-construction surveys found 22 burrows on the restored Destin corridor. While tortoises were removed from the right-of-way only in Greene and Wayne counties, they were found on the right-of-way in all four counties during the post-construction survey. Because occupancy could not be ascertained in all of the burrows, the occupancy rate may range between 41 and 77% (9–17 tortoises). In addition, there were 42 additional active/inactive burrows seen in adjacent habitat beyond the right-of-way. Probably more important than just the number of tortoises on the right-of-way is their demographic profile. The presence of at least four tortoise colonies utilizing the Destin corridor is important, as is the presence of juvenile burrows within these colonies. Isolated tortoises may be reproductively unsuccessful, and may be indicative of a decline in tortoise populations in that area. If pipeline corridors serve to link isolated tortoises by providing travel corridors, these tortoises may again have opportunity to become reproductively viable. It is therefore encouraging to see that tortoises have moved onto the pipeline corridor in areas in which they were not previously seen.

There is evidence that tortoises have begun using the Destin Pipeline for more than burrowing. Adult female tortoises were seen on or in the vicinity of the pipeline corridor at MP's 172.9 and 159.9. The tortoise at MP 159.9 had been relocated prior to construction and was marked number 106. The period prior to this survey was unusually dry, allowing tortoises movement beyond normal environmental constraints. There was also evidence of an unfortunate aspect of pipeline corridors. Pipelines often give humans easy access into areas frequented by gopher tortoises. The skeletal remains of a gravid female tortoise were found just west of the corridor at MP 156.5 in Greene County, possibly shot by hunters.

The concentrations of burrows on and near the Destin Pipeline and movements along the corridor indicate that tortoise populations have begun taking advantage of the improved habitat provided by the corridor. While never considered plentiful along the route, in subsequent years tortoise numbers are expected to increase within the Destin right-of-way. Using the conservative number of 9 tortoises already on the right-of-way and 17 immediately adjacent to it (42 active/inactive × 0.41 corrective factor) (Burke, 1989), the number of tortoises already is approaching pre-construction levels. It would appear that the construction of the Destin Pipeline had little negative impact on gopher tortoise populations, and may serve to increase their numbers and viability. Ideally, future surveys will indicate gopher tortoise recruitment from less optimal habitat onto the pipeline, and tortoise reproduction will bring numbers to near carrying capacity for each area.

REFERENCES

Auffenberg, W. and R. Franz. 1982. The status and distribution of the gopher tortoise (*Gopherus polyphemus*). In: R.B. Bury, ed. North American Tortoises Conservation and Ecology, pp. 95–126. US Fish and Wildlife Service, Wildlife Resource Report 12.

Burke, R. 1989. Burrow-to-tortoise conversion factors: Comparison of three gopher tortoise survey techniques. Herpetological Review, 20: 92–94.

ENSR. 1998. Destin Pipeline Project Sensitive Species Mitigation Plan. Prepared for Destin Pipeline Company, 1900 Fifth Avenue North, Birmingham, AL. FERC Docket No. CP96-655-000. 21 pp.

ENSR. 1998a. Final Report. Gopher tortoise (*Gopherus polyphemus*) relocation for the construction of the Destin Pipeline Project. Prepared for Destin Pipeline Company, LLC, 1900 Fifth Avenue North, Birmingham, AL. FERC Docket No. CP96-655-001, et al. 29 pp.

Estes, T. and T. Mann. 1996. State land 16th section gopher tortoise survey. Mississippi Technical Report No. 43, Mississippi Department of Wildlife, Fisheries, and Parks. 37 pp.

Federal Energy Regulatory Commission (FERC). 1997. Final Environmental Impact Statement, Destin Pipeline Project. FERC/EIS-113, Docket Nos. CP96-655-001, et al. CP97-291-000. Washington, DC.

Jacobson, E. 1992. The desert tortoise and upper respiratory tract disease. Special Report (rev. November 1992) prepared for the Desert Tortoise Preserve Committee, Inc., and US Bureau of Land Management.

Lohoefener, R. and L. Lohmeier. 1981. Comparison of gopher tortoise (*Gopherus polyphemus*) habitats in young slash pine and old longleaf pine areas of southern Mississippi. Journal of Herpetology, 15(2): 239–242.

Mann, T. 1995. Tortoise densities and burrow occupancy rates for gopher tortoises on selected sites in Mississippi. Mississippi Museum of Natural Science, Museum Technical Report No. 24. 48 pp.

Mount, R.H., ed. 1986. Vertebrate animals of Alabama in need of special attention. Ala. Agr. Expt. Sta., Auburn University. 124 pp.

US Fish and Wildlife Service (USFWS). 1997. Biological Opinion for the Proposed Destin Pipeline Project. US Department of the Interior Doc. No. C4-3-97.

Wester, E. 2000. Alabama annual state report. The Tortoise Burrow, Newsletter of the Gopher Tortoise Council, 19(4): 2.

Wester, E. and T. Haas. 1995. Distribution of the threatened gopher tortoise (*Gopherus polyphemus*) on priority soils DeSoto National Forest, Mississippi. Technical report prepared under US Forest Service contract numbers 00-447U-1026 and 53-447U-5-32. 18 pp. + appendices.

BIOGRAPHICAL SKETCH

David P. Thomas
ENSR International, 4155 Shackleford Road, Suite 245, Norcross, GA 30093, USA

David Thomas is a graduate of David Lipscomb University in Nashville, Tennessee, where he was awarded a Bachelor of Science degree in Biology. He was awarded a Master of Science degree in Zoology from Auburn University, where he worked with the federally listed gray bat, *Myotis grisescens*. He has over seven years of experience in the pipeline construction industry, in which he has done extensive field survey work, biological assessment for threatened and endangered species, project coordination, field construction supervision, and project management. He has been a biological consultant for ENSR International for the past five years, and has worked extensively with protected species.

Effects of Brushmat/Corduroy Roads on Wetlands within Rights-of-Way after Pipeline Construction

Joseph M. McMullen and Scott D. Shupe

Brushmat roads and commercial mats are used to support equipment and lessen impacts to wetlands during the construction of pipelines. Removal of brushmat from wetlands and the disposal of the removed material, which is usually required by regulators, can create wetlands disturbance and is very expensive. A five-year research effort was implemented to assess the effect of brushmat roads on wetland vegetation, hydrology, and habitat in different wetlands within a gas pipeline right-of-way. The portion of the research project presented in this paper concentrates on changes in physical parameters and vegetation to assess whether the brushmat area was converted to upland. The research was conducted on eight different wetlands in upstate New York. Both organic soil and mineral soil wetlands were assessed. Varying lengths of brushmat road were left in the wetlands to establish different "percent leave." Scattering of brushmat was also tested. Results of the study indicated that brushmat height above wetlands soil surface decreased in time. Decay was higher in areas of smaller stems, greater mutilation, higher soil/debris on mat, less bark, and vegetation cover. Observations indicated that brushmat totally submerged under water decays more slowly than brushmat under wet and dry moisture regimes. Scatter areas had an initial rapid decline in mat thickness, likely as a result of settling, but case hardening of exposed stems slowed decay and mat thickness declined little in the latter portion of the study. With sectional removal in obvious channels, brushmats did not impact wetland water levels. Such sectional removal is considered necessary. Removal of brushmat segments adjacent to uplands and other points of access is important to restrict vehicular access. Vegetation was sampled on and off the brushmat to test dominance by wetland species. Vegetation established rather quickly on the mat or grew up through the mat. Vegetation on-mat and off-mat in organic soil wetlands and mineral soil wetlands with prolonged inundation or saturation were dominated by wetland species. Vegetation on mat in certain mineral soil wetlands with limited saturated conditions was dominated by upland species. Results of the study question the need and benefits of regulatory agencies' request to remove brushmat roads from most wetlands.

Keywords: Wetland restoration, wetland impacts, pipeline construction, woody debris, woody decay, rights-of-way

OBJECTIVE

The objective of the study was to determine the effect of five different amounts of brushmat "leave" on wetland vegetation and hydrology in different wetlands within a recently-constructed gas pipeline right-of-way.

Environmental Concerns in Rights-of-Way
Management: Seventh International Symposium
J.W. Goodrich-Mahoney, D.F. Mutrie and C.A. Guild (editors)
© 2002 Elsevier Science Ltd. All rights reserved.

INTRODUCTION

A natural gas pipeline constructed in 1993 crossed many areas of wetlands regulated by the New York State Department of Environmental Conservation (NYSDEC) and the US Army Corps of Engineers (Corps). Brushmat roads were installed for construction access across wetlands to support equipment and lessen impacts. Corps permit conditions usually require that brushmats be removed after construction, because they consider brushmats to constitute fill and the area over the brushmat to develop into an upland.

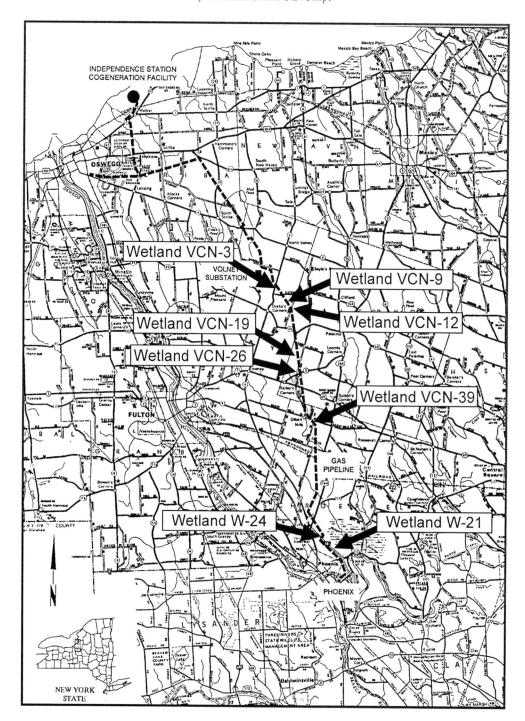

Fig. 1. General location of wetland study areas used for brushmat roads research project along natural gas transmission pipeline no. 63.

Such removal creates excessive soil and wetland disturbance and can be very expensive. It is difficult to find locations to dispose of this woody material, and where disposal occurs, impacts to upland habitats result.

The long-term effects of brushmats on wetlands has never been assessed. To address these concerns, Niagara Mohawk Power Corporation (NMPC) supported a five-year research effort to assess the effects of brushmat roads on wetlands. The complete results of this study are found in TES (1999).

METHODS

Eight different wetlands along Natural Gas Pipeline No. 63 in southcentral Oswego County, New York, USA were studied (Fig. 1). The pipeline was constructed in 1993 and the wetlands were initially characterized in 1994 and sampled in 1995, 1997, and 1999.

Five types of brushmat treatment were studied: four involved leaving various lengths of brushmat in wetlands (based on a percent "leave"), and one involved the scattering of removed brushmat material in wet-

Table 1. Brushmat treatments, lengths, widths, and number of sampling transects

Wetland area	% Leave[a]	Brushmat lengths (Feet)			Avg. width (Feet)	Number of sampling transects[b]
		Total	Leave	Remove		
VCN-12	0	430	0	430	25	6
VCN-39	0	431	0	431	25	6
VCN-9N	20–25	464	115	349	37	2
W-24	20–25	812	224	588	25	8
VCN-3	70–80	1851	1256	595	23	14
VCN-19N	70–80	614	380	234	24	4
VCN-26	90–100	529	465	64	30	4
W-21	90–100	373	318	55	23	6
VCN-9S	Scatter	265	N/A	N/A	N/A	4
VCN-19S	Scatter	92	N/A	N/A	N/A	2

[a] Amount of leave established by removing segments of brushmat relative to total brushmat length.
[b] Each sampling transect contains 10 sampling intervals.

lands (Table 1). The four amounts of brushmat "leave" assessed included: 0% leave, 20–25% leave, 70–80% leave, and a 90–100% leave. Zero percent leave was a complete removal of brushmat. Twenty to twenty-five percent leave involved removal of segments of brushmat equaling 75–80% of the total brushmat length. Ninety to one hundred percent leave entailed leaving almost the entire brushmat intact, except for the removal of smaller segments of material approximately every 150 feet to facilitate the flow of water and at the ends of the brushmat to restrict unauthorized access. Scattering involved the spread of brushmat across the wetland adjacent to the pipeline to resemble a "drop and lop" forest clearing operation.

Removal of brushmat was performed using brush rakes, tracked excavators, and bulldozers. Brushmat removed from wetlands was transported to approved NMPC owned upland sites for disposal. Removed logs could not be salvaged for timber, fuel, or chipping for they were contaminated with soil. Similarly, landfills would not accept removed brushmat. All areas where brushmat segments were removed were broadcast seeded with annual ryegrass (*Lolium* sp.) at a rate of 1 lb./1000 ft.^{2} within 72 h of removing brushmat.

An initial baseline characterization was made of the brushmat, soils, and hydrology in September and October 1994. Data on brushmat parameters and vegetation were collected in the three monitoring years 1995, 1997, and 1999 along permanent transects established on the brushmat in each study area. A schematic representation of a transect is presented in Fig. 2.

Each transect was 30 feet in length, and was established parallel to the long axis of the brushmat. By using permanent stakes, the same transects were sampled each year. One pair of transects was established approximately every 150 linear feet of brushmat, "leave" or "scatter." A pair of transects consisted of one transect located near the edge of the brushmat referred to as "edge," and one transect located in the center, referred to as "center." The "center" of the brushmat received most of the equipment traffic and was much more disturbed than the brushmat "edge."

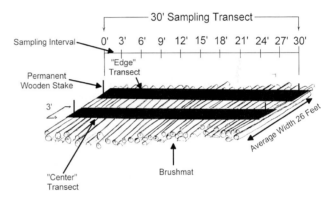

Fig. 2. Schematic representation of sampling transects.

Data on the characteristics of the brushmat were collected along the 30-foot transect in ten, 3-foot intervals (Fig. 2). Each interval was three feet long by three feet wide.

Total percent cover of vegetation in categories of high, medium, or low was recorded in each of the ten, 3-foot sampling intervals of each transect throughout the entire study. During the 1995, 1997, and 1999 samplings, species composition and vegetation cover data by dominant plant species were recorded in three of the ten intervals along the brushmat sampling transects. The three intervals of each transect sampled for vegetation included the 1'–3', 12'–15', and 27'–30' segment. The line-intercept method was used to sample the species composition and cover in each interval (Lindsey, 1956; Kisslinger et al., 1960; Cox, 1972). In addition, to compare vegetation on the brushmat (on-mat) to that growing adjacent to the brushmat (off-mat), a parallel transect was established 10 feet from the brushmat transect towards the area over the pipeline and vegetation sampled in a similar manner.

In each brushmat transect, data were collected on several variables related to the nature and characteristics of the woody material, various decay parameters, as well as total vegetation cover, as follows:

Initial characterization	Monitoring years
Brushmat thickness above wetland surface	Brushmat thickness above wetland surface
Depth of brushmat into wetland	Percent bark on brushmat material
Brushmat species composition and size	Soil/debris on surface of brushmat
Amount of mutilation of woody material	Surface decay
Percent bark remaining on stems	Insect infestation
Woody debris/soil on brushmat	Presence of fungi
Total vegetation cover	Total vegetation cover

Brushmat thickness above the wetland soil surface was measured. In several wetlands, the brushmat was pushed into the wetland and this depth was estimated. Tree and shrub species that comprised the brushmat were identified, with the three most common species in each 3-foot interval recorded. Diameter and number of stems in each sample interval were estimated.

Amount of mutilation was a qualitative assessment of the disturbance or "chewed-up" nature of the woody material comprising the brushmat. Amount of mutilation was recorded was high, medium, or low based on percentage of wood surface disturbed. Percent of bark remaining on the woody stems was recorded. Mutilation and percent bark were recorded because of their likely influence on decay rates. Soil and woody debris (bark and chips) were frequently deposited on the surface of the mat, and the amount and depth of each was recorded. Surface decay, insect infestation, and presence of fungi were also recorded in percent class categories of high (>75%), medium (25–75%), and low (<25%).

DESCRIPTION OF WETLAND STUDY AREAS

The eight wetland study areas selected for the brushmat road research are labeled as VCN-3, VCN-9, VCN-12, VCN-19, VCN-26, VCN-39, W-24, and W-21 (Fig. 1 and Table 1). VCN-9 and VCN-19 received two different treatments resulting in ten sample areas.

All the wetland study areas are within the Erie-Ontario Lake Plain physiographic province of New York, characterized by receding waters of Pleistocene Lake Iroquois. The area is underlain by slightly tilted layers of Ordovician and Silurian sedimentary formations, overlain with a variety of glacial deposits (Jones et al., 1983). Topography of the area was largely shaped by direct glacial action and the erosional forces that followed the glacial retreat. Soils in these wetlands have developed from glacio-lacustrine deposits and deposits of decomposed organic material.

Wetlands formed in depressions between low ridges of glacial till and drift where drainage was blocked by glacial deposits (Jones et al., 1983). Many of these wetlands consist of impermeable or slightly permeable drift deposits. Over top these layers exists a relatively thick accumulation of organic matter. Other wetlands in this region are a result of lacustrine silt and clay deposits within interdrumlin lowlands.

LITERATURE REVIEW

Only minimal literature is available on the decomposition of access roads such as brushmat roads and log corduroy roads. However, there is an abundance of literature available on the decomposition of coarse woody debris (CWD). Brushmat roads resemble CWD because the roads were made from a variety of sized logs, chunks of wood, and branches.

Many authors have studied individual components of the decay process. The basic components are leaching and fragmentation, but settling, seasoning, and biological factors are also involved.

Leaching occurs when water percolates through CWD and dissolves parts of the woody material, resulting in weight loss. Fragmentation works in conjunction with leaching as it increases the surface area-to-volume (SA/V) ratio of wood for the leaching process (Harmon et al., 1986).

Fragmentation of wood takes two forms, physical and biological. Physical fragmentation can occur by gravitational forces, such as flowing water, freezing and thawing activities, exposure to sun, and by mechanical means. Gravitational forces cause elevated CWD to break and fall to the ground. Flowing water can erode the exposed surface of the wood. Freezing and thawing activities can cause wood to split apart during freezing activities. Exposing more surface area of the wood to weathering forces increases the rate of gas and liquid exchange, resulting in an increase in the rate of decay (Harmon et al., 1986).

Settling increases the degree of contact between soil and CWD and increases the suitability of CWD as microbial, vertebrate, and invertebrate habitat (Harmon et al., 1986). During settling, the cross-sectional profile of logs changes from circular to elliptical and the contact between soil and CWD increases.

Seasoning is the series of changes that CWD goes through in dry environments. During seasoning, CWD decreases in moisture, shrinks, and the formation of checks and cracks begins, which increases access to microbes. In wet periods water also fills the checks and cracks. During cold weather conditions this water can freeze, thus increasing the size and amounts of checks and cracks, thereby increasing the SA/V ratio.

Case hardening may also occur to the outer ring of wood a few centimeters deep as the sun bleaches and dries the surface wood. If case hardening occurs, the wood will be initially protected from fragmentation losses and moisture from the interior (Harmon et al., 1986).

Rate of wood decay differs considerably between hardwoods and softwoods. Allison and Murphy (1962) demonstrated that, in the presence of available nitrogen, the rate of decomposition of hardwoods was six times higher than that of softwoods.

RESULTS AND DISCUSSION

Baseline characterization of brushmats

All soils in wetland study areas were classified as hydric or as having potential hydric inclusions. Mineral soils were present in wetland study areas VCN-3, VCN-9 South, VCN-12, VCN-39, W-24, and W-21. Organic soils were present in wetland study areas VCN-9 North, VCN-19 North, VCN-19 South, and VCN-26.

Data collected along the transects during the 1994 baseline characterization for the various brushmat variables are presented in Tables 2 and 3, respectively. Data on the thickness or height of the brushmat indicate that average heights in the different leave categories ranged from 3 to 14 inches. In this study, brushmat height was greatest in the one scatter area. In many instances, it was observed that soil types and associated stability greatly influenced visible brushmat thickness. In wetland study areas that contained muck soils, the brushmat was often pressed well into the substrate. Use of commercial mats over top of the brushmat and amount of vehicular traffic on the brushmat also affected its height, as well as the depth that the brushmat was below the wetland surface.

The tree and shrub species that comprised the brushmat are also indicated on Tables 2 and 3. Red maple (*Acer rubrum*) and green ash (*Fraxinus pennsylvanica*) were the most common species. Other species were: aspen (*Populus tremuloides*), willow (*Salix* sp.), black cherry (*Prunus serotina*), and yellow birch (*Betula alleghaniensis*). Rate of decay can be affected by the species present. In this study, the dominant species were relatively consistent and they were all hardwoods. Variation between hardwood and softwood decay rates is noted in the literature, but was not considered a factor in this study.

The average stem diameter ranged from 2 to 7 inches, but varied as did the number of stems in the brushmat per unit area. Smaller stems decay faster than larger stems as noted in the later discussion.

Disturbance of the surface of the brushmat material was reflected in the data recorded under "amount of mutilation." Amount of mutilation was mostly in the low (<25%) category, although there was some variation (Tables 2 and 3). Mutilation was usually higher in the center transects, and also tended to be higher where the brushmat was comprised of small diameter material. Where the percent mutilation was high, the amount of bark remaining on the stems was low (Tables 2 and 3). It was observed that where there was high vehicular traffic, soil and woody debris on the brushmat was high.

Brushmat parameters and decay

A comparison of mean values for various brushmat parameters (including total vegetation cover) is presented in Table 4. Graphical comparisons over the monitoring years by percent brushmat leave are presented on Figures 3–8. To test whether wetland or upland vegetation dominated the brushmat, the percent of the dominant species considered hydrophytic are summarized in Table 5.

Mat thickness

Mat thickness, or height of the mat above the soil surface, decreased in each wetland study area over five years. The decrease in mat thickness did not appear to be affected by "leave" treatment. Mat thickness decreased in both the organic and mineral soil study areas and was lower in organic soil areas.

The decrease in mat thickness was likely the result of many decomposition factors at work simultaneously. These factors include: fragmentation, leaching, settling, seasoning, respiration, and biological transformation (Harmon et al., 1986). It is likely that fragmentation and settling were the two factors responsible for the initial (between 1995 and 1997) decrease in mat thickness, particularly in the scatter areas. In the scatter areas, these factors likely resulted in the sharp initial decrease in mat thickness, but there was no decrease in mat thickness in the latter portions of the study as the more exposed stems became case hardened.

Weathering forces such as wind, rain, ice, and heat were reported as the primary cause of bark removal. Harman et al. (1986) and TES (1998) alluded to the fact that these weathering forces would enhance the decay of woody debris, such as brushmat. Furthermore, heavy equipment travel while working from the brushmat surface increased the fragmentation of the bark on brushmat stems.

Surface decay

Surface decay increased from 1995 to 1999 in both organic and mineral soil study areas (Fig. 6). The amount of decay was low in 1995 in both organic and mineral soil study areas. By 1997, surface decay was slightly higher in mineral soil study areas than in organic soil study areas. By 1999, the greatest amount of surface decay existed in mineral soil wetlands.

As the study proceeded from 1995 to 1999, observations were made regarding the relationship between soil/debris and decay of the brushmat, with surface decay observed to be higher where there was a greater

Table 2. Summary of 1994 brushmat characterization data collected in transects on "edge" of brushmat

Wetland study area	Amount of leave	Average mat thickness above wetland surface (inches)	Average depth of mat into wetland (inches)	Mat composition frequency of occurrence — Species	Mat composition frequency of occurrence — Times species recorded (%)	Size — Avg. diameter (inches)	Size — Predominant # of stems in each interval	Amount of mutilation H, M, L	Amount of mutilation Avg. % bark on stem	Avg. soil on surface Depth (in)	Avg. soil on surface H, M, L	Woody debris Avg. depth (in)	Woody debris H, M, L	Total veg. cover overall H, M, L
VCN-12	0%	NA	NA	NA NA NA	NA NA NA	NA	NA	NA	NA	NA	NA	NA	NA	NA
VCN-39	0%	NA	NA	NA NA NA	NA NA NA	NA	NA	NA	NA	NA	NA	NA	NA	NA
VCN-9N	20–25%	4	7	Green Ash / Red Maple / Hemlock	30 / 20 / 20	6	<5	L	41	0.5	M	0.3	L	H
W-24	20–25%	8	4	Green Ash / Red Maple / Aspen	85 / 52 / 30	4	5–10	H	15	2	H	2	H	L
VCN-3	70–80%	9	2	Red Maple / Yellow Birch / Green Ash	73 / 44 / 19	5	<5	L	42	1	M	0.5	L	L
VCN-19N	70–80%	13	>18	Red Maple / Green Ash / Yellow Birch	100 / 15 / 15	4	10–20	L	64	1	L	0	NA	L
VCN-26	90–100%	5	3	Red Maple / Green Ash / Black Cherry	75 / 20 / 5	3	<5	L	37	1	M	1	L	L
W-21	90–100%	7	2	Green Ash / Willow / Aspen	100 / 17 / 17	2	30–50	H	34	2	L	2	L	L
VCN-9S	Scatter	11	2	Green Ash / Red Maple / Aspen	85 / 40 / 15	4	<5	L	64	5	H	2	H	L
VCN-19S	Scatter	14	>24	Red Maple / Yellow Birch / Black Cherry	100 / 10 / 10	5	5–10	L	52	0	NA	1	L	L

#Stems/3' Interval: <5, 5–10, 10–20, 20–30, 30–50, >50.
H, M, L: high >75%, med. 25–75%, low <25%.
NA = not applicable.

Table 3. Summary of 1994 brushmat characterization data collected in transects on "center" of brushmat

Wetland study area	Amount of leave	Average mat thickness above wetland surface (inches)	Average depth of mat into wetland (inches)	Mat composition frequency of occurrence		Size		Amount of mutilation		Avg. soil on surface		Woody debris		Total veg. cover overall H, M, L
				Species	Times species recorded (%)	Avg. diameter (inches)	Predominant # of stems in each interval	H, M, L	Avg. % bark on stem	Depth (in)	H, M, L	Avg. depth (in)	H, M, L	
VCN-12	0%	NA	NA	NA NA NA	NA NA NA	NA	NA	NA	NA	NA NA		NA NA		NA
VCN-39	0%	NA	NA	NA NA NA	NA NA NA	NA	NA	NA	NA	NA NA		NA NA		NA
VCN-9N	20–25%	4	>12	Black Cherry Green Ash Red Maple	40 20 20	4	<5	L	30	0.2 L		1 M		L
W-24	20–25%	12	5	Green Ash Red Maple Aspen	85 52 30	4	5–10	H	8	3 H		1 H		L
VCN-3	70–80%	8	3	Red Maple Yellow Birch Green Ash	56 23 15	5	<5	L	33	2 H		2 L		L
VCN-19N	70–80%	7	>24	Red Maple Green Ash Aspen	75 35 25	7	<5	H	25	1 L		1 H		L
VCN-26	90–100%	3	1	Red Maple NA NA	55 NA NA	2	<5	L	34	0.2 H		0.5 M		M
W-21	90–100%	7	3	Green Ash Willow Aspen	100 17 17	2	30–50	L	17	2 H		2 H		L
VCN-9S	Scatter	11	1	Green Ash Aspen Red Maple	80 40 20	3	5–10	L	56	1 L		1 M		H
VCN-19S	Scatter	26	>24	Red Maple Black Cherry Green Ash	100 40 20	6	5–10	L	79	0.4 M		4 M		L

#Stems/3' Interval: <5, 5–10, 10–20, 20–30, 30–50, >50.
H, M, L: high >75%, med. 25–75%, low <25%.
NA = not applicable.

Table 4. Comparison of 1995, 1997, and 1999 brushmat data mean values for various parameters

Wetland study area		Mat thickness (inches)	Amount of bark (%)	Soil/debris[a]	Depth of soil debris (inches)	Surface decay[a]	Insect evidence[a]	Fungi evidence[a]	Vegetation cover[a]	Amount of water (%)	Water depth (inches)
VCN-9N	1995	3.6	2.3	0.2	0.1	0.8	0.0	0.0	2.0	0.0	0.0
	1997	2.9	0.5	2.6	1.5	2.9	0.0	0.1	3.0	0.0	0.0
	1999	2.5	0.0	2.5	b	3.0	0.0	0.1	3.0	0.0	0.0
W-24	1995	12.8	4.4	2.5	2.1	1.7	0.0	0.2	2.0	0.0	0.0
	1997	9.5	0.0	2.4	2.4	2.4	0.0	0.3	3.0	0.0	0.0
	1999	6.3	0.1	2.7	b	3.0	0.2	0.1	3.0	0.0	0.0
VCN-3	1995	8.0	19.9	0.6	0.7	1.1	0.0	0.3	2.5	0.0	0.0
	1997	6.4	4.7	1.8	1.4	2.7	0.0	0.3	2.9	0.0	0.0
	1999	5.1	8.9	2.0	b	2.9	0.1	0.4	2.9	0.0	0.0
VCN-19N	1995	10.4	22.6	1.0	0.5	1.4	0.0	0.3	1.3	5.5	0.0
	1997	8.4	10.5	0.8	1.3	2.8	0.1	0.9	3.0	0.0	0.0
	1999	4.5	1.0	1.5	b	2.9	0.1	0.6	3.0	0.0	0.0
VCN-26	1995	2.7	6.0	0.2	0.5	0.7	0.0	0.1	2.2	34.3	0.4
	1997	1.2	1.5	0.9	0.8	0.7	0.0	0.1	3.0	0.0	0.0
	1999	0.6	0.0	2.9	b	0.6	0.0	0.0	2.9	0.0	0.0
W-21	1995	10.0	14.0	1.8	2.0	0.1	0.0	0.1	1.3	0.0	0.0
	1997	7.6	2.8	1.5	1.4	3.0	0.3	0.2	2.8	0.0	0.0
	1999	6.0	0.0	2.3	b	3.0	0.3	0.0	2.9	0.0	0.0
VCN-9S	1995	10.6	33.8	0.8	2.2	1.1	0.0	0.3	1.6	0.0	0.0
	1997	6.0	22.8	0.1	0.1	2.1	0.0	0.5	3.0	0.0	0.0
	1999	7.4	3.3	2.2	b	2.9	0.0	0.2	3.0	0.0	0.0
VCN-19S	1995	22.0	13.5	0.0	0.0	1.1	0.0	0.3	1.3	15.5	0.4
	1997	16.9	14.5	0.4	0.7	2.5	0.0	0.2	2.5	0.0	0.0
	1999	14.2	8.0	0.7	b	2.6	0.4	0.5	2.4	0.0	0.0

[a] Represents rank data where: 0 = none, 1 = low (<25%), 2 = medium (25–75%), 3 = high (>75%).
[b] Data not collected.

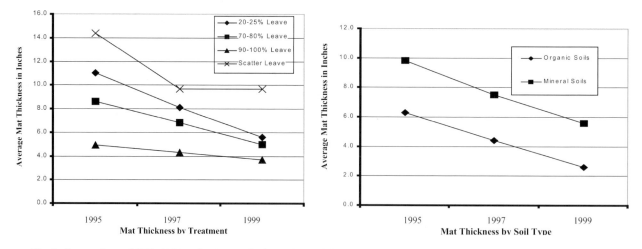

Fig. 3. Comparison of 1995, 1997, and 1999 mat thickness for each brushmat treatment and organic versus mineral soil wetlands.

amount of soil/debris on the surface. Decay was also greater on brushmat that was in contact with soil than on brushmat without soil contact. This response was likely a result of the soil maintaining a moisture constant suitable for decomposing organisms within the area surrounding the brushmat (Harmon et al., 1986).

Size of the brushmat stems was observed to influence the amount of decay. In 1997, small diameter stems (less than three inches) were usually decayed into the center of the stem. By 1999, brushmat in nearly all leave treatments were highly decayed. Stems that were highly mutilated due to heavy equipment travel also had extremely high rates of decay (TES, 1998). This decay response is due to the increased surface area available for decomposition activities (Harmon et al., 1986).

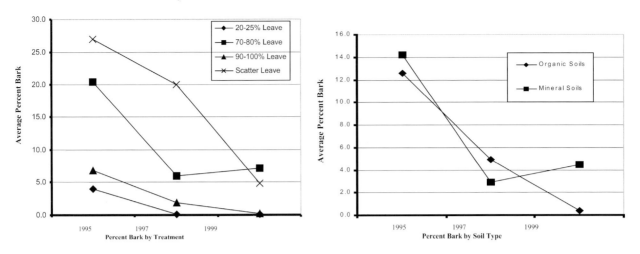

Fig. 4. Comparison of 1995, 1997, and 1999 percent bark for each brushmat treatment and organic versus mineral soil wetlands.

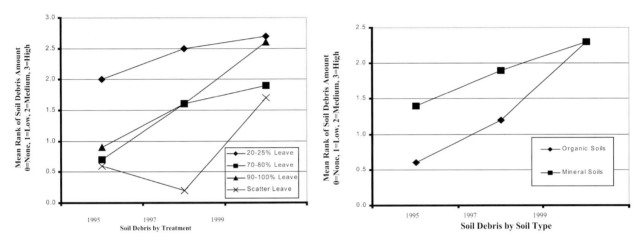

Fig. 5. Comparison of 1995, 1997, and 1999 soil debris for each brushmat treatment and organic versus mineral soil wetlands.

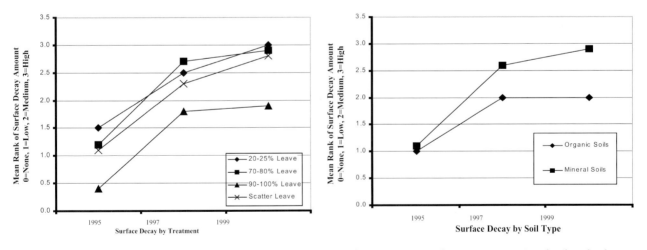

Fig. 6. Comparison of 1995, 1997, and 1999 surface decay for each brushmat treatment and organic versus mineral soil wetlands.

Insect activity

During the 1999 sampling, insect activity was noted in five of the eight study areas. Insect activity consisted of the presence of carpenter bees and ants. Ants were abundant in brushmat stems in close contact with the soil, whereas bee activity was greatest in elevated stems that were dried out, such as in scatter areas. Such insect activity is an important part of the decomposition of brushmat because the insects increase the surface area of mat to be decomposed. This material will decompose quicker because it has a greater surface area. These openings also allow

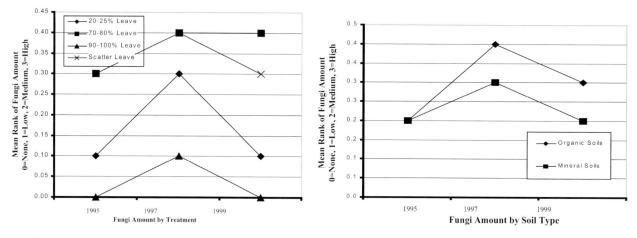

Fig. 7. Comparison of 1995, 1997, and 1999 fungi amount for each brushmat treatment and organic versus mineral soil wetlands.

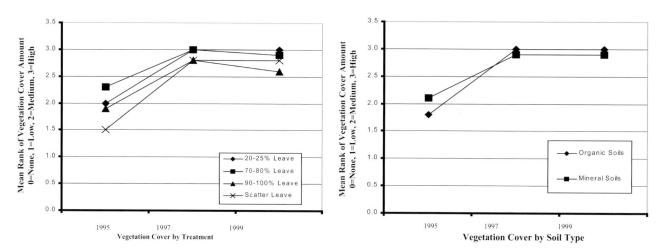

Fig. 8. Comparison of 1995, 1997, and 1999 vegetation cover for each brushmat treatment and organic versus mineral soil wetlands.

microbes to colonize the woody material and aid in the decomposition process (Harmon et al., 1986).

Vegetation cover/species composition
Overall, the brushmat did not impede vegetation cover. After the second growing season, vegetation cover was nearly 100% in most areas (Fig. 8). Vegetation grew up through the brushmat material and invaded soil and fine material deposited on the brushmat.

The brushmat areas were usually dominated by wetland vegetation (Table 5). All brushmat segments in organic soil study areas were dominated by wetland vegetation. Brushmat segments in two of the six mineral soil wetlands were dominated by upland vegetation after five years. However, these were areas of marginal wetlands. These areas had limited water near the surface and contained a mix of upland species in off-mat portions. Conditions favoring a dominance of upland vegetation may have been exacerbated by two dry years during the study. This study does conclude that in wetlands areas that are only seasonally wet and contain a mix of upland species (these marginal wetlands usually are on mineral soils), brushmats left in place may create upland conditions. In such areas,

Table 5. Comparison of on-mat versus off-mat dominant plant species, five years after mat placement

Wetland study area	Brushmat leave (%)	Species FAC or wetter (%)	
		On-Mat	Off-Mat
VCN-12	0	100	100
VCN-39	0	75	90
VCN-9N	20–25	100	100
W-24	20–25	25	70
VCN-3	70–80	89	100
VCN-19N	70–80	100	100
VCN-26	90–100	100	100
W-21	90–100	40	50
VCN-9S	Scatter	75	67
VCN-19S	Scatter	100	100

an elevation change of 4–8 inches created by brushmat may make a difference between an upland and a wetland. In all other wetlands studied, no wetland conversion was noted by this minor elevation change.

Vegetation species data recorded on and off the mat presented in TES (1999) for this study provide evidence of the lack of change in hydrology in areas adjacent to the brushmat. These data and observations made indicated little to no alteration in hydrologic regimes because of the brushmat.

Comparison of varying amounts of brushmat leave
Various percentages of brushmat "leave" were developed by removing varying segments of brushmat road. Segments of brushmat were always removed from two areas: (1) the ends of the brushmat road where it connected to an upland or structure pad, and (2) where there were visible drainageways or water channels. Removal of "end" segments restricted access to the brushmat by ATVs and other unwarranted vehicular activity. Removal of segments in water channels permitted unrestricted hydrological conditions.

In general, there was great variability with little to no evident difference in the parameters measured among the amount of brushmat leave among wetlands of a similar nature. An organic soil wetland, with water near the surface for much of the year, would not be more greatly affected by 75% brushmat leave than by 25% brushmat leave. Such a difference in brushmat leave created more of a slightly different habitat, and perhaps diversified the area, but it was not seen as detrimental.

This conclusion can also be made for mineral soil wetlands where there was relatively abundant water. However, in marginal wetland areas where a slight change in elevation can make the difference between an upland and a wetland, brushmat leave can have a negative impact and a greater percentage of brushmat in such a wetland can increase the impact.

Brushmats in wetlands can take up space (until they decay) that cannot be occupied by standing water. And, the more brushmat, the greater the volume of water that would be displaced. However, it should be noted that most of the wetlands where brushmats were utilized were originally forested or scrub-shrub habitat where the woody material, although standing, also occupied space.

The scattering of removed brushmat within the wetland was one of the different brushmat "treatments" assessed; it has several drawbacks and is not recommended. Scattering may increase the height of the brushmat. Logs and other woody material elevated above the ground did not decay readily. Such logs became "case hardened" where the outside of the wood hardens and encases the stem. This decreased the rate of decay. More of a problem with scattering was the restrictions to access and potential future equipment use in these areas. For pipelines where maintenance mowing is normally required every three years, such scattering can be very restrictive.

CONCLUSIONS

Upon completion of five years of research it has been determined that the five amounts of brushmat leave tested (0% leave, 20–25% leave, 75–80% leave, 90–100% leave, and scatter of brushmat) did not have an overall negative effect on vegetation or the classification of the brushmat area as a wetland in most wetland areas.

Segments of brushmat were always removed adjacent to uplands and other points of access in order to restrict unwanted vehicular access. This removal practice is considered prudent. Brushmat was also removed from any evident drainageway or channel at the initiation of the study. Brushmat did not appear to restrict water movement or alter water regimes in any wetland areas.

In general, although there was variability in the data, differences in the amount of brushmat leave among wetlands of a similar nature were not evident. An organic soil wetland, with water near the surface for much of the year, did not appear to be more greatly affected by 75% brushmat leave than by 25% brushmat leave. Such a difference in brushmat leave created more of a slightly different habitat, and perhaps diversified the area, but this was not seen as detrimental.

Decay of brushmat increased over the five-year study and, along with settling, reduced mat thickness. Brushmat that had high amounts of soil/debris and mutilation and a low amount of bark on stems at the time of establishment was observed to have a high rate of decay during the study. Increased vegetation cover likely also contributed to increased decay. It is speculated that high soil/debris conditions and vegetation cover maintained optimal moisture conditions within the brushmat stems for decomposing organisms, while the high amount of mutilation and low amount of bark provided openings for water and insects to enter.

Scattering of brushmat had several drawbacks and is not recommended. Scattering increased the height of brushmat in this study. Logs and other woody material elevated above the ground did not decay as rapidly as brushmat in contact with soil/debris. Elevated stems of brushmat became case hardened, where the outside of the wood hardens and encases the stem, which decreased the rate of decay. Likely the greatest problem with scattering is the restrictions it creates for access and future equipment uses in pipeline, rights-of-way where maintenance mowing is required.

Vegetation quickly established on all brushmat areas. In organic and mineral soil wetlands with relatively abundant water throughout the growing season, hydrophytic vegetation grew on the mat regardless of treatment. However, in marginal wetland areas usually found in seasonably wet mineral soils, a change in elevation of 4–8 inches, which can be caused by brushmat, created an upland vegetation island in two of the six mineral soil wetlands. The creation of an upland on brushmat in a wetland can have a negative impact. Allowing a greater percentage of brushmat leave in such marginal wetlands can increase this impact. Therefore, it is recommended that construction managers and resource managers negotiate, on a case-by-case basis, the need to remove brushmat from mineral soil wetlands of marginal hydrology.

The effects of brushmat in wetlands, especially organic soil wetlands, is not necessarily negative, and therefore the high costs of complete brushmat removal from these wetlands is not warranted. In mineral soil wetlands with limited available water, complete removal of brushmat may be warranted so that upland brushmat islands are not created within the wetlands.

Cost of brushmat removal is one of the primary concerns for industries requiring brushmat use. However, it should be noted that removal of brushmat roads and their disposal can also be a significant impact, particularly to the area of disposal. Material removed from brushmat roads are usually deposited in upland areas and can create impacts to these habitats.

Complete decay of brushmat will occur at some time after placement. This time interval is projected to likely be in the range of 8–12 years. However, in areas where the brushmat is submerged under water, or in areas where the stems are exposed and case hardened, this time interval may be longer.

ACKNOWLEDGEMENTS

TES would like to acknowledge the efforts of Niagara Mohawk Power Corporation in the support of this research effort.

REFERENCES

Abbott, D.T. and D.A. Crossley, Jr. 1982. Woody litter decomposition following clear-cutting. Ecology, 63: 35–42.

Allison, F.E. and R.M. Murphy. 1962. Comparative rates of decomposition in soil of wood and bark particles of several hardwood species. Soil Sci. Soc. Proc., 461–466.

Cox, G.C. 1972. Laboratory manual of general ecology. Wm. C. Brown Company Pub., Dubuque, IA.

Harmon, M.E., J.F. Franklin, F.J. Swanson, P. Sollins, S.V. Gregory, J.D. Lattin, N.H. Anderson, G.W. Lienkaemper, K. Cromack Jr., and K.W. Cummins. 1986. Ecology of Coarse of Woody Debris in Temperate Ecosystems. Adv. Ecol. Research., 15: 133–276.

Jones, S.A., M.E. Corey, and L. Zicari. 1983. The wetlands of Oswego County, New York: The interrelationships of glaciation, surficial geologic deposits, and wetland formation. Oswego County Planning Board, Oswego, NY.

Kisslinger, F.E., R.E. Eckert, and P. Currie. 1960. A comparison of line-intercept, variable plot, and loop methods as used to measure shrub cover. J. Range Manage., 13: 17–21.

Lindsey, A.A. 1956. Sampling methods and community attributes in forest ecology. For. Sci., 2(4): 287–296.

TES. 1998. Interim status and progress report, evaluation of alternatives to brushmat removal, natural gas transmission pipeline no. 63. Terrestrial Environmental Specialists, Inc. Phoenix, NY.

TES. 1999. Final report, evaluation of alternatives to brushmat removal, natural gas transmission pipeline no. 63. Terrestrial Environmental Specialists, Inc. Phoenix, NY.

BIOGRAPHICAL SKETCHES

Joseph M. McMullen

Principal Environmental Scientist, Terrestrial Environmental Specialists, Inc., 23 County Route 6, Suite A, Phoenix, NY 13135, USA, Telephone: (315) 692-7228, Fax: (315) 695-3277, E-mail: TES@dreamscape.com

has a BS in biology from Saint Francis College and a MS in biology with a concentration in botany from West Virginia University. He has worked for 27 years on all aspects of vegetation and wetland study, including wetlands restoration and numerous projects for electric and gas right-of-way permitting and maintenance.

Scott D. Shupe

Environmental Analyst, Niagara Mohawk Power Corporation, 300 Erie Boulevard West, Syracuse, NY 13202, USA, Telephone: (315) 428-6616, Fax: (315) 428-3549, E-mail: Scott.Shupe@us.ngrid.com

holds a BS in biology and a MS in water resource management from SUNY College of Environmental Science and Forestry, and a MS in science management from the University of Alaska-Anchorage. His career has spanned the planning-construction-operations spectrum, including high-voltage powerline construction management, small hydropower and navigation planning, and is currently supporting non-nuclear generation, gas, and electric system operating and licensing groups.

Designing Railroads, Highways and Canals in Protected Areas to Reduce Man–Elephant Conflicts

A.P. Singh and Dr. S.M. Satheesan

Construction of Eco-friendly linear developments in and around Protected Areas and forests has become a reasoned necessity in light of evidence that poorly designed network of railroads, highways, and canals in existence has adversely affected the foraging and migratory movements of larger wild animals including elephants. One of the root causes of this trend is the fragmentation and shrinkage of major wildlife habitats. This has lead to man-wildlife conflicts, confrontations among wild animals, and high rate of accidental deaths due to collisions with speeding motor vehicles and trains. After imposition of Forest Conservation Act, 1980 and Wildlife (Protection) Act, 1972 of the Government of India, constructions have been banned in Protected Areas and forests. But the ever-increasing heavy vehicular traffic on the existing railroads and highways in and around protected areas and forests has made wild animals irritable, restless, and accident-prone. This paper examines case histories of the Haridwar–Rishikesh/Dehradun rail-road and highway, the channel of Garhwal–Rishikesh–Chilla Hydroelectric Project and the canal of the Eastern Ganges Irrigation Project in Rajaji National Park area in Haridwar, Pauri, and Dehradun districts of Uttranchal State in India. The railroad, the highway and the channel/canal affect the movement of elephants in Chilla Motichur Corridor where the corridor width has shrunk from 20 km between Haridwar and Rishikesh to 1–2 km. The highway divides the natural habitat on one side and the legendary Ganges River on the other, the irresistible attraction for the Asian Elephants, which they have to visit daily for drinking, bathing and cooling in the summer months. Hence elephants trapped on one side of the road due to heavy traffic will look for alternate sources of water and food. Man–elephant conflict results when these animals cannot conveniently forage or drink in natural habitats and are forced to enter human habitation and croplands. Unavoidable or negligent crossing of railroad and highway by elephants have caused their accidental deaths, and at times, also of man, in addition to damage to vehicles colliding with them. About 16 elephants have been killed due to collisions with trains in this area. This paper discusses the disastrous effect of the inefficient design of existing linear developments on elephants and how they can be rectified in an animal-friendly way. Then the sustainability of viable populations of the largest terrestrial mammals living on the land can be ensured, reducing man–animal conflicts and confrontation among animals for ecological requirements in a habitat shrunk by human alterations.

Keywords: Designing, linear developments, railroads, highways, channel, canal, man–elephant conflicts, protected areas, forests, accidental deaths, vehicular traffic, confrontation among animals

INTRODUCTION

The populations of the Asian Elephant *(Elephas Maximus)* in the wild, presently, have a discontinuous distribution in the northern, eastern, and southern ranges in India. In the past, elephant populations of the north from the Yamuna River to the Brahmaputra River used to migrate freely from one end to the other, travelling a maximum distance of approximately 1300 km to meet ecological requirements in the foothills of the Himalayas. But ecologically unplanned linear developments such as railroads, highways, and canals, industrial establishments as well as human encroach-

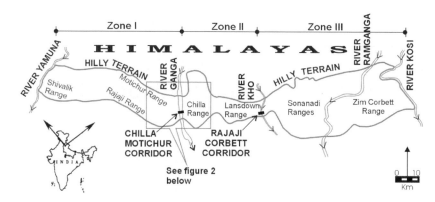

Fig. 1. Rajaji — Corbett elephant conservation unit.

ment on the original habitats and migration corridors have adversely effected their free movements and fragmented this 1300 km long migratory route into isolated zones. A sizable number of elephants (≈1600), are found between Yamuna River and Indo-Nepal border in the foothills of Himalayas, Uttranchal State, India. This belt of about 300 km long, is itself fragmented in several zones. Of these, 3 major zones which harbors 90% of the elephant population in the Rajaji — Jim Corbett conservation area are between (I) Yamuna River and Ganges River (II) Ganges River and Kho River (III) Kho River and Kosi River (Ram Nagar town). The present study and the discussion that follows focus on the man-elephant conflicts observed in Rajaji National Park in Haridwar and Dehradun districts of Uttranchal State due to linear developments (Fig. 1. Rajaji — Corbett Elephant Conservation Unit).

The main topographical features of the area bounded by Rajaji National Park are hilly torrents that link the river through deep forests. These torrents are not very steep and thus facilitate the movement of wild elephants. As long-distance and short-distance migration of wild elephants in the habitat is generally along torrents, the structures made at the junctions of torrents and railroads, highways, and canals play a significant role in their movement.

In this context, the aim of this paper is to find ways to make these structures eco-friendly at the new location or modify the existing ones so that elephants can walk across with ease and restore the lost continuity of their fragmented habitat. If corrective measures on the lines suggested in this paper are delayed any further, this largest and most majestic terrestrial mammal will slip into history like the Dinosaurs.

THE STUDY AREA — RAJAJI NATIONAL PARK

The National Park is located in the foothills of Shivalik Range and Garhwal Himalayas between 29°52′ to 30°16′N and 77°52′ to 78°22′E in Haridwar, Pauri, and Dehradun districts of Uttranchal State. The altitude of the main portion of the park lies around 365.0 m above mean sea level. The Ganges flows 24 km through the park dividing it into 2 unequal halves, with a core area of 820 sq. km. The larger western portion occupies 571 sq. km (right bank) and the smaller eastern portion covers 249 sq. km (left bank). The park has significant conservation values. It includes a large area of the fragile Shiwalik ecosystem. The fauna and flora of this region have affinities to those of the Himalayan and the Gangetic Plains Biogeographic Zones (2 and 7 categories of classification of Rodgers and Panwar, 1988). It is important to note that the park is home to a good population of the Asian Elephant (*Elephas maximus*).

The area is largely "Moist Deciduous Forests" (Champion and Seth, 1968) with the subtypes, moist Shiwalik Sal (*Shorea robusta*), moist Bhabhar Dun Sal and dry Shiwalik Sal which cover about 75% of the park area. The remaining area is under mixed forests along torrents and on the hills. Riparian forests exist along the Ganges. On higher slopes, the area around the ridgelines usually has a sparse cover of pine tree (*Pinus roxburghii*) and an abundant grass cover in flat areas. Commensurate with the considerable diversity of habitat types, the National Park harbors rich faunal diversity. The Elephant is the most important flagship species found in this Protected Area. There are approximately 453 elephants in the Park according to the latest census by the authorities. Among the common herbivores are the Sambar (*Cervus unicolor*), Chital (*Axis axis*), Barking deer (*Muntiacus muntjak*), Goral (*Nemorhaedus goral*), Nilgai (*Boselaphus tragocamelus*), Common Langur (*Presbytis entellus*), and Rhesus Monkey (*Macaca mulatta*). Omnivores are the Sloth Bear (*Melurus ursinus*), Wild Boar (*Sus scrofa*), and Indian Palm Civet (*Paradoxurys Hermaphroditus*). The carnivores present are the Tiger (*Panthera tigris*), Leopard (*Panthera pardus*), Wild Dog (*Cuon alpinus*), Jackal (*Canis aureus*), and Hyaena (*Hyaena hyaena*). Reptiles in Rajaji National Park are represented by a number of snakes including the Python (*Python molurus*), King Cobra (*Ophiophagus hannah*), Common Krait (*Bungarus careruleus*), and Indian Cobra (*Naja naja*). There are some 315 bird species in the Park, which include residents and migratory, terrestrial, and water birds.

THE PSYCHOLOGY AND HABITS OF ELEPHANTS

Elephants are long distance migratory animals. The migration is very important for elephants fodder and water requirement and maintaining gene flow. Elephants devote about three fourth of their lifetime towards feeding or moving towards a food or water source. They stay in an area for a few days and then move to another area. They like to take baths daily in summers in deep water. It has been observed that during warm weather, groups of elephants try to reach the water spots at noon or in the afternoon. As the availability of water and fodder changes seasonally in the park, the short distance migration also plays an important role in the life of elephants.

Being a sensitive and intelligent animal, the elephant requires a free environment without any hindrance. If the herd finds any obstacle on the movement track, it tries to avoid the route even at the cost of travelling long distances to fulfil the same requirement elsewhere. The elephant moves very cautiously in the group for the safety of their younger ones. There is an intense bonding and love between elder/parent elephants and their calves. Normally, to achieve a sense of security, the baby elephant moves under its mother and at the time of crossing any deep ditch or obstacle, the mother lifts the infant with its trunk. They do not tolerate any man made structure with a roof because none exists in the natural environment. They normally move in herds in a spread pattern but within visible range. The elephants consume 75–150 kg of food and 80–160 l of water every day. Their food consists mostly of grass, tender shoots, twigs, barks, leaves, and fruits (Shoshani, 1992). At times the herd walks into fields of sugarcane, rice situated in the vicinity of the park.

THE LINEAR DEVELOPMENTS-OBSTACLES IN ELEPHANTS' PATHWAY

The migration of elephants and their gene flow are threatened by following major linear developments in the study area. The alignment of railroads, highways, canals, and Chilla–Motichur corridor in Rajai National Park is shown in Fig. 2.

Haridwar–Rishikesh/Dehradun highway and railroad

The Haridwar–Rishikesh/Dehradun highway and railroad run across the narrow Chilla–Motichur corridor in Motichur Range on the right bank of the Ganges River. These obstacles divide the Park in 2 segments. Initially it was a forest road and the traffic intensity was low. With the passage of time, lucrative tourism, hydroelectric potential and the strategic importance of the India–China border, converted this road into a lifeline to Garhwal Hills and forced on it a high intensity

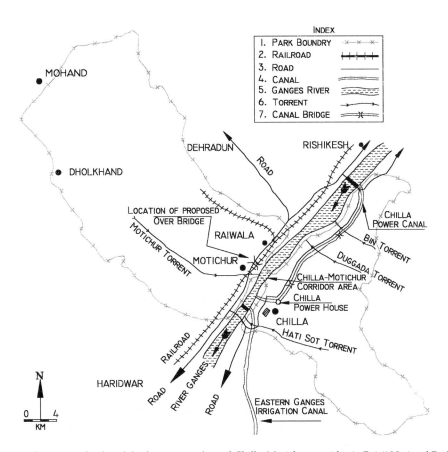

Fig. 2. Alignment of railroad, highways, canals, and Chilla–Motichur corridor in Rajaji National Park.

of mixed traffic, round the clock. A one hundred year old single lane broad gauge rail track runs parallel to the highway (about 50–150 m apart) between Motichur and Raiwala. It has become a busy route with the introduction of many fast moving trains. Both, the railroad and the highway cross the main migration track of elephants in the narrow Chilla–Motichur corridor.

Garhwal–Rishikesh–Chilla Hydel Project

Garhwal–Rishikesh Chilla Hydel Project is a run-of-the-river scheme on the left bank of the Ganges River. It utilizes a drop of 33 m in the river, from Veerbhadra to Chilla (4 km upstream of Haridwar Barrage, the head works of Upper Ganges Canal). The river discharge available at Veerbhadra has been diverted by a barrage into a 14.3 km long hydropower canal. After generating power at Chilla Power House, the water is discharged back into the Ganges River through a 1.2 km long tailrace canal. This project was commissioned in 1982.

Among the important features of the project, a 312 m long barrage is located on the Ganges at Veerbhadra, about 4 km downstream of Rishikesh. It has 15 bays (4 under sluice and 11 other bays). A 14.3 km long power canal with discharge capacity of 20,000 cubic feet per second runs almost parallel to the Ganges on the left bank through hilly terrain. Its bed width is 12.5 m and depth 9.1 m. The complete canal is lined with cement concrete tiles with side slopes of 1.75:1 (V:H). There is a powerhouse with 4 turbines of 36 MW each, generating 725 million watts per year. This power is supplied to the State grid. The whole project is in the high-intensity zone of wild elephants in the Rajaji National Park.

Eastern Ganges Canal Irrigation Project

The Eastern Ganges Canal with a capacity of 4850 cubic feet per second, takes-off from the left bank of the Ganges from the Haridwar barrage and carries water to the districts of Bijnor and Moradabad Uttar Pradesh State for irrigation. The bed width of the canal is 12 m, the water depth 4.5 m and the side slopes are 1.5:1 (V:H). The canal is partly cement concrete tile-lined and partly stone-pitched in the head-reach. The head-reach of the canal is also in high intensity zone of wild Asian elephants.

Kotdwar Landsdown Road

The road traverses the Rajaji — Corbett Corridor and runs parallel to the Kho River. Kotdwar is the base station for Pauri Garhwal hills and this road caters to a mixed-traffic (pedestrians, cycles, motorcycles, jeeps, cars, trucks, buses) of medium intensity, round the clock.

LINEAR DEVELOPMENTS-THE ARISING CONFLICTS

The intra-zone migration of elephant herds in the conservation area has almost been stopped due to man-made barriers such as railroads, highways, and canals, but the genetic exchange between populations is still carried on, by bull elephants migrating across these artificial barriers. The gene flow however cannot continue for long in the existing fragile habitat corridors between the zones, if it is not immediately strengthened by planned conservation. The confrontation of elephants with moving traffic on railroads and highways has made them irritable, restless, and prone to accident. It is shocking that elephants, water-loving animals, are not able to reach the Ganges River in Rajaji National Park, which has been their lifeline since time immemorial and are forced to use water from alternate sources such as artificial tanks and natural ponds.

Haridwar–Rishikesh/Dehradun highway and railroad

Elephants have to cross the twin railroad and highway (12 m wide) obstructions through a narrow width of 1–2 km forest to drink and bathe in the Ganges River and to go to other side of the park in Chilla–Motichur range. These days, there is high-density mixed-traffic on this route, round the clock. The herds are unable to cross the road during the day. Rarely do they cross the road at night through gaps in the traffic. Lone bull elephants at times are seen crossing the road even during the day.

There are number of trains between 5 and 11 p.m. on the Haridwar–Rishikesh/Dehradun rail track. This is also the time that most herds cross the track. Sixteen elephants have died in train accidents in the last 13 years (Table 1). Normally one would feel that any train can hit an elephant crossing the track, but it is not the case. There is an intense bonding and love between elder/parent elephants and their calves. On several occasions when a train passes through the park, while an elephant herd is crossing the rail track, members of the herd become divided in 2 groups by the moving train. This situation creates confusion in the elder members of the herd (particularly the elder females) who think that the younger members of the group on the other side of the train were killed by the running train, because they are out of their sight. So this situation creates confusion leading to their accidental deaths. In most of these rail accidents, dead elephants were mothers and their calves. Train workers have frequently spotted baby elephants at accident sites. In a recent accident on 2nd May 2000, the dead elephant was a female and the forest officer who first reached the accident site observed milk in her breasts. This meant that the weaning mother might have performed an attack on the moving train thinking that it had killed her young one. It establishes that the bondage between the mother and the calf, as well as herd psychology accounts for most of the rail

Table 1. Elephants death in train accidents on Haridwar–Dehradun rail track, in Rajaji National Park, Uttranchal, India

S. No	Date	Time	No. of deaths	App. age (years)	Sex	Name of the train	Remark
1	28/4/87	22:00	1	13	F	Mussoorie Express	
2	16/3/88	2:18	1	30	F	Goods Train	
3	24/2/89	20:45	1	4	M	Ujjain Express	
4	1/1/92	5:30	1	80	F	Haridwar Passenger	
5	2/5/92	2:10	4	45	F	Goods Train	A calf, named Raja, recovered from the accident site, is now in the custody of forest department at Chilla.
				45	F		
				40	F		
				4	M		
6	22/11/92	12:00	1	35	F	Goods Train	
7	10/5/94	22:00	1	8	M	Mussoorie Express	
8	17/5/94	20:40	1	55	M	Ujjain Express	
9	29/9/98	19:50	3	35	F	Janta Express	
				6	F		
				1	F		
10	3/4/99	22:30	1	35	F	Mussoorie Express	
11	2/5/00	21:45	1	25	F	Howrah Express	Milk observed in the breasts of the dead elephant suggest the passing train separated the weaning mother from the calf.

Total 16 Elephants have died in last 14 years.
Source: U.P. Forest Department and News Papers.

accidents inside the Protected Area. Due to the heavy traffic on the road and death of elephants in train accidents — the movement of the herds from forest to river (long distance migration) has almost stopped along the Motichur–Chilla corridor. As a result the elephant population ($\approx$300) on the right bank of the Ganges River is trapped in the zone.

Canal of Garhwal–Rishikesh–Chilla Hydro Electric Project and irrigation canal of Eastern Ganges Project on the left bank of the Ganges River

As a result of the construction of the canal on the left bank, 20.0 km long forest bank touching the river has been reduced to only 1.0 km upstream of Veerbhadra Barrage and 4–5 km between Chilla Power House and Haridwar Barrage for free movement of elephants to the Ganges River. There are 7 major cross drainage works on the junction of the power canal and torrents/streams. At a few locations, provisions are made for the movement of elephants through these structures. Unfortunately, the provisions made at these locations are insufficient and non eco-friendly, as elephants have not accepted these structures, even after 17 years of the construction of the project. Details of the critical structures on the canal are given below:

- **Bin super passage:** The structure is such that the torrent passes over the canal. Also, the appearance of the entire structure merges with the forest background (Fig. 3). This is readily acceptable to elephants. The width of the structure is 120 m, good enough for the movement of elephants. But the rows of cement concrete blocks, just downstream of the barrel of the canal, used for energy dissipation are placed at a level-difference of 1 m. This creates problems for elephants (Fig. 4). Elephant calves are not able to cross four parallel obstructions each 1 m high, side by side. Before the construction of the project, this was a major migration route for elephants.

Fig. 3. Bin super passage over Bin Torrent.

Fig. 4. Energy dissipation works downstream of Bin super passage barrel.

- **Duggada drainage crossing:** Here the canal passes over the torrent where six barrels, each 5.0 m wide and 5.25 m high, have been constructed. Though the size of barrels is appropriate, the "tunnel syndrome" of the barrels repels most of the elephants. However, lone bull elephants have been observed crossing these barrels (Fig. 7).
- **Bridges on canal:** There are 2 road bridges on the power canal at the sixth and eighth kilometer stones (Fig. 10). Wildlife and traffic moving on the canal inspection roads commonly use these bridges. It has been observed that herds seldom cross these bridges during night only. They avoid moving during the day due to traffic on the inspection roads on either side of the canal. Another reason for not using the bridge in daytime is that the sight and sound of turbulent water gushing below the bridge is horrifying to the elephants. Once again, it is only the lone bull elephant, which have been observed using this bridge in daytime.
- **Artificial water tanks:** Four water tanks were connected with the canal as alternate water source to the river for the water requirements of elephants. In time, the water in these tanks grew putrid. The tanks are located very close to the canal inspection road and there is not much forest between the canal and the tanks. The elephants get disturbed by the moving traffic on the road and the element of safety that elephants need while drinking and bathing has been denied. On several occasions it was observed that the elephants returned to the forest without using the water tanks due to the disturbance on the road, even on very warm days.

Canal of Eastern Ganges Irrigation Project

The head-reach to this canal is in the high-density zone of elephants. The movement of elephants to the Ganges River is almost halted due to construction of this canal in the head reach. Currently the canal is running only during monsoons. The details of the critical structures are discussed below.
- **Hathi Sot torrent:** A famous torrent named *Hathi Sot* (*Hathi* means elephant and *Sot* means torrent) is situated on the head reach of the canal. As part of the project, a drainage crossing (aqueduct) was constructed at the junction of canal and the torrent. Before construction of the canal, this torrent was one of the main routes for elephants to go to the river. In the evenings, the elephants could easily be sighted at this spot from January to May. After the completion of the Eastern Ganges Canal Project, this age-old migratory route to the river has been blocked. These days, the herds move to the road causeway from this torrent and then move along the road towards the river, and that too, only at night.
- **Sidh Sot torrent super passage:** Before construction of the canal, the elephants used this torrent to go to the Ganges River. Now a cross drainage structure (super passage) on the canal and a road causeway just downstream of super passage has been constructed at the torrent crossing. The appearance and shape of the super passage and causeway are apparently acceptable to the elephants, but the traffic on the Bijnor–Haridwar highway and the vertical drops of "launched" cement concrete blocks (used as an energy dissipation device) just downstream of the road causeway has restricted the movement of elephants from forest to the Ganges River (Fig. 5).

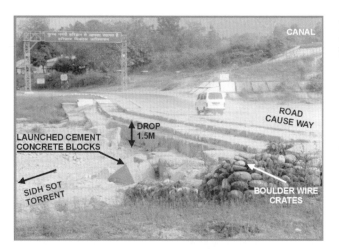

Fig. 5. Road cause way on Haridwar–Bijnor highway and Sidh Sot torrent.

As of now, the movement of elephants is not much disturbed on the left bank of Ganges River between Haridwar barrage and Chilla, because the intensity of traffic on the forest roads is low. But in future, if the intensity of traffic increases it may become hazardous for elephants, thus isolating the entire left bank of the Ganges River in the Park. Other important animals of the park such as tiger, leopard, and deer use the openings made in the cross drainage structures on the canals to go across without any problem. On several occasions, leopards and tigers have been observed resting in the barrels of syphon of the cross drainage works during summer.

Due to blockage of migration routes, herds are forced to live off the food-plants available in their zone and are not able to forage other plants available in other parts of the forest. They are also not able to reach the Ganges and instead have to use alternate sources of water. This may eventually cause problems for them because there is a difference in the quality and nature of alternate sources of water. In the last few years, the mortality rate of elephants due to infighting among herds has also increased. The group-clashes ensue due to assemblage of large number of elephants near the only available passage from the forest to the river, when the water sources dry up in the upper reaches of the park area.

Another non eco-friendly feature is the use of boulder wire crates (Gabions) for guiding the water flow in the torrents/rivers. The single wire edge in the side/top of the wire crate pierces the legs of elephants when they move on the wire crates. Being sensitive animals they never reuse the same path in which such hurdles exist.

Kotdwar–Lansdown Road

The presence of vehicular traffic on the road round the clock, the steep hillside and valley side walls/edges of the road and presence of local population near the migration route, have completely stopped the migration of elephant herds between the parks.

MITIGATION MEASURES

Considering the conservation implication of arrested migratory movements of elephants between population of 2 unequal halves of Rajaji National Park and within the larger Rajaji — Corbett conservation area, there is an urgent need to develop a sound conservation plan to reopen the identified blocked migratory routes/corridors by modifying existing structures and by constructing new alternative structures as per requirements of wild animals. There is also a need to avoid mistakes of the past in the ecological planning and designing for future engineering structures/activities. By doing so, the developmental activities and the wild life can continue in tandem in the desired direction without confrontation.

Measures for improved conservation planning

Considering that whatever damage from linear developments such as railroads, highways and canals that has been done cannot be undone, restorative strategies should be adopted for an improved conservation planning of the area. Restoration of degraded habitats and attempts to control future damage resulting from resource extraction and incompatible land use practices as well as fast-progressing developmental activities in the corridors are perhaps the only possible means to regain some levels of lost corridors among the adjacent elephant habitats (Johnsingh, 1990). A balanced utilization of resources between the elephants and the resident human population by careful planning the location of artifical water sources and promoting regeneration of species of fodder plants would eliminate to a great extent the stress on the basic ecological requirements of food and water for elephants and other wild animals.

Design alternates for engineering structures

A careful blend of ecological considerations in the planning of engineering structures on railroads, highways, and canals such as cross-drainage works, bridges, causeways, etc. satisfying the requirements of the wild animals of the area, can play a major role on their movement. The psychology of the wild animals living in the area also has to be considered while designing structures. For instance, elephants are not ready to accept any type of structures, which have a roof because of the "tunnel syndrome." However tigers, leopards, and deer were observed to use these structures without any problem. Likes and dislikes of different wild animals towards various engineering structures and activities should also be studied in detail and considered when planning their shape, size, and general appearance. The existing designs of engineering structures on the power canal are not very conducive to animal movements. Alternative structures or modifications to the existing ones are discussed below:

Energy dissipation works at downstream end of road causeway or super-passage on canals

If the topography of the area permits and the traffic intensity is low then road causeways are better than bridges for making the road-crossing structure on the torrent. Similarly a super-passage (torrent passing above the canal) is better than an aqueduct or a syphon (canal crossing over the torrent). As road causeways or barrels of canal cross-drainage works (super passage) are made straight across the torrent, a vertical drop is formed just downstream of the structure. In general cement concrete blocks or boulder wire crates are used at this spot for energy dissipation of flow of stream. The "launching" of these cement concrete blocks or boulder wire crates creates vertical drops creating serious hurdles for the movement of wild animals along the torrent. If sloping *glacis* type energy dissipation arrangement is provided at this spot then both the requirements can be the fulfilled, that is, dissipation of energy of water in the torrent and the movement of wildlife due to easy slope. A photograph of sloping *glacis* type energy dissipation system at downstream end of road causeway on Haridwar–Bijnor highway is shown in Fig. 6. If similar arrangement is made at downstream of *Bin* super-passage on the Chilla Canal

Fig. 6. Sloping glacis type energy dissipation system at downstream end of road causeway on Haridwar–Bijnore highway.

Fig. 7. Duggada drainage crossing.

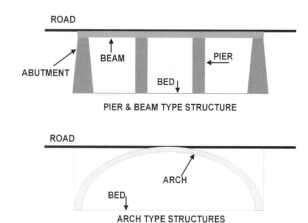

Fig. 9. Pier and beam type and arch type bridge.

Fig. 8. Perspective view of eco-friendly alternate Duggada drainage crossing.

Fig. 10. Bridge on Chilla power canal.

and at downstream of road causeway on *Sidh Sot* torrent on the Eastern Ganges Canal, then the elephants can move along these structures without any problem.

Construction of aqueducts on canal

When the topography of the area does not permit construction of super passages (torrent/drainage passing over canal), the other alternate engineering structures like aqueducts (canal passing over the torrent/drainage) are constructed (Fig. 7). While designing aqueducts, the following points should be considered for making the structure eco-friendly. The width of the structure should be approximately equal the width of *nala*/drainage/torrent so that the barrier effect is minimum. The headroom in the structure should be as large as possible so that the forest on the other side of the structure is visible to the moving animals in the torrent. A perspective view of eco-friendly alternate *Duggada* drainage crossing is shown in Fig. 8. This will have less barrier effect and no tunnel type appearance or effect in comparison to the existing structure shown in Fig. 7.

Construction of bridge on road

When the topography of the area does not permit the construction of road causeways, then bridges are made for crossing the torrent. In bridges, instead of pier and beam type structures, arch type structures with large headroom will be more acceptable to wildlife on the move (Fig. 9).

Construction of over bridges on canal for crossing of wildlife

As observed in the case of the Chilla Canal, bridges can be a good alternative for crossing of the canal by elephants, if design satisfies their requirements. Existing bridges on the canal are common for vehicular traffic as well as wildlife. The width of the roadway and the height of side railing in the existing bridge are less. Photograph of an existing bridge on the Chilla power canal appears in Fig. 10. If the bridges are designed with the following considerations then the elephants will accept them for crossing the canal: (1) The width of the bridge should be at least 25–30 m for movement of big herds. (2) The side wall or railing should be blind up to a height of at least 3.6 m or blind up to 1.5–2.0 m with camouflaging up to a height 3.6 m with some locally available creeper

Fig. 11. Carcass of elephants killed in train accidents in September 1998.

Fig. 12. Carcass of elephant killed in train accident in May 2000.

so that the elephants will not be visually disturbed while using the bridge by the sight of the turbulent water in the canal. (3) The side walls of the bridge should be constructed in an eco-friendly manner, such as making artificial earth pockets on the wall surface to grow some creepers or local vegetation to make the appearance of wall surface match the surrounding forest.

Artificial water tank fed from canal

The major draw backs in the present design are that they are small and located very close to the canal inspection road. Moreover, they lack any forest cover between the road and the canal. This can be rectified with the following provisions. The tank should be sufficiently large to accommodate big herds. There should be sufficient forest cover between the canal inspection road and the tank so that the elephants are not disturbed by the moving traffic on the road. There should be circulation of water by providing an outlet so that the quality of water is maintained and the tanks should be cleaned periodically, at least twice a year, to maintain the quality of water.

Death of elephants in train accidents

As discussed earlier, about 16 elephants have died due to collision with trains in the last 13 years (Figs. 11 and 12). These collisions can be avoided in 2 ways — wider eco-friendly over-bridges along the established migration routes of elephants for crossing the railroad, righway and adequate training to train drivers. Guided paths should be developed from forest to the over-bridge entry point to blend-in these structures with the forest. This would enable the animals to lead upto and use these over-bridge without a problem. If the elephants use the structure once without any discomfort, then it is assured they will use it regularly in the future. A computer generated perspective view of the eco-friendly over bridge on railroad and highway is shown in Fig. 13. Also, the train drivers should be

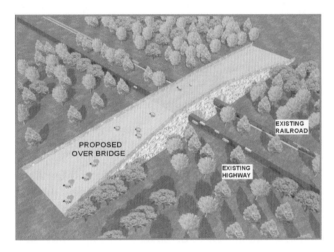

Fig. 13. Perspective view of proposed eco-friendly over bridge on existing railroad and highway.

taught the herd psychology and they should be vigilant while driving the train through the park area. If the drivers see elephants by the side of the railway track, it should be made mandatory for them to stop the train so that the elephants can adjust to the presence of train. The driver should restart the train only when he is convinced that all the members of the herd have moved to the forest. Two powerful side lamps should also be provided in addition to the headlamp for better vision in the forest area because all the train accidents took place in night only.

CONCLUSION

Remedial measures

Rajaji National Park is a typical example of pursuit for conservation in which the ecological requirements had to be compromised at the time of its declaration as a protected area, because of the major developments already in place. Not much can be achieved to mitigate the irreparable damage already caused by the construction of canals, railroads, and highways, therefore the following measures need to be implemented. First, wherever possible attempts should be made to modify the existing structures/activities matching the requirements of a friendly environment for the wildlife to prosper. Second, when an option to modify the designs is not available at a later stage, conservation planning should incorporate the principles and practices of restoration ecology.

For new constructions inside the protected areas

Careful planning of engineering and infrastructure projects should be done in the wildlife areas to avoid ecological disasters. In future, the design of the bridges, other cross-drainage structures on railroads, highways, canals, and over bridges, or subways for wildlife in a protected area, should integrate the findings of this study so that the movement of wildlife is not disturbed and the barrier effect and visual impacts are minimum. These measures can also be applicable to other similar species as well. The authors believe that if the structures erected on the migratory route of wild animals satisfy the requirements of wildlife, developmental activities will have much less adverse impact on wildlife and *vice versa*.

ACKNOWLEDGEMENTS

We thank Dr. S.K. Mukerjee — Director and Dr. Asha Rajvanshi — Faculty in charge Environment Impact Assessment cell, Wild Life Institute of India, Dehradun, India, Mr. S. Janardhan. Rao — Corporate Executive in New Delhi, Mr. S.M. Saxena — Superintending Engineer, Mr. Radhey Shyam-Executive Engineer and Mr. Rajvir Singh-Junior Engineer of U.P. State Irrigation Department, India, Mr. Manu Rajvanshi for their guidance and help in the preparation of this paper, Ms Aditi Singh and Ms S. Swati, student National Institute of Fashion Technology, New Delhi, for the preparation of graphics, Mr. Neeraj Sharma CAD consultant and Mr. Vinay Shishodia, M.E (civil) for preparation of drawings.

REFERENCES

Champion, H.G. and S.K. Seth. 1968. A Revised Survey of the Forest Types of India. Govt. of India Press, New Delhi. 404 pp.

Johnsingh, A.J.T., S. Narendra, Prashed, and S.P. Goel. 1990. Conservation Status of the Chilla–Motichur Corridor for Elephant Movement in Rajaji-Corbett National Park Area, India. Biological Conservation, 51: 125–138.

Johnsingh, A.J.T. 1992. Elephant Corridor in Uttar Pradesh. In: Proceeding of the Asian Elephant Specialist Group Meeting held in Bogor. Indonesia, 20–22 May.

Rodgers, W.A. and H.S. Panwar. 1988. Planning a Wildlife Protected Area Network in India. Vol. I and II. A Report of Department of Environment, Forest and Wildlife, Government of India and Wildlife Institute of India. 608 pp.

Shoshani, J. (Consulting Editor). 1992. Elephant, Majestic Creature of the Wild. R.D. Press Australia. pp. 1–171.

BIOGRAPHICAL SKETCHES

A.P. Singh

S.D.O., Ganges Canals, IV/50, Peerbaba Officers Colony, Roorkee, District-Haridwar, Uttranchal, India, Phone +91-1332-78743, E-mail: apsingh1957@yahoo.com

A.P. Singh is Bachelor of Technology in Civil Engineering (1976) from Institute of Technology, Banaras Hindu University, India. Working in U.P. State Irrigation Department, from 1977. Mostly worked in construction and maintenance of major and medium hydroelectric Projects. Worked at Tehri Dam Project, from 1977 to 1988 and was responsible for construction of underground tunnels in the Himalayas. From 1990 to 1996 was responsible for maintenance of civil engineering structures of Chilla Hydro Electric Project inside the Rajaji National Park-world famous habitat of wild Asian elephants. During this posting, studied in depth the liking and disliking of wild Asian elephants towards the different civil engineering structures on canals and roads. Now working on the topic "Ecological Planning of Civil Engineering Structures-Mitigation Passages in Wild Life Areas." Presently posted as Sub Divisional Officer in Muzaffernager Division Ganges Canal, Muzaffernager, U.P., looking after the maintenance of irrigation canals of the Ganges Canal system.

Dr. S.M. Satheesan

Bird Aircraft Strike Prevention Specialist, Vulture Expert and Environmental Consultant, B-15/5, A.A.I Colony, Sahar Road, Andhari East, Mumbai-400499, India, Phone +91-22-8302833, E-mail: smsatheesan2001@yahoo.com

Dr. S.M. Satheesan is Ornithologist, Ecologist, and Consultant on Bird-Aircraft-Strike prevention, has worked with the Bombay Natural History Society (1978–1994) and with the World Wide Fund for Nature — India (1995–2000), which monitors wildlife projects including on Elephants and Rhinos. India's and Asia's correspondent for *Vulture News* (*Vulture Study Group*), honorary member of the *Endangered Wildlife Trust*, South Africa, India's Main Contact person for *Bird Strike Committees* and Indian member of the *Standing Committee on Raptors* to the *International Ornithological Congress*, and has represented India and Asia in several Conferences including that of Electric Power Research Institute.

Part VII
Biodiversity

Environmental Issues Associated with the Cuiabá Natural Gas Pipeline in Bolivia

Bruce D. Barnett

Enron constructed a 630-km, 18-inch gas pipeline from the Bolivia-to-Brazil pipeline at Ipias, Bolivia to a 480 MW power plant in Cuiabá, Brazil. The pipeline crosses a large (160-km) tract of sensitive "Chiquitano" dry forest in eastern Bolivia, of particular concern to regional conservation. Following several Environmental Assessments (ENTRIX, 1998; ENTRIX, 1999; Fundacion Amigos de la Naturaleza et al., 1999) of the project, The Overseas Private Investment Corporation (OPIC) determined that detailed routing surveys were still necessary to assure avoidance of "high quality" Chiquitano forest and wildlife habitat along the route alternatives, and to minimize engineering constraints of pipeline construction on slopes subject to severe erosion. A field evaluation of the environmental characteristics of alternative route recommendations in the SEA concluded that: (1) the tropical dry (Chiquitano) forest along nearly the entire length of the route has been significantly altered by human influences related to fire, selective timber harvest, mining, and cattle grazing; (2) four minor route modifications avoided all remaining, significant ecological and topographical sensitivities with no net increase in construction costs; (3) managing induced access along the right-of-way during construction (through ROW access control) and post-construction revegetation can help to minimize cumulative, indirect impacts on the regional ecosystem; and (4) a $30 million Conservation Fund, administered by local and international conservation organizations, will contribute to long-term regional protection.

Keywords: Pipeline routing, tropical forest, Latin America

INTRODUCTION

The Cuiabá Pipeline is located in the western and central part of the Department of Santa Cruz in eastern Bolivia. Also referred to as the Río San Miguel–San Matías Pipeline, it begins at kilometer post (KP) 242 of the existing 32-inch Bolivia-to-Brazil natural gas pipeline, and runs in a northeasterly direction for 361 km to San Matías, Bolivia. The 18-inch pipeline then continues on to Cuiabá, Brazil, where it will provide natural gas to a 480 MW combined-cycle, thermal power plant in Cuiabá, Mato Grosso, Brazil (Fig. 1). The construction right-of-way (ROW) is a maximum of 30 m in width, with a maximum ROW width during pipeline operation of 15 m. Assuming a 30-m construction ROW, the Cuiabá Pipeline Project (Bolivian portion) directly disturbed an area of approximately 1050 ha.

Following preparation of an Environmental Impact Assessment (EA) of the project in June of 1998, it was determined that additional environmental information was required to more closely evaluate the impacts of pipeline construction on sensitive, tropical, dry (Chiquitano) forest habitat in the region. A Supplemental Environmental Assessment (SEA) was subsequently prepared for OPIC by a consultant/NGO team of 31 scientists in May of 1999.

The SEA considered three areas along approximately 160 km of the originally proposed pipeline route to be of sufficient ecological sensitivity to require alternative route recommendations. These route alternatives were presented in order to:

1. Avoid "high quality" Chiquitano Forest,
2. Avoid valuable wildlife habitat associated with ridges (Serranias) in the region, and

Environmental Concerns in Rights-of-Way Management: Seventh International Symposium
J.W. Goodrich-Mahoney, D.F. Mutrie and C.A. Guild (editors)
© 2002 Elsevier Science Ltd. All rights reserved.

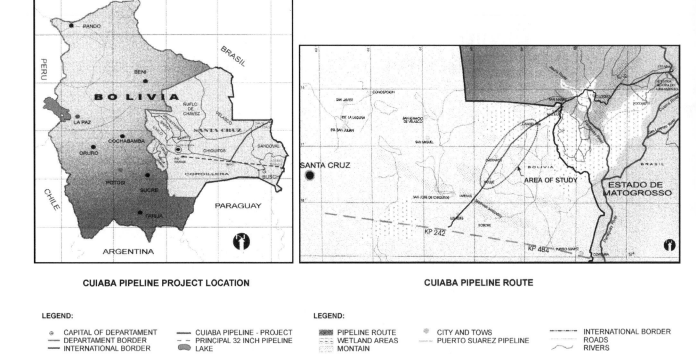

Fig. 1. Project location.

3. Minimize engineering constraints of pipeline construction on steep slopes, subject to severe erosion potential.

The present study was commissioned in July of 1999 to evaluate the geological, biological, and archaeological characteristics of the proposed pipeline reroutes recommended in the SEA and to make minor modifications to these alternative routes, based on environmental sensitivities observed.

Chiquitano Dry Forest and Serranía Cerrado Vegetation of Eastern Bolivia

The pipeline passes through approximately 160 km of Chiquitano Dry Forest in eastern Bolivia. This forest type is listed by the World Wildlife Fund (WWF) as one of the world's 200 most important ecosystems. With an area of almost three million hectares, it is one of the largest expanses of dry tropical forest in the Neotropics. This semi-deciduous forest type occurs between a vegetation gradient separating evergreen Amazonian forest and the dry forest of the Gran Chaco in eastern Bolivia, between the headwaters of the Rió San Miguel and the Bolivian pantanal, at an altitudinal gradient between 300 and 1200 m above mean sea level. This forest type has a nearly continuous forest canopy, is generally 20–25 m tall, and contains an average of 65 tree species per hectare and a dense representation of lianas, which appears to be a standard feature of the transition between dry and moist forests to the west (Parker et al., 1994).

The pipeline route also passes several, isolated sandstone ridges (Serranías), uplifted along this southwestern fringe of the Brazilian Shield during the Mezozoic, which support a distinctive vegetation and flora known as "Cerrado", similar to that found in the Cerrado biogeographic region of central Brazil. The mountain Cerrado vegetation in this region, subject to harsh microclimatic and edaphic conditions that lead to specialization and reproductive isolation, also contains numerous regional endemic species (Fundacion Amigos de la Naturaleza et al., 1999). This distinct set of plant communities interfaces with the valley bottom dry forest (with little floristic overlap) at an elevation of about 400 m. Most of the slopes of these ridges are dominated either by a: (1) fire-tolerant open woodland with widely separated, small trees with twisted trunks and thick bark and an grassy understory, or (2) dense woodland with an almost continuous canopy and no grass below, that intergrades into closed-canopy dry forest toward the base of the slopes. This is a conspicuously species-rich habitat, with over 30 woody plant species. The tops of the ridges support an open, campo rupestrine (rocky) formation with a distinct vegetation association of grasses, sedges, and low herbs with scattered bushes and small trees (Parker et al., 1994).

Seasonal wetlands associated with rivers in the region make up another unique geomorphologic landscape, known as "Lagunillas." More than 800 separate marshes and ponds (curiches) are scattered across the alluvial fan formed by the three streams that traverse the area (Fundacion Amigos de la Naturaleza et al., 1999).

Table 1. Dry and Chiquitano forest timber species along the survey route

Scientific name	Common name	Habitat	Commercial value
Amburana cearensis	Roble	DCF tall	High
Anadenanthera colubrina	Curupau	DF disturbed	Low
Aspidosperma pyrifolium	Jichituriqui	DF to disturbed sub humid	Low
Aspidosperma rigidum	Jichituriqui blanco	DF disturbed	Low
Astronium urundeuva	Cuchi	DCF disturbed	High
Calycophyllum multiflorum	Palo blanco	DCF on poorly drained soils	Construction
Cedrela fissilis	Cedro	DCF disturbed	High
Ceiba samauma	Mapajo	DCF tall	Construction
Chorisia speciosa	Toborochi	DF	Construction
Curatella americana	Chaaco	Pampas y savannas	Construction
Gallesia integrifolia	Ajo	DF to semi humid	Construction
Hymenaea courbaril	Paquió	Tall forest on poorly drained soils	Construction
Jacaranda cuspidifolia	Jacaranda	DCF	Construction
Machaerium scleroxylon	Morado	DCF tall	High
Pseudobombax marginatum	Peroto	DCF short and savannas	Construction
Schinopsis brasiliensis	Soto	DCF tall	High
Sterculia apetala	Sujo	DCF short	Construction
Tabebuia heptaphylla	Tajibo Negro	Savannas and flooded pampas	Low
Tabebuia impetiginosa	Tajibo	DF	High

DCF = Dry Chiquitano Forest, DF = Dry Forest.

The region's diverse habitats, including upland and wet savannas, flooded marsh, gallery forest, and rocky outcrops, also give it a rich vertebrate fauna. At least 257 bird species, as well as caimans, land tortoises, tapirs, peccaries, brocket and marsh deer, jaguars, pumas, ocelot, maned wolves, bush dogs, river otters, coatis, kinkajous, howler monkeys, marmosets, capuchin monkeys, armadillos, anteaters, and capybara live in the Chiquitano. Twenty vertebrate species are classified as endangered or vulnerable and nearly 90 mammal, bird and reptile species — including the hyacinth macaw and ocelot — are protected under the Convention on International Trade in Endangered Species (CITES). Cerrado vegetation provides important habitat for a variety of birds and mammals. The cliffs and rock outcrops associated with the ridges where this community occurs along the pipeline route provide critical nesting habitat for several rare bird species, including the orange-breasted falcon, cliff flycatcher, and hyacinth macaw.

Archaeological resources

The pipeline route passes through the ancestral lands of the Chiquitano people, who have occupied the region since pre-Hispanic times. Though there have been no formal archaeological studies of Chiquitano communities, artifacts recovered from the area — ceramic vessels, worked stone, bone ornaments, and what appears to be ritual offerings consisting of complete ceramic vessels and other objects — are the only remaining evidence of the numerous agricultural settlements that once dotted the alluvial plains. Today, the indigenous Chiquitano population numbers approximately 20,000–40,000 individuals.

Protected areas

Ninety-three kilometers of the pipeline route crosses the northeastern portion of the *San Matías Integrated Management Natural Area*, which was created in 1997 to conserve Chiquitano Forest, protect the cerrado vegetation of the Serranías, develop eco-tourism activities, establish a biological corridor to the Brazilian Pantanal and promote sustainable production activities. Human settlement is permitted in the Natural Area, as is "mining, energy utilization, and/or infrastructure development in exceptional cases and in cases of national interest" (Supreme Decree 24734, 1997).

Human activity in the region

Logging

Legal and illegal forest exploitation has occurred in the region for approximately 30 years and numerous logging roads and skid trails are evident throughout the area. The Chiquitano forest is rich in timber, and while it supports only moderate levels of tree diversity when compared to humid tropical forests, it contains a greater abundance of species with high wood density (hardwoods). The structure and composition of the dry deciduous (Chiquitano) forest along the survey route suggests the ongoing, selective extraction of commercial hardwood species (see Table 1).

Forest exploitation in Bolivia has been subject to specific regulations and guidelines only for the past several years. All timber companies operating in the country (see Fig. 3) are now required to develop and comply with an Annual Forest Operations Plan.

While some studies indicate that the area disturbed in the region is generally small (Fredericksen, 2000; Fredericksen and Licona, 2000; Fredericksen and Mostacedo, 2000), the previously uncontrolled harvest of commercial timber has led to a consistent reduction in the stock of hardwoods in the region. Primary forest vegetation in the vicinity of the proposed pipeline now occurs only in infrequent patches (forest fragments), due in part to the opening of roads, skid trails, and lumber yards associated with harvest activities.

Years of selective logging in the region with little subsequent forest management have led to a proliferation of secondary vegetation and the conversion of the forest to other uses. Due to increased settlement and conflicting land use claims in the region, many of the forest concessions in this portion of the Chiquitano Forest have been abandoned. Logging by landowners continues, however, in the vicinity of the pipeline, whether legal or illegal. Timber extraction remains highly selective and rarely follows any sustainable management guidelines. Our survey crews frequently came upon areas of fresh-cut Soto, Roble, Morado, and Cedro. In many cases, the fallen trees have been left in place, apparently due to low market value and elevated transport costs (according to local information sources).

Mining

The pipeline route crosses 10 out of a total of 45 mining concessions in the region (see Fig. 3), totaling 68,500 ha (ENTRIX, 1999 — Don Mario Project–E.M. Paititi–ORVANA). All mining activity is concentrated in the central portion of the study area.

Exploration studies in these concessions have shown concentrations of copper, gold, and silver. The "Don Mario" Gold Mine, used as a base camp for the present study, has temporarily suspended activity, due to a drop in world gold prices and high cost of production.

Cattle ranching

Subsistence-based cattle ranching in the region has occurred since the colonial period. On the Chiquitano Shield, livestock feed on the local short grasses and graze extensively throughout the region. In the pampas and the pantanal zone, livestock feed more intensively on the more abundant natural grasses of the region.

A total of 14 cattle ranches exist along the proposed pipeline survey route (see Fig. 3). One ranch alone covers over 50,000 ha. Families in the southern portion of the study area maintain an average of one to 10 cattle, with approximately 2000 head grazing in the vicinity of the local villages. Cattle ranching is even more ubiquitous in the flat, pantanal zones in the northern portion of the study area, where approximately 150,000 head graze on unmanaged grasslands. Almost 20% (30,000) of these cattle graze on 25,000 ha in the vicinity of the village of Candelaria. The high concentration of cattle grazing in this area severely stresses this fragile grassland ecosystem.

A continued increase in cattle production, combined with increasing land demand for agriculture and poor land management, has resulted in the steady degradation of the local, natural ecosystem through conversion to agricultural uses.

Hunting

Subsistence hunting by indigenous communities is *not* prohibited by Bolivian law, though hunting by colonists *is* prohibited. Consequently, enforcement of this selective prohibition is nonexistent and poaching continues to supply bush meat to local markets, as a subsidy to logging operations, or for sport. As the population in the region increases, either naturally or by the continued immigration of ranchers and miners, uncontrolled exploitation of the local wildlife becomes a more serious problem.

Fire

The Chiquitano region in the southern portion of the study area is characterized by dry and semi-humid forest vegetation. The climate in the southern portion of the study area is tropical, with dry winds (sometimes up to 80 km/h), seasonal rainfall and an average daily temperature of 25°C. Between May and September, fire danger increases as the forest becomes drier, and fires can easily get out of control. While fires in this region can be of natural origin, it is highly unlikely during the dry season when very few storms occur. More likely, the fires are intentionally set, but poorly managed. During drought periods, it is common for local residents to burn old grasslands in order to control weeds, renew the soil and encourage the growth of new seedlings, ultimately to increase forage and graze production for cattle. Local residents also burn the forest understory to open inaccessible areas for timber exploitation. It is also possible that such forest fires originate from campfires of poachers or at logging camps.

STUDY METHODOLOGY

The field surveys were conducted between 17 July and 19 August 1999. Four survey teams of approximately 20 individuals each were mobilized along the 160-km pipeline route through the Chiquitano Forest region to evaluate the geological, biological, and archaeological characteristics of the proposed reroutes recommended in the SEA and to make minor modifications to these alternative routes. Each team included a biologist, archaeologist, topographer, and engineer, along with 10–15 logistical support personnel (paramedic, cook, field camp assistant, and support laborers [porters and brush cutters]). The responsibilities of each team specialist are indicated in Table 2.

Logistical support for the field teams was centralized at a base camp midway along the pipeline survey

Table 2. Survey team specialist responsibilities

Role (team leader)	Responsibilities
Biologist	Biological/ecological route characterization, sensitive area identification, route modification recommendation, data entry, and database management. Coordination with project leaders, Base Camp and team topographer. Health, safety, security, and environmental policy compliance. MEDEVAC and heli-support coordination.
Archaeologist	Identification of sites with potential archaeological value and establishment of construction monitoring requirements.
Engineer	Identification of engineering and geological constraints during construction, route modification recommendation and establishment of preventive measures to be applied during construction to minimize environmental impacts.
Topographer	Identification of topographical constraints for construction and surveying and staking of pipeline ROW centerline. Coordination with Base Camp for delivery of field supplies. Reporting of daily progress. Coordination of daily team activities with biologist.

route (Don Mario Gold Mine; Empresa Minera Paititi S.A. — ORVANA). The camp maintains an airstrip, direct road access to the nearest village, San Juan de Chiquitos, an electric power supply, dormitories, dining room and kitchen facilities, telephone, fax, and computer support and replenishable storage of 50,000 l of potable water. The base camp was used to store and ship food, water, and equipment and to coordinate the movements of field personnel.

Air support for the supply and transfer of food, water, camps and personnel throughout the field survey period was provided by an Alouette helicopter stationed at the Don Mario base camp.

Each field team was outfitted with (Iridium and Satellite 1) satellite telephones, an HF multi-band radio and a portable, VHF transceiver. Satellite telephones were used to communicate with project personnel in Bolivia, Brazil, and the US. HF radios were used to communicate with the Base Camp and among field teams. VHF transceivers were used for communication between field personnel and the helicopter pilot for coordinating supply drops and camp relocations.

Prior to the field survey, all available project and regional information was collected, compiled and reviewed. The majority of baseline information on the project and study area was drawn from the (June 1998) Environmental Assessment (EA), the May 1999 Supplemental EA, the May 1999 Independent (NGO) Supplemental EA and a 1993 Conservation International RAP Evaluation of the area, entitled *The Lowland Dry Forests of Santa Cruz, Bolivia: A global conservation priority* (Parker et al., 1994).

Additional information used during the field surveys included:
- Topographic base maps of the pipeline corridor (at both 1:250,000 and 1:50,000 scales), from the Geographic Military Institute of Bolivia; and
- Vegetation, Sensitive Areas and Pipeline Alternatives maps from the May 1999 Supplemental EA.

A decision matrix (Table 3) was developed to classify environmental sensitivities along the pipeline survey route by addressing a range of soil/geological,

Table 3. Environmental decision matrix — factors considered

Issue	Environmental characteristic	Code
Archaeology		
	Cultural artifacts *in situ*	AR-1
	Archaeological site	AR-2
	Topographic indicators of strategic zone	AR-3
	Potential for permanent habitability	AR-4
	Potential for temporary habitability	AR-5
	Resource availability for human settlement	AR-6
Soils/Geology/Geomorphology		
	Potential for erosion due to runoff	SG-1
	Potential for landslide	SG-2
	Potential for eolic erosion	SG-3
	Potential for flooding	SG-4
	Poorly drained areas	SG-5
	Low revegetation potential	SG-6
	Slopes	SG-7
	Exposed rock	SG-8
	Salt deposits	SG-9
Fauna		
	Breeding/nesting area	FA-1
	Wildlife movement/migration route	FA-2
	Dry season feeding/watering area	FA-3
	Cover/protective area	FA-4
	Endemic species potential	FA-5
	Wildlife concentration area	FA-6
	Riparian/riverine habitat	FA-7
	Frugivore feeding area	FA-8
Flora		
	Natural disturbance	FL-1
	Anthropogenic disturbance	FL-2
	Presence of common species	FL-3
	Relative plant diversity	FL-4
	Structural richness/complexity	FL-5
	Capacity for natural regeneration	FL-6
	Endemic species potential	FL-7
	Special vegetation community	FL-8
	Ravine or hill micro-habitat	FL-9
	Palm stands	FL-10
	Intact forest fragments	FL-11
	Ecotones	FL-12
	Wetlands	FL-13
	Swamps/marshes	FL-14
	Presence of introduced (weed) species	FL-15

Table 4. Explanation of environmental features

Feature code	Explanation
AR-1	Direct surface observation of cultural artifacts
AR-2	Direct indication of archaeological sites
AR-3	Likelihood of "strategic" zone, based on topographic features (e.g., observation, defense, storage, housing, communication, transportation, etc.)
AR-4	Likelihood of permanent habitability based on topographic features
AR-5	Likelihood of temporary habitability, based on topographic features
AR-6	Food and water resources locally available for human settlement
SG-1	Potential for severe erosion
SG-2	Potential for landslides
SG-3	Potential for eolic erosion
SG-4	Potential for periodic to regular flooding
SG-5	Limited drainage
SG-6	Limited revegetation potential, due to poor soils, compaction, rock substrate, dry conditions, etc.
SG-7	Steep slopes
SG-8	Exposed rock substrate with low revegetation potential
SG-9	Salt deposits with significance for local wildlife populations
FA-1	Important breeding/nesting area for wildlife (e.g., rivers, lakes, islands, cliffs, large trees, exposed banks, etc.)
FA-2	Important movement or migration corridor for wildlife (e.g., river, riparian vegetation, intact forest fragment, etc.)
FA-3	Important feeding/watering habitat, not otherwise available in the immediate vicinity
FA-4	Important cover/protective habitat, not otherwise available in the immediate vicinity
FA-5	Presence (or potential) for endemic, endangered, or otherwise unique species
FA-6	Wildlife concentration area (e.g., roosting, migration, breeding, etc.)
FA-7	Riverine/riparian environments with important wildlife resources
FA-8	Important, year-round food source for frugivorous species
FL-1	Existing level of natural disturbance (reflects regeneration capacity)
FL-2	Existing level of human-caused disturbance (reflects conservation potential)
FL-3	Presence of common species vs. rare/endemic species (reflects conservation priority)
FL-4	Relative plant diversity (higher being more sensitive)
FL-5	Level of structural richness/complexity (reflects ecological capacity, habitat availability)
FL-6	Capacity for natural regeneration of vegetation (lower capacity = more sensitive)
FL-7	Presence of endemic or rare/endangered species
FL-8	Presence of unique or uncommon vegetation community
FL-9	Important/rare micro-habitat (supporting rare or unique species)
FL-10	Presence of stands of palm trees
FL-11	Presence of intact forest fragments (islands) — provide important microclimatic/physical environmental conditions for plants
FL-12	Ecotones — usually support a higher diversity of species and communities
FL-13	Wetlands — usually support unique floral associations
FL-14	Swamps and marshes — usually support unique floral associations
FL-15	Presence (and relative abundance/frequency) of introduce, weed species — indicate secondary/tertiary vegetation community.

botanical, wildlife, and archaeological parameters. The use of a decision matrix approach permitted quantification of the relative degree of environmental sensitivity at a given location. The matrix was originally developed to evaluate a similar gas pipeline routing in Peru and was revised and improved by the team specialists involved in the present surveys, all of who were familiar with the study area. Tables 3 and 4, describe the environmental variables considered in the sensitivity assessment.

A numeric ranking (0–3) was proposed to quantify each specialist's observations of relative environmental sensitivity at a given location. A rank of "3" for a given parameter indicated the need for a modification of the proposed route. A rank of "2" indicated the need for special monitoring during construction at that location. A rank of "0–1" reflected a moderate to significant level of *existing* disturbance of the area (i.e., no environmental sensitivity).

349 observation points were recorded within a 100–300 m wide corridor along the entire 163-km pipeline route (depending on topographical and vegetation constraints). Data entered for each observation location included:

1. Date,
2. Position (in degrees, minutes, seconds),
3. Elevation (meters above mean sea level),
4. Kilometer Post (KP),
5. General environmental description,
6. Sensitivity observations,
7. Feature code,
8. Sensitivity rank,
9. Whether a route modification was required, and
10. Whether the July/August 1999 forest fire, affected the area.

Photographs of the immediate vicinity of the survey route were also taken at each observation point. Apart from general environmental observations, archaeologists examined all exposed soil under fallen trees and areas rooted by peccary for artifacts, as well as areas around exposed rock outcrops. All pottery fragments encountered during the surveys were collected, cleaned, packaged, and marked with the appropriate KP for later laboratory analysis in La Paz.

Field observations were compiled using an MS Access$_{tm}$ database. Photographs were taken at each observation point along the survey route for a visual record of representative habitat. Each photograph was identified by KP. Of the over 200 photographs taken along the survey route, 80 were scanned in JPG format (75 dpi resolution) and used to illustrate representative habitats. CADD maps of the alternative pipeline routes (1:100,000 scale) recommended in the SEA were overlaid onto topographic base maps. Observation points were then plotted onto these maps (Fig. 2). Maps of existing timber, mining, and agriculture concessions within the project area were also prepared to indicate officially sanctioned human activity in the region (Fig. 3).

RESULTS

Field observations (both photographic and database) were compiled into a web-based document, which will soon be available online at www.aspeneg.com or by request from the author. To view this document, one can click on the document title on the EA "Documents" web page. Clicking on the pipeline route on the first screen, will access a detailed map of the survey route. Each survey "Spread" is indicated by different color kilometer points (KPs). Clicking on any given Spread will bring up a detailed map of that Spread. Clicking on an individual KP on the detailed Spread maps will access specific photographic/database information for the areas at and around these points. Clicking on the map icons at the top of any of the photo/database screens will return to the individual Spread map or map of all three Spreads. Clicking on the "home" icon above the photographs will return to the title screen. To view previous or successive photo/database screens without returning to the Spread map, click on the ▶ or ◀ icons above the photographs.

In addition to the results of this study, project information for the Cuiabá Pipeline Project is also available online at www.cuiabaenergy.com or www.opic.gov/cuiaba/cuiabahome.htm.

Pipeline route modifications

The survey teams made specific modifications to the alternative routes recommended in the Supplemental EA at four locations, as a result of perceived topographical or ecological sensitivity. These route modifications are shown in Table 5 and are discussed below.

Modification 1 (KP 121.327) was made to avoid the hillsides and steep slopes associated with Cerro Capurú. The hill also supports an "island" of undisturbed, Chiquitano dry forest. These hillsides are subject to severe erosion and landslide. For these reasons, the route was moved one kilometer to the northwest in order to completely avoid the area.

Modification 2 (KP 149.277) was made to avoid the steep slopes and system of creeks and drainages on an unnamed hill west of the La Aventura Gorge. The steeper slopes of this hill also support relatively undisturbed Chiquitano dry forest vegetation. Construction of the pipeline along the initially proposed route alternative could cause severe erosion and landslides. To avoid these impacts, the pipeline route was moved one kilometer to the northeast, to an area with gentler slopes and supporting more disturbed forest vegetation. This modification will also reduce the length of the line somewhat and allow for more effective slope stabilization, runoff, and sediment control.

Modification 3 (KP 224.200) was made to avoid a "curiche" or circular pond that supports important habitat and resources for wildlife (see Table 6). Even late in the dry season, this pond contained water, and the surrounding habitat provided an important source of food and refuge for the wildlife that concentrates in the area. For these reasons, the route was moved to provide a 150-m buffer zone around this "curiche" habitat (Fig. 4).

Modification 4 (KP 253.400) was made to avoid an area that drains water during the rainy season toward a system of nearby "curiches" (see Table 7). Though not a clearly defined waterway, the drainage function of the terrain is obvious from the apparent system of small mounds, which reflect the movement of water across the landscape. The route was moved approximately 150 m to avoid a serious impact on the nearby "curiches" from disruption of this drainage pattern (Fig. 5). An example of the database (Decision Matrix) entry for this location is shown in Table 7.

Areas of low to moderate sensitivity along the pipeline route

A number of areas with low to moderate environmental sensitivities (database values of 1 and 2) were noted along the route. The pipeline route was *not* modified in these instances for reasons discussed below:
- *Vegetation* — areas with low to moderate environmental sensitivities correspond to relatively intact (relatively low level of disturbance) vegetation, but not unique or uncommon in the region.
- *Wildlife* — areas with low to moderate environmental sensitivities correspond to a noticeable presence of wildlife species, though these are not unique or singular to this region. Moreover, the region does not present unique habitat characteristics or vegetation communities/habitats of crucial importance.

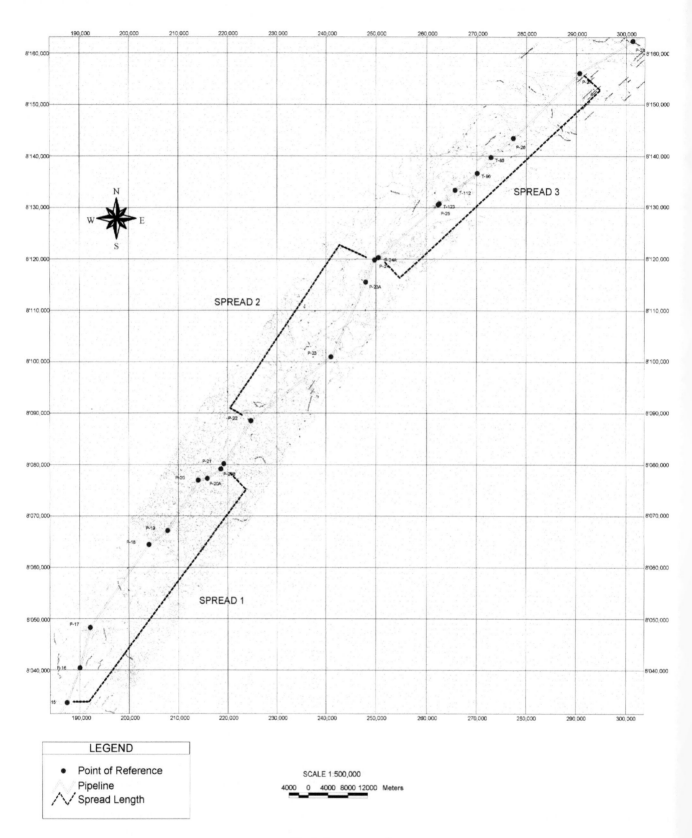

Fig. 2. Survey spreads.

Environmental issues

Fig. 3. Timber, mining, and agricultural concessions in the pipeline vicinity.

Table 5. Pipeline route modifications

Spread	KP	Sensitivity	Reason for reroute
Spread 1	121.327	Topographic/Ecological	Minimize the impact of steep slopes and on relatively intact forest
Spread 1	149.277	Topographic/Ecological	Minimize the impact of steep slopes and on relatively intact forest
Spread 2	224.200[*]	Ecological	Avoid seasonally ponded area (curiche)
Spread 3	253.400[**]	Ecological	Avoid important drainage system

[*]See Table 6.
[**]See Table 7.

Table 6. Decision matrix entry for route modification 3

Geographic position	Date	Km	Ecological/ archaeological feature(s)	Additional notes	Code	Sensitivity rank	Route change	Elevation	Fire
W 59°20'44" S 16°59'32"	14/08/99	224.200	Natural circular pond ("curiche"), with water (late in season).	Poorly drained area — important dry season watering area.	SG5 FA3 FA2 FA6 FL7	1 3 3 3 2	√	228.78 m	
			Wildlife concentration and watering area.	Wildlife migration route.					
			Route moved approximately 130 m to the NW to avoid this ponded area.	Special species potential area.					

Table 7. Decision Matrix Entry for Route Modification 4

Geographic position	Date	Km	Ecological/ archaeological feature(s)	Additional notes	Code	Sensitivity rank	Route change	Elevation	Fire
W 59°08'13" S 16°49'17"	9/08/99	253.400	Dry deciduous forest — 15 m canopy, understory dense, dominated by vines.	Construction will alter natural drainage pattern and affect existing wildlife water sources.	SG 9 FL 12	3 3	√	132.20 m	
			Numerous mounds (30 cm high) along >600 m of ROW in this area. Formed by running water, which feeds the ponds (curiches).	Route moved approx. 150 meters to south to avoid curiches					
			Formations a result of natural drainage along gradient between upper and lower forest formations.						

Fig. 4. Curiche.

Fig. 5. Drainage mounds.

– *Archaeology* — Registered sites/locations with a low to moderate sensitivities suggest a relatively low potential for pre-Hispanic artifacts, but are being monitored during construction.

DISCUSSION

The controversy surrounding the construction of a pipeline through this portion of Bolivia stems from the high biological sensitivity of the tropical dry forest vegetation in the region and the concern by conservation organizations that disturbance of the ecosystem from the mounting cumulative impacts of human activity will lead to a further disruption of ecosystem function and integrity.

There has been much controversy over whether this portion of the Chiquitano Dry Forest is truly primary in nature or has been converted over many years of human intervention to predominantly secondary habitat. During our surveys, we noted considerable and widespread forest disturbance from timber harvest, cattle grazing, and fire along the entire ROW.

Evidence of timber harvest (stumps, felled trees, log piles, logging roads, skid trails, and abandoned log-

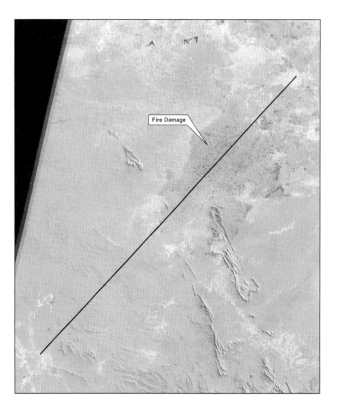

Fig. 6. Satellite image of the fire of 1999. (—) Pipeline location.

ging camps) was apparent and several saw mills (some fairly large in the PONTONS and MAKO concessions) exist just a few kilometers from the survey ROW. The commercial timber species that have been exploited in this area now occur in very low numbers and have been replaced by several secondary, indicator species including: *Cordia alliodora*, *Chlorophora tinctoria*, several species of *Casearia*, *Prockia crucis*, and *Zanthoxylum fagara*, among others.

Cattle grazing was ubiquitous along the entire northern portion of the route in this region, and several large cattle ranches occur in the area. There was also considerable evidence of past forest fires all along the route, including burned lower portions of trees, burned snags, and fallen trees. It is a common practice in the region to burn off the forest understory to control weeds, renew the soil and encourage the growth of new seedlings, in order to increase forage and graze production for cattle and/or open inaccessible areas for timber exploitation. During (and subsequent to) the current field survey (August–October 1999), human-caused fires in the Department of Santa Cruz destroyed over 3.6 million hectares of forests and grasslands (see Figs. 6 and 7). Of this loss total, 1.7 million ha of pampas with dispersed trees were destroyed; 1.3 million ha of Chiquitano Forest, 200,000 ha of shrub-scrub vegetation and 500,000 ha of palm and hill vegetation (El Mundo, 9/11/99; Figs. 6 and 7). The chance that these fires were of natural origin is slim to impossible, as survey personnel or local residents in the region observed no clouds or storms during the period.

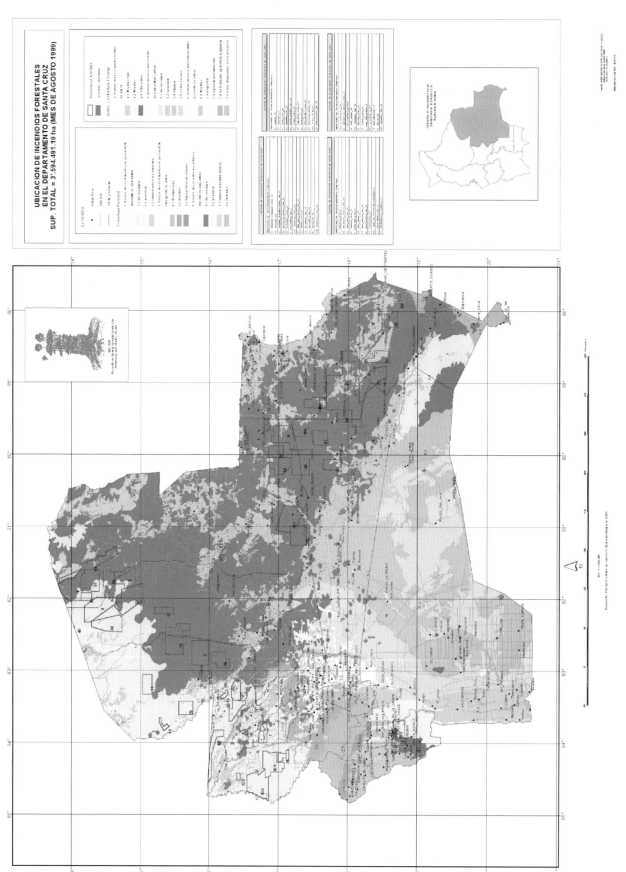

Fig. 7. 1999 fire damage in the department of Santa Cruz.

Because much of the region along the proposed ROW continues to be disturbed by human activity, there is clear evidence that the one-time "primary" nature of this forest has been replaced by predominantly, secondary vegetation. The destruction of most of the northern portion of the pipeline route in this area by fire also suggested that the timing of pipeline construction is fortuitous, in that natural, post-fire regeneration would help to quickly restore the localized construction impacts to vegetation.

To facilitate habitat restoration following construction, the Cuiabá Project awarded a revegetation contract to the Noel Kempff Natural History Museum of Santa Cruz, Bolivia. The four objectives of the Revegetation Plan include erosion control, accelerating forest cover restoration, access control, and collection of additional scientific information. In most of the ROW however, the vegetation cover will *not* be recovered by means of assisted revegetation. In general, natural vegetation, including trees, will be allowed to occupy the entire area, except for 10 m of the 30 m of the temporary construction ROW. In these 10-m areas, an herbaceous soil cover will be developed, either naturally or artificially, to prevent erosion.

Also, in recognition of the ecological significance of the Chiquitano Forest, project sponsors have committed funds to help initiate, in conjunction with the environmental community, a broad-based, long-term conservation program for the Chiquitano Dry Forest region. The plan was originally developed with participation from the World Wildlife Fund, Missouri Botanical Garden, the Bolivian Friends of Nature Foundation, and the Noel Kempff Natural History Museum. The Cuiabá Project has committed to support the long-term conservation of the Chiquitano Forest and the surrounding eco-systems with up to US$ 20 million over the next 15 years with a further US$ 10 million of matching funds expected from the NGOs.

Private parties, including the Project sponsors and local and international NGOs, agreed to implement the conservation program, with input from indigenous groups, representatives of the government, private industry, and other stakeholders to define priorities and objectives. In June of 1999 however, The World Wildlife Fund (WWF) decided not to join the Conservation Plan consortium, following pressure from environmental and human rights groups condemning the conservation organizations for pursuing a plan that is perceived to "green wash" an environmentally and culturally destructive fossil-fuel infrastructure project (World Wildlife Fund-US Decision not to Sign Chiquitano Agreement, 9 September 1999).

Irregardless of this setback and the general politics and controversy surrounding this project, the Overseas Private Investment Corporation (OPIC) awarded the Cuiabá Project $250 million in June of 1999 to assist with pipeline construction.

ACKNOWLEDGEMENTS

Many thanks to: Edwin Saravia of Dames and Moore and Carlos Reynel, Moisés Cavero, Diego Rivera, and Javier Zumarán of Walsh Peru for their fine efforts in this field survey; to Sr. Roberto Ibatta of IPE, Bolivia for his crucial support and coordination of the field effort; to Mr. Michael Molocsay of ORVANA (Empresa Minera Paititi, S.A.) for coordinating the use of the Don Mario base camp; to Thierry Vorms and Pierre Galipon of HeliAmerica for their air support throughout the field effort; and to Dr. Marco Gomez-Barrios, Ana Maria Olivares, Vladimir Garcia, and Elario Valle for all of their help in the preparation of this report.

REFERENCES

ENTRIX. 1998. Environmental Assessment (EA) for the Cuiabá pipeline project, Bolivian portions. La Paz, Bolivia.

ENTRIX. 1999. Supplemental Environmental Assessment (SEA) for the Cuiabá pipeline project, Bolivian portions. La Paz, Bolivia.

Fredericksen, T.S. 2000. Logging and conservation of Bolivian forests. International Forestry Review, 2: 271–278.

Fredericksen, T.S. and J.C. Licona. 2000. Encroachment of non-commercial tree species after selection logging in a Bolivian tropical forest. Journal of Sustainable Forestry, 11: 213–223.

Fredericksen, T.S. and B. Mostacedo. 2000. Regeneration of sawtimber species following selective logging in a Bolivian tropical forest. Forest Ecology and Management, 131: 47–55.

Fundacion Amigos de la Naturaleza, Missouri Botanical Garden, Museo de Historia Natural Manuel Kempff Mercado, Wildlife Conservation Society, and World Wildlife Fund. 1999. The San Miguel — Cuiabá Pipeline Project. Independent Supplemental Environmental Assessment (ISEA). Santa Cruz, Bolivia. 79 pp.

Parker, T.A., et al. 1993. The Lowland Dry Forests of Santa Cruz, Bolivia: A global conservation priority. Conservation International. RAP Working Paper # 4.

Supreme Decree, No. 24734. July 31, 1997. Establishment of the San Matías Natural Area of Integrated Management. La Paz, Bolivia.

BIOGRAPHICAL SKETCH

Bruce Barnett, Ph.D.

Aspen Environmental Group, 1760 Creekside Oaks, Suite 170, Sacramento, CA 95833, USA, (916) 646-3869, E-mail: bbarnett@aspeneg.com

Dr. Bruce Barnett is a consultant with over 20 years experience in the application of wildlife biology, community and population ecology, and habitat assessment, management and monitoring to development projects involving: government installations; energy and natural resource development (hydroelectric, petroleum, natural gas, geothermal, wind, mining); water management systems (flood control, dams, reservoirs); linear facilities (pipelines, transmission lines, fiber-optic cables, transportation corridors); forest products and wildlife refuges/natural areas in the United States, Europe, Latin America, Africa, and the Pacific Rim.

Direct Relevance to the Natural Gas Industry of the Habitat Fragmentation/Biodiversity Issue Resulting from the Construction of New Pipelines

Raymond Hinkle, Sherri Albrecht, Eric Nathanson, and Jim Evans

There has been an increasing interest on the part of federal and state regulators to evaluate linear project impacts on otherwise unfragmented blocks of habitat. Habitat fragmentation has two components: (1) reduction in total habitat area, which may affect population size and (2) reorganization of areas into disjunct fragments, which may affect dispersal and immigration rates. Concerns over these impacts have led to alterations in the selection of right of way (ROW) alignments that avoid large blocks of unfragmented habitat at significant additional cost to industry. A literature review found that linear projects have the potential to modify wildlife habitats in a variety of ways, both beneficial and adverse. A survey of regulatory agencies and industry representatives showed that habitat fragmentation is addressed indirectly by regulations aimed at protection of the environment and sensitive species and by a multitude of federal and state policies and guidelines. It is most commonly an issue in forested habitats, but has also been a concern in grasslands, deserts, wetlands, and riparian habitats. Habitat fragmentation is a complex issue with specific concerns ranging from the obvious (e.g., breaking large habitat blocks into smaller areas; general habitat disturbance) to the more subtle (e.g., invasion of exotic species; facilitation, or hindrance of movement; nest predation). Species that have been of concern include aquatic species, amphibians, reptiles, insects, migratory and resident birds, raptors, and large and small mammals. With proper planning and construction implementation, many adverse impacts associated with habitat fragmentation can be avoided and benefits can be maximized.

Keywords: Habitat(s), habitat fragmentation, rights-of-way (ROW), linear projects, pipeline(s)

INTRODUCTION

Linear projects such as gas pipelines have the potential to modify wildlife habitats in a variety of ways, both beneficial and adverse. Such projects have long been recognized as providing edge habitat that is of value to many wildlife species. Maintained rights-of-way (ROW) corridors can also increase habitat diversity by providing herbaceous and shrub vegetation in areas that would otherwise lack such habitats. On the other hand, it has also been demonstrated that linear projects, especially roads, can have adverse impacts on wildlife. Such impacts can affect either individuals or populations. In the latter case, the effect is usually the result of what is defined as habitat fragmentation.

The objective of this study was to summarize available literature and regulations related to habitat fragmentation, and using this information, to determine the relevancy of the habitat fragmentation issue to the natural gas pipeline industry.

AN OVERVIEW OF HABITAT FRAGMENTATION

Habitat fragmentation occurs when a large expanse of habitat is transformed into a number of smaller patches of less total area than the original. When the landscape surrounding the fragments is inhospitable to species of the original habitat and dispersal is low, remnant patches can be considered "habitat islands" (Wilcove, 1986). Corridors, which are defined as reasonably similar areas that differ from their surroundings, can influence habitat fragmentation.

Natural gas pipelines (NGPs) can act as corridors since they are linear in nature and their construction and maintenance requires vegetative clearing; therefore, they may potentially cause habitat fragmentation. The nature and extent of the fragmentation will depend on factors such as the width of the ROW, the type of vegetation being cleared (the habitat), and the wildlife species utilizing the habitat. Surrounding land uses may also contribute to whether or not pipeline development constitutes a legitimate habitat fragmentation impact.

A SUMMARY OF HABITAT FRAGMENTATION RELATED LITERATURE

A comprehensive literature search was conducted to identify research on habitat fragmentation as it relates to linear projects such as natural gas pipelines and electric transmission lines (GRI, 1999a). There has been very little research specific to habitat fragmentation resulting from natural gas pipelines.

Information relating to the effectiveness of measures instituted to avoid or minimize adverse habitat fragmentation impacts from pipeline development was also compiled. The information obtained through this literature search was summarized for each major animal group (i.e., birds, mammals, amphibians, reptiles, and invertebrates) as well as for plants. A summary of articles describing potential positive effects of linear corridors was also prepared.

Birds

Birds, particularly neotropical migrants, were most commonly studied in relation to habitat fragmentation. Related issues that were evaluated concerning neotropical migrants included habitat area requirements, edge effect, nest predation, and nest parasitism.

Nest predation and nest parasitism are components of the edge effect. Edge effects, or higher predation/parasitism rates, were found to be dependent on landscape context and edge type. Edge effect is not limited to the immediate corridor vicinity, but can extend for some distance into the forest interior.

The types of habitat fragmentation in a forested habitat created by small well clearing sites (~1 acre) and narrow pipeline corridors (10–65 feet wide) do not appear to significantly affect avian species composition or abundance (Hartzler, 1999).

Mammals

Linear corridors can act as barriers to movement for both large and small mammals. Without concealing vegetative cover, both large and small mammals may be unwilling to cross a cleared corridor. This is dependent on the width of the corridor, the species, and the degree of vegetative cover. Small mammal abundance has been documented to be higher along edges and wooded areas, as opposed to cleared areas (Allen, 1998). Limiting the degree of clearing and establishing vegetated travel lanes across the corridor can lessen the barrier effect. Elevated pipelines present a clear physical barrier. Raised "windows" or sections of buried pipe are necessary to allow animal movements across elevated pipelines.

In some instances, corridors can act as conduits to facilitate movement. For example, several species of bats have been documented using natural gas pipeline corridors for travel and foraging (Bearer, 1999). While corridors can facilitate movement, this may be a detriment to some species (e.g., game species or small mammals) since animals utilizing corridors can be more susceptible to hunting or predation.

Amphibians, reptiles, and invertebrates

Only a few studies were identified that evaluated the effects of habitat fragmentation on amphibians, reptiles, and invertebrates. The microclimate changes along the ROW can prohibit movement or may benefit some species (Sheldon, Capen 1995; Kamsura, et al., 1993). Amphibians, for example, which generally require moist environments, may be prevented from migrating across a hot, dry ROW. Some reptiles, however, may benefit from the warmer temperatures and sparse vegetation that make hunting for prey easier.

Plants

Very few studies were identified which discussed the impacts of habitat fragmentation on plants. Much more frequently, vegetation has been utilized to reduce fragmentation. The initial ROW clearing for pipeline construction negatively impacts native vegetation in the ROW. Re-planting with native shrubs and herbs can minimize fragmentation impacts. Additionally, the ROW may also provide habitat for threatened or endangered plant species. In some cases, however, the microclimate changes in the cleared ROW and/or maintenance activities can prevent the re-establishment of desired vegetation and may allow invasive species to become established.

Positive effects of right-of-way corridors

ROW corridors can serve as greenways and/or wildlife travel lanes. They can also increase habitat diversity. As greenways, ROW corridors can serve to link urban and rural landscapes. Wildlife can utilize these corridors to migrate between isolated habitat patches and as habitat in developed areas that are otherwise incompatible with their survival. Vegetation management within ROW corridors can enhance their attractiveness to wildlife as travel lanes and habitat.

Mitigation measures

Mitigation measures for habitat fragmentation fit into two broad categories: avoidance and vegetation management. Avoidance is not as much a mitigation measure as it is a siting policy applied prior to pipeline construction.

Vegetation management is a means to minimize the changes to the original habitat and can enhance wildlife use of the ROW. Measures such as creating small shrub patches in a corridor and maintaining shrubs along the corridor-forest edge are aimed at reducing the edge effects. A variety of native shrub and herbaceous vegetation should be selected. Cutting edges in a zig-zag pattern in order to create softer edges is another technique.

Minimizing ROW width can lessen impacts associated with edge associated predator species such as the brown-headed cowbird since these predators are less likely to enter narrow corridors. Elevated sections (windows) of pipe or buried pipe are two types of mitigation techniques that may be employed to reduce impacts to large mammals.

The consolidation of corridors (i.e., co-alignment) along forest boundaries has also been suggested as a mitigation measure. In addition to avoiding the habitat fragmentation, the wide corridor would provide suitable habitat for early successional birds, especially those that prefer shrubland and thickets. Most corridor widths for solitary powerlines or pipelines are not wide enough to create suitable habitat for these birds. However, co-alignment may become a concern if the corridors become prohibitively wide.

AN OVERVIEW OF FEDERAL, STATE, AND LOCAL REGULATIONS

Existing policies and regulations that address habitat issues were identified through direct and indirect contact with government agencies and natural gas pipeline companies. Direct contact methods included the distribution of a questionnaire, telephone contact, and meetings with agency personnel. Indirect contact consisted primarily of reviewing agency web sites and relevant documents for pertinent information.

While habitat fragmentation has been an issue for linear development, federal, state, provincial, and local regulations that specifically address habitat fragmentation were not identified. However, habitat fragmentation is addressed indirectly by legislation aimed at overall environmental protection such as the National Environmental Policy Act (NEPA) as well as legislation intended to protect sensitive species such as the Endangered Species Act and the Migratory Bird Treaty Act. The federal law that most directly addresses habitat fragmentation is the Endangered Species Act. Under this act, protection of Critical Habitat is required and indirect impacts to listed species must be evaluated.

A multitude of federal and state policies and guidelines address habitat fragmentation, both directly and indirectly. These guidelines or guidance documents have been developed to assist agency personnel in regulatory enforcement and decision making. In fact, pipeline developers and oversight managers often refer to these guidance documents because they address habitat fragmentation more specifically than the regulations.

All of these regulations, policies, and guidelines call for a minimization of environmental impacts. In one form or another, they support the preservation of natural habitats and biodiversity by calling for avoidance of habitat fragmentation and habitat disturbance. For example, US Fish and Wildlife Service recovery plans address the protection, and promote habitat management to boost the recovery of individual Threatened and Endangered Species. These recovery plans are frequently consulted by federal agencies when proposed gas pipeline development projects raise habitat fragmentation issues.

The Federal Energy Regulatory Commission (FERC) is the regulatory agency that oversees natural gas pipeline development. In general, FERC prefers looping or co-alignment with existing corridors, as opposed to new pipelines that fragment undisturbed habitat. Current pipeline projects under review by FERC are subject to specific environmental conditions. Generally, these conditions pertain to frequently employed mitigation techniques including avoidance of sensitive areas (e.g., high quality wetlands, mature growth forests, habitats used by threatened and/or endangered species, etc.) and surveying for the presence of species of concern (i.e., threatened and/or endangered species).

While habitat fragmentation resulting from gas pipeline development is not explicitly the subject of regulation, sufficient regulation and policies on inherently related subjects (e.g., conservation of critical habitats and threatened and endangered species) exist to demand that the issue be addressed by the gas pipeline industry.

RELEVANCY

As illustrated by previous sections, habitat fragmentation is a very broad issue that cannot be ignored by the NGP industry. The nature of linear facilities, such as gas pipelines, demands that habitat impacts be addressed. However, not all of the various components of habitat fragmentation will be of concern for all NGP projects.

In evaluating which components of habitat fragmentation present a concern for a particular project, many variables must be considered. The habitat type,

Table 1. Habitat type and related fragmentation issues

Habitat type	Issues										
	Human intrusion	Nest parasitism	Hinder movements	Facilitate predator movements	Breaking large habitat into smaller areas	Row size	Impacts to T&E species habitat	Avian mortality due to powerlines	Spread of exotic species	Habitat disturbance	Road kills
Forested Areas	•	•	•	•	•	•	•	•	•	•	•
Forested Wetlands	•	•		•	•			•	•		
Wetland/Pocosin/Swamp	•		•		•						
Aquatic & Riverine	•	•	•		•		•			•	
Grassland/Prairie	•	•	•		•		•			•	
Desert	•	•	•								
Scrub–Shrub	•		•		•						
Sagebrush Steppe			•		•						

landscape, region, species of concern, duration of impact, and mitigation measures implemented are some of the main variables that will determine whether habitat fragmentation constitutes a valid issue for a NGP project. Applicable laws, regulations, and policies must also be considered.

The relevancy of habitat fragmentation is highly dependent on the species of concern in a particular habitat. The same habitat changes that adversely impact some species will benefit others. For example, fragmentation that adversely impacts neotropical migrants can benefit brown-headed cowbirds. Therefore, it is important to identify which species should be protected at the possible detriment of other species. Obviously, federal or state listed Threatened or Endangered species will be afforded the most protection in accordance with relevant laws and regulations. In the absence of listed species, habitat management decisions must be made. In the case of neotropical migrants versus brown-headed cowbirds, the decision is clear-cut. However, this may not always be the case.

Whether or not habitat fragmentation constitutes a significant issue is highly dependent on habitat type and landscape characteristics. Habitat fragmentation is a major issue in the forested areas of the northeast. On the other hand, natural gas pipelines do not create a significant long-term habitat fragmentation concern in western habitats (e.g., high desert, scrub-land, mountainous regions) since pipelines are typically below ground and the disturbed area is re-graded and allowed to recover to its natural state. Any fragmentation related disturbance is temporary during new pipeline installation. A summary of different habitat types and related fragmentation issues is provided in Table 1. This table is based on a compilation of agency and industry input (GRI, 1999b).

The degree of habitat fragmentation is often dependent on corridor width. For example, a 15-foot wide corridor may present a limited fragmentation issue to some species. On the other hand, a 400-foot wide corridor would likely constitute a major habitat fragmentation issue which could impact many species. Corridor width is therefore a relevant concern to the NGP industry.

In general habitat management decisions favor the preservation of large tracts of undisturbed habitat, particularly forested habitat, over the creation of edge habitat. The general consensus among regulatory agencies is that there is an abundance of edge. Edge is created by nearly every human disturbance of habitat. Large tracts of undisturbed habitat are at risk from all types of development pressure, including NGP development.

The various sub-issues that are components of habitat fragmentation are evaluated for relevancy to the gas pipeline industry in the following sections. An attempt is made to explain the situations and conditions under which habitat fragmentation issues may be considered relevant. For each situation, recommended mitigation measures intended to reduce habitat fragmentation impacts are discussed. Table 2 presents a summary of the determination of relevancy based on the various issues of habitat fragmentation.

Barrier to movement

Pipeline corridors can act as barriers both during and after project completion. Construction related impacts are basically short-term while those that persist after the pipeline is installed can be considered long-term.

Trenching and material stockpiling during pipeline construction can create physical barriers to different species. Small mammals, reptiles, amphibians, and flightless invertebrates can fall into and be trapped in open trenches. Instances of continuous piles of soil, rock, and debris over 10 feet high along long lengths of the pipeline route have been reported. Such continuous linear stockpiling presents a physical barrier to all species except those capable of flight. The degree of impact from this type of fragmentation is seasonally dependent in some areas. For example, some reptiles (e.g., turtles) and amphibians migrate during different times of the year either between wetland areas or from wetland areas to uplands.

Table 2. Relevancy determination for habitat fragmentation issues associated with the construction of linear projects

Habitat type	Species type affected	Landscape context	Mitigation measures	Effect of mitigation	Relevant Yes/No
Issue: Maintained ROW as a Barrier to Movement					
Forests, Forested Wetlands	Large and small mammals, amphibians	Not applicable	Retain vegetated corridors across the ROW; Avoid critical habitat; Limit clearing; Use existing ROWs; Install nest boxes (e.g., for flying squirrel)	Minimizes HF Impact	Yes
Issue: Construction Activities as a Barrier to Movement					
All Habitat Types	Herpetiles, small mammals, potentially large mammals	Not applicable	Trenching guidelines (re-seed area) backfill close to digging, cover trench overnight, place ramps in trench	Minimizes HF Impact	Yes temporary impact only
Issue: Elevated Pipeline as a Barrier to Movement					
Primarily Tundra, All Habitat Types	Large mammals	Not applicable	Elevated windows, sections of buried pipe	Minimizes HF Impact	Yes
Issue: Edge Effect (Including nest parasitism and predation)					
Forests, Forested Wetlands	Neotropical migrants	Primarily forested; or forested w/some agricultural areas	Feathered edges, selective ROW clearing	Minimizes HF Impact	Yes
	Neotropical migrants, small mammals	Forest patches in mainly agricultural or developed setting or w/i areas of clear-cuts (i.e., already fragmented habitat	Not Applicable	Not Applicable	No (neotropical migrants and most small mammals)
Grassland/Prairie	Neotropical migrants	Prairie/grassland with wooded or shrubby edges along sides of ROW	Maintain corridor with native grasses; Clear shrubs/saplings	Resolves HF Issue	No (with mitigation)
Issue: Habitat Disturbance — Short Term Construction Related					
Forests, Aquatic/Riverine, Grassland/Prairie	Birds, mammals, invertebrates, herpetiles	Not Applicable	Schedule work to avoid breeding/migration periods; Minimize ROW width	Minimizes HF Impact	Yes
Issue: Habitat Disturbance — Long Term ROW Maintenance					
Forests, Aquatic/Riverine, Grassland/Prairie	Birds, mammals, herpetiles, plants	Not Applicable	Consolidate corridors; Create irregular forest edges; Alternate ROW width, narrow to wide; Revegate ROW with native species; Implement habitat improvements	Minimizes HF Impact	Yes
Issue: Reduced Habitat Area					
Forests	Neotropical migrants	Primarily areas with large blocks of unfragmented habitat	Co-alignment with existing linear features	Minimizes HF Impact	Yes
Issue: Impacts to T&E Species Habitat					
All Habitat Types	Various threatened/ endangered species	Not Applicable	Manage ROW to avoid habitat disturbance	Resolves HF Issue	Yes[a]

Table 2. (continued)

Habitat type	Species type affected	Landscape context	Mitigation measures	Effect of mitigation	Relevant Yes/No
Issue: Facilitation of Predator Movements					
Forests, Forested Wetlands	Neotropical migrants, other avian species	Primarily areas with large blocks of unfragmented habitat	Feathered edges along corridor; Staggered or vegetated crossings at roadways or other clearing intersections	Minimizes HF Impact	Yes
Issue: Invasive Species Intrusion					
Forests, Forested Wetlands	Ecosystem impact	Not Applicable	Plant ROW with native species; ROW maintenance practices	Minimizes HF Impact	Yes
Issue: Human Intrusion					
All Habitat Types	Various	Not Applicable	Posting, fencing, patrolling	Minimizes HF Impact	Yes
Issue: Visual Impact					
Forests	Humans	Relatively undisturbed landscape	Feathered edges along corridor; Staggered or vegetated crossings at roadways or other clearing intersections	Minimizes HF Impact	Yes

[a] Some species, plants in particular, may be protected by the ROW.

Preventing this migration can prevent mating or may effect the viability of offspring.

These construction related impacts to wildlife are usually temporary and can be easily mitigated by:
- limiting the length of open trench at any one time in the construction process;
- placing wooden ramps in all areas of the trench overnight;
- placing plywood or other cover over the trench overnight;
- visually inspecting the trench for trapped animals and removing them prior to pipe installation and back-filling; and
- creating "breaks" in material stockpiles along the trench to allow passage through the area.

For some species, the difference in vegetative cover within a maintained ROW can act as a physical barrier. Wary species can be hesitant to leave the concealing vegetative cover of the forest to cross a comparatively bare ROW. For small mammals such as mice and voles, cleared areas can increase the chance of capture by predators.

The ROW as a barrier is probably most significant to small, relatively non-motile species. Salamanders, for example, require moist habitats and may be unable to cross a hot, dry ROW, or may only be able to make such a crossing during precipitation events. Movement can therefore be affected.

Avoidance of critical habitats is the most effective way to mitigate for potential long-term "barrier-related" impacts. Other recommended mitigation measures to minimize the impacts of ROWs include:

- limiting the amount of ROW clearing;
- minimizing ROW width;
- using existing ROWs whenever possible; and
- re-vegetating the disturbed ROW.

Edge effect

Edge effect is a multifaceted impact that includes potential increases in nest parasitism and predation, non-uniformity of vegetation, habitat preference, and suitability. In many cases, the regional landscape will determine whether this issue is relevant for a new NGP corridor.

Edge effect is most pronounced in forested habitats within a landscape that contains a mosaic of land uses. Farmland, small woodlots, and rural and suburban residential areas often provide ideal habitat for predators (e.g., raccoons, skunks, opossums, and American crows) and parasites (e.g., brown-headed cowbirds). A cleared ROW through this type of landscape into an otherwise unfragmented forest provides an entry corridor for these species. Once entry into the forest is made easier for these species, the nests of neotropical migrants are predated upon and parasitized. In addition to the regional landscape, the ROW width is a factor. Narrow ROWs create a less obvious opening and are not as appealing to predators as wider ROWs.

Creation of a narrow corridor through a uniform forested landscape or a forested landscape with patches of clear cut areas does not result in the same detrimental edge effect as in a diverse landscape. A possible explanation is that without farms and residential areas to provide food sources, predator species are not as concentrated. In a forested landscape, predators are dispersed throughout the region and a cleared corridor may not serve as a common travel route. Limiting the ROW width in this landscape can reduce the impact to species that prefer forest interior.

Although edge effect is typically associated with forested habitats, it may also be a relevant issue in grasslands or prairies. If shrubs or trees are allowed to flourish along the ROW in otherwise uninterrupted grassland, the shrubs can create an edge effect. To the likely detriment of native grassland bird populations, the shrub area can provide suitable habitat for various mammalian or avian predators that would otherwise not be present in the area. This unique type of edge effect is not likely to be particularly relevant to the NGP industry since ROWs are typically managed to prohibit shrub growth. Planting the ROW with native grasses and maintaining it to remove any shrub vegetation will successfully mitigate any impacts.

Due to ROW maintenance procedures, edge effect in general can be a valid issue throughout the life of the project. Employing the following mitigation techniques can minimize the effect:
- Create "feathered" ROW edges rather than abrupt edges,
- Selectively clear the ROW to minimize vegetation removal,
- Schedule ROW maintenance in such a way that allows higher vegetation in some areas,
- Maintain the corridor with native grasses, and
- Plant shrubs or small trees across the ROW in some areas to serve as travel lanes.

Miscellaneous

Miscellaneous habitat fragmentation issues that are relevant to the gas pipeline industry include:
- **General habitat disturbance.** Construction creates a short-term habitat disturbance. Subsequent maintenance can result in long-term habitat disturbance. All habitat types are affected by the short-term construction disturbance. Forested habitats are most affected by prolonged maintenance of the ROW in a cleared state. Locating pipelines along the periphery of a forested area and consolidating corridors are two recommended mitigation measures. Other measures include creating irregular forest edges, alternating between narrow and wide ROW widths, and general re-vegetation with species selected for habitat improvement.
- **Reduction in habitat area.** When considering individual pipeline corridors, it may not seem like this impact would be significant. However, the combined acreage of habitat disturbed for development of existing and future pipelines and associated gas well fields and compression stations amounts to a rather large area. This long-term impact primarily affects neotropical migrants and is an issue in nearly all habitat types, except desert.
- **Impacts to threatened and endangered species and associated critical habitat.** This is a genuine concern which is typically addressed through avoidance or site specific mitigation under the direction of the responsible state or federal agency. Plants, as well as animals, are covered under this issue.
- **Facilitation of predator movements.** Linear corridors can serve as unobstructed travel ways for ground and aerial predators. Birds, particularly neotropical migrants, and small mammals are negatively affected, while the predators (e.g., foxes, raccoons, feral cats, raptors, and owls) benefit, at least in the short term. This may be considered a component of edge effect.
- **Invasive species intrusion.** Prior to the re-establishment of native vegetation, pipeline ROWs can provide opportunities for invasive species to take hold. This is mainly a concern in forested habitats and wetlands. Minimizing ROW clearing, immediate replanting of a disturbed ROW, and an active invasive species control program can mitigate for this impact.
- **Human intrusion.** In nearly every habitat type, the presence of natural gas pipeline ROWs lead to human intrusion. In some areas the clearing provides easy access through habitat that otherwise could not be easily penetrated, particularly with motorized vehicles. In other areas, it is viewed not as private land, but as a ROW for access. Human disturbance can negatively impact wildlife and can increase hunting pressures. Attempts to minimize human intrusion include posting the area with no-trespassing signs, installing fences or gates at road crossings, and patrolling by project personnel.
- **Visual impact.** By breaking up the habitat continuity, ROWs can create a long-term visual impact. This is particularly obvious in forested habitats. Planting a vegetative screen at locations where the ROW crosses roadways can provide location specific minimization of visual impacts. Utilizing existing ROWs is a broad approach to mitigating for visual impacts.

Benefits of natural gas pipeline ROWs

There can be corresponding benefits associated with many perceived adverse impacts. Some beneficial functions of NGP ROWs include providing habitat for threatened and endangered species, providing edge habitat, serving as greenways, and enhancing habitat diversity.

One of the more well known potential benefits of ROWs is the creation of edge habitat. Small corridors through large tracts of contiguous forests can be beneficial by increasing habitat diversity along the corridor edges. Successive growth following corridor development provides this increase in habitat diversity, which in turn can benefit herbivore and subsequently omnivore and carnivore species.

There are documented instances of ROWs serving as habitat for threatened plant species. For example, an electric transmission line ROW in New Jersey serves as habitat for Swamp Pink (*Helonias bullata*), an endangered species.

Pipeline ROWs can serve as greenways for wildlife and humans. There is documentation that elk and deer in Pennsylvania utilize NGP ROWs for migration routes. Bear have been reported to use NGP ROWs for travel as well. There is also interest in potentially utilizing NGP ROWs as greenways for trail development to provide passive outdoor recreation.

The different vegetation and microclimate of a ROW increases habitat diversity that can benefit some species. Invertebrates and reptiles can benefit from the warmer temperatures resulting from the reduced vegetative cover than that found in surrounding forest areas. Hunting opportunities can then be improved for snakes and avian predators due to the fact that small mammals do not have dense cover in which to hide.

REFERENCES

Allen, J.M. 1998. Small mammal populations in wooded areas versus small gas well clearings in the Callen Run Research Area, Clear Creek State Forest, Jefferson County, PA. Master's Thesis. Clarion University of Pennsylvania.

Bearer, S.L. 1999. Use of natural gas well sites and pipeline corridors by bats in northwestern Pennsylvania. Master's Thesis. Clarion University of Pennsylvania.

GRI. 1999a. Final Report: Habitat Fragmentation Resulting from the Construction of Linear Projects: Literature Review, Phase 1. GRI-99/0034.

GRI. 1999b. Final Report: Habitat Fragmentation Resulting from the Construction of New Natural Gas Transmission Pipelines: Federal, State, and Local Regulation, Phase 1. GRI-99/0035.

Hartzler, I.C. 1999. Effects of pipeline corridors and well clearings on avian species composition and diversity in a forested landscape. Master's Thesis. Clarion University of Pennsylvania.

Kamsura, J., S. Hounsell, and W. Weller. 1993. Vulnerability of reptiles and amphibians to transmission corridors and facilities. In: Fifth International Symposium on Environmental Concerns in Rights-of-Way Management. September 19–22, 1993. Montreal, Quebec.

Sheldon, A. and D. Capen. 1995. Distribution of Redback Salamanders in a fragmented landscape. http://www.snr.uvm.edu/redback.html.

Wilcove, D.S., C. McLellan, and A. Dobson. 1986. Habitat Fragmentation in the Temperate Zone. In: Conservation Biology: The Science of Scarcity and Diversity. M. Soule, ed. Sinauer Associates, Sunderland, MA. pp. 237–256.

BIOGRAPHICAL SKETCHES

Raymond Hinkle

URS Corporation, 201 Willowbrook Blvd., Wayne, NJ 07470, USA. Phone: 973-785-0700. Fax: 973-785-0023. E-mail: ray_hinkle@urscorp.com

Ray Hinkle is a principal ecologist with 28 years experience in assessing the effects of project developments on terrestrial and wetland habitats. He holds a BS degree in forestry (1969) and a MS degree in wildlife management (1972) from the Pennsylvania State University and is a Certified Wildlife Biologist.

Jim Evans

Consultant, Environment and Safety, 615 West Maude Avenue, Arlington Heights, IL 60004, USA

Jim Evans was a Principal Project Manager with 19 years experience at the Gas Research Institute (GRI). At GRI he worked in areas of synthetic fuels, air emissions, pollution prevention, occupational health, and rights-of-way environmental issues, among others. He holds a BS degree in Chemistry from Amherst College and a BS degree in Chemical Engineering from MIT.

Sherri Albrecht

URS, 201 Willowbrook Blvd., Wayne, NJ 07470. Phone: 973-785-0700. Fax: 973-785-0023. E-mail: sherri_albrecht@urscorp.com

Sherri Albrecht is an assistant project scientist at URS, specializing in wetland delineation, permitting and ecological studies. Her graduate studies in environmental science were completed at Montclair State University. She has over 13 years of experience in the environmental field.

Eric Nathanson

URS Corporation, 201 Willowbrook Blvd., Wayne, NJ 07470. Phone: 973-785-0070. Fax: 973-785-0023. E-mail: eric_nathanson@urscorp.com

Eric Nathanson is a senior environmental scientist at URS, specializing in marine and freshwater ecology, wetland science, and ecological studies. He has over ten years experience.

Management of Native Prairie Fragments on Canadian Pacific Railway Rights-of-Way

Michelle Bissonnette and Scott Paradise

Remnant fragments of native prairie were identified and mapped along Canadian Pacific Railway (CPR) rights-of-way in Minnesota, USA. This work was part of a statewide prairie survey on railroad rights-of-way which was performed by the Minnesota Department of Natural Resources (DNR). Prairie fragments that were identified were graded based on presence of plant species and disturbance. CPR proactively worked with the DNR, both to monitor and enhance the quality and usability of the DNR study, and to provide technical support and field supervision during DNR fieldwork on CPR property. During the field survey, native prairie fragments were mapped with GIS tools relative to railroad mile posts using a global positioning system with sub-meter accuracy. Native prairie fragments along CPR rights-of-way are generally small and isolated. Larger prairie fragments were found between parallel railroad and highway rights-of-way. The Minnesota Department of Transportation was therefore identified as another landowner and stakeholder responsible for management of native prairie fragments. CPR and the DNR have used the survey results in conjunction with a review of historic railroad vegetation management plans to develop and validate new and existing best management plans (BMPs) for vegetation control and land use that promote the preservation of native prairies and protect threatened species.

Keywords: Best management plan, vegetation management, highway rights-of-way, endangered species, Minnesota

INTRODUCTION

Minnesota's prairie

Approximately eighteen million acres of native prairie covered the state of Minnesota, USA prior to the establishment of European settlements in the mid-1800s (Fig. 1). In the Ecological Classification system adopted by the Minnesota Department of Natural Resources (DNR), prairie was located in the Eastern Broadleaf Forest and Prairie Parkland Provinces (DNR, 1996). This landscape and this ecosystem underwent a dramatic transformation as homesteaders claimed land and put it to the plow; nearly every acre of land that could be farmed was. Today less than 1% of Minnesota's original prairie remains, and it is generally restricted to areas unsuitable for cultivation. Because of this loss of native prairie habitat, today more than one-third of Minnesota's endangered, threatened, and special concern species are native prairie plants (Pfannmuller and Coffin, 1989).

The DNR is commissioned by the Minnesota state legislature to preserve and protect endangered, threatened and special concern species. As part of this mission, the DNR initiated the Minnesota County Biological Survey Program (MCBS) in 1987. This survey systematically catalogs rare biological features, and identifies significant natural areas that are worthy of preservation. The DNR then works with local planning agencies to develop land uses that help preserve these natural areas. The DNR has also developed Scientific and Natural Areas (SNAs), permanently preserving significant sites through land acquisition. Many of these SNAs contain native prairie fragments.

Minnesota's rail network

Minnesota's railroad network was established in 1862, the same year that the Homestead Act was enacted. Railroad use peaked in the early 1900s. In the ensuing

Environmental Concerns in Rights-of-Way
Management: Seventh International Symposium
J.W. Goodrich-Mahoney, D.F. Mutrie and C.A. Guild (editors)
© 2002 Elsevier Science Ltd. All rights reserved.

ECS Provinces in Minnesota
■ Laurentian Mixed Forest
□ Eastern Broadleaf Forest

Fig. 1. Ecological Provinces in Minnesota. Prior to European settlement, native prairie was a major ecosystem within the Eastern Broadleaf Forest and Prairie Parkland Provinces (Merchant and Biederman, 1999).

years, rail passenger traffic dwindled and railroad systems were rationalized to maintain profitability. Still, in 1999 the state's rail network consisted of 9600 km of track and rights-of-way owned and operated by both large Class I railroads and smaller regional and short line railroads.

North American railroads are constructed on rights-of-way corridors that typically range from 15 to 122 m in width. Railroad rights-of-way typically consist of three distinct zones (Fig. 2). Tracks and underlying ballast are found in Zone 1, grading and drainage ditches on either side of the track are found and Zone 2, and generally unimproved land is found in Zone 3. Zones 1 and 2, the most active areas of rail operations, are typically 10 m wide. With 30-m wide rights-of-way common in rural portions of Minnesota's rail system, the Zone 3 portion of railroad rights-of-way often comprises 70% of a railroad corridor.

Zone 1 railroad track construction involves the placement of crushed rock ballast approximately 0.5 m in depth over relatively level grade of land. Since invasive plant root structures can weaken ballast strength, inhibit drainage and potentially increase the risk of train derailments, US Federal Railroad Administration (FRA) rules require railroads to maintain a plant-free ballast zone through vegetation management programs. Zone 2 contains ditches that maintain adequate drainage away from the track and ballast. Zone 3 is essentially a safety and buffer zone between the railroad and adjacent property owners. This area of generally undeveloped land is used to preserve sight lines and minimizes the potential for track obstructions. Railroad rights-of-way management practices in Zone 3 are generally limited to management techniques that limit the height and extent of vegetation.

Railroads and prairie: A historical co-existence

The historically limited access and usage of the Zone 3 portion of railroad rights-of-way led to the suggestion that these corridors have a potential to preserve portions of Minnesota's native prairie. Some of the railroad corridors were constructed on native prairie that had not been altered by the plow. While original grading and track construction processes may have affected Zone 3 plant species, adjacent prairie vegetation in places naturally re-seeded the disturbed portions of Zone 3 rights-of-way. While land adjacent to the rights-of-way was cultivated and developed, Zone 3 lands typically lay fallow, potentially preserving prairie plants. Brushfires potentially ignited in the past by the sparks from passing steam locomotives may have mimicked the natural wildfires and periodically rejuvenated the prairie by controlling invasive hardwood plant species.

Survey along active railroad corridors

DNR biological surveys through the MCBS had previously identified native prairie fragments along abandoned railroad rights-of-way; some of these fragments were large enough to warrant preservation though the creation of SNAs. The presence of prairie fragments along abandoned rights-of-way also led to the hypothesis that prairie fragments could exist along active railroad rights-of-way. Two previous field surveys along rail corridors supported this hypothesis. In 1978 Borowske and Heitlinger (1983) sampled 2673 km of

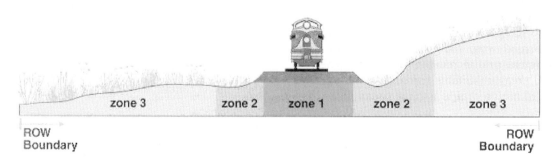

Fig. 2. Cross-sectional view of a typical railroad right-of-way (Merchant and Biederman, 1999).

rights-of-way in western Minnesota. Bolin et al. (1980) sampled 748 km of rights-of-way in the southeast portion of Minnesota. Both studies used regular sampling intervals of 1.6 and 0.8 km respectively to roughly assess the extent of prairie vegetation. Native prairie fragments were identified in both studies.

DNR survey objective
Given the potential for native prairie fragments to exist along Minnesota rights-of-way and the desire to preserve a piece of Minnesota's natural heritage, the 1997 Minnesota State Legislature directed the DNR to conduct a field review of active railroad rights-of-way and identify native prairie. The legislature also directed the DNR to identify and assess management practices used to control vegetation on railroad rights-of-way and to work cooperatively with railroads to develop voluntary best management practices for the preservation of identified prairies.

SURVEY METHODS

Initial review
In 1998, the DNR, through the MCBS, began identifying native prairie on 5213 km of active track that was operated by fifteen railroad companies. The track was located within portions of Minnesota that supported native prairie at the time of European settlement.

Initial efforts included prescreening areas with the highest potential for prairies by reviewing aerial photos, topography maps, and the data from the two previous field surveys. The DNR also hired and trained seven MCBS botanists for the inventory of railroad property. The prescreening attempted to systematically survey areas for native prairie communities and rare biological features. Field inventory efforts were then based on prescreening results and employed methods used elsewhere by MCBS.

Railroad involvement
Fifteen of the 24 railroad companies that operate in Minnesota own or operate track throughout those portions of Minnesota that supported native prairie or mixed forest and native prairie vegetation at the time of European settlement. The level of involvement by each railroad in this prairie survey varied. Prior to initiation of field inventory activities, a meeting between CPR, DNR and certain other Minnesota railroads was held in May of 1998. Proposed DNR field work, insurance issues, and railroad safety concerns were discussed at the meeting. Before inventory efforts began, Burlington Northern Santa Fe Railway Company voluntarily conducted safety training on behalf of all Minnesota railroads for DNR and contract personnel that would be working on railroad property. Other railroads cooperated on an individual basis by granting access to their property for survey work.

CPR project objectives
CPR was proactive during the inventory of native prairie species along its rights-of-way and provided oversight during DNR survey efforts. CPR staff facilitated communication between the DNR and the railroad industry, proposed survey methods that helped the DNR achieve time and budgetary goals, and reviewed and commented on DNR survey data and reports. Relative to its own rights-of-way, CPR retained HDR staff to provide technical support and environmental oversight during DNR surveys on CPR rights-of-way only.

Field survey methods
The 1998 DNR Railroad rights-of-way project systematically surveyed areas for native prairie communities and rare biological features based on methodology developed by MCBS. The majority of CPR rights-of-way was initially field surveyed from vehicles driven on roads that were parallel and adjacent to the rights-of-way. Areas lacking prairie vegetation were eliminated from further survey. On-site surveys of selected areas of CPR rights-of-way were performed when the rights-of-way was not visible from the road or when the DNR wanted to better delineate the extent of prairie species within certain segments of the rights-of-way.

The rights-of-way were inspected by walking along areas with prairie vegetation. DNR botanists identified the existence of native prairie species and prairie fragments and classified the quality of each segment. The prairie areas were then delineated on maps. Prairie data was collected in the field and recorded by the botanists on standard survey forms and maps. From the survey forms, tabular data was entered into an Access database. Rare species locations and prairies assessed as *Very Good* were entered into the DNR's Rare Features Database in the Natural Heritage Information System. All prairie fragments identified in the field inventory were mapped.

On behalf of CPR, HDR field staff coordinated with the DNR on scheduling inventory surveys. In the field, HDR staff surveyed prairie boundaries and the locations of individual state listed or special concern species using Ground Positioning System (GPS). DNR data sheets corresponding to the surveyed boundaries were completed that describe environmental conditions, disturbances of forbes, grasses and woody plants. HDR took field notes during the inventory from information discussed and noted on the standard survey forms that were filled out by the DNR. Quality control and review of DNR data collection efforts was also performed in the field.

Prairie classification
The data collected during the inventory was also reviewed to classify the quality of the observed prairie fragments. The DNR based quality assessments on the coverage of native prairie plant species, presence of

Table 1. Prairie quality classification system

	Native grass cover	Native wildflowers	Native trees and shrubs	Disturbance indicators
Examples	Big bluestem Switch grass Indian grass	Blazing star Asters Coneflower	Bur oak New Jersey tea Willows	Herbicide use Equipment storage ATV trail
Quality Rank	Percent cover	Number of species	Percent cover	Percent cover
Very Good	>70%	>15	<10%	<10%
Good	>55%	>10	<25%	<25%
Fair	>25%	>6	<50%	<50%

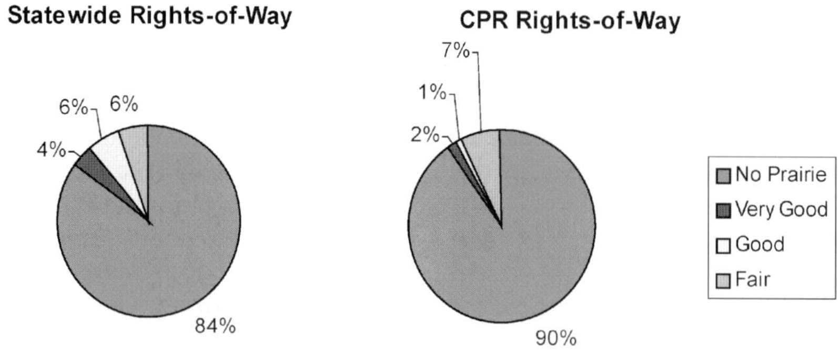

Statewide Rights-of-Way: No Prairie 84%, Very Good 4%, Good 6%, Fair 6%

CPR Rights-of-Way: No Prairie 90%, Very Good 2%, Good 1%, Fair 7%

Fig. 3. Comparison of prairie occurrence and quality between all Minnesota rights-of-way and CPR's rights-of-way in Minnesota.

disturbance indicators, and the abundance of woody plants. Examples of these criteria are shown in Table 1. For example, if a prairie had over 55% coverage of native prairie grasses, 10 species of prairie wildflowers and less than 25% disturbance, the prairie was rated *Good*.

SURVEY RESULTS

Limited extent of native prairie fragments

Of the 5213 km of surveyed railroad rights-of-way in Minnesota, 784 discontinuous km of native prairie were identified (Merchant and Biederman, 1999). Overall, prairies tended to be highly fragmental and variable in quality. Long corridors of undisturbed native prairie, especially stretches of *Very Good* prairie, were rare. The average length of an individual prairie fragment is 1 km, with a range of 0.05 to 6.31 km. Four percent of the total surveyed railroad rights-of-way contained *Very Good* prairie. *Good* and *Fair* prairie each are found on 6% of the rights-of-way. Eighty-four percent of the railroad rights-of-way surveyed did not support native prairie.

Native prairie fragments were identified in 95 km (9.7%) of the 980 km of CPR rights-of-way that was surveyed. Two percent of CPR rights-of-way contained *Very Good* prairie, 1% contained *Good* Prairie and 8% contained *Fair* prairie. The majority of *Very Good* prairie was located in northwestern Minnesota.

A relative comparison of CPR and statewide results is shown in Fig. 3. Historic vegetation management practices along CPR rights-of-way are not significantly different than those of other railroads involved in the survey. The fact that CPR rights-of-way contains less prairie on a percentage basis and poorer quality prairie is therefore more likely attributable to the location of CPR's track predominately within the Eastern Broadleaf Forest Province (Fig. 4).

Highway/railway rights-of-way relationships

Some of Minnesota's railroads were constructed along transportation corridors previously established by stagecoach, ox-cart and horse. A portion of Minnesota's highways, in turn, were constructed along established rail corridors. The result in both cases was parallel highway and railroad rights-of-way. The prairie survey determined that larger prairie fragments were often located on land between parallel railroad and highway rights-or-way. The average length of *Very Good* prairie fragments in these areas were 1.5 km in comparison to 1 km average length of a prairie not running parallel to highway rights-of-way. These areas were likely less accessible and otherwise unsuitable for agricultural or other development. As a result, the DNR identified the Minnesota Department of Transportation (MDOT) as an additional owner and steward of remnant prairie fragments.

PRAIRIE MANAGEMENT OUTCOMES

The DNR began discussions with railroads regarding prairie management soon after the completion of

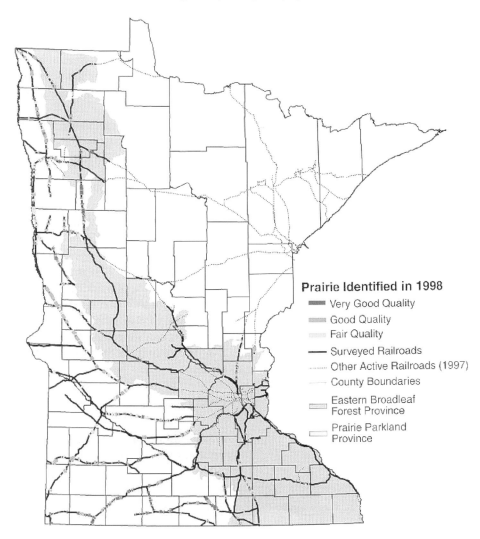

Fig. 4. Locations of native prairie fragments identified during the 1998 field survey of Minnesota railroad rights-of-way. Most of CPR's rights-of-way is located within the Prairie Parkland Province (Merchant and Biederman, 1999).

data collection. CPR provided input to help refine the format and content of the prairie management product. Discussions centered on voluntary management practices helpful in maintaining native prairie and the unique vegetation management requirements of railroads. These include state and federal regulations pertaining to safety, air quality, open fires, noxious weeds, field road access, and utility and ditch crossings.

Best management practices and other impacts on prairie resources

Vegetation management and other activities that may be conducted on railroad rights-of-way are illustrated in Table 2. These activities were evaluated to determine relative level of impact on native prairie vegetation. Where possible and practicable, these practices were refined to lessen the possibility of impacts in areas of native prairie.

Railroad rights-of-way management zones

The DNR learned that railroads necessarily practice distinct types of vegetation management within the three rights-of-way zones. As a result, focus was placed on Zone 3, where refinement of existing vegetation management practices held the greatest potential for improving the long-term maintenance of prairie resources. Table 3 identifies the distinct types of vegetation management practiced by railroads, and shows the refinements to Zone 3 practices that are enacted where native prairie fragments are found along CPR rights-of-way. All of these vegetation management activities conform with federal and state safety regulations.

Railroad BMP implementation

CPR's environmental protection policy commits to meeting or exceeding governmental requirements applicable to its operations. CPR believes that existing and past management practices along the railroad right-of-way are conducive to maintaining the prairie.

In response to data collected during the prairie survey, CPR is implementing the following Best Man-

Table 2. Impact of specific vegetation management activity on native prairie fragments

	Impact		
	Positive	Neutral	Negative
Vegetation management activities			
Fire		▓	
Haying		▓	
Mowing		▓	
Brush mowing		▓	
Volunteer management restoration	▓		
Tree removal, chainsaw	▓		
Long-term rest (no management)			▓
Cultivation			▓
Total vegetation removal			▓
Herbicide treatment (broadcast)			▓
Tree and shrub planting			▓
Tree removal, bulldoze			▓
Other activities			
Railroad tie stockpiling		▓	
Equipment storage		▓	
Ditch maintenance			▓
Utility construction			▓
Ditch construction			▓
Road construction			▓
Snowmobile trail		▓	

agement Practices (BMP):
- broadcast application of herbicides is managed using GIS-based prairie habitat location data;
- native prairie habitat areas are avoided for storage of track material, railroad equipment and other materials;
- implementation of Prairie Awareness Program for CPR rights-of-way maintenance employees and others working on CPR rights-of-way by the distribution of a prairie awareness flyer; and
- maintaining controls for ballast application in Zone 1.

The use of GPS has linked native prairie fragment locations along CPR rights-of-way to mile post locations. As a result, native prairie fragment locations can be presented to CPR rights-of-way maintenance employees and others working on CPR rights-of-way in a user-friendly format (Fig. 5). In addition to implementing BMP's, CPR officials and DNR have also informally agreed to continue the process of exploring cooperative prairie management opportunities.

CONCLUSIONS

A state and railroad-funded survey of active railroad rights-of-way in Minnesota, USA, identified isolated

Table 3. Zone-specific vegetation Best Management Practices on railroad rights-of-way

	Description	Practice	Objectives/methods
Zone 1	Ballast and Rails	Keep all ballast and rail free of any vegetation	• Provide surface drainage • Reduce fire potential • Provide visibility for maintenance of rail hardware • Prevent buildup of wind blown debris and snow
Zone 2	Grade and Ditch	Maintain existing herbaceous vegetation on grade and ditches to support railroad operations	• Provide sight distances for safe operations • Eliminate trees capable of interfering with train traffic • Maintain hydraulic capacity of ditches and culverts • Prevent erosion • Control weeds
Zone 3	Safety buffer	Maintain low maintenance vegetation without disrupting railroad operations	• Provide sight distances for safe operations • Provide access for track maintenance • Maintain ROW boundaries • Accommodate utilities • Prevent erosion • Control noxious weeds
Refined Zone 3	Native Prairie	Adhere to Zone 3 objectives while conserving native plant communities	• Avoid storage of track material and equipment • Avoid broadcast application of herbicides • Avoid bulldozing or removing vegetative cover • Use locally adapted native plant materials for revegetating disturbed sites.

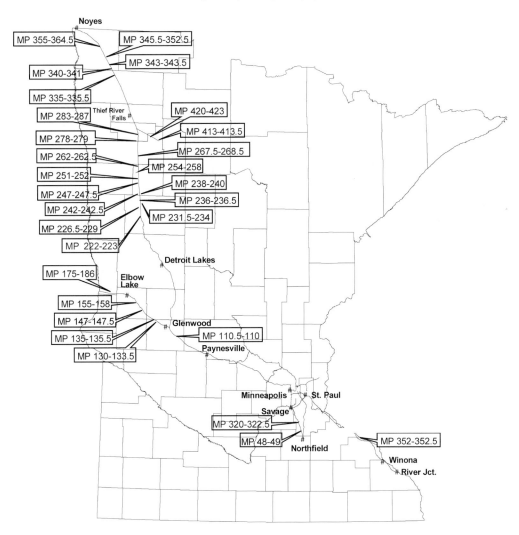

Fig. 5. CPR rights-of-way in Minnesota. Native prairie fragments are identified by mile post locations to facilitate location recognition by railroad maintenance of way employees and others performing work on CPR rights-of-way.

fragments of native prairie. These native prairie locations were generally located in Zone 3 of active rights-of-way, and the quality and size of prairie was generally better in the northwestern portion of the state. State and railroad officials identified refined best management plans for areas of native prairie that promote preservation efforts without compromising safety requirements associated with active railroad use of the rights-of-way. As a result, railroads are able to meet their commitment to be responsible environmental stewards without compromising a long-standing commitment to providing a safe working environment for railroad employees and the communities they serve.

ACKNOWLEDGEMENTS

We thank Dan Schmidt and Jennifer Kamm for their work in the field during this project. We would like to thank Steve Merchant and the DNR for their help in preparing this manuscript and for granting permission for use of previously published material. Thoughtful and constructive reviews by Mark Wollschlager strengthened this manuscript. This project was funded in part by Canadian Pacific Railway and HDR Engineering.

REFERENCES

Bolin, K.E., J. McCoughlin, and R. Soderberg. 1980. A survey of southeastern MN railroad rights-of-way. Unpublished.

Borowske, J.R. and M.E. Heitlinger. 1983. A survey of native prairie on railroad rights-of-way. In: Proceedings from the Seventh North American Prairie Conference. C.L. Kucera and J. Bielefelt, eds. Springfield, MO.

Coffin, B. and L. Pfannmuller. 1988. Minnesota's Endangered Flora and Fauna. University of Minnesota Press, Minneapolis.

Merchant, S. and L. Biederman. 1999. Minnesota's Railroad Rights-of-Way Prairie: A Report to the 1999 Legislature. Department of Natural Resources Biological Report No. 61, St. Paul.

Minnesota Department of Natural Resources. 1996. Ecological Classification System.

BIOGRAPHICAL SKETCHES

Michelle Bissonnette (Corresponding author)
 HDR Engineering, 6190 Golden Hills Drive, Minneapolis, MN 55416, USA, Tel: 763/591-5400, Fax: 763/591-5413

Michelle Bissonnette is a senior environmental consultant with the *Minneapolis office of HDR Engineering*, where she leads environmental assessment and permitting efforts as well as designs, manages and conducts land reclamation and wetland restoration activities. Her work focuses on permitting and compliance requirements for large linear corridor projects, and her client base includes railroads, roadways pipelines and utility companies. Michelle received a BS in Landscape Architecture from the University of Minnesota in 1982. Prior to joining HDR Engineering, Michelle was senior environmental consultant with *Braun Intertec Corporation*, Minneapolis, and worked for the Minnesota State Planning and Land Management Information Center.

Scott Paradise
 Canadian Pacific Railway, 11306 Franklin Ave, Franklin Park, IL 60131, USA

Scott Paradise, PE, is an environmental engineer and structures specialist with *Canadian Pacific Railway*, and manages environmental compliance, environmental infrastructure upgrades and natural resource projects; develops and manages internal environmental awareness, communication and compliance training for railroad personnel; and performs environmental incident response and response planning. Scott received a BS in Civil Engineering with an Environmental Emphasis from the University of Minnesota. Prior to joining CPR, Scott worked for the Minnesota Pollution Control Agency, and was a staff engineer for Remediation Technologies, Inc, where he managed environmental compliance and remediation projects for *North American railroads*.

Part VIII
Geographic Information Systems

Using GIS Tools to Conduct Environmental and Asset Analyses Along Rights-of-Way

E. Alkiewicz, J. Wingfield, D. Frazier, and L. Khitrik

Due to the inadequacy of existing mapping, a decision was made to acquire natural color digital orthophotographic base maps of a 200-mile, double-circuit, 345-kV right-of-way. A 6000-foot corridor along the right-of-way was mapped to identify off right-of-way access roads and adjacent landowners, as well as land use characteristics. After obtaining current low altitude aerial photographs, natural color digital orthophotographs were created. Since the accurate location of the transmission structures was not well known, true horizontal coordinates were obtained for point-of-intersection tower centers along both circuits. This work was accomplished with differential global position systems (GPS) within one meter. A right-of-way environmental inventory consisting of field evaluations to identify vegetation characteristics (species, height, density, and distribution) was conducted by ground-based crews using pentop, weather-resistant computers loaded with digital orthophotographic base maps. Other information collected included access roads, foreign utilities, stream crossings, land use, and landowner information. The automated process significantly improved the accuracy of the data collected and the delivery time for the completed inventory data. All data were delivered in a GIS-ready format into an in-house GIS integrated with a workforce management system that issues work-orders for required maintenance work. NYPA groups that benefit from the data collected during this process include: transmission, environmental, real estate, and licensing.

Keywords: Rights of way (ROW), vegetation inventories, New York Power Authority, digital orthophotographic base maps

INTRODUCTION

The New York Power Authority (NYPA) is one of the major producers of power in New York State. Its generating facilities produce a quarter of the electricity in the state. The power is sold to large industrial and municipal customers and through the Independent System Operator (ISO) network. NYPA does not operate any distribution systems. The bulk of NYPA's transmission system is composed of 230-kV, 345-kV, and 765-kV lines. These result in large rights-of-way (ROWs) that traverse many different physiographic regions of the state (see Fig. 1).

ROW MANAGEMENT

The 1400-miles of transmission lines are divided into three statewide management regions (Western, Central and Northern). These regions were established by NYPA to identify maintenance and budgeting responsibility for all of its assets. The Northern Region contains direct connections to the Canadian electric system, allowing imports of Canadian power to be mixed with NYPA-generated power and transmitted into the New York system.

NYPA also has developed a ROW management program that includes cost-effective and environmentally-sensitive vegetation management and land stewardship. The goal of NYPA's ROW management program is to support the safe and reliable transmission of electrical power in an economically and ecologically sound manner. This goal builds upon the present state of knowledge concerning the strategies and techniques that will minimize labor and equipment costs, while

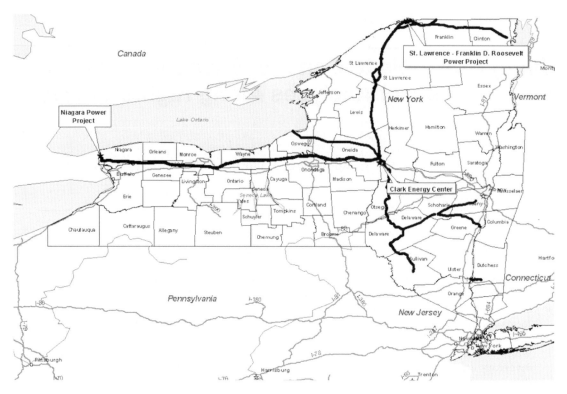

Fig. 1. The fourteen hundred miles of transmission lines crosses the New York state from north to south and west to east. They are divided into three statewide management regions: Niagara Power Project, Clark Energy Center, and St. Lawrence — Franklin D. Roosevelt Power Project.

maximizing the stability and extent of the compatible plant communities maintained through vegetation management and land management practices. The ROW management program takes into account regulatory compliance. The New York State Public Service Commission requires that ROW management plans be prepared under the terms of the Article VII Certificates of Environmental Compatibility and Public Need issued for three transmission facilities built in the late 1970s and early 1980s. These management plans were required to describe the vegetation conditions along the ROW, the management techniques proposed, and the measures to protect sensitive resources.

The traditional process

One of the cornerstones for achieving the ROW management goal was the development of a process of regular inventory and documentation of maintenance activities to allow for analysis, evaluation, and continuous improvement in the overall ROW management program. Historically, the inventory process consisted of ground-based field inventories conducted by biologists and experienced ROW managers that would survey existing vegetation conditions and propose treatment recommendations. Inventory information included: non-compatible vegetation, density, height and distance below the conductor, compatible vegetation and relative density, land use, and techniques proposed for treatment as well as year of proposed treatment.

This process was very time consuming and relied on existing post-construction plan and profile drawings as base maps for delineating vegetation inventory data. Copies of these drawings were then used by maintenance crews to identify the location of "treatment" sites. Although this system worked, it had its drawbacks. The major concern was that the drawings used for the inventory process did not reflect current conditions along the ROW. Additionally, the delineated vegetation sites were depicted as zones that perpendicularly crossed the entire ROW, with offset distances from the nearest structure. There was no effective way to faithfully delineate the actual vegetation configuration within the ROW. This resulted in inaccurate estimates of "brush acres" or vegetation that actually needed maintenance. Since not all ROW vegetation is incompatible, it is important to be able to differentiate species and physical configuration in order to apply the most effective maintenance solution. Without accurate information about vegetation conditions, it was also difficult to determine treatment costs per acre. Finally, although a tabular database system was developed to manipulate the inventory and maintenance data, it relied on the previously-mentioned plan and profile drawing for spatial information. The user had to go back and forth between the tabular database and the hard-copy drawing to plan the work and determine what maintenance had been done at each vegetation site. Information regarding maintenance activities performed on site were recorded manually on paper forms and brought back to the office for later compilation and analysis.

The Maintenance Resource Management (MRM) work order system is used to track the status of any particular site through the process of proposal for treatment, scheduling, and actual treatment. In addition, periodic line patrol information related to vegetation management is also included in the MRM system. These periodic line patrols update current conditions and assist in refining work plans. Treatment plans are entered into the MRM work order system so that work progress and costs can be monitored and tracked. The work order system drives the collection of treatment information, a portion of which is used to meet regulatory requirements related to pesticide use.

Treatment records are another key component of the ROW vegetation management program. These records tie the work back into the MRM work order system and add to the overall inventory system so that follow-up work can be planned and effectiveness of treatment can be assessed. Treatment records are specifically required by regulatory statutes governing the use of herbicides and become the building blocks for reports that must be submitted to regulatory agencies on an annual basis. Treatment data must be collected to satisfy regulatory reporting requirements. Although this type of vegetation maintenance information was being entered into the MRM system, it was still subject to the same drawbacks discussed earlier regarding mapping data.

Finally, New York State laws require that a landowner on or adjacent to the ROW be notified before pesticides are applied to their premises. Since most of NYPA's ROW rights have been acquired through easement, properly identifying the current owner of the property is a challenge. In many cases, property lines and owners are not shown on existing plan and profile drawings. When maintenance plans are prepared, proposed treatment areas are usually identified by structure/span numbers or stationing. Since the only reliable means of identifying current ownership is through county tax maps that do not show the structure/span numbers, the task resulted in a substantial pretreatment season workload for NYPA's real estate staff.

The improved process

Due to the needs expressed by various staff members involved in all aspects of ROW vegetation management, a small group of NYPA staff began looking into solutions that involved the rapidly evolving field of GIS. From the start, it was envisioned that any solution would have to result in a multipurpose, multidiscipline, and easy to use tool that would achieve across-the-board acceptance.

One of the first decisions to be made involved choosing an appropriate base map to replace the plan and profile standard used previously. In an effort to balance scale, accuracy, currency, and cost, only one effective solution became apparent: 1:4800 or $1'' = 400'$ digital orthophotographs. This type of imagery clearly provides the most information for the least cost of all the existing alternatives. At appropriate scales, data can be vectorized on the screen. This allows the user to work with data attributes associated with the images (lacking in raster images), while serving as a kind of "library" of features which can be added later. In most cases, human interpretation of the raster images is sufficient and eliminates the need for comprehensive vector mapping. In addition, updates are far simpler and less expensive than with other base map alternatives.

Since specific environmental features affect the selection of a technique for vegetation management, it was decided the ROW vegetation inventory would continue as the primary means of collecting the necessary data. The inventory would benefit from using current natural color orthophotographs by allowing photo interpretation before beginning field work. Additionally, existing GIS data layers, such as structure location, ROW edges, roads, regulated wetlands, hydrology, and tax maps could be superimposed on the orthophotographs to provide additional information in the field during the inventory process.

Site vegetation was delineated using the same vegetation criteria (species, density, and heights) as in the past, but with new tools. Sites could now be drawn to depict the vegetation site boundaries as they really existed. Creating these vegetation "polygons" allowed the location and acreage for each site to be determined on the orthophotographic base map. Since field computers were being used for the inventory, vegetation sites were delineated on top of the base map in the field. All the other existing GIS layers were available to assist the inventory crews in their work.

The information collected in the field computers subsequently were brought back to the office for post-processing and quality control. The data was provided as GIS layers and stored on a central server where it was accessible to internal users. This data was then used to prepare treatment plans, perform landowner notification, act as support material to MRM work orders, and provide location information and site characteristics to maintenance crews.

NYPA completed a GIS inventory pilot study for its Western Region in 1999 using the Niagara Adirondack Tie Line (NATL). The success of this pilot has let to the adoption of this approach for the remainder of the transmission system. It will be completed by 2001.

GIS DEVELOPMENT

Data requirements

Upon receiving funding for an enterprise-wide GIS implementation focused on transmission ROW management, NYPA established an internal GIS Users

Group. Members of this group were carefully chosen to ensure representation of all segments of the end-user community. This group developed a list of data requirements for various transmission ROW applications which was reviewed, modified, and finally adopted through meetings with selected transmission maintenance, environmental, and real estate staff. This process was carefully managed to ensure that all data elements necessary to support the proposed applications were included, while discouraging requests entailing potentially budget-breaking costs or development time.

The data layers necessary to support the proposed applications, along with the approach for obtaining them and rationale for including them, included:

- *Digital Orthophotographic Base Maps*: A base map is necessary in any GIS in order to put the other database elements into context. NYPA's long experience with this technology (since 1989) led it to adopt natural color, 1.25 foot pixel, 1:4800 nominal scale digital orthophotographs as the base map for its transmission system.

- *Scanning of Existing Records*: Originals or legible copies of all existing real estate division acquisition and conveyance maps and all systems operations plan/profiles were scanned. The plan/profiles are NYPA's only current source for determining conductor clearances. The real estate acquisition and conveyance maps describe the property rights acquired or conveyed for each parcel in more detail than is practical to capture in a database.

- *Transmission Tower Centers*: Transmission tower centers were generated internally by NYPA's GIS staff from company survey records for most of its system. For those lines where such data were unavailable, true horizontal coordinates (sub-meter accuracy) were obtained for every point-of-intersection tower using GPS survey techniques. The remaining tower centers were calculated using the existing plan/profiles database so that the two databases could be linked.

- *Transmission Line Centerlines and ROW Edges*: The transmission line centerlines and ROW edges were created from the tower centers data. These data form the framework for NYPA's vegetation management sites and provide the links for the asset maintenance data in the computerized maintenance management system (MAXIMO).

- *Access Routes*: Access routes were digitized from hard copies of the digital orthophotographs. In addition to enabling the efficient planning of routine maintenance tasks and the dispatch of emergency vehicles, these data will permit a more complete evaluation of the legal status of NYPA's transmission access routes.

- *Vegetation Sites, Wetlands, Foreign Utilities, and ROW Improvements*: A ROW environmental inventory was conducted consisting of field evaluations to identify vegetation sites and wetlands along the transmission corridors. The additional following features were collected and attributed: parking lots, public and private recreation facilities (pools, golf courses, miniature golf courses, swing sets, volleyball courts, etc.); chain-link, board, and other substantial fences (specifically excluding barbed wire fences); public and private paved or gravel driveways; buildings including tool sheds; wells, well houses, and spring houses; and commercial use of any kind other than agricultural use. Foreign utilities were identified where there was physical evidence of a utility crossing. The ROW improvement inventory provides a means to document and evaluate the compatibility of fixtures placed in NYPA's ROWs by others. The foreign utilities inventory has a similar purpose, but with a special focus on system safety and reliability.

- *Digital, Attributed Tax Maps*: Digital tax map parcels attributed with assessors' data (New York State Real Property Services data) was or developed for all parcels within 100 feet of the subject transmission corridors or that were affected by or contiguous to any parcel which NYPA owns in connection with its transmission corridors. These data were used by NYPA's real estate staff to track special landowner conditions (wells, organic farms, etc.) which affect vegetation management plans and to track permitted uses of NYPA's ROWs.

- *Special Conditions*: Special regulatory conditions were captured from the plan profiles and developed as a polygon coverage, while special landowner conditions were captured from existing real estate division records and linked as to the appropriate tax parcel and/or acquisition parcel polygons. These data will ensure that ROW managers are aware of existing regulatory and landowner commitments.

- *Acquisition of Existing Data — NYSDEC-Regulated Wetlands, Native American (Indian) Reservations, Soils, Federal Wetlands, State Parks Data*: Existing data sets and metadata from various sources (e.g., the New York State Department of Environmental Conservation, State GIS Clearinghouse, US Department of Agriculture, and US Census Bureau) were obtained. These data sets will be used to plan routine maintenance and to evaluate future system improvement plans and permit applications.

- *Roads*: New York State Department of Transportation (NYSDOT) 1:24,000 road data were used in conjunction with digital orthophotographic base maps. These data are necessary to provide orientation to the end users, and to enable maintenance and emergency vehicle dispatch and routing.

- *Land Use*: The digital orthophotographic base maps were used to delineate standard land use categories within and 100 feet adjacent to the transmission ROW. Photogrammetric efforts were augmented by data gathered in the field vegetation inventory.

- *Hydrology*: NYSDOT existing hydrologic coverages were obtained. The wetland delineation results from the vegetation inventory were used to adjust the final hydrology coverage. These data sets will be used to ensure compliance with various environmental laws and regulations.
- *Real Estate Acquisition Parcels*: All acquisition and conveyance parcels for the subject corridor(s) were developed as a polygon coverage. Since the existing real estate division tabular database is predicated on parcel numbers, it was linked to this polygon coverage to facilitate real property inventory analysis and maintenance.
- *Cultural Resources*: Attributed point data describing cultural resources (historical sites, sites of archaeological significance, etc.) were obtained from the New York State Office of Parks, Recreation, and Historical Preservation.
- *Spans*: This coverage integrated the vegetation site coverage and span identifications. These data enable the integration of the GIS with the existing MRM database (MAXIMO).
- *Stations*: This coverage consists of a point file for each 500-foot station (5+00, 10+00, 15+00, etc.).

GIS STRUCTURE

The current dedicated GIS staff is composed of two GIS administrators/analysts (one each in the environmental and real estate divisions) whose work is coordinated by a GIS manager, located in the real estate division. This minimal core staff is augmented by an environmental scientist with special expertise in GIS support of ROW management and hydro relicensing, and an additional contract GIS technician working primarily in support of environmental programs. The management concept is that this core staff will handle basic system maintenance and database administration, and provide analyses and general GIS support for specialized projects. GIS support of routine tasks (e.g., ROW management) will be handled by the staff that is already responsible for these tasks. Overall coordination of ongoing GIS applications, and the identification and evaluation of new applications will be handled through the GIS Users Group, chaired by the GIS Manager.

The two administrators/analysts use Arc Info on an NT platform primarily to create and manage coverages and for special analyses and data manipulation where its inherent power is required. Virtually all routine GIS work by the core staff is done with ArcView, also on an NT platform. The current end users with sufficient expertise and/or special needs use ArcView (primarily Windows95, some NT) with some casual users employing ArcExplorer. Existing data are resident on shared servers at six different locations. These local databases are updated periodically and reconciled both over the wide area network (WAN) and, when data size warrants it, by personal visits. Training and user help have been handled by the core staff on an ad hoc basis.

The schedule calls for full implementation for transmission ROW support in two years, building on the foundation built by the previously described pilot project. NYPA's information technology department has assigned a project manager and other staff (database analysts, database administrators, programmers) to guide the effort and ensure successful completion of the initial phase, which is focused on transmission ROW applications and support. Contracts have been issued to URS Corporation (Buffalo, NY office) for data collection and conversion, general GIS consulting and support, and specialized application development. Current emphasis is on data collection/conversion and specialized application development. These tasks require integration with NYPA's MRM system, MAXIMO.

DATA COLLECTION

While the primary objective for the GIS was to provide detailed mapping of vegetation sites and features both on and off the ROW, the GIS also provided ROW inventory crews with an efficient tool for collecting field data. The GIS was set up in two stages. The first stage consisted of creating a digital orthophotographic base map and readily available GIS coverages (i.e., roads, streams, and state/national wetlands). It was completed before the ROW inventory crews mobilized to the field and was loaded on pentop weather-resistant computers used by the field crews. The second stage consisted mainly of post-processing the ROW inventory GIS field data and enhancing the previously developed coverages (e.g., NYSDEC stream classifications were added to the stream coverage). The second state also involved developing some new coverages (e.g., real estate acquisition parcels and tax map data).

As with any electrical transmission ROW vegetation inventory, it is necessary to gather information and maps that will be used in the field. These data, such as road maps, topographic information, access rights, regulated wetland maps, plan and profile maps, ROW edges, tower nomenclature, compatible/noncompatible species and information on sensitive landowners, are necessary to bring to the field but can also be quite cumbersome. The approach for this inventory was to collect as much of these data as possible in electronic format before heading to the field. As noted earlier, existing electronic data were procured, where possible, from governmental agencies. The GIS coverages obtained from governmental agencies were compiled at a much smaller scale than the 1:4800 NYPA base map. In order to create a consistent data set, the

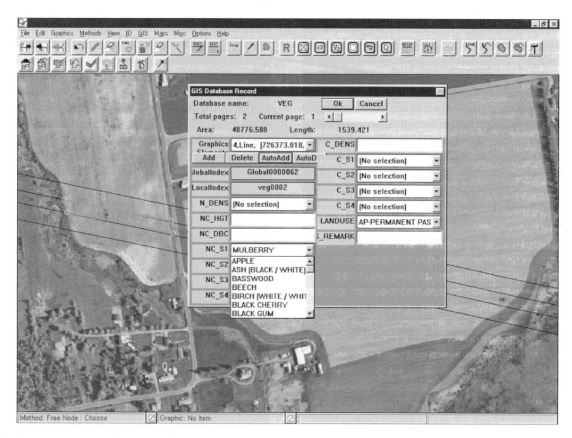

Fig. 2. The inventory crews could see the vegetation sites on the digital orthophotographs loaded in their field computers. Vegetation sites (or land use sites) were traced directly on the computer screen and attributed with information from the pull-down menus.

roads and stream coverages were adjusted to match visible features on the digital orthophotographic base maps. However, due to their regulatory nature, the state and federal wetlands coverages were not modified in any way.

More specific GIS coverages for the ROW were also created prior to field inventory efforts. These coverages include: transmission tower centers, ROW edges, access roads, and special conditions (i.e., landowner concerns, areas with difficult site access, etc.). To top-off the electronic data set, ROW plan-profile maps for the entire ROW were converted to raster images and color TIF images of 7.5-minute series United States Geological Survey (USGS) topographic maps were obtained.

PenMap GIS was selected as the base software for field data collection. A custom application was developed in PenMap that was specifically designed for collecting ROW information in accordance with NYPA's standard environmental inventory procedures. The data collection application incorporates integrated functions for GPS mapping which was used during this project for verifying tower center coordinates.

In the PenMap data collection application, field crews can create points, lines, or polygons and attribute these features through pre-programmed pull-down menus. The pentop computers were setup so that the field crews had all the data necessary to efficiently execute the inventory work.

Vegetation sites (or land use sites) were traced directly on the computer screen to produce a polygon with true spatial coordinates. The polygons were subsequently attributed with information from the pull-down menus and crews were free to move onto their next site (Fig. 2). From time-to-time, the field crews would obtain true coordinates (using GPS with submeter accuracy) of tower centers. The speed and efficiency of the data collection technique coupled with reliable all-terrain vehicles enabled the two environmental inventory field crews to cover approximately 200 miles of ROW in 14 days. Yet this was not the only time savings — since the field data were collected electronically in a well-designed database, post-processing efforts were only a fraction of what would be expected from a conventional paper-based ROW inventory.

GIS SYSTEM IMPLEMENTATION

Once data collection and post-processing were complete, the GIS contained 25 coverages with a wealth of up-to-date environmental inventory data. However, in order for users to access the data, a fair degree of GIS software training was needed. In keeping with the underlying strategy of promoting internal use of the GIS data, NYPA began evaluating the feasibility of implementing an end-user application that would streamline the training process and provide a customized tool for ROW management functions.

The concept of a customized software system was evaluated and it was determined that in this case, the advantages of a custom application outweighed the feasibility of implementing off-the-shelf traditional software applications. These advantages include:

Ease of Access — Training times for users of customized applications are generally much lower than those for non-customized software products, while users' understanding of content in customized systems is generally higher.

Simplicity — Custom systems can be configured to perform relatively complex tasks that simplify commonly performed end user tasks and in turn save time.

Centralized Data Access — All data are maintained and accessed through a central location. Moreover, all parties have access to current information, avoiding duplication and synchronization problems inherent in local systems.

Security — Central data access allows centralized data control, with system- and database-level security provided through the use of user IDs, passwords, and data encryption.

The custom software application was designed for two main end user groups — ROW managers and real estate professionals. In general, ROW managers were interested in evaluating ROW vegetation conditions and required access to the geographical data sets in order to examine treatment techniques in light of ROW conditions (e.g., wetlands, landowner issues/agreements, site access, regulatory commitments, tracking landowner complaints, etc.). ROW managers also wanted a function for automating the treatment plan review process and a link for creating work orders through the existing MAXIMO work order generation and tracking system.

Real estate professionals, on the other hand, required support for the following business functions: notifying land owners of herbicide application, acquiring danger tree cutting rights, issuing various land use permits, tracking conveyances of NYPA land to other parties, and tracking property acquisition by NYPA. Real estate professionals also provide a quality assurance check for treatment plan work orders. As such, due to the considerable overlap in ROW management processes for ROW managers and real estate professionals, a single software application was designed with some elements specifically targeted at one or the other user groups, while other elements provided a bridge for interactions between the two groups.

NYPA assessed the available systems that could be used to create the custom application and identified two viable options: ArcView GIS Version 3.2 and MapObjects Version 2.

Ultimately, it was determined the best system for this custom application was MapObjects due to its unrestricted flexibility for custom programming through VisualBasic, low cost for end user deployment, and ESRI's impending migration away from ArcView's current program language (Avenue). However, ArcView (and ArcInfo) will continue to be used by GIS administrators and other advanced GIS users to maintain and update system fields, and conduct high-end statistical and data analyses. At this time, NYPA has a Beta version of the custom software in-hand and is testing system functionality (Fig. 3).

CONCLUSIONS

Although the implementation of GIS as an enterprise system at NYPA is still in progress, the benefits of the technology to assist in conducting environmental and asset inventories and analyses are already becoming evident. At the request of the Northern Region, the vegetation inventory and related data (e.g., tower centers, spans, NYSDEC wetlands) for the Moses Adirondack 230-kV transmission line were acquired on an accelerated schedule in the fall of 1999. The region transmission staff planned to use these data in support of outsourcing vegetation maintenance for this corridor in the spring/summer of 2000. They have reported anecdotally that the level of detail of the information provided through the use of the GIS to the prospective bidders resulted in costs so much lower than past experience that the investment in the inventory and related work (~$90,000) was completely offset.

The GIS core staff and information technology staff are currently identifying system and data maintenance issues, and working on cost effective solutions. It appears that tax parcel updates may be acquired in a timely manner from a single source — the New York State Office of Real Property Services. Although investigation at individual county clerks' offices will still be required in the event of parcel subdivisions, total staff time devoted to maintaining current property owner information will decrease. The State GIS Clearinghouse has initiated a pilot study for a planned multi-resolution, ongoing digital orthophotographic base map acquisition program which may significantly defray NYPA's estimated base map update costs of about $100,000 per year. NYPA recently centralized transmission maintenance in a single group reporting to the Central Regional Manager. This move will make the implementation of consistent and uniform maintenance practices across the organization more certain, thereby making GIS implementation and maintenance simpler. It also puts GIS in an even more important role, as the central transmission maintenance staff comes to depend on it for accurate, current information on the status of NYPA's transmission corridors.

As the ROW management application is deployed over the next few years, it is expected that enhancements will be suggested. Even as the application is being developed, additional implementation concepts,

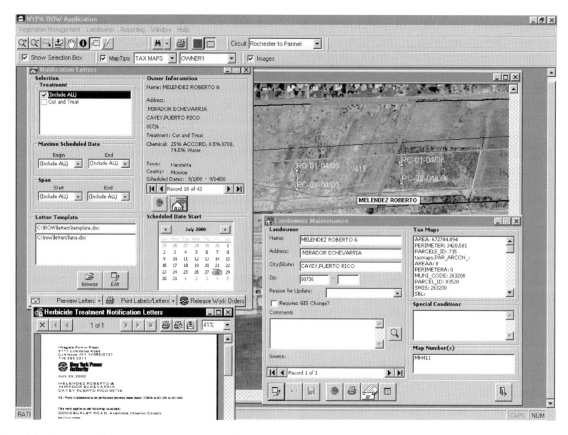

Fig. 3. One of the functions of the ROW Management GIS application is the ability to identify the location of the application for herbicide notification, obtain the addresses to whom to send the notification, and generate notification letters without duplication.

such as spatial database engine data migration are being evaluated. This migration promises more tightly integrated applications, as the migration of GIS data to Oracle will join MAXIMO and other enterprise data sets in a common format. Some additional enhancements being investigated are the use of integrated cell phones/GPS technology to facilitate danger tree location and general database update functions, high resolution LIDAR terrain and conductor catenary modeling for conductor clearance analysis and danger tree detection.

The future of GIS at NYPA is promising. The challenge will be, as always, to stay far enough ahead of the curve to provide a competitive advantage while avoiding the "bleeding edge."

BIOGRAPHICAL SKETCHES

Ed Alkiewicz
New York Power Authority, 123 Main St., White Plains, NY 10601, USA

Ed Alkiewicz is a Senior Environmental Scientist with the New York Power Authority. He is a graduate of the SUNY College of Environmental Science and Forestry. Since 1977 he has been involved in transmission line siting and construction, rights-of-way vegetation management, GIS application development and hydroelectric project relicensing.

John Wingfield
New York Power Authority, Blenheim-Gilboa Power Project, P.O. Box 200, Gilboa, NY 12076, USA

John Wingfield is the Survey Coordinator and GIS Manager for the New York Power Authority. He is responsible for maintaining the GIS Real Estate database, coordination of enterprise wide GIS implementation and application development. He also supports various groups within the New York Power Authority with survey data as needed.

Lana Khitrik
URS Corporation, 282 Delaware Avenue, Buffalo, NY 14202-1805, USA

Ms. Khitrik has 18 years of experience in civil/environmental engineering and GIS including designing and managing systems for planning, environmental studies, statistical calculations and data collection. Ms. Khitirik has a BS in Civil Engineering from the Institute of Railway Engineers, Lenningrad, Russia, 1981 and an AAS in Microcomputer System Management, Bryant & Stratton Business Institute, 1993. Ms. Khitrik has initiated, successfully developed, and implemented a variety of comprehensive GISs across many applications such as environmental assessments, groundwater impact studies, 3D models, sewer and waterworks facilities, flood mitigation studies, land use, GPS and pen computer data collection.

David Frazier
 URS Corporation, 282 Delaware Avenue, Buffalo, NY 14202-1805, USA

Mr. Frazier has 17 years of experience as a project manager and hydrogeologist. His educational background includes an MA in Geochemistry from SUNY at Buffalo and a BS in Geology from Ohio University. With a strong background in environmental sciences, and technical expertise in database systems and GIS, Mr. Frazier's diverse experience provides a sound foundation in his role as a manager.

Using GIS to Support Environmental Stewardship Objectives in Maryland Rights of Way

Mark T. Southerland, Donald E. Strebel, Allison Brindley,
A. Morris Perot, Jr., and Sandra Shaw Patty

The Power Plant Research Program (PPRP), a division of the Maryland Department of Natural Resources (DNR), is charged with addressing the environmental consequences of electric power generation and transmission within Maryland. At the same time, DNR has embraced an ecosystem approach to natural resources management and is seeking new tools to help meet more ambitious environmental stewardship goals. Geographic information systems (GIS) are powerful tools for overlaying electric utility infrastructure management needs and biodiversity conservation opportunities. PPRP has recently assembled a comprehensive GIS data base of transmission line routes and rights-of-way (ROWs) attributes throughout Maryland. PPRP has also used rare, threatened, and endangered species data on a watershed scale to identify priority regional biodiversity hotspots. In a separate initiative, DNR has identified hubs and corridors of contiguous forests and wetlands as part of a statewide "green infrastructure" program. PPRP is now using these layers in GIS to: (1) assess the impacts of current ROWs management practices, (2) recommend improved practices in specific areas, (3) facilitate optimal siting of new transmission lines, and (4) promote ecosystem-based restoration and planning that minimizes the costs and maximizes the benefits of landscape changes. For example, utility ROWs in the vicinity of biodiversity hotspots are being targeted to enhance habitat for rare plants and animals, ROWs within proposed green infrastructure corridors are being proposed for compatible vegetation management to link fragmented habitats, and utility properties within existing green infrastructure hubs or biodiversity hotspots are being considered for purchase or management as "core" preserved lands.

Keywords: Geographic information systems (GIS), rights-of-way, transmission lines, power plants, biodiversity, endangered species, greenways, land use, conservation, environmental stewardship

INTRODUCTION

The goal of the Power Plant Research Program (PPRP) of the Maryland Department of Natural Resources (DNR) is to effectively manage the natural resources of the State affected by the generation and transmission of electric power. Rights of way (ROWs) for transmission lines and other linear facilities are located throughout the State and provide unique challenges for stewardship of natural resources. The need for effective management decisions affecting these ROWs will likely increase as electric power is deregulated.

In 1996, Maryland DNR adopted a new paradigm for managing Maryland's natural resources founded on the concept of ecosystem-based management (Maryland DNR Ecosystem Council, 1996). This ecosystem-based approach to natural resources stewardship poses special challenges for managing electric utility ROWs. PPRP is enlisting geographic information system (GIS) technologies to meet this challenge. This paper describes the ongoing research efforts at PPRP to develop the necessary data and build the requisite GIS tools to implement ecosystem-based management of ROWs through a spatial analysis approach.

GIS APPROACH

The benefit of using GIS-based spatial analysis for management is that it provides specific geographic locations for facilities and natural resources that vary in their attributes and conditions. Because these locations are known, the spatial relationships of the facilities and natural resources can be determined and ROW management conducted in a specific and integrated fashion. The difficulty posed by GIS-based spatial analysis is that it requires extensive locational data. PPRP's approach to conducting spatial analysis using GIS is twofold: (1) to develop the statewide transmission line and ecological data to support GIS applications and (2) to build several GIS-based tools that can support Maryland DNR and electric utility decisionmaking. Potential outcomes of these tools are impact evaluation, impact minimization through siting and facility management, and ecological restoration targeting.

MAP DATA TO SUPPORT THE GIS APPROACH

Two kinds of data are needed to support PPRP's GIS approach to managing ROWs: (1) a complete GIS data base of transmission line locations and attributes across Maryland and (2) relevant locational data on ecological conditions at site and watershed scales.

Transmission Line Data Base

The PPRP Transmission Line Data Base Project has compiled a comprehensive data base of transmission line locations within the State of Maryland using a variety of source maps. Data sources include digital and hardcopy USGS topographic maps augmented by transmission line location maps provided by the Public Service Commission and the electric utility companies (BGE, SMECO, PEPCO, Allegheny Power, and DPL/Conectiv). The data base is believed to be current and accurate, but an independent quality assurance check by the utilities is underway.

The spatial data base was created by digitizing map information and adding line attributes manually from the service territory and other maps. The data are fully transferable to ArcView and other GIS packages and can be displayed using the ArcExplorer freeware tool. Fig. 1 illustrates the pattern of transmission lines across Maryland. Currently the project not only includes the line locations, but also indicates the owners of the lines, their capacities (kV), and the substations between which the lines run. Future work will expand these attributes (e.g., adding land use and ROW width) and link the spatial data to historical permit application information.

Ecological maps

A variety of ecological maps are available to use in conjunction with the PPRP Transmission Line Data Base. They vary in scale and the natural resources they depict. A number of maps are available for any location in Maryland and have traditionally been used, in conjunction with site surveys, to evaluate potential impacts of transmission lines. The most important of these maps describe land use/land cover, soils, streams, wetlands, historical and archeological areas, agricultural preservation areas, and parks. These can generally be obtained from the US Geological Survey or state agencies, although the effort to obtain and format the data for spatial analysis can be substantial.

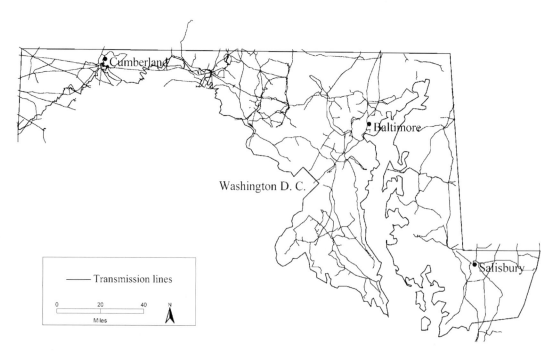

Fig. 1. Distribution of transmission lines (greater than 69 kV) in Maryland.

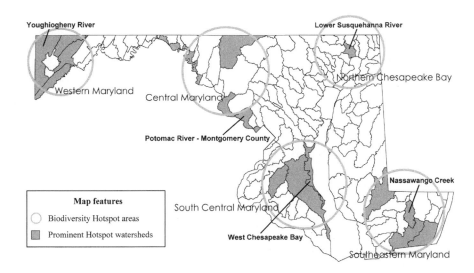

Fig. 2. Priority hotspots for biodiversity conservation in Maryland.

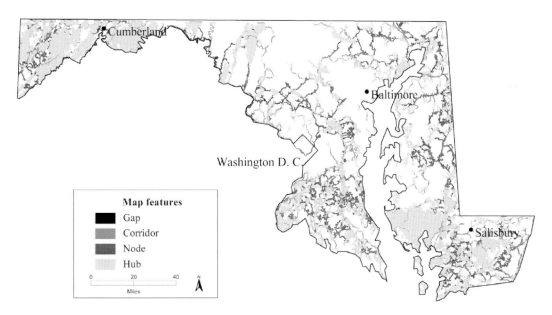

Fig. 3. Map of green infrastructure hubs and corridors in Maryland.

At the same time, new ecological maps are being created to more accurately represent the range of habitats and species distributions across Maryland. Two are of special interest for ecosystem-based management of ROWs:

- *PPRP's Provisional Biodiversity Hotspots in Maryland* — Phase Two of a project describing the patterns of biodiversity among Maryland watersheds using rare, threatened, and endangered species records for 12 major taxonomic and ecological categories (Fig. 2).
- *Maryland DNR's Green Infrastructure* — A statewide landscape assessment of hubs (large contiguous forest and wetland habitat areas) and corridors (compatible habitat connecting hubs) developed to facilitate targeting of conservation easements, ecosystem restoration, and land use planning (Fig. 3).

GIS TOOLS AND PRELIMINARY RESULTS

PPRP is currently developing two kinds of tools to support ROW decisionmaking: (1) a method for evaluating the potential impacts of specific transmission line ROWs using their coincidence with ecological attributes and (2) a method for targeting restoration opportunities within ROWs by overlaying them on high-value natural areas (as described by biodiversity hotspots and the green infrastructure). Once targeted, vegetation and habitat management options can help minimize impacts or promote restoration in ROWs.

ROW Impact Evaluation Method

PPRP has developed a draft Transmission Line ROW Impact Evaluation Method (Harriott et al., 1997) to facilitate licensing reviews traditionally conducted independently by the mandated agencies. The goal of

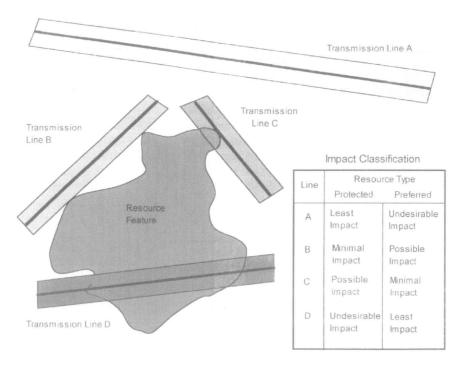

Fig. 4. Schematic illustrating impact categories derived from spatial analysis of ROW Impact Evaluation Method.

this project is to provide a computer tool that will augment the best professional judgement routinely used in reviewing a new transmission line route. The Evaluation Method is a computerized decision tool that can be used to calculate the ecological impact or "cost" of a new route and provide the user with a rapid, unbiased ranking of the potential environmental impacts from proposed transmission lines.

The Evaluation Method uses digital data to represent natural and cultural resources that have been incorporated into and enhanced in a GIS coupled with an analytical, algorithmic processing program. Initially, seven resource layers representing landscape features known to affect routing decisions for transmission lines were selected for the development of the Evaluation Method. Data layers were generated for forests, streams, roads, and other utility corridors; wetlands (forested and non-forested were treated separately); agricultural preservation districts; and historic properties. Each resource layer was given a set of weighted buffer zones based on State regulations or best professional judgement. The weights were designed to account for the impacts associated with a 200-foot right-of-way, based on each resource's vulnerability and the ROW's route near or through the features (Fig. 4). The base features and their buffer zones were compiled in a GIS and converted from vector to raster format; the summed weight at each pixel provides a point-for-point computerized ecological landscape for the quantitative evaluation of superimposed transmission line ROWs. For each proposed route, the algorithmic program is applied to this landscape to calculate total cost per line and average cost per pixel (in terms

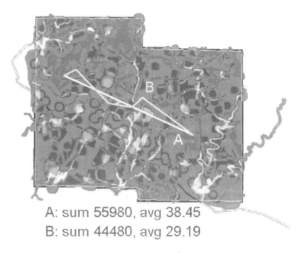

A: sum 55980, avg 38.45
B: sum 44480, avg 29.19

Fig. 5. Environment impact (cost) landscape resulting from two alternative transmission line ROWs using ROW Impact Evaluation Method.

of environmental impact) (Fig. 5). Because the Evaluation Method was designed to incorporate GIS data representing different natural or cultural resources, the user can select different sets of resources (and apply customized weighting schemes or variable buffer widths) to address agency or regional concerns. Additionally, the Evaluation Method allows the user to investigate the proposed line's influence on individual resources, providing a tabular result describing the relative amount of impact on each resource (e.g., using the number of pixels contacted by the line).

A separate program has been designed that can seek out the least environmentally damaging route across the computerized landscape. This program takes the starting and ending points (supplied by the user), and plots the path of lowest pixel values. The information gained from the results of such a program may assist the user in evaluating proposed routes by comparing their values against the values associated with the "best" line generated by the computer. This program provides the ability to compare multiple alternative routes objectively and select the "least environmentally damaging" route. The combination of this "optimal" computerized landscape and the resource-specific tabular output provides the user with a powerful tool for ROW impact research and mitigation. Ultimately, this tool should reduce the time and effort needed to evaluate proposed transmission line routes and decrease the likelihood of project delays during the review process.

Restoration targeting at ROWs
While rigorous evaluation of potential impacts from specific transmission line ROWs will continue to be an essential activity for avoiding or minimizing adverse effects, spatial analysis through GIS also offers the opportunity to target management at the scale of watersheds and landscapes. This was not possible until comprehensive GIS data on ROWs and natural resources became available for large areas. Now that the Transmission Line Data Base and the Provisional Biodiversity Hotspots and Green Infrastructure maps are available for the entire State, effective targeting of restoration opportunities can be done.

The method for identifying targeting priorities is simple: spatial overlays of ROWs are done on high-value natural areas described at the watershed level (Biodiversity Hotspots) and across the whole landscape (Green Infrastructure). Each of these ecological maps provides a different picture of Maryland's natural resources: the Biodiversity Hotspots describe the pattern of rare species most at risk of extirpation, while the Green Infrastructure describes the pattern of contiguous habitat best able to support area-dependent species.

Biodiversity hotspots
The PPRP Biodiversity Hotspots Project (Southerland et al., 1999) is applying spatial analysis through GIS to existing biological data on the distribution and abundance of organisms in Maryland. PPRP has identified three key sources of biodiversity data within DNR that will be incorporated into the Project in phases: (1) the Maryland Biological Stream Survey (MBSS) is a recently completed source of probability-based, statewide information on aquatic species, (2) the Heritage and Biodiversity Conservation Programs (HBCP) have long been the primary source of data on rare, threatened, and endangered species throughout all Maryland's natural communities, and (3) the Gap Analysis Program (GAP) is an ongoing initiative that will provide complete coverage of predicted species ranges in Maryland based on remotely sensed vegetation and species habitat models.

The specific objectives of the project are to identify species-rich areas, areas that support rare species, and other areas or "hotspots" that make the greatest contribution to regional and state biodiversity as defined below:

Biodiversity is the variety of life and its processes. It includes the variety of organisms, the genetic differences among them, the communities and ecosystems in which they occur, and the ecological and evolutionary processes that keep them functioning, yet ever changing and adapting (Noss and Cooperrider, 1994).

PPRP has recently completed Phase Two of the project, while incorporating the lessons of Phase One. Specifically, spatial analysis methods have been applied to determine the distribution of rare species richness for 12 taxonomic and ecological categories at the scale of Maryland 8-digit watersheds (138 in the State). While the HBCP data improve on the MBSS data by focusing on rare species and including terrestrial taxa, these data still represent an incomplete sample of biodiversity, both taxonomically and geographically. Our knowledge of geographic patterns will be further improved by incorporating the finer resolution of the GAP data in Phase Three.

The hotspots analyses of the rare, threatened, and endangered species data from DNR's HBCP, in conjunction with the MBSS hotspots results, provide information that should be useful to land managers in Maryland, including the electric utility industry. The two primary conclusions are as follows:
- Rare, threatened, and endangered species, especially plants, can be found in all regions of Maryland and, therefore, provide **numerous opportunities** for biodiversity conservation for major land managers in the State.
- The pattern of these rare, threatened, and endangered species, taken across all taxonomic and ecological categories, reveals **five hotspot areas** that can form the basis for priority biodiversity conservation efforts.

While opportunities for biodiversity conservation exist statewide, these analyses reveal hotspots of rare, threatened, and endangered species richness in five areas of Maryland (Fig. 2). These regional hotspots are logical priorities for conducting larger scale biodiversity conservation efforts. Each regional hotspot has a central watershed that is especially rich in rare, threatened, and endangered species. Several watersheds in that region may also be species rich depending on the taxonomic or ecological category. Biogeographical processes would predict the separation of hotspots by major regions, but the benefit of these analyses is to restrict the hotspots to a small set of watersheds in each region. The following five regional hotspots comprise

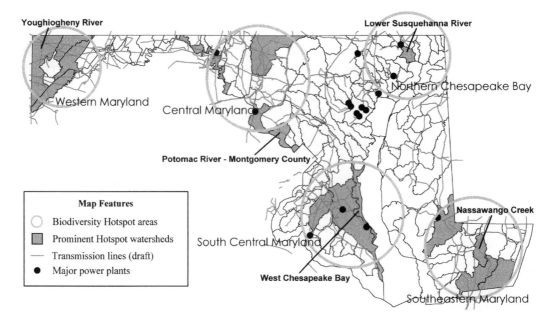

Fig. 6. Overlay of transmission lines and major power plants on priority hotspots for biodiversity conservation.

15 watersheds or only 11% of the 138 watersheds in Maryland:
- *Western Maryland*. Far northwestern Maryland centered on the Youghiogheny River watershed, but including the neighboring Upper North Branch Potomac River, Savage River, and Casselman River watersheds.
- *Central Maryland*. The middle of the State north of Washington, DC centered on the Potomac River-Montgomery County watershed, but including the nearby Upper Monocacy River and Potomac River-Washington County watersheds.
- *Southeastern Maryland*. Far southeastern Maryland centered on Nassawango Creek, including two neighboring watersheds (Chincoteague Bay and Lower Pocomoke River) and the Nanticoke River watershed.
- *South Central Maryland*. The southern western shore centered on the West Chesapeake Bay watershed, including the neighboring Lower Patuxent River and Zekiah Swamp watersheds.
- *Northern Chesapeake Bay*. The northern part of Maryland above the Chesapeake Bay centered on the Lower Susquehanna River watershed.

Electric utilities and other organizations interested in biodiversity conservation can use these priority, regional biodiversity hotspots to initiate watershed-scale biodiversity conservation efforts. Both large and small watershed stewardship groups are forming throughout the State. Effective partnerships among the US EPA, State agencies, local governments, private organizations, and electric utilities could be based on these provisional hotspots. In an era of declining funding for environmental management at utilities, land management activities can be targeted to those properties that make the largest contribution to statewide biodiversity conservation. Similarly, when utilities are faced with the need to divest properties, their biodiversity value can be factored into decisions to sell. For example, conservation trust organizations may be sought as prospective buyers or environmental credits may be sought from regulatory agencies for conservation efforts on these lands.

More immediately, utilities can use these hotspots to focus their current land management efforts in their ROWs and other properties. Fig. 6 shows an overlay of power plants and transmission lines on the five priority biodiversity hotspot areas. Table 1 lists the total miles of transmission lines (and proportion per watershed area) in each of the prominent watersheds of each biodiversity hotspot area. On average, there are 0.04 miles of transmission line per acre of State land; the range of transmission line density in the prominent watersheds varies from 0.007 in Chincoteague Bay to 0.093 in Potomac River-Washington County. In each of the five priority hotspot areas (but less so in the Northern Chesapeake Bay), there are many miles of transmission lines that provide opportunities for rare, threatened, and endangered species management. Many electric utilities already maintain such programs, especially for rare grassland plants.

Green infrastructure

Maryland's Green Infrastructure Assessment (Weber, 1999) is a tool being developed to help identify and prioritize areas in Maryland for conservation and restoration. It uses GIS technology to identify large, ecologically valuable areas (hubs) and a potential system of connecting corridors. These areas are further ranked according to their relative ecological importance, as

Table 1. Miles of transmission line ROWs in prominent watersheds within priority biodiversity hotspot areas of Maryland

SHEDNAME	MD8DIGIT	SHEDAREA (acres)	PH_AREA	TL_LENGTH (miles)	PROP_TL
Youghiogheny River	5020201	153543.0938	Western Maryland	79.2163	0.0516
Potomac River (Upper North Branch)	2141005	67064.1094	Western Maryland	22.4292	0.0334
Casselman River	5020204	58408	Western Maryland	22.2166	0.038
Savage River	2141006	74219.4375	Western Maryland	25.2341	0.034
Potomac River (Washington County)	2140501	58039.3789	Central Maryland	54.1642	0.0933
Potomac River (Montgomery County)	2140202	87914.2031	Central Maryland	19.2351	0.0219
Upper Monocacy River	2140303	155934.4844	Central Maryland	96.3069	0.0618
Zekiah Swamp	2140108	69725.3828	South Central Maryland	56.3833	0.0809
Patuxent River (Lower)	2131101	239273.6563	South Central Maryland	116.462	0.0487
West Chesapeake Bay	2131005	52661.4258	South Central Maryland	21.2185	0.0403
Lower Susquehanna River	2120201	24352.2813	Northern Chesapeake Bay	3.6047	0.0148
Nanticoke River	2130305	127292.6094	Southeastern Maryland	41.2175	0.0324
Lower Pocomoke River	2130202	100977.5938	Southeastern Maryland	32.8839	0.0326
Nassawango Creek	2130205	43780.1914	Southeastern Maryland	19.7759	0.0452
Chincoteague Bay	2130106	89009.1016	Southeastern Maryland	6.415	0.0072

PROP_TL is calculated as [tl_length/shedarea) * 100].
Maryland average [tl_length/state area) * 100 = 0.04033.

well as the potential risk of loss to development. Ranking is done on two scales: by entire hub or corridor and by individual cell (approximately a third of an acre). Two tiers of hubs are identified: those of statewide significance (at least 2000 ac) and smaller hubs (500–2000 ac) that may be of local concern. Counties or other local governments with little or no unprotected statewide core area might be interested in preserving these smaller ecological hubs. These would be linked by corridors to the statewide hub and corridor network. "Nodes" are patches of interior forest, wetlands, sensitive species areas, or protected areas along corridors. These serve as "stepping stones" for wildlife movement along corridors. Buffers around core areas are identified. Finally, gaps, which are developed, agricultural, or mined areas within ecological hubs, corridors, and nodes, are identified, and ranked for potential restoration.

While the results of the Phase Two Biodiversity Hotspots Project are limited to ecological conditions projected over the 138 watersheds in Maryland, the Green Infrastructure provides a landscape map based on 30-meter resolution land cover data. This finer scale allows PPRP to evaluate more subtle associations between transmission line ROWs and natural resource values (although they contain less information on the rare species composition of each area). In particular, PPRP can address forest fragmentation issues and identify locations where transmission line ROWs impacts to natural habitat corridors may be minimized. PPRP's current Greenlines Project (Perot et al., 2000) focuses on targeting ROW locations where compatible vegetation management can improve their condition as wildlife corridors. The Green Infrastructure provides the best ecological map for identifying critical gaps in contiguous habitat caused by ROWs.

The Greenlines Project has conducted spatial analysis to identify locations where transmission line ROWs intersect natural habitat corridors that are of local or state-wide importance as defined by the Green Infrastructure. Initially, GIS was used to find the intersection of transmission lines and habitat corridors, producing the base data set for subsequent analysis. The intersections identified in the spatial analysis were then visually evaluated to select sites that had less complex intersections and higher degrees of ecological importance. Intersections not meeting these qualitative attributes were removed from further consideration. The goal was to identify, in priority order, the transmission line ROW locations where enhanced vegetation management would effectively connect the most hub and corridor habitat.

The spatial analysis produced 19 transmission line ROW-habitat corridor intersections (Fig. 7). Sites were identified in 13 counties, with the greatest number (4 sites) in western Maryland's Garrett County. Other concentrations were in south-central Maryland (7 sites), northern Chesapeake Bay (7 sites), and southeastern Maryland (3 sites). This distribution corresponds well to the priority biodiversity hotspots identified using rare, threatened, and endangered species occurrences. This may be a result of greater ecological values in these areas and/or greater ROW densities, but nonetheless indicates that substantial opportunities exist to minimize ROW impacts and link contiguous habitat.

CONCLUSIONS

GIS-based spatial analysis can be an important tool for managing Maryland ROWs and supporting stewardship based on ecosystem principles. Within PPRP,

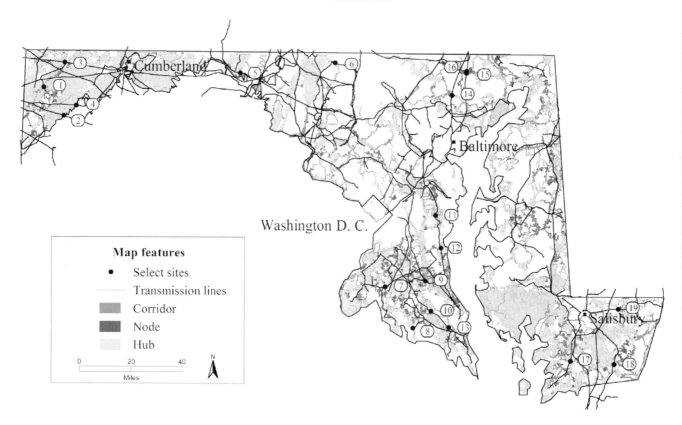

Fig. 7. Priority intersections of transmission line ROWs and gaps in the green infrastructure.

GIS is currently being used to improve impact evaluation of ROWs and better target ROWs for ecological restoration and planning. Specifically, the ROW Evaluation Method, while still in draft form, has the potential to expedite environmental reviews and build consensus among reviewers by providing standard data in an objective format. Both regulatory review agencies and electric utilities have shown an interest in this method. At the same time, it is important that the method not become a "black box" that confounds the evaluation of individual resource impacts by combining results into a single output. GIS-based spatial analysis is also being used by PPRP for restoration targeting of ROWs within priority biodiversity hotspots and green infrastructure landscapes. Electric utilities are being encouraged to focus their current land management efforts on these targeted ROWs to create habitat for rare, threatened, and endangered species, and to reduce fragmentation in large areas of contiguous habitat. Utilities may also seek environmental credits for ecologically friendly management or prospective buyers (e.g., conservation trust or government organizations) for surplus utility lands in targeted areas.

Maryland DNR will continue to develop these and other GIS-based tools for ROW management, so they can be used effectively by DNR, other agencies, and the electric utilities. In particular, the Transmission Line Data Base will be reviewed and updated as necessary and the biodiversity hotspots will be refined using GAP data. Where feasible the spatial analysis procedures and their GIS output will be made available to all interested parties, including other states.

ACKNOWLEDGMENTS

This work is supported by Maryland Department of Natural Resources Contract No. PR-96-055-001 to Versar, Inc., as the Biology Integrator for the Power Plant Research Program under the direction of Sandra Patty. The ecological data used in the research comes from many sources and we are indebted to them for their cooperation and support, including the Maryland DNR Monitoring and Non-Tidal Assessment Division (especially Ron Klauda, Paul Kazyak, and Scott Stranko), University of Maryland (especially Ray Morgan and Lenwood Hall), Heritage and Biodiversity Conservation Programs of DNR (especially Lynn Davidson, Ann Rasberry, and Glenn Therres), Watershed Management and Analysis Division (especially Bill Jenkins, John Wolf, and Ted Weber), and Geographic Information Service (especially Bill Burgess and Ken Miller). Information on the status and locations of transmission lines were obtained from the Maryland Public Service Commission and electric utility companies (BGE, SMECO, PEPCO, Allegheny Power, and DPL/Conectiv).

REFERENCES

Harriott, S., D. Strebel, and A. Brindley. 1997. A Quantitative Transmission Line Placement Methodology for the Maryland Department of Natural Resources' Power Plant Research Program — Phase I Report. Versar, Inc. for the Maryland Department of Natural Resources, Power Plant Research Program, Annapolis.

Maryland Department of Natural Resources (DNR) Ecosystem Council. 1996. Ecosystem-Based Management: Recommendations of the Ecosystem Council. Maryland Department of Natural Resources, Annapolis.

Noss, R.F. and A.Y. Cooperrider. 1994. Saving Nature's Legacy: Protecting and Restoring Biodiversity. Island Press, Washington, DC.

Perot, M., M. Southerland, and A. Brindley. 2000. Mitigating Cumulative Effects of Power Plants: Turning Transmission Lines into Greenlines. Draft report. Versar, Inc. for Maryland Department of Natural Resources, Power Plant Research Program, Maryland Department of Natural Resources, Annapolis.

Southerland, M.T., N.E. Roth, and G. Mercurio. 1999. Biodiversity Hotspots in Maryland: Provisional Targets for Conservation Management. Versar, Inc. for Power Plant Research Program, Maryland Department of Natural Resources, Annapolis.

Weber, T. 1999. Draft. Maryland's Green Infrastructure Assessment: An Ecological Framework for Land Protection and Restoration. Maryland Department of Natural Resources, Annapolis.

BIOGRAPHICAL SKETCHES

Dr. Mark Southerland (corresponding author)
Versar, Inc., 9200 Rumsey Road, Columbia, MD 21045, USA, Fax: 410-964-5156, southerlandmar@versar.com

As a senior ecologist with Versar, Inc., Dr. Mark Southerland has been supporting PPRP since 1993 on the use of integrative science to address the implications of power plant activities on ecosystems and landscapes. With 20 years of ecological research experience and 95 publications, Dr. Southerland has established himself as a national expert on biocriteria development (including Maryland streams and Hudson River Estuary) and ecological analysis under NEPA (preparing guidance and representing CEQ and EPA across the country).

Dr. Donald Strebel
Versar, Inc., 9200 Rumsey Road, Columbia, MD 21045, USA, Fax: 410-964-5156

Dr. Donald Strebel is a senior scientist and program manager at Versar, Inc. He has developed state-of-the-art scientific information systems to support numerous environmental projects for federal, state, and private clients.

Miss Allison Brindley
Versar, Inc., 9200 Rumsey Road, Columbia, MD 21045, USA, Fax: 410-964-5156

Miss Allison Brindley has over 13 years of experience providing support to environmental and ecological studies with Versar, Inc. As a GIS analyst, she contributes to projects with spatial analysis, decision support, graphic interpretation of environmental data, and data base management.

A. Morris Perot, Jr.
Versar, Inc., 9200 Rumsey Road, Columbia, MD 21045, USA, Fax: 410-964-5156, perotmor@versar.com

Mr. Morris Perot is an environmental scientist with Versar, Inc., and has 10 years of experience researching human impacts on aquatic and terrestrial ecosystems.

Sandra Shaw Patty
Power Plant Research Program, Department of Natural Resources, 580 Taylor Avenue, Tawes State Office Building, B-3, Annapolis, MD 21401, USA, 410-260-8668, spatty@dnr.state.md.us

Ms. Patty is an Energy Resources Manager for the Maryland Power Plant Research Program, in the Department of Natural Resources in Annapolis, Maryland, where she serves as the transmission program manager, responsible for conducting studies assessing all aspects of the electric transmission network in Maryland. Prior to joining PPRP, she was employed by Allegheny Power Service Corporation, now Allegheny Energy as an Environmental Analyst. Ms. Patty received her BS in Biology from California State College in 1973 and a Masters of Energy Resources from the University of Pittsburgh in 1983.

Using GIS for Right-of-Way Vegetation Maintenance and Landowner Notification

Craig Nyrose and Terry MacNeill

ATCO Electric Ltd. operates and maintains over 8600 km of transmission lines and associated rights-of-way. Effective vegetation management is key to ensuring that ATCO Electric's facilities are free of any potential hazard. The Forest Operations section is responsible for ensuring that proper limits are maintained between vegetation and electrical equipment, for both electrical transmission and distribution lines, and performs vegetation control on transmission lines according to a three year cycle. This work involves initial patrol, landowner notification, maintenance operations, and inspection. The effective utilization of vegetation maintenance and management information is critical to the success of their program, and it is important that this information be made available to field staff in a simple and effective way. The Forest Operations section, in association with Applied GeoProcessing Inc., has developed an innovative approach to managing and maintaining vegetation information. This approach uses GIS (Geographic Information Systems) technology to provide a simple, intuitive tool for its Forest Operations office and field staff. This paper provides an overview of the ATCO Electric's Vegetation Maintenance and Landowner Notification GIS application and includes a discussion of initial requirements, issues related to the development of the application, and the identification of benefits to the company and its customers.

Keywords: Geographic Information Systems

BACKGROUND

ATCO Electric Ltd. is an investor owned electric utility that provides service to over 160,000 customers in the southeastern and northern portions of the province of Alberta, Canada. The company operates and maintains over 8600 km of transmission lines and 80,000 km of distribution facilities. The effective management of vegetation within and around transmission rights-of-way is critical, in order to ensure that ATCO Electric's facilities are free of any potential hazards, and that they operate in a safe and reliable manner.

The company's Forest Operations section is responsible for ensuring that proper limits are maintained between vegetation and electrical equipment, for both transmission and distribution lines.

In support of its mandate, the Forest Operations section performs vegetation control on transmission lines according to a three year cycle. Activities related to the management of vegetation along electric transmission line rights-of-way include:

– Line patrols — during this activity ATCO Forest Operations staff or external contractors visit and examine the right of way and determine the appropriate vegetation management operations that are required. Typical operations include tree cutting, trimming or the application of herbicides by spraying. During the patrol, the forester completes a powerline tree survey report that identifies for each span, the existing conditions and the type of vegetation operation required. Additional items are noted, such as the presence of danger trees, beehives, organic farms, and other items that may affect the type of vegetation management operation that may be applied.
– Landowner notification — based on the line patrol, affected landowners and occupants are contacted to

Environmental Concerns in Rights-of-Way
Management: Seventh International Symposium
J.W. Goodrich-Mahoney, D.F. Mutrie and C.A. Guild (editors)
© 2002 Elsevier Science Ltd. All rights reserved.

notify them of planned vegetation management operations within and along the right of way. ATCO Forest Operations staff physically visit each property where operations will be performed. This includes lands were ATCO Electric has a registered interest (right-of-way), as well as adjoining lands. During this field visit, field staff update records related to landowner, occupant name, address, etc., and ownership status. A Landowner Notification form is completed which includes the types of operations that will be performed on the property, as well as any special conditions that may be specified by the landowner in order to obtain their approval to proceed. Typically, special conditions may require a modification to the original patrol recommendations. For example, selective tree trimming may be required in certain areas. The Landowner Notification form typically includes a sketch plan, showing the location of the property, other base information such as the location of access roads, buildings, streams, as well as the location of powerlines and poles. Prior to proceeding with any vegetation maintenance work, the landowners' signature or a verbal approval is required to indicate that they have been notified, and that they consent to the work that will be done on their property.

- Maintenance operations — this work is typically contracted on a line by line basis. Prior to initiating the work, bid packages are prepared and the work is tendered to several contractors that are capable of performing the vegetation maintenance work. The bid packages typically include the original patrol reports, landowner notification/permission forms, maps showing the line and property locations, as well as other supplementary data. This information forms the basis of a fixed price tender. Once awarded the work, the maintenance contractor performs the required operations on each property according to the information on the Landowner Notification/Permission form. If the actual work performed varies from that originally authorized, then a notation is required by the contractor indicating that a different operation was performed, and the reasons for doing so.

- Final inspection — this work is performed by ATCO Forest Operations staff, prior to the approval of the work done by the vegetation maintenance contractor. The inspector physically inspects the line to examine the work done by the contractor to ensure that it has been done according to specifications, as well as what was authorized and acknowledged by the landowner. During this activity, the inspector checks for compliance with information on the Landowner Notification/Permission form, as well as any modifications that may have been performed by the contractor. This final inspection forms the basis for the approval of the work by ATCO.

ISSUES ASSOCIATED WITH A "PAPER-BASED" SYSTEM

In the past, information related to these activities has been created, managed, and maintained using paper forms, hardcopy maps, and other documents. Issues associated with managing and maintaining this information in a 'paper-based' world included:

- Difficulties in storing, managing, and maintaining information — vegetation maintenance information was kept in large binders within numerous file cabinets. Multiple copies of patrol and other information may exist, with each having potentially different notations on them. Landowner Notification forms were typically stored in ATCO regional offices. Often, the regional offices would have different information than head office staff, due to the number of different copies of documents that were in circulation. A method to synchronize information collected at a regional level with information at head office was required. Changes to landowner and other information were only made on a line by line basis, according to the three year patrol cycle. Often, properties would contain more than one powerline, resulting in inconsistencies with basic landowner information.

- Difficulties in responding to landowner and occupant inquiries pertaining to past vegetation management operations on their property. In many cases, landowners may be applying to have their land organically certified and need to know whether herbicides had been applied and when the work was done. Responding to these inquiries often resulted in significant time and effort being expended to search and find documents due to problems associated with efficiently accessing information that is stored in binders, file cabinets, etc. Often this information was not readily available to other users within the company.

- Lack of integration between textual data and mapping information related to vegetation management operations. Typically map and textual data were maintained in different formats and stored in different physical locations, making it a difficult and time consuming task to geographically reference various operations that were performed along the right-of-way and adjoining properties. Landowner Notification forms contained sketch information that had to be manually re-drawn for each maintenance cycle. There was no direct link between vegetation management information and the electrical system maps, nor was there a way to effectively link to other base map data sources.

A NEW APPROACH TO MANAGING INFORMATION

To improve on operating efficiency and the utilization of information, the application of a custom GIS application was investigated. Applied GeoProcessing Inc.,

(AGP) provided the technical expertise to match the application to ATCO Electric's requirements. The objective was to create an application that was able to maintain vegetation management records in an easily accessible fashion, to directly link and utilize existing electrical system maps, provide direct access to aerial video footage, and produce custom forms and reports. It would also have to link other information such as herbicide application, base feature mapping, vegetation inventories, and company work standards. The application had to be usable from a laptop computer and be end user friendly.

APPLICATION COMPONENTS

Technology

The ATCO Electric Vegetation and Landowner Notification application was developed using the following software components:
- User interface — Visual Basic 6.0;
- Database — Microsoft Access;
- GIS — ESRI's MapObjects.

The application was developed to operate in the office and in the field running on a minimum configuration consisting of Pentium 166 MHz laptops, with 32 MB of RAM. The chosen operating system for the application is Windows 95/NT.

Textual data

Textual data is managed through a database implemented using Microsoft Access. The database manages and maintains patrol, notification, maintenance, and inspection information through related database tables. As vegetation operation data is entered into the application from line patrols, it is stored in both the patrol and notification database tables. During the notification stage, operation information may be modified based on input from landowners. Under these circumstances, the operations are modified in the affected notification tables only. The result is an "audit trail" of changes to operations through the various stages of the work process, from patrol to the work that was actually performed.

In order to ensure consistency between data stored and managed in head office and data that was maintained in the field, a custom database synchronization process was developed by AGP to manage updates and changes in the field through each project stage. This process extracts a field copy from the master database and flags these records as "out for update." After the data is returned from the field, prior to loading into the master database, a record by record matching process is initiated that detects new records, changed records, and deleted records. The process also identifies any data inconsistencies or conflicts and provides a mechanism for resolving them prior to updating the master database.

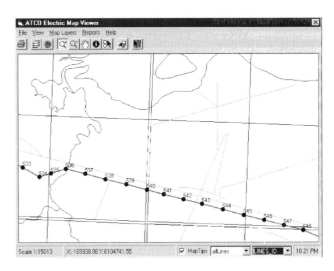

Fig. 1. Map viewer.

Map viewer

Patrol and notification information is accessed using simple to use map viewer (see Fig. 1). The viewer provides the capability for ATCO field and contract staff to quickly orient themselves by accessing a location by powerline and pole number, legal description, or by locating it in the map window. Patrol, vegetation operation or other data can then be entered in the appropriate textual forms.

The data managed by the application includes:
- Province of Alberta digital topographic and cadastral land base in Arc/Info, shape and Intergraph design file format;
- ATCO transmission facilities — this data includes pole and line locations determined to a 1 m accuracy using airborne GPS (Global Positioning System) technology, as well as associated video imagery in MPEG format;
- Map and sketch information entered by ATCO field staff. The application provides sketch and red-lining tools that provide the capability of adding user-defined features, such as buildings, streams, lakes, roads, danger trees, hot spots, etc.

Within the map viewer, the user has the capability of identifying and querying information about any geographic feature managed by the application. Using the red-line capabilities of the map viewer, ATCO field staff can add other features and sketch information. This information is stored with each project and can be used on subsequent projects. The sketch information is used by the application to create the detailed sketch component of the Landowner Notification form, thereby eliminating the need to manually re-draw the sketches for each property.

Video viewer

The map viewer also provides access to video imagery for each line in the transmission system. The user

Fig. 2. Video viewer.

has the option of interactively selecting a line and pole number using the map interface, or by simply keying it in. This activates a video viewer (see Fig. 2) which queues the image to the appropriate powerline and pole number. Video imagery is stored on CD-ROM, and is in MPEG format. The video viewer, in combination with the map viewer provides ATCO Electric staff with a simple and intuitive method to access line and right of way information as well as associated imagery, thereby reducing the number of potential trips to the field to verify information.

Textual data entry

The application provides a number of forms for the entry of textual information in support of vegetation maintenance and landowner notification. These forms include:
- A landowner information form — for the entry and maintenance of landowner name, address, phone number, ownership status, etc.
- A patrol information form — this form provides the capability to enter and edit operation, patrol notation, and patrol comments;
- A notification form — this form provides the capability to update and edit operation data, and to add landowner comments and conditions. Additional information pertaining to the status of permission or authorization to perform proposed vegetation management operations can also be managed.
- Status forms — various forms are available to indicate both contractor status (completed or not completed) and inspection status (approved or not approved) by property.

Reporting functions

Using the data managed and maintained by the textual and GIS databases, the application provides the capability to generate a number of standard forms and reports in support of ATCO's Forest Operations business. These reports can be generated either in the field or in head office and output to a standard laser or inkjet printer. In addition to the standard Landowner Notification form (on an individual property basis), various summary and statistical reports (on a line by line basis) can be generated as required. These reports include:
- Duplicate and problem landowners;
- Patrol summary reports — mechanical operations only, spray operations only, and special areas;
- Notification summary reports — mechanical operations, spray operations, etc.

BENEFITS

The implementation of this application for right of way vegetation maintenance operations and landowner notifications has resulted in the following benefits to ATCO Electric Ltd. They are:
- More effective management of information — data is available for field staff in a simple intuitive way for review and update. All data is managed and maintained in a central database repository that is updated using a sychronization process between the central database and field copies;
- All data is digital — this results in improved quality of information, the elimination of multiple copies, and reduced costs to manually photocopy and reproduce information;
- Improved integration of data — the application provides the capability to integrate and geo-reference vegetation maintenance and other information with provincial base mapping, ATCO system maps, imagery, and other geographic information;
- Improved availability of data — vegetation maintenance, landowner, and geographic data can be made available in digital form to other potential users within the company.

FUTURE PLANS

Future plans for this application include broadening its scope to include electrical distribution facilities in addition to transmission lines. Other enhancements include the addition of ad-hoc textual and map reports and the generation of digital documentation in support of the preparation of tender documents.

BIOGRAPHICAL SKETCHES

Craig Nyrose
 ATCO Electric Ltd., 1006 15 Ave, Nisku, Canada, T5K 2J6, ph. 780-955-6225, e-mail: craig.nyrose@atcoelectric.com

Craig Nyrose is a Utility Forester with ATCO Electric Ltd. He is a graduate of the University of Alberta in Forestry, 1985. He has worked with ATCO for over 15 years, as a brushing inspector and maintenance supervisor. He is responsible for the brushing operation and maintenance of over 88,000 km of powerline right of way in the Province of Alberta.

Terry MacNeill
 Applied GeoProcessing Inc., 10302 121 Street, Edmonton, Alberta, Canada, T5N 1K8, ph. 780-453-2292, e-mail: tmacneill@geoprocessing.com

Terry MacNeill is the President and senior consultant with Applied GeoProcessing Inc., an Edmonton, Alberta consulting company specializing in GIS projection management and implementation. He has over 25 years experience in GIS with clients in the government, utility and private sector.

GIS as a Tool to Address Environmental Issues in Rights-of-Way Planning and Management: The Example of Rural Road Networks

Dr. Ir. Catharinus F. Jaarsma[1] and Ir. Geert P.A. Willems

Planners must find a balance between maximising accessibility and minimising traffic impacts. Therefore, impacts of roads and their traffic on, for example, energy consumption, emissions, noise and habitat fragmentation for the fauna must be identified. This paper shows the opportunities of a GIS, developed for this purpose. To promote traffic safety, in the Netherlands a concentration of present diffuse traffic flows on minor roads within an area on a limited number of trunk roads is pursued. Several alternative network solutions may realise this concentration, each with its own impacts. The GIS enables both an overview per road link and on a regional scale. In a case study, energy consumption and emissions increased on a regional scale. Noise and habitat fragmentation decreased by concentration of traffic flows. Because of the impacts on habitat fragmentation strongly depend on the location within the region, both scales, regional and on the link level, should be taken into account. It is well known that a GIS is a powerful instrument in traffic planning. This paper shows that an enlargement in the wider context of environmental issues may be helpful to include such impacts in the rights-of-way planning and management of rural road networks.

Keywords: Minor rural roads, noise, emissions, ecology, modeling

INTRODUCTION

The road network is a form of land use, which planning strongly depends on other land uses. Simultaneously, all human land uses are strongly depending on this network. An accurate road network provides good accessibility, which leads to economic development and an efficient use of land resources.

Traffic flows showed a considerable growth, due to an increase of the prosperity and an increase of spare time. Nevertheless the present road network seems to be sufficient in industrialized, densely populated countries, at least from a quantitative point of view. However this is not the case from a qualitative point of view (Jaarsma, 1997). Many roads are no longer adapted to their current function. This leads to traffic accidents and higher costs for the road management due to damage of the verges and the road construction.

With expanding road networks in the recent past and increasing traffic flows also the effects of the networks and their traffic on the environment have increased. Although these effects sometimes can be positive (a verge can function as a corridor for some species), most effects are harmful and affect local people and the fauna. The question arises in which way these harmful effects can be reduced, without affecting accessibility. The impact of the harmful effects is related to the traffic volumes and the technical layout of the road and its verges. Moreover the structure of the road network plays an important role in the impact of harmful effects.

While a reduction of a harmful effect on one road link may cause new problems or enlarge existing problems on another neighboring road link one has to develop a comprehensive network approach on a regional scale. Therefore often several variants of road networks can be developed. These variants differ

---

[1] Corresponding author: Tel.: +31 317 482 050; fax: + 31 317 482 166; E-mail: rinus.jaarsma@users.rpv.wau.nl.

Environmental Concerns in Rights-of-Way Management: Seventh International Symposium
J.W. Goodrich-Mahoney, D.F. Mutrie and C.A. Guild (editors)
© 2002 Elsevier Science Ltd. All rights reserved.

in suitability for higher volumes and speeds. In this broad range of variants on one end very diffuse traffic flows are spread completely over the whole road network. On the other end traffic flows are concentrated at a few trunk roads. All these variants have got a different impact.

To find a balance between maximizing good accessibility and minimizing traffic disadvantages (especially environmental disadvantages) one needs a good overview of all possible effects for alternative variants of a rural road network. For this purpose Jaarsma and Kessels (1999) have developed the GIS-model ITEM. In this particular paper we will question if this model can be used as a helpful tool for road management especially with regards to environmental effects, like habitat fragmentation for the fauna, traffic emissions, noise disturbance, and fuel consumption.

In the next section we will give a brief introduction about general problems of minor rural roads. In section three we will discuss the concept of traffic calming. In the fourth section the GIS model ITEM will be discussed which can visualize different results of environmental effects for several variants. In section five the GIS model will be demonstrated with an example of a region, where the ITEM has been applied. The paper finishes with conclusions.

PROBLEMS OF MINOR RURAL ROADS (MRRS)

Many industrialized countries have a dense network of paved rural roads, which is intensively used by motorized traffic. The rural road network in the Netherlands can be distinguished into three categories: motorways (2200 km; dual carriageways with limited access), rural highways (7400 km; two lanes, with limited access) for other road-users (for instance prohibited for bicycles) and minor rural roads, MRRs (48,700 km; mostly one lane, unlimited access for all modes). Each category has its own function and specific technical layout. Related to this paper two types of problems of the rural road network appear: habitat fragmentation, and a low level of traffic safety.

Fig. 1 illustrates three adverse effects of roads and their traffic on species. Firstly the traffic on the road causes disturbance by noise, emissions and visual impacts. This decreases the quality of the habitat alongside the road. Secondly the road itself may act as a barrier. When the barrier is absolute, the original habitat is divided into two smaller parts by the road. Thirdly if animals can cross the road, they may get killed during the crossing of the road. Van der Fluit et al. (1990) call this the barrier effect of traffic.

Traditionally, research on habitat fragmentation for the fauna focuses on motorways. The heavy flows and broad construction of this type of roads can explain this. However it is evident that an animal, that crosses

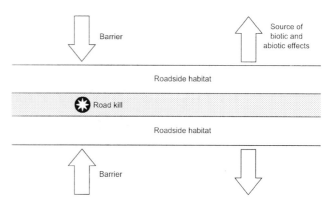

Fig. 1. Relationships between roads and their environment (Bennett, 1991).

the countryside will find much more MRRs than motorways on its way. Looking at their presence all over the rural area in combination with often considerable traffic flows, MRRs are a serious problem for a lot of species, especially smaller mammals and amphibians (Derckx, 1995; Van Apeldoorn and Kalkhoven, 1991). Moreover according Forman and Alexander (1998) the impact of acute disturbance by individual vehicles periodically passing on roads with little traffic (like MRRs) might be bigger than the impact of chronic disturbance along busy roads.

Traffic safety differs considerably between the three categories of road networks. Accident risks per kilometre on MRRs are a tenfold of those on motorways. Accident risks on rural highways are in between. The policy of the Dutch national government is to reduce the amount of traffic kills with 50% in 2010 compared to 1986 (Wegman, 1997). To achieve this goal, several traffic measures are necessary.

Traditionally, the assignment of road functions and the resulting technical lay-out are implicitly based on appearing or planned traffic flows. In practice, this frequently requires relatively high technical standards for minor rural roads. As a result, diffuse flows of through traffic are spread all over the rural area. Fig. 2(A) illustrates this phenomenon. Through traffic on local access roads may conflict with local bound traffic, including slow vehicles, such as bicycles and agricultural vehicles. Because of the high risk of traffic accidents on MRRs, it is better to concentrate traffic flows on a limited number of roads with a more suitable design. To achieve this, roads with a function for through flows are upgraded, if their present layout is insufficient. This means adjustment to higher volumes and/or speeds by, for example, road widening or construction of bicycle paths. The other way around is also possible. If a road with only a local access function is too well equipped for its function, this may lead to unwanted use. To avoid this one can decide to downgrade the road, for example by road narrowing or removing junctions. Fig. 2(B) shows the traffic flows after such a combination of upgrading (the rural highways around the region) and downgrading (the MRRs within the region).

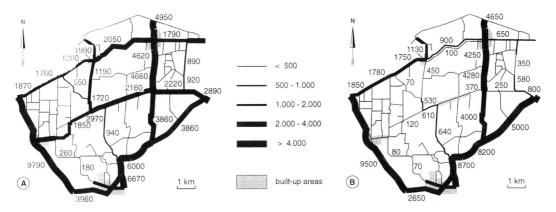

Fig. 2. Average annual daily traffic (AADT) in the Ooststellingwerf area in (A) autonomous and (B) planned situation (TCRA) (Jaarsma et al., 1995).

To avoid rat-run traffic and causing new traffic problems at other places, one has to look at a regional scale to the complete road network. The concept of "Traffic Calmed Rural Area" (TCRA) seems suitable for this purpose (Jaarsma and Van Langevelde, 1997).

THE CONCEPT OF THE 'TRAFFIC CALMED RURAL AREA' (TCRA)

The concept of TCRA has been developed to improve traffic safety. Traffic calming refers to the adaptation of existing road layouts in urban areas in order to reduce the speed of vehicles travelling through areas where they are likely to come into conflict with other road users (Macpherson, 1993). The concept of the TCRA transfers these ideas from built-up areas to the rural area (Jaarsma, 1997). The underlying idea is a clear separation between space for living and staying (for inhabitants and recreationists, but also for local fauna) and space for traffic flows (Jaarsma and Van Langevelde, 1997).

This concept uses the principles of "sustainable safety," a road traffic system adapted to the limitations of human capacity. A proper road design and properly educated, informed and controlled road users must contribute to these principles (Wegman, 1997).

The TCRA-concept tries to regulate traffic flows instead of to follow them. The region will be surrounded and be accessible by rural highways with a flow function for through traffic, on which traffic flows will be concentrated (as in Fig. 2). Within the region roads will mainly have an access function for rural bound traffic, with a belonging modest technical layout. In this way one wants to achieve lower traffic flows and lower speeds on these roads and create a kind of rural residential area within the region (Jaarsma, 1997). This will increase traffic safety.

The concept however has got much more impacts than at traffic safety alone. It also affects the accessibility of the region, habitat fragmentation and other environmental effects. To be able to choose the best variant of the road network all these (environmental) effects have to be known.

THE "INTEGRAL TRAFFIC EFFECT MODEL" (ITEM)

To evaluate all possible effects of different variants of a road network the "Integral Traffic Effect Model" (ITEM) has been developed. In this paper we will only focus on the impact of environmental effects (noise pollution, fuel consumption, traffic emissions and habitat fragmentation). However with this model also other effects can be calculated like the capacity of the road, related to the actual traffic volume, accessibility and traffic safety.

Explanation of the model in general

With the ITEM physical relationships between traffic volumes and speeds of rural traffic flows and their environmental impacts are visualized with a GIS for each link in a regional road network. By adding all these particular links one can obtain the total environmental impacts at a regional scale. This provides a tool to compare different variants by repeating this process for alternative road network solutions.

The ITEM — model can be divided into three parts. In the first part of the model the input of the network variants takes place. Input data, such as traffic volumes, road widths and prohibition orders have to be known for each variant. Moreover the road sections in the present situation or autonomous development have to be present in a digitized version. Either the present situation or the autonomous development can be used as reference for a comparison of the different variants (Jaarsma and Kessels, 1999). The second part of the model consists of the calculations of the effects for each variant. Based on the input data and by users specified variables different effects can be measured, like environmental effects. In the final part the results of the calculations can be presented, either in a map or in a table. The results can be presented for one specific variant, but one can also make a comparison with the present situation or the autonomous development.

Explanation of calculation-methods of environmental effects

The calculation of environmental effects of different variants of a road network in ITEM is based on several formulae. In this section we briefly discuss the calculation of these environmental effects. Kessels (1998) gives a more extended description and formulae. Section 4.3 gives an overview of the effects and their explaining variables.

Noise pollution

Traffic flows inevitable produce noise. Depending on the nearness of noise-sensitive functions and objects problems will arouse. By changing traffic flows the impact of the noise pollution can change. This impact depends on:
1. the noise emission by motor vehicles, depending on engine characteristics, traffic volume, speed and composition by mode (cars, trucks and motorbikes);
2. the interaction between tire and road, depending on road surface material (brick paved roads cause more noise than asphalt);
3. the transfer of noise between road and observation point, depending on sound reduction (by soil and air) and reflecting objects (walls, screens and/or buildings close to the road).

The Dutch Traffic Pollution Law distinguishes two critical noise levels. In especially designated silence areas no noise levels above 35 or 40 dB(A) may occur. In attention areas (situated around noise distributors, like roads) special attention is given to noise sensitive buildings (like houses, college-buildings and hospitals). Finally outside these zones there is the "normal" noise level, which may not exceed 50 dB(A).

Calculations of the noise effects of different traffic flows are based on a standard method, introduced by the Dutch Ministry of Public Health and Environment. By taking into account the traffic characteristics, road characteristics and the transfer of noise (mentioned above) the noise-load contour (40 or 50 dB(A)) can be determined in an iteration process. The final results can be presented in a map with the noise load contour or in a table with the total acreage of the noise load contour (Jaarsma and Kessels, 1999).

Fuel consumption and traffic emissions

Change of traffic flows and speed limits changes fuel consumption and traffic emissions, like CO_2, CO, C_xH_y, and NO_x. These emissions contribute to acidification (NO_x), global warming (CO_2) or can be harmful for the public health (CO, C_xH_y). While traffic emissions are strongly related to the fuel consumption both calculation methods are discussed together.

The traffic speed and the road-dynamic (amount of (un)disturbed driving conditions by more or less de- and accelerating of vehicles) are the most important determinants for fuel consumption (Kessels, 1998). Road-dynamic will be lower on roads with constant speeds, which mostly occurs on major roads. This seems not the case for minor rural roads. According to Förster (1980) an average speed of approximately 80 km/h would be the optimal speed in terms of fuel consumption. The fuel consumption and the road-dynamic together with the traffic volumes form the input of the model, which calculates the fuel consumption and traffic emissions.

The calculation method of fuel consumption and traffic emissions of cars and trucks is based on the Versit-model developed by TNO (Van Helden, 1995). With some system parameters (like vehicle weight and several kinds of resistance) the model can calculate the driving energy for each road link. Next, the model calculates the fuel consumption ($MJ\,km^{-1}$) and the emissions of CO, NO_x, and C_xH_y ($g\,km^{-1}$). Finally, the total fuel consumption and emissions on a road link can be calculated by multiplying fuel consumption and emission of one car/truck with traffic volumes and the length of the road link.

While fuel consumption varies according the fuel type, the fuel consumption for the whole region can not automatically be obtained. For this reason the fuel consumption has to be converted into the energy-consumption with the fuel-density.

Habitat fragmentation for the fauna

To calculate habitat fragmentation by the road and its traffic different methods can be used. Jaarsma and Willems (2000) discuss some methods taking the road as starting point (road-density, mesh-size and continuous landscape unit sizes). Here we will discuss three methods, which are more suitable for GIS. This type of methods takes the traffic as point of view for looking at the issue.
1. Traffic performance (expressed in vehicle kilometres a day, $vh\,km\,day^{-1}$). This is simply a product of the length of a road link with the traffic volumes. This method can be improved by making a distinction between the three categories of roads (motorways, rural highways and MRRs). A further improvement would be to take into account the relevance of a road (only roads above certain AADT, and/or roads crossing ecological corridors).
2. Traversability of a road. This can be calculated with the crossing formula, which calculates the probability of successful road crossing for a species. The crossing formula is based on pedestrian traffic. It assumes that a road crossing of an animal will be successful if an "acceptable" gap in the traffic flow appears at the start of the crossing (Van Langevelde and Jaarsma, 1997). With this formula one can calculate the crossing risk of roads and traffic for animals and their mortality-effect. The chance of a successful crossing depends on the characteristics of the species, the road and its traffic. According the size and speed of the animal and the width of the road one can calculate the crossing-time. Next,

with the (Poison-distributed) traffic flow one can calculate the chance of a successful crossing of a roadlane. This leads automatically to the chance of a roadkill by a car accident. Once you multiply this with the amount of crossings for the road section the amount of roadkills can be calculated. To be able to make a comparison and judge different variants finally one can calculate the relatively change of the traversability. Only looking at roads above a certain AADT, and/or crossings with ecological corridors can refine this method.

3. Noise-load contour. In this method zones are determined with a noise load above the critical value (40–50 dB(A)). After concentrating traffic on main roads the size of these zones will decrease in terms of percentages. Calculations of this noise-load contour are already discussed before.

An overview of the environmental effects and their determinants

In Table 1 we present an overview of the environmental effects discussed in the previous sections. We make a distinction between determinants related to traffic and related to the road itself. Traffic determinants are volume, speed and composition by mode (cars, trucks or motorbikes). Road determinants can be distinguished by the road network category (motorway, rural highway or MRR), the pavement width and the surface (bricks, asphalt, concrete).

Traffic volume is a determinant for all environmental effects. In planned situations volumes per road link will adjust by applying measurements. Because this can have big environmental effects, the impacts of traffic regulation have to be considered in advance. ITEM is developed for this purpose.

ITEM: AN APPLICATION IN NOORD-LIMBURG WEST

Introduction

To demonstrate ITEM we discuss the example of a region situated in the northern part of Limburg, a southern province of the Netherlands (see Fig. 3). Its acreage is about 180 km². It consists of three municipalities (Horst, Sevenum, and Venray), with approximately 65,000 inhabitants. The study area is bounded on the east by the A73 and on the south by the A67, both motorways. The western boundary is the N277 and the northern boundary is the N270, both national rural highways.

The Provincial Mobility Plan of Limburg aims at a concentration of diffuse traffic flows on trunk roads (motorways and rural highways). For this purpose two network variants are developed (see Fig. 4). For both variants, the intended function of each road link is specified. To achieve a concentration of motorised traffic on the bounding trunk roads, within the study area speed reducing measures are taken (from 80 to 60 or sometimes even 40 km h^{-1}), depending on the road function. Variant 1 is primarily based on safety concerns and aims for a nearly total concentration of flows on trunk roads. Variant 2 allows for flows on a limited number of MRRs within the study area, connecting villages and hamlets with the trunk roads. As a result of this concentration, not only traffic volumes but also environmental effects will change. The ITEM identifies these "new" effects. By comparing the results of each variant, the user can make a proper selection out of the variants. Table 2 and the Figs. 5–8 in paragraph 5.2, adapted from Jaarsma and Hoogeveen (1999), present the overall results. Table 2 shows the calculated relative impacts for the variants 1 and 2 in relation to the present situation. The Figs. 6–8 present for one or both variants the relative alteration of an environmental impact, in respect to the present situation. An alteration of +60% (class +50–+100%) means an increase of this particular environmental effect on that specific road link with 60% compared to the present situation.

RESULTS

In the planned situations the speeds on several roads within the region are reduced (Fig. 4). This changes traffic flows, because drivers try to avoid roads with lower speed limits. In this way people are forced to use surrounding trunk roads, where traffic flows will concentrate. This increases traffic performance with 8.1% in variant 1 and with 6.9% in variant 2. This also leads to several environmental effects, which will be discussed below.

Noise pollution

The new calculated noise load contours of 40 and 50 dB(A) do not show big differences between both

Table 1. Environmental aspects and their determinants

	Traffic related			Related to the road		
	Volume	Speed	Composition	Category	Width	Surface
Noise pollution	X	X	X			X
Fuel consumption and traffic emissions	X	X	X	X		X
Traversability	X				X	

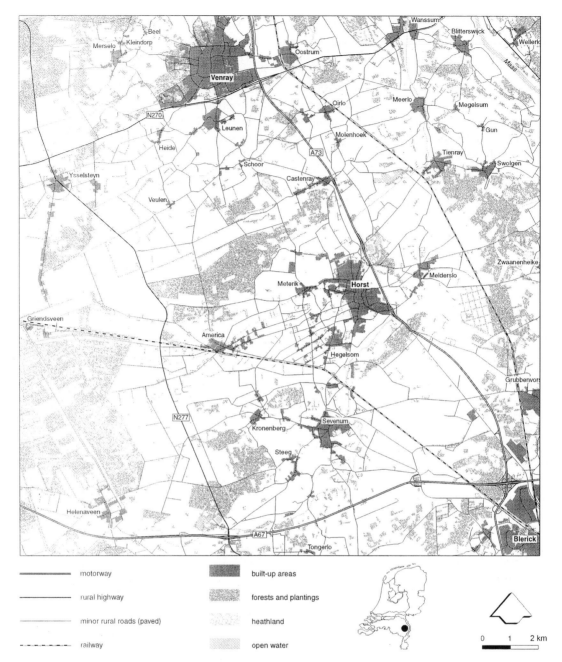

Fig. 3. The study area Noord-Limburg West (Jaarsma and Hoogeveen, 1999).

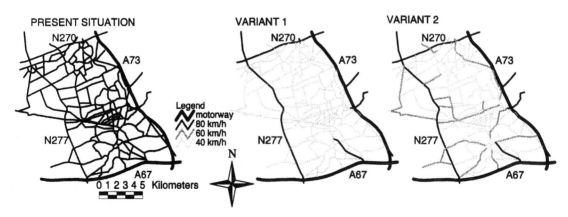

Fig. 4. The differences in road category between the present situation and variant 1 and 2 (Jaarsma and Kessels, 1999).

Table 2. Relative impacts in relation to the present situation for the variants 1 and 2 — an overview

	Present situation	Variant 1	Variant 2
Vehicle kilometrage	100 (454×10^3 vh km day^{-1})	108.1	106.9
Noise load			
≥ 40 dB(A)	100 (1.58 km^2)	98.7	97.6
≥ 50 dB(A)	100 (0.49 km^2)	99.0	97.9
Fuel consumption	100 (6.431×10^3 MJ day^{-1})	106.6	104.8
Emission			
CO	100 (272 kg day^{-1})	110.5	107.1
C_xH_y	100 (83 kg day^{-1})	109.0	106.2
NO_x	100 (769 kg day^{-1})	107.6	105.4
Traversability for the fauna[a]			
roe deer	100[b]	78.9	82.0
badger	100	78.8	81.9
toad	100	80.8	76.7

[a]Expressed by the change of a roadkill within the traffic calmed rural area, excluding through traffic on the surrounding rural highways and motorways.
[b]For traversability only relative numbers are availabe.

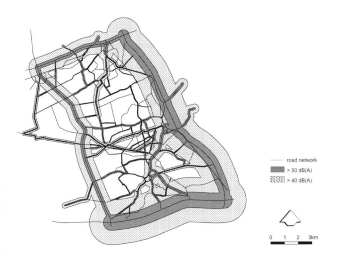

Fig. 5. Noise load contours in variant 1.

variants. For this reason only variant 1 will be shown (see Fig. 5). From Table 2 we conclude the impact on noise pollution of new speed limits and resulting new traffic flows is in variant 1 less extended than in variant 2. Compared to the present situation, especially in the central part of the study area (mainly access roads) zones with high noise levels decrease substantially, while it just slightly increases at the border of the study area (trunk roads). This can be explained as follows. The width of a zone hardly increases when already present high volumes further increase, which is the case on trunk roads. When, on the contrary, lower volumes on access roads drastically reduce by the concentration of flows on the trunk roads, a considerable reduction of the zone appears. Therefore, a concentration of traffic flows is advisable.

Fuel consumption
Fig. 6 illustrates the alteration of the fuel consumption of both variants compared with the present situation for each road section. In variant 2 this consumption is lower than in variant 1. This can be explained by the proposed speed limits. In both variants the speed limit on the minor rural roads is reduced. In variant 1 the reduction is more extended (from 80 to 40 km h^{-1}) than in variant 2 (from 80 to 60 or 40 km h^{-1}), see also Fig. 4. Because of this the increase of the fuel consumption in variant 2 is lower than in variant 1, see also Table 2. For this aspect visualisation of the alteration on the level of a road section is not necessary. It is more interesting to see the overall results of the alteration within the whole region, as presented in Table 2.

Traffic emissions
The increase in fuel consumption of a motor vehicle, caused by lower speed limits, induces higher CO and C_xH_y emissions and lower NO_x emissions. From Table 2 it can be concluded that for the total emissions also NO_x emissions increase in both variants. This can be explained by the increase in the total travelled distance. This compensates the originally decrease of the NO_x-emission of one vehicle due to lower speeds. Nevertheless almost half of the NO_x-emissions are produced by heavy traffic and NO_x-emissions occur more easily with high speeds, as on motorways. So, demonstration of this emission is not particular appropriate for this study area with mostly MRRs.

Only with high traffic volumes problems can be expected for the air pollution. Based on the European Pollution Norm, a critical volume occurs for CO at 12,000 vehicles a day. For C_xH_y problems will already occur with a traffic volume of 5000 vehicles a day. For

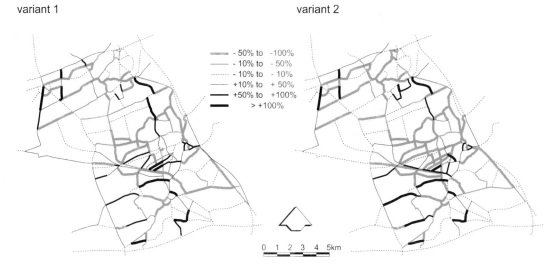

Fig. 6. Relative alteration of fuel consumption in variant 1 and 2 in respect to present situation.

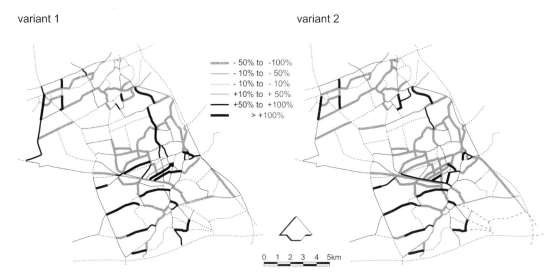

Fig. 7. Relative alteration of C_xH_y emission of variant 1 and 2 in respect to present situation.

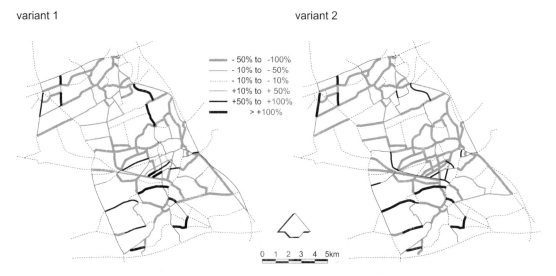

Fig. 8. Relative alteration in traversability for the roe deer in variant 1 and 2 in respect to present situation.

this reason in Fig. 7 the alteration in C_xH_y-emission is presented for both variants. Besides this figure doesn't differ much from the alteration in CO-emissions for the region, although the CO-emission in absolute numbers is higher.

Visualisation on the level of a road section is more interesting for the alteration of emissions than for the fuel consumption. This is especially the case when sensitive functions are present in the area.

Habitat fragmentation for the fauna
For the effects on habitat fragmentation three calculation methods were discussed in Section 4.2. Here we will mainly focus on the results for the traversability. The increase in vehicle kilometrage in both variants does not necessarily lead to new habitat fragmentation problems. Traffic flows will concentrate on the edge of the study area. So, within the region more quiet areas will occur. (This was also the conclusion after analysing the new noise load contours.) For some smaller species this can be very positive, because their relatively small habitat maybe can be extended.

In this application traversability is expressed by the alteration in the chance of road kills for three different species: the toad (*Bufo bufo*), the badger (*Meles meles*) and the roe deer (*Capreolus capreolus*). It is not possible (yet) to take into account in ITEM mitigating measures, such as fences, which will be erected around motorways. We therefore in Table 2 present the traversability data for the traffic calmed rural area only. One can conclude that here the traversability shows a considerable increase. Differences between both variants are small.

An increasing traversability means a decreasing number of road kills. This is illustrated in Fig. 8 for the roe deer. For the traversability a presentation of the alteration of traversability on the level of a single road section is relevant due to occurring species and nature areas or corridors.

An overview of the environmental impacts

The case study shows an increase of the emissions and energy consumption, mostly caused by the increase in travel distance and kilometers. Looking within the traffic calmed region, traversability increases evidently. The slight decrease in the overall **noise** pollution in both variants is another positive environmental effect. These conclusions hold for a regional scale. The effects on the level of a single road link sometimes can be contrary.

DISCUSSION AND FINAL CONCLUSIONS

While maximising accessibility often also involves an increase of negative environmental impacts by roads and its traffic it is necessary to find a good balance between the accessibility and environmental sustainability. In order to make proper management decisions for roads a comparison of all possible effects of different variants of a road network is required. In this paper we demonstrated ITEM can be a useful tool to visualise several environmental effects for alternative road networks, despite it is still in development.

The impacts for both variants in the case study presented in this paper only show slight differences. This is an important conclusion, because of the big differences in accessibility between both variants. It is possible to serve the environment in the study area, without disadvantaging accessibility too much.

Concluding, concentration of diffuse rural traffic flows on trunk roads to improve safety has got several environmental effects. Some of these effects contribute to a better environment, but there are also harming effects. ITEM visualises these effects on both a regional scale and on the level of a single road link. This facilitates a deeper understanding of the effects and so a better process of decision making in rights-of-way planning and management for rural road networks.

REFERENCES

Bennett, A.F. 1991. Roads, roadsides and wildlife conservation: A review. In: Nature Conservation 2: The Role of Corridors. Saunders, D.A. and R.J. Hobbs, eds. Surrey Beatty & Sons Pty Limited, Chipping Norton (Australia): pp. 99–116.

Derckx, H. 1995. Dassen op weg. (Badgers on their way.) Landschap, 12: 39–44. (in Dutch).

Forman, R.T.T. and L.E. Alexander. 1998. Roads and their major ecological effects. Annual Reviews Ecological Systems, 29: 207–231.

Förster, H.J. Der Einfluss der Strasse auf den Krafstoffverbrauch (The influence of the road on fuel consumption). Strasse und Autobahn, 31: 51–63 (In German).

Jaarsma, C.F. 1997. Approaches for the planning of rural road networks according to sustainable land use planning. Landscape and Urban Planning, 39(1): 47–54.

Jaarsma, C.F. and A. Hoogeveen. 1999. Pilotstudie bundeling autoverkeer. Realiseringsmogelijkheden en effecten van een samenhangend Duurzaam Veilig infrastructuur-concept in Noord-Limburg West (Pilotstudy possibilities and effects of an integral infrastructure concept "Sustainable safety" in the study area Noord-Limburg West). Nota vakgroep Ruimtelijke Planvorming nr. 76, Wageningen (in Dutch).

Jaarsma, C.F. and J.C.H.M. Kessels. 1999. Environment and rural roads: A GIS supported integral planning. International Conference on Agricultural Engineering AgEng Oslo 98, Oslo (N), 24–27 August 1998, CD-ROM: pdf\g\98–G-010.pdf (9 pp).

Jaarsma, C.F., J.O.K. Luimstra, and T.J. De Wit. 1995. De kortste weg naar een verkeersleefbaar platteland. Onderzoek ruraal verblijfsgebied Ooststellingwerf (The shortest way to a livable rural area. A traffic and transportation plan for a residential rural area in Ooststellingwerf). Nota vakgroep Ruimtelijke Planvorming 58, Wageningen (in Dutch).

Jaarsma, C.F. and F. Van Langevelde. 1997. Right-of-way Management and habitat fragmentation: an integral approach with the spatial concept of the Traffic Calmed Rural Area. IN: 6th International Symposium Environmental Concerns in Rights-of-way Management, New Orleans (LA), 24–26 February. Elsevier Science, pp. 383–392.

Jaarsma, C.F. and G.P.A. Willems. 2000. Fragmentation and landuse planning: reducing the role of minor rural roads. Third

International Workshop on Sustainable Land Use Planning. Fragmentation and land use planning: analysis and beyond, Wageningen University, the Netherlands, June 19–21. CD-ROM: papers\pdf\d4JAARSMA.pdf (12 pp).

Kessels, J.C.H.M. 1998. IVEM: Het integrale verkeers effect model. Een eerste invulling voor het kwantificeren en visualiseren van verkeerseffecten, met een toepassing in Noord-Limburg (ITEM: The integral traffic effect model). Wageningen Universiteit. 70 pp (in Dutch).

Macpherson, G. 1993. Highway and transportation engineering and planning. Longman, Harlow, UK. 385 pp.

Van Apeldoorn, R. and J. Kalkhoven. 1991. De relatie tussen zoogdieren en infrastructuur: de effecten van habitatfragmentatie en verstoring (The relation between mammals and infrastructure: the effects of habitatfragmentation and disturbance). Intern rapport 91/22. Rijksinstituut voor Natuurbeheer, Leersum. (in Dutch).

Van der Fluit, N., R. Cuperus, and K.J. Canters. 1990. Mitigerende en compenserende maatregelen aan het hoofdwegennet voor het bevorderen van natuurwaarden (Mitigating en compensating measures of the road network to stimulate ecological values). CML mededelingen 65, Centrum voor Milieukunde, Rijksuniversiteit, Leiden, 98 pp. (in Dutch).

Van Helden, M. 1995. Modelbeschrijving/gebruikershandleiding Versit Versie 1.0) (Users manual Versit Version 1.0). TNO wegtransportmiddelen, Delft (in Dutch).

Van Langevelde, F., and C.F. Jaarsma. 1997. Habitat fragmentation, the role of minor rural roads and their traversability. In: K.J. Canters, A. Piepers, and D. Hendriks-Heersma, eds. Habitat fragmentation & infrastructure. Proceedings of the international conference "Habitat Fragmentation, infrastructure and the role of ecological engineering," Maastricht/The Hague, 17–21 September 1995: pp. 171–182.

Wegman, F. 1997. The concept of a sustainably safe road traffic system. A new vision for road safety policy in The Netherlands. SWOV-report D-97-2. Netherlands Institute for Road Safety Research, Leidschendam, The Netherlands.

BIOGRAPHICAL SKETCHES

Catharinus Freerk (Rinus) Jaarsma

Wageningen University and Research Centre, Department for Environmental Sciences, Land Use Planning Group, Generaal Foulkesweg 13, 6703 BJ Wageningen, the Netherlands, Telephone +31-317-482050, Fax +31 317 482166, e-mail: rinus.jaarsma@users.rpv.wau.nl

Rinus Jaarsma is a senior lecturer at the Wageningen University, Land Use Planning Group. He investigates rural road and traffic planning for several types of land use. The improvement of traffic safety is an important motive for this research. For this purpose the urban concept of Traffic Calming was introduced in rural areas. Growing attention for environmental aspects and habitat fragmentation have given new impulses to rural traffic research, within the wider perspective of environmental circumstances.

Geert P.A. Willems

Wageningen University and Research Centre, Department for Environmental Sciences, Land Use Planning Grou, Generaal Foulkesweg 13, 6703 BJ Wageningen, the Netherlands, Telephone +31-317-482050, Fax +31 317 482166, e-mail: geert.willems@guests.rpv.wau.nl

Geert Willems graduated in Land Use and Spatial Planning at Wageningen University in 1999. In 2000 he joined the Land Use Planning Group of Wageningen University as a research fellow. His research focuses on the ecological, environmental and safety impacts of infastructure in the rural areas.

Innovative Airborne Inventory and Inspection Technology for Electric Power Line Condition Assessments and Defect Reporting

Mark Ostendorp

A cost-effective and innovative airborne inventory and inspection patrol system for distributed assets such as transmission lines, pipelines, and roadways has been developed and evaluated. Results show that aerial high-resolution digital visual and spectral images tagged by Global Positioning Satellite (GPS) coordinates can be successfully used to cost-effectively identify the majority of conditions/defects on electric power lines. Experiments show that the condition and defect detection rate of the airborne inventory and inspection system is significantly higher than rates derived from traditional aerial patrols and comparable to values achieved from driving patrols. Geographic Information Systems (GIS) based mapping tools can be used to quickly and efficiently interpret digital images collected from aerial platforms. Digital images provide an archival record of the condition of the distributed assets to estimate the long-term performance of the assets and to define cost-effective maintenance and replacement schedules.

Keywords: Aerial patrol, inventory, inspection, condition, defect, assessment, GPS, GIS, digital images, digital video

INTRODUCTION

Traditionally, electric utilities use a combination of aerial patrol, walking/driving line patrol, climbing or bucket truck inspection, and detailed aerial inspection to inspect their assets at regular intervals. In the past, high-speed aerial patrols have shown to be ineffective in detecting all but the larger line defects, such as right-of-way-encroachments and breakage of major components. While the high speed (100–160 km/h) at which these aerial patrols are conducted results in a relatively low per mile cost, it also makes the recognition of smaller conditions extremely difficult or impossible. Contrary to the traditional high speed aerial patrols, detailed aerial patrols from rotary winged airframes at low speeds (2–15 km/h) are effective in detecting a noticeable number of line defects but may be cost prohibitive in most remote areas. Based on experiments performed by the Electric Power Research Institute [Stewart et al., 1995(a,b)] on a number of electric power lines, either of the traditional airborne inspection methods, when normalized with respect to the cost, resulted in comparable ratios of cost per condition/defect.

Recent advances in digital video and still image technology coupled with new developments in high speed, high-resolution, visual geographic imagery, and photogrammetry, make it now possible to conduct Computer Aided Mass Surveying (CAMS) of distributed installations such as transmission lines, pipe lines, and road ways in remote areas. Additionally, recent improvements to Global Positioning Systems (GPS) and Inertial Navigation Systems (INS) allow images to be tagged with accurate location and camera angle information.

Each frame of the digital images and videos can be tagged using corrected values from the airframe's Differentially Corrected Global Positioning System (DGPS). Based on the capability and accuracy of the on board system, images and individual video frames can be spatially located without requiring the collected data to be post-processed or spatially corrected. Consequently, distributed assets such as transmission lines

Environmental Concerns in Rights-of-Way
Management: Seventh International Symposium
J.W. Goodrich-Mahoney, D.F. Mutrie and C.A. Guild (editors)
© 2002 Elsevier Science Ltd. All rights reserved.

are mapped while high-resolution digital images are collected for subsequent in-office evaluation and interpretation [Ostendorp et al., 1998 and 1999(b)].

The integration of high-resolution, digital imagery from an aerial patrol in the utility's inventory and inspection process, as suggested in this paper, combines the advantages of the traditional fast fly-by aerial inspection patrols with the advantages of the more labor-intensive walking/driving inspections or more costly detailed aerial patrols. The use of DGPS tagged high-resolution digital images provides an inspection process with a condition/defect detection rate similar to the rate achieved by traditional walking/driving or detailed aerial patrols at a significant reduction in cost.

Based on comparisons [Stewart et al., 1995(a,b)] developed for electric power lines located in the United States, the airborne patrol method presented in this paper is ~40–60% less expensive than the detailed aerial patrol commonly used for electric power line inspections. Similarly, experiments performed in the United States comparisons [Stewart et al., 1995(a,b)] show that the aerial patrol method presented in the paper is ~30–50% less expensive than the traditional walking/driving inspection.

It should be noted that the cost reductions presented in this paper assume that the transmission lines are located on the North American Continent, that the electric power lines mostly traverse rural/remote terrain rather than metropolitan areas, and that incidental cost for materials and labor are comparable to United States standards. Significantly lower labor rates are likely to reduce the cost difference between the presented airborne patrol method and traditional walking/driving inspections. However, the relative cost difference between detailed aerial inspections and the presented method remains unaffected by different cost for materials and labor.

BACKGROUND

Traditionally, high-speed aerial transmission line inspections have been conducted by either fixed or rotor winged airframes staffed by a team of three people, the pilot, the inspector, and the recorder. The effectiveness of these inspections in determining damage conditions and defects has generally been rated low [Stewart et al., 1995(a,b)]. Consequently, high-speed aerial patrols have typically only been used to identify the most visible (i.e., of sufficient size and severity) conditions on transmission lines.

Recognizing the advantages and disadvantages associated with the traditionally used fast fly-by and detailed aerial inspection methods, EPRI [Ostendorp, 1999(a) and 2000] members promoted the development of a more cost-effective (i.e., based on cost per condition/defect) airborne inspection method for the inventory and inspection of electric power lines. It was anticipated that the development of an improved aerial inspection system would lower the overall cost of the inspection, improve the quality of the data collected, and facilitate the 'just-in-time' replacement of components to optimize the cost of preventive maintenance. Based on this premise, EPRI developed and evaluated the airborne inventory and inspection system presented in this paper.

OBJECTIVES

The objectives of the project were to identify, develop, and evaluate an airborne inventory and inspection system capable of acquiring DGPS tagged high-resolution digital images. More specifically, the objectives were:
– To develop an airborne inventory and inspection system capable of acquiring DGPS tagged digital visual and spectral high-resolution still images at high speeds and low altitude.
– To develop an airborne inventory and inspection system capable of acquiring DGPS tagged digital visual and spectral videos at high speeds and low altitude.
– To identify and evaluate currently available GIS based image processing and manipulation tools to cost-effectively interpret high-resolution digital images and video from high-speed aerial patrols to perform an In-Office Inspection.
– To identify and evaluate the digital visual and spectral image resolution required for the correct recognition and assessment of standard transmission line components and associated conditions and/or defects.

AIRBORNE INVENTORY & INSPECTION SYSTEM

The airborne system constitutes an aerial platform that is used to acquire high-speed, high-resolution digital video and still images (both, visual and spectral bands) at speeds ranging from 80 to 160 km/h (depending on terrain altitude). Digital images are typically obtained in low level flight at altitudes ranging from 10 to 60 m above the ground (at ~1.5–5 m above the asset to be inspected).

The aerial platform typically used for the acquisition of the digital images is a highly modified fixed wing aircraft with an exceptionally low stall speed and a reasonably high top end performance. The digital image acquisition system can also be fitted for helicopter operation with a significantly higher operating cost relative to the fixed wing alternative. Fig. 1(a) shows the aerial patrol plane in mid-flight of an ongoing inspection above a lattice tower transmission line. Fig. 1(b) shows a close up of the fixed wing aircraft, the housing for the forward and rearward looking digital video cameras, and the housing for the rearward-looking

Fig. 1. (a) Aerial patrol platform and digital image and video acquisition equipment. (b) Aerial patrol platform and digital image and video acquisition equipment.

high resolution digital still cameras, identified as the dark colored housing located at the center of the wings aft of the wheel struts.

The aerial patrol plane is equipped with a differentially corrected GPS unit that continuously references to at least 7 different satellite signals and radio beacons. Coupled with a proximity sensor based automatic trigger, the plane's data acquisition system records the DGPS coordinates of each structure while providing a time stamp for the fully automated digital image acquisition.

Based on experiments at the EPRI test facility (on full scale test lines), the accuracy of the DGPS coordinates collected by the plane's navigation and radar based proximity sensor systems is plus or minus 1.5 m for three standard deviations. Essentially, GPS coordinate corrections are performed real-time by the on-board computer system that also controls the image acquisition and data storage.

The image acquisition module can be equipped with multiple digital still picture and video cameras to provide forward and rearward looking views as well as a straight down view of the transmission line corridor. Each digital still and video image is tagged with DGPS coordinates and the viewing angles of the appropriate camera by the on-board computer control system.

Acquisition of the digital images (the timing of the picture acquisition of each camera) has been automated to allow the on-board computer to trigger the high-resolution digital still and video cameras based on the current DGPS coordinate, the speed above ground, and the altitude above the transmission line. Acquired images are DGPS tagged and stored by the on-board computer. Digital images are then transferred to digital tapes or disks upon completion of the aerial patrol.

Up-to-date digital visual and spectral images provided by the aerial patrol are processed and sorted with respect to the viewing coordinates and angles of each of the images. The digital images are transferred to digital tapes or disks for review at the office upon completion of the aerial patrol. Digital images and video are not reviewed during the patrol because of the extremely large size of each image and to allow the plane to be operated autonomously with a single pilot.

All images are transferred to the utility's computer after the conclusion of the airborne patrol. Digital images are then viewed and interpreted by the inspector at the office to identify any conditions/defects that may adversely affect the performance of the asset currently being inspected. Conditions/defects are then recorded for immediate or future action in the company's work management system.

SYSTEM APPLICATION AND FIELD EXPERIENCES

Field evaluations were performed on different transmission lines to assess the reliability of the aerial inventory and inspection system. Five different transmission lines were included in the proof-of-concept field evaluations. These lines were a 69 kV, double circuit, wood pole line, a 230 kV, single circuit, wood H-frame line, a 345 kV, single circuit, lattice tower line, a 345 kV,

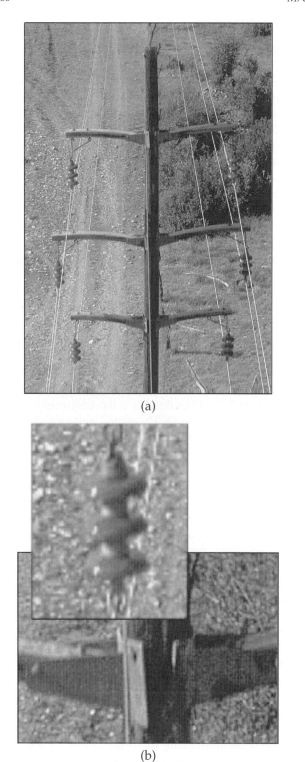

(a)

(b)

Fig. 2. (a) Aerial inspection — 69 kV wood pole (double circuit).
(b) Close up — 69 kV wood pole (double circuit).

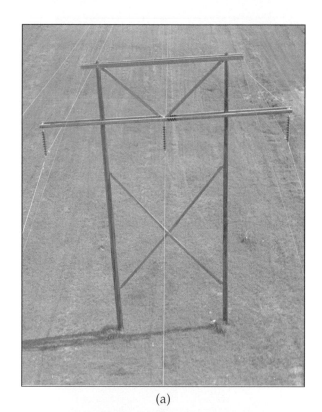

(a)

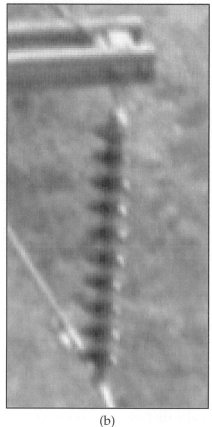

(b)

Fig. 3. (a) Aerial inspection — 230 kV H-frame (single circuit).
(b) Close up — 230 kV H-frame (single circuit).

double circuit, lattice tower line, and a 345 kV wood H-frame transmission line.

The 69 kV line inspected was in excess of 32 km in length and was located within a mountainous region of the Western United States. The 230 kV line segment used in the evaluation is approximately 1.6 km in length and is located in the plains region of the Southwestern United States. The 345 kV single circuit

Fig. 4. (a) Aerial inspection — 345 kV lattice (single circuit). (b) Close up — 345 kV lattice (single circuit).

line is approximately 3.2 km in length and is also located in the plains region of the Southwestern United States. The 345 kV double circuit line is in excess of 50 km in length and is also located in the Southwestern United States. Finally, the 345 kV single circuit line constitutes a test line of less than 4 km in length that is located at a testing center in the Southwestern United States.

Typical suspension structures present on each of the four transmission lines are shown in Figs. 2–5, respectively. Images of each of the structures shown were collected at speeds ranging from 125 to 150 km/h above ground, recorded with medium resolution digital cameras (1550 by 1280 pixels). High resolution digital images were also recorded (>3000 by 2000 pixels) and are included as Fig. 6(a) and 6(b).

Fig. 2(a) shows an overall view of the suspension structure. Fig. 2(b) shows a close-up of the top cross-arm to pole connection and the upper left insulator assembly. Clearly, based on the image shown in Fig. 2(b), the presence of individual bolts can be confirmed and the condition of each item can be assessed from the close-up view of the connection. At the same time, the image in Fig. 2(b) shows that each individual ceramic insulator bell can be identified in its entirety to identify any units that may be broken or chipped. However, it

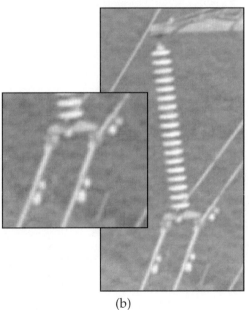

Fig. 5. (a) Aerial inspection — 345 kV lattice (double circuit). (b) Close up — 345 kV lattice (double circuit).

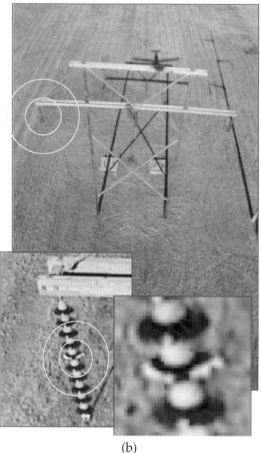

Fig. 6. (a) Aerial inspection & close up — 345 kV H-frame (test line).
(b) Aerial inspection & close up — 345 kV H-frame (test line).

should be noted that proper illumination of the shaded areas is required to collect the highest quality images. As a result, strobe lights were added to the patrol plane to provide synchronized illumination of shaded areas, provide a patrol process independent of the position of the sun and the angle with the structure.

Fig. 3(a) shows an overall view of the single circuit 230 kV wood H-frame suspension structure and Fig. 3(b) shows a close-up of the insulator string on the right side of the structure. The length of the insulator string on the 230 kV structure is approximately 2.25 m. In Fig. 3(a), one can identify that the ground wire and conductor cross-arm each consist of two sawn lumber sections and that the conductor cross-arm has been spliced on the right side of the center phase insulator attachment point.

Fig. 3(b) shows a close-up of the right outside phase insulator assembly. Based on the image, one can conclude that none of the ceramic insulators are significantly broken or chipped (otherwise they would show as a missing unit or as discoloration not matching the coloration of the other units). Similarly, one can conclude that the damper is present and not fatigued (the ends are not drooping). Again, the need for better illumination is apparent since the illumination of the insulators by the sun does not guarantee the highest quality of image. Also, to maximize the time spend in the air it is imperative to provide sufficient illumination of each asset regardless of location or height of sun above the horizon. Again, the addition of high powered strobe lights to the patrol plane eliminated the problem by providing a sufficient amount of illumination regardless of the time of day and position of the sun.

Fig. 4(a) shows an overall view of the 345 kV single circuit, lattice tower structure and Fig. 4(b) shows a close-up of the cross-arm insulator attachment point of the left conductor phase. Based on the image shown in Fig. 4(b), the inspection clearly reveals the presence of a broken insulator unit on the string. Furthermore, the close-up of the structure in Fig 4(b) shows that standard vibration dampers are not used on these spans of the transmission line at either of the three phase conductors. Finally, Fig. 4(a) shows that the color of the v-string center phase insulators is different than the color of the outside phase insulators. Based on this finding it is likely that the outside phase insulators are of different vintage or manufacturer than the center phase units.

Fig. 5(a) shows an overall view of the 345 kV double circuit lattice tower supporting a twin conductor bundle at each phase of the two circuits. Fig. 5(b) shows a close-up of the left circuit, upper phase insulator assembly that supports the twin conductor bundle. Each of the two images clearly shows that there are no broken insulators on that phase support assembly. Fig. 5(b) also shows each of the four standard dampers on the bundled conductors. Based on the image one can conclude that the dampers are not fatigued. Further examinations show no discoloration on the yoke indicating no corrosion on the insulator caps.

Fig. 6(a) shows an overall view and various close-ups of a 345 kV single circuit wood H-frame located on the test line at the Engineering and Testing Center in Haslet, TX. The close up on the ground wire peak clearly shows the 2.5 cm diameter lag bolt assembly. Additionally, the image shows that the nut of the lag bolt assembly has backed off and is in danger of falling to the ground. Similarly, a close inspection of Fig. 6(b) shows that the fifth ceramic insulator counting from the top of the assembly is severely damaged.

CONCLUSIONS

The aerial inventory and inspection patrol system described in this paper constitutes a cost-effective method to collect information on distributed assets such as transmission lines, oil and gas pipelines, and roadways. The cost of the automated fixed wing aerial patrol system is significantly less than the cost of traditional aerial inspection technologies while the detection rate of conditions/defects nearly equals the detection rate achieved by common walking/driving patrols.

Based on our experiences, the time required to review an individual aerial high-resolution image varies greatly depending on the type of structure, the terrain the transmission line traverses, and the tool used for the handling, manipulation, and interpretation. Typically, it takes 1–10 min to interpret each digital image. Review times were significantly shorter for structures of small size and number of components. Overall, review times were equivalent to inspection times observed for traditional driving patrols.

Condition or defect detection rates achieved with high-resolution digital images (>3000 by 2000 pixels) were comparable to detection rates achieved with traditional driving patrols at a significantly lower cost per record. Preliminary indications are that the resolution of ultra-high resolution digital cameras (>8000 by 6000 pixels) will be sufficient to identify most conditions that have a geometric extent of more than 0.5 in. Ultra-high resolution digital cameras are currently being developed by manufacturers.

In conclusion, low altitude digital image acquisition provides detailed high-resolution visual and spectral images at high speeds that are identified by DGPS coordinates and viewing angles. Digital images can be interpreted by qualified personnel at the office using commercially available GIS software. Comparisons between conditions recorded in previous inspections and recent inspections can be compared to determine the rate of change of conditions on the electric power line. Digital records can be archived to document the condition of the asset at specific times for planning, operational issues, and long term performance evaluations.

ACKNOWLEDGMENT

This study was performed under a research grant from the Electric Power Research Institute (EPRI) and EPRI member utilities. The author wishes to thank Paul Lyons of the EPRI Energy Delivery and Utilization Center — Haslet for his guidance and support.

REFERENCES

Stewart, A.H., E.A. Franke, and W.G. Eisinger. 1995a. Assessment and Inspection Methods (AIM) Field Experiment — Volume 1: Results of Transmission Line Inspection Experiment, TR-104449-V1. Technical Report. Electric Power Research Institute.

Stewart, A.H., E.A. Franke, and W.G. Eisinger. 1995b. Assessment and Inspection Methods (AIM) Field Experiment — Volume 2: Inspection Limitations, Enhancements, Technology Gaps, and Recommendations, TR-104449-V1. Technical Report. Electric Power Research Institute.

Ostendorp, Mark. 1998. Transmission Line Post Storm Damage Assessment and Vegetation Monitoring Using Remote Sensing Techniques, TR-111838. Technical Report. Electric Power Research Institute.

Ostendorp, Mark. 1999a. Airborne Inventory and Inspection of Transmission Lines — Unmanned Airborne Vehicles (UAV), TR-113682. Technical Report. Electric Power Research Institute.

Ostendorp, Mark. 1999b. Airborne Inventory and Inspection of Transmission Lines — Airborne Patrol System (APS), TR-114229. Technical Report. Electric Power Research Institute.

Ostendorp, Mark. 2000. Airborne Inventory and Inspection of Transmission Lines — AVCAN Systems Corporation's Helicopter Patrol System (HPS), TR-114345. Technical Report. Electric Power Research Institute.

BIOGRAPHICAL SKETCH

Mark Ostendorp

Engineering and Testing Center — Haslet, EPRIsolutions, Inc., 100 Research Drive, PO Box 187, Haslet, TX 76052, USA, E-mail: mostendo@eprisolutions.com

Mark Ostendorp is a registered licensed professional engineer in the State of Texas. He has a BS, MS, and PhD in Civil/Structural Engineering and Systems Science from Portland State University in Portland, OR. Working for EPRIsolutions, Inc., a wholly owned subsidiary of the Electric Power Research Institute (EPRI), Mark Ostendorp currently manages the engineering, inspection, and testing services group at the structural and mechanical engineering and testing center in Ft. Worth, TX. He has more than ten years experience in the power delivery industry, is a member of the American Society of Civil Engineers (ASCE), the Structural Engineering Institute (SEI), the Institute of Electrical and Electronics Engineers (IEEE), the International Electrotechnical Commission (IEC), and Conference Internationale Des Grandes Reseau Electrique a Haute Tension (CIGRE). He has authored or co-authored more than 100 publications that include trade magazine articles, conference proceedings, technical journal contributions, and research reports published by the Electric Power Research Institute (EPRI).

Part IX
Wetlands

Identifying Wetland Revegetation Goals in Pipeline Construction Rights-of-Way

Bill Magdych

An approach is described to evaluate wetland functions that are affected at pipeline crossings. Construction of pipeline crossings in wetlands by cut and trench methods results in removal and/or disturbance of vegetation within portions of pipeline rights-of-way (ROW). These crossings have received increased permitting scrutiny with an emphasis placed on more costly mitigation requirements and alternative crossing methods that may not be justified based on the actual functional effects of a cut-and-trench crossing. Evaluation of wetland functions affected at a specific crossing should lead to appropriate goals and techniques for wetland revegetation that would maintain or enhance key wetland functions. In many situations, this evaluation process will result in identification of a relatively small number of management considerations for individual crossings or groups of crossings, identification of appropriate revegetation goals, identification of performance standards to measure attainment of desired goals, and selection of appropriate revegetation techniques to meet these goals. In some cases, this process may allow for shifts in biological habitat type within the ROW while still maintaining key wetland functions in a manner consistent with the wetland revegetation goals.

Keywords: Wetland, permitting, functions, revegetation, performance standards

INTRODUCTION

This paper describes a standardized approach that the natural gas pipeline industry and others can use to evaluate the effects of cut-and-trench construction methods used during crossings of wetlands within pipeline rights-of-way (ROW). This paper also describes how to establish appropriate goals for wetland revegetation, including use of construction Best Management Practices (BMPs), at specific crossings based on evaluation of the actual observed effects. The results of this approach may help the pipeline industry avoid costly revegetation or alternative construction requirements that are not justified based on the functional effects of the cut and trench crossing. This proposed approach may be very important for projects that cross many and diverse types of wetlands.

The Federal Energy Regulatory Commission (FERC), as well as other federal, state, provincial, and local agencies, administers regulations and guidance that set requirements for cut and trench crossings of wetlands, such as the FERC Wetland and Waterbody Construction and Mitigation Procedures. In practice, potential effects on all wetlands crossed by a project, including effects that are unlikely to occur because of the nature of the crossing, are often lumped together during initial environmental review and permitting. This practice may result in mitigation and revegetation requirements for use on all wetland crossings, regardless of whether or not the specific requirements are justified in individual cases. Complex and potentially irresolvable issues may also arise as a result of requirements by multiple agencies that are in conflict with each other, overly prescriptive in nature, based on "one-size-fits-all" approaches to regulation, or inflexible relative to engineering feasibility and cost constraints (GRI, 1999). These issues may result in permit and construction delays, and in some cases, multiple requirements from different agency jurisdictions that are difficult to track and properly implement. Also, environmental issues that are most relevant at a specific wetland crossing may be overlooked.

Environmental Concerns in Rights-of-Way
Management: Seventh International Symposium
J.W. Goodrich-Mahoney, D.F. Mutrie and C.A. Guild (editors)
© 2002 Elsevier Science Ltd. All rights reserved.

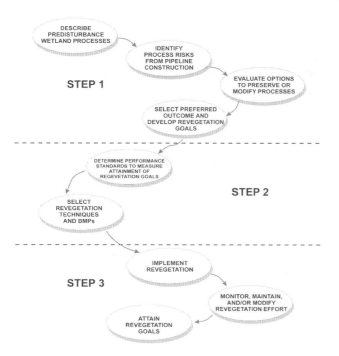

Fig. 1. Flow chart of the approach to setting and attaining wetland revegetation goals.

OVERVIEW OF THE APPROACH

The intent of the proposed approach is to determine wetland revegetation goals for pipeline crossings that are based on desired preservation, re-establishment, and/or modification of predisturbance functions of primary concern for a specific crossing. A more detailed description of this approach with examples is presented in GRI (2000). This overall approach attempts to answer two basic questions:

1. What goals for wetland revegetation are appropriate at a crossing or group of crossings?
2. Once wetland revegetation goals are selected, how should they be attained?

The proposed approach to determining wetland revegetation goals and techniques for a pipeline construction ROW consists of three basic steps (Fig. 1):
- Step 1: Functional Evaluation and Goal Setting
- Step 2: Determination of Performance standards and Selection of Revegetation Practices
- Step 3: Wetland Revegetation Implementation, Monitoring, and Maintenance

These steps are consistent with guidance recommended by the US Army Corps of Engineers (Corps), Waterways Experiment Station (WES) (Bill Streever, personal communication) for determining wetland mitigation requirements, although experience from the pipeline industry indicates that this guidance from WES is not universally applied (GRI, 1999). Each step of this approach identifies a conceptual decision process to make required determinations. This approach is intended to incorporate data that is routinely collected during a pipeline project's impact assessment phase, and to provide for a thorough evaluation of project effects in the short and long term. The proposed approach provides for evaluation of these issues to determine which specific requirements are necessary.

Performance standards for wetland revegetation provide a basis for determining if a wetland revegetation effort has been successful and usually provide measures for determining when long-term monitoring and maintenance can be terminated (Streever, 1999). This proposed approach stresses identification of ecologically based performance standards that reflect the revegetation goals for a project as exactly as possible. As long as the revegetation goals have been determined to be appropriate and attainable, then it should not matter how they are met. Therefore, it should be possible to develop performance standards that clearly define desired end-points, including reasonable time periods for meeting revegetation goals, and allow the use of a variety of available BMPs and revegetation techniques to meet the overall revegetation goals.

The final step in the proposed approach is to implement the revegetation program. This step may seem obvious; however, it is very important that the concepts from the previous two steps be carefully integrated in the wetland revegetation process. Implementation should consider requirements for pre-construction, construction, and post-construction activities, monitoring of activities, and ultimate performance, as well as maintenance activities (including "Plan B" types of options) that may be required to ensure attainment of performance standards and wetland revegetation goals.

STEP 1: FUNCTIONAL EVALUATION AND GOAL SETTING

Functional evaluation and goal setting is the most important aspect of the proposed approach. This step is where information on effects will be developed that should be most useful in building consensus among potentially interested parties, including pipeline companies and regulators. This step will identify the issues that are most important and that should be dealt with as part of the wetland revegetation process. This step should also eliminate inappropriate and/or generic issues that tend to get lumped into traditional evaluation and decision-making processes, even though they do not really apply to this type of project or at a specific crossing location. This first step of the proposed approach involves four substeps shown in Fig. 1.

Describe predisturbance wetland functions
The environmental setting serves as an organizational basis for describing wetland functions using descriptor groups for hydrology, geomorphology, climate, biology, and land use (Table 1). This approach draws upon the Corps' Hydrogeomorphic (HGM) approach (Brinson, 1995 and 1996) and the Bureau of Land Management's (BLM) process for assessing Proper Functioning

Table 1. Primary descriptors used in functional evaluation and goal setting

Descriptor group	Descriptor class	
Hydrology	Water Sources	Seasonal Duration
Geomorphology	HGM Class	Topsoil Type
	Hydraulic Class	Subsoil Type
Climate	Temperature Regime	
Biology	Vegetation Type	Key Processes
Land Use	Potential for Conflict	

Condition (PFC) (BLM, 1993 and 1994); however, the proposed approach is not as complex as HGM and does not require use of reference wetlands. The pre-disturbance conditions form the reference points for this approach. These descriptor groups should cover most wetland functions that could be affected by a cut-and-trench pipeline crossing, although additional descriptors could be added or substituted if deemed appropriate by an investigator.

Hydrology
The key descriptor classes in this group are Water Sources and Seasonal Duration. Water Sources create wetlands, and specific sources are important in evaluating the potential for a crossing to affect a water source, which ultimately drives all wetland functions. Examples of types of water sources are overbank flow, groundwater, tidal flow, direct rainfall, and surface runoff. Seasonal Duration describes when wetland hydrology is present, which may help determine how construction at a specific time will affect wetland functions. Construction during the dry season, for instance, may result in less disturbance of soil structure and the wetland processes associated with the soil structure.

Geomorphology
The key descriptor classes in this group are HGM Class, Topsoil Type, Subsoil Type, and Hydraulic Class. These classes are aimed at evaluating functions associated with a landform and its stability, and soil processes that may affect wetland vegetation. HGM Class (e.g., riverine or depressional) serves as an all-purpose descriptor that most wetland professionals can use to identify broad processes that may be present in a given wetland. Knowing that a wetland is associated with a river, rather than a perched depression, provides substantial information regarding the potential effects that a crossing may have on the wetland. Topsoil Type and Subsoil Type are important in evaluating the potential to affect landform stability, as well as the potential to affect certain types of vegetation planned for establishment after construction. Hydraulic Class includes consideration of water flows, subsurface flows, and potential for erosion or deposition that may affect the wetland stability in the short or long term.

Climate
The key class in this group is the Temperature Regime, which may affect construction conditions, growing periods, and potentially the relative importance of certain functions or processes in a wetland.

Biology
The major classes in this group are Vegetation Type and Key Processes. Vegetation Type [e.g., Cowardin et al. (1979) wetland class] serves a similar role as does HGM Class in that the Vegetation Type can provide a wetland professional with substantial insight into the biological processes that may occur in a given wetland. However, Vegetation Type is likely to be based on a general classification system, and thus, will provide only general information about the wetland. This approach discourages the sole use of acre-by-acre (or hectare-by-hectare) accounting methods for determining mitigation requirements and wetland revegetation goals. Key Processes are expected to provide the primary information that should drive revegetation goals in most cases. Consideration of the local, regional, and possibly global relevance of a key biological process, such as breeding in an area for special management species, is the primary aspect of this approach that is recommended for determining wetland revegetation goals. This type of evaluation may result in many potential outcomes such as requirements to re-establish predisturbance vegetation using rigid specifications, or to allow substantial changes in vegetation types within the construction ROW. The intent of this approach is to determine the relevance of the potential change in a key biological process resulting from the pipeline crossing, and then to determine wetland revegetation goals that minimize effects on processes determined to be significant at a specific crossing. As with all descriptor groups, effects on a certain biological process may not be significant, and may not result in a decision to preserve that process in the wetland following disturbance.

Land use
This descriptor group includes consideration of potential effects on wetland revegetation that may result from future land use on, or adjacent to, the construction ROW. Conflicts with revegetation goals could arise from either human interference, such as expansion of agriculture by landowners or increase in off-road vehicle use, or non-human interference, such as intense herbivore grazing of plants targeted for establishment onsite. Land Use is an important consideration that should be made when determining revegetation goals to ensure that they can actually be achieved. It may also be possible to determine that certain vegetation types or habitats can be established to help ensure that desired future land uses ultimately develop.

Identify process risks from pipeline construction
This approach recommends that actions be taken to compensate for effects on wetland functions that are at risk, and are determined to be of concern at a specific crossing. Not all wetland functions exist at a specific crossing, and no compensatory actions should be required for functions that are not present, for functions that are not significant at a crossing, or for other functions that may be present, but are not at risk.

Specific requirements are often placed in project permits for BMPs that apply to hydrological and geomorphological processes that may not be at risk at a specific crossing. For example, impermeable trench breakers or plugs are often required by the Corps and FERC at the entry and exit points of wetland crossings with the stated purpose to prevent drainage of the wetland. Most wetlands crossed by pipelines are at the bottom of depressions relative to pipeline trench entry and exit slopes; therefore, it is highly unlikely that water could drain through the trench out of the wetland in these cases. A more important consideration for construction at this type of crossing may be stabilization of the slopes on each side of the wetland to prevent landform destabilization, control of runoff down the trench line towards the wetland, and slumping or sedimentation into the wetland. The wetland may be at risk from partial conversion to upland as a result of hydraulic and geomorphological processes rather than hydrological processes; therefore, goals should focus on stabilizing the upslope landform, which would suggest the need for land stabilization BMPs in appropriate adjacent areas. In this case, the general requirement for trench breakers at wetland entry and exit points would provide no substantial environmental benefit and the excess cost for the trench breakers would be wasted.

Evaluate options to preserve or modify processes
Once wetland processes or functions of concern that are at risk from pipeline construction are identified, options that are available to either preserve or modify each wetland process should be evaluated. In some cases, there may be a strong desire by users of this proposed approach to maintain the wetland process in its predisturbance condition, while allowing change in the process may be desirable in other cases. Some changes may be neutral, without significant effect on overall wetland function. This type of evaluation strongly involves professional judgment and conceptual methods of evaluation, or quantitative measures.

For example, a crossing of a forested wetland may affect certain bird species that use the forest canopy for nesting and foraging at that location. Construction of a cut-and-trench crossing would require removal of trees within the construction ROW. In this case, bird nesting and foraging in the ROW may be key biological processes that would be at risk from construction. Options to preserve or modify these key processes could include establishment of predisturbance levels of nesting and foraging, random changes in these processes, or some other alternative such as a specified reduced level of nesting or foraging. It is important that mitigation options identified in this substep be practicable with regard to project requirements, cost, engineering logistics, and likelihood of achieving potential desired outcomes.

Select preferred outcomes and develop revegetation goals
The final substep involves choosing a desired outcome, and setting revegetation goals that reflect the desired outcome. In most cases, there should be several potential outcomes including preservation of the predisturbance process, changes in the predisturbance process, and potential loss of the process. Some common outcomes and goals may be identified more often than others. For instance, maintaining general predisturbance landforms on slopes around wetlands that are stable after construction and able to accommodate patterns of natural fluvial processes at the crossing location may be routinely determined to be desired outcomes and goals. Even though these types of goals may apply to most wetland crossings, they do not require that the same techniques or BMPs be applied to each wetland.

Some preferred outcomes may allow for changes to a key process or function. Using the forested wetland example described above, one potential outcome may allow for some reduced level of function within the wetland crossing relative to bird nesting as long as bird foraging is maintained at a relatively high level. In this case, there may be sufficient nesting habitat adjacent to the ROW that is not otherwise at risk, and that will maintain predisturbance bird populations in the area. Simple provision of suitable habitat to maintain foraging by key bird species to ensure that nesting success offsite continues may be sufficient in this case. A goal for this example could be to maintain bird foraging at, or greater than, predisturbance levels within the ROW. This goal could be refined depending on the key bird species of concern and special foraging requirements for these species. Again, this goal would not dictate specific revegetation techniques, although this goal should lead to selecting a range of techniques that may be applied in Step 2 of this approach.

STEP 2: DETERMINATION OF PERFORMANCE STANDARDS AND SELECTION OF REVEGETATION PRACTICES

Once specific goals are identified, performance standards need to be developed to provide a basis for measuring the attainment of revegetation goals. Selection of performance standards helps to narrow the range of suitable revegetation techniques and BMPs that are available for a crossing because only some techniques or BMPs are likely to meet the performance standards.

Determine performance standards to measure attainment of revegetation goals

A performance standard should provide discrete measures to evaluate the progress of revegetation efforts. Streever (1999) evaluated performance standards developed for wetland mitigation pursuant to Clean Water Act, Section 404 permitting, and found that, when present, performance standards in permits often use some specific measure (e.g., density or cover), comparison to reference wetlands, or include specific requirements (e.g., control of exotic species). These types of performance standards may be consistent with the proposed approach; however, the proposed approach emphasizes developing performance standards that measure attainment of specific revegetation goals. Therefore, performance standards that are developed as part of the proposed approach should be closely related to the functional goals for a wetland. As such, performance standards selected for a given project should be clearly associated with specific wetland processes or functions.

A general revegetation goal to maintain predisturbance landforms to avoid potential mounding or subsidence over the trench and associated habitat shifts would likely result in a performance standard that measures post-construction grades in comparison to predisturbance grades. Grading could be accomplished immediately after construction to set proper grades in consideration of edaphic factors, and monitored to ensure that the landform is stable. Potential longer term mounding, subsidence, or other factors could be determined through visual inspection. For instance, sedimentation caused by entrainment of flows and associated movement of soils along the trench line toward the wetland may result in observable deposition in the wetland and subsidence over the trench line at some point upslope from the wetland. Formal performance standards to address these issues could be stated as:

- Post-construction grades shall closely approximate predisturbance grades as demonstrated by post-construction inspection
- Erosion, subsidence, and deposition along the trench line, except from natural migration of wetland boundaries, shall be minimized. The trench line will be determined to be stabilized if no significant landform changes along the trench line are observed within five years.

The goal to maintain bird foraging in the wetland could result in performance standards that measure bird species observed foraging in the ROW after construction. Observed numbers of certain target bird species foraging could be identified. Standards based on indirect measures of foraging potential may also be desirable. For instance, establishment of shrubs or trees of a certain average height, specific density, or percentage of aerial cover may indicate that sufficient habitat is available to support foraging for key bird species. This latter type of performance standard may allow earlier determination of success than would be allowed by performance standards that rely on only a few species, whose populations in the local area may be affected by factors other than those associated with recovery of vegetation within the ROW. Performance standards should also provide for suitable periods of time to allow for revegetation to occur. Examples of potential formal performance standards for this case are:

- Three pairs or six individuals of four of the bird species observed in the wetland prior to construction must be observed foraging in the post-construction ROW during spring surveys within five years of construction. Specific species and different numeric values may be required depending upon the situation.
- Revegetation shall result in the establishment of native shrub and/or tree species in the post-construction ROW that will allow foraging of target bird species within five years. To meet this goal, native shrubs and/or trees that are greater than 3 feet in height shall be established at a minimum of 25% cover in the second year, 75% cover in the fourth year, and 90% cover within 5 years. Foraging by the target bird species shall be documented during spring surveys within 5 years of construction. Specific species of plants or birds could be specified depending upon the specific goal for the crossing. In other cases, the standard to only require establishment of desired vegetation cover may be sufficient.

The relationship between performance standards and revegetation goals should be documented to avoid confusion when determinations are made as to whether or not revegetation goals have been attained. One particular problem that can arise with performance standards is the possibility that the overall goal has actually been achieved even though a performance standard has not yet been met. For example, target bird species may not be observed during the prescribed monitoring period. These bird species may be absent for a variety of reasons that are unrelated to the effects of the pipeline crossing. A determination that the overall revegetation goals have been met based on diversity, density, and/or percent cover of the established vegetation may be possible if the vegetation is of sufficient quality to support the target bird species and there is a reasonable expectation that these bird species will ultimately use the habitat at some future time. A clear statement of the overall intent of the goal and how the performance standard relates to the goal should be helpful in assisting monitors and agencies to make appropriate determinations in this situation, especially when several years have passed and new staff may be involved in the project. The use of multiple performance standards with success determined by some combination of a subset of these standards may also help avoid this type of problem.

Select revegetation techniques and BMPs

There will be many approaches available to meet revegetation goals in most cases. The primary goal in this substep is to select practicable techniques that will attain the wetland revegetation goals. This process involves evaluating the technique's cost, how well the technique will work in the given situation, whether or not the technique will make a difference in the final outcome, and how the technique stacks up to other available techniques in an objective comparison. Techniques available for evaluation in a specific situation should also be limited to those that are likely to allow attainment of the wetland revegetation goals.

For example, the performance standard for shrubs and trees associated with bird foraging allows substantial latitude with regard to the shrub and tree species that should be established. This latitude, in turn, allows consideration of a wide range of approaches to revegetation, and may also allow a wider range of approaches to construction practices. This standard may be met by allowing natural recolonization, by establishing key species using cuttings, or through more extensive plantings. Disturbance of soils and root systems in the construction ROW may be allowable if sufficient vegetation can be later established and overall wetland hydrology is maintained.

STEP 3: WETLAND REVEGETATION IMPLEMENTATION, MONITORING, AND MAINTENANCE

This step is important because this is the stage where errors can directly affect the revegetation effort. Errors often occur during implementation of revegetation; however, they may also occur during maintenance. Errors generally consist of two types: (1) errors that affect attainment of revegetation goals, and (2) errors that may not be consistent with administrative requirements, but that do not affect the attainment of revegetation goals. The proposed approach focuses on selection and attainment of appropriate goals for revegetation, and emphasizes avoidance of errors that adversely affect the attainment of selected goals. Although the proposed approach recommends compliance with administrative requirements, the inability to meet certain administrative requirements should not result in penalties if revegetation goals are met. For example, administrative requirements may exist in a permit that require some irrigation and seeding to establish vegetation. With suitable rainfall and local seed sources, desired vegetation may be established by natural recolonization, thus making the requirements for seeding and irrigation unnecessary. Similarly requirements for trench breakers at a specific wetland's entry and exit points to prevent drainage may not require construction of trench breakers if the native soil is sufficiently impermeable and replaced in the trench to provide the desired seal to prevent drainage of the wetland. The ultimate revegetation goals could be met in both cases even if the specific administrative requirements were not implemented. Potential conflicts can be avoided by careful application of Steps 1 and 2 to select appropriate revegetation goals and techniques that do not result in administrative requirements that are excessive or difficult to comply with.

The intent of the proposed approach is to produce wetland revegetation goals that are attainable, and to select techniques that can be feasibly implemented in a cost-effective manner, which should make implementation as simple as possible. Regardless of how simple the requirements, proper implementation of all techniques is still important. To achieve proper implementation, revegetation plans should be developed that are clear and concise. Inclusion of specific requirements in the construction specifications, especially on construction plans that are map-based such as construction alignment sheets, will also be helpful. Geographic Information System (GIS) mapping can be a valuable tool for this type of documentation, as can other means of displaying construction requirements on maps, and they provide the basis for long-term monitoring of revegetation requirements and maintenance activities.

Regardless of how many mapping and other planning tools are available, revegetation is a hands-on process that requires involvement by the revegetation manager. Monitoring, with appropriate ongoing maintenance, is important in the implementation phase beginning with ROW preparation and extending through final ROW stabilization. Early monitoring is necessary to ensure that site preparation and construction occurs according to plans consistent with attainment of revegetation goals. Monitoring may play an important role in evaluating changes in techniques used during construction with appropriate documentation, thus allowing flexibility in construction methods. Longer term monitoring and maintenance will help ensure successful attainment of wetland revegetation goals within desired time periods.

DISCUSSION

Table 2 provides a comparison of some common permit requirements for pipeline projects with goals and recommendations that may be developed using the proposed approach. In some cases, the common permit requirements will be deemed appropriate and associated with a goal. However, a variety of options are expected to be available in most cases that will either avoid the use of unnecessary methods or provide methods that are more practicable. Several issues from Table 2 that are commonly encountered in pipeline permitting projects include the use of trench breakers, topsoil segregation, and establishment of key plant

Table 2. Examples of common pipeline construction requirements for wetland crossings compared to potential goals and recommendations using this approach

Common permit requirements	Potential alternative goals/outcomes	Potentially recommended techniques and BMPs
Place trench breakers at wetland entry and exit points	Prevent drainage from the wetland along the trench	Use suitable trench breakers or impermeable soil plugs at the edges of wetlands where lateral drainage may occur Re-establish wetland seals using compatible, impermeable materials within the trench for perched wetlands
Use water bars and trench breakers on slopes (along wetlands)	Maintain stable landforms on slopes to prevent damage to wetland	Options should be evaluated to provide practicable stabilization of slopes Potential BMPs include water bars and trench breakers, as well as other, state-of-the-art BMPs
Segregate and replace 12 inches of topsoil over the trench	Maintain topsoil over the trench that is suitable for establishing target vegetation	Topsoil segregation may or may not be appropriate. Maintenance of seed and root stock may not be appropriate in forested wetlands if trees are prohibited over the trench. Topsoil segregation should only be used in situations where subsoils are incompatible with the desired vegetation
Use mats when operating equipment in wetlands to avoid disturbance of soils in the construction ROW	Maintain grades and soil conditions in the construction ROW to promote establishment of desired vegetation	A variety of BMPs may be available depending on local conditions including: use of construction mats in unconsolidated soils; construction on frozen ground; construction during the dry season; and controlled disturbance of soils with post-construction restoration
Avoid placement of soil augments or materials in wetlands	Maintain grades and soil conditions in the construction ROW to promote establishment of desired vegetation	Restoration of the construction ROW may include augmentation with compatible soils or other materials
Provide active plantings of trees in forested wetlands	Re-establish similar forest and shrub species in the construction ROW within five years	A variety of BMPs may be available to meet this goal depending on site-specific considerations including: natural recolonization; use of unrooted or rooted cuttings; or container stock
Establish specific plant species in the construction ROW, and control exotic species	Re-establish plant species similar to predisturbance conditions	See prior example. Exotic control may or may not be feasible. If the site or adjacent land was already infested with exotics, then exotic species control may not be possible or desirable

species excluding exotic plants. Problems often arise when these seemingly sound requirements are enforced without flexibility.

The use of trench breakers at the entry and exit points for every wetland crossed has already been described above as an issue because the requirement is usually intended to prevent drainage of wetlands, and most wetlands crossed by pipelines are at topographic depressions relative to surrounding lands such that drainage down the entry and exit trench lines is unlikely to occur. A more suitable approach focusing on the goal of preventing drainage of the wetland would only require that trench breakers be used when they would actually provide some value in preventing drainage (i.e., they would only be required when the threat of drainage exists, and when other methods are less practicable) (Table 2). This could result in substantial cost savings during construction. For instance, a savings of $360,000–1,200,000 in construction costs may occur if a new pipeline project that is 400 miles (645 km) long crosses 700 wetlands and trench breakers (assume two per wetland at a cost of $300–1000 each) are not required at 600 of the wetlands.

Topsoil segregation is another requirement that may be inappropriate in consideration of specific goals for wetland revegetation in pipeline ROW (Table 2). Topsoil segregation is often required for wetland crossings with the intent of preserving seed and root material, and in providing suitable topsoil for re-establishment of vegetation. The need to preserve seed and root material over the trench line may be questionable in some cases, especially when the project involves forested wetlands and natural gas pipelines. The need for aerial safety inspections of natural gas pipelines often results in requirements that prohibit the growth of tree species over the trench line and include maintenance to prevent such growth. Therefore, requirements for topsoil segregation that promote tree growth over the trench line may not be desirable if suitable vegetation can be established without topsoil segregation. Topsoil segregation may also be of very limited value in situations where the topsoil and subsoil are not strongly differentiated, such as with deep sandy or deep organic soils. In these cases, mixing of similar subsoil with the topsoil over the trench line may not substantially affect revegetation within the wetland.

Control of exotic plants is a common requirement that may also be inappropriate in some cases (Table 2). A goal to re-establish plants within the ROW that are similar to predisturbance conditions or conditions off the ROW may result in identification of a requirement for control of exotic plants. This requirement would likely be necessary if exotic plants were absent or at very low densities in the predisturbance wetland and surrounding areas. However, this requirement may also be determined to be impractical in areas where exotic plants are more abundant, and control of such exotics within the pipeline ROW would be nearly impossible. In this case, the initial functional evaluation would include consideration of the presence of exotic species on- and offsite, and should lead to identification of wetland revegetation goals that include consideration of these exotic species.

The proposed approach is intended to be relatively straightforward and easy to apply, even on large projects that cross many wetlands. Many of the wetlands crossed on large projects are likely to be very similar in nature and can be placed in groups based on similar features related to geographic area, geomorphology, hydrology, soils, habitat types, and land uses. Evaluation of wetlands within each group of similar wetlands should lead to determination of common wetland revegetation goals that could be applied on a group basis. Development of appropriate goals and options for performance standards could accommodate potential minor variations among individual wetlands within such groups that could be addressed on a case-by-case basis during construction, with appropriate documentation.

Most project planning and impact assessment phases of pipeline projects involve the collection of detailed wetland information that can be used for evaluation and goal setting. GIS or other mapping databases greatly facilitate management of this information and required planning, construction, and post-construction documentation. Special case wetlands with unique requirements are still likely to occur with large projects. GIS can also help track and facilitate implementation of requirements for individual wetlands. Therefore, the proposed approach should be useful on both small and large projects.

CONCLUSION

Identifying wetland revegetation goals within pipeline construction ROW provides a way to focus on wetland issues that are of concern and actually affected by the cut-and-trench method of pipeline construction at wetland crossings. Most environmental regulations support this type of approach, although it is common practice for mitigation and revegetation permit requirements for pipeline ROW to be prescriptive, especially when dealing with local permits (GRI, 1999). The proposed approach should provide a useful framework that can be applied in both general and specific situations to build consensus among regulators, permit applicants, and other appropriate parties.

The proposed approach is important to the pipeline industry because many mitigation requirements that are developed in normal permit processes are often viewed by industry as rigid, prescriptive, inappropriate, costly, causing delays, and potentially in conflict with other requirements (GRI, 1999). A common request from industry is for flexibility in providing suitable environmental protection. The proposed approach encourages flexibility because several options will usually be available to meet performance standards, and the performance standards are intended to measure overall goals, not prescriptive requirements. The proposed approach should also improve overall environmental protection because the approach focuses on achieving goals, and has the potential to identify goals that are appropriate but that may have been missed using conventional processes.

ACKNOWLEDGEMENTS

This research was funded by GRI (formerly the Gas Research Institute). Many people at URS, GRI, and GRI's member companies provided input and support in preparing this document. I would like to specifically thank the following people for their help with this project: Krista Bartsch, Richard Bausell, Scott Moorhouse, Ray Hinkle, and Sherri Albrecht of URS; James Evans, the GRI Project Manager; the GRI Technical Assistance Group; and Bill Streever of the Corps' Waterways Experiment Station. Additional input was provided during the early stages of this work by numerous federal and state agency representatives, over 30 participants at a workshop held as part of this research at the Society of Wetland Scientists Conference held in Norfolk, Virginia in June, 1999, and representatives from the FERC at a GRI meeting held in Washington, DC in March, 2000. Although the recommendations in this paper may not reflect the opinions of these people and agencies, all comments received from them were evaluated and appreciated.

REFERENCES

BLM. 1993. Process for Assessing Proper Functioning Condition. Riparian Area Management, TR 1737-9, 1993.

BLM. 1994. Process for Assessing Proper Functioning Condition for Lentic Riparian — Wetland Areas. Riparian Area Management, TR 1737-11, 1994.

Brinson, Mark. 1995. The HGM Approach Explained. National Wetlands Newsletter. November–December 1995.

Brinson, Mark. 1996. Assessing Wetland Functions Using HGM. National Wetlands Newsletter. January–February 1996.

Cowardin, L.M., V. Carter, F.C. Golet, and E.T. LaRoe. 1979. Classification of Wetlands and Deepwater Habitats of the United States. US Department of the Interior, Fish and Wildlife Service, Washington, DC FWS/OBS-79/31.

GRI. 1999. Summary and Evaluation of Literature Reviewed and the Results of the Outreach Program for Wetland Revegetation Practices on Pipeline Rights of Way. GRI-97/1704.

GRI. 2000. An Approach for Determining and Meeting Wetland Revegetation Goals in Pipeline Construction Rights of Way. GRI-00/0112.

Streever, Bill. 1999. Performance standards for wetland creation and restoration under Section 404. National Wetlands Newsletter, 21(3): 10.

BIOGRAPHICAL SKETCH

Bill Magdych

URS, 1615 Murray Canyon Road, Suite 1,000, San Diego, CA 92108, USA. Phone: 619-294-9400. Fax: 619-293-7920. E-mail: bill_magdych@urscorp.com

Bill Magdych, PhD, is a senior manager, ecologist, and permitting specialist at URS. His graduate work was conducted at the University of Oklahoma, and he performed Post Doctoral research on wetlands at San Diego State University. He has over 20 years experience working with wetlands and permitting for pipeline and other projects in the United States, Canada, Mexico, Caribbean, and Pacific Islands.

Effects of Soil Segregation Treatments on Revegetation of Wetlands Affected by Pipeline Construction

Stephen A. Compton, David J. Santillo, and Patrick G. Fellion

Revegetation success was assessed in three wetlands six years after being affected by natural gas pipeline construction. Two soil handling treatments (mixed and segregated) were used in two of the wetlands to assess the effects of wetland construction technique on restoration success. Revegetation success was also assessed in three areas within each right-of-way including the working area, trench line, and control area (existing powerline right-of-way). Nine vegetation characteristics were analyzed, including percent cover, height and richness of herbaceous and woody species, percent wetland species, species quality rating index, and Shannon–Wiener index. There are few differences in the nine vegetation characteristics between mixed and segregated soil treatments. However, herbaceous height and percent cover were generally lower in the trench line area than in either the working or control areas. Furthermore, woody height and percent cover were higher in control areas than either the working or trench line areas in two of the three wetlands. Although soil segregation methods apparently had little impact on plant restoration success six years after construction, the trench line area of the natural gas pipeline right-of-way generally had lower herbaceous and woody height and percent cover than either the working or control areas.

Keywords: Soil segregation, wetlands, revegetation, natural gas pipeline

INTRODUCTION

Soil removed from trenches excavated during pipeline construction in wetlands is commonly segregated. Specifically, topsoil and subsoil are typically removed separately, segregated, and then replaced, as practicable, in their original horizon following pipe installation. Although segregation of soils in unsaturated wetlands is an accepted procedure, it is unclear whether this method offers clear advantages over other methods of soil treatment (e.g., mixing of topsoil and subsoil) in terms of the success of post-construction revegetation.

This report presents results from the 1999 growing season, which is year 6 of a 10-year monitoring project being conducted by ANR Pipeline on the Empire State Pipeline, located in central New York State. Year 6 research was completed by Northern Ecological Associates, Inc. (NEA), and follows year 4 research performed in 1997 by NEA (1999), year 2 research performed in 1995 by the State University of New York, College of Environmental Science and Forestry (O'Reilly, 1996), and year 1 research performed in 1994 by Beak Consultants, Inc. (1995). Final sampling will occur in 2003, which corresponds to year 10.

The specific objectives of the study were to:

1. Determine the effect of mixing topsoil and subsoil on the regeneration of the post-construction vegetation community; and
2. Conduct a multiple-year comparison of nine vegetation indices to determine the degree of restoration success in segregated and mixed soil treatments in different areas of the right-of-way.

METHODS

Study locations

Three wetlands, each with a different underlying soil texture class, hydrologic regime, and vegetation community were selected for this study, as described below.

Wetland Wn-56a. Wetland Wn-56a is located in the Town of Rose, Wayne County, New York. This wetland is a semi saturated emergent marsh underlain by silty to silty clay soils. At year 3, dominant post-construction vegetation in the right-of-way portion of Wetland Wn-56a included reed canary grass (*Phalaris arundinacea*), boneset (*Eupatorium perfoliatum*), and goldenrods (*Solidago altissima, E. graminifolia*).

Wetland Ca-4b. Wetland Ca-4b is located in the Town of Conquest, Cayuga County, New York. This wetland is a semi-permanently flooded emergent marsh/shrub swamp underlain by clay soils. At year 3, dominant post-construction vegetation in the right-of-way portion of Wetland Ca-4b included purple loosestrife (*Lythrum salicaria*), arrow arum (*Peltandra virginica*), cattail (*Typha latifolia*), duckweed (*Lemna spp*), and bur reed (*Sparganium eurycarpum*).

Wetland Ca-19. Wetland Ca-19 is located in the Town of Cato, Cayuga County, New York. This wetland is a semi-permanently flooded emergent marsh underlain by organic soils. At year 3, dominant post-construction vegetation in the right-of-way portion of Wetland Ca-19 included purple loosestrife, cattail, bur reed, and reed canary grass.

Control areas. Separate control areas were located within each of the three wetland communities studied. Control area exhibited the same pre-construction vegetation composition and structure as the treatment sites located on the pipeline construction right-of-way. Control areas were located adjacent to the pipeline construction right-of-way and were not disturbed by pipeline construction. Control areas also were located adjacent to a New York Power Authority electric transmission line right-of-way.

Data collection

Two separate soil treatments were established in two of the three wetlands (Wn-56a and Ca-4b), one for segregated soils and one for mixed soils. For each soil treatment, three 200-ft-long transects were established parallel to the trench line, one in each of three right-of-way areas (Fig. 1). The three right-of-way areas included the trench area, where soil segregation or mixing took place and where the pipeline was installed; the working area, trafficked by heavy construction equipment; and the control area, a pre-existing New York Power Authority powerline right-of-way. Along each right-of-way transect, 12 1-m² quadrat samples were taken at equal intervals. The sampling design was identical in Wetland Ca-19, except that soil mixing was the only soil treatment.

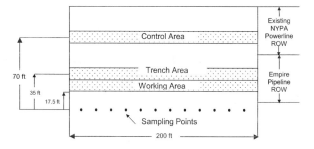

Fig. 1. Generalized sampling design.

Field measurements recorded from each 1-m² quadrat sample included mean herbaceous canopy height (cm), mean woody canopy height (cm), percent herbaceous cover by species; and percent woody cover by species. From the above field measurements, percent wetland species (Reed, 1988), Species Quality Rating Index (USACE, 1993), herbaceous species richness, woody species richness, and Shannon–Wiener Index (Barbour et al., 1993) were calculated.

Data analyses

1999 field season

Due to the limited sample size and inherent differences in the soils, hydrology, and plant communities of the three wetlands used in this study, most comparisons for both the soil treatments (e.g., segregated vs. mixed) and the right-of-way areas (e.g., working, trench, and control) were conducted within but not among the three wetlands. For the soil treatments, t-tests were used to determine whether there were significant differences between segregated and mixed soil within the working, trench, and control areas for each of the nine variables of interest. Soil treatment effects were investigated in only two of the three wetlands (Wn-56a and Ca-4b) because the third (Ca-19) had only the mixed soil treatment. Differences between the working trench, and control areas within each of the soil treatments were examined using one-way Analysis of Variance (ANOVA). Duncan's new multiple range pairwise comparisons were used to determine differences among the three right-of-way treatments. Minimum significance level for statistical tests was 0.05.

Multiple-year comparison

Multiple-year comparisons of the nine vegetation indices by soil treatment and right-of-way treatment were performed to determine the degree of restoration success in the three different wetlands. Data were compiled from this report and from the three previous field season reports (Beak Consultants, Inc., 1995; O'Reilly, 1995; and NEA, 1999) to establish a 6-year post-construction sequence of wetland revegetation. Mean control values were determined for each variable using data from all four sampling events, except in Wetland Ca-4b, where 1994 control data were not used because a different area was sampled as the control treatment.

RESULTS

1999 field season

Comparison of segregated vs. mixed soil treatment

Wetland Wn-56a — Silty to silty clay soil. There were few significant differences for the nine vegetation indices between the segregated and mixed soil treatments in the working, trench, or control areas in Wn-56a (Table 1). In the working and trench areas, percent woody cover and woody species richness were significantly higher in the mixed soil treatment than in the segregated soil treatment. There were no significant differences in the nine vegetation indices between control areas.

Wetland Ca-4b — Clay soil. There were few significant differences between the segregated and mixed soil treatments for the working and trench areas in Wetland Ca-4b (Table 2). In the working area, percent woody cover was significantly higher in the segregated soil treatment. In the trench area, both percent woody cover and woody canopy height were significantly higher in the segregated soil treatment. There were no significant differences in the nine vegetation indices between the segregated and mixed soil treatments for the control area.

Comparison of right-of-way areas: Working, trench, and control

Wetland Wn-56a — Silty to silty clay soil. Herbaceous canopy height and percent wetland species were significantly lower in the trench area than in the working area for the segregated soil treatment of Wn-56a (Table 3). Herbaceous species richness and Shannon–Wiener index were significantly lower in the control area than in the trench area of the segregated soil treatment. Also, the control area had a taller woody canopy, shorter herbaceous canopy height, and lower percent wetland species and herbaceous species richness than the working area.

In the mixed soil treatment of Wetland Wn-56a, herbaceous canopy height, percent wetland species, and herbaceous species richness were significantly lower in the trench area than in the working area (Table 3). The woody canopy was higher and percent wetland species lower in the control as compared to both the working and trench areas. The control area also had significantly lower herbaceous canopy, herbaceous species richness, woody species richness, and Shannon–Wiener index than the working area of the mixed soil treatment of Wetland Wn-56a.

Wetland Ca-4b — Clay soil. For the segregated soil treatment in Wetland Ca-4b, the trench area had a significantly lower herbaceous canopy than the working area (Table 4). There were no other differences between the trench and working areas in the segregated soil treatment. The control area had a lower herbaceous canopy, percent herbaceous cover, and woody species richness than the working area. The trench and control areas differed only in percent herbaceous cover (lower in control).

Table 1. Mean (± Standard Error) of nine vegetation characteristics in segregated and mixed soil treatments (for each right-of-way area) in Wetland Wn-56a

	Working		Trench		Control	
	Segregated	Mixed	Segregated	Mixed	Segregated	Mixed
Herbaceous Canopy Height (cm)	76.67 (3.86)	68.18 (4.49)	61.25 (4.53)	43.63 (2.70)	62.92 (4.37)	50.45 (7.82)
Woody Canopy Height (cm)	25.42 (5.85)	34.09 (6.35)	36.25 (6.86)	22.00 (6.88)	59.58 (14.78)	93.63 (8.84)
Herbaceous Cover (%)	128.33 (4.28)	109.60 (7.09)	112.00 (5.58)	118.36 (10.11)	110.79 (9.70)	111.13 (6.98)
Woody Cover (%)	1.83* (0.85)	7.09* (3.73)	2.33* (0.69)	5.18* (2.21)	3.50 (1.94)	3.55 (1.71)
Wetland Species (%)	54.86 (6.84)	59.09 (6.88)	20.42 (9.14)	22.58 (9.64)	20.83 (8.97)	87.88 (6.39)
Quality Index	5.88 (0.33)	6.59 (0.59)	6.59 (0.73)	5.07 (0.72)	6.95 (0.51)	5.82 (0.43)
Herbaceous Species (#/m^2)	9.75 (0.57)	12.00 (0.77)	9.58 (0.57)	9.27 (0.43)	7.58 (0.58)	7.73 (0.59)
Woody Species (#/m^2)	0.67* (0.19)	1.36* (0.45)	1.25* (0.25)	2.27* (0.54)	0.58 (0.23)	0.73 (0.30)
Shannon–Wiener Index	1.50 (0.09)	1.89 (0.10)	1.73 (0.08)	1.64 (0.06)	1.42 (0.11)	1.16 (0.16)

*Statistically different at the 0.05 level of significance using the t-test and/or χ^2 test.

Table 2. Mean (± Standard Error) of nine vegetation characteristics in segregated and mixed soil treatments (for each right-of-way area) in Wetland Ca-4b

	Working		Trench		Control	
	Segregated	Mixed	Segregated	Mixed	Segregated	Mixed
Herbaceous Canopy Height (cm)	154.58 (7.96)	155.42 (13.36)	125.83 (4.56)	141.67 (3.55)	135.42 (3.56)	148.75 (4.36)
Woody Canopy Height (cm)	26.25 (15.72)	15.83 (15.83)	2.50* (0.75)	0.25* (0.25)	1.25 (0.65)	0.00 (0.00)
Herbaceous Cover (%)	124.75 (7.84)	95.17 (7.01)	126.33 (10.26)	104.46 (10.78)	99.58 (3.91)	88.96 (6.23)
Woody Cover (%)	7.25* (4.67)	1.33* (1.33)	0.83* (0.41)	0.13* (0.09)	0.25 (0.13)	0.08 (0.08)
Wetland Species (%)	100.00 (0.00)	100.00 (0.00)	100.00 (0.00)	100.00 (0.00)	100.00 (0.00)	100.00 (0.00)
Quality Index	5.42 (0.96)	5.05 (1.11)	4.74 (1.25)	5.31 (1.31)	3.41 (1.06)	5.71 (0.88)
Herbaceous Species (#/m^2)	6.92 (0.29)	7.08 (0.42)	7.50 (0.50)	8.42 (0.31)	7.50 (0.50)	8.50 (0.53)
Woody Species (#/m^2)	0.75 (0.18)	0.17 (0.17)	0.50 (0.15)	0.17 (0.11)	0.25 (0.13)	0.08 (0.08)
Shannon–Wiener Index	1.32 (0.08)	1.45 (0.10)	1.45 (0.09)	1.56 (0.06)	1.28 (0.08)	1.61 (0.08)

*Statistically different at the 0.05 level of significance using the t-test and/or χ^2 test.

Table 3. Mean (± Standard Error) for nine vegetation characteristics in three right-of-way areas for both segregated and mixed soil treatments in Wetland Wn-56a

	Segregated			Mixed		
	Working	Trench	Control	Working	Trench	Control
Herbaceous Canopy Height (cm)	76.67[a] (3.86)	61.25[b] (4.53)	62.92[b] (4.37)	68.18[a] (4.49)	43.63[b] (2.70)	50.45[b] (7.82)
Woody Canopy Height (cm)	25.42[a] (5.85)	36.25[ab] (6.86)	59.58[b] (14.78)	34.09[a] (6.35)	22.00[a] (6.88)	93.63[b] (8.84)
Herbaceous Cover (%)	128.33[a] (4.28)	112.00[a] (5.58)	110.79[a] (9.70)	109.60[a] (7.09)	118.36[a] (10.11)	111.13[a] (6.98)
Woody Cover (%)	1.83[a] (0.85)	2.33[a] (0.69)	3.50[a] (1.94)	7.09[a] (3.73)	5.18[a] (2.21)	3.55[a] (1.71)
Wetland Species (%)	54.86[a] (6.84)	20.42[b] (9.14)	20.83[b] (8.97)	59.09[a] (6.88)	22.58[b] (9.64)	87.88[c] (6.39)
Quality Index	5.88[a] (0.33)	6.59[a] (0.73)	6.95[a] (0.51)	6.59[a] (0.59)	5.07[a] (0.72)	5.82[a] (0.43)
Herbaceous Species (#/m^2)	9.75[a] (0.57)	9.58[a] (0.57)	7.58[b] (0.58)	12.00[a] (0.77)	9.27[b] (0.43)	7.73[b] (0.59)
Woody Species (#/m^2)	0.67[a] (0.19)	1.25[a] (0.25)	0.58[a] (0.23)	1.36[a] (0.45)	2.27[ab] (0.54)	0.73[b] (0.30)
Shannon–Wiener Index	1.50[ab] (0.09)	1.73[a] (0.08)	1.42[b] (0.11)	1.89[a] (0.10)	1.64[a] (0.06)	1.16[b] (0.16)

[ab]For comparisons among the three right-of-way areas, within each soil treatment (i.e., segregated or mixed), mean values with the same superscript letter are not significantly different at the 0.05 level.

Table 4. Mean (± Standard Error) for nine vegetation characteristics in three right-of-way areas for both segregated and mixed soil treatments in Wetland Ca-4b

	Segregated			Mixed		
	Working	Trench	Control	Working	Trench	Control
Herbaceous Canopy Height (cm)	154.58[a] (7.96)	125.83[b] (4.56)	135.42[b] (3.56)	155.42[a] (13.36)	141.67[a] (3.55)	148.75[a] (4.36)
Woody Canopy Height (cm)	26.25[a] (15.72)	2.50[a] (0.75)	1.25[a] (0.65)	15.83[a] (15.83)	0.25[a] (0.25)	0.00[a] (0.00)
Herbaceous Cover (%)	124.75[a] (7.84)	126.33[a] (10.26)	99.58[b] (3.91)	95.17[a] (7.01)	104.46[a] (10.78)	88.96[a] (6.23)
Woody Cover (%)	7.25[a] (4.67)	0.83[a] (0.41)	0.25[a] (0.13)	1.33[a] (1.33)	0.13[a] (0.09)	0.08[a] (0.08)
Wetland Species (%)	100.00[a] (0.00)	100.00[a] (0.00)	100.00[a] (0.00)	100.00[a] (0.00)	100.00[a] (0.00)	100.00[a] (0.00)
Quality Index	5.42[a] (0.96)	4.74[a] (1.25)	3.41[a] (1.06)	5.05[a] (1.11)	5.31[a] (1.31)	5.71[a] (0.88)
Herbaceous Species (#/m^2)	6.92[a] (0.29)	7.50[a] (0.50)	7.50[a] (0.50)	7.08[a] (0.42)	8.42[b] (0.31)	8.50[b] (0.53)
Woody Species (#/m^2)	0.75[a] (0.18)	0.50[ab] (0.15)	0.25[b] (0.13)	0.17[a] (0.17)	0.17[a] (0.11)	0.08[a] (0.08)
Shannon–Wiener Index	1.32[a] (0.08)	1.45[a] (0.09)	1.28[a] (0.08)	1.45[a] (0.10)	1.56[a] (0.06)	1.61[a] (0.08)

[ab] For comparisons among the three right-of-way areas, within each soil treatment (i.e., segregated or mixed), mean values with the same superscript letter are not significantly different at the 0.05 level.

In the mixed soil treatment, the only significant difference was the working area had a lower herbaceous species richness than either the trench or control areas (Table 4).

Wetland Ca-19 — Organic soil. In Wetland Ca-19, where there was only a mixed topsoil/subsoil treatment, the control area is distinguished from both the working and trench soil areas due to a significantly higher herbaceous canopy, higher species quality index, and higher herbaceous species richness (Table 5). The trench had a significantly lower herbaceous canopy than both the working and control treatments. The trench treatment was further distinguished from the working treatment by its lower herbaceous canopy.

Multiple-year comparison
Wetland Wn-56a — Silty to silty clay soil. In both the working and trench areas, six of the nine vegetation indices (percent herbaceous cover, percent wetland species, species quality index, herbaceous species richness, woody species richness, and Shannon–Wiener index) equaled or exceeded the mean control value (used as a measure of restoration success) by the first growing season (1994). Furthermore, herbaceous canopy height in the working and trench areas reached the mean control value by the second growing season (1995). Only woody height and percent woody

Table 5. Mean (± Standard Error) for nine vegetation characteristics in three right-of-way areas in Wetland Ca-19

	Working area	Trench area	Control area
Herbaceous Canopy Height (cm)	167.08[a] (5.13)	135.83[b] (3.07)	188.75[c] (3.90)
Woody Canopy Height (cm)	5.42[a] (5.42)	12.92[a] (8.71)	51.25[a] (25.32)
Herbaceous Cover (%)	121.00[a] (4.50)	89.42[b] (4.34)	107.25[a] (7.86)
Woody Cover (%)	0.08[a] (0.08)	1.25[a] (0.90)	10.67[a] (8.10)
Wetland Species (%)	100.00[a] (0.00)	100.00[a] (0.00)	100.00[a] (0.00)
Quality Index	4.64[a] (0.29)	3.37[a] (0.59)	8.41[b] (0.84)
Herbaceous Species (#/m^2)	3.50[a] (0.23)	3.42[a] (0.26)	4.75[b] (0.28)
Woody Species (#/m^2)	0.08[a] (0.08)	0.17[a] (0.11)	0.33[a] (0.14)
Shannon–Wiener Index	0.78[a] (0.05)	0.80[a] (0.04)	0.89[a] (0.06)

[ab] For comparisons among the three right-of-way areas, mean values with the same superscript letter are not significantly different at the 0.05 level.

cover did not reach the mean control value by the sixth growing season (1999). Also, there was a general decline in percent wetland species, species quality index, herbaceous and woody species richness, and Shannon–Wiener index after the first growing season in both working and trench areas.

Wetland Ca-4b — Clay soil. In both the working and trench areas of Wetland Ca-4b, three of the nine vegetation indices (percent wetland species, species quality index, herbaceous species richness, and woody species richness) equaled or exceeded the mean control value by the first growing season (1994). Herbaceous canopy height, percent herbaceous cover, and Shannon–Wiener index all reached the mean control value by the sixth growing season. In the working area/mixed soil treatment, only one vegetation index (percent woody cover) did not reach the mean control value by the sixth growing season. Indices that did not reach the mean control value in the trench line area included woody height, percent woody cover, and woody species richness (except in the mixed soil treatment/first growing season).

Wetland Ca-19 — Organic soil. In the first growing season, three of the nine vegetation indices (species quality index, herbaceous species richness, and woody species richness) in Wetland Ca-19 had reached or exceeded that of the mean control value. Between the second and sixth growing seasons herbaceous canopy height, herbaceous cover, percent wetland species, and Shannon–Wiener index also reached the mean control value in both the segregated and mixed soil treatments. Two vegetation indices, woody height and percent woody cover, did not reach the mean control value by the sixth growing season (1999).

DISCUSSION

1999 field season
Comparison of segregated vs. mixed soil treatment
Wetland Wn-56a — Silty to silty clay soil. Data from the 1997 growing season suggested that the control areas for the segregated and mixed soil treatments differed in their woody vegetation characteristics and, therefore, possibly in their underlying hydrology and soil characteristics (NEA, 1999). In contrast to the 1997 growing season, data from the 1999 growing season suggests that there were no significant differences in the nine vegetation characteristics between the control areas for the segregated and mixed soil treatments. Variability in the vegetation characteristics of the control areas is likely to have been introduced by NYPA powerline right-of-way maintenance activities.

The segregated and mixed soil treatments of Wetland Wn-56a differed most significantly in their woody vegetation characteristics in the working and trench areas. Specifically, the mixed soil treatment had a higher percentage woody cover and woody species richness. Although it is possible that topsoil/subsoil mixing enhances woody species revegetation, 1999 growing season data from Wetland Ca-4b exhibit the opposite trend, suggesting that soil treatment differences in woody vegetation growth may be the result of other, unknown factors.

Wetland Ca-4b — Clay soil. As with Wetland Wn-56a, there were no differences between the control areas for the two soil treatments in Wetland Ca-4b in the 1999 growing season, although there were significant differences between the two control areas in the 1997 growing season. Right-of-way management activities would not have been a factor in this wetland; however, observed differences in herbaceous vegetation between the control areas for the two soil treatments in 1997 may be the result of inherent seasonal variability.

The segregated soil treatment for both the working and trench areas of Wetland Ca-4b had a more significant woody vegetation component. As with Wetland Wn-56a, these differences are most likely attributed to factors other than soil treatment because, as mentioned in previous section, the woody vegetation component of Wetland Wn-56a is greater in the mixed soil treatment, which is opposite to the trend observed in Ca-4b.

Right-of-way areas: Working, trench, and control
Wetland Wn-56a — Silty to silty clay soil. In the segregated soil treatment area of Wetland Wn-56a, the control and trench areas were similar to each other, differing only in their herbaceous species richness and Shannon–Wiener index (both were higher in the trench area). Higher herbaceous species richness and Shannon–Wiener index may be attributed to the use of the trench area as an all-terrain-vehicle (ATV) travel corridor. This disturbance has introduced typical invasive herbaceous species such as path rush (*Juncus tenuis*) and bull thistle (*Cirsium vulgare*) to the trench treatment area. In comparison, the working area differs considerably from both the trench and control areas. In general, the working area, which was adjacent to the undisturbed forested wetland had a higher percentage of wetland species and a more significant herbaceous component than either the trench or control treatment area, suggesting that these two areas are in a drier part of the wetland.

Wetland Ca-4b — Clay soil. The most important difference among the three right-of-way areas in the segregated soil area of Wetland Ca-4b is the more vigorous herbaceous community in the working area as compared to both the trench and control areas. The difference in herbaceous canopy height between the working and trench areas may reflect a shift in plant community composition as a result of wetter conditions in the trench area resulting from construction. Although the plant communities of the two areas were similar in their dominant species (i.e., purple loosestrife and cattail), the trench area had a greater occurrence of shorter vegetation common to permanently flooded areas such as duckweed and bur reed. The less vigorous herbaceous community of the control area, as compared to both the working and trench areas, likely reflects shading effects from the adjacent forested wetland community.

Although the only significant difference among the three right-of-way areas of the mixed soil treatment area was the lower herbaceous species richness in the working area, closer inspection of the data shows a similar pattern to that of the segregated area of Wetland Ca-4b. The herbaceous canopy was consistently low in the trench area; however, differences between the herbaceous canopy height in the trench and working areas were masked by high variability in heights among plots in the working area.

Wetland Ca-19 — Organic soil. As in both Wetlands Wn-56a and Ca-4b, the trench treatment of Wetland Ca-19 had the lowest herbaceous canopy. Furthermore, the control area of this wetland had the highest herbaceous canopy, species quality index and herbaceous species richness of all three treatments. Although the causal relationship is unclear, this decreasing gradient in herbaceous canopy height from control to working to trench area may reflect the degree of disturbance due to construction. Nonetheless, changes in hydrology are likely to have occurred during construction restoration (regrading) activities, resulting in a shift in plant community composition in the working and, especially, the trench areas.

Multiple-year comparison
Wetland Wn-56a — Silty to silty clay soil. Multiple-year comparison of the nine vegetation indices in Wetland Wn-56a demonstrates that the overall herbaceous community structure (i.e., species richness, canopy height, and percent cover) had become reestablished by the end of the second growing season (1995) in both mixed and segregated soil treatments. Not surprisingly, however, woody canopy height and percent woody cover is returning more slowly and, by the end of the sixth growing season (1999), had not yet reached the levels of the control area.

Wetland Ca-4b — Clay soil. Similar to Wetland Wn-56a, the overall herbaceous community of both the mixed and segregated soil treatments had become reestablished within the first six growing seasons. Diversity indices, species quality, and wetland species composition had also recovered. Also, similar to Wetland Wn-56a, the woody community structure was not fully reestablished in either the working or trench areas by the sixth growing season.

Wetland Ca-19 — Organic soil. Again, similar to both Wetlands Wn-56a and Ca-4b, the overall herbaceous community structure had become reestablished by the end of the sixth growing season in both the mixed and segregated soil treatments. Diversity indices, species quality, and wetland species composition had also recovered. Woody height and percent cover had not yet reached control levels by the end of the growing season, probably due to the inherent slower recovery of woody vegetation.

CONCLUSIONS

The vegetation communities in three wetlands, which varied in their underlying soil texture, were studied to determine the effects of two different soil treatments (segregated and mixed) in three right-of-way areas (trench, working, and control). The vegetation communities of wetlands under both silty to silty clay (Wetland Wn-56a) and clay soils (Wetland Ca-4b) did not differ significantly as a result of soil treatment after six years of post-construction recovery. Results from the 1999 growing season suggest that, in all three wetlands, herbaceous canopy height, and to a lesser degree percent herbaceous cover, are lower in the trench areas than in the working or control areas, probably due to a shift in plant community composition resulting from a drier hydrology caused by construction.

Multiple-year comparisons demonstrated that the herbaceous community structure of all three wetlands had become reestablished by the sixth post-construction growing season and, in some cases, as early as the second growing season. Multiple-year comparisons also revealed that, in all three wetlands, woody vegetation structure in the working and trench treatments was not fully restored when compared to that of the control treatment.

ACKNOWLEDGEMENT

ANR Pipeline is conducting this research project in selected wetlands along the Empire State Pipeline to monitor the success of wetland restoration efforts involving two different soil treatments (segregated and mixed) in accordance with Special Condition #54 (iii) of US Army Corps of Engineers Permit 92-976-282.

REFERENCES

Barbour, M.G., J.H. Burk, and W.D. Pitts. 1993. Terrestrial Plant Ecology, 2nd ed. Benjamin/Cumming. Menlo Park, CA.

Beak Consultants, Inc. 1995. Empire State Pipeline, Wetland Research Study, 1994 Field Report. Prepared for ANR Pipeline Company, 500 Renaissance Center, Detroit, MI 48243.

Northern Ecological Associates, Inc. 1999. Empire State Pipeline, Wetland Research Study, 1997 Field Report. Prepared for ANR Pipeline Company, 500 Renaissance Center, Detroit, MI 48243.

O'Reilly, J. February 1996. Empire State Pipeline, Wetland Research Study, 1995 Field Season Report. State University of New York, College of Environmental Science and Forestry, Syracuse, NY.

Reed, P.B. 1988. National List of Plant Species that Occur in Wetlands: Northeast (Region 1). US Fish and Wildlife Service. Washington, DC.

US Army Corps of Engineers. 1993. Report of Potential Impacts to Waters of the United States. USACE, Buffalo District., Buffalo, NY.

BIOGRAPHICAL SKETCHES

Stephen A. Compton

Northern Ecological Associates, Inc., (315) 386-3704 (P), (315) 379-0355 (F), scompton@neanewyork.com

Mr. Compton has over 13 years of relevant environmental work experience, including the management and execution of comprehensive environmental impact analysis and development of mitigation measures at both the state and federal level. Mr. Compton has managed and/or prepared Environmental Assessments (EAs) and Impact Statements (EISs) for various federal actions and recreational, roadway, and natural gas pipeline development and expansion projects. Mr. Compton's areas of expertise include NEPA analysis and compliance; comprehensive environmental permitting and mitigation planning; and environmental compliance monitoring of construction activities.

David J. Santillo

Northern Ecological Associates, Inc.

With over 14 years experience conducting ecological investigations and comprehensive analysis of environmental impact and mitigation measures at both the state and federal level, Mr. Santillo specializes in the design, implementation, and management of environmental assessments and ecological resource analyses including wetland studies, ecological inventories, and habitat mitigation and restoration plans. In particular, he has extensive experience in all phases of natural gas pipeline planning and construction. As Principal Ecologist for Northern Ecological Associates, Mr. Santillo is responsible for supervising and participating in the planning and implementation of environmental and ecological analysis projects, including development and implementation work plans, principal review of reports, supervision of staff, and budget control.

Patrick G. Fellion

Northern Ecological Associates, Inc.

Mr. Fellion is a terrestrial and aquatic biologist with five years experience conducting ecological and wetland field investigations and assisting in data collection for interdisciplinary environmental assessment projects. Mr. Fellion has assisted with numerous plant and animal inventories in upland, wetland, and aquatic ecosystems, as well as assisting with preparation of numerous environmental permitting and environmental impact assessment projects.

Rapid Approach to Required Post-Construction Wetland Vegetation Monitoring after Pipeline Construction

Brett M. Battaglia, J. Roger Trettel

Federal and state authorizations for construction of pipeline projects through wetlands typically require 2–5 years of post-construction monitoring to assess the long-term condition of wetlands. The standard wetland monitoring condition imposed by the Federal Energy Regulatory Commission (FERC) typically requires qualitative cover assessments along with quantitative sampling to calculate pre-construction and post-construction community diversity. Due to the large number of wetlands crossed by large pipeline projects, a rapid, yet scientifically valid sampling methodology is desirable. Northern Ecological Associates, Inc. (NEA) has implemented a modified version of an established qualitative/quantitative assessment technique that provides a means of rapidly documenting wetland characteristics. In order to obtain both qualitative and quantitative data, the established plant sampling technique, the Braun–Blanquet Releve' Method (Bonham, 1989) was used. The qualitative component involves a walkover of the wetland to visually assess the overall condition of the site and documentation of a variety of parameters on a checklist-type data form. The quantitative component of the program involves determination of percent cover in accordance with a variable-sized quadrat sampled at a representative location within the wetland as per the Releve' Method. Data collected with the Releve' Method may be used to calculate diversity by means of the Shannon–Weaver diversity index.

Keywords: Wetland monitoring, Releve', quadrat, diversity, cover

INTRODUCTION

This paper presents a methodology for performing required post-construction qualitative and quantitative monitoring of wetlands following pipeline construction. Because of the large numbers of wetlands typically crossed by large-scale pipeline projects, required monitoring can be time consuming and costly. Furthermore, completing surveys and summarizing data in report form for submittal to regulatory agencies is typically required by early fall, thus necessitating rapid data collection, processing, and reporting. The methodology developed by Northern Ecological Associates, Inc. (NEA) addresses these issues of timing and cost, while generating valid, comprehensive qualitative and quantitative data to fulfill permit condition requirements.

This methodology has been utilized on several recent natural gas pipeline projects in the northeastern US including, most recently, the Portland Natural Gas Transmission System (PNGTS) and PNGTS/Maritimes & Northeast, L.L.C. (Maritimes) Joint Facilities projects. The combined PNGTS and PNGTS/Maritimes Joint Facilities projects (Projects) involved pipe installation and heavy equipment operation through a total of over 1500 wetlands through portions of Massachusetts, New Hampshire, Maine, and Vermont. These Projects will be used as a case study in describing the wetland monitoring methodology.

Authorization for the Projects included permits to allow pipeline construction through wetlands issued by the Federal Energy Regulatory Commission (FERC), US Army Corps of Engineers (COE), the Maine Department of Environmental Protection

(MDEP), the New Hampshire Department of Environmental Services (NHDES), the Massachusetts Department of Environmental Protection (MADEP), and the Vermont Agency of Natural Resources (VTANR). In issuing these permits, the various regulatory agencies required that wetlands be restored to approximate original condition and the wetlands be monitored over time to ensure satisfactory revegetation. In general, conditions of each of these permits are summarized as follows:
- restore the grade, hydrology, and vegetation of impacted wetland communities;
- provide for no net loss of wetland acreage;
- adequately assess the condition and vegetation diversity of the restored wetlands; and
- link monitoring to management or maintenance actions that will be taken when performance criteria are not attained.

In compliance with its permit conditions, PNGTS implemented the procedures specified in the Program and described in this paper. During July and August, 1999, NEA field ecologists implemented the first year of the Program and performed qualitative and quantitative assessments of all 1400 wetlands crossed by the Projects.

Specific wetland monitoring permit conditions and success criteria

Each of the state and federal permits issued for the project included conditions relating to post-construction wetland monitoring and reporting. Specific post-construction monitoring and reporting permit conditions were as follows.

Federal Energy Regulatory Commission
"Monitor the success of wetland revegetation annually for the first 3–5 years after construction. Revegetation should be considered successful if the cover of native herbaceous and/or woody species is at least 80% of the total area, and the diversity of native species is at least 50% of the diversity originally found in the wetlands. If revegetation is not successful at the end of 3 years, develop and implement (in consultation with a professional wetland ecologist) a remedial revegetation plan to actively revegetate the wetland with native wetland herbaceous and woody plant species. Continue revegetation efforts until wetland revegetation is successful."

US Army Corps of Engineers
"A restoration monitoring report shall be submitted to the Corps of Engineers and the US EPA at the end of the growing season for at least five consecutive years or until the restoration is successful. The restoration monitoring reports for the FERC may be used to satisfy this condition if they contain at least: the estimated percentage of foliage cover at each restored site by non invasive hydrophytes; a summary of inspections and corrective actions to control erosion, sedimentation and invasive species of hydrophytes; and, any relevant recommendations or suggestions."

New Hampshire Department of Environmental Services
"Company shall monitor wetland revegetation efforts annually until successful as per NHDES success standards described as follows. Revegetation shall be considered successful if (1) at least 80% of the total cover is native species and (2) the level of diversity of the native species present after construction is at least 50% of the level originally found in the wetland. If the area is not showing signs of re-establishing native wetland vegetation during the first growing season following construction, Company shall develop and implement (in consultation with a professional wetland ecologist) a plan to revegetate the wetland with native wetland species. If the NHDES-specified level of percent cover and diversity is not achieved after the third growing season, Company shall consult with the NHDES to develop a strategy for achieving successful revegetation."

"Monitoring reports related to wetland vegetative restoration shall be submitted annually no later than September 1st each year, for a period of three growing seasons following the completion of construction." Due to on-going construction/restoration work during the 1999 growing season, the NHDES granted an extension for the submittal of the First Year Report to October 15, 1999.

Maine Department of Environmental Protection
"Company will monitor the success of wetland revegetation annually for the first three to five years after construction. Revegetation should be considered successful if (1) at least 80% of the total cover is native species and (2) the level of diversity of the native species present after construction is at least 50% of the level originally found in the wetland. If the area is not showing signs of re-establishing native wetland vegetation during the first growing season following construction, Company will develop and implement (in consultation with a professional wetland ecologist) a plan to revegetate the wetland with native wetland species."

Massachusetts Department of Environmental Protection
"Company will monitor the success of wetland revegetation annually for the first three to five years after construction. Revegetation should be considered successful if (1) at least 80% of the total cover is native species and (2) the level of diversity of the native species present after construction is at least 50% of the level originally found in the wetland. If the area is not showing signs of re-establishing native wetland vegetation during the first growing season following construction, Company will develop and implement (in consultation with a professional wetland ecologist) a plan to revegetate the wetland with native wetland species."

Vermont Agency of Natural Resources
"The applicant shall monitor both wetland and riparian buffer revegetation efforts (see Condition #29 below) annually until successful. Re-vegetation shall be considered successful if (1) at least 80% of the total cover is native species and (2) the level of diversity of the native species present after construction is at least 50% of the level originally found in the wetland or riparian buffer. If the area is not showing signs of re-establishing native vegetation during the first growing season following construction, the applicant shall develop and implement (in consultation with a professional ecologist) a plan to revegetate the wetland or riparian buffer with native species."

"Immediately following construction across stream channel AST003, temporary erosion controls and bank restoration and stabilization techniques described in the Applicant's Environmental Construction Plan shall be implemented. As soon as practicable following construction across stream channel ST003, the full 25-foot riparian buffer zones shall be re-planted with native willows (*Salix spp.*) and speckled alder (*Alnus rugosa*). Restoration efforts shall be monitored annually until 'successful' as outlined in Condition #19 above."

Success criteria

Based on the various permit conditions for the Projects, the following criteria were used to evaluate wetland restoration success:
- the affected wetland must be the same size as the pre-disturbance wetland as documented in permit applications;
- the restored wetland must meet the US Army Corps of Engineers 1987 soils, vegetation, and hydrology criteria for wetland designation; and
- initial revegetation of wetlands shall consist of annual rye grass. With time, the cover of native herbaceous and/or woody wetland species shall be at least 80% of the total area, and the diversity of native species shall be 50% of the diversity originally found in the wetlands.

MONITORING METHODS

Field ecologists performed the required wetland vegetation monitoring. Wetlands were monitored during the peak-growing season, which coincides with the mid-summer months (July–August). In order to obtain both qualitative and quantitative data to achieve permit condition compliance, NEA utilized the established plant sampling technique, the Braun–Blanquet Releve' method (Bonham, 1989). The Releve' method involves the qualitative description and quantitative documentation of plant community characteristics, including species richness and vegetation structure, within plots that are representative of particular plant communities or cover types, which are identified through preliminary reconnaissance of a site. This approach provides a formal characterization of the wetland community, while avoiding excessively labor-intensive field sampling commonly associated with randomized sampling designs. The following provides the procedures of the Releve' method that were implemented to perform qualitative and quantitative wetland vegetation monitoring. At each site, a Qualitative/Quantitative Wetland Assessment Form and a Species Inventory Report Form are completed. In addition, representative photographs are taken at each wetland and documented in a photographic record.

Qualitative assessment

The qualitative component of the monitoring program involves a detailed site reconnaissance of the entire wetland and a visual assessment of the overall condition of the site. Parameters evaluated include grade, hydrology, soils, percent vegetative cover, vegetation vigor, dominant species community composition, and evidence of nuisance weed invasion. The wetland community on the disturbed ROW is compared with undisturbed portions of the same wetland located adjacent to the disturbed ROW. Care is taken to compare appropriate similar communities on- and off-ROW. The field teams are also instructed to use best professional judgement to assess whether the wetland appears to be successfully revegetating to a hydrophytic vegetation community, or whether corrective actions may be warranted.

Where a wetland complex is defined by several separate segments, similar community types are combined and represented by a single data plot. Where separate segments of the same wetland are dissimilar from each other in vegetation community type (e.g., scrub-shrub wetland in one section of the wetland and wet meadow in another), a separate data plot was established within each representative wetland area.

At each site, a Qualitative/Quantitative Wetland Assessment Form and a Species Inventory Report Form were completed. In addition, representative photographs were taken at each wetland and documented in a photographic record.

Quantitative assessment

Permit conditions addressing long-term monitoring all contain a component calling for quantitative assessment. Specifically, the FERC, COE, MDEP, NHDES, VTANR, and MADEP permit conditions all require assessing the total "percent cover" of wetland vegetation and the "diversity" of the plant community in comparison to pre-construction conditions. In order to determine these quantitative values, the following procedures were implemented at each wetland.

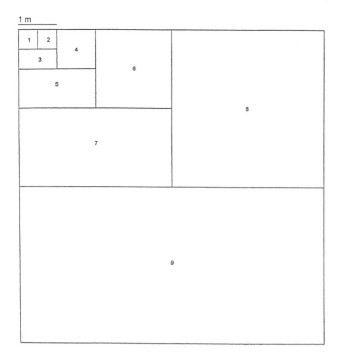

Plot number	Size (m²)	Plot number	Size (m²)
1	0.25	6	8.0
2	0.5	7	16.0
3	1.0	8	32.0
4	2.0	9	64.0
5	4.0		

Fig. 1. Nested quadrat diagram.

Table 1. Cover classes of Braun–Blanquet

Class	Range of % Cover	Median
5	75–100	87.5
4	50–75	62.5
3	25–50	37.5
2	2–25	15.0
1	1–5	2.5
t[a]	<1	0.1
r[a]	≪1	*

[a]Individuals occurring seldom or only once; cover ignored and assumed to be insignificant.
Source: Mueller-Dombois and Ellenburg, 1974.

Table 2. Sociability scale of Braun–Blanquet

Value	Meaning
5	Growing in large, almost pure stands
4	Growing in small colonies or carpets
3	Forming small patches or cushions
2	Forming small but dense clumps
1	Growing singly

Source: Barbour et al., 1987.

Percent cover

In accordance with the Releve' Method, a variable-sized quadrat was sampled at a representative location within the wetland in the approximate center of the construction ROW. The quadrat is a minimum of one square meter and sized to contain at least 90–95% of the dominant plant species identified within the community during the general site reconnaissance. The actual size of the Releve' plot is determined by sampling a series of nested quadrats (Fig. 1). Successively larger quadrats, each of which contains the smaller, previously sampled quadrat, are to be sampled until the required 90–95% of the dominant species are encountered.

Within each quadrat, two parameters are measured: percent cover of each species present, and the sociability of each plant species. Percent cover estimates are visually estimated within cover classes defined by the Braun–Blanquet cover scale (Table 1) (Mueller-Dombois and Ellenburg, 1974). The sociability of each plant species is estimated according to the Braun–Blanquet sociability scale (Table 2). The data are recorded on a Wetland Qualitative/Quantitative Wetland Assessment Form (Fig. 2). Each quadrat is photographed from above to visually document vegetative cover conditions.

For each quadrat that is measured on the ROW, a control quadrat is measured in an adjacent representative area off-ROW. This off-ROW quadrat is used to estimate pre-construction cover and vegetative diversity conditions. Note that this off-ROW control quadrat is not necessary if this method is utilized within the wetland during the pre-construction phase.

Following field data collection, the data are analyzed to determine overall percent cover between the on-ROW and off-ROW samples. Measured percent cover for individual species are summed and extrapolated as appropriate across the site. Quantitative results measured from quadrats are combined with the qualitative visual assessment to determine an overall assessment of the condition and percent cover of the wetland plant community.

Vegetation community diversity

Diversity, in its simplest form, is a measure of the number of species within a unit area. Simple diversity based on species counts can be undesirable because it fails to consider the relative abundance of the species present. A more meaningful estimate of the overall diversity of a plant population incorporates the number of species ("species richness") and the relative abundance or distribution ("evenness") of the species into a diversity model.

Due to the magnitude of large pipeline projects and the numerous wetlands encountered, it is not possible to identify and count every individual plant in each wetland vegetation community. In such cases, it is necessary to take a random sample of individuals from the population of all species present as described above for the percent cover quadrat sampling. Under these circumstances, the Shannon–Weaver Index is

PNGTS North-Section Facilities	
Wetland Monitoring Form	
Field Team:	Date:
Wetland No.:	Town/State/County:
MP/Station:	Alignment Sheet #:
Photo Roll/Frame:	

QUALITATIVE ASSESSMENT

General Condition of Wetland On ROW:
Grade: Percent Veg. Cover:
Hydrology: Veg. Vigor:
Soils: Nuisance Weed Invasion:

On-ROW Species				Off-ROW Species			
Species Code	% Cover	Species Code	% Cover	Species Code	% Cover	Species Code	% Cover

QUANTITATIVE ASSESSMENT

On-ROW Species				Off-ROW Species			
Plot #	Species Code	% Cover	Sociability	Plot #	Species Code	% Cover	Sociability

COMMENTS/RECOMMENDATIONS

Success Criteria Met? Yes   No

Fig. 2. Qualitative/Quantitative Wetland Assessment Form.

an appropriate model for measuring diversity. The Shannon–Weaver Index is one of the simplest and most extensively used diversity indices in plant ecology, and incorporates the concepts of species richness and evenness into the model.

The formula for the Shannon–Weaver function is:

$$H' = \frac{C}{N(N \log_{10} N - \sum n_i \log_{10} n_i)},$$

where H' is the diversity index, C is the constant for conversion of logarithms, N is the total number of species, and n_i is the number individuals of the ith species.

Using data collected from the Releve' plots, the Shannon Weaver diversity index is calculated for the wetland vegetation community on the restored ROW and for the off-ROW control. The on-ROW wetland diversity is then compared with the off-ROW or pre-construction control. The wetland is considered successful for diversity if the restored wetland diversity is at least 50% of the control wetland diversity.

CASE STUDY RESULTS

Using the methodologies described above, the monitoring crews were able to successfully monitor all 1500 wetlands crossed by the Project within a three-month time period during the summers of 1999, 2000, and 2001. Use of the Releve' sampling technique enabled each 2-person sampling team to survey and collect qualitative and quantitative data on approximately 10–15 wetlands per day.

Weather conditions during the field surveys consisted of above average temperatures and near drought precipitation conditions. Due to the unusually low precipitation, many wetlands showed little evidence of wetland hydrology. Evidence of dry cracked soil and concentrated mineral deposits in wetland depression areas were visible throughout the right-of-way. Despite the dry conditions, the vegetation along the right-of-way was readily identifiable with a number of wetlands reaching nearly 100% cover with a diverse hydrophytic plant community.

The field surveys revealed the right-of-way to be generally stable and well vegetated. The grade and hydrology of the wetlands exhibited mostly pre-construction contours, with little variation in wetland vegetation diversity compared to off right-of-way data points located in similar vegetatative community types. The vigor of the wetland vegetation was good despite the near drought conditions. Some wetlands indicated signs of plant stress due to the lack of normal seasonal precipitation, however, overall the wetlands appeared to be properly restored and progressing toward revegetation success.

Overall, the results after three years of field surveys determined that 1275 (85%) wetlands contained at least 80% cover by hydrophytes with 50% or greater species diversity compared with the off right-of-way control plot. An additional 225 wetlands (15%) had greater than 50% diversity, but were just under the 80% cover threshold.

SUMMARY

Implementation of the Wetland Vegetation Monitoring Program was successful in evaluating the revegetation success of wetlands along the PNGTS–Maritimes Joint Facilities Project with regard to specific state and federal permit requirements that require both qualitative and quantitative assessment. The sampling technique was effective in that it provided an efficient means for sampling a large number of wetlands in relatively little time. This was achieved through comparison of similar vegetation community types that exist on and off the right-of-way. Through comparison of similar community types, the sampling technique provides an accurate measure of species diversity, percent cover, sociability, and plant vigor.

The general right-of-way conditions were reported as stable and no significant erosion problems were evident based on the monitoring surveys described in this report. Approximately 85% of the wetlands were observed to be successfully revegetated to a hydrophytic vegetation community. The majority of the remaining 15% of the wetlands contained hydrophytic vegetation, however, the calculated species diversity and/or percent vegetative cover was not yet high enough to meet the success criterion. It is estimated from review of the results and from general visual observations conducted along the ROW, that the majority of the wetlands will achieve the success criteria by the end of the next growing season.

ACKNOWLEDGMENTS

We gratefully acknowledge PNGTS Operating Company, and Maritimes & Northeast Pipeline for supporting the use of data from their projects as a case study. We also acknowledge and thank the team that contributed to the development of the wetland monitoring program and concepts presented in this manuscript, as well as the field crews for their careful identification of plant species and rapid collection of the field data.

REFERENCES

Barbour, M.G., J.H. Burk, and W.D. Pitts. 1987. Terrestrial Plant Ecology, 2nd ed. Benjamin/Cummings, Menlo Park, CA. 634 pp.

Bookhout, T.A., ed. 1996. Research and Management Techniques for Wildlife and Habitats. 5th ed., rev. Wildlife Society, Bethesda, Md. 740 pp.

Bonham, C.D. 1989. Measurements for Terrestrial Vegetation. John Wiley & Sons, New York, NY. 338 pp.

Cowardin, A.P., et al. 1979. Classification of Wetlands and Deepwater Habitats of the United States. US Fish and Wildlife Service, Washington, DC.

FWS/OBS-79/31.

Gosselink, J.G. and J.W. Mitsch. 1993. Wetlands, 2nd ed. Van Nostrand Reinhold, New York, NY.

Magee, D.W. and H.E. Ahles. 1999. Flora of the Northeast: A Manual of the Vascular Flora of New England and Adjacent New York. University of Massachusetts Press, Amherst, MA.

Mueller-Dombois, D. and H. Ellenburg. 1974. Aims and Methods of Vegetation Ecology. John Wiley & Sons, New York, NY.

BIOGRAPHICAL SKETCHES

Mr. Brett M. Battaglia

Northern Ecological Associates, Inc., 451 Presumpscot Street, Portland, Maine 04103, Fax: (207) 879-9481, Email: bbattaglia@neamaine.com

Mr. Battaglia is an environmental scientist with over nine years of experience with wetland investigation/delineation, qualitative and quantitative vegetation sampling, wetland mitigation planning, wetland restoration, development of rapid assessment wetland monitoring programs, and inventory of riparian areas. Mr. Battaglia's is a Certified Wetland Scientist (New Hampshire), and a member of the Maine Association of Wetland Scientists (MAWS) and the New Hampshire Association of Natural Resource Scientists (NHANRS). Mr. Battaglia also is experienced with rare, threatened, and endangered plant and animal species and communities surveys, habitat surveys and mapping, biological sampling and analysis, and environmental impact studies, assessments, and permitting. His background also includes marine science, fish identification/sampling, and wildlife species population studies.

Mr. J. Roger Trettel
Northern Ecological Associates, Inc., 451 Presumpscot Street, Portland, Maine 04103, Fax: (207) 879-9481, Email: rtrettel@neamaine.com
As a Principal of Northern Ecological Associates, Inc. (NEA) and a specialist in environmental impact assessment and restoration ecology, Mr. Trettel has over 19 years experience in the environmental field. Mr. Trettel's experience includes management of comprehensive environmental programs for the planning, assessment, permitting, construction, inspection, restoration, and monitoring of natural gas pipeline development projects. A certified Professional Wetland Scientist (PWS), Mr. Trettel also has extensive experience performing wetland, vegetation, and biological analyses and developing wetland and wildlife habitat mitigation and restoration plans. In addition, Mr. Trettel manages and prepares Environmental Impact Statements (EISs), Environmental Assessments (EAs), and Environmental Reports (ERs) for proposed development projects.

Evaluating the Effects of Muds on Wetlands from Horizontal Directional Drilling (HDD) Within Natural Gas Transmission Line Rights-of-Way

David Cameron, Carl Tammi, Emily Steel, Jon Schmidt, and James Evans

Horizontal Directional Drilling (HDD) has emerged as an innovative technology for providing alternative solutions for installing natural gas transmission lines under wetlands, waterways, and ecologically-sensitive areas. Bentonite drilling muds are utilized in HDD applications to keep cutting tools cool, as a lubricant, to remove cuttings, and to confine liquids by creating an impervious coating on the inside wall of a drill hole. However, drill muds can seep up through fractures in the upper soil profile (inadvertent returns), and, in the case of wetlands, potentially into the saturated or inundated root zone. This may present significant implications from a wetlands impact perspective, both physically and functionally, which may ultimately trigger increased scrutiny under wetlands regulatory programs as the seeping bentonite may be mildly toxic or constitute a deposit of *dredged or fill material*. The purpose of this research was to evaluate the potential effects that bentonite-based drilling muds may have on wetlands, and to assess whether these muds can be naturally attenuated within the wetland ecosystem. The research included a literature review, as well as a survey of industry, contractors, and the regulatory community to assess permit conditions and perceived environmental impacts and to identify mitigation measures for effectively managing inadvertent returns. Screening criteria for permit relevancy included scientific and technical validity, implementation, and cost factors. Five study sites in Michigan, Ohio, and Alabama were evaluated to further assess the scope of environmental concerns and the efficacy of mitigation measures. Field parameters assessed included monitoring wetlands vegetation, observation of hydrologic condition, soils, and select functional parameters through periods of seasonal succession to evaluate recuperative processes. None of the five field sites displayed significant long-term impacts as a result of the bentonite discharges. However, in some instances, minor structural changes were observed. The level of impact was in part due to the nature and extent of the clean-up procedures. Discrepancies exist between perceived impacts from the inadvertent return of HDD drill muds and field data recorded at study locations.

Keywords: Drill fluid, inadvertent returns, bentonite, impacts, pipeline

INTRODUCTION

This research project was developed to investigate existing knowledge and provide technical information relative to the rapidly growing implementation of Horizontal Directional Drilling (HDD) technology for natural gas transmission line crossings of vegetated wetlands. Use of HDD crossing methods for ecologically sensitive areas including vegetated wetlands is increasingly common, however, prior to this research project little data had been gathered to determine potential environmental impacts associated with inadvertent returns of bentonite muds into vegetated wetlands when these muds are used as fluids in HDD applications.

Bentonite is a term used to describe any natural material composed primarily of the clay minerals of the smectite group. Bentonite has a wide variety of physical properties making it a suitable substance for several commercial uses and applications. Sodium or Wyoming bentonite is a high-swelling variety used in

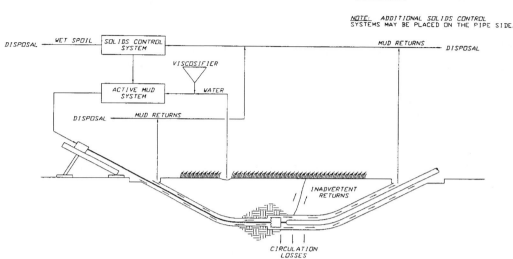

Fig. 1. HDD Drilling Fluid Flow schematic.

drilling muds to cool cutting tools, remove cuttings, lubricate the drill bit, and to confine liquids to the borehole, helping to prevent releases or "frac-outs" by creating an impervious coating on the wall of the drill hole (Hosterman and Patterson, 1992). A schematic cross-section depicting the set-up of a directional bore procedure is shown in Fig. 1 (GRI Topical Report 99/0132).

The research program was designed to assess existing information on HDD and drill mud returns as they relate to vegetated wetlands and to investigate actual sites where bentonite returns have occurred in wetlands, with a goal of supplementing available literature with actual project-specific data. Several discrete tasks were conducted to achieve the research target, including a literature search, a survey of industry professionals and regulatory personnel who use or permit HDD technology, evaluation of typical permit conditions stipulated for HDD crossings and mitigation measures implemented in the event of an inadvertent release, and comprehensive field investigations.

METHODS

At the inception of this research program, it was anticipated that there was little published data directly addressing the potential impacts of bentonite on wetlands. Therefore, a comprehensive research program was adopted to evaluate available information and data and design the field investigation component to address informational gaps or discrepancies.

Literature search

The literature search was conducted using the Internet and a database search system to locate articles and papers addressing the impacts on wetlands from HDD muds. Initially, over 1000 potentially relevant article titles from the database and Internet searches were identified. Initial screening of these titles resulted in the incorporation of approximately 200 of the most relevant titles into a database, and the subsequent formal review of 110 abstract or full text items.

Survey

Following the literature search, a matrix of professionals from Natural Gas Transmission Line (NGTL) companies, HDD contractors, and regulatory agencies was developed. A questionnaire was forwarded to the contacts to collect information relative to their experience with HDD and wetlands and to obtain data about potential effects of bentonite releases in wetlands. Individuals whose responses to the survey questionnaires indicated they had significant experience with HDD were contacted for detailed follow-up interviews. Information obtained from these individuals included geographic location, type of crossing, geotechnical data, wetlands classification, size of borehole, and estimated volume of drill mud release.

The follow-up interviews requested examples of typical permit conditions or mitigation measures for inadvertent bentonite returns to a wetland and an assessment of the efficacy of the permit condition or mitigation measure. This information was evaluated pursuant to the federal guidelines for Section 404(b)(1) of the Clean Water Act (*Guidelines for Specification of Disposal Sites for Dredged or Fill Material — 40 CFR 230; 45 FR 85344, July 1, 1991*), the most applicable federal regulations available for use in the context of an inadvertent release.

Field investigations

Following the gathering of background data described above, field investigations were conducted in 1998 and 1999 at five sites that experienced inadvertent returns of bentonite in wetlands from HDD. NGTL companies in the US provided access to sites in both coastal and freshwater vegetated wetlands located in coastal and central Alabama, southeastern Michigan, and north-central Ohio. Field study sites were selected based on several factors, including surface area of returns, wetland type, available property access, geographical location, cleanup operations, and date of inadvertent return. Sites were selected that had experienced relatively sizable returns (greater than or equal to 10,000 ft^2) to a depth of six or more inches in most cases. In addition, sites were selected based on relative dates of bentonite return events, allowing for comparison of site recovery based on time elapsed since the inadvertent return. Deposition of drill muds occurred at the sites in 1994, 1996, and 1998 (3 sites).

Vegetation and soils monitoring plots were established within linear belt transects where practicable, however, the presence of surface water at two of the five sites precluded the establishment of linear transects. Random plots were established to avoid inaccessible open water areas. Multiple 1 m × 1 m (m^2) monitoring plots were established at each site encompassing the extent of visible impact for the semi-quantitative documentation of total and relative percent areal cover of vegetation, species richness, and soil profile analyses. Plot locations were selected to reflect severe impact, moderate impact, and the periphery of visible impact from drill muds. In addition, control plots were established at each site in areas reflective of conditions undisturbed by the drill mud release, but within close enough proximity to the impact area to encompass vegetative communities and hydrology. The overall vegetative community at each site was evaluated for signs of stress (e.g., dieback, stunted growth, leaf wilt, etc.), and a qualitative wetlands functional assessment was conducted. Wetland functions evaluated included wildlife and aquatic species habitat; flood storage and attenuation; nutrient removal and transformation; sediment stabilization and entrapment; and water quality.

Vegetation assessment

Vegetational assessment included determining the percent areal cover of all defined strata (tree, liana, sapling, shrub, and seedlings and herbs) using the *Ocular Estimation of Cover Technique* (Hays, et al., 1981). During vegetation monitoring, special attention was given to documenting areas of the study sites that appeared structurally impaired (evidence of vegetation smothering, compaction, removal, or other alteration) based on inadvertent drill mud returns. Impacts were considered apparent when live wetlands vegetation was smothered by returns, displaced by upland or invasive species, or where growth was impaired relative to control plots due to surficial bentonite deposits.

Soil profile evaluation

Where possible, soils at each plot were examined to a depth of 18–20 in. (45 cm), using a hand auger. Soil colors were recorded using *Munsell Soil Color Charts* (Kollmorgen Corp., 1975) and the USDA/SCS soil textures were also determined for each soil boring. Hydric soils were considered to be present when the mandatory technical criteria of the 1987 US Army Corps of Engineers (Corps) Manual were satisfied, such as evidence of an aquic or peraquic moisture regime, sulfidic material, or gleyed, mottled, and/or low chroma soils. Each soil sample was examined for the presence of bentonite clay, disturbance, or inconsistencies within the soil profile that may have been related to displacement of subsoils to the surface from HDD mud intrusion in the subsurface.

Functional impact assessment

A qualitative wetlands functional assessment was conducted at each site during each inspection. Potential impacts were based on direct evidence that certain wetland functions may be affected as a result of inadvertent returns. A brief description of the functions considered during this evaluation are described below and have been adapted from the US Army Corps of Engineers *Wetlands Functions & Values: A Descriptive Approach* (WES) (US ACOE, 1987) and *A Rapid Procedure for Assessing Wetland Functional Capacity Based on Hydrogeomorphic Classification* (Magee and Hollands, 1998):

Wildlife and aquatic species habitat

This function considers the ability and resultant effectiveness of a wetland to provide habitat for various types of populations of animals typically associated with both the aquatic and wetland edge habitats. This function was considered to be affected by HDD returns if large expanses of hardened clays were observed over formerly organic wetland soils, if features such as a bank were altered by mud deposits, if significant areas appeared unvegetated due to returns, or if expected (common) wildlife species were not present or evident.

Flood storage and attenuation

Wetlands function to reduce flood damage to areas of social importance by attenuating floodwaters for prolonged periods following precipitation events. Each site was inspected for large expanses of hardened spoils and returns to determine whether a change in infiltration of floodwaters resulted from deposition of inadvertent returns. Documentation also included areas where returns occupied potential flood storage space, or potentially acted to obstruct or divert high flows.

Nutrient removal and transformation
Excess nutrients may be prevented from entering aquifers or surface waters such as ponds, lakes, streams, rivers, or estuaries by first being transported through wetlands. Nutrient removal and transformation in wetlands is largely a function of the abundance of emergent vegetation which acts as a medium for nutrient uptake. During each monitoring event, areas were documented within the study sites which had experienced significant dieback of vegetation due to smothering from bentonite.

Sediment stabilization and entrapment
This function relates to the ability of a wetland to stabilize stream bank shorelines against erosion, and to protect downstream receiving waters from the effects of turbidity and suspended particles. As such, observations were made at each site relative to vegetation adjacent to streambanks that may have been impaired due to inadvertent HDD returns. In addition, areas were documented where of the vegetative community had been damaged thereby reducing the wetland's ability to trap sedimentary particles within emergent or aquatic vegetation.

Water quality
This function is inclusive of a wetland's potential to serve as a groundwater recharge and/or discharge area as well as the effectiveness of a wetland to reduce or prevent the degradation of water quality by trapping toxicants and pathogens (Ehrlich and Roughgarden, 1987). Organic wetland soils significantly contribute to a watershed's ability to trap and/or uptake toxicants. Consequently, areas were noted at each site where unmitigated returns of bentonite had displaced (buried) such soils. In addition, turbidity of surface waters present at each site was assessed to determine whether the turbidity was associated with bentonite returns.

RESULTS

Results of the Literature Survey indicated a scarcity of published information regarding potential effects of bentonite HDD fluid deposition on palustrine wetlands. Of the 110 abstracts or full-text items reviewed, a total of 30 were determined to be directly related to the project. Relevant articles concluded that bentonite drilling fluids are biologically and chemically inert and non-toxic, and that deposition of bentonite in vegetated wetlands generally does not create structural impacts (vegetative structure or condition changes) for the long-term if proper cleanup operations are implemented. However, some literature suggested that the deposition of bentonite in standing or flowing water may affect the egg and larval development of amphibians, smother fish spawning beds (or other habitats sensitive to sedimentation), or negatively impact benthic macroinvertebrate populations (Land and Bernard, 1974). Although temporary impacts to wetlands will occur during typical HDD project mobilization activities, as well as during removal of inadvertent returns, the use of HDD technology can be generally less environmentally intrusive than using conventional trenching methods to install pipelines across a wetland (Luginbuhl and Gartman, 1995).

The results of the questionnaire and interview component of the project indicated that among contacts with demonstrated relevant experience and who have developed an informed opinion, bentonite mud as used in HDD applications is not considered to be especially hazardous to wetlands. The majority of responses indicated that HDD is perceived as the least damaging crossing technology, although there are some associated environmental concerns. Contacts primarily believed that bentonite is non-toxic, but may present other types of impacts (i.e. physical and functional) such as alteration of wetland microtopography, sedimentation and physical smothering of wetland vegetation. Concerns expressed by several individuals included chemical and biological impacts such as clogging of fish gills, facilitating the toxicity of certain metals, or the impairment to certain amphibian life stages. Contacts in regulatory agencies generally were under the impression that inadvertent returns are relatively uncommon (less than 25% of the time) in HDD operations while NGTL contacts estimated frequencies of 50% or greater. Only one contractor of four believed that inadvertent returns occurred greater than 50% of the time. The distribution of perceived frequency of inadvertent returns from HDD at a regulatory level has direct implications relative to its required implementation as a crossing method. However, the overall consensus of interviewed contacts was that the primary environmental concern relative to inadvertent bentonite returns in wetlands is from siltation, sedimentation, smothering, and turbidity concerns.

Examples of commonly encountered or issued permit conditions included installation of silt fence and hay bales around the bore entry and exit pits, monitoring for loss of mud during drilling operations, indication of minimum drilling depth, water quality monitoring during bore advancement, prohibition of discharge of drill fluids to wetlands or waterbodies, and removal of released muds through vacuuming or shoveling. Many of the suggested or commonly issued permit conditions are justified relative to applicable regulatory guidelines, while some appear to be excessive and not technically based. Permit conditions determined to be relevant correspond closely to the general requirements placed on any type of project associated with the potential disturbance of jurisdictional wetlands. No standard Federal Energy Regulatory Commission (FERC) or Corps permit conditions were identified with respect to HDD and wetlands. A list of mitigation measures that were generally

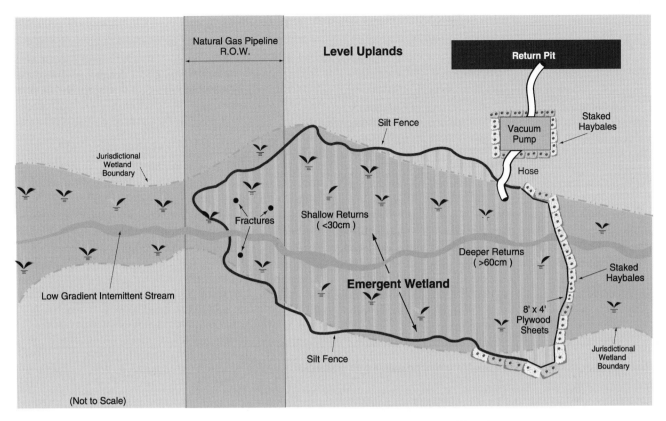

Fig. 2. Representative inadvertent returns mitigation measures: Plan view.

deemed appropriate was synthesized and formulated into a generalized pre-construction Contingency Plan. If a pre-approved Contingency Plan is in place, ambiguities associated with mitigation and cleanup measures will theoretically be eliminated, saving NGTLs time and resources, and reducing impacts to wetlands and aquatic resources. Relevant mitigation measures consist of reasonable regulatory requests that would typically be associated with any project proposed in or in the immediate proximity of wetlands, such as removal of released muds by shoveling or vacuuming, dilution of bentonite returns by washing with water, and construction of containment areas by using hay bales, booms or sandbags. Fig. 2 (GRI Topical Report 99/0132) depicts commonly used mitigation measures in the event of an inadvertent return to a vegetated wetland as would be typically implemented during installation of a natural gas pipeline.

Results of the field investigations at the five sites selected for this study provide a technical basis which supports and supplements the information gathered in the preliminary background tasks. All of the sites experienced surface deposits of bentonite which were subsequently removed, and one site additionally experienced significant volumes of subsurface deposits which resulted in the upheaval of the wetland surface soils. Based on the investigations of the five sites studied, the following observations were made regarding potential impacts to wetlands vegetation, soils, and functions.

Vegetation

Table 1 summarizes the results of vegetation monitoring at each of the five study sites. Following removal of drill muds from the surface of vegetated wetlands, the floral community generally rebounds fully within one to several growing seasons. Vegetative recovery occurs in terms of general diversity, total percent areal cover, and density of the overall plant community. Impact areas within all wetland sites displayed a dominance of hydrophytic vegetation. Upland and/or invasive pioneer species did not displace pre-existing wetlands vegetation at any of the sites as a result of HDD returns, and pre-existing species generally remained present.

Vegetative colonization and success of hydrophytic vegetation does not appear to be impaired by bentonite drill muds. These parameters were especially evidenced at an upland drill mud disposal/dispersal area at one of the field sites. At the subject site, total areal cover and percentage of hydrophytes was significantly greater within the deposit area compared to similar data collected within the control transect. It is interesting to note that the bentonite in this disposal area appeared to be contributing to a proliferation of hydrophytes within an upland field. This phenomenon is likely due to cleanup measures resulting in the collection of hydrophytic plant material, and the soil moisture retaining capabilities of the deposited bentonite clays.

Table 1. Summarized results of vegetation monitoring

Site ID	Year of bentonite deposit and removal	Prevalent species	Average percent areal cover of m^2 study quadrats during final monitoring event	Average percent areal cover of m^2 control quadrats during final monitoring event
#1 — Dauphin Island, Alabama	1998	Panicum repens Hydrocotyle bonariensis	66	104
#2 — Portersville Bay, Alabama	1998	Juncus romerianus Spartina alterniflora	42	88
#3 — Perry County, Alabama	1998	Juncus effusus Leersia oryzoides Polygonum pensylvanicum Carex spp.	94	120
#4 — Macomb County, Michigan	1996	Impatiens capensis Verbena hastata Carex lacustris Carex stricta	105	88
#5 — Lorain County, Ohio	1994	Lysimachia nummularia Viburnum recognitum Cornus racemosa Juncus effusus	116	N/A*

*Data used from historic study conducted by others; no control plots established.

Table 2. Soils monitoring results from select monitoring plots

Site ID	Soils data from representative m^2 monitoring quadrats			
	Sample depth (cm)	Munsell color	USDA texture	Residual bentonite present in soil profile?
#1 — Dauphin Island, Alabama	0–1	10YR 2/1	Sapric	No
	1–16	10YR 3/2	Sandy, clay loam	No
	16–40	10YR 3/1	Sandy loam	No
#2 — Portersville Bay, Alabama	0–2	10YR 2/1	Sapric	No
	2–16	10YR 3/2	Sandy, clay loam	No
	16–40	10YR 3/1	Sandy loam	No
#3 — Perry County, Alabama	0–10	Gleyed	Clay (bentonite)	Yes
	10–30	10YR 2/1	Sapric	No
	30+	10YR 5/3	Sandy, clay loam	No
#4 — Macomb County, Michigan	0–30	10YR 2/2	Hemic	No
	30–45	10 YR 2/1	Sapric	No
#5 — Lorain County, Ohio	0–25	10YR 5/1	Silt loam	Yes
	25–30	10YR 4/1	Silt loam	Yes

Soils

Table 2 provides the soils data for selected profiles at each of the five study sites. With the exception of site #3, residual bentonite was virtually undetectable at the wetland surfaces, as well as within the soil profiles. One site experienced displacement of the soil profile due to a significant change in the wetland surface elevation. The topographical rise was the result of subsurface pressure created by drill mud releases, and changed the hydrology of the shallow root zone. Although the relative landscape position and soil profile was altered at this site, the jurisdictional wetland boundary did not change (the soil remained hydric). At another site, small isolated pockets of bentonite mud up to 10 cm remained at the site even after one full growing season of the initial release. These areas became naturally and densely vegetated rapidly. Wetland areas at each site subject to disturbance from cleanup machinery showed no discernable long-term impacts to soils and vegetation.

Wetland functions

In general, wetland functions did not appear compromised at the study sites as a result of HDD returns. However, the site at which the ground elevation was changed due to upheaval from drill mud intrusion

Table 3. Summarized results of wetland functional assessments

Site ID	Wildlife and aquatic species habitat	Flood storage and attenuation	Nutrient removal and transformation	Sediment stabilization and entrapment	Water quality	Comments/ rationale
#1 — Dauphin Island, Alabama					Possible downstream sedimentation due to hurricane influence	No long-term impacts. Small site with rapid cleanup. Washing away of muds by Hurricane Georges.
#2 — Portersville Bay, Alabama			X	X		Large area of marsh vegetation gradually rebounding from impacts of mud deposition, but cover still sparse.
#3 — Perry County, Alabama						No visible impairment as a result of HDD activities.
#4 — Macomb County, Michigan		X				Only negligible influences on flood flow. Small section of creek diverted as a result of HDD impact.
#5 — Lorain County, Ohio						No visible impairment as a result of HDD activities.

X — indicative of *potential* functional impairment.

displayed minor impacts relative to flood storage and attenuation, as a "mound" was heaved up within the wetland and a section of a pre-existing stream channel was effectively dammed and diverted. Table 3 summarizes the results of the wetland functional assessments conducted at the five study sites.

CONCLUSIONS

A lack of widespread quantitative data or case study literature exists documenting potential short or long-term effects of bentonite on vegetated wetlands. Literature reviewed generally indicated that bentonite is chemically and biologically inert, but may have physical impacts to sensitive wetlands biota. Site-specific review of individual wetlands crossings is recommended prior to selection of crossing technology.

Concerns expressed by the professionals contacted for the survey are supported by information from the literature search which indicated that bentonite apparently does not stay in suspension for long periods of time, and the settling of bentonite and other drilling fluids solids has been determined to be a concern for benthic fauna. There is an overall perception that short-term impacts to vegetated wetland communities can occur from inadvertent returns of bentonite drilling muds. However, there is an acknowledgement that there is a lack of reliable, quantitative monitoring data to support this assertion. Many contacts knowledgeable and experienced with HDD inadvertent returns had different opinions and perceptions about the potential for short and long-term impacts to wetlands. Despite varied opinions, there is little available quantitative data to provide technical backup to the opinions expressed. Certain mitigation measures identified as commonly used or required are relevant to the federal guidelines, while others are not.

Based on the data collected during the field component of this study it does not appear that significant long-term impacts are incurred on the vegetative community or soils from inadvertent bentonite releases to vegetated wetlands, provided that the bentonite is removed. Pre-existing vegetative species are not necessarily displaced as a result of drill mud releases. Vegetative colonization and success of hydrophytic vegetation does not appear to be impaired by bentonite drill muds. In general, wetland functions did not appear compromised at the study sites as a result of HDD returns.

RECOMMENDATIONS

From a research standpoint, a data gap still exists as all removable bentonite deposits were dealt with at sites investigated under this research program, and no data were acquired from sites that had not been cleaned. In addition, under this study little differentiation can be made relative to the recovery of herbaceous versus woody vegetation, as each study site was largely composed of herbaceous vegetation. Another relevant parameter not investigated under this research, but worthy of study is benthic infauna. As inadvertent returns are deposited and in many cases displace, bury, or otherwise disturb surface sediments in wetlands, the macroinvertebrate community may be affected, at least in the short term. Sampling and analysis of surface soils with the intent to document gradual changes in the benthic infaunal community would augment the data collected thus far under this research.

ACKNOWLEDGEMENTS

This research was conducted by ENSR Corp. under contract with and funding by the Gas Research Institute (GRI, Chicago, IL), through the program *Evaluating the Effects of Muds on Wetlands from Horizontal Drilling*. Mr. James Evans serves as the GRI Project Manager; Mr. Jon Schmidt, PhD, as ENSR Principal-in-Charge; Mr. Carl Tammi, CWD, PWS as ENSR Project Manager; Mr. David Cameron, PWS as ENSR Principal Scientist; and Ms. Emily Steel as ENSR Project Specialist. Mr. John Hair of J.D. Hair & Associates is the Sr. Technical Advisor for certain components of the research.

REFERENCES

Ehrlich and Roughgarden. 1987. The Science of Ecology. Macmillan, New York.

GRI. 1999. Evaluating the Effects of Muds on Wetlands from Horizontal Drilling: Professional Screening Survey/Permit Condition Review Topical Report. ENSR Corporation under contract with the Gas Research Institute. Document # GRI 98/0350.

GRI. 1999. Evaluating the Effects of Muds on Wetlands from Horizontal Drilling: Permit Condition and Mitigation Measures Review and Alternatives Evaluation Topical Report. By ENSR Corporation under contract with the Gas Research Institute. Document # GRI 99/0132.

Hays, R.L., C. Summers, and W. Seitz. 1981. Estimating Wildlife Habitat Variables. US Fish and Wildlife Service. FWS/OBS-81/47. 111 pp.

Hosterman, J.W. and S.W. Patterson. 1992. Bentonite and Fuller's Earth Resources of the United States. US Geological Survey Professional Paper 1522. US Government Printing Office, Washington.

Kadlec and Knight. 1996. Treatment Wetlands. CRC Press.

Kollmorgen Corporation. 1990. Munsell Soil Color Charts. Munsell Color Division, Baltimore, MD. Revised Edition.

Land and Bernard. 1974. Toxicity of Drilling Fluid Components to Aquatic Biological Systems: A Literature Review. Canada Department of the Environment R&D Directorate Technical Report #487.

Luginbuhl and Gartman. 1995. Pipeline Construction in Wetlands: Lessons Learned. Pipeline and Utilities Construction Journal.

Magee, D. and Garry Hollands. 1998. A Rapid Procedure for Assessing Wetland Functional Capacity Based on Hydrogeomorphic Classification.

Reed, P.B., Jr. 1988. National List of Plant Species that Occur in Wetlands. US Fish and Wildlife Service, National Wetlands Inventory. Biological Report 88 (26.1) May, 1988.

US Army Corps of Engineers. 1987. Wetland Functions & Values: A Descriptive Approach.

BIOGRAPHICAL SKETCHES

David J. Cameron, PWS

ENSR International Corporation, 2 Technology Park Drive, Westford, MA 01886, USA, 978/589-3000 Phone, 978/589-3035 Fax

David J. Cameron is a Senior Ecologist and Wetland Scientist in the Water Resources Department of ENSR, Inc. Mr. Cameron has over 9 years experience in wetland evaluation, permitting and wildlife habitat assessment. He is a Certified Professional Wetland Scientist.

Carl E. Tammi, PWS, CWD

ENSR International Corporation, 2 Technology Park Drive, Westford, MA 01886, USA, 978/589-3000 Phone, 978/589-3035 Fax

Carl E. Tammi is a Senior Wetlands Project Manager in the *Water Resources Department* of *ENSR*, Inc. He has over 13 years of professional experience in multidisciplinary wetlands program management throughout the US Mr. Tammi directs wetland assessments, delineation, permitting, mitigation, and restoration design, construction, long-term monitoring, and treatment design. Mr. Tammi is the author of 2 chapters in the national-released Lewis Publishers textbook *Applied Wetland Science and Technology* as well as numerous technical publications on wetlands restoration. He is a Certified Professional Wetland Scientist, and received his Professional Wetland Delineator Certification from the US Army Corps of Engineers, Baltimore District.

Emily Steel

ENSR International Corporation, 2 Technology Park Drive, Westford, MA 01886, USA, 978/589-3000 Phone, 978/589-3035 Fax

Emily Steel is a *Wetland Scientist* and Geologist with 4 years of experience. Ms. Steel has conducted field surveys and prepared reports and permit applications in support of dozens of natural gas pipeline projects in the eastern US.

John A. Schmidt PhD

ENSR International Corporation, 1538 Metropolitan Blvd., Suite C1, Tallahasee, FL 32308, USA, 850/309-0264

John Schmidt is Director of Energy Services for ENSR, Inc. and is the client manager for three international energy companies. Dr. Schmidt has managed large natural gas projects both domestically and overseas, from 700+ mile, large-diameter natural gas pipelines in the midwestern and southeastern United States, to Category A Environmental Impact Assessments in Chile. Dr. Schmidt has worked on oil and natural gas pipelines in Venezuela, Columbia, Argentina, and the United States. Dr. Schmidt has over 12 years experience managing and directing large, multi-disciplinary projects for the oil and gas industry. He has managed the siting, environmental field surveys, permitting, licensing, and NEPA document preparation for over 8000 miles of natural gas and oil pipelines, liquefied natural gas plants, marine terminals and marine pipelines, compressor stations, and hydroelectric facilities.

James Evans
Gas Research Institute (Gas Technology Institute), 1700 South Mount Prospect Road, Des Plaines, IL 60018-1804, USA, 847/768-0500, 847/768-0501

James Evans is Senior Project Manager at the *Gas Technology Institute* (formerly Gas Research Institute). Mr. Evans has directed dozens of research projects in support of the natural gas industry.

A Comparative Assessment of Horizontal Directional Drilling and Traditional Construction Techniques for Wetland and Riparian Area Crossings in Natural Gas Pipeline Rights-of-Way

John Hair, David Cameron, Carl Tammi, Emily Steel, Jon Schmidt, and James Evans

Horizontal Directional Drilling (HDD) is increasingly advocated as the preferred, and often required, construction method (as opposed to traditional trenching) for natural gas transmission line crossings of ecologically-sensitive areas including wetlands and riparian areas. As a result, a closer look at the technical rationale, environmental and cost implications, and construction procedures in these areas is required to determine the benefits and drawbacks of these crossing techniques. The focus of this evaluation was to examine crossing techniques such as the traditional open-cut trenching and HDD in the context of the above-mentioned criteria. Variables common to both crossing technologies which were evaluated included assessing physical elements such as landform and subsurface conditions and limitations; operational components such as workspace requirements, staging area locations, and equipment mobilization; engineering design; manpower requirements; and ecological restoration. Representative cost comparisons were developed and correlated with matrices of potential environmental concerns. This comparative analysis can be used as a template to assist planners, designers and permitting specialists in decision-making relative to application and implementation of these construction techniques.

Keywords: Drill method, inadvertent returns, bentonite, engineering limitations, cost

INTRODUCTION

This research project was initiated to compare Horizontal Directional Drilling (HDD) with conventional trenching methods for pipeline crossings of vegetated wetlands in terms of potential environmental impact, technical rationale, and cost implications. Crossing methods investigated included Trench and Lay, Trench and Push, and HDD. Use of HDD as a crossing method is increasingly common and is frequently required by regulatory agencies. As HDD technology evolves and is increasingly required by agencies, it is necessary to evaluate this technology relative to existing crossing methods to determine the optimal construction method to use at a given wetland crossing. The primary differences in the aforementioned technologies are presented, demonstrating that a certain construction method may be appropriate for each project.

BACKGROUND OF PIPELINE INSTALLATION METHODS AND RESEARCH METHODOLOGY

The pertinent aspects of HDD, conventional trench and lay, and conventional trench and push construction methods for wetland crossings are briefly described herein, to provide a basis for the crossing method comparison.

Horizontal directional drilling
Installation of a pipeline by HDD is generally achieved in three stages: pilot hole drilling, reaming, and pulling back (Fig. 1). Pilot hole drilling involves directionally

Environmental Concerns in Rights-of-Way
Management: Seventh International Symposium
J.W. Goodrich-Mahoney, D.F. Mutrie and C.A. Guild (editors)
© 2002 Elsevier Science Ltd. All rights reserved.

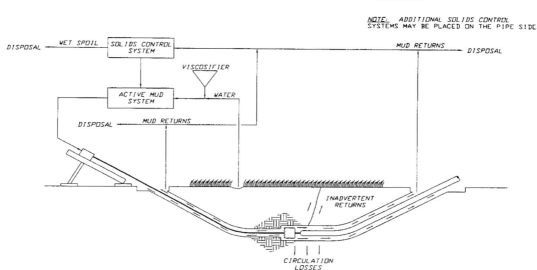

Fig. 1. HDD drilling fluid flow schematic.

drilling (from an upland location) a small diameter pilot hole along a designated directional path. The drill path can be changed after the drill is advanced, if necessary. In soft soils, drilling progress is often achieved by hydraulic cutting with a jet nozzle. For harder soils, downhole hydraulic motors (mud motors) provide mechanical cutting action by converting hydraulic energy from drilling mud pumped from the surface to mechanical energy at the bit. The actual path of the pilot hole is monitored during drilling by periodic readings of a probe inserted in a drill collar as close as possible to the drill bit. Readings of the inclination and azimuth of the leading edge of the drill are taken in conjunction with measurements of the distance drilled since the last survey. These are used to calculate the horizontal and vertical coordinates along the pilot hole relative to the initial entry point on the surface. The pilot hole path may also be tracked using a surface monitoring system which determines the location of the probe downhole by taking measurements from a grid or point on the surface.

The second stage of HDD involves enlarging the pilot hole to a diameter which will accommodate the pipe (reaming). The pilot hole is enlarged using one or more reaming passes prior to pipe installation. In a typical reaming pass, reamers are attached to the drill string at the exit point of the directional drill and are rotated and drawn back through the pilot hole to the drilling rig, enlarging the pilot hole. The exit point is located in uplands on the opposite side of the wetland from the entrance point. A string of pipe is always maintained in the drilled hole. It is also possible to ream away from the drill rig, in which case, reamers fitted into the drill string at the rig are rotated and pulled away from it by a piece of equipment at the exit point of the pilot hole.

The third stage of HDD consists of pulling the pipe back into the reamed hole. After reaming is completed, a prefabricated pipeline pull section is attached behind a reaming assembly at the exit point of the pilot hole, and the reaming assembly and pipeline section are pulled back to the drilling rig. For smaller diameter lines in soft soils, the pipeline can be pulled back directly after completion of the pilot hole, skipping the reaming step. The pull section is supported using a combination of roller stands, pipe handling equipment, or a flotation ditch to minimize tension and prevent damage to the pipe.

Trench and lay

Trench and lay is the most common form of pipeline construction. It is utilized to install pipelines in all types of terrain where dry or otherwise "drivable" land access is available. This pipeline installation method consists of excavating a trench, welding a pipeline along and above the trench, lowering the pipeline into the trench, and backfilling the trench (Fig. 2). Trench and lay installation across a wetland is generally accomplished with six distinct construction operations: clearing and grading, ditching, hauling and stringing, welding, lowering-in, and backfilling.

Clearing and grading involves preparing the right-of-way for equipment access. A substantial amount of grading is usually not required in wetlands as they are typically physiographically low and have negligible relief. The amount of vegetation clearing required in wetlands is largely dependent on the wetland type. Required clearing is greater in wetlands characterized by forested and/or scrub-shrub vegetative communities compared to wetlands colonized with emergent or otherwise herbaceous species.

Trench excavation is accomplished with either a ditching machine or a track-mounted backhoe. Trench

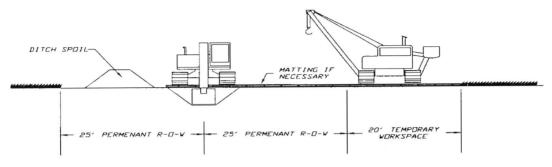

Fig. 2. Typical trench layout and right-of-way cross section.

spoil is placed to the side of the ditch for use as backfill. Blasting may be required if rock is encountered which cannot be mechanically removed, although near-surface rock is not generally found beneath vegetated wetlands.

In the trench and lay method, the pipeline is welded together above the ditch. Joints of pipe, typically 40 feet in length, are set in place above the ditch by stringing trucks in preparation for welding. The trucks drive, or are towed, down the right-of-way. As they progress, a side boom lifts the individual joints of pipe off of the trailers and places them in line above the ditch. Pipe welding is completed in place, and the pipe is subsequently lowered into the ditch by two or more side boom tractors. The side booms travel down the right-of-way lifting the pipeline from the ditch bank and setting it in place on the ditch bottom.

Backfilling involves placing excavated spoil on and around the pipe. If the spoil cannot be recovered or is not suitable for backfill, appropriate material must be imported. Backfilling can be accomplished by bulldozers or specialized machines designed specifically for that purpose.

Trench and push

Trench and push is a specialized form of pipeline construction developed to install pipelines across emergent wetlands and shallow open water areas. The presence of surface water allows the pipeline to be floated into the ditch, which in turn reduces space requirements for operations along the right-of-way (ROW). In contrast to the trench and lay method, welding takes place at a stationary location at one end of trench and the welded pipeline is pushed into the ditch. Three operations are required for trench and push: ditching, welding and pushing, and backfilling. Clearing and grading is generally not required due to the flat and open nature of emergent wetlands.

Excavation is accomplished by equipment, commonly specialized "marsh" backhoes, capable of working in standing water or high water table conditions. Marsh backhoes are hydraulically operated backhoes mounted on very low ground-pressure tracked vehicles capable of operating in very soft ground conditions, and will float if moved into standing water. Excavation in standing water is typically carried out by backhoes or draglines supported on small barges. The size of the ditch must be increased to allow movement of the barge, therefore barge size is kept to the minimum possible to keep workspace requirements as small as possible. Ditching machines cannot be used in high water table conditions.

All welding operations take place at one push site. The basic operations are the same as those involved with trench and lay with the exception that the assembly line is stationary with single joints of pipe moving in one end and a continuously welded pipeline being pushed out the other. Pushing typically takes place via rollers from a suitable upland location at one end of the crossing (Fig. 3).

Backfilling is accomplished by the same specialized marsh backhoes used to excavate the ditch, due to standing water or high water table conditions. Achieving good backfill in standing water conditions can be complicated because of the difficulty involved with recovering wet excavated spoil.

Representative costs

Installation cost estimates for the three construction methods and cost estimates of inadvertent return clean-up operations were examined as part of this research. Installation cost estimates were produced for typical wetland crossings in three diameters (12-, 24-, and 36-in) and four lengths (1000, 2000, 3000, and 4000 feet). Variance of diameter and length allows

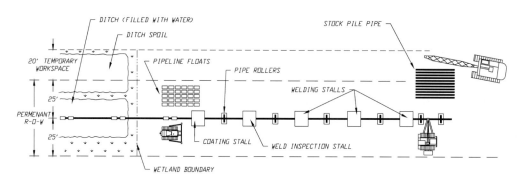

Fig. 3. Typical trench and push right-of-way plan view.

comparison of each method's cost over the majority of foreseeable applications. Inadvertent return clean-up operations have been estimated for three differing scenarios, including typical contractor's cost. Typical owner's costs, such as line pipe, engineering, right-of-way, permits, etc. are not included. HDD and trench and push wetland crossings on a cross-country pipeline are separate operations from the pipeline installation. Therefore, the cost estimate for these methods includes establishment tasks such as mobilization and site preparation. A trench and lay wetland crossing on a cross-country pipeline does not need to be mobilized separately from other pipe installation operations. Therefore, the comparative cost estimate developed for this crossing method does not account for establishment tasks such as mobilization and site preparation. Costs are generally estimated as an extension of the adjacent cross-country pipe laying operations.

Inadvertent fluid release clean-up

For the purposes of estimating cost of drill fluid clean-up operations, three options for mud removal related to access limitations and clean-up urgency were evaluated. Certain assumptions were made relative to the inadvertent release in order to compare the different removal methods:

- The inadvertent fluid release occurs during pilot hole drilling;
- Sixty percent of the fluid used during drilling is lost to the ground surface during a 10-hour shift;
- The inadvertent fluid release location is 500 feet away from the working location;
- The inadvertent release initially goes unnoticed and spreads to an area of 50 feet by 50 feet prior to containment;
- The general wetland characteristics are fixed;
- The drill fluid release is moved from the area of concern to an excavated sump or holding tank at the work site; and
- The sump is accessible to heavy equipment for final disposal using land farming or mix and bury methods.

RESULTS

Potential environmental impacts

Environmental impacts were evaluated relative to each of the three wetland crossing construction methods.

Horizontal directional drilling

In many cases, crossing a wetland using HDD has significantly less environmental impact than that associated with construction by trench and lay or trench and push. Nevertheless, impact due to HDD occurs and is related to workspace and drilling fluids. Workspace requirements for HDD require clearing and grading to allow movement along the ROW and equipment staging areas. Approximately seven tractor-trailer loads and a workspace of 150 feet by 250 feet is adequate for most typical large horizontal drilling rig operations. It is possible to decrease the workspace for the rig assembly to 60 feet by 150 feet if necessary. However, minimal workspace restricts the size and capacity of the drilling rig. HDD equipment is typically supported on the ground surface in uplands adjacent to the area to be drilled. Timber mats may be used where soft ground is encountered, but if the sensitive area to be crossed is a wetland, staging of the drill rig will be limited to uplands.

Pipe pull section fabrication is accomplished using the same construction methods used to lay a pipeline. Therefore, similar workspace is required with the exception that no space is required for the ditch and spoil. The location of pull section fabrication workspace is determined by the drilled segment exit point, as space must be available to allow the pipe to be fed into the drilled hole. It is preferable to have workspace in line with the drilled segment and extending back from the exit point two hundred feet further than the length of the pull section, allowing the pull section to be prefabricated in one continuous length prior to installation. If space is not available, the pull section may be fabricated in two or more sections that are welded together during installation. The pull section fabrication workspace must be cleared but need not be graded level. Equipment is typically supported on the ground surface and timber mats may be used where soft ground is encountered.

The primary impact of HDD on the environment is due to the uncontrolled subsurface discharge of drilling fluids. Drilling fluids flow in the path of least resistance, which can mean dispersal into the surrounding soils or discharge to the surface at a random location. Drilling parameters may be adjusted to maximize circulation and minimize the risk of inadvertent returns, however, the possibility of lost circulation and inadvertent returns cannot be totally eliminated. Inadvertent returns are more likely to occur in soils with low-permeability or pre-existing flow paths, such as fractured rock. Coarse-grained, permeable soils tend to absorb circulation losses, while manmade features such as exploratory boreholes or piles may serve as conduits to the surface for drilling fluids.

Drilling fluids utilized in HDD applications are largely composed of bentonite clay and fresh water (AGA, 1994). Based on the research available to date, the primary impacts to wetlands associated with HDD drilling fluids appear to be from sedimentation and turbidity increases incurred on surface water bodies. Although bentonite is chemically non-toxic to aquatic life, large volumes of drilling mud returns to sensitive ecological areas can smother vegetation and macroinvertebrate habitat, affect the filter-feeding processes utilized by certain aquatic organisms, and interfere with reproduction and larval development of fish and amphibians (Falk and Lawrence, 1973).

In comparison to the other two construction technologies evaluated under this task, the relative environmental impact from HDD is largely a factor of the frequency of which sizable returns occur, and whether or not they are removed from the affected area. No available data exist relative to the frequency of inadvertent returns, as their chance of occurrence is determined by multiple factors. However, anectodal evidence from NGTLs and HDD contractors suggests that sizable mud returns may occur in more than 50% of all drills. In terms of clean-up operations, evidence suggests that the long-term impacts of mud returns in wetlands are reduced by prompt and complete removal of muds. This contention is based on consideration of the wetland functions of water quality, flood storage and attenuation, wildlife and aquatic species habitat, floodflow alteration, and nutrient removal and transformation. Cleanup of HDD muds in wetlands typically involves the use of heavy equipment, which may result in surface soil disturbance and compaction, vegetation clearing, or other physical damage to the vegetative community. In addition, introducing heavy machinery into wetlands for cleanup operations may pose the potential for fuel oil releases.

Trench and lay
The trench and lay method produces the greatest impact to the wetland being crossed in that all construction activities occur within the wetland. The equipment typically operates on the ground surface, and the right-of-way must be cleared. Topsoil may be stripped and stockpiled for post-construction restoration. The widths of the ditch and spoil pile depend on soil conditions. In a vegetated wetland setting, timber or swamp mats must be used to support construction equipment used to excavate the trench and lay the pipe. Soils generated from the excavation are typically sidecast next to the trench and then used again as backfill material. Impacts resulting from a wetland crossing using the trench and lay construction method include potential sedimentation of surface waters from the dispersal of sidecast materials, soil compaction due to the placement of swamp mats and movement of heavy equipment in the wetland, and soil profile disturbance from excavation and backfill activities. Sedimentation of surface waters may not be problematic in seasonally saturated wetlands, but could pose substantial impacts to a wetland that is periodically flooded, or if the wetland is subject to sudden storm events. Vegetation clearing in wetlands for this construction method is dependent on the wetland type; wetlands characterized by forested and/or scrub-shrub vegetative communities are subject to greater impacts from clearing than are wetlands dominated by emergent species. In addition, aquatic impacts may result in the event of an inadvertent fuel/lubricating oil release from construction vehicles. Impacts to uplands as a result of staging equipment and workspace requirements are similar to those of HDD.

Trench and push
Environmental impact is comparatively less in the trench and push method than in trench and lay in that only ditching and backfilling activities occur within the wetland. Equipment is employed that can operate in standing water or on the ground surface. Grading and topsoil stripping along the ditch line is typically not performed in wetlands, and in some cases ditching can be performed from a barge. Trees and other large woody vegetation are typically not present in permanently inundated wetlands, therefore, impacts

to the vegetative community may be less severe during a trench and push operation as compared to trench and lay. In general, the impacts to wetlands resulting from this construction method are similar to that of the trench and lay method. Impacts resulting from a wetland crossing using the trench and push construction method include sedimentation of surface waters from the dispersal of excavated and sidecast materials, potential soil compaction due to the movement of heavy equipment in the wetland, and soil profile disturbance from excavation and backfill activities. Sedimentation of surface waters can be minimized through the use of floating protective booms or silt curtains, but is unavoidable due to the nature of this construction method. In addition, the same potential impacts exist relative to the presence of heavy machinery (e.g., fuel oil release).

Typically, an upland workspace of 70 feet by 250 feet is required for pipeline welding and the push staging area (Hair, 1999). The workspace must be cleared and graded level. Equipment is typically supported on the ground surface and timber mats or sand fill may be used where soft ground is encountered. As soil conditions in wetlands can be less stable than in upland or drier conditions, the ditch and spoil pile associated with trench and push operations require more room than the typical trench and lay requirements. Ditch slopes in moist soils can exceed a 1:2 ratio, and maximum spoil pile stability will equal that of the ditch. The construction ROW configuration should be sufficient to accommodate a larger ditch and spoil pile.

Engineering and geophysical limitations

While the three wetland crossing methods examined in this report are widely applicable, each has its own limitations. Specific geophysical and engineering considerations associated with each construction method are described below.

Horizontal directional drilling

Drilled length, pipe diameter, and subsurface soil condition limit the feasibility of HDD. These three factors work in combination to restrict what can be accomplished at a given location. The longest drilled crossings to date have been recorded at approximately 6000 feet, and typically consist of smaller diameter crossings installed through alluvial deposits. The largest diameter drill successfully completed on record is 48 inches outer diameter (OD). Crossings for this diameter pipeline are fairly rare, however, and rarely extend over lengths of approximately 2500 feet through alluvial deposits.

Limitations with respect to borehole length and diameter are primarily due to limits on the capacity of existing tools and drill pipe. The flexibility of relatively slender drill pipe does not allow an unlimited amount of pressure to be applied. In addition, control of the leading edge diminishes over long lengths. Present technology also involves rotating pipe at the surface to rotate reamers downhole, however the capacity of drill pipe for the transmission of torsion is limited. Installation of a 48-inch OD pipe typically requires completion of a 60-inch reaming pass. While development of new tools and techniques to increase load bearing and energy transmission capacities of drill pipe is possible, economic factors must be considered. The market for HDD installation of pipe over longer lengths or larger diameters than those cited above has not yet developed.

The primary technical limitation of HDD is the subsurface soil material at the proposed crossing. The two main soil characteristics potentially impairing the use of HDD are a high percentage of coarse-grained materials (i.e., gravel, cobbles) and excessive rock strength and hardness. Soils consisting principally of coarse-grained material present a serious restriction to the feasibility of HDD, as coarse material cannot be readily fluidized by the drilling muds. It also cannot be cut and removed in a drilling fluid stream through an open hole as would be the case in a crossing drilled through competent rock. A boulder or cluster of cobbles will remain in the drilled path and present an obstruction to a bit, reamer, or pipeline. Exceptionally strong and hard rock will hamper all phases of an HDD project. Experience has shown that competent rock with unconfined compressive strengths in the neighborhood of 15,000 psi and Moh's Scale of Hardness factors ranging somewhat above 7 can be negotiated with today's technology. However, encountering such materials at depth usually presents difficulty as the directional drilling string tends to deflect rather than penetrate. Conversely, extensively fractured or jointed rock can present the same problems as coarse granular deposits (Hair, 1999).

Trench and lay

There are no physical limitations on the application of the trench and lay method to wetland crossings as long as standard tracked construction equipment can operate within the wetland. If standing water is present, or the natural ground is so soft that it cannot support standard tracked equipment, than an alternate crossing method must be employed.

Trench and push

Trench and push can only be applied where a flotation ditch can be constructed. The terrain must be flat and the ditch must hold water. The pipeline alignment can contain bends, but they must be of a long enough radius to allow the pipe to conform with a free elastic bend (Hair, 1999). Push sections several miles in length are not uncommon.

COST

Figs. 4–6 compare crossing construction costs for three pipeline diameters: 12, 24, and 36 in. Both lump sum and unit prices are listed for each construction method over the four crossing lengths estimated. No estimates were prepared for a 1000 foot 36-inch crossing as standard HDD industry design criteria generally requires the drilled length for a 36-inch installation to exceed 1000 feet. The unit cost of all of the crossings generally increases as the length and diameter increase for the range of lengths under consideration. However, the rate of increase is much greater for an HDD crossing. Overall, trench & lay is the least expensive method for installing a pipeline across a wetland.

In general, HDD is two to three times as costly as trench and lay construction for pipes 12–36 inches ID. HDD is 25–80% more expensive than trench and push construction, depending on the pipe diameter. Trench and push construction is approximately 30–50% more expensive than trench and lay construction, and too, increases in cost as the diameter of the pipe being installed increases.

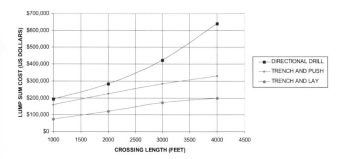

Fig. 4. Wetland crossing comparative assessment 12 inch pipe.

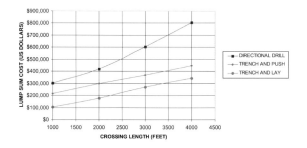

Fig. 5. Wetland crossing comparative assessment 24 inch pipeline.

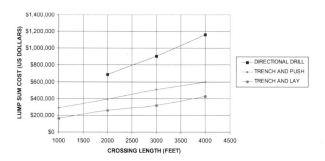

Fig. 6. Wetland crossing comparative assessment 36 inch pipeline.

Inadvertent fluid release cleanup costs

Scenario 1. The location of this inadvertent fluid release is such that no vehicular or equipment access is possible. Access is by foot only and narrow plywood pathways may be used if soil conditions require. The drill fluid does not need to be removed immediately, so it eventually gels to a moist clay material. In this case drill fluid is shoveled manually into wheelbarrows and transported to a sump at the drill site. The estimated cost for a clean-up similar to this is $23,725.

Scenario 2. This case involves a situation in which access to the inadvertent fluid release is permitted only to pick-up trucks and small rubber-tired backhoes. Regulations force the contractor to remove the material before it dries. Here, a contractor utilizes pumps to transport the fluid to the sump at the rig site. The estimated cost for a clean-up similar to this is $14,328.

Scenario 3. This scenario allows equipment access to the inadvertent fluid release via board road only. Standing water exists at this location such that fill dirt must be hauled in to elevate the board road. The drill fluid must be removed immediately, so vacuum trucks are used to suck the mud from the surface. In this case, it is assumed that a large enough sump pit could not be excavated at the drill site so holding tanks are utilized for storage. The estimated cost for a clean-up similar to this is $28,097.

The estimates for these three scenarios do not include cost for actual mud disposal operations such as land farming or mix and bury, which occur on almost all directionally drilled crossings since there is usually excess drill fluid to dispose of after drilling is complete.

CONCLUSIONS

HDD is theoretically the least intrusive method for constructing pipelines across sensitive areas such as wetlands, waterways, cultural, historic, and archaeological sites. If executed without incident in a wetland setting, a horizontal drill will install the pipeline without the need for heavy machinery to access the wetland, essentially creating no environmental impacts and therefore environmental cleanup costs will not be incurred. However, if sizable volumes of drill muds are deposited in a wetland, water quality, aquatic species/habitat and the vegetative community can be impaired, at least in the short-term. Impacts will likely be less if returns are removed from the wetland area, although potential additional damage to the wetland vegetation and soils as a result of cleanup operations must be considered. Engineering limitations to HDD exist, and in certain substrates HDD is not the optimal construction method. In addition, HDD crossings are limited to linear distances of less than 6000 ft. and the success of the drill and integrity of the pipe are related to the length and diameter of the bore.

Trench and lay construction involves the clearing of vegetation and grading of surface features of the right-of-way. In wetlands, water quality, aquatic species/habitat, and vegetation will all be compromised, at least locally and for the short-term. Trench and lay technology is essentially free of engineering limitations relative to the other two technologies reviewed, and has fewer variables involved in terms of overall cost, as construction and restoration operations are easier to forecast than in the other two technologies.

Trench and push construction is a feasible pipeline installation alternative for wetland crossings where sufficient standing water is present to create a flotation ditch. The trench and push method will incur comparable impacts to uplands as HDD and trench and lay construction. In terms of environmental impacts in a wetland setting, this method will result in at least short-term, localized impacts to water quality, aquatic species/habitat, and vegetation. Water quality will likely be affected more through this method than in trench and lay, as a wetter hydrologic regime is required to facilitate the trench and push method. However, as the vegetative community at a trench and push wetland site will likely be absent or limited to floating or submerged aquatic plants, impacts to site vegetation will be less than with trench and lay. However, soil disturbance and compaction will occur from marsh excavator movement. In terms of cost, trench and push technology is significantly less costly than HDD and approximately twice the cost of trench and lay construction.

In order to determine the appropriate wetland crossing method, multiple factors need consideration, including the geology of underlying soils, site topography, hydrology, and length of pipe to be installed. HDD may not be the optimal crossing method where underlying soils consist of cobbles, boulders, or bedrock, or if the pipe to be installed is greater than one mile in length.

All three of the crossing techniques reviewed under this study have advantages under certain situations, and it should be noted that the increased requirement and use of HDD for wetlands and waterway crossings has prompted this research. HDD can be effective at minimizing certain environmental impacts but it is not without limitation. In addition, HDD can be extremely costly and even cost-prohibitive. The probability of inadvertent return occurrence to vegetated wetlands must be a serious consideration prior to HDD being selected as the crossing method for a given project. One aspect not included in this study was the timeframe for implementation of HDD relative to conventional methods, based on the permitting process, and actual time requirements for project set-up. As this research suggests, the initial costs, potential impacts, and additional damage that can be incurred from cleanup activities may not coincide with the overall goals of the project or the goals of the associated jurisdictional environmental agency.

ACKNOWLEDGEMENTS

This research was conducted by ENSR Corp. under contract with and funding by the Gas Research Institute (GRI, Chicago, IL) through the program Evaluating the Effects of Muds on Wetlands from Horizontal Drilling. Mr. James Evans serves as the GRI Project Manager; Mr. Jon Schmidt, PhD as ENSR Principal-in-Charge; Mr. Carl Tammi, CWD, PWS as ENSR Project Manager; Mr. David Cameron, PWS as ENSR Principal Scientist; and Ms. Emily Steel as ENSR Project Specialist. Mr. John Hair of J.D. Hair & Associates was the Sr. Technical Advisor for this component of the research.

REFERENCES

AGA. 1994. Drilling Fluids and Pipeline Installation by HDD: Directional Drilling Muds Characteristics. American Gas Association Pipeline Research Committee Contract to J.D. Hair & Associates, Tulsa, OK.

API Bulletin D11, 1st ed. December 1965.

Drilling Mud, Unit II, Lesson 2, 3rd ed. Rotary Drilling Series. Austin, Texas; Petroleum Extension Service, University of Texas at Austin, 1984.

Falk and Lawrence. 1973. Acute Toxicity of Petro-Chemical Drilling Fluid Components to Fish. Canada Dept. of Environment.

GRI. 1998. Evaluating the Effects of Muds on Wetlands from Horizontal Drilling: Literature Survey Topical Report. ENSR Corporation under contract with the Gas Research Institute. Document # GRI 98/0190.

GRI. 1999. Evaluating the Effects of Muds on Wetlands from Horizontal Drilling: Professional Screening Survey/Permit Condition Review Topical Report. ENSR Corporation under contract with the Gas Research Institute. Document # GRI 98/0350.

GRI. 1999. Evaluating the Effects of Muds on Wetlands from Horizontal Drilling: Permit Condition and Mitigation Measures Review and Alternatives Evaluation Topical Report. ENSR Corporation under contract with the Gas Research Institute. Document # GRI 99/0132.

Hair. 1999. Personal Communication between ENSR Corp. and J.D. Hair & Associates.

IADC Drilling Manual, 11th ed. Houston, Texas; International Association of Drilling Contractors, 1992.

BIOGRAPHICAL SKETCHES

John D. Hair

J.D. Hair & Associates, Inc., 2121 South Columbia Avenue, Suite 101, Tulsa, OK 74114-3502, USA, 918/747-9945 Phone, 918/742-7480 Fax

John Hair is Principal of J.D. Hair & Associates, Inc. (JDH&A), a professional corporation which was established in 1987 with the objective to focus creative engineering talent on projects involving the installation of buried utilities by trenchless construction methods. In the thirteen years since its founding, JDH&A has been involved in over 50 miles of trenchless utility construction covering pipe diameters from four to forty-eight inches. Mr. Hair has conducted work world-wide.

David J. Cameron, PWS
   ENSR International Corporation, 2 Technology Park Drive, Westford, MA 01886, USA, 978/589-3000 Phone, 978/589-3035 Fax

David J. Cameron is a Senior Ecologist and Wetland Scientist in the Water Resources Department of ENSR, Inc. Mr. Cameron has over 9 years experience in wetland evaluation, permitting and wildlife habitat assessment. He is a Certified Professional Wetland Scientist.

Carl E. Tammi, PWS, CWD
   ENSR International Corporation, 2 Technology Park Drive, Westford, MA 01886, USA, 978/589-3000 Phone, 978/589-3035 Fax

Carl E. Tammi is a Senior Wetlands Project Manager in the *Water Resources Department* of *ENSR*, Inc. He has over 13 years of professional experience in multidisciplinary wetlands program management throughout the US. Mr. Tammi directs wetland assessments, delineation, permitting, mitigation, and restoration design, construction, long-term monitoring, and treatment design. Mr. Tammi is the author of 2 chapters in the national-released Lewis Publishers textbook *Applied Wetland Science and Technology* as well as numerous technical publications on wetlands restoration. He is a Certified Professional Wetland Scientist, and received his Professional Wetland Delineator Certification from the US Army Corps of Engineers, Baltimore District.

Emily Steel
   ENSR International Corporation, 2 Technology Park Drive, Westford, MA 01886, USA, 978/589-3000 Phone, 978/589-3035 Fax

Emily Steel is a *Wetland Scientist* and Geologist with 4 years of experience. Ms. Steel has conducted field surveys and prepared reports and permit applications in support of dozens of natural gas pipeline projects in the eastern US.

John A. Schmidt PhD
   ENSR International Corporation, 1538 Metropolitan Blvd., Suite C1, Tallahasee, FL 32308, USA, 850/309-0264

John Schmidt is Director of Energy Services for ENSR, Inc. and is the client manager for three international energy companies. Dr. Schmidt has managed large natural gas projects both domestically and overseas, from 700+ mile, large-diameter natural gas pipelines in the midwestern and southeastern United States, to Category A Environmental Impact Assessments in Chile. Dr. Schmidt has worked on oil and natural gas pipelines in Venezuela, Columbia, Argentina, and the United States. Dr. Schmidt has over 12 years experience managing and directing large, multi-disciplinary projects for the oil and gas industry. He has managed the siting, environmental field surveys, permitting, licensing, and NEPA document preparation for over 8000 miles of natural gas and oil pipelines, liquefied natural gas plants, marine terminals and marine pipelines, compressor stations, and hydroelectric facilities.

James Evans
   Gas Research Institute (Gas Technology Institute), 1700 South Mount Prospect Road, Des Plaines, IL 60018-1804, USA, 847/768-0500, 847/768-0501

James Evans is Senior Project Manager at the *Gas Technology Institute* (formerly Gas Research Institute). Mr. Evans has directed dozens of research projects in support of the natural gas industry.

Part X
Soils

Influences of Soil Acidity Levels on Vegetative Reclamation and Wildlife Habitat on Rights-of-Way Transecting Drastically-disturbed Lands

Jeanne C. Jones

Utility rights-of-way may transect drastically disturbed lands, such as public works projects, water resources projects, and reclaimed mine sites. Many of these lands have acid overburden, such as pyrite (iron sulfide), incorporated in their upper soil layers due to disturbance of parent material and soil horizon mixing. Acidifying overburden, such as iron pyrite, oxidizes to produce sulfuric acid and highly acid soil conditions upon exposure to atmospheric oxygen and water. Occurrence of these compounds near the soil's surface can limit success with vegetative reclamation of rights-of-way, and subsequently, limit wildlife habitat quality. Research conducted over an eleven-year period on upland disposal areas of the Tennessee–Tombigbee Waterway in Mississippi revealed active soil pH levels of 3.9 and less on sites where pyrite occurred 3–35 cm from the soil's surface. These pH levels, in conjunction with exchangeable acidity and metal cation concentrations, caused phytotoxic soil conditions and loss of vegetation. Seeded and native plant biomass was less than 1.3 kg/ha during the summers of 1991 and 1992. Phytotoxic soil conditions were minimal on sites where acid overburden was buried beneath at least 40 cm of topsoil soils brought from undisturbed areas that exhibited near neutral pH levels. On these sites ($N = 30$), biomass of native and seeded agronomic plants generally exceeded 3000 kg/ha. With proper management, rights-of-way on disturbed lands can support vegetation and wildlife. However, planners and resource managers should be aware of problems produced by exposure of acid overburden during powerline or pipeline construction and maintenance.

Keywords: Soil acidity, pyrite, reclamation, ecological restoration, rights-of-way

INTRODUCTION

Drastically disturbed lands can be defined as lands on which vegetation has been removed or destroyed, soil horizon structure has been destroyed or intermixed, and in some cases, where parent material is exposed or intermixed with upper horizon layers (Pettry et al., 1980). Land uses that create this type of disturbance include, but are not limited to, surface mining, public works projects, military training areas used for artillery and tracked vehicle maneuvers, and subterranean pipeline construction (Pettry et al., 1980). Depending on the underlying parent material and the degree of disturbance, reclamation challenges that may be encountered on these areas are loss of plant cover and species diversity, destruction of wildlife habitat, creation of phytotoxic substrate conditions, exposure of substrates with high compaction or high rock content, and soil erosion. Aquatic and terrestrial habitats near disturbed lands can also be negatively affected by sedimentation and toxic chemical leachates arising from the disturbed sites. Without proper treatment, disturbed sites and adjacent habitats can exhibit loss of productivity over the long term due to degradation of soil, water, floral, and faunal resources.

Timely reclamation of disturbed lands is necessary to restore habitats over the short term, prevent habitat degradation on adjacent lands, and to initiate ecological restoration of native biological communities. Although most of the available data on drastically disturbed lands is derived from research conducted

---

Environmental Concerns in Rights-of-Way
Management: Seventh International Symposium
J.W. Goodrich-Mahoney, D.F. Mutrie and C.A. Guild (editors)
© 2002 Elsevier Science Ltd. All rights reserved.

on mine sites, the concepts are directly applicable to soils crossed by utility rights-of-way. Many disturbed lands can be reclaimed over time with proper substrate amelioration, revegetation, management, and monitoring (Wade and Tritton, 1997). With proper liming and fertilization, reclaimed mine sites can support high vegetative productivity of seeded herbaceous plants (Barnhisel and Krupe, 1985; Pettry and Wood, 1986). Although seeded plant biomass can be high, many studies of reclaimed surface mine and upland disposal sites have reported delayed reforestation, low native plant species diversity, limited A-horizon development, and delayed recolonization by macroinvertebrate detritivores in the first 20 years following reclamation (Jones, 1995; Curry and Cotton, 1983; Pettry et al., 1980). There is evidence that site age is related to the degree of soil formation, detritivore colonization, and native plant succession. Pettry et al. (1980) reported that mine sites may require up to 50 years for development of topsoil layers. Studies from >50 year-old surface mine sites in Kentucky reported high diversity of native and planted species (Wade and Tritton, 1997). Most studies of reclaimed mine and upland disposal sites of less than 50 years of age have reported low reforestation rates and limited native plant diversity due to edaphic conditions and seeded plant cover (Skousen et al., 1994; Byrnes and Miller, 1973). On many surface mine and disposal sites, high soil acidity and the associated metal salt contents were primary factors limiting vegetation establishment during the first 10 years following reclamation (Jones et al., 1996; Skousen et al., 1994).

Despite the restoration challenges, many public agencies in the United States manage reclaimed disturbed lands for fish, wildlife, and outdoor recreation (Department of Energy, 1984). Because of the preponderance of herbaceous and shrub-type plant communities during the first 10–20 years following reclamation, these areas can provide habitat for many grassland and old-field wildlife species, such as northern bobwhite (*Colinus virginianus*), rabbits (*Sylvilagus* spp.), and white-tailed deer (*Odocoileus virginianus*) (Jones et al., 1994). To maintain the productivity of these habitats, land managers must understand the existing edaphic conditions and how these conditions can influence flora, fauna, and habitat quality. Because utility and gas line rights-of-way often transect disturbed land bases, access may be required for line construction, vegetation management, monitoring, and line maintenance. Since some activities may result in soil disturbance and vegetative manipulation, utility company personnel should be aware of soil conditions that influence degradation, amelioration, and restoration of these sites. Proactive measures that prevent vegetation loss, acid substrate exposure, and erosion can prevent on-site and adjacent-site damage.

The objectives of this paper are as follows: (1) to provide a summary of literature on soil conditions that cause vegetation loss and planting failures on drastically disturbed lands, (2) to report the findings of a case study on a drastically disturbed land base in Mississippi, and (3) to present proactive reclamation approaches for utility rights-of-way transecting disturbed land bases.

SOIL CONDITIONS AND RESTORATION

The degradation of soil horizon structure, exposure of parent material, and incorporation of phytotoxic overburden in spoil substrates on severely disturbed areas can produce harsh edaphic conditions that limit plant establishment and survival. On sites where vegetation has been lost, soil stabilization and plant community establishment are essential for short-term reclamation and long-term ecological restoration.

Physical soil factors

Physical soil characteristics that may impact soil stabilization and revegetation success include soil texture, coarse fragment content, and bulk density (Hons et al., 1978). Percent coarse fragment can influence root development and water availability to plants. Low water-holding capabilities and droughty nature of substrates with high rock content can limit plant survival, especially during years of low rainfall (Jones, 1995). Research performed on reclaimed lignite mines in Texas reported that soil textural classes of loam, silt loam, and sandy loam were suitable growing media for reclamation plantings. In this study materials containing high coarse fragment content (60–99% >2 mm in size) were found in core samples. According to Feagley (1985), cores containing >95% coarse fragment content were unsuitable growing media for plants unless mixed with finer textured material. Data recorded on upland disposal sites in Mississippi indicated that coarse fragment content of <45% had little effect on plant cover during years of normal rainfall (Jones, 1995).

Bulk density, which represents the combination of soil particle size and pore space, can be utilized as an indicator for soil compaction. High bulk density can impede plant survival and growth by limiting the amount of water available to the plant and limiting root growth and zone. The bulk density of granulated clay surface soils will generally be 1.0–1.3 g/cc with coarse textured sandy soils ranging from 1.3–1.8 g/cc. (Foth, 1984). Organic soils (Histosols) have low bulk densities that commonly range from 0.1–0.6 g/cc. when compared to mineral soils (Foth, 1984). In general, parent materials exhibit greater bulk densities due to substrate density, limited weathering, and subsequent low pore space structure (Foth, 1984). Bulk densities on disturbed lands may exceed undisturbed natural areas due to compaction from heavy equipment, sandy content of substrate, and exposure of parent material. Bulk densities reported for a reclaimed surface mine in Alabama ranged from 1.45–1.86 g/cc and were higher on spoil substrates than undisturbed natural areas (Pettry et al., 1980). Bulk density values increased with depth due to less weathering and higher coarse fragment content. Highest bulk densities were reported on ridges and were attributed, in part, to compaction by heavy equipment and rainfall impact. Lowest bulk density values were found at the bottom of slopes in drainages where alluvium and colluvium accumulated (Pettry et al., 1980). Bulk density can be expected to decrease over time with progressive weathering and deposition of organic matter from vegetation (Pettry et al., 1980). Amelioration of high bulk density and compaction may be necessary for successful revegetation. Application of topsoil and manures can increase organic matter and lower bulk density on compacted areas of high sand and parent material content, creating better growing conditions for vegetation (Foth, 1984).

Soil chemistry factors

Nutrient and organic matter content on disturbed substrates may be influenced by parent material, substrate origin, reclamation treatment, vegetative cover, and colonization by detritivores. Phosphorous and nitrogen deficiencies have been reported on reclaimed overburden in the southeastern United States; however, these nutrient problems were corrected for forage and row crop production with proper fertilization and liming maintenance (Feagley, 1985). Research indicates that newly reclaimed disturbed lands lack easily oxidizable organic matter and the microflora and fauna associated with oxidized organic matter (Jones, 1995; Skousen et al., 1994; Feagley, 1985).

Surface mine spoil in Alabama exhibited low organic matter content compared to undisturbed areas with lowest contents of 0.4% being recorded in subsoil horizons and higher contents of 3.4% being found in upper horizons. Undisturbed sites averaged 5% organic matter content (Pettry and Wood, 1986). Upland disposal sites in Mississippi exhibited organic matter contents ranging from 0.3% in soil depths of >10 cm on pyrite oxidation sites to 4.6% in the upper 10 cm of substrate beneath planted shrubs eleven years following construction and reclamation (Jones, 1995). Formation of A horizons, melanin substrate coloration, and incorporation of organic matter to level of 5% and greater may require up to 50 years (Pettry and Wood, 1986). These processes can be expedited by topsoil and manure application; introduction of earthworms (annelids); and selection of reclamation plantings, such as annual legumes, that create favorable microhabitats for detritivores (Jones, 1995; Lee and Skogerboe, 1984).

Many researchers have reported problems with high soil acidities and high concentrations of metal salts on mine and upland disposal sites underlain by acid overburden materials (Jones et al., 1996). Bauxite, coal, and lignite deposits are generally associated with acid overburden originating from unweathered parent material layers. Common overburden materials found on these areas are iron-sulfur compounds, such as pyrite (FeS_2). Pyrite, when exposed to oxygen and water near the soil's surface, oxidizes to produce sulfuric acid (H_2SO_4) and metal ions, and metal salt complexes (Hons et al., 1978). Factors that may accelerate pyrite oxidation rates include exposure of pyrite near the soil's surface, pooling of water, presence of autotrophic Fe- and S-oxidizing bacteria, and morphological form of pyrite (Singer and Strumm, 1969; Pugh et al., 1984).

Acidity levels and metal salt solutions produced by pyrite oxidation processes can deter establishment and growth of vegetative cover, create bare soil areas which expand over time, increase erosion potential, and limit site productivity for forage crops, wildlife habitat, and reforestation (Jones et al., 1996; Jones et al., 1994; Hons et al., 1978). Exposed complexes of iron sulfide have been reported as major sources of acid mine drainage from and as the primary cause of unsuccessful revegetation on surface mines and civil works projects in the eastern United States (Jones et al., 1996; Ammons et al., 1983). Soil pH levels associated the oxidation of iron sulfide are generally ≤4.5 and are associated with high levels of soluble salts of aluminum, iron, and manganese (Pugh et al., 1984).

CASE STUDY — UPLAND DISPOSAL SITES OF THE TENNESSEE–TOMBIGBEE WATERWAY

Approximately 7,981 ha of upland disposal sites were created during the construction of the Tennessee–Tombigbee Waterway in Mississippi and Alabama (USACE, 1983). In the northerly most section, up to 156,000,000 m^3 of spoil were excavated from a 64-km canal to construct a waterway that connects the Tombigbee and Tennessee Rivers (Jones et al., 1996). Due to edaphic and vegetative characteristics, disposal sites in this region were similar to reclaimed coal surface mines and were classified as drastically disturbed land bases (Ammons and Shelton, 1991).

Our study area was located on upland disposal sites of the 4424-ha Divide Section Wildlife Management Area that occurrs along the northern canal section of the Tennessee-Tombigbee Waterway in Tishomingo, Mississippi. This land base is managed cooperatively by the US Army Corps of Engineers and the Mississippi Department of Wildlife, Fisheries, and Parks for game and nongame wildlife with emphasis on northern bobwhite quail (*Colinus virginianus*) (Jones et al., 1994). Upland disposal sites in this section were created by the deposition of excavated spoil material from the canal cut into woodland ravines adjacent to the waterway canal. Excavation depths were as deep as 54 m and reached into Cretaceous Age Formation layers and the Tombigbee sands of the Eutaw Formation, the latter of which is comprised of massive, glauconitic sands that contain acidic overburden.

Geologic cores and soil samples collected from the canal channel during pre-project studies verified the presence of the soil acidifying pyrite, within proposed excavation depths (Ammons et al., 1983). Incorporated into the disposal area soils during construction, this acid material was expected to cause problems with surface soil quality, vegetative reclamation, and wildlife habitat restoration (Jones et al., 1996; Ammons et al., 1991). To ameliorate these conditions, soil amendments were applied to disposal area substrates at prescription levels to neutralize soil acidities. Soil pH levels ranged from 2.5 to 7.5 prior to soil amendment treatments. Following treatment, pH levels on most sites ranged from 5.5 to 7.5 (Krans, 1981). Most soil textures were classified as sandy and sandy loam with sand contents ranging from 47 to 90% (Krans, 1981). Construction and vegetative reclamation of disposal areas were completed in 1981 by the US Army Corps of Engineers, (Nashville District) (Krans, 1981).

Short-term restoration objectives on disposal areas were similar to those of disturbed surface mines (Jones et al., 1996). Initial reclamation included resurfacing for soil stabilization, application of soil amendments, and seeding of reclamation plantings (Krans, 1981). Proper coverage and application of soil amendments were required on substrates containing acid overburden to prevent overburden oxidation, increased soil acidification, and vegetation failures (Pugh et al., 1884; Hons et al., 1978).

METHODS

Data presented in this paper are part of an eleven-year study on plant successional trends on upland disposal sites from 1982 through 1992 (Jones, 1995). Thirty-five disposal areas were selected in 1990 by stratified, random sampling within five dominant cover types: seeded legumes [sericea lespedeza (*Lespedeza cuneata*)], seeded grasses [fescue (*Festuca elatior arundinacae*), weeping lovegrass (*Eragrostic curvula*), Bermuda grass (*Cynodon dactylon*)], planted shrubs (*Eleagnus umbellata*), native herbaceous plants, and bare soil areas. A cover type was considered dominant if it comprised at least 60% of the surface ground coverage. Only disposal areas that had been completed and received reclamation plantings by June, 1981 were included in this study.

Four permanently located 15.0-m line transects radiating from one center point were established on each site. This design resulted in a total of 60.0 m of sampled transects on each site. A total of 30, 1-m² quadrats were clipped along line transects on each study site during July–August, 1991 and 1992. (Plots were not clipped on the planted shrub cover type.) Plants were clipped to within 2.5 cm above ground level, bagged, and returned to the university where samples were dried in an plant drier at 54–60°C for 72 h (Hayes et al., 1981). Samples were weighed using a digital Metler Scale.

Soil samples were collected by core sampling at each transect center point on each disposal area during February, 1991 and 1992. Each 20-cm core sample was divided in 2 subsamples of 0–10 cm and >10–20 cm for analysis. Soil samples were sieved and air-dried prior to physical and chemical analysis. Samples were air-dried and coarse fragment (>2 mm) was separated using a 2 mm sieve (Foth, 1984). Active soil pH was measured in water using a 1:1 soil/liquid ratio (Foth, 1984). The vertical depth to overburden was determined with auger sampling (10 cm diameter) and visual identification based coloration and texture (Foth, 1984). Statistical analyses used included correlation and regression analyses and Signed-rank Wilcoxon tests (Daniel, 1990; Myers, 1990).

RESULTS AND DISCUSSION

Covering of acidic spoil material with 2 m of sandy loam was a specified amelioration requirement during disposal area construction for successful of the project area (USACE, 1983). Depth of the acidic pyrite material on disposal areas was considered important due to upward vertical leaching, subsequent acidification, and vegetation failures. Despite coverage requirements in 1981, vertical depths to acidic pyrite measured in 1991 varied among disposal sites, ranging from 2.5 cm to 152 cm in depth. Proximity of overburden to the soil surface influenced soil pH levels and vegetative biomass production ($P < 0.001$, $R^2 = 0.53$). In general, disposal areas supporting vegetation exhibited pyrite that was buried at depths of 40 cm or greater. These sites also lacked pockets of pyrite-containing substrate in the upper 40 cm of substrate (Table 1). Highest active soil acidities were detected on bare pyritic sites where pH levels ranged from 2.9 to 3.9 over the two year period. Layers and pockets of pyrite were found intermixed in the upper 36 cm of substrate on these sites. Plant cover and herbaceous biomass were limited during both study years ranging from 0 to 6.4 kg/ha on the four sites in 1991 and 1992 (Table 1). PH levels of the >10–20 cm samples were significantly lowered than pH levels of the <10 cm soil samples ($P < 0.01$). Proximity of overburden to the surface influenced soil pH levels in the >10–20 cm soil depths ($P < 0.0001$; $r^2 = 0.81$; $R^2 = 0.66$; $P < 0.0001$; df = 32). However, soil pH levels in sample depths of ≤10 cm were not related to depth of overburden ($r^2 = 0.21$; $P = 0.10$) (Jones et al., 1996). Covering pyritic layers with substrates having pH levels of 5.0 or greater at depths of at least 40 cm appeared to be sufficient for long term survival of vegetation. However, deeper coverages and prescription liming are recommended for optimizing

Table 1. Ranges, means and standard errors of depth (cm) to acid pyrite substrate and active soil pH, and herbaceous plant biomass on five cover types of upland disposal areas of the Tennessee–Tombigbee Waterway in Tishomingo, Mississippi in July of 1991 and 1992

Cover type	Depth to pyritic substrate (cm)		Active soil acidity (pH)		Plant biomass dry weight (kg/ha)
	Range	Mean (SE)	Range	Mean (SE)	Mean (SE)
Seeded Legume ($N = 10$)	48.3–152.4	103.5 (11.3)	<10 cm 5.0–7.8 >10–20 cm 4.1–8.1	6.7 (0.3) 5.8 (0.4)	1991 3256.8 (556.0) 1992 1927.0 (624.5)
Seeded Grasses ($N = 6$)	86.0–152.0	100.8 (13.8)	<10 cm 6.4–7.9 >10–20 cm 4.1–8.0	7.3 (0.2) 5.8 (0.6)	1991 3170.0 (1854.4) 1992 3372 (1131.1)
Planted Shrubs ($N = 5$)	46.0–152.4	121.9 (19.5)	<10 cm 5.0–7.8 >10–20 cm 4.1–7.0	7.0 (0.4) 5.8 (0.5)	1991 no clip plots sampled 1992 no clip plots sampled
Native Herbaceous ($N = 10$)	15.2–147.3	104.7 (16.3)	<10 cm 5.3–7.8 >10–20 cm 3.2–7.5	6.4 (0.5) 5.0 (0.5)	1991 3460.0 (493.8) 1992 3906.5 (560.3)
Pyritic Sites (Bare) ($N = 4$)	2.5–35.6	23.4 (6.6)	<10 cm 3.0–3.9 >10–20 cm 2.7–3.7	3.6 (0.1) 3.2 (0.1)	1991 1.3 (1.3) 1992 0

reclamation and ecological restoration success. These actions are recommended due to potential soil acidity released over time, the upward movement of acid-forming complexes and metal salts facilitated by capillary water movement in the soil, and the potential for erosion and soil disturbance to expose overburden materials over time.

Overburden and soil acidity properties of disposal area substrates were similar to conditions found on lignite, coal, and bauxite mines of the Midwestern and Southeastern United States (Johnson and Skousen, 1995; Hons et al., 1978; Hossner et al., 1965; Feagley, 1985). High soil acidities that exhibit active soil pH level of 4.5 or less can cause loss of vegetation, degradation of fish and wildlife habitat, and damage to soil resources productivity. Although these conditions would generally be the responsibility of the land manager or owner, utility companies often require easements on and access to disturbed lands for construction and maintenance of utility powerlines and pipelines. Construction and maintenance activities that require digging substrate, pipe burial, or general soil disturbance may expose acid overburden if these complexes are near the soil's surface. Erosion control plantings on disturbed soils with oxidizing acid overburden will generally fail reducing cost effectiveness of revegetation treatment. Additionally, acid soil conditions and sedimentation arising from bare soil sites created by high acidities may damage natural resources featured on the land base, such as timber, agronomic plantings, wetlands, aesthetic quality, fish and wildlife habitat, and outdoor recreation features.

MANAGEMENT IMPLICATIONS

Utility rights-of-way managers should be aware of the soil characteristics on disturbed lands that may cause loss of vegetation and degradation of natural resource quality. In some cases, pipeline construction may cause exposure of soil acidifying substrates on undisturbed lands depending on the nature of the parent material, the proximity of this parent material to the soil's surface, and the excavation depths required for pipeline construction. Pre-emptive knowledge and proactive treatment of phytotoxic soil conditions can enable managers to develop cost-effective approaches to revegetation and vegetation management on utility line construction and maintenance sites. General recommendations are as follows:

1. Acquire information on past land use practices, soil, and geological resources. If proposed pipelines or utility lines transect drastically disturbed lands managed by public agencies, industries, or organizations, consultation with these personnel is recommended to acquire information on past and current land use and reclamation history. In the United States, environmental assessments of proposed actions may be necessary on public lands, especially if wetlands and endangered species are in close proximity to the proposed project area. Restoration and mitigation of project effects may also be required.
2. Collection of geologic core samples should be accomplished through the assistance of certified geologists and soil scientists if acidifying substrate or parent materials are expected to occur on the site.

3. Soil samples should be collected at sites that remain devoid of vegetation. Soil samples should be collected at a minimum of two depths — 0–10 cm and >10–20 cm. Upper and lower soil samples should be kept separate for analysis to detect upper and lower soil acidity levels. Deeper soil samples may provide insight into the proximity of unweathered acidic substrate to the soil's surface. If pH levels are less than 4.5 in the upper or lower sample depths, precautions and special ameliorations may be necessary.
4. Measuring the vertical depth to acidic substrate layers is recommended on drastically disturbed sites so that managers will know the likelihood of reaching these layers during construction and maintenance activities.
5. Soil sample analysis should include measurement for lime requirements and active soil acidity (soil pH) (Jones et al., 1996; Skousen, 1987). In substrates containing unweathered parent material or acidic substrates, more extensive tests may be needed to measure exchangeable and nonexchangeable acidity. These measurements determine the presence of unweathered acid-forming complexes and the acid-production potential of a substrate over time (Jones et al., 1996; Skousen, 1987). Techniques for measuring these parameters include acid-base accounting, potassium chloride extraction, and barium chloride triethanolamine method (Skousen, 1987).
6. Reclamation treatment for pyritic sites may include burial of acidic substrates by covering with topsoil or nontoxic soil, prescription liming based on soil tests, and minimization of sites that might pool water. Prescription liming required to stabilize pyritic disposal sites in Mississippi were 27 mg/ha over the short term with a rate of 44 mg/ha being recommended to neutralize acid potential over the long term (Ammons and Shelton, 1991). However, Skousen (1987) recommended rates of 11.2 mg/ha of lime or less for surface application of lime where no incorporation is planned. Skousen (1987) recommended that lime be incorporated into the top 15.2 cm of soil on sites where pH is low and large amounts of lime are needed.
7. Following soil amelioration, acid-tolerant, erosion control plantings should be considered to limit erosion. Selection of plants that are acid tolerant and withstand high levels of salts in the soil solution are recommended. Recommended plants will vary with locales. On upland disposal sites in Mississippi, native grasses (*Androgon virginicus*), native shrubs (*Rhus copallina and R. glabra*), and kobe lespedeza (*Lespedeza striata*), exhibited high ground coverages on ameliorated acid soil sites (Jones, 1995). Feagley (1985) reported that Dallas grass (*Paspalum dilitatum*) and common Bermudagrass (*Cynodon dactylon*) exhibit moderate to high salt tolerance to acid soil conditions.

Management of drastically disturbed lands offers unique challenges due to edaphic and vegetative characteristics. Cooperative management and proactive approaches to treatment and maintenance on these lands can provide fish and wildlife habitat, recreational benefits to many human users, and unique areas for ecological research and education. Utility companies may own these lands or easements and operations may transect these lands, therefore, professionals from these companies are an important part of the cooperative effort to restore and maintain ecological productivity on drastically disturbed land bases.

REFERENCES

Ammons, J.T. and P.A. Shelton. 1991. Monitoring chemical properties on a pyritic disposal area after liming. Soil Science Society of America Journal, 55: 368–371.

Ammons, J.T., P.A. Shelton, and G.G. Davis. 1983. A detailed study of five overburden cores and six disposal areas along the divide section of the Tennessee–Tombigbee Waterway. Final Rep US Army Corps of Eng., Nashville, TN. 63 pp.

Barnhisel, R.I. and R.R. Krupe. 1985. Oil shale revegetation research at the Hope Creek project. Proceedings. 1985 Eastern Oil Shale Symposium. Kentucky Center for Energy Research Laboratory. pp. 157–167.

Byrnes, W.R. and J.H. Miller. 1973. Natural revegetation and cast overburden properties of surface mined coal lands in southern Indiana. In: Ecology and Reclamation of Devastated land. R.J. Hutnik and G. Davis, eds. Gordon and Breach, New York, NY, USA. pp. 285–306.

Curry, J.P. and D.C.F. Cotton. 1983. Earthworms and land reclamation. In: Earthworm Ecology — from Darwin to Vermiculite. J.C. Satchell, ed. Chapman and Hall, London. 370 pp.

Daniel, W.W. 1990. Applied nonparametric statistics. PWS-KENT Publishing Co. Boston, MA. 635 pp.

Feagley, S.E. 1985. Chemical, physical and mineralogical characteristics of the overburden lignite surface mine reclamation of the Gulf Coast Region. S. Coop. Series Bulletin 294. Arkansas Agricultural Experiment Station. Fayetteville, AK. pp. 33–53.

Foth, H.D. 1984. Fundamentals of Soil Science. John Wiley and Sons, New York, NY. 435 pp.

Hays, R.L., Summers, and C.W. Cietz. 1981. Estimating wildlife habitat variables. U.S.D.I. Fish and Wildlife Service FWS/OBS-81147. 111 pp.

Hons, F.M., P.E. Askenasy, L.R. Hossner, and E.L. Shiteley. 1978. Physical and chemical properties of lignite spoil material as it influences successful revegetation. In: Proc. Gulf Coast Lignite Conference: Geology, Utilization, and Environmental Aspects, Report No. 90. W.R. Kaiser, ed. Bureau of Econ. Geol., University of Texas at Austin. pp. 209–217.

Hossner, L.R., J.S. Ahlrichs, and A.L. Senkayi. 1965. Physical and chemical properties of east Texas overburden as related to successful reclamation. Soc. of Mining Engineers of AIME. Transactions Vol. 274.

Johnson, C.D. and J.G. Skousen. 1995. Minesoil properties of 15 abandoned mine land sites in West Virginia. Journal of Environmental Quality, 24: 635–643.

Jones, J.C. 1995. Vegetative succession, edaphic factors, and annelid densities on reclaimed disposal areas of the Tennessee–Tombigbee Waterway. PhD Dissertation. Miss. State Univ., MS. 224 pp.

Jones, J.C., D.H. Arner, and C.H. Bucciantini. 1996. Soil sampling for the detection of acid overburden on small game management areas located on severely disturbed land bases. Proceedings of

Annual Conference of Southeastern Association of Fish and Wildlife Agencies, 50: 583–591.

Jones, J.C., D.H. Arner, and C.H. Bucciantini. 1994. Primary foods of northern bobwhites inhabiting disposal areas of the Tennessee–Tombigbee Waterway. Proceedings of Annual Conference of Southeastern Association of Fish and Wildlife Agencies, 50: 583–591.

Krans, J.V. 1981. Vegetative erosion control studies, Tennessee–Tombigbee Waterway. Final Report. Department of Agronomy, Mississippi State University, MS. 134 pp.

Myers, R.H. 1990. Classical and modern regression with applications. PWS-KENT Publishing Co. Boston, MA. 488 pp.

Pettry, D.E. and C.W. Wood. 1986. Reclamation and crop growth in a drastically disturbed prime farmland soil in the Mississippi Delta. In: New Horizons for mined land reclamation. Am. Soc. for surface mining and reclamation. Jackson, MS. pp. 73–77.

Pettry, D.E., W.F. Miller, and J.W. Darden. 1980. Reclamation of the Knob surface mine, Alabama, using selected overburden material. In: Symposium on Surface Mining Hydrology, Sedimentation and Reclamation. Lexington, KY.

Pugh, C.E., L.R. Hossner, and J.B. Dixon. 1984. Oxidation rate of iron sulfides as affected by surface area, morphology, oxygen concentration and autotrophic bacteria. Soil Science, 137(5): 314.

Singer, P.C. and W. Strumm. 1969. Oxygenation of ferrous iron: the rate-determining step in the formation of acidic mine drainage. US Environmental Protection Agency, No. 14010-06/70. US Government Printing Office, Washington, DC.

Skousen, J.G., C.D. Johnson, and K. Garbutt. 1994. Natural revegetation of 15 abandoned mine land sites in West Virginia. J. Envir. Qual., 23: 1224–1230.

Skousen, J.G. 1987. Acid soils and liming principles. Green lands, 17: 33–39.

US Army Corp of Engineers. 1983. Wildlife Mitigation Feasibility Study, Volume III, Tennessee–Tombigbee Waterway, Alabama and Mississippi. Final Report. Mobile and Nashville District, Mobile, AL. 516 pp.

US Department of Energy. 1984. Ecological studies of disturbed landscapes: A compendium of five years of research aimed at the restoration of disturbed ecosystems. Office of Scientific and Technical Information. US D.O.E. 358 pp.

Wade, G.L. and L.M. Tritton. 1997. Evaluating biodiversity of mineral lands. Proceedings. 1997 Annual Meeting of the American Society for Surface Mining and Reclamation, Austin, TX. pp. 336–343.

BIOGRAPHICAL SKETCH

Jeanne C. Jones
Professor of Wildlife and Fisheries at Mississippi State University, Forest and Wildlife Research Center, Box 9690, Mississippi State, MS 39762, USA, Phone: 662-325-2219, Email: jjones@cfr.msstate.edu.

A native of Vicksburg, Mississippi, Jeanne is currently an associate professor in the Department of Wildlife and Fisheries at Mississippi State University. She teaches courses in wildlife and plant ecology, wildlife habitat management, and restoration ecology and received 7 outstanding teaching awards. She has authored and co-authored over 45 publications, technical reports, and book chapters on eco-tourism, native species diversity, reptile and amphibian conservation, and restoration ecology. Her primary research interests include restoration of degraded ecosystems and management strategies for conservation of sensitive plant, amphibian, bird, and reptile communities. Her hobbies include botanical and wildlife illustration, nature photography, organic gardening, horseback riding, backpacking and fly-fishing.

The Union Gas Crop Yield Monitoring Program: An Evaluation of Pipeline Construction Practices on Agricultural Lands

E.E. Mackintosh, E.J. Mozuraitis, and R.C. Rowland

Union Gas has developed an extensive crop yield monitoring database for assessing the impact of pipeline construction activities on agricultural lands in southern Ontario. The 227 km Dawn-Trafalgar pipeline easement contains up to four pipelines and crop yield data has been collected since 1976 for the NPS 42 pipeline constructed between 1975–1989 and the NPS 48 which started construction loops in 1990. Upwards of a thousand crop yield samples have been collected during this period. Numerous changes have been made to pipeline construction and clean up practices over this period, and in particular, the implementation of policies dealing with wet soil shutdown, trench line management, soil construction inspection and post-construction clean-up has had a significant positive impact on restoration of agricultural lands. Average on easement crop yields have improved over 23% during the period from 1980 to 2000. In particular, there have been significant improvements in average crop yields from construction of the NPS 48 over to the NPS 42 with average crop yields being 91 and 80% of controls, respectively. The major changes implemented during construction of the NPS 48 during the 1990s has been more stringent environmental pipeline inspection and more extensive post construction clean-up. With present construction practices in southern Ontario, it is reasonable to expect average on easement crop yields greater than 90% for year after construction.

Keywords: Pipeline impacts, historical, crop yield

BACKGROUND

The Union Gas Trafalgar System extends from the Dawn Compressor Station in Lambton County to the Trafalgar Compressor Station in the Regional Municipality of Peel, a distance of about 227 km (Fig. 1). The system contains a minimum of two and up to four pipelines within the easement: a 26 inch diameter pipeline constructed in 1957; a 34 inch diameter pipeline constructed from 1964 to 1970; a 42 inch diameter pipeline constructed from 1974 to 1989; and a 48 inch diameter pipeline which began construction in 1990.

The pipeline primarily crosses prime agricultural lands and, consequently, many of the environmental issues that have surfaced during construction are focused on mitigation and restoration of agricultural lands. A crop monitoring program was initiated by Union Gas in 1976 on the Dawn/Kerwood pipeline loop to assess the level of crop damage for payment of compensation packages to farmers over time. The program has been expanded to include: research into techniques for improving restoration of agricultural lands; refinement of crop sampling design for improved measurements; and the inclusion of soil monitoring. Significant changes have also been made to pipeline construction techniques on agricultural lands, since the initial construction of the NPS 42 Dawn/Kerwood pipeline in 1975.

Union Gas has developed a substantial soil/crop monitoring database since 1976 and it is the purpose of this paper to highlight some of the conclusions arising from the program with respect to the impacts of pipeline construction on agricultural lands.

Environmental Concerns in Rights-of-Way Management: Seventh International Symposium
J.W. Goodrich-Mahoney, D.F. Mutrie and C.A. Guild (editors)
© 2002 Elsevier Science Ltd. All rights reserved.

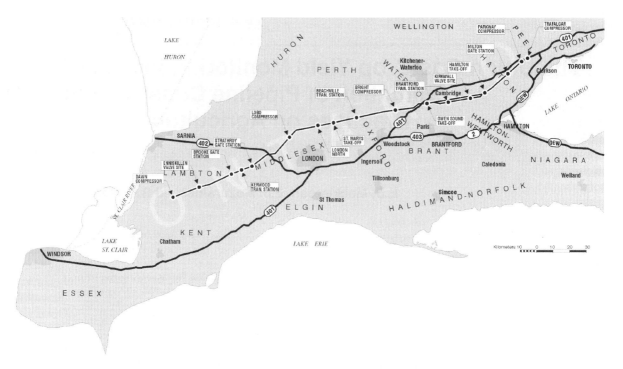

Fig. 1. Trafalgar pipeline system corridor.

Table 1. Pipeline loops constructed since 1975

Pipeline loop	Length of loop (km)	NPS 42		NPS 48	
		Year constructed	Year(s) sampled	Year constructed	Year(s) sampled
Dawn/Enniskillen	15.8	1975	1976–1985	–	–
Enniskillen/Brooke	19.4	1975	1976–1985	1994	1996
Brooke/Kerwood	10.0	1976	1977–1985	–	–
Kerwood/Strathroy	8.1	1982	1983–1987	–	–
Strathroy/Lobo	18.1	1989	1991, 1993, 1995	–	1993, 1995
Lobo/London	30.7	1979	1981–1985	1991	1993, 1995
London/St. Mary's		1981	1982–1986	1991	1993, 1995
St. Mary's Beachville	17.5	1984	–	1993	1995, 1997
Beachville/Bright	19.9	1989	1991, 1993, 1995	–	–
Bright/Owen Sound	18.4	1982	1983–1987	1996	1998
Owen Sound/Brantford	15.9	1985	–	–	–
Brantford/Kirkwall	13.9	1988	–	–	–
Kirkwall/Hamilton	10.2	–	–	1990	1993, 1995
Milton/Parkway	11.0	–	–	1991	1993, 1995, 1997

HISTORICAL PERSPECTIVE

Dawn — Trafalgar pipeline system

Construction of the NPS 42 and 48 pipelines was undertaken by construction loop (Table 1). The choice and length of the construction loop is determined by gas demand and related engineering design parameters. A typical cross-section of an easement used in construction of the pipelines is shown in Fig. 2.

Each successive construction easement is overlapped with the previous easement so that the spoil area of the NPS 48 is usually located over the workspace and trench area of the NPS 42.

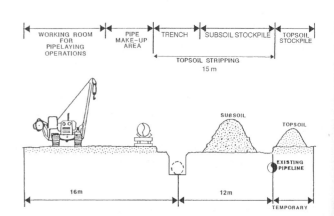

Fig. 2. Typical cross section of an easement for construction of NPS48 pipelines.

Pipeline construction practices

Environmental construction practices and post-construction compliance monitoring used on all the construction since 1976 follow the Ontario Energy Board guidelines, Union Gas specifications, and recommendations arising from the environmental assessments.

Numerous changes have been made to pipeline construction and cleanup practices over the years and some of the more important changes have been as follows:

- *Wet Soil Shutdown* — Formerly called wet weather shutdown, Union Gas implemented a policy on wet soil shutdown on the NPS 42 Lobo/London pipeline loop in 1979. It involves suspending most construction activities on the pipeline easement as a result of wet soil conditions that may lead to excessive rutting, soil compaction or mixing of topsoil/subsoil.
- *Trench Line Management* — Crowning the trench to offset subsidence of soil backfilled around the pipe was initiated in 1979. Further amendments to this practice were made in 1993 and involved hauling away excess trench materials as opposed to feathering the material over the spoil pile side of the trench. Rerouting the stringing trucks over the trench line was implemented as a standard practice in 1989. Up to that time, stringing trucks used the workspace or the trench area for travel.
- *Soil Construction Inspection* — A topsoil conservation inspector is responsible for agronomic aspects of topsoil conservation, such as topsoil removal based on soil horizon depth rather than uniform depth, and appropriate stockpiling and topsoil replacement to its original location. In addition, the soil inspector addresses issues of easement compaction.
- *Construction Clean Up* — Clean up includes construction activities related to soil tillage for ameliorating soil compaction on easement, stone picking and repair of tile drainage, among others. During the 1980s, most tillage operations were completed using a chisel plough to a depth of 15–20 cm. The use of subsoilers on easement was limited. In 1993, subsoiling was introduced as a standard construction clean up practice. As well, the environmental inspectors also inspected the clean up operations in greater detail using soil penetrometers or related equipment to assess soil compaction.

Crop monitoring program

The Union Gas crop monitoring program began in 1976 following construction of the NPS 42 Dawn/Kerwood pipeline. Construction of the Dawn–Kerwood section actually began in 1974; however, due to technical problems with the pipe and field welding, construction on the Dawn/Enniskillen loop was postponed until 1975. Wet weather resulted in adverse conditions during construction, post-construction cleanup and soil restoration which resulted in significant loss of topsoil, severe soil compaction and degradation of soil structure across the easement.

Due to the significant crop yield losses along the Dawn/Kerwood loop, Union Gas undertook a three year soil restoration research program in fall, 1981. The study resulted in a recommendation to subsoil the entire easement and implement a green manure program. A majority of the farmers along the easement accepted the subsoiling program which was completed in the fall of 1984. Although a crop compensation program was included as part of the green manure program, there was limited implementation by farmers due to the crop rotation system in use at the time (i.e., corn/soybean/winter wheat).

Crop monitoring data was collected on a five year program for loops constructed from 1976–1982 (Table 1). The Dawn to Kerwood loop contains 10 years of data (i.e., 2 five year programs). Crop monitoring data was changed to a 1, 3, and 5 year program following construction in 1989. As well, the sampling design for crop monitoring was also modified as a result of detailed field studies (Ecological Services for Planning, 1990). The main modifications made to the sampling procedures consisted of increasing the minimum number of field replications from 3 to 6 and subsampling the easement as work space, trench area and spoil area. The width of the area in workspace, trench and spoil pile is then used to calculate the average yield for the entire easement.

Throughout the crop monitoring program, yield information on easement has always been expressed as a percentage of the off easement control sample. A control site, paired with each on easement sample, was located 10 m off easement in the farm field.

CROP YIELD TRENDS

General

The overall improvement in on-easement crop yields for corn, soybeans and winter wheat during the period 1976 to 1997 is shown in Fig. 3. The data show a clear trend toward higher crop yields on easement and a reduction in impacts related to pipeline construction over time. Fit of a straight line through the data indicates an increase of 0.83% per year over the period 1976–1997 and is significant at $p < 0.05$.

Due to the number of variables that impact on crop yield, it is difficult to ascribe an actual per cent to anyone factor. For example, one would expect that the impact of climate would average out over time. Although farm management and crop rotation practices have changed in response to new innovations and research, one would expect the relative impact of these practices on the control and easement yields to be similar. Field sampling design was modified in 1991 to increase the minimum number of sample replications per field from 3 to 6. A sample size of 6 was chosen

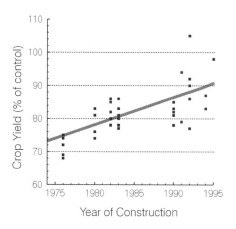

Fig. 3. General crop yield trends for NPS 42/48 pipelines (1976–1997).

following field studies that varied sample size from 4 to 12 per field (ESP, 1990). These results suggest that a sample size of 4 per field tended to over estimate average crop yield losses relative to larger sample sizes by less than 10 percent which would not significantly change the slope of the line in Fig. 3. This primarily leaves the changes to pipeline construction and clean up practices as the major factors influencing overall yield trends.

A more detailed breakdown of average yields and the related range in crop yield is shown for each construction loop in Table 2. There is a significant improvement in on-easement crop yields for construction loops built in the 1990s as compared to those constructed from 1976 to 1989.

Variations in crop yield across the easement

Prior to 1989, on-easement yields were measured by sampling across the easement; hence, an average crop yield for the entire easement was obtained. Crop sampling design was modified in 1991 to correspond with the construction activity on easement (i.e. work space, trench area and spoil area (Fig. 2). Average crop yield for the workspace, trench and spoil areas are 91, 81 and 84% of the control, respectively (Table 3).

Table 2. Average crop yield for whole easement* (expressed as percent of control) for all crops by pipeline loop

Pipeline loop	Year constructed/ diameter	Year program started	Year 1 Average yield	Year 1 Range	Year 2 Average yield	Year 2 Range	Year 3 Average yield	Year 3 Range	Year 4 Average yield	Year 4 Range	Year 5 Average yield	Year 5 Range	Average
Dawn/Enniskillen	1975/NPS 42	1976	32	**	41	**	48	**	54	**	65	**	48
Dawn/Kerwood	1975/NPS 42	1981	72	12–97	69	23–100	74	24–116	75	41–96	72	26–116	72
Lobo/London	1979/NPS 42	1981	83	32–136	76	37–100	74	27–122	81	47–95	81	60–102	79
London/St. Mary's	1981/NPS 42	1982	78	38–100	80	60–102	85	60–99	82	54–92	86	65–100	83
Kerwood/Strathroy	1981/NPS 42	1983	77	52–99	83	33–118	78	46–97	86	56–108	80	49–92	81
Bright/Owen Sound	1982/NPS 42	1983	80	51–103	78	42–105	80	57–92	81	60–103	78	45–100	80
Beachville/Bright	1989/NPS 42	1991	82	48–99	†	†	78	68–94	†	†	83	78–88	81
Strathroy/Lobo	1989/NPS 42	1991	78	49–104	†	†	81	59–99	†	†	85	70–100	81
Kirkwall/Hamilton	1990/NPS 48	1991	**	**	†	†	94	77–121	†	†	79	79	91
Lobo/St. Mary's	1991/NPS 48	1993	90	63–136	†	†	86	32–116	†	†	86	62–102	88
Milton/Parkway	1991/NPS 48	1993	105	63–129	†	†	77	58–106	†	†	92	82–108	93
St. Mary's/Beachville	1993/NPS 48	1995	87	76–100	†	†	83	44–107	†	†	†	†	85
Enniskillen/Brooke	1994/NPS 48	1996	98	84–115	†	†	†	†	†	†	†	†	98
Bright/Owen Sound	1996/NPS 48	1998	75	65–87	†	†	†	†	†	†	†	†	75

*Changes made to field data design in 1991 do not impact average crop yield figures for whole easement.
**Data not available.
†Program changed to 1, 3, 5 year after crop monitoring.

Table 3. Average crop yield on easement by construction activity (expressed as % control for all crop/properties)

Construction loop	Year constructed/diameter	Year sampled	Spoil area	Trench area	Workspace	Whole easement*
Strathroy–Lobo	1989/NPS 42	1991	–	73	80	78
		1993	76	77	90	81
		1995	82	80	92	85
Beachville–Bright	1989/NPS 42	1991	–	79	83	82
		1993	77	75	81	78
		1995	84	63	90	83
Kirkwall–Hamilton	1990/NPS 48	1993	98	92	90	94
		1995	80	59	82	79
Lobo–St. Mary's	1991/NPS 48	1993	90	89	91	90
		1995	83	86	91	86
		1997	85	85	86	86
Milton–Parkway	1991/NPS 48	1993	93	111	115	105
		1995	72	60	85	77
		1997	82	92	101	92
St. Mary's–Beachville	1993/NPS 48	1995	81	74	96	87
		1997	78	71	90	83
Enniskillen–Brooke	1994/NPS 48	1996	94	103	102	98
Average			84	81	91	86

*Calculated using width of respective easement areas.

Clearly, the trench and spoil pile areas are the most affected by construction activities. The trench area is the most affected since soil structure is destroyed during trenching operations and subsoils are mixed to the bottom of the topsoil layer. As well, soils over the pipe are compacted to minimize subsidence and are often not subsoiled during construction clean up.

Along most of the NPS 48 pipeline easement, the spoil area is the work space and trench line area of the previously constructed NPS 42 pipeline. The reduced crop yields on the spoil area are, therefore, related to residual impacts associated with the construction activities and clean up practices used on the work space of the previous construction easement.

Variations in crop yield over time
Further reference to Table 2 suggests that the average crop yield for any particular construction easement does not change markedly over the duration of the sampling program. Consequently, modifying the crop sampling program from a continuous 5 year program to a 3 year one consisting of 1, 3, 5 year after sampling provides one with a reliable set of data with cost savings.

Farm management practices
Crop yield response varies markedly from farm to farm (Table 4). Although farm management practices were not specifically evaluated for each farm, the detailed crop yield data indicates that the highest crop yield losses are usually associated with controls that have the lowest crop yields. Such variations are typical for all the easements and are further illustrated in Table 2 which shows the range in crop yield losses by year and pipeline loop for the duration of the study.

Table 4. Variation in average soybean yield (% of control) by property NPS 42 Strathroy/Lobo

Property	Workspace	Trench line	Spoil side	Total easement
1	103	76	79	87
2	75	50	51	59
3	96	98	80	88
4	80	57	73	73

Within a pipeline loop, the same farms are usually sampled over the duration of the monitoring program. On occasion, it may be necessary to drop a farm or select a new one for a variety of reasons. Since there are no indications that variability in crop yield losses among farms is decreasing over time, it is unlikely that changes in farm management practices are contributing significantly to the improved trends shown in Fig. 3.

Construction practices
Continuous changes to and improvements in construction and cleanup practices have occurred throughout the duration of the crop monitoring program. Due to the large number of variables involved in determining annual crop yield, it is impossible to attribute or allocate percentage improvements in crop yield to anyone specific construction practice. However, it is clearly evident that average crop yields on easement have gradually improved over the past twenty years (Fig. 3). A considerable amount of this improvement must rest with the changes in construction practice

Table 5. Average on easement crop yield by construction activity for the NPS 42 and 48 pipelines (% of control for all crops)

	Spoil area	Trench area	Workspace	Whole easement
NPS 42	79	75	85	81
NPS 48	86	86	93	89

(e.g., implementation of wet soil shutdown policy and, in particular, in construction cleanup). As an example, average on easement crop yields (Table 5) for NPS 48 spreads constructed in the 1990s is about 89% as compared to the NPS 42 constructed in the 1970/80s which is about 81%. These differences are statistically significant at $P < 0.001$.

The benefit accrued from changes in policies and practices is also evident from direct comparisons of crop yield data obtained from construction of the NPS 42 and 48 pipelines. Table 5 uses the same data as Table 3, but is recalculated to compare the results for the NPS 42 and 48 pipelines. Average crop yields for the NPS 48 pipeline show significant improvements on all areas of the easement compared to the NPS 42. As well, the NPS 48 Lobo/St. Mary's Loop (constructed in 1991) has an average on-easement yield of 88% based on the 1 and 3 year after crop monitoring program (Table 2). The comparable NPS 42 loops, i.e., Lobo/London and London/St. Mary's constructed in 1979 and 1981, respectively, averaged 81%. The averages are statistically significant at $P < 0.05$. More dramatic improvements are noted for the Enniskillen Brooke loop. Average easement yield (from the second 5 year crop monitoring program) for the NPS42 built in 1975 is 72% whereas comparable figures for the NPS48 constructed in 1994 is 98%.

Impact of subsoiling practices
Research undertaken during the soil restoration program 1981–1984 demonstrated that significant benefits could be accrued from subsoiling the NPS 42 pipeline easement. The practice of subsoiling was evaluated on twelve farms. Crop yield for cereal, corn and soybean improved considerably in the year following the subsoiling operation from ~64–101%. Subsequent interviews with farmers suggested that the beneficial impacts of subsoiling lasted up to 3 years.

Subsoiling was also included as a standard practice in construction clean up during the 1990s. The noticeable improvements in average on-easement crop yields for construction loops completed after 1990 (Table 2) also suggest that changes to post construction clean up practices have had a significant benefit.

CONCLUSIONS

The Dawn to Trafalgar pipeline easement is approximately 220 km long and contains up to four pipelines in some sections ranging from NPS 26 to 48. The pipeline largely passes through prime agricultural lands, with the exception of lands in the eastern section of the system where shallow depth to bedrock is encountered.

Since construction began on the NPS 42 in 1974/75, Union Gas has developed one of the most comprehensive databases available to assess the impacts of pipeline construction on agricultural lands. This paper presents the results of the crop monitoring program, and to the extent possible, assesses the impact that changes in pipeline construction practices have had on the restoration of agricultural lands.

Due to the large number of variables inherent in field studies of this nature, it is impossible to assign actual quantitative values in terms of improved crop yield performance to specific changes in pipeline construction and clean up practices during the period. However, the data clearly show a set of trends that are helpful in reaching some conclusions with respect to the past and establishing future direction.

1. Average on easement crop yields show a 23% improvement over the 25 year period. These improvements reflect major changes made to pipeline construction practices over this period including implementation of wet soil shutdown policies and improved construction clean up practices, among others.
2. Average crop yield levels expressed as a percent of control for the NPS 48 and NPS 42 construction loops are 89 and 81%, respectively. Clearly, construction and clean up practices used on the NPS 48 pipeline have led to significant improvements in crop yield performance as compared to NPS 42 construction. The major changes implemented during construction of the NPS 48 have been more stringent environmental pipeline inspection and more extensive post-construction clean-up.
3. The impact of pipeline construction varies on easement depending on the construction activity. Crop yields indicate that the greatest residual impact of construction on agricultural land occurs immediately over the trench area, followed by the spoil pile area and is least for the workspace. Average crop yield levels for all crops and properties sampled over the trench area, spoil pile and workspace areas are 81, 84, and 91%, respectively. The low values for the spoil pile area represents a cumulative (or residual) impact as the spoil pile areas are usually located on the workspace of the NPS42. The depth of clean-up over the trench is often reduced for safety reasons due to proximity of the pipe.
4. Analysis of the data supports changing the crop yield sampling frequency from the 5 year program to a 3 year consisting of 1, 3, and 5 year.
5. Although the data are limited, inclusion of subsoiling as an ongoing component of construction clean up appears to be improving overall crop yield performance on easement.

ACKNOWLEDGEMENT

We would like to thank Union Gas Limited for permission to present this manuscript.

REFERENCE

Ecological Services for Planning, Limited. 1990. Crop Monitoring Program, Dawn Kerwood. Prepared for Union Gas Ltd. pp. 71

BIOGRAPHICAL SKETCHES

Erven Mackintosh
ESG International Inc., 361 Southgate Dr., Guelph, ON, Canada N1G 3M5

Erven Mackintosh has been president of ESG International, an environmental science consulting firm, since 1975. He has worked extensively on environmental impacts of linear facilities, and in particular, on the impacts of pipeline construction on agricultural soils.

Edward Mozuraitis
ESG International Inc., 361 Southgate Dr., Guelph, ON, Canada N1G 3M5

Ed Mozuraitis has worked as a soil specialist for ESG International for over ten years. For much of that time, Ed has worked as an environmental inspector on pipeline construction, and in particular, has worked extensively on assessing the impacts of pipeline construction on agricultural soils and on implementation of mitigation measures.

Robert Rowland
ESG International Inc., 361 Southgate Dr., Guelph, ON, Canada N1G 3M5

Robert Rowland has worked as a soil specialist/geomorphologist for ESG International for ten years. He has worked extensively on environmental impacts of linear facilities on agricultural lands and as an environmental inspector on pipeline construction.

Repairing Eroded Gas Lines

Scott D. Shupe

Erosion has exposed dozens of New York State's high-pressure gas transmission lines, presenting operational hazards. Multiple agency permits were negotiated before individual repairs could be effected. Several repair techniques were used to rebed and rebackfill the pipeline trenches. Summarized herein are lessons learned; contemporary repair methods; vintage planning and design considerations that contributed to the exposures; and GIS-based solutions to expedite permitting agency requirements.

Keywords: Stream dynamics, sediment control, right-of-way maintenance, stream restoration, pipeline protection

OBJECTIVE

This paper reviews basic hydrologic principles that illustrate the relationship of sediment transport, peak erosive discharges, and pipeline armor repair methods. Preventive maintenance questions can be raised at the onset of new installations, and situation-appropriate strategies and permits can be developed.

INTRODUCTION

Most northeast operations managers are maintaining gas line rights-of-way (ROW's) that were expediently constructed — straight as an arrow — in an era when agriculture was big and rural was still sharply distinct from urban. Today that distinction is gone in upstate New York. Today we continue to safely maintain 60-year-old assets that retain economic value, as well as new facilities that cross the suburban landscape as crooked as a dog's hind leg. This maintenance, however, is performed with an environmental ethic and regulatory climate that did not exist when most lines were constructed. The net result is that, to conform, spot repairs are more costly and are undertaken with techniques and measures laughable when old-timers bulldozed arrow-straight trenches across the open landscape and through stream channels.

One increasingly common problem exemplifies the current issue of "urban sprawl" — washouts (Fig. 1). As infrastructure extends from the cities, development follows. Drainage basin impervious surface area increases, and hydrographs evolve shorter durations but taller peaks. Channels are 'managed' and natural vegetation removed. Snowmelt and storm runoff has more energy. Undersized highway devices concentrate flow

Fig. 1. Washout of 8″ gas line in Willow Creek following a July 4, 1999 thunderstorm. Although bedded and buried well, the disturbed trench in bed of the stream was unconsolidated in relation to the naturally packed hardpan of the streambed, and cover was scoured. A concrete cap was installed to make the repair.

Environmental Concerns in Rights-of-Way Management: Seventh International Symposium
J.W. Goodrich-Mahoney, D.F. Mutrie and C.A. Guild (editors)
© 2002 Elsevier Science Ltd. All rights reserved.

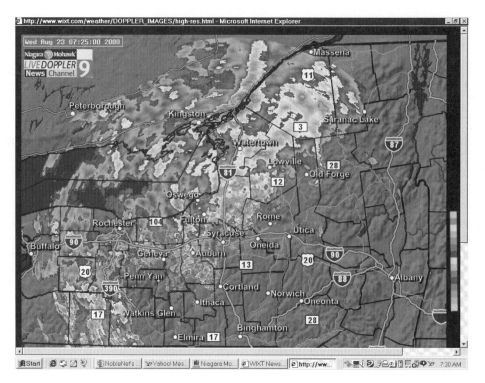

Fig. 2. Online services, such as Doppler Radar, provides Niagara Mohawk with real-time prognostication capability to estimate catastrophic events that influence right-of-way maintenance, such as erosion and repair of exposed gas lines, all across upstate New York.

at pipelines that were installed inside the highway easements, a location typically favored by regulators. Streambeds and banks erode. Code requires 36″ of cover over pipelines that may now have as much air space beneath.

Service area location description

Niagara Mohawk's (NM) namesakes are the two rivers spanning the width of New York State. To the south, strata derived from erosion of northerly older rocks incline into Appalachia. The Adirondacks to the north include Pre-Cambrian outcrops, shaved by at least three glaciations. Water, flowing and frozen, has sculpted nearly every imaginable geomorphic form within the area we serve. These areas present engineering, environmental, cultural and stewardship opportunities and challenges to our rights-of-way management programs. Repairs have been concentrated in three geologic areas of the state.

Tug Hill is a cuesta — a sloped mudstone plateau rising eastward to the Black River valley 90 miles to the lee of Lake Ontario. Tug Hill gets more snow — 300 inches — than any place east of the Mississippi River. "Lake effect" storms arise from moisture picked up over the warm Great Lakes that orographically cools as it rises over Tug Hill (Fig. 2). This precipitation runs off west via a dozen tributaries to Lake Ontario. Eight pipeline exposures have been repaired in these tributaries.

South of Syracuse, in the glacial U-shaped Onondaga valley, eight pipeline exposures were repaired. These resulted from hydrologic events that may have been exacerbated by glacial rebound and land subsidence following decades of salt water extraction. Crevasses now ring the valley, and nickpoints in the streams have moved upstream. A nickpoint is a sharp inflection in stream profile of the where hydraulics are typically concentrated and erosive; that is, a waterfall. Additionally, urban sprawl has moved into the hills, causing dramatic increases in impervious surface area thus increasing the severity of runoff events.

Changing land use and steep hillside developments in mid-Hudson Valley removed vegetation, altered wetlands, compressed hydrographs, and resulted in pipeline several exposures in both intermittent and permanent streams.

Basic hydrology

Fluvial processes, the classic study of dynamic equilibrium, shape a stream's cross sectional and longitudinal profiles. Resistance, from a rocky bed, vegetated banks, and depth of flow define stream shape, giving a range of velocities imparted by a streambed gradient. Over time, if the amounts of water and sediment that leave a particular reach of stream equal the volumes that entered it, the stream is said to be in dynamic equilibrium — the "natural" goal of a stream. If not, erosion or deposition will occur.

As Hunter (1991) puts it, "if something in the watershed puts the stream out of whack, such as a dramatic increase in sediment from soil and debris washed off a hillside from either natural or man-caused events,

Fig. 3. Nickpoint is a box culvert. Highway culverts are nominally sized for the 25-year discharge event. Sediment is trapped upstream and the outfall erodes as the undernourished stream seeks a new sediment load. Banks then collapse as the bed incises and headcuts. Pipe cover below culvert failed from turbulence, cattle traffic, and inadequate armor to match storm events.

the stream's velocity, depth, and/or slope will begin to naturally adjust to maintain dynamic equilibrium." Excavate a trench to bury a gasline and you (1) disturb sediment, (2) concentrate or redistribute bypassed flow, (3) alter the depth, and (4) generally change the flow dynamics in that reach of stream, resulting in movement of the nickpoint or meander.

A stream "wants" to flatten its slope, increase its length, and meander downstream. Fig. 3 shows the nickpoint in Budlong Creek, in this case it is artificial in the form of a highway box culvert, and the plunge pool that eroded the gas distribution line between Utica and Herkimer, NY. The highway altered the longitudinal profile of the creek, causing the upstream side to accrete level with the floor of the culvert, but the streambed eroded six feet lower. A July 4, 1999 thunderstorm carried away sufficient material to fully expose and undermine the 8-inch steel pipe the full width of the stream. The dynamic equilibrium in this reach was further perturbed by cattle traffic that trampled grasses. Plant roots in the soil serve two functions: (a) they increase the rate of decomposition of surficial rock and decrease the size of the sediment produced, (b) they bind this sediment and retard its erosion, decreasing the denudation rate (Blatt, 1972).

Dominance of large cobbles in this streambed and the undermined concrete slab indicate regular, periodic high-energy discharges. The lesson here, and in other crossings, is to use all available resources to anticipate the potential of floods (Fig. 2), catastrophic erosive forces, potential failures, and anticipate scheduling repairs. Resources available to you not only include computing power and design aids, but also those old geology, engineering, and physics texts.

Variables in the realm of fluid mechanics are all relative to Newton's second law:

force = mass × acceleration.

Fluid viscosity, variable drag coefficients, shear stress, unit discharge, specific weight, (Blatt, 1972; Heisler, 1984; Linsley, 1958) and some 175 equations describing stream regimes can be more simply interpreted for construction foremen. The larger the stone in the creek, the greater the discharge; a good storm will wash away anything finer. The extreme case is exposed bedrock. A shingled bed of tightly packed stones tilting up at the downstream face indicates a steady, but significant stream flow. A bed of sand or mud indicates the lower end of the energy spectrum. By reading the geomorphology of the reach of stream to be crossed, the experienced turnkey can reasonably approximate appropriate levels of pipeline protection.

Meandering streams tend to be slow moving, flat water. Streams with a sinuousity (centerline length divided by straight line distance) of over 1.5 are meandering, while a lower number indicates a stream with a greater slope. In a hillside drainage, the concern becomes more of gradient-induced vertical erosion, rather than lateral erosion (meandering) as a cause of pipeline exposure. In the former case, we tend to recommend that a directional bore pipeline installation be nominally 10 feet below the thalweg. Where bank erosion may be suggested over the pipeline's life, directional bore termini should be at least one stream width from either bank.

Northern pipeline engineers should consider the effects of ice on stream flow. When ice covers a stream, a new friction surface is formed and the stream becomes a closed conduit with lower discharge because of the decreased hydraulic radius (Linsley, 1958). If ice is thick and confines flow, a greater velocity can erode a perforation in the ice cover near an obstacle such as a bridge abutment near the pipe. Scour could occur. Over ice flow (glaciation) could excise bank material or armor where the ice cover is breached. A built-up ice coating on bank debris upstream of a pipeline crossing could be a serious current deflection point in the proverbial "January thaw". Intense power of water flowing past such an obstruction (for instance a fallen tree, boulder, or deformed gabion wall) can erode pipeline cover. But if the original pipeline installation was, for instance, downstream of a meander's outlet, a wing or triangular deflector could be placed to reorient a portion of a high-energy (stage) flow away from the pipeline cover. Overbank river ice moves more easily compared to meandering reaches (Smith, 2000). So if there is low channel sinuosity in the reach upstream of your pipeline crossing, anticipate scouring and debris if the sinuosity changes at or downstream of the crossing.

Also anticipate the affects of aspect. A south-facing slope receives more direct sunshine, has a higher evaporation loss, experiences more frequent freeze-thaws and retains snow/ice cover for a shorter period than will a north-facing slope (Thornbury, 1969). Higher temperatures and less soil moisture usually result in less vegetation. Weathering, sheetwash, and mass-wasting will be more aggressive on south-facing slopes, delivering more sediment to the stream.

Because water does not flow naturally in a straight line, particular attention should be paid during the planning of a gasline crossing, to the location of the thalweg — the line of maximum water depth. A stream's thalweg shifts laterally from bank to bank over time, as the natural tendency is for stability. Even in a straight section of stream, the thalweg meanders within the channel, creating pools, riffles, runs, and bars in 5–7 stream widths (Hunter, 1991). Cumulative deposition of storm event debris and normal bedload accumulation both alter patterns of flow, causing the thalweg to meander. Sinuosity increases length of flow, the net result of which is dissipation of energy over that of a straight stream reach.

Rigid vs flexible repair materials

New England and New York extend preference to so-called "hard" armor (Fig. 4), while mid and southwestern states favor bioengineering and geotextile "soft" armor when restoring streams and protecting waterside infrastructure. Coastal engineers long ago learned that large rigid walls deflect energy, while porous materials (such as rubble breakwaters and gabions) absorb the erosive power of penetrating waves and currents. European hydrologist's consider riprap a permanent scour countermeasure for stream instability measures in protecting bridges and facilities (CE, 1999). These countries do not have a problem with scour because they incorporate countermeasures into their original design, generating long-term savings generally absent expensive repairs. While geotextiles and fascine mats are incorporated, Europeans are partial to using carefully placed individual stones. Partially grouted riprap is used instead of the American propensity to grout the entire surface — again in an effort to absorb and dissipate energy that would undercut a solid wall. The key is a design that enables the transformation of destructive water forces into energies that can be managed to reinforce the armor itself.

NY has rock; NM has favored riprap and gabions because we can buy stone at $11–13 a ton. While flexible revetment mats have long been used on southern river levees and coasts, transportation of small quantities from Dixie has been cost-prohibitive. In 1996 NM located a NY vendor, and first used mats for protecting

Fig. 4. Hard armor system used on Pipeline 33 crossing Salmon River. To retain toe subject to 18-foot stage increase and ice/debris erosion in floods when currents are directed into this bank, repairs integrate boulders, concrete, gabions and a soil mesh system along with up-slope site grading. Southern aspect requires porous media to cope with freeze-thaw of ground and surface water infiltration.

Fig. 5. Concrete mat used to stabilize the bankside drainage ditch from the highway and also the bed of the stream at Budlong Creek in Utica, NY.

a pipeline deep on the bed of the Hudson River. Articulated concrete mats (Fig. 5) we used are designed for bed velocities up to 18 fps, which correlates to a design equivalent of 30-inch riprap rock. The 4 × 16-

Fig. 6. Yellow rock shield mesh and sand bedding beneath graded crushed stone, then fabric lined concrete block mats, with anchors. Subsequent runoff vibrated the blocks, shredded the stainless steel cable, and debris carried dislodged several blocks from the mat. Settlement and loss of bedding material by undercurrents is accelerating deterioration. Note the temporary diversion pipe.

foot mats are 35-pound blocks 4.5 inches high and 12 inches square, cabled by 1/8 inch stainless wire rope and weighing 2240 pounds. This low profile is advantageous in maintaining the pipeline's original vertical position without altering the streambed grade. Costing about $400 per mat, they are easy to transport on site, quick to install, and generate minimal turbidity during installation. These are advantages over gabions and Reno mats which may fail in acidic waters, where cement leaching will occur, or in streams where local labor and rock costs are lower or where dump trucks have easy access.

However, based on our experiences at Budlong Creek and Willow Creek, inadequately sized bedding beneath the mat, failure to accommodate settlement, a flat bank-to-bank installation, and extreme flow events reduced the mat lifetime. One year after installation another 100-year discharge rotated mat blocks in Willow Creek enough to break the cable. Conventional rip-rap was used in the second repair. While the Budlong Creek mat installation is still functional two years later, the complete integrity of the mat was compromised, and it too will have to be replaced or the pipe relocated. The mat system (Fig. 6) incorporates a synthetic mesh pipe wrapping (rock shield), trench backfill, compacted layers of #3 and #6 stone, a geotextile blanket (attached by the mat manufacturer), the concrete, and adequate bed-to-bank anchoring by cable dogs (duckbills) or heavy armor. It appears that these articulated mats are fine for low gradient installations, emulating revetments and levee designs where nominal settlement is allowable. The 12-inch mats will hold banks and work well to line ditches, but do not withstand placement in the beds of streams that are subject to extreme, periodic and "flashy" discharges.

Regardless of which material is used:
- install protection with a slightly concave bank-to-bank profile,
- carry the material above the maximum high water line,
- align outflow with the downstream thalweg, and
- install in the longitudinal profile in a manner that creates a series of small baffles or other form of energy dissipation so that nickpoint and plunge pool formation is retarded.

Sediment

A stream must have sediment in the water for equilibrium. Contrary to expectations, a sediment-laden stream tends to have a higher velocity (Blatt, 1972). These are the storm-related, erosive conditions. Protection should err on the "larger" size, whether using "hard" or "soft" armor. Many older lines were put in lands no one else wanted — commonly because these lands are wet, at least seasonally. Consequently, trench excavation exposes bed materials, disrupts drainage patterns, decompacts soils, and unbalances the waterway's dynamics. Sediment is America's most common water pollutant, so apply five principles of erosion and sediment control:

1. Keep the disturbed area small. Minimal clearing and grading preserves natural cover, especially important on erodible soils, steep slopes, or streambanks.
2. Stabilize disturbed area as soon as practicable. Employ either vegetation suitable to the region, soils, and season, or design a structural plan for diversion, storage, and infiltration.
3. Keep water runoff velocities low. Removal of vegetation and grade changes generally increases the impervious surface area.
4. Protect disturbed areas from runoff. Install diversions to intercept water before it enters the work area, and provide stable outlets.
5. Retain sediment within the site. Filter it or detain it with fabrics, hay bales, finely graded gravel, and/or a basin that allows precipitation and settling.

The Gas Research Institute (1998) reports that excess sediment in rivers and stream is the largest and most pervasive water pollution problem faced by aquatic systems in North America. It is important to know that turbidity and suspended sediment are specifically related to the parent geology and basin type, and therefore are not transferable between river systems. Each situation will be different, and you must be able to recognize when sediment and erosion may be an issue. GRI (1998) reports pipeline installations increase the sediment load within watercourses as a result of
- instream construction/installation activity,

- disposal of dredged or fill material directly into the stream,
- erosion and run-off from adjacent upland worksites,
- discharge of hydrostatic testing waters,
- discharge of waters during trench dewatering,
- backfill of the installed pipeline, and
- ongoing erosion until the ROW is reclaimed.

Sediment is also derived from the "restored" in-stream excavation area and continues until the stream reaches natural hydrologic and hydraulic stability. Regardless, controlling sediment may be the key to regulatory negotiations.

Fisheries

Most pipeline repairs will invite regulatory scrutiny and staff may dwell on turbidity limits. Understand and educate your permit administrators. Turbidity is but a coarse approximation of the sediment deposition potential in a stream, and does not represent a biologically relevant threshold for protection of aquatic habitats and organisms (GRI, 1998). Limits to allowable sediment deposition, or construction windows that prevent sedimentation during critical lifestages, are more defensible. Monitoring should be unnecessary, for direct effects to fish communities are usually undetectable, and fisheries are quick to recovery. Immobile life stages and species immediately adjacent to the crossing are at greatest risk, but represent a proportionately small biomass of the stream.

Elect to work during low flow periods, but recognize that higher discharges may "dilute" the adverse biological affects of sediment. Recognize that a crossing may have short-term adverse affects, but the long-term change in streambed structure at the crossing can be a benefit. Post-construction fish and invertebrate communities may find the armored pipeline a new riffle in otherwise flat water. The hard substrate hosts different insects, and the turbulence increases dissolved oxygen for a short distance downstream. Benthic shredders and grazers, indicating high quality waters, can enhance the midge population that dominate mud bottoms.

GENERAL PERMIT AND STANDARD ACTIVITY PERMIT

Culminating three years of negotiations with New York State Department of Environmental Conservation (NYSDEC), Niagara Mohawk's Environmental Affairs Department (NM-EAD) in 1998 obtained two permits that enabled crews to proceed with routine O&M activities with minimal advance regulatory notification. With the new General Permit, activities that were at or below the NYS "minor action" threshold could proceed with as little as 15 days notice, while "major actions" exceeding protective thresholds (although then below Corps Nationwide Permit limits) were candidates for the new Standard Activity Permit.

The permit enables specified activities (e.g., wetlands herbicide applications) an accelerated review period, and has pre-agreed conditions. Both permits were "firsts" for a NYS utility, and carried 5 and 10-year renewals, respectively. While framed as permits, these are remarkably similar to the Great Lakes' Hiawatha National Forest Operations and Management Plan discussed at this symposium by John Muehlhausen (2001). In both cases the intent is to secure a predictable timeframe in which the utility can proceed with defined-scope maintenance activities, and do so with mutual understanding of and by the agencies.

Geographic Information Systems (GIS) are integral with this permit model. Initially NM-EAD uses GIS as a mapping tool to locate the pipeline and stream crossings in relationship to features to which all parties can relate. GIS will be used, as appropriate, to calculate sinuosity, drainage area, apply a factor to estimate the range in seasonal flows, size stone and materials, and generate statistics as may be needed to complete the design and permit. GIS, simply as a "where is this place?" tool has shaved weeks off our application process. GIS has also increased our credibility.

A last word on permits. Permits are needed to destroy beaver dams. Don't create a hydraulic jump or constriction beavers will adopt. Discourage beavers by maintaining a "regular" bed and bank profile in the affected reach of stream. Moreover, draining a wetland above a beaver dam (for instance, if your operations crew breeches a dam to facilitate mowing the ROW) probably contravenes Corps of Engineers §401 regulations or maybe the Migratory Bird Treaty Act if nests are disturbed.

LESSONS LEARNED

The exposure of a pipe, or the presence of a noticeable bank failure near a crossing, indicates that fluvial processes at work in this stream reach should be modified. Ask some questions and evaluate the repair assessment.

Did operations check for "jeeps" and corrosion? Is the pipe really worth saving, or is a new installation appropriate? Why waste money recovering an exposure if the pipe itself is damaged, fails to meet contemporary code, or is at replacement age? Should you install a spare bypass while the trench is open? Is the pipe really buried as deep as the as-built drawings depict? If the root cause cannot be corrected, should the crossing be relocated?

Many stream systems will "heal" themselves. Given time, will your infrastructure still be threatened? Is this really performing preventive maintenance or correcting a deficient design? Does the project warrant collecting data and arguing a Rosgen classification or HEC modeling outcomes? Or is a field design (not overlooking the concepts of these analytical methods)

Fig. 7. Porous outfall protection (stepped gabions) absorb and dissipate energy that is undercutting an interceptor culvert that diverts water from the pipeline running directly upslope. The original installation left a 6-foot free fall that scoured and undermined the headwall placed to hold the drain pipe.

the better business decision? Who is the appropriate team to fix the problem? Will an archeologist be required? What web, organizational, agency, and commercial expertise can be queried? Is new directional boring and pipeline abandonment an option? What are the materials choices and logistical options? What permitting is required, with how much lead-time?

Does the stream channel need to be restored? What is the bed/bank composition and erodibility? Can the velocity (energy) be dissipated? Should currents be deflected? Is an upstream debris obstruction creating a hydraulic jump that contributes to the pipeline exposure? Can fish protection measures be accommodated? Can native materials and plants be used to restore the area effectively?

Then consider some responses:

1. Install pipes on the *upstream* side of highway culverts, bridges, or other features that obstruct or alter flow dynamics. Outlet plunge pools (Fig. 3) tend to develop.
2. Installations downstream of nickpoints should have outfall protection (Fig. 7).
3. Cross the stream/thalweg at the best angle to avoid future stream migration (Fig. 8). Anticipate erosion below Reno mats or stream deflectors oriented perpendicular to flow.
4. Provide debris catchment and avoidance measures. Do not create an obstacle that will trap debris and frazil ice at the pipeline. Installation of a shelter rock for fisheries can be considered, but an improperly placed boulder will induce scour, and may adversely affect nickpoints and bank erosion.
5. Place rip-rap and cover materials that will not (1) dislodge with floods, and (2) obstruct flow patterns in such a way that undermines the bed or banks in the vicinity of the pipeline crossing.
6. Consider directional boring (at $11–22/LF, nominal) instead of open trenching that requires permit, dewatering, and more time in permitting and probably in the field (risk of weather).

Fig. 8. Deer Creek exposure from meander migration into south bank, compounded by upstream debris/shoaling that diverted currents. Hydraulic capacity increased by widening channel, debris cleared upstream and down, trees removed that would capture flotsam, and gabions installed to move south bank back over the pipe.

7. Get well below the bed.
8. Pay attention to cultural sensitivities. An onsite archeologist may add $1500/day for artifact collecting, cleaning, photographing, cataloging, and reporting.
9. Work with farmers/landowners to keep cattle out of streams.
10. Incorporate bank stabilization, but avoid degrading the bed.
11. Extend trench protection of the meandering stream up-bank to beyond the crest, or at least as high as the extraordinary high water mark. An excavated trench, even if "compacted to 95%" as many contracts specify, is much less resistant to erosion than the undisturbed native materials that have naturally compacted over eons (Fig. 1).
12. Install trench breakers up-pipe to reduce pore pressure behind streambank armor.
13. Allow for settling of trench backfill in the streambed and banks as fines are washed out. Do not backfill to the degree that fish passage (Fig. 7) is obstructed or that a hydraulic gradient is generated.
14. Backfill should be compacted in thin lifts. Grade lifts upward with increasingly coarser-screen materials. Bedload sediments will become trapped in interstices over time. Use a top cover of a size that matches or exceeds the most prevalent larger natural onsite stone. This in situ material reflects the stream's natural bedload range.
15. Armor the slopes. In high water events the disturbed trench soils will erode first. Carry armor

Fig. 9. Pipeline E-30 and tower leg exposures resulted from a narrow gully, which made tight turns, to intermittently divert its storm discharge along the disturbed earth of the pipeline backfill in a wetland. Hydraulic radius and capacity was increased, sinuosity redefined, and banks at turns armored with stone and mats. Allowances were made to let the stream go out-of-bank in floods.

Fig. 10. Tully Farms Road stream intersected the broken shale of the original trench cover, and began to follow the pipe. The stream was redirected, stepped gabions installed, but the radius of curvature for the bend below the gabions was too tight. Longitudinal forces scoured the riprap on the outside curve that was premature, demonstrating that meanders tend to migrate downstream. Water flowing over an obstruction leaves the obstructing surface flowing at right angles to it.

Fig. 11. Pipeline E-30 and tower leg exposures resulted from a gully intermittently diverting its storm discharge along the disturbed earth of the pipeline backfill in a wetland. Hydraulic capacity was increased, sinuosity redefined, and banks at turns armored with stone and mats.

(rip rap or geotextile systems) well above the top of bank to delay catastrophic failure during the flood of record (Fig. 4). Armor also deters, or protects from, the ATV traffic inherently drawn to utility ROW's!

16. Open riparian wetlands to floods (Fig. 9). Bank berms that were intended to confine the stream can induce either inappropriate aggradation or incision. Streams and wetlands are natural sponges. Flood attenuation (reduction in velocity and energy, and erosive currents) may be influenced by past land management activities. Consult with landowners to remove relic berms that no longer protect abandoned agriculture. This may allow the stream to go overbank, recreate riparian wetlands, and reduce erosion. The benefit may be a raised water table in adjacent lands that halts downcutting of the streambed. The downside may be maintenance access through another wetland.

17. Learn to use GIS for permit mapping *and* project evaluations; interpret the big view.
18. Calculate sinuosity and decide if meander migration will threaten your installation.
19. Concentrate on getting the slope right in the restored reach (sinuosity calculation). A correct local channel length, in proportion to the slope, will keep your repairs from blowing out (Fig. 10).
20. Observe presence of nickpoints and project the bed erosion rate.
21. Plan for dislodged soils; several repairs were due, in part, to decompacted soils (Fig. 11).
22. Manipulate conditions that induce bed aggradation, if beneficial.
23. Install materials, adequately graded and bedded, that reflect dynamic equilibrium conditions within that reach of stream.
24. Design for high flow — not the stable flow. Look for terraces at and above the bank-full (witnessed or perceived) condition.

25. Logically present all considerations to your permit administrator.
26. Explain environmental and natural resource benefits of your project design.
27. Make a business decision: identify the problem, determine if it should/can be fixed.
28. Optimize installation on height-of-land. Try to install as much of your pipeline on high ground, staying on the ridges, rather than striking across the gullies or breaks in slope where mass wasting and erosion are more likely to erode cover and bedding. Try to accommodate gentle terrain breaks by crossing contours at a moderate angle.

Lesson summary

More important than applying these lessons to repairs, is to plan and design new gas line facilities from the onset to avoid conditions that may result in the need to repair exposures. Keep your regulator stations out of the wetlands and away from the banks of rivers and streams. An adequately designed installation, located with an understanding of runoff, hydrology, and soils/surficial geology may preclude later repairs due to backfill or armor displacement. As we saw in the Pipeline 33 cases on the Salmon River (Fig. 3) and Sandy Creek, the crossing is aligned directly below the confined discharge exiting bends in the water course. If the alignment could not have been moved up/downstream to transect perpendicularly the high flow pattern, the initial armor design could be made to compensate for anticipated erosive events.

ACKNOWLEDGEMENTS

Thanks to M. Corbett, C. Sheldon, J. Sullivan, and the Gas Operations staff who gave me the opportunity to help, for the quality construction services of B. Newton, R. Ray, and B. Hunter, and to K. Finch for negotiating their contracting rate.

REFERENCES

Blatt, Harvey, Gerard Middleton, and Raymond Murray. 1972. Origin of sedimentary rocks. Prentice-Hall, Englewood Cliffs, NJ. 634 pp.

Civil Engineering. July 1999. Hydrology: Europeans offer bridge scour and stream stability solutions. P22.

Gas Research Institute. February 1998. Topical Report 97/0244: Suspended sediment and turbidity conditions associated with instream construction activities — An assessment of biological relevance. Chicago, IL. 331 pp.

Heisler, Sanford I. 1984. The Wiley engineer's desk reference. Wiley Interscience. NYC, NY. 567 pp.

Hunter, Christopher J. 1991. Better trout habitat — A guide to stream restoration and management Montana Land Alliance. Island Press, Washington, DC. 320 pp.

Ibid. April 1998. Topical Report 97/0243: Sediment entrainment due to pipeline watercourse crossing construction. Chicago, IL. 48 pp.

Linsley, Ray K., Jr., Max A. Kohler, and Joseph L.H. Paulhus. 1958. Hydrology for engineers. McGraw-Hill, New York, NY. 340 pp.

Muehlhausen, John. 2001. Operation and maintenance activities on public lands. In: Proceedings 7th International Symposium on Environmental Concerns in Rights-of-Way Management.

Smith, Derald G. and Cheryl M. Pearce. June 2000. River ice and its role in limitig woodland development on a sandy braid-plain, Milk River, Montana. Wetlands, 20(2): 232–250.

Thornbury, William D. 1969. Principles of geomorphology. John Wiley & Sons, New York, NY. 594 pp.

BIOGRAPHICAL SKETCH

Scott D. Shupe

Environmental Affairs Department, Niagara Mohawk Power Corporation, 300 Erie Boulevard West, Syracuse, NY 13202, (315) 428-6616 (desk), (315) 428-3549 (FAX), E-mail: Scott.Shupe@us.ngrid.com

Scott D. Shupe, Environmental Analyst at Niagara Mohawk, holds a BS in Biology and a MS in Water Resource Management from SUNY College of Environmental Science and Forestry, and a MS in Science Management from the University of Alaska-Anchorage. His career has spanned the planning-construction-operations spectrum, including powerline construction, small hydropower and navigation planning, emergency management, hydroelectric relicensing, gas pipeline licensing and operations, and is currently involved with other regulatory issues associated with utility ROW management.

Part XI
Pesticides

Human Health Risk Assessment for the Use of Herbicides on Electric Utility Rights-of-Way on the Allegheny National Forest, USA

Logan A. Norris, Frank Dost, and Rufin VanBossuyt Jr.

Herbicides were a commonly used tool for managing tall-growing vegetation on electric utility ROW on the Allegheny National Forest in Pennsylvania until 1990. Between 1990 and 1998, vegetation management was restricted to manual and mechanical methods. An EIS that complied with NEPA provided the basis on which herbicide use could resume. A key part of the EIS was the risk assessment for human health and impact on other organisms for glyphosate, picloram, fosamine ammonium, imazapyr, metsulfuron methyl, and triclopyr herbicides. The assessment showed these herbicides could be used safely when mitigating measures such as signage, limited operations on steep slopes and no-spray buffers around sensitive sites were employed. Successful ROW vegetation spray operations were conducted in 1998, 1999, and 2000. The specific buffer zone strategies protected water quality, with no detectable herbicide reported.

Keywords: Picloram, triclopyr, metsulfuron methyl, imazapyr, fosamine ammonium, glyphosate, toxicity, vegetation management

INTRODUCTION

Allegheny Power and GPU Energy have 125 miles (955 acres) of electric utility ROW (both transmission and distribution) that cross portions of the Allegheny National Forest (USDA Forest Service) in Pennsylvania, USA. The utilities had used herbicides on the ROW on the Forest prior to 1990, but since 1990 only manual and mechanical methods have been used. The utilities felt that they needed to return to the use of herbicides to reduce long-term costs and the management intensity needed, as these sites were becoming increasingly dominated by dense sprout clumps of tall growing trees. However, the USDA Forest Service determined that there was no National Environmental Policy Act (NEPA) basis for the use of herbicides on these ROW, and that an Environmental Impact Statement (EIS) must be approved before herbicide use could occur.

Working collaboratively with the utilities and the Allegheny National Forest, Environmental Consultants, Inc. (ECI) prepared a site-specific EIS that was accepted by the USDA Forest Service in 1997 (USDA Forest Service, 1997; Norris, 2000). It successfully withstood appeals and was the basis for the vegetation management program that followed in 1997–2000. This paper provides a brief introduction to NEPA but concentrates on the technical basis for the use of herbicides as part of a program of integrated vegetation management. The dominant focus is on the behavior of chemicals in the environment, human health risk assessment and effects of herbicide use on the environment.

NATIONAL ENVIRONMENTAL POLICY ACT (NEPA)

The National Environmental Policy Act, or NEPA, is the basic public law governing federal programs that may impact the environment. This includes the management of ROW of all kinds (electric utility, pipelines, roads and highways, rail lines, etc.) on federal property. NEPA was established as law in 1969. It was amended in 1975 and 1982, but the law remains fundamentally the same. The purpose of the act is to "develop a policy that will (a) encourage productive and enjoyable harmony between man and his environment, (b) promote efforts which will prevent damage to the environment and stimulate the health and welfare of man, and (c) enrich the understanding of ecological systems and natural resources important to the Nation."

The key elements of the National Environmental Policy Act are that *all federal agencies shall*:

1. Utilize a systematic, interdisciplinary approach that will ensure the integrated use of the sciences and environmental design arts in planning and decision-making (means no "seat of the pants" estimates in planning).
2. All federal agencies shall give appropriate consideration in planning to presently unquantified environmental amenities and values (means more than economics is to be considered).
3. The Act establishes specific responsibilities for designated "responsible officials" for what are called "major federal actions affecting the quality of the human environment" (means a specific individual is responsible/accountable for the decision).

If ROW management activities occur on federal property, they are subject to NEPA. The implementation of NEPA is still highly structured, very public, vulnerable to delays, and to appeals and litigation. In addition, it takes time, costs money and does not necessarily have a certain outcome. All of this sounds terribly complex, but operating on federal lands is possible as long as you know and understand the rules. Here are some resources that may help:

– On the World Wide Web: http://ceq.eh.doe.gov/nepa/nepanet.htm. You will find a full-text copy of NEPA and many other useful materials at this site.
– If you are considering operating on a particular piece of federal property, ask the agency managing this property for a copy of their NEPA regulations. The USDA Forest Service calls this the Environmental Policy and Procedures Handbook and it details the Council of Environmental Quality regulations needed for compliance. It will also be helpful to examine an EIS relevant to your type of operations.
– Norris (1999) described NEPA and how it operates with respect to ROW management on federal properties.

PREPARING AN EIS

The EIS evaluates the appropriateness and environmental effects of various vegetation management alternatives, including the use of six specific herbicides. The EIS provides an extensive review of scientific information on the movement and persistence in the environment, toxicity to humans and other mammals, birds and aquatic species, and effects on soil, water and vegetation. The herbicides included were:

– Fosamine ammonium (Krenite UT®)
– Glyphosate (Accord®)
– Imazapyr (Arsenal®)
– Metsulfuron methyl (Escort®)
– Picloram (Tordon K®)
– Triclopyr (Garlon 3A® and Garlon 4®).

The 133-page Appendix A of the EIS reports in detail what is known about the movement, persistence and fate of these herbicides, and provides the details of the human health risk assessment. Appendix C (28 pages) includes the risk assessment for non-human mammals, birds and aquatic species (USDA Forest Service, 1997).

The USDA Forest Service Record of Decision was finalized in May of 1997, with the use of selected herbicides, alone or in combination, and alone or in combination with manual and/or mechanical methods as the preferred alternative. The approval was appealed in writing by members of the public, but the appeal was denied by the Forest Supervisor and the Regional Forester (the next higher level of authority). Under this EIS, the utilities are allowed to resume the use of herbicides, as described in the EIS, until significant new information is available that might require a change in the EIS or the decision. Allegheny Power resumed their use of herbicides in 1998, and GPU Energy did so in 1999 and 2000.

RISK ASSESSMENT

Risk assessment is the process by which the likelihood of adverse effects from the use of a herbicide is determined. The process is not unique to herbicides and their use on ROW. It is also used to determine the likelihood of adverse effects from food additives, medications, household and industrial chemicals, and environmental contaminants. It is soundly based on widely accepted theory and practice in toxicology, chemistry and biology.

Risk is not determined solely by the toxicity characteristics of the chemical, or only the exposure organisms may receive in a particular pattern of use. It is a combination of both of these distinct items. Risk assessment has three components:

– *Hazard analysis* — in which the critical toxicity characteristics of each compound are identified. The hazard is expressed as the response of organisms to varying levels of exposure of herbicide, usually in controlled laboratory experiments. The exposure in these tests is usually expressed as milligrams per kilograms per day ($mg\ kg^{-1}\ d^{-1}$). Most importantly, the hazard analysis identifies the lowest reliable no-observable-effect-level (NOEL), which is crucial to the risk assessment for humans, other mammals, birds, and aquatic species (Fig. 1).
– *Exposure analysis* — in which the level of exposure a human or other organism is likely to receive is quantified. This requires knowing the routes by which

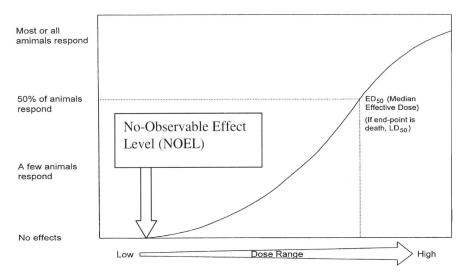

Fig. 1. The relationship between the level of toxic response to the size of the dose.

Table 1. Laboratory determined LD_{-50} and no-observed-effect-levels (NOEL)[1]

Chemical	Acute oral LD_{-50}, rat (mg kg^{-1})	Lowest systematic toxicity NOEL (mg kg^{-1} d^{-1})	Lowest reproductive maternal fetotoxic or teratogenic toxicity NOEL (mg kg^{-1} d^{-1})
Fosamine ammonium	7000	10 (90-days, rat)	1000 (maternal rat) >3000 (fetal rat)
Glyphosate	>5000	362 (2-year, male rat)	175 (fetal and maternal rabbit)
Imazapyr	>5000	500 (1-year, rat)	300 (maternal rat)
Metsulfuron methyl	>5000	25 (2-year, rat)	25 (maternal rabbit)
Picloram	3000	7 (180-day, dog)	400 (fetal and maternal rabbit)
Triclopyr	300 → 2000	5 (rat reproductive)	5 (rat reproductive)

[1] From Tables 7 and 8, Appendix A, USDA Forest Service, 1997.

exposure may occur: ingestion of contaminated food and water, exposure through the skin or inhalation of contaminated air. The information on the movement, persistence and fate of an herbicide in the environment is used to estimate exposure (Appendix A, USDA Forest Service, 1997). As examples:

- *Leaching and persistence characteristics in soil* determine the potential for impact on ground water quality, and the tendency to *drift or runoff* determines the impact on surface water quality, both of which determine the possibility organisms could be exposed by ingestion of this water,
- *Persistence in vegetation* determines the potential exposure of organisms that eat the vegetation, and
- *Volatilization* determines impacts on air quality and the potential for inhalation exposure.
- Risk analysis — in which the expected exposure (from the exposure analysis) is compared to the NOEL (from the hazard analysis) and the risk described as the margin of safety.

What constitutes safety? A margin of safety that is 100 or greater than the NOEL is the commonly accepted criterion (regulatory standard) for human safety. If the exposure that is expected or possible from the specific proposed use of a specific herbicide is 100 times less than the NOEL, the margin of safety is 100. Risk analysis is more complicated if the chemicals in the analysis are carcinogens. None of the herbicides included in the EIS are carcinogens. If they had been, a cancer risk analysis would be required to determine the probability of causing cancer. The common regulatory standard for this is one excess cancer in one million lifetimes. Cancer is a very common human disease, occurring naturally approximately 250,000 times in a population of one million. The standard allows an increase in the incidence of cancer from the natural level of 250,000 to 250,001 in a population of one million.

For each of the six herbicides included in the EIS, the following section summarizes the environmental behavior and the results of the hazard analysis, exposure analysis and risk analysis from the EIS (USDA Forest Service, 1997). The essential quantitative measures of toxicity, exposure and risk are in Tables 1–3.

FOSAMINE AMMONIUM (KRENITE UT®) MOVEMENT, PERSISTENCE AND FATE IN THE ENVIRONMENT

Fosamine ammonium is used for post-emergence control of woody plants. It is adsorbed to soil particles,

Table 2. Estimated typical exposure of the public and workers, mg kg^{-1} d^{-1} [1]

	Krenite	Accord	Arsenal	Tordon K	Escort	Garlon 3A	Garlon 4
Public							
Dermal[2]	0.0046	0.0003	0.00045	0.00001	0.0001	0.0004	0.0004
Water	0.0002	0.00004	0.00002	0.00002	0.00001	0.0001	0.0001
Food[3]	0.01	0.001	0.001	0.0009	0.0003	0.004	0.004
Workers							
HV foliar	0.007	0.004	0.0037	NA	0.0005	0.0059	NA
LV foliar	0.205	0.051	0.051	0.00037	NA	0.012	0.0085
Cut-surface	NA	0.033	NA	NA	NA	0.0046	NA
Spill[4]	0.31	8.2	11.4	0.49	NA	8.9	12.3

[1] From Tables 27–34, Appendix A USDA Forest Service, 1997.
[2] Dermal exposure levels are from contact with treated vegetation just after treatment. Dermal exposure from drift is typically 5–10 times less.
[3] Food includes the sum of possible exposure to contaminated fish, meat, produce and berries.
[4] The spill is not considered a typical exposure. It is considered a maximum exposure scenario.

Table 3. Representative margins of safety for systemic effects, typical exposure[1]

	Krenite	Accord	Arsenal	Tordon K	Escort	Garlon 3A	Garlon 4
Public							
Drift	>10,000	>10,000	>10,000	>10,000	>10,000	>10,000	>10,000
Water	>10,000	>10,000	>10,000	>10,000	>10,000	>10,000	>10,000
Food	6575	>10,000	>10,000	>10,000	>10,000	>10,000	9000
Workers							
HV foliar	7150	>10,000	>10,000	NA	>10,000	5100	NA
LV foliar	244	7000	>10,000	>10,000	NA	2500	3500
Cut-surface	3125	>10,000	NA	NA	NA	6500	NA
Spill[2]	3	44	44	14	NA	3	24

[1] From Tables 27–34, Appendix A, USDA Forest Service, 1997.
[2] The spill is not a typical exposure. It is a worst case, maximum exposure scenario.

rapidly degraded in soil (half-life <7 days) and is relatively unstable in water. It is absorbed by plant stems, buds and foliage. Absorption through young stems appears to occur more readily than through foliage. Laboratory studies indicate that fosamine ammonium is translocated throughout the plant; however, in practice, effective action requires complete coverage of all aerial parts of woody plants. Fosamine ammonium has a short persistence in plants and is metabolized to products that in turn have a relatively short half-life. It does not bioaccumulate in animals. The movement, persistence and fate of fosamine ammonium are reviewed in detail in Appendix A, USDA Forest Service (1997).

HAZARD ANALYSIS

Most of the information on the toxicology of fosamine ammonium is unpublished registration data reviewed by USDA Forest Service (1984) and discussed below without reference. Later unpublished registration data and published reports are specifically referenced.

Acute toxicity

The acute oral LD$_{50}$ for fosamine ammonium is 24,000 mg kg^{-1} in the rat and 7400 mg kg^{-1} in the guinea pig. When administered by injection under the skin, the LD$_{50}$ was 3000 mg kg^{-1}. The difference from the oral LD$_{50}$ demonstrates the poor absorption from the gut.

The acute dermal LD$_{50}$ of the formulation, including surfactant, in rabbits is greater than 5000 mg kg^{-1}, apparently the highest dose tested. Ten daily doses of 2200 mg kg^{-1} produced no toxic effects. Dermal application to rabbits for 6 h d^{-1} over 21 days at doses of 50, 500, and 1500 mg kg^{-1} d^{-1} caused no clinical changes, no changes in blood or urine chemistry or morphology, and no cellular pathology (Mackenzie, 1991). It does not cause allergic sensitization.

The active ingredient is not an eye irritant, but with surfactant the formulation causes transient irritation and corneal opacity. Inhalation exposure to full formulation for four hours indicated a median lethal dose results from a concentration in air of 3 g M^{-3} for rats.

In neurotoxicity testing, male rats were given 2000 mg kg^{-1} d^{-1} for 5 days. Cholinesterase activity of plasma, serum and three regions of the brain were not changed by the treatment. There was no other indication of toxicity (Mackenzie, 1993). Fosamine ammonium does not produce delayed neurotoxicity, or inhibition of neurotoxic esterase or acetylcholine esterase after acute intoxication of hens (Fletcher, 1993). A subchronic neurotoxicity assay in rats at dose rates up to 1000 mg kg^{-1} d^{-1} for 96 days caused no changes in motor activity or functional parameters and no neural pathology (Christoph, 1993a). Acute neurotoxicity at single oral doses of 0, 500, 1000, 2000 mg kg^{-1} also caused no observable changes in the test battery administered prior, 2–3 h, 8 and 15 days after administration (Christoph, 1993b).

Chronic toxicity

Feeding of diets containing up to 10,000 ppm fosamine ammonium for 90 days produced equivocal renal tubular effects in rats; the US Environmental Protection Agency (USEPA) has judged the NOEL to be 200 ppm or 10 mg kg^{-1} d^{-1}. Dogs fed up to 10,000 ppm (280 mg kg^{-1} d^{-1}) for six months were unaffected except for greater stomach weights in females at the highest dietary concentration (Kaplan, 1993).

A developmental toxicity assay in rats at doses of 0, 50, 350, 1000, 3000 mg kg^{-1} d^{-1} over days 7–16 caused diarrhea, erratic weight gain and depressed feed consumption at the highest dose, and marginal effects at 1000 mg kg^{-1} d^{-1}.

Reproductive toxicity

In rats at 3000 mg kg^{-1} d^{-1}, pregnancy rate, miscarriage, resorption, litter size, and fetal death did not differ from control. The NOEL for maternal toxicity was 1000 mg kg^{-1} d^{-1}; the fetal NOEL was in excess of 3000 mg kg^{-1} d^{-1} (Alvarez, 1992).

In an earlier rat teratogenicity study, a dietary concentration of 10,000 ppm of the 42% formulation (about 210 mg kg^{-1} d^{-1}) fed from days 6–15 of gestation produced no birth defects, and no fetal or maternal toxicity. A single generation, two litter reproduction assay indicated no adverse effects at 10,000 ppm in the diet (DuPont, 1983).

Mutagenicity and carcinogenicity

Fosamine ammonium is not mutagenic in *S. typhimurium* bacterial assays (Reynolds, 1991). A point mutation assay in Chinese hamster ovary (CHO) cells was negative, as was an *in vivo* bone marrow cytogenetics assay in rats. An *in vitro* test for chromosome damage in CHO cells was positive. Fosamine ammonium does not induce unscheduled DNA synthesis (USDA Forest Service, 1989).

The weight of evidence indicates that fosamine ammonium does not have mutagenic potential. Because it has no uses on food crops, and no characteristics suggesting carcinogenic potential, fosamine ammonium has not been assayed for carcinogenicity.

EXPOSURE ANALYSIS

Ingestion

Fosamine is absorbed by stems, buds and foliage of plants. In forage plants, it dissipates rapidly with time after application, showing a half-life of seven days, and none detected one year later (USDA Forest Service, 1984). This indicates the duration of exposure of humans due to ingestion of treated vegetation will be only a short period of time after application. Fosamine is rapidly excreted from animals in feces and urine, and shows no tendency for bioaccumulation. In water, microbial decomposition is believed to be the dominant mechanism of dissipation, although in moving water systems it is likely that dilution and movement with the water are also important. Analysis of the human exposure via this mechanism focuses on the period shortly after application.

Inhalation

The vaporization of fosamine is negligible because of its low vapor pressure (USDA Forest Service, 1984). Thus, the opportunity for inhalation exposure is limited to the time that spray droplets may be in the air.

Dermal exposure

The low solubility of fosamine in fatty solvents indicates there is little potential for movement across the skin, making the potential for human dermal exposure quite limited. It will be highest when an individual comes in direct contact with the wet spray.

RISK ANALYSIS

Fosamine ammonium (Krenite UT®) presents a very low level of risk to the public in typical exposure scenarios. The margin of safety is greater than 6000 in every case, and in all but two cases is greater than 10,000. For workers (applicators), the margins of safety are lower but are greater than 200 in every instance and are greater than 1000 in all but one case for typical exposures. In a worst-case scenario, the direct spill of herbicide concentrate on the skin can result in a margin of safety of 3, which is significantly less than 100, emphasizing the importance of careful handling, the use of protective gear and rigorous sanitation.

GLYPHOSATE (ACCORD®) MOVEMENT, PERSISTENCE AND FATE IN THE ENVIRONMENT

Glyphosate is absorbed by plant foliage and is then readily translocated throughout the plant to roots and rhizomes where it inhibits further growth and sprouting. It is not metabolized by plant tissue. Glyphosate has a very low lipid solubility and thus has little tendency to bioaccumulate in animals. Cows fed glyphosate had undetectable levels of residue in their milk.

Glyphosate is completely and rapidly degraded in soil by microbiological activity but is resistant to chemical degradation in the soil environment (soil half-life <60 days). It is stable to sunlight, is resistant to leaching, has a low tendency to runoff, is strongly adsorbed to soil particles, has a negligible volatility, and has a minimal effect on soil micro flora. Soil micro flora degrade glyphosate to aminomethyl phosphonic acid (AMPA), which is somewhat more stable than glyphosate but is degraded over time.

In aquatic systems, glyphosate is strongly adsorbed to both organic and mineral matter and is degraded primarily by microorganisms. The rate of degradation of glyphosate in water is generally slower than it is in most soils because there are fewer microorganisms in water than in soil. Only very small amounts of applied glyphosate are removed in runoff. The movement, persistence and fate of glyphosate are reviewed in detail in Appendix A, USDA Forest Service (1997).

HAZARD ANALYSIS

A Reregistration Eligibility Decision Document has been issued for glyphosate (USEPA, 1993). Information in this section comes from that document and the toxicology information summary (Monsanto, 1983); see also Syracuse (1996b).

Acute toxicity
Acute oral LD_{50} in the rat is >5000 mg kg^{-1}. The acute dermal LD_{50} for rabbits is >2 g kg^{-1}. Glyphosate is a mild eye irritant and slight skin irritant, and does not cause skin sensitization.

Chronic toxicity
In a 90-day study, rats were fed diets containing 0, 1000, 5000, and 20,000 ppm, equivalent to 0, 63, 317, and 1267 mg kg^{-1} d^{-1} for males and 0, 84, 404, and 1623 mg kg^{-1} d^{-1} for females. Serum glucose was increased in males at the two higher doses but not in a dose-related manner, and not in excess of normal limits. In a subsequent chronic study, however, the effects on serum phosphorous and potassium were not seen, suggesting that they were not related to treatment. In a similar study of mice given 0, 250, 500, and 2500 mg kg^{-1} d^{-1}, body weight was decreased in the high dose group, but no other change was detected.

A chronic dietary study of male rats given 0, 89, 362, or 940 mg kg^{-1} d^{-1} and females given 0, 113, 457, or 1183 mg kg^{-1} d^{-1} indicated effects only in the high dose group. Females gained less weight than controls, and males were found to have increased frequency of cataracts and increased liver weight. The NOEL was 362 mg kg^{-1} d^{-1} for males and 457 mg kg^{-1} d^{-1} for females.

Dermal exposure of rabbits to 100, 1000, and 5000 mg glyphosate kg^{-1} d^{-1}, five days per week for three weeks caused minor skin irritation at the highest doses, but no systemic effects. The systemic NOEL was 5000 mg kg^{-1} d^{-1}.

Mice on diets providing dose rates of 0, 150, 750, and 4500 mg kg^{-1} d^{-1} were fed for 18 months. At the highest dose rate, weight loss occurred, along with cellular effects that were determined to be nontreatment related. The no-effect level was determined to be 450 mg kg^{-1} d^{-1}. Male beagle dogs given up to 500 mg glyphosate per kg daily for a year were unaffected at any dose rate.

Reproductive toxicity
In an early three-generation reproduction study in rats, kidney lesions were found in males of the second litter in the third generation at the highest dose, 30 mg kg^{-1} d^{-1}. A second study, employing doses of 0, 100, 500, or 1500 mg kg^{-1} d^{-1}, did not produce the kidney effects seen in the earlier work. The systemic and developmental NOELs were 500 mg kg^{-1} d^{-1}, and the reproductive NOEL was 1500 mg kg^{-1} d^{-1}.

Developmental toxicity in rats was assayed at dose rates of 0, 300, 1000, and 3000 mg kg^{-1} d^{-1} by stomach tube during days 6–19 of gestation. Maternal and fetal toxicity appeared at the highest dose rate, and there was no effect on either fetal development or maternal health at a dose rate of 1000 mg kg^{-1} d^{-1}. Rabbits were administered 0, 75, 175, or 350 mg glyphosate kg^{-1} d^{-1} through days 6–27 of gestation. Severe maternal toxicity occurred at the highest dose. The NOEL for both maternal and fetal effects was 175 mg kg^{-1} d^{-1}.

Mutagenicity and carcinogenicity
Glyphosate is considered to have no mutagenic or carcinogenic activity (Syracuse, 1996b). Specifically, gene mutation assays with several strains of Salmonella with and without metabolic activation were all negative. A gene mutation assay in CHO cells (HGPRT assay) with and without metabolic activation was negative up to a concentration of 10 mg ml^{-1}. Hepatocyte DNA repair was not induced by glyphosate, and an *in vivo* bone marrow cytogenicity assay was also negative (Li and Long, 1988; USEPA, 1993).

A bone marrow structural chromosome aberration assay in the rats (dose, 1000 mg kg^{-1}), and bone marrow micronucleus tests in the mouse, was done with both Roundup® formulation (high dose 200 mg kg^{-1} as glyphosate IPA; 24 h assay) and glyphosate IPA (high dose 200 mg kg^{-1}; 24 and 48 h) Rank et al. (1993). Unlike other studies, Rank et al. (1993) found a weak response to glyphosate with tester strains TA 98 without, but not with, activation and weak response in TA 100 with activation. Neither finding was dose-related and neither was found in other laboratories at higher concentrations.

An 18-month study of mice at a maximum dose rate of 4500 mg kg^{-1} d^{-1} produced some systemic pathology in the high dose group but no carcinogenic response. In high dosage exposures in rats, no increase in tumor incidence occurred (USEPA, 1993).

EXPOSURE ANALYSIS

Ingestion

Glyphosate is absorbed by plant foliage and readily translocated throughout the plant. It is not readily degraded by plant metabolism, so residues in the plant remain available for ingestion by humans and other animals as long as the plant material is suitable for consumption. Glyphosate has very low tendency to be incorporated into animal tissues due to its low octanol:water partition coefficient (0.017) and very limited tendency to cross gastrointestinal membranes. Residues that do occur in the body are rapidly eliminated (USDA Forest Service, 1984). These characteristics minimize the exposure of humans and other animals due to eating of animals that may have been areas treated with glyphosate. In aquatic systems, glyphosate is strongly adsorbed to organic and mineral matter and is degraded primarily by microorganisms, although the rate of microbial decomposition is slower in water than in soil. The concentration of glyphosate remaining in water is influenced primarily by the amount of herbicide that enters the water, the volume of water exposed and its rate of movement.

Inhalation

Glyphosate has a low vapor pressure so it does not volatilize into the atmosphere. Any residues in air dissipate by dilution and movement with wind. Human exposure via inhalation includes this aspect of glyphosate environmental fate in air.

Dermal absorption

The tendency of glyphosate to bind tightly to soil and other organic materials limits dermal exposure to herbicide deposited directly on the skin in connection with the application. Direct exposure of skin is included in the dermal exposure analysis.

RISK ANALYSIS

Glyphosate (Accord®) presents a very low level of risk to the public in typical exposure scenarios. The margin of safety is greater than 10,000 in every case. For workers (applicators), the margins of safety are lower but are greater than 7000 for typical exposures in every instance. In a worst-case scenario, the direct spill of herbicide concentrate on the skin the margin of safety is 44, which is significantly less than 100, emphasizing the importance of careful handling, the use of protective gear and rigorous sanitation.

IMAZYPYR (ARSENAL®) MOVEMENT, PERSISTENCE AND FATE IN THE ENVIRONMENT

The isopropylamine salt of imazapyr has a calculated half-life in soil at a forest study site of 19–34 days. The major route of degradation is photolysis with some contribution by aerobic microbes. Field studies with radioactive imazapyr showed that loss of radioactivity was primarily from the top three inches of the soil profile, indicating that imazapyr has low potential for leaching. Imazapyr has low potential for bioaccumulation. The hydrolytic half-life of imazapyr at pH 7.0 was calculated to be 325 days, indicating that hydrolysis is not a major route for environmental degradation. A half-life of <30 days is expected in many forest soils. The movement, persistence and fate of imazapyr are reviewed in detail in Appendix A, USDA Forest Service (1997). USEPA (1985) is also a useful reference for imazapyr.

HAZARD ANALYSIS

Available data on the toxicology of imazapyr is summarized in a background statement (Weeks et al., 1988) prepared in 1987 for USDA Forest Service, and from an undated summary of test results provided by American Cyanamid (the registrant).

Acute toxicity

The acute oral LD_{50} for imazapyr is greater than 5000 mg kg^{-1}. The acute dermal LD_{50} is in excess of 2000 mg kg^{-1}. The compound caused eye irritation in the rabbit with recovery in seven days. It is a mild skin irritant. The acute oral LD_{50} of the formulation was greater than 5000 mg kg^{-1}. The acute dermal LD_{50} for the formulation was 2148 mg kg^{-1}. The formulation affected the eyes and skin in the same way technical imazapyr did.

An inhalation study of rats maintained in a concentration of 5.1 gm technical imazapyr per cubic meter of air for four hours caused nasal irritation that was resolved by the second day. In 14 days of observation, there was no effect on body or organ weight. A similar assay of the formulation provided a similar result.

Chronic toxicity

Neither imazapyr nor the IPA formulation caused dermal sensitization in guinea pigs.

Twenty one-day dermal toxicity studies were conducted with both imazapyr and its formulation in rabbits. Dose rates were 100, 200, 400 mg kg^{-1} d^{-1}, 6 h each day, five days a week for three weeks. There was no toxicity associated with the treatment.

No treatment-related effects have been found in rats maintained on dietary levels of imazapyr up to 500 mg kg^{-1} d^{-1} (10,000 ppm).

Reproductive toxicity

Developmental toxicity (teratogenicity) studies have been conducted in rats and rabbits. Rats were administered by gavage 0, 100, 300, or 1000 mg imazapyr

kg^{-1} d^{-1} on gestation days 6–15. There were no teratogenic or other pathological findings. The dose rates for rabbits were 0, 25, 100, and 400 mg kg^{-1} d^{-1}, during gestation days 6–18. In this assay, no effects on fetal development were found.

Mutagenicity and carcinogenicity

Ames tests for reverse mutations with strains of Salmonella with and without metabolic activation were negative (American Cyanamid, 1986a). Other mutagenicity assays reported in an imazapyr background statement prepared for USDA Forest Service by Labat-Anderson, Inc. (Weeks et al., 1988) include an *in vitro* Chinese hamster ovary (CHO) cell mutation assay, an *in vitro* CHO chromosomal aberration assay, dominant lethal assay in mice, and unscheduled DNA synthesis assay in rat hepatocytes. USEPA has classified imazapyr in Group E, "no evidence of carcinogenicity in at least two adequate animal tests in different species" (USEPA, 1995a).

EXPOSURE ANALYSIS

Ingestion

Imazapyr is absorbed readily through foliage and roots, translocates rapidly throughout the plant and tends to concentrate in meristematic regions. It dissipates fairly quickly from plant tissues, with a half-life reported to be 12–40 days. Mechanical loss due to wind erosion and wash-off by precipitation are also important factors in reducing the residue levels of picloram in and on vegetation (USDA Forest Service, 1984). Imazapyr is rapidly excreted by animals (87% in 24 h, with elimination virtually complete in 6 days). The bioaccumulation factor is less than one, meaning the opportunity for exposure via ingestion of animals is limited to animals taken within a few days of the time they would have consumed treated vegetation. Imazapyr can occur in water due to direct application to water, or in areas where storm generated runoff may move residues to water channels. It is subject to rapid photolysis in water and this, combined with dilution, limits the opportunity for exposure by ingestion of water. Mitigation measures that limit initial entry to water help minimize human exposure via this mechanism.

Inhalation

The vapor pressure of imazapyr is very low (2×10^{-7} mmHg at 45°C), meaning there will be little or no vaporization of imazapyr after it has been applied. Exposure via inhalation will be limited to the period when spray droplets are in the air.

Dermal exposure

The octanol:water partition coefficient for imazapyr is 1.3, meaning there will be little absorption of this chemical through the skin, and no substantive exposure via dermal absorption.

RISK ANALYSIS

Imazypyr (Arsenal®) presents a very low level of risk to the public with margins of safety greater than 10,000 in every case in typical exposure scenarios. For workers (applicators), the margins of safety are also greater than 10,000 for typical exposures in every instance. In a worst-case scenario, the direct spill of herbicide concentrate on the skin the margin of safety is 44. Careful handling, the use of protective gear and rigorous sanitation are useful mitigation measures.

METSULFURON METHYL (ESCORT®) MOVEMENT, PERSISTENCE AND FATE IN THE ENVIRONMENT

Metsulfuron methyl has a half-life in soil of one to two months, depending on soil moisture, temperature, pH, and organic matter content. In alkaline soils, degradation is somewhat slower. Mobility in soil is positively correlated with net movement of soil moisture. Less mobility occurs if soil pH is less than 6.0. Initial degradation of the molecule is through chemical hydrolysis, followed by degradation to lower molecular weight metabolites by means of soil microbial metabolism. Loss of this chemical from photodecomposition and volatilization in the field is negligible. The movement, persistence and fate of metsulfuron methyl are reviewed in detail in Appendix A, USDA Forest Service (1997).

HAZARD ANALYSIS

The toxicity of metsulfuron methyl has been reviewed by Labat-Anderson, Inc. (undated). Other data are specifically referenced in the following paragraphs.

Acute toxicity

The oral acute median lethal dose (LD_{50}) in the rat is greater than 5000 mg kg^{-1}. Acute dermal toxicity is also low; the LD_{50} in the rabbit is greater than 2000 mg kg^{-1}. Higher doses were not practical to apply. Concentrated formulation (70%) was moderately irritating in rabbits. Metsulfuron methyl is moderately to severely irritating to the eyes if not washed. A 95.8% pure technical product caused slight corneal opacity and mild conjunctivitis in rabbits, with recovery in 72 h. *In vivo* ophthalmologic examination showed no corneal injury (Brock, 1987). All effects were reversed in two weeks.

Sub acute (21 consecutive days) dermal treatment of rabbits with 2000 mg metsulfuron methyl kg^{-1} d^{-1} produced no effect on body or organ weight, hematology, blood chemistry, or organ pathology. At the site of application, there was reddening, edema and grossly evident dermatitis at 2000 mg kg^{-1} d^{-1}, and microscopically visible dermatitis at 500 mg kg^{-1} d^{-1}. The

NOEL was 125 mg kg^{-1} d^{-1} (Sarver, 1987). A repeat-insult-closed-patch dermal sensitization assay in guinea pigs produced no dermal irritation and no delayed hypersensitivity or allergic response at doses high enough to cause diarrhea.

Chronic toxicity

The NOEL for systemic toxicity after 90-day feeding of rats was established at 50 mg metsulfuron methyl kg^{-1} d^{-1} (1000 ppm in the diet). The next higher dose was 375 mg kg^{-1} d^{-1}, which caused reduced weight gain and change in serum protein pattern. Ninety-day dietary treatment of dogs was without effect at 125 mg kg^{-1} d^{-1} (5000 ppm), the highest dose rate tested.

Chronic toxicity tests were conducted concurrently with cancer bioassays at dietary concentrations of 0, 5, 25, 500, and 5000 ppm. The dose rate for rats was 0, 0.25, 1.25, 25, and 250 mg kg^{-1} d^{-1}, and for mice was 0, 0.75, 3.75, 75, and 750 mg kg^{-1} d^{-1}. The NOEL for rats was 25 mg kg^{-1} d^{-1}, based on weight loss at a tenfold higher dose. The systemic NOEL for mice was greater than 750 mg kg^{-1} d^{-1}, which caused no evidence of toxicity.

Reproductive toxicity

Metsulfuron methyl is not a reproductive or developmental toxicant at dose rates that can be tolerated by pregnant females. A two-generation rat reproduction study at dose rates up to 250 mg kg^{-1} d^{-1} resulted in no reproductive or fetal toxicity at any dose. There was evidence of maternal toxicity, however, in the form of lower body weight gains at the highest dose rate. The maternal NOEL was 25 mg kg^{-1} d^{-1}.

Teratogenicity (birth defects) assays were negative in rats at doses up to 1000 mg kg^{-1} d^{-1} through the period of greatest sensitivity. In rabbits, the NOEL for teratogenicity and fetal toxicity was greater than 700 mg kg^{-1} d^{-1}, but for maternal toxicity the NOEL was 25 mg kg^{-1} d^{-1}.

Mutagenicity and carcinogenicity

Mutagenicity assays of metsulfuron methyl have been generally negative Labat-Anderson, Inc. (undated). Vincent (1990) reports no effect on *in vitro* unscheduled DNA synthesis in primary rat hepatocytes at concentrations up to 3000 ug ml^{-1} (the limit of solubility). There was no cytotoxic effect. Vlachos (1984) also reports a negative mouse bone marrow micronucleus test in which the maximum dose was 5000 mg kg^{-1} by gavage. These findings indicate that metsulfuron methyl is not mutagenic.

Eighteen-month mouse and 24-month rat feeding studies showed no carcinogenic response. To date, there is no evidence to indicate carcinogenic activity with metsulfuron methyl. USEPA is considering the carcinogenicity group for this chemical, but has not made a ruling to date.

EXPOSURE ANALYSIS

Ingestion

Metsulfuron methyl is readily absorbed by plants and is extensively translocated throughout the plant. Plant metabolism is the dominant factor in dissipation in plants that are resistant to this herbicide. This means metsulfuron methyl residues will dissipate quickly from those species. Plants that are susceptible may retain the herbicide while they are alive, with residues remaining likely to be lost to soil and other decomposition factors after plant death. These factors are incorporated into the exposure analysis involving the ingestion of vegetation. In water, metsulfuron methyl dissipates primarily by dilution, although at pH values below 5.0, hydrolysis will reduce residue levels. Thus, dilution due to water movement is the dominant factor influencing human exposure through ingestion of water. Reports are not available on the behavior of this herbicide in animals, making an analysis of exposure through consumption of animals taken from treated areas less certain. However, metsulfuron methyl is quite soluble in water (9500 parts per million at pH 7.0 and 25°C), and has only very limited solubility in hexane (0.8 ppm at 20°C), meaning it will have very limited tendency to accumulate in animals. When exposure decreases or stops, imazapyr will clear rapidly from the body, meaning the potential for exposure is very limited by eating animals from treated areas.

Inhalation

There are no published data on metsulfuron methyl in air. It has a relatively low vapor pressure, meaning the tendency to vaporize is limited, limiting human exposure via inhalation to the period when spray droplets are suspended in air in locations where humans could inhale it.

Dermal exposure

There is no data on absorption of metsulfuron methyl across skin. Its solubility, however, indicates that skin absorption should be limited.

RISK ANALYSIS

Metsulfuron methyl (Escort®) presents a very low level of risk to the public in typical exposure scenarios. The margin of safety is greater than 10,000 in every case. For workers (applicators), the margins of safety are greater than 7000 in every instance for normal exposure scenarios. Because of the form of Escort®, there will be no spill in which the chemical can be absorbed by the skin. However, rigorous sanitation remains important to minimize ingestion while eating, drinking or smoking.

PICLORAM (TORDON K®) MOVEMENT, PERSISTENCE AND FATE IN THE ENVIRONMENT

Picloram is readily absorbed by plant roots and translocated throughout plant tissues. It is particularly prone to accumulate in new plant growth, where it is quite stable and remains largely intact. In animals, picloram does not bioaccumulate. Picloram that is ingested by animals is rapidly excreted unchanged, primarily in the urine.

Picloram is moderately to highly persistent in soil, with a half-life of approximately one month under highly favorable conditions of moisture, temperature, and organic conditions, and a half-life of more than four years in arid regions. It is a relatively mobile herbicide. The potassium salt and acid formulations of picloram are easily leached from sandy soil. Picloram, especially in salt formulations, is water-soluble and thus has a potential for runoff following heavy rainfall soon after applications where the soil infiltration capacity is low. Under such conditions, concentrations of 0.4–0.8 mg l^{-1} have been detected. However, studies have indicated that runoff accounts for less than 3% of the total quantity of picloram applied to soil where the soil surface has a relatively intact litter or organic layer, runoff has not been a problem. In most forested settings, we expect a soil half-life of 90 days and no detectable leaching below 30 cm. The movement, persistence and fate of picloram are reviewed in detail in Appendix A, USDA Forest Service (1997).

HAZARD ANALYSIS

Much of the information on the toxicology of picloram is unpublished registration data (USEPA, 1984), reviewed by USEPA Office of Drinking Water in a Health Advisory (USEPA, 1988) and the Reregistration Eligibility Decision (picloram) (USEPA, 1995b), and is discussed below without reference.

Acute toxicity

Acute toxicity is low, with an LD$_{50}$ range between 2000 and 4000 mg kg^{-1}. Doses of 400, 800, or 1600 mg kg^{-1} d^{-1} for seven days caused body weight loss at the two higher doses but no effects at 400 mg kg^{-1} d^{-1}. A similar evaluation in dogs indicated a NOEL of 200 mg kg^{-1} d^{-1}. In mice, the NOEL for a 30-day feeding exposure was 900 mg kg^{-1} d^{-1}.

Picloram formulations are not sensitizing in dermal exposure tests. Interestingly, a formulation of picloram and 2,4-D caused sensitization in several individuals, but neither is active alone.

Chronic toxicity

In feeding studies over three to six months, the predominant effect at high doses has been increased liver weight. The 13-week NOEL in rats was 50 mg kg^{-1} d^{-1}. The lowest dose administered to mice was 1000 mg kg^{-1} d^{-1}, so a NOEL was not found. A six-month feeding trial in dogs indicated NOEL of 7 mg kg^{-1} d^{-1}. EPA uses this figure as the overall NOEL for picloram (USEPA, 1995b).

Over a two-year feeding schedule of 0, 20, 60, or 200 mg kg^{-1} d^{-1}, liver effects, including histological changes, were evident at the two higher levels, but there was no effect at 20 mg kg^{-1} d^{-1}. Another rat study at 370 and 740 mg kg^{-1} d^{-1} showed evidence of thyroid hyperplasia and adenomas, parathyroid hyperplasia and testicular atrophy. Apparently, the lower dose was not a NOEL.

Reproductive toxicity

In a three-generation, two-litter reproduction assay, at daily doses of 0, 7.5, 25, or 75 mg kg^{-1}, there was reduced fertility in the second litter of the first generation at the highest dose level, but apparently no effects in other segments at that dose. On the basis of that finding, the NOEL was considered to be 25 mg kg^{-1} d^{-1}. The third litters from each generation were examined for birth defects; none was found at any dose level.

In a later study with larger numbers of rats, fetal and maternal toxicity was substantial at dose rates of 750 and 1000 mg kg^{-1} d^{-1}, and there was some evidence of toxicity at 500 mg kg^{-1} d^{-1}, the lowest level studied. There was no evidence of teratogenic effect. A rabbit teratology study was reported to have shown no fetotoxic or teratogenic response at doses up to 400 mg kg^{-1} d^{-1} (John-Greene et al., 1985).

Mutagenicity and carcinogenicity

Picloram has been generally negative in mutagenicity assays, but a forward mutation test with Streptomyces coelicolor was positive (USEPA, 1988).

Carcinogenicity assays of picloram have been negative. A study in rats by the National Cancer Institute (NCI) suggested a weakly positive response but the assay was found to have been compromised and was repeated by the registrant. The highest dose was 200 mg kg^{-1} d^{-1} over two years and was negative (Stott et al., 1990). A mouse study by NCI at high daily doses for males of 417 mg kg^{-1} and for females of 723 mg kg^{-1} was negative. Picloram has been placed in carcinogenicity Group E "Evidence of non-carcinogenicity in humans" (USEPA, 1988).

EXPOSURE ANALYSIS

Ingestion

Picloram is readily absorbed by plant roots, but less well by foliage. Once absorbed, it is translocated throughout the plant. It undergoes little decomposition in the plant, and thus initial internal plant residues are likely to continue to be available to animals through ingestion for as long as the vegetation remains palatable. This pattern is incorporated into the exposure analysis. In water, both dilution and photodegradation increasingly limit exposure by ingestion. Picloram is both persistent and mobile in soil, resulting in an increased potential for a longer period of entry to water through leaching or runoff, and thus an increased opportunity for exposure by ingestion of water. In animals, picloram clears the body very rapidly (97%), primarily in urine. There is little tendency to accumulate in body tissues (none detectable after 12 h), so the opportunity for human exposure via ingestion of animals from treated areas is low (USDA Forest Service, 1984).

Inhalation

Picloram has no substantive vapor pressure, thus exposure via inhalation is limited to the period when spray droplets may be in air shortly after application.

Dermal exposure

Based on its physical properties, there is little tendency for picloram to transfer to and be absorbed through the skin. The dermal exposure scenario is limited to the period of time when humans would be in or near areas being treated with picloram.

RISK ANALYSIS

Picloram (Tordon K®) provides margins of safety greater than 10,000 in every case. For workers (applicators), the margins of safety are greater than 7000 in every instance for normal exposure scenarios. In a worst-case scenario, the direct spill of herbicide concentrate on the skin the margin of safety is 14, which is significantly less than 100, emphasizing the importance of careful handling, the use of protective gear and rigorous sanitation.

TRICLOPYR (GARLON 3A® AND GARLON 4®) MOVEMENT, PERSISTENCE AND FATE IN THE ENVIRONMENT

Triclopyr is absorbed by both plant leaves and roots and is readily translocated. It appears to interfere with normal plant growth processes. It is rapidly absorbed by animals and subsequently completely excreted by the kidney, mostly in an unmetabolized form. Triclopyr does not bioaccumulate in fish.

In soil, triclopyr does not strongly adsorb and is potentially mobile. It is rapidly degraded by microorganisms and has a short persistence in soil environments. Rapid photo degradation is the major means by which triclopyr is degraded in aquatic environments. The movement, persistence and fate of triclopyr are reviewed in detail in Appendix A, USDA Forest Service (1997).

HAZARD ANALYSIS

Much of the information on the toxicology of triclopyr is unpublished registration data, reviewed in USDA Forest Service (1984), Syracuse (1996a) and in a summary of toxicological studies provided by Dow Chemical Co. (1988) (now DowElanco) under confidentiality agreements. Later unpublished registration data and published reports are specifically referenced.

Acute toxicity

The oral LD_{50} of triclopyr acid is just over 700 mg kg^{-1} in rats and 300 mg kg^{-1} in rabbits. In dermal toxicity tests with the rabbit, doses of 2000 mg kg^{-1} caused some short-term weight loss but no mortality. Undiluted technical triclopyr caused modest eye irritation, but the condition persisted for more than seven days. Eye washing immediately was shown to mitigate the injury. Triclopyr acid is not a primary skin irritant. Exposure to the highest concentration aerosol that could be produced, 1.84 g M^{-3}, caused transient eye irritation and no other adverse effects.

Acute oral LD_{50} of the butoxyethyl ester formulation, Garlon 4®, was in excess of 2000 mg kg^{-1}. There were various non-specific signs of toxicity in survivors, but no weight loss. Application of almost 4000 mg Garlon 4® kg^{-1} to shaved areas of the skin of rabbits and bandaged in place for 24 h caused edema, irritation and some cell damage, with transient loss. No other evidence of systemic toxicity appeared. Inhalation of aerosols containing 0.82 g formulation M^{-3} (maximum practicable) was without effect other than nasal irritation. Repeated application of undiluted formulation was moderately irritating, but the formulation is not a skin-sensitizing agent.

The triethylamine salt of triclopyr (Garlon 3A®) is also of limited acute toxicity. Oral LD_{50}s in rats were in excess of 2000 mg kg^{-1}. The dermal lethal dose after 24 h of contact is known only to be in excess of 3980 mg kg^{-1}, as no animals on test died. Aerosol exposure at a concentration of 5.34 g M^{-3} for one hour produced no response. The triethylamine salt is a moderate skin irritant, and is considered hazardous to the eyes on the basis of severe conjunctivitis and corneal injury. It is not a skin-sensitizing agent.

Chronic toxicity

A thirteen-week feeding study of rats at daily doses of 0, 3, 10, 30, or 100 mg kg^{-1} produced no effects in males at 30 mg kg^{-1} d^{-1} and no effects in females at 100 mg kg^{-1} d^{-1}. The animals were subjected to complete clinical biochemistry, hematology, urinalysis, and pathological examination. In a subsequent study at daily doses of 0, 5, 20, 50, or 250 mg kg^{-1}, there were dose-related changes in the kidney tubules; males were more sensitive than females, and the NOEL was 5 mg kg^{-1} d^{-1}. There were moderate liver effects at the highest dose level that may have been adaptive changes.

Beagle dogs were maintained for 288 days at dose levels of 0, 5, 10, or 20 mg kg^{-1} d^{-1}. At all dose rates, females lost weight relative to controls. Weights of males were less affected. Clinical biochemistry findings suggested marginal liver and kidney toxicity. While changes were of modest extent, some deviation from controls was seen at all dose levels, which precluded setting of a NOEL.

A similar study at dose rates of 0, 0.1, 0.5, and 2.5 mg kg^{-1} d^{-1} led to a conclusion that the NOEL is 0.5 mg kg^{-1} d^{-1}. It is likely that the apparent sensitivity of the dog to triclopyr is a function of the much lower capacity for renal excretion of organic acids by this species. A USEPA Peer Review Committee has concluded that in the case of triclopyr, the dog is not the appropriate animal model for kidney effects (USEPA, 1996).

A dietary chronic toxicity assay in rats provided daily doses of 0, 3, 12, or 36 mg kg^{-1} over a two-year period. Full clinical and pathology examinations disclosed minor differences in pigmentation of kidney tubules and increased kidney weights. The NOEL was 3 mg kg^{-1} d^{-1}.

Reproductive toxicity

A three-generation single-litter reproduction test in rats at doses of 3, 10, or 30 mg kg^{-1} d^{-1} did not cause decreases in fertility, litter size or neonatal survival. A reduction in body weights at weaning for the second generation, but not the first or third, was seen. The NOEL was determined to be in excess of 30 mg kg^{-1} d^{-1}. In a more recent reproductive toxicity study in rats, the NOEL was established as 5 mg kg^{-1} d^{-1}. As a result of a recent decision by USEPA, the NOEL of 5 mg kg^{-1} d^{-1} is to be used for systemic risk assessment, a ten-fold increase over the prior figure (USEPA, 1996).

Teratogenicity in rabbits was assessed at daily doses of 0, 10, or 25 mg kg^{-1} through days 6–18 of gestation. Triclopyr was not teratogenic at any dose, but a NOEL for maternal toxicity could not be determined. A following study established a NOEL for fetal toxicity of 75 mg kg^{-1} d^{-1}, and a maternal NOEL of 50 mg kg^{-1} d^{-1}. A similar study in rats produced fetal toxicity at daily doses of 200 mg kg^{-1}, and no effect at 100 mg kg^{-1} d^{-1}.

Mutagenicity and carcinogenicity

Mutagenic assays of triclopyr have been reviewed by Dow Chemical Co. (1988) and Syracuse (1996a).

Triclopyr was not mutagenic in Ames tests. A host-mediated assay in the mouse with three bacterial strains was negative. A bone marrow cytogenetic test for chromosome damage in rats at doses up to 70 mg kg^{-1} d^{-1} for five days, and mouse bone marrow micronucleus test at a maximum single dose of 270 mg kg^{-1} were also negative.

A dominant lethal assay in rats given doses up to 70 mg kg^{-1} d^{-1} for five days showed weak evidence of an effect in the fourth and fifth week. A later similar test in mice was negative. Triclopyr does not induce unscheduled DNA synthesis, indicating that DNA repair is not required after intoxication.

Triclopyr is not considered to be carcinogenic on the basis of three assays. A combined chronic carcinogenicity assay in rats utilized daily intakes of 3, 12, or 36 mg kg^{-1} d^{-1}. There was a small apparent increase in combined mammary adenomas and adenocarcinomas in the high dose females, compared to the control animals for this experiment. However, the incidence in those control animals was zero, which was at variance with historical controls of that strain. Incidence in the treated groups was not different from the historical incidence in untreated rats of that strain. Other cancer biology information also suggests that the finding was an anomaly.

Two mouse studies have been done. The first employed approximately 0, 3, 10, and 30 mg kg^{-1} d^{-1}. The conclusion of the pathologist was that no carcinogenic response was shown. Curiously, survival was highest in the high dose group. Because of questions raised by the original mouse observations, another assay was conducted at dose rates of about 6, 31, and 156 mg kg^{-1} d^{-1}. There was no evidence for a carcinogenic effect.

Triclopyr is presently classified as Group D "not classifiable as to human carcinogenicity." This classification is unclear, because USEPA has stated that in both the mouse and rat cancer assays there were "no carcinogenic effects observed under the conditions of the study" (Federal Register 60:4093-4095, Jan. 20, 1995). All other experimental findings are also consistent with an absence of carcinogenic or mutagenic potential. Syracuse (1996a) concludes none of the cancer studies are adequate to support a quantitative risk assessment for carcinogenicity.

EXPOSURE ANALYSIS

Ingestion

Triclopyr is readily absorbed and translocated throughout the plant. Field studies show residue levels decrease with time, meaning the opportunities for exposure via ingestion of treated vegetation decreases with time as well. Triclopyr residue data are available for foliage and berries, meaning the basis for exposure analysis due to ingestion of vegetation is good. In animals, triclopyr is rapidly absorbed but also rapidly excreted via the kidneys. This data provides a good basis for estimating human exposure via consumption of animals that have been in treated areas.

Inhalation

Triclopyr is more volatile in the ester form (Garlon 4®) than in the amine form (Garlon 3A®), but the ester form is rapidly hydrolyzed. Both forms are converted rapidly to a neutral salt when they are in the environment. Thus, volatilization of either form is not expected to result in appreciable human exposure via inhalation. The inhalation exposure scenario is limited to the period of time spray droplets may be in air after application.

Dermal exposure

The physical properties of triclopyr amine (Garlon 3A®) will largely preclude its absorption through the skin. The ester form will be more likely to penetrate the skin, but it exists for only a short period of time in the environment as the ester due to hydrolysis. Thus, the exposure scenario for dermal exposure is limited to the period of time when spray droplets are likely to be in the air in or near the treated areas.

RISK ANALYSIS

The risk analysis for the general public shows triclopyr in either formulation has margins of safety greater than 10,000 for typical exposure scenarios. The results for workers are similar but show some minor differences between formulations. Garlon 3A® provides margins of safety that range from 2500 to 6500 in typical exposure scenarios, while the margin of safety for Garlon 4® is 3500 for the type of application included in the EIS. In the case of a spill of the concentrate on the skin, the margin of safety for workers is much less than 100, being 3 for Garlon 3A® and 4 for Garlon 4®. Careful attention to sanitation, the use of protective gear and careful handling procedures can eliminate this risk.

TOXICITY OF FORMULATED HERBICIDES AND BIOACUMULATION

Much of the toxicity testing is done with the active ingredient of commercial herbicide formulations, and there is often concern that the commercial product may differ significantly in its effect on non-target organisms. USEPA requires acute toxicity data for formulated products, which permits evaluation of the acute toxicity of the pesticide formulations' inert ingredients. Table 4 compares various toxicity findings for active ingredients and their full formulations. It shows that the

Table 4. Comparison of acute toxicities of active ingredient and formulation[1]

Herbicide	Technical grade acute oral LD_{50} values for rats	Formulation acute oral LD_{50} values for rats
Imazapyr	Acute oral LD_{50}, rat >5000 mg kg^{-1}	Arsenal® 5000 mg kg^{-1}
Fosamine	>5000 mg kg^{-1}	Krenite® 24,400 mg kg^{-1} (USDA, 1984) Krenite® >5000 mg kg^{-1} (USDA, 1984)
Glyphosate, IPA	4320 mg kg^{-1} (EPA, 1986)	Accord® >5000 mg kg^{-1}
Imazapyr	>5000 mg kg^{-1} (EPA, 1985)	Arsenal® >5000 mg kg^{-1} (Weeks et al., 1988)
Picloram	8200 mg kg^{-1} (EPA, 1984c)	Tordon® K- 8440 mg kg^{-1}
Triclopyr	Acute oral LD_{50}, rat (F) 630 mg kg^{-1} Acute oral LD_{50}, rat (M) 729 mg kg^{-1}	Garlon 3A® 1087 mg kg^{-1} (F) Garlon 3A® 2574 mg kg^{-1} (M) Garlon 4® 2140 mg kg^{-1} (F) Garlon 4® 2830 mg kg^{-1} (M)
Metsulfuron methyl	>5000 mg kg^{-1}	Escort® >5000 mg kg^{-1}

[1] From Table 15 Appendix A, USDA Forest Service, 1997.

formulations are less acutely toxic than their active ingredient.

Bioaccumulation is the tendency of a chemical to be retained and concentrate in body tissues. If bioaccumulation occurs to a significant degree, the potential for biomagnification in the food chain increases. These are the characteristics that caused serious problems with many of the early insecticides, such as DDT.

None of the herbicides reviewed in this paper show significant tendency to bioaccumulate. This reflects their high water solubility and low solubility in fat. While organisms will show measurable levels of these herbicides during the time they are actively exposed, the concentration will not be greater than the substrate from which they receive the exposure, and as exposure decreases or stops, rapid elimination occurs (Table 5).

WATER QUALITY CRITERIA

Unfortunately, there are no water quality standards for any of the herbicides included in the EIS, hence there is no established basis for judging the protection of water quality. In the absence of standards, we used USEPA procedures to identify the levels of each herbicide that could be in the water without harming aquatic species or other organisms likely to use the water. These are called water quality protection criteria, and are the "standard" against which water quality protection was judged in the Allegheny National Forest project (Table 6). The toxicological bases on which these criteria

Table 5. Elimination rates of the chemicals[1]

Chemical	Test animal	Elimination rate
Fosamine	Rat	99–100% within 72 h (USDA, 1984)
Glyphosate	Rabbit	92% within 5 days (USDA, 1984)
	Rat	94% within 5 days
Imazapyr	Rat	87% within 24 h (American Cyanamid, 1985)
Metsulfuron methyl	Rat	90% in 72 h; excretion half-life was 9–16 h for low dose
Picloram	Human	75% in 6 h, half time for remainder 27 h (Nolan et al., 1984)
	Dog	90% within 48 h (USDA, 1984)

[1] From Table 12, Appendix A, USDA Forest Service, 1997.

Table 6. Water Quality Protection Criteria[1]

Herbicide	Water quality[2] (mg l^{-1})	Inspection[3] (mg l^{-1})
Picloram	0.07	0.03
Fosamine ammonium	1.0	0.5
Glyphosate	0.7	0.3
Triclopyr amine	0.5	0.2
Imazapyr	5.0	2.0
Metsulfuron methyl	6.9	3.0

[1] From Table 2, Chapter V, USDA Forest Service, 1997.
[2] Provides protection for organisms that live in or consume the water.
[3] The maximum level of water contamination that might occur if the label directions and good practice are followed. Exceeding this criterion results in inspection of the operation and the site to determine the reason the criterion was exceeded, and future practice adjusted accordingly.

are based are in Appendix C of the EIS (USDA Forest Service, 1997).

The water quality protection criteria will protect aquatic species and water users, but in our experience represent a higher level of water contamination than should normally occur if current standards of "good practice" are used. Therefore, we identified an "inspection criterion" for each chemical (Table 6). This is the level of water contamination that should be easily avoided with normal careful practice. The purpose of this criterion was to prompt a careful on-site inspection to determine what "went wrong" if water-monitoring data showed the inspection criterion has been exceeded.

MITIGATION MEASURES

The EIS also identified sensitive sites such as wetlands, streams, houses, wells, road and recreational trail crossings, and visually sensitive travel ways. Mitigation measures were developed to provide protection of these sites. These measures included signage containing specific information about the application posted 30 days in advance around areas to be treated to permit the public to make an informed decision about entering an area that has been treated. No herbicide applications except by the cut surface method (with glyphosate) were permitted within 100 feet of houses or recreational trail crossings. For visually sensitive areas and road crossings, only cut surface or low volume basal is permitted, and if low volume basal is used, dead material must be cut and scattered before the Memorial Day weekend.

Buffers were an important mitigation measure used to achieve protection of water quality. These included (a) no herbicide use within 10 feet of water, (b) the use of cut stump applications within 10 feet of intermittent streams, (c) no high volume herbicide within 75 feet of water, (d) no picloram or triclopyr within 75 feet of water, (e) only cut-surface applications (glyphosate) were permitted in wetlands, (f) no-spray buffers were used to protect other sensitive sites, and (g) only cut-surface application (glyphosate) was permitted within 100 feet of wells and springs that are a domestic water supply.

STREAM BUFFER EFFECTIVENESS

We monitored the buffer effectiveness around streams each year by two methods. In one method, water samples were collected and analyzed before and after application and after the first rain, and in the second method, stream buffers were visually inspected for signs of herbicide damage which would indicate entry of herbicide into the buffer area. Automatic water sampling equipment was used and composite samples were gathered to reduce the cost.

Water monitoring

Monitoring the water for herbicide residues is a direct method of evaluating the effectiveness of the buffer strategy. ISCO automatic water samplers were installed downstream but relatively close to the ROW where the herbicide will be applied and a short distance upstream from the area. The latter is to detect herbicide in the surface water that is not from the ROW treatment (serves as a control). The samplers were operated on a 24-day cycle (one sample per day, composed of four or more separate "pumpings" to get an average daily sample).

The following samples from the down-stream sites were sent for chemical analysis:
– one sample collected during a 24-h period ending at least 24 h before any herbicide application,
– one sample for the first 24-h period immediately following the application (day 1),
– one sample for the next 24-h period (day 2),
– one sample composed of equal parts of three of the 24-h samples collected over the next 72-h (days 3, 4, and 5),

- one sample for the first 24-h period within which more than 0.25 inches of rain falls, and
- one sample for the next 24-h period following 0.25 inches of rain.

If herbicide is detected in any of the samples from the downstream sampler, a composite sample for the same time period from the upstream control sampler is sent to determine if the source of the herbicide is from the ROW treatment or from a different source upstream.

Water sampling results

Careful analysis of samples showed no detectable herbicide. If herbicide had been detected, the concentration would be compared to the water quality criterion (Table 6). If the concentration was less than the criterion, then the water quality protection goal had been achieved. If not and a composite sample is involved, analysis of the individual components of the composite are done to characterize the pattern of contamination. If the concentration exceeds the "inspection criterion", an on-site evaluation is done to determine why, since it is our experience that the inspection criterion should normally be easily attained when instructions on the label are followed and "good practice" is used. The results of the water quality monitoring program are used to adjust the application procedures and the mitigation measures if needed.

Buffer strip monitoring

We visually monitored the vegetation for signs of herbicide damage in the 10-foot portion of the buffer closest to the water at 34 locations. The condition of the vegetation in this portion of the buffer was rated on a damage scale of 1–5 at the water's edge, in the middle of the zone and at a point 10 feet from the water's edge. Herbicide damage is easily detected by an experienced observer, and indicated incursion of herbicide into the buffer zone.

We used the following criteria in evaluating the effectiveness of the buffer in achieving water quality protection goals:
- Buffers with less than 25% of the area closest to the water (within 3 feet) in a damage class of 2 or less are considered to be effective in achieving water quality objectives.
- Buffers with less than 25% of the middle zone (4–6 feet from the water's edge) in damage class 3 or less are considered to be effective in achieving water quality protection objectives.
- Buffers with less than 50% of the far edge (8–10 feet from the water's edge) in damage class 4 or less are considered to be effective in achieving water quality protection objectives.
- After the visual inspection of 34 buffers, there was only one point of minor vegetation damage found.
- Based on both the water sampling and the visual inspection of buffer zones we conclude that the buffers worked. Water quality was protected, and the integrity of riparian buffers was maintained.

CONCLUSIONS

The development of the EIS and return to use of herbicides on the Allegheny National Forest is a success. Specifically (a) the utilities were able to resume the use of herbicides with no adverse effects measured, (b) the local officials of the Allegheny National Forest observed the professional and responsible approach taken by utilities to the management of tall-growing vegetation on ROW, (c) the utilities gained experience in working with USDA Forest Service officials and the National Environmental Protection Act, and (d) the public was involved with the decision process and was able to see the detail and the technical base for vegetation management on electric utility ROW.

The EIS is a valuable technical document for those considering the use of fosamine ammonium (Krenite UT®), glyphosate (Accord®), imazapyr (Arsenal®), metsulfuron methyl (Escort®), picloram (Tordon K®) or triclopyr (Garlon 3A® and Garlon 4®).

The human health risk analysis shows there is a significant margin of safety for each of these chemicals when used in the manner proposed. The greatest risk to the public is from ingestion of berries shortly after treatment, but even this provides a margin of safety far greater than that used for regulatory purposes. The greatest risk to applicators is from the spill of herbicide concentrate directly on the skin with no subsequent clean up. In this scenario the margins of safety are below 100 in every case, emphasizing the importance of careful handling so that spills don't occur, the use of protective gear to shield the skin if a spill does occur, and rigorous sanitation to remove the material from the skin promptly. With these mitigation measures, the level of protection for workers is satisfactory.

REFERENCES

Alvarez, L. 1992. Developmental toxicity study of DPX-R1 108-100 to rats. DuPont Proprietary Report HLR 43-92.

American Cyanamid Company. 1985. Arsenal® herbicides for brush control and forest management. Agricultural Research Division. Princeton, New Jersey. 12 pp.

Brock, W.J. 1987. Primary eye irritation study with IN T6376-41 in rabbits. DuPont Proprietary Report HLR 630-87.

Christoph, G.R. 1993a. Acute neurotoxicity study of DPX-RI 108-100 (fosamine ammonium) in rats. DuPont Proprietary Report HLR 431-93.

Christoph, G.R. 1993b. Subchronic neurotoxicity study of DPX-R1 108-100 (fosamine ammonium) in rats. DuPont Proprietary Report HLR 438-93.

Dow Chemical Company (North American Agricultural Products Department). 1988. Summary of toxicological studies on triclopyr (3,5,6-trichloro-2-pyridinyloxyacetic acid).

DuPont Chemical Company. 1983. Technical data sheet for fosamine ammonium. Biochemicals Department. Wilmington, DE. 5 pp.

Fletcher, D.V. 1993. 21-day acute delayed neurotoxicity study in mature white leghorn hens. DuPont Proprietary Report HLR 434-93.

John-Greene, J.A., J.H. Ouellette, T.K. Jeffries, K.A. Johnson, and K.S. Rao. 1985. Teratological evaluation of picloram potassium salts in rabbits. Food Chemistry and Toxicology, 23(8): 753–756.

Kaplan, A.M. 1993. Subchronic oral toxicity: Six-month study with DPX-R1 108-100 (fosamine ammonium) feeding study in dogs; revision 1. DuPont Proprietary Report HLR 406-78; Rev. 1.

Labat-Anderson. ND (not dated). Metsulfuron methyl: A review of its toxic properties and environmental fate characteristics. Undated report by Labat-Anderson, Incorporated, 2200 Clarendon Boulevard, Suite 900, Arlington VA 22201. 12 pp.

Li, A.P. and T.J. Long. 1988. An evaluation of the genotoxic potential of glyphosate. Fund. Appl. Toxicol., 10: 537–546.

Mackenzie, S.A. 1991. Repeated dose dermal toxicity; 21-day study with DPX-R1 108-100 (fosamine ammonium) in rabbits. DuPont Proprietary Report HLR 431-91.

Mackenzie, S.A. 1993. Cholinesterase inhibition study with DPX-R1 108-100 (fosamine ammonium) in rats. DuPont Proprietary Report HLR 599-93.

Monsanto. 1983. Rodeo® Herbicide Bulletin No. 1, January. Monsanto Company, St. Louis, MO.

Norris, L.A. 1999. ROW on federal lands and NEPA. UAA Quarterly, winter 1999. Vol. 8. No. 2. pp. 1–5.

Norris, L.A. 2000. Returning to herbicide use on the Allegheny National Forest. UAA Quarterly, spring 2000. Vol. 8. No. 3. pp. 1–5.

Rank, J., A.G. Jensen, B. Skov, L.H. Pederson, and K. Jensen. 1993. Genotoxicity testing of the herbicide Roundup® and its active ingredient glyphosate isopropylamine using the mouse bone marrow micronucleus test, Salmonella mutagenicity test, and Allium anaphase telephase test. Mutation Res., 300: 29–36.

Reynolds, V.L. 1991. Mutagenicity testing of DPX-R1 108-100 (fosamine ammonium) in the Salmonella typhimurium plate incorporation assay. DuPont Proprietary Report HLR 221-91.

Sarver, J.W. 1987. Repeated dose dermal toxicity: 21-day study with IN T6376 in rabbits. DuPont Proprietary Report HLR 35-87.

Stott, W.T., K.A. Johnson, T.D. Landry, S.J. Gorzinski, and F.S. Cieziak. 1990. Chronic toxicity and oncogenicity of picloram in Fischer 344 rats. Jour. Toxicol. Envir. Health, 30: 91–104.

Syracuse. 1996a. Selected commercial formulations of triclopyr — Garlon 3A® and Garlon 4® risk assessment final report. Syracuse Environmental Research Associates, Inc., Fayetteville, NY and Syracuse Research Corporation, Syracuse NY. March 31, 1996.

Syracuse. 1996b. Selected commercial formulations of glyphosate — Accord®, Rodeo®, Roundup® and Roundup Pro® risk assessment final report. Syracuse Environmental Research Associates, Inc. Fayetteville, NY and Syracuse Research Corporation, Syracuse NY. June 30, 1996.

USDA Forest Service. 1984. Pesticide Background Statements. Volume 1, Herbicides. Agricultural Handbook 633. Washington, DC.

USDA Forest Service. 1989. Final Environmental Impact Statement Vegetation Management in the Coastal Plan/Piedmont, Volumes and III. February 1989. Atlanta, GA.

USDA Forest Service. 1997. Final Environmental Impact Statement, Vegetation Management on Electric Utility Rights-Of-Way. Allegheny National Forest, Warren PA. 187 pp. plus appendices.

USEPA Office of Pesticides and Toxic Substances. 1984. Summary of results of studies submitted in support of the registration of picloram. Washington, DC.

USEPA. 1985. Pesticide Fact Sheet: Imazapyr. Fact Sheet Number 63. Issued September 5, 1985. Washington, DC. 5 pp.

USEPA Office of Pesticides and Toxic Substances. 1986. Summary of results of studies submitted in support of the registration of triclopyr. Washington, DC.

USEPA. 1988. Picloram. Health Advisory, Office of Drinking Water.

USEPA. 1993. Reregistration Eligibility Decision Document: Glyphosate. EPA 738-R-93-014.

USEPA. 1995a. Memorandum from W. Dykstra and E. Rinde, Health Effects Division, USEPA to R. Taylor, Registration Division and K. Davis, Special Review and Reregistration Division, USEPA. October 3, 1995.

USEPA. 1995b. Office of Prevention, Pesticides and Toxic Substances (1995). Reregistration Eligibility Document (RED). Picloram.

USEPA. 1996. Memorandum from R.J. Taylor, US Environmental Protection Agency, Office of Pesticides and Toxic Substances to S.A. McMaster, Dow Elanco.

Vincent, D.R. 1990. Assessment of IN T6376-74 in the in vitro unscheduled DNA synthesis assay in primary rat hepatocytes. DuPont Proprietary Report HLR 574-90.

Vlachos, D.A. 1984. Mouse bone marrow micronucleus assay of IN T6376-22; revision. DuPont Proprietary Report HLR 433-84.

Weeks, J.A., G.H. Drendel, R.S. Jagan, T.E. McManus, and P.J. Sczerzenie. 1988. Imazapyr Background Statement. Report prepared for USDA Forest Service, Washington DC.

BIOGRAPHICAL SKETCHES

Logan A. Norris
Oregon State University and Environmental Consultants, Inc., 4045 NW Dale Place, Corvallis, OR 97330, USA, Phone 541/737-6557, FAX 541/737-5814, E-mail: logan.norris@orst.edu

Logan Norris is Professor and Department Head, Emeritus, Department of Forest Science, Oregon State University. He also served on the Board of Governors of Environmental Consultants, Incorporated. Since the early 1960's he has been active in research involving the movement, persistence, and fate of herbicides, and with the health and environmental risks associated with their use. His work focuses on forested settings, including rights-of-way.

Frank Dost
Environmental Consultants, Inc., 5944 Sundown Lane, Freeland, WA 98249, USA

Frank Dost is Professor, Emeritus, Department Environmental and Molecular Toxicology, Oregon State University. His specialization is toxicology. He has focused on exposure and human health risk assessments for workers and the general public as it relates to the use of herbicides and other chemicals in forestry, agriculture and in rights-of-way management.

Rufin VanBossuyt, Jr.
Environmental Consultants, Inc., 125 Westboro Road, Upton, MA 01568, USA

Rufin VanBossuyt was System Forester, New England Electric until his retirement in 1993. He also served on the Board of Governors of Environmental Consultants, Incorporated. Long active in ISA and the Utility Arborists Association, he received the Lifetime Achievement Award for his leadership in the management of electric utility rights-of-way.

Chondrostereum purpureum: An Alternative to Chemical Herbicide Brush Control

Paul Y. de la Bastide,[1] Hong Zhu, Gwen Shrimpton, Simon F. Shamoun, and William E. Hintz

Fast-growing hardwood species pose a hazard to power lines, hence hydroelectric companies must ensure that rights-of-way are kept clear of trees in order to maintain uninterrupted power service. Many of these species propagate by resprouting from cut stumps. The application of chemical herbicides to the cut stumps has proven to be effective in suppressing resprouting, however, herbicide use is increasingly encountering public opposition. Where herbicide use is prohibited, the lack of stump treatment quickly leads to extremely high stem densities. The fungus Chondrostereum purpureum provides an attractive alternative to chemical herbicide use in industrial vegetation management. Living cultures of C. purpureum are placed on cut stumps in a formulation that will protect the fungus from desiccation and UV irradiation, as well as provide nutrients for establishment. The fungus invades the lower stem and prevents resprouting by killing adventitious shoots or branches. We have been working towards the development of new application technologies to better integrate this biocontrol into operational trials. We have optimized a two-phase fermentation process that is capable of producing viable mycelial biomass with a minimum titer of 1×10^7 cfu kg^{-1} of solid substrate (active ingredient). A newly formulated C. purpureum has been field tested in the Nanaimo Lakes region of Vancouver Island.

Keywords: Biocontrol agent, mycoherbicide, basidiomycete, riparian zone, integrated vegetation management

INTRODUCTION

On productive forestlands in Canada, over 400,000 ha of burned or logged forestlands are planted to tree seedlings every year to ensure softwood production. Prior to planting, over 300,000 ha annually require some type of site preparation (e.g., mechanical brush removal, scarification, or chemical herbicide treatment). In addition, nearly 400,000 ha annually of plantations and young naturally regenerated stands receive some form of stand tending (e.g., weeding, cleaning, pre-commercial thinning) to reduce the impact of competing vegetation on productivity (Statistics Canada, 1996–1997; Natural Resources Canada, 1996). In addition to forested lands, there are other areas where the control of weed trees and brush is required, including industrial rights-of-way, industrial parks, military ranges and roadsides. In British Columbia alone, there are 73,000 km of hydroelectric rights-of-way that require regular maintenance, including the removal and suppression of interfering tree growth (BC Hydro and Power Authority, 1996). Vegetation management is therefore an essential component of effective forest resource management.

Much of the vegetation that requires control in both forestry and right-of-way management consists of deciduous hardwood trees, such as alder (*Alnus* spp.), birch (*Betula* spp.), maple (*Acer* spp.), and poplar (*Populus* spp.) species. On forested lands, these fast growing species suppress the more economically desirable softwood species that are the foundation of our lumber and pulpwood industries (MacLean and Morgan, 1982; Haeuschler and Coates, 1986; Smith, 1988). They

---

[1] Corresponding author (Fax: 250-721-7120, e-mail address: pdelabas@uvic.ca).

Environmental Concerns in Rights-of-Way
Management: Seventh International Symposium
J.W. Goodrich-Mahoney, D.F. Mutrie and C.A. Guild (editors)
© 2002 Elsevier Science Ltd. All rights reserved.

are also the most likely species to interfere with electrical power transmission on power line rights-of-way. Although some hardwoods are increasing in importance as crop species, their control remains necessary in softwood plantations, naturally regenerating conifer forests and in industrial rights-of-way (Cuthbert, 1991; Peterson and Peterson, 1992; Peterson et al., 1996). In order to both control and utilize these species, sometimes on the same sites, selective control agents with minimal non-target effects are essential.

Control of hardwood species in forests and industrial rights-of-way in Canada and adjacent regions of the US presents several problems. The weed species are often native pioneer species that normally occupy disturbed sites and are essential components of the forest ecosystem. It is not always necessary or desirable to completely eliminate these tree species from the site. There exist several options for hardwood weed control, namely mechanical removal, use of fire, manual cutting, and application of herbicides. The relative merit of each method depends on the site conditions and the objective of the weed control program.

Mechanical brush control is less expensive than other methods, but can contribute to soil erosion, may favour the regrowth of weed vegetation and limit natural regeneration of crop tree species. Prescribed burns can control weed vegetation regrowth when an adequate fuel load is present, or be employed subsequent to herbicide application. However, burns may also contribute to soil erosion, favor recolonization by weed vegetation, and destroy natural regeneration of crop species. The manual cutting of hardwoods is more selective than mechanical treatment or fire. It allows the natural regeneration of crop trees and limits soil erosion. However, it is a more labor intensive and hence an expensive method of control. In addition, most hardwoods re-sprout vigorously after cutting, producing a hardwood cover that is often more dense than the original (D'Anjou, 1990). In spite of the disadvantages, manual brushing is practiced widely (Canadian Council of Forest Ministers, 1993). Much research has been devoted to improve methods and timing of manual brushing in Canada and elsewhere (Harrington, 1984; Johansson, 1987; Pendl and D'Anjou, 1990).

Chemical herbicide use is the most common solution to vegetation control in Canadian forestry (Canadian Council of Forest Ministers, 1993) and on industrial rights-of way. Glyphosate (e.g., Roundup™ and Carbopaste™) is the most widely used chemical herbicide in Canadian forestry (Campbell, 1990) and is generally considered the most effective against the major forest brush species in BC (Coates and Haeussler, 1986). Herbicide use is favoured for a number of reasons; they may be applied to large areas within a short time, they can be selective, or broad spectrum, and can therefore be used for site preparation prior to planting, as well as for conifer release in established plantations (Malik and Vanden Born, 1986; Campbell, 1990). Chemical herbicides have one major disadvantage; the risk of contamination of soils, water courses, vegetation, and fauna. In some cases this risk is real and in others it is questionable, but the net effects of these perceptions of risk are increasingly stringent restrictions on herbicide use and a renewed search for environmentally acceptable alternatives (Conway-Brown, 1984; Halleran, 1990). Such restrictions also discourage the development and registration of new and better herbicides (Campbell, 1991). Restrictions on aerial spraying has led to increased use of manual stem injection, foliar sprays using vehicle mounted sprayers, or backpack sprayers, and stump treatments for the application of herbicides. A lack of permissible broadcast treatments means that weed control must become more selective, while maintaining/increasing environmental and worker safety.

BIOLOGICAL CONTROL AND CHONDROSTEREUM PURPUREUM

An alternative to the use of chemical herbicides is the application of natural pathogens of weed species to obtain a biological control of vegetation. Biological control is defined as the deliberate use of one or more organisms to suppress the growth or reduce the population of another organism to a level where it is no longer an economic problem (Hawksworth et al., 1995; Templeton et al., 1979). The preferred control organism is a native species that has been thoroughly characterized and is easily employed as an inundative control strategy. The inundative method of biocontrol involves single or multiple applications of sufficiently high levels of the control agent to the weed population, under conditions that favour disease onset (Daniel et al., 1973; Templeton et al., 1979; Charudattan, 1991). This typically results in a locally elevated population of the biocontrol agent that declines to normal endemic levels, once the target weed species has been suppressed. Following the initial inundation of the target species with the biocontrol agent, the population of the biocontrol is not self-sustaining and new inoculum is required for each control situation. This situation is most desirable, since it will help to minimize the likelihood of effects on non-target species.

The phytopathogen *C. purpureum* is a good candidate for development as a biological control agent of hardwoods in reforestation sites and industrial rights-of-way as it is an indigenous basidiomycete fungus that occurs naturally in all of the ecozones of Canada. It is usually the primary invader of fresh wounds of trees and, as such, has a unique role among the wood inhabiting basidiomycetes (Rayner and Boddy, 1986). Its only reported habitat is in living or recently killed trees and on recently cut logs, stumps or logging slash (Rayner, 1977; Hintikka, 1993; Duncan and Lombard, 1965; Ginns, 1986). Although it has a broad host range among the woody angiosperms, non-target hosts are not likely to be affected unless they are wounded during inoculum (basidiospore) dispersal (Dye, 1974; de Jong et al., 1990).

The use of C. purpureum will offer several advantages over current efforts in vegetation management. This biocontrol agent is selective and will not affect other vegetation on site. This is advantageous to vegetation managers in rights-of-way, who wish to maintain a low understory of vegetation to prevent soil erosion. On reforestation sites, it may be desirable to maintain a small hardwood component to aid in nitrogen fixation, nutrient cycling, and improve soil quality, as well as increase biodiversity for the benefit of other components of the forest biota. The non-living components of the biocontrol agent formulations are non-toxic and biodegradable; the active ingredient is a plant pathogen that will only infect wounded trees and is not toxic, infectious or pathogenic to the pesticide applicator or to animal species in general. The risk of non-target effects on plants, animals, soils, and watercourses should be much reduced, as compared to chemical methods of control. The use of C. purpureum in vegetation management can significantly reduce chemical herbicide use and thus minimize any possible detrimental effects associated with their application.

SCALE-UP AND MANUFACTURE

The development of a successful biological control agent relies on the satisfaction of a number of criteria. These include the evaluation of the effectiveness of the control agent against the target species (Templeton, 1992; Wall, 1992; Yang and Tebeest, 1993), an evaluation of the potential impact of the control agent on non-target species (Wapshere, 1974; Wall, 1991; Yang and Tebeest, 1993), an assessment of the safety (Templeton, 1992; Cook et al., 1996) and environmental fate of an inoculated strain in natural ecosystems (Anderson and May, 1986; Teng and Yang, 1993). Many of these criteria have already been met for C. purpureum (Becker, Ball, and Hintz, 1999; Ramsfield et al., 1999; Hintz et al., 2000). Other factors which must be considered include the development of an effective formulation and application method for the control organism (van Drieshe and Bellows, 1996), and the development of a reliable method of inoculum preparation that may be scaled up for the commercial production of the control agent. For the production of C. purpureum to be commercially viable, it is necessary to have a reliable, inexpensive method of producing the active ingredient. Ideally, the inoculum must be of consistently high level of titer (colony forming units, or cfus g^{-1}), contain an acceptably low level, of microbial contaminants, maintain a high level of infectivity/pathogenicity for the target tree species, exist in a form that may be stored for prolonged periods and easily transported, and be easily adaptable to new formulations suitable for different application technologies.

Chondrostereum purpureum grows well both in a stirred liquid culture and on solid substrate, but even though the fungus will grow quickly in liquid culture, it is not a suitable medium for the long-term storage of the fungus. This is due to the rapid decline of culture viability and the impracticality of storing large volumes of liquid cultures. Because C. purpureum is a filamentous fungus, it is also difficult to estimate the titer of liquid cultures and measure out consistent quantities of biomass for addition to the formulation. Fortunately, the fungus will readily colonize a solid substrate, amended with a nutrient solution, and retain a high viability for a long period. This form of inoculum is more suitable for storage in large quantities, is easy to measure for titer and can be easily mixed into a formulation to produce batches of the end-use product (EUP) as required. These features of C. purpureum have prompted us to manufacture the fungus by a two-stage fermentation process.

The two-stage fermentation process begins with the inoculation of a malt extract based broth contained in a 10 l BioFlow fermenter (New Brunswick Scientific) with a sheared liquid culture. A high rate of agitation and aeration produces a liquid C. purpureum culture with a large number of small mycelial fragments of high viability and titer (500–700 g fresh weight). This liquid culture is diluted in a nutrient broth and provides an ideal inoculum for a peat-based substrate, contained in sterile bags. Solid matrix fermentation proceeds for 4–6 weeks to allow adequate colonization of the substrate and this uniform material is subsequently used as the active ingredient in the EUP. Quality control at all stages of this manufacturing process is important in detecting the occurrence of microbial contaminants and identifying sources of contamination. The substrate must be free of human and animal pathogens and may contain no more than 1×10^2 cfus kg^{-1} of microbial contaminants. Contaminants will reduce the titer of the substrate and may include organisms that pose a risk to worker health, or non-target species. As well, quality control is essential in monitoring the titer of inoculum and detecting abnormal growth of the fungus, that may be indicative of physiological changes or genetic abnormalities (Horgen et al., 1996).

Upon completion of the solid matrix fermentation, the titer of the active ingredient is well above the minimum standard of 1×10^7 cfus kg^{-1} (Table 1). When stored at room temperature (22–26°C), the minimum standard is maintained for at least twelve months (Table 1). It has proven to be of consistently high purity and maintains its pathogenicity for the target hosts. The solid matrix is used as the active ingredient in different formulations of the biocontrol agent as required,

Table 1. Titer and long-term storage of peat- and clay-based active ingredients

Active ingredient	Titer over time (cfus kg^{-1})[a]			
	4 weeks	4 months	8 months	12 months
Peat-based	1.4 to 4.4 × 10^8	1.1 to 4.4 × 10^8	4.7 × 10^7 to 3.5 × 10^8	1.5 × 10^7 to 1.2 × 10^8
Clay-based	1.5 to 2.5 × 10^8	1.9 to 7.3 × 10^7	1.3 to 3.2 × 10^7	5.8 to 7.7 × 10^6

[a] Range of titers determined by cfu assays of independent samples taken from five separate batches each of clay- and peat-based inoculum over time.

and can also be easily transported in dry form, prior to mixing with the other ingredients of a formulation. Since the fungus C. purpureum does not produce conidial spores during vegetative growth, the fungal inoculum consists of small fragments of fungal mycelium growing on the peat-based substrate. The larger and variable size of this biomass, as compared to fungal spores, presents some challenges to the development of an effective formulation and an efficient application method.

EVALUATION OF DIFFERENT FORMULATIONS OF THE BIOCONTROL AGENT

A commercially successful formulation must be inexpensive, easy to prepare and apply, as well as demonstrate a reliable efficacy under operational field conditions. With these criteria in mind, the growth characteristics of the fungus C. purpureum must be accommodated when developing a suitable formulation and application method.

The solid matrix inoculum consisted of fine fragments colonized by the mycelium. These fragments were then diluted and mixed in a suitable carrier to provide a formulated product. We developed and tested two formulations of the EUP; the first is a paste-like formulation which is applied by hand from a squeeze bottle, and the second formulation is a liquid preparation that may be applied to cut stumps using a portable backpack sprayer.

Paste formulation
Using a paste formulation of glyphosate (Carbopaste™) as a model for a suitable carrier for a biocontrol, researchers at the Canadian Forestry Service (Pacific Region) developed a clay-based formulation for C. purpureum. Carbopaste™ was being used by BC Hydro as a spot treatment to minimize herbicide application. The CFS paste formulation consisted of the active ingredient mixed with a clay-based carrier that provided protection from dessication and UV irradiation, as well as sufficient nutrients to support the fungus until an infection was established. The paste was applied to the living sapwood of a stump, immediately after cutting. The Canadian Forestry Service (Pacific Region) has recently been awarded a patent covering the preparation and application of C. purpureum in this formulation as a mycoherbicide for the control of weed trees (Wall et al., 1996). The efficacy of the clay paste EUP has been demonstrated in a number of field trials against several weed tree species (Pitt et al., 1996; Harper et al., 1998) (Table 2). Results to date indicated the greatest efficacy is obtained with the tree species of red alder (Alnus rubra), Sitka alder (Alnus sinulata), and aspen (Populus tremuloides). The minimum titer of the paste EUP is 1×10^2 cfus g^{-1} and an average application rate of 5 g per stem provides a minimum of 500 infection units stem^{-1}.

The composition of the clay paste EUP has since been modified to improve the efficiency of formulation production with the current two-stage fermentation process. One of the disadvantages of the clay-based inoculum was the relatively low titer and short shelf life. The clay-based inoculum used previously for the clay paste EUP maintained the minimum titer (1×10^7 cfus kg^{-1}) for eight months of refrigerated storage. In contrast, the peat-based inoculum maintained a higher titer over a longer period and could be stored at room temperature, thus reducing costs tremendously (Table 1). The peat paste requires a much smaller quantity of inoculum to obtain the same titer as the clay paste, also reducing EUP production costs. The clay-based inoculum must be kept at 4–8°C for long-term storage, while the peat-based inoculum may be stored at room temperature (22–26°C). The former is also more costly to prepare. The peat paste EUP is easier to prepare and apply, and has a similar efficacy (Table 3).

The improved peat paste formulation still has several limitations, namely, a limited shelf life once formulated as an EUP and a requirement of cold storage prior to use, a greater cost of manufacture than simpler formulations (spray formulation), due to the inclusion of several ingredients, and a labour intensive method of application that contributes to the cost of vegetation control. These limitations have spurred further refinement of our application technology.

Spray formulation
The spray formulation was developed to permit the use of the biocontrol product on a larger scale, employing more conventional application technologies. This liquid EUP contains a carrier that protects the fungus, while at the same time maintaining the active ingredient in suspension. The viscosity of the suspension

Table 2. Summary of field efficacy of clay paste formulation

Location and year	Target tree species	Treatments	First year assessment (%, mortality)	Second year assessment (%, mortality)
Duncan, BC 1994[b]	Red alder	Paste	92	100
		Glyphosate	97	99
		Brush control	65	86
Prince Rupert, BC 1995	Red alder	Paste	99	Not assessed
		Brush control	68	
Ripperto Creek, BC 1995[a]	Sitka alder	Paste	80	88
		Release[c]	100	98
		Brush control	16	11
Chetwynd, BC 1996	Aspen	Paste	36	Not assessed
		Carbopaste[d]	98	
		Garlon 4[c]	100	
		Brush control	15	
Grand Forks, BC 1995[a]	Aspen	Paste	Not assessed	84
		Release[c]		97
		Brush control		31

[a] Harper et al. (1998).
[b] Pitt et al. (1996).
[c] Triclopyr.
[d] Glyphosate.

Table 3. Comparative efficacy of peat- and clay-based formulations

Formulation	Re-isolation of fungus from stumps[a]	Efficacy in 1999 Coppices with no re-sprouting (%)	Efficacy in 2000 Coppices with no re-sprouting (%)	Titer of EUP (cfus g^{-1})[b]
Peat paste (1×)	Yes	90	78	1×10^2
Peat paste (0.5×)	Yes	95	94	0.5×10^2
Peat paste (0.25×)	Yes	81	93	0.25×10^2
Clay paste	Yes	85	75	1×10^2
Untreated control	NA	40	22	NA

[a] Identified by PCR-based genetic markers (Becker, Ball, and Hintz, 1999).
[b] Minimum estimated titer of EUP.

is low enough to permit it to pass easily through the modified nozzle of standard backpack sprayers, and is likely suitable for vehicle mounted sprayers, or other methods of general broadcast application. The relatively large size of inoculum fragments (as compared to fungal spores) necessitates a larger nozzle aperture to produce a stream of inoculum rather than a mist. The minimum titer that will yield infection frequencies greater than 95% is currently being determined through field trial testing. A patent application has been filed recently (2000) for this innovative spray formulation.

FIELD TRIALS OF BIOCONTROL AGENT EFFICACY

Paste trials

Operational testing of both the paste and spray formulations is being conducted in a right-of-way on Vancouver Island in the Nanaimo Lakes district (East Circuit 2L 128), with the cooperation of BC Hydro-electric Power Co. Stem density averaged 30–40,000 stems ha^{-1} on this site and the primary species present was red alder. An area of 7 ha was cut and treated with the peat paste formation, using methods to simulate normal operational vegetation management. As in past trials, we have been testing a local dikaryotic isolate of C. purpureum, originally collected from a canker on red alder (Alnus rubra Bong) near Duncan, British Columbia in 1994 (isolate PFC2139). The fungal mycelium of this isolate is the active ingredient contained in our formulations applied to target trees.

Treatment plots were set up to compare the efficacy of the standard clay paste with the newly developed peat paste formulation. Peat paste was prepared at $1 \times (1 \times 10^2$ cfus g$^{-1})$, $0.5 \times (0.5 \times 10^2$ cfus g$^{-1})$, and $0.25 \times (0.25 \times 10^2$ cfus g$^{-1})$ active ingredient in the EUP and a single concentration of clay paste (1 ×

10^2 cfus g^{-1}) was also prepared and applied to cut alder coppices in separate 50 × 114 m blocks. For efficacy measurement, six 50 m^2 circular plots were established along transect lines running through each treatment block. The effectiveness of these treatments were assessed in the summer of 1999 by comparing the extent of re-sprouting from cut stumps in each of the treatment areas, involving counts of at least 100 coppices in each. A second assessment was done for re-sprouting in the summer of 2000 (Table 3).

The estimated titers of the clay paste and the 1× peat paste were of the same order of magnitude, while the lower concentrations of peat paste were lower titer. The efficacy of the peat paste at all concentrations was similar to that seen with the clay paste in this trial and in previous field assessments (Table 2). The vigorous regrowth of other vegetation in the second year of assessments made the detection of dead coppices difficult and likely contributed to an under estimate of efficacy. This is the first report of field efficacy for the peat paste and these favorable results support the future use of the peat-based paste, in place of the clay paste. The other advantages of the peat-based inoculum (longer shelf life, reduced cost, reduced contamination, reduced quantity of inoculum required in EUP) also support this choice.

Spray trials

It is important that the development of any new biocontrols consider the existing requirements of the applicator (e.g., ease of application and cost) and the constraints of the site conditions. With these factors in mind, our spray formulation was developed for testing in large-scale applications, where mechanized brushing is often chosen over manual brushing to reduce costs. Although the paste formulation provides good efficacy, it is likely to be better suited for more strategic use, for example, in riparian areas where the selective treatment of coppices is required. In other situations, such as mechanized brushing, a formulation suitable for broadcast application is most suitable. For these trials, local contractors were hired to ensure that the tests emulated true application conditions.

In November of 1999, an area of 2.3 ha was mowed by Hydro-Ax and then treated with the spray formulation, applied from backpack spayers. In these tests, the formulation was applied to a shattered stump rather than a clean-cut surface, as with the paste. The average application rate of the formulation was 7.7 × 10^3 cfus m^{-2}, which is in the same order of magnitude as the average application rate of peat paste (at least 500 cfus stump^{-1}), if applied to a coppice with multiple cut stumps. In these trials, the time elapsed before application was much greater, about 2–3 h, than in trials of the paste formulation, about 10–15 min. The greater time to treatment was due to logistical and safety constraints with the mower on site. This method of mowing and treatment would prove to be more cost effective than brushing by hand, if the biocontrol agent efficacy is acceptable. The efficacy of the spray application will be determined in the summers of 2000 and 2001. Should this formulation and application method provide sufficient infection for good efficacy, it will likely become the prefered strategy for large-scale treatment of weed trees.

GENERAL DISCUSSION AND SUMMARY

Our field trials so far have demonstrated that C. purpureum can serve as an effective alternative to chemical or manual methods of brush control, for several important weed tree species. Our continued improvement of the production and application technologies will also make this method of vegetation control a financially viable/competitive approach. Future trials will be initiated in collaboration with vegetation managers operating in industrial rights-of-way, municipal and in the forestry sectors. The commercial success of this biocontrol agent may provide a needed impetus for the development of other control agents, for vegetation management and other sectors of pest control.

We have improved our paste formulation by reducing the cost of inoculum production and improving shelf life, while maintaining standards of quality control and product efficacy against the target weed species. The paste formulation has demonstrated an efficacy comparable to the herbicide glyphosate on red alder. The ongoing development of the spray formulation should identify the best composition of this formulation, the minimum titer required and the optimal methods of application. The optimization of the spray formulation should provide a more competitive alternative to herbicide application and will hopefully prove to be useful for large-scale vegetation management.

This biocontrol agent could be an important component of an integrated vegetation management strategy, incorporating manual, mechanical, and biological control treatments. The use of safe vegetation control methods in the vicinity of riparian zones is of increasing concern; a safe and selective control agent will permit the strategic control of weed trees in these areas, with a minimum of soil disturbance and a reduced impact upon aquatic organisms. The use of conventional chemical herbicides on species resistant to C. purpureum will still be required in some situations. However, the use of C. purpureum on susceptable plant species can reduce chemical herbicide use/dependence overall in vegetation management. The use of C. purpureum will also result in a reduction in the frequency of manual/mechanical brush control measures required in a given area, due to the prevention of resprouting by the fungus. This attribute of the biocontrol agent will contribute to reduced costs of vegetation management for susceptible species, especially on sites where management is an ongoing concern.

REFERENCES

Anderson, R.M. and R.M. May. 1986. The invasion, persistence and spread of infectious diseases within animal and plant communities. Phil. Trans. R. Soc. Lond., B 314: 533–570.

BC Hydro and Power Authority. 1996. Vegetation management in powerline corridors. Environment Home Page. http://ewu.bchydro.bc.ca

Becker, E.M., A. Ball, and W.E. Hintz. 1999. PCR-based genetic markers for detection and infection frequency analysis of the biocontrol fungus *Chondrosterem purpureum* on Sitka alder and trembling aspen. Biological Control, 15: 71–80.

Campbell, R.A. 1990. Herbicide use for forest management in Canada: Where we are and where we are going. For. Chron., 66: 355–360.

Campbell, R.A. 1991. Silvicultural herbicides in Canada: Registration status and research needs. For. Chron., 67: 520–527.

Canadian Council of Forest Ministers. 1993. Compendium of Forestry Statistics. Forestry Canada, Communications Division, Ottawa, ON. 122 pp.

Charudattan, R. 1991. The mycoherbicide approach with plant pathogens. In: Microbial Control of Weeds. D.O. TeBeest, ed. Chapman and Hall, New York. pp. 24–57.

Coates, D. and S. Haeussler. 1986. A preliminary guide to the response of major species of competing vegetation to silvicultural treatments. BC Ministry of Forests, Land Management Handbook No. 9. 88 pp.

Conway-Brown, M. 1984. Alternatives to herbicides in forestry. In: Pesticide Policy — The Environmental Perspective. R. Vles and T. Schrecker, eds. Friends of the Earth, Ottawa, ON, Canada. pp. 183–216.

Cook, R.J., W.L. Bruckart, J.R. Coulson, M.S. Goettel, R.A. Humber, R.D. Lumsden, J.V. Maddox, M.L. McManus, L. Moore, S.F. Meyer, P.C. Quimby, Jr., J.P. Stack, and J.L. Vaughn. 1996. Safety of microorganisms intended for pest and plant disease control: A framework for scientific evaluation. Biological Control, 7: 333–351.

Cuthbert, J. 1991. The future for mixedwood management in BC. In: Northern Mixedwood 89, Proceedings of a Symposium Held at Fort Saint John, BC, Sept. 12–14th, 1989. A. Shortreid, ed. Canada-BC Forest Resource Development Agreement (FRDA) Report 164. pp. 132–134.

D'Anjou, B. 1990. Growth response of several vegetation species to herbicides and manual cutting treatments in the Vancouver Forest Region. Canada-BC Forest Resource Development Agreement (FRDA) Report 135. 8 pp.

Daniel, J.T., G.E. Templeton, R.J. Smith, Jr., and W.T. Fox. 1973. Biological control of northern jointvetch in rice with an endemic fungal disease. Weed Science, 21: 303–307.

de Jong, M.D., P.C. Scheepens, and J.C. Zadoks. 1990. Risk analysis for biological control: A Dutch case study in biocontrol of *Prunus serotina* by the fungus *Chondrostereum purpureum*. Plant Dis., 74: 189–194.

Duncan, G.C. and F.F. Lombard. 1965. Fungi associated with principal decays in wood products in the United States. US For. Serv. Res. Pap. WO-4. 31 pp.

Dye, M.H. 1974. Basidiocarp development and spore release by *Stereum purpureum* in the field. NZJ. Agr. Res., 17: 93–100.

Ginns, J.H. 1986. Compendium of plant disease and decay fungi in Canada, 1960–1980. Agric. Can. Publ. 1813. 416 pp.

Haeuschler, S. and D. Coates. 1986. Autecological characteristics of selected species that compete with conifers in British Columbia: A literature review. Canada-BC Forest Resource Development Agreement (FRDA) Report 001. 180 pp.

Halleran, M. 1990. Forest vegetation management and the politics of environment. For. Chron., 66: 369–371.

Harper, G.J., P. Comeau, W. Hintz, R. Wall, R. Prasad, and E. Becker. 1998. *Chondrostereum purpureum* as a biological control agent. Part 1: Efficacy on Sitka alder and aspen in eastern Canada.

Harrington, C.A. 1984. Factors influencing initial sprouting of red alder. Can. J. For. Res., 14: 357–361.

Hawksworth, D.L., P.M. Kirk, B.C. Sutton, and D.N. Pegler. 1995. Ainsworth & Bisby's Dictionary of the Fungi, 8th ed., CAB International, Wallingford.

Hintikka, V. 1993. Occurrence of edible fungi and other macromycetes on tree stumps over a sixteen-year period. (Abstr.). Hort. Abstr., 64(6): 610.

Hintz, W.E., E.M. Becker, and S.F. Shamoun. 2000. Development of genetic markers for risk assessment of biological control agents. In: Proc. Canadian Phytopathological Society, Annual Meeting, Victoria, BC, Canada. June 18th–21st, 2000.

Horgen, P.A., D. Carvalho, A. Sonnenberg, A. Li, and L.J.L.D. Van Griensven. 1996. Chromosomal abnormalities associated with strain degeneration in the cultivated mushroom, *Agaricus bisporus*. Fungal Genet. Biol., 20: 229–241.

Johansson, T. 1987. Development of stump suckers by *Betula pubescens* at different light intensities. Scand. J. For. Res., 2: 77–83.

MacLean, D.A. and M.G. Morgan. 1982. Long-term growth and yield response of young fir to manual and chemical release from shrub competition. For. Chron., 59: 177–183.

Malik, N. and W.H. Vanden Born. 1986. Use of herbicides in forest management. Can. For. Serv. Inf. Rep. NOR-X-282. 18 pp.

Natural Resources Canada. 1996. Compendium of Canadian Forestry Statistics. Can. For. Serv., National Forestry Database Program. http://nrcan.gc.ca

Pendl, F. and B. D'Anjou. 1990. Effect of treatment timing on red alder regrowth and conifer response. Canada-BC Forest Resource Development Agreement (FRDA) Report 112. 21 pp.

Peterson, E.B. and N.M. Peterson. 1992. Ecology, management and use of aspen and balsam popular in the prairie provinces, Canada. Special Report 1, Forestry Canada, Northwest Region, Northern Forestry Centre. 252 pp.

Peterson, E.B., G.R. Ahrens, and N.M. Peterson. 1996. Red alders managers handbook for British Columbia. Canada-BC Forest Resource Development Agreement (FRDA) Report 240. 124 pp.

Pitt, D.G., D.G. Thompson, P.G. Comeau, M. Dumas, W. Hintz, L. Lanteigne, G. Sampson, R.G. Wagner, and R. Wall. 1996. A national field trial of *Chondrostereum purpureum* as a woody weed-control agent: Objectives, design and methods. Expert committee on weeds. Proceedings of the 1996 National meeting. Dec. 9–12, 1996, Victoria, BC.

Ramsfield, T.D., S.F. Shamoun, Z.K. Punja, and W.E. Hintz. 1999. Variation in the mitochondrial DNA of the potential biological control agent *Chondrostereum purpureum*. Can. J. Bot., 77: 1490–1498.

Rayner, A.D.M. 1977. Fungal colonization of hardwood stumps from natural sources. II. Basidiomycetes. Trans. Brit. Mycol. Soc., 69(2): 303–312.

Rayner, A.D.M. and L. Boddy. 1986. Population structure and the infection biology of wood-decay fungi in living trees. Adv. Plant Pathol., 5: 119–160.

Smith, S.M. 1988. Regeneration delays and natural yields on untreated backlog forest land in British Columbia. Canada-BC Forest Resource Development Agreement (FRDA) Report 043. 130 pp.

Statistics Canada. 1996–1997. Canadian Statistics — The Land. http://www.statcan.ca

Templeton, G.E. 1992. Regulations and Guidelines: Critical Issues in Biological Control. In: Proceedings of the USDA/CSRS National Workshop, June 10–12, 1991, Vienna, USA. 63 pp.

Templeton, G.E., D.O. TeBeest, and R.J. Smith, Jr. 1979. Biological weed control with mycoherbicides. Annu. Rev. Phytopathol., 17: 301–310.

Teng, P.S. and X.B. Yang. 1993. Biological impact and risk assessment in plant pathology. Annu. Rev. Phytopathol., 31: 495–521.

Van Driesche, R.G. and T.S. Bellows, Jr. 1996. Biological Control. Chapman and Hall, New York.

Wall, R., R. Prasad, and E. Sela. 1996. Biological control for weed trees. United States Patent No. 5,587,158.
Wall, R.E. 1992. Wound pathogens and control of woody vegetation. (Abstr.) In: Proc. 8th Int. Symp. Biol. Cont. Weeds. E.S. Delfosse and R.R. Scott, eds. 2–7 Feb. 1992, Canterbury, New Zealand.
Wall, R.E. 1991. Pathological effects of *Chondrostereum purpureum* in inoculated yellow birch and beech. Can. J. Plant Pathol., 13: 81–87.
Wapshere, A.J. 1974. A strategy for evaluating the safety of organisms for biological weed control. Ann. Appl. Biol., 77: 201–211.
Yang, X.B. and D.O. TeBeest. 1993. Epidemiological mechanisms of mycoherbicide effectiveness. Phytopathology, 83: 891–893.

BIOGRAPHICAL SKETCHES

Paul Y. de la Bastide
Mycologic Inc., University of Victoria, PO Box 3020, STN CSC, Victoria, BC V8W 3N5, Canada

Paul de la Bastide is currently a research scientist at Mycologic Inc., beginning his work with the company as an NSERC Industrial Postdoctoral Research Fellow (1998–2000). His work has been concerned with the optimization of inoculum production and the field evaluation of bioherbicide formulations, so as to provide supporting data towards the registration of a formulation of *Chondrostereum purpureum* as a commercial bioherbicide product. Areas of research interest include the development of production and application systems for new biocontrol fungi and bacteria, as well as the study of gene regulation and expression in fungal pathogens, with a view to develop effective biocontrol methods.

Hong Zhu
MetaBios Inc., R-Hut, McKenzie Ave, University of Victoria, Victoria, BC V8W 3W2, Canada

Hong Zhu is an industrial microbiologist with expertise in fermentation and the formulation of biological pesticides. He is currently the president of MetaBios Inc., a biotech company specializing in disposable fermentation and cell culture technologies applicable to both laboratory and industrial scales of production.

Gwen Shrimpton
BC Hydro, 6911 Southpoint Drive, Burnaby, BC V3N 4X8, Canada

Gwen Shrimpton works for BC Hydro developing Integrated Vegetation Management programs for the over 70,000 km of powerlines that the corporation maintains. Gwen is particularly interested in researching new products and techniques that will reduce environmental impact, while improving program effectiveness. She has supported projects to develop fungi for the biological control of deciduous weed trees and insects for the biocontrol of broom. She has also developed an Environmental Management System for vegetation management at BC Hydro.

Simon Francis Shamoun
Natural Resources Canada, Canadian Forest Service, Pacific Forestry Centre, 506 West Burnside Road, Victoria, BC V8Z 1M5, Canada

Dr. Shamoun is a Research Scientist at the Canadian Forest Service, Pacific Forestry Centre. He is an adjunct professor at the University of British Columbia, Department of Forest Sciences and at the University of Victoria, Department of Biology, Centre for Forest Biology. In addition, Dr. Shamoun is Research Leader of the "Biological Control of Forest Diseases and Weeds Research Program" at the Pacific Forestry Centre. Currently, Dr. Shamoun leads major research studies, including biological control of invasive forest weeds (*Rubus* spp., Salal, and weedy hardwood species) with indigenous fungal pathogens. Recently, Dr. Shamoun initiated a new project to develop biological control agents for the management of dwarf mistletoes. Dr. Shamoun has a wealth of expertise in the Etiology, Epidemiology, Population Structure and Genetic Diversity of biological control agents.

William E. Hintz
Mycologic Inc., University of Victoria, PO Box 3020, STN CSC, Victoria, BC V8W 3N5, Canada

In addition to being a faculty member in the Biology Department at the University of Victoria, William Hintz is also the director of research for MycoLogic Incorporated, a university spin-off company that specializes in the development of biological controls for vegetation management. His main areas of research include the use of fungi and bacteria for the control of agricultural, forest and industrial pests, as well as studies of fungal gene regulation and expression. He has brought his experience in molecular genetics to address questions of environmental fate and safety of biocontrols.

Risk Analysis for Tree Growth Regulators (TGR) Used on Electric Utility Rights-of-Way

Logan A. Norris, Frank Dost, Rufin VanBossuyt Jr., and Jeffrey Jenkins

Paclobutrazol and flurprimidol tree growth regulators are useful for lengthening the trim cycle for trees in electric utility rights-of-way. The results of an analysis of the human health risks show that with appropriate precautions these materials can be used safely. The safety results from the limited exposure humans and other organisms receive due to the restricted distribution of the chemicals and their lack of mobility in the environment. Comparing the exposure information to the no-observable-effect-level (NOEL) shows nearly all exposure scenarios have adequate margins of safety. In those few instances where the margins of safety are less than 100, simple mitigation procedures will help. The most important are to (a) restrict the access of children to the flurprimidol pellets, (b) limit the soil injection of paclobutrazol in areas where sand is the dominant component of the soil, (c) use protective gear in handling paclobutrazol concentrate, and (d) if paclobutrazol concentrate is spilled, immediately remove contaminated clothing and wash affected skin. The risk to other organisms is small, requiring no mitigation.

Keywords: Paclobutrazol, flurprimidol, human health risk

INTRODUCTION

Modern electric utility distribution systems require a program of management to provide space between tree-parts and electrical conductors and equipment. Tree growth regulator chemicals (TGRs) such as paclobutrazol (Profile® 2SC) and flurprimidol (Cutless®) are approved by the US Environmental Protection Agency (USEPA) for this purpose. Decisions concerning the use of these materials must include specific consideration of the effects of their use on the environment and various life forms. A human health-risk assessment, including the risk to the general public and to utility workers (applicators), is a critical part of this.

As part of a process to consider the use of paclobutrazol and flurprimidol in New York, Empire State Electric Energy Research Corporation (ESEERCO) commissioned Environmental Consultants, Inc. (ECI) to prepare a Generic Environmental Impact Statement (GEIS). TGRs have been used on a trial basis in New York, and the purpose of the GEIS was to compile information related to its further use in the State, drawing on research and experience in other places. The GEIS evaluates and summarizes what is known about paclobutrazol and flurprimidol, including human health risk and the risk to other life forms, to aid in the decision making process. The GEIS is being submitted to the New York regulatory authorities (Norris et al., 2000).

RISK ASSESSMENT

Risk assessment is the process by which the likelihood of adverse effects from the use of a TGR such as paclobutrazol or flurprimidol is determined. The process is based on widely accepted theory and practice in toxicology, chemistry and biology, and is not unique to TGRs. The risk assessment process used here is the same one used to determine the likelihood of adverse effects from food additives, medications, household and industrial chemicals, and environmental contaminants (Fig. 1). It is applicable to human health risk and the risk to other organisms.

Environmental Concerns in Rights-of-Way Management: Seventh International Symposium
J.W. Goodrich-Mahoney, D.F. Mutrie and C.A. Guild (editors)
© 2002 Elsevier Science Ltd. All rights reserved.

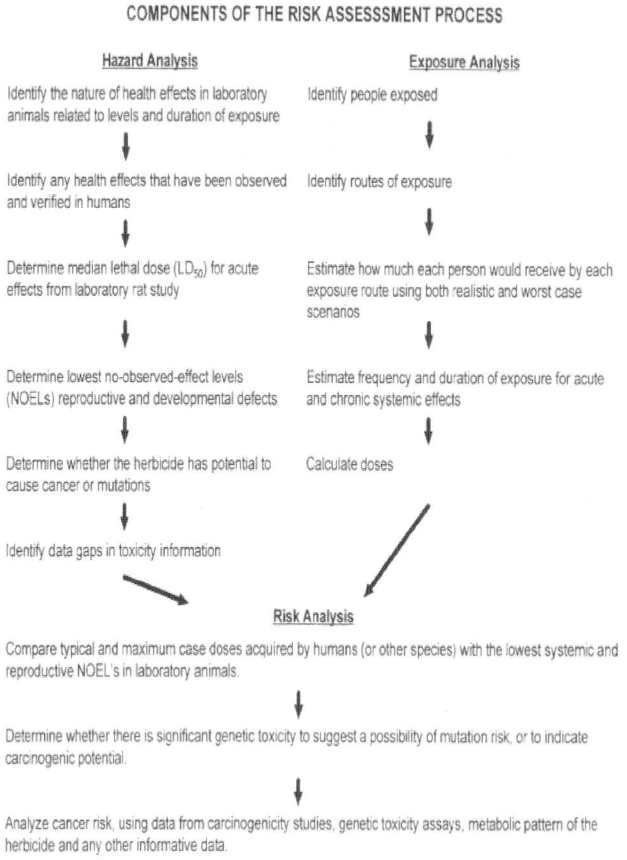

COMPONENTS OF THE RISK ASSESSMENT PROCESS

Hazard Analysis

Identify the nature of health effects in laboratory animals related to levels and duration of exposure

↓

Identify any health effects that have been observed and verified in humans

↓

Determine median lethal dose (LD_{50}) for acute effects from laboratory rat study

↓

Determine lowest no-observed-effect levels (NOELs) reproductive and developmental defects

↓

Determine whether the herbicide has potential to cause cancer or mutations

↓

Identify data gaps in toxicity information

Exposure Analysis

Identify people exposed

↓

Identify routes of exposure

↓

Estimate how much each person would receive by each exposure route using both realistic and worst case scenarios

↓

Estimate frequency and duration of exposure for acute and chronic systemic effects

↓

Calculate doses

Risk Analysis

Compare typical and maximum case doses acquired by humans (or other species) with the lowest systemic and reproductive NOEL's in laboratory animals.

↓

Determine whether there is significant genetic toxicity to suggest a possibility of mutation risk, or to indicate carcinogenic potential.

↓

Analyze cancer risk, using data from carcinogenicity studies, genetic toxicity assays, metabolic pattern of the herbicide and any other informative data.

Fig. 1. The risk assessment process.

Risk is determined by both the toxicity characteristics of the chemical and the exposure organisms may receive in a particular pattern of use. This TGR risk assessment has three components:

- *Hazard analysis*. Hazard analysis identifies the critical toxicity characteristics of each compound. The hazard is expressed as the response of organisms to varying levels of exposure to the subject chemical, usually in controlled laboratory experiments. The exposure in these tests is usually expressed as milligrams kilograms^{-1} day^{-1} (mg kg^{-1} day^{-1}). Hazard assessment identifies such measures of toxicity as the acute oral LD_{50}, dermal toxicity, reproductive effects, and such chronic toxicity characteristics as mutagenicity and cancer. Importantly, the hazard analysis identifies the lowest reliable no-observable-effect-level (NOEL) that has been reported for each compound. Since the goal is not to have adverse effects on non-target organisms, the NOEL is crucial to the risk assessment.
- *Exposure analysis*. Exposure analysis quantitatively determines the level of exposure a human or other organism is likely to receive. This requires knowing the routes by which exposure may occur and then quantifying the levels expected to occur in a particular practice or pattern of use. The routes of exposure include *ingestion* of contaminated food and water, *absorption* through the skin, and *inhalation* of contaminated air. Information on the movement, persistence and fate of a TGR in the environment is used in estimating the exposure. For instance:
  - *Leaching and persistence characteristics in soil* determine the potential for impact on ground water quality, and the tendency to *drift or runoff* determines the impact on surface water quality. In combination, these determine the possibility humans could be exposed by ingestion of this water,
  - *Persistence in vegetation or animals* determines the potential exposure of humans from eating the vegetation or animals, and
  - *Volatilization* determines impacts on air quality and the potential for inhalation exposure.
- *Risk analysis*. Risk analysis combines the information from the hazard analysis and the exposure analysis to determine the toxicological impact. This is done by comparing the expected exposure (from the exposure analysis) to the NOEL (from the hazard analysis). For systemic or reproductive effects, the risk is described as the margin of safety. The margin of safety is simply the ratio of the NOEL:exposure.

To illustrate, if paclobutrazol has a NOEL for systemic effects of 7.0 mg of paclobutrazol per kg of body weight per day (abbreviated mg kg^{-1} day^{-1}) and the expected exposure is 0.0002 mg kg^{-1} day^{-1}, then the margin of safety is the result of the ratio of $(7.0)(0.0002)^{-1}$ which is 35,000. In this illustration the margin of safety is 35,000, which means that the level of expected exposure is 35,000 times lower than the level of exposure shown to produce no observable effects in laboratory testing.

What constitutes safety? In the human health risk assessment process, a margin of safety that is 100 or greater is the commonly accepted criterion (regulatory standard) for human safety. It provides a 100-fold margin to accommodate uncertainty, differences in sensitivity among individuals, and the possibility there may be adverse effects that have not yet been observed or reported.

Risk assessment is more complicated if the chemicals in the assessment are carcinogens. If they are, then a cancer risk assessment is done to determine the probability of causing cancer. Cancer risk assessment is complicated, but has been well developed and is widely used as part of the regulatory process. The common regulatory standard for cancer is one excess cancer in 1 million lifetimes. Cancer is a very common human disease, occurring naturally approximately 250,000 times in one million lifetimes. It is believed that roughly one in every four people will have cancer sometime in their lifetime, not as the result of exposure to cancer-causing human-made chemicals, but due to the normal stressors of life and our genetic makeup. The standard of one excess cancer allows an increase in the incidence of cancer from the natural level of 250,000 to 250,001 in a population of one million people.

In the following sections we describe the environmental behavior of each chemical, then report the results of the hazard analysis, the exposure analysis and the risk analysis.

TREE GROWTH REGULATORS

Moore (1998) provides a useful review and discussion of plant growth regulation. His discussion includes the role and function of the various natural plant hormones (auxins, gibberellins, cytokinins, absicic acid, and ethylene). Flurprimidol and paclobutrazol exert their biochemical action though influence on the biosynthesis of some of the natural plant hormones. Breedlove, Holt, and Chaney (1989) have published an annotated bibliography on tree growth regulators.

PACLOBUTRAZOL

Paclobutrazol was reported as a plant growth regulator by Lever et al. (1982). It was first introduced by ICI Agrochemicals (now Zeneca Agrochemicals). Now paclobutrazol is sold by Dow Agro-Sciences as the specialty growth regulator named Profile® 2SC. Paclobutrazol is also sold under the label name of Bonzi® for floriculture crops, and TGR Turf Enhancer® 2SC by another manufacturer for use on fine turf grasses. Cultar® is another paclobutrazol formulation.

Paclobutrazol was first registered with the USEPA on March 1, 1989, for use as a tree growth regulator to be applied by a tree trunk injection application method. It was then registered for the currently-used soil injection and basal soil drench application methods on June 29, 1992. Profile® 2SC contains 21.8% (2 pounds/gallon) paclobutrazol as active ingredient and 78.2% inert ingredients.

Paclobutrazol

IUPAC name: (2RS,3RS)-1-(4-chlorophenyl)-4,4-dimethyl-2-(1H-1,2,4-triazol-1-yl)-pentan-3-ol.

Chemical abstracts name: (R*,R*)-(±)-β-[(4-chlorophenyl)methyl]-α-(1,1-dimethylethyl)-1H-1,2,4-triazole-1-ethanol.

Molecular weight: 293.8.
Melting point: 165–166°C.
Vapor pressure: 1×10^{-3} mPa (20°C), 8×10^{-3} mPa (30°C).
K_{ow}: $\log P = 3.2$.
Solubility: water (distilled, 20°C) 26 mg l^{-1}, hexane 10 g l^{-1}, methanol 150 g l^{-1}.

Stability: stable for more than 2 years at 20°C. Stable to hydrolysis (pH 4–9), not degraded by UV light (pH 7, 10 days).

Paclobutrazol is absorbed by stems, leaves and roots and moves in the xylem to growing sub-apical meristems. It is used on fruit trees to inhibit vegetative growth and to improve fruit set. It is also used on container-grown ornamentals and flower crops (i.e., chrysanthemum, begonia, poinsettia) to inhibit their growth, and on grass seed crops to reduce height and prevent lodging. The biochemical mode of action is through inhibition of gibberellin and sterol biosynthesis. When used as a tree growth regulator, paclobutrazol reduces stem elongation and lengthens the period of time between trimmings required to keep plants within a desired size. Paclobutrazol has been reported to have a wide range of effects on plant anatomy, physiology, and biochemistry. It is likely most or all of these effects are secondary, and result from the primary effects of paclobutrazol on the biosynthesis of plant hormones.

ENVIRONMENTAL BEHAVIOR OF PACLOBUTRAZOL

Soil persistence and leaching

Paclobutrazol is quite persistent in soil but shows little tendency to leach in the soil profile. This suggests it binds strongly to soil particles. British Crop Protection Council (1997) summarized the soil half-life as between 0.5 and 1 year in general, with a half-life of 42 days in a clay loam (pH 8.8, 14% organic matter content), and half-life of 140 days in a coarse sandy loam (pH 6.8, 4% organic matter content).

Harvey and Hill (1985) studied the fate of paclobutrazol in soil following broadcast application as it might be done for turf grass. They reported a half-life in soil of 25–32 weeks under field conditions in North Carolina, Mississippi, Illinois, and California for paclobutrazol and its major soil metabolite (ketone oxidation product). Francis (1986) studied the behavior of paclobutrazol where it was used in a broadcast application, which we use to estimate paclobutrazol behavior in soil after leaf-fall from trees treated in the fall of the year. He found the half-life is 6–7 months, and no residues (<0.01 mg kg^{-1}) were found at depths below 6 inches.

Mak, Crook, and Atreya (1987) conducted a detailed field study of the persistence and movement of paclobutrazol in soil following soil injection in US orchard soils in several states. The material was injected at two rates, 0.6 and 6.0 g of chemical per lineal horizontal-foot of injection trench. Soil samples were taken using the open box technique at various time intervals up to twelve months, and to various depths. Paclobutrazol remained highly localized at the points of application up to twelve months after treatment, with the majority remaining in the top 40-cm layer of

Table 1. Paclobutrazol residues at 12 months[1]

Depth in soil (cm)	Florida		West Virginia		California	
	(mg kg^{-1})[2]	% of zero time[3]	(mg kg^{-1})	% of zero time	(mg kg^{-1})	% of zero time
0.6 grams paclobutrazol						
0–20	11	55	35	76	14	50
20–40	1.3	6.5	0.35	0.8	1.3	4.6
40–60	0.27	1.4	0.03	0.1	0.64	2.3
60–80	0.21	1.1	NA[4]	NA	0.19	0.68
80–100	0.09	0.5	NA	NA	0.1	0.36
100–120	0.07	0.4	NA	NA	0.05	0.18
6.0 grams paclobutrazol						
0–20	108	120	447	109	177	54
20–40	25	28	1.0	0.24	3.3	1.0
40–60	6.3	6.9	0.1	0.02	1.4	0.43
60–80	3	3.3	NA	NA	0.4	0.12
80–100	2.4	2.7	NA	NA	0.05	0.02
100–120	1.8	1.8	NA	NA	0.05	0.02

[1] After Mak, Crook, and Atreya, 1987.
[2] mg kg^{-1} is for paclobutrazol plus ketone metabolite.
[3] % of zero time is for paclobutrazol alone.
[4] NA — no data reported.

the soil at all sites. A very small percentage (generally <5%) was found at depths between 40 and 122 cm. Paclobutrazol dissipated from both rates in California, and from the lower rate trial at West Virginia, with an estimated half-life of 1–3 years (Table 1).

Summarizing the work of several others, Atreya, Skidmore, and Lewis (1990) reported the following concerning the behavior of paclobutrazol in field studies of persistence and mobility in soil:

United Kingdom — Apple trees were treated at 2.0 kg a.i. ha^{-1} and soil samples were taken underneath trees to a depth of 30 cm over a one-year period after application. Paclobutrazol had a half-life of 6–7 months under alkaline soil conditions with 70–72% of the applied chemical dissipated at 12 months. The half-life was longer (10 months) under acidic soil conditions, and 59% of the applied chemical dissipated at 12 months. Extremely low residues of paclobutrazol were measured in the 10–20 cm soil profile (0.05 mg kg^{-1}), and non-detectable residues (<0.02 mg kg^{-1}) were found in 20–30 cm soil profile. These trials showed little evidence of leaching.

Italy — Peach orchards in Northern Italy were treated with paclobutrazol at 0.75 kg a.i. ha^{-1} and soil samples to a depth of 30 cm were taken for one year. Paclobutrazol had a half-life of three months and less than 5% remained after one year. Generally, no detectable residues (<0.01 mg kg^{-1}) of paclobutrazol were measured in the 15–30 cm soil profile (Mak and Atreya, 1990).

Malaysia — Paclobutrazol was applied at 2.0 kg a.i. ha^{-1} and soil samples to 40 cm were taken for 183 days. The half-life was approximately one month, and only 1% remained after 183 days. No detectable residues (<0.01 mg kg^{-1}) of paclobutrazol were found below 20 cm (Crook, Mak, and Atreya, 1989).

Canada — Paclobutrazol was applied at a rate of 1.0 kg a.i. ha^{-1} to a loamy fine sand and to a silty clay, and soil samples were taken to a depth of 30 cm for a period of 366 days. 25 and 29% of zero-time residues remained after three months. Dissipation slowed during the winter months, resuming in spring. 10 and 17% of the applied dose remained after 366 days. No paclobutrazol was found below the 10 cm soil depth.

United States — Four trials were set up at various locations in the USA on a variety of soil types (silty loam, silty clay loam, loamy fine sand, and fine sandy loam with range of pH 5.6–8.0). Paclobutrazol (applied at 2.24 kg ha^{-1}) exhibited half-lives of between 4 and 8 months. 87–98% of the applied chemical dissipated in 18–24 months, and no residues (<0.01 mg kg^{-1}) were measured at depths greater than 15 cm (Pearson, 1984).

Summarizing their conclusions, under temperate climatic conditions the half-life of paclobutrazol in a variety of soil types and environmental conditions is 4–11 months with up to 30% remaining in soil after one year.

Atreya, Skidmore, and Lewis (1990) also summarized field studies of paclobutrazol persistence and mobility in soil following repeated applications of this material in apple orchards in the United Kingdom, providing a basis for evaluating the potential for accumulation of this material following repeated applications over time.

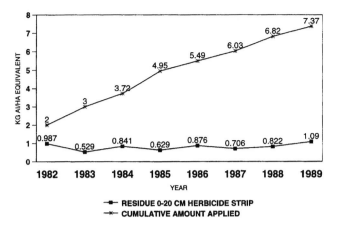

Fig. 2. Paclobutrazol residues in soil in the UK apple orchards following repeated annual applications of Cultar®, 1982–1989.

Paclobutrazol was applied annually as foliar spray using commercial equipment to established apple orchards. In the first year, rates up to twice the maximum annual use rate were applied but subsequent treatments were within the label guidelines. Soils were sampled annually in November. Residue levels remained constant, showing no buildup over time (Fig. 2). Similar results were found over a three-year period in a peach orchard in Italy, indicating that repeated applications of paclobutrazol will not result in a progressively higher accumulation over time.

Ground water
The pattern of persistence and mobility in soil of paclobutrazol as it is used by electric utilities is such that it is highly unlikely to contaminate groundwater. However, because of the concern expressed about this by reviewers, a more detailed analysis was made by modeling the leaching of paclobutrazol in New York soils using the PATRIOT Model System used by USEPA (Appendix 11.3, Norris et al., 2000).

In each simulation, the depth to the water table was assumed to be 200 cm or greater, and the persistence in soil to be represented by a half-life of 270 days. The climatic variables are for the specific geographic location. A sample of ten soils for the county was included in each model analysis. The soils were selected from a list of soils of the county, arrayed by their clay content. The soils chosen were evenly distributed by clay content and were arable.

The modeling simulations of paclobutrazol leaching in 60 soils found in six New York counties show no paclobutrazol leaching below 200 cm at the 0.5 kg ha^{-1} application rate. At the 1.8 kg ha^{-1} application rate, the model results show paclobutrazol at a level of 0.1 parts per million (ppm) at 200 cm in three soils (one soil in each of three counties) out of the 60 tested. The leaching predicted by the model is conservative because it is based on annual applications for 10 years, and paclobutrazol is generally used only once in a period of three to eight years in electric utility vegetation management.

Table 2. Concentration of paclobutrazol in apple after exposure via soil drench (from Reed et al., 1989)

Weeks after exposure	Dry weight (mg kg^{-1})		
	Shoot	Apex	Leaf
1	9	5.5	20
3	10	8.5	35
5	4.5	4.5	18
7	5.5	4	22
9	4	5.5	22
11	3	2	9
13	2.5	2	9

Based on these results and the results of leaching and persistence studies in other locations (cited above), we conclude the likelihood of paclobutrazol leaching to contaminate ground water is remote. Further, the pattern of use by electric utilities is unlikely to result in entry of paclobutrazol to surface water; therefore, we conclude that ingestion of contaminated water is not a meaningful route of exposure for humans or animals.

Vegetation
Stems, leaves and roots can absorb paclobutrazol (British Crop Protection Council, 1997) but when applied as a soil drench or soil injection the vast majority of absorption will be by the roots in the uppermost layers of the soil profile. While application is focused on a particular tree, any plant with their roots in the zone of soil containing the growth regulator is likely to absorb some of the material as well. The extent of such absorption will be a function of root density in the zone.

Once absorbed into the plant, paclobutrazol moves in the xylem to growing sub-apical meristems. Dow AgroSciences (1997) indicates paclobutrazol is not accumulated in fruits or nuts, although the label has a general use precaution against treating fruit or nut trees that will be harvested within one year, or trees that are or might be tapped for sap in the production of sugar.

Early and Martin (1988, 1989) reported on the distribution and fate of C-14 labeled paclobutrazol in peach seedlings (roots exposed through a nutrient solution). 41% of the material absorbed by the plant was found in the roots and 49% in the leaves. Nine days after treatment, the remaining radioactivity was distributed 71% in roots, 41–68% in the stem and 8–12% in the leaves. The concentrations were higher in the leaves but the rate of degradation was also higher in the leaves, with 88–92% of the paclobutrazol being converted to other forms after nine days.

Reed et al. (1989) reported on the concentration of paclobutrazol that occurs in foliage and other plant parts following exposure via a hydroponic solution, a trunk paint application, or a soil drench. Table 2 shows the residue data for foliage and stem apex tissues as a function of time after exposure for the soil drench treatment.

Table 3. Residue of paclobutrazol in stone fruits after soil drench applications (from FAO, 1988)

Country, year, crop	Application rate (kg ha^{-1})	Time since application (weeks)	Paclobutrazol (mg kg^{-1})	Reference
Australia, 1983–1984, cherries, nectarines, peaches	1–2	11–19	<0.01	Mitchell, 1987
New Zealand, 1985–1987, cherries	1.6, plus 0.2 following year	18	0.01	Hawthorne et al., 1987
	1.25 each for 2 years	18	<0.01	
	5.0	18	0.01	
peaches	0.75–1	23	0.01–0.02	
France, 1985, peaches	1	7–15	<0.02	Culoto, 1985
UK, 1983, cherries, plums	4	15–21	<0.02	Freeman and Pay, 1985
UK, 1985, cherries	0.75	23–29	<0.01	Cavell and Mak, 1986b
plums	0.75	14–19	<0.01–0.04	Cavell and Mak, 1986b
USA, 1982, cherries, plums, apricots, nectarines, peaches	4.5	8–12	<0.01	French and Atreya, 1983b

The Food and Agriculture Organization (FAO) of the United Nations, jointly with the World Health Organization (WHO), extensively reviewed the residue data for paclobutrazol in connection with its use as a tree growth regulator in certain tree fruit crops (FAO, 1988). The patterns of use they considered include a soil drench application where the rate of application is 0.5–1.0 kg ha^{-1}, a rate consistent with that used for maintenance functions in electric utility line clearance. FAO summarized results of trials with stone fruits in several countries (Table 3). Studies done with radiocarbon-labeled paclobutrazol provide similar data (FAO, 1988).

From these studies, we conclude that the concentration likely to occur in leaves will vary from 9–35 ppm dry weight, and about 3–11 ppm fresh weight in foliage. The level of paclobutrazol that might occur in fruit that could be consumed by humans, domestic animals or wildlife is <0.04 ppm.

Air

When used as a tree growth regulator, paclobutrazol is not applied as a spray, therefore the potential for its occurrence in air in the form of droplets is nil. The vapor pressure of paclobutrazol (1×10^{-3} mPa) is such that it has little tendency to evaporate under normal environmental conditions. When it is applied by soil injection, the opportunity for evaporation is nearly eliminated. Due to its strong adsorption by soil, it is not expected to vaporize from the soil. When it is applied as a soil drench, the liquid is exposed to the air during the period of time before it is covered, fully absorbed by surface soil and organic matter, or has entered the soil profile. This period is brief (a few minutes), and the surface to volume ratio of the material is very small compared to spray droplets, resulting in little opportunity for evaporation. As a result of these factors, we conclude that there will be little or no residues of paclobutrazol in the air, and we therefore eliminate inhalation as a route of exposure.

HAZARD ANALYSIS

The most important aspect of a hazard analysis is to identify the most sensitive measures of response of organisms. It is a key element of the human health risk process. Thus, while the LD$_{50}$ is a useful value for some purposes, for purposes of risk assessment it is more important to know the no-observable-effect-level (NOEL) for acute, sub acute and chronic patterns of exposure. This section is organized to provide this information. The findings are summarized in Tables 4 and 5.

There is very little published research on the toxicology of paclobutrazol. Acute and chronic toxicology and metabolic fate of paclobutrazol has been reviewed in summaries prepared by ICI Americas (now Zeneca) and provided by Dow Agro-Sciences, the current registrant (Smith, 1988, 1989). A review of residues and toxicology of paclobutrazol was published by FAO/WHO (FAO, 1988), and USEPA reviewed data necessary to establish a reference dose for systemic toxicity (USEPA, 1997a). Except where specific sources are noted, this discussion of the toxicology of paclobutrazol is based on those reviews.

Table 4. Summary of critical toxicity values for paclobutrazol

Acute lethality (LD$_{50}$)	Oral exposure (mg kg^{-1})	Dermal exposure (mg kg^{-1})	Intraperitoneal exposure (mg kg^{-1})	Inhalation exposure (mg l^{-1})
Rat, female	1300	>1000	100	3.13
Rat, male	2000	>1000	200	4.79
Mouse, female	490			
Mouse, male	1200			
Guinea pig	500			
Rabbit, female	840	>1000		
Rabbit, male	940	>1000		
Chronic effects, NOEL*			Effect**	
90-day dietary exposure, rat	8 mg kg^{-1} day^{-1}		liver enlarged, weight loss	
6-week dietary exposure, dog	15 mg kg^{-1} day^{-1}		increased liver weight	
3-week dermal, rabbit	>1000 mg kg^{-1} day^{-1}			
2-year, rat	6.8 mg kg^{-1} day^{-1}***		fatty liver,	
2-year, mouse	15 mg kg^{-1} day^{-1}		weight loss	
1-year, dog	75 mg kg^{-1} day^{-1}		fatty liver liver cell swelling	

*NOEL is the no-observed effect level.
**Effect is the effect noted at the next highest level of exposure.
***This is the most sensitive NOEL, and is the value used in the risk assessment.

Table 5. Reproductive toxicity of paclobutrazol

Type of test animal	Developmental NOEL (mg kg^{-1} day^{-1})	Maternal NOEL (mg kg^{-1} day^{-1})
Teratogenicity, rat*	10	40
Teratogenicity, rabbits	125	25
	Reproductive effect (mg kg^{-1} day^{-1})	Parental toxicity (mg kg^{-1} day^{-1})
Two-generation reproductive study, rat	>34	6.8
Dominant lethal assay, male rat	>300	100

*Effects probably fetotoxic rather than teratogenic.

Oral and intraperitoneal exposure

When given orally, paclobutrazol is of low acute toxicity to rats. The median lethal dose (LD$_{50}$) was greater than 1000 mg kg^{-1}. The LD$_{50}$ for mice, guinea pigs and rabbits were, respectively 490, 500, and 940 mg kg^{-1}. When injected intraperitoneally into rats the LD$_{50}$s were lower, on the order of 100 mg kg^{-1} for females and 200 mg kg^{-1} for males. The differences between intraperitoneal and oral toxicities indicate relatively poor absorption from the digestive tract.

Effects on the eye and skin

Paclobutrazol is a slight irritant to the skin of rats and rabbits. The rats received a 12.5% suspension in propylene glycol held in place under a bandage for 24 h, removed, the skin washed, and the material reapplied 24 h later. The cycle repeated five times and the animals observed for an additional nine days. Transient slight reddening and scabbing occurred in some animals. Rabbits are more sensitive — a single treatment of 500 mg paclobutrazol in olive oil applied to shaved skin under a bandage for a single 24-h treatment caused well-defined redness. Paclobutrazol did not cause allergic sensitization of skin of guinea pigs, even at concentrations that resulted in slight irritation. There was no evidence of systemic toxicity in any of the animals.

Paclobutrazol is classified as a moderate irritant to the eye. The eyes of all animals were normal seven days later. Washing the eyes 30 s after treatment markedly reduced the effects.

Inhalation toxicity

While the methods of application make inhalation exposure unlikely, paclobutrazol can vaporize to a very limited extent. Rats were exposed for four hours and observed for 17 days. Females were more sensitive, with a median lethal concentration of 3.13 mg l^{-1}. Such concentrations are vastly greater than can be achieved outside the laboratory in the workplace or the environment.

Subchronic toxicity

Paclobutrazol was fed in the diet to rats at concentrations of 0, 50, 250, and 1250 ppm for 90 days (equivalent to a dose of 1.6, 8, and 40 mg kg^{-1} day^{-1}). At the highest dose, weight gain and food consumption decreased, and liver weight increased. At the intermediate dose, only a slight effect was seen (females only) and was considered to be toxicologically insignificant. There was no evidence of pathological change at terminal examination. The no-observed-effect level (NOEL) was considered to be 250 ppm (about 8 mg kg^{-1} day^{-1}).

USEPA has published a reference dose for paclobutrazol of 0.013 mg kg^{-1} day^{-1}, based on these data (USEPA, 1997a). The reference dose (RfD) is the lifetime daily intake that is considered to have no potential for harm. USEPA considers the no-effect level to be 12.5 mg kg^{-1} day^{-1} on the basis of default assumptions for food consumption of 1 ppm, equal to 0.05 mg kg^{-1} day^{-1}.

A similar study was conducted in dogs over a six-week period at daily oral doses (by capsule) of 0, 15, 75, and 225 mg kg^{-1} day^{-1}. There was no evidence of overt toxicity and no histopathologic changes. Animals at the higher doses were found to have dose-related increased liver weight. The NOEL may be considered as 15 mg kg^{-1} day^{-1}.

Chronic toxicity and carcinogenicity

Evaluation of the ability of a chemical to cause cancer is carried out with two species, usually rats and mice, treated with the test substance over a two-year period, which approaches the life span of these species. Cancer studies are combined with lifetime studies of general toxic effects through the use of a broad range of clinical laboratory assays, which provide the most thorough picture of adverse responses. The assays described below indicate that paclobutrazol has no carcinogenic potential and produces a limited spectrum of systemic responses.

Fifty male and 50 female rats had dietary exposure of 0, 50, 250, and 1250 ppm (equivalent to 1.4, 6.8, and 34 mg kg^{-1} day^{-1} in males, and 1.8, 8.8, and 44 mg kg^{-1} day^{-1} in females). Treatment was continuous over 104 weeks. There was no evidence of carcinogenic potential at any dose rate, and only systemic effects at rates greater than 6.8 mg kg^{-1} day^{-1} in males and 8.8 mg kg^{-1} day^{-1} in females. The effects were minor and this exposure level was proposed as the no-effect level.

A similar study in mice utilized groups of 51 animals of each sex fed diets containing paclobutrazol concentrations of 15, 125, and 750 ppm, representing daily doses of 3, 15, and 45 mg kg^{-1} day^{-1}, respectively. There was no evidence of carcinogenic potential. Systemic toxicity appeared in a comparable pattern to the rat and the no-effect level was established at 125 ppm, or 15 mg kg^{-1} day^{-1}.

A year-long assessment of dogs given 0, 15, 75, and 300 mg kg^{-1} day^{-1} allowed more detailed study of clinical and biochemical abnormalities that might result from intoxication. Six male and six female beagles were on study. The highest dose rate caused a decrease in weight but general condition remained good. The no-effect level was considered to be 75 mg kg^{-1} day^{-1}; changes at this dose rate were adaptive only.

Effects on reproduction and development

Two assays have been done in rats with dose rates ranging from 2.5 to 250 mg kg^{-1} day^{-1} during days 7–16 of gestation. The highest dose caused overt toxicity and some maternal deaths. At 100 mg kg^{-1} day^{-1}, there were some minimal signs of toxicity in the first study but none at that dose in the second study. In both assays, there was no effect on litter size or weight of offspring, and no evidence of loss of embryos either before or after implanting on the wall of the uterus. The evidence indicates that paclobutrazol is not a direct teratogen, but is fetotoxic. The no-effect level for these experiments was established at 10 mg kg^{-1} day^{-1}.

With rabbits (much less sensitive to the fetotoxic effects) at dose rates up to 125 mg kg^{-1} day^{-1}, there was no evidence of increased visceral or skeletal defects other than a single cardiac anomaly even though the highest dose caused maternal toxicity. There were also no changes in rates of pre- or post-implantation of embryos, intrauterine deaths or fetal weights. The cardiac defect occurs at low frequency in these animals without treatment and was probably spontaneous rather than treatment-related.

The multi-generation reproduction assay is designed to respond to any injury to either males or females that may affect fertility or ability to carry and support offspring. It also seeks to identify changes that may affect the ability of offspring to reproduce. The study used 15 male and 30 female weanling rats on diets containing 0, 50, 250, or 1250 ppm paclobutrazol (approximately 1.4, 6.8, and 34 mg kg^{-1} day^{-1} in adults). The animals were mated after 12 weeks on the diets to produce a first set of litters, and re-mated later to produce a second set of litters. The offspring were maintained on the same diet, mated, and their offspring evaluated.

At the highest dose rate, both generations of parents exhibited decreased weight gain and increased fat in the liver, which was consistent with findings in animals at high doses in other experiments. There was no evidence of pathological change in reproductive organs at any dose, and no adverse effects on reproductive parameters, even with evident systemic toxicity at the highest intake.

Genetic toxicity and mutation

Genetic toxicity usually refers to structural damage to DNA or chromosomes (making them nonfunctional), and mutation is a change in DNA that can potentially cause a cell to behave abnormally and give rise to daughter cells with the same defect. The normal background for offspring with genetic defects is above 1%; most cannot be attributed to a specific cause. The normal frequency of occurrence of cancer in humans is one in every three to four lifetimes. The obligation of the testing process is to avoid any additions to those burdens.

The Ames test and related assays utilize a series of strains of Salmonella bacteria. The mouse lymphoma assay is done with a specific cell line that has been standardized in culture over many years. If the test material causes a mutation, it enables the cells to utilize and grow on a substance that is lethal to normal cells. Paclobutrazol was not mutagenic in the several strains of Salmonella or in mouse lymphoma cells.

Rats were administered paclobutrazol in single doses of 0, 30, 150, or 300 mg kg^{-1}, and the chromosomes of bone marrow cells were evaluated at intervals up to 48 h. There was a small increase in aberrations 12 h after treatment with 300 mg kg^{-1} but at no other time. It was not considered related to treatment, indicating that paclobutrazol does not cause chromosomal damage at these levels of exposure. Paclobutrazol at doses of 40, 200, and 400 mg kg^{-1} to rats did not induce DNA synthesis, an indication that it does not damage DNA.

The sum of the genetic toxicity and mutagenicity data lead to a conclusion that paclobutrazol is not genetically active. These findings also support the carcinogenicity data that indicate that paclobutrazol is not carcinogenic.

EXPOSURE ANALYSIS

Worker exposure, typical operations

The usual dilution for soil placement is 1:12 (18.2 g l^{-1}). Application rates range from 50 to 200 ml of diluted formulation per 2.5 cm DBH. Trees of 25 cm diameter at the maximum rate would require a total of 2000 ml dilute formulation. It is estimated that each tree requires 15 min per application. In an 8-h day, a worker may be assumed to mix and apply 64 l of solution containing 1.2 kg active ingredient, treating 32 trees.

The nature of application indicates that exposure and intake incidental to work will be limited almost entirely to the mixing activity. However, direct field studies of applicator exposure or absorbed dosage have not been made. Measurements have been made for mixing and loading of other pesticides, of which work with phenoxy herbicides is most useful. A study of skin absorption of paclobutrazol by rats over 24 h indicates that absorption is not rapid (1% of concentrate and 16% of a 1:450 dilution of the concentrate). The low rate of absorption of concentrate is consistent with absorption factors known for herbicides, which have been extensively studied in the field, and suggests that excretion rates will be reasonably consistent as well. For purposes of estimating mixer and applicator risk associated with routine use of paclobutrazol, a daily absorption of 0.0002 mg kg^{-1} body weight, twice the rate suggested by the Frank et al. (1985) studies, is assumed.

Exposure through accidental spillage

As with any kind of pesticide, a worker may somehow accidentally spill either concentrated or dilute paclobutrazol on clothed or bare body surfaces. A severe case scenario would be spillage of 0.5 l of concentrate directly on the worker. Most of such a volume would drip from the subject, and most of that reaching clothing would be bound to fabric and not immediately available for absorption.

While we expect that contaminated clothing would be removed and the skin washed, preventing absorption of almost all of the spilled material, for this analysis we assume 100 ml (21.8 g) reaches the skin. With a 1% absorption factor, the exposure dose with the concentrate would be 4.4 mg kg^{-1} for a 50 kg person and for the diluted material the estimated dose would be 0.36 mg kg^{-1}.

Public exposure

Many of the exposure scenarios typical of herbicide application do not occur in the use of paclobutrazol. There is no spraying, which means no exposure of workers or the public to airborne droplets, and there will be no contact with the skin because the TGR is buried.

Exposure via water contamination is not a significant factor because the potential for entry to water is so low and the extent of use is limited, providing for extensive dilution to occur if entry to water should occur.

Dietary exposure is imaginable though unlikely. The possible but unlikely routes of exposure via ingestion are (1) ingestion of leaves or fruits from treated trees, and (2) ingestion of soil from the back fill of an application site.

Existing data suggests that soil concentration may be as high as 200–400 ppm, and dissipation from the site or microbial metabolism is slow. Ingestion of 1 g of soil by a 15-kg child would provide a dose of 0.027 mg kg^{-1}, assuming complex extraction by the gut. USEPA assumes that 95% of children ingest less than 200 mg of soil daily, but some individuals have been observed to consume as much as 60 g in a day (Calabrese et al., 1997; Calabrese, 1978), an amount that would carry a dose of about 1.6 mg paclobutrazol kg^{-1}.

A child might eat leaves from a treated tree out of curiosity. We consider this to be highly unlikely because foliage from treated trees will generally be out of reach, and the taste of leaves is unattractive.

However, we provide the following assessment of exposure via ingestion for the risk analysis. Assuming a 15-kg child consumes 50 g of green leaves containing 4 ppm paclobutrazol, the exposure of the child is to 0.2 mg of paclobutrazol, or 0.013 mg kg^{-1}.

There is a possibility that a child or adult might handle treated soil. There is a body of literature in which incidental skin contact is estimated, but discussions of handling bulk soil have not been found. We assume contact with 10 g of soil, in the absence of better information.

A summary of the exposures used in the risk analysis is in Table 6.

RISK ANALYSIS

A summary of the risk assessment and human health risk margins of safety are in Table 7.

Cancer or genetic effects

Paclobutrazol does not exhibit genetic activity, and assays for carcinogenicity show that it is highly unlikely that it may induce cancer. The relatively rapid excretion of paclobutrazol with only limited change to make it more soluble is consistent with absence of carcinogenic activity.

Human health risk to applicators, under typical conditions

The NOEL used is 7 mg kg^{-1} day^{-1}, based on two-year studies in rats. The no-effect-levels in all other assays (including reproductive assessments) were higher. For purposes of estimating worker risk associated with routine use of paclobutrazol, we assume a daily absorption of 0.0002 mg kg^{-1}. This leads to a margin of safety that is (7.0 mg kg^{-1} day^{-1})(0.0002 mg kg^{-1} day^{-1})$^{-1}$ = 35,000.

Human health risk to applicators, as a result of spills

A spill on the body of 0.5 l of paclobutrazol concentrate results in an exposure of 4.4 mg kg^{-1}. The margin of safety is (7.0 mg kg^{-1} day^{-1})(4.4 mg kg^{-1} day^{-1})$^{-1}$ = 1.6, which is far below the standard of 100; however, exposure is very brief, compared to the NOEL which is based on lifetime exposure. For a spill of 0.5 l of paclobutrazol diluted for application, the margin of safety is (7.0 mg kg^{-1} day^{-1})(0.36 mg kg^{-1} day^{-1})$^{-1}$ = 19.

We expect, however, that a competent and well-supervised crew will follow proper procedures and will remove contaminated clothing and wash the affected skin. In this case, we consider it highly unlikely that adverse systemic effect will result although skin irritation may occur.

Human health risk to the public

Given the method of application of paclobutrazol, there is no likely route of exposure other than direct contact with soil at the treatment site or possibly a child eating leaves.

There are three scenarios for soil-mediated exposure to paclobutrazol:
- A. An individual is assumed to retain 10 g of soil containing 0.4 mg g^{-1} (400 ppm) on the skin. Assuming intimate contact, no hand washing for 2 h and a 1% absorption rate, the absorbed dose for a 50-kg individual would be 80 ug, or 0.0016 mg kg^{-1}. This leads to a margin of safety in this case that is (7.0 mg kg^{-1} day^{-1})(0.0016 mg kg^{-1} day^{-1})$^{-1}$ = 4375.

Table 6. Exposure to paclobutrazol

	Expected dose to workers* mg kg^{-1} body weight	
	Paclobutrazol handled (kg^{-1})	32^{-1} 25 cm trees treated
Mixing and application, normal	0.000083	0.0002
	per incident	
Spill of concentrate, 0.5 l	4.4	
Spill of treatment mixture (diluted concentrate), 0.5 l	0.36	

*Estimates are based on comparison with excretion of herbicides following mixing and loading for aerial application, and therefore represent dosage, not exposure.

	Public exposure*	
	Amount of soil or leaves ingested (g)	Dose** body weight (mg kg^{-1})
Ingestion of soil, 15-kg child	1	0.027
	5	0.135
	60	1.6
Ingestion of leaves	50	0.013

*No exposure through consumption of food and water, no surface deposition.
**Assumes complete extraction by the gut.

Table 7. Summary of risk assessments and margins of safety associated with use of paclobutrazol as a tree growth regulator[a]

Systemic effects	(NOEL mg kg^{-1} day^{-1})(Dose mg kg^{-1} day^{-1})$^{-1}$	Margin of safety
Workers		
Mixer and applicator	(7.0 mg kg^{-1} day^{-1})(0.0002 mg kg^{-1} day^{-1})$^{-1}$	35,000
Spill of 0.5 l concentrate	(7.0 mg kg^{-1} day^{-1})(4.4 mg kg^{-1})$^{-1}$	1.6
Spill of 0.5 l diluted	(7.0 mg kg^{-1} day^{-1})(0.36 mg kg^{-1})$^{-1}$	19
Public, adult: The nature of application of paclobutrazol in this use is such that exposure of adults in normal activities will be zero.		
Adult handling 10 g treated soil (400 ppm) for 2 h, absorption 1%/h	(7.0 mg kg^{-1} day^{-1})(0.0016 mg kg^{-1})$^{-1}$	4300
Public, 15-kg child		
Playing in treated soil for 2 h. 30 g soil (400 ppm), dermal absorption 2%/h	(7.0 mg kg^{-1} day^{-1})(0.032 mg kg^{-1} day^{-1})$^{-1}$	219
Ingests 1 g soil, absorption complete	(7.0 mg kg^{-1} day^{-1})(0.027 mg kg^{-1} day^{-1})$^{-1}$	260
Ingests 5 g soil, absorption complete	(7.0 mg kg^{-1} day^{-1})(0.133 mg kg^{-1} day^{-1})$^{-1}$	52
Ingests 60 g soil, absorption complete	(7.0 mg kg^{-1} day^{-1})(1.6 mg kg^{-1} day^{-1})$^{-1}$	4
Ingests 50 g green leaves	(7.0 mg kg^{-1} day^{-1})(0.013 mg kg^{-1} day^{-1})$^{-1}$	538

[a] Assays for carcinogenicity and mutagenicity of paclobutrazol have been negative, and metabolic changes possibly suggestive of activation to genetic activity do not occur. A cancer risk assessment is therefore not necessary. Reproductive NOEL's are higher than those for systemic effects; systemic margins of safety therefore apply.

– B. A 15-kg child playing in treated soil for two hours per day is assumed to have 30 g of soil containing 0.4 mg g^{-1} on the skin. Assuming the rate of absorption is twice that of an adult, the dose over 2 h would 12 mg × 0.04% absorbed = 0.48 mg 15 kg^{-1} = 0.032 mg kg^{-1} day^{-1}. This leads to a margin of safety of (7.0 mg kg^{-1} day^{-1})(0.032 mg kg^{-1} day^{-1})$^{-1}$ = 219.
– C. Ingestion of 1 g of soil containing 400 ppm paclobutrazol will provide a dose of 0.4 mg. For a 15-kg child, the exposure level is 0.027 mg kg^{-1}. Assuming all of the paclobutrazol is absorbed from the gut, the margin of safety is (7.0 mg kg^{-1} day^{-1})(0.027 mg kg^{-1} day^{-1})$^{-1}$ = 259. If the ingestion level is 5 g of soil, the margin of safety is (7.0 mg kg^{-1} day^{-1}) (0.135 mg kg^{-1} day^{-1})$^{-1}$ = 52. These amounts of soil ingestion are high; it is estimated that 95% of children consume less than 200 mg of soil per day (Calabrese et al., 1997).

While unlikely, it is possible a child might ingest green leaves from a treated tree. The exposure assessment of 0.013 mg kg^{-1} day^{-1} is based on a 15-kg child ingesting 50 g of green leaves. In this instance, the margin of safety is (7.0 mg kg^{-1} day^{-1})(0.013 mg kg^{-1} day^{-1})$^{-1}$ = 538.

FLURPRIMIDOL

Flurprimidol is a plant growth regulator. It is absorbed by plant leaves and roots, and exhibits translocation primarily in the xylem. It is used to decrease the rate of growth in a wide range of plants, including deciduous and coniferous trees. It acts by inhibiting gibberellin biosynthesis.

Flurprimidol

IUPAC name: (RS)-2-methyl-1-pyrimidin-5-yl-1-(4-(trifluoromethoxyphenyl)=propan-1-ol.

Chemical Abstracts name: α-(1-methylethyl)-α-[4-(trifluoromethoxy)phenyl]=5-pyrimidinemethanol.

Molecular weight: 312.3.
Melting point: 93.5–97°C.
Boiling point: 264°C.
Vapor Pressure: 4.85 × 10^{-2} mPa (25°C).
K_{ow}: log P = 3.34 (pH 7, 20°C).
Solubility: water (distilled, 20°C) 114 mg l^{-1}, hexane 1260 mg l^{-1}, methanol 1990 g l^{-1}.
Stability: <10% hydrolysis after 5 days at pH 4, 7, and 9. Photolytically decomposes in water, half-life 4.3 h in the laboratory, with an estimated half-life in the field of 1.8 h at 40 degrees latitude in summer and 7.5 h in winter (Saunders and Mosier, 1985).

ENVIRONMENTAL BEHAVIOR OF FLURPRIMIDOL

Soil and ground water

In the Cutless® formulation, flurprimidol is applied as a pellet inserted directly into the stem of the tree. As a result, little flurprimidol should enter the soil directly. It is possible some may enter soil through leaf- or litter-fall, although this has not been quantified. Root exudation or release of residues through root decomposition seems unlikely given the primary movement of this material upward with the water stream in the xylem.

Should flurprimidol enter the soil, it is strongly adsorbed by the soil, is not readily desorbed and shows negligible leaching (British Crop Protection Council, 1997). It is somewhat persistent in soil, showing a field dissipation half-life of 5–55 days (British Crop Protection council, 1997). USEPA fact sheet shows an estimated soil half-life of 1.5 years in unvegetated loam, but a half-life of only 5–21 days in turf (USEPA, 1989).

Jackson (1994) applied ^{14}C-labeled flurprimidol to soil and peat in the laboratory (field application rate of 45 g ha^{-1}). The soils were incubated at 40% moisture holding capacity (80% for the peat) under aerobic conditions in the dark at 20 ± 2°C, and evolved ^{14}C-carbon dioxide was quantified. ^{14}C-flurprimidol was also applied to the surface of peat soil in open pots that were then exposed to sunlight in a glasshouse. He reported a degradation half-life of 119 days in the Marcham sandy loam, 138 days in the Standard 2.2 loamy sand, 157 days in the Marcham sandy clay loam, and 187 days in the peat.

Figure 3 shows the results for loamy sand. The others are similar. The regression equations are in Table 8.

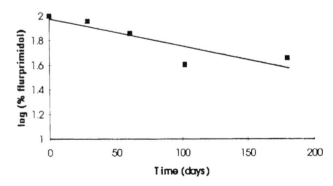

Fig. 3. Concentration of flurprimidol in loamy sand (percent remaining with time).

Table 8. Regression equations and regression coefficients for the concentration of flurprimidol with time in different soils

	Regression equation	Regression coefficient
Loamy sand	$Y = 0.0021795X + 1.974133$	$R = 0.87$
Sandy loam	$Y = 0.0025278X + 1.956868$	$R = 0.96$
Sandy clay loam	$Y = 0.0019124X + 2.000198$	$R = 0.99$
Peat	$Y = 0.0016123X + 1.884128$	$R = 0.97$

From these findings, we conclude that little flurprimidol will enter the soil environment other than the degree to which it is present in senescent leaves when they fall. Any flurprimidol entering the soil by this mechanism will exhibit only moderate persistence, and will dissipate due to the microbial decomposition. It is strongly adsorbed by soil and will exhibit only very limited mobility.

Vegetation

Flurprimidol is absorbed into the woody tissues in the area of the implant. It is transported passively with water in the xylem moving to the growing points of the stem. It does not accumulate preferentially in fruits or nuts (Dow AgroSciences, 1996), although the label indicates a use precaution against the use of this material on trees that will be used for fruit or nut harvesting for food or feed, or trees that are or might be tapped for sugar. Plants do not readily metabolize Flurprimidol, so it is likely to persist in the tissues to which it moves for an extended period of time. However, the concentration in this tissue will decrease over time due to growth dilution (the increasing volume of the tissue due to growth).

Sterrett and Tworkoski (1987) used C-14 labeled flurprimidol to determine the fate of the chemical in one-year old apple seedlings. Thirty-five days after injection, 10% had moved into the new shoots, 1.5% into the scion phloem and 80% remained near the site of injection. There was little metabolism of the material, with unmetabolized flurprimidol accounting for 95% of the material in xylem, 86% in phloem and 75% in the shoots. Using data they report for leaf weight from another experiment and adjusting for plant age, we calculate that the concentration of flurprimidol in leaves to be 24 mg kg^{-1}.

Relying on the same data and an application rate of 22 g tree^{-1} (25 cm diameter sycamore tree, sycamore is a group-two species, requiring the higher rate of application for effectiveness), we calculate 2 g would be contained in all of the foliage and shoots of the tree. For purposes of this analysis, we assume 100 kg of foliage and stems in a tree this size or, alternatively, that all of the flurprimidol that has translocated to the crown is concentrated in the foliage or fruits of this total weight. Based on this, we estimate the concentration of flurprimidol in this material would be approximately 24 ppm.

Vandervoort et al. (1997) studied the fate of flurprimidol in composted turf grass residues and found little decline in the residue level in the first 128 days. There was no flurprimidol detected one year after application.

Based on these findings, we conclude that the concentration of flurprimidol in plant material might be 24 ppm. Additionally, we conclude that residue levels of flurprimidol in leaf litter from treated trees will decrease only slowly with time, and will likely be incorporated into the soil with the decomposing organic matter of the leaves. Once in the soil, it is expected to exhibit the patterns of persistence and mobility previously described for soil behavior.

Air

In the Cutless® formulation, flurprimidol is applied as a pellet inserted directly into the stem of the tree. This method of application nearly eliminates any exposure of the chemical to the air. This, combined with its low vapor pressure (4.85×10^{-2} mPa), will nearly eliminate any possibility of evaporation to air. As a result of these factors, we conclude that there will be little or no residue of flurprimidol in the air, and we therefore eliminate inhalation as a route of exposure.

HAZARD ANALYSIS

The information in this section is from animal toxicology studies prepared by the original registrant, a review by USEPA scientists in the Integrated Risk Information System (IRIS) last revised in 1990, and the USEPA Pesticide Fact Sheet for flurprimidol, dated 1989. It is relevant to the human health risk assessment process. The scientific literature does not include published research on the toxicology of flurprimidol.

Systemic toxicology

The acute median lethal oral dose (LD$_{50}$) for the rat is 709 mg kg^{-1} in females and 914 mg kg^{-1} in males. In mice, the male is slightly more sensitive; the LD$_{50}$ is 602 mg kg^{-1} in males and 702 mg kg^{-1} in females. The intraperitoneal LD$_{50}$s are 489 and 390 mg kg^{-1} for male and female rats, and 352 and 364 mg kg^{-1} for male and female mice, respectively (Kehr, 1982).

There were no systemic effects and little local inflammation caused by a single 500 mg kg^{-1} dermal application of flurprimidol. Abrading the skin of the treatment area prior to application enhanced potential effects (Pierson, 1982). There was no evidence of systemic toxicity over the two weeks of post-treatment observation, and dermal irritation was limited to a slight reddening of the skin in one animal.

Flurprimidol does not cause allergic sensitization in guinea pigs. To sensitize the animals, they were treated on the skin three times weekly for two weeks with 50 mg crystalline flurprimidol. The material was held under a bandage for 6 h at each application. Ten days later, flurprimidol was applied as a challenge to a different area; there was no indication of sensitization or irritation (Brown, 1986). A similar evaluation at an applied dose of 400 mg also produced no evidence of sensitization (Berdasco, 1992).

Flurprimidol was applied to the skin of rabbits at rates of 0, 500, and 1000 mg kg^{-1} day^{-1} on five animals per group per sex. Treatment was repeated, apparently daily, for 21 days. No systemic effects were observed at any application rate; the NOEL for systemic effects was considered to be greater than 1000 mg kg^{-1} day^{-1}. Slight transient irritation was evident at both treatment levels; a NOEL for skin irritation was not established (USEPA, 1997b).

Application of 0.1 ml of undiluted flurprimidol (64 mg) to one eye of each of a similar group of rabbits caused corneal dullness and slight conjunctivitis, which cleared in 3 days (Pierson, 1982).

Subchronic toxicity

A three-month feeding study of rats indicated a NOEL of 1.68 mg kg^{-1} day^{-1} in females and 1.98 mg kg^{-1} day^{-1} for males. There were significant increases in the activity of a liver enzyme at 6.04 and 7.13 mg kg^{-1} day^{-1} in females and males, respectively, with hypertrophy of liver cells at higher dose rates. There was evidence of increased ovarian weight and elevated white blood cell counts at the higher treatment levels. All effects were reversible (Kehr, 1982). In a 90-day mouse assay, dose rates were 0, 15, 67.5, and 300 mg kg^{-1} day^{-1}. The NOEL was 15 mg kg^{-1} day^{-1}. Higher doses caused induction of liver enzymes, increased liver weight and cellular hypertrophy.

In a three-month study with the dog, dose rates of 0.5, 1.5, and 30 mg kg^{-1} day^{-1} were used to measure the ability of the adrenal cortex to produce its hormones. At the highest dose rate, the cortisol levels in the plasma of treated animals were significantly decreased. In some of the animals the adrenal cortex was atrophied. There was no effect at the two lowest doses. The effect occurred in the first few days of treatment and did not progress with further treatment, which indicates that non-effective doses would probably not cause changes with the longer exposures (Kehr, 1986).

Reproduction and development

The multigenerational reproduction assay is designed to respond to any injury to either males or females that may directly or indirectly affect fertility or ability to carry and support offspring. It also identifies changes that may affect the ability of offspring to reproduce. Assays of this kind also provide sensitive non-specific indications of cumulative non-reproductive effects.

Hoyt (1986) placed 25 male and 25 female weanling rats on diets containing 0, 25, 100, and 1000 ppm flurprimidol (0, 1.8, 7.3, and 74 mg kg^{-1} day^{-1}) for 70 days until they were of breeding age. The same diets were maintained through production of 2 l, and offspring from the first set of litters were placed on the same diets at weaning through mating and production of 2 l, which were evaluated.

Mating performance and fertility were not affected at the two lower doses (1.8 and 7.3 mg kg^{-1} day^{-1}); the reproductive NOEL was therefore 7.3 mg kg^{-1} day^{-1}. The latter dose rate did produce some evidence of parental toxicity, however. The NOEL for parental toxicity was 1.8 mg kg^{-1} day^{-1}. The highest dose rate resulted in substantial effect, both on reproduction and general toxicity.

In rabbits, at dose rates of 0, 1.7, 9, and 45 mg kg^{-1} day^{-1} through the period of organogenesis, there was no teratogenic effect. At the highest dose rate, maternal body weight and food intake were decreased; the NOEL for maternal toxicity was 9 mg kg^{-1} day^{-1} (Hagopian, 1985). Dose rates in the rat teratology study were higher: 2.5, 10, 45, and 200 mg kg^{-1} day^{-1}. Maternal toxicity was evident at 45 mg kg^{-1} day^{-1} in the form of decreased body weight and food intake. There was no maternal effect at the two lower dose rates and developmental effects were also absent at the two lower rates (Byrd, 1985).

Genetic toxicity and mutation

Flurprimidol has shown no evidence of genetic toxicity in a variety of assays. An extensive bacterial mutagenicity-testing scheme produced no effect at concentrations up to 1000 ug ml^{-1}, at which level cellular toxicity became evident. There was no evidence of increased DNA repair activity in cultured liver cells at a concentration of 100 nmole ml^{-1}. An intraperitoneal dose of 300 mg kg^{-1} IP was negative in the Chinese hamster bone marrow sister chromatid exchange assay (Kehr, 1982; Thompson, 1982; USEPA, 1989).

Chronic toxicity and carcinogenicity studies

Assays have been conducted over two year periods with rats and mice, which approaches the life span of these animals. The studies show no oncogenic potential.

In the two-year rat study, the males received 0, 1.0, 3.6, 12.1, and 41.2 mg kg^{-1} day^{-1}; the dose rate for females was 0, 1.2, 4.4, 14.5 and 49.3 mg kg^{-1} day^{-1}. The NOEL was 3.6 mg kg^{-1} day^{-1}, or 90 ppm in the diet. Effects seen at higher dose rates were primarily in the liver, with enzyme induction, accumulation of fat and eosinophils (a type of white blood cell) and foci of altered cell structure. At the highest dose rate, cholesterol and serum triglycerides were increased in both sexes. The dose rates in mice were 0, 1.4, 10.5, and 79.9 mg kg^{-1} day^{-1}. The NOEL for systemic toxicity was 1.4 mg kg^{-1} day^{-1}. Higher dose rates caused increased liver weight in males.

EXPOSURE ANALYSIS

Properly used, the implants containing flurprimidol (Cutless® tablets) are placed in the boreholes in the tree trunk where they dissolve in a short time, and absorption into the transpiration stream of the tree takes place. Removal of an implanted tablet after placement is difficult because of the rapid dissolution of the implant. In other words, if a small child were to peel away the material covering the implant site, the material in the borehole would be very difficult to access or handle. Exposure would probably be limited to any residue that could be absorbed or licked from the fingers. If the implants remain in place, exposure may be expected to be essentially zero for all worker or public groups.

Exposure potential is limited to (1) the possibility that a person or animal might ingest a tablet, (2) careless handling by a worker with moistening, crumbling of the tablet and possible absorption across the skin, and (3) ingestion of foliage from a treated tree.

Worker exposure

As a dry solid, the Cutless® tablets can be handled with negligible transfer to skin of workers, who should wear gloves in any case. Flurprimidol is slightly water soluble ($\sim$130 mg l^{-1}; 130 ppm); surface wetting of the tablets would mobilize only a small amount of the material. The tendency of the tablets to crumble when moistened could cause the material to distribute on bare hands, which would increase the available surface area. Although skin absorption of flurprimidol is quite limited and no systemic toxicity resulted from heavy experimental skin exposure, workers should not handle the implants if they should become moist. It is unlikely that a properly informed and equipped worker would be significantly exposed on the skin. As a general case, worker training, education and proper equipment can adequately deal with exposure. Based on this, we conclude that there will be no worker exposure to flurprimidol.

Public exposure

The most likely exposure of the public would result from the ingestion of a Cutless® tablet by a child. Exposure of an adult by this route is virtually nil. A 1 g tablet ingested by a 20-kg child represents a total dose of 50 mg kg^{-1}, assuming complete absorption. Distribution of an entire moistened tablet on the skin seems highly unlikely, but if it did occur and absorption of 1% of the content of the tablet occurred, a 50-kg person would thereby acquire 10 mg of flurprimidol. As a practical matter, if a tablet were to be crushed against the skin, most of the material would fall away. Absorption is not likely to be more than 1 mg of flurprimidol.

To estimate exposure from ingestion of leaves from treated trees, we used data from Sterrett and Tworkoski (1987). We calculate the concentration of flurprimidol in leaves might be 24 mg kg^{-1}. Assuming a 15-kg child were to ingest 50 g of green leaves, the exposure would be 1.2 mg for the child, or 0.08 mg kg^{-1}.

RISK ANALYSIS

We conclude that there is no human health risk to workers because there is no exposure. Human health risk assessment for the public is possible, using the exposure scenarios outlined above.

Ingestion of a tablet with complete absorption would deliver 50 mg kg^{-1} to a 20 kg child. This is many times the NOEL of 1.68 mg kg^{-1} day^{-1}, established for a 90 day oral exposure. This results in a margin of safety of 0.03, much less than one and far from the accepted margin of safety of 100. If a single tablet is accessible, many are likely to be, and the dose and risk increases with multiple ingestion. This level of human health risk is preventable, and calls for mitigation measures that prevent access of the general public to the Cutless® tablets.

A moistened, crumbling tablet distributed over the surface of the bare hand is unlikely without deliberate intent. However, the 1% estimated absorption would deliver 10 mg of flurprimidol, or a dose of 0.2 mg kg^{-1} to a 50-kg person. A more likely dose is based on delivery of 1 mg of flurprimidol, or a dose of 0.02 mg kg^{-1} to a 50 kg person. The margins of safety for these two scenarios are: $(1.68 \text{ mg kg}^{-1})(0.2 \text{ mg kg}^{-1})^{-1} = 8.4$ and $(1.68 \text{ mg kg}^{-1})(0.02 \text{ mg kg}^{-1})^{-1} = 84$.

Adopting the hypothetical scenario for exposure of a child through ingestion of leaves, the risk assessment shows a level of exposure of 0.08 mg kg^{-1} day^{-1}, contrasted with a NOEL of 1.68 mg kg^{-1} day^{-1}. This leads to a human health risk margin of safety $(1.68 \text{ mg kg}^{-1})(0.08 \text{ mg kg}^{-1})^{-1} = 21$.

DOMESTIC ANIMAL AND WILDLIFE RISK ASSESSMENT FOR PACLOBUTRAZOL AND FLURPRIMIDOL

The risk assessment for domestic animals and wildlife follows the same form as the risk assessment for humans. The hazard analysis provides the following toxicity values:

	Paclobutrazol	Flurprimidol
Mammals: rat, or mouse LD_{50}	490 mg kg^{-1}	709 mg kg^{-1}
Bird: acute oral LD_{50} mallard or quail	7900 mg kg^{-1}	>2000 mg kg^{-1}
Fish: LC_{50} 96 h rainbow	27.8 mg l^{-1}	18.3 mg l^{-1}
Aquatic invertebrate: Daphnia LC_{50} (48 h)	33.2 mg l^{-1}	11.8 mg l^{-1}
Bee: acute oral NOEL	0.002 mg bee^{-1}	0.1 mg bee^{-1}

Analysis of exposure potential shows it is limited to consumption of foliage or fruits from trees treated with flurprimidol and paclobutrazol, with the additional route of exposure for paclobutrazol involving contact with treated soil or the external portions of the stem of the tree when the soil drench method of application is used. There is no exposure of aquatic species.

Comparison of the exposure levels with the critical toxicity values for all of the classes of organisms identified above shows adequate margins of safety. Example values include:

	Margin of safety	
	Paclobutrazol	Flurprimidol
Mammals: oral exposure	44.5	29
Bird: oral exposure	144	208
Earthworms: environmental exposure	5	42

From this analysis, we conclude there will be no adverse effects on domestic animals or wildlife as a result of the use of paclobutrazol or flurprimidol when used according to label directions as provided for Profile® 2SC or Cutless® tree growth regulator products.

MANAGEMENT AND MITIGATION TO MINIMIZE RISK TO ENVIRONMENT, HUMANS, AND WILDLIFE

There are so few risks with the use of the Profile® 2SC or Cutless® tree growth regulator products that few unique management or mitigation steps would be helpful in reducing risk, assuming applications are done in accordance with the label and state regulations.

The primary concern about environmental effects from the use of paclobutrazol relates to contamination of ground water. Normal patterns of use will not result in ground water contamination. Special care should be used in planning applications of paclobutrazol to prevent entry to wells located within the drip-line of trees to be treated. This will prevent misapplication into a well, or rapid translocation of soil-applied material through air pockets in soil along the side of a well casing. Applications of paclobutrazol should also be avoided where (a) soils are heavily compacted such that soil-applied material might not penetrate the soil and be washed in surface runoff into surface water, (b) there is evidence of a very high water table (such as seeps, springs or areas that qualify as wetlands), or (c) in areas with very sandy soils.

The human health risk assessment for workers and the general public shows that there are adequate margins of safety involved with the use of Profile® 2SC and Cutless® tree growth regulator products if care is taken in handling. Risk to workers can be reduced by adhering to the standards of good practice outlined on the label. We conclude that the best approach to risk management is prevention of exposure.

For the general public, the key is to minimize or prevent contact with the commercial products. Covering soil-drench areas or areas where soil-injected material has been forced to the surface with fresh soil will minimize exposure of the public to Profile® 2SC. Sealing the injection holes where Cutless® tablets have been implanted will prevent access by children. Careful security of the Cutless® tablets at all times is necessary to prevent ingestion of one or more tablets by a child. While ingestion of leaves is possible, we believe this avenue of exposure can also be mitigated through a program of notification.

There are no special mitigation or management techniques required for protection of domestic animals or wildlife.

REFERENCES

Atreya, N.C., M.V. Skidmore, and F.J. Lewis. 1990. Paclobutrazol: An overview of behavior in soil and effects on soil organisms. Unpublished report. ICI Agrochemicals, Bracknell, Berkshire, United Kingdom. 7 pp.

Berdasco, N.M. 1992. Cutless® 0.5%: Dermal sensitization potential in the Hartley albino guinea pig. The Toxicology Research Laboratory, The Dow Chemical Company. Study ID 0329-4608-001.

Breedlove, D.A., H.A. Holt, and W.R. Chaney. 1989. Tree growth regulators: An annotated bibliography. Purdue Univ. Agric. Exp. Sta. Bull., 989. 135 pp.

British Crop Protection Council. 1997. The pesticide manual, 11th ed. C.D.S. Tomlin, ed. British Crop Protection Council, Farnham, Surrey, United Kingdom.

Brown, G.E. 1986. A guinea pig sensitization study of flurprimidol (EL-500, Compound 72500). Toxicology Division, Lilly Research Laboratories. Study GO1485.

Byrd, R.A. 1985. A teratology study of flurprimidol (EL-500, Compound 72500) administered orally to Charles River CD rats. Toxicology Division, Lilly Research Laboratories. Study R14584.

Calabrese, E.J. 1978. Pollutants and high risk groups. John Wiley and Sons, New York.

Calabrese, E.J., E.J. Stanek, R.C. James, and S.M. Roberts. 1997. Soil ingestion: A concern for acute toxicity in children. Environ. Health Perspect, 105: 1354–1358.

Crook, S.J., C. Mak, and N.C. Atreya. 1989. Paclobutrazol: Dissipation in Malaysian soils from trials carried out during 1987. Unpublished report RJ0690B. ICI Agrochemicals, Bracknell, Berkshire, United Kingdom.

Dow AgroSciences. 1996. Cutless® tree implant. Dow AgroSciences, Indianapolis, IN, USA. 5 pp.

Dow AgroSciences. 1997. Profile®, the tree-growth regulator. Dow AgroSciences, Indianapolis, IN, USA. 5 pp.

Early, J.D. and G.C. Martin. 1988. Translocation and breakdown of C-14 paclobutrazol in peach seedlings. HortScience, 23: 196–200.

Early, J.D. and G.C. Martin. 1989. Transport and accumulation of paclobutrazol in peach seedlings. Acta Horticulturae, 239: 73–76.

FAO. 1988. Pesticide residues in food. Evaluations. 1988. Part 1 — Residues. FAO Plant Production and Protection Paper 93/1. Food and Agriculture Organization, United Nations. pp. 147–164.

Francis, P.D. 1986. Short-term dissipation and movement following a broadcast spray TMU1953. ICI America.

Frank, R., R.A. Campbell, and G.J. Sirons. 1985. Forestry workers involved in aerial application of 2,4-dichlorophenoxyacetic acid: Exposure and urinary excretion. Arch. Environ. Contam. Toxicol., 14: 427–435.

Hagopian, G.S. 1985. A teratology study in Dutch belted rabbits given oral doses of flurprimidol (EL-500, Compound 72500). Toxicology Division, Lilly Research Laboratories. Study BO2584.

Harvey, B.R. and I.R. Hill. 1985. Paclobutrazol: Degradation in aerobic and flooded soils. Unpublished report RJ0370B. Plant Protection Division. ICI. Bracknell, Berkshire, United Kingdom.

Hoyt, J.A. 1986. A one-year two-generation reproduction study in CD rats maintained on diets containing flurprimidol (EL-500, Compound 72500). Toxicology Division, Lilly Research Laboratories.

Jackson, R. 1994. The degradation of flurprimidol in soil. Study 2R, Unpublished Report GHE-P-3515. Dow AgroSciences, Wantage, Oxon, United Kingdom. 54 pp.

Kehr, C. 1982. A summary of laboratory animal toxicology studies and a human health safety assessment of EL-500 (Compound 72500) for a proposed experimental use permit program with Cutless® 50W, a formulation of EL-500. Toxicology Division, Lilly Research Laboratories. Greenfield, IN, USA.

Kehr, C.C. 1986. The three-month subchronic oral toxicity of flurprimidol (EL-500, Compound 72500) in beagle dogs. Toxicology Division, Lilly Research Laboratories. Study DO9585.

Lever, B.G., et al. 1982. Proc. Br. Crop Prot. Conf. — Weeds, 1: 3.

Mak, C. and N.C. Atreya. 1990. Paclobutrazol: Dissipation in Italian soils from trials carried out during 1986. Unpublished report M0722B. ICI Agrochemicals, Bracknell, Berkshire, United Kingdom.

Mak, C., S.J. Crook, and N.C. Atreya. 1987. Paclobutrazol: Field dissipation following subsurface application in US orchard soils up to 12 months. Unpublished report RJ0574B. ICI Agrochemicals, Bracknell, Berkshire, United Kingdom. 25 pp.

Moore, G.M. 1998. Tree growth regulators: Issues of control, matters of management. J. Arboriculture, 24: 10–18.

Norris, L., F.N. Dost, R. Van Bossuyt, and M. Browning. 2000. Use of the registered tree growth regulators paclobutrazol (Profile® 2SC) and flurprimidol (Cutless®) in the state of New York. Generic Environmental Impact Statement. Enviromental Consultants, Inc. Southampton PA. 114 pp. and appendices.

Pearson, F.J. 1984. PP333 and PP333 ketone: Residue profile in soils. Unpublished report TM.

Pierson, C.L. 1982. Acute dermal and ocular toxicity testing of EL-500 (Compound 72500) in New Zealand white rabbits. Toxicology Division, Lilly Research Laboratories. Studies B-D-63-79 and B-E-68-79.

Reed, A.N., E.A. Curry, and M.W. Williams. 1989. Translocation of triazole growth retardants in plant tissues. J. Amer. Soc. Hortic. Sci., 114: 893–898. U1514B. ICI Agrochemicals, Bracknell, Berkshire, United Kingdom.

Saunders, D.G. and J.W. Mosier. 1985. Photolysis of flurprimidol in aqueous solution. Study number EWD8201. Accession number 264253. Eli Lilly and Company. Greenfield, IN, USA.

Sterrett, J.P. and T.J. Tworkoski. 1987. Flurprimidol: Plant response, translocation and metabolism. J. Amer. Soc. Hort. Sci., 112: 341–345.

Thompson, C.Z. 1982. The effect of EL-500 on the induction of bacterial mutation using a modification of the Ames test. Toxicology Division, Lilly Research Laboratories. Study 811109-GPA-1694.

USEPA. 1989. Flurprimidol. Pesticide Fact Sheet 202. US Environmental Protection Agency. Washington, DC, USA. 10 pp.

USEPA. 1997a. Paclobutrazol. Integrated Risk Information System. 7 pp.

USEPA. 1997b. (Last revised 1990) Flurprimidol. Integrated Risk Information System. 7 pp.

Vandervoort, C., M. Zabik, B. Branham, and D. Lickfeldt. 1997. Fate of selected pesticides applied to turfgrass: Effects of composting on residues. Bull. Environ. Contam. Toxicol., 58: 38–45.

BIOGRAPHICAL SKETCHES

Logan A. Norris
Oregon State University and Environmental Consultants, Inc., 4045 NW Dale Place, Corvallis, OR 97330, USA, Phone 541/737-6557, FAX 541/737-5814, E-mail: logan.norris@orst.edu

Logan Norris is Professor and Dept. Head, Emeritus, Dept. of Forest Science, Oregon State University. He also served on the Board of Governors of Environmental Consultants, Incorporated. Since the early 1960's he has been active in research involving the movement, persistence, and fate of herbicides, and with the health and environmental risks associated with their use. His work focuses on forested settings, including rights-of-way.

Frank Dost
Environmental Consultants, Inc., 5944 Sundown Lane, Freeland, WA 98249, USA

Frank Dost is Professor, Emeritus, Dept. Environmental and Molecular Toxicology, Oregon State University. His specialization is toxicology. He has focused on exposure and human health risk assessments for workers and the general public as it relates to the use of herbicides and other chemicals in forestry, agriculture and in rights-of-way management.

Rufin VanBossuyt, Jr.
Environmental Consultants, Inc., 125 Westboro Road, Upton, MA 01568, USA

Rufin VanBossuyt was System Forester, New England Electric until his retirement in 1993. He also served on the Board of Governors of Environmental Consultants, Incorporated. Long active in ISA and the Utility Arborists Association, he received the Lifetime Achievement Award for his leadership in the management of electric utility rights-of-way.

Jeffrey Jenkins
Department of Environmental and Molecular Toxicology, Oregon State University, Corvallis, OR 97331, USA

Jeffrey Jenkins is Professor, Department Environmental and Molecular Toxicology, Oregon State University. His specialization is environmental chemistry and toxicology. Current research activities include field and laboratory studies to examine the impact of pesticide use on air and water quality, and studies designed to investigate human and wildlife exposure as a result of pesticide use in both agricultural and urban settings.

Groundline Decay Prevention without Toxic Materials

Chad Roper, Fred Pfaender, and John Goodman

Amendment of the soil adjacent to a utility pole or similar buried wood with a time-released carbohydrate source slows decay dramatically, without the environmental and safety hazards associated with the introduction of toxins. Consumption of the readily degradable carbohydrate source accelerates the depletion of oxygen from the soil during saturated conditions. Because decay occurs in anaerobic conditions at 1/5th to 1/10th the rate of aerobic conditions, increases in the length of time the soil around a pole is anaerobic produce decreases in the overall rate of degradation. The addition of a simple carbohydrate source also alters the microbial community around the pole to one, which favors bacteria over wood decay fungi. Bacteria are incapable of degrading lignin and are competing with wood decay fungi for mineral and organic nutrients in the soil. Data on oxygen depletion in soil and water systems is presented to support these mechanisms. In accelerated laboratory decay studies, carbohydrate amendment allowed southern yellow pine test strips to have no loss of strength in the same time period that strips without amendment decayed completely (280 days). In the field, application of a time-released carbohydrate source slowed the rate of decay for southern yellow pine stubs (as measured by Pilodyn) to roughly 1/3 of their un-amended counterparts.

Keywords: Carbohydrate, groundline, decay, wood

INTRODUCTION

Biological degradation of wood in the environment is mediated by three major groups of organisms (Brock and Madigan, 1991). Filamentous fungi use their hyphae and extra-cellular enzymes to penetrate and degrade the wood structure. Bacteria of many genera have the ability to utilize the cellulose and hemicellulose components of wood, generally using the material to support their growth and reproduction. Finally, wood boring insects and insect larvae also participate in wood biodegradation.

Wood consists of interlocked layers of cellulose and lignin. The rigidity and structural integrity of wood depends on maintaining the lignin backbone and supporting cellulose materials. Bacteria are probably the most important in cellulose degradation, while fungi, particularly the Basidiomycetes are the most important for lignin degradation. As each layer of lignin is compromised, more cellulose becomes available (Krik and Highley, 1973). Thus, it is the action of wood decay fungi in concert with bacteria which allows for the degradation of wood in nature.

Generally, the organisms responsible for degrading the structure of wood are obligate aerobes, that is, they require oxygen for their metabolism. Ground line decay in utility poles is an example of the convergence of oxygen, fungi, and bacteria causing accelerated wood decay. A model of this process was given by the authors in an earlier publication (Pfaender et al., 1996).

For decades, humankind has looked for ways to treat wood that slow wood decay processes. Current technology has been based almost entirely on treating the wood with materials toxic to the bacteria, fungi, and insects. While this strategy has been quite effective if done properly, it has led to potential environmental problems at each pole, and major hazardous waste problems at sites where wood is treated. In addition to inhibiting microorganisms and insects, most of the chemicals also are toxins or carcinogens for humans and other animals. All of the major wood treating materials currently used (i.e., creosote, pentachlorophenol, and CCA) represent potential human and environmental health hazards. Currently EPA lists over 3000 present and former wood treating operations as hazardous waste sites (www.EPA.gov, 2000). The clean up of these sites represents a major liability for the wood treating industry and railroads, as well as society in general.

If we start with the premise that decay is inevitable, then our goal is to delay the onset or slow the progress of the decomposition process. One common requirement for wood decay is oxygen and another is water. In contrast to their cooperation in the degradation of wood, bacteria, and fungi are in competition for oxygen and other resources (mineral and organic nutrients, water) in the area adjacent to the surface of the wood.

Competition for available resources is a fundamental tenet of biology and is visible on all levels of life. This competition can be used to control the activity of wood decay organisms. When a readily bioavailable carbohydrate source can be added adjacent to the pole's surface, the limiting factor in the degradation of the carbohydrate source will, in fact, be another limited resource for which bacteria compete with fungi, namely oxygen. Competition for oxygen creates conditions, which are described as anaerobic (defined as extremely depleted oxygen). Anaerobic conditions cause a rapid dominance of bacteria and subsequent, slower rise of anaerobic bacteria (Swindoll et al., 1988). Bacteria are also favored over the wood decay fungi in this system because the bacteria are more readily adaptable, are able to consume the carbohydrate source and grow at a faster rate than the wood decay fungi.

Microbially mediated processes are many times slower in the absence of oxygen (Brock and Madigan, 1991). The amount of energy available to an aerobe is approximately 19 times greater than can be extracted by anaerobes from the same food materials. This will be especially true of wood decay organisms because of the unique nature of wood and its constituents. Since it is a complex polymer, cellulose, like almost all polymers, is slowly degraded anaerobically (Zeikus, 1981). Further, there are no known pathways for the anaerobic biodegradation of lignin (Colberg, 1988). A detailed review of anaerobic degradation of lignin suggests it may be biochemically possible, but is very rare in nature (Kirk and Highley, 1973).

The anaerobic community induced by the addition of carbohydrate should be either greatly slowed or completely prevented from degrading the wood. In the presence of mineral sulfates, the anaerobic community formed is likely to be one of sulfate reducers. The reduction of the sulfate should also produce hydrogen sulfide (H_2S). H_2S is known to inhibit insect activity and repel larger animals.

This report presents evidence that carbohydrate amendment accelerates the formation of anaerobic conditions in water saturated systems. It will also show that carbohydrate amendment preserves the break strength of test stakes in accelerated laboratory studies and that time-released carbohydrate amendment slows the softening of full-size, untreated, southern yellow pine stubs in field studies near Charlotte, North Carolina. The product that has resulted from this research is currently being tested independently in a laboratory at Oregon State University.

METHODS

Laboratory tests: Oxygen depletion

Rates of oxygen depletion in an aqueous solution caused by the addition of soil alone and soil with carbohydrate amendments were determined. An aqueous system was used due to the limitations of the instrument used, a membrane-based dissolved oxygen (DO) probe (YSI Biological Oxygen Monitor). Oxygen depletion caused by the addition of 1 g of soil with and without 0.1 g/carbohydrate source to 10 ml deionized water was measured over time. This apparatus was interfaced with a PC and the data logged until the dissolved oxygen reached 0 mg/l.

Laboratory tests: Test stakes

Laboratory testing was performed on model stakes (0.5 inch × 0.5 inch × 10 inch, southern yellow pine). Model stakes chosen for the study were free from visible defect (knots, cracks, etc.) as per the clear timber testing standards described by ASTM (1954). Evaluation of the wood decay process is based on visual observation of the poles after incubation (as recorded in photographs) and the ASTM procedure for testing the Static Bending Strength of wood. As per this method, all test-poles were weighed, dried in a 55°C oven for 12 h and re-weighed. When constant weight was reached, the model poles were placed on the test apparatus, which was built as a scaled down version of the apparatus described by ASTM for the 'static bending' of small, clear, timber specimens (D143-52).

The bearing block was scaled down and the distance between the bearing plates was reduced to 4 inches. Because of this width, each 10-inch test-pole could be sampled twice, once at the ground line and once well above the ground line (the clean end of the test-pole). The ASTM method, which uses 2 inch width sections of wood has been scaled down for the model pole size used. The method was further modified in that rather than comparing sections of wood of equal distance from the pith, the modified method compares sections of wood to themselves by testing two sections along the same grain. These modifications serve to apply the method to our particular case rather than alter the parameter tested. In each test, the maximum pressure exerted by the bearing block was recorded as the breaking pressure.

Field testing

During the summer of 1996, we began a field test at Lake Wiley near Charlotte, NC. This plan involved the introduction of sixteen (16) 5 foot long, full (8–12″) diameter, untreated southern yellow pine utility pole timbers into the earth. These tests used the prototype RS21 (US Patent #5,770,265) treatment material. In 1998, a second round of testing was initiated. This time 24 timbers were used, improving the statistical significance of this test and also allowing sets of timbers under each treatment protocol to be left alone until the end of the study to determine the impact of sampling on the experimental results.

To avoid the cost of breaking full size utility pole sections and to allow for repeated testing of the same pole over time, the field test at Lake Wiley has relied on a Pilodyn 6J™ penetrometer method for evaluating wood decay. The Pilodyn™ penetrometer fires a pin into the pole surface with a uniform, constant force (6 joules) and then measures the depth of penetration. At the time of planting, baseline data for the penetrability of the timbers was obtained.

Beginning in 1998, Dr. Jeff Morrell at Oregon State University initiated a field trial of the effectiveness of RS21. The study was conducted in the same manner as described above except that Pilodyn readings were taken at multiple locations above and below the ground line. Also, plugs were collected for the identification of fungi colonizing the surface of the wood.

Fungal identifications

Cultivating and identifying fungi from a wood surface is a difficult technique that combines microscopy with the enrichment of selected organisms on growth media. By examining a wood plug under the microscope, fungal hyphae are selected for enrichment and subsequent identification. Fungi are identified most conclusively by the sporophore they produce when grown on laboratory media (Brock and Madigan, 1991). After the selected hyphae are inoculated on the laboratory media, they are allowed to grow until a sporophore is formed. The shape and appearance (morphology) of this sporophore allow for the identification of the fungi. The numbers of decay and non-decay fungi are then counted and the counts reported.

RESULTS

Laboratory results: Oxygen depletion studies

The amendment of soil with a carbohydrate source should accelerate the depletion of oxygen due to increased respiration by soil microorganisms. In Fig. 1, the addition of 0.1 g of a simple carbohydrate source caused the rate of oxygen consumption to increase nearly 8 fold. Amended samples were depleted of oxygen in an average of three hours while samples that were not amended took an average of 24 h to deplete

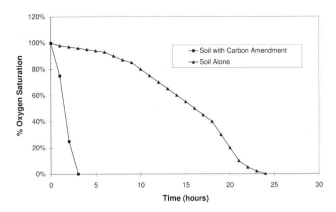

Fig. 1. Oxygen depletion in aqueous system.

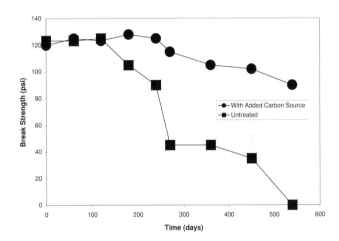

Fig. 2. Lab study of 0.5″ test strips.

their oxygen. In nature it is difficult to deplete the oxygen in the soil around a pole continually due to its contact with the atmosphere. However in conditions where the soil is moist or saturated with water, the presence of the simple carbohydrate source causes the oxygen to be depleted much more rapidly, and therefore extends the length of time the soil around the pole will be anaerobic. As was previously mentioned, anaerobic conditions mean slower degradation, bacterial domination of resources, and possibly the elimination of lignin degradation. The impact of these changes was observed in the laboratory and field efficacy tests.

Laboratory results: Test stakes

The results from the laboratory studies using model test stakes are given in Fig. 2. As can be seen, the periodic addition of a simple carbohydrate source to the stakes alters the rate at which they lose break strength. Without carbohydrate amendment, the stakes began to lose their strength very rapidly (around 180 days) and had lost all of their strength after about a year and a half. Carbohydrate amended stakes had no significant loss in strength for 270 days and retained an average of 75% of their initial break strength when the study was concluded after 18 months.

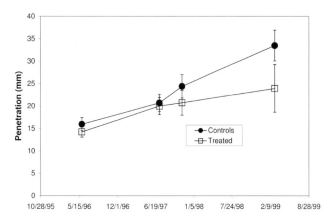

Fig. 3. Field study of time-release carbon source amendment.

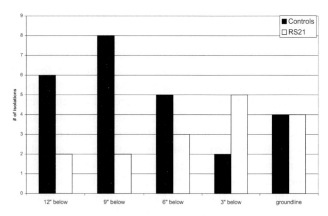

Fig. 4. Number of isolations of decay fungi from pole stubs with and without RS21.

To determine if this effect could be replicated in the field, it was necessary to modify the method of carbohydrate amendment. In the field, the direct addition of the carbohydrate source would be ineffective due to carbohydrate dilution in wet conditions. To overcome this limitation, a time-release mechanism was devised by which the carbohydrate is released whenever biological activity (and therefore the likelihood of decay) in the area is high. This technology, as well as the use of carbohydrate amendment to preserve wood in contact with soil have been patented by Triangle Laboratories (Durham, NC) and the University of North Carolina at Chapel Hill (US Patents #5,770,265 and #6,004,572).

Field results

The results of the field test of the time-release carbohydrate source amendment are given in Fig. 3. Pilodyn™ penetration increases with increasing decay and was used as a measure of wood softening for this study. Treatment material was added after decay had begun in order to simulate likely re-treatment conditions. Prior to June of 1997, the rate of decay was nearly identical in all stubs. Following the addition of the time release carbohydrate source, the rates of decay diverged significantly. Control samples (without carbohydrate source amendment) showed a 65% increase in Pilodyn™ penetration from July of 1997 to March of 1999. During the same time period, stubs with time-release carbohydrate sources added to the soil around them had an increase of penetration of only 20%. Extrapolated, this indicates a three-fold life extension caused by the addition of the time-release carbohydrate source assuming that the density of the outer wood is directly proportional to its overall strength.

External testing

RS21 is also under concurrent testing in the laboratory of Dr. Jeff Morrell at Oregon State University. In 1998, Dr. Morrell's research group established a stand of test stubs and initiated an annual sampling plan. Sampling consisted of Pilodyn measurements above and below the ground line and the collection of wood plugs for the cultivation and identification of fungi on the wood

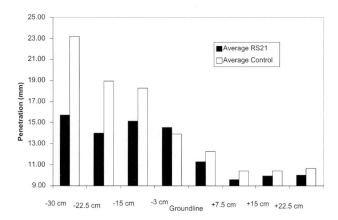

Fig. 5. Pilodyn penetration at 1 year.

surface. Results given are from the sampling, which occurred in the summer of 1999 (Figs. 4 and 5).

Fungal cultures

Although these results come from only one year of testing, the numbers of decay fungi cultivated from the pole's surface were generally lower in the presence of RS21 (Fig. 4). At a level 3" below the ground line, there were more decay fungi present with RS21 than with the untreated controls, but at all other depths below ground line, there were at least 20% more decay fungi culturable from the controls than were cultured from the poles which had RS21.

Pilodyn testing

The Pilodyn testing performed by Dr. Morrell's group was also conducted at multiple depths and closely mirrors the results of the fungal identifications (Fig. 5). At the ground line and just below, poles with RS21 are roughly equal in surface penetration to untreated poles. As the depth increases however, the advantage of the poles treated with RS21 begins to show. For comparison purposes, the Pilodyn measurement was taken 5–7" (12.5–17.5 cm) below groundline in the tests conducted at Lake Wiley. At 15 cm, the surface of the poles treated with RS21 retained approximately 10% greater resistance to penetration than the control.

DISCUSSION

The results of this research indicate that carbohydrate amendment will accelerate the depletion of oxygen under water saturated soil conditions. The depletion of oxygen is believed to cause three distinct effects that lead to the preservation of wood: (1) formation of anaerobic conditions under which all biodegradative processes occur more slowly, (2) alteration of the soil microbial community to one which is predominated by bacteria (which cannot degrade lignin), and (3) reduction of added sulfate to sulfide (which is known to inhibit insects). Carbohydrate amendment is demonstrated to preserve the break strength of wood test stakes in laboratory studies, and the addition of a time-released carbohydrate source slows the softening of untreated southern yellow pine stubs in a field study. Although the external testing is still in its early stages, the preliminary results seem to be in good correlation with the results from our trials. The additional information regarding the numbers of decay fungi present supports the presumed mode of action for carbohydrate amendment. Time-released carbohydrate amendment represents an alternative to using toxic methods of groundline decay prevention.

ACKNOWLEDGMENTS

The authors would like to thank Dr. Jeff Morrell for his permission to report on the data collected by his group. We would also like to thank Camille Freitag, one of Dr. Morrell's students for her work in culturing and identifying the fungi, as well as answering our questions about the process.

REFERENCES

American Society for Testing and Materials. 1954. ASTM Standards for Wood, Wood Preservatives and Related Materials, Committee D-7. American Society for Testing and Materials, Philadelphia, PA.

Brock, T.D. and M.T. Madigan. 1991. Biology of Microorganisms. Prentice-Hall, Englewood Cliffs, NJ.

Colberg, P.J. 1988. Anaerobic microbial degradation of cellulose, lignin, oligolignols, and monoaromatic lignin derivatives. In: Biology of Anaerobic Microorganisms. A.J.B. Zehnder, ed. John Wiley and Sons, New York. pp. 333–372.

Kirk, T.K. and T.L. Highley. 1973. Quantitative changes in structural components of conifer woods during decay by white and brown rot fungi. Phytopathology, 63: 1338–1342.

Pfaender, F.K., J.C. Roper, and D.J. Harvan. 1996. Pole Preservation Through Alteration of Wood Rot Microbial Community Activity. In: Proceedings of the 3rd International Conference on Wood Poles and Piles. L. Nelson, ed. Colorado State University, Fort Collins, CO. pp. 11–26.

Swindoll, C.M., C.M. Aelion, and F.K. Pfaender. 1988. Influence of mineral and organic nutrients on the aerobic biodegradation and adaptation response of subsurface microbial communities. Appl. Environ. Microbiol., 54: 212–217.

Zeikus, J.G. 1981. Lignin metabolism and the carbon cycle: Polymer biosynthesis, biodegradation, and environmental recalcitrance. In: Advances in Microbial Ecology, Vol. 5. M. Alexander, ed. Plenum Press, NY. pp. 211–243.

BIOGRAPHICAL SKETCHES

Chad Roper

Triangle Laboratories, Inc., 801 Capitola Dr., Durham, NC 27713, USA, (919) 544 5729 xt. 248, Fax (919) 544 5491, E-mail: Chad_Roper@compuserve.com

Dr. Chad Roper is the director of new technologies at Triangle Laboratories, Inc., Durham, NC. Dr. Roper is the primary point of contact for inquiries about RS21, a product based on carbohydrate amendment of soil for wood preservation. Triangle Laboratories has jointly licensed the patents related to RS21 with the University of North Carolina — Chapel Hill.

Fred Pfaender

University of North Carolina, Department of Environmental Science and Engineering, CB#7400, Chapel Hill, NC 27599-7400, USA, (919) 966 3842

Dr. Fred Pfaender is a professor in the department of environmental sciences and engineering at the University of North Carolina — Chapel Hill. Dr. Pfaender has more than 25 years of research experience in the field of biodegradation. His research has given him unique insights into microbial decay and the conditions controlling it. He is the inventor of RS21.

John Goodman

Duke Energy, PO Box 33189, TV02B, Charlotte, NC 28242, USA

John Goodman is an employee of Duke Energy Company. Mr. Goodman has been a research collaborator and has graciously provided facilities for some of the research in this paper.

Part XII
Aquatic Life

A Performance Measurement Framework for Pipeline Water Crossing Construction

S. Reid, A. Jalbert, S. Metikosh, and M. Bender

A lack of standardized construction monitoring data has limited the ability of the pipeline industry and regulators to evaluate the effectiveness of different water crossing methods in avoiding, or minimizing sediment related effects on stream and river ecosystems. This limitation needs to be addressed as some crossing techniques are selected based on the assumption that effectiveness varies among crossing techniques. In this paper, we present a retrospective approach developed by TransCanada Pipelines Limited to evaluate completed water crossings. The information collected within the Performance Measurement Framework (PMF) is used to evaluate the effectiveness of the construction design, associated Best Management Practices (BMPs) and other mitigation measures for individual crossings, and to develop a database of water crossing information. The database will allow for defensible judgements to be made on the effectiveness of given water crossing techniques and associated BMPs to limit potential negative effects on fish and fish habitat. The framework, its information requirements, a Microsoft Access^{TM} database capable of storing and querying past water crossing information and the role of the framework within the lifecycle of pipeline water crossing construction are discussed.

Keywords: Pipeline construction, streams rivers sediment, database, planning

INTRODUCTION

Pipeline water crossing construction has the potential to cause temporary adverse effects on stream and river ecosystems (Reid and Anderson, 1999). Generally, adverse effects can be avoided, or minimized through the selection of appropriate crossing methods, limiting the duration of instream work, and using Best Management Practices (BMPs). For the most part, the pipeline industry has been diligent in ensuring that these measures are incorporated in the design and construction of water crossings. However, there have been few attempts made to evaluate the effectiveness of a given crossing technique or to make comparisons among crossing methods. Additionally, members of the pipeline construction industry (TERA, 1996; Wolverton and Gray, 1996) have questioned the net environmental benefits of isolated crossing techniques. This deficiency is important to address as some crossing techniques: (1) are applied under the assumption that they will mitigate against environmental damage; and (2) have greater construction complexities, risks, cost, and durations of instream activity.

A performance measurement framework (PMF or framework) was developed by TransCanada PipeLines Limited (TransCanada) to determine the effectiveness of different crossing construction methods, associated BMPs and other mitigation measures. It is aimed at addressing the fundamental questions: "How well did we do?"; "Was the crossing technique appropriate?"; and, "How can we do better?" The framework includes a standardized approach for the collection and evaluation of water crossing construction monitoring information. The following paper will describe the framework, outline its information requirements, discuss its application to the planning of watercourse crossing construction, and present a database developed to compile and query historical water crossing information.

Environmental Concerns in Rights-of-Way Management: Seventh International Symposium
J.W. Goodrich-Mahoney, D.F. Mutrie and C.A. Guild (editors)
© 2002 Elsevier Science Ltd. All rights reserved.

PIPELINE WATER CROSSING CONSTRUCTION PERFORMANCE MEASUREMENT FRAMEWORK

The primary goal of the framework is to provide a standardized approach to assess completed pipeline water crossings. Information collected during construction is used to evaluate the effectiveness of the construction design, associated BMPs and other mitigation measures for an individual crossing, and, to develop a database of historical water crossing information. In order to achieve this goal, the framework has three main components: (1) a standard protocol for the collection of construction monitoring information; (2) performance based post-construction evaluations of constructed water crossings; and (3) a Microsoft Access™ database to compile and query historical water crossing information.

The primary measurement of performance is the magnitude and duration of increases in downstream suspended sediment concentrations during crossing construction: the lower the amount and duration, the higher the performance. This is based on the following assumptions: (1) sediment generated during water crossing construction (Table 1) is the primary vector through which adverse environmental effects occur (Goodchild and Metikosh, 1994; Reid and Anderson, 1999); and (2) crossings releasing the smallest amount of sediment over the shortest period of time have the least effect.

At this point, the framework is limited to open-cut (wet) and isolated (dry) crossing methods (e.g., dam and pump, or flumed). This is due to the limited applicability of the parameters used to measure performance to trenchless water crossings (e.g., bored or horizontal directionally drilled). However, as trenchless methods are often applied to environmentally sensitive water crossings and drilling mud releases or crossing failures do occur, an alternative (less intensive and more construction focused) PMF should be developed for trenchless crossings.

INFORMATION REQUIREMENTS

Past reviews of construction techniques and associated monitoring studies have used a wide variety of study designs, different monitoring parameters and have lacked physical watercourse and detailed construction information. This has made comparisons between crossing techniques and evaluation of performance difficult. Therefore, it is of paramount importance that the information is collected using consistent and scientifically defensible methods. Standard field data collection sheets and a sediment load monitoring protocol were developed for the PMF to provide a consistent method of collecting and recording water crossing data. Four general information categories are used in the framework to evaluate crossing performance (Table 2): watercourse attributes; water crossing design; construction specific observations and impressions; and environmental monitoring results (sediment and biological effects). It is also important to identify key internal and external contacts for the project to facilitate post-construction discussions.

Past pipeline water crossing reviews have been limited by a lack of case-studies with consistently recorded watercourse information. Physical and biological characteristics of the watercourse are important as they: (1) influence the sensitivity of the aquatic biota and habitat to suspended sediment and sediment deposition; (2) influence the level of sediment generation, transport and dilution during instream construction; and (3) define the suitability of available crossing techniques and mitigation, and the risk of failure.

Water crossing design information identifies the pathways (activities and equipment) through which sediment is released into the watercourse during construction. It also forms the basis for comparisons with other water crossings. All undertakings implemented, equipment, and materials used during construction to minimize or avoid the release of sediment into the watercourse, must be identified and recorded (e.g., crossing technique, sediment and erosion control, and reclamation measures). Observations and impressions by on-site staff or consultants regarding the success of the crossing from a construction standpoint are essential for linking performance measurement indicators to components of the installation that did, or did not perform satisfactorily. Each of these examples of such observations, or impressions include whether the number of pumps used during a dam and pump crossing were of sufficient capacity, whether the construction contractor was experienced with a given isolated

Table 1. Examples of sediment inputs during pipeline water crossings

Timing	Source
Preparation	equipment bridge installation
	fording of watercourse by equipment
	bank and/or bed contouring[a]
	installation of trench isolation structures (e.g., sandbag dam)[a]
	installation of flow diversion structures (flume) or equipment (pumps)[a]
Installation	trench excavation
	scour of bed material by diverted flow[a]
	trench scour during pipe-laying
	trench backfilling
	overflow of retention ponds/sumps[a]
	erosion from ROW
Post-installation	removal of flow diversion structures (flumes) or equipment[a]
	removal of equipment bridges
	bank and bed restoration
	erosion from ROW

[a] Applicable to isolated or partial diversion methods only.

Table 2. Examples of information to be collected during the construction of water crossings and applied to the performance measurement framework

Watercourse description	Crossing design	Construction monitoring	Environmental monitoring
Legal land location	Start and completion dates	Completion timing	Suspended sediment concentration
Watercourse type	Crossing method	Pre-construction data not collected	Sediment deposition rate
Fish community	Type of equipment bridge	Contractor experience	Streambed embeddedness
Ambient suspended sediment concentrations	Equipment used	Performance of materials and structures	Channel morphology
Water depth	Trench dimensions	Equipment performance	Benthic invertebrate biomass
Watercourse width	Spoil storage	Difficult construction conditions	Benthic invertebrate species diversity
Water velocity	Crossing length	Difficult BMPs or construction practices	Fish density
Discharge	Pipe diameter	Permit compliance	Fish species diversity
Streambed gradient	Blasting	Regulatory feedback	Fish egg survival and alevin emergence
Surficial streambed material	Burial depth		Habitat use and selection
Groundwater flow	Flume capacity		Fish health indicators
Approach slopes	Isolation materials, or structures		
	Backfill material		
	Number and capacity of pumps		
	Upland erosion control		

crossing technique, or if unseasonable warm temperatures occurred during winter pipeline construction. Such situations can lengthen the duration of instream activity, or result in the failure of instream structures (e.g., aquadams). It is critical that a detailed record of construction related information (crossing design and time-referenced logbook) is kept so that sediment monitoring data can be cross-referenced to construction activities. Failing to identify such crossing-specific observations or impressions limits opportunities to learn from past crossings.

Environmental monitoring data provide the measurements used to evaluate the performance of an individual water crossing or to compare it with past water crossings. Past monitoring studies of pipeline water crossing construction have identified the following effects downstream of water crossings (Reid and Anderson, 1999): (1) increases in suspended sediment concentrations and sediment deposition rates for the duration of construction; (2) temporary (<2 years) changes in streambed composition; (3) temporary (<2 years) reductions in the biomass and species diversity of benthic invertebrate communities; (4) temporary (<2 years) reductions in fish abundance; and (5) direct mortality or internal damage of fish due to instream blasting. Within the PMF, the primary performance measurements are suspended sediment concentration and duration of instream activity. The inclusion of additional performance measures may be appropriate for crossings of highly sensitive watercourses and/or during sensitive time periods (e.g., just after spawning).

The names and contact numbers of all involved parties (TransCanada, regulators, consultants, contractors) are recorded in order to facilitate the identification and discussion of issues with individuals familiar with, and/or responsible for a specific crossing during water crossing evaluations.

PERFORMANCE EVALUATION OF INDIVIDUAL WATER CROSSINGS AND CROSSING METHODS

The goal of post-construction performance evaluations of individual crossings is to identify conditions or components of crossing construction that did, or did not minimize sediment generation. Although not all pipeline crossings can be success stories, difficulties encountered during water crossing construction need not be repeated. Key findings and recommendations can be identified and future water crossing site selection, design and construction can be improved based on a defensible performance measurement. Fig. 1 provides a perspective regarding how the PMF fits into the planning lifecycle for pipeline water crossing construction. These evaluations are based on information collected during construction monitoring and discussions between TransCanada staff, their consultants and construction contractors, regulators and other key stakeholders. Specifically, evaluations link measured suspended sediment concentrations to activities and factors such as:

1. Construction related activities (e.g., flume installation, or how the trench was back-filled);
2. The performance of structures, or materials (e.g., material used to build berms);
3. The abilities/experience of the contractor;
4. Environmental conditions (e.g., rained for 5 out of the 6 days instream); and,
5. Watercourse specific conditions (e.g., high groundwater flows).

Such evaluations require the review of all the information components collected for the water crossing. For comparisons of different phases of construction, time weighted averages should be calculated from suspended sediment monitoring data. Fig. 2 illustrates

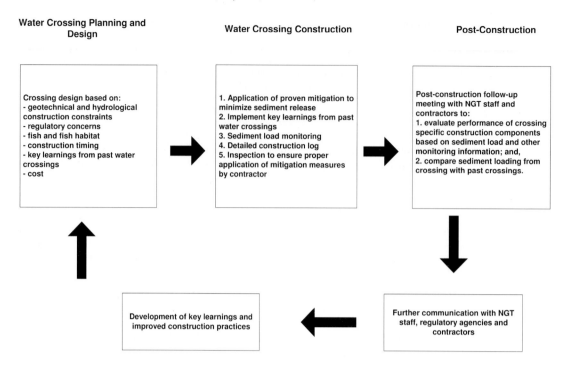

Fig. 1. Application of the performance measurement framework in the life-cycle of pipeline water crossing construction.

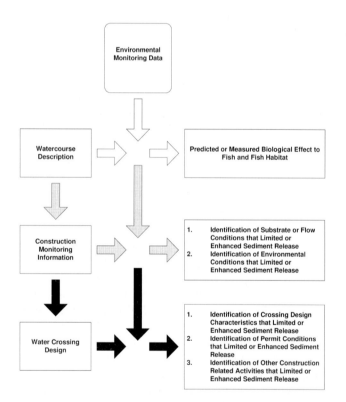

Fig. 2. Framework for performance measurement of individual pipeline water crossings. Shading of pathway arrows indicates which information categories (on the left side of the figure) are integrated to drive different crossing performance measures or key learnings (on the right side of the figure).

how the collected information could be applied to evaluate individual water crossings.

Over the past 20 years, TransCanada has collected construction monitoring information during the construction of pipeline water crossings. Table 3 outlines examples of key learnings from these past water crossings and how subsequent water crossing planning, contracting, and construction practices were changed based on these learnings.

EVALUATING CROSSING METHODS AND THE PERFORMANCE MEASUREMENT DATABASE

While evaluations of individual crossings will help improve the design and construction of individual crossing techniques, comparisons between crossing techniques are necessary to ultimately improve crossing design and route selection. The strength of these comparisons will be dependent on a sufficiently sized database of water crossings across watercourse types and crossing techniques and the collection of data in a standardized manner. The next step in the development and refinement of the performance measurement framework is its application across a wide variety (geographically and technically) of watercourse crossings. Once a database of past water crossings has been compiled, the following sets of performance comparisons are made:

– Between watercourses of similar flow characteristics and bed material: (1) different water crossing methods (e.g., open-cut vs. flumed); and (2) different approaches to the same construction component (e.g., aquadam vs. sandbag dam).
– Between different water crossings using the same crossing method: (1) different flow conditions and, or bed material; and (2) different construction timing (e.g., summer vs. winter).

Table 3. Key learnings from past water crossings in Alberta and improved construction practices

Method	Watercourses	Key learnings from monitoring data	Improved construction practices
Open-cut	Smoky River Wildhay River Brazeau River Little Smoky River	• Lowering of the bucket into the water before emptying reduces sediment loading during backfilling • Using clean backfill can minimize sediment levels • Poor planning can prolong the duration of sediment loading • Drilling of blasting holes and blasting causes only minor increases in downstream sediment levels	• Where the sensitivity of the habitat is a concern and certain stream conditions exist (e.g., high flow), the backhoe bucket is lowered into the water before emptying backfill material • Reduce the time instream by ensuring all equipment is on-site prior to construction • The number of contingency plan options is restricted and properly communicated to avoid confusion during construction
Dam and pump	James River Brewster Cr Deep Valley Cr Dogpound Cr	• Very effective method for meandering watercourses or where terrain is uneven and difficult for flume installation • Steel plate dams are very effective at isolating the crossing area • Removal of the upstream dam first followed by pumping out turbid water in crossing areas is very effective at reducing sediment loading during dam removal • Isolation dams constructed with clean washed gravel are only temporarily effective • Pumping trench water into dry side channels does not allow for sufficient settling before water re-enters the channel • Meter bags do not work well to get a seal • Bentonite sock works well to get a seal but can break	• Dam and pump method has become a more common practice and is often the preferred method of certain contractors • As a standard practice, the upstream dam is removed first and the turbid water that was within the isolation is pumped into a sump or vegetated area prior to removing the lower dam • Sumps are constructed prior to instream construction to ensure they are in place when and if required
Superflume	Berland River Simonette River	• The superflume in association with aquadams is an effective method for crossing sensitive medium sized watercourses • Lengthy construction periods should be avoided, as sumps may be unable to contain the high volumes of pumped ditch water	• A contingency plan is developed for all crossings to deal with changes in site conditions, or if the original method is not feasible • Contingency plans (including construction of sumps) are now incorporated into the contract for all crossings • Depth of cover is verified prior to pulling pipe to ensure it is adequate and to minimize time in-stream

The development and maintenance of such a data set requires an increased management effort. A Microsoft Access™ styled database was developed to assist in the compilation, administration, and interpretation of collected water crossing information. In addition to assisting TransCanada staff in identifying the linkages between potential sources of sediment generation and measured increases, and identifying common features of crossing methods, the database will help to preserve water crossing construction knowledge. Figs. 3 and 4 are examples of input and output screens within the database.

DISCUSSION

Continuous improvement of pipeline water crossing construction is a key component of the environmental protection of rivers and streams. As a part of the life-cycle approach that TransCanada applies to its management of pipeline water crossing construction (Fig. 1), the PMF facilitates continuous improvements to TransCanada's pipeline construction practices. Key learnings identified after construction by project staff and other involved parties from construction monitoring information are an integral part to these improvements. Considering the variety of expertise applied during the planning and construction of pipeline water crossings, the successful identification of key learnings and future application requires the involvement of construction design engineers, environmental inspectors, construction contractors, fisheries biologists, and environmental planners.

By preserving key learnings and construction monitoring information, the PMF database can assist construction and environmental planners in the future to identify crossing methods and mitigation that will be effective at avoiding or minimizing adverse effects. As with most databases and decision support tools, the usefulness of output from the PMF database to con-

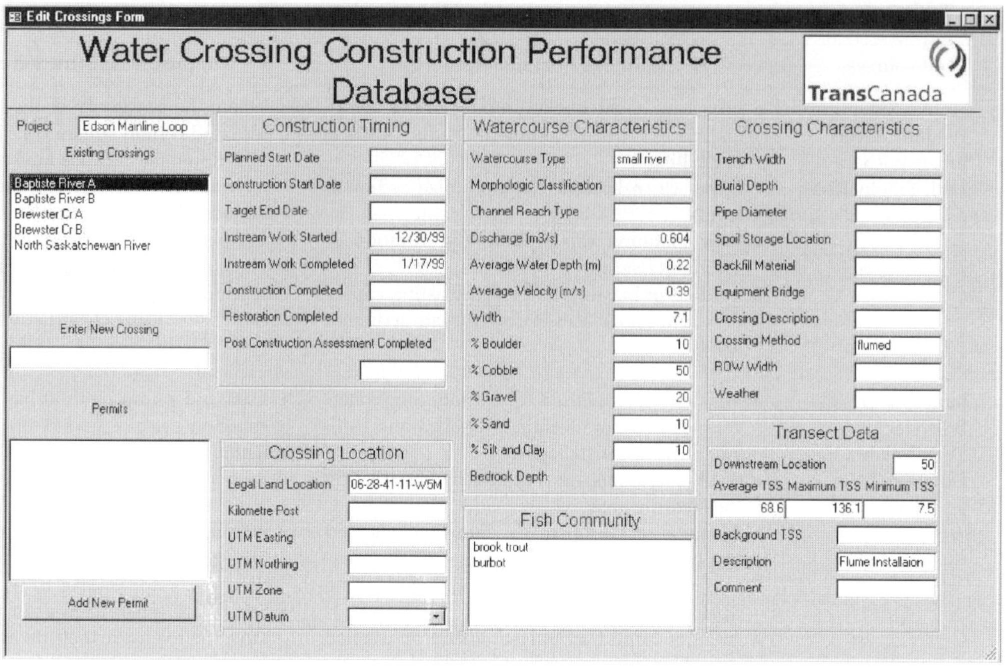

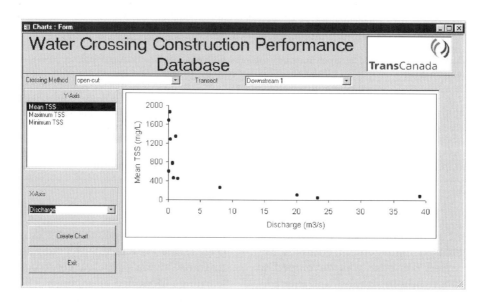

Fig. 3. Data input screen, TransCanada water crossing construction performance database.

Fig. 4. Data output screen displaying results of TSS — discharge query for Open-cut pipeline water crossings.

struction planning is restricted by the data input or stored. A small data set of water crossing monitoring information will restrict the scope of questions that can be answered and limit the defensibility of the answers. Once a database of sufficient size and geographic coverage is developed, defensible queries regarding the relative effectiveness of different crossing methods to minimize sediment related effects can be undertaken. The PMF and associated database presents an opportunity for industry to work together to improve BMPs, to resolve issues identified by regulators and key stakeholders, and to clarify misconceptions related to water crossing construction.

ACKNOWLEDGEMENTS

The authors would like to acknowledge the contributions of the following people to the development of this framework: T. de Grosbois, D. McNeely, A. Lees, R. Hunter, R. Fletcher, J. Ness, H. Klassen, C. Newcombe, J. Nixon, R. Morrison, J. Allen, K. McDougall, C. Briggs, and P. Anderson.

REFERENCES

Goodchild, G.A. and S. Metikosh. 1994. Fisheries-related information requirements for pipeline water crossings. Canadian Manuscript Report Fisheries and Aquatic Sciences, 2235: 17 pp.

Reid, S.M. and P.G. Anderson. 1999. Review of the effects of sediment released during open-cut pipeline water crossings on stream and river ecosystems. Canadian Water Resources Journal, 24: 23–39.

TERA Environmental Consultants (Alta.) Ltd. (TERA). 1996. Water crossing case history review. Prepared for Westcoast Energy.

Wolverton, T. and L.A. Gray. 1997. Lengthy, candid talks result in successful stream crossing. Pipeline and Gas Industry. January 1997. pp. 71–75.

BIOGRAPHICAL SKETCHES

Scott Reid
Golder Associates Ltd. 2180 Meadowvale Boulevard, Mississauga, ON L5N 5S3, Canada

For the past 5 years, Scott Reid has been a fisheries biologist with Golder Associates Ltd. He has a BSc in Ecology from the University of Calgary and a MSc in Watershed Ecosystems from Trent University. Mr. Reid's has been involved in numerous projects investigating the effects of sediment on fish and fish habitat in stream and river systems and developing related assessment and planning tools.

Andrea Jalbert
TransCanada Pipelines Limited. 450-1st Street SW, Calgary, AB T2P 5H1, Canada

Andrea Jalbert is currently an Environmental Advisor with TransCanada PipeLines Limited in Calgary. Andrea has been working in the pipeline industry for seven years and her main focus has been on issues related to pipeline water crossings and undertaking the environmental planning for pipeline projects.

Serge Metikosh
Golder Associates Ltd., 10th floor, 940 6th Avenue S.W., Calgary, AB T2P 3T1, Canada

Mr. Metikosh joined Golder Associates in September 1997 after 25 years as a biologist with various federal government departments, most recently as the Senior Habitat Biologist with the Department of Fisheries and Oceans in Burlington, Ontario. Main professional interests include affects of sediment and fish and fish habitat, effects of pipelines on fish and fish habitat, fish habitat assessment, protection and restoration.

Effects of Pipeline Rights-of-Way on Fish Habitat at Two Alberta Stream Crossings

Christine M. Brown, Richard D. Revel, and John R. Post

A field study was conducted to investigate the physical and biological effects of pipeline watercourse crossings on fish habitat, in two streams in southwestern Alberta. The effects of the crossing were assessed using selected variables that are standard measures of fish habitat quality: water temperature, flow rates, water depth, substrate composition, benthic macroinvertebrates, and fish cover. The effects of the crossing include a substantial reduction in available fish cover, a reduction in the diversity of cover types, and the lack of specific cover types, such as deep pools and undercut banks; an alteration in the substrate composition in the right-of-way and the subsequent loss of structural heterogeneity in the physical habitat; channelization of the stream; and an alteration in the community structure of benthic macroinvertebrates. These findings will be of particular interest to individuals responsible for the assessment or regulation of pipeline crossings under legislation such as the Canada Fisheries Act, which requires a determination whether a river crossing will cause "Harmful Alteration, Disruption or Destruction of fish habitat" (HADD).

Keywords: Pipeline crossing, watercourse crossing, right-of-way (ROW), brook trout, brown trout, fish habitat, fish cover, Fisheries Act, Harmful Alteration, Disruption or Destruction of fish habitat (HADD)

INTRODUCTION

The construction of watercourse crossings in Alberta is widespread. Although the regulatory agencies do not specifically track the number of watercourse crossings constructed each year, approximately 700–900 crossing applications are received in a given year, the majority of which are pipeline crossing applications, many containing multiple crossings. Despite their frequency and the potential for in-stream and riparian activities to effect fish habitat, there has been very little research on such effects to date, apart from studies on the effects of sedimentation which have been well documented.

The issues associated with pipeline crossings are relatively complex, involving regulatory requirements and guidelines, corporate goals and policies, and ecological considerations. From a regulatory perspective, both the federal and provincial governments are responsible for protecting and managing Canada's water resources. One of the most powerful pieces of legislation in water resource management is the Federal *Fisheries Act*, as it contains a significant provision for fish habitat protection. As established by Section 35(1) of the Act, it is an offence for any person to "carry on any work or undertaking that results in the harmful alteration, disruption or destruction of fish habitat" (HADD).

OBJECTIVES

The objective of this study was to evaluate the effects of the removal of riparian vegetation associated with the construction of the watercourse crossing, and the effects of the in-stream construction techniques on the physical and biological quality of fish habitat at two streams in Southwestern Alberta. The findings were then used to develop recommendations for improvements in current practices.

DESCRIPTION OF STREAM STUDY SITES

Two streams were investigated: Prairie Creek (south fork) and Alford Creek. Both streams are located in the District of Clearwater and are tributaries to the Clearwater River (Fig. 1). Both creeks are located in the Boreal Cordilleran ecoregions, the dominant vegetation being aspen, balsam poplar, lodgepole pine, white and black spruce (Strong, 1992). Annual precipitation is approximately 450–550 mm, most of which falls in the summer (Strong, 1992). The watercourses in the vicinity support a number of fish species including brown trout (*Salmo trutta*) eastern brook trout (*Salvenius fontinalis*), rocky mountain whitefish (*Prosopium williamsoni*), northern pike (*Esox lucius*), and white perch (*Etheostoma exile*) (Alberta Recreation, Parks, and Wildlife, 1976).

METHODS

Three reaches in each stream were selected for investigation: the section of the stream crossed by the pipeline right-of-way (ROW) and sections located 100 m upstream and downstream of the ROW. The upstream reach was unaffected by the watercourse crossing or any other observable anthropogenic disturbance and was used as the control site, representing the natural physical and ecological conditions of the stream. The ROW had undergone a specific type of alteration, the effects of which should manifest as physical or biological differences relative to the control site. The downstream reach was used to evaluate the downstream effects of the watercourse crossing and the linear extent and nature of those effects. The reaches were sampled using a standard transect design (Fig. 2). Each reach contained three transects. Transects in the ROW were located at evenly spaced intervals within that reach. In the reaches upstream and downstream of the ROW, one transect was located immediately adjacent to the ROW and the other transects were located at intervals of 50 m. Sampling for the following parameters was conducted at evenly spaced intervals within each transect and were chosen because they are widely accepted as being among the most important components of habitat quality (Platts et al., 1983):

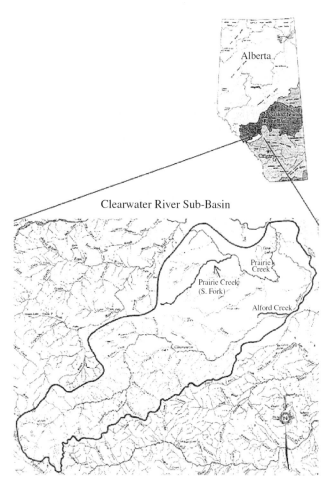

Fig. 1. Map of the stream study sites, and their locations relative to Calgary.

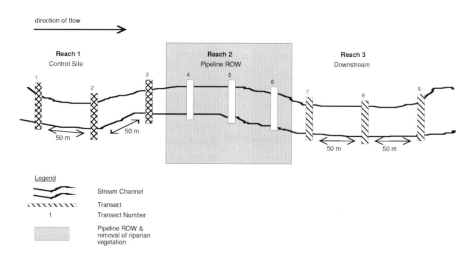

Fig. 2. Schematic representation of the stream study sites, illustrating the sampling design.

stream width, depth and discharge; stream water temperature; substrate composition; benthic macroinvertebrates; and fish cover. The data were analyzed using SYSTAT (DOS version) (Wilkinson, 1990). Analyses of variance (ANOVA) were used to test the differences among means. If the differences were significant, Least Square Difference (LSD) hypothesis tests were used to establish which means were different. For the analysis of two or more dependent variables, multivariate analyses of variance (MANOVA) were used. As a significant difference for a MANOVA does not indicate the relative importance of the dependant variables, univariate statistics were also calculated, as were LSD tests. The probability level used to reject or accept the hypothesis for all analyses was $p = 0.05$. The data were assessed for compliance with the assumptions associated with each test and outliers were treated on a individual basis.

The wetted width of the stream was measured using a calibrated surveyor's tape. Depth was measured using a metre stick and stream flow measurements were taken using either a Teledyne Gurly current meter or a Teledyne Pygmy Gurly current meter depending on stream depth. Data collected from the three sampling periods were pooled for the analysis of stream width and depth to allow for a more powerful statistical analysis of the results. Discharge was calculated according to the following formula (Johnston and Slaney, 1996):

$$\text{discharge } (m^3/s) = R_m \cdot D \cdot V \cdot W_w,$$

where R_m is a bottom roughness adjustment factor (≈ 0.75), D is a mean depth, V is a water velocity and W_w is a mean wetted width. Water temperature was measured directly using Hobo® Temp thermographs (Onset Computer Corporation). Each transect contained one thermograph which was placed at approximately the same depth and in equitable water flows at each location. Hourly measurements of the water temperature were obtained for both streams; from July 11 to September 18, 1997 for Prairie Creek, and from August 1 to October 2, 1997 for Alford Creek.

Five substrate samples were taken in each transect at equally spaced intervals across the stream channel. Samples were obtained by digging into the stream bottom using a shovel to a depth of approximately 10 cm. The samples were then sorted into the following particle-size categories using a wet-sieve method (Brower et al., 1990; Johnston and Slaney, 1996; MacDonald et al., 1992): pebbles and cobbles (>31.5 mm); coarse gravels (16–31.5 mm); medium gravels (9.5–16 mm); fine gravels (2–9.5 mm); silts and sands (<2 mm); and detritus. After the substrate was sorted the samples were dried to 150°C and weighed to the nearest tenth of a gram. Substrate composition weights were converted to percent of total sample weight that passed through each sieve (Scrivener and Brownlee, 1982). The habitat diversity of the reaches was also analyzed using the Shannon–Wiener Diversity Index, a standard index for assessing the structural diversity within a habitat (Brower et al., 1990).

Quantitative benthic macroinvertebrate samples were collected twice from each stream in mid and late summer (July 28–31 and August 22–24 for Prairie Creek, August 6–8 and September 5–7 for Alford Creek). Sampling for macroinvertebrates was conducted using a Neil cylinder sampler at Prairie Creek (0.1 m^2, 210 µm) and a modified Surber sampler at Alford Creek (0.1 m^2) to a depth of approximately 10 cm. The equipment differences reflect the difference in depth at each stream and the subsequent selection of the most appropriate technique. Sampling was timed to ensure equal sampling effort. Identification of the taxa was made to family level using standard keys (Clifford, 1991; Edmunds et al., 1976; Jewett, 1959; Merritt and Cummins, 1996). In the laboratory, the samples were rinsed through a 250 µm sieve and sorted in a 75% ethanol solution. Samples with large amounts of detritus were split into extra coarse (>4 mm), coarse (1–4 mm) and fine (<1 mm) fractions. The extra coarse and coarse fractions were sorted and enumerated as above and the fine fraction was subsampled as described by Wrona, Culp, and Davies (1982) for the purposes of subsampling chironomid larvae (Chironomidae) and mayfly larvae (Baetidae) where appropriate. The remainder of the sample was processed to enumerate all other taxa. Quality control measures were taken to ensure that the processing and identification procedures were consistently thorough for all samples.

Elements of fish cover were also estimated during the field season. Cover was defined as "a structural element in the wetted channel... that serves to visually isolate fish and/or to provide suitable microhabitats where fish can hide, rest or feed" (Johnston and Slaney, 1996). The percentage of the total surface area in the transects that was covered by each of the following cover types was estimated (modified from Johnston and Slaney, 1996): large woody debris (LWD), small woody debris (SWD), boulders, undercut banks, deep pools, overhanging vegetation, and in-stream vegetation.

RESULTS

The wetted width and depth of the stream were significantly different between the three reaches in each stream ($P = 0.01$ for Prairie Creek, and $P < 0.05$ for Alford Creek) (Table 1). Stream discharge was not significantly different for Prairie Creek, but was significantly different for Alford Creek ($P < 0.05$) (Table 1). For Prairie Creek, the mean wetted width decreased significantly downstream of the ROW and the ROW was significantly shallower than the other reaches. For Alford Creek the ROW was significantly

Table 1. Mean wetted width, depth, and discharge, with standard error, of the three reaches in Prairie and Alford Creek, and the results of the statistical analysis

	Sample size (n)	Mean wetted width (m)	MANOVA/ pairwise tests	Mean stream depth (cm)	MANOVA/ pairwise tests	Mean discharge (m^3/s)	ANOVA/ pairwise test
Prairie Creek							
Reach 1	9	14.2 ± 1.08	$P = 0.001$	49.4 ± 1.94	$P = 0.001$	2.12 ± 0.41	
Reach 2	9	12.7 ± 0.35		34.6 ± 3.38		1.47 ± 0.12	NS
Reach 3	9	10.7 ± 0.32	$R_3 < R_1 \approx R_2$	55.8 ± 7.47	$R_2 < R_1 \approx R_3$	1.52 ± 0.12	
Alford Creek							
Reach 1	9	4.7 ± 0.24	$P < 0.05$	18.0 ± 3.97	$P < 0.05$	0.08 ± 0.02	$P < 0.05$
Reach 2	9	3.6 ± 0.17		24.6 ± 1.90		0.18 ± 0.03	
Reach 3	9	4.2 ± 0.33	$R_2 < R_1$	26.0 ± 2.84	NS	0.13 ± 0.02	$R_2 > R_1$

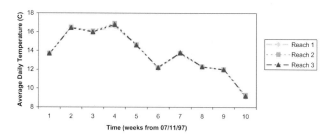

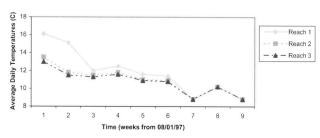

Fig. 3. Average weekly maximum temperatures at Prairie Creek and Alford Creek during the sampling period.

narrower that the first reach and had significantly higher discharge.

As shown in Fig. 3 there was very little difference in stream water temperature among the reaches in Prairie Creek. Although the repeated measures ANOVA resulted in no statistically significant difference, the mean weekly maximum temperatures were consistently higher between the third and control reach by a very small amount (less than 1°C) and the daily maximum temperature in the seventh transect was higher than any of the other transects in either the control or ROW twelve times out of seventy by an average of approximately 0.4°C. The daily maximum temperatures in the eighth transect were higher than that recorded in the ROW approximately 11% of the time. The highest temperature recorded during the field season was 19°C in the ROW and it was 0.8°C higher than the temperatures recorded in other transects. Stream water temperature among the reaches differed much more in Alford Creek, in which the stream temperature decreased downstream of the first reach consistently for all weeks during the entire sampling period. There was a statistically significant difference in temperature among the reaches for Alford Creek for the first six weeks the thermographs were in place while the last three weeks showed no significant difference in temperature.

With respect to substrate, Prairie Creek had an abundance of cobbles in all three reaches. Differences among the reaches included a 10% increase in the amount of silts and sands downstream of the ROW, a 6% increase in the amount of coarse gravels in the ROW and a decrease in the amount of detritus in the ROW and downstream of the ROW by 30% and 44%, respectively (Fig. 4). In Alford Creek the substrate composition in the ROW was quite different from the first and third reaches. The primary differences included a 30% increase in the proportion of cobbles in the ROW and a 25% decrease in the proportion of silts and sands. The proportion of silts and sands increased by 10% in the third reach relative to the control. The amount of detritus decreased in the ROW by 10%. Using the Shannon–Wiener Diversity Index the structural diversity of each reach was assessed, for each sampling period (Table 2). The habitat diversity in the ROW at Prairie Creek was approximately equal to that in the first and third reaches. At Alford Creek the ROW scored consistently lower than the control reach by a moderate amount.

Prairie Creek and Alford Creek had similar responses to the pipeline ROW with respect to macroinvertebrate abundance and community structure. First, the average number of individuals per sample increased considerably in the ROW, such that it contained the largest number of macroinvertebrates (Table 3). This difference was statistically significant in Prairie Creek ($P < 0.05$), but not in Alford Creek ($P > 0.05$) (Tables 3 and 4). Although the average number of invertebrates decreased in the third reach, macroinvertebrates were still considerably more abundant in the third reach relative to the control. A number of families of invertebrates were more abundant in the ROW than in the control, including mayfly larvae (Order Ephemeroptera; Families Baetidae, Epehemerellidae, Leptophlebiidae, and Heptageniidae), stonefly

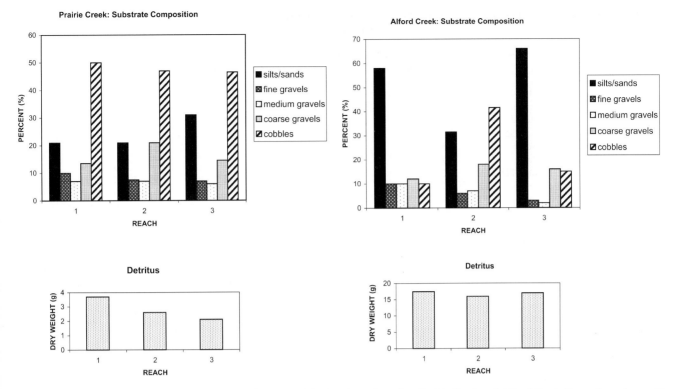

Fig. 4. Comparison of the substrate composition and amount of detritus in each reach at Prairie Creek and Alford Creek. For each reach, $n = 45$ (5 samples * 3 transects * 3 sampling periods).

Table 2. Shannon–Wiener Diversity Index scores for the three reaches at Prairie Creek and Alford Creek

Stream	Reach	Sampling time	SW-DI
Prairie Creek			
	1	1	0.59
	1	2	0.48
	1	3	0.58
	2	1	0.56
	2	2	0.51
	2	3	0.65
	3	1	0.52
	3	2	0.48
	3	3	0.59
Alford Creek			
	1	1	0.70
	1	2	0.70
	1	3	0.69
	2	1	0.51
	2	2	0.59
	2	3	0.64
	3	1	0.60
	3	2	0.63
	3	3	0.59

larvae (Order Plecoptera; Families Perlidae, Perlodidae, Nemouridae, and Chloroperlidae), caddisfly larvae (Order Trichoptera; Family Brachycentridae), and midgefly larvae (Order Diptera; Family Chironomidae). This difference was statistically significant for Ephemeroptera Leptophlebiidae and E. Heptageniidae at Prairie Creek, and E. Baetidae and E. Ephemerellidae at Alford Creek. The increase in the caddisfly larvae Trichoptera Brachycentridae in the ROW was highly statistically significant at Alford Creek ($P < 0.01$), and there were significantly more midgefly larvae (Diptera Chironimidae) in the ROW at Prairie Creek, although both streams contained considerably more midgefly larvae in the second reach. The total number of families in each reach was higher in the ROW than in the control for both streams.

The individual streams also had distinct results. First, the mean number of invertebrates per sample was much higher at Prairie Creek than Alford Creek. Within Prairie Creek, the increase in the number of worms (Order Oligochaeta; Family Naididae) in the second and third reach was highly significant ($P < 0.001$). There were also statistically significant increases in the number of mites (Order Arachnidia; Family Hydrachnidia), crane fly larvae (Diptera Tipulidae), and a caddisfly larvae (Trichoptera Hydroptilidae) in the second reach. At Alford Creek, the number of blackfly larvae (Diptera Simuliidae) was significantly higher in the ROW whereas blackflies were completely absent in the control reach. The number of EPT taxa [Ephemeroptera (mayflies), Plecoptera (stoneflies), and Trichoptera (caddisflies)] was significantly lower in the control than the second or third reach.

With respect to fish cover, there were a number of trends evident in both streams. The ROW had the least amount of cover available to fish, averaging 46% less cover in Prairie Creek and 54% less cover in Alford Creek relative to the control reach (Fig. 5). The primary

Table 3. Mean density (no./0.1 m^2) and standard error of dominant taxa, and total density of all taxa in each of the three study sections in Prairie Creek.

Order	Family	Prairie Creek			MANOVA	Pairwise tests
		Reach 1	Reach 2	Reach 3		
Oligochaeta	Naididae	3.7±1.4	58.8±14.7	102.7±51.8	***	$R_1 < (R_2 \approx R_3)$
	Lumbriculidae	3.5±2.2	4.2±1.3	3.2±2.0	ns	
	Nematoda	1.0±0.2	3.71±1.1	4.8±1.8	ns	
Arachnida	Hydrachnidia	41.8±7.0	124.8±18.0	59.2±20.3	*	$R_2 > (R_1 \approx R_3)$
Crustacea	Ostracods	1.8±0.9	2.0±1.2	2.8±1.9	ns	
Ephemeroptera	Baetidae	17.7±3.3	83.5±39.6	87.2±61.5	ns	
	Ephemerellidae	27.5±5.8	87.8±29.7	65.7±25.9	ns	
	Siphlonuridae	1.7±0.7	0.0±0.0	0.8±0.4	ns	$R_1 > R_2$
	Leptophlebiidae	2.3±0.4	8.2±1.6	1.5±1.1	**	$R_2 > (R_1 \approx R_3)$
	Heptageniidae	0.7±0.5	5.3±1.7	1.7±1.4	*	$R_2 > (R_1 \approx R_3)$
Plecoptera	Perlidae	1.0±0.5	3.3±1.1	0.8±0.5	ns	
	Perlodidae	1.8±1.2	14.5±7.5	4.7±2.2	ns	
	Nemouridae	2.8±1.8	5.5±2.7	2.0±0.8	ns	
	Chloroperlidae	3.0±1.4	7.7±2.1	3.2±1.8	ns	
Trichoptera	Brachycentridae	8.2±6.3	15.7±6.3	12.5±6.5	ns	
	Rhyacophilidae	0.2±0.1	3.8±1.7	1.8±1.2	ns	$R_1 < R_2$
	Hydroptilidae	4.3±3.7	23.8±7.3	9.2±5.5	*	$R_1 < R_2$
Diptera	Simuliidae	2.5±0.6	8.0±1.9	5.7±2.9	ns	$R_1 < R_2$
	Chironomidae	288.0±52.5	805.3±147.8	490.0±171.0	*	**$R_1 < R_2$**
	Psychodidae	2.2±1.0	2.5±0.3	1.5±0.6	ns	
	Tipulidae	20.0±6.2	50.2±5.9	40.3±14.2	*	$R_1 < R_2$
Coleoptera	Elmidae	26.2±12.0	56.8±17.1	29.2±13.4	ns	
	Dytiscidae	0.5±0.2	0.7±0.3	1.8±1.6	ns	
	No. indiv.	464.0±41.4	1379.0±249.1	935.0±352.3	*	$R_1 < R_2$
	No. of families	17.3±1.1	21.7±0.9	18.7±1.7	ns	
	EPT taxa	72.3±17.7	259.8±92.4	191.7±102.0	ns	
	Chir. (%)	62	58	52		
	EPT/Chir.	0.08	0.11	0.13		

ns = not significant.
*Sig. 0.05.
**Sig. 0.01.
***Sig. 0.001.
Bold font depicts data with the outliers removed.

cover type in the ROW was in-stream vegetation, comprising 42% of the available cover in Prairie Creek and 81% of the cover in Alford Creek, whereas in-stream vegetation comprised only 15% of cover in the control in Prairie Creek and 9% in Alford Creek. Overhanging vegetation decreased by 20% in Prairie Creek and by 38% in Alford Creek in the ROW relative to the control. There were no deep pools, nor any undercut banks in the ROW of either stream, although these cover types were present in varying amounts in the other reaches. The ROW at Alford Creek had more boulders, which were absent elsewhere. In Prairie Creek, the ROW also had more boulders. There was less woody debris overall in the ROW of both streams. The amount of woody debris decreased in the ROW by 14% in Prairie Creek and by 41% in Alford Creek, most of which represented large woody debris. Within Prairie Creek there were specific observable trends. The control reach was the only reach to have some representation of all of the cover types selected for consideration. Deep pools were an important cover type in the first and third reaches of Prairie Creek, although they were absent in the ROW. Within Alford Creek specific trends were also apparent. In-stream vegetation accounted for less than 20% of the available cover in the control reach and over 60% in the second and third reaches. There were no boulders or deep pools in the control reach, although it had a larger amount of undercut banks than either of the other two reaches.

DISCUSSION

The results of this study show that a number of physical and biological attributes of fish habitat were altered in the ROW relative to the control reach, to varying degrees in both of the streams under investigation. With respect to the physical attributes of fish habitat, there is evidence that the structural complexity of the stream has been reduced in the ROW. Stream width decreased significantly downstream of the control reach, while depth was almost homogeneous across the channel, providing evidence of channelization. The substrate

Table 4. Mean density (no./0.1 m^2) and standard error of dominant taxa, and mean density of all taxa in each of the three study sections in Alford Creek

Order	Family	Alford Creek			MANOVA	Pairwise tests
		Reach 1	Reach 2	Reach 3		
Oligochaeta	Naididae	27.3±13.8	19.0±11.8	6.8±2.6	ns	
Pelecypoda	Sphaeriidae	184.8±62.7	83.5±43.7	134.7±82.8	ns	
Arachnida	Hydrachnidia	2.0±0.9	2.7±0.5	2.3±0.5	ns	
Crustacea	Ostracods	1.3±0.8	4.7±3.9	23±21.4	ns	
Ephemeroptera	Baetidae	22±7.2	126±35.3	106.5±59.5	*	$R_1 < (R_2 \approx R_3)$
	Ephemerellidae	3.5±1.9	18.3±3.0	9.0±3.7	**	$R_2 > (R_1 \approx \underline{R_3})$
	Leptophlebiidae	1.3±0.7	1.17±0.6	2.2±0.7	ns	
Plecoptera	Perlidae	1±1.0	3.7±1.6	2.2±1.1	ns	
	Perlodidae	2.8±2.2	2.2±0.9	2.0±1.0	ns	
	Nemouridae	17.2±11.6	25.8±6.5	61.3±38.9	ns	
Trichoptera	Brachycentridae	10.3±9.1	56.3±17.3	17.3±8.0	**	$R_2 > (R_1 \approx R_3)$
Diptera	Simuliidae	0.0±0.0	25±15.2	29.5±24.7	*	$R_1 < (R_2 \approx R_3)$
	Chironomidae	158.2±72.0	219.2±55.5	160.5±52.4	ns	
	Psychodidae	0.8±0.5	0±0.0	2.7±2.6	ns	
	Tipulidae	10±4.1	5.5±1.7	6.2±1.8	ns	
Coleoptera	Elmidae	11±8.4	9.5±2.2	9.0±5.4	ns	
	No. indiv./sample	918±144.2	605.7±122.5	582.3±216.2		
	No. indiv. (w/o Spha)	274.1±85.2	522.2±96.1	447.7±147.2	ns	
	No. of families	12.5±1.3	14.8±0.9	15.8±1.5	ns	
	EPT taxa	123±27.4	235.2±40.2	204.8±0.2	*	$R_1 < (R_2 \approx R_3)$
	Chir. (%)	34	36	28		
	Chir. (%) (w/o Spha)	58	42	36		
	EPT/Chir.	0.39	1.07	1.28		

ns = not significant.
*Sig. at $P < 0.05$.
**Sig. at $P < 0.01$.
Underline indicate differences that are almost significant (0.05–0.555).

composition in both rights-of-way was almost uniform across the channel, with the bankside samples containing similar proportions of particles as the mid-channel samples. There were no deep pools or undercut banks in either ROW. The impacts of such an alteration may result in a reduction in habitat complexity due to the elimination of riffles and pools and other non-uniformities in the stream channel (Brookes, 1988). The loss of habitat diversity and the pool-riffle sequence may result in the reduction or elimination of fish cover, which in turn can affect fish movement, predation, feeding, breeding, migration, and the amount of suitable shelter available for resting and cover (Brookes, 1988; Gregg and Rose, 1985). This may be particularly important for salmonids which require morphological variability in stream channels for shelter while they wait for prey (Brookes, 1988). Rivers that have had channel alterations on lengths of stream have been shown to produce less trout on the channelized reaches relative to the unmodified channel lengths (Brookes, 1988).

Another variable under investigation was stream water temperature, which generated quite different results in each of the two streams. There are a number of factors controlling the temperature of water as it flows downstream. Among these factors, the input of direct solar radiation is the primary source of heat causing water temperatures to increase (Brown, 1969). In his studies predicting the effect of clearcutting on streams, Brown (1969) found that solar radiation accounted for over 95% of the heat input on small, unshaded streams. The amount of solar radiation that is exposed to the stream is controlled by the quantity and quality of riparian vegetation (Brown, 1983). The removal of riparian vegetation or its replacement by vegetation that is less effective in providing shade can cause significant increases in stream temperatures (Beschta et al., 1987; Brown and Krygier, 1970). Thus, the shading effect of riparian vegetation is very important in maintaining acceptable stream temperatures, which in turn maintain the stream biota. At Prairie Creek there was a small increase in the stream water temperature downstream of the ROW, however it was within the range of normal variability. The increase in temperature was so small that it would be unlikely to have a significant, detrimental effect on the fish or other biota that comprise fish habitat unless temperatures were above or within close range of the thermal limits for the target species, which was the case for Prairie Creek. Temperatures reached 19°C in the ROW, thus approaching the lower range of the thermal tolerance limits for brown and brook trout (Schmitt et al., 1993). These temperatures are highly unlikely to

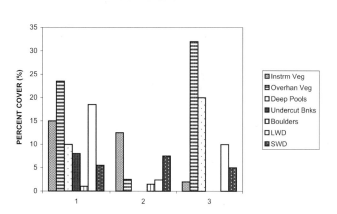

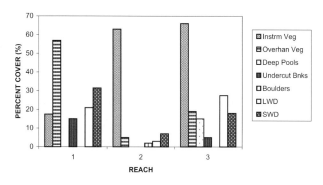

Fig. 5. Estimate of fish cover (% by type) in the three reaches at Prairie Creek and Alford Creek, respectively. For each reach, $n = 3$ (whole reach * 3 sampling periods).

be lethal to fish, but they may result in habitat avoidance until stream water temperature decreases, or in the reduction of fitness of the aquatic biota. Providing fish cover elements in the ROW, such as deep pools or overhanging structures, would benefit fish by providing protective areas with cooler water and shade. Although the removal of riparian vegetation did not substantially affect the water temperature in Prairie Creek, it may have a more significant effect on other streams. The physical and hydrological characteristics of Prairie Creek, specifically its depth and relatively fast current, cause it to be less susceptible to changes in water temperature as a result of incoming heat compared to shallow streams with low flows (Brown and Krygier, 1967). Therefore, stream water temperature should be carefully considered in the development of successive or large crossings, or if the watercourse in consideration is small and has low flows. Alford Creek was more likely to be affected by the removal of riparian vegetation because it is a shallow, low-flow stream, however the stream temperature in Alford Creek consistently decreased downstream of the control. This is caused by the introduction of another source of cooler water, called advection, as heat cannot be that readily dissipated from a stream (Brown, 1969). The source at Alford Creek was most likely groundwater that mixed with the main streamflow, as other potential sources of water such as a tributary were absent. This explanation is supported by the increase in stream discharge downstream of the control reach, likely the result of the additional input of groundwater which is also an indicator of advection (Brown, 1969). The input of cooler water hinders the determination of the effects of the removal of riparian vegetation on the stream that is most likely to be affected (Brown, 1970). However, it does demonstrate the influence that such factors may have in the determination of stream temperature. Consequently, the potential effects of the removal of riparian vegetation may be superseded by the inflow of groundwater or a tributary thereby eliminating, reducing or adding to the effects.

The results of the benthic macroinvertebrate sampling show an alteration in abundance and community structure in the ROW, although it is difficult to evaluate the nature of the alteration as being either detrimental or beneficial. Some of the results are seemingly beneficial, particularly the increases in the EPT taxa that are usually associated with clean, cool streams and are often used as biological indicators for evaluating environmental quality (Merritt and Cummins, 1996; Resh and Rosenberg, 1993). On the other hand, there were also increases in other invertebrates that are known to be disturbance tolerant, such as Oligochaeta Naididae, Diptera Chironomidae and Simuliidae (Cairns and Pratt, 1993). Other biological measures of environmental quality include family richness, the ratio of EPT taxa to Chironomidae abundance and the ratio of Chironomids relative to the total number of individuals (Resh and Jackson, 1993). With regards to these measures, there was no statistically significant difference for either stream.

There are a number of possible interpretations of these results. The macroinvertebrates may be responding to the increase in aquatic macrophytes, particularly in Alford Creek where the increase in in-stream vegetation was considerable. Increases in algal production as a result of increased exposure to solar radiation have been shown to lead to higher invertebrate production (Beschta et al., 1987; Shortreed and Stockner, 1982). Macrophytes have also been shown to have a significant influence on benthic macroinvertebrates by altering the microhabitats in the stream (Gregg and Rose, 1985). They reduce current velocity, which will subsequently affect substrate composition and distribution and they increase the physical heterogeneity of the microhabitats as they grow vertically into the water column providing potential living spaces where none existed above unvegetated substrate (Gregg and Rose, 1985). Other studies investigating the effects of the removal of riparian vegetation on macroinvertebrates have found similar results (Murphy and Hall, 1980; Murphy et al., 1981). In these studies, it was demonstrated that the increase in primary production in streams due to increased light availability following canopy removal resulted in greater biomass, density, and species richness of insects. Another possible explanation is the change in substrate composition in the ROW in both streams. Substrate composition may be a factor in determining the taxonomic composition of macroinvertebrates in the stream as macroinvertebrate distribution and abundance has been correlated to substrate composition (Culp et al., 1983). The substrate composition changed in the ROW to some degree in both streams towards larger sized substrata, which is generally beneficial to macroinvertebrates (Brookes, 1988). These increases may be beneficial to fish as benthic macroinvertebrates are the primary food source for the fish species under consideration, thus it represents an increase in food availability. However, the corresponding increase in disturbance tolerant invertebrates may also indicate environmental stress.

Alterations in the abundance, diversity, and type of fish cover were also evident in the ROW. The ROW had the least amount of cover for fish, resulting in a loss of approximately 50% of available cover relative to the control, for both streams. The diversity of cover elements was also reduced in the ROW. In Prairie Creek two cover types comprised 67% of the available cover and in Alford Creek one cover type comprised 81% of the available cover and the amount and diversity of other cover elements were low. In the control reaches of both rights-of-way the proportion of cover types was distributed more equitably. The proportion of woody debris available in the ROW decreased by 14% in Prairie Creek and 41% in Alford Creek relative to the control reach, most of which represented a loss of large woody debris. Furthermore, the ROW lacked specific cover elements such as pools and undercut banks in both streams. The considerable reduction of fish cover may contribute to the loss of habitat diversity that is important to fish and other aquatic biota (Hartman et al., 1987). Numerous studies (Boussu, 1954; Calkins, 1989; Hunt, 1976; Lamberti, 1992; Lewis, 1969; Butler and Hawthorne, 1968; Schmitt et al., 1993; Wootton, 1992) have shown that fish cover, and deep pools in particular, are among the most important factors for fish and are crucial in influencing fish densities and community structure. There may also be indirect effects of changes in the amount of woody debris, including changes to the bank stability and channel form, as well as reducing the amount of cover provided to young fish (Hartman and Holtby, 1982; Towes and Moore, 1982). This may be particularly important in the winter, when fish populations are reduced substantially and stream sections containing adequate habitat in the form of deep pools, logjams, debris, and undercut banks maintain more fish than sections without this habitat (Tschaplinski and Hartman, 1982).

In addition to the alterations in the substrate composition already mentioned, other changes were apparent. There was also a 10% increase in the amount of silts and sands downstream of the ROW at Prairie Creek and an increased proportion of fines in the bankside habitats. Studies have shown that the deposition of sediments on stream bottoms will reduce egg and alevin survival and negatively affect juvenile fish (Berg, 1982; Cordone and Kelly, 1961). Therefore, some concern should be given to this finding. That aside however, the changes in the substrata at Prairie Creek were not that substantial. In Alford Creek there was a 30% increase in the proportion of cobbles in the ROW and a 24% decrease in the proportion of silts and sands. Though this represents a departure from the typical substrata of the stream, it is potentially beneficial to the aquatic biota as it provides for a more diverse benthic community, as invertebrate abundance and distribution is highly correlated with the substrate composition (Culp and Davies, 1982; Vinson and Hawkins, 1998).

CONCLUSIONS

The structural habitat in the ROW has become more homogenous as a result of the physical alterations to the stream channel which is likely attributable to the construction and installation of the pipeline. The shape and dimensions of the channel have changed to become more homogenous, fish cover has been considerably reduced and the substrate is relatively uniform across the stream channel. Consequently, the niche potential is reduced which will affect the amount, type, and composition of the species occupying the system (Brookes, 1988; McCulloch, 1986). Furthermore the loss of diversity may interfere with the ability of the ecosystem to function effectively and to remain resilient to other disturbances, such as floods (Christensen, 1996; Lamberti, 1992; Lewis, 1969). The degree to which this change in the habitat will affect the ability of the stream to produce or maintain fish is difficult to determine. It is unlikely that the channelization of such a small section of the stream will have a significant, detrimental effect on the fishery however it may influence other physical aspects of the stream and subsequently the biota (Carter et al., 1996). Furthermore, the reduction of fish cover and the loss of diversity in the structural habitat is likely to have an effect on the capacity of the habitat to support the stream biota, as these are all important aspects of fish habitat (Ralph et al., 1994). Given the number of watercourse crossings that are constructed in Alberta each year however, the potential cumulative effects resulting from such crossings is significant. Techniques that would increase habitat complexity in the ROW effectively would be beneficial to reducing alterations caused by the crossing.

Thus, there is evidence of an alteration to the physical and biological attributes of fish habitat as a result of the pipeline watercourse crossing. The majority of alterations seem to be attributable to the physical construction and installation of the pipeline rather than as a result of the removal of riparian vegetation, although the loss of cover elements such as overhanging vegetation may contribute to this alteration. These changes may result in a reduction of the habitat to support the life processes of fish including spawning, rearing, nursery, overwintering, feeding and migration (DFO, 1998). The assumption, as given by the DFO (1998) is that "as a result of the reduced capacity of the habitat to support the life processes of fish, there will *also* be a loss in the capacity of the habitat to *produce* fish." Hence, the alteration of the stream at the ROW could be construed as causing a harmful alteration, disruption or destruction of fish habitat. Furthermore the cumulative effects of multiple or successive rights-of-way may compound the impact, particularly if the removal of riparian vegetation is large enough to cause water temperature increases beyond the thermal tolerances of the target species or is significantly higher than in undisturbed reaches.

Many of the measures to reduce crossing impacts would be relatively inexpensive and easy to implement. These could include: restoring the ecological attributes of the stream back to its original state following the construction of the crossing; conducting a full and accurate baseline study of the area prior to construction; developing site-specific restoration plans rather than a generic plan; implementing trenchless construction techniques wherever possible; restoring the bankside habitat such that it provides an equitable ecological function as it originally had; restore fish habitat attributes such as stream channel meanders and fish cover elements; monitoring and continuing to conduct research to evaluate the success of implementing these measures; and considering the potential cumulative effects that may result from a project. Should such measures be implemented, there would be little to no concern regarding the loss of habitat as a result of pipeline rights-of-way.

REFERENCES

Alberta Recreation, Parks, and Wildlife. 1976. Fish of Alberta.

Berg, L. 1982. The effect of exposure to short-term pulses of suspended sediment on the behaviour of juvenile salmonids. In: Proceedings of the Carnation Creek Workshop, a 10 year review. G. Hartman, ed. Nanaimo, BC. pp. 177–196.

Beschta, R.L., R.E. Bilby, G.W. Brown, L.B. Holtby, and T.D. Hofstra. 1987. Stream water temperature and aquatic habitat: Fisheries and forestry interactions. In: Streamside Management: Forestry and Fishery Interactions. E.O. Salo and T.W. Cundy, eds. Institute of Forest Resources, University of Washington. Seattle. Contribution No. 57. pp. 191–231.

Boussu, M.F. 1954. Relationship between trout populations and cover on a small stream. Journal of Wildlife Management, 18(2): 229–239.

Brookes, A. 1988. Channelized Rivers: Perspectives for Environmental Management. John Wiley and Sons Ltd. Toronto, Canada.

Brower, J., J. Zarr, and C. von Ende. 1990. Field and laboratory methods for general ecology. Wm. C. Brown Publishers. Dubuque, IA.

Brown, G.W. 1969. Predicting temperatures on small streams. Water Resource Research, 5(1): 68–75.

Brown, G.W. 1970. Predicting the effect of clearcutting on stream temperature. Journal of Soil and Water Conservation, 25: 11–13.

Brown, G.W. 1983. Forestry and water quality. D.S.U. Book Stores, Inc. Corvallis, OR.

Brown, G. and J.T. Krygier. 1967. Changing water temperature in small mountain stream. Journal of Soil and Water Conservation, 22(6): 242–244.

Brown, G. and J.T. Krygier. 1970. Effects of clear-cutting on stream temperature. Water Resources Research, 6(4): 1133–1139.

Butler, R.L. and V.M. Hawthorne. 1968. The reactions of dominant trout to changes in overhead artificial cover. Transactions of the American Fisheries Society, 97(1): 37–41.

Cairns, J. Jr. and J.R. Pratt. 1993. A history of biological monitoring using benthic macroinvertebrates. In: Freshwater Biomonitoring and Benthic Invertebrates. D.M. Rosenberg and V.H. Resh, eds. New York, NY. pp. 10–27.

Calkins, D.J. 1989. Winter habitats of Atlantic salmon, brook trout, brown trout and rainbow trout. US Army Corps of Engineers Special Report 89-34.

Carter, J.L., S.V. Fend, and S.S. Kennelly. 1996. The relationship among three habitat scales and stream benthic invertebrate community structure. Freshwater Biology, 35: 109–124.

Christensen, N.L. (Chair). 1996. The report of the Ecological Society of America Committee on the scientific basis for ecosystem management. Ecological Applications, 6(3): 665–691.

Clifford, H.F. 1991. Aquatic invertebrates of Alberta. The University of Alberta Press. Edmonton, AB.

Cordone, A.J. and D.W. Kelley. 1961. The influences of inorganic sediment on the aquatic life of streams. California Fish and Game, 47: 189–228.

Culp, J.M. and R.W. Davies. 1982. Effect of substrate and detritus manipulation on macroinvertebrate density and biomass: Implications for forest clearcutting. In: Proceedings of the Carnation Creek Workshop, a 10 year review. G. Hartman, ed. Nanaimo, BC. pp. 210–216.

Culp, J.M., S.J. Walde, and R.W. Davies. 1983. Relative importance of substrate particle size and detritus to stream benthic macroinvertebrates microdistribution. Canadian Journal of Fisheries and Aquatic Sciences, 40: 1568–1573.

Department of Fisheries and Oceans. 1998. Decision framework for the determination and authorization of harmful alteration, disruption or destruction of fish habitat. Communications Directorate. Ottawa, ON.

Edmunds, G.F. Jr., S. Jensen, and L. Berner. 1976. The mayflies of North and Central America. Burns and MacEachern Limited. Don Mills, ON.

Fisheries Act. RSC 1985, c. F-14.

Gregg, W.W. and F.L. Rose. 1985. Influences of aquatic macrophytes on invertebrate community structure, guild structure, and microdistribution in streams. Hydrobiologia, 128: 45–56.

Hartman, G. and L.B. Holtby. 1982. An overview of some biophysical determinants of fish production and fish population responses to logging in Carnation Creek. In: Proceedings of the Carnation Creek Workshop, a 10 year review. G. Hartman, ed. Nanaimo, BC. pp. 348–374.

Hartman, G., J.C. Scrivener, L.B. Holtby, and L. Powell. 1987. Some effects of different streamside treatments on physical conditions and fish population process in Carnation Creek, a coastal rain forest stream in British Columbia. In: Streamside Management: Forestry and Fishery Interactions. E.O. Salo and T.W. Cundy, eds. Institute of Forest Resources, University of Washington. Seattle. Contribution No. 57. pp. 330–372.

Hunt, R.L. 1976. A long-term evaluation of trout habitat development and its relation to improving management-related research. Transactions of the American Fisheries Society, 105(3): 361–364.

Jewett, S.G. Jr. 1959. The stoneflies (Plecoptera) of the Pacific Northwest. Oregon State College. Corvallis, OR. No. 3.

Johnston, N.T. and P.A. Slaney. 1996. Fish habitat assessment procedures. Watershed Restoration Technical Circular No. 8.

Lamberti, G. 1992. Influence of habitat complexity on resistance to flooding and resilience of fish assemblages. Transactions of the American Fisheries Society, 121: 427–436.

Lewis, S.L. 1969. Physical factors influencing fish populations in pools of a trout stream. Transactions of the American Fisheries Society, 98(1): 14–19.

MacDonald, J.S., J.C. Scrivener, and G. Smith. 1992. The Stuart-Takla Fisheries/Forestry Interaction Project: Study Description and Design. Canadian Technical Report of Fisheries and Aquatic Sciences no. 1899.

McCulloch, D.L. 1986. Benthic macroinvertebrate distributions in the riffle-pool communities of two east Texas streams. Hydrobiologia, 135: 61–70.

Merritt, R.W. and K.W. Cummins. 1996. An introduction to the aquatic insects of North America. Kendall/Hunt Publishing Company. Dubuque, Iowa.

Murphy, M.L. and J.D. Hall. 1980. Varied effects of clear-cut logging on predators and their habitat in small streams of the Cascade Mountains, Oregon. Canadian Journal of Fisheries and Aquatic Sciences, 38: 137–145.

Murphy, M.L., C.P. Hawkins, and N.H. Anderson. 1981. Effects of canopy modification and accumulated sediment of stream communities. Transactions of the American Fisheries Society, 110: 469–478.

Platts, W.S., W.F. Megahan, and G.W. Minshall. 1983. Methods for evaluating stream, riparian, and biotic conditions. United States Forest Service General Technical Report IN-138.

Ralph, S.C., G.C. Poole, L.L. Conquest, and R.J. Naiman. 1994. Stream channel morphology and woody debris in logged and unlogged basins of Western Washington. Canadian Journal of Fisheries and Aquatic Sciences, 51: 37–51.

Resh, V.H. and J.K. Jackson. 1993. Rapid assessment approaches to biomonitoring using benthic macroinvertebrates. In: Freshwater Biomonitoring and Benthic Invertebrates. D.M. Rosenberg and V.H. Resh, eds. New York, NY. pp. 195–233.

Rosenberg, D.M. and V.H. Resh. 1993. Introduction to freshwater biomonitoring and benthic macroinvertebrates. In: Freshwater Biomonitoring and Benthic Unvertebrates. D.M. Rosenberg and V.H. Resh, eds. New York, NY. pp. 1–9.

Schmitt, C.J., A.D. Lemly, and P.V. Winger. 1993. Habitat suitability index model for brook trout in streams of the southern Blue Ridge Province: Surrogate variables, model evaluation, and suggested improvements. US Fish and Wildlife Service, Washington.

Scrivener, J.C. and M.J. Brownlee. 1982. An analysis of the Carnation Creek gravel-quality data 1973 to 1981. In: Proceedings of the Carnation Creek Workshop, a 10 year review. G. Hartman, ed. Nanaimo, BC. pp. 154–176.

Shortreed, D.S. and J.G. Stockner. 1982. The impact of logging on periphyton biomass and species composition in Carnation Creek. In: Proceedings of the Carnation Creek Workshop, a 10 year review. G. Hartman, ed. Nanaimo, BC. pp. 197–209.

Strong, W.L. 1992. Ecoregions of Alberta. Provincial Base Map. Alberta Forestry, Lands and Wildlife.

Towes, D.A.A. and M.K. Moores. 1982. The effects of three streamside logging treatments on organic debris and channel morphology of Carnation Creek. In: Proceedings of the Carnation Creek Workshop, a 10 year review. G. Hartman, ed. Nanaimo, BC. pp. 129–152.

Tschaplinski, P.J. and G.F. Hartman. 1982. Winter distribution of juvenile coho salmon (*Oncorhynchus kisutch*) in Carnation Creek and some implications to overwinter survival. In: Proceedings of the Carnation Creek Workshop, a 10 year review. G. Hartman, ed. Nanaimo, BC. pp. 273–286.

Vinson, M.R. and C.P. Hawkins. 1998. Biodiversity of stream insects: Variation at local, basin and regional scales. Annu. Rev. Entomol., 43: 271–293.

Wilkinson, L. 1990. SYSTAT: The system for statistics. SYSTAT Inc. Evanston, IL, USA.

Wootton, R.J. 1992. Fish Ecology. Blackie. Glasgow.

Wrona, F.J., J.M. Culp, and R.W. Davies. 1982. Macroinvertebrate subsampling: A simplified apparatus and approach. Canadian Journal of Fisheries and Aquatic Sciences, 39: 1051–1053.

BIOGRAPHICAL SKETCHES

Christine M. Brown (corresponding author)

Alberta Energy and Utilities Board, Environment Section, Compliance and Operations Branch, 640-5th Avenue SW, Calgary, AB T2P3G4, Canada, e-mail: christine.brown@gov.ab.ca, fax: (403) 297-2691.

Christine Brown works at the Alberta Energy and Utilities board as an Environmental Science Specialist and Advisor. Her responsibilities are quite diverse, ranging from policy development and implementation, to reviewing and advising on Environmental Impact Assessments for large-scale energy developments. The work conducted for this study represents part of the work undertaken for her Master's at the University of Calgary.

Richard D. Revel

Faculty of Environmental Design, University of Calgary, 2500 University Dr. NW, Calgary, AB T2N1N4, Canada

Dr. Richard Revel is a Professor of Environmental Science at the Faculty of Environmental Design at the University of Calgary. His research interests lie in the areas of resource management and planning, reclamation, range management, forest management and plant ecology. Dr. Revel has been actively involved in regulatory functions in the energy industry, both in Alberta, Canada and internationally. Dr. Revel acted as the Supervisor for the work conducted for this Master's Project.

John R. Post

Department of Biology, University of Calgary, 2500 University Dr. NW, Calgary, AB T2N1N4, Canada

Dr. John Post is an Associate Professor in the Department of Biological Sciences at the University of Calgary. His primary research interests included energy dynamics and bioenergetics models, fish biology and aquatic food web dynamics. Dr. Post acted as a Committee Member for the Master's project presented in part in the following paper.

Effects of Natural Gas Pipeline Water Crossing Replacement on the Benthic Invertebrate and Fish Communities of Big Darby Creek, Ohio

Scott Reid, Scott Stoklosar, Serge Metikosh, Jim Evans, and Tracy Huffman

During the fall of 1998, two exposed natural gas pipeline crossings of Big Darby Creek, Ohio were removed and then replaced using open-cut (wet) and flumed (dry) crossing techniques. Big Darby Creek, a national and state scenic river, supports a diverse warmwater fish community that includes several state-listed threatened and endangered species. Instream construction resulted in short-term increases to downstream suspended sediment concentrations, sediment deposition rates, and the amount of fine sediment in riffle habitats. Jersey barrier and sandbag dams, used during the flumed crossing provided a poor seal from the creek flow. Therefore, a similar amount of sediment was released downstream as the open-cut replacement. Increased fine sediment in riffle habitats immediately downstream of the crossing coincided with short-term (<1 year) changes in the abundance and community structure of benthic invertebrates. Small post-construction changes of the abundance and species composition of fish communities were measured at riffles and runs upstream and downstream of construction and therefore, are not considered due to sediment released during instream construction. No long-term (>1 year) changes to benthic invertebrate and fish communities were observed.

Keywords: Sediment, construction, open-cut crossings, flumed crossings, aquatic effects

INTRODUCTION

Two parallel exposed natural gas pipelines crossing Big Darby Creek, Ohio were replaced using both open-cut (wet) and isolated (dry) methods during the fall of 1998. Big Darby Creek, a National and State Scenic River, supports a diverse warmwater fishery including several state listed threatened and endangered fish species. Pipeline water crossing construction can result in temporary increases in downstream sediment loads. While it has been recognized that warmwater riffle fish species are sensitive to increased sediment loading (Trautman, 1981; Berkman and Rabeni, 1987), the effects of pipeline water crossing construction on these particular fish communities were not known. Secondly, few case studies have evaluated the effectiveness of isolated crossing methods in mitigating the adverse effects of water crossing construction (Bandaloo, 1978; Reid and Metikosh, 2001). The pipe replacement work at Big Darby Creek provided an opportunity to compare sediment loading associated with two different crossing techniques and to study its effect on habitat condition, benthic invertebrates and warmwater fish.

METHODOLOGY

Study area
Big Darby Creek, a tributary of the Scioto River in Central Ohio, drains 1443 km^2 in the Eastern Cornbelt Plains Ecoregion (Hambrook et al., 1997). It supports a diverse warmwater fish assemblage (86 species) including several state-listed threatened and endangered fish species. The study area, located several kilometers upstream of Darbyville, Ohio, consisted of a 3.1 km reach that extended from 0.6 km upstream of the crossing to 2.5 km downstream.

Monitoring stations were established along this reach upstream and downstream of the exposed pipelines. Riffle habitats were selected to monitor sediment deposition rates, habitat alteration and the responses of benthic invertebrates and riffle fish communities. Run habitats were chosen to measure the responses of fish not dependent on riffle habitats.

Over the study area, the channel gradient is flat (<0.1%). Fish habitat predominately consisted of long stretches of placid runs with occasional riffles found at areas of channel constriction and downstream of meander bends. Flow levels during construction ranged between 1.4 and 2.1 m^3 s^{-1}. At the crossing location, the wetted width of the channel was 37 m. Based on sieve analysis, bed material excavated from Big Darby Creek during construction was 26% gravel sized material, 34% sand and 40% silts and clay. Riffles were approximately 9 m wide, with mean water depths and velocities of 0.2–0.5 m, and 0.2–0.3 m s^{-1}, respectively. The surficial bed material of riffle habitats was dominated by clean gravel and cobble material. Run habitats were ≈0.5–1.5 m deep with hard packed sand and gravel substrates.

Sampling methodology

The study included: (1) monitoring of suspended sediment concentrations (TSS) during instream construction; (2) measurement of sediment deposition rates; and, (3) pre- and post-construction sampling of surficial creek bed material, benthic invertebrate communities; and fish inhabiting run and riffle habitats. Field work was conducted between September 14th, 1998 and September 24th, 1999. Sampling of habitat conditions, and benthic invertebrates occurred before (September 14th–16th, 1998), immediately after (October 4th–6th, 1998); one month after (November 5th, 1998); and, one year after construction (September 23rd–24th, 1999). Fish communities were sampled during all site visits except in November 1998.

Suspended sediment

Water samples were taken at mid water column for the duration of instream construction (September 16th to October 5th, 1998) to document TSS (mg l^{-1}) upstream and downstream of construction. Water sampling stations were established 50 m upstream, and 50, 500, and 1600 m downstream of instream construction. A site-specific TSS–turbidity relationship was then derived from field turbidity measurements and a subsample (50) of water samples representing a range of turbidities that were analyzed for TSS concentration. Turbidity measurements taken in the field were converted to TSS (mg l^{-1}) using the following regression equation where NTU is nephelometric turbidity units:

$$\log_{10}(\text{TSS}+1) = \frac{0.7568 e^{0.5455(\log_{10}\text{NTU}+1)}}{r^2} = 0.87. \quad (1)$$

The ranges of NTU and TSS measurements in the subsample were 0.1–853 NTU and 4–3360 mg l^{-1}, respectively.

Sediment deposition and habitat alteration

Sediment deposition and associated habitat alteration downstream of the crossing was determined by: (1) measurement of the amount of material captured in sediment traps; and (2) the characterization of surficial bed material using the pebble count method. Three monitoring stations were established at riffles 600 m upstream, 50 and 500 m downstream of the crossing. To measure sediment deposition, modified Whitlock–Vibert boxes filled with washed 25 mm diameter gravel were buried in the creek bed flush with the surface before construction (Clarke and Scruton, 1997). After construction, traps were removed and captured sediment was analyzed for dry weight and particle size distribution. A one-way ANOVA and Tukey's HSD multiple comparisons were used to test for differences in sediment deposition rates between riffles (Zar, 1984). Surficial bed material and the amount of fine sediment were characterized using the pebble count method (Kondolf, 1997). D_{16}, D_{50}, D_{84} (sediment particle diameter at which 16, 50, and 84% of the sample is finer) and the percentage of particles less than 4 mm in diameter were calculated from pebble count data for each riffle and sampling event to identify changes in surficial bed material.

Benthic invertebrates

Benthic invertebrate communities in riffles were sampled with a Surber sampler (0.1 m^2 sampling area and 250 μm mesh). Five samples were taken at each riffle. Samples were preserved in a 70% alcohol solution in 1 l bottles and identified to the lowest possible taxonomic level. Changes to benthic invertebrate communities in relation to instream construction were evaluated using five biological indicators: total density, abundance of individual taxa, species richness, Ephemeroptera, Plecoptera, Trichoptera (EPT) richness (number of mayfly, stonefly, and caddisfly taxa), and the ratio of EPT individuals to total density. EPT metrics were used as these species are considered to be sensitive to fine sediment related changes to habitat condition.

Fish community

Fish in Big Darby Creek were sampled using seine nets (7.0 m × 1.9 m with 6 mm mesh) and backpack electro-fishing units. Three areas of run habitat (50 m upstream, 90 and 1600 m downstream) were sampled with multiple seine hauls (5 at each run). Areas seined were approximately 0.5–1.5 m deep with hard packed sand and gravel substrate. ANOVAs and Tukey's HSD multiple comparisons were used to test for differences in capture rates and species number at each site and sampling event (Zar, 1984). Proportional similarity indices (PSI) were calculated, to assess the similarities between pre- and post-construction species assemblages in run habitats. PSI values range from 0 (completely different) to 1 (identical). PSI values greater than 0.7 are considered to indicate very similar fish assemblages (Paller, 1997).

Two riffles (600 m upstream and 500 m downstream) were sampled using three depletion passes through a 35 m reach of each riffle with a backpack electro-fishing unit. Each reach was isolated with upstream and downstream blocknets and sampled by a three person crew. Methods outlined in Zippen (1958) were used to generate population estimates. PSI values were calculated to assess the similarity of pre- and post-construction species assemblages in riffle habitats.

RESULTS

Overview of instream construction activities at Big Darby Creek

The old 18 and 20 inch exposed lines (457 and 508 mm diameter) were removed and then replaced with two 508 mm concrete coated lines during September and October of 1998. Instream construction was authorized pursuant to Sections 401 and 404 of the Clean Water Act (33 USC 1344), a Flood Hazard Building Permit and a National Pollution Discharge Elimination System general permit for construction site stormwater. Each replacement and accompanying tie-in was done independently and in succession in order to maintain gas supply to nearby consumers.

Replacement of the first pipe required nine days of instream activity. Initially, the workspace was to be isolated with aqua-barriers and a flexible flume. However, due to a tear along a seam, the upstream aqua-barrier failed before trench excavation commenced and the replacement was instead completed as an open-cut crossing. The second line replacement was completed over a six day period using the flumed crossing method. The workspace was isolated from the creek by concrete jersey barrier and sandbag dams and the flow was diverted through a flume (508 mm diameter pipe). Turbid water from the isolated work area was pumped to an upland discharge location. During both replacements, the trench was excavated and backfilled by backhoe and spoil was stockpiled instream. After the lines were replaced, creek banks were recontoured and stabilized using soil bioengineering procedures; including rootwad placement, live-stakes, and cribbing.

Suspended sediment
First line replacement (open-cut)
During the first replacement, the mean background TSS concentration was 7.1 mg l^{-1} (range 4.7–14.6 mg l^{-1}). TSS concentrations 50 m downstream increased slightly above background (mean 8.9 mg l^{-1}: range 4.7–44 mg l^{-1}) during aqua-barrier and flexible flume installation and removal. However, during trench excavation (September 25th–26th), TSS concentrations were measured up to 2723.7 mg l^{-1}, 50 m downstream of construction. TSS concentrations remained high during backfilling (mean 773.0 mg l^{-1}, 50 m downstream) with the peak TSS concentration of 5100 mg l^{-1}. This was the highest concentration measured over the entire project. Six hours after backfilling had been completed (September 27th), downstream TSS concentrations had decreased markedly (15 mg l^{-1}). By the following morning, TSS concentrations were equivalent to background (7.8 mg l^{-1}).

Second line replacement (flumed)
During the second line replacement, the mean background TSS concentration was 9.2 mg l^{-1} (range 7.7–9.2 mg l^{-1}). Removal of the second exposed pipe caused a temporary (<2 h) increase in downstream TSS concentrations. Installation of the flume and dam structures resulted in larger increases in TSS concentrations above background (mean 131.7 mg l^{-1}, 50 m downstream). Dams were ineffective at isolating the work area as water flowed underneath the concrete jersey barriers. Accordingly, downstream TSS concentrations were high during both trenching (mean 290.9 mg l^{-1}, 50 m downstream) and backfilling (mean 1487.9 mg l^{-1}, 50 m downstream). The peak TSS concentration was measured during backfilling on October 5th (13120 mg l^{-1}).

Partway through trench excavation, spoil stockpiled on either side of the trench improved the seal of the isolation dams. Consequently, TSS concentrations measured 50 m downstream during pipe-laying, and the initial stages of backfilling were relatively low (9.5–77 mg l^{-1}). However, as stockpiled material was used up during backfilling, the seal deteriorated and isolation structures were again ineffective at keeping the work area dry. As a result, after 1 h of backfilling, TSS concentrations downstream increased from 134 to 1306 mg l^{-1}. Downstream TSS concentrations remained high during dam and flume removal. Over the 5.5 h required to remove the dams and flume, TSS concentrations measured 50 m downstream averaged over 840 mg l^{-1} above background.

During both line replacements, TSS concentrations decreased as the plume of turbid water moved downstream. During trenching and backfilling, mean TSS concentrations measured 500 m downstream were 89% and 96% lower than 50 m downstream. TSS concentrations of water samples collected at the bridge crossing at Darbyville (3 km downstream) during trenching (8.3 and 9.4 mg l^{-1}) and backfilling (6.5 and 7.6 mg l^{-1}) were equivalent to background levels.

Sediment deposition and habitat alteration
A significantly greater amount of silt and clay (<0.75 mm diameter) was deposited at the first downstream riffle (50 m downstream of the pipeline crossings) than at the riffle monitored upstream of the

crossing (ANOVA $p < 0.001$; Tukey HSD $p < 0.001$). Deposition of silt and clay was 6.6 times greater than at the upstream riffle (12.6 vs. 1.9 g m^2). Sediment traps were not removed from the riffle 500 m downstream of the crossing until one month after construction and were therefore not used in this analysis. However, for the following reasons, it is suggested that most of the deposition occurred within 500 m downstream of the crossing. TSS concentrations measured during construction 500 m downstream were 89–96% lower than 50 m downstream and, unlike the first downstream riffle, there was no measurable change in surficial bed material due to silt and clay deposition at the second downstream riffle (see below).

Before instream construction, the surficial bed material of riffles was gravel and cobble (D_{50}: 55–71 mm) with a low level of fine sediment (3–9%). The high rate of deposition of silt and clay at the first downstream riffle resulted in: a 36% increase in the amount of surficial fine sediment (<4 mm); and, a shift in surficial bed material from gravel-cobble (D_{50}: 71 mm) to a mixture of clay, silts, gravel and cobble (D_{50}: 33 mm). Changes to habitat conditions were still evident one month after construction. After construction, the amount of fine sediment measured at the upstream and the second downstream riffles increased by only 3 and 1%, respectively. One year after construction, the bed material at the first downstream riffle had recovered to its pre-construction condition.

Benthic invertebrates

Over the fall of 1998, post-construction changes in abundance and community structure of benthic invertebrates were evident at the first downstream riffle. Benthic invertebrate density was 46% lower, one month after construction [Fig. 1(a)]. In contrast, benthic invertebrate density increased from September to November at both the upstream and second downstream riffles. The proportion of EPT individuals relative to total abundance was greater at all riffles immediately after construction [Fig. 2(a)]. However, while the proportion of EPT species relative to all species continued to increase at the upstream and second downstream riffles, it decreased from October to November (one month post-construction) at the first downstream riffle. Both the number of individual taxa and EPT taxa collected from both downstream riffles increased within one month of construction [Figs. 1(b) and 2(b)]. Alternatively, the number of benthic invertebrate and EPT taxa collected from the upstream riffle was relatively constant.

Specific taxonomic level changes observed at the first downstream riffle included: (1) an increase in oligochaete (aquatic worms) and Neuroeclipsis (caddisfly) abundance from September to November to a density greater than the two other riffles; and (2) an initial increase in the abundance of several species of

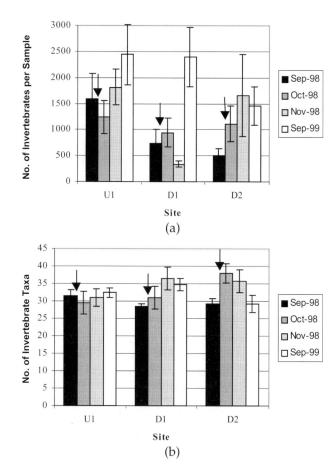

Fig. 1. (a) Mean (SE) densities and (b) number of benthic invertebrate taxa collected from riffles along Big Darby Creek (arrows indicate the timing of construction). U1: 600 m upstream; D1: 50 m downstream; D2: 500 m downstream.

mayflies (*Stenonema* sp., Tricorythidae sp.), midges (Chironomidae sp.) and a species of web-spinning caddisfly (Hydropsychidae sp.) immediately after construction followed by a reduction in abundance by November. At the other riffles, the densities of these taxa had remained constant, or had increased slightly.

One year after construction (September 1999), benthic invertebrate densities and number of taxa at the first downstream riffle were equivalent or greater than before construction.

Fish community

Twenty-seven fish species were collected from riffle habitats of which ninety-five percent were either darters (Percidae sp.) or minnows and shiners (Cyprinidae sp.). One state-listed endangered species (spotted darter, *Etheostoma maculatum*), and two state-listed threatened species (Tippecanoe darter, *Etheostoma tippecanoe* and bluebreast darter, *Etheostoma caeruleum*) were captured. The most frequently captured species were the central stoneroller (*Campostoma anomalum*), banded darter (*Etheostoma zonale*), bluebreast darter, rainbow darter (*Etheostoma caeruleum*), Tippecanoe darter and the variegate darter (*Etheostoma variatum*). After construction, fish abundance (including numbers of the

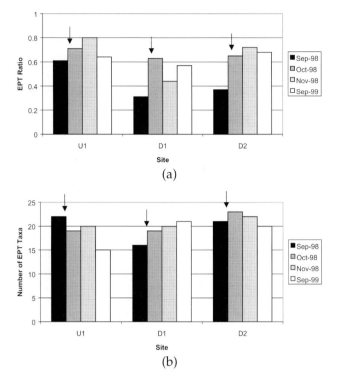

Fig. 2. (a) EPT (mayflies, stoneflies, caddisflies) ratios and (b) number of EPT taxa collected from riffles along Big Darby Creek (arrows indicate timing of construction). U1: 600 m upstream; D1: 50 m downstream; D2: 500 m downstream.

two-state listed threatened species Tippecanoe and bluebreast darters) increased substantially at both upstream and downstream riffles (Table 1).

PSI values calculated from pre- and post-construction electro-fishing data indicate that the post-construction fish assemblage at the downstream riffle (0.62) was slightly different than before construction. Three additional species were collected in October of 1998. The relative abundance of dominant species (central stonerollers, Tippecanoe darters, rainbow darters, and variegate darters) changed between 10 and 16%. The post-construction fish assemblage at the upstream riffle was similar to the pre-construction assemblage (PSI: 0.73)

In total, 21 different species were seined from run habitats. The most frequently captured species belonged to the sunfish and bass (*Centrarchidae* sp.), sucker and redhorse (*Catostomidae* sp.), and shiner and minnow (*Cyprinidae* sp.) families. There were no statistical differences in the number of fish (ANOVA: $p = 0.18$), or species captured (ANOVA: $p = 0.38$) before and after construction at any of the sampling locations [Fig. 3 (a) and (b)]. However, PSI values calculated for each run indicated changes in the composition of upstream and downstream fish assemblages immediately after construction (0.28–0.59). The relative abundance of golden redhorse (*Moxostoma erythrurum*) at each run decreased between 14 and 23%. Other species including smallmouth bass (*Micropterus dolomieui*), silver shiner (*Notropis photogenis*), and longear sunfish (*Lep-

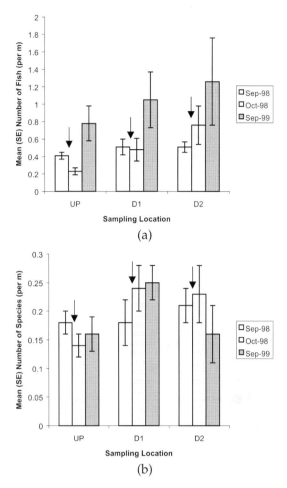

Fig. 3. Mean numbers (±SE) of (a) fish and (b) fish species in seine hauls in run habitats along Big Darby Creek (arrow indicates timing of construction). UP: 50 m upstream of crossing; D1: 90 m downstream; D2: 1600 m downstream.

omis megalotis) were also caught less frequently along the study reach after construction.

DISCUSSION

The flumed crossing method has been successful in minimizing sediment entrainment from pipeline water crossing construction (Baddaloo, 1978; Reid and Metikosh, 2001). Successful application of the method is strongly dependent on watercourse size, bed material, channel characteristics, and materials used to construct isolation dams. Dam leakage and failure, insufficient sump storage volume, insufficient pump capacity, poor maintenance of sediment control measures, and inadequate planning can all limit the effectiveness of this method to control sediment loading (TERA, 1996). The flumed crossing of Big Darby Creek took longer than the open-cut crossing (22.7 h of instream work over 6 days vs. 16.8 h over 3 days) and resulted in only slightly lower mean downstream TSS concentrations (523 vs. 771.6 mg l^{-1}). The use of concrete jersey barriers with sandbags and plastic sheeting has been effective in minimizing sediment release during flumed crossings of watercourses much smaller

Table 1. Pre- and post-construction fish population size estimates and species number at sampled riffles. Upstream riffle: 600 m upstream of crossing; downstream riffle: 500 m downstream of crossing

Riffle	Date	Species number	Pop. estimate	95% CI	Tippecanoe darter	Bluebreast darter	Spotted darter
Upstream	15-Sep 98[1]	17	187	22	2	9	0
Downstream	16-Sep 98[1]	18	349	49	24	46	1
Upstream	5-Oct 98[2]	16	507	33	42	38	0
Downstream	7-Oct 98[2]	23	980	132	133	101	0
Upstream	24-Sep 99[2]	15	671	49	14	36	0
Downstream	23-Sep 99[2]	22	518	62	6	31	2

[1] Pre-construction.
[2] Post-construction.

(discharge <0.3 m^3 s^{-1}) than Big Darby Creek (Reid and Metikosh, 2001). However, downstream of the flumed crossing of Big Darby Creek, high TSS concentrations resulted from the poor seal between concrete jersey barriers used to isolate the work area and the unconsolidated creek bed material underneath. The use of these materials during crossings of watercourses with similar flows and readily erodible bed material is therefore not recommended.

Increased sediment deposition resulted in short-term (<1 year) changes to riffle habitat immediately downstream of instream construction. Increases in embeddedness and the amount of silts and clay coincided with shifts in benthic invertebrate density and community structure observed over the fall of 1998. Observed increases in oligochaete (aquatic worms) densities and decreases in the numbers of mayflies, stoneflies and caddisflies (EPT taxa) have been reported in other studies of pipeline water crossing construction effects on benthic invertebrates (Tsui and McCart, 1981; Anderson et al., 1998). The clay and silt deposits at the first downstream riffle likely created habitat conditions more suitable for burrowing forms such as oligochaetes than other benthic taxa that prefer clean coarse bed material as habitat. The short time frame for recovery (1 year) is consistent with previous studies of the effects of sediment released during open-cut pipeline water crossing construction on downstream benthic invertebrate communities (Reid and Anderson, 1999).

Despite the extended period of elevated sediment loading during instream construction and the expected sensitivity of resident fish, more fish were collected from riffles during post-construction electro-fishing than prior to construction. While substantial sediment deposition and habitat alteration occurred immediately downstream of instream work, habitat conditions at the riffle 500 m downstream were unaffected. Secondly, mean and peak TSS concentrations measured during instream construction at this riffle (mean concentrations <70 mg l^{-1} and peak concentration <150 mg l^{-1}) were well within the natural range of TSS concentrations for Big Darby Creek (USGS 1992–1997: 1–844 mg l^{-1}). Large reductions in the occurrence of darters likely requires a greater degree of habitat alteration (i.e., smothering of riffles by sediment) and/or a more prolonged exposure to turbid water than that reported downstream of these water crossings (Branson and Batch, 1972; Trautman, 1981). Although not captured by electro-fishing, darter and cyprinid species were observed using the first downstream riffle at Big Darby Creek during the fall of 1998. Electrofishing of the same riffle the following September indicated that it was being used by seven different riffle species including the bluebreast, Tippecanoe, and spotted darters.

Post-construction increases in darter abundance at both upstream and downstream riffles may be related to fall downstream migrations. Trautman (1981) reported that between its confluences with the Scioto River and Little Darby Creek, large downstream migrations of bluebreast darters occur along Big Darby Creek during September. The study reach is within this area and therefore, the large post-construction increase of bluebreast darters may be due to this behaviour. The observed increase in bluebreast darter abundance at the downstream riffle suggests that instream pipeline construction did not obstruct this migratory behaviour. Changes in the relative abundance of dominant riffle species at the upstream riffle (± 7–20%) suggest that such changes at the riffle 500 m downstream of the crossing reflect natural levels of variation and are not related to instream construction. Post-construction changes to the fish assemblages in run habitats were restricted to shifts in the relative abundance of a few species. Some of the observed species shifts (e.g., golden redhorse) may also be related to fall migrations to lower reaches of the Big Darby Creek drainage (Trautman, 1981).

In summary, although pipeline replacements resulted in increased downstream TSS concentrations and sediment deposition, adverse effects were limited to short-term (<1 yr) changes to riffle habitats and benthic invertebrates within 50 m downstream.

ACKNOWLEDGEMENTS

We would like to acknowledge the support and funding of this project by the Gas Research Institute (Chicago) and Columbia Gas Transmission Corporation. Fish species identification assistance by Mark Hughes and David Etnier (University of Tennessee, Knoxville) was invaluable. Valuable comments on earlier versions of the manuscript provided by Don Gartman, Dean Mutrie, and members of the GRI Technical Advisory Group greatly improved the content of this review.

REFERENCES

Anderson, P.G., C.G.J. Fraikin, and T.J. Chandler. 1998. Natural gas pipeline crossing of a coldwater stream: Impacts and Recovery. In: Proceedings of the International Pipeline Conference. Vol. 2. American Society of Mechanical Engineers. June 7–11, 1998. Calgary, AB. pp. 1013–102.

Baddaloo, E.G. 1978. An assessment of effects of pipeline activity in streams in the Durham and Northumberland counties of Ontario. Journal of the Canadian Society of Petroleum Geologists, 4: 1–8.

Berkman, H.E. and C.F. Rabeni. 1987. Effect of siltation on stream fish communities. Environmental Biology of Fishes, 18: 285–294.

Branson, B.A. and D.L. Batch. 1972. Effects of strip mining on small-stream fishes in East-Central Kentucky. Proceedings of the Biological Society of Washington, 84: 507–518.

Clarke, K.D. and D.A. Scruton. 1997. Use of the Wesche method to evaluate fine-sediment dynamics in small boreal forest headwater streams. North American Journal of Fisheries Management, 17: 188–193.

Hambrook, J.A., G.F. Koltun, B.B. Palcsak, and J.S. Tertuliani. 1997. Hydrologic disturbance and response of aquatic biota in Big Darby Creek Basin, OH, US. Geological Survey. Water-Resources Investigations Report 96-4315.

Kondolf, G.M. 1997. Application of the pebble count: Notes on purpose, method, and variants. Journal of the American Water Resources Association, 33: 79–87.

Paller, M.H. 1997. Recovery of a reservoir fish community from drawdown related impacts. North American Journal of Fisheries Management, 17: 726–733.

Reid, S.M. and P.G. Anderson. 1999. Effects of sediment released during open-cut pipeline water crossings. Canadian Water Resources Journal, 24: 235–252.

Reid, S.M. and S. Metikosh. 2001. Effects of pipeline water crossing construction on the Otter Creek Fish Community. Gas Research Institute, Chicago, IL. NTIS. GRI-01/35.

TERA Environmental Consultants (Alta.) Ltd (TERA). 1996. Water crossing case history review. Prepared for Westcoast Energy.

Trautman, M. 1981. Fishes of Ohio. The Ohio State University Press.

Tsui, P.T.P. and P.J. McCart. 1981. Effects of streamcrossing by a pipeline on the benthic macroinvertebrate communities of a small mountain stream. Hydrobiologia, 79: 271–276.

Zar, J.H. 1984. Biostatistical Analysis, 2nd ed. London: Prentice Hall.

Zippen, C. 1958. The removal method of population estimation. Journal of Wildlife Management, 22: 82–90.

BIOGRAPHICAL SKETCHES

Scott Reid

Golder Associates Ltd. 2180 Meadowvale Boulevard, Mississauga, ON, Canada, L5N 5S3

For the past 5 years, Scott Reid has been a fisheries biologist with Golder Associates Ltd. He has a BSc in Ecology from the University of Calgary and a MSc in Watershed Ecosystems from Trent University. Mr. Reid has been involved in numerous projects investigating the effects of sediment on fish and fish habitat in stream and river systems and developing related assessment and planning tools.

Scott Stoklosar

Golder Associates Ltd., 10th floor, 940 6th Avenue S.W., Calgary, AB, Canada, T2P 3T1

Mr. Stoklosar has worked as a fisheries biologist with Golder Associates Ltd. in Calgary for the past five years. He has a diploma in Fish and Wildlife Technology (Fleming College), and a BSc and MSc in Biology and Watershed Ecosystems (Trent University), respectively. His work primarily consists of aquatic impact assessments of oil sand, pipeline, road, and energy projects in western Canada. He is particularly interested in stream ecology and aquatic habitat restoration.

Serge Metikosh

Golder Associates Ltd., 10th floor, 940 6th Avenue S.W., Calgary, AB, Canada, T2P 3T1

Mr. Metikosh joined Golder Associates in September 1997 after 25 years as a biologist with various federal government departments, most recently as the Senior Habitat Biologist with the Department of Fisheries and Oceans in Burlington, Ontario. Main professional interests include affects of sediment and fish and fish habitat, effects of pipelines on fish and fish habitat, fish habitat assessment, protection and restoration.

James M. Evans

Consultant, Environment and Safety, 615 West Maude Avenue, Arlington Heights, IL 60004, USA

Mr. Evans is a Chemical Engineer with 25 years experience in the management of environmental and safety related research. This work at Gas Research Intitute has ranged from research to eliminate groundwater contamination from Underground Coal Gasification operations, to studies on the toxicity of saline waters to fresh water and to marine organisms, to fate and transport of mercury from mercury contaminated soil. During the past 6 years he has managed rights-of-way environmental research studies on wetland revegetation, the effects of pipelines on habitat fragmentation and biodiversity, the effects of horizontal directional drilling mud on wetlands and the effect of sediment from pipeline river crossings on fish and biota, which led to the development of the CROSSING Software.

Natural Resources that May Be Affected if Your Horizontal Directional Drill Fails: Open Cut Analysis of A Coastal Maine River

Paul D. Martin and Mike Tyrrell

The Joint Pipeline Project (a 100-mile natural gas pipeline) located in Maine, New Hampshire, and Massachusetts has recently been constructed. The route includes a crossing of the Piscataqua River, which forms a portion of the border between Maine and New Hampshire. Installation of the pipeline occurred by horizontal directional drill (HDD) under the river. During permitting of the project, the contingency plan identified open cut construction (dredge and blasting) if the drill failed. The need for mitigation of potential open cut impacts arose during discussions with regulators. The very high velocity reversing tidal flows were of special concern. To develop appropriate mitigation, an analysis was undertaken to determine the probable nature and extent of impacts to biotic resources should an open cut occur. Potential impacts to eelgrass, finfish, lobsters, and shellfish were quantified using hydrodynamic and sediment transport modeling in conjunction with biological survey data. Numbers of target organisms and area of eelgrass beds that might be affected by an open cut were determined. Between 0.8 and 1.3 acres of eelgrass loss was predicted. A loss of 27,500 lobsters and 800,000 shellfish (3 species) was predicted from direct impacts. Impacts to finfish were limited to indirect effects on larvae, which could not be quantified. Pipeline installation was successfully completed with the HDD with no adverse impacts to Piscataqua River habitats.

Keywords: Sedimentation, estuarine, fisheries, pipeline, construction, HDD, open cut

INTRODUCTION

The Joint Pipeline Project was developed and constructed as a teaming arrangement between El Paso Energy and Maritimes and Northeast Pipeline Company. During US Army Corps of Engineers permitting, a contingency plan was requested in the event that the horizontal directional drill (HDD) of the Piscataqua River failed and the crossing needed to be completed by open cut (a trench dug/dredged across the river bottom). In agency discussions about the contingency plan, the need for mitigation for impacts to habitats in the Piscataqua River/Great Bay estuarine system arose. To develop appropriate mitigation, the nature and extent of potential impacts that could be realistically anticipated from an open cut were investigated. Of particular concern were impacts to eelgrass beds, fisheries, lobsters, and shellfish (oysters, clams, and mussels).

Impacts were classified as near-field (within 100 m of the crossing location) and far-field beyond 100 m. Near-field impacts could include direct excavation and sidecasting of spoil. Far-field impacts could occur from bedload transport, suspended solids re-deposition and elevated TSS levels.

Given the magnitude of the effort and the importance of the resources involved, the study had a number of objectives:
- assess river bottom and sediment characteristics in the pipeline crossing vicinity;
- assess sediment transport and deposition that could result from open trench construction;
- characterize existing eelgrass, lobster, shellfish, and finfish resources in the pipeline crossing vicinity;

Environmental Concerns in Rights-of-Way Management: Seventh International Symposium
J.W. Goodrich-Mahoney, D.F. Mutrie and C.A. Guild (editors)
© 2002 Elsevier Science Ltd. All rights reserved.

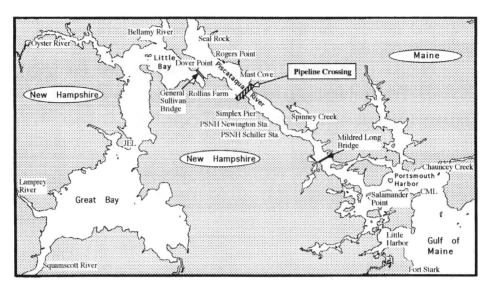

Fig. 1. Great Bay Estuary and project location map.

- determine the nature and extent of potential impacts to eelgrass, lobster, shellfish, and finfish; and
- provide a basis for discussions on potential mitigation measures.

SITE DESCRIPTION

The Piscataqua River is part of the 4400 ha Great Bay estuary (Fig. 1), a component of the National Estuary Reserve program. Seven tributary rivers provide freshwater input, contributing 1140 cfs to the estuary. The estuary is characterized as having extensive shallow mudflats with narrow and deeper channels cut into the sediment by river inflow.

At the pipeline crossing location the River is 730 m wide, 13 m deep at mean high water (MHW), and has an average tidal range of 1.5 m. There is a 270 m wide navigation channel maintained from the mouth of the river to about 1000 m upstream of the pipeline crossing location. The northern (Maine) shoreline is relatively straight and the river bottom slopes relatively steeply into the navigation channel. The southern shoreline (New Hampshire) has a shallow embayment with a 180-m wide mud flat before the top of the navigation channel is encountered.

River sediments consist primarily of sand and coarse material within channels and mudflats in shallow areas. Bedrock outcrops also occur in the area, and sub-bottom sonar showed that outcrop occurs in several locations along the pipeline centerline. The geology of the area is dominated by past glacial activity, including the presence of moraine and drumlin deposits, glacio-marine deposits such as the Presumpscot clay, old beach elevations, and buried river channels.

Hydrodynamics and water quality

River flow varies seasonally, the greatest volumes occurring as a result of spring runoff. However, the tidal exchange component in the river is large and storms throughout the year may also create runoff and sediment load peaks. Average maximum current speeds are 1.5–2.3 m s^{-1} and spring tide currents can be as great as 2.5–3 m s^{-1}. The strongest currents are confined to a central "core" in the river, with near shore areas having lower current speeds and even weak counter-currents. The observed flushing time for water entering the head of the Great Bay Estuary is 36 tidal cycles (18 days) during high river flow.

Tides cause considerable fluctuations of water clarity, temperature, salinity, and current speed with suspended loads highest in the upper estuary, and seasonally highest in the spring. Turbidity values are higher on the ebb than the flood tide. Freshwater contribution to Great Bay from seven rivers can be substantial, particularly in the spring and after storm events. Salinity typically drops to levels approaching 10 ppt in the spring (vs. 30 ppt just off the coast) but may drop to 1 ppt after spring storms. In summer the temperature is about 10°C warmer than the Gulf of Maine while both coastal and estuarine waters approach 0°C in the winter.

Estuarine flora and fauna

The Great Bay Estuary is a typical New England well-mixed estuary with extensive intertidal mud flats, eelgrass beds, rocky zones, and deep, narrow channels. American lobsters are common in the Great Bay Estuary. The Great Bay Estuary is ideal habitat for a number of molluscan shellfish species. The primary species of ecological and economic importance are the softshell clam (*Mya arenaria*), the Eastern oyster (*Crassostrea virginica*), the razor clam (*Ensis directus*), the blue mussel

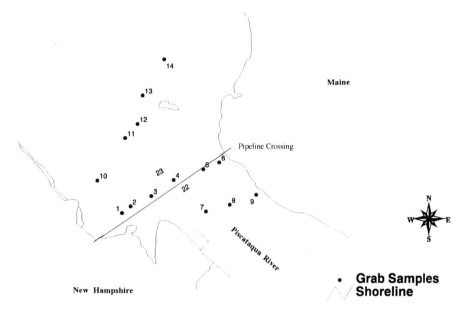

Fig. 2. Sediment sampling locations.

(*Mytilis edulis*), the sea scallop (*Placopecten magellanicus*), and the Belon oyster (*Ostrea edulis*).

Juveniles and adults of twenty-eight species of resident and migratory fish have been collected in the Piscataqua River in the vicinity of the open cut (NAI, 1974; Nelson, 1981, 1982). Resident as well as anadromous fishes utilize the estuary either as spawning grounds or as a nursery. Dominant resident species include silversides, killifish, winter flounder, tomcod, sticklebacks, and grubby. Anadromous fish include smelt, blueback herring, alewives, striped bass, Atlantic herring, and menhaden.

Eelgrass, *Zostera marina* L., is a submerged marine flowering plant that forms underwater beds or meadows in coastal and estuarine waters, contributing to the health and productivity of these areas. Eelgrass habitats cover 10 km^2 within the estuary, but varies from year to year as eelgrass is a dynamic habitat. Eelgrass communities are valuable sediment traps (Thayer et al., 1975) and filter estuarine waters, removing both suspended sediments and dissolved nutrients (Jackson, 1944; Short and Short, 1984).

STUDY METHODS

A number of tasks were completed to assess potential open cut impacts to Piscataqua River resources, including sediment and subbottom characterization, hydrodynamic modeling, sediment transport and deposition analysis, an eelgrass survey, and impact assessments of eelgrass, finfish, lobster, and shellfish. This work was performed under subcontract by researchers at the University of New Hampshire, all of who have had extensive experience working in the Great Bay estuary.

Sediment and subbottom characterization

Sampling occurred at 6 stations along and 8 stations adjacent to the pipeline crossing (Fig. 2). Because of shallow water along the New Hampshire shoreline, the first station was 160 m from shore while the first Maine station was 35 m from shore. A Shipek bottom grab sampler was used to obtain surficial samples (~10–15 cm of the bottom) at each station. After viewing the contents of the grab sampler, a gravity corer was used at three of the 14 stations in an attempt to obtain deeper samples. Gravity cores can obtain relatively undisturbed bottom sediment samples in soft sediments up to several meters. Coarse or compacted sediments prohibit gravity core penetration. Grab samples were taken at 13 of 14 stations, with the bottom at station 11 too rocky to retrieve a sample. Coarse sediments allowed collection of gravity cores only at stations 1 (50 cm penetration) and 2 (10 cm penetration) along the open cut and station 14 upstream (1.1 m penetration). The cores were photographed, examined and described, and subsampled for grain size and carbon content by loss-on-ignition (LOI).

A sub-bottom profile survey was performed along the centerline of the pipeline (in water over 3 m deep) crossing using CHIRP sonar. This sonar is able to determine sediment horizons potentially to depths of 30 m below the river bottom. Of particular interest was depth of sediment and depth to bedrock to aid in the calculation of the amount of sediment involved in trenching operations. Survey transects were run parallel to the pipeline centerline as well as perpendicular, in order to get coverage of the entire study.

Hydrodynamic modeling

Great Bay Estuary was modeled with the BOSS International Surfacewater Modeling Systems (SMS) program. SMS is a pre- and post-processor for two-dimensional finite element and finite difference models

Fig. 3. Hydrodynamic model grid and bathymetry.

of contaminant migration and sediment transport. The finite element mesh and associated boundary conditions were created with mean high water level defined as the shoreline boundary and depths were digitized from NOAA nautical charts. The final Great Bay Estuary mesh consisted of a total of 41,105 nodes and 19,613 quadratic triangular elements. The mesh in the immediate area of the pipeline crossing is shown in Fig. 3. Flow conditions were established for two tidal cycles (24 h) for mean (2.65 m), neap (2.4 m), and spring (3.05 m) tidal heights. Hydrodynamic analysis linked the SMS mesh with RMA2, a hydrodynamic modeling code, that supports flow analysis including wetting and drying models. Given the complexity of the model, each run took 24 h computing time and the complex estuary geometry required repeated corrections of the mesh due to insufficient elements.

Sediment transport and deposition analysis

Sediment characteristics were determined using the project's sediment sampling and subbottom survey, and additional core data from prior geotechnical investigations at five locations along the horizontal directional drill path. Using the seismic reflection profiles, sediment sampling and geotechnical cores, the stratigraphic cross section thickness and textural characteristics of the sedimentary layer was developed. Volumes of sediment material to be dredged were calculated. Dredge sediment volume and characteristics were linked with the results of the hydrodynamic model to analyze sediment transport and deposition. Based on river flow and sediment characteristics an estimate was made of the extent, nature and location of sediment deposition and total suspended solid (TSS) concentrations.

Eelgrass survey

Intertidal and shallow subtidal areas were surveyed from a shallow draft boat and by walking the shoreline at low tide. Subtidal areas deeper than −1 m MLW were surveyed by SCUBA divers. The dive surveys were conducted by anchoring a 180 m long transect line on the bottom, with markers every 7.5 m, parallel to the shoreline. Transect lines were placed 6 m apart along the depth gradient at the site. Surveys were conducted by two divers swimming parallel to the transect lines, each about 1.5 m from the transect line and surveying a 3 m wide strip. The extent and health of eelgrass and other vegetation within the interval was noted along with the occurrence of crustaceans or bivalves.

Eelgrass impact assessment

Eelgrass impacts were determined using a quantitative model that relates total suspended solid (TSS) concentrations to the density and health of eelgrass. The model calculates light extinction from TSS (based on Dennison et al., 1993), % light reaching eelgrass plants from light extinction coefficients (Short, 1980), and eelgrass growth and/or density from the % light available (Short et al., 1995). The relation between TSS and light extinction coefficient is based on a linear regression of simultaneous measurements of TSS and change in the light extinction coefficient (Kd) where:

$$\text{change in } Kd = 0.0491 \times \text{TSS}.$$

Table 1. Sediment grain size analysis results

Sample type	Station	Depth (cm)	Classification (based on G/S/M)[a]	% G/S/M	% (G+S)/S/C[b]	% LOI
Core	1	8–10	Sandy Mud	1/33/66	34/53/13	3
		24–26	Sandy Mud	2/19/79	21/38/41	21
		31–33	Muddy Sand	0/57/43	57/34/9	2
		40–42	Muddy Sand	0/54/46	54/40/6	3
		50–52	Muddy Sand	0/50/50	50/32/18	2
	2	4–6	Sandy Gravel	44/54/2	98/1/1	1
	14	0–2	Muddy Sand	1/66/33	67/21/12	3
		24–26	Sandy Mud	0/44/56	44/44/12	4
		49–51	Sandy Mud	0/19/81	19/57/24	4
		74–76	Sandy Mud	0/23/77	23/54/23	5
		99–101	Sandy Mud	0/47/53	47/52/1	5
Grab	1	Surface	Sandy Mud	4/82/14	86/9/5	2
	2	Surface	Sandy Mud	0/89/11	89/6/5	3
	3	Surface	Sand	0/96/4	96/3/1	2
	4	Surface	Gravel	100/0/0	100/0/0	–
	5	Surface	Gravely Sand	9/91/0	100/0/0	1
	6	Surface	Gravely Sand	11/89/0	100/0/0	–
	7	Surface	Gravely Sand	22/75/3	97/2/1	1
	8	Surface	Sandy Gravel	33/66/1	99/0.5/0.5	1
	9	Surface	Gravely Sand	22/76/2	98/1/1	1
	10	Surface	Gravely Sand	21/76/3	97/2/1	1
	11	Surface	No Sample	–	–	–
	12	Surface	Gravel	90/10/0	100/0/0	–
	13	Surface	Gravely Sand	29/69/2	98/1/1	1
	14	Surface	Muddy Sand	1/87/12	88/7/5	1

[a] G = Gravel, S = Sand, M = Mud.
[b] G + S = Gravel + Sand, S = Silt, C = Clay.

The reduction of light reaching the plants (% L) is determined from the calculated change in Kd, according to the light extinction equation, where:

$$\%L = \exp(-Kd \times depth).$$

These equations together evaluate the effects of increased water turbidity, or increased TSS, on eelgrass growth and density to ±10% accuracy. Studies have shown that a reduction in light reaching the plants, caused by increased turbidity, will result in a reduction in eelgrass shoot density and a decreased growth rate, leading to a loss in eelgrass bed health status and areal coverage (Dennison et al., 1993; Short et al., 1995).

Sediment deposition effects on areal cover of eelgrass beds were determined by comparing sediment transport model output to maps of eelgrass distribution in the Piscataqua River. Direct dredging and spoil smothering of eelgrass beds was assessed within the pipeline corridor (100 m either side of the proposed center line). Any dredged eelgrass would be destroyed, leading to loss of eelgrass habitat. Any eelgrass within 100 m upstream or downstream of the trench area would also likely be buried by dredge spoil, resulting in eelgrass habitat loss.

Finfish, lobster, and shellfish impact assessment

Assessment of potential impacts to lobsters, molluscan shellfish, and finfish species was based on: (1) previous studies in the Great Bay Estuary; (2) similar studies of the target species conducted in other temperate estuarine locations; (3) documentation of effects derived from the scientific literature; an (4) investigations conducted for this project. Since potential effects differ for each specie or group of species, the assessments are presented in the results as such.

RESULTS

Sediment and subbottom characterization

Results of the grain size and LOI analyses are shown in Table 1. Typical of glaciated and estuarine environments in northern New England, the samples are extremely poorly sorted with grain sizes ranging from mud to gravel. Along the proposed trench, except for station 1, the surficial sediments are relatively coarse grained, being composed of muddy sand or gravel. With station 1 located on a broad shallow flat, the sediments consist of sandy mud or mud to a depth of about 30-cm, then a muddy sand down to 50 cm. There was a peat deposit from 20 to 30 cm, most likely an old transgressive marsh deposit. All other grab samples were sand, gravel or some combination of the two, the exception of station 14. At station 14, in the upstream cove in Maine, sediments were composed of muddy sand to sandy mud in the 100 cm core.

The Loss On Ignition (LOI) contents were generally low, being less than 3% for all the surface grab samples. Typically, coarser grained estuarine sediments have low organic contents. The station 1 core had a higher LOI content (21%) in the peat deposit located in the depth interval at 20–30 cm below the surface. The

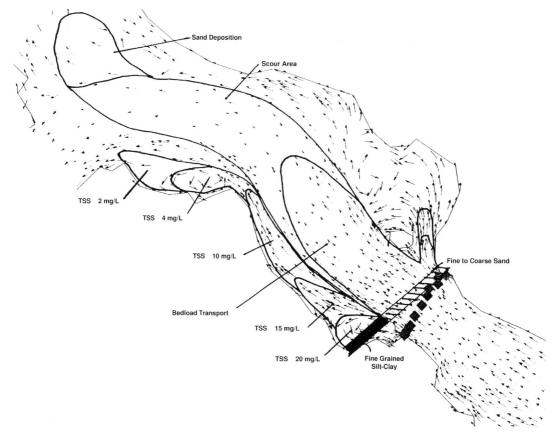

Fig. 4. Suspended sediments and bedload transport — incoming tide.

station 14 core sample had slightly higher LOI values (5%) than the other samples.

Hydrodynamic modeling

Although several tidal ranges and tidal stages were run with the hydrodynamic model, the two conditions with maximum velocities are the mid-outgoing (ebb) tide on high tidal range and mid-incoming (flood) tide on high tidal range. Eddy currents form in coves both upstream and downstream on the New Hampshire shore depending on tidal direction. A large eddy forms in the upriver cove on the Maine shore on incoming tides while downriver flow is linear given the straighter shoreline. The center of the channel has strong linear currents in both tidal directions. Maximum current velocities at the crossing location are slightly in excess of 1 m s^{-1} on the incoming tide. Current vector arrows are shown on Figs. 4 and 5.

Sediment transport and deposition analysis

Examination of stratigraphy and sediment data indicates that the New Hampshire sediments are thin (typically less than ~16 feet and less than ~12 feet at a number of locations), and contain some fine grained sediments (estimated to be less than 3 feet thick) underlain by sand and gravel deposits. Bedrock is encountered several times at a depth of less than 13 feet (proposed open cut depth). From the Maine shoreline across the navigation channel the sediment layer thickens and appears to be composed of fine to coarse sand with gravel with depth to bedrock exceeding 13 feet. Dredge spoil volume in cubic yards was estimated at 31,775 for sand, 208 for gravel, 450 for mud, and 4283 for bedrock.

The settling velocities of medium to coarse sand size particles are relatively fast (~2.5 to ~15 cm s^{-1} at 10°C) resulting in bedload transport that will only affect turbidity of nearbottom water. Very fine to fine sands have lower settling velocities (~0.25 to ~2.5 cm s^{-1} at 10°C) and will result in far-field sediment deposition. The mud fraction has very low settling velocities (fine silt/clay of ~0.004 mm diameter settles at 0.0014 cm s^{-1}) and will result in a turbidity plume that gradually disperses far from the pipeline crossing. Areas of elevated TSS concentrations as well as areas of bedload and suspended sediment transport are shown for flood tide conditions in Fig. 4 and ebb tide in Fig. 5.

Eelgrass survey and impact assessment

Healthy eelgrass at an average density of 200 shoots per square meter was found in patches and as scattered individual shoots on the Maine side of the river, corresponding to the 0.34 acre area ME-3 on Fig. 6. No eelgrass was found in New Hampshire, however a several hectare mussel bed was observed at a −4 to −5.0 m depth range along with occupied lobster burrows. Based on prior investigations, other known eelgrass habitats were incorporated into the study and are shown on Fig. 6.

Open cut analysis of a coastal Maine River 731

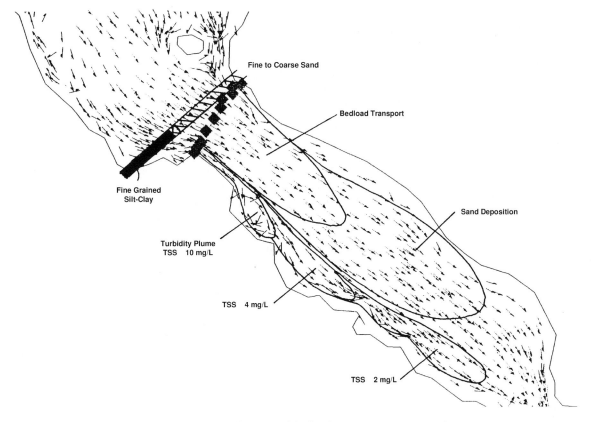

Fig. 5. Suspended sediments and bedload transport — outgoing tide.

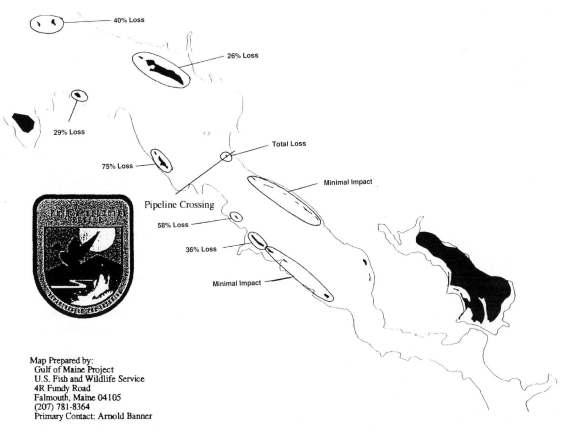

Fig. 6. Eelgrass impact assessment.

Effects of dredging on eelgrass

Direct disturbance from open cut activities includes excavation and burial with dredged sediments while indirect disturbances include interference with photosynthesis due to high suspended sediment loads and burial by sediment re-deposition. If open cut, pipeline construction would destroy the 0.34 acres of the ME-3 habitat by dredging and dredge spoil burial. Indirect and far-field impacts from sediment transport and deposition would impact a number of the eelgrass area in the vicinity of the crossing. Estimates of the loss of these other eelgrass habitats is provided on Fig. 6 and can be related to the TSS levels presented in Figs. 4 and 5. In total, from direct and the more severe indirect impacts it was estimated that 1.3 acres of eelgrass habitat would be lost if an open cut crossing were completed.

Finfish, lobster, and shellfish impact assessment

The following assessment was performed using both existing available information and relied heavily on the expertise of the UNH investigators who have been working on the Great Bay Estuary for years and information collected for this study. Table 2 presents the estimated impacts by faunal group. Estimates were derived by comparison of known densities or extrapolated densities of organisms to the habitat area to be affected by the project. In certain instances, no suitable habitat and therefore no members of that species exist within the area to be influenced by open cut construction.

Table 2. Faunal impact assessment

Species (group)	Lifestage	Direct impacts	Indirect impacts	Total
Lobster	Juvenile and adult	8610	2500	11,110
	Larval	0	0	0
Softshell clam	Adult	98,780	0	98,780
	Larval	0	0	0
Eastern Oyster	Adult	0	0	0
	Larval	0	0	0
Belon Oyster	Adult	0	0	0
	Larval	0	0	0
Razor Clam	Adult	185,000	0	185,000
	Larval	0	0	0
Blue Mussel	Adult	6300	0	6300
	Larval	0	0	0
Sea Scallop	Adult	0	0	0
	Larval	0	0	0
Finfish	Juvenile and adult	0	0	0
	Larvae	ND[a]	ND	ND
	Anadromous species	0	0	0

[a] ND indicates no data is available on which to make a determination either because the likelihood of occurrence is unknown or because the nature of impacts has not been adequately studied in the scientific literature.

CONCLUSIONS

Shortly following completion of the open cut contingency study, construction of the Piscataqua River crossing commenced with HDD technology and after nearly three months the 30 inch pipeline was successfully installed across the river. A small release of drilling mud occurred and was contained at the New Hampshire shoreline, and during one of the reaming passes the drill became temporarily stuck. No impacts to the estuarine resources of the Great Bay estuary occurred.

Results of the study suggest that in the immediate area of the open cut, localized impacts to eelgrass habitats, lobsters, and molluscan species would occur. Impacts to finfish were anticipated to be negligible, primarily as a result of their mobility. Further afield, impacts from suspended sediments and bedload transport would be directly related to hydrodynamic conditions. Greater increases in TSS would be limited to shoreline areas resulting from the development of tidal eddy currents. Bedload transport was strongest in mid-channel and resulted in the dispersal of coarser sediments into shoaling areas were flow velocity decreased.

This project reveals the potential benefits of HDD crossing of sensitive waterbodies if the geology of the crossing location supports success since essentially no impacts occur to aquatic resources. Conversely, the study also revealed that open cut crossings have the potential for predominantly localized impacts, even in reversing tidal flow situations, and that at population levels these impacts are negligible. Impacts to eelgrass habitat would most likely have required mitigation under wetland protection provisions of the Clean Water Act.

REFERENCES

Dennison, W.C., R.J. Orth, K.A. Moore, J.C. Stevenson, V. Carter, S. Kollar, P.W. Bergstrom, and R.A. Batuik. 1993. Assessing water quality with submersed aquatic vegetation. Bioscience, 43: 86–94.

Hart, R.C. 1988. Zooplankton feeding rates in relation to suspended sediment content: Potential influences on community structure in a turbid reservoir. Freshwater Biology, 19: 123–149.

Jackson, C.F. 1944. A biological Survey of Great Bay, New Hampshire: No. 1 Physical and Biological Features of Great Bay and the Present Status of its Marine Resources. Marine Fisheries Communication Durham NH. 61 pp.

Jury, S.H., W.H. Howell, and W.H. Watson. 1995. Lobster movements in response to a hurricane. Marine Ecological Progress Series, 119: 305–310.

NAI 1974. Newington Generating Station 316 Demonstration. Report No. 4, Monitoring Studies. Normandeau Associates, Inc. Bedford NH.

Nelson, J.I. 1981. Inventory of the Natural Resources of the Great Bay Estuarine System. NH Fish and Game Department.

Nelson, J.I. 1982. Great Bay Estuary Monitoring Survey, 1981–1982. NH Fish and Game Department.

Short, F.T. 1980. A simulation model of the seagrass production system. In: Handbook of Seagrass Biology: An Ecosystem Perspective. R.C. Phillips and C.P. McRoy, eds. Garland STPM Press NY. pp. 275–295.

Short, F.T. and C.A. Short. 1984. The seagrass filter: purification of estuarine and coastal waters. In: The Estuary as a Filter. V.S. Kennedy, ed. Academic Press, pp. 395–413.

Short, F.T., D.M. Burdick, and J.E. Kaldy. 1995. Mesocosm experiments quantify the effects of eutrophication on eelgrass *Zostera marina* L. Limnology and Oceanography, 40: 740–749.

Thayer, G.W., Wolff, D.A, and R.B. Williams. 1975. The impact of man on seagrass. American Scientist, 63: 288–296.

Wahle, R.A. 1993. Recruitment to American lobster populations along an estuarine gradient. Estuaries, 16(4): 731–738.

BIOGRAPHICAL SKETCHES

Paul D. Martin

TRC Environmental Corporation, Boott Mills South, Foot of John Street, Lowell, MA 01852, USA, 978-656-3631 (phone), 978-453-1995 (fax), e-mail: pmartin@trcsolutions.com

Paul Martin has a BA in Biology from Carleton College and an MS in Zoology from the University of New Hampshire. Mr. Martin has provided natural resource investigations, permitting and construction support on numerous natural gas pipeline projects. Mr. Martin's expertise encompasses wetlands and aquatic resources, focusing on minimizing adverse impacts associated with pipeline construction while expediting permit acquisition.

Mike Tyrrell

TRC Environmental Corporation, Boott Mills South, Foot of John Street, Lowell, MA 01852, USA

Michael Tyrrell has a BA in Natural Resources Science from the University of Rhode Island and is a certified wetland scientist. Mr. Tyrrell has provided project management and natural resource assessments for numerous natural gas pipeline projects in the northeastern United States. Mr. Tyrrell specializes in wildlife and wetland habitat assessments, pipeline permitting, and construction mitigation.

Evaluation of Isolated Water Course Crossings during Winter Construction along the Alliance Pipeline in Northern Alberta

Scott Reid and Paul G. Anderson

Isolated (dry) crossing techniques (i.e., dam and pump, or flumed) are required by many government agencies to minimize the effects of instream construction during pipeline water crossing installation. Although there is considerable anecdotal information regarding the effectiveness of these techniques, limited empirical data has been collected to document their effectiveness to minimize the release of sediment into watercourses. The construction of the Alliance Pipeline from northwest Alberta to the Canada/USA border near Elmore, Saskatchewan required the crossing of 505 watercourses, of which more than 70 were classified as sensitive to instream construction. Pipeline construction during the winter of 1999/2000 required the crossing of 18 sensitive watercourses supporting coldwater fish species (Arctic grayling, bull trout, and mountain whitefish). These crossings were constructed using isolated crossing methods. A series of monitoring studies were undertaken to evaluate the effectiveness of the applied crossing techniques, to limit sediment release into the watercourse and subsequent changes to habitat conditions during, and after instream construction. Results indicate that dam and pump and superflume methods can be very effective at limiting sediment release during the crossing of small to medium sized watercourses and thereby protect downstream fish habitats.

Keywords: Sediment, fish habitat, Horizontal Directional Drill, dam and pump, superflume

INTRODUCTION

Construction of the Alliance Pipeline mainline system over the past two years required crossing a number of sensitive watercourses between Whitecourt and Grand Prairie, Alberta. Due to the large areas of muskeg encountered in this area of Alberta, pipeline construction had to occur during winter (i.e., frozen) conditions. Winter construction conflicts with the preferred instream timing window for sensitive watercourses as they support fall spawning fish species such as bull trout (*Salvelinus confluentus*) and mountain whitefish (*Prosopium williamsoni*). Isolated (dry) crossing techniques (dam and pump and "superflume") were applied to limit the release of sediment during instream construction.

Environmental Concerns in Rights-of-Way
Management: Seventh International Symposium
J.W. Goodrich-Mahoney, D.F. Mutrie and C.A. Guild (editors)
© 2002 Elsevier Science Ltd. All rights reserved.

In theory, isolated crossing techniques minimize the amount of sediment released into the watercourse by diverting flow around the construction site. Few case studies have evaluated the effectiveness of isolated crossing methods in mitigating the adverse effects of water crossing construction. Given that pipeline construction in northern environments often requires winter construction time schedules and that trenchless crossing methods are not always feasible, practical, or cost effective, documentation of the effectiveness of isolated crossing methods is important to ensure an appropriate level of environmental protection.

A monitoring program was undertaken during the winter of 1999/2000 to evaluate isolated water crossings constructed by Alliance. Components of the program included the monitoring of total suspended sediment (TSS) and dissolved oxygen levels during crossing construction and pre-and post construction assessments of habitat condition. This paper presents the results, key learnings and recommendations from the study.

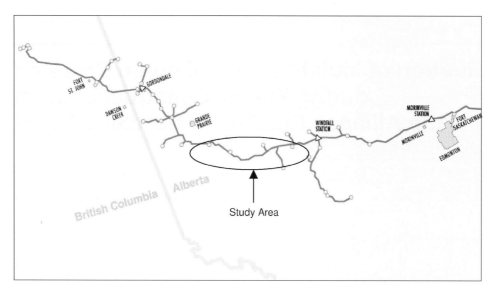

Fig. 1. Study area.

METHODS

Study area

The Canadian portion of the Alliance Pipeline System traverses six ecoregions between Fort St. John, British Columbia and Elmore, Saskatchewan. Numerous sensitive watercourses were crossed between in northwestern Alberta (between Whitecourt and Grand Prairie, Alberta) (Fig. 1). The mainline pipeline through this area traverses the Lower Boreal-Cordilleran and Mid Boreal Mixedwood ecoregions of Alberta. The rolling to deeply incised terrain is covered by mixedwood and coniferous forests as well as muskeg. Forestry and oil and gas production are the dominant industries within the region.

The watercourses crossed lie within the Athabasca River watershed and the Smoky, Little Smoky subwatersheds of the Peace River watershed. Important coldwater species found in these watercourses include Arctic grayling, bull trout, mountain whitefish, northern pike (*Esox lucius*), rainbow trout (*Oncorhynchus mykiss*), and walleye (*Stizostedion vitreum*). In most cases, the Alliance watercourses crossing location was adjacent, or in relatively close proximity, to existing pipeline watercourse crossings.

Alliance was required to undertake a water quality monitoring program at sensitive watercourses that were being crossed outside of the preferred timing windows for in-stream construction. Characteristics of the watercourses monitored are provided in Table 1. These watercourses ranged between 2.0 and 42 m wide (summer wetted width). Only the Simonette and Little Smoky rivers are greater than 16.0 m in width. Habitat conditions in the vicinity of the crossings were generally run and riffle habitats with clean gravel and cobble bed material.

Suspended sediment

At each water crossing, water samples were taken at mid water column through holes augered in the ice cover to document total suspended sediment (TSS) concentrations (mg l^{-1}) during construction (Fig. 2). Water sampling stations were established upstream and downstream of instream construction. Downstream monitoring transects ranged between 40 and 160 m downstream of the ditchline. Site-specific TSS-turbidity relationships were derived from field turbidity measurements and subsamples of water samples (15–48 samples) representing a range of turbidities that were analyzed for TSS concentration. Turbidity measurements taken in the field were then converted to TSS. Correlation indices (r^2 values 0.88–0.98) from the regression analyses indicate that field NTU measurements provide a good proxy for TSS.

Dissolved oxygen

Dissolved oxygen concentration (mg l^{-1}) was also monitored during the construction of the Simonette River, Shell Creek, Deep Valley Creek, Little Smoky River, and Sakwatamau River crossings. Dissolved oxygen concentrations were measured from grab water samples collected three times daily from transects upstream and downstream of the crossings.

Fish habitat

Riffles along eight watercourses were monitored to assess alteration of downstream habitats due to sediment deposition (Table 1). The watercourses selected represent four size-classes of watercourse (≤4.0, 4–10, 10–20, and >20 m). Riffle habitats were monitored as shallow water depths allowed for sampling and secondly, because of their sensitivity to sediment deposition. Habitat condition at riffles upstream and downstream of each crossing was characterized using either: (1) visual assessments of embeddedness (1–100%)

Table 1. Summary of watercourses crossed by the Alliance Pipeline Project (mainline) during winter 2000, crossing methods and monitoring activities

Watercourse	Discharge ($m^3 s^{-1}$)	Wetted width (m)	Crossing method	Monitoring activities
Patterson Creek	No measurable flow	n/a	Dam and pump	Habitat alteration
Latornell River	0.02	3.0	Dam and pump	TSS monitoring
Simonette River	0.29	5.6	Superflume	TSS monitoring Dissolved oxygen Habitat alteration
Unnamed Tributary to Simonette River	No measurable flow	n/a	Dam and pump	Habitat alteration
Shell Creek	0.06	1.5	Dam and pump	TSS monitoring Dissolved oxygen Habitat alteration
Deep Valley Creek	0.47	10.2	Superflume	TSS monitoring Dissolved oxygen Habitat alteration
Waskahigan River	0.1	11.7	Dam and pump	TSS monitoring
Little Smoky River	2.2	20.4	Superflume	TSS monitoring Dissolved oxygen Habitat alteration
Iosegun River	0.02	12	Dam and pump	TSS monitoring
Two Creek	0.04	7.2	Dam and pump	TSS monitoring
Chickadee Creek	0.02	1.3	Dam and pump	TSS monitoring
Unnamed Tributary to Chickadee Creek	0.04	1.4	Dam and pump	TSS monitoring Habitat alteration
Sakwatamau River	0.35	10.5	Dam and pump	TSS monitoring Dissolved oxygen Habitat alteration

Fig. 2. Depth and water velocity measurements at holes augured in the ice downstream of the crossing of Two Creeks.

(Platts et al., 1983) and composition of bed material (i.e., sand, gravel, cobble, boulder) at 10 evenly spaced locations along a transect at each monitoring site; or (2) the pebble count method (Kondolf, 1997). Pre-construction habitat characterizations were done between October 15th and 17th, 1999. Post-construction visits were done shortly after ice-out (April 24th–27th, and May 17th, 2000). At Shell Creek, cross-sectional monitoring transects across pools (400 m upstream and 140 m downstream of the crossing) were surveyed with a survey level and rod, before and after construction.

RESULTS

Summary of water crossing construction

Between January 17th and March 4th, 2000, the 1067 mm OD pipeline was installed underneath eighteen watercourses considered as sensitive in the fisheries assessment. Fourteen crossings were constructed using the dam and pump method. Five of these crossings used steel plates installed into the bed as isolation dams. The other dam and pump crossings used sandbag dams and plastic sheeting. Flow was diverted around the crossings using bypass pumps (7.6–25 cm diameter). Dam and pump crossings required between 1 and 9 days of instream activity. Flows during construction were generally low (0.02–0.35 $m^3 s^{-1}$). Six of the fourteen dam and pump crossings were constructed in the "dry" (i.e., no flows were present at the time of construction).

Fig. 3. Aquadams™ (centre of photo) diverting flow of the Little Smoky River into the 30 m long superflume. Crossing successfully installed by Marine Pipeline Construction.

The Simonette River, Deep Valley Creek and the Little Smoky River pipeline crossings were constructed using the "superflume" method. During crossing construction, flow was carried across the crossing area through a large flume (30 m long with 2.4 m × 1.5 m openings) (Fig. 3). Water structures (Aquadams™) were used to isolate the workspace from the flow. Superflume crossings required between 4 and 10 days of instream activity. Flow levels ranged between 0.29 and 2.2 $m^3 s^{-1}$.

Suspended sediment

Over the course of crossing construction, isolated water crossings resulted in mean downstream TSS concentrations that ranged from 4 to 100 $mg l^{-1}$ above background (Table 2). Increases in mean downstream TSS concentrations were substantially lower than that measured downstream of open-cut crossings of similarly sized watercourses (Table 3). No patterns relating to watercourse size, or flow and increases to downstream TSS level were evident from the monitoring data.

Increases to downstream TSS concentrations were generally limited to the installation and removal of dams and the flume, or bypass pumps (Figs. 4 and 5). Increases to downstream TSS concentrations during the dam and pump, or superflume and aquadam installation were on average less than 76 $mg l^{-1}$ above background. The duration of these increases was between 2.0 and 16.5 h. Dam and pump installation during the Latornell River crossing, however, increased average downstream TSS concentrations by 520 $mg l^{-1}$ for 3 h. Ice removal at the crossing before installation lengthened the period of instream disturbance.

Increases to downstream TSS levels were generally greater during dam and pump removal (1.0–703 $mg l^{-1}$ above background) than during installation. Measured increases were also temporary (20 min to 6.5 h).

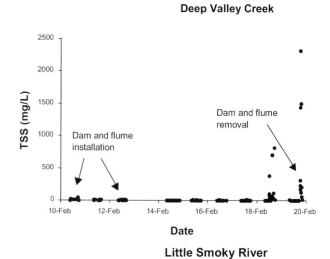
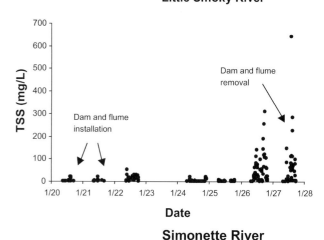
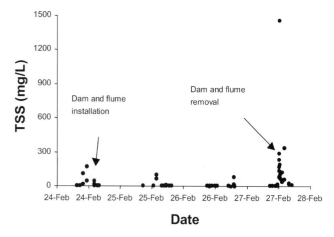

Fig. 4. TSS data downstream of superflume crossings.

Generally, during other phases of construction (i.e., trench excavation and backfill of native material), mean downstream TSS levels were less than 8 $mg l^{-1}$ above background. However, at the Latornell, Simonette, and Little Smoky river crossings, turbid ditch water pumped to dry side channels, or upland locations flowed back into the channel. As a result, TSS levels within several hundred meters downstream of the crossings increased by up 30 to 172 $mg l^{-1}$ for

Evaluation of isolated water course crossings during winter construction

Table 2. Duration and TSS concentrations measured during winter isolated water crossings

Watercourse	Distance downstream (m)	Duration (h)	Days instream	Background TSS (mg l^{-1})	Mean TSS (mg l^{-1})	Peak TSS (mg l^{-1})
Latornell River	80	16.5	3	10.0	112.8	1537.4
Simonette River	50	24.9	4	4.6	74.4	1458.2
Shell Creek	80	34.3	5	6.8	47.1	855.7
Deep Valley Creek	50	75.6	7	4.8	48.0	1497.5
Waskahigan River	40	37.6	5	2.4	16.5	110.3
Little Smoky River	40	54.7	10	3.8	22.5	643.6
Iosegun River	80	23.9	7	12.3	32.8	311.7
Two Creek	50	15.1	2	5.1	20.7	150.2
Chickadee Creek	140	11.8	4	7.4	11.8	22.0
Unnamed Tributary to Chickadee Creek	160	27.4	5	14.6	27.2	359.5
Sakwatamau River	160	93.8	9	7.5	12.6	29.1

Table 3. Duration and mean TSS concentrations during past open-cut installations of similarly sized watercourses

Watercourse	Distance downstream (m)	Duration (h)	Days instream	Background TSS (mg l^{-1})	Mean TSS (mg l^{-1})	Reference
Hodgson Cr, NWT	75	18	2	1.0	608.9	McKinnon and Hnytka, 1988
Archibald Cr, BC	10	–	2	2.1	6247	Tsui and McCart, 1981
Little Cedar R, IA	45	27	4	21.6	451	Reid and Metikosh, 1999
Coxes Cr, Penn.	35	12	2	24.4	781	Reid and Metikosh, 1999

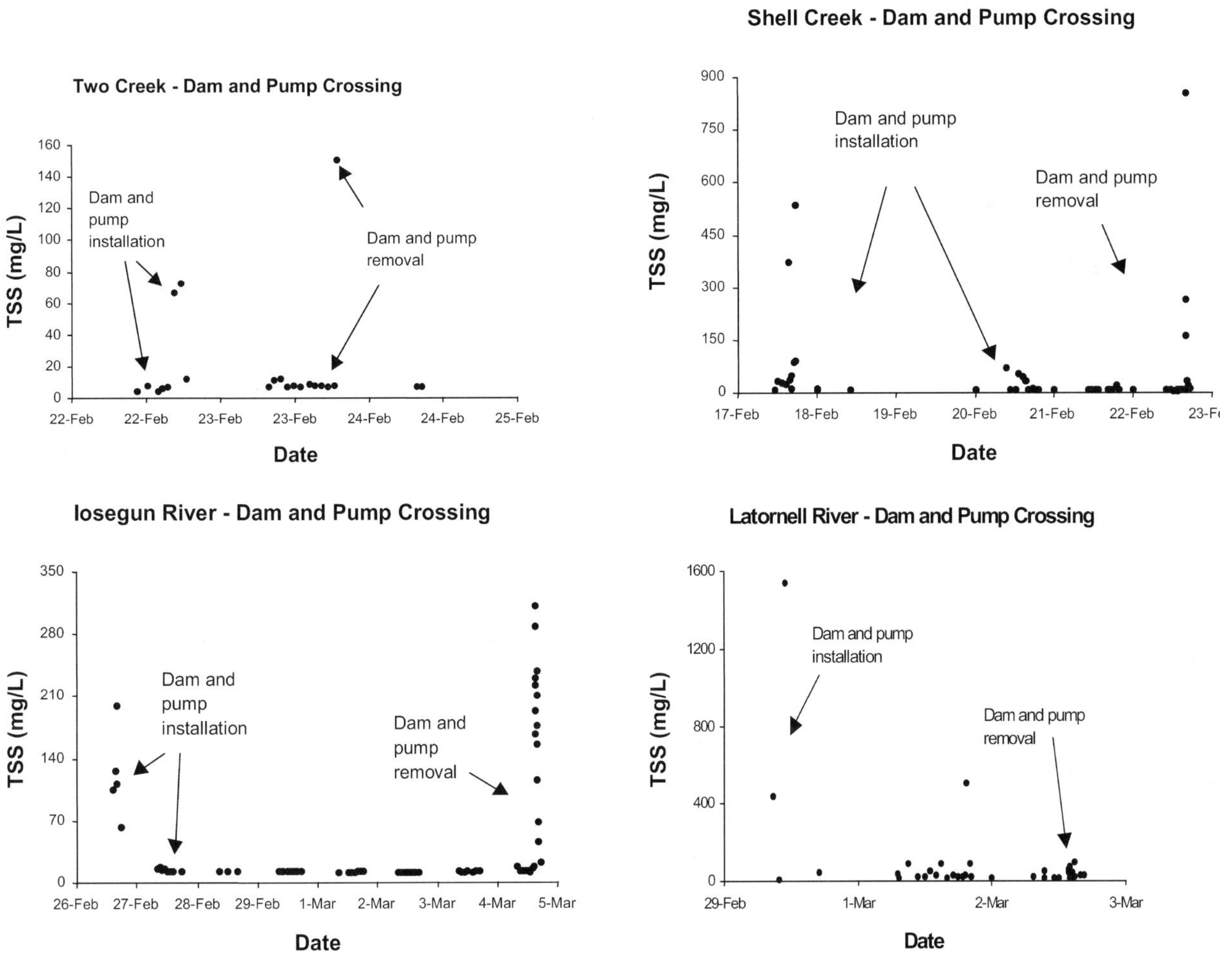

Fig. 5. TSS data collected downstream of selected dam and pump crossings.

Table 4. Difficulties and associated remedial actions encountered during isolated winter water crossings

Watercourse	Difficulty	Remedial action
Latornell River	Ditchwater pumped to upland location flowed back into creek 70 m d/s of crossing	Moved discharge to a different upland location
Simonette River	During backfilling, turbid ditch water pumped to an oxbow-side channel flowed back into the river 50–250 m d/s of crossing	None
Deep Valley Creek	When groundwater input from trench greater than pumping capacity, turbid water seeped out through poor seal between aquadams and superflume	Stop backfilling until water level pumped down
Little Smoky River	During backfilling, pumped turbid ditch water overflowed a beaver dam blocked dry side channel	Moved to discharge to an upland location

Table 5. Dissolved oxygen concentrations measured during isolated winter water crossings

Watercourse	Location	Mean DO level (mg l^{-1})	Range
Simonette River	Upstream	12.2	11.0–13.4
	Downstream	12.5	11.4–13.6
Shell Creek	Upstream	11.3	10.2–11.8
	Downstream	12.7	11.0–13.8
Deep Valley Creek	Upstream	12.3	11.6–13.5
	Downstream	12.3	11.2–13.7
Little Smoky River	Upstream	9.3	8–11.5
	Downstream	9.7	6.5–11.5
Sakwatamau River	Upstream	7.1	6.0–8.5
	Downstream	10.1	6.8–12.6

Table 6. Summary of pre- and post-construction pebble count data collected at riffles upstream and downstream of eight water crossings

Watercourse	Riffle	Fines (<4 mm) Oct 99	Fines (<4 mm) Apr 00	D_{50} Oct 99	D_{50} Apr 00
Simonette River	U/S	0	0	110	101
	DS1 (50 m d/s)	3	0	78	65
	DS2 (380 m d/s)	0	0	102	81
Shell Creek	U/S	2	5	80	72
	DS1 (120 m d/s)	4	1	62	69
	DS2 (330 m d/s)	3	3	65	58
Deep Valley Creek	U/S	0	1	82	92
	DS1 (110 m d/s)	3	1	78	93
	DS2 (600 m d/s)	1	1	64	60
Little Smoky River	U/S	1	2	62	62
	DS1 (40 m d/s)	2	1	62	64
	DS2 (270 m d/s)	0	1	57	69
Tributary to Chickadee Creek	U/S	12	16	81	82
	DS1 (40 m d/s)	10	14	53	48
	DS2 (160 m d/s)	13	10	82	73
Sakwatamau River	U/S	0	6	63	79
	DS1 (270 m d/s)	1	1	68	81
	DS2 (450 m d/s)	2	3	62	65

periods of 4–12 h. During backfilling across Deep Valley Creek, pumps used to de-water the trench were unable to keep the crossing area dry. Turbid water seeped through the seal between the downstream aquadams and the superflume and downstream TSS levels increased up to 820 mg l^{-1} for a period of 5.5 h. Co-ordination between monitoring staff and onsite Alliance environmental inspectors allowed for remedial actions to be implemented quickly once problems were identified during these crossings and therefore limited sediment loading (Table 4).

Dissolved oxygen

Dissolved oxygen levels during the winter can be naturally low due to ice cover preventing aeration. The addition of sediment (especially that containing organic material) during instream construction could further reduce downstream dissolved oxygen concentrations by increasing biological oxygen demand (McKinnon and Hnytka, 1988). Dissolved oxygen concentrations measured downstream of five Alliance water crossings were either equal or greater than upstream concentrations (Table 5). These observations agree with past studies that measured dissolved oxygen levels downstream of winter pipeline crossing construction (McKinnon and Hnytka, 1988; Golder, 1993). Higher dissolved oxygen concentrations downstream of Sakwtamau River crossing likely resulted from bypass water being discharged into an ice-free side channel where aeration could occur.

Fish habitat

Pebble count data did not indicate that water crossing construction resulted in any changes to the amount of fine sediment (<4 mm diameter) in the surficial bed material of riffles downstream of the Simonette River, Shell Creek, Deep Valley Creek, Little Smoky River, Tributary to Chickadee Creek, and Sakwatamau River crossings (Table 6). Except for the Tributary to Chickadee Creek, the amount of fine sediment measured at all riffles and sampling visits was low (<6% composition).

Visual assessments of riffle habitats along Patterson Creek and Tributary to Simmonette River also indicate no effect of water crossing construction on downstream habitats (Table 7). The amount of fine sediment (sand, silts and clay) and the degree of embeddedness of riffles upstream and downstream of the Patterson Creek crossing was significantly less after construction (April 24th, 2000) than before construction (October

Table 7. Summary of pre- and post-construction habitat assessments at riffles upstream and downstream of the Patterson Creek and unnamed tributary to the Simonette River water crossings. Mean (standard error) values are reported

Transect	October 99					April 00				
	Embeddedness	% Boulder	% Cobble	% Gravel	% Fines	Embeddedness	% Boulder	% Cobble	% Gravel	% Fines
Patterson Creek										
Upstream	3.9 (0.1)	20 (4.4)	46 (6.3)	21 (4.9)	14 (4.4)	4.3 (0.2)	36 (7.2)	43 (7.5)	16 (2.8)	6 (3.0)
D1	4.2 (0.1)	11 (2.1)	60 (3.6)	22 (3.3)	7 (1.5)	4.4 (0.2)	27 (5.4)	46 (7.4)	24 (4.6)	4 (1.5)
D2	4.0 (0.2)	22 (4.2)	36 (5.2)	34 (9.8)	8 (2.3)	4.4 (0.2)	18 (5.5)	52 (3.7)	25 (4.8)	6 (1.9)
Unnamed Tributary to the Simonette River										
Upstream	4.1 (0.2)	10 (3.6)	51 (5.2)	34 (6.4)	6 (1.7)	4.3 (0.2)	2 (1.1)	56 (5.1)	35 (6.7)	7 (2)
D1	4.4 (0.2)	0	43 (6.7)	55 (6.6)	3 (1.1)	4.4 (0.2)	5 (4)	47 (5.7)	42 (6.0)	7 (2.4)
D2	4.2 (0.3)	2 (1.1)	53 (3.4)	38 (3.3)	8 (3.2)	4.3 (0.2)	0	25 (5.3)	70 (5.3)	(0.9)

Embeddedness scale: (1) greater than 75%; (2) 50–75%; (3) 25–50%; (4) 5–25%, (5) less than 5%.

15th, 2000) (ANOVA $P < 0.01$). There were also no significant differences in the amount of fine sediment (sand, silts, and clay) or the degree of embeddedness at riffles upstream and downstream of the Tributary to Simonette River crossing.

The cross-sectional area of the pool surveyed 140 m downstream Shell Creek crossing was 24% greater in the spring of 2000 than before construction. Before construction, the cross-sectional area was 13.8 m². After ice-out, it increased to 18.1 m². Therefore there was no reduction in pool habitat. The cross-sectional area of the upstream pool was unchanged (19.5 vs. 19.7 m²).

DISCUSSION

In many areas of the boreal forest of northern Canada, pipeline construction must be constructed during winter as these areas are largely inaccessible during other times of the year. As many of the rivers and streams contain cold water fish habitat and fall spawning species, construction must often occur outside of the preferred timing construction windows identified by provincial regulatory agencies. Sediment released during winter open-cut pipeline crossings has been observed to result in deposits of fine sediment on downstream habitats, especially in slower flowing areas such as pools and back eddies (Wendling, 1978). Sediment deposited downstream of pipeline water crossings has the potential to adversely affect fish populations by smothering incubating eggs, or reducing the availability of critical over-wintering habitats.

TSS and habitat monitoring information collected during this study illustrates that winter isolated water crossings can be effective at reducing the risk of sediment related adverse effects on downstream fish and fish habitat. Properly constructed, increases to downstream TSS levels are limited to the installation and removal of isolation dams and bypass pumps, or flumes. Poor containment of turbid water pumped from the isolated workspace, insufficient pump capacity and poor seals between aquadams and the superflume can reduce the effectiveness of isolated crossing techniques.

The superflume is a newly developed approach to cross sensitive watercourses larger than that suitable for conventional isolated methods (i.e., dam and pump and flume). Watercourses with anticipated flows in excess of 4 $m^3 s^{-1}$ are generally not considered good candidates for conventional isolation techniques. The capacity of the superflume is estimated to be 10 $m^3 s^{-1}$, however, construction personnel who have used this crossing technique consider it to work best at flows less than 7 $m^3 s^{-1}$. The effectiveness of the superflume method to minimize sediment release has been monitored during winter crossings of rivers with flows ranging from 0.29 to 5.0 $m^3 s^{-1}$ (Jaron, 1996; Golder, 1998, this study). Generally, the superflume method is very effective. However, a common problem associated with superflume crossings is the large volume of seepage water that occurs during crossings with porous bed material. The large volumes of water pumped from the work area have resulted in containment failures and the flow of turbid water back into the watercourses. Proper pre-construction planning and diligent monitoring of containment ponds or discharge locations is crucial for the successful application of the superflume method.

Environmental protection regulatory agencies and environmental non-government organizations apply considerable pressure on the proponents of pipeline construction to utilize horizontal directional drilling (HDD) when crossing sensitive watercourses. HDD is an important and useful crossing technique, but is not appropriate for all situations. This is especially true with large diameter pipeline crossings, as the associated risk and added costs of HDD may not be warranted. Along the Alliance Pipeline project, there were 40 HDD water crossings, 22 of which were in Canada. HDD was implemented at crossings with highly sensitive fish species, life stages or habitat, exceptionally steep approach slopes within the valley, extensive existing pipeline infrastructure or other special environmental considerations. In virtually all cases there were inadvertent returns of drilling fluids to the surface and in some situations, these drilling fluids entered surface waters.

As demonstrated in this paper, isolated crossing techniques provide effective mitigation of potential aquatic environmental effects. Isolated crossing techniques should be considered as a viable alternative to HDD if the primary consideration is protection of sensitive aquatic species and/or habitat.

Similar to horizontal directional drilling, isolated crossing techniques are not applicable at all watercourse crossings. The risk of construction related failures is less than HDD, provided adequate contingency (e.g., additional pumps, aquadams and/or clean fill material) are onsite to address unanticipated events such as increased water flow, dam leakage, trench sloughing, or pump failure. However, insufficient information is available to predict if an isolated crossing technique will be successful. Further research could be directed at determining the factors influencing success or failure of isolated crossing techniques and developing best management practices to maximize the potential for success of isolated crossings.

ACKNOWLEDGEMENTS

The authors wish to thank the biologists and technicians at Golder that conducted the field work during the winter of 1999–2000 and the Alliance Environmental Inspectors who assisted in field logistics and data collection.

REFERENCES

Golder Associates Ltd. 1993. Suspended sediment monitoring for pipeline crossings of the Sukunka River and Rocky Creek. Prepared for Talisman Energy Inc., Calgary, AB.

Golder Associates Ltd. 1998. Sediment load monitoring study of the Berland River pipeline crossing. Prepared for NOVA Gas Transmission Ltd., Calgary, AB.

Jaron, K.B. 1996. Superflume crossing of the Telkwa River. March 1995. Pacific Coast Gas Association. 1996 PCGA Transmission/Distribution Conference. Diversity, Fuelling Our Success. Sparks, Nevada, February 21–23, 1996.

Kondolf, G.M. 1997. Application of the pebble count: Notes on purpose, method, and variants. Journal of the American Water Resources Association, 33: 79–87.

McKinnon, G.A. and F.N. Hnytka. 1988. The effect of winter pipeline construction on the fishes and fish habitat of Hodgson Creek, NWT. Canadian Technical Report of Fisheries and Aquatic Sciences No. 1598.

Platts, W.S., W.F. Megahan, and G.W. Minshall. 1983. Methods for evaluating streams, riparian and biotic conditions. USDA. General Technical Report. INT-138., Ogden Utah.

Reid, S.M. and P.G. Anderson. 1999. Effects of sediment released during open-cut pipeline water crossings. Canadian Water Resources Journal, 24: 23–39.

Tsui, P.T.P. and P.J. McCart. 1981. Effects of streamcrossing by a pipeline on the benthic macroinvertebrate communities of a small mountain stream. Hydrobiologia, 79: 271–227.

Wendling, F.L. 1978. Final report on gravel porosity studies along the Trans-Alaska Pipeline. Special Report Number 18. Joint State/Federal Fish and Wildlife Advisory Team.

BIOGRAPHICAL SKETCHES

Scott Reid, MSc

Golder Associates Ltd., 2180 Meadowvale Boulevard, Mississauga, ON L5N5S3, Canada

For the past 5 years, Scott Reid has been a fisheries biologist with Golder Associates Ltd. He has a BSc in Ecology from the University of Calgary and a MSc in Watershed Ecosystems from Trent University. Mr. Reid has been involved in projects investigating the effects of sediment on fish and fish habitat in stream and river systems and developing related assessment and planning tools.

Paul Anderson, MSc, P Biol

Manager, Health, Safety and Environment, Alliance Pipeline Ltd., 400, 605-5 Avenue S.W., Calgary, AB T2P 3H5, Canada

Paul Anderson is the Manager, Health, Safety and Environment for Alliance Pipeline Ltd., responsible for managing environmental affairs and health and safety related issues on the pipeline project. Paul has a Bachelor of Science degree in Watershed Ecosystems from Trent University.

Methods and Results of A Comprehensive Monitoring Program to Document Turbidity and Suspended Sediment Generated During Pipeline Construction

J. Roger Trettel, Stephen A. Compton and David J. Santillo

Northern Ecological Associates, Inc. (NEA) conducted a comprehensive turbidity (nephelometric turbidity unit [NTU]) and suspended sediment (Total Suspended Sediment [TSS]) monitoring program (Program) during construction of the Portland Natural Gas Transmission System (PNGTS) and PNGTS/Maritimes Joint Facilities Pipeline Projects (Project) in New Hampshire. The Program was developed and conducted to monitor NTU/TSS generated during pipeline construction, and to use this data to assess pipeline construction impacts on fishery resources. Monitoring crews collected NTU/TSS data on over 300 stream crossings in New Hampshire. Water samples were collected using automatic water samplers and manually, from each crossing according to spatial and temporal sampling schedules identified by the New Hampshire Department of Environmental Services (NHDES). Crews also collected streambed sediment samples, and complementary ecological data for each crossing. NEA personnel compared NTU and TSS measurement to develop stream specific relationships between the two parameters, and determined that NTU is not an accurate proxy for TSS. NEA documented that the majority of stream crossing had a minimal impact (within the sublethal effects class) on fishery resources as predicted by Newcome and Jensen's 1996 mathematical model. Crossings with a significant fishery impact were typically ones with unique environmental conditions that resulted in extended crossing duration. NEA analyzed streambed sediment samples to determine grain size distribution to correlate with TSS magnitude and duration, and found that grain size distribution was useful in predicting potential fishery impacts. NEA's Program successfully added substantial new information describing construction impacts in aquatic systems.

Keywords: Stream, water, fish, turbidity, suspended sediment

INTRODUCTION

Construction of the Portland Natural Gas Transmission System (PNGTS) and PNGTS/Maritimes & Northeast Pipeline Projects (hereafter referred to as the Project) through the State of New Hampshire involved pipe installation across a total of 179 perennial and 155 intermittent waterbodies.

In order to protect the existing and designated uses of surface waters affected by construction of the Project, the New Hampshire Energy Facility Site Evaluation Committee (EFSEC) together with the New Hampshire Department of Environmental Services (NHDES) developed a series of special conditions. Special Condition 12, which was issued to PNGTS as part of the EFSEC Certificating Order, was developed to address compliance with the state water quality standard for turbidity. This standard states that an activity cannot create a turbidity value that exceeds 10 nephelometric turbidity units (NTU) above background. To enable the project to be constructed, the NHDES modified Special Condition 12 to include provisions for a mixing zone and specific detailed monitoring requirements. The PNGTS/Maritimes & Northeast turbidity

Environmental Concerns in Rights-of-Way Management: Seventh International Symposium
J.W. Goodrich-Mahoney, D.F. Mutrie and C.A. Guild (editors)
© 2002 Elsevier Science Ltd. All rights reserved.

monitoring program was developed to fulfill turbidity monitoring requirements outlined in the condition.

This paper provides a summary of the methods and results of the turbidity monitoring program. Included herein is an introduction to the types of data collected, methods and equipment used for monitoring, and a summary of turbidity (NTU), total suspended solids (TSS), and severity of ill effect (SEV) values obtained from each crossing.

Turbidity and total suspended solids

NHDES Special Condition 12 stipulated that the company monitor turbidity during all flowing stream crossings. In addition, the Condition required the applicants to estimate the potential effect of construction activities on fisheries using Newcombe and Jensen's (1996) severity of ill effects model. This mathematical model generates a severity of ill effect value (SEV) based on the dose (i.e., the product of average TSS in mg/L and exposure duration) of elevated suspended sediment.

Measurements of turbidity, measured in NTU, were necessary to determine when downstream turbidity levels were 10 NTU or less above background, at which time water sample collection could stop. For purposes of determining TSS, the NHDES gave PNGTS the option of using NTU as a proxy for determining TSS, or measuring TSS directly (absolute determination). Because the indirect relationship between turbidity (NTU) and TSS is usually dependent on both the substrate material and basin type of the waterbody, using NTU measurements as a proxy for TSS could lead to gross over- or underestimation of TSS and therefore an inaccurate estimate of SEV. Consequently, PNGTS measured turbidity (NTU) in the field to determine when sampling could stop, and collected water samples so that TSS could be measured in a laboratory for more accurate results used in SEV calculation.

TURBIDITY MONITORING PROTOCOL

On site documentation

On the day that in-stream construction began, field crew(s) produced a diagrammatic sketch in their field books that documented stream crossing location, active construction activity, and any equipment that could potentially affect stream turbidity levels. The sketch included the location of trench dewatering filter bags or any other structures/activities on or off the right-of-way that could affect turbidity. Crewmembers also recorded the following stream characteristics for each crossing:

- Vegetative overhang[1] — A qualitative visual estimation of the percentage of the stream channel that was covered with vegetation at the time of crossing.

- Streambed substrate[1] — A visual estimate of sediment substrate particle size. Particle size classification followed the following guidelines: large boulder (>1024 mm), small boulder (256–1024 mm), large cobble (128–256 mm), small cobble (64–128 mm), and gravel (2–64 mm). Grain sizes smaller than gravel were not determined in the field.
- Bank-height[1] — The distance from stream water surface to the top of the bank.
- Channel width[1] — Average wetted stream channel width within the construction area.
- Water depth[1] — Average stream depth within the construction area.
- Approximate Flow Rate[2] — Velocity (meters/sec) of stream flow, measured by recording the mean time necessary for a floating object (ideally one with sufficient subsurface mass) to progress 3 meters down a representative stream reach.
- Water Temperature — Temperature (F) at the time of sample collection. Note: temperatures were not taken at each overnight sampling event.

Sample collection

Three stream depth-dependent sampling protocols were developed to collect water samples during stream crossings in New Hampshire. Sampling protocol specifics are outlined below.

A one-liter water sample was collected from streams with adequate depth (≈20 ml was collected from shallow or low-flow streams) according to the schedules outlined in NHDES Special Condition 12. All water samples were collected according to 40 CFR Part 136 and Standard Methods 2130B-Turbidity. Water samples were held on site pending potential quality assurance checks by the NHDES Environmental Inspectors (EIs). Sampling locations were selected to ensure that pre-construction turbidity at upstream and downstream sampling locations were as similar as possible. When possible, sampling stations were located where up- and downstream flow conditions were similar (e.g., pools and pools, or riffles and riffles). The first water sample taken from each crossing was a grab sample taken prior to in-stream activity. This grab sample was used to determine inter-station background turbidity variability. Using measurements from the grab sample, up- and downstream sampling stations were positioned in similar environments as much as practicable, with the upstream sampling station located in an area of representative ambient turbidity.

Sampling, at the intervals described below, was initiated after the grab sample had been taken. Replicate samples were taken from each station every 10 samples as a QA/QC measure. Samples were analyzed for turbidity immediately after collection, and then stored in clean one-liter polyethylene bottles. Following turbidity analysis, bottles were labeled with labels placed

---

1 Methodology as described by Hunter (1991).

2 Methodology as described by Lind (1985).

over the mouth of the bottle to ensure that samples were not opened in transit. Samples were then transported to a storage facility, inventoried, and delivered weekly or biweekly to the Forestry Analytical Laboratory at the University of New Hampshire in Durham, NH for TSS analysis.

Collection intervals
Dry crossings
In order to minimize impacts to aquatic resources and facilitate construction, all relatively small and low flow coldwater streams (approximately three meters wide or less) were crossed using one of two "dry crossing" methods (or a combination thereof): Method 2A — Flumed Crossing, or Method 2B — Dam & Pump Crossing. These methods involve maintaining downstream flow and isolating the construction zone from the streamflow by channeling the flow through a flume pipe(s) or culvert(s), or by damming the flow and pumping the water around the construction area. The overall objective is to minimize siltation of the stream and facilitate trenching and excavation of saturated trench spoil. Streams crossed using one of the dry crossings described below are referred to as "Category I" crossings.

As required in Condition 12 (c), all Category I crossings were sampled at two sites ($\approx$15 m upstream and 30 m downstream of the crossing area, respectively). Sampling was performed every two hours during water barrier installation, and again at one, two, four, eight, and twelve hours following water barrier removal, until downstream turbidity was 10 NTU or less above background.

Regardless of sampling protocol, background sample collection was initiated at the beginning of water barrier installation, and again at the beginning of water barrier removal. For purposes of turbidity monitoring, water barrier installation began the moment a flume or sandbag was placed in the stream (whichever came first) as part of a water barrier installation (i.e., dam & flume or dam & pump). Any in-stream construction activity that generated turbidity and occurred prior to placement of the flume or first sand bag, was considered part of water barrier installation, and was determined the beginning of water barrier installation. Water barrier installation was considered complete when all in-stream activity associated with the installation was finished. Water barrier removal was interpreted to be either the beginning of physical water barrier removal, or when the flume was lifted during pipe installation. Water barrier removal was considered to be complete when all equipment associated with the water barrier had been completely removed from the stream.

Wet crossings
A wet crossing (i.e., open cut) construction technique is used to cross warmwater streams that do not support significant fisheries, and streams with substantial flow that cannot be effectively culverted or pumped around the construction zone, and where the directional drill crossing technique is not warranted or feasible. The fundamental objective in using this method is to complete the waterbody crossing as quickly as possible so as to minimize the duration of impacts to aquatic resources and the associated floodplain.

As required in NHDES Special Condition 12(d), for wet crossings, samples were collected from the following sampling stations: Station #1 — 15 m upstream of construction activity; Station #2 — 30 m downstream of construction activity, and Station #3 — 150 m downstream of construction activity.

Sampling protocol and equipment
PNGTS was required to obtain water samples from all perennial and those intermittent streams where water was present at the time of construction. Pre-programmed automatic water samplers that collected continuous, representative, samples at the precise intervals outlined in Special Condition 12 were used to obtain samples at perennial streams. Many of the intermittent streams were too shallow and/or too slow moving to allow water collection using autosamplers. Consequently, PNGTS developed two new sampling protocols, the cuvette and syringe methods. These methods allowed collection of the most representative water sample possible from streams with low flow, or shallow depth.

Ultimately, three primary (Isco Model 6700 automatic sampler, Hach Model 2100P and HF Scientific Model DRT-15CE portable turbidimeters) and two secondary (20 ml glass sampling cuvette, 50 ml plastic syringe) pieces of field equipment were used to collect water samples. Autosamplers were used to collect samples from streams greater than 5 cm deep, the cuvette method was used to collect samples at streams that were too shallow for autosamplers, and the syringe method was used to collect water from streams that were too shallow for the cuvette method. Autosamplers were programmed to collect individual one-liter water samples at the time intervals outlined in Condition 12; the cuvette and/or syringe methods were used to hand-collect sufficient water for turbidity analysis (typically 10–20 ml). The Hach and HF Scientific turbidimeters were used to determine turbidity (NTU) for all water samples.

Autosampler collection method
Isco Model 6700 Autosamplers were used to obtain water samples at all streams that were greater than 5 cm deep at the time of crossing. The terminal end of the autosampler intake line contained a 3 cm diameter polypropylene "strainer" that prevented extremely

large particles from entering the line that could interfere with sample collection. Note: the "strainer" avoided biased samples because holes in the strainer walls allowed collection of all grain sizes that could affect turbidity. Water samples were repeatedly collected from static sampling platforms to minimize sampling bias resulting from heterogeneous turbidity dispersion. At streams less than 1.5 m deep, the autosampler intake was securely fastened to an aluminum post, which in turn was inserted into a steel-sampling platform positioned appropriately in the stream channel. At streams greater than 1.5 m deep, the autosampler intake was securely fastened to a rope that was anchored to the streambed with a weight, and held taut using a float tied to the opposite end. In both cases, the sample intake line was positioned to obtain water samples from the middle to lower third of the water column.

Autosamplers were pre-programmed with the following three sampling programs: Dry 1 — which takes one, 1000 ml water sample every two hours until the program is terminated; Dry 2 — which takes one, 1000 ml water sample immediately upon initiation, a second sample one hour after the initiation of sampling, and future samples every three hours thereafter until the program is terminated (i.e., when turbidity is measured to be 10 NTU or less above background); and, Wet 1 — which takes one, 1000 ml sample every two hours until the program is terminated (i.e., when turbidity is measured to be 10 NTU or less above background). Dry 1 was initiated at the beginning of water barrier installation, Dry 2 was initiated at the beginning of water barrier removal, and Wet 1 was initiated at the beginning of in-stream activity at wet crossings.

Cuvette sampling method
The Cuvette Sampling Method was employed at intermittent or perennial stream crossings when, due to extremely low flow, there was only enough water present in the stream channel to fill the 20 ml glass cuvette that is inserted into the turbidimeter to obtain a NTU measurement. Cuvette water samples were taken by placing the 20-ml glass turbidimeter cuvette into a portion of the stream with sufficient depth to allow sample collection. During sample collection, the cuvette was positioned such that its opening was facing stream flow (when present), and no sediment would be collected from the streambed. Three replicate samples were obtained from each site; the final reported turbidity measurement was the mean of these replicates.

Syringe sampling method
The syringe sampling method was used at streams that were too shallow to allow collection of a sample using the cuvette method. The syringe consisted of a rubber bulb attached to the end of a 100 ml volumetric syringe. Samples were collected by siphoning water from the upper 5 mm of the stream surface without disturbing the stream sediment. Three samples were taken where possible; the final turbidity value was the mean from these three samples. Since the same amount of water was collected using the syringe and cuvette methods, and water collected using the syringe was transferred to a cuvette for analysis, streams sampled using the syringe method are listed as cuvette method streams in all summary tables.

Sample analysis
Turbidity
Turbidity measurements were made immediately after collection using either a HF Scientific Model DRT-15CE or Hach 2100 portable turbidimeter, both of which meet EPA (Method 180.1) design criteria. Turbidimeters were operated according to the manufacturer's specifications. Calibration was performed as per manufacturers specifications, weekly, and oftentimes daily, using factory supplied Formazin standards.

Samples obtained using the cuvette or syringe methods were inserted directly into the turbidimeter for analysis. Samples collected using the Isco autosampler were vigorously agitated prior to obtaining a sub-sample for analysis. Following agitation, a sub-sample was poured directly from the sample bottle into the turbidimeter cuvette. Three measurements were made from each water sample and the mean value recorded according to the EPA (1993) reporting guidelines. Note, turbidity measurements from cuvette and syringe method streams are the mean of three separate water samples while all other values represent the mean of triplicate subsamples from the same initial water sample. Sampling was terminated when downstream turbidity was 10 NTU or less above background.

Water samples with turbidity greater than 10 NTU were sealed, labeled, and transferred to a storage facility following turbidity determination. Water samples were delivered weekly, or biweekly, to UNH for TSS determination. Turbidity results were entered into a spreadsheet, electronically transferred into the master Turbidity Monitoring Database Management System (TMDMS). The data were then plotted against time for each stream crossing, and provided to the NHDES as per Condition 12 (e) of the SEC order.

Total suspended solids
TSS analyses were conducted under the direction of Dr. William H. McDowell at the Forestry Analysis Laboratory (FAL) of the University of New Hampshire. At FAL, TSS analysis was conducted following the procedures described in Standard Methods for the Examination of Water and Wastewater (APHA, 1995; 19th edition), Method 2540 D-Total Suspended Solids Dried at 103–105°C. Results were reported as milligrams of suspended solid per liter of filtered water, and were transmitted periodically to PNGTS. TSS results were paired with the corresponding turbidity measurements in the TMDBS, and used in SEV calculations.

Severity of ill effects values

Severity of ill effects (SEV) values were calculated for all stream crossings where one-liter water samples were collected. SEV values were determined using "model one" developed by Newcombe and Jensen (1996).

Model One assigns a severity of ill effect (SEV) value to adult and juvenile salmonids based on exposure duration (hours) and concentration (mg/l) of suspended sediment (TSS). The model is based on a multiple regression of SEV values and logarithmic transformations of exposure duration and suspended sediment concentration. The result is a predictive model of the form:

$$z = 1.0642 + 0.6068(\ln x) + 0.7384(\ln y)$$

where z is SEV, x is an estimate of exposure duration in hours (ED), and y is the concentration of suspended sediment (mg SS/liter).

To qualify SEV values, Newcombe and Jensen (1996) scored qualitative response data along a semi-quantitative ranking scale. Superimposed on a 15-point scale (0–14), where 0 is no effect and a 14 is greater than 80–100% mortality, were four major classes of effect (i–iv). On this scale, a seven represents "moderate habitat degradation and impaired homing", a subset of the "sublethal" (a classification that included effects such as short-term reduction in feeding success) effect class.

With respect to damage assessment, habitat degradation can be characterized in biological or physical terms or both. Biological manifestations of habitat damage include the following from Newcombe and Jensen (1996): under-utilitzation of stream habitat (Birtwell et al., 1984), abandonment of traditional spawning habitat (Hamilton, 1961), displacement of fish from their habitat (McLeay et al., 1987), and avoidance of habitat (Swenson, 1978). Physical manifestations include degradation of spawning habitat (Slaney et al., 1977; Cederholm et al., 1981), damage to habitat structure (Newcomb and Flagg, 1983; Menzel et al., 1984) and loss of habitat (Menzel et al., 1984; Coats et al. 1985).

SEV was calculated for the background (upstream), 30-m, and where appropriate, 150-m stations. Since water samples were collected at different time intervals, and turbidity and TSS fluctuated throughout the crossing, the most appropriate duration for SEV calculations was determined to be the total crossing duration (i.e., the total duration of active in-stream construction and/or turbidity greater than or equal to 10 NTU above background). Periods when turbidity was less than 10 NTU above background and construction was inactive were typically not included in the total crossing duration.

The TSS value used in calculating SEV was the average TSS that the stream "experienced" during the total construction duration described above. This TSS value was determined by computing the average sampling station TSS (arithmetic mean of samples collected from each of the 1–3 sampling sites per station) for each sampling period, and then averaging sampling station TSS for the total crossing duration. The result was a single TSS value for the upstream, 30-m, and 150-m (where appropriate) downstream sampling stations that represented the average in-stream TSS during the crossing.

Sediment sampling

Monitoring personnel collected streambed substrate samples from all perennial stream crossings to determine if turbidity values could be correlated to substrate type. A representative sample (>50 g) of streambed substrate was collected from the streambed spoil pile. Samples were sent to the University of New Hampshire where a gravimetric analysis was performed to determine grain size distribution (i.e., percentage of sand, silt, and clay). This data was later analyzed to elucidate relationships between turbidity and streambed substrate characteristics. Samples were not collected at perennial stream crossings where the streambed was dominated by bedrock or where personnel could not obtain a representative sample.

RESULTS

Monitoring crews actively monitored turbidity at all streams that were flowing at the time of construction. A number of crossings were dry or frozen at the time of crossing and were not able to be monitored for turbidity.

Project summary

Turbidity monitoring and SEV results for perennial and intermittent stream crossings were compiled in tabular form and individual turbidity summary graphs, stream crossing narratives, and photo documentation were prepared. Where possible, potential causative factors of elevated turbidity reading(s) were described using a call-out box. Crossing narratives provide a physical stream description, a construction and turbidity monitoring summary, elevated turbidity and SEV discussions, and a stream sediment composition chart for select perennial streams. Mean SEV values for perennial streams, and corresponding effect class descriptions from Newcombe and Jensen (1996) were summarized. Length constraints for this paper do not allow inclusion of this detailed information, but may be requested from the authors.

Crossing method and SEV

A random sub-sample of 75 perennial streams (30 dam and pump, 24 flume, 16 combination of dam and pump and flume, and 4 wet crossings) were evaluated to assess mean severity of ill-effects values (SEV). Analyses showed a negligible difference between calculated mean SEVs for dam and pump (6.42) and flumed crossings (6.47). Eleven of the dam and pump crossings (36%), and eight of the flumed crossings (33%), equaled or exceeded an SEV of 7.0. The lowest mean SEV (6.35) was calculated for the 17 crossings that were conducted using a combination of dam and pump and flume methods. The highest mean SEV (7.41) was calculated for the four wet crossings; three of the four wet crossings (75%) equaled or exceeded an SEV of 7.0. Ninety-nine percent of perennial crossing SEV values fell within the Sublethal Effect category, while the remaining 1% were within the lowest grade Paralethal Effect.

Mixing zone compliance

As defined in NHDES's Special Condition 12, a mixing zone for any water body crossed using a dry method is "that volume of water subject to increased turbidity as a result of and immediately following installation and removal of water barriers...." Special Condition 12 specified that within four and twelve hours following water barrier installation and removal, respectively, turbidity levels at a sampling point 30 m downstream of the crossing shall not exceed 10 NTUs above natural background levels. In addition, Special Condition 12 defined a mixing zone for a wet water body crossing as "that volume of water subject to increased turbidity as a result of trenching, pipe installation, and backfilling, so long as total in-stream time...does not exceed forty-eight hours."

On the PNGTS-North Project, the four- and twelve hour mixing zones were exceeded 25 and 34 times, respectively, out of a total of 108 perennial crossings that were monitored for turbidity. Four perennial water bodies were crossed using the wet method; two of which exceeded the forty-eight hour mixing zone. A total of 42 intermittent water body crossings were monitored for turbidity; the four and twelve hour mixing zones were exceeded at 13 and 16 of these crossings, respectively.

In completing the perennial stream crossings on the PNGTS-Joint Facilities Project, the four- and twelve hour mixing zones were exceeded sixteen and seven times, respectively, out of a total of 23 perennial streams that were monitored. Four perennial water bodies crossed using the wet method exceeded the forty-eight hour mixing zone. Out of a total of four intermittent streams that were monitored for turbidity during construction, three of the crossings exceeded the four and twelve hour mixing zones.

DISCUSSION

As indicated in the introduction, the primary objective of NHDES Special Condition 12 was to maintain and protect existing and designated uses of New Hampshire surface waters while permitting construction of the PNGTS-Maritimes Joint Facilities Project. The objective, as stated in Special Condition 12, is as follows:

"...to maintain and protect all existing and designated uses of the surface waters impacted by the construction of the pipeline, during the entire period of construction. New Hampshire water quality standards, including specifically, but not limited to, the standards for turbidity provided in New Hampshire Administrative Rule Env-Ws 430, shall be maintained at all times during construction."

Additionally, Special Condition 12 (paragraph f) included a provision for after-the-fact compensatory mitigation as a result of impairment to designated uses of New Hampshire surface waters or adverse effects to fisheries. The provision, as stated in Special Condition 12, is as follows:

"The applicant will be responsible for providing appropriate after-the-fact compensatory mitigation for any impairment to designated beneficial uses of New Hampshire surface waters caused by exceedence of the 10 NTU turbidity standard outside of a designated mixing zone. The applicant will also be responsible for providing compensatory mitigation for any adverse effects to fisheries within a mixing zone, to the extent that sampling demonstrates predicted effects which exceed a severity level of seven (7) on the scale developed by Charles Newcombe and Jorgan Jensen..."

Water samples were collected upstream and downstream of river and stream crossings at specified intervals to quantify and assess turbidity (NTU) with respect to New Hampshire water quality standards. These samples were further analyzed to determine TSS, which was used in calculations to predict adverse effects to fisheries. These acts fulfilled all turbidity monitoring requirements promulgated in NHDES Special Condition 12. However, turbidity monitoring program effectiveness is probably best evaluated in terms of both the number of waterbody crossings that were successfully monitored and whether the crossing affected existing or designated uses or resulted in adverse affects to fisheries. The following sections provide explanations and interpretations of turbidity monitoring results, and summaries the results with respect to water quality standards and fishery impacts. Recommendations for designing future monitoring programs are provided at the end of the document.

The following sections provide a brief overview of sampling effort, SEV and fishery impacts, and recommendations for future turbidity monitoring programs. The conclusions and recommendations do not include an exhaustive analysis and review of available scientific literature. Such a study may be forthcoming if requested by PNGTS and the NHDES.

Turbidity, total suspended solids

Data analyzed showed that turbidity (NTU) was a poor predictor of TSS and in turn SEV. As originally hypothesized, the relationship between NTU and TSS varied considerably between stream types and was significantly influenced by sediment grain size distribution.

Based on data collected from streams greater than 10 cm deep, the magnitude and duration of elevated turbidity and TSS generated during pipeline construction appears to be the dependent on a variety of interrelated physical stream characteristics. Among these, stream substrate particle size distribution and flow rate appeared to have the greatest effect on turbidity, TSS, and indirectly, SEV. In general, streams that were swiftly-flowing and/or had substrate dominated by coarse textured soil material (i.e., sand, gravel, cobble, boulder) had considerably lower turbidity and TSS levels during construction than slow moving streams with sediment dominated by fine textured soil material (i.e., silt and clay). Swift flowing streams rapidly transported fine textured soil material out of the sampling area, while coarse sediment material quickly settled out of the water column. Conversely, low flow streams were often dominated by sediment consisting of fine-textured material, which is characterized by having a large surface area for scattering light (i.e., elevated NTU levels) and low settling velocities. Furthermore, streams dominated by fine textured soils often took extended time to cross due to the logistical difficulties created by their lack of structure.

SEV and fishery impacts

Another important consideration in reviewing SEV results is the effect of different sediment grain size distributions on downstream SEV values. Analysis of project-wide, sediment grain size distribution from 103 streams allowed determination of the following:
- if streambed substrate soil texture class was sand or boulder, 100% of the streams had a downstream SEV < 7;
- if streambed substrate soil texture class was 80–100% sand, 80% of the crossings had a downstream SEV < 7;
- if streambed substrate soil texture class was loamy sand, 81% of the crossings had a downstream SEV < 7;
- a greater percentage of silt leads to a greater probability for exceeding a downstream SEV of 7 during the crossing; specifically,

    0–20% silt composition, 29% of crossings with a downstream SEV > 7,

    21–40% silt, 42% of crossings with a downstream SEV > 7, and

    41–60% silt, 89% of crossings with a downstream SEV > 7.

Based on these results it is apparent that grain size has a profound effect on SEV. In this case, the effect is probably a result of two factors:
1. silt particles that have an optimum surface area to mass ratio such that they remain suspended in water for an extended duration (up to 48 h) and weigh enough to significantly increase TSS, and
2. streams with a high percentage of silt are predestined to extended crossing duration due to the structural properties of silt.

Since SEV is calculated using average TSS and crossing duration, it is not surprising to find that the majority of stream crossings where SEV exceeded seven were places where the synergistic, and in many cases interdependent, effects of low flow and fine textured soil material were realized. As a result of this interaction, any conditions mandating crossing streams during periods of "low flow" probably resulted in crossings with an increased probability of exceeding an SEV of seven.

Newcombe and Jensen (1996) indicate that their SEV scale ranges from moderate to severe habitat damage, which "can be characterized in biological or physical terms." The scale is based on a meta-analysis of 80 published, and adequately documented, reports on fish responses to suspended sediment in streams. It begins with nil effect and progresses to 100% mortality. One of the model's assumptions is that the SEV scale represents "proportional differences in true effects." While effects might be progressive and proportional, it is unlikely that a singular SEV value can be chosen and applied uniformly to a variety of species and habitats to represent the onset of adverse habitat impacts. Newcombe and Jensen (1996) state, "the distinction between moderate and severe habitat damage is a matter of degree that still has not been delineated exactly" and continue by indicating that the "boundary between short-term and long-term reductions in feeding success (the major difference between an SEV of 4 and 8) is two hours."

Regardless of the threshold SEV where "adverse impacts" are realized, it is unlikely that an SEV of 7 caused long-term damage to fish populations or habitats. As previously stated, "long term reductions in feeding rate," an SEV of 8 on Newcombe and Jensen's scale, could actually be reductions that persist for as little as two hours. Furthermore, based on visual observations, streambed composition typically returned to pre-construction conditions within one week or less, or following the first significant storm event. Repeated visits to completed stream crossings indicated that observable construction generated sedimentation was not present two-weeks to one month after a crossing was completed. Given these observations, it follows that while a calculated fishery impact might have temporarily exceeded a seven, long-term impact to fish or their habitat was highly unlikely. Based on visual observations, and empirical SEV data, it is likely that long-term impacts would not be observed until at least an SEV of 8 or 9 is reached.

RECOMMENDATIONS AND CONCLUSIONS

The objective of the NHDES turbidity monitoring criteria (Special Condition 12) was to determine compliance with state water quality standards and to minimize and predict fishery impacts. The monitoring program was successful in meeting these objectives. While the turbidity monitoring program confirmed that in-stream construction causes short-term increases in turbidity, consideration should be given to revising future monitoring programs to collect potentially more significant data. For example, instead of equal resources being devoted to all sites, even greater resources might be devoted to identified waterbodies that support significant fisheries, while less significant fish or aquatic resources might be the subject of lesser efforts and expenditures.

The results of this monitoring program revealed that turbidity is not an appropriate surrogate for total suspended solids. The relationship between turbidity (NTU) and TSS varied by at least one order of magnitude depending on the stream, and rarely followed the approved algorithm $TSS = 1.6 * NTU$. The NTU/TSS relationship was particularly poor at shallow (<5 cm), low-flowing watercourses where collection of a representative sample was problematic. In order to accurately assess fishery impacts, monitoring must be conducted at streams characterized by adequate depth (>5 cm) and flow rates such that representative samples can be obtained. TSS measurements should always be taken in favor of turbidity (NTU), and used in management decisions.

An SEV value of 9, the beginning of Paralethal Effects according to Newcombe and Jensen (1996), seems to better represent the threshold where suspended sediments begin to have a significant effect on fish. We base this observation on species-specific scientific literature, visual estimation of how quickly sediment flushes from an area following initial sedimentation, and results from this study.

Pipeline construction across a given waterbody usually follows an orderly sequence of events. However, waterbody crossing dynamics can be differentially affected by channel substrate, surrounding hydrology (e.g., wetland complexes and water table height), and other variable factors such as weather. Any of these factors, operating independently or synergistically, can complicate construction activities, which may result in unpredictable and/or prolonged in-stream disturbance. Consequently, any monitoring program intended to assess construction disturbance on fishery resources must allow enough flexibility to accommodate dynamic field conditions. More specifically, rigid spatial and temporal specifications for sample collection (i.e., collecting samples at one or two hour intervals) can result in an under- or overestimation of actual impacts because sampling is not frequent enough to detect periodic disturbances. To accurately assess construction impacts, sampling protocol should be developed with the recognition that sample collection must be closely tied to field observations of in-stream construction disturbances.

Turbidity monitoring personnel, environmental inspectors, and third party inspectors acknowledge that every reasonable effort should be made to expedite waterbody crossings and minimize the overall duration of in-stream disturbance. As evidenced by SEV values and visual observations, waterbody crossings that occurred over an extended duration had the greatest observable effect on fishery resources and in-stream turbidity. Activities designed to mitigate impacts, but which create longer instream disturbances, are counter productive.

The individual efforts of pipeline personnel to minimize in-stream disturbance cannot be overemphasized. Increased attention to insure that dam and pump-around discharge is adequately diffused is one example where right-of-way construction personnel can play an integral role in minimizing impacts to fishery resources. In addition, increased communication between foremen, spread supervisors, and turbidity monitoring personnel enhances the ability to effectively monitor in-stream construction disturbances and ultimately protect valuable fishery resources.

REFERENCES

APHA. 1995. Standard Methods for the Examination of Water and Wastewater, 19th edn. American Public Health Association, Washington, DC.

Birtwell, I.K., G.F. Hartman, B. Anderson, D.J. McLeay, and J.G. Malick. 1984. A brief investigation of Arctic grayling (Thymallus arcticus) and aquatic invertebrates in the Minto Creek drainage, Mayo, Yukon Territory: An area subjected to placer mining. Canadian Technical Report of Fisheries and Aquatic Sciences 1287.

Cederholm, C.J., L.M. Reid, and E.O. Salo. 1981. Cumulative effects of logging road sediment on salmonid populations in the Clearwater River, Jefferson County, Washington. In: Salmon Spawning Gravel: A Renewable Resource in the Pacific Northwest. Washington State University, Washington Water Research Center, Report 39, Pullman. pp. 38–74.

Coats, R., L. Collins, J. Florsheim, and D. Kaufman. 1985. Channel change, sediment transport, and fish habitat in a coastal stream: Effects of an extreme event. Environmental Management, 9: 35–48.

Hamilton, J.D. 1961. The effect of sand-pit washings on a stream fauna. Internationale Vereinigung fur theoretische und angewandte Limnologie Verhandlungen, 14: 435–439.

Hunter, C.J. 1991. Better Trout Habitat; A Guide to Stream Restoration and Management. Island Press, Washington, DC.

Lind, O.T. 1985. Handbook of Common Methods in Limnology. Kendall/Hunt, Dubuque, IA.

McLeay, D.J., I.K. Birtwell, G.F. Hartman, and G.L. Ennis. 1987. Responses of Arctic grayling (Thymallus arcticus) to acute and prolonged exposure to Yukon placer mining sediment. Canadian Journal of Fisheries and Aquatic Sciences, 44: 658–673.

Menzel, B.W., J.B. Barnum, and L.M. Antosch. 1984. Ecological alterations of Iowa prairie-agricultural streams. Iowa State Journal of Research, 59: 5–30.

Newcombe, C.P. and J.O. Jensen. 1996. Channel suspended sediment and fisheries: A synthesis for quantitative assessment of risk and impact. North American Journal of Fisheries Management, 16: 693–727.

Newcomb, T.W. and T.A. Flagg. 1983. Some effects of Mt. St. Helens ash on juvenile salmon smolts. US National Marine Fisheries Service Marine Fisheries Review, 45(2): 8–12.

Slaney, P.A., T.G. Halsey, and A.F. Tautz. 1977. Effects of forest harvesting practices on spawning habitat of stream salmonids in the Centennial Creek watershed. British Columbia. British Columbia Ministry of Recreation and Conservation, Fish and Wildlife Branch, Fisheries Management Report 73, Victoria.

Swenson, W.A. 1978. Influence of turbidity on fish abundance in western Lake superior. US Environmental Protection Agency, National Environmental Research Center, Ecological Research Series EPA 600/3-78-067 (not seen: cited by Gradall and Swenson 1982).

Sykora, J.L., E.J. Smith, and M. Synak. 1972. Effect of lime-neutralized iron hydroxide suspensions on juvenile brook trout (Salvelinus fontinalis Mitchill). Water Research, 6: 935–950.

United States Environmental Protection Agency (EPA). 1994. Water Quality Standards Handbook, 2nd ed. EPA-823-B-94-055a. Washington, DC.

United States Environmental Protection Agency (EPA). 1993. Methods for the determination of Inorganic Substances in Environmental Samples; Method 180.1, Determination of Turbidity by Nephelometry. EPA 600/R-93/100. Washington, DC.

BIOGRAPHICAL SKETCHES

J. Roger Trettel

Northern Ecological Associates, Inc., 451 Presumpscot St., Portland, ME 04103, USA, Fax: (207) 879-9481, E-mail: rtrettel@neamaine.com

As a Principal of Northern Ecological Associates, Inc. (NEA) and a specialist in environmental impact assessment and restoration ecology, Mr. Trettel has over 18 years experience in the environmental field. Mr. Trettel holds a BS in Forest Science and an MS in Wetland Ecology. Mr. Trettel's experience includes management of comprehensive environmental programs for the planning, assessment, permitting, construction, inspection, restoration, and monitoring of natural gas pipeline development projects. A certified Professional Wetland Scientist (PWS), Mr. Trettel also has extensive experience performing wetland, vegetation, and biological analyses and developing wetland and wildlife habitat mitigation and restoration plans. In addition, Mr. Trettel manages and prepares Environmental Impact Statements (EISs), Environmental Assessments (EAs), and Environmental Reports (ERs) for proposed development projects.

David J. Santillo, PhD

Northern Ecological Associates, Inc., 451 Presumpscot St., Portland, ME 04103, USA, Fax: (207) 879-9481

David J. Santillo, PhD, is a Principal Ecologist for Northern Ecological Associates with over 19 years experience designing and conducting biological and ecological investigations, and in environmental impact and restoration planning. Dr. Santillo has a BS in Environmental Biology, a MS in Wildlife Management, and a PhD in Environmental and Forest Biology. His specific research experience includes impacts of utility construction on wetland plants and birds, birds and mammals on herbicide-treated forest clearcuts, and a variety of avian research. Dr. Santillo's areas of expertise include terrestrial and aquatic ecology, wildlife biology, restoration of fresh- and salt marshes, and environmental permitting and NEPA compliance. Dr. Santillo is a certified Professional Wetland Scientist, and a qualified Professional Wildlife Biologist.

Stephen A. Compton

Northern Ecological Associates, Inc., Village Square, 33 Church St., Fredonia, NY 14063, USA, Fax: 315-379-0355, E-mail: scompton@neanewyork.com

With over 13 years of experience in the environmental field, Mr. Compton's expertise includes the management and execution of comprehensive environmental impact analyses, environmental permitting, development of mitigation measures, and environmental inspection at both the state and federal level. Mr. Compton holds a BS in Environmental Studies and an MS in Forest Ecology. Mr. Compton has managed and prepared NEPA documents for various federal actions, and natural gas pipeline, roadway, and recreational development and expansion projects. Mr. Compton's areas of expertise include NEPA analysis and compliance; comprehensive environmental permitting and mitigation planning; and environmental compliance monitoring of pipeline construction activities. In addition, Mr. Compton specializes in animal habitat quality assessment and impact analysis and development of forest wildlife habitat suitability computer models; design, implementation, and reporting of Threatened and Endangered (T&E) species and preparation of Biological Assessments (BAs) for federal T&E species.

Theoretical Modeling of Suspended Sediment, Turbidity Dynamics, and Fishery Impacts during Pipeline Construction across Streams

H. Wayne Harper and Roger Trettel

State water quality agencies typically impose turbidity standards on pipeline construction across waterbodies primarily because it is a widely used water quality measurement, is easy to determine in the field, and provides instantaneous feedback to regulatory personnel. Often, regulatory personnel will use turbidity data to infer fishery impacts. Turbidity, however, has a lesser biological effect on fish than does its often-related measurement, suspended sediment. Portland Natural Gas Transmission System (PNGTS)/Northern Ecological Associates, Inc. (NEA) used established engineering models and grain size analysis to conduct a detailed study of turbidity and suspended sediment dynamics caused by pipeline construction across streams. To predict total suspended sediment (TSS) distribution and transport, PNGTS/NEA developed scenarios for typical waterbody crossings by assuming representative stream characteristics including: width, cross-sectional area, bed composition, mean velocity, estimated transport distances, material lost during excavation, and the increase in suspended solids expected downstream of the crossing. PNGTS/NEA used sediment grain size analyses that were collected from representative stream crossings as input parameters in the model. PNGTS/NEA's estimates were then input into Trow's 1996 model to estimate sediment dispersion for three stream types: low, medium, and high energy. Predicted suspended sediment values were then used to determine lethal and sublethal fishery impacts using Newcombe and Jensen's mathematical model which assigns a Severity of Ill Effect (SEV) value for fish species guilds based on dose (TSS/ml) and duration (hours) of exposure. The results of this analysis were used in negotiations with state regulatory personnel to help describe potential realistic fishery impacts, rather than hypothetical effects that may be caused by elevated turbidity values.

Keywords: Water quality, stream disturbance, mixing zone, sediment grain size distribution, best management practices (BMPs), turbidity, TSS, sediment transport modeling

INTRODUCTION

The creation and expansion of linear facilities such as pipelines and roads necessitates traversing waterbodies, rivers, and streams and therefore normally requires some level of in-stream construction activity. Construction within a waterbody will inevitably suspend sediments in the water column. As a result, state and federal agencies often attach suspended sediment or turbidity water quality regulations to permits authorizing in-stream activity. With pipeline construction in waterbodies, crossing techniques have been developed to minimize the magnitude and duration of suspended sediment events. However, even with the implementation of Best Management Practices (BMPs), any in-stream construction operations will result in a temporary increase in sediment loads and turbidity within a waterbody higher than natural background levels for at least a short time period. This technical report has been prepared to convey the following key points:

- Normal pipeline construction through waterbodies creates short-term levels of suspended sediments and turbidity greater than that allowed by most state water quality regulations;

- Case studies of recent pipeline construction projects and basic sediment transport modeling demonstrate the realistic levels of turbidity that can be expected during construction; and
- Impacts to fisheries and aquatic biota will not be adversely affected by the short-term nature of the turbidity created by pipeline construction.

CHARACTERISTICS OF TURBIDITY AND SEDIMENTATION

Turbidity

The American Public Health Association defines turbidity as an optical property of water wherein suspended and some dissolved materials such as clay, silt, finely divided organic and inorganic matter, plankton, and other microscopic organisms cause light to be scattered and absorbed rather than transmitted in straight lines. More simply, turbidity is a measure of the "cloudiness" of water or other fluids. Turbidity is measured using a nephelometric method with turbidity values presented in nephelometric turbidity units ("NTUs"). Nephelometry is a measure of light extinction measuring the light scattered at a 90° angle by suspended particles.

Sedimentation

Suspended solids (or sediment) are the portion of the sediment load within a waterbody which can be transported via suspension (mainly clays, silts, and fine sands). The component of the suspended load that will settle out rapidly is defined as the settleable solids portion. Settleable solids refer to particles that settle out quickly from suspension. Settleable solids can either remain in-place indefinitely, or move downstream mainly via bedload transport processes. Suspended sediments are typically classified as silt-clay particles less than 62 microns in diameter. Conversely, particles larger than these are considered settleable solids.

Sediment suspension during construction

An impact of pipeline construction is the temporary generation of a plume of suspended solids and turbid water to downstream reaches of the watercourse. Levels of suspended solids increase rapidly at the onset of in-stream activity. However, pipeline installations do not generate uniform periods of high-suspended concentrations downstream. Instead, discrete peaks of high-suspended sediment concentrations occur corresponding to activities such as trench excavation, trench dewatering, and backfilling. During these time periods of peak suspended sediment concentrations, turbidity values may reach levels ranging from several hundred to several thousand NTUs. When construction stops and the streambed is no longer disturbed, suspended sediment levels typically recede to near ambient conditions. The magnitude and duration of downstream increases in suspended sediment concentrations and turbidity levels during in-stream construction are determined by:
- Size of waterbody crossing;
- Flow volume and velocity;
- Construction activity;
- Sediment particle settling rates.

REVIEW OF SEDIMENT-RELATED WATER QUALITY STANDARDS AND CRITERIA

Regulation of the input of sediment into waterbodies attributable to pipeline construction activities has been achieved through defining allowable construction methods and time frames within construction permits. In some states, numerical turbidity restrictions have been incorporated into permit conditions in order to ensure the application of permit conditions defined for a given watercrossing. These values are generally based on state water quality guidelines. However, most state water quality regulations pertaining to turbidity were originally developed for use with chronic long-term point-source discharge situations. The use of these criteria without some adjustment for the short-term nature of construction projects may be a mis-application of the basic concepts behind their original intent (Trow, 1996). Some states have recognized that during in-stream construction there are no practicable means to maintain turbidity levels to typical regulation levels developed for chronic exposure situations. Acknowledging that their water quality regulations do not appropriately address the short-term impacts associated construction activities within waterbodies, some states have modified their water quality standards and/or mixing zone criteria.

ANTICIPATED TURBIDITY DURING PIPELINE CONSTRUCTION

To document the magnitude of suspended sediments and turbidity that typically can be expected during pipeline construction, this section provides two recent case studies that review turbidity monitoring programs conducted during the construction of the Florida Gas Transmission–Phase III Expansion and the Pacific Gas Transmission–Pacific Gas & Electric Pipeline Expansion projects. The experience in these case studies, which were located in the southeast and western United States, reveals that exceeding chronic exposure turbidity threshold levels simply cannot be avoided during construction. Additionally, sediment transport analyses for "Wet" and "Dry" waterbody crossings were performed to simulate anticipated suspended sediment and turbidity levels that can be expected in New Hampshire.

Case study 1: Florida Gas Transmission — Phase III Expansion

The Florida Gas Transmission Company (FGT) — Phase III Expansion Project (Expansion) consisted of the construction of approximately 600-miles of natural gas pipeline throughout Florida during 1994 and 1995. Following existing ROWs to the greatest extent practicable, the mainline route, which was relatively parallel to the coastline, crossed hundreds of waterbodies through Florida.

Surface water quality regulation variance

During the permitting process, FGT petitioned the Florida Department of Environmental Protection (FDEP) for a variance of the existing state water quality standards for turbidity and criteria for mixing zones during the construction of its Phase III Expansion Project for Class B waterbodies (FDEP, 1993). The FDEP, acknowledging the fact as stated in the petition, that "there is no practicable means known or available for the adequate control of the pollution involved (turbidity)," granted the petitioner temporary variance from the Florida Administrative Codes regulating mixing zones and turbidity. The variance issued by the FDEP to FGT for pipeline construction activities within waterbodies had the following major components:

- The mixing zone to be utilized during pipeline construction activities within waterbodies shall be expanded from 150 to 800 m downstream of the crossing;
- Turbidity levels at the end of the mixing zones shall not exceed 1000 NTUs above natural background levels for more than 12 consecutive hours;
- Turbidity levels at the end of the mixing zones shall not exceed 3000 NTUs above natural background levels for more than 3 consecutive hours; and
- Within 5 days after the beginning of trenching, turbidity levels at sampling points located 150 m downstream of the crossing shall not exceed 29 NTUs above natural background levels.

It should be noted that the 1000 and 3000 NTU turbidity values were deemed necessary by both FGT and the FDEP due to fine sediment conditions typically encountered below grade throughout many portions of Florida. Turbidity resulting from these formations can be significant as the fine sediment has extremely small particle size and mass. Although the actual turbidity values utilized in the FGT variance may not necessarily be applicable to other states, the overall framework of stratified turbidity levels, time windows, and mixing zone lengths contained within this variance reflect a mechanism that allowed the construction to proceed while providing some level of environmental protection.

Turbidity monitoring program

Throughout construction of the Expansion, FGT was required to conduct a turbidity monitoring program. As documented in the "Intent to Grant Variance" issued by the FDEP, this monitoring program consisted of the following components:

- Turbidity sampling shall take place at the end of the mixing zone and within 150 m of the impact site (within the mixing zone), downstream of the construction activities, within the visible plume.
- Sampling at the end of the mixing zone shall be conducted twice daily, during the morning and afternoon work periods, and additionally during the daylight hours of each rainy day, during the rain event or within 3 h following the rain event. Sampling at 150 m shall be conducted once daily, during work periods. If any turbidity sample exceeds 600 NTUs within the mixing zone, hourly sampling shall continue at that site until turbidity levels drop below 600 NTUs.

PNGTS/NEA were able to obtain a small portion of this turbidity sampling data from the FDEP reflecting typical pipeline construction activities within minor waterbodies during October, 1994 (FGT, 1994). Data from four streams reveals that, upon initiation of construction activities, turbidity levels increased between 110 and 1100 NTUs above background conditions. Following completion of the in-stream activities, these elevated turbidity levels quickly dropped and approached background levels within a few hours.

Case Study 2: Pacific Gas Transmission–Pacific Gas & Electric Pipeline Expansion

During the summer of 1992, Pacific Gas Transmission ("PGT") and Pacific Gas & Electric ("PG&E") expanded their natural gas pipeline system by looping an approximate 700-mile section that ran from the Canadian–United States border near Eastport, Idaho to the Central Valley of California. The construction process involved numerous waterbody crossings including eight "wet" crossings of the Moyie River along a 13-mile section of pipeline immediately south of the Canadian–United States border in Boundary County, Idaho. The information provided in the following sections was obtained from the *Data Summary Report on Short-Term Turbidity Monitoring of Pipeline River Crossings in the Moyie River, Boundary County, Idaho: PGT-PG&E Pipeline Expansion Project, March 1994* ("Moyie-Report").

Surface water quality regulations for turbidity

As part of project's Section 401 Water Quality Certification, the Idaho Division of Environmental Quality ("IDEQ") established water quality monitoring requirements for turbidity, which included the following:

- Turbidity will be the water-quality parameter measured.

- Measurements will be taken immediately upstream and 600 feet downstream of the trenching activity. The upstream location will be far enough upstream to be unaffected by construction and will allow background turbidity to be measured. A best professional judgement of 600 feet downstream was determined by IDEQ as the distance required for dissipation on the basis of the permit for what the IDEQ considered to be an analogous river crossing in California (the upper Sacramento River crossing permit issued by the Army Corps of Engineers, Sacramento).
- The downstream turbidity is not to exceed background turbidity by more than 50 nephelometric turbidity units (NTUs) instantaneously or 25 NTU averaged over a 10-day period.

Revised IDEQ requirements

The turbidity plumes that were generated by construction of the first two crossings of the Moyie River (#8 and #6) did not behave as anticipated by the IDEQ, and revisions to the sampling protocol were developed to better characterize the sediment plumes. The following observations were documented by the Army Corps of Engineers and the IDEQ:
- The plume was more persistent than expected, distinguishable as far as the confluence with the Kootenai River, 9–23 miles downstream from the crossing activities (depending on the crossing location).
- Poor mixing 600 feet downstream precluded representative sampling of the plume at that location.
- Turbidity levels were much higher than the IDEQ 50-NTU instantaneous standard.

In response to these sediment distribution observations, IDEQ changed the sampling protocol to obtain more representative measurements. Additionally, in response to levels of turbidity in excess of the 50 NTU standard, experimental BMPs, which are typically not utilized during pipeline construction, were developed by the construction contractor and applicable federal and state agencies before the start of each of the remaining crossings.

Turbidity monitoring results

Turbidity levels were measured from samples collected at regular time intervals utilizing automatic samplers at each Moyie River crossing. Peak turbidity levels, which can be associated with excavation and backfilling, are summarized in Table 1.

A comparison of statistical analysis results, utilizing flow weighted averages, indicates a similar turbidity level verses time pattern between the FGT and PGT/PG&E projects. Turbidity values rose quickly with the initiation of pipeline construction activities and declined with the completion of the work efforts. Within 24-h of restoration of the stream banks, turbidity levels were generally the same as upstream background conditions.

Table 1. Moyie River pipeline crossing peak turbidity levels

Moyie river crossing number	Peak turbidity levels (NTUs) at ≃600' downstream of crossing	
	Associated with excavation	Associated with backfilling
8	214	155
6	743	225
4	1060	660
5	683	398
2	1181	1783
1	2652	424
3	1200	1400

Report conclusions

Provided below is a summary of the main components of the conclusions and recommendations documented in the Moyie Report.
- Mixing of suspended sediments across the river cross-section was not uniform 600 feet to up to 0.5 mile downstream of the crossings. This uneven mixing presents a problem when trying to take samples representative of the overall turbidity.
- The turbidity plumes observed were extremely persistent. The plumes generated at the northern crossings (#1, #2, #3, and #4) had turbidity levels far above the IDEQ standards, even after they had traveled several river miles downstream. Less is known quantitatively about the persistence of the plumes generated by the southern crossings (#5, #6, #7, and #8), but visual observations suggest that they were as persistent as the other plumes.
- Dissolved-oxygen concentration and temperature of the water downstream of the crossing construction were not affected by in-stream construction activities.
- However, several of the "experimental" BMPs appeared to be ineffectual when field tested and were, by consensus, discarded at later crossings.

Sediment transport analysis for "wet" waterbody crossings

In an effort to assess the magnitude of sediment transport and turbidity that would occur in New Hampshire waterbodies crossed by the proposed PNGTS North-Section Facilities and PNGTS/Maritimes & Northeast Joint Facilities (collectively herein referred to as the "Projects") using the open cut or "wet" method, the PNGTS/NEA have conducted sediment transport analysis using computer simulations. The computer model utilized was developed following the methodologies for sediment transport assessment as presented in the *Waterbody Crossing Design and Installation Manual - Appendix C*, ("Model") (Trow, 1996). This model predicts particle transport distances, zones of deposition, depth of sediment deposition per zone, and expected suspended solids increase at downstream zone intervals. Provided in the following sections are documentation of input data development,

Table 2. Summary of waterbodies crossed by the projects in New Hampshire

Waterbody type	Criteria definition	Number of waterbodies	Average width (feet)	Average depth (inches)	Average side slope ratio	Average cross-sectional area (ft)(2)
Major	width > 100'	6[1]	237.7	38.2	1:1	786.2
Intermediate	10' ≤ width ≤ 100'	46	22.7	16.9	1:1	37.7
Minor	width < 10'	227	4.5	6.5	1:1	3.3

Excludes the Piscataqua and Connecticut Rivers.

Table 3. Summary of sediment grain size distributions

Waterbody		Androscoggin river	Presumpscot river	Great works river
Number of crossing locations		3	2	2
Total number of samples analyzed		9	8	8
Clay composition	0.001–0.075 mm	0.88%	12.41%	15.28%
Silt composition	0.001–0.075 mm	6.46%	12.58%	18.80%
Fine-sand composition	0.075–0.420 mm	22.59%	29.54%	28.98%
Medium-sand composition	0.42–2.00 mm	20.76%	30.87%	34.19%
Coarse-sand composition	2.0–4.8 mm	8.91%	4.97%	1.42%
Fine-gravel composition	4.8–19.0 mm	26.78%	8.53%	1.26%
Course gravel composition	19–75 mm	13.62%	1.10%	0.07%
Computer model waterbody classifications with corresponding sediment grain size distributions		Major Waterbody "High-Energy"	Major Waterbody "Low-Energy"	Intermediate & Minor Waterbodies

sediment transport calculation methodologies, resulting output data, and interpretation of the results.

New Hampshire waterbody classifications

To develop scenarios of "typical waterbodies crossed" by the Projects in New Hampshire, a statistical analysis of the comprehensive waterbody crossing table was conducted. This Table was presented for the applicable portions of the Projects in the permit filings that were submitted to the New Hampshire Energy Facility Evaluation Committee ("EFSEC") and Federal Energy Regulatory Commission (FERC). This information is summarized in Table 2.

Sediment grain size distributions

In addition to the dimensional characteristics of the waterbodies crossed, substrate composition data was also needed as input to the computer model. Since existing substrate data from within these waterbodies was not available, the PNGTS/NEA substituted substrate composition data collected during a sediment sampling program performed on several rivers in Maine during August, 1997. The waterbodies sampled in Maine have characteristics similar to those crossed in New Hampshire. In general, most waterbodies in the region have substrates consisting of glacial till with surface characteristics determined by site-specific flow regimes. Therefore, waterbodies with comparable size and flow regime types can be expected to have similar substrate compositions. During the summer of 1997 the PNGTS/NEA conducted the *Maine Sediment Sampling Program* ("Program") at the proposed pipeline crossings of the Androscoggin, Presumpscot, and Great Works Rivers in Maine. Sediment grain size distribution was one of the parameters for which these waterbodies were analyzed. A summary of the particle distribution data from this Program is provided in Table 3. Comparative analysis of the size and flow regime type for these three waterbodies was also conducted for the purpose of assigning sediment grain size distributions to New Hampshire waterbody categories during computer modeling. Based on this representative comparison, each of the three major categories of waterbodies was correlated with a particle distribution as indicated in Table 3.

Major "High-Energy" and "Low-Energy" waterbodies are contrasted by their substrate compositions. "High-Energy" waterbodies contain higher proportions of heavy sediment particles such as cobbles and sands, while "Low-Energy" waterbodies contain higher proportions of light sediment particles such as silts and clays.

Particle settling velocities

Settling velocities for various particle sizes were presented in the Model. However, the data provided did not cover the entire sediment grain size distribution range that was documented from the Program. Therefore, a linear regression analysis of this relationship was conducted to develop an equation to expand the range for which data were available. The resulting equation, $Y = (0.122529)X - 0.003806$, had an R^2 of 0.9988 and a standard error of coefficient of 0.002999.

Sediment transport distances

Sediment transport distances were calculated within each waterbody category for each limiting particle size

Table 4. Summary of pipeline trench physical characteristics within waterbodies

Characteristic description	Value	Units
Average trench depth	3	m
Average trench bottom width	2	m
Average trench top width	6.8	m
Average trench side-slope ratio (horizontal:vertical)	0.8:1	–
Average trench cross-sectional area	13.2	square m
Average length for major waterbody	72.44	m
Average length for intermediate waterbody	6.91	m
Average length for minor waterbody	1.36	m
Major waterbody in-stream disturbance duration	30	h
Intermediate waterbody in-stream disturbance duration	12	h
Minor waterbody in-stream disturbance duration	8	h
Sediment volume lost from trench at $V_a = 0.2$ m/s	3.34[6]	%
Sediment volume lost from trench at $V_a = 0.4$ m/s	6.67[5]	%
Sediment volume lost from trench at $V_a = 0.6$ m/s	10.00[4]	%
Sediment volume lost from trench at $V_a = 0.8$ m/s	13.33[3]	%
Sediment volume lost from trench at $V_a = 1.0$ m/s	16.67[2]	%
Sediment volume lost from trench at $V_a = 1.2$ m/s	20.00[1]	%

utilizing the (Trow, 1996) equation $L = \{(D)(V_a)\}/V_s$, where: L is a transport distance (m); D is a depth of flow (m); V_a is an average streamflow velocity (m/s); and V_s is a settling velocity (m/s). Calculations for each waterbody category were generated with a range of streamflow velocities to simulate flow regimes that typically could be encountered in New Hampshire. The section of the waterbody between the "minimum particle size distance value" and the "maximum particle size distance value" for each defined particle type represents the zone of deposition for that particle type.

Sediment distribution characteristics
Utilizing the physical characteristics of each typical waterbody type, sediment transport distances, and physical characteristics of the pipeline trench, sediment distribution profiles were calculated as a function of streamflow velocity. Table 4 summarizes the physical characteristics of the pipeline trench and waterbodies, in-stream disturbance durations, and sediment loss percentages used for these calculations. Suspended solid values generated by the model are calculated as averages and do not reflect peak values associated with excavation and backfilling. Specifically, the model disperses the sediment loss volume evenly through the time period of construction disturbance within the waterbody.

Suspended solids concentration to turbidity level conversions
In an effort to expand the usefulness of the Model, the final output as suspended solids concentration was converted into turbidity levels (NTUs). Although direct correlation between suspended solids and turbidity must be determined on a site-specific stream basis, streams of similar substrate composition generally have similar correlations. The PNGTS/NEA obtained correlation equations (personal communication Scott Reid, Golder Associates, 1997), which are provided below, for waterbodies in western Canada that have similar glacial till substrate characteristics. These equations were developed by Golder Associates during extensive monitoring of eight pipeline construction crossings of five waterbodies. The resulting turbidity vs. suspended solids relationships from these equations were averaged and plotted. The averaging equation and plot were then modified to have a Y-intercept $\simeq 0$, which represents suspended solids concentration of 0 mg/l equal to turbidity level of 0 NTU. NTU = $\{(TSS)(0.880387)\} + 0.001946$ (modified averaging equation).

Summary and interpretation of computer modeling results
As previously mentioned, sediment distribution profiles were generated utilizing the Model for typical major "high-energy," major "low-energy," intermediate, and minor waterbodies crossed by the proposed Projects in New Hampshire. The integral components of this analysis consisting of:

Input Parameters:
– sediment grain size distributions;
– particle settling velocities;
– physical characteristics of the typical waterbody types;
– physical characteristics of the typical pipeline construction trench within a waterbody;
– average stream velocities representing various flow regimes; and
– proportional sediment loss ratios.

Output Parameters:
– a sediment transport distances for various particle sizes;
– sediment loss proportional to average stream velocity;

Table 5. Sediment transport characteristics calculated at various distances downstream of "wet" waterbody crossing

Parameter	Major "high-energy" waterbody						Major "low-energy" waterbody						Intermediate waterbody						Minor waterbody					
In-stream disturbance duration (h)[1]	30						30						12						8					
Average stream velocity (m/s)	0.2	0.4	0.6	0.8	1.0	1.2	0.2	0.4	0.6	0.8	1.0	1.2	0.2	0.4	0.6	0.8	1.0	1.2	0.2	0.4	0.6	0.8	1.0	1.2
6.56 feet (2 m) downstream of pipeline crossing																								
Turbidity levels (NTUs)	11	29	48	67	86	108	20	48	78	106	135	164	92	207	357	523	705	878	235	560	972	1421	1861	2316
Suspended solids concentration (mg/l)	13	33	54	76	98	123	23	55	89	121	153	186	105	254	406	595	801	998	267	636	1105	1615	2115	2633
Depth of sediment (mm)	25	46	58	77	92	110	23	43	46	48	50	68	50	88	101	89	74	61	22	78	154	198	224	243
Total sediment loss (metric tons)	54	107	163	217	270	325	54	107	163	217	270	325	5.2	10	16	21	26	31	1.0	2.0	3.1	4.1	5.1	6.1
1000 feet (304.8 m) downstream of pipeline crossing																								
Turbidity lvels (NTUs)	1	3	6	8	11	12	3	8	18	26	35	43	18	48	76	128	183	240	7	105	201	298	362	467
Suspended solids concentration (mg/l)	0.9	3.8	6.5	8.9	12	14	3.8	9.3	21	30	40	49	21	54	86	145	208	273	8.4	119	229	339	411	531
Depth of sediment (mm)	<0.1	0.7	1.0	1.3	1.4	1.5	0.1	0.5	1.4	1.6	1.8	1.9	0.1	0.2	0.7	1.2	2.1	2.6	0	0.2	0.3	0.3	0.4	0.4
2000 feet (609.6 m) downstream of pipeline crossing																								
Turbidity levels (NTUs)	1	2	4	6	9	11	3	7	12	20	29	37	8	37	66	95	123	153	—	15	112	209	304	383
Suspended solids concentration (mg/l)	0.8	2.8	4.3	6.8	9.7	12	3.1	8.5	14	23	33	42	9.5	42	75	108	140	174	—	17	127	237	346	435
Depth of sediment (mm)	<0.1	<0.1	0.2	0.6	0.9	1.0	0.1	0.1	0.2	0.8	1.1	1.4	<0.1	0.1	0.1	0..1	0.1	0.1	—	<0.1	0.2	0.2	0.3	0.3
3000 feet (914.4 m) downstream of pipeline crossing																								
Turbidity levels (NTUs)	0.5	2	3	4	6	10	2	7	11	15	22	31	—	27	55	85	113	143	—	—	22	120	218	297
Suspended solids concentration (mg/l)	0.6	2.6	3.8	5.0	7.3	11	2.4	7.7	12	17	25	35	—	31	63	97	128	162	—	—	25	136	248	338
Depth of sediment (mm)	<0.1	<0.1	<0.1	<0.1	0.3	0.6	<0.1	<0.1	0.1	0.1	0.4	0.8	—	0.1	0.1	0.1	0.1	0.1	—	—	<0.1	0.1	0.1	0.1

The data provided in this table represent average values calculated over the duration of construction disturbance. Actual in-stream values are expected to be instantaneously higher at some point during the construction process.
Shaded areas indicate sediment transport regimes which exceed turbidity levels of 10 NTUs.
(—) Turbidity plume dissipated before reaching indicated distance downstream of pipeline crossing.
[1] In-stream disturbance duration indicates the amount of time the equipment will actually be trenching and creating disturbance during the crossing. Actual pipe installation and restoration may take considerably longer.

- area of deposition for various particle sizes;
- depth of sediment for various deposition zones;
- suspended solids concentrations at downstream distances; and
- turbidity levels at downstream distances (obtained from correlation equations).

The results of the modeling effort for "wet" waterbody crossings, which are summarized in Table 5, represent average values calculated over the duration of construction disturbance. This table documents sediments transport characteristics at distances of 6.7, 1000, 2000, and 3000-feet, respectively. The 6.7-foot location represents conditions that occur at the pipeline crossing. The 1000-foot location represents the maximum allowable mixing zone length as stipulated in the Standards and Conditions. The 2000 and 3000-foot locations were generated for comparison purposes and represent conditions farther downstream of the crossing point. The actual in-stream turbidity values are expected to be instantaneously higher and lower at various points during the construction process. Specifically, the results indicate the following:

- Turbidity levels of ≤10 NTUs cannot be attained 2 m downstream of a pipeline crossing regardless of waterbody type or stream velocities.
- At the end of a 1000′ mixing zone, turbidity levels range from 1 to 467 NTUs. Turbidity levels of ≤10 NTUs can be attained at the slow to moderate stream flow regime major waterbody crossings, none of the intermediate waterbody crossings, and at only the slowest streamflow minor waterbody crossing.
- At the end of a 2000′ mixing zone, conditions improve only slightly over the 1000′ levels, with turbidity levels ranging from 1 to 383 NTUs. Turbidity levels of ≤10 NTUs attained at all but the fastest flow "high-energy" major waterbody, the two slowest flow regime "low-energy" major waterbodies, the slowest flow intermediate waterbody, and the slowest streamflow minor waterbody.
- At the end of a 3000′ mixing zone, conditions are similar to the 2000′ levels, with turbidity levels ranging from 0.5 to 297 NTUs. Turbidity levels of ≤10 NTUs attained at all of the "high-energy" major waterbodies, the two slowest flow regime "low-energy" major waterbodies, the slowest flow intermediate

Table 6. Summary of modified sediment transport analysis input parameters

Characteristic description	Value	Units
Intermediate waterbody "in-stream flush" duration	1	hours
Minor waterbody "in-stream flush" duration	1	hours
Sediment volume lost from trench at $V_a = 0.2$ m/s	0.11^6	%
Sediment volume lost from trench at $V_a = 0.4$ m/s	0.22^5	%
Sediment volume lost from trench at $V_a = 0.6$ m/s	0.33^4	%
Sediment volume lost from trench at $V_a = 0.8$ m/s	0.44^3	%
Sediment volume lost from trench at $V_a = 1.0$ m/s	0.55^2	%
Sediment volume lost from trench at $V_a = 1.2$ m/s	0.66^1	%

waterbody, and the two slowest streamflow minor waterbodies.

Based on the modeling results, the majority of the major, intermediate, and minor waterbodies proposed for "wet" crossings could not be crossed without exceeding the New Hampshire 10 NTU water quality standard at the end of the 1000-foot mixing zone at some point in the construction process. This would occur despite using approved industry standard techniques and BMPs.

Sediment transport analysis for "dry" waterbody crossings

Certain waterbodies, typically those less than 10-feet in width may be suitable for crossing using the flumed or pump-around "dry" crossing method. To assess the magnitude of sediment transport which would occur in New Hampshire waterbodies crossed using the "dry" method, the PNGTS/NEA modified the sediment transport analysis presented earlier. Because it is impracticable to conduct a dry crossing of a major waterbody, modeling for this size class was omitted. Although it is generally infeasible to conduct dry crossings of intermediate waterbodies, turbidity levels were calculated for comparison purposes. Although the same calculation algorithms were utilized, selected input parameter values were modified to represent the "quick-flush" which occurs after a "dry" crossing is complete and water barriers around the construction work area are removed. This "quick-flush" flow regime is very different from that which occurs during "wet" crossing and is characterized by very turbulent and high energy initial impact which suspends most of the sediments in a concentrated time period. A summary of the modified input parameters is provided in Table 6.

Summary and interpretation of computer modeling
Review of model outputs for the sediment transport characteristics between the "wet" and "dry" waterbody crossings, indicates they have very similar average turbidity values at comparable sediment transport distances. However, for "dry" crossings the volume of sediment loss and the duration of the turbidity plume is minimal in comparison. As previously stated, the results of the modeling effort for "wet" and "dry" waterbody crossings represent average values calculated over the duration of construction disturbance. It should be noted that the turbidity produced with either crossing method will have peak values associated with certain construction activities. These activities include excavation and backfilling for "wet" crossings and water barrier removal for "dry" crossings. Specifically, the modeling results for "dry" crossings, as summarized in Table 7 indicate the following:

– It is expected that New Hampshire water quality levels for turbidity *can* be maintained at the end of the 1000-foot mixing zone as per the Standards and Criteria during the trenching and pipe installation;
– Minimal amounts of total sediment removal as compared to "wet" crossings; and
– Turbidity levels will be elevated in manner similar to "wet" crossings, but only for the approximate 1-h "quick flush" period. Specifically, turbidity levels can be expected as follows:
– Turbidity levels of <10 NTUs cannot be obtained 2 m downstream of a pipeline crossing regardless of waterbody type or stream velocities.
– At the end of a 1000' mixing zone, turbidity levels range between 8 and 129 NTUs. Turbidity levels of <10 NTUs can be obtained at none of the intermediate waterbody crossings, and at only the slowest streamflow minor waterbody crossing. Results would be even less favorable at the end of a 500-foot mixing zone.

Based on these results, the Applicants believe that it may be possible to maintain the required turbidity standard during the construction process of typical minor waterbody crossing. However, the 10 NTU turbidity standard would typically be exceeded for a short period during the restoration period.

IMPACTS TO AQUATIC BIOTA

This section addresses potential impacts to aquatic biota caused by suspended solids and turbidity in a watercourse. Although substantial research has been done, impacts are variable depending upon nature of pollutant, duration of exposure, type of organism, water temperature, and season of the year. This section focuses on review of several recent studies performed

Table 7. Sediment transport characteristics measured at various distances downstream of "dry" waterbody crossing

Parameter	Intermediate waterbody[1]						Minor waterbody					
Post-disturbance "flush-time" (h)	1						1					
Average stream velocity (m/s)	0.2	0.4	0.6	0.8	1.0	1.2	0.2	0.4	0.6	0.8	1.0	1.2
6.56 feet (2 m) downstream of pipeline crossing												
Turbidity levels (NTUs)	36	88	140	204	275	343	62	107	251	370	484	603
Suspended solids concentration (mg/l)	41	100	159	232	313	390	70	121	285	420	550	685
Depth of sediment (mm)	1.7	2.9	3.2	1.7	3.3	2.1	0.7	2.6	5.0	7.0	8.0	8.0
Total sediment loss (metric tons)	0.15	0.35	0.50	0.70	0.85	1.0	0.05	0.05	0.10	0.15	0.15	0.20
1000 feet (304.8 m) downstream of pipeline crossing												
Turbidity levels (NTUs)	8	19	30	50	71	94	2	14	18	78	103	129
Suspended solids concentration (mg/l)	8.5	21	34	57	81	107	2.2	16	20	89	117	146
Depth of sediment (mm)	<0.1	<0.1	<0.1	<0.1	0.1	0.1	<0.1	<0.1	<0.1	<0.1	<0.1	<0.1
2000 feet (609.6 m) downstream of pipeline crossing												
Turbidity levels (NTUs)	3	15	26	37	48	60	—	4	29	53	79	105
Suspended solids concentration (mg/l)	3.8	17	29	42	55	68	—	4.5	33	62	90	119
Depth of sediment (mm)	<0.1	<0.1	<0.1	<0.1	<0.1	<0.1	—	<0.1	<0.1	<0.1	<0.1	<0.1
3000 feet (914.4 m) downstream of pipeline crossing												
Turbidity levels (NTUs)	—	11	22	33	44	55	—	—	6	32	56	82
Suspended solids concentration (mg/l)	—	12	25	38	50	63	—	—	6.5	36	64	93
Depth of sediment (mm)	—	<0.1	<0.1	<0.1	<0.1	<0.1	—	—	<0.1	<0.1	<0.1	<0.1

The data provided in this table represent average values calculated over the duration of construction disturbance. Actual in-stream values are expected to be instantaneously higher at some point during the construction process.
Shaded areas indicate sediment transport regimes, which exceed turbidity levels of 10 NTUs.
(—) Turbidity plume dissipated before reaching indicated distance downstream of pipeline crossing.
[1]Dry crossings of intermediate waterbodies are not typically feasible due to width and flow constraints.

specifically to attempt to quantify impacts to fishery resources caused by various levels of suspended solids and turbidity.

Introduction

Studies on the effect of sediments on fish and other aquatic organisms are extensively reviewed in Anderson et al. (1996). Various studies have shown that there is no easily defined concentration of suspended sediment above which fisheries are damaged and below which fisheries are protected (Alabaster and Lloyd, 1982; cf. Anderson et al., 1996).

Anderson et al. (1996) indicate that the response of biological receptors to environmental stresses is complex. Many factors may influence the actual severity of effect that are caused by a sediment release episode, including:
– characteristics of the particles suspended;
– temperature of the water; and
– the existing stress level within the receiving environment.

Despite the difficulties associated with quantifying impacts to aquatic resources, Newcombe and MacDonald (1991), Newcombe (1994), Newcombe and Jensen (1996), and Anderson et al. (1996) have developed theoretical models in an attempt to provide guidelines or criteria for the protection of fish populations.

Analysis and discussion
PNGTS/NEA utilized models and analytical techniques developed by the above-mentioned authors to attempt to quantify impacts to fisheries that may be created by construction of the proposed pipeline and its resultant suspended sediment and turbidity. The analysis attempted to evaluate impacts to fisheries that may occur immediately downstream of the construction zone and at the end of the New Hampshire Department of Environmental Services ("NHDES") proposed 1000-foot mixing zone. Suspended sediment concentrations calculated herein using sediment data from the PNGTS Maine sediment sampling program along with anticipated exposure duration data (24, 36, and 72 h) were used to predict the potential impact of suspended sediment episodes on fish life history stages. For each life history stage, Severity of Effect (SEV) classifications (Table 1 from Newcombe and Jensen 1996) were estimated for each of four age class/sediment size categories and one habitat category (Anderson et al., 1996):

– Juvenile and Adult Salmonids (particle sizes 0.5–250 µm);
– Adult Salmonids (particle sizes 0.5–250 µm);
– Juvenile Salmonids (particle sizes 0.5–75 µm);
– Eggs and Larvae of Salmonids and Non-Salmonids (particle sizes 0.5–75 µm);
– Adult Freshwater Non-Salmonids (particle sizes 0.5–75 µm);
– Habitat Effects.

Table 8. Scale of severity for ill effects associated with suspended solids

SEV #	Description of effect
Nil effect	
0	No behavioral effects
1	Alarm reaction
2	Abandonment of cover
3	Avoidance response
Behavioral effects	
4	Short-term reduction in feeding rates; Short-term reduction in feeding success
5	Minor physiological stress: increase in the rate of coughing; increased respiration rate
6	Moderate physiological stress
7	Moderate habitat degradation; Impaired homing
4	Short-term reduction in feeding rates; Short-term reduction in feeding success
5	Minor physiological stress: increase in the rate of coughing; increased respiration rate
6	Moderate physiological stress
7	Moderate habitat degradation; Impaired homing
8	Indications of major physiological stress: long-term reduction in feeding rate; long-term reduction in feeding success; poor condition
Lethal and paralethal effects	
9	Reduced growth rate; Delayed hatching; Reduced fish density
10	0–20% mortality; Increased predation; Moderate to severe habitat degradation
11	>20–40% mortality
12	>40–60% mortality
13	>60–80% mortality
14	>80–100% mortality

SEV estimates were made for multiple waterbody types (Major High and Low Energy, Intermediate, and Minor), stream velocity (0.2–1.2 m/s), and fish family (salmonid or non-salmonid) for each of the categories above using the multiple regression model developed by Newcombe and Jensen (1996). The model was run assuming the performance of a wet crossing, with periods of turbidity extending for up to 72-h. The model was not used to predict impacts associated with the 1-h turbidity event that would occur with a "dry" crossing. Generalized habitat effects were predicted using the multiple regression model developed by Anderson et al. (1996). Table 8 presents a 0–14 scale of the severity of ill effects in relation to four major classes of effect as presented in Newcombe and Jensen (1996). The four major classes of effect include: nil effect; behavior effects; sublethal effects; and lethal effects.

Results and conclusion

– The results of the modeling show that moderate behavioral effects to salmonids and non-salmonids may occur due to the levels of suspended solids and turbidity created by a typical wet crossing. However, no paralethal or lethal effects on salmonids and non-salmonids are anticipated 1000 feet from the source of disturbance.
– One of the assumptions of the models is that fish would remain in the turbidity plume and be subjected to the various levels of suspended sediments for extended periods of time. In reality, it can be expected that fish will display the avoidance response to the extent possible and vacate the areas of highest concentrations. Furthermore, it can be expected that peak levels of turbidity will not extend beyond 48 h, thus fewer effects are anticipated. In the case of "dry" crossings, turbidity plumes will be extremely brief in duration (<1 h), thus having an insignificant effect on fishery resources.
– Potential paralethal effects could occur to salmonid and non-salmonids eggs and larvae (Newcombe and Jensen, 1996). However, the construction window imposed by the FERC of June 1–September 30 avoids the period when most eggs or larval fish will be present in the waterbody, thus substantially minimizing the effect of suspended sediment and turbidity and habitat degradation due to silt deposition. Furthermore, sediment transport modeling indicates minimal silt deposition particularly for "dry" crossings.

SUMMARY AND CONCLUSIONS

States water quality standards and criteria related to turbidity and mixing zones are primarily applicable to long-term point discharges of pollutants that have the potential to result in significant degradation of water quality. Short-term discharges associated with temporary construction activities such as pipeline construction do not fit well with the standards and criteria related to turbidity and mixing zones.

Well-documented case studies on recent pipeline construction projects show that turbidity levels during normal stream crossing activities typically exceed the states turbidity standards even when applying all appropriate Best Management Practices. Various states have recognized the difficulty of applying turbidity standards designed for long-term point discharges to the short-term disturbances caused by pipeline construction, and have attempted to identify allowable tolerances, mixing zones, and time windows to enable the construction process to proceed.

The analysis contained herein demonstrates the following basic conclusions:
– Sediment transport modeling using sediment data and stream size/flow characteristics applicable to the New Hampshire project area predict temporary turbidity levels significantly higher than the New Hampshire turbidity standard at the end of the allowed mixing zone. Even when utilizing the most

protective dry crossing techniques, sediment transport modeling predicts exceeding on a short-term basis the 10 NTU turbidity standard.
- Recent research on predicted suspended sediment and turbidity impacts to fishery resources show that impacts to fishery resources can be expected to be generally minor and short term. The sediment transport modeling predicts that the turbidity levels generated during pipeline construction of the projects were not expected to have a significant effect on aquatic resources.

REFERENCES

Alabaster, J.S. and R. Lloyd. 1982. Finely divided solids. In: Water Quality Criteria for Freshwater Fish, 2nd ed. J.S. Alabaster and R. Lloyd eds. Butterworth, London. pp. 1–20.

Anderson, P.G., B.R. Taylor, and G.C. Balch. 1996. Quantifying the Effects of Sediment Release on Fish and their Habitats. Canadian Manuscript Report of Fisheries and Aquatic Sciences No. 2346. 109 pp.

Golder Associates Ltd. 1997. Suspended Sediment and Turbidity Criteria Associated with In-stream Construction Activities; An Assessment of Biological Relevance. Report submitted to the Interstate Natural Gas Association of America. Golder Associates Ltd. Calgary, Alberta, Canada.

Florida Gas Transmission–Phase III Expansion Project (FGT-III). 1994. Spreads 3b, 4, & 5: Monthly Report — November 14, 1994. FGT-III. Tallahassee, FL.

Newcombe, C.P. and J.O.T. Jensen. 1996. Channel suspended sediment and fisheries: A synthesis for qualitative assessment of risk and impact. North American Journal of Fisheries Management, 16: 693–727.

Newcombe, C.P. 1994. Suspended Sediments in Aquatic Ecosystems: Ill Effects as a Function of Concentration and Duration of Exposure. Habitat Protection Branch, British Columbia Ministry of Environmental, Lands and Parks. Victoria, BC, Canada. 298 pp.

Newcombe, C.P. and D.D. MacDonald. 1991. Effects of suspended sediments on aquatic ecosystems. North American Journal of Fisheries Management, 11: 72–82.

State of Florida Department of Environmental Protection (FDEP). 1993. Intent to Grant Variance–Florida Gas Transmission Company — File No. VE-03-646. FDEP. Tallahassee, FL.

Trow Engineering Consultants Inc. 1996. Waterbody Crossing Design and Installation Manual. Report submitted to the Offshore and Onshore Design Applications Supervisory Committee of the Pipeline Research Committee at the American Gas Association. Trow Engineering Consultants Inc. Tallahassee, FL.

BIOGRAPHICAL SKETCHES

H. Wayne Harper, PE

Portland Natural Gas Transmission System, 18 Commons Avenue, Windham, ME 04062, USA, (207) 892-0781, fax: (207) 892-4786, e-mail: WHarper@pngts.com

Mr. Harper is a professionally licensed environmental engineer with over thirteen years experience performing a variety of environmental studies, assessments, permitting, and inspection. His experience includes extensive activities with natural gas pipeline environmental design, permitting, training, construction inspection, quality assurance, restoration, and operations, as well as numerous natural surface water, groundwater, and stormwater quality monitoring projects. Over the past four years, Mr. Harper has been dedicated to the successful permitting, environmental construction implementation, and restoration of the Portland Natural Gas Transmission System (PNGTS) North-Section Facilities and PNGTS/Maritimes & Northeast Joint Facilities Pipeline Projects. Currently, Mr. Harper serves as PNGTS' Environmental, Health, & Safety Manager.

Roger J. Trettel

Northern Ecological Associates, Inc., 451 Presumpscot Street, Portland, ME 04103, USA, (207) 879-9496, fax: (207) 879-9481, e-mail: rtrettel@neamaine.com

As a Principal of Northern Ecological Associates, Inc. (NEA) and a specialist in environmental impact assessment and restoration ecology, Mr. Trettel has over 18 years experience in the environmental field. Mr. Trettel holds a BS in Forest Science and an MS in Wetland Ecology. Mr. Trettel's experience includes management of comprehensive environmental programs for the planning, assessment, permitting, construction, inspection, restoration, and monitoring of natural gas pipeline development projects. A certified Professional Wetland Scientist (PWS), Mr. Trettel also has extensive experience performing wetland, vegetation, and biological analyses and developing wetland and wildlife habitat mitigation and restoration plans. In addition, Mr. Trettel manages and prepares Environmental Impact Statements (EISs), Environmental Assessments (EAs), and Environmental Reports (ERs) for proposed development projects.

An Investigation into the Influence of Marine Pipelines and Cables on Benthic Ecology and Biodiversity

Randal G. Glaholt, Michelle Nunas, and Stacey Ong

Installation of bottom-founded marine pipelines and cables involves an initial disturbance usually resulting in the creation of a new linear substrate. The effect of these two elements on the ecology of benthic organisms and marine biodiversity depends on facility siting, design characteristics of the facility, construction methods and the receiving environment. While consideration is given to direct construction-related impacts, the biological consequence of the creation of new linear substrate on feeding, reproduction, predation, distribution and dispersal of benthic organisms has for the most part received little attention. This paper explores the potential for marine pipelines and cables to impact species movement and dispersal, habitat availability, boundary layer ecology, predation and the marine acoustic environment. Data are analyzed based on available literature, laboratory simulation, *in situ* field measurements and field inspection. Data from laboratory study suggests pipelines can act as barriers to the movement of some benthic species (e.g., crabs), an effect likely mediated by several biological and physical factors. The extent to which other residual ecological or hydrological barriers may occur is unclear. As a source of new hard substrate, pipelines are readily colonized by a variety of sessile marine organisms and so act as artificial reefs. During a reconnaissance of an exposed marine pipeline in temperate coastal waters of British Columbia, a minimum of 24 species of encrusting organisms and associated fish species were recorded. A case can be made that pipelines affect benthic communities through alteration of boundary layer processes, near bottom current dynamics and induced scour. Data obtained on pipeline noise and observed pipeline colonization by numerous benthic organisms suggest pipeline noise per se, is not a deterrent to certain invertebrate communities. The effect of electro magnetic radiation from cables is unresolved. Recommendations are made concerning facility siting, construction procedures and future research.

Keywords: Marine pipelines, benthic ecolosystem, biodiversity, Dungeness crab, sea cucumber

INTRODUCTION

Installation and operation of marine pipelines and cables has been undertaken globally for over 50 years. It is likely that well in excess of 200,000 km of marine pipeline and cable have been installed globally. Up to and including 1998, there were ≈46,046 km of marine pipeline installed in the Gulf of Mexico alone (Oil and Gas Journal, 1999). Marine pipelines occur in most offshore oil and gas producing areas while cables are more broadly distributed. Marine cables are typically small diameter (e.g., <10 cm), while marine pipelines can reach 122 cm in diameter and may be installed in water depths exceeding 2000 m. Pipelines are typically trenched or buried in shallow water to protect them from natural and human physical damage, for thermal protection as well as to reduce interference with coastal ecosystems and fisheries. In deeper waters pipelines and cables are typically laid on top of the substrate, this may also be done to minimize risk associated with seismic events. While typically avoided, unsupported "free spans" on marine pipelines can occur where there are irregular bottom contours. In some cases these spans require supports, which may include steel jack-up supports, grout bag supports and/or articulating concrete mattresses. Burial may involve replacement of trench spoil, allowing natural in-fill of the trench, rock dumps, or use flanges or "spoilers" which can facilitate self-burial in certain instance.

Concern over the environmental consequences of marine pipeline construction and related activities has primarily focused on the potential to physically remove or damage sensitive benthic communities (e.g., seagrass beds or corals), sediment generation, potential for accidental release of hydrocarbons or other contaminants and interference with commercially important fisheries (Essink, 1999; and US Environmental Protection Agency, 1980). Increasing concern over the maintenance of ecological integrity and biodiversity of marine environments as well as pipeline related issues raised by the public (e.g., suggesting pipelines may act as barriers) suggest further ecological examination of marine pipelines and cables is warranted. This paper explores the potential for marine pipelines and cables to act as barriers to the movement of benthic organisms, to act as artificial reefs, conduits for genetic exchange and species introduction, as well as their potential influence on marine ecosystems through boundary layer effects, pipeline scour and noise. Not withstanding their potential for generation of electro-magnetic field effects, cables can be considered essentially small diameter pipelines.

METHODS

This investigation relied on literature review, internet search, communication with other research institutions, laboratory simulation, *in situ* field measurements and field inspection. Details of the experimental component and field measurements are provided below.

Pipeline crossing experiment

A laboratory experiment was conducted at the Government of Canada, Fisheries and Oceans Canada (DFO) West Vancouver Laboratory, British Columbia to examine the response of Dungeness crab (*Cancer magister*), California sea cucumber (*Parastichopus californicus*) and green sea urchin (*Strongylocentrotus droebachiensis*) to segments of 53 cm, outside diameter (OD), concrete coated pipe. Of particular interest was to determine if Dungeness crab, California sea cucumber and green sea urchin were physically capable and or behaviorally inclined to cross pipe segments that were either 100% exposed or 50% exposed. The experimental test period was kept relatively short (e.g., 72 h for each experimental run) in order to maximize the opportunity for experiment replication. In regard to run duration, it was believed more germane that the organism in question did or did not cross the pipe within a relatively short period of time than a longer period of time. Crossing in a longer period of time would be less likely to rule out a potentially significant ecological effect caused by a delay in movement. The experiment was conducted between May 1, 2000 and June 28, 2000. Four, 4000-litre tanks were leased from the DFO West Vancouver Laboratory. Continuous water exchange was provided by a flow-through seawater system. A cylindrical pipe segment 2.1 m long was placed in the middle of three of the four tanks on a 10 cm sand base. Two of these pipes were left to lie on the sand surface to represent a 100% exposed marine pipe segment. In the third tank, additional sand was added to leave the pipe 50% exposed above the sand. The fourth tank was used as a control and had a 10 cm sand base. During an initial trial run of the experiment it was determined that the crabs would at times crawl on top of each other in the corner formed by the pipe and the curved wall of the tank and get over the pipe. In order to defeat this problem, plastic panels were placed against the pipe to create a wall, which extended 40 cm along the pipe from the tank wall and approximately 100 cm vertically.

Crabs were obtained from a commercial crab fisherman fishing in the vicinity of Cowichan Bay, Satellite Channel and Plumper Sound along the southeast coast of Vancouver Island, Canada. Collections of female crabs were done under a *Licence to Fish for Scientific, Experimental or Educational Purposes* issued by DFO. Males were significantly larger than females (Mann Whitney $U = 238.0$, $n = 244$ male, 103 female; $P < 0.001$). Each crab was given a identifying number, applied with permanent waterproof marker, and then randomly assigned to one of the four tanks. Ten crabs were placed on the same side of each tank. Four crab experiments were conducted: commercial-sized (carapace width > 16.5 cm, mean = 18.4 cm, SD = 1.15) male crabs with and without attractant and female crabs (mean carapace width = 14.9 cm, SD = 1.13) with and without attractant. Due to time limitations on facility availability, the female — attractant experiment was terminated after the first run. All tanks were kept covered throughout the experiment except when the viewing panels were opened to determine which side of the pipe each crab was on. Crabs were acclimated in the control tank for approximately 24 h before being assigned to a treatment. Each run lasted 72 h, with tanks monitored at 4-h intervals for the first 12 h and then at 6-h intervals thereafter. Each experiment was run three times using new crabs on each run. For the attractant experiments, fresh squid was placed in a perforated, sealed plastic container anchored to a concrete block placed in each tank.

Statistical analysis was done using SPSS Version 9. A Kolmogorov–Smirnov test was used to determine whether crab size and number of crossings were normally distributed. Crab size was not normally distributed where both genders were combined but was normally distributed where genders were separate.

The number of crossings was not normally distributed whether genders were combined or separate. Due to departures from normality associated with the number of crossings, non-parametric tests were used [Mann–Whitney, Kruskal–Wallis "test" (Sokal and Rohlf, 1981)]. Logistic regression was used to further examine the relationship between crab size and probability of an individual crossing the experimental pipeline segments while regression analysis was used to examine the relationship between crab size and total number of crossings.

The same experimental design was used to examine the response of California sea cucumber and green sea urchin to the pipe. It became very apparent these two echinoderm species were capable and inclined to readily traverse all surfaces in the tank including the pipe segment, tank walls and plastic corner guards. A suitable barrier material to force these two species to either cross the pipe or remain confined to one side of the tank was not found in the time the tanks were available. Data was obtained on substrate occupation for these 2 species over 12 observation periods for one 72-h experimental run. Observed vs expected frequency of substrate occupation was examined using Chi square analysis. Observations were corrected for available surface area. Area available for tank walls was 7.6 m^2, for 100% exposed pipe area 2 m^2 and for sand bottom 4.7 m^2. An underwater video camera was used to obtain video documentation of each species response at the end of the experiment.

Epifaunal colonization of an existing pipeline

An underwater survey was conducted of two existing 25.4 cm diameter, epoxy coated, marine pipelines located in the nearshore environment of the Strait of Georgia, British Columbia on June 22, 2000. Three divers examined an approximate 80 m segment of pipe at depths ranging from 25 to 43 m. A high-resolution color video camera was used to record the surveyed section and facilitate subsequent species identification and cover analysis.

Gas pipeline acoustic signature measurement

Measurements of acoustic frequency and energy were taken at 1, 5, 10, and 15 m above one of two high pressure pipelines referred to above, on June 21, 2000. Ambient water temperatures were in the range of approximately 12°C at the time of sampling. The pipelines acoustic signature was measured using a broadband acoustic sampler/data logger on loan from the DFO, Institute of Ocean Sciences in Sidney, British Columbia. The sampler and hydrophone assembly had a full bandwidth frequency range of 5.4 Hz to 22,050 Hz and a 44,100 Hz sampling rate. Full 22.5 dB gain was used for all recordings and ≈3–5 minutes of data were recorded at each location/depth. Reference ambient noise levels were recorded approximately 1000 m away and a similar distance offshore for comparative purposes.

RESULTS AND DISCUSSION

Pipeline crossing experiment

Results of the laboratory experiment to examine the response of Dungeness crab, California sea cucumber and green sea urchin to a 53 cm OD concrete coated pipeline are summarized in the sub-sections which follow.

Commercial-sized male crabs — No attractant

There was a slightly significant (Fisher's Exact Test; $P = 0.055$) decrease in the percentage of adult male crabs crossing the 100% exposed pipe (81.8%; 54) compared with the control tank (96.9%; 31) while there was no significant difference (Fisher's Exact Test: $P = 1.000$) in the number of male crabs crossing the 50% exposed pipe segment (93.9%; 31) compared with the percentage crossing the control tank (96.9%; 31). Follow-up tests indicate that there was significantly ($P < 0.001$) more crossings (includes multiple crossings by the same individual) of the control tank than for tanks with 100% ($P = 0.001$) and 50% exposed pipe segments ($P = 0.005$) by commercial-sized males. Similarly there was significantly more crossing of the 50% exposed pipe than 100% exposed pipe ($P = 0.013$).

Commercial-sized male crabs — Attractant vs. no attractant

There were no significant differences ($P > 0.05$) between number of crossings, the percentage of individuals crossing, or percentage of individuals crossing within the first 24 h vs. the remaining 48 h, for males when an attractant was and was not present for the 100 and 50% exposed pipe segments.

Female crabs — No attractant

A significantly smaller percentage (33.3%; 17) of female crabs crossed the 100% exposed pipe segment compared with the percentage crossing the control tank (96.3%; 26). Conversely there was no significant difference in the percentage of females crossing the 50% exposed pipe (88.0%; 22) when compared with the percentage crossing the control tank (96.3%; 26).

Males vs. females — No attractant

There were significantly more ($P < 0.05$) male crossings overall and individual males that crossed the 100% exposed pipe than females. For the 50% exposed pipe there were significantly more ($P < 0.05$) male crossings as well, however, the percentage of individuals that crossed was not significantly different (Fisher's Exact Test: $P = 0.642$). There were no significant differences ($P > 0.05$) between males and females for the number of crossings or the percentage of individuals crossing in the control tank.

Time to cross

For males in the 100% exposed pipe treatment, 61.5% (no attractant) and 60% (attractant) crossed in the first 24 h. For the 50% exposed pipe 75.9% (no attractant) and 82.1% (attractant) of crossed within the first 24 h. A slightly higher percentage crossed the control tank (76.7% with no attractant; 89.3% with attractant). For males in the absence of an attractant, there were no significant differences (Pearson statistic, $P = 0.265$) between treatments in the time to cross. With an attractant present there was a significant difference (Pearson statistic, $P = 0.011$) between treatments in time to cross.

In the case of females (only tested in the absence of an attractant), 57.9% crossed the 100% exposed pipe segment in the first 24 h compared with 45.8% for the 50% exposed pipe and 66.7% for the control tank. For females, differences in time to cross between treatments were not significant (Pearson statistic, $P = 0.323$ exposed pipe treatment (82.1%) compared with the 100% exposed treatment (60%).

Crab size as a predictor of crossing success and frequency

The results of the regression determined that for a 100% exposed 53 cm OD pipe segment, crab size was a highly significant ($P < 0.001$, Nagelkerke R-squared = 0.306) predictor of the probability of crossing such that the larger the crab, the higher the probability of crossing. The low Nagelkerke R-square value indicates other substantive factors likely also contribute to crossing success. The relationship is expressed by the following equation:

$$\text{Probability of a given crab crossing} = \frac{e^{[-9.630+0.607(w)]}}{1+e^{[-9.630+0.607(w)]}},$$

where w is a carapace width.

A 16 cm carapace width crab would, by this model, have a probability of crossing of $P = 0.52$. For the 50% exposed pipeline crab size is not a significant predictor ($P = 0.399$) for the probability of crossing. It is likely that both the significance and r-squared values would increase if a broader size range of crabs examined.

The data indicate that crab size is also a significant ($P < 0.001$, r-square = 0.258) predictor of the number of times a crab will cross a 100% exposed, 53 cm diameter pipe segment. The low r-square value suggests other substantive factors likely contribute to number of crossings by an individual. The relationship is given by the equation:

$$\text{No. Crossings} = -4.927 + 0.366(w).$$

Solving for zero suggests the minimum size to cross the pipe would be >13.5 cm carapace width. For the 50% exposed pipe segment the r-squared coefficient was substantively reduced though crab size was still a slightly significant predictor ($P = 0.0498$)

Fig. 1. Dungeness crab climbing the side of 100% exposed 53 cm OD (outside diameter) concrete coated pipe segment.

of the number of crossings by an individual. Again, experimentation on a broader size range of crabs would likely increase the significance and r-squared values.

Videotape taken of the Dungeness crabs at the end of the experiment documented both successful and unsuccessful attempts at climbing the pipe surface (Fig. 1). In addition to actively crossing the pipe many individuals used the sand-pipe interface and sand-tank interface for cover. Where the pipe was challenged, failure to climb the pipe appeared related to difficulty to obtain a claw hold on the concrete. It is anticipated that natural colonization of a newly installed pipeline by marine organisms (e.g., tubeworms, encrusting sponges, and corals) would reduce the significance of this effect on Dungeness crab over time. While possible, it is not a given that particularly small crabs will have more difficulty traversing a pipe or cable. Surface irregularities and roughness may be amplified for smaller crabs as their claw size and mass is reduced, and as such, they may have less difficulty within some size range. The overall barrier effect on crabs is likely mediated by diameter of the pipe, the amount of pipe exposed above grade, the inherent and acquired surface roughness and the size of crab involved. The consequence of any potential obstruction effect on Dungeness crab, and others, can also be expected to be tempered by the nature and frequency of "free span" sections that may develop as a result of scour or occur naturally as a result of seabed irregularities.

Sea cucumber and green sea urchin

An attempt was also made to experimentally examine whether a 53 cm OD concrete pipe, would inhibit the movement of California sea cucumbers and green sea urchins. It was apparent these two species could and would readily cross the exposed pipeline as well as traverse all tank surfaces. Sea cucumber exhibited a statistically significant ($P < 0.001$) greater frequency of association with the tank walls than either the sand bottom or concrete coated pipe while green sea urchins showed a significantly ($P < 0.001$) greater frequency of association with the concrete coated pipe than the sand bottom or tank walls (in all cases observations were corrected for an equal availability of surface area for each of the three options (tank walls, sand bottom and pipe segment). The tube feet associated with echinoderms provide these organisms with a capacity to climb both very smooth and rough surfaces. Organisms which rely on suction or surface tension for locomotion (e.g., echinoderms, nudibranchs and snails) are, in the absence of an ecological avoidance response to hard-bottom substrate, likely to have no difficulty traversing a pipe segment.

To the extent pipelines and cables are not colonized and/or are particularly smooth, a barrier effect may deter some organisms from optimizing their feeding, predator avoidance, and reproductive strategy. Soft-bottom adapted motile organisms would in certain instances have to "run the gauntlet" across substrate which may harbor predators. The pelagic nature of the reproductive cells/gametes and or eggs and larvae of most marine invertebrates and vertebrates suggests that they would be relatively unaffected by a linear, relatively low profile structure such as a marine pipeline or cable. However, where these biotic elements depend on either boundary layer phenomenon or near surface drift for dispersal or transport of essential nutrients (e.g., benthic algal drift) some effect could occur (see also the pipelines as corridors for genetic exchange and species dispersal section). The magnitude of this latter effect would be strongly mediated by a number of hydrological, biological and design elements. Given their typically much smaller diameter, marine cables and fiber optic lines can be expected to have a negligible barrier effect relative to large diameter pipelines.

Pipelines as artificial reefs

Bottom-founded marine pipelines and cables create a new source of hard-bottom substrate available for colonization by marine biota and share characteristics and issues in common with other artificial reefs and hard-bottom substrate community complexes. The two structural habitat types potentially associated with these installations involve an exposed pipe or cable segment and a nearshore segment typically covered by a rock dump layer. The latter may not be present where the pipeline has been deep buried in native sediments or installed using a horizontal directional drill.

This study examined a pair of exposed, epoxy coated steel pipelines off the coast of British Columbia using underwater video. The pipe was examined nine years after installation. During the reconnaissance, a total of 24 species of invertebrate, vertebrate and algal species were positively identified growing on and in close association with the pipeline (Fig. 2; Table 1). Sixteen species of conspicuous macro-benthos were recorded on the adjacent soft-bottom habitats. More

Fig. 2. Sponges and calcareous tube worms colonizing sections of two small marine pipelines, nine years after construction.

species of fish were recorded in association with the pipe than either the gravel/boulder cap or adjacent soft-bottom substrate. The most conspicuous biotic elements associated with the pipe were calcareous *Serpulid* tube worms, which were estimated to cover in excess of 50% of the lateral surface of the pipe segment from 25 to 43 m depth and encrusting coraline algae and sponges. Colonization by calcareous tube worms appeared restricted to the sides and bottom of the pipe. This may be attributable to sediment build up on the pipe, though this factor did not preclude colonization by anemones, boot and cloud sponge and crinoids.

The observed presence of cloud and boot sponges was likely contributing to habitat suitability along the pipe for fish species such as quillback rockfish (*Sebastes maliger*), copper rockfish (*Sebastes caurinus*) and cabezon (*Scorpaenichthys marmoratus*) which were also observed. The largest cloud sponges observed had grown to over 20 cm in the nine years since pipeline construction. The gravel and boulder cap areas observed at above 25 m depth were colonized by a slightly different assemblage of species. This area was notable in providing suitable substrate for a variety of seaweeds including sugar wrack kelp and an introduced *Sargassum* species. This area had been previously colonized by eelgrass. Even small diameter marine phone cables can provide sufficient hard substrate to promote establishment of alternate species assemblages. For example, the marine telephone cable located in an area dominated by fine sediments in the middle of the southern Strait of Georgia hosts the anemone *Metridium senile* and other epilithic organisms (Levings et al., 1983).

A number of researchers have reported that artificial reefs increase food, shelter, habitat availability, and provide a means for orientation for pelagic species (Grossman, et al., 1997; Love et al., 1994; Bohnsack, 1989; Alevizon and Gorham, 1989). Fish appear to be naturally attracted to suitable habitats that are less crowded (Coll et al., 1998), conversely fish that are inhabiting adequate environments spend little time

Table 1. Species observed in association with a marine pipeline in the Strait of Georgia, British Columbia

Common name	Latin name	Zones[1]		
		ADJ.	EXP.	G/B CAP.
eelgrass	*Zostera marina*	x		
sea lettuce	*Ulva complex*	x		
sugar wrack kelp	*Laminaria saccharina*	x		x
sea collander	*Agarum fimbriatum*			x
sargassum	*Sargassum muticum*			x
red spaghetti seaweed	*Sarcodiotheca gaudichaudii*			x
unknown bladed and branching red algae	*Rhodophyta*			x
cup and saucer sponge	*Constantinea simplex*			x
red rock crust	*Hildebrandia* sp.			x
pink rock crust	*Lithothamnium complex*		x	x
boot sponge	*Rhabdocalyptus dawsoni*		x	x
cloud sponge	*Aphrocallistes vastus*		x	
yellow boring sponge	*Cliona celata*			x
orange finger sponge	*Neoesperiopsis rigida*			x
Iophon sponge	*Iophon chelifer*		x	
velvety red sponge	*Ophlitaspongia pennata*			x
wine-glass hydroid	*Obelia* sp.			x
white sea pen	*Virgularia* sp.	x		
tube-dwelling anemone	*Pachycerianthus fimbriatus*	x		
crimson anemone	*Cribrinopsis fernaldi*		x	x
white-spotted swimming anemone	*Stomphia didemon*		x	x
tall plumose anemone	*Metridium giganteum*		x	x
jointed tubeworm	*Spiochaetopterus costarum*	x		
multicoloured calcareous tubeworm	*Serpula veermicularis*			x
pale calcareous tubeworm	*Crucigera* sp.		x	
giant white calcareous tubeworm	*Protula* sp.		x	
Lewis' moonsnail	*Polinices lewisi*			x
carinate dovesnail	*Alia carinata*	x		
western lean nassa	*Nassarius mendicus*	x		
swimming or pink scallop	*Chlamys* spp.		x	
Nuttall's cockle	*Clinocardium nuttallii*			x
common acorn barnacle	*Balanus glandula*	x		
common gray mysid	unknown			x
rough patch shrimp	*Pandalus stenolepis*		x	
threespine shrimp	*Heptacarpus tridens*		x	
Bering hermit	*Pagurus beringanus*		x	
miscellaneous bryozoans	*Bugula* sp.		x	x
feather star	*Florometra serratissima*	x	x	x
vermilion star	*Mediaster aequalis*	x		x
leather star	*Dermasterias imbricata*			x
rose star	*Crossaster papposus*			x
morning sun star	*Solaster dawsoni*			x
mottled star	*Evasterias troscheli*			x
long rayed star	*Orthasterias koehleri*		x	
purple star or ochre star	*Pisaster ochraceus*			x
sunflower star	*Pycnopodia helianthoides*			x
daisy brittle star	*Ophiopholis aculeata*			x
green sea urchin	*Strongylocentrotus droebachiensis*			x
armoured sea cucumber	*Psolus chitonoides*		x	x
white sea cucumber	*Eupentacta quinquesemita*			x
giant sea cucumber	*Parastichopus californicus*	x		x
transparent tunicate	*Corella willmeriana*		x	
glassy tunicate	*Ascidia paratropa*		x	x
broadbase tunicate	*Cnemidocarpa finmarkiensis*			x
blackeye gobie	*Coryphopterus nicholsi*	x		
northern ronquil	*Ronquilus jordani*	x		
copper rockfish	*Sebastes caurinus*		x	
quillback rockfish	*Sebastes maliger*		x	x
tiger rockfish	*Sebastes nigrocinctus*		x	
kelp greenling	*Hexagrammos decagrammus*			x
lingcod	*Ophiodon elongatus*		x	
scalyhead sculpin	*Artedius harringtoni*			x
cabezon	*Scorpaenichthys marmoratus*		x	

Table 1. (continued)

Common name	Latin name	Zones[1]		
		ADJ.	EXP.	G/B CAP.
spotfin sculpin	*Icelinus tenuis*	x		
rock sole	*Pleuronectes bilineata*	x		
Total Number of Taxa		16	24	39
Total Number of Unique Taxa		12	13	27

[1] ADJ is a soft bottom adjacent to pipeline; EXP is an exposed pipeline; G/B CAP is a gravel or boulder cap.

exploring. The suggestion being that a pipeline or cable may help offset density dependent constraints on certain species suited to hard-bottom substrates.

Although artificial reefs in low productivity areas are readily colonized (Armstrong, 1993; Bohnsack, 1989), some fear that they may only result in a redistribution and concentration of existing individuals, thereby rendering the stocks more susceptible to over fishing (Grossman, et al., 1997; Danner et al., 1994). Others believe that when fish migrate from natural areas to artificial reefs they create habitat openings for new fish to colonize in the natural reefs resulting in an overall increase in biomass (Love et al., 1994; Bohnsack, 1989). It is generally assumed that there are more larvae that are capable of settling on natural reefs than there are resources available for settlement (Bohnsack, 1989).

Where artificial reefs are placed can affect the productivity of the artificial reef as well as the natural habitats surrounding it (Carr and Hixon, 1997). It has been suggested that if larvae grow better on natural reefs but are intercepted by an artificial reef that is placed up-current of the natural reef then the natural reef's productivity may for a time decrease (Carr and Hixon, 1997). An artificial reef may also result in changes to the adjacent sediment through the introduction of the shells from fouling organisms onto the surrounding sediment. This phenomenon was observed during the pipeline reconnaissance reported above. Jones et al. (1991) provide a review of fish predation impacts on invertebrates of coral reefs and adjacent sediments. At the time of their study they observed that while many authors cite research showing fish having an impact on a broad range of benthic invertebrate assemblages, the methodologies were less than definitive. More conclusive results have been reported in regard to artificial reefs attracting piscivores, which in turn have reduced the abundance of resident fish prey species (Shulman, 1985; Hixon and Beets, 1989). This reduction may in part be offset from a human resource use perspective by the increase in potential abundance of piscivorous fish. Ambrose and Anderson (1990) found no evidence that foraging by reef-associated fishes caused a widespread reduction in infaunal densities near the reef and but did observe localized decreases in the number of some species and increases in others.

Given their geometry and surface area, pipelines and cables represent relatively simple and non-extensive reef structure compared with more purposefully built or installed artificial reefs. Based on experiments in the Florida Keys, Alevizon and Gorham (1989) concluded that at least in some contexts, artificial reefs can result in a marked increase in the numbers of local resident reef fishes, without notable effects on fishes dwelling in nearby non-reef habitats. Potts and Hulbert (1994) noted that fish abundance was directly proportional to artificial reef structural volume and complexity. They also noted that as structure size and shelter availability lessened (decreasing complexity), baitfish abundances decreased and predator abundance increased.

Pipelines that are trenched or buried using native fill will reduce the "artificial reef" effect and any benefits or concerns arising from it. To the extent pipelines and cables, as "artificial reefs," allow sequestering and recirculation of nutrients and provide potential habitat for spawn/larvae that would otherwise have been lost to the seabed, they should increase local productivity and biodiversity within a given area.

Pipelines as corridors for genetic exchange and species dispersal

By providing a continuous hard substrate from one area to another, the possibility exists that a marine pipeline could create a linear corridor for species dispersal and attendant flow of genetic material. In theory, this could result in an increase in distribution and range in certain species and the various implications associated with these changes (i.e., change in local fauna, niche competition, introduction of a new predator or grazer). In regard to a marine pipeline, the primary mode of transfer would be through extension of linear hard substrate or perhaps through transfer of hydrostatic test water. In regard to the former there are however, several limiting factors which would, for certain species and environments, limit the likelihood of this occurring. The primary limitations relate to the reproductive biology of many marine species and the physical and chemical barrier potentially imposed by oceanic conditions potentially traversed by a marine pipeline or cable.

Reproductive output and associated dispersal of marine species includes dissemination of fragments (e.g., many marine algae), daughter cells (diatoms), fission or clone production (e.g., sponges and bryozoans), rhizomes (e.g., seagrasses), production of adherent eggs, buried and or brooded eggs/larvae (many gastropods, fish and octopus), dissemination of pelagic gametes, eggs and larvae (numerous species of fish an invertebrates) (Robertson, 1991; Levinton, 1995).

In order for a pipeline to act as a potential agent for significant new extra-limital dispersal, the species involved would have to have a number of characteristics. These would include being an obligate associate of hard-bottom substrate, rely on adherent, buried or brooded eggs or larvae, have an adequate anti-predator and foraging requirement relative to the new environment, and have a reasonably wide range of tolerance for differences in its physico-chemical environmental. The second mode of transfer mentioned (i.e., via hydrostatic test water), would require the test section to be a significant length, and that the organism involved meet all the other requirements specified above as they pertain to the receiving environment.

Boundary layer, current and scour effects
Boundary layer effects in the marine environment occur at a range of scales, wherever seawater flows over or around a solid such as the seabed or a kelp blade, or for example, when a solid such as unicellular plankton falls through a fluid. The phenomenon describes the way in which the velocity of a media around or over an object tends to decrease closer to that surface. It is directly linked to the inertial and viscose forces at work between the object and the media that surrounds it. The ratio of these forces is referred to as the Reynolds Number. Typically the velocity of water around the organism or over the surface approaches zero as you near the surface. The thickness of the boundary layer varies according to the velocity of the media or organism and the viscosity of the medium. Within the marine environment, boundary layer phenomenon are most pronounced within the range of tens of centimeters above the bottom (Mann and Lazier, 1991). This phenomenon is important in the feeding and ecology of benthic organisms (Mann and Lazier, 1991).

The existence of a boundary layer influences the molecular diffusion of nutrients close to the surface of the seabed as well as the surface of sessile organisms inhabiting it. It also affects the movement of organisms (Mann and Lazier, 1991) and by extension, the dissemination of reproductive cells (gametes and spawn). Tidal currents have the effect of facilitating the dispersion and transport of organic and inorganic materials as well as organisms within the zone affected by boundary layer dynamics. Tube worms, while anchored within the boundary layer are adapted to optimally feed above it (Mann and Lazier, 1991). Baynes and Szmant (1989) suggest that organisms such as sponges may be positioned in such a manner in the boundary layer to experience passive pumping, which would increase feeding efficiency and growth rate. The growth and feeding efficiency of suspension feeding mussels (*Mytilus edulis*) has been shown to be strongly mediated by boundary layer processes (Frechette et al., 1989).

Bottom-founded pipelines and cables, like any other object on the seabed alter the flow of water across the seabed and the boundary layer profile. This effect will depend on numerous interacting factors. These factors include the size of the pipeline or cable, its angle relative to the ambient current regime, the amount of pipe exposed above the seabed surface, the roughness of the pipeline coating, ecological context (biota present) and time since installation (as it affects the organisms which may colonize the pipe surface and extent to which the pipe may settle). The predicted net effect is that the diversity, distribution and productivity of organisms in proximity to a pipeline or cable can be expected to change in response to boundary layer effects in addition to other factors discussed in this paper. Wilson (1991) identifies numerous studies demonstrating shifts in the biodiversity of benthic invertebrate communities in response to sediment disturbance and introduction or exclusion of certain species (as would occur with creation of new hard-bottom substrate and altered boundary layer regime). At scales above boundary layer processes it is clear that bottom-founded pipelines and cables, have potential to alter the near bottom current regime and with this the associated transport of nutrients and organisms.

Determining the ecological zone or magnitude of these effects has yet to be investigated and is complicated by the coincident creation of new hard-bottom substrate in the form of a pipeline or cable.

Scour effects
Jensen et al. (1990) observed that current flow over bottom-founded pipelines on erodible seabed substrate will commonly result in creation of "free spans" and "scour holes." Typically, this process is observed in shallow water less than 45 m (150 ft) deep and in tidal areas or deep water where "loop" currents are present (Exley pers. comm.). Scour has the potential to impact benthic marine ecosystems in several ways:
- physical scour of occupied soft-bottom habitats;
- scour induced re-suspension of sediment and any associated contaminants;
- increases exposed pipe surface for colonization by hard-bottom associated species;
- creation of free spans and scour holes that may offset potential barrier effects caused by the original pipeline; and
- alteration of boundary layer hydro-ecological processes.

The physical and ecological magnitude of these impacts can be expected to vary depending on a host of variables related to the characteristics of the pipeline, the time since installation and the environment in which it is placed. The physical scour effect can be expected to diminish with distance from the pipeline but can range from the scale of centimeters to tens of meters. At the same time it is not uncommon for the dominant upstream side to collect and build up sediment adjacent to the pipe. Studies have demonstrated relatively rapid recolonization of disturbed soft-sediment habitat, which similar to circumstance within terrestrial environments, leads to an initial successional pulse of opportunistic species (Wilson, 1991). Among the consequences of scour is the translocation of displaced sediments. Studies of response of marine infaunal communities to sediment inundation indicate certain species, such as mussels and oysters are relatively sensitive to sediment inundation while many others are less so. Essink (1999) observes that most macrozoobenthos will not be seriously affected as long as sediment deposition does not exceed 20 to 30 cm. Wulff et al. (1997) also concluded that the microbenthic community in sandy sediments has an inherent capacity to recover after moderate deposition of fine particle sediment. Low growing corals would likely be smothered through sediment translocation. While prolonged changes in turbidity can be a major problem for corals Bohnsack (1992) short-term changes in turbidity associated with a scour event would likely be less consequential.

Independent of concern over scour effects on marine benthic ecosystems, pipeline and cable companies have a strong desire to avoid the phenomenon as it also has an influence on pipeline integrity. In addition to efforts to avoid areas where scour may occur, other mitigation measures may be applied, including deep trenching, burial with coarse material, anchoring and installation of "spoilers" or fins on the pipe surface to offset current-driven bottom erosion and deposition.

Pipeline noise
Sound is a communication tool used by a wide range of aquatic and semi-aquatic animals including invertebrates, fishes, aquatic birds, aquatic reptiles and various mammals (Cowles et al., 1981; Gisiner, 1998). Present data on the effects of noise on marine life is far from definitive. Very few studies deal with the issue of noise and marine fishes. Available data supports the idea that fish could be affected by anthropogenic sounds (e.g., high intensity sounds can alter hearing sensitivity in goldfish); however, there is very substantial inter-specific variation in the structure of the ears of fish, thus extrapolating results between fish species is almost impossible (Gisiner, 1998). The effects of anthropogenic sounds on aquatic reptiles, birds and invertebrates is completely unknown (Gisiner, 1998).

Most research on the effects of noise in the marine environment has focused on marine mammals (Richardson et al., 1995). Communications frequencies, signal intensity and response thresholds vary considerably between species. Any noise made by a pipeline occurs against a background of both natural sources (e.g., tectonic activity, rain, waves, wind, marine vertebrates and invertebrates) and anthropogenic sources (e.g., shipping, ferry, commercial fishery boat and navy traffic). In general, ambient noise levels are greatest at low frequency (<100 Hz) and diminish with increasing frequency. Shipping noises are generally considered to be the single biggest factor contributing energy in the region of 20–500 Hz (Gisiner, 1998). At higher frequencies (1–100 kHz), noise is dominated by sea surface and wind action (Gisiner, 1998).

For the present investigation the acoustic signature was measured over two parallel high-pressure gas pipelines. The sound produced by the pipelines had an "organ pipe" quality and had a fundamental tone at 80 Hz and harmonics up to 480 Hz (Birch et al., 2000). The spectral intensities in the peak were approximately 72 dB (re uPa^2/Hz) and approximately 10 dB lower than the ambient level. The observed, close association of numerous invertebrates and fish with this existing pipeline discussed previously, tends to suggest pipeline noise in this case does not deter the species observed. The frequency and energy of the sound recorded appears to also be within the range of other biophysical processes in the marine environment. At equivalent pressures, larger pipe can be expected to produce lower resonant frequencies than smaller pipes.

CONCLUSION

The review and studies conducted above provide insight into some of the less explored areas concerning potential impacts of pipelines and marine cable following installation. The impacts identified may act cumulatively, be both small and or difficult to resolve against the myriad of other factors influencing benthic marine ecosystems and are likely of widely variable significance. The formulation of recommendations for facility siting and design around these issues is difficult due to this uncertainty and complexity. Implementation of any recommendation is likely to have substantive cost implications and require site-specific assessment. On the positive side, costs are routinely absorbed where they address issues that affect pipeline integrity and coincidentally these same measures can also address some of the environmental issues discussed. Measures and practices which physically and functionally promote a return of the benthic ecosystem to its former state and encourage stability are generally preferred unless there is a clear resource management consensus for enhancement or alteration. Responsible implementation of environmentally targeted mitigation measures must reconcile the perceived or known environmental sensitivity or value with the cost of the measure (e.g., for trenching, burial, directional drilled landfalls, scour "spoilers," crossing mats, etc.), the disturbance and risks associated with the measure, and the certainty around the measures effectiveness. For example, increasing surface roughness to temporarily facilitate traverse of new pipe or cable by benthic organisms in one location may increase pipeline vibration where there are free spans in another location. Project-specific conditions may also reduce the concern around a potential impact (e.g., numerous small free spans may reduce potential barrier effects). With these qualifications in mind, the following are some siting and design recommendations that should be considered.

RECOMMENDATIONS

Reconnaissance level surveys to identify unique or particularly productive benthic communities should be considered as part of any pipeline or cable route selection. These surveys should be conducted using a combination of side scan sonar, video recording and or SCUBA depending on site conditions. Where unique communities are identified, pipelines and cables should be routed some distance away (e.g. >100 m), depending on community significance, installation technique and pipeline design constraints. Pipelines routed over soft-bottom substrate, particularly larger diameter pipelines, should be installed in trenches, with, or without native backfill replacement, to reduce "reef effects" and potential interference with bottom currents and benthic drift. The benefits from this measure are likely greater in shallower, nearshore areas. Directionally drilled landfalls should be incorporated into the design wherever sensitive nearshore marine communities are encountered. Where more substantial migrations or concentrations of soft-bottom associated, bottom-traveling benthic organisms are known to occur and natural free spans or settlement are unlikely, some combination of trenching, trench backfill with native material or crossing mats should be considered, particularly with larger diameter installations. Employ design technologies which reduce scour and encourage burial. Future research should consider the potential for particularly large diameter installations to act as barriers or to significantly modify benthic drift and currents. Additional research on the acoustic and electro magnetic effects of pipelines and cables as well as on the variability in species colonization for various pipeline/cable coating alternatives would further improve understanding of benthic community interaction with marine pipelines and cables.

ACKNOWLEDGEMENTS

The authors would like to gratefully acknowledge the following contributors who variously provided advice, technical and physical assistance and/or equipment. The Government of Canada, Department of Fisheries and Oceans, Institute of Ocean Sciences and West Vancouver Laboratory, Williams Gas Pipeline, BC Hydro, Hannah Kim, Travis Ponky, Sam Bowes, Randy Haight of Vacilador Productions, Ken Ridgway, Shawn Thorstenson, Dr. Tak Fung, Dr. Larry Linton, Dr. Bob Devlin, Hector Chu-Joy, Karl Skold, Rick Birch, Dr. Mark Travarrow, Dr. David Farmer, Dr. Christine Erbe, Lois Pittaway, Captain Doug Hartley, Butch Exley, Sandor Karpathy, and Dr. Glen Jamieson.

REFERENCES

Alevizon, W.S. and J.C. Gorham. 1989. Effects of artificial reef deployment on nearby resident fishes. Bulletin of Marine Science, 44(2): 646–661.

Ambrose, R.F. and T.W. Anderson. 1990. Influence of an artificial reef on the surrounding infaunal community. Marine Biology, 107: 41–52.

Armstrong, J.W. 1993. A biological survey of an artificial reef at Newcastle Island, British Columbia. Canadian Manuscript Report of Fisheries and Aquatic Sciences No. 2212. Department of Fisheries and Oceans Habitat Management South Coast Division. 21 pp.

Baynes, T.W. and A.M. Szmant. 1989. Effect of current on the sessile benthic community structure of an artificial reef. Bulletin of Marine Science, 44(2): 545–566.

Birch, R., R. Glaholt, and D. Lemon. 2000. Noise measurements near an underwater gas pipeline at Secret Cove, British Columbia. Georgia Strait Crossing Pipeline Limited. 10 pp.

Bohnsack, J.A. 1989. Are high densities of fishes at artificial reefs the result of habitat limitation or behavioral preference? Bulletin of Marine Science, 44(2): 631–645.

Bohnsack, J.A. 1992. Reef resource habitat protection: The forgotten factor. In: Stemming the tide of coastal fish habitat loss. In: Proceedings of A symposium on Conservation of Coastal Fish Habitat. Baltimore, Maryland, March 7–9, 1991. pp. 117–129.

Carr, M.H. and M.A. Hixon. 1997. Artificial reefs: The importance of comparisons with natural reef fisheries. American Fisheries Society, 22(4): 28–33.

Coll, J., J. Moranta, O. Remunes, A. Garcia-Rubies, and I. Morena. 1998. Influence of substrate and deployment time of fish assemblages on an artificial reef at Formentera Island (Balearic Islands, western Mediterranean). Hydrobiologia, 385: 139–152.

Cowles, C.J., D.J. Hansen, and J.D. Hubbard. 1981. Types of potential effects of offshore oil and gas development on marine mammals and endangered species of the Northern Bering Sea and Arctic Ocean. Alaska Outer Continental Shelf Office Technical Paper Number 9. United States Department of the Interior, Bureau of Land Management. 23 pp.

Danner, E.M., T.C Wilson, and R.E. Schlotterbeck. 1994. Comparison of rockfish recruitment of nearshore artificial and natural reefs off the coast of Central California. Bulletin of Marine Science, 55(2–3): 333–343.

Essink, K. 1999. Ecological effects of dumping of dredged sediments; options for management. J. Coast. Cons., 5: 69–80.

Frechette, M., C.A. Butman, and W.R. Rockwell Geyer. 1989. The importance of boundary layer flows in supplying phytoplankton to the suspension feeder. Mytilus edulis L. Limnol. Oceanogr., 34(1): 19–36.

Gisiner, R.C., PhD, ed. 1998. Proceedings — Workshop on the effects of anthropogenic noise in the marine environment. February 10–12, 1998. 117 pp. + appendix.

Grossman, G.D., G.D. Jones, and W.J. Seaman Jr. 1997. Do artificial reefs increase regional fish production? A review of existing data. American Fisheries Society, 22(4): 17–23.

Hixon, M.A. and J.P. Beets. 1989. Shelter characteristics of Caribbean fish assemblages: Experiments with artificial reefs. Bull. Mar. Sci., 44: 666–680.

Jensen, B.L., B.M. Sumer, H.R. Jensen, and J. Fredsoe. 1990. Flow around and forces on a pipeline near a scoured bed in steady current. J. Offshore Mechanics and Arctic Engineering, 112: 206–213.

Jones, G.P., D.J. Ferrell, and P.F. Sale. 1991. Fish predation and its impact on the invertebrates of coral reefs and adjacent sediments. In: The Ecology of Fish on Coral Reefs. P.F. Sale, ed. Academic Press, Toronto. Chapter 7. pp. 156–179.

Levings, C.D., R.E. Foreman, and V.J Tunnicliffe. 1983. Review of the benthos of the strait of Georgia and contiguous fjords. Can. J. Fish Aquat. Sci., 40: 1120–1141.

Levinton, J.S. 1995. Marine Biology: Function, Biodiversity, Ecology. Oxford University Press New York. 420 pp.

Love, M., M.J. Hayland, A.A. Ebeling, T. Herrlinger, A. Brooks, and E. Imamura. 1994. A pilot study of the distribution and abundances of rockfishes in relation to natural environmental factors and offshore oil and gas production platform off the coast of Southern California. Bulletin of Marine Science, 55(2–3): 1062–1085.

Mann, K.H. and J.R.N. Lazier. 1991. Dynamics of marine Ecosystems: Biological-Physical Interactions in the Oceans. Blackwell Scientific Publications, Boston. pp. 52–60.

Minerals Management Service Gulf of Mexico OCS Region. 2000. Gulf of Mexico Deepwater Operations and Activities: Environmental Assessment. OCS EIS/EA MMS 2000-001. US Department of the Interior Minerals Management Service Gulf of Mexico OCS Region, New Orleans. May 2000.

1999. Vessel readied for ultra-deepwater work in Gulf of Mexico, Black Sea. Oil and Gas Journal, 59(6).

Potts, T.A. and A.W. Hulbert. 1994. Structural influences of artificial and natural habitats on fish aggregations in Onslow Bay, North Carolina. Bulletin of Marine Science, 55(2–3): 609–622.

Richardson, W.J., C.R. Greene Jr., C.I. Malme, and D.H. Thomson. 1995. Marine Mammals And Noise. Academic, Toronto. 576 pp.

Robertson, D.R. 1991. The role of adult biology in the timing of spawning of tropical reef fishes. In: The Ecology of Fish on Coral Reefs. P.F. Sale, ed. Academic, Toronto. Chapter 13. pp 356–386.

Scarborough Bull, Ann and James J. Kendall, Jr. 1994. An Indication of the Process: Offshore Platforms as Artificial Reefs in the Gulf of Mexico. Bulletin of Marine Science, 55(2–3): 1086–1098.

Shulman, M.J. 1985. Variability in recruitment of coral reef fishes. J. Exp. Mar. Biol. Ecol., 89: 205–219.

Sokal R.R. and F.J.Rohlf. 1981. Biometry, 2nd ed. W.H. Freeman and Company, San Francisco.

Wilson, W.H. 1991. Competition and predation in marine soft-sediment communities. Annu. Rev. Ecol. Syst., 21: 221–241.

Wulff, A., K. Sundback, C. Nilsson, L. Carlson, and B. Johnson. 1997. Effect of sediment load on the microbenthic community of a shallow-water sandy sediment. Estuaries, 20(3): 547–558.

PERSONAL COMMUNICATIONS

Exley, Butch. Williams Gas Pipeline. Houston, Texas.

BIOGRAPHICAL SKETCHES

Randal G. Glaholt, MEDes, PBiol

Biotechnics International Ltd., 6031 Bowwater Cr. N.W., Calgary, AL T3B 2E5, Canada, Tel: (403) 247-8945, Fax: (403) 266-6471, E-mail: rglaholt@biotechnics.ca

Randal Glaholt is a professional biologist and president of Biotechnics International Ltd. His areas of interest include applied aquatic and terrestrial ecology, biodiversity conservation, environmental planning and environmental assessment. He has worked on a variety of projects in Canada, the United States, Central America and Central Asia.

Michelle Nunas, BSc

TERA Environmental Consultants (Alta) Ltd., 205, 925 7th Avenue S.W., Calgary, AL T2P 1A5, Canada, Tel: (403) 265-2885

Michelle Nunas is an aquatic biologist with a BSc (Agr), major in Wildlife Biology. She has experience in both tropical and temperate habitats. Her expertise are in freshwater and marine habitat mapping and population studies, underwater surveys, electroshocking, environmental impact assessments and development of mitigation measures.

Stacey Ong, BSc

6231 Spender Drive Richmond, BC V7E 4B9 Tel: 604-274-3784

Stacey Ong is a marine biologist with a BSc who has provided research support on a range of fisheries related projects while working in the Fisheries and Oceans Coastal and Marine Habitat Science Section at their West Vancouver Laboratory. She has interests in invertebrate and vertebrate behavior and ecology as well as the effects of trawling and trapping on fisheries and the marine environment.

Evaluation of Low Technology Large Woody Debris as a Technique to Augment Fish Habitat in Streams Crossed by Transmission Corridors

Gregory C. Scarborough and Tasha Robertson

The suitability of low technology large woody debris (LWD) structures for fish habitat augmentation in streams crossed by transmission corridors was investigated at five stream sites (eight structures in total) in the Greater Vancouver Area, British Columbia (BC). The structure types included lateral logjams ($n = 2$), a log bank cover, a simulated root-wad, tree top revetments ($n = 2$), and an upstream and downstream facing log deflector. Year 2 biological assessments were conducted in the early and late summer of 2000. The Year 2 early summer catch results were significantly lower than Year 1 results but this was likely caused by high discharge conditions and poor sampling conditions. The Year 2 late summer catch results, however, are more comparable and showed an overall increase in relative fish abundance for the habitat units in which LWD structures were placed. Fish were found associated with six out of seven structures in the late summer sampling. One structure (lateral logjam) failed completely during winter floods and was not investigated further in Year 2. Year 2 physical assessments of the remaining structures found that most remained in good condition but two showed signs of deterioration and one suffered a failed anchor. Additional monitoring of structures in Year 3 will provide better evaluations of each structures overall success.

Keywords: Large woody debris, fish habitat augmentation, transmission corridors, stream crossings, habitat compensation, riparian habitat

INTRODUCTION

Construction of transmission corridors historically involved the removal of all vegetation from within the corridor, including riparian trees and sometimes even fallen timber and debris from stream channels (Scouras, 1999). Although this practice was acceptable at the time, it is now well known that removal of riparian vegetation and in-stream debris has many deleterious impacts on fish habitat. These include, but are not limited to, changes in temperature regime (Brown and Krygier, 1970; Meehan, 1970; Hetrick et al., 1998a), physical channel (Hartman et al., 1996; Murphy et al., 1986; Heifetz et al., 1986; Tschaplinski and Hartman, 1983), and food supply (Hetrick et al., 1998a, 1998b),

Environmental Concerns in Rights-of-Way Management: Seventh International Symposium
J.W. Goodrich-Mahoney, D.F. Mutrie and C.A. Guild (editors)
© 2002 Elsevier Science Ltd. All rights reserved.

and contribution of LWD (Bragg and Kershner, 1999; Bryant, 1985; Knutson and Naef, 1997; Murphy and Meehan, 1991).

Utilities are under increasing pressure from society and environmental agencies to remediate the impacts of on going maintenance programs on riparian habitat. In some instances, impacts of past work practices are also under scrutiny and habitat compensation is often used to address this scrutiny. Consequently, right-of-way (ROW) managers must find new ways to manage stream crossings in utility corridors. At BC Hydro, such new management techniques focus on protecting riparian habitat by limiting the one-time removal of vegetation, utilizing special vegetation management techniques and planting low growing vegetation. While these techniques benefit bank stability, water quality, and shading (given the correct circumstances), it is doubtful that they lead to recruitment of LWD into a stream.

LWD has several critical functions in a stream ecosystem which include sediment and nutrient storage, energy dissipation during high flows, channel stability, local bed and bank scour (i.e., creation of pools), habitat complexity, the provision of refuge habitat and cover for salmonids, and the provision of a complex substrate for microbial and invertebrate colonisation (Armantrout, 1991; Cederholm et al., 1997; Faush and Northcote, 1992; Gregory et al., 1991; Lisle, 1986; MacDonald et al., 1991; Scrivner and Brown, 1993). Studies have found that juvenile salmonids rearing in streams are often associated with LWD (Bryant, 1985; Cederholm et al., 1997; McMahon and Holtby, 1992; Murphy and Meehan, 1991) and fish abundance has also been correlated with the abundance and quality of instream cover (Bjornn and Reiser, 1991; Elliott, 1986; Fausch and Northcote, 1992; Lisle, 1986) although the exact mechanisms by which LWD causes increased fish abundance is unknown.

LWD is supplied from healthy riparian zones and where these areas are adversely affected, typically by past logging practices, many government agencies, stream stewardship groups and non-profit groups artificially add LWD into streams to replace lost habitat (see, for example, Anon, 1998; Hartman and Miles, 1995). Placement of LWD into streams is now a well developed science and the literature contains many manuals on installation techniques (see, for example, Abbe et al., 1997; Chapters 8 and 9 in Slaney and Zaldokas, 1997; Poulin, 1991) and reviews of LWD projects (see, for example, Anon, 1999; Koning et al., 1997; Chapman, 1996; Hartman and Miles, 1995; Fitch et al., 1994). Many of these LWD projects involve engineered LWD structures, heavy machinery and extensive site surveys, which are expensive and require special skills. There has been little research, however, into techniques for installing small scale, low technology LWD structures using inexperienced crews and hand tools only with little to no site investigation. Given the increasing fiscal constraints faced by ROW Managers, the need to mitigate impacts caused by ROW maintenance and the many benefits of in-stream LWD additions, a simple and cost effective method of successfully adding LWD into streams crossed by transmission corridors is greatly needed.

Effective small scale, low technology LWD structures will produce measurable biological and physical success. Therefore, research should investigate the site criteria, structure type(s) and installation technique(s) that provide significant biological (i.e., increase in fish abundance) and physical (i.e., structures survive freshet, increase pool area and pool depth) success. In order for this study to be useful to ROW managers, it should also focus on streams crossed by transmission corridors and should evaluate variables that are easy to quantify and use in a LWD structure installation manual. Overall, it is expected that the most suitable LWD structure type(s) are easily installed at minimal expense, survive freshet conditions without damage and provide measurable physical and biological benefits.

The following represents the results of the first year of a multi-year study to investigate LWD structures suitable for streams crossed by transmission corridors.

METHODS

The a priori criteria for candidate stream study sites were that a stream was fish bearing with an average channel width between 3 and 10 m, average stream gradient between 1 and 5%, and is crossed by a transmission corridor. Eleven (11) candidate streams in the Lower Mainland of BC met these criteria but following reconnaissance field investigations, the number of study streams was reduced to five (5) because some sites had poor access, signs of flashy discharge, were boulder dominated or already contained abundant natural in-stream LWD. The location of the five study sites is shown in Fig. 1.

Each study stream encompassed one or two enhancement sites and between three and nine habitat units (i.e., pools, riffles, glides, etc.). Where stream habitat units are not well defined, a minimum distance of 15 m upstream and 30 m downstream of the enhancement site(s) was included in the study area. The limits of the study area and its habitat units were marked with flagging tape and wooden stakes and the location was referenced to a permanent benchmark structure for follow-up monitoring.

Habitat surveys

Habitat surveys of each study area were conducted in Year 1 between September 28 and October 4, 1999. These studies obtained information on stream geomorphology, habitat type, bank height and width, wetted width, depth, and gradient. Observations of in-stream boulders, woody debris, erosion, undercut banks, and other outstanding stream characteristics were recorded. Photographs and detailed drawings of each study area were used to document key features. Stream habitat surveys began at the downstream end of the study area (+0.0 m), and continued to the upstream limit of the study area. The length of each study area varied, and each habitat unit was staked and labeled in the field as a distance in meters (i.e., +30.0 m) from the downstream end of the study area. All field measurements were taken facing downstream for consistency.

The intent of Year 2 habitat surveys was to determine if the LWD structures physically altered the stream habitat around them. These habitat surveys were carried out after freshet on June 26, 2000.

Fish distribution

Fish distribution surveys were conducted using single pass electro-shocking prior to LWD structure installation in Year 1 between September 28 and October 4, 1999. These surveys were repeated following freshet in

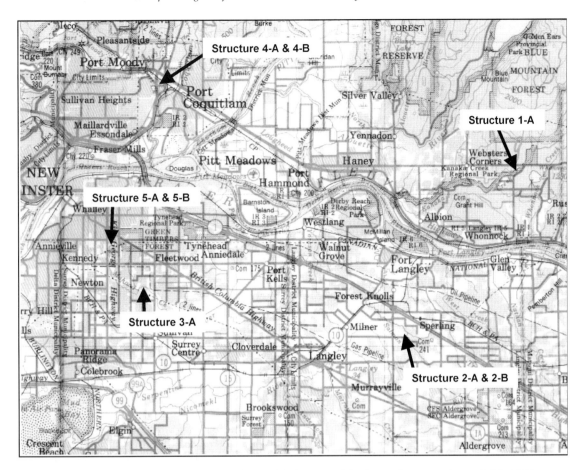

Fig. 1. View of the Lower Mainland of British Columbia and the location of the five study stream sites and eight LWD structures.

Year 2 (June 26, 2000) and in late summer (September 18 and 19, 2000). Catch and effort were recorded for each habitat unit separately. This method was chosen because of its ability to cover a variety of habitat types in a consistent and reproducible manner. Other studies investigated the response of fish to habitat alterations by determining population estimates through stop nets and multiple-pass electro-shocking (e.g., Keith et al., 1998; Riley and Fausch, 1995; Nickelson et al., 1992; House and Boehne, 1985). This approach was unsuitable for this project because of the extra time and cost involved and the small size of some of the study habitat units. Electro-shocking was conducted using consistent, even sweeps across the entire habitat unit and particular attention was given to observing the micro-scale fish use of habitat. Captured fish species were identified and their fork length was measured.

LWD structure assessments

The physical and biological success of each LWD structure was evaluated post freshet in Year 2 following the "operational monitoring" protocol in Koning et al. (1997). Monitoring included comparing the structures design objectives to an assessment of each structures structural condition, structural stability, physical performance and biological performance (Koning et al., 1997). This approach was useful because the small

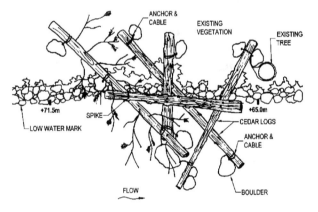

Fig. 2. View of plan drawing of LWD structure 1A in Kanaka Creek.

scale of the low-technology LWD structures in this study was expected to provide reduced results compared to large-scale, engineered structures. This also allows an evaluation of each structures success based on "realistic expectations" (Hartman and Miles, 1985).

RESULTS

Site distribution and habitat units

Eight LWD structures were installed into five study streams (Fig. 1). The study streams and their respec-

Table 1. Summary of stream habitat survey results from Year 1 investigations

Stream	Habitat type	Structure number	Location (m)[c]	No. of habitat units	Length (m)	Wetted width (m)	Bank width (m)	Wetted area[d] (m^2)	Ave. depth (cm)
Kanaka Creek	riffle	1-A	8		20.0	8.9	12.8	178.0	16.0
Totals and Averages[a]	AR[b]			2	80.0	9.7	13.1	802.0	14.5
	AP[b]			1	10.0	8.5	14.3	85.0	35.0
	AHU[b]			3	90.0	9.3	13.5	887.0	21.3
Salmon River	pool	2-B	32		13.0	4.5	7.6	58.5	38.0
	riffle	2-A	35		2.0	4.4	9.5	8.8	12
Totals and Averages[a]	AR			2	5.4	4.9	8.5	25.0	13.5
	ARu[b]			2	19.6	4.1	8.8	79.6	22.0
	AP			3	35.5	6.0	11.4	210.0	30.3
	AHU			7	60.5	5.1	9.8	314.6	23.1
Bear Creek	pool	3-A	50		14.5	3.3	6.0	47.9	13.0
Totals and Averages[a]	AR			2	15.5	3.4	4.6	51.5	17.5
	ARu			1	7.5	8.6	10.9	64.5	11.0
	AP			4	59.0	5.9	8.8	350.5	46.0
	AHU			7	82.0	5.6	7.9	466.5	32.9
Scott Creek	run	4-B	39		8.5	5.6	6.9	47.6	19.0
Totals and Averages[a]	run	4-A	73		5.5	6.6	10.5	36.3	32.0
	AR			2	20.0	5.7	7.1	114.0	8.0
	ARu			4	53.0	6.2	8.1	318.2	23.5
	AP			3	31.0	4.2	6.4	133.5	42.7
	AHU			9	104.0	5.4	7.3	565.7	26.4
Bear Creek Park	run[e]	5-B	27		6.5	3.9	6.2	25.4	13.0
Totals and Averages[a]	riffle	5-A	48.5		6.2	4.9	11.6	30.4	5.0
	AR			3	19.2	5.1	8.5	98.0	9.7
	ARu			4	48.2	4.8	8.3	243.7	23.5
	AHU			7	67.4	4.9	8.4	341.0	17.6
Maximum[f]				9	104.0	9.3	13.5	887.0	32.9
Minimum[f]				3	60.5	4.9	7.3	314.8	17.6
Average[f]				7	80.8	6.1	9.4	515.0	24.3

Data are grouped by individual habitat unit containing a LWD structure (row shown in italics), by each habitat unit type (e.g. pool), and for the entire study stream (indicated by AHU).

[a] Number of habitat units, length, and area are summed for each habitat unit type (e.g., pool) and for all habitat units measured in the stream. Wetted width, bank width and average depth are averaged among each habitat unit types (e.g., pools) and for all habitat units measured in the stream.

[b] AR — all riffles, AP — all pools, AHU — all habitat units surveyed in the stream, ARu — all runs.

[c] Indicates distance in meters from beginning at the downstream end of the study stream.

[d] Wetted area calculated as wetted width of habitat unit times its length. Note that values shown for AR, ARu, and AP are totals measured in the field, not the product of average wetted width and average habitat unit length for each habitat type.

[e] Includes a side-pool.

[f] Maximum, minimum and average values are for all habitat units (AHU) for each stream.

tive LWD structure numbers are: Kanaka Creek (1A); Salmon River (2-A, 2-B); Bear Creek (3-A); Scott Creek (4-A, 4-B); and Bear Creek in Bear Creek Park (5-A, 5-B). Fig. 2 provides an example of the installed orientation and design of the lateral logjam installed in Kanaka Creek (Structure 1-A). Habitat unit measurement summaries are provided in Table 1. The study area lengths ranged from 60.5 m (Salmon River) to 104 m (Scott Creek) and the number of habitat units investigated ranged from 4 (Kanaka Creek) to 9 (Scott Creek). The study stream sites ranged in total area from a minimum of 571.7 m^2 to a maximum of 1197 m^2 (Table 1).

Fish sampling

Electro-fishing was conducted in both Year 1 (September 28–October 4, 1999) and Year 2 (June 26, 2000 and September 18–19, 2000) sampling periods for all stream sites except Kanaka Creek because the LWD structure in this stream was destroyed by winter floods (see LWD structure results). Electro-shocking at this site was only conducted in Year 1. Eleven fish species were captured during Year 1 fish sampling (Table 2) including coho salmon (*Oncorhynchus kisutch*), cutthroat trout (*O. clarki*), steelhead trout (*O. mykiss*), chum salmon (*O. keta*), western brook lamprey (*Lampetra richardsoni*), river lamprey (*L. ayresi*), prickly sculpin

(*Cottus asper*), sculpins general (*Cottus sp.*), longnose dace (*Rhinichthys cataractae*), redside shiner (*Richardsonius balteatus*), and threespine stickleback (*Gasterosteidae aculeatus*). All but three of these fish species (chum salmon, western brook lamprey, and sculpins) were captured in the Year 2 follow-up sampling.

Since salmonids are the desired target species for most stream rehabilitation projects and to simplify summation of the results, only catch of salmonid species are discussed in the following summaries. Furthermore, because the Year 2 early summer sampling produced very small catch numbers compared to Year 1, and the late summer sampling period provides a consistent time-frame comparison among years, only late summer (i.e., September 18 and 19) catch results are discussed below and shown in Table 2.

Maximum and minimum sampling efforts (seconds) per stream in Year 1 and for late summer sampling in Year 2 were 1627 and 552, and 1268 and 556, respectively (Table 2). Corresponding maximum and minimum catch per unit effort (CPUE — fish per 100 s electro-shocking) in Years 1 and 2 were 6.7 and 0.8, and 4.5 and 1.3, respectively (Table 2). Moreover, maximum and minimum fish densities (fish per 100 m^2) in Years 1 and 2 were 12.2 and 2.8, and 13 and 2.1, respectively (Table 2). The average change in CPUE and density, from Year 1 to Year 2, for all streams was -1.8 and -4.6, respectively (Table 2). The catch results suggest that late summer catch effectiveness dropped slightly in Year 2. The reason for this decrease is unknown but it might reflect different stream discharge conditions, temperature, time of sampling and various other environmental variables that affect fish distribution and abundance.

Year 2 late summer fish sampling captured fish from six of the seven habitat units containing LWD structures. Year 2 Catch statistics (CPUE and fish/100 m^2) also increased compared to Year 1 in four of the seven habitat units containing LWD structures (Table 2). When pooled together, the catch statistics for habitat units containing LWD structures showed a slight increase in Year 2 compared to Year 1 but this result is strongly weighted by the significant increase in catch in the Salmon River's structure 2-A habitat unit (Table 2). Moreover, combined average Year 2 fish density (fish/100 m^2) for habitat units with LWD structures exceeded that for all habitat units per stream (Table 2).

LWD structure assessment

Biological, physical and structural assessments of all of the LWD structures, with the exception of Structure 1-A, were conducted in Year 2 as part of the operational monitoring program (Table 3).

LWD Structures 2-A, 4-B, and 5-A were designed to provide instream cover and create small scour pools (Table 3). The approximate dimensions of the scour pool associated with Structure 2-A were 1.6 m long × 0.9 m wide × 1.1 m deep at the time of the survey. The invert of the streambed had deepened by ≈0.3 m at the center of the pool. The approximate dimensions of the scour pool associated with Structure 4-B were 0.6 m wide × 0.5 m long and 0.5 m deep at the time of the survey. The invert of the streambed at the outer edge of the deflector had deepened by ≈0.2 m. Deposition of sand and gravels has occurred upstream and downstream of structure 4-B adjacent to the streambank. Structure 5-A was deflected onto the stream bank during high flows and was therefore unable to scour the streambed. The structure was put back into position several weeks before the Year 2 fish distribution surveys were conducted.

LWD Structures 2-B, 3-A, 4-A, and 5-B were designed to provide instream cover for salmonids (Table 3). LWD structure 2-B was in the exact position and condition as when it was constructed and provides instream cover in a pool. LWD Structures 3-A, 4-A, and 5-B shifted slightly in position and experienced wear and tear. These structures lost a significant portion of leaf/needles and small branches, however the main LWD logs are still present and they continue to function as cover. Structure 4-A accumulated a large amount of smaller woody debris in the form of branches and leaf litter. A small scour pool was also formed at the upstream end of this structure.

DISCUSSION

Year 2 fish sampling captured salmonids in six of seven habitat units in which LWD structures were placed (Table 2). Furthermore, salmonids were observed utilizing five of the seven structures sampled in the late summer of Year 2 (Table 3). Although average catch effectiveness (CPUE) for all study streams decreased in Year 2 by 1.8, Year 2 late summer CPUE increased in four of the seven habitat units and average CPUE from all habitat units containing LWD structures increased by 0.63 compared to Year 1. This suggests that LWD structures may have improved each habitat units ability to support juvenile salmonids.

Year 2 LWD structure assessments were also completed at the end of June 2000. LWD Structure 1-A failed completely and none of its LWD pieces were relocated. Although the exact reason for the structure failure is unknown, it is likely that the forces acting on the LWD structure outweighed the forces acting to keep the structure in place (i.e., boulder anchors, tree anchor, and cable). Detailed methods to compute anchoring requirements of LWD structures in streams exist (D'Aoust and Millar, 1999). However, these methods often require detailed hydrological studies to determine peak flow velocities: studies that are beyond the scope of the "low technology" fish habitat augmentation technique described in this study.

Pitch et al. (1994) suggest a more general rule that boulders used to create instream cover will have a

Table 2. Summary of fish sampling results from Year 1 and Year 2 (late summer only) investigations

Stream	Habitat type	Structure	Area (m²)	Year 1 fish sampling (Sept. 29–Oct. 4, 1999)						Year 2 fish sampling (Sept. 18–19, 2000)						
				Effort (sec.)	No.	Ave. FL (cm)	CPUE[b]	Fish/ 100 m²		Effort (sec.)	No.	Ave. FL (cm)	CPUE[b]	Difference from Y1	Fish/ 100 m²	Difference from Y1
Kanaka Creek	Riffle	1-A	178.0	268	3	11	1.1	1.7		—	—	—	—	—	—	—
Totals & Averages[a]	AR[c]		802.0	911	5	10	0.5	0.6		—	—	—	—	—	—	—
	AP[c]		85.0	121	3	8	2.5	3.5		—	—	—	—	—	—	—
	AHU[c]		887.0	1032	8	10	0.8	0.9		—	—	—	—	—	—	—
Salmon River	Pool	2-B	58.5	338	20	8	5.9	34.2		335	1	12	0.3	−5.6	1.7	−32.5
	Riffle	2-A	8.8	48	1	8	2.1	11.4		48	7	9	14.6	12.5	79.5	68.1
Totals & Averages	AR		25.0	104	2	8	1.9	8.0		104	11	9	10.6	8.7	44.0	36.0
	ARu[c]		79.6	433	18	7	4.2	22.6		420	8	8	1.9	−2.3	10.1	−12.5
	AP		210.0	752	54	8	7.2	25.7		744	22	9	3.0	−4.2	10.5	−15.2
	AHU		314.8	1289	74	7	5.7	23.5		1268	41	9	3.2	−2.5	13.0	−10.5
Bear Creek	Pool	3-A	47.9	99	3	5	3.0	6.3		97	7	7	7.2	4.2	14.6	8.3
Totals & Averages	AR		51.5	96	4	9	4.2	7.8		98	3	8	3.1	−1.1	5.8	−2.0
	ARu		64.5	48	0	—	0.0	0.0		49	0	—	0.0	0.0	0.0	0.0
	AP		350.5	408	21	9	5.1	6.0		409	12	10	2.9	−2.2	3.4	−2.6
	AHU		466.5	552	25	9	4.5	5.4		556	15	9	2.7	−1.8	3.2	−2.2
Scott Creek	Run	4-B	47.6	85	1	7	1.2	2.1		83	2	8	2.4	1.2	4.2	2.1
	Run	4-A	36.3	40	0	—	0.0	0.0		40	1	5	2.5	2.5	2.8	2.8
Totals & Averages	AR		114.0	220	1	8	0.5	0.9		216	4	5	1.9	1.4	3.5	2.6
	ARu		318.2	396	5	7	1.3	1.6		398	6	8	1.5	0.2	1.9	0.3
	AP		133.5	280	1	7	0.4	0.7		277	2	9	0.7	0.3	1.5	0.8
	AHU		565.7	896	7	7	0.8	1.2		891	12	7	1.3	0.5	2.1	0.9
Bear Creek	Run[e]	5-B	25.4	40	7	8	17.5	27.6		43	5	8	11.6	−5.9	19.7	−7.9
	Riffle	5-A	30.4	44	2	10	4.5	6.6		45	0	—	0.0	−4.5	0.0	−6.6
Totals & Averages	AR		98.0	191	5	8	2.6	5.1		191	0	—	0.0	−2.6	0.0	−5.1
	ARu		243.7	542	44	8	8.1	18.1		548	33	9	6.0	−2.1	13.5	−4.6
	AHU		341.0	733	49	8	6.7	14.4		739	33	9	4.5	−2.2	9.7	−4.7
Maximum[d]			887.0	1289	74	10	6.7	23.5		1268	41	9	4.5	−2.5	13.0	−10.5
Minimum[d]			314.8	552	7	7	0.8	0.9		556	3	7	1.3	0.5	2.1	0.9
Average[d]			514.8	900	33	8	3.7	9.1		864	25	9	2.9	−1.8	7.0	−4.6

Only catch of salmonid species (coho, chum, cutthroat trout and rainbow trout) are shown. Non-salmonids were removed from the analysis. Data are grouped by individual habitat unit containing a LWD structure (row shown in italics), by each habitat unit type (e.g., pool) and for the entire study stream (indicated by AHU).

[a] Area, effort and catch are summed per habitat unit type (e.g., pool) and for all habitat units measured in the stream. Average fork length represents the average fork length per habitat unit type and for the entire study stream.
[b] CPUE — catch per unit effort (number of fish caught per 100 s electro-shocking.
[c] AR — all riffles, AP — all pools, AHU — all habitat units surveyed in the stream, ARu — all runs.
[d] Maximum, minimum and average values are for all habitat units (AHU) for each stream.
[e] Includes a small side pool.

Technique to augment fish habitat in streams crossed by transmission corridors 783

Table 3. Summary of follow-up monitoring of LWD structures (from Koning et al., 1997) and comparative ranking of each structure.

Structure number[1]	Type of structure	Time to install (labour-hours)	Physical performance	Structure rating based on physical performance	Biological performance	Structure rating based on biological performance
			1 – Not meeting objectives 2 – Poorly meeting objectives 3 – Adequately meeting objectives 4 – Fully meeting objectives	Rank assigned to structures in numerical order from 1 (least successful LWD structure) to 8 (most successful LWD structure)	1 – Not meeting objectives 2 – Poorly meeting objectives 3 – Adequately meeting objectives 4 – Fully meeting objectives	Rank assigned to structures in numerical order from 1 (least successful LWD structure) to 8 (most successful LWD structure)
1-A	Large lateral log jam	11	1 Complete Failure	1 Anchors failed	N/A	1 Structure failed
2-A	Small lateral log jam	4	4 Scour pool created; provides instream cover	7 Provides localized scour and good refuge/cover for salmonids. Easy construction	3 Salmonids ($n = 2$) observed under the structure (September 18, 2000)	5 Provides good cover and refuge habitat for salmonids
2-B	Log bank cover	4	4 Provides cover for existing pool	4 Provides marginal cover for salmonids. Requires instream anchor boulders that are stable	1 No salmonids were observed or captured using the structure	3 Provides good cover for salmonids but no refuge from high flows. Salmonids were not observed using the structure
3-A	Simulated root-wad	3	3 Provides cover for existing side pool	3 Provides marginal refuge/cover for salmonids. Likely more effective if several root wads are utilized and anchored into the stream bank or a stable anchor boulder	4 CT ($n = 4$) captured under the structure (September 18, 2000)	8 Largest number of salmonids captured under the simulated root wad. Provides good instream cover and refuge for salmonids
4-A	Multiple tree revetment	3	4 Protects bank and provides cover	8 Provides good refuge/cover for salmonids and promotes channel scour and bank stability. Easy installation. Also promotes accumulation of other woody debris and leaf litter	4 CO ($n = 1$) captured under the structure (June 26, 2000) CT ($n = 1$) and other salmonids observed (September 19, 2000).	6 Provides good cover and refuge habitat for salmonids. Fish utilizing the structure at the time of the surveys were likely under-represented as electroshocking amongst the LWD was difficult
4-B	Upstream facing log weir	3	4 Scour pool created; provides instream cover	5 Provides marginal cover and scour due to its limited size. Promotes upstream and downstream deposition that alters channel morphology and increases habitat complexity in uniform reaches. Multiple deflectors would be more effective	3 CT ($n = 2$) captured using the structure (September 19, 2000)	4 Provides limited cover and refuge habitat for salmonids

Table 3. (continued)

Structure number[1]	Type of structure	Time to install (labour–hours)	Physical performance	Structure rating based on physical performance	Biological performance	Structure rating based on biological performance
5-A	Downstream facing log weir	2	2 Provides cover however structure needs to be stabilized to prevent shifting	2 Structure shifted in high flows that affected its performance. Additional anchor boulders were placed at the downstream end of the structure	1 No salmonids were observed or captured using the structure	2 Provides limited cover and refuge habitat for salmonids. Salmonids were not observed using the structure
5-B	Single tree top revetment	2	4 Provides cover	6 Provides good refuge/cover for salmonids. Easy installation. Promotes the accumulation of additional woody debris	4 CT ($n = 5$) and other salmonids observed using structure (June 26 and September 18, 2000)	7 Provides good instream cover and refuge habitat for salmonids

[1] See Fig. 1 for location of structures and Table 1 for detail on structures in-stream location.

higher likelihood of remaining stable if their diameter is ≈25 times the diameter of the average bed material size (D_{50}). This value was designed for individual boulder placement and does not consider additional forces that would act on the boulder if it was used as an anchor. It does, however, establish a minimum diameter for the selection of anchor boulders for LWD enhancement. Newbury and Gaboury (1993) also describe a simple method to estimate the tractive force exerted on bed materials and determine the maximum size class of substrate material that will be forced into movement at a site at different depths of flow. The tractive force (t) can be calculated with two simple field measurements, depth of flow (d) and slope of water surface (s), where $t = 1000 \times d \times s$, and tractive force (kg/m^2) = incipient diameter (cm).

Structures 1-A, 2-A, 4-B, and 5-A were designed to scour the streambed and provide cover (i.e., pool and LWD) for salmonids. Structure 1-A failed completely so its success could not be evaluated. Structure 2-A created a roughness element in the stream channel, which caused the formation of eddies that scoured material from the streambed. Structure 4-B constricted flow into a narrower channel, increasing the velocity of water flowing around the structure and causing scour. The angle of Structure 4-B (i.e., 45° upstream) repels flow away from the stream bank towards the center of the channel (Breusers and Raudkivi, 1991). Deposition of sand and gravels occurred upstream and downstream of structure 4-B, immediately adjacent to the bank, as expected with the deflection of flow towards the center of the channel. Structure 5-A was shifted onto the stream bank during high flows and was therefore unable to provide similar habitat. An anchor boulder should be added to the downstream end of this structure to maintain in position in the channel. Although the extent of effects of the LWD structures on stream morphology was limited, structures 2-A and 4-B did meet the expected physical performance for low-technology LWD. Lateral log jams and multiple log structures have a greater ability to scour streambeds and trap other small woody debris for cover than single log structures, and therefore may be preferred for ROW enhancement works.

LWD Structures 2-B, 3-A, 4-A, and 5-B were designed to provide cover for salmonids. All of the structures, with the exception of Structure 2-B, had been subjected to wear and tear in the form of lost branches and leaves/needles. All of the structures were, however, still functioning as intended. An accumulation of small woody debris against Structure 4-A has reinforced the structure creating a debris jam that dissipates the energy of the flow and reduces flow velocity against the eroding bank. Cover created by the multiple tree revetment (4-A) and the log bank cover (2-B) exceeded that of the other structures and provided a good surface for debris accumulation. The single tree top revetment (5-B) may have been more effective had it been constructed with coniferous wood that would have endured less wear and tear, or a tree top with larger branches with an ability to trap small woody debris. The simulated root-wad provided instream cover, but appeared less stable and provided less aerial cover than the other structures. A grouping of root-wads would likely provide better results.

In general, anchor rocks for LWD structures should only be chosen if they are abnormally large amongst the existing bed materials within the channel (e.g., 25 times the average bed material size). This will not guarantee structure stability but can provide information on the size of boulder or rock that is generally stable in that portion of the watercourse. Streams with an abundance of large cobble/rock/boulder material should in most cases be avoided for low-technology LWD as an abundance of larger materials generally indicates that high flows have the capability to move these larger particles. Where available, LWD structures should be cabled to a healthy tree or stable tree trunk (provided care is taken to avoid girdling the tree), or alternatively to a wooden stake located on the stream bank. Other anchors systems, although not used in this study, can also stabilize instream LWD. These include, but are not limited to: rebar or wood stakes that can be driven into the channel bank; duck-bill anchors that can be buried into the channel bank; and partially burying LWD in the channel bank.

Longevity of the LWD structures will vary between sites. Observations of natural tree fall into streams indicate that continuously submerged deciduous logs can last up to 10 years while those exposed to air over for several months were significantly deteriorated after 3 years (Armantrout, 1991). It should be noted that deciduous wood decomposes at a faster rate than coniferous wood (Cederholm et al., 1997). Therefore, the effect of deciduous trees on channel morphology will not be long-lived, but they will be more rapidly assimilated into the biological cycle than coniferous trees. All of the LWD structures in this study will eventually decompose yielding coarse-particulate organic matter to the stream that in turn, feeds invertebrates, fungi and bacteria. As a result, nutrients released from the decomposing woody debris are returned to the environment (Gregory et al., 1991 and Vannote et al., 1980) providing additional long-term benefits of LWD structures.

The results of this study indicate that the effects of low-technology LWD structures are limited to the area immediately surrounding the structures. Other minor changes in channel geomorphology within the study areas were observed, but were not likely a result of the LWD structures. Moreover, the limitations of the installation equipment permitted for this study, (i.e., hand tools), suggest that it is unlikely that the small-scale LWD structures will have any significant effects on channel geomorphology. In order to have greater scour capabilities, these structures would require larger diameter logs and have greater ballasting requirements. Therefore, the main objective of the low-technology LWD structures should be focused on the structures ability to provide cover, refuge, food, and nutrients to salmonids. The preliminary results of the fish distribution studies indicate that several of these structures are providing suitable cover for fish, including salmonids.

The implementation of instream low-technology LWD within BC Hydro rights-of-way can replace valuable woody debris within stream ecosystems, providing instream habitat complexing, important cover from predators and slow-velocity resting areas for juvenile salmonids (Angermeier and Karr, 1984; Armantrout, 1991; Cederholm et al., 1997; Murphy and Meehan, 1991), nutrients and sources of terrestrial insects (Bjornn and Reiser, 1991; Meehan et al., 1977), and providing structurally complex substrate for macroinvertebrate colonization (O'Connor, 1991; Meehan et al., 1977). The preliminary results of this study suggest that some LWD structures can create scour and are utilized by fish. However, to better understand the effects and design criteria for low technology LWD structures, additional research is needed. This research should investigate more LWD structures in different environmental settings and include more quantitative (e.g., population estimates) and repeated fish sampling and channel bottom assessments.

REFERENCES

Abbe, T.B., D.R. Montgomery, and C. Petroff. 1997. Design of stable in-channel wood debris structures for bank protection and habitat restoration: An example from the Cowlitz River, WA. In: Proceedings of the Conference on Management of Landscapes Disturbed by Channel Incision (MLDCI), S.S.Y. Wong, E.J. Langendoen, and F.D. Shields, eds. University of Mississippi. May. pp. 809–814.

Anonymous, 1999. Watershed Restoration Technical Bulletin, 4(3). Watershed Restoration Program, BC Ministry of Environment, Vancouver, BC.

Anonymous. 1998. Annual compendium of WRP Aquatic Rehabilitation Projects for the Watershed Restoration Program 1997–1998. Watershed Restoration Project Report No. 8. Watershed Restoration Program, Ministry of Environment, Lands and Parks and Ministry of Forests. British Columbia, Canada.

Angermeier, P.L. and J.R. Karr. 1984. Relationships between woody debris and fish habitat in a small warm-water stream. Trans. Am. Fish. Soc., 113: 716–726.

Armantrout, N.B. 1991. Restructuring Streams for Anadromous Salmonids. American Fisheries Society Symposium, 10: 136–149.

Bjornn, T.C. and D.W. Reiser. 1991. Habitat Requirements of Salmonids in Streams. In: Influences of Forest and Rangeland Management on Salmonid Fishes and Their Habitats. American Fisheries Society Special Publication, 19: 83–138.

Bragg, D.C. and J.L. Kershner. 1999. Coarse woody debris in riparian zones. Journal of Forestry, 97(4): 30–35.

Breusers, H.N.C. and Raudkivi, A.J. 1991. Scouring: Hydraulic Structures and Design Manual. A.A. Balkeman, Rotterdam, Netherlands.

Brown, G.W. and J.T. Krygier. 1970. Effects of clear cutting on stream temperatures. Water Resources Research, 6: 1133–1139.

Bryant, M.D. 1985. Changes 30 Years After Logging in Large Woody Debris, and Its Use by Salmonids. In: Proceedings of the Riparian Management Conference, Tuscan, AZ (April 16–18).

Cederholm, C.J., L.G. Dominquez, and T.W Bumstead. 1997. Rehabilitating Stream Channels and Fish Habitat Using Large Woody Debris. In: Fish Rehabilitation Procedures. Watershed Restoration Program, Ministry of Environment, Lands and Parks and Ministry of Forests, Vancouver, BC. Watershed Restoration Technical Circular, No. 9: 8.1–8.28.

Chapman, D.W. 1996. Efficacy of structural manipulations of instream habitat in the Columbia River basin. Rivers, 5(4): 279–293.

D'Aoust, S.G. and R.G. Millar. 1999. Large Woody Debris Fish Habitat Structure Performance and Ballasting Requirements. Ministry of Environment, Lands and Parks and the Ministry of Forests. Watershed Restoration Management Report No. 8. 119 pp.

Elliot, S.T. 1986. Reduction of Dolly Varden population and macrobenthos after removal of logging debris. Trans. Am. Fish. Soc., 115: 392–400.

Fausch, K.D. and T.G. Northcote. 1992. Large woody debris and salmon habitat in a small coastal British Columbia stream. Can. J. Fish. Aquat. Sci., 49: 682–693.

Fitch, L., M. Miles, J. O'Neil, R. Pattenden, and G. Van Der Vinne. 1994. Defining Variables that influence success of habitat structures in southwestern Alberta: A work in progress. In: Proceedings of the 9th International Trout Stream Habitat Improvement Workshop, September 6–9, Calgary, Alberta. Trout Unlimited Canada.

Gregory, S. V., F. J. Swanson, A. McKee, and K. W. Cummins. 1991. An ecosystem perspective on riparian zones: Focus on links between land and water. BioScience, 41: 540–551.

Hartman, G.F. and M. Miles. 1995. Evaluation of fish habitat improvement projects in BC and recommendations on the development of guidelines for future work. Report prepared for the BC Ministry of Environment, Lands and Parks, Fisheries Branch, Victoria, BC.

Hartman, G.F., J.C. Scrivener, and M.J. Miles. 1996. Impacts of logging in Carnation Creek, A high-energy coastal stream in British Columbia, and their implication for restoring fish habitat. Can. J. Fish. Aquat. Sci., 53(suppl. 1): 237–251.

Heifetz, J., M.L. Murphey, and K.V. Koski. 1986. Effects of logging on winter habitat of juvenile salmonids in Alaskan streams. North Am. J. Fish. Manage., 6: 52–58.

Hetrick, N.J., M.A. Brusven, W.R. Meehan, and T.C. Bjornn. 1998a. Changes in solar input, water temperature, periphyton accumulation, and allochthonous input and storage after canopy removal along two salmon streams in southeast Alaska. Trans. Am. Fish. Soc., 127: 859–875.

Hetrick, N.J., M.A. Brusven, T.C. Bjornn, R.M. Keith, and W.R. Meehan. 1998b. Effects of canopy removal on invertebrates and diet of juvenile coho salmon in a small stream in southeast Alaska. Trans. Am. Fish. Soc., 127: 876–888.

House, R.A. and P.L. Boehne. 1985. Evaluation of instream enhancement structures for salmonid spawning ad rearing in a coastal Oregon Stream. N. Am. J. Fish. Manage., 5: 283–295.

Keith, R.M., T.C. Bjornn, W.R. Meehan, N.J. Hetrick, and M.A. Brusven. 1998. Response of juvenile salmonids to riparian and instream cover modifications in small streams flowing through second-growth forests of southeast Alaska. Trans. Am. Fish. Soc., 127: 889–907.

Knutson, K.L. and V.L. Naef. 1997. Management Recommendations for Washington's Priority Habitats: Riparian. Washington Department of Fish and Wildlife, Olympia, WA. 172 pp.

Koning, C.W., M.N. Gaboury, M.D. Feduk, and P.A. Slaney. 1997. Techniques to evaluate the effectiveness of fish habitat restoration works in streams impacted by logging activities. In: Proceedings of the 50th Annual Conference of the Canadian Water Resources Association (CWRA), Footprints of Humanity, June 3–6, 1997, Lethbridge, Alberta.

Koski, K.V. 1992. Restoring stream habitats affected by logging activities. In: Restoring the Nations Marine Environment. G.W. Thayer, ed. Maryland Sea Grant College, College Park, MD. pp. 343–403.

Lisle, T.E. 1986. Effect of woody debris on anadromous salmon habitat, Prince of Wales Island, southeast Alaska. North Am. J. Fish. Manage., 6: 538–550.

MacDonald, L.H., T.W. Smart, and R.C. Wissmar. 1991. Monitoring Guidelines to Evaluate Effects of Forestry Activities on Streams in the Pacific Northwest and Alaska. United States Environmental Protection Agency, Seattle, WA. 166 pp.

McMahon, T.E. and L.B. Holtby. 1992. Behavior, habitat use, and movements of coho salmon (Oncorhynchus kisutch) smolts during seaward migration. Canadian Journal of Fisheries and Aquatic Sciences, 49: 1478–1485.

Meehan, W.R. 1970. Some effects of shade cover on streams in southeast Alaska. US Forest Service Research Note PNW-113.

Meehan, W.R., F.J. Swanson, and J.R. Sedell. 1977. Influences of Riparian Vegetation on Aquatic Ecosystems with Particular Reference to Salmonid Fishes and Their Food Supply. In: Importance, Preservation and Management of Riparian Habitat: A Symposium. USDA Forest Service General Technical Report RM-43.

Murphy, M.L., J. Heifetz, S.W. Johnson, K.V. Koski, and J.F. Thedinga. 1986. Effects of clear cut logging with and without buffer strips on juvenile salmonids in Alaskan streams. Can. J. Fish. Aquat. Sci., 43: 1521–1533.

Murphy, M.L. and W.R. Meehan. 1991. Influences of forest and rangeland management on salmonid fishes and their habitats. American Fisheries Society Special Publication, 19: 17–46.

Newbury, R.W. and M.N. Gaboury. 1993. Stream Analysis and Fish Habitat Design: A field Manual. Co-published by Newbury Hydraulics Ltd. and the Manitoba Habitat Heritage Corporation. Newbury Hydraulics Ltd., Gibsons, BC.

Nickelson, T. E., M.F. Solazzi, S.L. Johnson, and J.D. Rodgers. 1992. Effectiveness of selected stream improvement techniques to create suitable summer and winter rearing habitat for juvenile coho salmon (Oncorhynchus kisutch) in Oregon coastal streams. Can. J. Fish. Aquat. Sci., 49: 790–794.

O'Connor, N.A. 1991. The effects of habitat complexity on the macroinvertebrates colonizing wood substrate in a lowland stream. Oecologia, 85: 504–512.

Pitch, L., M. Miles, J. O'Neil, R. Pattenden, and G. Van Der Vinne. 1994. Defining the Variables that Influence Success of Habitat Structures in Southwestern Alberta: A Work in Progress. In: Proceedings of the 9th International Trout Stream Habitat Improvement Workshop (September 6–9), Calgary, Alberta.

Poulin, V. A. and Associates Ltd. 1991. Stream rehabilitation using LOD placements and off-channel pool development. Land Management Report Number 61, BC Ministry of Forests.

Riley, S.C. and K.D. Fausch. 1995. Trout populations response to habitat enhancement in six northern Colorado streams. Can. J. Fish. Aquat. Sci., 52: 34–53.

Scouras, J. 1999. Integrating Riparian Zones with Rightofway Management. MSc Thesis. University of Northern British Columbia, November.

Scrivner, J.C. and T.G. Brown. 1993. Impact and complexity from forests practices on streams and their salmonid fishes in British Columbia. In: développement du saumon Atlantique au Québec: connaître règles du jeu pour réussir. Schooner and S. Asselin, eds. Colloue international de la Fédération québecoise pour le saumon atlantique. Québec, PQ. pp. 41–49.

Slaney, P.A. and D. Zaldokas, eds. 1997. Fish Habitat Rehabilitation Procedures. Watershed Restoration technical Circular No. 9. Watershed Restoration Program, Ministry of Environment, Lands and Parks, Vancouver, BC.

Tschaplinski, P.J. and G.F. Hartman. 1983. Winter distribution of juvenile coho salmon (Oncorhynchus kisutch) before and after logging in Carnation Creek, British Columbia, and some implications for over winter survival. Can. J. Fish. Aquat. Sci., 40: 452–461.

Vannote, R.L., G.W. Minshall, K.W. Cummins, J.R. Sedell, and C.E. Cushing. 1980. The river continuum concept. Can. J. Fish. Aquat. Sci., 37: 130–137.

BIOGRAPHICAL SKETCHES

Greg Scarborough, RPBio (corresponding author)
Fisheries Biologist, BC Hydro, T&D Environment, 6911 Southpoint Dr. (E05), Burnaby, BC, V3N 4X8. Tel: 604.528.1721, fax: 604.528.2940, e-mail: greg.scarborough@BCHydro.bc.ca

Mr. Scarborough has eight years of experience managing natural resources with a focus on the environmental aspects of linear corridors. He specializes in mitigating environmental impacts of small and large projects, fish biology and aquatic ecology.

Tasha Robertson, MSc, RPBio
Fisheries Biologist, ECL Envirowest Consultants Ltd., Suite 130-3700 North Fraser Way, Burnaby, BC, V5J 5J4. Tel: 604.451.0505, fax: 604.451.0557

Ms. Robertson has extensive experience: conducting watershed assessments, fish and fish habitat, vegetation, water quality and lake surveys; habitat restoration and compensation projects; performing literature reviews and writing reports; and conducting environmental impact assessments. Ms. Robertson completed her Thesis, as well as various other projects, on salmon pool restoration/enhancement projects during her stay in New Brunswick. Ms. Robertson currently works for ECL Envirowest Consultants Limited where she has been involved in the design and implementation of various stream habitat restoration/enhancement projects throughout watercourses in the Lower Mainland.

Part XIII
Public Participation

Right-of-Way Communication Strategies

Teri L. Vierima and John W. Goodrich-Mahoney

The increasing demand for electricity and the resulting need for additional power delivery systems, combined with an increasing public reluctance to have those power delivery systems in its back yards, has made the siting and maintenance of power lines a significant public issue for transmission and distribution companies. This study identifies and analyzes the key public issues associated with power line siting and maintenance and applies modern risk communication knowledge and techniques to developing strategies and suggestions for successfully communicating about right-of-way issues. Among the resources used are interviews with transmission and distribution company engineers and communications experts. The key steps in developing an effective public communications program are discussed. These key steps are: understand the basis of public perception; establish the project need; integrate public issues into site selection; identify audiences and plan communications; and expect to accommodate and plan accordingly. The study also examines how public issues are likely to affect right-of-way siting and maintenance in the future.

Keywords: Public, communications, strategy, siting, maintenance

THE BUSINESS CASE FOR PUBLIC COMMUNICATION STRATEGIES

In the energy industry, "communicating with the public" brings to mind two extremes: (1) the warm, fuzzy images that companies put in their annual reports and television ads, and (2) the room full of hostile people they face when they announce that they want to put something in someone's back yard. This first case — promoting the company's public image to shareholders — is treated as a vital element of the corporate strategy: every image used in the annual report is professionally done and approved at the highest levels of the organization. Rarely, however, is the second case — communicating with the public about the impact of business operations on their lives — considered to be a strategic activity. Most commonly, it is an afterthought — after the business decisions have been made, after the need for the power line has been determined, after the route has been chosen and after design of the line has been engineered. It is then that companies begin thinking about how they will explain to [not necessarily discuss with] the public why what is being done is right for them. And, again in contrast to other significant corporate communications, the person sent to talk to the public has rarely had any training in public communication.

In business, in order for something to be elevated from an activity to a strategy, it must be linked to the business objectives, that is to say, it must be shown to have a direct financial impact. In this case, a picture says a thousand words (Fig. 1).

In the "good old days" the route from substation A to substation B was a straight line. Today, most new power lines are a jagged route of compromise. This

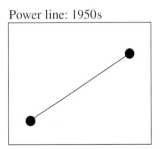 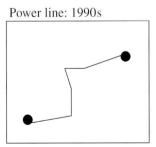

Fig. 1. The evolution of power line siting.

Environmental Concerns in Rights-of-Way Management: Seventh International Symposium
J.W. Goodrich-Mahoney, D.F. Mutrie and C.A. Guild (editors)
© 2002 Elsevier Science Ltd. All rights reserved.

illustration is, of course, a symbolic one, but it is based on examples of real power lines. If you compare the routes of lines in your company over time, you will see the same evolution.

No cost analysis is necessary to tell you that the second power line is much more costly than the first.
– The line is longer, with a proportionately greater construction and materials cost. Chances are there are also more costly pole designs or landscaping along portions of the route. Some of it may be underground.
– The time it takes to site is longer, and time is money.
– And typically, the lawyers' fees are immense.

The difference is not in technology. The difference between these two pictures is due solely to the influence of the public and changes in public values.

Companies have done much to reduce the technical risk associated with power lines, and EPRI research has been a major contributor to that success. Companies also do their best to reduce the financial risk associated with owning and operating a transmission and distribution system. But little attention is paid to reducing the public risk — the risk that a well designed, much-needed project will never be completed because of public outrage — and that risk is growing.

The EPRI project on communicating with the public on issues associated with rights-of-way is a first step in attempting to find ways to make the siting and maintaining of rights-of-way more acceptable, or perhaps better stated, less objectionable. In this paper we report on the first element of this study, which involves soliciting the views of those people within electric utilities who have spent a significant amount of time interacting with the public on these issues. They included design and construction engineers, right-of-way operations and maintenance personnel, foresters, environmental permitting and compliance personnel, real estate managers and corporate public communications experts. For this purpose, we developed a brief questionnaire, to which 37 people in 18 companies responded. Their views will help us to target communication strategies and technical research on those areas that create the greatest controversy and that pose the greatest public risk to right-of-way projects.

One question that was posed to these people was, in their best guess, of all the people in the company who participated in their most recent transmission line siting or upgrade project, what percentage of their time was spent addressing public issues and concerns. The average response was 35%. If 35% of the human resources that a company delegates to developing and maintaining rights-of-way are being spent on public issues, as much attention should be paid to planning and professionally managing the public issues associated with power lines as is paid to designing the annual report.

The following suggestions for managing public risk as an element of business strategy come from discussions with utility experts and observations of communication successes and failures.

STEP ONE: UNDERSTAND THE BASIS OF PUBLIC PERCEPTION

Because of the tremendous influence that public concerns have had on the nuclear power industry, and because of the potential for concerns about electric and magnetic fields (EMF) to have similar impacts on the ability to site power lines, EPRI was among the first to sponsor research aimed at understanding public perception of risk. There is now a wealth of literature on the factors that affect public perception and hence, public acceptance, of risk (see, for example, Trudell and Tikalsky, 1997; Sandman, 1994). Five of these common factors are familiarity of the risk, the voluntary nature or the amount of personal control one has over the risk, the fairness of the risk (that is who bears the risk versus who benefits from the risk), the level of fear that the potential outcome incites, and the level of trust placed in the person or institution who imposes or controls the risk. Many of these factors weigh in negatively against rights-of-way and power lines: rights-of-way are inherently unfair in that most of those who benefit do not live near them, nearby residents feel very little control over the siting process, the potential impacts from EMF, stray currents or the use of herbicides are frightening to the general public, and it is probably safe to say that public members have very little trust in utility companies when it comes to siting rights-of-way in their back yards. The first step in addressing public concerns about rights-of-way is to identify and understand the underlying causes of these concerns. It cannot be emphasized enough that those people who will be interacting with the public on right-of-way issues — whether it be in the context of a large public meeting or in one-on-one interactions with landowners — need to be able to identify the fundamental values that create these issues.

STEP TWO: ESTABLISH THE PROJECT NEED

In our survey, we asked the respondents what advice they would give others in dealing with the public regarding power line rights-of-way. By far the most common response was "start early." When asked what they would do differently next time, many of them answered "start even earlier." When asked what issues they had the most difficulty in explaining to the public, respondents frequently cited the need for the line and the benefits to the local community. These are issues that can be made easier by putting in place a strategy to communicate with the public about the way the grid works, the need for new lines into the area, the local benefits of a more reliable transmission and distribution system (which is more important to locals than the company's ability to make money by selling power elsewhere) and the process that will be used to site new lines. All of this can be begun well in advance

Table 1. Common public concerns associated with rights-of-way and power lines

Local concerns about corridors	Local concerns about power lines	State or regional concerns
✓ Property values	✓ Electric and magnetic fields	✓ Wetland impacts
✓ Equity/fairness	✓ Stray voltage/currents	✓ Biodiversity/habitat fragmentation
✓ Restrictions on use of easements	✓ Visual impact of the poles	✓ River/stream crossings
✓ Compensation for easements	✓ Electrical safety	✓ Avian interactions
✓ Impacts of construction	✓ Need for the line	✓ Pesticide use
✓ Use of eminent domain	✓ Ozone/odor	✓ Impacts on endangered/threatened species
✓ Tree trimming/removal	✓ Noise	✓ Impacts on the viewshed
✓ Use of herbicides	✓ Electromagnetic interference	✓ Impacts on archeological/historic sites
✓ Maintenance and use of access roads/routes	✓ Impacts on agriculture	✓ Co-location with other facilities
✓ Illegal trespass/use by outside parties	✓ Chemically treated poles	✓ Relative impact on low-income/minority populations
	✓ Proximity to schools/day care centers	

of any siting efforts. Media articles, presentations to civic groups and schools, conversations with civic and industrial leaders can all be useful in changing the public consciousness about energy issues. This takes time, but it will give the siting process a smoother beginning. In fact, an audience of citizens who have come to accept the need for a line can become positive contributors to the solution.

STEP THREE: INTEGRATE PUBLIC ISSUES INTO SITE SELECTION

The standard process used in siting rights-of-way has been (1) select the best routes from a technical perspective and then (2) deal with the public issues when they arise. But if the public risk to the project is as great or greater than the technical risk, then assessment of the public risk should be built into the site selection process from the beginning. Someone who is familiar with public issues should be on the site selection team.

We all know what the issues are. Table 1 lists the most common causes of public concerns about new rights-of-way.

In the first column are issues associated with the creation of any right-of-way, regardless of what is being sited; the second column lists concerns associated with having a power line in that right-of-way; and the third lists those issues that are likely to generate concern among broader groups, beyond just the landowners and residents who live next to the right-of-way. A simple process for assessing the public risk associated with a proposed route is to break the line into segments, according to the characteristics of the adjacent property (e.g., agricultural, urban, suburban residential), and to use Table 1 as a checklist to anticipate what issues are likely to create the greatest opposition along each segment. The geographic information systems that are increasingly being used in planning power-line routes can be applied to and integrated with this process. By systematically analyzing the potential public risk associated with the route, changes can be made to the route or the line design in advance of creating public opposition. The more you can anticipate and prepare for public issues before you ever announce the project, the better you will be at managing the public risk.

In our gathering of the views of utility personnel who deal with public issues, we asked them to rank the importance of these issues in their most recent power line siting or upgrade project. On a scale of one to four, with one being "not raised" and four being "became a major issue," the following issues topped the list.
- Property values (3.3)
- Visual impact/aesthetic appearance of the towers/poles (3.3)
- Impacts on the viewshed (scenic aesthetics) (3.0)
- Electromagnetic fields (2.8)
- Equity/fairness (i.e., those who must live next to the line vs. those who benefit) (2.8)
- Compensation for easements/tax implications (2.8)
- Need for the line (e.g., use of conservation or distributed generation instead) (2.5)

STEP FOUR: IDENTIFY AUDIENCES AND PLAN COMMUNICATIONS

Just as you can usually identify what issues are likely to be of greatest concern, you can also identify in advance what audiences with whom you will need to communicate. Before your proposed action hits the newspaper, you should have developed an in-depth, detailed plan for notifying, educating and involving each of these audiences. A simple table, like Table 2, can be used to identify specific communication initiatives for each audience during each stage of the siting process.

The entries shown in this table are the responses we received from the power company experts when asked at what stage in the project did they first notify key groups of interested parties. In a true communication

Table 2. A structure for planning communications. (Entries indicate the percentage of respondents who indicated the stage at which they first notified key interest groups.)

	Project stages								
	Needs assessment	Preliminary design	Selection of primary and alternative routes	Assessment of impacts	Application to regulatory agencies	Regulatory review and approval process	Final design	Construction	Maintenance
State or federal environmental regulators and public utility commissions	62%	7%	7%		21%	3%			
Landowners/ neighbors	9%	26%	50%	6%	3%		6%		
Local officials (e.g., legislators, city councils)	20%	29%	45%		3%		3%		
Local, regional and national environmental groups	8%	20%	44%	8%	12%	4%	4%		
General public	10%	17%	46%		17%	7%	3%		
Media	NA								

plan, there would be entries in each cell of the table, including the key communication points, the most effective communication vehicles, and the responsible individuals at each stage. Communication vehicles can range from simple brochures to very involved public advisory groups.

STEP FIVE: EXPECT TO ACCOMMODATE AND PLAN ACCORDINGLY

Anticipating public issues, as described in Step Two, can enable you to make accommodations for issues that you know will be controversial before they become a controversy, but others will always arise once your intended actions become known. The questionnaire respondents were asked about the means of accommodating public interests or improving public acceptance of a power line. The following list shows the percentage of respondents who said that their company had used the following means of accommodation. (Note that some companies had more than one respondent and therefore may be represented more than once in these percentages.)
– Relocation of some portion of the line (86%)
– Special clearing techniques to save vegetation (76%)
– Change in pole design/height/color (76%)
– Landscaping (68%)
– Agricultural use of the corridor (e.g., tree farming) (65%)
– Wildlife or endangered/threatened species habitat or wetlands preservation or creation (59%)
– Accommodations for bird nesting (59%)
– Research projects (46%)
– Recreational use of the corridor (41%)
– Financial incentives (30%)
– Undergrounding all or a portion of the line (22%)
– Enlarging the corridor (16%)
– Change in construction techniques (e.g., flying the towers in, rather than using trucks) (3%)

As the EPRI project progresses, we will learn more from these individuals about innovative and effective ways of making rights-of-way and power lines less objectionable.

WHAT THE FUTURE HOLDS

At the end of the questionnaire, we asked our respondents to put their feet up on their desks, look into the future and give us their opinion of how power-line right-of-way siting, operation and maintenance will evolve. They do not see the situation getting any easier. They see greater restrictions on overhead lines and more pressure to put lines underground. They see landowners and public activists becoming more sophisticated and assertive, and more skilled at using the Internet as a tool to organize opposition. Regulatory agency involvement will increase, as will the lead times necessary to site new lines. With the increasing number of players in the energy scene and the increasingly monetary motives of those players, they predict that the public will become more suspicious. The new independent transmission companies, and even the new breed of larger, geographically dispersed utilities, may not develop the community relations that utilities have traditionally had in the past. And as power-line owners tighten their right-of-way maintenance budgets, they see public and regulatory attention to right-of-way maintenance issues increasing.

Not only will it become more difficult to site new rights-of-way, it will become more costly. The cost of acquiring new easement rights will escalate with increasing population, property values and community demands for compensation. Companies are now beginning to think of and treat existing corridors as assets with escalating value. More facilities will be forced to site within these existing corridors. One respondent, in fact, recommended that new corridors be designated and obtained now for future use, as they may be profitable investments.

Lastly, technology development can assist in easing public issues. While the EMF issue will never go away, EPRI health effects research has had a major impact in mitigating the pressure to impose strict EMF-related regulations on power lines. At the same time, EPRI has developed low-EMF line designs that are cost-effective and accommodate the public's concern regardless of any actual health risks. More selective vegetation management techniques and improved pole materials and treatment can make power-line rights-of-way of less concern to those who worry about chemical contamination. New line designs that reduce the visual impact would be welcome. And a study of ways to turn rights-of-way into environmental assets by using them to benefit bird nesting and endangered plants is being conducted by EPRI and is reported on elsewhere in these proceedings. When respondents were asked what future EPRI research would be of most use to them, the most frequent answers were research into public perceptions, research on the impact of rights-of-way on property values and the development of public information materials on rights-of-way.

CONCLUSIONS

This EPRI study of public issues associated with rights-of-way and actions that can be taken to improve communications about rights-of-way is just the first step in attempting to bring public issue management into the framework of business management. Understanding and planning for public issues will not make them go away, as most would wish. But a company that learns to communicate well with the public and to reduce public opposition to right-of-way activities is likely to become a better communicator in all aspects of its business. The public image that companies promote in their annual reports is important and encompasses a broad audience. But equally important to the business over the long run is the quality of the daily, local communications they have with the public about the energy business and its impacts.

NOTE

Subsequent to this presentation, the results of this study have been published. See (Vierima, 2001).

REFERENCES

Trudell, K.A. and S.M. Tikalsky. 1997. Risk Communication for the Natural Gas Industry. Gas Research Institute, Chicago.

Sandman, P. 1994. Responding to Community Outrage: Strategies for Effective Risk Communication. American Industrial Hygiene Association, Fairfax, VA.

Vierima, T.L. 2001. Communicating with the Public About Rights-of-Way: A Practitioner's Guide. EPRI, Palo Alto, CA.

BIOGRAPHICAL SKETCHES

Teri L. Vierima

Resource Strategies, Inc., 22 N. Carroll St., Suite 300, Madison, WI 53703, USA. (608) 251-8767

Dr. Vierima has been involved with the utility industry for over twenty years as an analyst with the Wisconsin Public Service Commission, as scientific advisor and director of regulatory programs for radiation sources for the State of Wisconsin, and as the manager of research and development for Wisconsin Power and Light Company. For the past five years she has been a consultant to the energy industry. Her expertise is in assisting the industry in analyzing and planning for emerging safety and environmental health issues, and in communicating complex technical information to lay audiences. Dr. Vierima holds a PhD degree in physics from Yale University.

John W. Goodrich-Mahoney

EPRI, 2000 L Street, NW, Suite 805, Washington, DC 20036, USA

Mr. Goodrich-Mahoney is the Target Manager for EPRI's right-of-way and water quality research programs. He is responsible for the development and management of research to help reduce surface water, vegetation management and other regulatory compliance costs for the energy industry, and to help promote beneficial uses of rights-of-way. Mr. Goodrich-Mahoney holds a BS degree in chemistry and geology from St. Lawrence University and a MSc degree in geochemistry from Brown University.

Infographic Simulations using Photographs as a Method to Gain Greater Social Acceptance for Projected Lines and Substations

Jorge Roig Solés, Leticia González Cantalapiedra, Roberto Arranz Cuesta, and Javier Arevalo Camacho

One of the greatest stumbling blocks in developing projects for new power transmission lines and substations is the opposition to such structures on the part of the affected individuals and organizations. One of the main reasons for this opposition is the difficulty people have in evaluating how a new line, substation or related infrastructure may affect the landscape they are used to. The aim of the infographic simulations is to help people visualize the effects, especially visual or scenic, likely to be produced on the landscape of the proposed line. This paper gives a description of the method used and shows infographic simulations carried out by Red Eléctrica on several of its lines. Since the medium involved is photographic those affected can easily recognize the territory featured in the simulation. As regards new line projects, examples are given of two alternative routes studied for a line passing close to a castle, and the visual impact of replacing a single-circuit line by a double-circuit line. In the case of substations, three simulations are shown for the different phases of locating of a new substation: Before the work is started; the substation's switchgear at the end of the construction and assembly work and, finally, the substation's appearance after the surrounding area has been landscaped, with simulations of plant screens, embankment treatment and other treatments. The results of this method have in general been satisfactory, allowing the opinion of all those involved to be taken into account and helping to make the new lines and structures more readily acceptable.

Keywords: Public acceptance, business communications, view shed, visual simulation, visual impact, infography

INTRODUCTION

One of the difficulties faced in projects involving the installation of new power lines is the opposition from organizations and individuals that might be affected by such installations. It is therefore appropriate to analyze the reasons why electrical installations are rejected. Rarely, no one is prepared to deny the need for electrical installations or to argue the convenience of building airports, railways, schools, or hospitals. The objective is to ensure that their location is suitably distant from one's home. "All right, but not here." The second reason is related to the very nature of electric energy, about which the public is quite ignorant.

In decisions related to the location of a new transformer station or the alignment of a power line, it is an error to consider only the technical and economic factors because any location or alignment will inevitably affect the owners of the land involved and their neighbors. Studies show that both country and urban land has a greater value if there is no nearby electrical installation.

From the point of view of the national government, the needs of the electricity sector are validated by the procedures of the corresponding ministry. Regional governments are absolved from responsibility "by a higher authority" because the majority of installations have been classified as being in the public interest. However, at local government levels, the complaints

Environmental Concerns in Rights-of-Way
Management: Seventh International Symposium
J.W. Goodrich-Mahoney, D.F. Mutrie and C.A. Guild (editors)
© 2002 Elsevier Science Ltd. All rights reserved.

have a more direct effect. Those who are allegedly affected are residents of the municipalities in question and in many cases councilors support protests by the local public — proposing alternative alignments that are difficult or impossible to accept in the majority of cases.

The point of view of the environmentalists is the easiest one to predict. As they have no executive responsibility, they can ask for the impossible with the appearance of being reasonable. They want power lines to be located in areas that do not affect the environment and they want all other electrical installations to be located far away from centers of population, without the opposition of their neighbors. It need not be said that they rarely offer any explanation on how to resolve this problem and if they offer any suggestion at all it is in the realms of utopia. Their messages on the other hand are strongly supported by the inhabitants of the affected areas.

The attitude of the media is deeply influenced by their social nature. Most journalists are reporters with limited technical knowledge and a high degree of sensitivity with regard to the abuse and might of the political and economic powers. Consequently, the information provided by groups of environmentalists and neighborhood associations, are generously received by the newspapers. This could be due to the sporting instincts of the younger reporters and to the assumption that these reports will be broadly accepted by a wide majority of readers.

OBJECTIVES

Business communications should not be considered merely from the utilitarian point of view. They are an activity that should be carried out daily and therefore active public acceptance programs should be established. These programs should provide an effective means of internal communication leading subsequently to an understanding of the need to establish a close relationship with the local inhabitants, institutions, local government, neighborhood associations, environmental movements, and the media.

A relationship with the inhabitants of a particular area must be based on the good neighbor principle. There are small owners and small companies that might be affected by large installations. The proponents should visit them and explain the project. Perhaps this will not be sufficient to neutralize their protests but, in most cases, it will moderate the protests and limit them to specific aspects, which are much easier to handle than general and undocumented complaints.

The relationship with the local authorities is also important. Within a constituency, a mayor is an authority and his or her capacity to jeopardize a project is infinitely greater than his or her capacity to promote it or support it. Ignoring these people because they initially have no official responsibility with regard to a project, which affects their municipality, is a grave error that may have disastrous consequences in the short and medium term. They are probably not in a position to prevent an installation going ahead but they can hold it up for years — which can be economically dangerous.

The proliferation of neighborhood associations of all kinds makes it necessary to find out which are active in the area of influence and to approach them. They should be given information about the plans and aided with their problems while maintaining frequent contact with their activities and members. This may or may not be of direct benefit to the company, but it will certainly do no harm and may even contribute to resolving certain problems effectively.

Although this may come as a shock, it is also necessary to establish a close relationship with the environmental movements in the area. Providing them with complete and truthful information may prevent them from requesting information from national or international environmental movements and, in the best case, it will serve as a real comparison and mitigate many of the arguments that might arise.

Lastly, it is essential to maintain a flexible, continuous, and sincere relationship with the media. They act as loudspeakers in the case of any protest and they are a vehicle for accusations and complaints because they exercise great influence on public opinion.

Therefore, an active policy of communication must start by accepting that the installation of substations and power lines will cause people to feel they are legitimately affected. In many cases, these facilities have an obvious impact on the landscape and efforts should be made to minimize this.

Landscape considerations are a growing concern. This is due to the desire to reduce negative impacts and involves preventive and corrective measures to integrate the installations with their natural surroundings. The interpretation of these preventive and corrective measures, which lack visual realism, is limited to technical staff. In these matters it is difficult for the public to evaluate the effect of a new installation, power line, or substation, on a landscape to which they are accustomed.

What does visual simulation mean? The area of information technology that deals with graphic representation — in its widest sense — is called infography. The definition of visual simulation is the application of infographic techniques to obtain images or scenes of things, which do not exist or which are removed from the user in space or time. The objectives of visual simulation in engineering work are as follows:

– To obtain representations of the project, which provide an approximate idea of its aspect in the future, showing the main components and its integration in its surroundings.

- To facilitate the public's perception of the effect, especially the visual and landscape effect, which the new installation will produce.

It is the importance of the project or its effect on the landscape, which determines whether or not it is necessary to produce a visual simulation. However, the simulation is a document of unquestionable value, both for technical staff and customers, and this indicates that visual simulations should be carried out systematically.

Infographic simulation in photo format is the most widely used technique at the present time for visual simulation in engineering design work and architecture. This is due to the fact that in recent years highly realistic effects have been achieved with three-dimensional models of the project components and these can be effectively integrated with real photographs, resulting in images with a high degree of realism. Alternative methods of visual simulation are limited almost exclusively to use by technical personnel who can interpret synthetic images lacking in visual realism. When it is necessary to convince the public by visual means, these synthetic images may result in confusion, especially in the case of those who are not accustomed to interpreting computer-generated images.

The principle of infographic simulations in photo format is very simple. It involves images that represent the future reality of the different project alternatives using photocomposition of the elements, which make up the project. These images are obtained by synthesizing three-dimensional images on a real scene, which is photographed from specific viewpoints. As can be seen, the principle is simple but in practice it requires a series of skills that are described below.

METHODOLOGY

The viewpoints of interest are determined in the office based on the design of the future power line

The viewpoints from which the photographs will be taken are selected by following a specific process:

Fig. 1. Determination of possible view points using existing maps.

- Existing maps are used to determine the position of possible viewpoints. Once these have been selected, their UTM co-ordinates are noted for subsequent location in the field. (See Fig. 1)
- In the field, GPS and the maps are used to locate the points from where the photographs will be taken – taking into account the existence of obstacles which might interfere with the view and in which case alternative points will be used which have previously been determined in the office.

The photographs are taken from the selected points

The photographs in the field are taken under strict controls with regard to position, lighting, and transparency of the air, apart from photography parameters. All the details are noted on a form and used later to simulate the characteristics of the synthetic scene with great precision.

- Photographic details: numbering of photographs, film details, lens, exposure and aperture, use of filters, and polarizes.
- Position and angle of the camera: UTM co-ordinates of the points, map location, the bearing (taken with a compass), vertical angle, camera height, and the reference of the object.
- Environment: date and time, height of the sun (shadow length), sun azimuth (shadow bearing), and lighting (degree of cloudiness). (See Fig. 2)

Fig. 2. Taking the photographs.

Fig. 3. Storing the photograph on digital media.

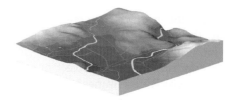

Fig. 5. A digital model of the terrain.

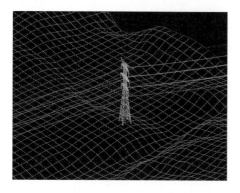

Fig. 4. Modelling the power line components in 3D.

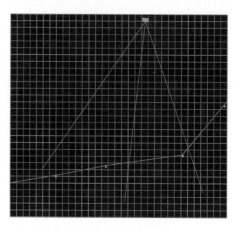

Fig. 6. Locating the virtual camera in the digital model of the terrain.

The topography of the area in question is determined in digital format

The process of preparing photographic material for computer use starts after the film has been developed and it can take two directions:
– Direct scanning of the film.
– Scanning of photographic enlargements.

In either case, once the final result has been obtained, it is stored on a suitable medium, such as CD-ROM and optical disk, for later use during the incorporation of the digital model. (See Fig. 3)

A three-dimensional model is prepared of the project components

Using the digital data of the detail drawings of the project elements, these elements are digitally recreated in three dimensions. This process is called "modeling." The result is a graphic database, which contains the coordinates of the vertices that describe each object.
– In the case of power lines the elements which must be modeled and which will be included later in the final model are, towers and insulator strings, cables, and a digital model of the ground. (See Fig. 4)
– In the case of substations the elements which must be modeled and which will be included later in the final model are compound platform, access roads, internal roads, leveling and side slopes, fencing, buildings, portal frames, bus bars, transformers (voltage, current, etc.), power transformers, other vertical elements in the compound (support insulators, etc.), compound entry towers, cables, and the digital model of the terrain.
– From the point of view of simulation, natural elements are reduced to different strata of vegetation.

These strata (grass, bushes, and trees) have different degrees of simulation. However, only the tree stratum is susceptible to three-dimensional modeling.

A Digital Model of the Terrain (DMT) is prepared

From the point of view of simulation the terrain has two specific functions. It supports the objects in the simulation and the digital model of the terrain is used as a three-dimensional body that blocks vision. (See Fig. 5)

The digital model of the terrain is simply another three-dimensional object. It must be constructed using contour information, which on many occasions is the only data available. The different heights in a scene are reflected by contours which are lines joining points of equal height. These details of relief are essential in any visual impact evaluation and obviously they are essential for the visual simulation of alternatives.

Integration and photocomposition is carried out in two dimensions

In the integration and photocomposition stage, the goal is to superimpose the elements of the project on the base scene.
– The models of the supports and the cables of the power line are located over the digital model of the terrain in their real position.
– The next step is to position the virtual camera in the model, adjusting the view point and the focal distance to match that of the real photograph. (See Fig. 6)

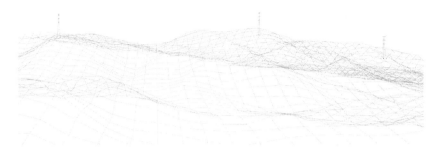

Fig. 7. Adjusting the digital model of the terrain to the photograph.

Fig. 8. Generating the visual simulation with the photograph as a background.

Fig. 9. Alternative 1.

- This provides a view of the model that matches that of the photograph. (See Fig. 7)
- The final step is to generate the visual simulation using the photograph as a background and to carry out final rendering. (See Fig. 8)

RESULTS

Infographic simulations made by Red Eléctrica for some of its installations are shown below. As these have a photographic format, the people involved have no trouble recognizing the area in simulation and this facilitates their perception of the effect that will be produced by the new installation.

Examples of new power line projects

1. An example of two alternative routes for a power line near a castle (see Figs. 9 and 10).
2. An example of the replacement of a single-circuit line by a double-circuit line (see Figs. 11 and 12).
3. An example of two alternative alignments (see Figs. 13 and 14).
4. An example of the visual impact caused by different types of supports (see Figs. 15 and 16).

Fig. 10. Alternative 2.

Fig. 11. Single circuit tower (current situation).

Fig. 12. Double circuit tower (simulated situation).

Fig. 13. Alternative 1.

Fig. 14. Alternative 2.

Examples of new substation projects

1. An example of the simulation of a new substation (see Figs. 17 and 18).
2. An example of alternative forms of substation construction (see Figs. 19, 20, and 21).
3. An example of a simulation of a new substation site in different phases of construction (see Figs. 22, 23, 24, and 25).

CONCLUSIONS

During a project this methodology can represent the visual impact, which each alternative will have on the

Fig. 15. Project with standard towers.

Fig. 18. Simulated substation.

Fig. 16. Project with tubular towers.

Fig. 19. Air insulated substation — metal fencing.

Fig. 17. Original situation.

Fig. 20. Enclosed substation — metal fencing.

area surrounding the project. This feature facilitates the choice of an acceptable solution in the case of different alternatives. The use of this method so far has generally obtained good results. It allows the opinion of those affected to be taken into account and it fosters acceptance of new installations.

At the present time any company, which wishes to achieve excellence must pay the same level of attention and care which it applies to the drawings and designs of its engineers, to the design and development of communication plans and strategies. Any refusal to accept this will ignore the evidence and the medium and long term consequences may be negative.

Fig. 21. Air insulated substation — surrounded by a wall.

Fig. 22. Original situation.

Fig. 23. Simulated substation.

Fig. 24. Recently planted.

Fig. 25. Mature vegetation.

Macia, P. 1996. Strategic importance of communication. A paper at the Second Conference on Power Lines and Environment. Red Eléctrica de España, Madrid, Spain.

Sanders, G.A., et al. 1993. Visual simulation analysis. In: Proceedings of the 1993 Simulation Multiconference on the Simulation in Military and Government Conference. USA.

Visual Simulation Lab. 1997. Methodology for visual simulation of electrical facilities. Red Eléctrica de España, Spain.

REFERENCES

Blanco, A. and M. Aguilo. 1981. The evaluation of landscape. In: The Encyclopaedia of the Environment. CEOTMA and UPM, Madrid, Spain.

Booche, F. 1993. Automatic DTM generation from spaceborne KFA 1000 images — A contribution to the establishment of a digital landscape model. In: Proceedings of IGARSS '93 — IEEE International Geoscience and Remote Sensing Symposium. USA.

Broadbent, D. E. 1987. Perception and communication. USA.

Chiba, N., et al. 1994. Visual simulation of botanical trees based on virtual heliotropism and dormancy break. Journal of Visualization and Computer Animation, 5(1). UK.

Ecker, R. 1992. Digital orthophoto generation based on a high-quality DTM. ITC Journal, 1. The Netherlands.

BIOGRAPHICAL SKETCHES

Jorge Roig Solés

Environmental Department, Red Eléctrica de España, S.A., P° del Conde de los Gaitanes, 177, 28109 Alcobendas-Madrid, Spain (Red Eléctrica is the company in charge of the spanish transmission grid management)

Head of the Environmental Department, he is dealing with the environmental issues of Red Eléctrica de España since its constitution in 1985. He has over 20 years experience in environmental control in industry. Jorge is a Mining Engineer from the Universidad Politécnica de Madrid and holds a Diploma in Environmental Engineering from the University of Strathclyde (Glasgow).

Leticia González Cantalapiedra
Environmental Department, Red Eléctrica de España, S.A., P° del Conde de los Gaitanes, 177, 28109 Alcobendas-Madrid, Spain (Red Eléctrica is the company in charge of the spanish transmission grid management)
Member of the Environmental Department, Red Eléctrica de España, Leticia holds a degree in Biological Sciences from the Universidad Complutense de Madrid and a Master in Environmental Engineering and Management from the Escuela de Organización Industrial (Madrid).

Roberto Arranz Cuesta
Environmental Department, Red Eléctrica de España, S.A., P° del Conde de los Gaitanes, 177, 28109 Alcobendas-Madrid, Spain (Red Eléctrica is the company in charge of the spanish transmission grid management)
Technician at the Environmental Department of Red Eléctrica de España, S.A. Roberto holds a Degree in Geology from the Universidad del País Vasco, a Graduation in Environmental Engineering and a Master in Environmental Engineering and Management from the Escuela de Organización Industrial, Madrid.

Javier Arévalo Camacho
Environmental Department, Red Eléctrica de España, S.A., P° del Conde de los Gaitanes, 177, 28109 Alcobendas-Madrid, Spain (Red Eléctrica is the company in charge of the spanish transmission grid management)
Technician at the Environmental Department of Red Eléctrica de España, Javier is a Forestry Engineer from the Universidad Politécnica de Madrid. He is specialized in Environmental Impacts and is an active member of several Associations such as the Spanish Forest Sciences Association, the Spanish Earth Environment Association and the Spanish Landscape Engineering Association. He has over 20 years experience in environmental issues.

Public-Private Cooperation in Electric Transmission Line Siting, The Dorchester to Quincy Cable Project: A Case Study

F. Paul Richards, Frank S. Smith, John Amodeo, and Margaret Mills

The Dorchester to Quincy Cable Project was initially a classic "not in my backyard" confrontation between the electric company and the affected communities. The first part of the paper documents our presentation of the need case; the importance of our understanding the local political-social climate existing at the time; the process of consensus-building; the eventual turnaround by the affected communities; and the ultimate routing concept that won whole-hearted community endorsement. The second part of the paper deals with the process of using a necessary easement agreement for the cable route through public land to structure a park plan, in lieu of cash payment, that had direct community benefit. A series of community meetings led to the consensus for a park plan incorporating the cables in its design. The initial phase of the park is due to open in the spring of 2001.

Keywords: Transmission, siting, public participation, cables, park

NEED FOR THE PROJECT

Quincy, Massachusetts, a city of about 90,000 inhabitants, is on the coast adjacent to and south of Boston. It is the primary commercial and industrial center in the South Shore area of Massachusetts Bay. Prior to the year 2000, Quincy with its 137 megawatts (MW) of electrical load, was supplied by two 115,000 volt (115 kV) underground electric cables and a number of lower voltage cables which are owned and operated by New England Power Company (NEP) and Massachusetts Electric Company (MEC).[1] No electrical generating sources other than small private generators are located within the load center. The existing 6.5 mile long 115 kV cables cross Quincy in public streets and feed the only two supply substations in the city. It was necessary to retire lower voltage, back-up cables late in 1999. Because the two 115 kV cables are in close proximity to each other, they are vulnerable to a very unlikely, but possible, coincident failure which could take several days to repair and return to service. Following retirement of the lower voltage cables, and without some major additions to the electrical system prior to 2000, loss of the two 115 kV transmission cables could interrupt Quincy's entire electrical supply for several days. In 1996, following a study of several options NEP and MEC concluded that the reliability of Quincy's electric supply could be maintained best by installing two 115 kV underground electric cables between an NSTAR (aka Boston Edison) Company substation in Dorchester, a neighborhood of Boston, and a MEC substation in Quincy (the Dorchester to Quincy Cable Project; Fig. 1).

PROJECT DESCRIPTION

The Dorchester to Quincy Cable Project involved the installation of two 115 kV pipe-type electric cables in 8-inch diameter steel pipes and two fiberoptic control cables in 2-inch diameter conduits. The cables and conduits were primarily installed in a $5\frac{1}{2}$-foot wide and deep open trench. In two special situations open trenching was replaced by use of horizontal directional drilling techniques for installation of the steel pipes.

---

1 New England Power Company and Massachusetts Electric Company are subsidaries of National Grid USA.

Environmental Concerns in Rights-of-Way Management: Seventh International Symposium
J.W. Goodrich-Mahoney, D.F. Mutrie and C.A. Guild (editors)
© 2002 Elsevier Science Ltd. All rights reserved.

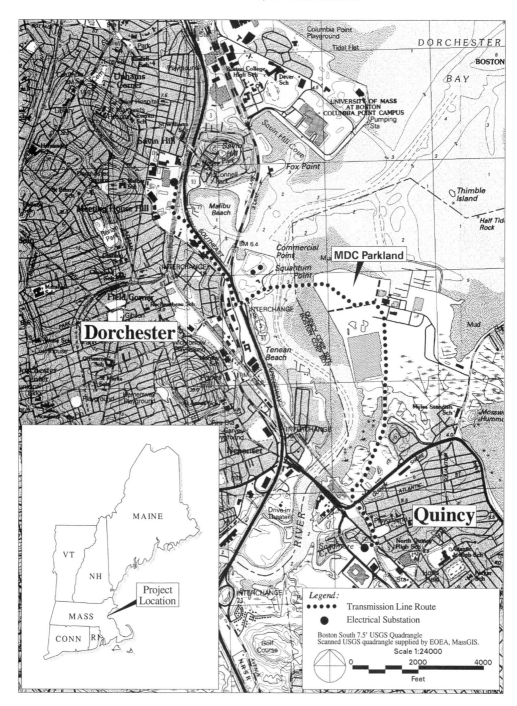

Fig. 1. Project locus map.

THE PROJECT CONTEXT

The principal contextual elements of the Dorchester to Quincy Cable Project are land use, political processes, Boston's construction explosion and the regulatory framework.

Land use

Approximately two square miles of Dorchester and Quincy were studied for possible cable routes. The Dorchester portion of the area studied has mixed land use with residential, commercial, light industry and major transportation uses predominating. The Quincy portion of the area studied is also mixed use with park land, commercial, light industrial and condominium complexes dominating. The Neponset River, with its extensive shellfish flats, marshes, and estuarine environment, is the major natural environmental resource in the area. Because the Neponset River forms the border between Boston and Quincy it had to be crossed by the cables. During the route selection process, the Neponset River was designated an Area of Critical Environmental Concern (ACEC) by the Massachusetts Department of Environmental Management (DEM).

This designation substantially limited the environmental impact allowed for any new land uses proposed in the vicinity of the Neponset River.

Political processes

It was the late Speaker of the US House of Representatives, Thomas "Tip" O'Neill of Cambridge, Massachusetts, who said "All politics is local." Politics is truly a way of life in Massachusetts, especially in and around Boston. Not only are local executive and legislative elected officials vitally interested and involved in the planning of what goes on in their spheres of interest, but so are the state legislators. Political interest doesn't stop with elected officials. Numerous active, formal and informal neighborhood associations exist in the areas of Dorchester and Quincy considered for the cables. While planning for the cable project, the project team worked with twenty elected officials or their representatives, and seventeen neighborhood associations and environmental advocacy groups.

Boston's construction explosion

Boston has been experiencing the effects of a construction explosion for the last several years. The largest of these projects, the "Big Dig," a $13 billion federal highway project to depress I-93 through the city, has generated traffic impacts throughout the city including in the Dorchester neighborhood. In the same time period ten other major projects have taken place, are under construction, or are being planned for the area that was being considered for the route of the transmission cables. Of course, in addition to the "megaprojects" there have been numerous ordinary projects that inconvenience the public on a regular basis. Who could fault the neighborhoods for their initial message to the project team: "Enough is enough — Go away!"

Regulatory framework

Large, capital, utility projects in the Commonwealth of Massachusetts are faced with a battery of federal, state and local rules and regulations — many with overlapping areas of responsibility — to be satisfied during the permitting and licensing phase of such a project. Massachusetts is generally considered one of the most heavily regulated states[2] with an extremely informed and active environmental community. The added factor that the cables would have to cross the local transit authority lines, an Interstate highway, a tidal river, a parkway and possibly state park land only served to make the regulatory picture more complicated.

---

2 The Dorchester to Quincy Cable Project required an environmental impact report, one federal permit, nine major state permits and licenses, consultative review by six other state agencies or jurisdictions and two local permits. Additional construction related licenses and permits were also required for much of the work.

CONSENSUS BUILDING

Given the project context, it was apparent to project management that a smooth licensing and permitting process was critical to having the new cables ready for service by the year 2000. This could not be accomplished with opposition to the proposed project. Project management felt that in order to keep the schedule, it had to be able to demonstrate to the regulatory agencies that not only was there no opposition but that there was full support for the project in both the Dorchester and Quincy communities. Given the expected strong interest of the neighborhood groups, the political leadership, and the environmental advocacy groups and regulators, full support was needed from a variety of stakeholders[3] with potentially varying points of view. NEP and MEC felt that support for the project could be best achieved through extensive public participation in the selection of a preferred route for the cables; by selecting a route where the property owners could feel that they would benefit from allowing the cables to be installed; and, by selecting installation methods that would minimize the potential for construction impacts.

The first step in the public participation effort was to meet with elected officials in each community and with leading federal, state and local regulators to describe the project, explain the need for it, seek their response to some initial routing concepts and obtain their advice on how best to solicit community input for the route selection process. Based on those initial meetings, the project team began meeting with numerous neighborhood groups, area business people, local property owners, environmental regulators and environmental advocacy groups to describe the project and its need, project construction, schedule, permitting and licensing needs, and to seek input on routes and to identify concerns about the possible impacts of construction. Brochures for distribution at all meetings and visual aids were developed and maintained current as routes were revised and as the project design matured. Because Quincy and Dorchester have large Asian populations, bilingual brochures were also developed in Chinese/English and Vietnamese/English formats. All public meetings were advertised in local newspapers. The project was represented at most public meetings by a team of experts, including the project manager, the cable or substation engineer (depending on the subject of the meeting), the project manager of environmental studies, an expert on electric and magnetic fields and a community liaison. All

---

3 The major stakeholders were seen to be the people that live and work in the routing study area, public officials from Dorchester and Quincy, several environmental groups interested in Boston Harbor and the Neponset River, numerous civic associations, the environmental regulators, the utility regulators, the major property owners in the area and the management of New England Power Company and Massachusetts Electric Company.

questions raised at the meetings were answered as forthrightly as possible and all routing suggestions were taken seriously and investigated for feasibility of implementation. Notes taken at the meetings served as a reference for future project planning. To further gain an understanding of community concerns and issues, members of the project team frequently attended business association and community meetings on other proposed projects in Dorchester and Quincy.

Through the public participation process, which involved over one hundred meetings during a two year period, the project team was able to eliminate routes that would have caused substantial community opposition or that had significant construction constraints, even though they initially seemed to be good choices from a strictly technical perspective. The public participation process also brought to light opportunities for routing and for partnering with property owners in a way that would address public needs as part of the compensation for permanent location rights.

PARTNERSHIPS WERE THE KEY

The initial proposed routes were primarily located within city streets. In meetings in both communities, the project team was strongly encouraged to investigate a route which made use of a relatively narrow strip of undeveloped land adjacent to, but not on, the Southeast Expressway (I-93), one of most heavily traveled highways in the Commonwealth. That route would then cross the Neponset River through one of the most productive shellfish flats in the Commonwealth and would cross undeveloped park land owned by the Metropolitan District Commission (MDC). Lastly, it would traverse along more than a mile of private road which cut across coastal wetlands and served as a private roadway to an industrial facility and as access to a waterfront commercial and residential development. On the surface, this route seemed doomed to failure. However, through a series of partnerships, the project team was able to make it work. Ultimately, it became the route of first choice for all stakeholders. A description of each of these partnerships follows.

Massachusetts Highway Department

By locating about 56% of the Dorchester portion of the cable route on vacant land owned by the Massachusetts Highway Department (MHD) adjacent to the Southeast Expressway, a route could be established which would avoid major streets in Dorchester. However, the construction technique of horizontal directional drilling would have to be used to avoid use of private property adjacent to the MHD parcel while installing about 1000 feet of the cables. MHD was receptive to the idea of realizing some income from previously unused land, provided the project team would work closely with the agency during the design and construction phases of the project to ensure that construction would not affect traffic along the Expressway. Both parties readily agreed to the terms of this partnership.

Environmental regulators

The partnership with the environmental community came about primarily through the project's early recognition of the environmental community's major interests in the Neponset River and acceptance of its guidance. After investigating several methods of cable installation, the project team felt that crossing the Neponset River, an underwater distance of about 1200 feet, with the horizontal directional drilling technique would be the most environmentally benign method and that it could address all of the concerns of the environmental community. The environmental community agreed. However, because the Neponset River and its adjacent wetlands were in the process of being designated an ACEC by the Massachusetts DEM, the project team felt that it would be important to be able to demonstrate that some direct and tangible environmental benefit could result from installing the cables across the Neponset River at the proposed location. The project team felt that if it could be a partner with the MDC in the development of a park on MDC's park land while crossing through it, the project would be able to show that environmental benefit.

Metropolitan District Commission

Normally one would strive to avoid park land when selecting a preferred route for a linear facility such as an underground transmission line. However, circumstances in this instance led the project team to explore this option with the MDC. Coincident with the planning for the new transmission cables to Quincy, the MDC was developing a master plan for a park system along the Lower Neponset River. One of the sites included in the Lower Neponset River Master Plan (for development at some undesignated future time) was park land on Squantum Point, through which the project team wished to locate the cables. Further, many local Quincy residents used the undeveloped park lands for passive recreation, and they had expressed an interest in the establishment of permanent amenities which would better accommodate use of the park land. Discussions between the MDC and the project team led to a partnership agreement in which NEP would receive a right to install, operate and maintain the underground transmission cables in exchange for the development of the initial phase of the park. That would meet some of the goals of the MDC's Master Plan, provide many of the amenities desired by the nearby Quincy residents and establish a direct and tangible environmental benefit resulting from the installation of the cables in that location.

Owner of a private roadway

The last major link in this improbable route involved establishing a partnership with the owner of 3500 feet of private, two-lane roadway. This last link would complete most of the route from the MDC park land to the MEC substation. Although a private roadway, it is used by travelers to an adjacent multi-use waterfront development and other abutters as if it was a public street. Because the roadway was in need of repair, a number of community leaders and area residents had been advocating for its improvement. NEP gained project support from the owner of the road and area residents when NEP committed to resurfacing the full width of the roadway, rather than just the lane affected by the construction. An additional potential benefit for the community brought about by NEP's commitment was that the owner of the roadway and the City of Quincy began discussions to explore the possibility of undertaking further road improvements while the road was under repair following the cable installation.

Acting on routing possibilities identified through the public participation process, no matter how improbable, guided the project to a route that could be actively supported by the public, environmental and political leadership. The most visible and complex partnership was with the MDC and the development of Squantum Point Park.

CULTURAL AND ENVIRONMENTAL RESOURCES AT SQUANTUM POINT

The section of land called Squantum Point is located between Quincy and Boston, a highly urbanized area (Fig. 1). Squantum Point contains existing open space and natural resources, uncommon in a location so close to a major metropolitan area.

It had been host to varied activities over the past century. In the late 1800s, this parcel was within a larger area known at the time as Squantum Meadows, and contained undeveloped salt marshes and uplands owned by many individual farmers. The Harvard Boston Aero Association's use of a portion of Squantum Point as an airfield in 1910 marked the beginning of Squantum Point's significant involvement in aviation industry. In 1917, the Massachusetts Naval Militia set up a naval aviation program at Squantum Point, establishing a military presence that lasted until the 1950s. During that time, the site on Squantum Point served as a naval training facility, a US Naval Reserve Air Station (NRAS), and a US Naval Air Station. Over the years, Squantum aviation operations hosted many industry luminaries including Amelia Earhart, Wilbur Wright and Joe Kennedy. In addition to its aviation history, a private shipbuilding facility occupied the site during World War I, producing a record number of destroyer ships for the war effort. During the period of military occupation, the US Navy altered the site significantly in several phases, filling it with marine clays and dredge spoil to accommodate runway development, and expanding and stabilizing the natural shoreline with a 1700 lineal foot steel bulkhead.

The Squantum Point NRAS was deactivated in 1953 and there have been few comprehensive uses of the site since. In the 1960s, a department store warehouse, one of the largest of its day, was constructed in the southwest portion of the site extending beyond its southern boundary. The northernmost tip of land was acquired by the MDC in the late 1960s, but was not formally developed as a park. In the 1970s, the Marina Bay Company developed upscale housing just beyond the park land's eastern boundary. The Massachusetts Water Resources Authority (MWRA) constructed a temporary parking lot and ferry terminal in a portion of the park land for one of the major projects of the Boston Harbor cleanup. During recent years, the strong economy has spurred further development of the area, such as market-rate townhouse construction and varied living facilities for seniors. Currently, the Squantum Point park land is completely undeveloped, except for the MWRA parking lot, and consists of a relatively quiet, level piece of land, dominated by scrub-shrub communities and surrounded by sandy beaches and tidal flats. Remnants of an abandoned runway and taxiway serve as reminders of the previous uses of the site.

A natural resources investigation of Squantum Point identified fourteen wetland resource areas within the park land. Nine wetlands are salt marsh areas lining the northern and western sides of the site. Five interior wetlands exist in disturbed areas altered by the placement of fill. Some of these wetlands are the result of filling activity (i.e., perched), especially when marine clays and compacted materials were placed as fill material. Other areas exhibit remnant hydrologic characteristics of original wetland communities. Habitat mapping indicated that the area is dominated by a scrub-shrub community, with little variation in shrub species throughout the site. Areas of special ecological importance in the vicinity of the site are salt marsh and mud flat. A wildlife inventory within each habitat indicated much avian activity was present on the site. Bird sitings indicated heavy use of the tidal flats and scrub-shrub habitat type. Over 185 bird species have been recorded from the area. Fifteen state-listed bird species protected by the Massachusetts Endangered Species Act have been noted at the Squantum Point area through the Massachusetts Natural Heritage Program. The site is known as a major resting area for spring and fall migrations for a number of bird species. Shellfish flats bordering both Dorchester Bay and the Neponset River were inventoried. A broad band of extemely productive soft shell clam flats was documented, as were extensive mussel beds nearer to the low water zone.

PUBLIC PROCESS FOR SQUANTUM POINT PARK

To address the park improvements agreed upon between NEP and the MDC for the cable easement through Squantum Point Park, NEP retained a local landscape architecture firm to develop a master plan and construction documents for an initial phase of site improvements for the park. With such high project visibility, a public participation process would be essential in building consensus for the park design.

Before the design was begun, NEP/MDC held a workshop by invitation, where park abutters, harbor advocates, environmentalists, regulatory agencies, and public officials met to outline the anticipated regulatory requirements, and identify design issues that might be of concern to the public. Issues cited ranged from the pragmatic needs for parking, soccer fields, and a boat ramp, to environmental concerns for migratory bird habitat, coastal bank erosion and salt marsh preservation. Park use issues such as development of a Visitor Center, local and regional multi-use path circulation, maintenance and operations were also addressed. Input from this meeting became the foundation on which the conceptual park design was developed.

During the design process for the master plan and the initial phase site improvements, three well-attended public meetings were held. Various concept alternatives for the park were presented, and one was chosen that balanced the public needs for parking and active recreation with concerns for wetlands and migratory bird habitat (Fig. 2). An arrangement of parking, walkways, overlooks, and open space was proposed during this process and received full pub-

Fig. 2. Squantum Point Park, concept alternative.

lic consensus. The public also supported the proposed interpretive program concept, emphasizing the importance of recognizing the site's unique aviation history.

SQUANTUM POINT PARK DESIGN

The Squantum Point Park Master Plan addressed the entire 45-acre parcel (Fig. 3). The most significant improvement shown in this Master Plan is a coastal esplanade with intermittent overlooks focusing on harbor views, and a major overlook at the Point featuring a dramatic view of the Boston skyline. The Point overlook is at the confluence of the coastal esplanade and a wide linear meadow that traces the path of the former US Naval Air Station runway. Paths along the former runway and taxiways provide small and large walking loop alternatives within the site, addressing community concerns for a loop circulation system. A system of crosspaths frame wide bands of wildflowers that together trace the existing overhead flight paths to Logan International Airport. Along former air base taxiways,

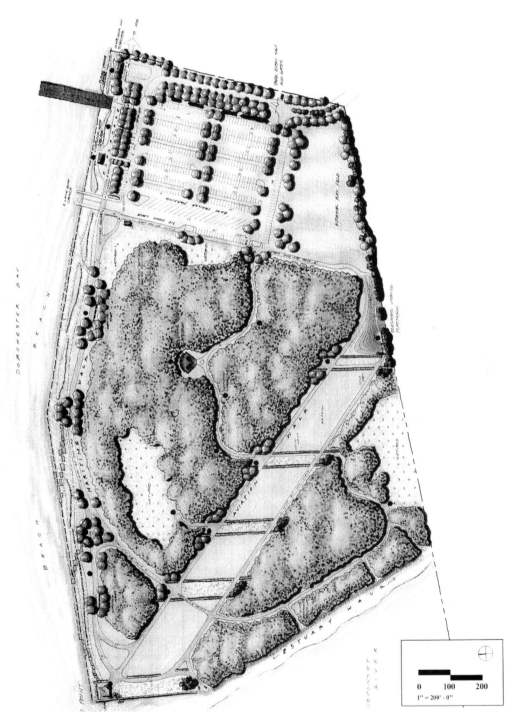

Fig. 3. Squantum Point Park, master plan.

a nature trail system was added to allow for bird watching and closer observation of natural features. The disintegrating steel and concrete bulkhead along the bay will be eventually replaced by a bioengineered system that would stabilize the eroding coastal bank in a more natural way. A reconfigured site entryway and parking lot simplifies vehicular circulation, focuses views on the water, and allows for informal field games in an open green space south of the parking lot, satisfying community recreation concerns. Public interest in the site's history was met by an interpretive marker system featuring maritime history along the coastal path, aviation history along the former runway, and ecological features along the nature path. A boat ramp was briefly entertained, but later eliminated from this Master Plan because it would be only 25% usable without dredging, which is not allowed in an ACEC.

The initial phase of this Master Plan is being constructed by NEP and roughly follows the route of the cable installation. The Aviation Walk and the Point construction are major features of this phase. There is also an elevated overlook at the southern end of the former runway. Ten interpretive markers featuring aviation, cultural and natural features are included at overlooks and gathering places, including a map of the harbor engraved in granite at the Point overlook. Restoration of the runway meadow, and introduction of wildflower bands with only native plant materials enhance aesthetics as well as improve wildlife and avian habitat. The bulkhead at the Point overlook is reconfigured with bleacher seat terracing, offering improved appreciation of the beach flats and harbor views. With Phase I park improvements underway, NEP has taken a major step toward facilitating future site improvements at Squantum Point Park.

SUCCESS — REGULATORY AND COMMUNITY ACCEPTANCE

The effectiveness of the public participation process and the building of partnerships was demonstrated during the hearings before the Massachusetts Energy Facilities Siting Board, when in Dorchester and Quincy a number of community leaders, property owners and elected officials or their representatives spoke in favor of the project and commended the National Grid Companies on how well they involved the community in the process of route selection. No one spoke in opposition to the project at those public meetings. As a result, the adjudicatory portion of the hearings took only half of the time initially planned.

MEC's and NEP's inclusion of the public in planning the project was acknowledged on the record by the Energy Facilities Siting Board hearing officer during her concluding remarks, when she said, "I would also like to comment on the effort the company expended in working with the people of the community and disseminating information regarding this project. The record demonstrates that the company held over 100 community meetings about the project. Further, the Siting Board received numerous letters of community support for the company to construct the proposed transmission line along the primary route." One of the most significant contributors to this feeling of good will and support by the public was the commitment by MEC and NEP to undertake the initial development of Squantum Point Park which is due to be completed by spring 2001.

POSTSCRIPT

MEC's and NEP's commitment to community involvement extended throughout construction of the project by placing special emphasis on keeping the communities informed about construction plans and progress. This was done in four ways. First, project management established the position of "Project Community Liaison" whose primary responsibilities were to keep the people who might be affected by construction activities informed about project plans, and to keep the contractors informed about public concerns that would have to be addressed during construction. Second, a 24 h call line was established through an answering service so that emergency calls could be addressed immediately and other calls could be addressed as soon as possible, but within 24 h. Third, in addition to establishing face-to-face and telephone communications, NEP published a monthly project newsletter (distribution about 200) which was mailed to community leaders and others living in the vicinity of the project. Fourth, NEP maintained a project web site, www.cableproject.com, which was updated on a regular basis.

The project team proudly reports that the two new cables were installed and were available for use by November 1999 and January 2000, respectively.

ACKNOWLEDGEMENTS

We wish to acknowledge the time and effort expended on behalf of this project by the MDC, most notably Julia O'Brien, Rich Kleiman, and Cathy Garnett. Their guidance was greatly appreciated. National Grid provided financial and technical support. Ms. Susan Brochu typed the manuscript.

BIOGRAPHICAL SKETCHES

F. Paul Richards
National Grid USA Service Company, 55 Bearfoot Road, Northborough, MA 01532, USA

F. Paul Richards has a BS in Zoology from the University of Massachusetts at Amherst and an MS in Marine

Biology from the University of Massachusetts at Dartmouth. He currently serves as Principal Environmental Engineer for National Grid USA Service Company. He had worked previously as an environmental consultant to the electric power and natural gas industries throughout the United States for over 25 years.

Frank S. Smith
  National Grid USA Service Company (Retired),148 Ashland Street, Melrose, MA 02176, USA

Frank Smith has a BS in Engineering from Trinity College, a BCE from Renssalaer Polytechnic Institute, and an MCE from Northeastern University. He retired as Consulting Engineer from National Grid in 1999 where he was employed for 40 years and where he managed major electrical transmission and generation projects. He is now self-employed as a consultant to the electric industry.

John Amodeo
  Carol R. Johnson Associates, Inc., 115 Broad Street Boston, MA 02110, USA

John Amodeo has a BS in Landscape Architecture from Cornell University and a MLA from Harvard University. He serves as a Senior Associate for Carol R. Johnson Associates, Inc. He has 20 years of professional experience and manages site-planning projects domestically and internationally.

Margaret Mills
  Earth Tech, Inc., 300 Baker Ave., Concord, MA 01742, USA

Margaret Mills has a BA in Biology from Hood College and an MS in Zoology from the University of New Hampshire. She is a Senior Project Manager for Earth Tech. She has more than 20 years experience in biological research and environmental consulting. Her specialties are aquatic ecology and marine biology.

Part XIV
Regulatory Compliance

Recent Advances in Evaluating, Selecting, and Training Environmental Inspectors

Lynette Curthoys

The role of the environmental inspector on linear construction projects has evolved into a unique job description that requires both technical and interpersonal skills. Evaluating and selecting qualified environmental inspectors and adequately training them on project-specific requirements and procedures is critical to a successful environmental compliance management program for large-scale linear construction projects. Drawing from lessons learned on recent linear construction projects and a survey of 20 environmental managers from the electric, gas, transportation, and water industries, this paper discusses key evaluation criteria for selecting qualified environmental inspectors. The paper also provides recommendations for providing comprehensive, project-specific training for environmental inspectors that covers relevant agency jurisdictions, mitigation requirements, communication standards, environmental management systems, and team building. As this paper demonstrates, environmental managers should consider using strategic evaluation criteria and comprehensive, project-specific training in selecting and preparing their environmental inspection team.

Keywords: Construction, pipeline, vector, maritimes, alliance

INTRODUCTION

Over the past 10 years, environmental inspection (or some form of environmental oversight during construction) has become the norm on most large-scale linear construction projects in the United States. Project proponents typically hire environmental inspectors to oversee their construction contractor's environmental performance and ensure compliance with the numerous permit conditions and mitigation measures that are commonly required on construction projects. In some cases, permitting agencies, such as the Federal Energy Regulatory Commission (FERC) or the United States Bureau of Land Management, require project proponents to employ environmental inspectors to oversee environmental compliance in the field. In addition, regulatory agencies and permitting authorities often employ their own monitors to enforce compliance, either through a "third party" inspection firm or by using in-house agency enforcement personnel.

Training has played an important role in the environmental inspection field since its inception. When the field was in its infancy, environmental managers sought common-sense individuals with environmental degrees and trained them in construction procedures and mitigation practices. Alternatively, companies hired individuals with a construction inspection background and provided training on the environmental aspects of the job.

However, the environmental inspection field has matured over the last 10 years, and the growing pool of professional environmental inspectors and monitors now includes individuals with significant expertise and experience. As a result, the role of the environmental inspector has evolved into a unique job that requires both technical and interpersonal skills. The stereotypical "environmentalist" who writes up non-compliance reports has been largely replaced by environmental inspectors with several years of construction experience, strong negotiation and communication skills, and specialized expertise in erosion control and stream and wetland crossing procedures.

For environmental managers tasked with assembling inspection teams, the selection criteria and training needs for environmental inspectors have changed

Environmental Concerns in Rights-of-Way
Management: Seventh International Symposium
J.W. Goodrich-Mahoney, D.F. Mutrie and C.A. Guild (editors)
© 2002 Elsevier Science Ltd. All rights reserved.

as the environmental inspection field has matured and standards have risen. Training programs for experienced environmental inspection staff can assume a base level of knowledge and can focus on project-specific requirements and procedures. However, as is the case with most employment sectors in today's booming economy, the applicant pool for qualified environmental inspectors appears to be limited in the face of growing demand. While many environmental managers can now select from a pool of experienced environmental inspectors, there remains a strong need to bring new inspectors into the field and train them to the higher standards that have been established.

The purpose of this paper is to share information on recent advances in evaluating, selecting, and training qualified environmental inspectors. The paper includes specific recommendations for environmental managers who are tasked with assembling effective environmental inspection programs for construction of linear utility or infrastructure projects. The paper concludes with a discussion of the need to increase the pool of qualified environmental inspectors through industry training and certification programs. While the selection criteria and training needs of today's environmental inspectors have changed, one thing has not changed: evaluating and selecting qualified environmental inspectors and providing them with appropriate training remains critical to a successful environmental management program.

METHODS

This paper represents observations and recommendations based on the experience of seven recent successful environmental management and inspection programs on linear construction projects across the United States, as well as the results of an informal survey of 20 environmental managers in the United States and Canada.

The projects
The environmental management and inspection programs of the following projects were evaluated based on post-project lessons learned documents and/or interviews with key project staff from: Vector Pipeline (2000), Alliance Pipeline (1999–2000), Maritimes and Northeast Phase II (1999), Alturas 345 kV Intertie (1999), TransColorado Pipeline (1998), Express Pipeline (1996), and Tuscarora Gas Transmission (1995). Project proponents for all seven of these projects established comprehensive environmental compliance management programs, which involved both environmental inspection programs managed by the proponent, as well as regulatory agency monitoring and oversight.

The survey
A two-page, nine-question survey was distributed to 30 environmental managers from the gas, oil, electric, water, fiber optics, and transportation industries. Twenty surveys were returned, for a response rate of 67%. While the sample size of the survey is small, the responses provide valuable insight into the state of the industry.

RESULTS/CONCLUSIONS

Qualified environmental inspectors are a rare commodity
Although the environmental inspection field has grown significantly over the past decade, environmental managers still perceive there to be a limited pool of qualified inspectors. In fact, over 45% of the environmental managers surveyed believed there were less than 200 qualified environmental inspectors in the United States and Canada; 70% believed there to be less than 600. This is a small number, given that over 60 environmental inspectors were employed at the peak of construction in 1999 on just two projects in the gas industry alone (Maritimes and Alliance).

Environmental inspection experience is critical
Seventy-five percent of the environmental managers surveyed indicated that past environmental inspection experience is the first thing they look at on an environmental inspector's resume. Previous construction project experience was a distant second at 25%. While past environmental inspection experience is critical, several survey respondents (as well as the experience of recent construction projects) indicated that staff without direct environmental inspection experience can be very effective if they receive proper training and work under the direction of a qualified lead/chief environmental inspector.

Construction experience is more important than environmental expertise
Environmental inspectors are expected to have a background that combines environmental expertise with past construction project experience. However, when asked to rank several possible selection criteria for hiring environmental inspectors, prior construction experience ranked substantially higher than education/environmental expertise as the most important criteria. Prior experience with the company, education/environmental expertise, and reputation/reference were all ranked approximately second as selection criteria, while communication skills and costs were considered the least important selection criteria.

While it is not surprising that companies are willing to pay a premium for qualified environmental inspectors (given the perceived shortage of qualified staff reported above), communication skills were ranked surprisingly low, given the experience of recent construction projects. All of the seven projects that were evaluated for this analysis considered communication skills to be a critical selection criteria for environmental inspectors. In fact, applicants with significant construction and environmental inspection experience were rejected if they lacked proven communication and teamwork skills.

Environmental managers expect inspectors to arrive trained in the basics

Over 60% of environmental managers surveyed expect environmental inspectors to come to their project with knowledge of environmental best management practices, environmental inspection skills, communication skills, and computer skills — without providing additional training. The vast majority (over 95%) expected to provide some level of project-specific training, although 35% expected environmental inspectors to also have some familiarity with the project's requirements on their own. Just 10% believed it was important to provide training on communication skills. Half of the environmental managers surveyed indicated that their expectations for existing qualifications of new environmental inspectors had increased in the last five years, while half indicated no change in their expectations.

The seven projects considered in this assessment provided some level of formal training for their environmental inspectors, ranging from two to five days. The environmental inspector training programs included technical topics, such as project-specific environmental requirements, as well as skills training (e.g., communication skills, training skills, and environmental inspection skills). Perhaps most importantly, all seven projects provided training on both the project's environmental management *procedures* (i.e., variance process, non-compliance levels, reporting requirements), as well as the company's environmental management *approach*. As an example, the Maritimes Project trained both its environmental and construction inspectors on an approach that emphasized teamwork, communication, looking ahead of construction to anticipate problems, strong agency relationships, and zero tolerance for environmental non-compliance. This approach was communicated and supported from the highest level of the project, setting clear expectations for all project staff.

Preconstruction preparation time is critical

Another important aspect of environmental inspector training and preparedness is allowing adequate time prior to construction for inspectors to study project documents and familiarize themselves with the right-of-way. The amount of time needed varies depending on the complexity of the project and can range from one to four weeks or more. Fifty percent of environmental managers surveyed indicated that environmental inspectors should report to the job site two weeks before the construction start date, while 30% believed only one week was needed and 20% indicated three or more weeks were needed. The seven projects considered for this assessment also demonstrated a wide range in preparation time for environmental inspectors, ranging from two to eight weeks.

In addition to project complexity, this significant range in environmental inspector preconstruction preparation time may also be attributed to differing expectations for the role of environmental inspectors prior to construction. Some projects expect the environmental inspection staff to assist in final routing and permitting, install resource flagging and signage, conduct preconstruction biological surveys, and prepare variance requests. These activities can take significant time, requiring inspectors to arrive at the job site much earlier than is necessary if their preconstruction responsibilities are limited to individual preparation tasks (e.g., reading project documents, reviewing right-of-way conditions).

Assembling spread teams

Because many large-scale construction projects typically require more than one environmental inspector per spread, assigning effective and cohesive spread inspection teams is often just as important as selecting qualified individual inspectors. While technical expertise is an important factor in making spread assignments, other factors such as "team chemistry" and individual preference should also be considered.

Seventy percent of environmental managers surveyed consider technical expertise as the most important criteria for spread team assignments (e.g., assigning erosion control experts to the spread with steep slopes), while 30% ranked team chemistry as the most important criteria (i.e., assembling a group that will work well together). Individual preference was ranked the least important criteria to consider when making spread team assignments.

RECOMMENDATIONS

Environmental managers are encouraged to consider the following recommendations when selecting and training environmental inspectors:

1. When evaluating an individual's prior environmental inspection and construction experience, environmental managers should not just consider the *number* of projects that are listed on a resume, but also *which* projects are listed and whether or not the projects were successful. Full analysis of an individual's experience often requires looking beyond their resume, including reference checks.
2. Environmental managers need to consider more than just resume qualifications to determine if an individual is a good fit for their environmental inspection team. Communication and teamwork skills can

be equally important — and a lack of these skills can quickly negate years of experience in terms of an inspector's overall effectiveness in the field. Communication skills may have been under-ranked in the survey results because they are difficult to measure and assess during the hiring process. Environmental managers should consider using scenarios and role-play activities to assess communication and teamwork skills during in-person interviews with potential candidates. For example, a candidate could role-play their response to a resistant construction foreman or an irate agency inspector. Scenarios can also help assess an inspector's judgment, another key factor in selecting inspectors. If the scenarios and role-play activities give any indication that the individual would not be a right fit for the team, the applicant should be rejected.

3. Total years of experience should not be used as a surrogate for evaluating actual knowledge of environmental best management practices. Environmental managers should consider using a verbal or written test to assess applicants' familiarity with standard environmental practices. Some form of testing is particularly critical if the manager does not intend to provide training on basic environmental requirements. The test can be "open book" with project documents, but should be taken during the interview (i.e., not mailed).

4. Even qualified, experienced environmental inspectors need at least one or two days of formal training before beginning work. Some very simple projects can do just one day, but most require at least two. Training topics should include project-specific requirements, resources, and agency jurisdictions. To be effective, the content should focus on information that the environmental inspectors need to know for the construction phase of the project (e.g., discuss sensitive resources that were found during preconstruction surveys, not resources that will be avoided). Perhaps most importantly, the training must provide clear direction and set expectations for the project's environmental management procedures, organization, and approach. It is critical to have high-level project staff speak at the training to emphasize the importance of the environmental program and demonstrate a strong organizational commitment to compliance. Finally, the training should be highly interactive, including activities that test knowledge of the requirements and help calibrate judgment and approach.

5. Environmental inspectors need to report to the field at least two weeks ahead of the construction start date for projects with any degree of size or complexity. The inspectors need enough time to study the project documents (including mitigation plans, permits, contract specifications, alignment sheets, and line lists), attend training, and perform detailed reconnaissance of the right-of-way and access roads. Even relatively small-scale, simple projects typically require at least two days to read through the project documents and review the right-of-way, plus one day of training. If the environmental inspectors are expected to have a larger role prior to construction (i.e., installing flagging and signs, conducting preconstruction surveys, etc.), they will likely need more than two weeks.

6. Environmental managers should consider team chemistry and personal preference, in addition to technical skills, when making spread team assignments. Sometimes details like geographical location, anticipated duration of construction, and surrounding environment can be important to individual job satisfaction and staff retention. While individual preference was ranked the least important criteria to consider when making spread team assignments, the importance of this criterion should not be underestimated. Environmental inspectors often work long hours under stressful conditions, making team morale and employee satisfaction a significant challenge that environmental managers face. When an environmental inspector leaves a project for professional or personal reasons, it can be very disruptive to the environmental inspection program. Sometimes making the extra effort to assign inspectors to the spread of their choice can make all the difference in staff retention.

7. Regardless of whether they hire individual employees or out-source inspection services to a consultant team, environmental managers should look beyond individual hiring decisions and focus on building and maintaining an effective organization. While the first step is to hire individuals with good communication and teamwork skills, environmental managers must also set clear expectations during the initial training and continue to support their staff throughout the duration of the project to maintain a strong team. This requires managing the people problems before they become project problems. In addition, small gestures like barbecues, hats, t-shirts, newsletters, and the like can go a long way towards maintaining a solid and effective team.

CLOSING

Environmental managers should consider the specific recommendations provided above in light of the complexity and size of their projects, however, the concepts discussed in this paper can be effectively applied to any linear construction project. Environmental compliance management programs are only as effective as the people who implement them on the ground. A project's environmental inspectors are the program's daily representatives in the field with contractors, construction managers, and agency representatives. Successful environmental managers must take an active role in the strategic hiring, training, and support of their environmental inspection teams.

In closing, industry organizations have an important role to play attracting new environmental inspectors to the field and training them on basic inspection skills. As discussed above, environmental managers expect to hire experienced environmental inspectors who do not require training on environmental best management practices, environmental inspection skills, communication skills, and computer skills. However, energy companies will be installing a significant amount of infrastructure in the coming years, and the pool of experienced environmental inspectors is limited.

Existing industry training programs include the Southern Gas Association's annual Environmental Inspection and Construction Compliance Workshop, which offers both a basic track for new environmental inspectors and an advanced track for more experienced inspectors and environmental managers (Southern Gas Association, 2001). The Calgary-based Petroleum Industry Training Service also offers a semi-annual basic pipeline environmental inspection course (Petroleum Industry Training Service, 2001). The FERC also offers a Post-Certificate Environmental Compliance course for the industry. In the coming years, an optional certification program for professional environmental inspectors may be the answer to ensuring environmental managers can continue to select environmental inspectors from a qualified applicant pool. While a mandatory certification program could potentially decrease the pool of qualified environmental inspectors, an optional program could provide environmental managers with an additional avenue for identifying and selecting qualified inspection personnel.

ACKNOWLEDGEMENTS

The author would like to acknowledge and thank all the environmental managers who participated in the survey and shared their invaluable insights: Tom Acuna, Mark Bisett, Paul Brown, Tim Cass, John Cassady, Sheila Castellano, Bill Chilson, Jim Easton, Dave Flaim, Colin Guild, Rick Hall, Howard Heffler, John Hopkins, Lynne Hosley, Bill Huhtala, Janice Hutton, Carol Irwin, Carey Johannesson, Mark Johnson, Bill Kendrick, Sandra Marlin, Joe Martinez, Bob Masouka, Gus McLachlan, Doug Mithcell, Larry Purcell, Don Rose, John Schafer, Mary Smith, Jim Thompson, and Terry Wolverton.

REFERENCES

Petroleum Industry Training Service. 2001. Pipeline Environmental Inspection Course Manual.

Southern Gas Association. 2001. Environmental Inspection and Construction Compliance Workshop Course Manual.

BIOGRAPHICAL SKETCH

Lynette Curthoys

Essex Environmental, Inc., 637 Main Street, Half Moon Bay, CA 94019, USA. Tel: (650) 726-8320. Fax: (650) 712-1190. E-mail: lcurthoys@essexenv.com

Lynette Curthoys is the *Director of Planning and Training Services* at *Essex Environmental* in Half Moon Bay, California. She has nine years of experience in environmental management program development and implementation, including staff supervision, agency relations, construction reporting, and environmental inspection. Lynette has particular expertise in developing and delivering environmental training programs for environmental inspectors on large-scale construction projects, including Vector Pipeline, Alliance Pipeline, Maritimes, and Northeast Phase II, Alturas 345 kV Intertie, TransColorado Pipeline, Express Pipeline, and Tuscarora Gas Transmission Project. Prior to joining Essex Environmental, Lynette developed environmental training programs for Pacific Gas and Electric Company. She is a graduate of Stanford University, with a bachelor's degree in Human Biology.

Emergency Transmission Line Repair and Reinforcement Project: Environmental Management Overview

Franck Berry, Lauren Caldwell, Cameron Hiebert, and Bill Poirier

The winter of 1999 produced record snow pack levels in high-elevation areas of coastal British Columbia. Snow-pressure caused major structural damage to towers along two high voltage transmission corridors integral to the supply of electrical service to Vancouver Island and the Sunshine Coast. Although interim repairs were undertaken to limit the risk of circuit failure, the system required major reconstruction and upgrades to reduce the risk of future damage. A project team was formed to commence planning, coordination and execution of the repairs. Restricted access, due to heavy snow conditions, did not allow for a full evaluation of the extent of tower damage until close to the start of construction when snow had melted. It also hindered the assessment of proposed access roads, work area ground type and drainage characteristics in the work zone. To address environmental concerns, BC Hydro prepared an Environmental Management Plan (EMP) identifying potential impacts relating to the works and mitigation procedures to be implemented during the project. To expedite agency and stakeholder approval, an agreement was made between BC Hydro and the Ministry of Environment to work cooperatively, use a one-window lead agency approach to make timely decisions. An environmental monitor was used during the project to consult with the project team on unforeseen issues and implement the EMP. The purpose of this paper is to present the challenges encountered and solutions sought to address environmental issues resulting from a challenging construction project: the emergency repair and reinforcement of transmission line circuits 5L30/32/45. The paper discusses the strategy used to ensure successful completion of the required tasks in the short timeline available and under unknown and evolving site conditions.

Keywords: Emergency, British Columbia, environmental management, impact mitigation, regulatory compliance, environmental monitoring

INTRODUCTION

The BC Hydro Electric Generation System extends throughout the various regions of the province. It is an integrated network of 29 hydroelectric generating stations, one conventional thermal station and two combustion turbine stations with a total installed generating capacity of 10,762 MW. Most of British Columbia's energy is provided by hydroelectric generation and is transmitted and distributed via a province-wide system of transmission and distribution lines.

An unusually large snow pack during the winter of 1998/99 caused significant damage to BC Hydro's 5L30, 5L32, and 5L45 high voltage circuits in the Squamish–Sunshine Coast area resulting in an emergency situation. The three circuits run along two corridors, 5L30/32 in the Sechelt Creek/Tantalus Mountain Range and 5L45 in the Stawamus and Indian River Watersheds, near Squamish, BC as shown in Fig. 1.

In the Tantalus Mountains the snow pack was 200% of normal, measuring 8–12 m deep in some locations. Regular helicopter patrols identified numerous damaged towers in high elevation areas. Snow pressure caused major structural damage to tower metalwork, foundations, and anchors resulting in a high risk to the security of electrical service to Vancouver Island and the Sunshine Coast.

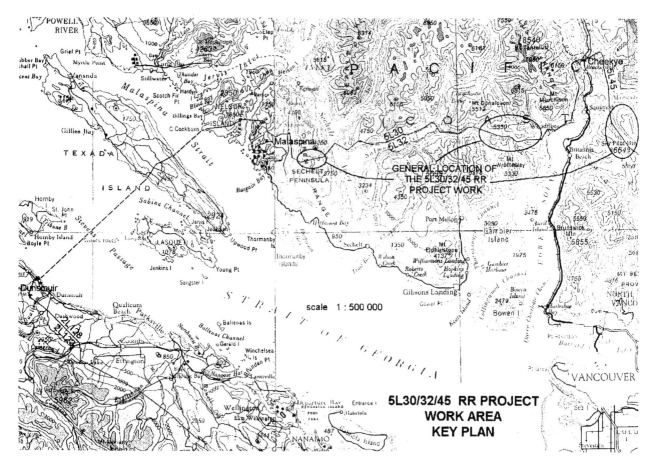

Fig. 1. 5L30/32/45: Project Work Area, Key Plan.

The project was considered non-traditional because site conditions were unknown and work strategies evolved during the course of the project. In addition to the short construction season, complicating factors included restricted outages, difficult access, environmentally sensitive sites, multiple stakeholders and multiple agency approval. To protect the transmission system and minimize the potential for future snow damage, BC Hydro executed an extraordinary project during the summer of 1999 to repair damaged towers and complete upgrades at critical locations.

Location

Two parallel 500 kV circuits, 5L30 and 5L32 (5L30/32), connect Cheekye Substation in Squamish and Malaspina Substation on the west coast of the Sechelt Peninsula. From Squamish, the corridor follows the coast around Howe Sound, ascends to a high-elevation pass in the Tantalus Mountain Range and follows the Sechelt Creek valley to Salmon Inlet. After crossing Sechelt Inlet, the corridor ascends and crosses over Caren Mountain Range and terminates near Pender Harbor. This corridor is environmentally sensitive due to its high elevation, proximity to a number of fish-bearing creeks, steep slopes, previous logging activities and associated access roads.

The second transmission line corridor, the 5L45, connects Meridian Substation in Coquitlam to Cheekye Substation in Squamish. The corridor runs adjacent to Buntzen Lake, Indian Arm, Indian River and Stawamus River. Near the boundary of the Stawamus and Indian River watersheds, it passes over a high-elevation area and descends as it follows the Stawamus River to the terminus near Squamish. Its high elevation, avalanche tracks, proximity to the Stawamus River, and designation as a municipal water supply makes this corridor sensitive.

Stakeholders

The following list of the agencies and organizations were contacted and involved in the project decision-making process:

– BC Environment — Section 9 Water Act Approval and appointment of representative to Environmental Management Project Team
– District of Squamish — entry into Stawamus Watershed and City of Squamish water supply area
– Ministry of Forests — removal of vegetation on crown lands, danger trees and slashing
– Centra Gas — use of right-of-way for access and crossing pipeline near 5L30/32 and 5L45
– Canadian Forest Products Limited (Canfor) — use of their forest service access roads and entry into timber area under their jurisdiction

- Terminal Forest Products — use of their forest service access roads and entry into timber area under their jurisdiction
- First Nations — work within traditional territories

SCOPE OF WORK

Project planning

A major amount of planning and public consultation was required prior to the initiation of the construction project. BC Hydro immediately notified potentially affected communities and large industrial customers about the risk of power outages. The 5L30/32 system is designed to accommodate the loss of one line with no impact to customers, but simultaneous failure of both 500 kV circuits would cause outages to customers on the Sunshine Coast and Vancouver Island. Meetings were held with industrial customers to keep them informed of on-going developments.

Contingency plans were developed to address all conceivable outage scenarios and minimize length of service disruption. Electricity supply to affected residential and commercial customers could likely be restored within hours using generating facilities on Vancouver Island and other transmission facilities serving the Sunshine Coast and Vancouver Island. To ensure power restoration and minimize impacts, BC Hydro commenced and completed a by-pass line to the Sunshine Coast, thereby enabling power to be re-connected to all Sunshine Coast customers within hours.

A project team was formed from experts across BC Hydro's strategic business units. Their objective was to minimize the potential for damage to the lines by repairing and upgrading the system to withstand future "one-in-a-hundred year" snowfall events. Planning tasks included developing strategies for interim stabilization, preparing contingency plans, obtaining regulatory approvals, designing system modifications, and scheduling and procuring of materials. The planning of virtually all construction activities was also significantly affected by the rigorous safety standards required to work under the harsh conditions associated with this project.

Emergency response (temporary repairs)

To minimize failure of each of the circuits, experts made aerial assessments of the damaged structures and coordinated emergency stabilization efforts on towers deemed most threatening to system integrity. Reconnaissance of other 500 kV circuits in the province was conducted following the discovery. To address the emergency, personnel from the operations, communications and environmental departments formed an immediate response team.

Snow removal and temporary repairs were undertaken over a 12-week period starting in April 1999.

Emergency repairs consisted primarily of the installation of temporary steel reinforcement ("tinker toys") to towers that had been damaged by heavy snow pack. Rough terrain and extreme weather conditions made access to the towers difficult and dangerous. As a result, crews could only access the towers by helicopter and a staging area was established at Lions Bay in Howe Sound to move crews and materials to the lines. Hot water snow removal techniques were tested to melt tonnes of snow and ice surrounding twenty damaged transmission towers. Ultimately, snow was cleared from the damaged towers by hand digging and backhoe in accessible locations. To ensure worker safety while these repairs were made, one circuit remained in service while the other was de-energized during critical stages of the emergency response work. The snow removal and temporary repairs cost some $1.6 million.

Major construction activities (permanent repairs)

Critical tower locations required major reconstruction efforts and structural modifications to minimize risk of catastrophic snow damage in future years. Due to the high elevation and remote location, repairs to the damaged towers had to be completed by late October to avoid heavy snowfalls and extreme weather conditions. Initially, the permanent repairs were estimated at $10 million. The budget was increased to $23.7 million to complete the 1999 phase of permanent repairs and system upgrades. BC Hydro's Construction Business Unit (CBU) and two independent contractors performed the work. Upwards of 80 people worked extended hours, seven days a week, in an effort to complete the work before the first heavy snowfall.

On 5L30/32 work consisted of major repairs (new foundations and tower legs) on ten towers; replacement of two guyed towers with heavier rigid structures; replacement of damaged steel members on nine towers; and replacement of 124 anchors on 31 additional towers. Trees were removed in several locations where they were previously burned and/or snow damaged and potentially hazardous to the transmission line and at the location of marshalling/helicopters sites and access trails to towers. Existing forestry logging roads and stream crossings required upgrading to facilitate access requirements and subsequent decommissioning following completion of work. Material required for the work included 400 m^3 of concrete for reinforcement of anchors and tower footings, 450 t of steel, lumber for forms, hardware, fuels and maintenance supplies for machinery.

On 5L45, work consisted of: reinforcement and replacement of tower steel members on five towers; additional minor repairs; reinforcement of an existing avalanche-deflection berm and construction of two new berms utilizing local materials; upgrading of existing forestry logging roads and stream crossings with subsequent decommissioning following completion of work. Removal of trees was also required; snow-damaged trees potentially hazardous to transmission lines and trees located at marshalling/helicopters sites and access trails to towers. Other materials required for the work included 150 t of steel, lumber for forms, hardware, fuels and maintenance supplies for machinery.

Access development

Since many of the work sites were remote, a significant amount of work was required to upgrade and maintain roads in order to allow passage by crews and equipment. Decisions regarding road access and construction methods were developed with input from the environmental monitor, forestry consultants and construction personnel. Many of the sites could be accessed by helicopter only.

Existing logging roads were used to transport personnel and equipment working on the portion of the transmission line in the Sechelt Creek headwaters. Portions of these roads required re-activation including bridge reinforcement; installation of culverts and cross ditches; and regrading. New access roads and work pads were constructed to reach two new rigid tower locations. An existing trail along the Centra Gas pipeline right-of-way (which parallels the corridor right-of-way) was used as a heavy equipment track to provide equipment access to several structures. For remote locations in steep terrain, only foot trails were constructed to access towers with all equipment and structural components being flown in via helicopter.

Avalanche deflection berms

Protection of transmission towers from avalanches was required at three locations along the 5L45 corridor. It was determined that bedload movement had resulted in the deposition of significant amounts of boulders and woody debris near each tower. It was decided that this material should be removed from the stream channel and used to build up the avalanche deflection berms protecting the towers. Environmental guidelines for in-stream work were established with input from related government agencies and were strictly adhered to, given the sensitivity of the area.

ENVIRONMENTAL RESOURCES

The majority of the project area is in high elevations with the terrain being of two types: (1) steep, rocky cliffs, and talus slopes or (2) sub-alpine forest. These types of terrain have unique biophysical characteristics that provide habitat specific for certain flora and fauna. They also serve as the headwaters to very important watersheds.

The 5L45 transmission line parallels the Stawamus River. The Stawamus River Watershed is a protected watershed, which provides a domestic water supply to the District of Squamish through surface intakes. For this reason extreme care was required to ensure a continued supply of uncontaminated drinking water and that works undertaken do not compromise the integrity of water quality and quantity or the integrity of the intake structure. All work in the watershed was subject to approval by the District of Squamish.

High elevation areas provide extremely important habitat for birds, ungulates and other mammals. Valleys provide important migration corridors during the spring and fall and also provide nesting habitat for a variety of birds. Traffic; particularly in the Tantalus Mountain range (helicopter, vehicles and people) could adversely impact the wildlife in the areas by changing seasonal movements and hindering access to higher elevations areas along the corridor. For the most part, impacts were localized and the wildlife populations in the area were likely not significantly affected.

Water bodies affected during the project included; Indian River, Stawamus River, Anderson Creek, and Sechelt Creek. These watersheds contain productive fish streams with anadromous and resident salmonid populations. The headwater lakes, wetlands and small drainages affected by the project were also considered important as functional fish and wildlife habitat. Protection of downstream water quality was the top environmental protection priority throughout the project.

PROJECT IMPACTS AND MITIGATION

The potential environmental impacts were defined as:
– Work in and about a stream for wet crossing, bridge construction, or creek channeling/tower protection
– Sedimentation of streams due to activities associated with clearing, site excavation, access road development, road decommissioning, installation and removal of drainage crossing structures, site restoration and avalanche berms construction
– Fuel, oil or chemical spills (including concrete/grout leachate)
– Waste management and refuse disposal
– Contamination of drinking water supply
– Damage to sensitive high elevation wildlife habitat and wetlands
– Loss of habitat related to tree/vegetation removal and ground disturbance

Impact mitigation strategies were employed at various stages of the project as follows.

Sedimentation and erosion control

Controlling siltation and run-off during site construction work and access development was a concern during the project. All lakes and wetlands encountered were considered functionally important fish and wildlife habitat and were treated accordingly. In addition, disturbance to dry channels was minimized, as these often serve as important drainage channels during the wet season.

Efforts were made to control silt-laden runoff from all construction areas. This involved utilizing a combination of several techniques on a site-specific basis. Upslope drainage interception ditches and cross-slope site swales were installed to remove clean uncontaminated water and reduce amount of water flowing through site. Sensitive sites were marked with fencing; ribbon or rope to prevent accidental intrusion and silt fencing was installed on the downslope side between construction site and any drainages or wetlands. During construction, materials such as straw bales and filter cloth were stored at all marshaling areas for use at the individual sites should the need arise. To prevent erosion and sedimentation of nearby watercourses, silt fencing and/or a polyethylene cover were used to contain soil excavation stockpiles.

General conditions were applied to the development of road access to maximize environmental protection. These included: restricting the construction and use of access roads/trails/vehicle tracks and marshalling sites to that detailed in the contract documents; any additional access required prior approval by BC Hydro's representative and the Environmental Monitor. The access upgrades were completed such that washouts and stream contamination were avoided, sidecasting on the downslope side was minimized, and riparian vegetation protected along stream channels. Appropriate methods and locations for spoiling excess material were assessed in the field. Culverts were installed and removed in the dry, using dams and pumping when necessary. Clean native material was used whenever possible for installation of culverts in drainage channels. Access by machinery and trucks was limited where it was deemed inappropriate to use culverts to access wetlands areas and streams.

Due to the environmental sensitivity of many of the work areas, the maintenance of water quality was critical during the course of the project. A sediment and erosion control plan was prepared detailing best management practices and mitigation procedures. The contractor and BC Hydro's Construction Business Unit in the prejob meeting signed off the plan. Water quality criteria, established by the regulatory agencies, were adhered to at all times. Sediment control berms and ponds were installed and maintained at various locations to ensure that introduction of silt or sediment into local drainages was minimized. Berms were constructed using straw bales, gravel, filter cloth and lumber, which caused water to pond, thus allowing fines to settle out and not be carried downstream. Water samples were collected downstream of each avalanche berm construction site in the Stawamus watershed. These samples were taken during all work activities and analyzed for TSS levels to ensure compliance with specific criteria. At no time were TSS levels above the established limits.

Oil and fuel management

Construction activities and the operation of machinery required the use of fuels, lubricating oils and hydraulic fluids. The migration of these compounds either from spills during construction or later through seepage from saturated soils can negatively impact both terrestrial and aquatic environments.

To reduce the risk of these fluids entering streams, various methods were employed An Emergency Spill Response Plan was posted at all marshaling locations and all staff were made aware of its content and the location of response materials. Clean-up materials and equipment such as sorbent pads, booms and leak proof containers were kept at all marshaling stations and equipment locations in sufficient quantities. Appropriate fuel storage facilities were constructed to ensure containment of the entire contents in the event of a catastrophic spill. Equipment operators and personnel responsible for oil spill response reviewed the plan regularly, ensuring it was up to date and all required materials were on-site and easily accessible. During the course of the project all machinery employed was inspected for leaks, worn hoses or fittings and appropriate repairs completed prior to access onto the site.

Compressors were required for some of the equipment being used at helicopter access sites. These large compressors and the fuel required to run them (in 45 gallon drums) were stored on wooden pads with impervious containment.

Environmental management plan (EMP)

Prior to the initiation of the project, an Environmental Management Plan (EMP) was completed. The purpose of the EMP was to identify potential environmental impacts related to project implementation and to detail mitigative measures to negate these impacts. Generally, in order to produce an EMP, a detailed site assessment of access upgrade requirements, ground type and drainage characteristics is required. In this case, a preliminary EMP was developed as a working document based upon best management practices. The document served to reduce the impact to the environment, while allowing for changes to the scope of work and site conditions. Due to the short construction season and the need to proceed quickly with the emergency repairs, a cooperative relationship was formed between the project team and Ministry of Environment, Lands and Parks (MELP) and the District of Squamish to evaluate the EMP and grant project approval.

The preliminary EMP addressed project-related issues and included generic environmental protection principles to be implemented during the project. To ensure the plan was updated to incorporate unforeseen issues and site-specific details, the project used a qualified environmental specialist to implement and monitor adherence to the plan. In several instances, agency representatives were onsite with the project team to assist in key decision-making. Conditional acceptance of the preliminary EMP and approval to proceed with the project was granted on the understanding that BC Hydro would involve stakeholders and cooperate with the regulatory agencies to address unforeseen issues during the project.

Environmental monitoring

An on site Environmental Monitor was used throughout the course of the project. The Monitor had the authority to stop construction work if there were any potential for harm to the environment. Work plans were reviewed to ensure the conditions of the EMP were met and recommendations (both verbal and written) were provided to address any deficiencies. It was also the responsibility of the monitor to act as liaison officer between government agencies, BC Hydro representatives, and all contractors. In the field, the monitor reviewed and oversaw the implementation of the sediment and erosion control plan, monitored various contractor work activities including clean-up and restoration activities and ensured that emergency response supplies and equipment were onsite.

In-stream work

In-stream work was required on the 5L45 corridor in order to construct the avalanche protection berms. Re-construction of two of the avalanche berms was conducted under dry conditions, thereby resulting in no sediment mobilization into the Stawamus River. Adjacent to a third avalanche berm, a tributary to Indian River was flowing during channel excavation activities. Prior to work taking place, a meeting was conducted with an agency representative to assess and determine the best plan for conducting the work. Based on the recommendations, sampling was conducted in this tributary and the Indian River downstream of the work site to determine fish presence in the area. Rainbow trout were sampled in the Indian River and in the lower 20 m of the tributary. No fish were observed upstream of this location, likely due to the high gradient of the stream.

Work in isolation of water flow was conducted by excavating a temporary diversion channel along the right bank. Once this temporary channel was constructed, stream flows were diverted into it so that the bedload material and old culverts could be removed in relatively dry conditions. Upon completion, water flows were diverted back into the original channel. Although there were pulses of siltation when the creek was diverted into newly excavated areas, this diversion method significantly reduced downstream siltation.

In-stream work in the Upper Sechelt Creek drainage was restricted to road maintenance and drainage improvements. New culverts and french drains were installed in dry weather during the summer months. Through the use of culverts and other drainage controls, surface water was diverted around disturbed areas.

Concrete and grouting

Virtually all concrete required for the repair work for the 5L30/32 line was obtained from a plant located in Squamish. The concrete was transferred into a 1-m^3 bucket and delivered to the individual work locations by helicopter. Equipment washout and spoiling of waste concrete occurred at sites designated by the environmental monitor, thus ensuring appropriate containment and protection of the aquatic environment. Grout used for setting of the anchor rods and rock anchors was mixed on-site with a small mixer and water.

On November 5, 1999 a bucket of ready mix concrete (~900 kg/0.5 yd) was accidentally dropped into Howe Sound from a Bell 212 helicopter. The environmental impact of this incident is negligible given the enormous buffering capacity of Howe Sound, however, it was a preventable accident resulting from equipment malfunction.

Sewage and refuse disposal

All waste steel and or other construction related materials (wood forms, hardware, plastics, etc.) were removed from each site and brought to the central marshaling areas for appropriate disposal. Near the end of the project, when weather conditions were favourable (i.e., cold and wet), concrete forms were burned at some of the helicopter access sites.

Portable toilets were provided at each work site, including marshalling sites and helicopter sites. These facilities were properly secured against collapse from wind and animals and were maintained and emptied on a regular basis.

SITE RECLAMATION AND RESTORATION ACTIVITIES

To ensure that all restoration and cleanup work was not left to the end of the project, a *progressive restoration program* was implemented. Once work was completed at each individual site, it was recontoured and drainage patterns were restored, fully cleaned up and reseeded.

Road deactivation

Once all sites requiring road access were completed, an extensive deactivation program was undertaken. Over 40 culverts installed during the project were carefully removed and stockpiled for recycling.

Canadian Forest Products Limited (Canfor) had undertaken significant amounts of restoration and road deactivation work in the Sechelt Creek watershed in recent years. Many of the roads required to access the 5L30/32 towers requiring repair were slated for deactivation during the summer of 1999. Since BC Hydro required access to these roads for the duration of the project, a road use agreement was developed between Canfor and BC Hydro to ensure that all roads used during the project were appropriately upgraded or deactivated. Road deactivation work was conducted at the termination of the 1999 work. Instances of short-term sedimentation to Sechelt Creek tributaries occurred as a result of the removal of culverts and the subsequent channel modifications.

In order to reduce the risk of road failure and sedimentation of local drainages, all 5L45 access roads used during the course of the project (with the exception of the forest service main line) were deactivated. The degree of deactivation of these roads varied depending on the steepness of the slopes and the stability of the road material. Relatively stable portions of road received minor drainage improvements such as cross ditching. Other sections of road showing signs of extreme instability were completely pulled back.

Seed application

Due to the risk of sedimentation to drainages affected by construction activities, seed was applied to all disturbed soils. As a result of the drinking water concerns in the Stawamus River, hydroseed was applied to order to provide rapid germination and establishment of ground cover vegetation. Along the 5L30/32 corridor where road access was limited, hand seeding was conducted utilizing a manual spreader. As per the seed supplier's advice, two types of seed were applied: fall rye for quick root mass growth and a coastal grass/legume mix which provides long term erosion protection and relatively natural looking ground cover vegetation.

CONCLUSIONS

The potential for environmental issues and impacts to arise during the project was high. Environmental issues played a major role in the planning and execution of work. The good design and on-site decisions that were made and the best management practices that were adhered to, resulted in minimal impacts to the environment and ensured regulatory compliance. The environmental management process was effective because of the commitment from agencies and the project team and the implementation of an evolving environmental management plan and comprehensive environmental monitoring. Execution of this emergency project was achieved through the team of dedicated BC Hydro project staff and construction crews working in a consultative process with customers, stakeholders and agency personnel.

BIOGRAPHICAL SKETCHES

Franck Berry
   White Pine Environmental Resources Inc. 564 Windermere Street, Vancouver, BC, Canada, V5K 4J2. fcberry@telus.net

Franck Berry is the principal of White Pine Environmental Resources Inc., contracted to undertake the environmental impact assessment, Environmental Management Plan (EMP) preparation and environmental monitoring throughout the project. Mr. Berry is a registered professional biologist with extensive expertise in environmental management, impact assessment, construction impact mitigation, stream habitat restoration and fisheries biology. He has been working in his profession since 1977 and since 1988 has been working as an independent consultant.

Lauren Caldwell
   BC Hydro, Transmission and Distribution, Environmental Sciences Support Services, 6911 Southpoint Drive, Burnaby, BC, Canada, V3N 4X8. lauren.caldwell@bchydro.bc.ca

Lauren Caldwell is a Senior Environmental Coordinator at BC Hydro and is responsible for environmental tasks of various transmission, substation and distribution capital projects. Ms. Caldwell oversees such disciplines as management of waste, vegetation, wildlife, heritage, fish and aquatic issues on new construction projects. Ms. Caldwell is a registered Landscape Architect.

Cameron Hiebert
   White Pine Environmental Resources Inc. 564 Windermere Street, Vancouver, BC, Canada, V5K 4J2. chiebert@direct.ca

Cameron Hiebert provided support as a backup environmental monitor assisting with the Sechelt Creek portion of the project. Mr. Heibert has a Bachelor of Science degree with a background in water quality related issues and has also been involved with several large-scale construction related projects.

Bill Poirier
   White Pine Environmental Resources Inc. 564 Windermere Street, Vancouver, BC, Canada, V5K 4J2. bill.poirier@home.com

Bill Poirier acted as the primary environmental monitor for the Sechelt Peninsula, Sechelt Creek, and Stawamus Watershed portion of the project. Mr. Poirier is a registered professional biologist with 9 years experience in the monitoring of large-scale construction projects and fish habitat enhancement.

Comparison of Canadian and US Regulatory Review Processes for the Alliance Pipeline

Howard R. Heffler

Environmental regulatory processes in Canada and the United States are constantly evolving. The Alliance Pipeline project has been a part of this evolution. The Alliance Pipeline system, built in 1999 and 2000, is a high-pressure, natural gas pipeline comprising 2988 km (1857 miles) of 36" diameter mainline and 698 km (434 miles) of smaller diameter laterals. The pipeline crosses three Canadian provinces and four American states. Alliance began the regulatory review process in 1996, receiving final regulatory approval from the two federal authorities: the Federal Energy Regulatory Commission (FERC) in the United States in September 1998, and the National Energy Board (NEB) in Canada in December 1998. This paper provides a review of the federal environmental regulatory process in both countries and presents a comparison of the major milestone dates and key document requirements. The application was the first to be considered by the National Energy Board as a Comprehensive Study under the provisions of the *Canadian Environmental Assessment Act* (*CEA Act*). This fact resulted in considerable regulatory uncertainty for the project. By contract, the FERC review process in the United States is quite well-defined, although the information requirements for the environmental assessment (a formal Environmental Impact Statement to satisfy the requirements of the *National Environmental Policy Act*), often require the applicant to complete environmental surveys before the pipeline route is certain and land access obtained. As a consequence, the environmental surveys may have significant gaps in coverage at the time the EIS must be completed. From the applicant's perspective, the federal environmental review process in Canada and the United States are similar in duration and in the level of protection afforded to sensitive resources. The two processes differ in the extent of public input and the clarity of information requirements. Some changes to the environmental approval processes that have occurred since the Alliance project was approved in 1998 are also described. The most significant changes relate to how the NEB fulfills its requirements under the *CEA Act*. Changes to the FERC procedures are more subtle; relating to minimum filing requirements and landowner notification.

Keywords: Pipelines, Canada, United States, permitting, National Energy Board, Federal Energy Regulatory Commission, environmental assessment

INTRODUCTION

This paper compares the federal environmental regulatory review process in Canada by the National Energy Board (NEB) and in the United States by the Federal Energy Regulatory Commission (FERC). The experiences described were gained on the Alliance Pipeline project (Alliance) from its inception in 1995 through to issuance of the Certificates of Public Convenience and Necessity in late 1998. The focus of the paper is on the federal, rather than provincial or state, authorizations up to and including the Certificate Order, and briefly mentions the subsequent post-certificate regulatory filing requirements to begin construction and to demonstrate compliance during construction. A brief postscript, describing the changes to the regulatory processes that have occurred since Alliance was approved, is also provided. The paper is intended to assist pipeline planners to better understand the time and information requirements for large, international (Canada–US) and interprovincial/interstate natural gas Pipelines.

Previous authors (Mutrie, 1993; Mutrie and Gilmore, 1993; Mutrie and Gilmore, 1997) also compared the environmental regulatory process in Canada and the United States. Those comparisons were based on experience gained with the Altamont, Express and Tuscorora pipeline projects, among others. In 1993 the authors concluded that the level of environmental protection during construction of Canadian Pipelines was roughly equivalent to comparable projects in the US, but was achieved in a more pragmatic, expeditious, and cost-effective fashion. This was seen principally as a result of the regulatory process in the US that was about three times longer and considerably more expensive compared to that in Canada. The authors also noted that Canada was moving closer to the US regulatory process. In 1997 the same authors concluded that there was a high degree of environmental protection achieved on pipeline projects in both countries, but that the regulatory process was becoming increasingly complicated, particularly in Canada which had recently passed the *Canadian Environmental Assessment Act* (*CEA Act*).

This paper follows the theme established by Mutrie and Gilmore by discussing the continuing evolution of the regulatory process where, especially in Canada, significant changes have occurred since their papers were published.

THE ALLIANCE PIPELINE PROJECT

Project description

The Alliance Pipeline system is a 3686-km (2290-mile) pipeline system which will transport natural gas from northeastern British Columbia and northwestern Alberta to the Chicago, Illinois area where it will interconnect with five existing pipelines in the North American pipeline grid. The Canadian portion of the Alliance system includes:
- 339 km (211 miles) of 42-inch and 1220 km (758 miles) of 36-inch diameter pipe,
- 36 receipt points connecting with lateral pipelines totaling about 698 km (434 miles), and
- 7 mainline compressor stations.

In the US the pipeline consists of 888 miles (1429 km) of 36-inch diameter pipe, and 7 compressor stations. The initial throughput volume is designed to be 37.5×10^6 m^3 (1.325 billion cubic feet per day) of natural gas at a maximum allowable operating pressure of 12,000 kpa (1740 psi). In addition to the pipeline, the Alliance system includes the Aux Sable Liquid Products facility, a natural gas liquids extraction and fractionation facility designed to recover 11.1×10^3 m^3 (70,000 barrels) per day of ethane, propane, and butane from the natural gas. Construction of the Alliance Pipeline system occurred over two years, 1999 and 2000.

Route selection and environmental setting

A key element in the overall environmental protection strategy was selection of a general pipeline routing concept and definition of the precise route for environmental resource surveys. Both the NEB and the FERC require the applicant to identify the location of the pipeline and to conduct site-specific environmental surveys. The width of the corridor for these surveys may vary from as narrow as the pipeline construction easement (32 m or 105 feet); in the order of 100 m (300 feet) for disciplines such as cultural resources, wetlands or endangered species; to as much as 5 km (3 miles) for noise, emissions or cumulative effects assessment.

The principal control points in the overall routing strategy were to connect:
- the Westcoast Energy Inc. gas plant near Fort St. John, British Columbia;
- the Fort Saskatchewan, Alberta area for access to natural gas liquids; and
- the Chicago area for connection to existing pipelines.

With the overall routing concept decided, the next level of pipeline routing criteria included objectives, such as:
- minimize overall length and corresponding construction and environmental costs;
- avoid areas designated as environmentally-sensitive, such as parks, etc.;
- follow existing pipeline rights-of-way wherever possible;
- minimize the number, and optimize the location, of crossings of major watercourses;
- minimize crossing complex terrain or areas posing reclamation difficulties; and
- accommodate reasonable landowner, agency or other routing requests where possible.

After consideration of alternative routing schemes and site-specific study, the selected route parallels existing pipelines in Canada for ≈80% of its overall length and over 90% in the US portion of the system. The lateral pipelines follow existing pipeline rights-of-way for approximately 60% of their overall length. In Canada the pipeline is located within the provinces of British Columbia, Alberta, and Saskatchewan. In the US, Alliance passes through North Dakota, Minnesota, Iowa, and Illinois (Fig. 1).

The Alliance Pipeline system traverses several different landscapes in Canada and the US. These varied landscapes differ in biophysical characteristics, wildlife, plant and aquatic habitat, settlement patterns, and land uses. As a result, potential environmental impacts vary somewhat from region to region. Measures to protect the environment of each unique region were given special consideration during pipeline construction. The northern portion of the Alliance system passes through the boreal forest in northeastern BC and northwestern Alberta, where the dominant land use is petroleum and forest industry activities. The

Fig. 1. Map of Alliance Pipeline System.

remainder of the pipeline route, throughout much of Alberta and essentially all of Saskatchewan and the four US states, crosses land that is developed for agriculture. Most of the route crosses the central North American plains, with relatively moderate terrain features that present few difficulties for pipeline construction. The Alliance project faced a wide variety of environmental resource protection issues (cold water fishery streams, endangered species, cultural resource features, etc.) but the dominant concern was mitigation of disturbance to agricultural lands. Over 100 intermediate or major rivers were crossed by conventional open-cut pipeline installation procedures. Horizontal directional drilling was employed at a total of 36 rivers.

CANADIAN ENVIRONMENTAL APPLICATION AND REVIEW PROCESS

The National Energy Board

Canadian natural gas pipelines crossing national or provincial boundaries fall under the jurisdiction of the National Energy Board, pursuant to the *National Energy Board Act (NEB Act)*. Board jurisdiction also encompasses oil and petroleum products and was extended in 1997 to cover essentially all federally-regulated commodity pipelines. Major projects are required to apply for a Certificate of Public Convenience and Necessity, pursuant to Section 52 of the *NEB Act*. The Board is required to consider matters in the public interest, including environmental protection. The NEB is a quasi-judicial board with strict procedures for public and private intervention and opportunities for public hearing and written interventions.

The NEB's *Guidelines for Filing Requirements*, GFR (NEB 1995) provide detailed information requirements addressing environmental issues that can potentially arise during the construction and operation of a pipeline. Section 9 of the GFR provides particulars as to the level of detail required in an environmental and socio-economic assessment submitted in support of an application. Sections 10–13 of the GFR require the filing of a detailed description of the mitigation and restoration information to be filed as a part of the application, as well as commitments and policies of the applicant to undertake mitigation measures proposed. Sections 14–18 require development of waste management and contingency plans and preparation of an Environmental Issues List. Section 18 requires the applicant to describe its environmental inspection program, policy, and procedures. In addition to the scientific and technical information required by Part VII of GFR, the NEB also requires applicants to implement a proactive program of Early Public Notification (EPN) and consultation.

The NEB's environmental protection mandate, under the *NEB Act*, is reinforced and supplemented by its duties as a "Responsible Authority" (RA) pursuant to the *Canadian Environmental Assessment Act (CEA Act)*. This Act was promulgated in 1995 and the Alliance Pipeline system was the first major project to be filed after the *CEA Act* was enacted. (The Act had been passed part way through the regulatory review phase of the Express Pipeline Project.) This paper considers the manner in which the NEB fulfilled the requirements under the *CEA Act* with respect to the Alliance system. It is important to note that future projects will undoubtedly face a different regime. A brief postscript is provided at the end of this paper to update the reader on recent changes to procedures with respect to an NEB application pursuant to the *CEA Act*.

An environmental assessment is required if a federal agency (such as the NEB) exercises a regulatory duty, such as issuing a permit. The level of environmental assessment is determined by the magnitude of the project. The highest level of environmental assessment, a Comprehensive Study, is required for a pipeline project which requires more than 75 km of new right-of-way. The federal authority, termed "Responsible Authority" or RA, must either ensure a Comprehensive Study Report (CSR) is prepared and provided to the Minister of Environment and to the Canadian Environmental Assessment Agency (CEAA), or refer the project to the Minister for referral to a mediator or a panel review. Some previous NEB projects have been considered by a joint review panel between the NEB and CEAA. In the case of the Alliance system, the CEAA directed the NEB to prepare the CSR and to fulfill the other requirements of a RA by consulting with other federal authorities.

After the CSR is complete, the Minister of Environment may approve the project or refer the project to a panel review if it is deemed there are significant adverse environmental impacts. This uncertainty presents applicants before the National Energy Board with a substantial risk because, after completing the environmental assessment, they may then be required to carry on to a panel review. The CEAA has issued a "Guide to Preparation of Comprehensive Study" (CEAA 1996). These requirements include public consultation, scoping, consideration of alternatives, cumulative effects assessment and the full range of environmental resource impact assessment and mitigation.

Other federal agencies
Although the CEA Act does not clearly provide for the role of "lead" Responsible Authority, it is expected that the NEB would act in that capacity. It is also expected that the Board would seek the input of other federal agencies with a regulatory role (Responsible Authority) or specialist agency for expert advice (Federal Authorities).

In the case of Alliance this consultation included Fisheries and Oceans Canada — Habitat Management Division and Habitat Enhancement Branch with respect to the Fisheries Act and the Prairie Farm Rehabilitation Administration (PFRA) regarding land managed by the PFRA. In addition, Fisheries and Oceans — Canadian Coast Guard was involved in approvals of water crossing designs on navigable watercourses pursuant to Section 108 of the National Energy Board Act. (Note that on federally-regulated pipeline projects, the Coast Guard's mandate under the Navigable Waters Act is captured by Section 108 of the NEB Act.) Environment Canada provided expert advice regarding air emissions from compressor stations and wildlife/endangered species information was provided by Canadian Wildlife Service.

US ENVIRONMENTAL APPLICATION AND REVIEW PROCESS

The Federal Energy Regulatory Commission
The environmental regulatory regime for federally regulated natural gas pipelines in the US is similar in scope, intent and timing to that in Canada. However, a comparison of the two regulatory regimes shows substantial differences in specific procedural matters and information requirements. These contrasts will be discussed in a subsequent section of this paper, but the two most significant differences are:
1. the environmental impact document is prepared by the agency rather than the applicant; and
2. while both jurisdictions provide opportunity for written interventions by the public and other pipelines, only the NEB routinely conducts a public hearing inviting oral testimony, interventions and cross-examination.

Construction of interstate and international gas (but not oil or other commodity) pipelines are regulated by the FERC. The proponent of a new pipeline is required to file for a Certificate of Public Convenience and Necessity under Section 7(c) of the Natural Gas Act. The FERC at 18 CFR, Part 157.14 requires the applicant to file Exhibit F-IV which is a statement regarding how the applicant proposes to comply with the National Environmental Policy Act NEPA of 1969. The application shall include a statement concerning the following factors:
1. the environmental impact of the proposed actions;
2. any adverse environmental effects which cannot be avoided should the proposal be implemented;
3. alternatives to the proposed action;
4. the relationship between local short-term uses of the environment and the maintenance and enhancement of long-term productivity, and
5. any irreversible and irretrievable commitment of resources which would be involved if the proposed action is implemented.

The FERC may also consider the environmental impact of directly connected facilities. In the case of the Alliance system, the Aux Sable Plant was considered in the EIS as a non-jurisdictional facility.

The environmental information required in the application is described in Guidance Manual for Environmental Report Preparation (FERC, 1995). The Environmental Report required in the 7(c) application is comprised of 12 Resource Reports:
- General Project Description;
- Water Use and Quality;
- Vegetation and Wildlife;
- Cultural Resources;
- Socio-Economics;
- Geological Resources;
- Soils;
- Land Use, Recreation, and Aesthetics;
- Air and Noise Quality;
- Alternatives;
- Reliability and Safety; and
- PCB Contamination.

The applicant is also required to describe how pipeline construction will comply with:
- Upland Erosion Control, Revegetation, and Maintenance Plan (FERC, 1994a);
- Wetland and Waterbody Construction and Mitigation Procedures (FERC, 1994b);
- Guidelines for Reporting on Cultural Resources Investigations (FERC, 1994c).

As mentioned, the federal agency (in this case the FERC) is required to satisfy the provisions of the NEPA. This task is undertaken by Commission staff, although it is becoming more common to see preparation of the EIS by a third-party contractor. The FERC (1994d) described these procedures in Handbook for Using Third-Party Contractors to Prepare Environmental Assessments and Environmental Impact Statements (Handbook), which allows for selection and hiring of a third-party environmental contractor working under the direction of commission staff, but at the expense of the applicant, to prepare the environmental documents. In compliance with ex parte rules, the third-party contractor prepares information requests and undertakes appropriate background studies to supplement material provided by the applicant for preparation of a draft and then a final Environmental Impact Statement (EIS). The procedures and timeline for this process are described in the Handbook. A Notice of Intent to prepare an EIS is sent by the FERC to landowners and other interested parties. During the preparation of the EIS, an initial scoping meeting is held to invite interested parties to submit written or oral interventions or comments on the proposed action. A second round of comment meetings is held following publication of the draft EIS. All comments are considered and incorporated into the final EIS. In the case of the Alliance project, an initial scoping meeting was held in each of the four states crossed by the pipeline route. A comment meeting, following publication of the DEIS, was similarly held in each state.

Other federal agencies

While the FERC is clearly the lead agency, other federal agencies may also play a significant role in review of federally-regulated pipeline projects. Depending on the location of the project, this could include the Bureau of Land Management, Forest Service, and others. In almost all cases, consultation and authorization from federal agencies concerned with preservation of historic resources, protection of endangered species and mitigation of impacts to wetlands and waterbodies are required.

Section 106 of the *National Historic Preservation Act* (1996) as amended, requires federal agencies to consider the effect of their undertakings on historic properties. All sites that are listed or eligible for listing on the National Register of Historic Places must be identified as a part of pipeline planning and the Advisory Council of Historic Preservation must be provided an opportunity to comment on plans designed to mitigate impact on eligible sites. The applicant is required to complete the necessary field surveys and seek concurrence from the State Historic Preservation Offices (SHPO) in each state.

The US Fish & Wildlife Service (USFWS) is responsible for determining compliance with the *Endangered Species Act* (1973). The applicant is required to consult with appropriate USFWS offices and state agencies regarding potentially affected species.

The US Army Corps of Engineers (COE) is responsible for reviewing projects and issuing permits for work affecting wetlands under Section 404 of the *Clean Water Act* and work in navigable waters under Section 10 of the *Rivers and Harbors Act*. Section 401 of the *Clean Water Act* requires that a water quality certification accompany nation-wide and individual permit applications. These authorizations allow construction across wetlands, waterbodies and provision for water withdrawal and discharge for pipeline hydrostatic testing, and includes discharge of water from dewatering the construction work areas.

COMPARISON OF CANADIAN AND US CERTIFICATE PROCESSES

As can be seen from the preceding description, the environmental aspects of the NEB and FERC Certificate processes have many similarities. Clearly, both agencies have a strong mandate to consider environmental matters in deciding the merits of a pipeline application. The information required to prepare supporting material for either an NEB or a FERC application are relatively well defined. Both agency staff and industry personnel generally have good experience with either the NEB's Guidelines for Filing Requirements (NEB, 1995) or the FERC's Guidance Manual for Environmental Report Preparation (FERC, 1995). As well, the information requirements for a Comprehensive Study are relatively clear, as are the NEPA requirements for an EIS in the US.

The principle difficulty encountered by the Alliance project (and probably other projects) in compiling the required environmental or cultural resource information was the site-specific nature of many survey requirements versus the lack of precise route location. Cultural resource survey, wetland delineation, soil survey and other studies were required on the actual, applied-for route, yet the project had not yet advanced far enough to have engineering survey or landowner permission for access. Both project proponents and regulators must deal with the reality of compiling a complete application at an early enough stage in project planning to facilitate proper environmental assessment. Of necessity, the application may be deficient in areas where survey permission is denied or route variations are still being considered.

In general, however, environmental information requirements in support of project applications for either the NEB or the FERC are reasonable and commensurate with the magnitude of a particular project. A potentially greater source of frustration from the applicants' perspective is the lack of procedural clarity in the preview process. Applicants should be expected to provide proper and complete environmental support information. The agencies, on the other hand, should be expected to provide a relatively clear roadmap that allows applicants to understand what information is required at each stage of the project. Prior to the *CEA Act*, the NEB process was well understood and the FERC process has been, and still is, relatively well defined. Alliance faced significant challenges as the NEB determined how to fulfill its requirements under the *CEA Act*. It is inevitable that new legislation will lead to confusion during the transition period. Along with the lack of procedural clarity, the applicant in Canada may be faced with further delay while appeals or challenges to either the process or the final authorizations are considered by the courts. Alliance faced substantial the possibility of delay as a result of procedural uncertainty with the NEB/CEAA process in Canada.

Table 1. Comparison of Canadian and American application and review process on the Alliance Pipeline Project

	Canada (NEB/CEAA)	United States (FERC/NEPA)
Strength of regulatory mandate to consider environmental matters	Strong, clear mandate	Strong, clear mandate
Potential for redundancy or conflict with other federal or provincial/stakeholders	High	None on Alliance
Clarity of procedural aspects of review process	Poor because of CEAA	Process is well defined
Clarity of information needs for application	Good	Good
Clarity of interrogatory process during application review	Fair	Good
Opportunity for public and landowner input to environmental assessment	Many opportunities for public input	Public scoping and comment meetings plus written interventions are common
Legal finality of procedures and outcome	Process and outcome is regularly challenged by opponents	Procedures for dealing with legal challenges and appeals is clear
Protection of endangered species	No legislated protection but specialist agencies provide advice	Applicant must consult with agencies and undertake survey per federal act
Protection of cultural/historical resources	Provincial regulations are clear and effective	State administered federal regulations are strict, but implementation is challenging
Protection of streams and fisheries resource	Legislation is strong but approval procedures unclear. Ultimate resource protection is excellent	Federal guidelines clear and effective. State processes are confusing. Ultimate resource protection is excellent
Protection of wetlands	No regulatory definition or protection of wetlands	Clear, strong federal procedure and outcome
Protection of agricultural soils	Site-specific survey plus mitigation measures are extensive	FERC Plan 1994a provides reasonable performance standards. State driven Agricultural Impact Mitigation Agree-ments created much difficulty

Since the date of Alliance's approval, the NEB has developed further refinements to their procedures to accommodate the *CEA Act* and the author is optimistic that both the regulators and the industry will find a more effective path through this maze.

Table 1 summarizes the author's observations gained from the Alliance project. In comparing the regulatory process in Canada and the US it is tempting to elect one as superior. Both have attributes that have evolved to serve particular needs of particular jurisdictions. Attempting to reach a "bottom line" conclusion is unrealistic. Table 1 presents a qualitative comparison for selected criteria. Because of the recent introduction of the CEAA process, the Canadian Certificate process was in a significant state of flux at the time of the Alliance application, so it is unfair to compare it with an established, stable process in the US with the FERC. While the two countries have different legislation and have placed different priorities on resources (the US, for example, have more definitive protection measures for wetlands and endangered species), in both countries pipeline construction practices are undertaken with a strong commitment from both the industry and the regulator to achieve high standards of environmental mitigation. In attempting to evaluate the final effectiveness of either process with respect to environmental protection, the author concludes both are successful in achieving their ultimate goal. With careful planning, thorough environmental survey and assessment and comprehensive environmental mitigation measures, supported by diligent application during construction, the consequences of pipeline disruption are relatively short term and restoration of upland, wetland, and waterbodies is effective.

The NEB review process offers substantially more opportunity for intervention and comment by other parties. Both the NEB Early Public Notification requirements and the public hearing format provide more frequent and more lenient venues than are available to the public in the FERC procedures. While the NEB hearings are formal, quasi-jurisdictional procedures, the Board members have a tradition of being tolerant and generous in allowing evidence from members of the public. (Perhaps less so with opposing intervenors represented by counsel.) This difference is still greater after the introduction of scoping and public consultation requirements of the *CEA Act*. The importance of public input and opportunity to object cannot be denied. However, the requirements of the *CEA Act* superimposed on the established NEB procedures has created confusion and redundancy.

COMPARISON OF APPROVAL TIMES

In late 1995, Alliance began to visit relevant federal and provincial/state agencies to understand their information needs, the scope of their authority and the expected schedule for review and approval. It was clear from the outset that the overall project schedule to implement the Alliance project was dictated by the information needs and review time required by the various environmental agencies.

The necessary work to undertake all environmental resource surveys, public consultation, and preparation of project applications began in earnest in March, 1996. Many environmental surveys required a precise location of the pipeline route and landowner permission for access. Coordination of the efforts of engineering, environment and right-of-way personnel was a vital component of success. As well, survey data or landowner requests sometimes dictated route variations, so it was often necessary to revisit areas to undertake the same type of survey a second or even a third time.

Another factor to be considered in project scheduling is to accommodate the biological season for field studies; for example, identification of flowering plants, nesting times of birds, or frost-free periods for soil sampling. An application to NEB requires project-specific field work that may encompass all biological seasons, so Alliance allowed approximately 14 months for preparation of a complete application. An application to the FERC allows for some supplemental field surveys to be submitted after the initial application, so approximately eight months was allocated for preparation of this application.

A study by the US General Accounting Office (GAO, 1992) considered 171 applications to the FERC for construction of natural gas pipelines between 1987 and 1991. Considering projects of a magnitude that required a full EIS, the average approval time was approximately 19 months. In developing its overall project schedule, Alliance reviewed several recent major project applications to the FERC and noted the time required from initial application to issuance of the final Certificate ranged from 18 to 44 months with 20 to 22 months being the norm. The overall project review milestone dates of the Alliance application are shown in Table 2. The initial application to the FERC was filed on December 24, 1996 and the Certificate Order issued on September 17, 1998, a total of 21 months.

Applications before the NEB also range in size, complexity, and other factors that might affect the time required for approval. The author is not aware of any study analyzing past NEB applications, however, Mutrie and Gilmore (1997) cited typical review periods ranging from 9 to 15 months. As stated earlier, Alliance recognized the need to allow 12 to 14 months for preparation of a complete environmental and socio-economic impact assessment to the National Energy Board. The resulting date of filing would not have allowed adequate time for NEB staff to conduct proper review and hearing of the application prior to the target construction start date. Consequently, Alliance took the initiative to submit a "Preliminary Submission" on December 29, 1996, enabling the NEB to initiate necessary actions to fulfill its obligations under the *CEA Act*. The concept of a Preliminary Submission has been adopted by subsequent projects and is now standard practice. Other major regulatory milestone dates are shown in Table 2 to facilitate comparison with the US FERC review process. While the two processes differ in detail, it is interesting to note the similarity between the milepost events. As noted by Mutrie and Gilmore (1997), the Canadian process is evolving to become similar to the US process.

POSTSCRIPT — CHANGES SINCE ALLIANCE

As noted by Mutrie and Gilmore (1993 and 1997), the environmental regulatory and application review process is continually evolving. This observation is still true as evidenced by changes since the Alliance application was filed in 1996 and approved in 1998. These changes have been more significant in Canada than in the US.

Changes to the NEB/CEAA process

The Alliance project was the first major application considered by the NEB after the *CEA Act* was enacted. Consequently, Alliance faced considerable uncertainty regarding procedural matters as the NEB determined how it would fulfill its requirements under the *CEA Act*. Previously, NEB information requirements and the review process had been well understood by the pipeline industry and by NEB staff. In Alliance's case, the NEB decided to use its interrogatory process and hearing procedures to fulfill its requirements under the *CEA Act* regarding scoping of environmental assessment and public input to environmental review as a "Comprehensive Study." If there had been a finding of significant adverse environmental impact, or if the Minister of Environment had considered public opposition to be significant, the Minister could have directed the NEB to conduct a panel review of the Alliance project. Although a panel review did not occur, this possibility did pose significant concern to project proponents since such a panel review would occur after the NEB hearing and would have resulted in significant delay to the entire project.

Subsequent to the Alliance approval, the NEB has issued *Guide to the Comprehensive Study Process for National Energy Board Regulated Pipeline Project Proposals* (draft December, 1998). These procedures have been applied, with some variations, to two approved projects and a third, Georgia Strait Crossing Project, that is still in progress. The process adopted by the

Table 2. Comparison of NEB and FERC approval milestone dates

Canada		Calendar		United States
Alliance filed Preliminary Submission requesting NEB to initiate scoping activities under CEA Act	Dec. 31	**Dec. 96**	Dec. 24	Alliance filed 7(c) application[a]
		Jan. 97		
		Feb. 97	Feb. 21	FERC issued Notice of Intent to prepare EIS
NEB issued news release announcing initiation of scoping activities	Mar. 14	**Mar. 97**		
		Apr. 97		
		May 97		
NEB issued final scope of environmental assessment	June 19	**June 97**		
Alliance filed completed application	July 3	**July 97**		
		Aug. 97	Aug. 1	FERC issued Preliminary Determination that, subject to completion of environmental review, the proposed pipeline is in the public interest
NEB issued Hearing Order setting out procedural matters for public involvement and public hearing	Sep. 3	**Sep. 97**		
		Oct. 97		
		Nov. 97		
		Dec. 97	Dec. 24	FERC published Draft EIS for comment.
NEB began public hearing	Jan. 6	**Jan. 98**		
		Feb. 98		
		Mar. 98		
		Apr. 98		
NEB concluded public hearing (77 hearing days total)	May 21	**May 98**		
NEB issues Draft Comprehensive Study Report (CSR)	June 30	**June 98**		
		July 98		
		Aug. 98	Aug. 24	FERC released Final EIS
NEB submits Final CSR to Minister of Environment and Agency for CEA Act public comment	Sep. 30	**Sep. 98**	Sep. 17	FERC issued Order granting Certificate of Public Convenience and Necessity
		Oct. 98		
NEB issued Reasons for Decision recommending issuance of Certificate of Public Convenience and Necessity	Nov. 23	**Nov. 98**		
Governor General in Counsel issued Certificate of Public Convenience and Necessity	Dec. 3	**Dec. 98**		

[a]It is important to note that both the NEB and the FERC applications were supplemented with further filings in response to information requests or further survey data pursuant to normal review procedures.

NEB requires that the proponent first submit scoping information in a Preliminary Submission. The NEB will assume the lead Responsible Authority role in accordance with *Regulations Respecting the Coordination by Federal Authorities of Environmental Procedures and Regulations* (CEAA, 1997). The Board may either ensure a Comprehensive Study is conducted, or it might refer the project to the Minister of Environment for mediation or panel review. It is expected that most major projects would follow the Comprehensive Study path. The NEB delegates conduct of the Comprehensive Study and preparation of the Comprehensive Study Report to the proponent. Interestingly, delegation of the CSR preparation to the proponent, in some ways, parallels the FERC process of third-party EIS preparation. With the NEB in the role of lead Responsible Authority, the CSR will be submitted to the Minister of Environment. Unless the Minister refers the project to a panel review, the Responsible Authority (the NEB) will have then completed its requirements under CEA Act and will begin its own hearing process. Information requirements for the NEB environmental review process are unchanged as described in the *Guidelines for Filing Requirements* (NEB, 1995).

These new procedural steps by the NEB, under the *CEA Act*, are being implemented on the Georgia Strait Crossing Project application. Time will tell if this process becomes the norm since the NEB continues to modify its procedures to deal with the *CEA Act* on each subsequent project received. The scoping process being implemented by the NEB, in some ways, also parallels that used by the FERC under NEPA.

Changes to the FERC process

On April 29, 1999 the FERC issued Order No. 603. The stated purpose was to conform FERC regulations with current practices. In effect, the new rule adopted the existing guidance manual for environmental report preparation (August, 1995). However, it also sets out *Minimum Filing Requirements for Environmental Reports* under the *Natural Gas Act*, which it considers to be the *minimum* environmental information necessary for it to begin its review. Applications that do not contain items provided in the checklist will be (and some have been) rejected.

The FERC has also issued Order No 607 to modify its regulations governing *ex parte* contacts in contested proceedings, which, in general, make communication with FERC staff less restrictive. Order No. 609 and 609(a), which expand the requirements for landowner notification, have also been issued.

POST-CERTIFICATE PROCEDURES

Both the NEB and the FERC, after issuing a Certificate, require substantial material to be filed that essentially serves two purposes: (1) to ensure that Certificate Conditions are satisfied prior to authorizing construction to begin; and (2) to ensure construction occurs in compliance with approved mitigation measures.

There is a tendency by environmental staff to underestimate the level of effort required to support construction activities. In fact, the volume of post-certificate material filed to either the NEB or the FERC and the manpower efforts for environmental inspection and construction support are greater than that required during the planning/regulatory phase. A detailed description of the post-certificate document and procedural requirements is beyond the scope of this paper. However, pipeline planners are cautioned not to underestimate this phase of a pipeline project.

CONCLUSIONS

This paper offers a comparison of the Canadian and US regulatory review processes based on experience gained with the Alliance Pipeline project. The author concludes that both the National Energy Board in Canada and the Federal Energy Regulatory Commission in the US have evolved environmental review processes that result in high standards of environmental protection during pipeline construction in either country. In evaluating the final effectiveness with respect to environmental protection, the author is of the opinion that both are successful in achieving their ultimate goal. With careful planning, thorough environmental survey and assessment, and comprehensive environmental mitigation measures supported by diligent application during construction, the consequences of the pipeline disruption are relatively short-term and restoration is effective.

The information requirements for environmental assessment in support of an application to either the NEB or the FERC are relatively clear and reasonable with respect to the potential for environmental impact. There is, however, difficulty in compiling site-specific survey information early enough in the planning process to fully satisfy the information requirements. The need for supplemental submission of data in areas of route variations or prohibited land access is inevitable.

Alliance filed its application to the NEB when the Canadian certificate process was in a state of flux because of the recent introduction of the *Canadian Environmental Assessment Act*. Consequently, there was significant confusion and some delay in the procedural aspects of the approval process. In contrast, the FERC process was relatively well established and stable so a critical comparison between the two processes is unfair. It is clear that in the case of the Alliance project, and presumably future such applications, the NEB/CEAA process will take at least as much time as the FERC process. The author is optimistic that the uncertainty in the procedures faced by Alliance will be resolved as more experience is gained with the requirements of the *CEA Act*.

ACKNOWLEDGEMENTS

The views expressed in this paper are those of the author, however, he wishes to express his thanks to Dr. Richard Skarie of Natural Resource Group, Inc., Minneapolis and Mr. Dean Mutrie of TERA Environmental Consultants, Calgary for their review of an initial draft.

REFERENCES

Canadian Environmental assessment Agency. 1997. Guide to Preparation of a Comprehensive Study. Ottawa, Canada.
Canadian Environmental assessment Agency. 1997. Regulations Respecting the Coordination by Federal Authorities of Environmental assessment Procedures and Requirements. Ottawa, Canada.
Environment Canada. 1994. *Migratory Birds Convention Act, 1994*.
Federal Energy Regulatory Commission. 1998. Alliance Pipeline project Final Environmental Impact Statement. Washington, DC.
Federal Energy Regulatory Commission. 1998. Order issuing certificates [to Alliance], granting Natural Gas Act section 3 authorization. Washington, DC.
Federal Energy Regulatory Commission. 1994a. Upland erosion control, revegetation, and maintenance plan. Washington, DC.
Federal Energy Regulatory Commission. 1994b. Wetland and waterbody construction and mitigation procedures. Washington, DC.
Federal Energy Regulatory Commission. 1994c. Guidelines for Reporting on Cultural Resources Investigations. Washington, DC.

Federal Energy Regulatory Commission. 1994d. Handbook for Using Third-Party Contractors to Prepare Environmental assessments and Environmental Impact Statements. Washington, DC.

Federal Energy Regulatory Commission. 1995. Guidance Manual for Environmental Report Preparation. Washington, DC.

General Accounting Office. 1992. Factors Affecting Approval Times for Construction of Natural Gas Pipelines, GAO/RCED-92-100. Washington, DC.

Illinois Department of Agriculture. 1997. Agricultural Impact Mitigation Agreement between Alliance Pipeline L.P. and the Illinois Department of Agriculture.

Iowa Department of Agriculture and Minnesota Department of Agriculture. 1997. Agricultural Impact Mitigation Agreement between Alliance Pipeline L.P. and the Iowa Attorney General's Office, Iowa Department of Agriculture and Land Stewardship and the Office of Consumer Advocate, and the Minnesota Attorney General's Office and Minnesota Department of Agriculture.

Mutrie, D.F. and K.B. Gilmore. 1993. Pipelining in Canada and the United States: An environmental comparison. Pipelines, 234–242.

Mutrie, D.F. 1993. Pipelining in Canada and the US: An environmental comparison. Pipeline Technology, V-B: 535–542.

Mutrie, D.F. and K.B. Gilmore. 1997. Environmental comparison of pipelines in Canada and the US. In: Proceedings of the Sixth International Symposium in Rights-of-Way Management. New Orleans, LA.

National Energy Board. 1998. Certificate GC-98 [Alliance Certificate]. Calgary, AB.

National Energy Board. 1995. Guidelines for Filing Requirements. Calgary, AB.

North Dakota Department of Agriculture. 1997. Agricultural Impact Mitigation Agreement between Alliance Pipeline L.P. and the North Dakota Department of Agriculture.

US Fish & Wildlife Service. 1973. Endangered Species Act of 1973. Washington, DC.

BIOGRAPHICAL SKETCH

Howard R. Heffler, MEng, PEng

Alliance Pipeline Ltd., #400, 605-5 Avenue S.W., Calgary, AB T2P 3H5, hefflerh@alliance-pipeline.com, Phone: (403) 517-6301 Fax: (403) 266-1604

Howard Heffler graduated with a BEng (Chem) from the University of New Brunswick in 1969 and obtained a MEng (Environmental) from McMaster University in 1970. He has 30 years experience as an environmental engineer, the past 25 years in the oil and gas industry in Calgary, Alberta. Howard has worked as an environmental manager within major resource companies and as a consultant for a wide variety of oil and gas and pipeline firms. Much of Mr. Heffler's experience over the past 25 years has related to environmental work in support of pipeline projects. He joined Alliance Pipeline at its inception and is Manager of Environmental Affairs. Alliance is a new company currently nearing completion of construction of a major new pipeline system serving North American gas markets.

'Facts' Point to Reduced ROW Land Use Projections

Sandra Patty, Andrew Cressman, and Deborah L. Kowalczyk

In Maryland, electric utilities must obtain a Certificate of Public Convenience and Necessity (CPCN) from the Maryland Public Service Commission before constructing new transmission lines greater than 69,000 volts. Maryland's Power Plant Research Program (PPRP) within the Department of Natural Resources coordinates the interagency reviews of CPCN applications and development of conditions issued with the CPCN that minimizes effects to the State's resources associated with ROW clearing, transmission line construction, and ROW maintenance. PPRP is currently evaluating the potential impact of innovative, high-voltage power flow control technology to Maryland's transmission system and ROWs. Flexible Alternating Current Transmission System (FACTS) technology, utilizing silicon-based thyristors in an integrated circuit arrangement, has been utilized in several applications to increase the efficiency of existing transmission systems by up to 40%. Wide-spread application of FACTS technology on existing transmission systems could result in a corresponding decrease in the demand for new transmission line and ROW development. This paper will examine the current and projected rate of transmission line ROW development in Maryland, and evaluate the potential impact of FACTS on the projected rate and cumulative land use savings. The findings presented will have important implications with respect to Maryland's economy and natural resources, and will support Maryland's Smart Growth Initiative.

Keywords: Cumulative environmental effects, habitat fragmentation, land conservation, innovative technology, planning

FOREWORD

This study was conducted under the direction of Ms. Sandra Patty of the Maryland Department of Natural Resources Power Plant Research Program (PPRP). The work was performed by Environmental Resources Management (ERM) under direct contract with PPRP.

INTRODUCTION

In 1999 the United States consumed approximately 3,200,000,000 megawatt-hours of electric power. Demand is expected to grow at a rate of 1.8% (NERC, 2000) annually over the next 10 years due increasing reliance on electric-powered technology. Meanwhile, the transition from a regulated to an open power market is resulting in power flow patterns that today's high-voltage transmission infrastructure was not designed to handle. The combination of demand growth and changing power flow patterns is causing serious concerns to be raised about the continued reliability of electric power supplies. In some areas of the country an already overloaded transmission system is struggling to keep up with present (peak) demand.

In May 2000, the North American Electric Reliability Council (NERC) published *"The Reliability of Bulk Electric Systems in North America"* (NERC, 2000). This report summarized findings for the assessment period 1999–2008, including the following:

– Capacity margins are at the lowest levels in many years, particularly in the Eastern Interconnection (roughly, the eastern US and Canada).

Environmental Concerns in Rights-of-Way
Management: Seventh International Symposium
J.W. Goodrich-Mahoney, D.F. Mutrie and C.A. Guild (editors)
© 2002 Elsevier Science Ltd. All rights reserved.

- The Eastern Interconnection is importing significantly more power than it is exporting; transfer capability must keep pace with this trend or capacity shortfalls will occur.
- Reactive power support is needed to prevent low-voltage episodes.
- Market driven changes in transmission usage patterns and the number and complexity of transactions are causing new transmission limitations to appear in different and unexpected locations.
- As the demand on the transmission system continues to rise, the ability to deliver energy from remote resources to demand centers is deteriorating.
- The majority of proposed transmission projects are for local system support. It is yet unknown whether appropriate incentives exist to prompt transmission system additions and reinforcements to support the needs of a competitive market.

To meet increasing demand, construction of 51,600 MW in additional generating capacity is planned by the end of 2001 (NERC, 2000). Approximately 7000 miles of new high-voltage (230 kV and above) transmission lines are planned (NERC, 2000). However, these lines are primarily intended for local support and are not expected to contribute toward a solution of the issues identified in the NERC report. Construction of new transmission facilities designed to meet the new challenges is generally being put off due to weak economic returns and regulatory uncertainty. Therefore, the actual number of new transmission lines required to handle increasing demand and evolving power flow patterns could be significantly greater than the current projections.

In light of this (some would say alarming) state of affairs, this paper reviews the potential impacts on transmission transfer capability and reliability of a powerful, emerging class of power flow controllers, collectively known as Flexible Alternating Current Transmission Systems (FACTS). This class of technology holds the promise of dramatically upgrading transmission systems to meet today's evolving power flow challenges. Transmission efficiency gains achieved through the widespread use of this technology could eliminate the need for a substantial number of new transmission lines and result in significant ROW land use and natural resource conservation.

TRANSMISSION LIMITATIONS

The electrical power system consists of generating stations, high-voltage transmission systems, and low-voltage distribution systems connected, ultimately, to consumers (homes, industrial plants, etc.). The efficient transmission of power from remote points of generation over long distances is a critical link in this system. Interconnected transmission facilities allow local and regional utilities to pool their resources to reduce the amount of capacity they must hold in reserve, as well as gain access to energy imports from other regions.

For a specified transmission line, there are actual and practical limits to the amount of power that can be transmitted. In establishing a practical limit, the actual limit is adjusted downward to provide safe operating margins against line damage and outages. The actual limit must be further adjusted downward to account for the fact that electric power travels through all parallel paths of an interconnected system, affecting all interconnected lines. Transmission system limitations are generally classified into three main groups:
- Thermal Limits: Resistance heat losses cause the temperature of transmission conductors to increase; this temperature increase can lead to sagging of overhead lines, short circuiting, and permanent damage to the conductors. Seasonal load ratings establish maximum current magnitude limits for a range of load duration scenarios.
- Voltage Limits: Throughout the transmission system, voltages must be maintained within acceptable ranges at all times. The flow of power through a transmission line generally results in a voltage drop due to line reactance. If large amounts of power are transferred over long distances, the bulk transmission system may not be capable of maintaining adequate voltage. In addition, sudden outages on interconnected lines will result in the fault current flowing over less efficient alternative parallel paths. As a result, the voltage drop occurring on the transmission system will increase, and there will be an abrupt change in the voltages at the receiving end.
- Stability Limits: Generating stations connected on an interconnected system are synchronized to operate at the same frequency (60 Hz), with the total system load evenly allocated among the operating generators. In the event of a fault on one of the interconnected transmission lines, the fault load will be picked up by the remaining lines. The nearest generators will respond by increasing output to the lines in the immediate vicinity of the fault, and in so doing will slow down and may fall out of step. The generators that slow down the least will then attempt to pick up the greatest share of the load and fault current, which will cause them to slow down, while the others, thus relieved, may tend to regain speed and pick up more of the load. If the system continues to oscillate in this manner, large fluctuations on line loadings and system voltages may occur. In the extreme case, this can lead to other lines becoming overloaded, and a cascading effect resulting in a blackout (Pansini, 1991). To maintain system stability, the system must have rapid system response capabilities and must be operated within acceptable contingency scenarios.

The great majority of utilities in the US normally operate so that the sudden loss of any component of the system will not result in unacceptable system conditions that threaten reliability. This is referred to as the "N-1 operating principle." The N-1 principle is intended to improve system reliability by ensuring that the thermal, voltage, and stability limits of the system will not be exceeded under any single contingency condition. That is, under the N-1 operation principle, there is no single component in the system the loss of which will cause voltage collapse or system breakup.

Under the N-1 operation principle, a portion of the transmission system is held in reserve for emergencies. The portion of the system capacity held in reserve to satisfy the N-1 principle is effectively another downward adjustment of the actual transfer limit. The "available" transfer capability of the system is what remains after subtracting the transmission reliability margins from the actual transfer capability.

FACTS TECHNOLOGY

Reliability margins and redundancies must be adequate to accommodate conventional, mechanical power flow controllers (switches, phase shifters, etc.) that are limited in their ability to respond to operating signals — rapid-response power flow control, in terms of power-frequency electrical circuitry, is not possible with mechanical switches. Transmission reliability margins (unused capacity) therefore represent assets that, to some degree, can be "recovered" with the use of rapid-response controllers.

FACTS is the name given to an emerging class of rapid-response power flow controllers developed by the Electric Power Research Institute (EPRI). FACTS devices can supplement or replace conventional, mechanical power flow switches with solid-state electronics. FACTS technology is thus emerging as an innovative tool for overcoming transmission limitations and improving system performance. Efficiency increases due to the installation of FACTS devices have been estimated at up to 50% (EPRI, 1996).

Design basis and functions

The key to this technology is the development of silicon-based (semiconducting) thyristors capable of handling high-power applications. These devices are solid-state switches analogous to integrated circuits. Previously, solid-state integrated circuit electronics devices were limited to low-power (mV and mA) applications. With recent innovations in silicon-based thyristors, solid-state applications are now possible at the level of thousands of volts and amps. Putting several such thyristors in series, EPRI researchers began in the 1980s constructing integrated circuits capable of handling high-voltage power transmission flows. These integrated circuit devices are capable of providing transmission circuit response within a fraction of a cycle, as opposed to conventional electromechanical switchgear that requires several cycles to act.

The quick response of the FACTS device enables precise tuning, switching, and control of entire transmission networks as a single circuit. The devices are therefore able to compensate for power flow inefficiencies before they can affect the transmission system. Elimination of reactive power loss, power flow bottlenecks, and other such disturbances, can dramatically increase the available transmission capacity.

Types of FACTS devices and attributes

FACTS devices can be installed in shunt, series, series-series, and series-shunt configurations, depending on the needs of a particular line and its interconnections. In these varied configurations FACTS devices can provide a wide array of power flow capabilities and efficiency improvements. Table 1 lists the control attributes for the FACTS Controllers developed to date.

FACTS devices have been installed at strategically located substations to alleviate bottlenecks, improve load leveling on interconnected lines, provide reactive power support, and generally increase the available transmission capacity without constructing new lines. The following example (from Hingorani and Gyugyi, 2000) illustrates the utility of FACTS technology.

For the three interconnected lines of Fig. 1(a), lines AB, BC, and AC have continuous ratings of 1000 MW, 1250 MW, and 2000 MW, respectively, and sites A and B are sending power to a load center, site C. The emergency (short-term) ratings are twice the normal ratings in case of a loss on one of the lines. If generator A is generating 2000 MW and generator B 2000 MW, a total of 3000 MW would be delivered to the load center at site C. For the impedances shown, the three lines would carry 600, 1600, and 1400 MW respectively. Line BC would be overloaded, and therefore generation would have to be decreased at B and increased at A in order to meet the load for any extended period of time without damaging BC or causing an outage.

The performance of the system can be dramatically improved by using a FACTS device. The addition of a Thyristor-Controlled Series Capacitor in line AC as shown in Fig. 1(b), for example, would increase the transfer capability of line AC, and prevent the overload situation on BC without any reduction in generation. Another approach would be to use a Thyristor-Controlled Series Reactor (inductor) in line BC that would serve to adjust the steady-state power flows as well as damp unwanted oscillations. Key FACTS installations currently in use are briefly reviewed below.

Existing applications

Tennessee: Static synchronous compensator (STATCOM)
The first STATCOM installation was commissioned in 1995 at the Sullivan Substation in Tennessee which is supplied by a 500 kV bulk power load and four 161 kV lines. This substation lies at the edge of the Tennessee Valley Authority (TVA) service area, and problems were arising due to increased power demand

Table 1. Control attributes of FACTS devices

FACTS controller	Control attributes
Static Synchronous Compensator (STATCOM)	Voltage control, VAR compensation, damping oscillations, voltage stability, transient and dynamic stability
Static VAR Compensator (SVC, TCR, TCS, TRS)	Voltage control, VAR compensation, damping oscillations, voltage stability, transient and dynamic stability
Thyristor-Controlled Braking Resistor (TCBR)	Damping oscillations, transient and dynamic stability
Static Synchronous Series Compensator (SSSC)	Current control, damping oscillations, transient and dynamic stability, voltage stability, fault current limiting
Thyristor-Controlled Series Capacitor (TCSC, TSSC)	Current control, damping oscillations, transient and dynamic stability, voltage stability, fault current limiting
Thyristor-Controlled Series Reactor (TCSR, TSSR)	Current control, damping oscillations, transient and dynamic stability, voltage stability, fault current limiting
Thyristor-Controlled Phase-Shifting Transformer (TCPST or TCPR)	Active power control, damping oscillations, transient and dynamic stability, voltage stability
Unified Power Flow Controller (UPFC)	Active and reactive power control, voltage control, VAR compensation, damping oscillations, transient and dynamic stability, voltage stability, fault current limiting
Thyristor-Controlled Voltage Limiter (TCVL)	Transient and dynamic voltage limit
Thyristor-Controlled Voltage Regulator (TCVR)	Reactive power control, voltage control, damping oscillations, transient and dynamic stability, voltage stability
Interline Power Flow Controller (IPFC)	Reactive power control, voltage control, damping oscillations, transient and dynamic stability, voltage stability

Source: Adapted from Hingorani & Gyugyi, 2000.

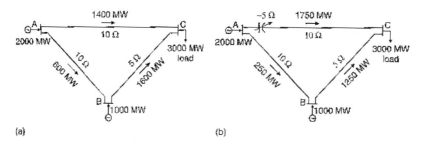

Fig. 1. FACTS example.

and weak interconnections to adjacent grids. A connection to the American Electric Power (AEP) network also exists at the Sullivan substation, and oscillations experienced by AEP were subsequently passed on to Sullivan and the rest of the TVA grid (Hingorani and Gyugyi, 2000).

A STATCOM device was installed to regulate voltage on a 161 kV line, and prevent failures in the 500 kV transformer banks. The alternative for TVA was to install another transformer and construct a new 161 kV line in the area (Till, 2000). In addition to eliminating the need for ROW land development for the 161 kV line, TVA has estimated savings of $10 million in cost avoidance for a new transformer and construction of the 161 kV line (EPRI, 1996). Fig. 2 is a photo of the STATCOM installation.

Fig. 2. STATCOM installation.

Fig. 3. UPFC installation.

Kentucky: Unified power flow controller (UPFC)
In the Inez area of eastern Kentucky, serviced by AEP, long 138 kV lines were relied upon to provide power to this rural area. Due to increased demand, heavy loadings on the 138 kV line over long distances resulted in excess voltage gradients. During peak loading times, contingency outages were predicted to cause voltage and thermal overload conditions.

To remedy the potential problems, a UPFC was installed (see Fig. 3) to provide voltage support and distribute power flow more evenly over the line. The UPFC enabled the 138 kV line to act as a 345 kV line and eliminated the need for construction of new facilities and associated land use development (Hingorani and Gyugyi, 2000).

New York: Convertible static compensator (CSC)
Increasing demand on the New York Power Authority (NYPA) transmission system connecting New York City and southeastern New York with generating facilities in the north was causing extreme congestion; this line was operating at maximum load for approximately one-quarter of the time. The solution to this problem needed to address the north-south power flow bottlenecking problem. Conventional electromechanical devices were deemed inadequate to keep pace with the rapidly evolving power flow patterns, and the construction of new lines was not an option (Zelingher, 2000).

The CSC Controller is currently being installed in the Marcy Substation in central New York. The CSC will be able to control both power flow and voltage, subsequently minimizing line disturbances and power interruptions. The system is expected to be in operation by July 2002, and will increase transfer capability by 240 MW (Reason, 1999). With the installation of the CSC, NYPA will meet its dual objectives of providing needed upgrades to the transmission system and eliminating the need for additional lines.

Economic considerations
Because FACTS technology is relatively new and the number of existing applications are limited, capital costs are high. For example, the cost of the NYPA project was $48 million (Reason, 1999). In a few cases, utilities and other interested parties may be interested in contributing to pilot projects to foster the development of this technology (as was the case with the NYPA project). In general, however, the current high cost of the technology is likely to be a barrier to widespread use. For now, FACTS installations make the most sense where:
– the transmission system must be upgraded to ensure a reliable supply, but new transmission lines are not an option due to sociopolitical or other factors (e.g., the NYPA project); or
– the installation of FACTS results in sufficient reductions in the cost of impedance and opportunity losses to offset high capital costs in life-cycle cost calculations (e.g., the TVA and Kentucky projects).[1]

In the future, it is anticipated that capital costs will decrease, perhaps dramatically, as FACTS technology matures. As this happens, FACTS devices should play an increasing role in system design and economic considerations. It is expected that the transmission efficiency increases associated with widespread use of FACTS will translate into significant ROW land use savings and/or reduced rates of land use development.

POTENTIAL IMPACT OF FACTS IN MARYLAND AND THE MID-ATLANTIC REGION

The Power Plant Research Program (PPRP) was established in the State of Maryland to ensure that the demand for electric power could be met in a timely manner and at a reasonable cost, while protecting the State's natural resources. PPRP is monitoring the emergence of FACTS technology with great interest because of its potential utility as a tool for furthering these goals.

Overview of PJM service area
Maryland lies within the Mid-Atlantic Area Council (MAAC) transmission system which is serviced by the Pennsylvania–New Jersey–Maryland (PJM) Interconnection. PJM is responsible for planning and maintaining reliability of the transmission grid and for the operation and control of the bulk electric power system in the Mid-Atlantic Area.

The PJM service area is the largest centrally dispatched electric control area in North America. It consists of 8000 miles of high voltage transmission lines

---
1 The utilities estimate that it takes 28.5 years to recover the cost of building a transmission line, versus the 3–5 years to recover the cost of building a generation project (EEI, EXNET, 2000).

and handles 8% of the total power generated in the US. Approximately 23 million people are served in this area. Interconnections between the PJM service area and adjacent systems allow for the importation of an additional 3500 MW on average to handle periods of peak demand or contingency situations (PPRP, 1999).

Summary of reliability assessments

In January 1999 PPRP published *"An Assessment of the Transmission Grid of Maryland Utilities and Some Potential Consequences of Retail Competition."* This report discussed PJM transfer capability limitations identified based on power flows during the 1994–1996 time period, and evaluated potential transfer capability issues associated with deregulation. This study concluded that significant new construction of transmission facilities could be needed to address the number and direction of power transactions under an open market.

On 6 July 1999, and again on 19 July, the PJM system approached or exceeded record peak load conditions. Extreme heat and humidity on these days led to record usage of electricity, equaling PJM's projected peak usage for 2004. Low-voltage conditions occurred on these days because reactive demand exceeded reactive supply. On 21 March 2000, PJM published a Root Cause Analysis Report of this event. Several recommendations for improving system operation have been implemented to improve reliability.

In December 1999, PJM published the 1999 Baseline Regional Transmission Expansion Plan (RTEP) Report, covering the period 2001–2006. This report summarizes the findings of a baseline analysis of PJM system adequacy and security for use in conducting Feasibility Studies for any proposed facility connection projects and subsequent Impact Studies.[2] This report lists transmission limitations and concerns with respect to import transfer capabilities, and notes that installed reserve margins are decreasing.

In May 2000, the MAAC–ECAR–NPCC (MEN) Study Committee published the *2000 Summer MEN Interregional Transmission System Reliability Assessment*. This report summarized transfer capability limitations with respect to interregional transfers and cited the need for close coordination among interconnection users and system operators.

Each of these reports cite the need for improvements in system operation and transfer capabilities, consistent with the May 2000 NERC report.

System upgrades

A potential maximum of 21,000 MW of new power generation capacity is planned for the PJM service area by 2004 (NERC, 2000). As on the national level, planned transmission upgrades are intended for local support and don't address issues associated with bulk transfers occurring over long distances in previously unforseen directions, as a deregulated open market will likely demand. Several specific points of concern have been identified in previous studies — in particular, interconnections to adjacent transmission grids — where FACTS technology could potentially provide an immediate and economical means of enhancing the PJM system performance and transfer capability.

While FACTS represents a potentially powerful new tool to system planners and operators, there are concerns about how this technology would be introduced to the existing grid. Such concerns include the potential for inadequate contingency capabilities in the event that power must be redistributed from a faulted, high-capacity, FACTS-equipped line to conventionally equipped connected lines. In addition, the concern exists that owners of FACTS-equipped lines may be able to influence power flow routing to the benefit of themselves and at the expense of optimal system operation. These issues require further study to ensure that the use of this technology does not result in any unintended, negative consequences. This situation, it should be noted, is not uncommon where new technology must be integrated, or phased in, with existing systems.

ROW land use impacts

For the purpose of this study, potential land use impacts were evaluated using assumed transfer capability efficiency increases and corresponding land use development rate decreases. Even using conservative potential efficiency increases, this evaluation shows that FACTS technology has the potential to result in significant ROW land use savings.

Table 2 and Fig. 4 present the potential ROW land use savings for various scenarios. The energy demand growth rate in the PJM service area is estimated to be 1.8% (NERC, 2000). There are currently 8000 miles of high voltage lines in the PJM service area (and approximately 2500 miles in Maryland). The growth rate in number of miles of transmission lines has been assumed to be proportional to the growth in installed generating capacity. It has also been assumed, for simplicity, that Maryland's land use and power production will be directly proportional to the PJM growth rates. The baseline land use in the PJM service area and Maryland was determined by using an assumed average ROW width of 150 feet.

Using these assumptions, it is estimated that PJM's generating capacity will grow from 77,000 MW by 2004 to 102,000 MW by 2020. Similarly, it is assumed that Maryland's generating capacity will grow from 18,500 MW by 2004 to 24,600 MW by 2020.

Potential transmission efficiency gains from the use of FACTS devices have been estimated by EPRI to be as high as 40–50% (EPRI, 1996). As a basis for this study, however, a 20% increase was assumed to reflect

---

[2] A new baseline analysis is conducted prior to the conduct of impact studies for a new group of facility connection requests (known as a Queue).

Table 2. Projected land use savings for the PJM service area

Scenario	Total land used (acres) 2004	ROW land saved (acres) 2004	Total land used (acres) 2020	ROW land saved (acres) 2020
BASE CASE	199,998	N/A	418,182	N/A
FACTS Applied to new t-lines	190,600	9398	371,192	46,990
FACTS Applied to New and Limiting t-lines	180,992	19,006	323,152	95,030
FACTS Applied to all t-lines	166,359	33,639	249,987	168,195

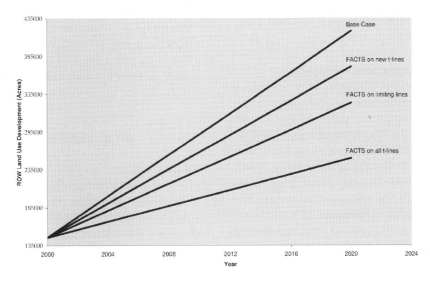

Fig. 4. Land use comparison in the PJM service area.

practical and technical limitations to the application of this technology.

The scenarios used in the analysis were as follows:
- *Base Case* — continuation of the status quo with respect to transmission facilities, with no usage of FACTS technology.
- *FACTS applied to new lines* — assumed FACTS would only be used on new transmission facilities. 20% of new ROW land development (compared to base case) would be avoided.
- *FACTS applied to new and limiting lines* — FACTS would be used on all new transmission facilities, and 30% of the current facilities.
- *FACTS applied to all lines* — assumes all existing and new transmission facilities would become 20% more efficient than the base case efficiency.

For the PJM service area, potential land use savings of nearly 170,000 acres are estimated, and in Maryland, 58,000 acres by 2020. These figures are dramatic and could play an important role in providing utilities needed impetus for committing to the high capital costs (at least in the short term) of FACTS installations.

These results, and similar evaluations performed for other states, could also be valuable to community/state land use planners. Planners and officials confronted with sprawl issues could use the results of such an evaluation to aid in identifying priority funding projects. Maryland's Smart Growth Initiative program, for example, has identified priority funding areas for which land use conservation and "smart growth" projects may be eligible for State funds.

OUTLOOK FOR THE FUTURE

FACTS and transmission reliability

Various options are being weighed to ensure that in the future the supply of electric power in the US will be adequate and reliable. Among these options are policy and legislative proposals to improve the coordination of planning and operation issues, market-based proposals designed to affect pricing schemes and demand patterns, and, of course, engineering upgrades to physically enhance the capabilities of transmission systems. The latter is essential if an unregulated, open market is to reach its potential as a low-cost efficient supplier of power. Otherwise, transmission limitations will be serious impediments to a robust transmission system and a healthy electric power market.

FACTS technology represents a potentially powerful tool for system planners and operators to overcome power flow limitations. As FACTS devices and other technological advances, such as low-resistance conductors, continue to emerge and mature, they need to be included for consideration in system design planning.

In the short term, FACTS devices represent a potential solution to interconnection tie bottlenecks, load leveling on parallel paths, and perhaps other applications. Although there is an immediate need to assess contingency and operator influence concerns, these issues will likely be overcome with proper planning.

In the long term, capital costs are expected to decrease as FACTS technology matures. As this happens it seems likely that the use of FACTS will become widespread and result in significant expansion of the available transfer capability for both intra- and inter-regional transfers.

FACTS and cumulative environmental impacts

The positive impacts of FACTS technology and other transmission efficiency advances on land conservation have received little attention to date. As the results of this study indicate, the widespread use of FACTS has the potential to result in substantial land use savings. Land conservation would consequently result in a reduction of habitat impacts, ROW fragmentation effects, and other ROW management issues. The potential positive cumulative impacts to natural resources in Maryland, the PJM service area, and indeed the nation, are substantial. At a minimum, FACTS technology warrants a long look from utilities, system planners, and operators, power industry consultants, and lawmakers.

REFERENCES

Electric Power Research Institute (EPRI). 1996. Electric Utility Power Flow Controller Wins R&D 100 Award. Available URL: www.epri.com/news/releases. September.

Hanger, John, et al. 2000. PJM: Record peaks mandate demand-side bidding. Penn Future, 2(6). March.

Hingorani, Narain G. and Laszlo Gyugyi. 2000. Understanding FACTS. IEEE Press.

MAAC–ECAR–NPCC Study Committee. 2000. 2000 Summer MEN Interregional Transmission System Reliability Assessment. May.

MAAC Homepage. 2000. Available URL: http://www.pjm.com/maac/maac_default.html.

North American Electric Reliability Council (NERC). 2000. Reliability Assessment 1999–2008. May.

Pansini, Anthony J. 1991. Power Transmission and Distribution. PennWell Publishing Company.

Pennsylvania–New Jersey–Maryland Interconnection (PJM). 1999. 1999 Baseline RTEP Report. December.

PJM Homepage. 2000. Available URL: http://www.pjm.com.

PJM (Prepared by the Root Cause Analysis Review Team). 2000. Heat Wave 1999: July 1999. Low Voltage Condition. March.

Power Plant Research Program (PPRP). 1996. Electricity in Maryland: Fact Book. January.

PPRP (Prepared by Exeter Associates, Inc.). 1999. An Assessment of the Transmission Grid of Maryland Utilities and Some Potential Consequences of Retail Competition. PPRP-PPSE-T-41. January.

Priest, Ken. 1997. FACTS in an Open Access Environment. Grid Operators & Planning News. Available URL: http://www.epri.com/newsletter.asp?issueid=4829&marketnid=207811&targetnid=207896&value=. September.

Reason, John. 1999. New York State Acts to relieve growing network congestion. Electrical World, 216(1). January/February.

Till, David. Tennessee Valley Authority (TVA). 2000. Telephone conversation. April.

Zelingher, Shalom. New York Power Authority (NYPA). 2000. Telephone conversation. April.

RELATED INTERNET SITES

PJM: www.pjm.com
MAAC: www.pjm.com/maac/maac_default.html
NERC: www.nerc.com
NYPA: www.nypa.gov
EPRI: www.epri.com
Siemens (Power Transmission & Distribution Division): www.ev.siemens.de/en/pages/futurere.htm

---

BIOGRAPHICAL SKETCHES

Sandra S. Patty

Power Plant Research Program, Department of Natural Resources, 580 Taylor Avenue, Annapolis, MD 21401, USA, 410-260-8668, spatty@dnr.state.md.us

Ms. Patty has been a project manager with the Maryland Power Plant Research Program (PPRP) of Maryland's Department of Natural Resource (DNR) since 1991. Ms. Patty provides technical and administrative direction on a wide variety of environmental assessment projects and tasks performed by PPRP staff and consultants related to generating facility and transmission line issues. Prior to joining PPRP, Ms. Patty was employed by Allegheny Power Service Corporation as an environmental analyst from 1974 to 1991. In that position, Ms. Patty was responsible for conducting environmental assessments of electric utility transmission projects, substations, and power stations.

Andrew W. Cressman, PE, CHMM

Environmental Resources, Management, 2666 Riva Road, Suite 200, Annapolis, MD 21401, USA, phone 410-266-0006, fax: 410-266-8912.

Mr. Cressman is an environmental engineer with over 11 years of diverse experience working with public and private sector clients. From 1995 to 2000 Mr. Cressman was a project engineer/manager with the Annapolis, MD office of Environmental Resources Management, Inc. In this capacity Mr. Cressman worked under contract to the Maryland Department of Natural Resources, Power Plant Research Program (PPRP), to evaluate potential impacts to the natural resources and environment of the State of Maryland caused by the construction, operation, and maintenance of high voltage transmission lines. Mr. Cressman has extensive experience in new transmission line siting, construction methods, ROW management, and power flow issues on a system-wide basis.

Mr. Cressman is a Professional Engineer and Certified Hazardous Materials Manager. He is currently an

Environmental Project Manager in the Baltimore, MD office of Dewberry & Davis LLC, and can be contacted at acressman@dewberry.com.

Deborah L. Kowalczyk
Environmental Resources, Management, 2666 Riva Road, Suite 200, Annapolis, MD 21401, USA, phone 410-266-0006, fax: 410-266-8912.
Ms. Kowalczyk is a chemical engineer with two years of experience in the environmental field. Ms. Kowalczyk has been employed with Environmental Resources Management, Inc. since March, 2000 as a project engineer. Ms. Kowalczyk works under contract to the the Maryland Department of Natural Resources, Power Plant Research Program (PPRP), to evaluate potential impacts to the natural resources and environment in the State of Maryland from transmission lines and power facilities. Ms. Kowalczyk can be contacted at deborah_kowalczyk@erm.com.

FERC Regulated Third-Party Compliance Monitoring and Variance Request Program — A Case Study during Construction of the Alliance Pipeline Project

Douglas J. Lake and Howard Heffler

The Federal Energy Regulatory Commission (FERC) generally monitors construction of natural gas pipelines on a periodic basis to document compliance with the environmental conditions and requirements of the Certificate issued for the project. Because monitoring is only occasional, the FERC staff is not always aware of site-specific conditions that affect construction on a daily basis. As such, decisions regarding variance requests by the pipeline company to apply alternative mitigation often require time for the FERC staff to become familiar with the conditions that may cause or initiate the requests. To increase environmental compliance during construction, and to reduce the time required for decisions regarding variance requests and alternative mitigation, Alliance Pipeline L.P. (Alliance) developed and implemented a third-party Compliance Monitoring Program in conjunction with the FERC staff. The overall objective of the program was to monitor environmental compliance during construction of the Alliance Pipeline in order to achieve a high level of environmental compliance. From Alliance's perspective, it was also important to minimize the time required for review and approval of variance requests. This was accomplished by providing a third-party compliance manager and monitors, as representatives of the FERC staff, a limited, predetermined level of decision-making authority to approve requests for variances and implementation of alternative mitigation measures. Other objectives of the program were to assist in the timely resolution of compliance issues in the field and to provide fast and accurate information to the FERC staff regarding construction conditions and progress, as well as noncompliance issues and their resolution. Implementation of this program resulted in a higher, more continuous level of compliance monitoring by the FERC staff during construction. It also allowed the staff to objectively consider and assess changes in site-specific conditions that affected construction, and apply these considerations to the assessment of environmental compliance and the review of variance requests.

Keywords: Regulations, mitigation, monitor, inspector, compliance, variance

INTRODUCTION

A third-party environmental monitoring program was developed for use during construction of the Alliance Pipeline to help keep the Federal Energy Regulatory Commission (FERC or Commission) staff apprized of environmental compliance issues during construction and to provide a level of FERC decision authority directly to people in the field.

There were several objectives in developing and implementing the third-party compliance monitoring program used during construction of the United States portion of the Alliance Pipeline Project. Since the project in the United States was 890 miles long and consisted of up to six mainline construction spreads at one time, continuous and objective environmental monitoring by a third-party contractor was a primary objective of the FERC environmental staff. The FERC staff typically monitors, assesses, and documents com-

Environmental Concerns in Rights-of-Way Management: Seventh International Symposium
J.W. Goodrich-Mahoney, D.F. Mutrie and C.A. Guild (editors)
© 2002 Elsevier Science Ltd. All rights reserved.

pliance with environmental requirements and mitigation measures specified in the FERC Certificate of Public Convenience and Necessity (Certificate) and commitments made by the pipeline company during the environmental permitting process. This is usually achieved by the FERC staff conducting intermittent environmental inspections of pipeline projects during construction, with each inspection effort generally occurring only once every 3–6 weeks and lasting from one to several days during active construction of the project.

Depending on the size of the project, only specific areas and construction activities are typically inspected during a single trip. Between trips, the FERC staff depends on weekly environmental inspection and construction status reports prepared by the pipeline company to obtain information regarding compliance issues as well as environmental conditions on site that may affect construction and environmental compliance issues. By having full-time compliance monitors in the field that can monitor, document and report directly back to the FERC staff in Washington, the staff would be continuously aware of conditions and compliance during pipeline construction, and could more closely monitor resolution and follow-up of noncompliance issues. Further, as questions arise from the pipeline company, affected landowners, or other regulatory agency staff, the FERC staff can utilize the third-party compliance monitors in the field to obtain current, site-specific information that addresses such issues.

Another objective of the program was to reduce the time required for the review and approval of variance requests made by Alliance Pipeline Company, L.P. (Alliance) field staff during construction. The third-party Compliance Monitoring Program used during construction of the Alliance Pipeline addressed this objective when the FERC Director of the Office of Energy Projects delegated a limited, predetermined level of decision-making authority to the third-party monitors in the field, and at a higher level to the third-party compliance manager, to approve or deny certain types of variance requests without requiring a formal filing to and review by the FERC. These included requests to vary or implement alternative site-specific performance-based mitigation measures, and to use additional temporary construction workspace or access roads that were not anticipated during the project planning process. Other objectives of the program were to assist in the timely resolution of compliance issues in the field and to provide fast and accurate information to the FERC staff regarding construction conditions and progress, as well as noncompliance issues and their resolution.

This paper describes the details of both the compliance monitoring and variance request components of the program developed and used throughout the Alliance Pipeline Project, including the:
- level of monitoring effort required;
- roles of the third-party compliance monitors and manager;
- criteria for decision-making authority; and
- variance request and review process and how it was used on the Alliance Pipeline Project.

THIRD-PARTY COMPLIANCE MONITORING

Staffing levels

The number of compliance monitors required to effectively monitor construction became an important issue to resolve early in the program. Pipeline construction activities during the Alliance Pipeline project in the United States involved up to six mainline construction spreads and a delivery segment. During the 1999 construction season the six mainline spreads varied in length from 85 to 159 miles long, averaging about 121 miles in length. In 2000, four mainline spreads were used to complete the project, each averaging about 30 miles in length. To provide an adequate level of monitoring coverage, the FERC required three full-time compliance monitors during the 1999 construction season and one full-time and one part time monitor during the 2000 construction season. Throughout the 1999 construction season, each full-time compliance monitor worked six, 10-h days per week and was responsible for monitoring two adjacent mainline construction spreads, or about 240 miles of pipeline construction. In 2000, the full-time compliance monitor was responsible for monitoring 81 miles on three spreads while the forth spread (38 miles long) was monitored on a part-time basis.

The role of the third-party compliance monitor was not to provide full-time environmental inspection, but to conduct "spot" compliance monitoring, similar to typical FERC staff inspections. The staffing levels described above provided adequate coverage and allowed time for travel between spreads and for preparation of daily and weekly reports. Another consideration was that, although 240 miles of pipeline construction was a large area for one monitor to cover, this area was constructed over 7 months and only a portion of this was under construction or restoration at any given time.

Role of the compliance monitor

Similar to the role of FERC staff conducting an inspection visit, the primary responsibility of the compliance monitor was to review implementation of required mitigation measures during construction. Monitoring concentrated on implementation of environmental mitigation measures that were either proposed by Alliance as part of its application to the FERC, committed to in supplemental filings subsequent to its application (i.e., data responses, comments on the Draft Environmental Impact Statement, and Post-Certificate filings), or included in conditions that had been stipulated by the Commission in its Certificate.

Examples of commitments and conditions to be monitored included:
- implementation of the mitigation measures in the FERC's Upland Erosion Control, Revegetation and Maintenance Plan (Plan) (FERC, 1994a) and the Wetland and Waterbody Construction and Mitigation Procedures (Procedures) (FERC, 1994b);
- ensuring construction disturbance was limited to the width of the approved construction right-of-way, contractor yards, and extra work space areas;
- methods of topsoil segregation;
- compliance with Agricultural Impact Mitigation Agreements required by each state;
- proposed trench and hydrostatic test section dewatering methods;
- adherence to filed Spill Prevention, Containment and Control Plans; and
- adherence to site-specific waterbody crossing plans.

The monitors were not responsible for compliance with commitments or conditions stipulated by other regulatory agencies that had not been reviewed or discussed in the FERC Environmental Impact Statement or included in the FERC Certificate.

The compliance monitors also provided Alliance's Environmental Inspectors (EIs) with interpretation and clarification in the field regarding specific, FERC-related issues (e.g., site-specific implementation of mitigation measures in the Plan and Procedures, whether or not a linear wetland could be treated as a waterbody instead of a wetland). Finally, the compliance monitors reviewed and approved or denied requests for implementation of limited variations to performance-base mitigation measures previously agreed to by Alliance or conditioned by the FERC.

Field logistics

Portions of each spread were monitored every week. Because of the size of most of the spreads, the monitors used their judgment in determining what part of the construction spread to review at any given time, rather then trying to inspect the entire spread during every visit. The decision on where to monitor took into account the status and schedule of construction activities during the visit, and/or direction received from the third-party compliance manager or the FERC Project Manager. Before each review trip, the monitor called Alliance's Lead EI prior to arriving at the construction spread, which allowed the Lead EI and the compliance monitor to exchange information on the status of construction and any significant construction events scheduled over the next 2–3 days. This communication also gave the Lead EI the opportunity to request review of variance requests or clarification of FERC requirements. The compliance monitor would then begin review of the spread with the Lead EI or, more often, would work alone. During each weekly review of the spread, the compliance monitor was required to call the Lead EI to discuss compliance issues as they were identified during the review. This allowed Alliance to quickly respond to the issue and provided the Lead EI an opportunity to communicate the corrective action to be taken, and any follow-up actions that may be required.

During review of the spread, and to assist in accurate and complete monitoring, the compliance monitor used the same field checklists for environmental mitigation procedures that the FERC staff uses during compliance inspections. The monitors also developed line lists containing site-specific resources for each spread that could be affected during construction. During inspections, the monitors recorded observations and took photographs to document construction progress and compliance issues. These photographs and notes were used to prepare reports submitted to the FERC Project Manager on a weekly basis. To facilitate monitoring, report writing, and electronic transfer of information to the FERC staff, the field checklists were incorporated into hand-held data computing devices and all photographs were digital.

Third-party compliance management

Management of the compliance monitoring program was conducted by the third-party contractor from its home office. Support documents, including previously filed environmental reports, construction alignment sheets, and site-specific construction plans were forwarded to the compliance manager for use in supporting the monitors. Management personnel were kept to a minimum and consisted of the compliance manager and occasional support staff as needed. The compliance manager was responsible for the day-to-day management and coordination of the compliance monitoring program, including the field monitoring effort. The manager provided guidance on, and review of, compliance issues; directed and advised the monitors; reviewed and approved or denied variance requests that exceeded the authority of the compliance monitors in the field; reviewed weekly inspection reports and noncompliance reports submitted by the monitors; and prepared the weekly Compliance Monitoring Reports that were submitted to the FERC Project Manager. The compliance manager had direct communication with the FERC staff and with Alliance's Environmental Construction Manager.

VARIANCE REQUEST PROGRAM

Program rational

Requests for variances from previously proposed or stipulated mitigation measures due to unforeseen or unavoidable site conditions are a common occurrence during pipeline construction. Typical requests include variances from proposed mitigation measures (including measures from the Plan and Procedures), from construction workspace requested by the pipeline company and previously approved by the FERC, or from environmental conditions stipulated in the FERC Certificate. Typically, the pipeline company would have to file the request and supporting information with the Commission for review and approval, a process that could take from several days to several weeks depending upon the workload of the FERC staff, the site-specific circumstances of the request, and the adequacy of the supporting information.

Requests for variances can differ from relatively simple and straightforward interpretations of the Plan and Procedures to more complicated issues resulting from unexpected site conditions. Variance requests may also require a determination of compliance with federal regulations under the National Historic Preservation Act or the Endangered Species Act, for which the FERC has regulatory responsibility as the lead federal agency. Depending on the number of requests being submitted and the workload of the FERC staff, review and approval time for variances can take several days and often result in unnecessary and costly construction delays. Under unusual circumstances, the time required to approve variance requests could also result in inadvertent environmental impact associated with inappropriate implementation of stopgap mitigation by construction personnel.

Due to the large size of the project, and because Alliance did not have previous experience constructing within this right-of-way corridor, the potential to move or add construction workspace, on a site-specific basis, was high. Alliance also anticipated that there could be many instances during construction that would involve unforeseen or unavoidable site conditions requiring the implementation of alternative forms of mitigation other than that which was originally proposed. Consequently, Alliance believed that an alternative to the typical variance request process would be beneficial.

Decision-making authority
From the outset, the objectives of the monitoring program focused on assisting the FERC staff by reducing the number of formal variance requests filed with and reviewed by the staff and by reducing the time and concomitant construction delays associated with approvals to implement appropriate alternative mitigation measures or to request new workspace. To accomplish this, criteria were jointly developed with the FERC to provide limited levels of FERC-authorized decision-making authority to the third-party compliance monitors and compliance manager, facilitating the approval or denial of variance requests made by Alliance's construction staff.

The requests were categorized into three distinct groups: those that could be reviewed and approved or denied by the third-party compliance monitor while in the field (Level 1 requests); those that would require review and approval or denial by the third-party compliance manager (Level 2 requests); and those that would require review and approval or denial only by the FERC staff (Level 3 requests). Level 3 requests would be handled by the standard procedure of filing a written request with the FERC.

These levels of decision-making authority offered several distinct advantages. If the compliance monitor was on the spread at the time of the request, it allowed site conditions and the need for the request to be reviewed, evaluated, and, if approved, implemented immediately in the field. If the request exceeded the decision-making authority of the compliance monitor, it would be submitted as a Level 2 request to the third-party compliance manager for review and approval or denial. In most instances, the time required to receive and respond to a request for a variance was significantly shortened compared to the typical procedure. Another advantage was that relatively simple and sometimes numerous requests pertaining to unanticipated site-specific conditions could be reviewed in the field or in the third-party contractor's office rather than all requests being formally filed and channeled through the FERC staff. From the FERC's perspective, this significantly reduced the paper work, Commission letter writing, and workload of the FERC staff.

Level 1 requests — Compliance monitor
Review and approval of some types of requests for variances can be relatively straight forward, such as those pertaining to many of the mitigation measures outlined in the FERC's Plan and Procedures which are intended to achieve a particular performance standard. In some instances, the FERC has delegated decision-making authority to EIs for performance-based issues, such as the need to stop construction in agricultural areas during wet weather, approval of the use of imported soils in agricultural and residential areas, and approval of stump-removal in wetlands due to safety-related issues associated with construction. As representatives of the FERC, the compliance monitors working on the Alliance Project had similar, but more inclusive, review and approval authority than Alliance EIs for issues that arose during construction that were:
– performance-based issues;
– relatively straight-forward requests;
– modifications to previously approved mitigation due to site-specific conditions; and
– did not contradict other federal or state agency requirements.

Requests for variances were considered and approved by the compliance monitor if the performance resulting from implementation of the requested variance would be similar or more environmentally protective (i.e., as good or better results) than the original

mitigation measure. Examples of Level 1 variances included:
- using alternative methods, or alternative placement, of erosion control devices;
- avoiding installation of permanent slope breakers at the base of angled grades leading into a wetland or waterbody if the angle of the slope drained water off the right-of-way before entering the wetland or waterbody;
- changing site-specific river crossing plans to reflect differences in site conditions from those that were anticipated when the plan was developed (e.g., location of a spoil storage areas or method of crossing);
- using alternative topsoil storage or handling procedures; or
- changing extra workspace setback distances from waterbodies, particularly in active agricultural lands.

All requests approved by the compliance monitor were documented on a Variance Request form that included a description of the requested variance, site-specific circumstances associated with the request, one or more digital photographs that clearly depicted the area where the variance would be implemented, and associated conditions to the approval, if applicable. The approved variance request form was then forwarded to the compliance manager and the FERC Project Manager, with a signed copy to Alliance.

Level 2 requests — Compliance manager

Requests for variances that exceeded the limits described above required the review and approval or denial by the compliance manager. Requests of this type often involved the review of supplemental documents, correspondence, and records and included requests that generally:
- involved more complex issues than performance-based mitigation; and/or
- required the use of additional or modified workspace or access roads outside of the previously approved work areas but within areas that had been surveyed for wetlands, protected species, and cultural resources.[1]

Common examples of this type of variance included:
- requests to increase the size of an extra workspace to accommodate additional spoil;
- requests to increase the width of the right-of-way at specific locations for additional topsoil storage, side-slope construction, or where unstable soils, landowner requests, or other conditions required slight realignments of the pipeline; or
- requests to use or modify access roads not previously identified to the FERC.

For requests that involved the use of construction workspace or access roads not previously approved, Alliance's Lead EI obtained the appropriate request information from the contractor, sign-off from the spread right-of-way foreman indicating that Alliance had landowner approval to use the additional lands, and sign off approval from the Spread Supervisor. The Lead EI would then submit a Level 2 variance request form to Alliance's Environmental Construction Manager, with the appropriate supporting information (e.g., description and digital photos of the additional or different lands to be used, including exact location by stationing, size, and the current use and cover) and a detailed explanation of why the variance was needed and the urgency of the request. A dimensioned sketch on a copy of the construction alignment sheet was also included to be certain of the requested lands to be used.

Alliance's environmental management staff reviewed this information using project aerial photo-based construction alignment sheets that showed all previously approved extra workspaces. Cultural resource, wetland, and protected species records, reports, and agency correspondence were reviewed to determine if these areas had been previously surveyed and whether their use would affect protected resources. If a requested workspace or access road had not been surveyed for cultural resources prior to construction (i.e., during the environmental permitting stage), a survey of the requested area could be conducted immediately. The Level 2 request, however, could not be submitted until the State Historic Preservation Officer (SHPO) concurred in writing that no potential sites within the requested area would be affected. Because of the lead-time needed for SHPO review, it was critical to identify new access roads and work areas that fall outside of previously surveyed areas well in advance of the time they would be needed for construction.

When reviewing the Level 2 request from the field, Alliance management also considered justification of the requested workspace or access road, the level of environmental effect, urgency of the request, and landowner approval to ensure compliance with the FERC's standard conditions. All requests for variances that met the above criteria and were determined by Alliance's Environmental Construction Manager to be appropriate were forwarded, via e-mail and fax, to the third-party compliance manager. The compliance manager conducted a review of the request and supporting information before approving or denying the request. The total time required for Alliance's internal variance request review and submittal, and review and approval by the compliance manager averaged about 1 to 3 days.

Level 3 — FERC staff

Variance requests that exceeded the compliance monitor or compliance manager's decision-making authority, as described above, were made directly to the FERC

---

1 Each request for additional workspace required attached documentation of agency clearance for protected species and cultural resources.

using the standard process for filing information or requests with the Commission. These included requests that involved:
- changes to Certificate Conditions;
- significant reroutes;
- potentially eligible cultural resource sites;
- protected species habitat;
- construction of *new* access roads;
- new landowners; or
- project-wide variances.

The FERC staff conducted review and approval of these types of requests, with support from the third-party contractor as needed.

RESULTS AND DISCUSSION

Use of this compliance monitoring and variance request program increased the overall level of environmental compliance during construction of the Alliance Pipeline. The continuous presence of the compliance monitors on each spread was recognized by all construction personnel on site. This presence, and direct reporting of noncompliance situations to the FERC staff within 24 h, provided Alliance's construction personnel and contractors with additional awareness of the environmental requirements and an incentive to achieve and maintain a higher level of environmental compliance.

Continuous monitoring resulted in other benefits as well. From the FERC's perspective, documentation of environmental compliance was much improved over the intermittent inspections that are usually conducted by the FERC. Construction on each spread was monitored during about 50% of the actual time (i.e., each full-time monitor divided his or her time between two spreads) while typical FERC inspections generally cover only about 5% or less of a project's total construction activity. Because reporting was automated, the monitors could inspect four to five different locations each day and quickly complete and electronically submit a site-specific FERC field checklist for each inspection completed. During construction, the third-party monitors completed and submitted to the FERC more than 3000 individual inspection reports.

During construction, Alliance's EIs used a powerful daily reporting program that allowed compliance inspections to be recorded and entered into a master database (Lake et al., 2000). More than 25 EIs submitted over 25,000 individual environmental inspection reports. Analysis of these reports indicated an overall environmental compliance level of 94%. This level of compliance was verified by review of the third-party monitoring records. With more than 3000 inspections completed, the FERC third-party monitors documented a virtually identical 93% compliance rate.

Full-time monitoring also allowed the FERC Project Manager to take site conditions, as reported by the monitors, into account when assessing compliance situations and when considering variance requests. Several times throughout construction, Alliance's contractors encountered temporary, site conditions (e.g., saturated unconsolidated sandy soils, extraordinarily severe rainfall events) where it was literally impossible to comply with the environmental requirements of the FERC Certificate without approval of additional workspace. The alternative was to either temporarily shut down construction in these areas or to request additional workspace to achieve compliance. In these instances, the FERC Project Manager depended on information, including real-time digital photos and personal communication from the third-party compliance monitors to depict site conditions and efforts by Alliance's contractors to achieve compliance. In many cases, significant and often critical requests for additional construction workspace were approved expeditiously, but only after the monitors could verify site conditions and justification for the requests. For example, in one instance an additional 50 feet of temporary construction right-of-way width for a distance of 15 miles was approved within 24 h based on verification of severe site conditions by the monitor. This avoided a costly full-spread move-around, provided the contractor sufficient room to complete construction without the mixing or loss of topsoil, thereby achieving a higher level of compliance, and helped to maintain the construction schedule. Clearly full-time monitoring was a benefit to Alliance as well as to FERC.

The variance request program was also considered successful. Over 100 Level 1 variance requests were reviewed and approved during construction. The Level 1 request process allowed implementation of appropriate mitigation to meet the specific requirements of each site where it was applied. In many cases, such as where installation of erosion control devices or slope or trench breakers were technically required but would not have helped to control erosion, variances were obtained not to install them. Although there was no decrease in the level of environmental protection, the variance reduced the time and cost associated with the installation of these unit price pay items. Requests for the same variance, but at multiple locations, were often identified by the EI and bundled into a single request that could be submitted to the monitor. The sites could then be inspected and approved or denied over the course of several days and implemented immediately after notification of approval.

The Level 2 request process was extremely beneficial to Alliance. The requests focused on the need for additional and/or modified extra workspace to meet unexpected field conditions and to address areas where landowner access for surveys prior to construction could not be obtained. During construction, the following Level 2 requests were approved:
- 216 requests for new or enlarged extra workspace areas, totaling 60 acres;

- 30 requests for increased construction right-of-way width, totaling 42 acres;
- 54 requests for the use of new access or shoofly roads, totaling 160 roads; and
- 11 requests to increase the size of contractor yards, totaling 48 acres.

The approval rate of Level 2 variance requests was high for specific reasons. Prior to implementation of the program, Alliance made a commitment to the FERC to not make frivolous requests. To achieve this, implementation of the variance request program was covered very thoroughly during environmental training, specifically indicating that unjustified requests would not be submitted to the third-party contractor. During construction, 286 Level 2 requests were received from the different construction spreads. As requests were received and reviewed internally by the environmental management team, 57 (20%) were rejected as being unnecessary, lacking appropriate surveys or clearances, or because implementation would result in unacceptable impact. Of the remaining 226 that were approved internally and submitted to the third-party compliance manager, 221 (98%) were approved within 1 to 2 days.

The ability to request and receive permission to use additional construction workspace to meet changing conditions was extremely valuable to the Alliance Project. When faced with record high rainfall and groundwater levels during 1999, and unconsolidated sand soils unknown of during planning, the need for additional workspace was often critical to maintain the construction schedule. This program allowed the contractors to proceed with construction through difficult conditions and problem areas without costly delays. The ability to quickly obtain more workspace when justified by site conditions, such as collapsing trench walls during river crossings, prevented numerous and extremely expensive crew and spread move-arounds. It also allowed construction crews and equipment to keep working and often avoided the use of expensive alternative construction methods, thereby helping to maintain work within budget and avoiding delays. In many instances, the avoidance of construction delays actually resulted in lower levels of environmental impact to sensitive resources.

Not all variance requests were generated under problematic or urgent conditions. The need for new access roads, shooflys around extensive wet areas in remote North Dakota, or additional workspace throughout the project area was identified through ground inspections made by the contractor. On-site inspections were often only completed once landowner permission was granted and access to the right-of-way had been obtained, or as construction progressed along the right-of-way. For this project, conditions changed drastically between the preconstruction planning process and the first year of construction, resulting in many unknown conditions.

CONCLUSIONS

No matter how much effort is expended during the project-planning phase, changing or unexpected conditions occur during almost all pipeline construction projects. The FERC Third-Party Monitoring and Variance Request Program provided a mechanism for the company to address changing conditions and additional workspace needs, while allowing the FERC to have independent monitors on site to verify conditions and justifications and to process variance requests in a timely manner. Timely approval of variance requests allowed construction to proceed in a more orderly and cost-effective manner with no decrease in environmental protection. The monitoring program also provided the FERC staff with improved compliance documentation and appears to have had a positive effect on the overall level of compliance. At date of publication the FERC has approved use of this program on four other pipeline construction projects totaling over 1,260 miles of new pipeline.

REFERENCES

Federal Energy Regulatory Commission. 1994a. Upland Erosion Control, Revegetation, and Maintenance Plan.

Federal Energy Regulatory Commission. 1994b. Wetland and Waterbody Construction and Mitigation Procedures.

Lake D., E. Dolezal, and T. Antoniuk, 2000. Electronic reporting as a tool for effective compliance management during pipeline construction. In: Proceedings of the Seventh International Symposium on Environmental Concerns in Right-of-Way Management, Calgary, AB, Canada. Accepted for Publication.

BIOGRAPHICAL SKETCHES

Douglas J. Lake

Natural Resource Group, Inc., 1000 IDS Center, 80 South Eight Street, Minneapolis, MN 55402, USA

Douglas Lake is a Vice President and Principal with Natural Resource Group, Inc., in Minneapolis, Minnesota. Mr. Lake received his BS degree in Biology from Marietta College and an MS degree from the University of New Hampshire. He has worked for over 21 years conducting environmental impact assessment studies, directing environmental permitting efforts, and managing environmental construction and compliance programs for major electric transmission lines, natural gas pipelines, LNG facilities, and reservoir projects across the country. Mr. Lake has worked during the past 13 years for both natural gas pipeline companies and as an environmental contractor to the Federal Energy Regulatory Commission. Most recently, Mr. Lake was the Environmental Construction Manger for the United States portion of the Alliance Pipeline Project.

Howard R. Heffler
Manager, Environmental Affairs, Alliance Pipeline Ltd., 400, 605 – 5 Ave. S.W. Calgary, AB T2P 3H5, Canada
Howard Heffler graduated with a BEng (Chem) from the University of New Brunswick in 1969 and obtained a MEng (Environmental) from McMaster University in 1970. He has 30 years experience as an environmental engineer, the past 25 years in the oil and gas industry in Calgary, Alberta. Mr. Heffler has worked as an environmental manager within major resource companies and as a consultant for a wide variety of oil and gas and pipeline firms. Much of Mr. Heffler's experience over the past 25 years has related to environmental work in support of pipeline projects. He joined Alliance Pipeline at its inception and is Manager of Environmental Affairs.

Electronic Reporting as a Tool to Effectively Manage Compliance During Pipeline Construction

Douglas J. Lake, Elizabeth Dolezal, and Terry Antoniuk

During peak construction of the Alliance Pipeline Project in the United States, six mainline construction spreads, 4800 construction workers, and up to 28 environmental inspectors (EI) worked simultaneously. To document, monitor, and effectively manage environmental compliance on a daily and weekly basis, Alliance Pipeline L.P. (Alliance) developed and implemented the United States Environmental Inspectors Reporting System (USEIRS). The USEIRS program was used by each EI to complete a construction activity report (e.g., erosion control, waterbody crossing, clearing, grading, trenching), which documented levels of environmental compliance for each inspection made throughout the day. Activity reports were automatically rolled into a daily report generated by each EI, which was submitted via e-mail to a central database at the end of each day. A daily "newspaper" summarizing, by spread and EI, the results of environmental inspection conducted during the previous day was generated from the database for the entire project and distributed electronically to construction and environmental management staff and to each construction spread by 6 AM daily. Included as part of the daily newspaper, summary matrix tables generated by USEIRS were used to keep Alliance's management staff aware of environmental compliance issues on a daily basis. Summary compliance information was organized by spread, construction activity, and level of compliance. This information was used to monitor construction progress and environmental inspection activities by spread and to rapidly (within 24 h) identify both minor and significant compliance issues and compliance trends across the 890-mile-long construction area. Environmental management and construction staff used this information to work with the contractors directly to clarify or resolve compliance situations and to determine the need for additional environmental training. By maintaining a centralized database of all inspection records, environmental management staff was also able to easily and quickly search, identify, and report on trends in non-compliance activities, to determine relationships of non-compliance trends to outside factors such as rainfall, and to effectively track, monitor, and document resolution of non-compliance issues. Finally, the reporting system was used to rapidly condense daily events, incidents, landowner contacts, agency notifications and other specific information into weekly environmental reports required by the Federal Energy Regulatory Commission.

Keywords: Software, database, inspection, environmental, regulatory

INTRODUCTION

The United States portion of the Alliance Pipeline is 890 miles long, from the Canada border in North Dakota, through Minnesota, Iowa, and Illinois. Construction activities involved six mainline construction spreads, up to 4800 construction workers, and 28 full time environmental inspectors working simultaneously. While overall project management was centered in Calgary, construction was managed primarily from Houston and environmental compliance was managed from Minneapolis. To monitor and document construction activities associated with implementation of environmental mitigation specified in the Federal Energy Regulatory Commission (FERC) Certificate of Public Convenience and Necessity and other regulations and permits, Alliance Pipeline L.P. (Alliance) developed an effective electronic environmental inspection reporting program that was used daily by each of the environmental inspectors in the field. The program allowed members of the project team to quickly communicate and discuss environmental compliance issues between Calgary, Minneapolis, Houston, and each construction spread.

To accommodate the size of the project, a major objective of the reporting program was to allow Alliance's environmental construction management team to quickly and efficiently monitor environmental inspection and compliance activities daily across the entire area of active construction. During implementation of this reporting program, we found that we were able to more effectively track, discuss, react to, and manage environmental compliance issues between construction spread personnel, contractor personnel, and each management center. This paper describes the components of the reporting program, how it was implemented in the field, and how it was used to effectively manage environmental compliance.

REPORTING PROGRAM DESCRIPTION

An electronic environmental inspector reporting system was developed for use by Alliance's environmental inspectors during construction of the project facilities in Canada. The reporting program was modified to address regulatory differences between Canada and the US. The modified reporting program, referred to as the United States Environmental Inspectors Reporting System (USEIRS), was used during Alliance's construction activities in the United States. USEIRS is an easy-to-use reporting and referencing program that runs in Microsoft Access®. It consists of both program files and a replicated database that was loaded onto each environmental inspector's laptop computer.

In addition to the traditional form of environmental inspection where the environmental inspector conducts an ongoing or "continuous" inspection of construction activities while interacting with the contractor, Alliance required its environmental inspectors to conduct multiple and specific "spot" inspections of distinct construction activities each day. This system, similar to the way FERC's environmental staff conducts environmental compliance inspections, allowed Alliance to specifically document and quantify levels of compliance by specific construction activity. The reporting program allowed each environmental inspector to complete multiple environmental inspection reports during each day of active construction. These inspection reports were then automatically rolled into a "daily report" for that individual inspector which was downloaded electronically via e-mail at the end of each day to the centralized master database in Minneapolis.

An objective in developing the program was to make environmental reporting simple and fast to complete in the field. This was achieved by incorporating pre-programmed drop-down menus specific to the project and construction spread and by using simple, descriptive text entry boxes, on-screen tips, and fail-safe mechanisms that directed the environmental inspectors to complete certain required data fields before logging out of the program. Proper training and user support throughout construction proved to be critical to successful reporting as many project personnel had limited experience with computers. Ongoing involvement of environmental construction management staff reinforced the importance of accurately completing and filing reports on time and helped to solve technical problems when they arose. Electronic communication, including Internet connections from remote areas, and other unique data transfer problems were encountered periodically by field staff and resulted in the most frequently needed support.

TYPES OF REPORTS

The environmental inspectors were required to fill out an inspection report for each construction activity that they inspected. The inspectors could select from four different types of inspection reports, including general inspection, non-compliance, non-compliance follow-up and incident reports.

General activity reports were completed by the environmental inspector when inspections indicated that, from an environmental perspective, work at a specific location was acceptable and within regulatory compliance. General activity reports were by far the most common report submitted on a daily basis and made up about 94% of all reports filed during construction. Once the report was electronically downloaded into the master database, these reports clearly documented compliance with environmental conditions and requirements at site-specific locations on each spread.

Non-compliance reports documented, on a site-specific basis, construction activities that did not comply with regulatory requirements or environmental specifications provided by Alliance. Notice of a stop work order, if issued by the environmental inspector, and recommended corrective actions were recorded in each non-compliance report. These reports also documented follow-up actions agreed to with the contractor, schedules to complete follow-up actions, persons contacted relative to the follow-up action, and supporting photo-documentation. Once a non-compliance report was entered into the system, a non-compliance follow-up report was automatically required by the program to document implementation of recommended follow-up actions that were agreed to in the field.

Each environmental inspector regularly searched his or her individual database to identify non-compliance actions that had not yet been closed out. The en-

Alliance Pipeline L.P.:
USA Environmental Inspection Reporting System

NONCOMPLIANCE REPORTS

Inspector: Paul Shrum	All NCR issues resolved	Shut down order given
Inspection Date: 23-Jul-1999		
Level: Minor Problem		Date of Incident: 23-Jul-1999
Subject: Minor topsoil mixing due to rutting		Time of Incident (if known):
Activity: Welding		Photo:
Location MP: 108.7 to 108.7	Station:	5745.00 to 5745.00
Facility/Location Name: South of HWY 3		Video:
Suggested completion Date:		Sketch:

The contractor rutted a small area and caused minor mixing of the topsoil in the area. Spoke to the welder foreman about rerouting the equipment around the area, which was done and no further impact to the area occurred. The ROW conditions overall are drying out and improving.

NCR FOLLOW-UP REPORTS

Inspector: Chris Duncan	All NCR issues resolved	Start up order given
Inspection Date: 23-Jul-1999		Photo:
NCR Inspector: Chris Duncan		Video:
NCR Date: 11-Jun-1999		Skecth:
NCR Subject: Topsoil mixing and working outside approved ROW		
Description of Follw-up:		

Recommended Follow-up Inspection and Monitoring: Contractor abandoned area after EI informed them of violation. No further rutting or working off ROW took place.

ACTIVITY REPORTS

Inspector: Chris Duncan	Inspection Date: 23-Jul-1999
Activity: Grade Final	Photo:
Location MP: 131.49 to 131.78	StationL: 6943.76 to 6965.21
Facility/Location Name: South of Hwy 30	Video:
	Sketch:
Description of activity:	Effect of Weather on Construction

Contractor restoring ROW topographical features to preconstruxtion condition. Replacing all topsoil and redistributing it across the ROW. Installing permanent slopebreakers in accordance with FERC and environmental alignment sheets.

Fig. 1. Typical page of daily newspaper showing noncompliance, noncompliance follow-up and activity report format.

vironmental compliance management team also routinely searched the master database to identify unresolved non-compliance issues by spread to discuss with the environmental inspectors and for inclusion into weekly reports to the FERC staff and monthly reports to Alliance's construction management.

Incident reports were used to document unexpected events that occur during construction (e.g., flooding, hazardous material spills, fire, and severe weather) and the actions required or corrective actions taken to respond to such events. Although an incident by itself was generally not considered a non-compliance action, it could lead to a non-compliance action and needed to be documented as such in the event of future actions or claims by regulatory agencies or landowners, respectively.

Each of the reports described above are presented in Fig. 1 as they appeared from a typical page of the daily newspaper. Each report required four different types of information to be entered, including:

General information
- Construction activity inspected
- Specific inspection location
- Landowner tract number
- Time and date
- Specific subject of inspection

Inspection information
- Inspection description
- Effect of weather on construction

Reference information
- Photo
- Video
- Sketch

Field contact information
- Name
- Organization
- Notes of contact

INFORMATION TYPES

To track the type of construction activities that were being inspected on a daily basis, all inspection reports were tied to over 22 different types of construction activities (e.g., grading, topsoil stripping, trenching, waterbody crossing, wetland construction). This allowed tracking of construction progress and environmental inspector activities by spread as well as environmental compliance by construction activity. Identification of trends in non-compliance during a particular construction activity, such as keeping topsoil and subsoil separated during trenching, became readily apparent during review of the inspection reports. Through use of the search function described below, reasons for non-compliance actions could often be correlated to spread conditions (i.e., weather, saturated subsoil conditions) and solutions to achieve greater compliance could be shared with other spreads. The need for additional crew-specific training could also be identified through tracking by construction activity.

Digital photo documentation was used regularly during inspections and played a major role in communicating and documenting compliance and resolution of non-compliance actions with regulatory agency personnel. When the environmental inspector took digital photographs, the digital photograph file was given a specific coded file name that incorporated site-specific location, date, and subject information, which was cross-referenced electronically in the site-specific inspection report. The photographic files were not incorporated directly into the reporting database, but sent electronically as a zipped batch file, together with the daily report, to the environmental compliance supervisor. Digital photographs were stored in a directory by spread and date and could be easily searched by date, spread, subject, or environmental inspector name when needed for reference to a specific inspection report.

PROGRAM UTILIZATION

The inspection information recorded and downloaded into the master database was used in a variety of ways to monitor and manage environmental inspection activities, to ensure timely follow-up of corrective actions, and to increase levels of environmental compliance during construction. After each environmental inspector submitted his or her daily report, a daily newspaper was automatically printed out and distributed by 6 AM the following morning to each spread's management team, as well as management personnel in Calgary, Minneapolis and Houston. The daily newspaper contained summary tables for the entire project and for each spread, as well as a descriptive summary of each inspection made the previous day.

Because each daily newspaper for a project of this size often exceeded 40 pages, the cover page of the newspaper contained a project-wide matrix table that summarized the total number of environmental inspections conducted on each spread from the previous day (see Fig. 2). From that total, the number of inspections that were acceptable, in non-compliance, or were non-compliance follow-up inspections was identified. This table allowed management personnel working on the project to quickly determine the level of environmental inspection activity from the previous day and where environmental problems, if any, were reported from the entire project area.

The project-wide matrix table was followed by detailed inspection information for each spread. This information included a spread-specific table that enumerated construction activity inspected during the previous day on that spread. This allowed separate, spread-specific newspapers containing information for individual spreads only to be generated and distributed to each respective spread.

Using the newspaper, environmental and construction managers could easily scan the cover page to review the environmental activities from the previous day and to determine from which spread they wanted additional information. By turning to the first page of that spread, they could quickly review the number of inspections completed the previous day, the types of construction activities that were being inspected, and the level of environmental compliance that was being achieved. Detailed information regarding specific inspections was then easily obtained by reviewing the following printed individual inspection reports.

The newspaper kept Alliance's construction management staff informed on a daily basis of all environmental as well as many non-environmental issues. In doing so, it provided the basis for conferences between environmental construction management staff, environmental inspectors, spread construction staff, and contractor management, as necessary, to help resolve noncompliance issues in a timely manner. Most importantly, it provided a means for non-environmental management staff to become actively involved in achieving a higher level of compliance.

The newspaper also allowed trends in non-compliance activities (e.g., poor topsoil segregation, failure to install erosion controls) by a particular contractor or crew to be identified promptly so that the need for additional crew training could be discussed with the environmental inspectors.

Non-compliance issues were tracked by each individual environmental inspector on their laptop computer and were periodically searched to ensure that follow-up on corrective actions were completed in a timely manner. The master database was also searched monthly for outstanding non-compliance items that required closeout by the inspector. Once the environmental inspector re-inspected the area in question, he

UsEIRS News — theDAILY Inspection MORNING EDITION

Alliance Pipeline L.P.: USA Environmental Inspection Reporting System

Inpection Date

Spread	Total Reports	Noncompliance	NCR Follow-up	Activity	Incidents
Spread 1	35	1	7	27	
Spread 2	18		2	16	
Spread 3	15		1	14	
Spread 4	3			3	
Spread 5	13	1		12	
Spread 6	60	2	2	56	
Delivery Segment	8			8	
Totals	152	4	12	136	

Spread Spread 1

Activity	Total Reports	In Compliance	Minor Problem	Noncompliance	Serious Noncompliance
Grubbing/Grading	1	1			
Backfilling	2	2			
Welding	2	1	1		
Training	1	1			
Stringing	3	3			
Pipe/Contractor Yard	1	1			
Trenching	1	1			
Notification/Coordination	2	2			
Wetland Construction	2	2			
Grade Final	1	1			
Flagging/Signage	1	1			
Facility Site Inspection	3	3			
Erosion Control	3	3			
Dewatering	1	1			
NCR Follow-up	7	7			
Other	4	4			
Incident	0	0			
Landowned Contact	0	0			
Agency Notification	0	0			
Totals	35	34	1		

Fig. 2. Typical cover page of the daily newspaper.

or she filled out a non-compliance follow-up report form, cross-referenced the original non-compliance report, and if the inspection was acceptable, the program deleted the non-compliance item from the electronic noncompliance report follow-up list. The noncompliance follow-up list in the master database was also automatically updated with the next daily electronic submittal from that environmental inspector. This system permitted careful tracking and documentation of all noncompliance follow-up actions and allowed environmental management to easily summarize follow-up activities for noncompliance situations. This information was included in weekly reports to the FERC, as discussed below.

OTHER APPLICATIONS

Once environmental inspection information was downloaded into the master database, it became readily available to the environmental construction management team for a variety of other applications.

The USEIRS program was used to record and document stormwater and erosion control inspections required by National Pollution Discharge and Elimination System (NPDES) Section 402 Stormwater Discharge Permits. Erosion control inspection reports of the construction right-of-way were typically made on a weekly basis or after storm events and were listed under the construction activity "Erosion Control." Milepost locations and descriptions of supplemental erosion control requirements were documented in these inspection reports. This record of inspection was used by Alliance to satisfy documentation requirements of the different states.

Another important function of the reporting program was the ability to search the database for any combination of data fields for which inspection information was collected, including landowner tract number, milepost, geographic feature, construction activity, date, or type of report. Typical searches included completion dates of waterbody crossings and documentation of agency contacts made by the environmental inspectors, such as the notification of hydrostatic test water withdrawals and releases, changes to stream crossing windows or crossing methods, or the reporting of hazardous materials spills. Database searches also played an important role in the location of photographic documentation records of right-of-way conditions prior to, during, and following construction, in tracking landowner contacts with the environmental inspectors to be included in weekly FERC reports, and in determining locations where environmental inspectors noted that contractor warranty work was required to complete or repair restoration work from the previous construction season.

Following the 1999 construction season, the construction contractors were required to complete followup restoration and warranty work on site-specific areas of the right-of-way. To help determine where additional restoration work was required, the database was searched for areas identified by the environmental inspectors during NPDES surveys over the winter shutdown period. The database was also searched by landowner, landowner tract, non-compliance report records, and by landowner contacts made with the environmental inspectors during construction to help determine the history of construction events on specific landowner tracts. The report information in the database has also been used as a basis for discussing damage claims brought forward by landowners after construction.

Database searches for non-compliance reports and follow-up activity, and landowner contacts and complaints made to the environmental inspectors were also conducted to help prepare the weekly environmental status report required by the FERC staff during construction. These weekly reports included updated information on construction and environmental events for each construction spread and were prepared in less than one day by inserting information from the daily reports downloaded from each construction spread from the previous week and tabulating searched information. Compliance issues were easily summarized by spread and construction activity.

CONCLUSION

Use of the USEIRS electronic reporting system described in this paper allowed Alliance's environmental construction management team to more effectively monitor and manage the daily activities of the environmental inspectors and the levels of environmental compliance recorded during construction of this large project. The reporting system allowed environmental information to be quickly distributed, reviewed, and acted upon by the entire project management team, which helped to increase the overall level of environmental compliance. The database software allowed documented information to be quickly retrieved to use in progress reports and to support other project team activities.

ACKNOWLEDGEMENTS

The authors would like to thank Brian Zelt (bzelt@e2canada.com) in Calgary for doing such an excellent job of writing the software for the USEIRS program in a short time frame and with so little problems.

BIOGRAPHICAL SKETCHES

Douglas J. Lake

Vice President and Principal, Natural Resource Group, Inc., 1000 IDS Center, 80 South Eight Street, Minneapolis, MN 55402, USA

Douglas Lake is a Vice President and Principal with Natural Resource Group, Inc, in Minneapolis, Minnesota. Mr. Lake received his BS degree in Biology from Marietta College and an MS degree in Entomology from the University of New Hampshire. He has worked for over 21 years conducting environmental impact assessment studies, directing environmental permitting efforts, and managing environmental construction and compliance programs for major electric transmission lines, natural gas pipelines, LNG facilities, and reservoir projects across the country. Mr. Lake has worked during the past twelve years for both natural gas pipeline companies and as an environmental contractor to the Federal Energy Regulatory Commission. Most recently, Mr. Lake was the Environmental Construction Manger for the United States portion of the Alliance Pipeline Project.

Elizabeth N. Dolezal

Senior Scientist, Natural Resource Group, Inc., 1000 IDS Center, 80 South Eight Street, Minneapolis, MN 55402, USA

Elizabeth N. Dolezal is a project manager with Natural Resource Group, Inc, in Minneapolis, Minnesota. Ms. Dolezal manages environmental permitting and regulatory compliance activities for pipeline construction projects. She has written environmental impact assessment studies, managed environmental permitting, and provided construction regulatory support for pipeline projects. She has assisted pipeline companies in working with federal, state, and local regulatory agencies to identify potential environmental impacts from construction and operation and developed appropriate mitigation plans. Ms. Dolezal received a MA in Public Administration from the George Washington University, Washington DC. Most recently, Ms. Dolezal was responsible for the coordination and implementation of Alliance's Third Party Monitoring Program, Variance Request Program, and its USEIRS daily environmental inspection reporting system for the United States portion of the Alliance Pipeline Project.

Terry Antoniuk
Principal, SALMO Consulting, Inc. Suite 230, 323-10 Avenue S.W., Calgary, AB T2R 0AS, Canada

Terry Antoniuk, the Principal of Salmo Consulting Inc., is a Professional Biologist registered in the provinces of Alberta and British Columbia. Mr. Antoniuk has more than twenty years experience in biological studies and research, environmental assessment and mitigation, and public involvement in federal, provincial, and territorial jurisdictions across Canada, and internationally. One of Terry's specialties is cumulative effect assessment (CEA); he has completed several assessments of cumulative and regional effects in northeastern British Columbia and Alberta, and prepared the CEA for the federally regulated Alliance Pipeline Project. Mr. Antoniuk also provides environmental planning and protection services including biophysical inventories, effects monitoring programs, environmental protection plans and operating guidelines. Terry coordinated development of the electronic reporting and computerized commitment databases for the Alliance Pipeline Project and co-authored the Watercourse Crossings guide issued by the Canadian Pipeline Water Crossing Committee.

The Value of a Third Party Inspection Program During the Construction of Natural Gas Pipelines in Maine

Linda Kokemuller

In 1998 and 1999, two major interstate natural gas pipelines were constructed in Maine. Prior to this construction, Maine had very few miles of gas pipeline located within the state and no experience with permitting interstate gas pipeline projects. Maine did have experience with the use of third party inspectors to monitor large construction projects for compliance with the approved plans and their impacts on protected natural resources. During the permitting process, the Maine Department of Environmental Protection (MDEP) determined that third party inspectors would be required for the construction of the two projects. MDEP worked with both companies to create the documentation that would be necessary to run the program and to hire the appropriate inspectors. The MDEP found the third party inspection program to be beneficial for several reasons, including the following:

1. The MDEP project manager was able to maintain direct daily overview of the pipeline construction and react quickly to resource issues that arose.

2. The third party inspector was immediately available to respond to specific landowner and/or public concerns.

3. MDEP was able to delegate certain specified functions to the third party inspectors, including the ability to grant variances from permit requirements based on site-specific conditions.

Keywords: Erosion, environmental, FERC, inspectors, natural resources

INTRODUCTION

In the mid-nineties, when two pipeline companies first approached the Maine Department of Environmental Protection (MDEP) to discuss the construction of two new natural gas pipelines, no one at the MDEP had any idea of just what such construction entailed. The only mainline natural gas pipeline in the state was originally constructed during wartime, in the early 1940s, to carry oil from Canada. At some point after that, this oil line had been converted to carry natural gas, but few of Maine's citizens were aware of its existence. Such would not be the case with the two new pipelines being proposed. These two pipelines would traverse the state from its southern border with New Hampshire to its northern border with Canada, utilizing a joint pipeline between Eliot and Westbrook. From Westbrook, the Western pipeline project would head for the western Maine border and Montreal, and the Eastern pipeline project would head for the eastern Maine border and Sable Island. In total, approximately 53 miles of 30″ diameter pipeline, approximately 273 miles of 24″ diameter pipeline and approximately 47 miles of 12″ diameter pipeline would be laid. Approximately 650 stream crossings would be constructed, including hundreds of cold water fishery stream crossings and approximately 3000 wetlands would be crossed. The Western and the Eastern pipeline projects, which were constructed in 1998 and 1999, respectively, represented the two largest infrastructure projects ever undertaken within the State of Maine, with the possible exception of the Maine Turnpike constructed fifty years earlier.

Environmental Concerns in Rights-of-Way Management: Seventh International Symposium
J.W. Goodrich-Mahoney, D.F. Mutrie and C.A. Guild (editors)
© 2002 Elsevier Science Ltd. All rights reserved.

PERMITTING PROCESS

Although the Federal Energy Regulatory Commission (FERC) has overlapping permitting authority for interstate pipeline projects, the two pipeline companies participated fully in the State of Maine's permitting process. The pipeline companies applied to the MDEP for Site Location of Development (Site Law) and Natural Resources Protection (NRPA) permits, and a Water Quality Certification, the issuance of which is delegated to the state by the EPA under the Clean Water Act. The Site Law requires permits to be obtained for all federal, state, municipal, quasi-municipal, educational, charitable, residential, commercial, or industrial developments that occupy a land or water area in excess of 20 acres. The NRPA requires permits to be obtained for activities located in, on or over any protected natural resource, or for activities located adjacent to a protected natural resource and operated in such a manner that material or soil may be washed into certain specified natural resources. Protected natural resources include coastal wetlands, significant wildlife habitats, fragile mountain areas, freshwater wetlands, great ponds or rivers, streams, or brooks. As part of the MDEP's permit process, alternative routes were analyzed, every stream to be crossed was identified and classified, historical sites were located, potential impacts to state-listed rare plants and animals were evaluated and every potential for impact to surface water quality was studied. Maine has widely varying soil types including one particular type (Presumpscot) composed of glacio-marine clay which is uniquely difficult to contain once disturbed, and which is found along large sections of both pipeline routes and at many stream and wetland crossings.

ESTABLISHING THE THIRD PARTY INSPECTION PROGRAM

Authorizing documentation

When a development is of substantial size and of a complex nature, the Site Law rules specifically allow the MDEP to make provision for a third party inspector to conduct on-site inspections, at the developer's expense, to ensure proper execution of the approved plans including any conditions imposed by the MDEP. Typically the MDEP has only required the use of third party inspectors on projects that would require large expanses of soil to be exposed for long periods of time, such as golf courses. In 1997 and 1998, while processing the pipeline applications, it became clear that the one project manager assigned to review both applications would be unable to effectively ensure compliance with the permits. The MDEP determined that the pipeline projects met the criteria for requiring a third party inspector and this requirement became a permit condition. The third party inspectors would contract directly with the applicant, but receive their direction from, and report to, the MDEP.

During the Western pipeline's review process, the applicant and the MDEP developed a document entitled "Independent Third Party Inspection Program" which was further refined during the Eastern pipeline's review process. The final version of this document was used during construction of the Eastern pipeline project. It contains nine sections. These are Introduction and Purpose, Selection of Independent Third party Inspector, Duties and Responsibilities, Activity Documentation and Communication, Communication and Coordination, Program Implementation, Wildlife and Fisheries, Dispute Resolution and Evidentiary Privilege. As stated in the Independent Third party Inspection Program document, the objectives of the program are:

– To monitor all construction and restoration activities to assure compliance with MDEP permits and conditions;
– To provide interpretation of MDEP conditions and standards at the request of the project Chief Inspector and Environmental Inspectors; and
– To participate in field decisions with respect to stream crossings based on conditions in the field at the time of construction.

Selection of inspectors

All parties agreed that it was crucial to hire the "right" individuals to be third party inspectors. The pipeline companies wanted to ensure that the inspectors had pipeline experience and the MDEP wanted to ensure that the inspectors were familiar with Maine's laws and standards for erosion control. Everyone wanted to ensure that the selected inspectors clearly understood their role in the pipeline construction process and had a suitable personality for functioning in this type of role. In the end, some of the individuals hired had extensive experience working with Soil and Water Conservation Districts in Maine and with the MDEP and others had extensive pipeline experience, having worked on various pipeline projects around the country.

On each pipeline spread, utilizing third party inspectors who could provide this combination of local and specialized experience worked extremely well. Each was able to learn from the other and all were able to quickly familiarize themselves with the expectations that the MDEP had for the third party inspectors' role. In addition, the MDEP was able to utilize the pipeline-savvy inspectors to provide independent verification of representations being made by the pipeline companies prior to construction, particularly in regard to stream crossing methodologies.

Training of inspectors

After the third party inspectors were selected, the MDEP project manager held numerous meetings with them to outline the MDEP's expectations for the pipeline construction. The third party inspectors were given the construction drawings for their assigned spread and, prior to construction, they walked the length of their spread to familiarize themselves with the terrain and the natural resources that would be impacted. Visits were made to the construction right-of-way with the MDEP project manager and discussions were held, on-site, about all the various aspects of the construction, particularly stream crossing methods. While construction was underway, the MDEP project manager continued to meet with the third party inspectors on the right-of-way, when necessary, to clarify permit conditions and MDEP expectations for such things as the granting of variances.

The third party inspectors were included in some of the pre-construction meetings held with the pipeline companies and in all of the environmental construction training conducted by the pipeline companies. At the environmental training sessions, the pipeline companies emphasized compliance with all of the federal and state permits and the necessity of working together as a team with the third party inspectors to successfully complete the project. The MDEP was represented at most of these training sessions and took part in the discussions.

Communication

For the third party inspection program to work, it was crucial that the inspectors were able to effectively access the right-of-way and communicate with the MDEP and the pipeline companies. The inspectors were supplied with four-wheel drive vehicles, cell phones, fax machines, computers and cameras. Standardized forms were created and utilized for submitting daily reports and for submitting more specific action requests. An organizational chart and telephone contact list was distributed. Discussions were held with the various parties and agreements were made to ensure that everyone knew what authority the third party inspectors had and who they were to contact.

PIPELINE CONSTRUCTION

Once underway, the actual construction of the two pipeline projects took very different routes, in both a literal and figurative sense. The MDEP found the third party inspection program to be invaluable during the construction of both projects. However the strengths of the program varied for each project. To understand this variability, it is important to note some very major differences between the two pipeline projects.

The Western pipeline project

When the Western pipeline project got under way in the spring of 1998, it was running weeks behind schedule and FERC had not yet granted clearance to construct on large sections of the right-of-way, mostly due to land acquisition issues. Also, the third party inspectors, who had walked the entire right-of-way prior to the start of construction, had identified numerous streams that were not shown on the approved construction drawings. When initial meetings were held with the contractors for the three construction spreads, it was readily apparent to the MDEP project manager that these contractors were not as familiar as they needed to be with the conditions that had been placed on the permits by the MDEP, with Maine's soils and with the vagaries of Maine's weather.

One of the spreads was voluntarily shut down almost immediately because of problems with the clearing crews; another was shut down approximately a month later because of poor erosion control and the unnecessary destruction of stream banks and habitat. At the end of June, a major rain event (nine inches in a few days) occurred across the entire state. The construction right-of-way, which contained numerous wetlands and streams, never quite dried out after that and then the fall rains arrived on schedule. Dewatering activities that caused sedimentation and siltation of streams, particularly the fisheries' streams, were a major problem and a major source of conflict between the Western Pipeline Company, the contractors and MDEP. Trenches were being left open for extended periods of time because the construction was not proceeding in an orderly manner.

As a result, in the summer of 1998, the Western Pipeline Company requested that the MDEP allow construction, which was supposed to have been completed by November 30, to extend into the winter. They also requested an extension of the crossing completion date for numerous coldwater fishery streams. The MDEP was faced with a major dilemma and input from the third party inspectors was crucial to the decision that was made-to allow construction to continue until it was completed.

The Eastern pipeline project

When it came time to start construction of the Eastern pipeline project, the Eastern Pipeline Company both benefited from the Western pipeline's experiences and suffered from them. During the year before construction was to start, the Eastern Pipeline Company completed a final walkover of their entire right-of-way to ensure that no streams or wetlands had been missed, and included this information in their construction drawings. The Eastern Pipeline Company emphasized to their contractors that the contractors were responsible for complying with MDEP permit conditions and that, in general, those conditions were not negotiable. Many of the conditions had been specifically placed in the Eastern Pipeline Company permit as a direct consequence of MDEP experiences with the Western pipeline construction.

When construction started in June 1999 on the Eastern pipeline project, it was generally on schedule for all three spreads and FERC clearance had basically been obtained for the entire right-of-way. Construction of the pipeline, June through October, took place under almost ideal weather conditions with very little rain. Most wetlands were unusually dry. By the time many fishery streams were ready to be crossed, they were dry or nearly so, allowing the use of dam and pumps instead of flumed dry crossings, thereby reducing the amount of time it took to complete the crossings and reducing environmental impacts to the resources.

There was one major sedimentation incident during an important stream crossing and several minor incidents that were brought to MDEP attention by the third party inspectors. This resulted in a very productive meeting between the Eastern Pipeline Company, the contractors and the MDEP in July. There were other minor problems and issues that arose during the remainder of the Eastern pipeline project, but, because of the ideal construction weather and the level of cooperation between all the responsible parties, they were quickly resolved. The pipeline was completed on time and with minimal environmental impacts.

BENEFITS OF THE THIRD PARTY INSPECTION PROGRAM

In the MDEP experience, all permitted projects benefit from some degree of oversight, if for no other reason than to ensure that permit conditions are properly interpreted. The applicant's number one priority is always the completion of their project. The MDEP's number one priority is to ensure that the applicant does not lose sight of the importance of the natural resources that could be impacted by their construction. There is no more effective way of accomplishing this than maintaining a presence at the construction site, even if only occasionally.

For the MDEP, the third party inspectors played a crucial role during the construction of both the pipeline projects. As discussed in the introduction, the two pipeline construction projects were so large, impacting so many natural resources, that the MDEP on its own, with its limited personnel resources would have been unable to effectively monitor their construction.

Although FERC and the Army Corps of Engineers also permitted the project and had inspectors on-site regularly during construction, the MDEP permits contained many requirements that were more stringent than the standard best management practices required by FERC. MDEP requirements included the following: (1) that clearing crews cross streams in the location where the permanent equipment bridge will be placed; (2) that an ungrubbed 25 foot wide buffer be maintained on both banks of a stream until the stream crossing crew arrived to construct the crossing; (3) that equipment bridges be constructed in such a way that soil cannot fall into waterbodies through cracks in the crossing or over the edge of the crossing; (4) that dry stream crossing methods be used for numerous coldwater fishery streams and streams with Class AA and A water quality greater than 10 feet in width; (5) that final restoration of the area within 100 feet of the stream bank for coldwater fisheries streams and streams with Class AA and A water quality be completed within 24 or 48 h of completing the stream crossing, depending upon the width of the stream (a pipe of adequate length had to be used for the crossing to ensure that tie-ins would be completed outside this 100 foot buffer); (6) that all trench dewatering completed within 250 feet of a stream had to use secondary containment; (7) that all trench dewatering structures had to be placed as far from the stream as possible to ensure that this water did not run directly back into the stream; and (8) that the final restoration crew could be no more than 45 days behind the pipe gang. The third party inspectors were specifically tasked with ensuring that the pipeline companies and their contractors complied with these requirements.

The third party inspectors' daily reports were submitted each evening by fax or e-mail to the appropriate parties and the required action reports, which documented specific items that should be addressed immediately to avoid violations, were submitted as needed. In this way, the MDEP project manager was able to keep abreast of the pipeline construction activities, while targeting visits to the most critical areas at the most critical times. This was particularly important during the construction of the Western pipeline project, because of the number of issues and problems that arose on all three spreads throughout an eight-month period of time. The Western Pipeline Company did receive several letters of non-compliance and one notice of violation from the state, but would have undoubtedly received many more if not for the daily overview that the third party inspectors provided. By their presence, the third party inspectors were able to prevent permit violations from occurring and minimize resource impacts.

The MDEP is quite aware that permitted construction projects seldom proceed according to plan and that acts of God do occur, in addition to acts of man. The MDEP does attempt to ascertain whether everything that could be done, in practical terms, has been done when determining the appropriate course of action, e.g., whether the contractor should be commended for taking all appropriate action or whether a letter of non-compliance or a formal notice of violation should be issued. The third party inspectors were invaluable in making this determination because they were on the project site every day.

The third party inspectors were frequently able to provide an explanation to the MDEP project manager, who could not visit the spreads on a regular basis, for why certain actions were either undertaken or omitted. They could explain why certain activities could appear to be a permit violation, but should not necessarily be perceived as a violation or cited as a violation. The third party inspectors saw what happened during a rainstorm and what attempts the contractors were making to control erosion. For example, the third party inspectors would be aware that, while it might not have rained in Portland that day, there was a thunderstorm in Saco (a town 15 miles away). They would know that this thunderstorm in Saco was the reason for the phone calls the MDEP project manager in Portland was receiving from concerned citizens in Saco about brown streams adjacent to the pipeline construction. The third party inspector would know whether or not, during the thunderstorm, all appropriate erosion control was in place and nothing else could be done, given the nature of the disturbed soils, the amount of rainfall and the flashiness of the streams. This type of explanation, given to the MDEP, by their inspectors went a long way in determining what action the MDEP took both immediately and in the future.

Although the pipeline companies and the contractors received the same standard reports that the MDEP received, the third party inspectors were able to supply the MDEP with specialized report documentation of permit violations, when requested, including photo documentation. When regulators are pursuing enforcement action, photo documentation can be even more helpful than written documentation. The MDEP required the third party inspectors to maintain photo documentation of daily activities and was able to make use of this photo documentation when discussing compliance issues with the pipeline companies. A picture is truly worth a thousand words when there are conflicting opinions and lack of first-hand knowledge on the MDEP's part.

In the ideal situation, the third party inspector and the environmental inspectors (EI) hired by the pipeline company work together as a team. This was the general situation that occurred during the construction of the Eastern pipeline project and it was very beneficial for everyone involved. It was also the situation at the beginning of the Western pipeline project. Because of the numerous problems on that project, a more adversarial relationship evolved over time between some of the EI, contractor personnel and the third party inspectors on the Western pipeline project. The third party program remained very valuable to the MDEP during the entire course of the Western pipeline project even with this adversarial relationship, but it was probably of less value to the Western Pipeline Company, or at least their contractors. Having this adversarial relationship also required the MDEP project manager to serve as a mediator between the Western Pipeline Company, the EI and the contractors and the third party inspectors in certain instances.

During construction of the pipeline projects, the third party inspectors participated in daily meetings with the EI and contractors. They served as another set of eyes for the EI who could not be everywhere and who had other responsibilities that were not as strictly tied to the permit conditions. The third party inspectors quite frequently notified the EI of developing situations that needed to be addressed before they turned into permit violations.

Since the MDEP allowed the third party inspectors to grant variances for certain specific activities, e.g., changing a stream crossing method from a dry flume crossing to a dam and pump based on site specific conditions at the time of the crossing, they could actually reduce the EI workload by signing the required forms on the spot and being the one to notify the MDEP of the change. The third party inspectors could help the EI and the contractors interpret permit conditions, and were readily accessible as opposed to the MDEP project manager who was more difficult to reach in a timely manner. With the third party inspectors in the field, construction was seldom slowed while waiting for variance approvals.

Although both the pipeline companies provided a toll-free telephone hotline number for landowners and the public to call, the Maine public was aware that the MDEP was responsible for protecting the state's natural resources and certain landowner rights as they related to the pipeline projects. During the permitting process, the public expressed many concerns about the pipeline construction, and in general seemed to be reassured by the implementation of the third party inspection program. They clearly liked the idea of having full-time inspectors representing the MDEP who would oversee the daily pipeline construction activities.

The third party inspectors were frequently called upon to respond to specific landowner and/or public concerns. They visited the affected property, explained the construction process and what was permitted, and contacted the EI and the pipeline companies to ensure that appropriate action was taken, if necessary. They reported these activities to the MDEP and followed up as needed. Every indication the MDEP has received points to the third party program being very well received by the public and individual landowners.

CONCLUSION

For all the reasons outlined above, the MDEP found the third party inspection program to be of immeasurable value during the construction of the two natural gas pipeline projects. For many of the reasons outlined above, some tangible and some not, MDEP also believes that the third party inspection program was of great value to the two pipeline companies.

BIOGRAPHICAL SKETCH

Ms. Linda Kokemuller
Maine Department of Environmental Protection, 312 Canco Road, Portland, ME 04103, USA, 207-822-6300 (phone), 207-822-6303 (fax), Linda.K.Kokemuller@state.me.us (e-mail)

Ms. Linda Kokemuller is currently the Southern Maine Regional Office Licensing Supervisor for the Division of Land Resource Regulation of the Maine Department of Environmental Protection. She was the project manager for the PNGTS and Maritimes pipeline projects. Ms. Kokemuller has worked for the MDEP for 12 years. She has been involved in the development of many MDEP land use policies including statewide stormwater rules, statewide erosion control BMP, and the use of third party inspection programs on large construction projects. She has an MA in Urban and Regional Planning and a BA in History from the University of Iowa.

The Implementation of an Environmental Management System for Distribution Pipeline Construction

Mario Buszynski

Most natural gas distribution pipelines are constructed in public rights-of-way such as road allowances. A common perception is that these rights-of-way have previously been disturbed and therefore construction will have minimal effect on the social and natural environment of these areas. In fact, there is a potential for significant impacts to the natural and social environment through possible erosion and sedimentation of watercourses, slope stability, damage to specimen trees, property damage and other issues. This paper describes the development and implementation of an Environmental Management System for pipeline projects by using the Orangeville Reinforcement Pipeline as a case study. It begins with a review of the environmental commitments made during the approval process and the mechanisms to ensure that these commitments are carried through the construction phase. A description of the pre-construction environmental activities is presented to illustrate the method by which environmental impacts are anticipated and remediated. The documentation and record keeping process is described and examples given to illustrate why this is a vital part of the management system. Examples are provided to illustrate how unanticipated environmental incidents are managed. Project completion activities are discussed, including recommendations for improvement and post-construction environmental monitoring studies.

Keywords: Environmental Management Systems, Orangeville reinforcement pipeline, audit, risk

INTRODUCTION

From the International Standard for Environmental Management Systems we learn that the rationale for a corporation developing an Environmental Management System ("EMS") relates to the improvement of the quality of the environment and protecting human health. Corporations are increasingly developing their EMS in response to internal and external stimuli. These stimuli may be both political and economic. A corporate commitment to a systematic approach and continual improvement is necessary to ensure the success of an EMS.

The Orangeville Reinforcement Pipeline construction program undertaken by Enbridge Consumers Gas is an example of how an EMS can be designed for an individual activity that can effectively contribute to the corporation's overall EMS. The key principles involved in this program include:
- high corporate commitment;
- communication with internal and external parties;
- clear assignment of accountability and responsibility;
- adherence to legislative aspects;
- ongoing environmental planning throughout the project;
- target setting for performance;
- appropriate resources and training on an ongoing basis to achieve targets;
- external audit of the process to identify opportunities for improvement; and
- encourage of contractors to establish an EMS.

The Orangeville Reinforcement Pipeline Project received approval from the Ontario Energy Board in July 1996. The 44 km NPS8 (8 inch diameter) extra high pressure steel distribution main originated from the Bond Head Gate Station in the Town of Bradford, West Gwillimbury, located north of the town of Orangeville in the County of Dufferin. Figure 1 provides both regional and detailed locations. Construction of the pipeline occurred during the months of August through November, 1996. The pipeline was located entirely within municipal road rights-of-way.

Roadside construction tends to have different impacts than cross-country construction. It would be inaccurate to characterize roadside construction as having little impact. Furthermore, since the local distribution company ("LDC") relies on adjacent residents and communities "hooking up" to the pipeline, it is imperative that these people are satisfied with the construction program and that the LDC is a "good neighbour".

CORPORATE COMMITMENT

Enbridge Consumers Gas has a high corporate commitment to environmental management. This commitment is reflected in their corporate environmental policy and in the environmental management that they use with respect to pipeline construction. The pipeline right-of-way is restored to "at least as good" condition as was found before construction and in some cases it is left in a better condition. In addition to natural environment considerations, social impacts are given a high regard and actions to avoid or mitigate these impacts are implemented as part of the pipeline EMS.

Prior to commencement of the construction project, a risk assessment is conducted to determine environmental issues. The results of this risk assessment are used to develop an audit protocol which will be discussed in the audit section of this paper.

CLEAR ASSIGNMENT OF RESPONSIBILITY AND ACCOUNTABILITY

On a project such as the Orangeville Reinforcement, company policy as well as regulatory requirements dictate that the responsibility for environmental management is assigned to an individual or individuals. Under the control of the Environmental Affairs Department, a third-party independent inspection company was retained to provide environmental inspection services. The duties of the environmental inspector were outlined in the scope of work as follows:
- provide day-to-day advice to the Project Manager, Construction Supervisor, and all construction personnel regarding compliance with environmental legislation, regulations and industry standards;
- provide advice regarding adherence to environmental specifications and commitments made in the previously mentioned documents and to regulatory agencies, including the Ontario Energy Board;
- provide advice on erosion protection measures to be taken in sensitive environmental areas along the pipeline route;
- act as liaison with environmental regulators, government agencies and interest groups;
- provide advice to the Project Manager to help resolve any identified landowner concerns and when required, maintain a log of those concerns, and the method of resolution;
- through appropriate noise and vibration level monitoring, ensure construction noise and vibration levels are within regulatory limits;
- provide immediate advice regarding spill prevention and contingency;
- ensure proper waste disposal of any hazardous construction wastes;
- ensure appropriate field documentation of environmental issues and their resolution;
- prepare a post-construction monitoring report; and
- review all agency correspondence and monitor agency conditions.

COMMUNICATION WITH INTERNAL AND EXTERNAL PARTIES

Constant communication between all members of the project was facilitated by the use of cellular phones and pagers. A "Contact List" containing the names and telephone numbers of all personnel involved with the project was distributed. This list included contacts at all regulatory agencies, government ministries, and the Tecumseth Arbor Committee. In addition, a listing of Emergency Response telephone numbers was also distributed to all personnel.

Contact with the general public was maintained on an ongoing basis. Notice of construction was provided to all landowners adjacent to the construction area and follow-up meetings provided information and addressed concerns. A "Contact Documentation" form (Fig. 2) was used to record all meetings and interviews with landowners or concerned parties along the pipeline route. These forms were completed, photocopies and distributed to all members of the management team so that everyone would be aware of issues and commitments made on behalf of the company.

Environmental inspectors recorded daily construction activities and related environmental concerns in a "Daily Field Report" (Fig. 3). This report documented the area of construction activity, equipment used, personnel involved in the activity, as well as the results of environmental inspection, monitoring, and testing. Included in the report were details of any verbal or

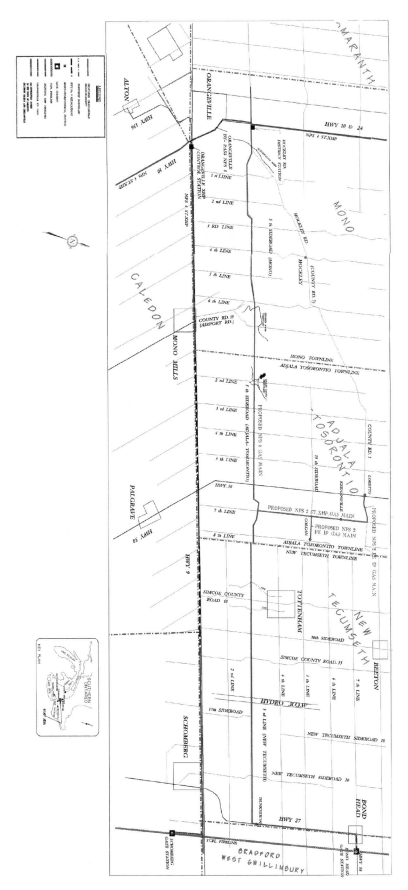

Fig. 1. Study area.

Fig. 2. Contact documentation form.

written instructions issued to construction personnel, as well as a description of their follow-up efforts.

In addition to daily logs, weekly "Evaluation of Environmental Measures Taken at Water Crossings" reports were also completed and submitted to the Project Coordinator. These reports outlined environmental mitigation measures taken at all 45 watercourse crossings along the route. Areas in which restoration activities were unacceptable were noted, as were recommendations and actions which should be taken. These reports were then photocopied and distributed to the contractor for action.

Periodic summaries of environmental deficiencies were provided to all management team members. Areas requiring further cleanup and restoration were closely monitored until mitigation was completed. These lists were prepared primarily in the later stages of the project to cover multiple areas. All deficiencies were attended to by the contractor after receipt of the lists.

ADHERENCE TO LEGISLATIVE ASPECTS

A number of conditions were placed on the company by the Ontario Energy Board. These conditions were adhered to and reported upon, before, during, and after the construction program.

There are numerous permits required in order to allow construction to commence. Examples include: water crossing permits; archaeological clearances; municipal road crossing permits; and permits to take and discharge water, to name a few. Since these permits take time to obtain, they were acquired early in the process. Permit conditions were closely followed.

ENVIRONMENTAL INSPECTION REPORT

Project ______ Project No. ______ Date ______
Client ______ Contractor ______
Nature of Work ______ Weather ______ Temperature ___°C→ ___°C

Construction Activity

Area	Equipment / Personnel

Inspection / Testing

Area	Details

Instructions Issued

Details	To	TIME ISSUED	WRITTEN	VERBAL	ACTED UPON

General Remarks

Signature: (Environmental Inspector) Signature: (Site Supervisor)

white – Environmental Inspector yellow – Site Supervisor

Fig. 3. Environmental inspection report form.

ONGOING ENVIRONMENTAL PLANNING THROUGHOUT THE PROJECT

Prior to the commencement of construction, environmentally sensitive areas were identified and recommendations made as to how they should be managed. General issues such as a wet soil shutdown policy were developed specifically for this project. The company's environmental management manual was reviewed and closely followed. An environmental implementation plan was developed and consisted of the following items:

Item 1 Pre-construction meeting involving Consumers Gas Inspectors and Contractor Supervisors.

Item 2 Meeting with Contractor Operators to discuss environmental issues.

Item 3 Construction Drawings to all Inspectors including copies of permit drawings (creek crossing — bore, flume & open cut, C.P.R., T.C.P.L.). Specific permit requirements — notification times.

Item 4 Permit summary issues to Inspector and Contractor. Copies of permits to all inspectors.

Item 5 Copy of mitigation recommendations to Inspectors.

Item 6 Wet weather shut down procedure issued to Inspectors and Contractor.

Item 7 Bore requirements marked on drawings.

Item 8 Creek crossings numbered on drawings and staked an numbered in the field.

Item 9 Specimen trees flagged in field.

Item 10 Review of route with Municipal and other local authorities (Arbor Committee) to discuss construction impact and mitigation (i.e., spoil placement, trees, creeks, bore areas).

Item 11 Review route with Contractor, Environmental Consultant and Inspector to discuss specific requirements.

Item 12 Environmental Inspection reports submitted daily, reviewed and copies issued to Contractor and Inspectors.

Item 13 Public Relations Inspector to make customer contact prior to construction and to relay specific customer concerns to Inspector and Contractor.

Item 14 Archaeologist on site during construction at Highways 88 & 27.

Item 15 Baseline noise and vibration monitoring on site.

Item 16 Test for hydrocarbon contamination prior to construction at site identified in the Environmental Assessment.

Item 17 Weekly review of sediment control by Environmental Consultant — issued to Contractor.

Item 18 Weekly meeting with Inspectors and Contract Supervisors.

During construction, activities in environmentally sensitive areas were closely monitored and the contractor was directed as to how to avoid or mitigate any serious impacts.

Once the project was completed, ongoing environmental monitoring of the pipeline right-of-way was carried out for two years after which time all impacts had been remediated.

TARGET SETTING FOR PERFORMANCE

Targets were established for environmental performance. Examples include:
- Watercourse Crossings — no erosion of banks and sedimentation
- Slopes — no erosion
- Vegetation — no damage to tree trunks, minimal root damage, restore cover crop as soon as possible
- Heritage Resources — no impact to heritage and archaeological resources
- Noise and Vibration — no damage to buildings, adhere to municipal noise by-laws
- Wells — no affect to water quality
- Contaminated Sites — clean up so pipeline is not affected
- Agricultural Land — avoid compaction and rutting
- Spills — avoid spills or if unavoidable, ensure rapid containment and clean-up.

Performance in meeting these targets was monitored on an ongoing basis through the daily reports and the project construction inspection report.

UNANTICIPATED ENVIRONMENTAL INCIDENTS

Even with all appropriate environmental mitigation in effect, it is possible that an environmental incident may occur. A true test of an effective EMS is to measure the length of time within which an appropriate response to the incident occurs. A rapid response and remediation is the sign of an effective EMS.

Fig. 4. Roadside directional drill showing sump pit for drill mud.

Two types of unanticipated incidents occurred on the Orangeville reinforcement project. The first had to do with a hydraulic hose rupture in a directional drill machine. Contractor equipment was previously inspected for leaks and worn materials. It was not possible to detect the hose rupture, however, the spill of hydraulic fluid was rapidly contained by the contractor who had a spill kit present. Spill Kits were present on site at all times in various vehicles and with most of the machines present.

Directional drills were used extensively on this project to drill under watercourses, roadways, and specimen trees. The bentonite clay used as a lubricant and to firm up the hole drilled is pumped out under pressure. Fig. 4 illustrates a drill in operation with a pit to contain excess bentonite.

Occasionally bentonite finds its way to the surface in the form of a frac-out. When this occurs in or adjacent to a watercourse it has the potential of harming fish or fish habitat. When any watercourse was being directionally drilled, the environmental inspector was present to ensure that if an in-water frac-out occurred, the drill was stopped and the bentonite contained and subsequently removed. Fig. 5 shows an in-stream bentonite frac-out that was contained and remediated.

RESOURCES AND TRAINING TO ACHIEVE TARGETS

A pre-construction meetings was held with contractor staff to provide them with an understanding of the environmental performance that they were expected to provide. Included in this discussion were health and safety issues.

On-site training of contractor staff (foremen and equipment operators) occurred on an ongoing basis. Environmental Inspectors demonstrated the proper installation of silt fences for use at erosion-sensitive areas and at all water crossings. Other training included tree and vegetation management.

Fig. 5. Instream containment of bentonite fracout.

Environmental Inspectors marked specimen trees with caution tape to indicate bore locations, and monitored pruning of branches and root cutting procedures. The practice of digging a sump pit to contain bentonite from bore machines was developed and enforced at all bore locations. All watercourse crossings were staked by environmental staff to make identification easy for the construction forces. Erosion control and bentonite containment measures were set up under environmental direction prior to construction activities at all watercourse crossings.

Since contractors tend to rotate staff on various distribution projects, ongoing training was required as new staff came to the job site.

EXTERNAL AUDIT

Risk identification was based upon a review of the 1996 Corporate risk assessment Report, 1996 Environmental Issues and Compliance Report, and a review of the environmental terms and conditions attached during the process of obtaining Ontario Energy Board, provincial, municipal, and third party approvals. Significant findings identified in previous environmental construction audit reports were also reviewed.

As a result, the following possible risk areas were identified and were addressed by the environmental audit of the pipeline construction project:
1. Project management may be insufficient to address environmental issues and concerns associated with pipeline construction, habitat protection, and right-of-way restoration activities. Project management may not have identified the existence of a potential environmental risk that could have a negative impact on the Company's image.
2. Project management may fail to obtain, or provide the timely acquisition of, required provincial, municipal or third party permits and approvals which could result in penalties and/or fines to the Company.
3. Inadequate communication, implementation, and monitoring of environmental terms and conditions attached to permits and approvals may result in environmental damage arising out of pipeline construction or restoration activities.
4. Untimely access to established emergency response systems for contaminated soils, spills, and natural gas releases may result in non-compliance with government regulations. A lack of appropriate on-site hazardous waste management procedures, sediment control, habitat protection, waste water management, and control of air emissions may also result in non-compliance with government regulations.

The risk assessment was used to determine the scope of the environmental audit. The scope included:
- a review of the project's Environmental Management System (EMS);
- verification through sampling that required permits and approvals were obtained;
- an examination of the process by which the project's environmental/socio-economic terms and conditions were identified, communicated, and monitored. Verification through sampling of the implementation of terms and conditions contained in the following documents:
  - the project's Route Selection and Environmental and Socio-Economic Impact Assessment Report as approved by the OEB,
  - required provincial and municipal approvals,
  - third party approvals such as Ontario Hydro and CNR/CPR requirements;
- a review of the construction and restoration activities related to the significant findings identified in previous construction audits such as environmental inspection, hydrostatic testing, and sediment control measures;
- a review of the hazardous waste management system, emergency response plans for spills, contaminated soils, construction waste water management, habitat protection, and control of air emissions such as noise and dust; and
- verification that a procedure to identify, resolve, and document public concerns associated with the project is established.

The objectives of the audit were to:
- identify areas of known or potential environmental risk so that action can be taken to minimize the risk of exposure to the Company in case of an incident;
- assess project management's awareness of environmental laws and their responsibilities under that legal framework;
- ensure that the company was complying with existing environmental practices and procedures with regards to the most significant requirements of known federal, provincial, and municipal environmental legislation, regulation, and standards; and

- ensure that construction procedures implemented address the environmental terms and conditions stipulated during the approval process and the findings identified in previous construction audits, and evaluate these procedures accordingly.

The results of the audit were to be reported to senior management only if there were significant issues such as:

- significant findings that pose unacceptable risk, such as non-compliance with legislation or corporate policies and procedures, were identified;
- any findings related to specific issues where client management did not implement the agreed upon action identified during previous audits;
- any findings identified where there was a disagreement with client management over the degree of significance or the feasibility of proposed recommendations; or
- a significant number of insignificant findings were identified in a variety of audited areas.

CONTRACTOR EMS

Gas distribution projects that are undertaken by pipeline contractors are increasingly becoming self-regulated. In order for contractors to be able to successfully bid for these projects they have to demonstrate that they have an EMS in place. As a result of the Orangeville Reinforcement Pipeline Project and a number of others we were able to develop an environmental code of practice for two pipeline contractors.

SUMMARY

The Orangeville Reinforcement illustrates how an EMS can be successfully applied to a pipeline construction project. The lessons learned from this project are directly transferable to other pipeline construction projects. In order to implement a successful pipeline EMS, a company needs to have a high corporate commitment to the environment. There must be a clear assignment of accountability and responsibility for environmental matters during all phases of the construction project. The environmental coordinator for the project must be clear on the targets that have been set and be able to make a clear determination on how they have been met. Internal and external communications have to be extensive to ensure that all stakeholders are aware of what the issues are, who is responsible for resolving them and when they have been resolved. Environmental training should be administered on a continuous basis throughout the project. An independent audit of the EMS should be carried out to determine if it is meeting its objectives. Recommendations for improvement should be made to ensure continuous improvement. The end result of the process should be that natural and social impacts are avoided and all those involved develop a greater appreciation for good environmental management. Hopefully, this will result in others developing an EMS for their activities.

BIOGRAPHICAL SKETCH

Mario Buszynski, MSc, MCIP, RPP
  SENES Consultants Limited, 121 Granton drive, Unit 12, Richmond Hill, ON L4B 3N4, Canada
Mr. Buszynski is presently Manager of Environmental Assessment and Energy Projects at SENES Consultants Limited. He has a MSc in forestry and over 25 years of environmental assessment and land use planning experience with the provincial government, Ontario Hydro and the private sector. Mr. Buszynski has spent 19 years working on over 6000 km of gas and electric transmission projects in Ontario, the United States and abroad. He has been an expert witness before the Ontario Environmental Assessment Board, the Ontario Municipal Board, the Consolidated Hearings Board (Ontario), the Ontario Energy Board and the Nova Scotia Utilities and Review Board.

Managing the Variance Process — Evaluation of Strategies Utilized on Two Major Pipeline Projects

Stephen Craycroft, Gus McLachlan, and Mike Tyrrell

Designing, planning, permitting, and constructing large-scale linear construction projects poses tremendous challenges with identifying every contingency or detail for regulatory consideration and approval. As a result, no matter how well the project is planned and designed, minor amendments to project specifications to meet site-specific conditions and project needs, and approval of additional access roads and extra workspaces are often needed quickly during construction to facilitate construction progress, and to minimize resource impacts. An effective variance process provides the mechanism for obtaining rapid approvals for minor project changes during project construction. This paper evaluates the variance processes utilized on two large-scale construction projects in the natural gas pipeline industry. The Maritimes & Northeast Phase II Pipeline Project (Maritimes) and the TransColorado Gas Transmission Project, Phase II (TransColorado) developed and implemented effective strategies for managing variances during the projects. A summary of effective components of variance processes and strategies is provided as a guide for future projects.

Keywords: Maritimes, compliance, inspection, TransColorado, constructability

INTRODUCTION

Designing, planning, and permitting oil, gas, and electric transmission projects poses tremendous challenges with developing environmental permits and plans that accurately identify resource protection measures and workspace needs for large-scale projects. Given the complexity of these projects and the immense variety of site-specific situations encountered in the field, standardized details and plans often cannot identify the full range of conditions and situations encountered during construction. Similarly, engineers and project designers cannot think of every approach the contractor would implement on the ground during construction.

For projects that are constructed in the United States, the environmental impact assessment and permitting process requires that the project — and project impacts — be clearly and specifically defined. Any change outside the specifically permitted project (including extra workspaces, access roads, and modification of mitigation measures or construction techniques) generally requires regulatory approval before the change is implemented. For these reasons and to meet site-specific conditions, minor amendments to project specifications or approval of additional access roads and extra workspaces are often needed quickly during construction to facilitate construction progress, and to minimize resource impacts. Over the past 10 years the variance processes on major pipeline projects have evolved to develop efficient and effective mechanisms for obtaining variances to project requirements during construction.

This paper evaluates the variance processes implemented on two recent large-scale natural gas pipeline construction projects. An overview of each project is given, followed by a discussion of the variance process implemented on each project. Characteristics of each project that contributed to effective information management and rapid regulatory approvals of variances are identified and discussed. Specific guidelines for developing and implementing effective variance management procedures on complex projects concludes

Environmental Concerns in Rights-of-Way Management: Seventh International Symposium
J.W. Goodrich-Mahoney, D.F. Mutrie and C.A. Guild (editors)
© 2002 Elsevier Science Ltd. All rights reserved.

this paper and provides readers with a model to apply on their own projects.

PROJECT OVERVIEWS

Maritimes & Northeast Pipeline Project

In 1995, Maritimes & Northeast Pipeline, L.L.C. began to develop plans to construct a natural gas pipeline in the northeastern United States and eastern Canada that would bring a new source of natural gas to the North American grid, and connect natural gas customers in New England with the Sable Offshore Energy Project off the coast of Nova Scotia, Canada. The United States portion of this project (the Maritimes & Northeast Phase II Pipeline Project) involved construction of approximately 205 miles of 24- and 30-inch diameter pipeline from Westbrook, Maine to Baileyville, Maine. The project was broken up into three construction spreads in Maine and was constructed in summer 1999.

The project was faced with many environmental challenges, including those associated with permitting and constructing one of the first large diameter natural gas pipelines in the state of Maine. In addition, numerous sensitive environmental resources and habitats were crossed by the project, including over 1700 wetlands and 325 sensitive streams, as well as significant coldwater fisheries habitat for trout and Atlantic salmon, waterfowl/wading birds, protected freshwater mussels, bald eagles, protected dragonflies and mayflies, sensitive plants, and numerous cultural resource sites. The project was reviewed and/or regulated by the Federal Energy Regulatory Commission (FERC) and the Maine Department of Environmental Protection (MDEP), as well as numerous other state, federal, local, and tribal agencies.

In keeping with a strong corporate commitment to the community and responsible construction practices, Maritimes took a proactive approach to permitting, planning, engineering, and designing the project, and incorporated public and agency concerns into the design and construction specifications. To communicate environmental responsibilities and project procedures to all project participants, Maritimes implemented a comprehensive environmental training program that was tailored to a number of different audiences, including project supervisory and management staff, project contractors, and individual construction workers. In addition, the project implemented an aggressive and effective field environmental compliance inspection effort during construction and restoration.

The Maritimes Project was constructed under intense public and agency scrutiny. The MDEP retained three full-time environmental monitors per spread (nine total) during construction of the 205-mile project, and one Field Services (MDEP enforcement) representative to each spread. Importantly, the MDEP monitors generally had previous experience with environmental issues associated with construction projects, and the lead MDEP monitors and Field Services representatives were given specific field variance approval authority during the project. The parameters of this field variance authority were negotiated during the permitting process. The FERC also maintained a full-time presence on the project with two FERC monitors per spread throughout construction. However, none of the FERC monitors in the field were given variance approval authority. A number of other federal (e.g., US Army Corps of Engineers) and state agencies (e.g., Land Use Regulation Commission) had regulatory authority over the project and reviewed field compliance intermittently throughout the project.

In addition, other environmental and tribal groups (e.g., the Atlantic Salmon Federation, the Sheepscot Valley Conservation Authority, and the Penobscot Indian Nation) reviewed the right-of-way (ROW) in a purely monitoring/oversight capacity during construction.

TransColorado

The TransColorado Gas Transmission Project, Phase II included the construction of approximately 270 miles of 24- and 22-inch mainline pipeline from Dolores County, Colorado to north of Bloomington, New Mexico. The project was regulated by the US Bureau of Land Management (BLM), the US Forest Service (USFS), FERC, and a number of other federal and state agencies. Key issues on the project included protection of cultural and biological resources, protection of water quality, implementation of effective erosion control measures, and restoration of high-elevation areas, including areas exceeding 10,000 feet in elevation. The project was divided into four construction spreads, with construction occurring on all four spreads simultaneously.

The TransColorado Project submitted its original FERC application in 1990, however, the project was put on hold and work on final permitting for the project was not re-initiated until 1997. During 1997 and early 1998, the environmental compliance management team conducted a comprehensive field-based constructability review of the pipeline alignment, prepared various environmental mitigation plans, conducted agency communications and negotiations, and designed a comprehensive reclamation program.

During the 1998 construction season, TransColorado implemented a thorough environmental inspection, reclamation, and compliance management program for the project. The environmental inspection effort (including 15 full-time on-site inspectors) was conducted in coordination with on-site agency monitors from the BLM, USFS, and FERC. In a somewhat unique, but highly successful effort, the environmental inspectors on the project represented both the land management and regulatory agencies, as well as the project proponent. This arrangement required increased communication and accountability of the environmental inspection staff to the agencies. Components of the environmental compliance management program included use of a computer-based inspection reporting database that posted daily inspection reports on a password-protected web site for project and agency staff. The project also implemented a comprehensive environmental training program that was tailored to a number of different audiences, including project supervisory and management staff, the project contractors, and individual construction workers. The open reporting system and thorough training program resulted in an elevated level of comfort and trust between the regulatory agencies and the project.

The BLM and USFS also had designated representatives (with variance approval authority) in the field essentially full-time during project construction. In addition, the FERC conducted a monthly compliance review of the project.

OVERVIEW OF THE PROJECTS' VARIANCE PROCESSES

Maritimes & Northeast Phase II Pipeline Project

The Maritimes Project took a proactive approach to environmental compliance throughout the permitting, planning, and construction phases of the project. The project provided strong management and corporate support for the project and for meeting environmental commitments. This included meeting early with regulators and the community, building an effective public relations effort into the process, and thoroughly incorporating environmental requirements into the construction process (including appropriate language in the contracts to ensure that the contractors provided adequate cost-considerations for the environmental mitigation requirements). Maritimes maintained a consistent project team from planning and permitting through construction. As a result, the Maritimes team understood agency concerns and permit requirements, which led to a consistent effort during construction of the project. Maritimes also implemented a strong environmental and safety incentives program, which recognized contractor and project staff for their efforts in helping the project maintain compliance. These approaches to environmental compliance contributed to the project's successful completion. The sections below address the variance efforts implemented before and during construction.

Preconstruction variance review
Maritimes' environmental inspectors and construction quality assurance staff conducted an in-depth review of the project alignment sheets and existing workspaces prior to construction in order to identify and document all areas of the existing project where variances were required from the FERC and MDEP requirements. Since the Maritimes Project had over 1700 wetland crossings and over 325 stream crossings, the majority of these variance requests represented areas where extra workspace could not be set back the required distance from streams and wetlands or where the project alignment ran parallel with an adjacent stream.

Additional variance requests were identified during a preconstruction walkthrough conducted with environmental inspectors and construction representatives. These variances ranged from minor route realignments to avoid parallel streams, to changes in the original stream or wetland crossing methods to better address site-specific construction or environmental requirements. Numerous site-specific variance requests or modifications were identified and submitted for approval as a result of the preconstruction variance and field "constructability" review. This detailed preconstruction review dramatically reduced the number of variances that needed to be approved during construction. The effort built confidence with the agencies that any remaining construction variances were truly needed — and that unforeseeable changes needed during construction were not just a result of poor planning.

Construction variance process
Maritimes developed a well-defined written variance procedure before the start of project construction. The variance process and strategies for meeting agencies' needs for complete variance requests, as well as the project's need for rapid turn-around of variance approvals were discussed with the major agencies to ensure that expectations were clearly established before construction of the project began.

The variance process during construction involved the contractor, construction managers and supervisors, land agents, environmental inspectors and the state inspectors in the field during construction, as well as the Maritimes permit coordinator and construction and environmental management staff as appropriate. To ensure that all appropriate clearances were received prior to submitting the variance request to the agencies, Maritimes utilized a simple variance form with signature lines to document biological and cultural resource clearances, landowner clearances, construction and environmental concurrence, and various supporting regulatory agency approvals. The form also provided lines for state and federal agency approval (with conditions, if necessary), and for a final project authorization once all appropriate regulatory approvals were obtained.

The process was designed so that the contractor or construction coordinator typically initiated variance requests for extra workspaces or additional access roads, while the LEI generally initiated variance requests for procedural changes (e.g., changes in stream crossing methods).

One of the most important components of the variance process was the internal review process. Each variance request was carefully analyzed to determine if the variance request (extra workspace, access road, or construction method) was justifiable and necessary. This review ensured that only the truly justified and necessary variance requests would be forwarded to the agencies for approval. On the Maritimes project, the MDEP and FERC had somewhat different regulatory authorities and resource protection requirements. This internal quality assurance effort ensured that conflicting requirements were adequately addressed in the variance process. Three major levels of variances were utilized during construction of the Maritimes Project.

Field variances
Minor changes were generally discussed in the field with the MDEP monitor and the agreed upon construction method was implemented in the field. The environmental inspector documented the field agreement on a field variance form, and provided a copy of the agreement to the MDEP monitor. These minor variances ranged from changes in erosion control measures based on site-specific conditions, extending time limits or restoration time frames for specific stream crossings, and certain stream crossing method changes. The FERC Project Manager and field monitors were generally copied on these minor field variance approvals.

Minor variances
Slightly more complex — but less than significant — variances were discussed in the field with the MDEP monitors and the lead MDEP monitor on the spread would sign the variance form indicating field approval of the change. The form with other appropriate signatures would then be faxed to the FERC Project Manager for review and approval. The turnaround time for these variances was generally less than 24 h. In several situations, the project permit coordinator or Environmental Manager would call the FERC Project Manager to communicate the details of the variance request. This procedure of faxing field variance forms to the FERC project manager (and at times the MDEP Project Manager) resulted in rapid approval of the majority of variances submitted. Of approximately 97 variance requests that went through this "fast-track" variance approval process, 96 were approved by the FERC and MDEP (most within 24 h). A key to the effectiveness of this approach was providing backup documentation of landowner approvals, resource clearances, and state field approvals on the variance request form.

Many stream crossing methods were changed during the Maritimes Project based on stream flow conditions at the time the construction crews reached the stream (e.g., changing from a flumed crossing to a dam and pump crossing to take advantage of low stream flow conditions). This approach reduced impacts to the streams significantly and led to highly effective stream crossing operations. At the outset of the project, the FERC was faxed a copy of the field agreement for approval for each of the stream crossing method changes. Later in the project, a general variance was approved by the FERC that provided approval for a change in stream crossing methodology based on the MDEP's field monitors concurrence. In these cases, the FERC would be sent a copy of the variance form showing the state monitor's approval, but the project was not required to wait for a subsequent FERC approval. This agreement was implemented approximately mid-project, after the state and the FERC developed confidence in the project's environmental inspection teams, the variance process, and in the project's continued commitment to meeting the environmental protection commitments.

Major variances
A limited number of more complex, potentially significant changes were filed with the FERC in the normal manner. These formal variance requests were generally much more significant in scope and typically required significant back-up documentation to support the variance request. Formal variance requests typically required three days to two weeks for approval. Examples of major variance requests include new staging areas, new access roads, or extra workspace areas located outside the previously surveyed corridor.

TransColorado
Constructability review
The TransColorado Gas Transmission Project, Phase II was a complex project from the start. The project had originally been routed and planned eight years earlier along an existing pipeline corridor for much of its route, but had not been previously reviewed for construction complications, environmental constraints, or extra workspace needs. In the summer of 1997, several teams, each composed of an environmental and a construction representative, reviewed the ROW on foot to evaluate the constructability of the route with respect to environmental and construction constraints, as well as to identify where extra workspace areas were needed along the route.

This "constructability review" proved to be a critical element in planning, final designing, and building the project. The field review identified numerous small route realignments that enabled the project to cross streams or wetlands at an alternate location that would have less impact, and many areas where a small modification in the route alignment would significantly reduce construction constraints and associated costs. In addition, during this review, the TransColorado construction and environmental representatives spent a significant amount of time discussing the project alignment and issues with the land management and regulatory agencies to address agency site-specific concerns and issues. These considerations were then built into the final construction design, alignment, and specifications.

The constructability review resulted in a project alignment that was still difficult — given the terrain and resource constraints — but one that was both constructable and acceptable to the various resource and land management agencies. As a result of this process, one large variance package was submitted to the agencies six months before construction to ensure approvals well in advance of project construction.

TransColorado Construction Variance Process

The TransColorado Pipeline Project utilized a streamlined construction variance process. The variance process was clearly defined in a written Environmental Compliance Management Plan that thoroughly described the roles and responsibilities of each group involved with the variances. Under this program, variance requests were initially identified in the field by the contractor, Construction Manager, or Lead Environmental Inspector. Signatures were obtained in the field from construction, environmental, land agents, and as appropriate, the land management agencies. This process ensured that the variances were discussed thoroughly in the field before they were submitted to the project office for review. Importantly, when variance requests were submitted to the project office, the Environmental Compliance Field Supervisor and Construction Manager evaluated each variance request carefully to ensure that the variance request was reasonable, justified, and complete. This internal quality assurance effort ensured that only complete applications were submitted to the FERC and other agencies for consideration, which resulted in more rapid review from regulatory agencies.

Similar to the Maritimes Project, the TransColorado Project utilized three general levels of variances. Since the majority of the TransColorado Project was constructed on federal BLM or USFS lands, the designated representatives for the BLM or USFS could approve the majority of minor changes in the field during construction. The same strategies that were implemented on the Maritimes Project (and numerous other recent large-scale projects across the United States) were initially developed on the TransColorado Project. It was clear during the TransColorado Project that the key to obtaining rapid regulatory approval for field variances was to provide complete, justifiable, and well-supported variance requests to the regulatory agencies. For the TransColorado Project, regulatory authorizations for minor and less than significant variances were obtained on the same day or within 24 h of the request, while potentially significant changes were generally approved (or denied) within three days to two weeks.

KEY COMPONENTS OF SUCCESSFUL VARIANCE PROCESSES

1. **Conduct a field constructability review**: Conducting a field constructability walk-over with environmental and construction representatives who understand construction requirements and capabilities, as well as environmental constraints and issues has been shown to be one of the most valuable efforts contributing to a smooth-functioning and successful project. The constructability review provides a final check on the route alignment, helps to identify difficult construction or environmental compliance concerns, and helps to identify any variances that may be needed — before the contractor gets on the ground and everyone gets busy — and changes become expensive to the project. This constructability review also provides final preconstruction variance information that can be submitted to the agencies for approval before the contractor starts construction.

   The qualifications of the staff conducting this field review are critical to the success of this effort. Ideal staff for this effort includes environmental inspectors who have significant experience with construction issues and environmental restrictions, soil characteristics, erosion control needs, and sensitive resource protection requirements for the region. Similarly, ideal construction representatives have significant construction experience and an understanding of environmental constraints and requirements for construction of pipeline projects.

   However, even with a thorough constructability review, a number of additional variances will be needed during construction of the project, due to site-specific soil conditions, weather conditions, stream flow levels at the time of construction, and the contractor's approach to the work.

2. **Develop and discuss the variance process before construction**: Discussing and developing agreements with the key regulatory agencies on the variance process, well before construction, is key to a successful variance process. Items to discuss with agencies should include:
   – the specific format for variance submittals;
   – the surveys/approvals and supporting documentation needed to ensure a complete variance package;
   – the types of variances that can be approved in the field, and those that require formal approval (i.e., establish different levels of variances);
   – the expected turn-around time for approval of complete variance requests; and
   – documentation procedures for variances of various levels.

3. **Develop a well-defined written variance procedure**: A well-defined variance procedure provides the map to guide the variance process during the

project. This written variance procedure also helps to ensure that all project participants and regulatory agencies develop similar and consistent expectations on the types of variances that will be considered, how variances will be handled and processed during construction, and the time frames for review and approval/denial of the variance requests.

4. **Provide appropriate staffing to support the variance process**: Managing the variance and documentation efforts on a large-scale construction project is a time-consuming task requiring significant attention to detail. A dedicated Permit Coordinator is critical during construction to assemble complete variance packages, ensure that appropriate surveys and supporting information is included with each submittal, track the status of variance approvals and distribute the approved/denied variances. Unfortunately, many projects put management of the variance process on the shoulders of the Lead Environmental Inspectors. This approach reduces the Lead Environmental Inspector's ability to manage the field compliance inspection program — a situation that may ultimately compromise the project's compliance management efforts.

5. **Review the variance requests internally before submitting to agencies**: An important step in the variance process involves an internal review of the variance request. The engineering and environmental project management staff should always review variance requests to ensure that they are justified and reasonable before submitting the requests to agencies. It is clear that some variances simply will not be approved by regulatory agencies. In these situations, it is far better to simply deny the variance request in-house, rather than burden the resource agencies with a review of a fatally flawed or impossible variance request. This internal review effort helps to prevent overloading agencies with variance requests and maintains the credibility of the project and its variance program.

6. **Implement effective variance tracking procedures**: Tracking the status of variance requests is a critical element of an effective variance process. The date the variance was submitted by the contractor, the date the environmental review was initiated, the date the variance request was submitted to the agencies, and the date approval or denial of the variance request was received should be documented clearly. During the construction phase, operations move quickly and requests for variances often need short turn-around times in order to prove useful for the project. In these situations, the tracking process provides an invaluable tool to identify variances that are delayed at some stage in the process and for keeping the field staff up-to-date on the status of each variance request. A simple database system can assist with successfully tracking variances during preconstruction and construction periods.

On most major projects, multiple agencies are required to review and approve variance requests. Therefore, it is critical that one central person within the project organization ensures that all of the appropriate agencies have approved the variance prior to releasing the approved variance to construction.

7. **Effective Document Distribution System**: An effective document or approval distribution system is critical to ensure smooth communication at the field level. It is important that the spread Construction Supervisor and the Lead Environmental Inspector receive notification regarding the status of a variance at the same time to prevent inaccurate communications or miscommunications with the contractor and inspection teams. A clear process must be in place where communication of the final project approval of a variance request comes from the main project office, to prevent premature use of an extra workspace area or modified procedure where the project had not yet obtained approval from all the necessary agencies.

8. **Provide appropriate training for the project team**: Large-scale construction projects move at a rapid pace, requiring close and effective communications and responsiveness. Prior to initiating construction, a thorough training program should be provided on all requirements, responsibilities, and the process for approval of the variances.

CONCLUSION — MANAGING CHANGE

Variance processes continue to be an important component of a project's environmental compliance management program. It is clear that even well-designed large-scale projects require a number of field variances during construction to address site-specific or weather-driven conditions. Managing the variance process effectively prior to and during project construction requires clear organization, early planning and communication with regulatory agencies, an effective organization for reviewing and processing variance requests from the field, appropriate manpower support to manage and implement the variance process, and an effective routing mechanism for communicating approved variances to the field. Implementing an effective variance process will contribute to the success of the environmental compliance program and can be a significant factor in facilitating project construction and maintaining effective agency relationships.

BIOGRAPHICAL SKETCHES

Steve Craycroft
Essex Environmental, Inc., 637 Main Street, Half Moon Bay, CA 94019, USA, Tel: (650) 726-8320, Fax: (650) 712-1190, E-mail: scraycroft@essexenv.com
Steve Craycroft is a Project Director with *Essex Environmental* in Half Moon Bay, California. Mr. Craycroft

has proven capabilities in environmental planning and on-site management of environmental programs for large-scale utility construction projects; including TransColorado and the Maritimes Project. Mr. Craycroft has been directly involved with developing and implementing environmental compliance, inspection, and training programs for well over 2300 miles of pipeline construction projects in the last ten years. Mr. Craycroft's expertise includes substantial experience on projects involving complex resource issues and multiple agency jurisdictions, with specific technical expertise in stream bank stabilization, sensitive resource mitigation, erosion and sediment control, and revegetation. Mr. Craycroft holds a Masters degree in Wildlife Ecology and Forest Management from the State University of New York and a Bachelor degree in Biology from Centre College of Kentucky.

George "Gus" McLachlan

Maritimes & Northeast Pipeline, L.L.C., P.O. Box 327, Hampton, NH 03842, USA, Tel: (207) 622-0073, Fax: (207) 621-8229, E-mail: gamclachlan@duke-energy.com

George "Gus" McLachlan has managed environmental field activities; local, state, and federal regulatory filings; and compliance programs on numerous construction and maintenance projects for *Duke Energy* over the past nine years. Currently, Mr. McLachlan is the Environmental Manager for *Maritimes & Northeast Phase II Pipeline Project* in Maine, as well as *Maritimes & Northeast/Portland Natural Gas Transmission System Joint Facilities Project* in Massachusetts and New Hampshire. Overall, the facilities include 305 miles of natural gas pipeline, compressor stations, and related facilities. In this capacity, Mr. McLachlan is responsible for all field studies, regulatory filings, and environmental inspection and compliance during and after construction. Mr. McLachlan holds a Bachelor degree in Natural Resources Conservation from the University of Connecticut.

Mike Tyrrell

Earth Tech, 300 Baker Avenue, Concord, MA 01742, USA, Tel: (978) 371-4240, Fax: (978) 371-7889, E-mail: mtyrrell@earthtech.com

Mike Tyrrell is currently the Program Director for *Linear Projects* and a senior wetlands ecologist in *Earth Tech's Environmental Sciences and Planning Group*. He has project experience involving over 1000 miles of natural gas pipelines throughout the United States and has been involved in the permitting of numerous power plants. Mike has over 11 years of experience in the environmental field and has completed numerous environmental permit applications including National Environmental Policy Act (NEPA) submittals, FERC applications, environmental impact reports, U.S. Army Corps of Engineers Section 404 submittals, and state water quality applications. Mike holds a Bachelors degree in Wildlife Biology from the University of Rhode Island.

Electronic Reporting for Environmental Inspection

Melissa Pockar, Paul Anderson, Julie Myhre, and Elizabeth Dolezal

Electronic reporting for environmental inspection on natural gas pipeline construction programs has been used in the past on projects such as the Tuscorora Gas Pipeline Project (McCullough, 1997). Electronic reporting provides for rapid information exchange and the development of a search-capable database that documents environmental compliance. In addition, electronic reporting systems allow field and management staff to direct construction activity effectively within and between construction spreads. An electronic Environmental Inspection Reporting System (EIRS) was developed for use during the construction of the Alliance Pipeline System. The Canadian version (CanEIRS©) and its US counterpart (USEIRS©) were developed to document compliance with Certificate Terms and Conditions, Federal Regulations and Provincial and State issued permit conditions, and to allow for efficient exchange of environmental information. Key tools of the environmental construction management program have been highlighted, including reporting forms, the Daily Inspection Newspapers, and construction photographs. Environmental inspection reporting systems produced a daily "newspaper" that provided both management and construction supervisory personnel on each spread with the summary of the previous day's environmental inspection reports. These reports allowed the construction management team to quickly respond to compliance issues, identify trends, and keep informed on the day-to-day issues associated with this large construction project. The electronic reporting of environmental inspection enabled a compliance database to be established. The database provided for trend analysis and documentation of compliance and monitoring as a tool for reclamation planning and environmental post-construction report compilation. Through the use of the electronic reporting systems, Alliance was able to maintain a high level of environmental compliance in three Canadian provinces (on nine mainline spreads and the construction of the lateral system in Canada) and in four US states (on seven construction spreads).

Keywords: Database, compliance, due diligence, environmental inspection

1. INTRODUCTION

The Alliance Pipeline system extends from northeastern British Columbia, Canada, to Chicago, IL, USA (Fig. 1). The Canadian portion of the system consists of:
- 339 km (211 miles) of 1067 mm (42-inch) and 1220 km (758 miles) of 914 mm (36-inch) diameter steel pipe;
- 36 receipt points connecting with lateral pipelines totaling about 698 km (434 miles), ranging in length from ≈0.3–142 km (0.2–96 miles) and in diameter 114–610 mm (4–24 inch);
- 7 mainline compressor stations of 23–30 MW (31,000–40,000 hp) each, spaced ~193 km (120 miles) apart; and
- mainline block valves spaced about every 32 km (20 miles).

The United States portion of the system consists of:
- 888 miles (1429 km) of 36-inch (914 mm) diameter steel pipe;
- 7 compressor stations of about 31,000 hp (23 MW) each, spaced about 120 miles (193 km) apart; and
- 7 mainline block valves spaced about every 20 miles (32 km).

The Alliance Pipeline was subject to federal regulatory approval processes in both Canada and the United

Fig. 1. Alliance pipeline system.

States. In Canada, the process primarily involved the National Energy Board (NEB) and the Canadian Environmental Assessment Agency (CEAA). In the US, it primarily involved the Federal Energy Regulatory Commission (FERC). In both countries, consultation was required to obtain local and regional approvals; permits and approvals were acquired from numerous agencies in three provinces and four states prior to construction.

One of the objectives of environmental inspection was to ensure that all environmental mitigation measures prescribed by Alliance and regulatory agencies were implemented, and that work proceeded in compliance with environmental regulations and Alliance Environmental Policy. In order to effectively manage the environmental inspection activities associated with a construction project of this magnitude, and to document compliance with NEB Certificate Terms and Conditions (National Energy Board, 1998), FERC regulations and provincial and state approvals, parallel Canadian and US electronic Environmental Inspection Reporting Systems (EIRS) were developed.

During peak mainline construction, the Canadian Environmental Inspection Team consisted of 22 Environmental Inspectors (EIs) working on six construction spreads, and the US team was comprised of 28 EIs working on the construction of seven spreads. Lateral pipeline construction in Canada peaked during the winter of 1999/2000 with the construction of 15 laterals. Lead Environmental Inspectors (LEIs) were designated on each spread, and both the Canadian and the US inspection programs were supervised by respective Supervisors of Environmental Inspection (SEI). The Alliance Environmental Policy and Environmental Compliance Management Program objectives were incorporated into the philosophy and design of the Environmental Inspection Reporting System (EIRS); however, the EIRS systems were modified to meet the regulatory requirements for the inspection programs on each side of the border. The two EIRSs have subsequently been referred to as CanEIRS© (Canada) and USEIRS© (US).

Traditionally, inspection data has been documented and transferred by means of hand-written notes. The EIRSs were designed to supplement inspection field notes and allow for the submission of final daily reports electronically in a consistent format that expedited report preparation in the field and automated the generation of the "Daily Inspection News." This newspaper was circulated to senior level management, construction offices, consultants, resource specialists and other construction personnel electronically or by fax the following morning. EIs were expected to submit electronic inspection reports by midnight of the inspection date in order to provide the summary by 6:00 a.m. the following morning to construction personnel. USEIRS© Daily Inspection News included all reports generated by the EI Team for a particular day. In contrast, the CanEIRS© Daily Inspection News consisted of only a "Daily Summary" report that was generated by the EIs as a synopsis of the days' activities in one report form, with a list of all activity inspection report forms attached for additional reference if required.

The inspection reports allowed EIs to document recommendations and actions taken on major decisions such as wet-weather shut-down, procedures implemented in the case of unforeseen environmental issues, or conflicting permit requirements. Standardized inspection reports provided an opportunity for documentation of contacts with government agency representatives and other project stakeholders, and the outcomes of any consultations. Unresolved issues or items identified for future follow-up could be recorded in

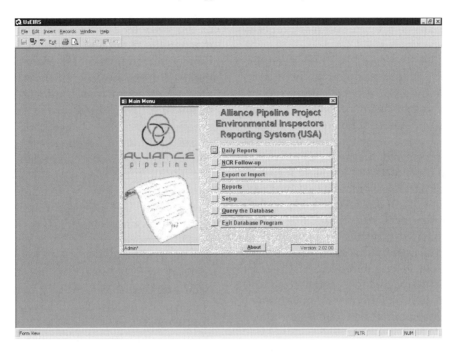

Fig. 2. EIRS Main Menu user interface.

a searchable database supported by keyword queries, and fields were available for referencing pertinent photos, videos, and sketches and for updating the status of environmental commitments.

METHODOLOGY

Program design criteria

Through consultation between the database programmers and Alliance environment personnel, the scope of the Environmental Inspection Reporting Systems and the desired data inputs and outputs from the proposed electronic programs were determined. Meetings were conducted with Alliance Environmental staff to incorporate the practical program attributes from a management point of view, as well as from a user (EI) perspective. The EIRS tool contained practical design elements that allowed for the creation and submission of Daily Inspection Reports, the permanent documentation and tracking of noncompliance events and other incidents, and the generation of summary documents for distribution to selected individuals and regulatory agencies. Design parameters also enabled the user to readily query and summarize the information contained in the database through data fields such as "inspection date," "EI," "activity," "location" or through keyword search results. Data fields for digital photos and other sources of documentation were incorporated to directly reference relevant materials to the respective inspection reports.

Both CanEIRS© and USEIRS© were developed in Microsoft Access© through the collaborative efforts of Salmo Consulting Inc., E2 Environmental Alliance Inc. and TERA Environmental Consultants (Alta.) Ltd. (here-after referred to as the "Design Team"). The EIRS programs were designed to be user friendly and incorporated as many drop-down menus and help messages as possible. Both Canadian and US systems consisted of the same main menu user interface as illustrated in Fig. 2. These menu options provided access to the basic functions required by Alliance.

To allow for efficient updates to the EIRS programs, the database was divided into two components: a "front-end" (the program) that includes the database program, reports and forms; and a "back-end" (the data), that includes completed daily reports. Front-end updates were typically forwarded to the EIs via self-extracting email files, CD or disk. An import function was developed for back-end updates of the EI databases from the Master Database in the event that additional data provision to EIs was required (for example, Non-Compliance reports from one Inspector could be forwarded to another for follow-up inspections and reporting). Back-end updates were designed to not overwrite existing data.

Required fields within the reports were designated with a red asterisk (∗). A report could not be closed or submitted without the entry of information in all required fields. This requirement provided for a base level of essential information in the activity reports (for example, spread location and activity were required data fields).

User levels

The EIRS programs were designed with four user and security levels. The default "Admin" level allowed for viewing of all records (daily reports) in the database, and provided the ability to prepare summary reports, such as the *Daily Inspection News.*

The "Inspector" level allowed a pre-defined list of authorized users (with pre-assigned passwords) to generate and edit daily reports, export daily reports and follow-up reports as they were prepared, view and print summary reports, delete daily reports created in error, and conduct searches within their databases. EIs maintained complete records of their individual reports on personal computers, which were synchronized with a "Master Database" maintained by Database (DB) Managers in both Calgary, Alberta and in Minneapolis, Minnesota on a daily basis. File export processes were automated from the EI computers to the respective DB Managers networks over the telephone lines via modem. Once submitted, these reports were used by the DB Managers to generate the Daily Inspection News, inspection summaries, government submissions and other summary or follow-up data as required.

In order to provide security and to ensure unauthorized individuals were not submitting reports, EIs were required to enter a pre-assigned user name and password to prepare, edit, delete, or export daily reports. EIs were able to edit daily reports for a period of two days after which time the files automatically converted into a read-only state. Daily reports of more than one EI could be retained on the same computer in the same back-end. All users of the same computer could view and print copies of the daily reports stored on the computer, but only an EI could edit or delete his or her own reports.

The DB Manager access level included the full ability to generate, edit and delete daily reports, create summary reports, and conduct searches. The DB Managers were responsible to ensure that the Daily Inspection News was generated from the previous day's inspection activities and distributed to the Supervisors of Environmental Inspection, construction field offices, senior Alliance management personnel, resource specialists, and other consultants as required. Copies of the original inspection reports and any reference photographs or sketches were archived for future reference. DB Managers were responsible for maintaining, updating, revising, and backing-up CanEIRS© and USEIRS© in the respective Alliance offices, and for providing program updates to the EIs.

The "Administrator" level had full access to modify the program code and design. This level was accessible by members of the Design Team. Hardware and software support for Canadian and US Inspectors was provided primarily by the Information Services Group at Alliance.

Training

A training program was implemented by the Design Team for all Alliance environmental staff. Environmental Managers and SEIs were trained on the utility of the EIRS as a search tool and how to effectively manage the records to ensure documentation of environmental compliance. DB Managers were trained on the structure of the program, how to generate pertinent reports and summaries, conduct searches, and provide technical software assistance to the Environmental Inspection teams.

EIRS training programs were conducted in the US and in Canada for the respective inspection groups. The training included a preliminary session on the hardware and software associated with the implementation of USEIRS© and CanEIRS©, as well as the logistical requirements for exporting daily reports to the DB Manager.

Follow-up surveys were conducted with the inspectors from both Canada and the US for feedback regarding the use of CanEIRS© and USEIRS©. The surveys were to encourage EIs to provide suggestions for improvements or additions to be incorporated into the programs and the philosophies behind their implementation.

CanEIRS© vs. USEIRS© — Design features

Minor differences in EIRS designs and philosophies were incorporated into CanEIRS© and USEIRS© as a result of the different regulatory requirements and the variations in approaches to inspection between the Canadian and US Environmental Inspectors. Basic "activity-based reporting" objectives varied between the US and Canada. The US Inspectors utilized Libretto™ or small notebook computers and inspection information was generally entered in the field as the activities occurred. In contrast, the Canadian inspectors preferred traditional laptop computers and reports were prepared at the end of an inspection day.

Menus and features differed slightly between CanEIRS© and USEIRS© due to requirements of the respective inspection teams. For example, the blank reports available under the "Daily Reports" button on the Main Menu (Fig. 2) of CanEIRS© include five additional reports that were not required by the inspectors in the US. These included "Wet Soils," "Equipment Inspection," "Extra Temporary Workspace," and "Watercourse Crossing" reports (Fig. 3). These blank reports were incorporated into CanEIRS© as a response to reporting requirements in the NEB Certificate Terms and Conditions applicable to the Canadian portion of the project.

The "Daily Summary" report was also unique to the Canadian version. The Daily Summary was utilized to pare down information captured in detail in other activity reports to the most significant issues of the day. An "issues checklist" was available to quickly denote noncompliance, incidents/emergencies, action items, trends, variances, etc. for the reader (Fig. 4). The completion of a Daily Summary report each day was mandatory for the Canadian Inspection Team as

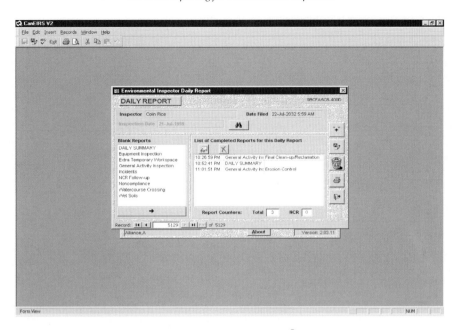

Fig. 3. CanEIRS© included blank reports additional to those found in USEIRS© (Equipment Inspection, Extra Temporary Workspace, Watercourse Crossing, and Wet Soils reports).

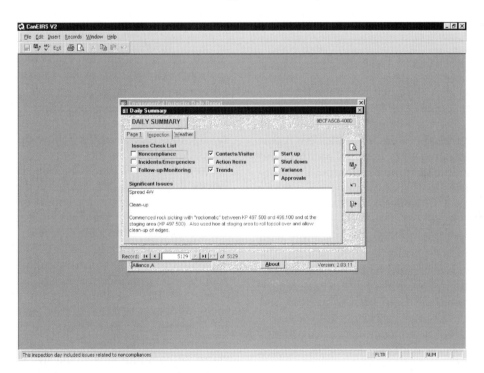

Fig. 4. CanEIRS© mandatory daily summary report was the source report for the Daily Inspection News in Canada.

this report was automatically incorporated into the Canadian Daily Inspection News.

"General Inspection," "Incidents," "Noncompliance," and "Noncompliance (NCR) Follow-up" reports are common to both CanEIRS© and USEIRS©; however, fields within these forms were further modified with respect to the requirements of each of the inspection teams.

The General Inspection reports were to be completed for construction activities that were in compliance with all applicable legislation, specifications, and policies. The "Acceptable Activity Report" (USEIRS©) or "General Activity Inspection" (CanEIRS©) topics were required fields available via drop down menus that varied between CanEIRS© and USEIRS© (for example, USEIRS© contained a "Wetland Construction" activity option that was not available in CanEIRS©). CanEIRS© also contained sub-forms that enabled site specific documentation of any variances to specifications or any further recommendations or follow-up.

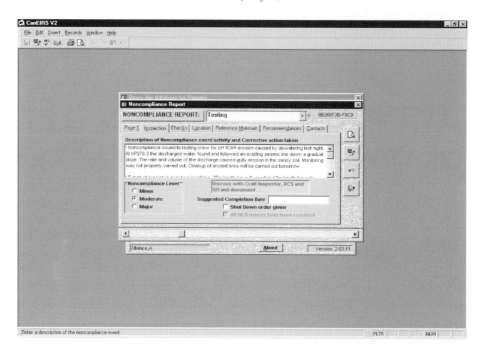

Fig. 5. A follow-up reminder is displayed in a yellow box to the right of the "Noncompliance Level" field that relates to the compliance level definitions pre-assigned by Alliance as guidance in submitting a Noncompliance Report.

These were not separate fields in the USEIRS© activity forms.

Incident reports were designed to document observations for an unexpected event such as a spill or an unanticipated discovery (endangered wildlife species, cultural or heritage resources, etc.). The Incident report event field was a required entry in both CanEIRS© and USEIRS©, although the items available from the drop-down menus varied slightly between systems.

EIs were required to complete a Noncompliance Report (NCR) to document observations for a construction activity or incident that did not comply with applicable legislation, specifications, or policies. Basic information fields such "incident date," "contacts," and "recommendations" were available in both reporting systems. Required fields in both CanEIRS© and USEIRS© included "activity," "spread," and "subject" of the NCR. The level of noncompliance was identified by selecting one of the three levels pre-defined by Alliance. A yellow box to the right of this field would display a follow-up reminder corresponding to the chosen noncompliance level (Fig. 5) as a guide to the EI filing the NCR.

The EIs were required to provide follow-up information regarding the status or resolution of a NCR through the NCR Follow-up Report. When a NCR was classified as either moderate or serious (major) in nature, the EI completed a NCR Follow-up Report documenting any action taken and identifying whether all issues and recommendations associated with the NCR had been resolved. NCR Follow-up reports could be filed at the EI's discretion for NCRs categorized as minor in nature. If a minor NCR issue had been resolved onsite, the EI had the option to check the box indicating that "All NCR issues have been resolved" (Fig. 5) within the NCR.

To track the status of a NCR, the NCR and Follow-up reports must be linked. EIs established this link during the creation of the Follow-up Report via selection of the NCR "Subject" from a drop-down menu in the report form. If the NCR "Subject" was not on the list, or if the EI was reporting on the NCR created by another EI, the Follow-up Report could subsequently be linked by the DB Manager. NCR resolution and status were tracked through the NCR Follow-up feature on the Main Menu (Fig. 2). Lists of all linked and unlinked NCRs and any corresponding NCR Follow-up reports were provided through this window.

In CanEIRS©, a data field for entry of commitment numbers identified in the Canadian Environmental Commitments Database (CanCommit©) was also available. This facilitated the communication of the status of commitments made by Alliance to various regulatory agencies and other stakeholder groups during the regulatory and approval phases of the project to the DB Manager to be recorded.

RESULTS

Environmental Inspection activities for the Alliance Project were first initiated in Canada during the pre-clearing program of Winter 1999. Four EIs mobilized for clearing activities in northwestern Alberta and utilized the initial version of CanEIRS© as a reporting tool. From this test phase, various front-end refinements were incorporated into CanEIRS© prior to full construction kick-off scheduled for June 1999 in Canada, and program adaptations were also completed for the creation of the USEIRS© version for June 1999 construction kick-off.

Activity inspection reports were generally fewer in number per individual in Canada, and tended to contain more detailed written explanations than those submitted by the US Inspectors. As of the end of July 2000, over 27,000 individual activity reports were submitted by US inspectors. During the same period, approximately 13,000 reports were submitted by the Canadian Inspectors.

Survey results received from the Canadian inspectors indicated that the mandatory submission of the Daily Summary reports for the Daily Inspection News was redundant with the submission of the General Activity Inspection reports. However, the Daily Inspection News generated on the Canadian side was typically less than half as long as the US Daily Inspection News, which was typically in excess of 40 pages per day.

Some of the General Activity Inspection reports were not utilized by the inspectors as they were intended for various reasons. For example, the Extra Temporary Workspace form in CanEIRS© was not widely utilized due to the unexpected volume of work associated with the workspace applications as a result of NEB requirements specified in Alliance's Certificate Terms and Conditions. The information volume in the optional fields was not consistent between inspectors. This limited querying abilities of the database in both the US and Canadian versions.

Additional information "Reference" fields (including photographs, videos, sketches) were not consistently utilized. The time requirements for re-labeling the default digital photo names and logging of digital photographs on a daily basis impeded this process to some extent. EIs tended to gather large volumes of digital photos and label them all at once, rather than on a daily basis which would allow for proper referencing in their daily reports.

As the electronic reporting system was a relatively new concept to many of the inspectors, some initial resistance was encountered as they were learning the program. However, the majority of the user issues were hardware related, and not EIRS software related. EI time requirements for reporting decreased markedly with system usage.

The master databases served as excellent search tools for the DB Managers and other environmental staff. Summary documents were easily generated from the systems for purposes of regulatory reporting, compliance monitoring, and follow-up documentation for due diligence purposes. Front-end changes were applied for report-generating features as both internal (Alliance) and external regulatory and stakeholder information requirements became standardized.

DISCUSSION

As construction progressed, refinements to the EIRS systems could be implemented relative to experience gained at the field level, as well as the data management level. However, front-end revision installation and set-up at the field level were sometimes complicated due to the varied computer knowledge levels of the users. Often front-end updates would result in software glitches that affected the transmission of the reports to the DB Manager. This could have been avoided by assigning someone with both software and hardware knowledge to install the front-end updates in the field and trouble-shoot any unique glitches that may arise on the EIs' computers. A more advanced level of training and familiarity with the EIRS software for the computer support personnel outside of the Environment group would have been beneficial to all program users.

EIs also experienced problems associated with data transfer from internet connections in remote areas, which would prolong the time requirements for exporting their reports. This long period of time interrupted by frequent disconnection from the phone lines was the primary source of frustration with the use of CanEIRS© and USEIRS© for the EIs.

Remote access issues also affected the transfer of digital photos on a regular basis. Plans for the construction trailers to have Alliance network access were not realized in time to benefit the Environmental Inspectors. As digital photo files were too large to transport via remote internet connections, many EIs chose to catalogue their photos onsite and send them in batches via "zip" disks. Pertinent photos were still distributed via email; however, typical photos were not forwarded on a daily basis as originally expected during the design of the EIRS. Electronic labeling and cataloguing of the digital photos proved to be an onerous task for many EIs. This again can be related to the individual computer skill sets. Labeling of photos was not always completed at the time of the relative inspection report; therefore this reference field was not consistently utilized.

The US inspectors opted to use the Libretto™ notebook computers, which were smaller than the traditional laptops that were chosen by the Canadian inspectors. The Librettos™ enabled the US inspectors to document activity inspection information on the site of a construction activity. In contrast, the Canadian inspectors maintained hand-written notes that were translated into the electronic report forms at the end of the day on their laptops. This modified the 'activity-based' reporting philosophy to some extent, as was evident through the different formats of the Daily Inspection News.

The inclusion of the "Daily Summary" report in CanEIRS© was beneficial in that it provided a method to summarize pertinent information into one report while documenting the activity details necessary for environmental post-construction reporting and reclamation planning in the activity inspection reports. This decreased the amount of information transmitted to senior management and construction personnel on a daily basis in the Daily Inspection News; however, it was considered a redundant exercise by the CanEIRS© inspector users. The Daily Summary report also provided an opportunity for the EIs to submit their daily activities without separating them into the respective activity reports, which ultimately affected the capabilities of the searching features within CanEIRS©. Although the USEIRS© Daily Inspection News was often in excess of 40 pages, a matrix table was provided on the first page to summarize the total number of environmental inspections conducted and the associated compliance levels. This allowed the reader to quickly identify areas where issues may have arisen, and reference the attached activity inspection reports for further details.

The distribution of the Daily Inspection News in the morning allowed senior level management to provide quick responses to compliance issues and to keep informed of day to day issues on each of the construction spreads. The Daily Inspection News would prompt issue resolution discussions between EIs, construction staff and management from different geographic centers. Through distribution of the environmental inspection news to non-environmental construction staff (for example Alliance Engineering and Land personnel), it instigated involvement of these parties and increased their awareness of and contributions towards environmental compliance.

The electronic reporting systems allowed for identification of trends in non-compliance during construction and provided the ability to identify compliance issues associated by Contractors, construction activities, and geographic locations that may prompt further environmental training for staff or additional follow-up in particular areas. The master database was a powerful tool that could be used to efficiently retrieve and summarize information related to environmental post-construction reporting, reclamation planning, as well as information requested by regulators. However, it was observed that reporting requirements and expectations must be clearly communicated during EI training and properly implemented at the field level in order for the search capabilities of the database to be effective and efficient.

In general, the inspectors responded positively to the use of the EIRS. Through feedback provided by the database users (Environmental Inspectors) surveys, the CanEIRS© system was rated an average of seven out of ten with respect to its efficiency and effectiveness as a tool for communication between the field and the Alliance corporate offices. Similar results were communicated by the US Inspectors. The majority of the inspectors communicated that it was a successful system for environmental inspection reporting; however, refinements to the activity inspection forms could be made to improve the system from a user's perspective and make it more time efficient. Such modifications might include the consolidation of all pipe activity reports (such as bending, welding, lowering-in) into one activity report as opposed to requiring the submission of several reports for activities that have potentially minimal environmental implications. Both CanEIRS© and USEIRS© Daily Inspection News formats had positive and negative attributes associated with them; however, both systems achieved the objective to effectively communicate environmental inspection information to construction staff, senior management, resource specialists, and other Alliance personnel.

CONCLUSION

Overall, the use of an electronic reporting system proved to be a successful means of transferring pertinent environmental information from the field to the corporate level at in a timely manner, and eliciting prompt responses from Alliance senior level management regarding compliance issues. Although not immediately well received by the environmental inspection teams, the CanEIRS© and USEIRS© systems were generally accepted as practical tools once the EIs had the opportunity to become familiar with the system as regular users. The majority of the problems for the inspectors associated with the systems were hardware issues. Training and manpower requirements at both the field and the support levels should not be under-estimated in order to address these issues.

The searchable attributes of the databases have proven to be extremely useful during both the construction and operations phases. Clear communication of expectations and requirements in report preparation is essential during training to ensure information is documented though standard methods for efficient and effective database queries.

ACKNOWLEDGEMENTS

The databases were designed and programmed by Brian Zelt, PhD of E2 Environmental Alliance Inc. — the authors wish to extend thanks for Dr. Zelt's technical expertise and innovation throughout the project. Recognition is also extended to the many members of Natural Resource Group Inc. and TERA Environmental Consultants (Alta.) Ltd., in particular Lorraine Blair, for program and hardware design and testing. A special acknowledgement is extended to Terry Antoniuk (Salmo Consulting Inc.) who held everyone together and facilitated the transformation of a concept to a functional tool with a smile.

REFERENCES

McCullough, J.A. 1997. We, they, us: A case study of environmental compliance. The Tuscarora Gas Transmission Project. In: The Sixth International Symposium on Environmental Concerns in Rights-of-Way Management. J.R. Williams, J.W. Goodrich-Mahoney, J.R. Wisniewski, and J. Wisniewski, eds. New Orleans, LA, USA, Elsevier Science Ltd.

National Energy Board. 1998. Certificate of Public Convenience and Necessity GC-98. Governor in Council Approval. December 3, 1998 by Order in Council P.C. 1998–2176.

BIOGRAPHICAL SKETCHES

Melissa Pockar, PBiol
Environmental Analyst, Alliance Pipeline Ltd., 400, 605-5 Avenue S.W., Calgary, AB T2P 3H5, Canada

Melissa Pockar graduated with a Bachelor of Science degree in Environmental Systems from the University of Lethbridge and joined Alliance Pipeline Ltd. in 1999. One of Ms. Pockar's responsibilities includes the "Database Manager" role for the CanEIRS© system. Ms. Pockar has had previous experience in environmental and reclamation planning in the coal mining industry, and has related experience in the agricultural research sector.

Paul Anderson, MSc, PBiol
Manager, Health, Safety & Environment, Alliance Pipeline Ltd., 400, 605-5 Avenue S.W., Calgary, AB T2P 3H5, Canada

Paul Anderson, is the Manager of Health, Safety & Environment at Alliance Pipeline Ltd. and is responsible for managing health, safety and environmental affairs in both the US and the Canadian portions of the pipeline project. Paul has a Bachelor of Science degree in Biology from the University of Waterloo and a Master of Science degree in Watershed Ecosystems from Trent University.

Julie A. Myhre, PE
Senior Environmental Engineer, Natural Resource Group, Inc., 1800 International Centre, 900 Second Avenue South, Minneapolis, MN 55402, USA

Julie Myhre graduated with a Bachelor of Science degree in Civil Engineering from the University of Minnesota in 1985. She has 15 years experience as an environmental engineer, the past 11 in oil, gas, and fiber optic industry in the United States. Ms. Myhre joined NRG at its inception and provides engineering perspective that bridges the gap between environmental requirements and engineering plans.

Elizabeth N. Dolezal
Senior Scientist, Natural Resource Group, Inc., 1800 International Centre, 900 Second Avenue South, Minneapolis, MN 55402, USA

Elizabeth N. Dolezal is a project manager with Natural Resource Group, Inc, in Minneapolis, Minnesota. Ms. Dolezal manages environmental permitting and regulatory compliance activities for pipeline construction projects. Ms. Dolezal received a MA in Public Administration from the George Washington University, Washington DC. Most recently, Ms. Dolezal was responsible for the coordination and implementation of Alliance's Third Party Monitoring Program, Variance Request Program, and its USEIRS© daily environmental inspection reporting system for the United States portion of the Alliance Pipeline Project.

Operation and Maintenance Activities on Federal Lands: The Great Lakes/Hiawatha National Forest Experience

John W. Muehlhausen and F. Jerry Kott

Operation and maintenance activities on utility rights-of-way frequently result in only minor disturbance and, therefore, require little or no environmental review. However, when they take place on federal land, even seemingly insignificant activities often require comprehensive and lengthy reviews, sometimes with unpredictable outcomes. Great Lakes Gas Transmission Company (Great Lakes) encountered such concerns on its natural gas pipeline right-of-way on Hiawatha National Forest land in the Upper Peninsula of Michigan. The Hiawatha National Forest generically denied authorization to conduct routine vegetation management for several years in the 1990s and indicated it would need to conduct an extensive environmental analysis before approving such activities. A number of factors contributed to this problem, including the agency's misunderstanding of the nature of the proposed activities and how the activities would impact the environment. To resolve this problem, Great Lakes approached the Hiawatha National Forest suggesting development and implementation of a comprehensive Operation and Maintenance Plan for pipeline activities within the Hiawatha National Forest. The plan defined typical operation activities (from vegetation maintenance to pipe dig-ups and replacements); categorized activities by amount of disturbance; identified environmentally sensitive areas along the pipeline route; described best management practices to be implemented in the field; and set time limitations for project notification and review. Prior to implementing the Operation and Maintenance Plan, the average project review time ranged between two and twelve months and had inconsistent results. After implementing the plan, the average review time decreased to about two weeks with all projects being approved. In short, the plan provided a streamlined and predictable approval process for Great Lakes and the Hiawatha National Forest. The Hiawatha National Forest has indicated it would like to use the plan as model for other utilities on its land in the Upper Peninsula. Moreover, the Regional Forest Service Office in Milwaukee, Wisconsin, will be assisting Great Lakes in implementing similar plans across Great Lakes' pipeline system in Minnesota, Wisconsin, and Michigan.

Keywords: Approval, notification, O&M, scope, turnover

INTRODUCTION

Obtaining approval to conduct operation and maintenance activities on federal land can be a time consuming process with unpredictable results. Utility companies often need approvals rather quickly in order to maintain their project schedules. This frequently does not allow sufficient time for agency review. A well designed Operation and Maintenance (O&M) Plan can solve this problem. By means of a case study, this paper will identify common problems with O&M Plans, and provide insight into the structure of a well-designed plan.

THE GREAT LAKES/HIAWATHA NATIONAL FOREST EXPERIENCE

The initial O&M Plan

Great Lakes Gas Transmission Company (Great Lakes) owns and operates a 36-inch-diameter 1000-mile-long

Environmental Concerns in Rights-of-Way Management: Seventh International Symposium
J.W. Goodrich-Mahoney, D.F. Mutrie and C.A. Guild (editors)
© 2002 Elsevier Science Ltd. All rights reserved.

pipeline system that extends from northern Minnesota to southeast Michigan. In 1991, Great Lakes completed a major expansion of its existing pipeline system in Minnesota, Wisconsin, and Michigan. The project involved constructing approximately 460 miles of loop pipeline parallel to an existing main pipeline. The loopline was constructed through a variety of landscapes, including several areas managed by the US Department of Agriculture, Forest Service (or National Forest).

As part of the approval process for the 1991 expansion project, Great Lakes was required to prepare O&M Plans for each of the National Forests crossed by the pipeline. The plans focused on how the upcoming construction would take place and briefly addressed maintenance activities that would be required after construction. At the time, the plans appeared complete because they addressed both construction of the pipeline and maintenance of the right-of-way. However, it later became apparent that the documents were too limited in scope and should have more thoroughly addressed post-construction activities.[1]

After construction of the new pipeline was completed, several years passed before maintenance activities were required within the National Forest. When the time came to seek approval for O&M activities, authorization was difficult to obtain and very time consuming. The National Forest viewed much of the O&M work as new construction and conducted rigorous environmental review of each proposed activity.

In addition to the problems of a narrowly defined O&M Plan, Great Lakes also experienced problems with staff turnover at the Hiawatha National Forest. Between the time the plan was written and the time O&M activities were required, a significant number of National Forest staff, who had worked on the construction project and helped develop the original O&M Plan, were no longer located at the Hiawatha National Forest. The new staff had little experience with utility companies and developed inaccurate ideas as to what had occurred during the construction project. For example, the National Forest was unhappy with the appearance of the pipeline right-of-way where it crossed a national wild and scenic river. The right-of-way was exceptionally wide at this location and the National Forest suggested that visual screening should

Table 1. Summary of project review and approval times from 1996 to 2000

O&M activity (in alphabetic order)	Review and approval times	
	Prior to the new O&M Plan[a]	After the new O&M Plan[b]
Anode Bed Installation		
Request No. 1	21 Weeks	n/a[c]
Civil Surveys		
Request No. 1	5 Weeks	4 Weeks
Erosion Repair/ROW Restoration		
Request No. 1	1 Week	n/a[c]
Request No. 2	1 Day	
Geotechnical Investigations		
Request No. 1	12 Weeks	n/a[c]
Request No. 2	9 Weeks	
Request No. 3	4 Weeks	
Request No. 4	2 Weeks	
Request No. 5	3 Weeks	
Pipe Inspection and Recoating		
Request No. 1	4 Weeks	n/a[c]
Request No. 2	20 Weeks	
Request No. 3	17 Weeks	
Routine Brushing and Clearing		
Request No. 1	Never approved	n/a[c]
Request No. 2	5 Weeks	
Test Wire Lead Installation/Repair		
Request No. 1	21 Weeks	5 Weeks
Request No. 2	10 Weeks	6 Weeks
Average Review and Approval Time	10 Weeks	5 Weeks

[a] From January 1, 1996 to April 21, 1999.
[b] From April 22, 1999 to September 8, 2000.
[c] A request to conduct these types of activities has not been submitted to the Hiawatha National Forest since implementation of the new O&M Plan.

have been planted immediately after construction. In truth, the corridor had been purposely widened at the direction of a National Forest landscape architect who, incidentally, was no longer employed at the Hiawatha National Forest.

Between the narrow scope of the initial O&M Plan and problems with staff turnover and institutional memory, Great Lakes had great difficulty obtaining approval to conduct O&M projects (see Table 1). For example, in 1996, Great Lakes requested approval under its existing O&M Plan to install two new cathodic test wire leads on its pipeline within the Hiawatha National Forest. A test wire lead installation involves excavating a hole approximately 10 feet in diameter by three feet deep over the pipeline and connecting wires to the top of the pipe. National Forest review and approval for the activities required over five months. Great Lakes requested permission for a similar activity in 1998 and approval took over two months to obtain. Between 1996 and the time a new O&M Plan was established (April 22, 1999), Great Lakes requested

---

1 It is understandable that many O&M Plans are somewhat limited in scope. O&M Plans are, after all, required as part of the permitting process for new construction and must discuss how new construction will take place. They therefore tend to focus heavily on the more immediate concerns of the upcoming construction, and touch only lightly on post-construction activities. In many cases, O&M Plans are actually closer to Construction Plans, and are not true O&M Plans. Some land managing agencies, such as the Bureau of Land Management, try to clarify this issue by making a distinction between construction and post-construction activities. They refer to their plans as Construction, Operation, and Maintenance Plans. In Great Lakes' case, this seemingly minor distinction led to regulatory problems in the years following construction.

approval to conduct twelve separate O&M activities. The projects ranged from routine brushing and clearing of the right-of-way corridor, to test lead repair, to excavation for pipe recoating. Some requests were approved within one or two weeks. Others took as long as 21 weeks. One was never approved (routine brushing and clearing were generically denied in 1996, even though such activities were addressed in the O&M Plan). The average review time was more than 10 weeks. Ironically, some of the simplest, least disruptive activities were denied after a long review time, and some of the more complex projects were approved rather quickly.

With variable review times and irregular approvals, neither Great Lakes nor the Hiawatha National Forest were having their needs met. Both Great Lakes and the National Forest were frustrated with the existing process, and both realized the O&M Plan needed to be revised.

The new O&M Plan

In 1996, Great Lakes approached the Hiawatha National Forest regarding permitting for a new pipeline construction project. At that time, Great Lakes' entire 1000-mile-long pipeline system had been entirely looped, except for approximately 25 miles located in the Upper Peninsula of Michigan. The new project involved looping the remaining 25 miles of pipeline, approximately 10 miles of which were located within the Hiawatha National Forest.

Great Lakes and the Hiawatha National Forest used the project as the means to revise the existing O&M Plan. Although the plan could have been revised at any time, the pending construction project prompted communication between the organizations and provided the momentum needed to facilitate the process.

The process of developing a new comprehensive O&M Plan allowed Great Lakes to more accurately define O&M projects. Up to that time, the National Forest's perception of what an O&M activity was comprised of was limited to routine brushing and clearing. The National Forest was somewhat surprised to learn that Great Lakes considered other, less frequent actions to be routine maintenance, such as pipe coating investigation digs, test lead installation, and stream bank repair. The fact that the National Forest did not consider these activities to be O&M was not unreasonable because the existing plan was far too limited in scope.

In developing the new O&M Plan it became readily apparent that the National Forest had many new staff with little or no exposure to pipeline maintenance issues. Also, the National Forest did not have sufficient resources to review the O&M requests submitted by Great Lakes in the level of detail they felt was necessary. Great Lakes was able to educate the National Forest on pipeline maintenance matters and establish trust with the new personnel. This was accomplished by spending significant amounts of time with specialists and management from the Hiawatha National Forest during the review and construction of the aforementioned construction project. Matters that were discussed and agreed upon were completed according to the terms of that agreement, even though they may have been thought to be excessive in the minds of construction personnel. Strict compliance with these measures helped establish the level of trust needed to make the new O&M Plan happen. In turn, the Hiawatha National Forest was able to express its concerns to Great Lakes, including the impacts of construction on wetlands, the visual appearance of a cleared corridor at critical viewpoints, all-terrain vehicle traffic, and staff availability to review the O&M requests.

The first major issue to be resolved was the limited scope of the previous O&M Plan. This was accomplished by agreeing to develop two separate plans — a Construction Plan and a true O&M Plan. The Construction Plan was developed first and addressed how construction of the new project would take place. Following construction, the O&M Plan was rewritten to address activities that would take place on the pipeline and right-of-way over the long term — true maintenance issues. The O&M Plan also included best management practices to make sure that O&M activities would not result in significant impacts on the environment and that they would occur in compliance with various land-use and environmental laws and policies. These include the Hiawatha National Forest Land and Resource Management Plan, the National Environmental Policy Act, and US Department of Agriculture guidelines. The new O&M Plan described the notification procedures to be followed by Great Lakes once an O&M project was identified and the review procedures to be followed by the Hiawatha National Forest to evaluate the project. The plan also discussed various standard mitigation measures to be implemented during O&M activities to ensure that they would not result in significant impacts on the environment. The plan was finalized and placed into service in April 1999. Table 2 summarizes the contents of Great Lakes' revised O&M Plan.

Since establishing the new O&M Plan, Great Lakes has submitted several O&M requests to the Hiawatha National Forest. All requests were approved with an average time of 5 weeks (see Table 1). By way of comparison, average review time was cut in half. The time spent revising the O&M Plan also improved Great Lakes' relationship with the Hiawatha National Forest and benefited Great Lakes in the planning and review of its next project in the National Forest.

Key elements in the new O&M Plan

The first and most important element in the new O&M Plan was a broader scope. The plan was expanded to include a discussion of a variety of typical O&M activities. Identifying and describing typical O&M activities

Table 2. Summary of contents of Great Lakes' O&M plan with the Hiawatha National Forest

Section titles in the O&M Plan
Introduction
Communication
Projection Notification, Review, and Approval Procedures
No Disturbance Activities
Minor Activities
Major Activities
Emergency Situations
Financial Account
Environmental Protection Measures
Environmental Inspection
Approved Work Area and Site Access
Noxious Weed Control
Right-of-Way Clearing
Soil Erosion and Sediment Control
Topsoil Segregation
Pipe Coating and Sand Blasting
Site Dewatering
Hydrostatic Testing
Restoration and Revegetation
Wetland Protection Measures
Stream Protection Measures
Road Protection Measures
Spill Prevention, Containment, and Control
Unanticipated Discover of Heritage Resources or Human Remains
O&M Plan Acceptance
O&M Plan History
Appendix A — Typical Operation and Maintenance Activities
Appendix B — Key Personnel
Appendix C — Operation and Maintenance Project Notification Form
Appendix D — Topographic Maps of the Permanent Right-of-Way

Table 3. List of typical O&M activities

O&M activity
All-Terrain Vehicle Barrier Installation and Repair
Cathodic Protection System Installation and Repair
Geotechnical Investigations
Global Positioning System Monument Installation and Repair
Pipe Coating Inspection, Pipe Lowering, and Pipe Replacement
Pipeline Integrity Surveys
Pipeline Marking Post Installation and Repair
Routine Right-of-Way Clearing
Soil Erosion Control Inspections and Repair
Test Lead Installation and Repair
Topographic and Civil Surveys
Washing and Painting Existing Facilities

provided National Forest staff with a practical reference for evaluating O&M projects, and helped new staff understand exactly what the O&M projects involve. A list of typical activities included in the O&M Plan is summarized in Table 3.

After defining the O&M activities, Great Lakes divided the activities into four main categories: (1) no disturbance, (2) minor projects, (3) major projects, and (4) emergency activities. Notification, review, and approval times were set according to category. A no disturbance project, as its name implies, involves no disturbance to the environment. No vegetation clearing, soil grading, or digging is involved. Additionally, work is not conducted in wetlands or near areas where endangered species are known to occur. Great Lakes provides advance notice of the activities to the Hiawatha National Forest, and, unless a written response is received from the National Forest stating the work cannot be conducted, the activity may be undertaken 72 h after notification. Examples of no disturbance activities include building or facility washing and painting, close interval surveys, and off-road vehicle barrier installation.

Minor projects involve only minimal disturbance — typically less than one or two acres of vegetation clearing, soil grading, or digging in upland areas. Work is not conducted in wetlands or near known endangered species sites. Great Lakes provides a 14-day advance notification of the activity to the Hiawatha National Forest, and must receive written confirmation before undertaking the work. Examples of minor O&M activities included brushing and clearing in upland areas, test lead repair, anode bed installation, and pipe inspection digs.

Major projects involve more disturbance or may involve work in wetlands or near endangered species. Great Lakes is required to provide a 30 day advance notice of the activity, and must receive approval from the National Forest before conducting the work. Examples of major activities include brushing or clearing in wetlands or any work involving extensive pipe excavation.

There is always a possibility that an emergency situation will arise which will require Great Lakes to respond to the situation immediately. In the event of an emergency situation, Great Lakes may, according to its Emergency Plan (a separate document filed with the National Forest), take remedial action to fix the problem, safeguard human health, and prevent damage to the environment. Activities conducted as part of an emergency situation are generally not subject to the conditions of the O&M Plan, except that Great Lakes must verbally inform the Hiawatha National Forest Emergency Contact of the situation within eight hours of undertaking remedial action. Written notification, including an explanation of the circumstances must be sent to the National Forest within 48 hours.

As stated, Great Lakes must receive approval from the Hiawatha National Forest before beginning work on minor or major projects. The Hiawatha National Forest is responsible for responding to Great Lakes within the review period to advise whether the project may proceed as proposed (including any additional mitigation measures that may be required), or whether the project cannot proceed, either because it is not within the scope of the plan, or would result in adverse environmental impacts. If the Hiawatha National Forest determines the project cannot proceed because it is

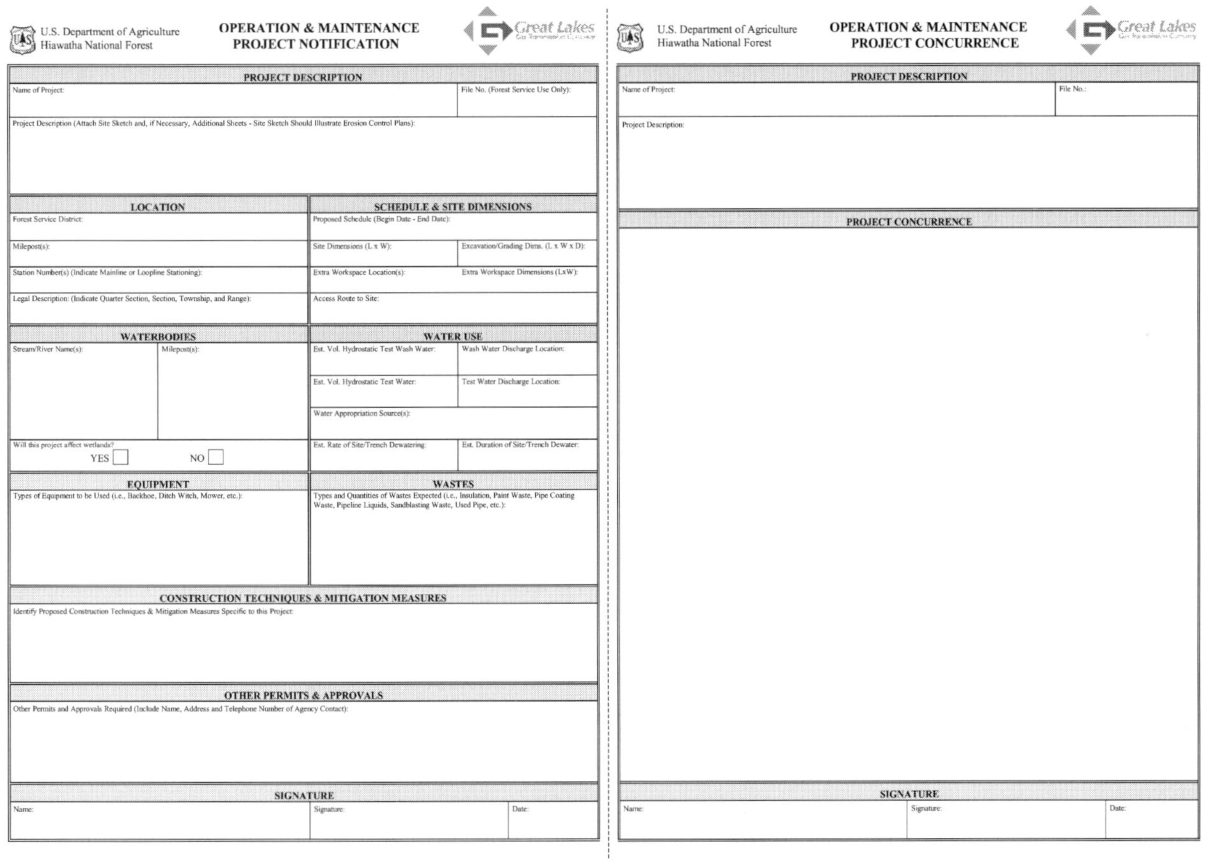

Fig. 1. Notification and approval forms.

not within the scope of the O&M Plan, or that it would result in adverse environmental impacts, the Hiawatha National Forest is required to provide a letter of explanation detailing why the project is not within the scope of this plan or why it believes the project would result in adverse environmental impacts.

Setting review and approval times for different types of O&M project was a significant improvement to the O&M Plan. To further improve the plan, Great Lakes and the National Forest developed a standard O&M project notification form. The notification form was incorporated into the plan and includes areas to describe the type, location, size, schedule, etc. of a proposed O&M activity. A National Forest approval form was also inserted into the document. The approval form provides the Hiawatha National Forest with a consistent method of responding to Great Lakes' O&M requests. Fig. 1 depicts the notification and approval forms.

Maps illustrating the pipeline route and environmentally sensitive features were also incorporated into the O&M Plan. The maps allow Great Lakes and the National Forest to consistently identify sensitive areas along the pipeline and plan work accordingly. The maps also provide the Hiawatha National Forest with a convenient reference for their environmental review. The maps are based on 7.5 minute USGS topographic maps and identify a wide variety of environmental features along the pipeline route. Features include: streams; wetlands; known cultural resources; known threatened, endangered, and sensitive species; highly erodible soils; visually sensitive areas; etc. The maps, which were developed using Geographical Information Systems, were attached as an appendix to the O&M Plan in hard copy and provided to the National Forest electronically. Information on cultural resources and protected species were available from field surveys performed for previous construction projects.

To ease the National Forest's concerns that O&M activities would be conducted in an environmentally responsible manner, environmental protection measures were integrated into the O&M Plan. Environmental protection measures actually comprise a bulk of the plan and describe in detail the procedures that Great Lakes will implement in the field. These measures are similar in nature to those found the Federal Energy Regulatory Commission's Plan and Procedures for pipeline construction. Examples of environmental protection measures include, requirements for annual walkovers of the pipeline right-of-way, restrictions on the width of clearing allowed within the permanent right-of-way, stipulations for bridging all streams, provisions for erosion control, etc.

Both Great Lakes and the Hiawatha National Forest also recognized that regular, ongoing communication would be integral to resolving problems associated with staff turn over. Great Lakes and the National Forest inserted a requirement in the O&M Plan to meet twice a year specifically to discuss O&M issues. At these meeting, discussions focus on Great Lakes' foreseeable O&M activities, anticipated Hiawatha National Forest activities that could affect Great Lakes' plans (e.g., road improvements and closures, Land and Resource Management Plan amendments, etc.), proposed amendments to the O&M Plan, and any other issues that warrant attention. This regular, ongoing communication keeps National Forest staff familiar with O&M activities and provides Great Lakes with an opportunity to address any questions or concerns they may have.

The new O&M Plan also contains a list of key personnel for both Great Lakes and the Hiawatha National Forest. Key personnel are contacts at Great Lakes and the Hiawatha National Forest who should be called regarding questions, comments, or concerns on the O&M Plan or specific activities. Having a list of key personnel keeps the appropriate people at both organizations in communication with each another, and help prevents misunderstandings that can occur when too many or the wrong individuals are involved in a process.

Staff and funding are always short at the National Forest, therefore, the O&M Plan incorporated a provision to allow the National Forest to be reimbursed by Great Lakes for time spent evaluating O&M activities. The O&M Plan required Great Lakes to establish a financial account to be used by the Hiawatha National Forest to resolve the staff and funding problem. At the beginning of each year, Great Lakes deposits funds into a financial account to maintain a predetermined level. Throughout the year, the Hiawatha National Forest draws on the account to cover costs associated with review of O&M projects and for any needed field inspection of the pipeline corridor.

CONCLUSIONS

Great Lakes' O&M Plan has been successful. It streamlined the notification, review, and approval process; it improved communication and trust; and it made the process predictable for both Great Lakes and the Hiawatha National Forest. Currently, the Hiawatha National Forest is asking other utilities crossing its boundaries to revise their O&M Plans to make them similar to Great Lakes' plan. In addition, other National Forests in the Region have become aware of the plan and are requesting Great Lakes to update their plans in those Forests.

ACKNOWLEDGEMENTS

The authors of this paper would like to thank Bob Walker, Bill Bowman, and Jim Phillips at Hiawatha National Forest for their tireless effort and vast contributions to the O&M Plan.

BIOGRAPHICAL SKETCHES

John W. Muehlhausen

Natural Resource Group, Inc., 1800 International Centre, 900 Second Avenue South, Minneapolis, MN 55402, USA, Phone: 612-347-6783, E-mail: jwmuehlhausen@nrginc.com, Fax: 612-347-6780

John W. Muehlhausen has worked as a consultant to the natural gas pipeline industry for nine years. Mr. Muehlhausen is a senior scientist for Natural Resource Group, Inc. and is responsible for environmental permitting and compliance activities for pipeline construction projects, including overall project management and the preparation of federal, state, and local permit documents. His background in archaeology and computer science also serves his clients in cultural resource management and the development and support of management information systems, including geographical information systems. Mr. Muehlhausen received a Bachelor of Arts in Anthropology from the University of Wisconsin, Madison, WI, in 1991.

F. Jerry Kott, PE

Great Lakes Gas Transmission Company, 5250 Corporate Drive, Troy, MI 48098, USA, Phone: 248-205-7451, E-mail: fjkott@glgt.com, Fax: 248-205-7475

Jerry Kott has worked in the pipeline industry for over 22 years. His responsibilities have included project management, construction administration and most recently environmental compliance for Great Lakes Gas Transmission Company. Jerry attended Michigan Technological University and holds a BS in Civil Engineering. He is a registered Professional Engineer in the state of Michigan.

The Iroquois Pipeline Operating Company Environmental Compliance Program

Kevin C. Owen and J. Tim Barnes

Between 1996 and 1999, the Iroquois Pipeline Operating Company (IPOC) overhauled the environmental compliance program of the company. Although most aspects of this revised environmental program were in place by 1999, this is a dynamic program that is being continually reviewed and, as needed, revised. The purpose of this paper is to discuss the different components of the IPOC environmental compliance program. This program includes:

1. A computerized database of the requirements that regulate IPOC;
2. A company-wide environmental procedure manual;
3. Computerized environmental compliance summary reports documenting the environmental controls that are in place;
4. A computerized environmental permitting database;
5. Environmental reviews within the computerized IPOC Work Order system;
6. An IPOC Environmental Compliance Committee to review and update the company compliance program;
7. Direct reporting of the IPOC Environmental Manager to management;
8. An in-house environmental training program; and
9. Internal and external audits and internal environmental compliance inspections.

IPOC is committed to environmental compliance and has developed a comprehensive program to ensure compliance. Now that the program is in place, IPOC continues to monitor environmental regulations and requirements to maintain compliance.

Keywords: Regulatory, permits, monitoring, procedures

INTRODUCTION

The Iroquois Pipeline Operating Company (IPOC) operates a 180 mile long pipeline system that runs from the St. Lawrence River to Long Island, New York. The gas transmission system, which includes three compressor stations and other facilities, passes through portions of New York State and Connecticut, including Long Island Sound. Like most interstate pipelines, the construction, operation and maintenance (O&M) of this gas transmission system are regulated by the environmental programs of a number of Federal, New York State (NYS), and Connecticut agencies. In some instances, the regulatory programs are administered through several different offices of the same agency. For example, portions of the IPOC system are regulated by the New York City and Buffalo Districts and New England Division of the Corps of Engineers (COE).

Tracking compliance with the myriad of environmental requirements administered by a host of agencies is a complicated task. In 1996, IPOC committed to establishing a comprehensive environmental compliance program for the company. This program was considered necessary to ensure that all activities were conducted in accordance with the applicable federal and states' laws and regulations and the conditions of the regulatory approvals obtained for the gas transmission system.

The development of the environmental compliance program consisted of several steps and involved most departments within the IPOC organization. These

steps included:
- Review of applicable laws, rules, regulations, permits, and court orders to create an environmental compliance manual and database;
- Development of environmental procedures to address all of the items in the environmental compliance database;
- Development of a company-wide training program on the environmental compliance program;
- Creation of a system to update the procedures to reflect changing regulatory requirements;
- Implementing the environmental compliance program on a company-wide basis; and
- Conducting audits of the environmental compliance program.

By 1999, all of the major components of the environmental compliance program were in-place and were being implemented. This paper provides an overview of this program and the steps IPOC is taking to maintain environmental compliance.

ENVIRONMENTAL COMPLIANCE MANUAL AND DATABASE

As a first step in the environmental compliance program, an environmental compliance manual (ECM) was developed for the company. The ECM was prepared mainly by the IPOC legal department with the assistance of outside law firms and attorneys. The ECM, in its present form, includes:
- A statement setting forth the environmental policy of the company with a commitment to conducting all company business in compliance with applicable laws;
- A review of the environmental regulatory documents including agencies' filings, permits, and regulations that pertain to the Iroquois system; and
- The environmental compliance summary database.

The environmental compliance summary database is a computerized database of specific conditions of permits and court rulings and other regulatory decisions that IPOC must comply with. The database includes each permit condition, the regulatory document the requirement comes from, and an identification of the procedures that have been developed to implemented that requirement. This database became the basis for the environmental compliance program that Iroquois has developed.

ENVIRONMENTAL PROCEDURES MANUAL

Once the compliance database was in place, IPOC then developed an Environmental Procedures Manual (EPM) to address each regulatory requirement in the compliance database. The EPM was developed primarily by the IPOC environmental department with the assistance of outside environmental consulting firms. All procedures were reviewed and approved by the IPOC legal, environmental, and engineering departments before implementation.

The EPM consists of five sections of procedures and a reference index. The sections of the EPM include procedures that address:
- Environmental permitting, monitoring, and compliance reviews;
- Environmental training requirements;
- Environmental requirements for construction and earth disturbances;
- Waste management; and
- ROW maintenance and emergency, and spill response plans.

Each individual procedure includes an introduction and sections on personal safety, notifications, equipment, and materials needed, references, instructions, and documentation or reporting. Currently, the EPM contains over 100 procedures.

ENVIRONMENTAL COMPLIANCE COMMITTEE

To ensure the EPM addressed all of the requirements in the compliance database, IPOC established an Environmental Compliance Committee (ECC). The ECC consists of the environmental department manager, the compliance coordinator from the legal department, and a representative for the director of engineering. The ECC also includes an office support person that serves as the ECC Administrator.

While the EPM was being developed, the ECC met on a regular basis to review and approve the environmental procedures being written. Since the completion of the EPM, the ECC meets at least once a month. At these meetings, the ECC reviews any new or revised procedures that may be proposed to ensure that accepted changes have been properly incorporated into the procedures. The ECC also reviews any new or amended regulations to ensure the procedures remain current. When a procedure or revision has been accepted, each member of the ECC (with the exception of the analyst) signs the procedure.

When new or amended procedures have been accepted by the ECC and revised, the ECC Administrator distributes the updates to all IPOC personnel that hold copies of the EPM. The manual holders sign a form acknowledging that they have read and understand the revisions and have updated their copy of the EPM. The ECC Administrator maintains a database of the changes to the EPM and the signed acknowledgement forms. These activities of the ECC are intended to keep the IPOC EPM current with regulatory changes that may occur.

ENVIRONMENTAL TRAINING

Implementation of the compliance program throughout the IPOC system is one of the most critical components of the program. To be successfully implemented, the procedures and manuals must be understood and used by IPOC personnel. Environmental training helps ensure that the users understand the compliance program. Accordingly, IPOC has implemented annual and pre-job training programs.

Three formats are used for the environmental training programs. These formats are:
- Videotaped training modules used both for orientation training of new personnel and pre-job training in long-duration projects;
- Computerized, web-based training for general awareness and annual training programs; and
- Classroom or field training most technical topics and project-specific pre-job training.

The amount of training each employee receives is determined by the ECC based upon each employee's job duties and description. A questionnaire is filled out by each employee on a yearly basis to confirm the job responsibilities of each person. The environmental department maintains records of the environmental training the personnel receive.

ENVIRONMENTAL AUDITING

IPOC conducts audits monitoring the implementation of the compliance program. Two types of audits are conducted; audits by the companies that form the ownership partnership of the Iroquois Gas system and audits by external third party companies. To date, either one or both types of audits have been conducted on an annual basis. Each audit has focused on a different aspect of the IPOC Compliance program; such as permits and compliance issues, random analysis of the compliance database; and specific procedures.

The results of the environmental audits are provided to IPOC for review. The ECC responds to audit issues and provides the response to the legal department. As required, aspects of the IPOC environmental compliance program are revised in response to the issues raised in the audits.

ENVIRONMENTAL PERMITS DATABASE

IPOC maintains a computerized environmental permits database. The database contains important information regarding each permit. The permits are scanned into the IPOC computer system and are electronically linked to the database. In this manner, the permits are routed to, and maintained in, one computer database. This system allows permit information and copies of the permits to be quickly accessed and retrieved.

ENVIRONMENTAL FILING SYSTEM

The environmental filing system is an important component of the compliance program. The environmental master files are divided into system-wide and project (or facility) specific files designated by a two letter identification (i.e., SW denotes system-wide topics). The system-wide and project specific files are then divided into topics using a numbering system. The topic numbering system is the same for all projects.

Environmental department personnel assign the filing number to each document filed. This system enables IPOC to file documents on a quicker and more consistent basis. Since the coding system is the same for all projects, there is less of a chance that the documents will be misfiled. The documents are more easily and quickly retrieved.

WORK ORDER SYSTEM

IPOC utilizes a computerized work order system for operational and maintenance (O&M) projects. As a work order is being prepared, the project initiator must complete a checklist that covers environmental compliance issues. If any of the environmental issues are marked, the work order is automatically sent to the environmental department for review and approval. The work cannot be initiated until the environmental department has approved the work order and informs the project manager that the necessary environmental approvals have been received. The work order contains a section for environmental cautions in which the environmental requirements for the work are listed. This approved work order is then sent into the field for implementation.

MONTHLY FACILITY INSPECTIONS

To help ensure the compliance program is being implemented, monthly environmental inspections of the compressor stations and warehouse facilities are conducted. A checklist is completed for each facility at each inspection. If compliance issues are identified, the inspector completes an action item checklist that identifies the actions to be taken and establishes target completion dates. Facility personnel are given a signed copy of the action item list and return a signed copy to the environmental department when the actions are completed. IPOC has developed a computerized database to track the action list items and document that the situations are resolved. The environmental department manager reviews these monthly inspection reports before the reports are filed.

CONSTRUCTION INSPECTIONS

Environmental inspectors are assigned to capital and O&M field projects. The inspectors may be either IPOC or contract personnel who typically conduct the environmental pre-job training for project personnel. The EPM contains instructions, forms, and checklists for the environmental inspectors to follow. The environmental inspectors are responsible for monitoring the field work and report to either the environmental project leader or the environmental department manager.

CONCLUSION

IPOC is committed to environmental compliance in all aspects of the company's operations. To achieve this goal, IPOC has committed considerable time and resources researching the applicable permits and regulatory requirements. An Environmental Procedures Manual has been developed to provide guidance and monitoring for the company's compliance efforts. IPOC has begun implementing the system-wide environmental compliance program. The environmental compliance program and procedures manual are both dynamic and are updated and revised as needed. IPOC continues to monitor environmental regulations and requirements to keep the Environmental Procedures Manual and compliance program current and up-to-date.

BIOGRAPHICAL SKETCHES

Kevin C. Owen (corresponding author)

Iroquois Pipeline Operating Company, One Corporate Drive, Suite 600, Shelton, CT 06484, USA, Fax # (203) 925-7213, E-mail: kc_owen@iroquois.com

Kevin C. Owen is a scientist with over 22 years of environmental experience. He is currently an E&HS Projects Leader at the Iroquois Pipeline Operating Company. Kevin has Bachelors' degrees in Biology and Geology, a MS in oceanography, a MS in Environmental Sciences and a MA in Biology. Kevin has over 20 technical publications and conference presentations to his credit.

J. Tim Barnes

Iroquois Pipeline Operating Company, One Corporate Drive, Suite 600, Shelton, CT 06484, USA

J. Tim Barnes is currently Manager of Environmental, Health, and Safety (EHS) for Iroquois Pipeline Operating Company, headquartered in Shelton, Connecticut. Prior to joining Iroquois, he was a member of the EHS staff of NorAm Gas Transmission (now a part of Reliant) and worked as a Landscape Architect for the Missouri Department of Natural Resources. Tim received his Bachelors of Science degree in Biology from Louisiana College and attended graduate school in Landscape Architecture at Louisiana State University in Baton Rouge, Louisiana. In 1998, he completed a Masters of Science degree in Environmental Science from the University of New Haven. Tim is currently working on a Masters' degree in Occupational Health and Safety Management through Tulane University.

Variability in Avoiding Impacts on Endangered Species: The Sault Looping Project Experience

Todd A. Mattson and F. Jerry Kott

The amount of information available on endangered species distribution and biology can directly affect the cost and schedule of a pipeline construction project. For many endangered species, this information is readily available and appropriate avoidance measures are generally not difficult to identify. For some species, however, the lack of available information makes it difficult to predict project-related effects and leads to variable approaches in avoiding impacts on endangered species. Great Lakes Gas Transmission Limited Partnership recently proposed to construct a 14.1-mile-long pipeline loop in the Hiawatha National Forest in the upper peninsula of Michigan. Twelve endangered species were known to occur in or near the project area. The treatment of two of these species, the American hart's-tongue fern and the Hine's emerald dragonfly, illustrates how the amount of information available for a species can affect a project. The fern is a readily identifiable species that had been found in the project area. Because the biology of this species is relatively well understood, it was possible to identify potential impacts on the species and develop appropriate measures to avoid those impacts. By contrast, less information is available on the biology of the dragonfly. Consequently, surveys to determine the species' presence were difficult to design and measures to avoid the species were, for the most part, found to be impractical or infeasible. Although ultimately not found in the project area, the potential occurrence of the dragonfly resulted in a one-year project delay. This paper examines how these species affected the regulatory and construction planning process and provides insights on managing endangered species compliance.

Keywords: Hine's emerald dragonfly, hart's-tongue fern, Endangered Species Act, biological assessments

INTRODUCTION

A large and growing number of plants and animals are protected by endangered species regulations in the United States. In general, life history and ecological information is more readily available for endangered species than for many non-game and/or economically unimportant species. However, because of their inherent rarity and other difficulties in studying endangered species, basic biological information is often lacking for many species. Construction projects being developed often adopt widely varying approaches when addressing mitigation for endangered species (e.g., temporal or spatial avoidance), due to the limited understanding of the biology and the vast differences in the life history characteristics of the species. This problem is further complicated because species are often being added or removed from endangered species lists. Several relatively complicated issues that illustrate the dynamic nature of handling endangered species concerns were identified during the permitting process for a small pipeline construction project in the Upper Peninsula of Michigan. The following discussion is presented to assist right-of-way project managers in dealing with the variability inherent in addressing endangered species concerns.

PROJECT BACKGROUND

Great Lakes Gas Transmission-Limited Partnership (Great Lakes) owns and operates a 36-inch-diameter natural gas pipeline system, which extends about 1000 miles in Minnesota, Wisconsin, and Michigan. In addition to its 36-inch mainline system, Great Lakes owns and operates a smaller 44-mile-long natural gas pipeline in the Upper Peninsula of Michigan known as the Sault Mainline. The Sault Mainline connects to Great Lakes' 36-inch mainline system near Brevort, Michigan, and extends northeast to Sault Ste. Marie, Michigan where it connects to a TransCanada Pipelines, Limited pipeline at the international border. For most of its route, the Sault Mainline consists of a 10.75-inch-diameter mainline paralleled by a 12.75-inch-diameter loopline. A loopline is a parallel segment of pipeline that is connected to the mainline at both ends. Within the project area, however, the Sault Mainline consists of a single 10.75-inch-diameter mainline with no loopline.

Great Lakes began agency consultations in late 1997 to construct 14.1 miles of 12.75-inch-diameter pipeline along this unlooped portion of the Sault Mainline. About 11 miles of the project is located on federal land within the Hiawatha National Forest (HNF). Although initially proposed for the spring of 1999, construction of the project did not begin until July 2000.

REGULATORY COMPLIANCE

During the fall of 1997, Great Lakes began consultation with the Federal Energy Regulatory Commission (FERC) and the HNF regarding environmental permitting requirements for the Sault Looping Project. Construction of the new loopline required a Certificate of Public Convenience and Necessity from the FERC and a Special Use Permit Amendment from the HNF. These federal actions required compliance with several environmental regulations including the National Environmental Policy Act (NEPA), the Endangered Species Act of 1973 (ESA), and the National Forest Management Act of 1976 (NFMA).

In order to comply with the above stated regulations, consultation with appropriate agencies was initiated in late 1997 to identify endangered or threatened species that could potentially be found in the project area. The US Fish and Wildlife Service identified the American Hart's-tongue fern (*Phyllitis scolopendrium* var. *americana*) as the only federally listed species potentially occurring in the project area. Additional consultations with the HNF and the Michigan Department of Natural Resources identified that the project area may have more than 76 plants and animals designated as state-listed endangered or threatened or Forest Service sensitive species.

Also during this time period, the HNF was designated the lead federal agency for purposes of compliance with NEPA. In early 1998, the HNF determined that an Environmental Assessment (EA) would be necessary for the project. Great Lakes' project planners estimated that environmental review and permitting should be initiated 18 months prior to beginning construction. This meant that all field surveys would need to be performed during the summer of 1998 to allow construction to proceed as scheduled in the summer of 1999.

SAULT LOOPING PROJECT ENDANGERED SPECIES ISSUES

A biological assessment was prepared by Great Lakes, and submitted to the respective state and federal agencies for their approval, in an effort to determine whether any protected species would be adversely affected by construction of the project. The assessment included a series of biological surveys for species potentially affected by the project, and included surveys for flowering plants, songbirds, and raptors. Species such as the federally listed endangered gray wolf (*Canis lupus*) and the state-listed threatened lake sturgeon (*Acipenser fulvescens*) were known to occur in the project area; but because no impacts were expected, further surveys for these species were not required.

During the botanical surveys, five protected plants were found within or adjacent to the construction right-of-way. These included the federally listed threatened American hart's-tongue fern, the state-listed threatened walking-fern spleenwort (*Asplenium rhizophyllum*) and flattened spike rush (*Eleocharis compressa*), and a Forest Service designated regionally sensitive species — the northern wild comfrey (*Cynogolossum virginianum* var. *boreale*). Although the life history and ecological requirements of these species are all unique, a fairly straight forward approach was used to expedite environmental review and permitting for these protected plants, as illustrated in the following example of the American hart's-tongue fern.

American hart's-tongue fern example
The distribution of the American hart's-tongue fern (see Fig. 1) is limited to a few sites in the eastern United States and Canada. These small, low-growing plants require a combination of high humidity, cool temperatures, shade provided by a mature forest canopy or overhanging rock cliffs, and a moist substrate (Doherty, 1993). Plants in Michigan have been found in rich, rocky woodlands in proximity to or on limestone boulders and outcrops at a few locations in the Upper Peninsula. Seven colonies of American hart's-tongue fern were discovered during the initial plant surveys in the summer of 1998. The colonies were observed to be growing on moss-covered boulders that were around 120 feet from the centerline of the proposed pipeline.

As originally proposed, installation of the loopline through the American hart's-tongue fern area would require widening an existing open right-of-way through a mature northern hardwood forest. Although the ferns would not be directly affected by construction, botanists with the HNF were concerned that changes to the canopy structure would change the microclimatic conditions where the ferns were found growing. Very little information is available regarding the long-term response of ferns to changes in overstory conditions and moisture regimes, however studies suggest that changes in overstory cover can result in the desiccation of individual ferns and reduced colony vigor (Penskar et al., 1997; US Fish and Wildlife Service, 1993). Consequently, a plan was developed to avoid additional forest clearing within 250 feet from any fern colony (see Fig. 2). Additionally, the plan included minor rearrangements to the route of the new pipeline to neck down, or minimize, the separation between the new and existing pipeline in the area of the ferns. Furthermore, refueling, concrete coating of the pipe, trench dewatering, and hydrostatic test water discharges would not be allowed within 250 feet of any colony. Establishing a conservative protective buffer around the ferns placed a relatively minor constraint on the construction — for a distance of less than 0.25 mile of the project. This approach adequately protected the plants and avoided the need for further, potentially time-consuming consultations with the HNF and the US Fish and Wildlife Service.

Based on even the most fundamental knowledge regarding habitat requirements of the American hart's-tongue fern, it was relatively straightforward to develop a plan that simply avoided impact on the species, either directly or indirectly, through alteration of its habitat. A similar approach was taken with several other protected plants on this project and proved equally successful. Conversely, it is more difficult to develop mitigation plans for protected species where

Fig. 1. American hart's-tongue fern (*photograph courtesy of Peterson Environmental Consulting, Inc.*).

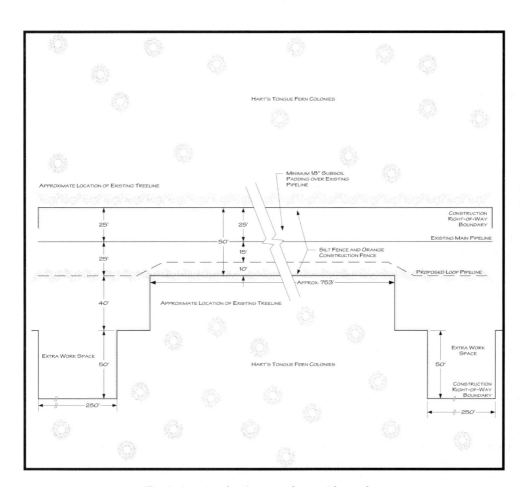

Fig. 2. American hart's-tongue fern avoidance plan.

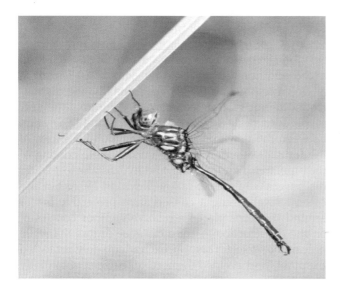

Fig. 3. Hine's emerald dragonfly (*photograph courtesy of E.D. Cashatt*).

detailed information on life history and/or distribution is lacking. The Hine's emerald dragonfly illustrates some of the difficulties associated with identifying the presence and avoiding impacts on an endangered species for which relatively little biological information is available.

Hine's emerald dragonfly example

During preliminary consultations with the US Fish and Wildlife Service, the Hine's emerald dragonfly (see Fig. 3) was not identified as a species potentially occurring in the project area. However, surveys being conducted within the HNF during this same time period, yet unrelated to the project, discovered several occurrences of this federally listed endangered species near the project area (Steffens, 1997). These occurrences were the first identified in Michigan and extended the range of this species by approximately 120 miles. Because the dragonfly was first discovered in Michigan during the summer of 1997, many of the resource agencies in the state did not become aware of its existence until 1998, when a report of the discovery was finalized and widely distributed. During discussions with HNF resource specialists in late 1998, the Hine's emerald dragonfly was finally identified as being potentially affected by the project. At this point in time, Great Lakes was expecting the imminent completion of the EA and subsequent issuance of permits and/or releases to allow construction in the summer of 1999.

Then current information regarding distribution of the Hine's emerald dragonfly limited occurrence to a few counties in Illinois, Wisconsin, and Michigan, although it formerly occurred in Indiana and Ohio as well. The species is typically associated with wetlands or streams with high water quality, often at calcareous marshes that overlay dolomite bedrock (US Fish and Wildlife Service, 1999). In Illinois and Wisconsin, it has been found in wetland complexes consisting of several natural communities such as marsh, sedge meadow, dolomite prairie, spring, seep, and pond. Very little information is available on the habitat requirements of this species in Michigan. Preliminary surveys indicate it is associated with calcareous fens and fen/conifer swamp complexes that appear to be spring-fed (Steffens, 1997).

Use of habitats by the Hine's emerald dragonfly depends on its life stage. Wetland communities are a critical habitat component because they provide appropriate conditions for larval development (Clemency, 1999). The Hine's emerald passes through three life-cycle stages: aquatic egg, aquatic larva, and terrestrial/aerial adult. The adults, or reproductive stage, may live for only a few months during the summer, at which time they breed and lay their eggs in wet sand, mud, or moss at water's edge. Although adults are able to fly, they tend to remain relatively close to the aquatic habitats where they lay their eggs. The larval stage is entirely aquatic and may live for several years. Unlike other dragonflies with a relatively long-life cycle, the larval stage of the Hine's emerald may survive in areas lacking permanent water. Hine's emerald larvae have been collected from streamlets that have been observed to dry up and appear uninhabitable (Soluk et al., 1998). The Hine's emerald survives over the cold winter months in the larval or egg stage.

Hine's emerald dragonfly larvae may become less active and/or crawl into tight spaces during cooler water temperatures in fall and spring (Soluk et al., 1998). Collectors have been unsuccessful in finding any larvae in streamlets during this time, even in streamlets that previously contained larvae. This overwintering behavior and possible shift in habitat is an important aspect of the larval life history, which effectively limits surveys to the summer months and makes assessment of impacts very difficult. Larval surveys and impact assessments are further complicated because Hine's emerald dragonfly larvae cannot be reliably distinguished from several non-protected dragonfly species (US Fish and Wildlife Service, 1999).

By the time that the Hine's emerald dragonfly was identified as potentially occurring in the project area it was too late in the year to conduct field studies. Consequently, the initial evaluation was limited to a review of existing resources — the wetland delineation report for the project, color infrared aerial photographs of the area, a soil survey report, topographic maps, and consultations with ecologists familiar with the pipeline route. Although no areas were identified as high potential habitat for Hine's emerald dragonflies, nearly 25% of the project route crossed wetlands that were at least marginally suitable for this species. Because the understanding of what constitutes suitable habitat for the Hine's emerald dragonfly is limited (particularly in Michigan); the evaluation took a very conservative approach. Avoidance of impact on the larval stages of this species, through the use of horizontal directional drill techniques, was not considered technically feasible for two major reasons. The potentially suitable habitats were found over such an extensive portion of the project that they extended beyond the capability of the drilling equipment. These areas were characterized by shallow non-consolidated bedrock, in which there is a high likelihood of drilling fluid escaping into the wetland.

Based on the initial habitat evaluation, the HNF concluded that more definitive information (e.g., site-specific surveys) would be needed before further proceeding with the environmental review for the project. Because of the lack of information on habitat requirements and the difficulty in accurately identifying larval stages, the additional data could only be reliably collected during the adult flight period the upcoming summer. The time window for the field studies, along with uncertainties surrounding the results and possible mitigation led to the decision to postpone construction for one year into the summer of 2000. It should be noted that all agencies involved in the review of the proposed field study plan worked with Great Lakes to expedite development and approval of the plan and assure that it was ready for the summer survey season.

The additional field surveys for the Hine's emerald dragonfly were conducted in two phases. The first phase included an early-season field visit to further refine the prior identification of potential Hine's emerald dragonfly habitats. The second phase included an adult flight survey to confirm the dragonflies' presence or absence in areas affected by the Sault Looping Project. Although biologists visited potential habitat on two separate occasions during the peak adult flight period, no Hine's emerald dragonflies were found in the vicinity of the project.

As part of the environmental review, the HNF determined that impacts on the vegetation and hydrology of potentially suitable, but unoccupied, dragonfly habitats would be short-term and that wetland vegetation and hydrology would return to preconstruction conditions within one to two growing seasons following construction. Consequently, the HNF determined the Hine's emerald dragonfly would not be adversely affected by the Sault Looping Project.

DISCUSSION

The lack of consistent, comprehensive data on the distribution, life history, and ecological requirements of rare and endangered species will continue to prove problematic for projects under development that are required to address potential impacts on endangered species. A further complication is the fact that the number of species being added to the federal list of threatened and endangered species is growing, and that the rate of new listings has increased over time (Flather et al., 1994). Of particular concern is

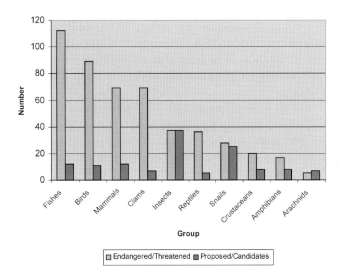

Fig. 4. Numbers of animals that are listed as endangered/threatened or that are proposed/candidates for listing under the Endangered Species Act of 1973 (*US Fish and Wildlife Service, 2000*).

the current list of 295 species that are candidates or proposed for listing under the ESA. These species are represented by a preponderance of more obscure and less ecologically well known species, particularly invertebrates (see Fig. 4). Although it is has been predicted that invertebrates will dominate the list of species at risk in the future, relatively little is known about the population status or life histories of most invertebrates.

Detailed biological information for the more obscure and less popularly known species will most likely continue to be deficient. The general public tends to show bias towards large, charismatic species and more funding is available for studying these species (Czech et al., 1998). Consequently, much more information tends to be available on the ecology, population status and distribution of the charismatic and readily identifiable birds and mammals compared to species such as insects and amphibians, which tend to hold less popular appeal (Breck, 2000).

It is not uncommon for some to view environmental regulations and natural resources agencies as a threat to economic development and landowner rights. Although attempts have been made to weaken the ESA, there is strong public support for species protection and conservation (Czech et al., 1998). Nevertheless, while legal mandates of the ESA remain largely unchanged and the number of species protected by the ESA continues to increase, yearly expenditures on endangered species research and recovery appears to be shrinking (US House of Representative Committee on Resources, 1998). Invertebrate research and recovery efforts, in particular, only receive a fraction of the money spent on mammals, birds, and fish (Czech et al., 1998). Our limited understanding of the biology of groups of organisms such as insects is likely to continue to complicate regulatory compliance. It should be stressed that although funding for endangered species is waning, the agencies are obligated to fulfill their requirements under ESA. The way that agencies fulfill that obligation is to fund this research as survey requirements for projects similar to the Sault Looping Project.

Given the linear nature of pipelines and other corridor-oriented development (i.e., power lines, water pipelines, roadways, etc.), these types of projects often cross a wide variety of ecosystems and/or habitat types. Although impacts may not always be viewed as significant or permanent in nature, there is a high potential for construction projects to encounter many different endangered species that may have quite different habitat and life history characteristics. Compliance with endangered species regulations is greatly complicated due to the ever-changing, dynamic nature of our knowledge of the species involved. As we learn more about an individual species' life history, ecological requirements, and distribution, the species may be added or removed from endangered species lists, and methods to avoid or mitigate impacts on the species may be updated. For example, during the two-year environmental review process for the Sault Looping Project the status of the Canadian lynx was changed from "proposed" to "threatened" under the ESA; the National Forest Service, Region 9, updated its sensitive species list to include 58 species not previously included and the state of Michigan updated its list of state-threatened and endangered species. Additionally, the Hine's emerald dragonfly was discovered in the Upper Peninsula of Michigan *during* the environmental review process for the project and added quite late in the process as a new study species.

CONCLUSIONS

Environmental compliance and permitting efforts are complicated by the variable nature of endangered species issues, whether due to biology, the quantity of available information, the regulations and/or interpretations of the available information/regulations by the regulators. Because endangered species issues can be dynamic, it is important to recognize that issues may change *at any point* during the review and approval process. Some species, like the American hart's-tongue fern raise predictable and manageable concerns, while the Hine's emerald dragonfly demonstrates how unpredictable and difficult endangered species issues can become. As the Sault Looping Project illustrates, late project changes can unavoidably lead to delays in project schedules. Although anticipating these types of concerns is difficult, steps can be taken to proactively address issues that have the potential to affect linear projects. In addition to following the guidelines and suggestions made by the US Fish and Wildlife Service (1998) when conducting endangered species consultations, project sponsors should consider making particular efforts to: (1) openly communicate with agency personnel throughout the environmental review process; and (2) thoroughly evaluate known or suspected issues early in the process.

Great Lakes went to considerable lengths to communicate with the respective governing agencies early in the planning process for the Sault Loop Project. Steps were taken to identify agency concerns and to communicate the company's goals to the agencies as well. A solid relationship was built between both groups by maintaining honest, ongoing communications. Despite these efforts, changes in personnel within the HNF and the unexpected discovery of the Hine's emerald dragonfly resulted in project delays. Nevertheless, the long-term implications of building positive working relationships with the HNF is expected to be important for completing construction and maintaining the right-of-way.

One additional aspect that has not been considered in this paper is that of the "cost" of delays due to dealing with an endangered species concern. This is because the cost implications for a delay can take on many forms and are different for each project. It can be a simple monetary outlay by the project proponent, or it can be more complicated, such as interruption of gas deliveries. In the example of the Sault Looping Project, the cost incurred to delay the project one year was minimal compared to the potential mitigation costs of dealing with the Hine's emerald dragonfly. Mitigation costs were high enough for the company to consider abandoning the project had the dragonfly been found within the project area.

REFERENCES

Breck S. 2000. The value of endangered species. Wildlife Society Bulletin, 28: 282–283.

Czech, B., P.R. Krausman, and R. Borkhataria. 1998. Social construction, political power, and the allocation of benefits to endangered species. Conservation Biology, 12: 1103–1112.

Doherty, R.G. 1993. Site characteristics and demography of *Asplenium scolopendrium* var. *americana* at two sites in Michigan. Unpublished MS thesis, University of Michigan, Department of Natural Resources and Environment. 48 pp.

Flather, C.H., L.A. Joyce, and C.A. Bloomgarden. 1994. Species endangerment patterns in the United States. General Technical Report RM-241. Fort Collins, CO: US Department of Agriculture, Forest Service, Rocky Mountain Forest and Range Experiment Station. 42 pp.

Penskar, M.R., S.R. Crispin, and P.J. Higman. 1997. Special plant abstract for *Phyllitis scolopendrium* (American hart's-tongue fern). Michigan Natural Features Inventory, Lansing, MI. 3 pp.

Soluk, D.A., B.J. Swisher, D.S. Zercher, J.D. Miller, and A.B. Hults. 1998. The ecology of Hine's emerald dragonfly (*Somatochlora hineana*): Monitoring populations and determining patterns of habitat use. Activity summary and report of findings (September 1996–August 1997). Illinois Natural History Survey, Champaign, IL. 111 pp.

Steffens, W.P. 1997. 1997 Hine's emerald (*Somatochlora hineana* Williamson) surveys in Michigan's upper peninsula. Unpublished report to the US Fish and Wildlife Service. 17 pp.

US House of Representatives Committee on Resources. 1998. The Endangered Species Act: How much does it cost the taxpayer? A study of ESA related expenditures and the Budget of the Fish and Wildlife Service as it relates to protecting endangered and threatened species prepared by the Majority Staff of the House of Representatives Committee on Resources. (http://www.house.gov/resources/105cong/fullcomm/esa_cost_98.htm#_1_7).

US Fish and Wildlife Service. 1993. American Hart's-tongue Fern Recovery Plan. US Fish and Wildlife Service, Atlanta, GA. 33 pp.

US Fish and Wildlife Service. 1998. Endangered Species Act Consultation Handbook: Procedures for Conducting Section 7 Consultations and Conferences. US Fish and Wildlife Service and the National Marine Fisheries Service. March 1998.

US Fish and Wildlife Service. 1999. Hine's Emerald Dragonfly (*Somatochlora hineana*) Draft Recovery Plan. Technical/Agency Draft. Fort Snelling, MN. 110 pp.

US Fish and Wildlife Service. 2000. Threatened and Endangered Species System: Summary of Listed Species (listing and recovery plans as of June 30, 2000). http://ecos.fws.gov/tess/html/boxscore.html.

BIOGRAPHICAL SKETCHES

Todd A. Mattson

Natural Resource Group, Inc., 1800 International Centre, 900 Second Avenue South, Minneapolis, MN 55402, USA, Phone: 612-337-3367, E-mail: tamattson@nrginc.com, Fax: 612-347-6780

Todd A. Mattson has eight years experience working as a natural resource specialist on a variety of environmental assessment projects as they relate to potential impacts on fish, wildlife, and plant communities. As an Environmental Scientist for Natural Resource Group, he specializes in compliance with threatened and endangered species regulations for construction of new pipeline or fiber optic projects. He holds a BA in Biology from Moorhead State University and a MS in Zoology and Physiology (wildlife ecology emphasis) from the University of Wyoming.

F. Jerry Kott, PE

Great Lakes Gas Transmission Company, 5250 Corporate Drive, Troy, MI 48098, USA, Phone: 248-205-7451, E-mail: fjkott@glgt.com, Fax: 248-205-7475

Jerry Kott has worked in the pipeline industry for over 22 years. His responsibilities have included project management, construction administration and most recently environmental compliance for Great Lakes Gas Transmission Company. Jerry attended Michigan Technological University and holds a BS in Civil Engineering. He is a registered Professional Engineer in the state of Michigan.

Husky Moose Mountain Pipeline

Carol J. Engstrom and Guy M. Goulet

In 1998, Husky Oil Operations Limited (with partner, formerly Rigel Oil) and Talisman Energy in 1999, constructed a 27.0 km pipeline in Kananaskis Country to transport sour oil, solution gas and produced water from Pad #3 on Cox Hill to the Shell Oil Jumping Pound Gas Plant for processing. Kananaskis Country is a 4160 km^2 "Planning Area" that has both prime protection and multiple use designations. Situated just west of Calgary, Alberta, Canada it has considerable recreational and environmental value, including significant wildlife habitat. The original exploration and subsequent pipeline construction applications required separate Alberta Energy & Utilities Board (AEUB) public hearings with both involving significant public consultation. Prior to drilling on the lands that had been purchased more than a decade ago, Husky adopted several governing principles to reduce environmental impact, mitigate damage, and foster open and honest communication with other industrial users, regulators, local interest groups, and local aboriginal communities. During planning and construction, careful attention was paid to using existing linear disturbances (seismic lines, roads, and cutblocks). A variety of environmental studies, that incorporated ecologically-integrated landscape classification and included the use of indicator species such as the Grizzly Bear, were conducted prior to and during the early stages of development. The results of these studies, along with the information gathered from the public consultation, historical and cultural studies, and engineering specifications formed the basis for the route selection. Watercourses presented particular challenges during pipeline construction. The pipeline right-of-way (ROW) intercepted 26 small water runs and 19 creeks. Fishery and water quality issues were identified as important issues in the lower Coxhill Creek and Jumpingpound Creeks. As a result, Jumpingpound Creek was directionally drilled at two locations and all other watercourses were open-cut using low-impact techniques. To minimize new ROW clearing, substantial portions of the pipeline were placed in the ditch of the existing road. Husky attributes the success of this project to planning, broad community input and the co-operation and buy-in by the project management team and construction companies.

Keywords: Kananaskis Country, pipeline, directional drill, sour gas, public consultation

INTRODUCTION AND HISTORY

Kananaskis Country encompasses an area of over 4160 km^2 located southwest of Calgary. It is an area of high peaks, flowing streams, and home to many important mammals and fish, as well as a heavily used recreation area. People from all over Alberta and Western Canada visit the area to hike, canoe, fish, snowmobile, cycle, quad, ski, and participate in a host of other outdoor pursuits. Industrial activities such as cattle grazing, logging and oil and gas development also occur in Kananaskis Country. Although it is not a park, it is managed by an Integrated Resource Plan (IRP) and is nicknamed "Calgary's playground" (Fig. 1). Husky's land is located in the Elbow/Jumpingpound Resource management area and is overlapped by two zones of the IRP, zone 5 (Multiple use) and zone 1 (Prime protection) (Alberta Forestry, 1986).

Project philosophy

Prior to Husky planning any oil and gas development in the area, six governing principles were adopted:

1. Consulting, openly, and early with all interested parties.

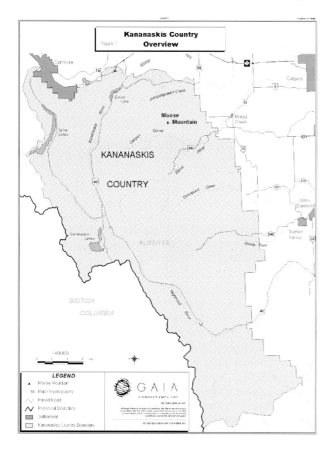

Fig. 1. Kananaskis Country overview.

2. Planning activities and facilities to allow co-existence with present and future uses of the area.
3. Preparing an environmental assessment for the development phase to ensure appropriate environmental measures are taken.
4. Reducing and where possible avoiding environmental impact through consultation, planning, design, innovation, and technology.
5. Minimizing access and ensuring any new access is compatible with future plans of Kananaskis Country.
6. Coordinating industry activities so as to minimize disturbance and duplication of infrastructure and activity.

In 1990, Husky conducted a seismic program, which led to a discovery well (02-23-12-07W5M) being completed in March 1993. A well test was conducted and the flow reached 125 m^3/day of oil and 70,000 m^3/day of gas and water. Following a public hearing and subsequent AEUB approval in 1994, a four-well drilling program was initiated. The program resulted in three oil wells (10-14-23-07W5M, Pad 1 and 02-27-23-07, 10-22-23-07W5M, Pad 3) and one gas well (12-12-23-07W5M, Pad 2) completed in late 1995. Following this, Husky applied to construct a pipeline to extract the oil from Pad 3 in 1997 (Husky Oil Operations Limited, 1997).

ENVIRONMENTAL SETTING

The proposed pipeline route lies within the Southern Foothills of the Rocky Mountains with the exception of Pad 3 which lies at the edge of the front range of the Rocky Mountains (Pettapiece, 1986). Elevations along the pipeline route range from 1356 m at Jumpingpound Creek to 1768 m at Pad #3.

The surficial deposits along the pipeline route are both glacial and post-glacial in origin. They consist mostly of coarse stream alluvium and glacial till. Additionally, there are small areas of colluvium, alluvial fans, and aprons, as well as outwash plains (Bayrock and Reimchen, 1975).

Soils that formed under forest vegetation are primarily Grey Luvisols. The textures vary from coarse sandy loam along the north end of the pipeline to a finer clay loam near the south (Wyatt et al., 1943). The soils in the vicinity of Jumpingpound Creek are Black or Eluviated Black Chernozems that were formed under grass and forb vegetation (Wyatt and Newton, 1943).

The two major watercourses that the proposed pipeline route crosses are Jumpingpound Creek and Coxhill Creek. Jumpingpound Creek originates on the Northwest slope of Jumpingpound Mountain and flows for approximately 80 km to where it joins the Bow River, near Cochrane, Alberta. Coxhill Creek flows down Cox Hill into Jumpingpound Creek and is classified as an intermittent stream (Anderson et al., 1997) (Fig. 2).

PRINCIPLES OF DEVELOPMENT

Consulting, openly and early with all interested parties

From the onset in 1988 Husky tried to be very open and straightforward about their plans for Moose Mountain. They held numerous kitchen table meetings with residents and scheduled meetings with environmental and recreational groups such as the Calgary Outdoor Council, Canadian Parks and Wilderness Society, and the Bragg Creek Environmental Coalition. First Nations were given tours and held spiritual ceremonies, blessings and inspections of the area. Newspaper ads were delivered to over 40,000 homes in Cochrane and Bragg Creek. In addition, nine Husky Oil Moose Mountain Updates were mailed to over 100 people from industry, Non-Governmental Organizations (NGO's) and area residents (Husky Oil Operations Limited, 1997).

The Alberta Energy & Utilities Board (AEUB) commissioned two public hearings to evaluate the projects. The delineation drilling hearing occurred in 1994, and the pipeline hearing was in 1997. In the 1994 hearing, two First Nation groups and five environmental groups voiced specific concerns with the proposed project. The concerns of the First Nations included the

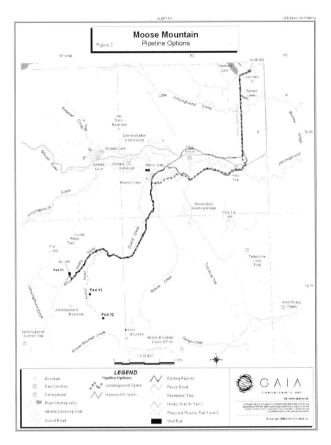

Fig. 2. Moose Mountain area pipeline options.

deterioration of their traditional hunting grounds and possible restrictions on the use of the mountain for spiritual ceremonies. Environmental concerns ranged from local environmental impact, greenhouse gases, wildlife and fisheries concerns to regional cumulative effects. As a result of the first hearing a Traditional Native Cultural Properties Study was completed by the Tsuu T'ina Nation and Husky Oil (Husky Oil Operations Limited and Tsuu T'ina Nation, 1995) as well as a comprehensive environmental assessment (Husky Oil Operations Limited, 1997). The results of these studies are discussed later in the paper.

Planning of activities and facilities to co-exist with present and future uses of the area

A recreational survey was conducted in the summer and fall of 1994 to determine the type of people who use Kananaskis Country (Usher and Jackson, 1995). The purpose was to determine what kinds of recreational activities occur in Kananaskis Country and the attitudes of the public towards oil and gas development within its boundaries. Two surveys were conducted targeting specific groups of Kananaskis Country users. The summer target group was a broad range of recreational users while the fall target group was hunters.

Data from the surveys showed that the four most frequent activities were sightseeing, hiking, picnicking, and camping. Of those who were classified as hikers and campers, 28.5% did not know oil and gas activities were occurring in Kananaskis Country and 61.6% of these people considered themselves to be poorly informed about the oil and gas activities occurring in Kananaskis Country. Forty two percent (42.5%) of the hikers and campers were of the opinion that oil and gas activities should not occur. In contrast, only 14.6% of the hunters surveyed stated that oil and gas activity should not occur in Kananaskis Country (Usher and Jackson, 1995).

This led Husky to believe that the hikers and campers were more sensitive to oil and gas activities than the hunters. In response to these concerns, Husky designed a pamphlet in the summer of 1998 and two signs to inform hunters, hikers, and campers about their activities during the construction phase of the project.

The pamphlet was created to detail the construction activity in the Moose Mountain area. It outlined Husky's governing principles and the conservation measures that were incorporated into the construction of the pipeline. One thousand copies of the pamphlet were printed and made available to the public in four key-areas around the Moose Mountain area. The two information signs were designed and permanently displayed in four areas of high traffic (both hiking and vehicular) to inform the public on the status of the project as well as some results of the environmental assessment that was completed prior to construction.

Preparing and incorporating an environment assessment into the development phase

In 1992 prior to the initial road construction an ecological inventory and several environmental studies were completed. From these studies a route for the exploration road and a possible future pipeline route was chosen. In 1992 geographical information system (GIS) technology was in its infancy. Several sections of the route would have been repositioned if the road were to be built today. In 1997 after the successful completion of the sour oil well on Pad 3 a new AEUB application and more environmental studies were commissioned. Upon completion of these studies, considerations given to engineering and production specifications, EUB regulations (i.e., sour gas pipeline setbacks) and existing disturbances, three pipeline routes were presented (Tera Environmental Consultants (Alta) Ltd., 1997) (Fig. 2):
- the proposed route,
- the south Jumpingpound variation, and
- the Hwy 68 variation.

The examples below demonstrate how Husky used the information to settle upon the actual pipeline route.

Vegetation

One of the surveys conducted prior to pipeline construction was a multi-scale ecological land inventory and classification study. The study had three goals

[Kansas and Collister, 1997(a)]:
- to classify the land into Ecologically Integrated Landscape Units (EILU),
- to evaluate habitat suitability for 12 indicator wildlife species using these EILU, and
- to characterize the vegetation and site conditions for the region.

A total of 117 unique EILU were classified and these were further grouped into 76 Wildlife Habitat Ecological Units (WHEU). Of the EILU's that were classified, several in the foothills parkland and lower foothills were rated as being in low supply. In the foothills parkland: Lodgepole pine forests of all slope and aspect, steep south-west facing white spruce and mixwood forests, and steep north-east facing grassland. In the lower foothills, native grasslands, gently sloping conifers and deciduous dominated mixwood [Kansas and Collister, 1997(a)]. The proposed route did not traverse any vegetative units that were in low supply.

The highest level of overall vegetative richness was found in the mixedwood forests especially in the foothills parkland and coniferous-dominated mixedwoods of the lower foothills [Kansas and Collister, 1997(a)].

A study was conducted to determine the presence and frequency of rare plants along the pipeline route. One provincially rare plant, the Dwarf Fleabane (*Erigeron radicatus*) which inhabits dry gravelly alpine habitat was found on Moose Mountain. There were four regionally rare plants found namely Simple Kobresia (*Kobresia simpliuscula*), Heart-leaved Twayblade (*Listera cordata*), Five-leaved Bramble (*Rubus pedatus*), and Alpine Mitrewort (*Mitella pentandra*). These plants were found in a small, wooded wetland located north of Pad #3 and within a fen on the Demonstration Forest Loop near Highway 68. The pipeline was deflected slightly near Pad #3 to avoid a rare plant community (Wallis and Usher, 1995).

Wildlife
A survey of the wildlife in the 11 vegetation categories found 199 bird species, 55 mammal species and ten species of reptile. Wildlife habitat suitability indices (HSI) were developed for four large mammals, two small mammals, and six bird species. Indicator species for the study were grizzly bear (*Ursus arctos horribilis*), moose (*Alces alces*), elk (*Cervus elaphus*), and black bear (*Ursus americanus*), meadow vole (*Microtus pennsylvanicus*), and the marten (*Martes americana*). The birds chosen were the northern goshawk (*Accipiter gentilis*), American pipit (*Anthus rubescens*), pileated woodpecker (*Dryocopus pileatus*), blue grouse (*Dendragapus obscurus*), ovenbird (*Seiurus aurocapillus*), and the alder flycatcher (*Empidonax elnorum*). In addition, the grizzly bear was chosen for a cumulative effects assessment [Kansas and Collister, 1997(b)].

During the evaluation of the three routes the proposed route was deemed more suitable because it avoided some very high spring, early fall and late fall habitat however it did transect some better denning grizzly habitat. In addition, the proposed route averted some very high black bear, elk, moose and alder flycatcher habitat [Kansas and Collister, 1997(b)].

Amphibian and reptile surveys were conducted and two species of frogs were found on the large clear-cut areas along the road; boreal toads (*Bufo boreas*) and wood frogs (*Rana sylvatica*). Additionally, wood frogs along with Chorus frogs (*Pseudacris triseriata*) were found in the wetland area of Fredrick and Darnell lakes (Powell, 1997).

Fish
There were fish studies conducted in 1994 (Golder Associates Ltd., 1996), 1997 and 1998 (Tera Environmental Consultants (Alta) Ltd., 1998). A total of seven fish species were encountered in the Study Area. They included brook trout (*Salvelinus fontinalis*), bull trout (*Salvelinus confluentus*), cutthroat trout (*Oncorhynchus clarki lewisi*), rainbow trout (*Oncorhynchus mykiss*), mountain whitefish (*Prosopium williamsoni*), and mountain sucker (*Catostomas platyrhyncus*) (Golder Associates Ltd., 1996; Tera Environmental Consultants (Alta) Ltd., 1998). There were no fish found in the upper reaches of Coxhill creek; however, near the confluence with Jumpingpound Creek brook trout and some cutthroat trout were found. All seven species of fish were found in Jumpingpound Creek at varying numbers throughout the season. To protect the fish habitat and the riparian zone two directional drills under Jumpingpound Creek were planned.

Archaeology
A comprehensive Historical Resource study was completed in 1997. Ten pre-contact sites, two historic sites and a number of historic structures were found within 1 km of the pipeline route (Fedirchuk McCullough & Associates, 1997). The results of the route evaluation determined that the south Jumpingpound variation avoided the archaeological site near Jumpingpound Creek (Tera Environmental Consultants (Alta) Ltd., 1997) while the proposed route crossed through the site and the Hwy 68 route came close to the sites.

As a result of the AEUB Public Hearing in 1994 a Traditional Native Cultural Properties Study was completed in 1995. This study identified several important traditional pursuits and associations with Moose Mountain. Another study was conducted with the first Nations in 1998. The First Nations have used the Moose Mountain area since the late 1800's for religious practice, hunting, trapping, fishing, plant collecting, and ethnobiology.

Route analysis
In the final analysis, the proposed route was chosen because it paralleled existing disturbances for 94% of its length, traversed more gentle terrain, and averted some important wildlife habitat. In addition it met all requirements for EUB sour gas pipeline setbacks. However, its disadvantages were two additional crossings of Jumpingpound Creek, the proximity to the Demonstration Forest Loop and the location of an archaeological site at Jumpingpound Creek (Tera Environmental Consultants (Alta) Ltd., 1997).

Integrating environmental planning, construction and technology

The Moose Mountain Pipeline project used fairly conventional construction techniques for much of the pipeline, but to lessen the environmental impact several variances from convention were implemented. Clearing was limited to less than 25.2 ha (from the planned clearing of 39.3 ha) by using existing linear features such as existing cut-lines, seismic lines, old logging trails, and placing the pipe in the bar ditch of the road (Goulet, 1999).

Environmental issues related to stringing and welding operations for conventional pipelines include disturbance to vegetation, mixing of soil types, surface rutting, soil compaction, and potential barriers to wildlife movement. Generally, the weight of the stringing truck/trailers combined with the high frequency of passes has the greatest environmental impact during pipeline construction. Because both the stringing and welding crews were quite small and construction proceeded at a low pace, overall impacts to vegetation were not observed (Goulet, 1999).

During construction, gaps in the welded pipe string were provided to maintain access across the ROW for wildlife and cattle. Along the Coxhill Creek Husky road, all pipe activities were compressed into 1-km sections and made concurrent, so that from the time the pipe was strung, welded, lowered-in, and backfilled, not more than 24 h passed (Goulet, 1999).

The ditching crew commenced at Kp 11 + 200 and worked towards kickoff at Pad #3, directly after welding, X-ray, and coating. Track hoes were used for all ditch advancements. Prior to ditching, additional upper surface material was salvaged and stored at the edge of the ROW, usually between trees for easy retrieval upon cleanup. Ditch spoil was placed on the road surface and used as the work surface by the pipe lower-in crew. This process limited most rubber-tired traffic to Pad #3 (Goulet, 1999).

Cleanup was initiated immediately following backfill activities to ensure that erosion control measures and watercourse restoration could take place. Slopes and watercourses were restored to original pre-construction contour. Swails were replaced on slopes to maintain cross ROW drainage and surface diversion berms were installed to prevent washouts and surface erosion (Goulet, 1999).

Directional drilling
Typically, watercourse crossings associated with pipeline construction can present environmental challenges, including the harmful alteration, disruption or destruction (HADD) of aquatic habitats and the impairment of water quality. Impacts on aquatic resources may result from in-stream and near-stream work, ineffective clean up and restoration near the watercourse, or from fuel or other hazardous material spills (Goulet, 1999).

The primary issues associated with the Moose Mountain Pipeline project included; maintaining clean flowing water by using isolation techniques, installing bridge spans on watercourses with confirmed fish presence, direct grading away from the watercourses, storing trench spoil beyond the wetted channel, and implementing sediment control for the watercourse crossing, as required (Goulet, 1999).

The Pipeline project intersected several watercourses including Coxhill Creek (13 times), Jumpingpound Creek (3 times) Little Jumpingpound Creek, Darnell Lake, and Frederick Lake drainage, and some additional minor drainages. The lower Coxhill Creek and Jumpingpound Creek were identified as having the most significant fisheries and water quality issues associated with pipeline construction. The upper Coxhill Creek, Little Jumpingpound Creek, and the two lake drainages (i.e., Darnell and Frederick) had no fisheries issues identified at the time of the initial assessment, and were deemed to be appropriate for simple open cut crossings (Goulet, 1999).

In order to protect local fish habitat, wildlife corridors, recreational space and important riparian habitat, the three Jumpingpound Creek crossings were assessed for geotechnical suitability for a trenchless crossing using a horizontal directional drill technique. This study indicated that two of three crossings were most suitable for directional drill, and the third crossing at the highway was unsuitable because of thick gravel seams on both sides of the creek. Husky committed to attempting the first two crossings of Jumpingpound Creek using the directional drill method, even though gravel seams were also found on one or both sides (Goulet, 1999).

All the watercourse crossings were constructed under an AEP Water Resources Act Permit. Planning included pre-construction preparation, construction methodology, site restoration, construction drawings and scheduling (Goulet, 1999).

To prevent frac-out of mud in the creek, the minimum depth of the drilling trajectory was calculated assuming a fracture gradient of 17 kPa/m. None of the drills experienced frac-out.

Jumpingpound Creek at Kp 11 + 600 and Kp 13 + 930
The geotechnical assessment for this watercourse crossing indicated suitable conditions to warrant an

attempt at a horizontal directional drill. The Crossing Company of Nisku, Alberta was commissioned to perform the drill. The Crossing Company compressed the drill set-up to accommodate a narrow and long configuration for a location on the Demonstration Forest Road. Workspace of 5 m × 40 m was acquired, but was not used. Therefore, no additional clearing was required. An Emergency Response Plan (ERP) was submitted to Husky in the event of a release of drilling fluids, to either the creek itself or the surrounding work area (Goulet, 1999).

Case pounding to bedrock and stringing of the 3″, 4″, and 6″ future blank line pipe for the creek section was initiated. The pilot hole exited successfully in a meadow beside the creek without incident after only seven days. The hole, which was eventually widened to a maximum diameter of 17″, was completed approximately 14 days later. Final cleanup, including topsoil replacement, seeding, and harrowing was conducted immediately after tie-ins and backfill (Goulet, 1999).

The second directional drill of Jumpingpound Creek was approved after the results of the fish assessment (REF) and the geotechnical assessment. However, the Crossing Company requested a change to the original drill path and length during an early pre-drill assessment. This increased the overall length of the drill, but it was believed to be an easier path and, therefore, more favorable for success. Fourteen days after the pilot hole, the creek section of pipe was pulled to the rig side (Goulet, 1999).

Coxhill Creek
Discussions about timing, procedures, and regulatory requirements between the Contractor and Husky Construction staff were conducted prior to any of the thirteen crossings of Coxhill Creek. The Environmental Protection Plan (EPP) indicated that relatively simple wet crossings (open cut) could be executed regardless of the flow regime of the upper Coxhill Creek. However Fisheries Management staff, requested that isolation or diversion techniques be implemented if any flow were present at the time of pipeline installation (Goulet, 1999).

To begin the diversions the contractor blocked off a culvert along the road to create a dam. An electric pump was placed upstream of the dam and pumped water around a rock outcropping and into an old meander of Coxhill Creek. This meander and natural streambed provided excellent opportunity for natural filtration of sediments by the many natural sumps and moss hummocks downstream. Eventually, approximately 250 m downstream, the old channel joined with the active channel and stream flow was maintained (Goulet, 1999).

Simultaneously, at a tributary crossing that originated uphill from the road, a dam and pump were placed in a natural hollow and water was pumped through the culvert in the road. Following this the contractor had control of all stream flow for approximately 300 m and water was diverted away from the ditching activities, leaving a relatively dry ditch. Ditching simultaneously from both ends at Kp 5 + 600 and Kp 5 + 300 using three track hoes allowed the entire 300 m section to be lowered-in and back-filled immediately. Creek sections were roughed in to approximate pre-construction bed and bank levels and dimensions with local material. Finally the upstream dam was removed and returned flow to the original, pre-construction watercourse (Goulet, 1999).

Sediment mitigation measures during the entire operation included the use of straw bales with filter cloth at outlets of culverts and in downstream placements. Additional protection measures included; minimum grading to approaches of creeks, no clearing for material storage and having all ditch spoil placed on the road and contained in-situ by proper material handling by experienced operators. Erosion control measures included rock armoring of large downstream culverts and bends. Creek beds were contoured and additional rock was placed where appropriate to prevent future erosion impacts (Goulet, 1999).

Historical resources
A number of mitigation steps were taken to protect the three historical and cultural resources sites which had been identified at Kp 5 + 300, Kp 13 + 930 and Kp 19 + 600 (Fedirchuk McCullough & Associates, 1997). A rock of cultural importance at Kp 5 + 300 was encircled with steel posts and chain to protect it during construction. The site at Kp 13 + 930 was averted by extending the directional drill of the second Jumpingpound Creek crossing while Kp 19 + 600 (intersection of Hwy 68) was avoided with a relatively minor re-route and a 35 m dry bore under the highway and the site at (Goulet, 1999).

Minimizing access and ensuring any new access is compatible with future plans of the Kananaskis Country
There are six priorities of Kananaskis Country, as stated in the IRP, which form the regulatory basis for operating in Kananaskis Country (Alberta Forestry, 1986). Table 1 describes what measures were taken to construct the pipeline in accordance with these principles.

General reclamation
As part of commitments made by Husky, a number of areas required tree planting along the Moose Mountain pipeline ROW and areas across Spray Lakes cut blocks to ensure reforestation was kept consistent with existing efforts. Seedlings were acquired from Water Valley Tree Nursery with approval from Spray Lakes. The two species planted were Lodgepole Pine (*Pinus contorta*) and White Spruce (*Picea glauca*). Approximately 5000 seedlings were planted. On one occasion a group of 40 students from Strathcona-Tweedsmuir School

Table 1. Mitigation measures taken to fulfill the priorities of Kananaskis Country

Priorities	Measures taken
1. To maintain water quality quantity and flow regime.	There were no measurable increases in sediment load to the streams during construction for the following reasons: isolation techniques were used, bridge spans on watercourses with fisheries capability were installed, grading was directed away from the watercourses, trench spoil was stored beyond the wetted channel, and sediment control was implemented for all crossings.
2. To provide a wide range of recreational, leisure and tourism opportunities.	The construction schedule was planned to minimize interference with peak recreational periods.
3. Maintenance of the abundance, diversity, distribution and recreational use of fish and wildlife resources.	The results of the environmental studies showed the study area contained important wildlife and fish habitat. As a result Husky routed the pipeline accordingly.
4. To provide for the management and development of renewable natural resources.	Used existing disturbances where feasible and worked co-operatively with other land users (Spray Lakes Sawmills) and government agencies to achieve this goal. To minimize access, controls were implemented: public motorized vehicles were prevented from using the road and logging slash and stumps were rolled back onto the ROW.
5. To protect historical and archaeological resources.	The pipeline was routed around/under areas of historical significance.
6. Maintenance and encouragement of research, educational and interpretation programs.	By creating public information signs and pamphlets Husky hoped to increase awareness and education about oil and gas activities in Kananaskis Country. Environmental Assessment and Ecologically Integrated Landscape mapping contributes significantly to knowledge of the study area. The co-operative Tsuu T'ina-Husky Cultural study adds knowledge of Native history in the Moose Mountain area.

participated in the planting of the seedlings. This gave them the opportunity to learn about pipelines and Husky's environmental responsibility when conducting operations in a sensitive area.

As part of Husky's commitment to reclaiming disturbed sites in association with its activities, Husky construction staff hydro-seeded the steep slopes and the cut and fill slope faces of Pad 3. This was partially successful and will be repeated in the summer of 2000.

The ROW was seeded with three native grass seed mixes, an agricultural zone mix, a forest zone mix and a steep slope and stream bank mix.

Coordinating industry activities to minimize disturbance and duplication of infrastructure and activity
Original construction planning and timing for scheduled pipeline activities had the project divided into three (3) sections. They were as follows:
- section 1 from Kp 0 + 000 to Kp 11 + 000 along the Coxhill Creek portion;
- section 2 from Kp 11 + 000 to Kp 18 + 000 to include the Demo Forest and the majority of the Green Area; and
- section 3 from Kp 18 + 000 to Kp 26 + 200 through the White (Public Lands and Private) Area.

Timing or scheduling for pipeline construction had section 1 from June 25 to July 29; section 2 from August 30 to September; and section 3 from July 30 to August 29. Changes to scheduling came into effect almost immediately. Section 2 was compressed to include only the Demonstration Forest portion with no time constraints on the Green Area portion from Homestead Road (Kp 13 + 3400) to the third crossing of Jumpingpound Creek #3 (Kp 19 + 350). Originally this section was to be constructed last so that construction activities and disturbance to tourists and other users might be minimized. However, the directional drill activity at the first Jumpingpound Creek crossing was on-going during late June to early August, so authorization was granted to close the Demonstration Forest Road (i.e., gate with information signage) to the public for both safety and environmental reasons, as construction of the pipeline proceeded. The only other stipulations for construction was that no pipeline construction, except the directional drill, could occur in the Demonstration Forest portion on the weekends during the summer months (Goulet, 1999).

CONCLUSIONS

Appropriate planning, environmental assessment, regulatory and public participation contributed significantly to the successful construction of the 26.2-km pipeline in this sensitive ecosystem in Kananaskis Country.

ACKNOWLEDGEMENTS

This project would not have achieved its goals without the onsite commitment of the Parkland Oilfield Construction, the project engineers, Tera Environmental Consultants (Alta) Ltd., Cottonwood Consultants Ltd., Fedirchuk McCullough & Associates Ltd., Ursus Environmental Inc., The Crossing Company, and the supervisory team Tridyne.

REFERENCES

Alberta Forestry. 1986. Kananaskis Country Sub Regional Integrated Resource Plan. Edmonton, AB.

Anderson et al. 1997. Assessment of Potential impacts to Fisheries Resources Associated with the Husky Oil Proposed Moose Mountain Pipeline. Golder Associates Ltd.

Bayrock, L.A. and T.H.F. Reimchen. 1975. Surficial Geology of the Foothills ands Rocky Mountains. 6 maps. Alberta Research Council.

Fedirchuk McCullough & Associates. 1997. Preliminary Historical Resources Impact Assessment.

Golder Associates Ltd. 1996. Fisheries Resource Inventory in the Moose Mountain Study Area. Golder Associates Ltd., Calgary.

Goulet, G. 1999. Environmental As-Built Report for Husky Moose Mountain Pipeline Project. Western Ecological System Management Consultant Inc.

Husky Oil Operations Limited and Tsuu T'ina Nation. 1995. Traditional Native Cultural Properties Study. Calgary, AB.

Husky Oil Operations Limited. 1997. Energy Development Application Proposed Moose Mountain Development.

Kansas, J. and D. Collister. 1997a. Ecologically-Integrated Landscape Classification and Mapping, Jumpingpound Pipeline Region. Ursus Ecosystem Management Ltd.

Kansas, J. and D. Collister. 1997b. Wildlife Habitat Assessment, Jumpingpound Pipeline Region. Ursus Ecosystem Management.

Pettapiece, W.W. 1986. Physiographic subdivisions of Alberta. Agriculture Canada. 1:1,500,000 map.

Powell, L. 1997. Amphibian and Reptile Occurrence, Moose Mountain Pipeline Assessment. GAIA Consultants Inc.

Tera Environmental Consultants (Alta) Ltd. 1997. Conservation and Reclamation Report for the Proposed Husky Oil Operations Limited Moose Mountain Pipeline Project.

Tera Environmental Consultants (Alta) Ltd. 1998. Alternate Open Cut for Jumpingpound Creek.

Usher, R. and E.L. Jackson. 1995. Recreational Activities and Attitudes to Oil and Gas Development in Kananaskis Country Moose Mountain Environmental Inventory. GAIA Consultants Inc.

Wallis, C. and Usher. 1995. Rare Plant Survey. Cottonwood Consultants Ltd. and GAIA Consultants Inc.

Wyatt, F.A. and D.J. Newton. 1943. Soil survey of Rosebud and Banff sheets. The University of Alberta, Alberta Soil Survey Report 12.

Wyatt, F.A. et al. 1943 Soil Survey of Blackfoot and Calgary Sheets. The University of Alberta. Alberta Soil Survey Report 11.

BIOGRAPHICAL SKETCHES

Carol Engstrom

Husky Oil Operations Limited, 707 8th Avenue SW, Calgary, AB T2P3G7, Canada

Carol Engstrom has worked at Husky Energy in Calgary, Alberta since 1998 in the Environmental Affairs Department. She is an Environmental Specialist at Husky and is responsible for ensuring high environmental performance for oil and gas production in most of Alberta. She holds a BSc in Ecology from the University of Calgary (1996). She is a member of the in Alberta Society of Professional Biologists (ASPB). Professional interests include public consultation, environmental protection planning, and wildlife and aquatic ecology.

Guy M. Goulet

Western Ecological Systems Management Consulting Inc., 424 Oakridge Way SW, Calgary, AB T2V 1T4, Canada

Guy M. Goulet is principal of Western Ecological Systems Management Consulting Inc., an environmental consulting company incorporated in Calgary, AB, in 1995. He holds a BSc in Forestry from the University of Alberta (1982) and a Masters in Natural Resources Management (MNRM) from the University of Manitoba (1992). He is a member in Alberta Society of Professional Biologists (ASPB) and The Alberta Registered Professional Foresters Association (ARPFA) since 1993. Professional interests include environmental protection planning for development projects, impact assessment and wildlife ecology.

Development of Pipeline Reclamation Criteria for Alberta

A.W. Fedkenheuer, W.W. Pettapiece, J.D. Burke, and L.A. Leskiw

Development of Alberta's oil and gas industry has led to a proliferation of pipelines in the province. All pipelines constructed in Alberta require a reclamation certificate before the proponent is released from further reclamation liabilities. In order for the land disturbed by construction, operation, or abandonment of the pipeline to be certified, the land must have equivalent land capability to that which existed prior to the disturbance. The approach that has been used for well site reclamation success evaluation is a parameter-by-parameter comparison and pass/fail system. In this case each parameter must pass or the site fails. In late 1996, NOVA Gas Transmission Ltd. undertook to assemble a group of government regulatory and non-regulatory personnel, industry and third party individuals to develop a more integrated capability-based evaluation system. Following a merger in 1998, TransCanada Transmission continued to be a major sponsor of this group. Various approaches were field tested in 1997, 1998, and 1999. A recommendation report was completed in late 1999. This paper reports on the process used, the results, and the current status of the criteria.

Keywords: Reclamation evaluation, reclamation criteria, reclamation standards, reclamation success, soil assessment, evaluation tool

INTRODUCTION

Pipelines are generally buried and rarely are seen because the soil over them continues to support pre-disturbance activities such as agriculture or forestry. However, even though most people are not aware of the presence of pipelines, concern about the environmental impacts from construction of pipelines has led to legislation governing their construction, operation, and decommissioning.

Within Alberta there was no legislated requirement for the reclamation of disturbed lands prior to 1963 when the Surface Reclamation Act was enacted (Brocke, 1988). Ten years later, in 1973, the Land Surface Conservation and Reclamation Act was proclaimed. This new Act required that environmental protection and reclamation be part of development planning (Landsburg and Fedkenheuer, 1990). A review and approval system that included Environmental Impact Assessments and Development and Reclamation Approvals was subsequently implemented. Regulatory changes were made in 1983 and again in 1993 with the passage of the Alberta "Environmental Protection and Enhancement Act" (Alberta Environmental Protection, 1994).

The 1993 legislation contained a requirement to return land disturbed by pipeline construction to an equivalent land capability at the time of abandonment (when the pipeline is no longer to be used, irrespective of whether the pipe is removed or left in place). Equivalent land capability is currently defined as, "The ability of the land to support various land uses after reclamation is similar to the ability that existed prior to any activity being conducted on the land, but that the individual land uses will not necessarily be identical" (Powter, 1998).

The requirement for equivalent land capability at the time of application for a reclamation certificate implies the need for criteria to measure equivalent land capability. Some documentation is required to enable the regulator to acknowledge that the area is suitably reclaimed and to release the proponent from further reclamation liability, as well as to assure

Environmental Concerns in Rights-of-Way
Management: Seventh International Symposium
J.W. Goodrich-Mahoney, D.F. Mutrie and C.A. Guild (editors)
© 2002 Elsevier Science Ltd. All rights reserved.

the public that a suitable reclamation job has been done. This documentation has been difficult to obtain agreement on and it has been the subject of discussions since the mid-1980s. The definition of reclamation success and how to measure it was the topic of a workshop in 1992 (Mahnic and Toogood, 1992). Following the workshop, focus shifted to well-site reclamation criteria development where a parameter-based checklist was developed and used. For these areas, specific individual parameters are compared on and off the well-site and each must pass or the site fails. For example, the soil pH on the well-site must closely match that on the adjoining control area. If it does not, the well-site site fails it's assessment, even if all of the other assessed parameters are as good or better than the control.

It has been suggested that the well-site system be used for pipeline rights-of-way assessments as well. It has also been suggested that a land capability rating system be used, such as has been used in Canadian agriculture for many years (Agronomic Interpretations Working Group, 1995). In either case, modifications may be required to each system if it is to be applied to pipelines. In 1996, NOVA Gas Transmission offered to take the lead in working to develop a land capability rating system, to demonstrate what it might contain, and how it might work for pipeline reclamation assessment. This paper addresses the approach, the results, and the current status of the approach.

PROCESS

In 1995, as interest in reclamation standards for pipelines again began to increase, several joint government/industry working groups were established. In mid-1996, a version of the well site reclamation criteria was modified and suggested for consideration as pipeline reclamation criteria. This was unacceptable to many industry representatives.

In fall, 1996, NOVA assembled a team to investigate developing a capability-based assessment tool for evaluating pipeline right-of-way reclamation success. This group, the NGTL (NOVA Gas Transmission Ltd.) External Soils Advisory Board consisted of representatives from government regulatory bodies, industry, and independent experts. NOVA provided much of the administrative support as well as the chair (A.W. Fedkenheuer) and assistant chair (J.D. Burke). A key component of this Board was that some members were not directly involved in oil and gas from an industry or government regulatory perspective. These individuals brought both a practical and scientific perspective to the Board, as well as considerable experience.

The Board's primary short-term objective was to develop a tool to evaluate the success of reclamation along pipeline rights-of-way. There was much discussion as to when this tool would be applied, either at post-construction or upon abandonment of the pipeline or at both times. It was agreed that the Board would focus on abandonment criteria that would be applied at the end of the life of a pipeline. In this way, the operator would know, in the planning stages of construction, what would be measured at the end. This approach would encourage good planning of soils handling and other environmental issues during construction in order to minimize reclamation costs and landowner concerns over the life of the pipeline.

In Alberta, the life span (time to abandonment) for a pipeline can vary from as little as three years (or less) to 50 or more years. The shorter three to ten year life span pipelines typically are those in gathering systems that come from a number of well-heads to a central collection area. When the well runs dry, the pipeline is abandoned. The much longer life span pipelines are those in the main line transmission systems that carry, for example, natural gas out of the province to Eastern Canada or into various areas in the United States. All pipeline rights-of-way, except those pipelines which are plowed in, are subject to obtaining a reclamation certificate upon their being abandoned (no longer to be used).

Important requirements of the reclamation evaluation tool as identified by the Board were:
- scientific validity,
- identification of important environmental parameters,
- a clear description of how to measure those environmental parameters,
- relatively easy usage,
- cost-effectiveness, and
- provision of reproducible results.

An initial decision was to evaluate systems and processes already available rather than build new systems. However, in the end, it was decided that a visual assessment needed to be developed. As well several others needed to be developed, one with a more detailed level than the visual, but not requiring laboratory analyses, and another requiring laboratory analyses. The Land Suitability Rating System (Agronomic Interpretations Working Group, 1995) and a version of the well-site reclamation criteria system (Well-site Criteria Working Group, 1995) were also tested. Along with these systems, a landowner reclamation evaluation form was also developed.

Following agreement on the systems to use, the Board retained three senior consultants to take the systems to the field and evaluate their performance. In October and November, 1997, the consultants were sent to three areas of central Alberta to test the systems on five pipeline segments in each area. The consultants were not at the same site at the same time, nor did they discuss their findings with each other until after their reports had been submitted to the Board. The Board visited each consultant individually at a different pipeline location. Subsequent to the receipt of the reports, three members of the Board summarized the consultant reports into one summary report.

The Board used the results of the 1997 field evaluation and the consultant recommendations to revise the evaluation tool into a three-step process for the 1998 field season. One step was a landowner reclamation evaluation form that reflects the parameters being assessed by consultants. The other two steps, a Phase 1 and a Phase 2 assessment, were conducted by consultants. In practice, only if an area failed the Phase 1 portion is the assessment to continue under a Phase 2 evaluation consisting of a more detailed soil assessment. However, for this field test, both the Phase 1 and 2 were conducted on all sites to provide information on whether parameters of importance were being missed in Phase 1.

FIELD PROTOCOL

The results of the 1997 field test led to the development of a general field protocol for system applications as well as a two-phase pipeline reclamation assessment process manual [NGTL External Advisory Board, 1999(b)]. In addition, a process was developed for obtaining the landowner's assessment of the reclamation on his property [NGTL External Advisory Board, 1999(a)].

The field protocol manual covers field procedures such as developing map units, how to handle problems or spot units, selection of controls, transect location, minimum size area to evaluate, how to deal with variability and how to handle with special circumstances where an over-ride may be appropriate. Also discussed is how to determine whether a transect, and also a pipeline segment, should pass or fail (see next section). Recommendations are included for what pre-field preparation should be undertaken as well as for field procedures and how to approach the final assessment and reporting.

The Phase 1 assessment involves a relatively quick overview of landscape, soils, and vegetation components. The factors evaluated in the landscape component are surface drainage, coarse fragments (number of stones, wood fragments, amount of gravel), and micro-topography. Factors to be evaluated in surface soil are soil color (estimate of soil organic matter content) surface aggregate size and strength (evaluation of compaction, soil admixing), and soil texture. Vegetation factors in Phase 1 are plant growth (plant density, cover, height, health) and species composition (focussing on unsuitable species including weeds).

In Phase 2 there is an emphasis on soil conditions to help determine both the specific causes for problems identified in Phase 1 as well as possible solutions. Phase 2 is to be implemented on those transects and pipeline segments that fail Phase 1. Both mineral and organic soils are addressed in the primary areas of water-supplying ability, various surface and sub-surface factors, and internal drainage. This phase is based on a modification of the Land Suitability Rating System (Agronomic Interpretations Working Group, 1995).

The landowner evaluation addresses similar factors to those in the Phase 1 level. Specific parameters are: surface drainage/ponding, stoniness, surface roughness, topsoil color, surface clods, tilth, plant cover or density, crop yield, crop growth, plant species, and weeds. The landowner is also asked for an overall assessment of the right-of-way on his land with respect to whether it is similar to the off-right-of-way or at least 20% better or worse.

The 1998 field study covered a range of ecological conditions in Alberta. This included approximately five pipeline sites in the dry Prairies, salt-affected and clayey soils in the Aspen Parkland region, the southern Boreal Forest, and the foothills Montane. All areas included both cultivation and grazing land uses.

RATING SYSTEMS

The explanation of the rating system in this section is, by necessity, a brief overview. For a more detailed explanation of the system, the reader should obtain a copy of the manual and see pages 15–17 [NGTL External Advisory Board, 1999(b)].

Phase 1
In the Phase 1 assessment the emphasis is on visible or surface attributes and a comparison between the right-of-way (and the trench if visible) and off-right-of-way control areas. The assessment includes documentation of both positive and negative differences between the areas, but only the negative values are considered for the determination of pass/fail. The conditional rating initiates a re-evaluation of the map unit and either a re-mapping into more units, a ratings change or a Phase 2 evaluation.

The conditions for pass or fail of a site by the Phase 1 rating are:

Pass — no negative results or one "−1" rating of any factor

Conditional — two "−1" ratings for any combination of factors

Fail — a "−2" rating for any factor or three (or more) "−1" ratings

Phase 2
For the Phase 2 assessment the emphasis is on a more detailed investigation of soil attributes that may be responsible for failures or for conditional passes. The right-of-way (and the trench if visible) is compared to an off-right-of-way control that is carefully selected to be representative. As with Phase 1, both the positive and negative differences between the right-of-way and

control sites are recorded, but only the negative values are considered for the determination of a pass/fail.

The conditions of pass/fail of a transect by Phase 2 are:

Pass — any rating that is within the defined tolerance of 20% of the Control ($\geq$80% of the Control)
Conditional — any rating that is just outside the equivalent tolerance (65–80% of the Control)
Fail — any rating that is significantly less than the Control (65% of the Control)

The location of the failures should be documented as to trench or the general right-of-way for segment rating and review purposes. There is a 20% buffer to recognize natural field variation in both the right-of-way and the adjacent field. That is, within a given field, there is expected to be natural variation of at least plus or minus 20% from any given sample point in the field.

Line segments

A line segment is any designated length of right-of-way, but it is normally 1/2 to 1 mile (0.8–1.6 km) to try and correspond to common legal ownership units. It may contain one to several map units or it could be related to natural features for tracts where ownership is not an issue.

For Phase 1, any line segment shall pass if there is:
– <50 m of continuous right-of-way (or trench) failure,
– <100 m of accumulated length of non-continuous failures (problem spots, small map units), and
– there are no areas (no size limit) that present a safety hazard.

If the above three requirements are met, but there is: >150 m of "conditional" rating in a line segment then a Phase 2 assessment must be conducted.

For Phase 2, any line segment shall pass if there is:
– <50 m of continuous right-of-way (or trench) failure,
– <100 m of accumulated length of non-continuous failures (problem spots, small units)
– <150 m of "conditional" rating, and
– there are no areas (no size limit) that present a safety hazard.

The 150 m of right-of-way represents about 20% of 1/2 mile (0.8 km) and any attribute causing a reduction of >50% of the control should be noted.

Landowner evaluation

The landowner evaluation is completed by the owner (or occupant) and includes an assessment of landscape, soils, and vegetation parameters similar to those in Phase 1 and 2. The landowner is requested to check the appropriate box corresponding to whether they thought the pipeline right-of-way was: "at least 20% better than," "as good as," or, "at least 20% worse than" the adjacent representative off-right-of-way control area. The landowner is also asked to provide an overall general assessment of the right-of-way using the same three categories.

RESULTS

1997 study

A result from the 1997 field study was that there was considerable variability in the rating systems, and also between consultants using the same system, when comparing the on-right-of-way areas to the off-right-of-way areas.

In 1997 particular attention was paid to topsoil depth and the variability of this parameter. Across the 18 quarter sections (65 ha or 160 ac) in the study, the average topsoil depth was 16 cm ($\pm$8 cm) both on and off the pipeline right-of-way. One consultant reported finding 10–26 cm of topsoil, another reported finding 10–19 cm and the third consultant reported 12–26 cm. Because these readings were all for the same 65 ha and were obtained by qualified soils professionals, these results are a reflection of the natural variability within a normal agricultural field. It was concluded that, because of this natural variability, topsoil thickness alone is a poor indicator of reclamation success. Systems that relied heavily on topsoil depth as a measure of reclamation success had failure rates of greater than 40%. This is because the on and off-right-of-way "paired" samples varied too much from each other. Removing the topsoil depth parameter resulted in failure rates of about 15%.

About 73% of the 183 right-of-way transect failures were the result of visual parameters. This means many of the failures were apparent to the evaluator before subsurface parameters were evaluated.

1998 study

In the 1998 field study, pipeline segments were evaluated in 32 quarter sections (160 acres/65 ha) by each of three consultant companies in August and September by applying both Phase 1 and Phase 2 to all areas. On 44% of the line segments all three consultants agreed on pass or fail for the Phase 1. Of the remaining areas, in 34% of the cases two of three consultants passed them and in the remaining 22%, two of three consultants failed them.

In 66% of the Phase 2 assessments, all three consultants agreed (all were passes). Of the remaining line segments 28% were rated as passes by two of three consultants and 6% were rated as fails. There were no cases where an area passing Phase 1 was failed under the Phase 2 assessment (note that for this testing both Phase 1 and 2 were done on all sites to provide insight as to whether the system was working. In practice, a Phase 2 would only be done where sites failed Phase 1). This supported a basic premise of the two-phase system which was that soil problems would be reflected in surface characteristics (landscape, vegetation and surface soil).

In the landowner input part of this process, the following results were obtained:
- In the 1998 study, 94% of the 31 landowners contacted responded, with some encouragement, by filling out the forms evaluating reclamation success as they saw it for the study pipelines on their land,
- 72% of the line segments were rated as passes by the landowners,
- the landowner evaluation and the Phase 1 rating by all three consultants agreed on 72% of the line segments (15 "pass" and 6 "fail" ratings, respectively), and
- on three line segments (10%) the landowners rated the area as "pass" and the Phase 1 ratings by all the consultants was a "fail."

1999 study

Following revisions to the reclamation evaluation tool in 1999, both of the manuals [NGTL External Advisory Board, 1999(a,b)] were forwarded to the Alberta Pipeline Environmental Steering Committee (APESC). They subsequently agreed to forward them to Alberta Environment for circulation to approximately 200 organizations and individuals for review and comment prior to releasing them for a widespread trial in the year 2000.

The widespread trial, recommended by the NGTL External Advisory Board for the 2000 growing season, has not taken place and the future of the pipeline reclamation evaluation tool is not clear. However, discussions have been taking place regarding implementing a two year trial beginning in 2001.

CONCLUSIONS

The general concept of a land capability based, relatively rapid Phase 1 "screening" assessment and an "as required" more detailed Phase 2 soil evaluation is workable and appears to address the proper concerns and issues. It appears that underlying soil problems are generally reflected by visible characteristics of landscape, vegetation or surface soil characteristics.

Landowners are willing to participate, there is generally good agreement between the ratings obtained by landowners and consultants. The landowner evaluation form can be a useful first evaluation of pipeline reclamation.

Orientation (training) sessions are expected to increase the level of agreement among evaluators.

The Phase I evaluation tool should include Landscape (drainage, coarse fragments and micro-topography), Soil (color, surface aggregate size and strength), and Vegetation (plant growth and species composition) parameters.

As a result of initial field studies, the authors believe that the protocol is ready for a broad-based trial. Alberta Environment, with the support of the Alberta Pipeline Environmental Steering Committee (APESC), sent the proposed criteria to various organizations and individuals for review and comment in early 2000. As of the fall of 2000, no broad-based field trial had taken place. However, there is discussion about a two year trial period starting in 2001.

ACKNOWLEDGEMENTS

Appreciation is extended to all members of the NGTL External Soils Advisory Board for their commitment of time and energy to this project.

Financial support for the project was provided by TransCanada Transmission (formerly NOVA Gas Transmission Ltd.), the Canadian Association of Petroleum Producers (CAPP), and Alberta Environment.

REFERENCES

Agronomic Interpretations Working Group. 1995. Land suitability rating system for agricultural crops: 1. Spring-seeded small grains. In: Tech. Bull. 1995-6E. W.W. Pettapiece, ed. Center for Land and Biological Resources Research, Agriculture and Agri-Food Canada, Ottawa. 90 pp. 2 maps.

Alberta Environmental Protection. 1994. Guide for pipelines pursuant to the Environmental Protection and Enhancement Act and Regulations. Alberta Environmental Protection, Land Reclamation Division. Edmonton, AB.

Brocke, L. 1988. Alberta legislation as it relates to soil reclamation and energy extraction. In: Energy Extraction: Concerns and Issues Related to Soil Reclamation. Partial Proceedings of the 34th Annual CSSS/AIC Meeting. University of Calgary, Calgary, AB. pp. 1–7.

Landsburg, S. and Fedkenheuer, A.W. 1990. Pipeline construction in NOVA's Alberta Gas Transmission Division. In: Proceedings of Planning, Rehabilitation and Treatment of Disturbed Lands Billings Symposium. Billings, Montana. March 25–30, 1990. Reclamation Research Unit Publication No. 9002, Montana State University, Bozeman. Vol. II, 9 pp.

Mahnic, R.J. and J.A. Toogood. 1992. Proceedings of the Industry/Government Pipeline Success Measurement Workshop. Alberta Land Conservation and Reclamation Council Report No. RRTAC 92-3. ISBN 0-7732-0886-0. 75 pp.

NGTL External Advisory Board. 1999a. Alberta landowner pipeline reclamation assessment manual. A.W. Fedkenheuer, ed. TransCanada Transmission, Calgary, AB. 8 p.

NGTL External Advisory Board. 1999b. Alberta pipeline reclamation assessment manual. A.W. Fedkenheuer and W.W. Pettapiece, eds. TransCanada Transmission, Calgary, AB. 126 p.

Powter, C.B. (compiler). 1998. Glossary of reclamation terms used in Alberta. 5th ed. Alberta Conservation and Reclamation Management Group Report No. RRTAC OF-1A. Alberta Conservation and Reclamation Management Group, Alberta Environmental Protection. Edmonton, AB.

Wellsite Criteria Working Group. 1995. Reclamation criteria for wellsites and associated facilities. Alberta Environmental Protection, Land Reclamation Division, Edmonton, AB.

BIOGRAPHICAL SKETCHES

Al W. Fedkenheuer
ALCLA Native Plant Restoration Inc., 3208 Bearspaw Dr. NW, Calgary, AB, Canada, T2L 1T2, e-mail: fedkenhp@cadvision.com

Al Fedkenheuer is president of ALCLA Native Plant Restoration Inc., a private environmental consulting firm involved in native plant propagation and sales, restoration of native areas, reclamation planning, and implementation. He has spent about 20 years in pipeline reclamation dealing with various soil, vegetation, and reclamation issues. His areas of interest are diverse and include reclamation success evaluation, general land reclamation, revegetation, native plant community restoration, forest ecology, and native plant propagation.

Wayne Pettapiece
Pettapiece Pedology, 11620-48 Avenue, Edmonton, AB, Canada, T6H 0E6, e-mail: pettapwi@aonet.com

Wayne Pettapiece is president of Pettapiece Pedology. Prior to this position Wayne spent 35 years with the Agriculture Canada Soil Survey unit. He has experience from the mixed grass prairies to the boreal forest, the sub-arctic plains, and the sub-alpine Rocky Mountains. His interests have been the application of soil survey/pedological information and the integration of ecological concepts into land management.

Leonard Leskiw
Can-Ag Enterprises Ltd., 14805-119 Avenue, Edmonton, AB, Canada, T5L 2N9, e-mail: lleskiw@telusplanet.net

Leonard Leskiw is president of Can-Ag Enterprises, a private soil consulting firm. He has over 25 years of experience in soil science with applications to agriculture, environment, and forestry in Canada and internationally. Leonard had been very active in developing soil capability assessment system for reclaimed agricultural and forest lands in Alberta. His interests are in pre-disturbance surveys, conservation and reclamation planning, environmental impact assessments, reclaimed soils investigations and agriculture and forest capability assessments for pipelines, mines, and wellsites.

Jim Burke
Jim Burke & Associates, 1216-18th Street N.E., Calgary, AB, Canada, T2E 4V9, e-mail: jimburke@cadvision.com

Jim Burke is president of Jim Burke & Associates, a private soil consulting firm. Previously Jim spent 8 years in the environmental department of NOVA Gas Transmission Ltd. He was responsible for pre-disturbance soil surveys, planning soils handling during pipeline construction, conservation and reclamation planning, reclaimed soil investigations, agricultural capability assessments, and investigating the impact of soils on pipe cracking and corrosion. In the course of his recent duties he is deeply involved in the remediation of contaminated soils at oil well-sites.

Symposium participants

Lawrence Abrahamson
SUNY-ESF
1 Forestry Drive
Syracuse, NY 13210, USA
E-mail: labrahamson@esf.edu
Fax: 315-470-6934
Phone: 315-470-6777

Hamid Aseshina Ade-Abolaji
Centre for Urban &
Regional Planning & Dev
PO Box 54338
Falomo, Ikoyi
Lagos, Lagos LOS, Nigeria
E-mail: eebong@yahoo.co.uk
Fax: 234-1-2641166
Phone: 234-1-2660600

Richard Yemi Afolabi
Centre for Urban &
Regional Planning & Dev
PO Box 54338
Falomo, Ikoyi
Lagos, Lagos LOS, Nigeria
E-mail: eebong@yahoo.co.uk
Fax: 234-1-2641166
Phone: 234-1-2660600

Markus Alapassi
Ministry of the Environment
PL 380
Helsinki 00131, Finland
E-mail: markus.alapassi@vyh.fi
Fax: 358-9-1991-9364
Phone: 358-9-19919367

Sherri Albrecht
URS
201 Willowbrook Blvd
Wayne, NJ 07470, USA
E-mail: sherri_albrecht@urscorp.com
Fax: 973-785-0023
Phone: 973-785-0700

Edward Alkiewicz
New York Power Authority
123 Main Street
White Plains, NY 10601, USA
E-mail: alkiewicz.e@nypa.gov
Fax: 914-287-3294
Phone: 914-287-3247

Bhuvan Kumar Amatya
Sulabh International Nepal
Bishalnagar, Kathmandu-5
Post Box 5083
Kathmandu, Nepal
E-mail: atharai@wlink.com
Fax: 977-1-432243
Phone: 977-1-432243

John Amodeo
Carol R. Johnson Assoc. Inc.
1100 Massachusetts Ave
Cambridge, MA 02138, USA
E-mail: jamodeo@crja.com
Fax: 617-354-9808
Phone: 617-868-6115

Chris Anderson
Asplundh Tree Expert Co.
7524 NE 175th Street
Bothell, WA 98011, USA
Phone: 206-255-5682

Paul Anderson
Alliance Pipeline, Ltd.
1200, 605 5th Avenue
Calgary, AB T2P 3H5, Canada
E-mail: paul.anderson@alliance-pipeline.com
Fax: 403-266-1604
Phone: 403-716-0389

Ted Anderson
Pioneer Land Services Ltd.
1729-12th Street SW
Calgary, AB T2T 3N1, Canada
E-mail: anderson@pioneerland.ca
Fax: 403-244-5104
Phone: 403-229-3989

Terry Antoniuk
Salmo Consulting Inc.
#230, 323-10 Ave SW
Calgary, AB T2R 0A5, Canada
E-mail: salmo@cadvision.com
Fax: 403-266-6363
Phone: 403-266-6363

Hans Arends
Inuvialuit Land Administration
PO Box 290
Tuktoyaktuk, NT X0E 1C0, Canada
E-mail: harends@irc.inuvialuit.com
Fax: 867-977-2467
Phone: 867-977-2202

Javier Arevalo Camacho
Red Electrica de Espana
PO Del Conde De Los Gaitanes, 177
LA Moraleja Alcobendas
Madrid 28109, Spain
E-mail: jarevalo@ree.es
Fax: 34-916594542
Phone: 34-91-650-8500

James Arndt
Peterson Environmental Consulting Inc.
1355 Mendota Heights Road
Suite 100
Mendota Heights, MN, USA
E-mail: jarndt@petersonenv.com

Dale Arner
Mississippi State University
209 Seville Place
Mississippi, MS, USA
Phone: 662-325-2617

Robert Arvedlund
Federal Energy Regulatory Comm.
888 First Street, N.E.
Washington, DC 20426, USA
E-mail: robert.arvedlund@ferc.fed.us
Fax: 202-208-0353
Phone: 202-208-0091

Brian Asmus
Minnesota Power
3215 Arrowhead Road
Duluth, MN 55811 4257, USA
E-mail: basmus@mnpower.com
Fax: 218-720-2781
Phone: 218-720-2758

Jann Atkinson
National Energy Board
444 7th Avenue S.W.
Calgary, AB T2P 0X8, Canada
E-mail: jatkinson@neb.gc.ca
Fax: 403-299-2785
Phone: 403-299-2796

John Auriemma
El Paso Energy
1001 Louisiana Street
Houston, TX 77009, USA
E-mail: auriemaj@epenergy.com
Fax: 713-420-6229
Phone: 713-420-7332

Jeff Back
Ecomark Ltd.
110, 1525-170 St
Edmonton, AB T5P 4W2, Canada
Fax: 780-914-3246
Phone: 780-444-0706

Evan Baker
Greystone Enviro Consultants Inc.
221, 2451 Dieppe Ave S.W.
Calgary, AB T3E 7K1, Canada
E-mail: baker.greystone@home.com
Fax: 403-271-7162
Phone: 403-271-7110

Benjamin Ballard
SUNY-ESF
218 Marshall Hall
1 Forestry Drive
Syracuse, NY 13210, USA
E-mail: bballard@esf.edu
Fax: 315-470-6956
Phone: 315-470-4821

Daniel Barghsoon
AXYS Environmental Consulting Ltd.
600-555 4th Ave S.W.
Calgary, AB T2P 3E7, Canada
E-mail: dbarghsoon@azys.net
Fax: 403-269-5245
Phone: 403-750-7661

James Barnes
Iroquois Gas Transmission
One Corporate Drive Suite 600
Shelton, CT 06484, USA
E-mail: Tim_Barnes@Iroquois.com
Fax: 203-925-7213
Phone: 203-944-7023

Bruce Barnett
Aspen Environmental Group
1760 Creekside Oaks, Suite 170
Sacramento, CA 95833, USA
E-mail: bbarnett@aspeneg.com
Fax: 916-646-3872
Phone: 916-646-3869

Krista Bartsch
URS Corporation
1615 Murray Canyon Road
Suite 1000
San Diego, CA 92108, USA
E-mail: krista_bartsch@urscorp.com
Fax: 619-293-7920
Phone: 619-683-6155

Brett Battaglia
Northern Ecological Assoc, Inc.
451 Presumpscot Street
Portland, ME 04103, USA
E-mail: bbattaglia@neamaine.com
Fax: 207-879-9481
Phone: 207-879-9496

Jayne Battey
Essex Environmental
637 Main Street
Half Moon Bay, CA 94019, USA
E-mail: jbattey@essexenv.com
Fax: 650-712-1190
Phone: 650-726-8320

Richard Bausell
URS Corporation
2318 Millpark Dr.
Maryland Hieghts, MO 63043, USA
E-mail: Richard_Bausell@URSCorp.com
Fax: (314) 427-0462
Phone: (314) 754-1035

Jean-Pierre Beaumont
Quebec Ministere des Transports
35 Port-Royal Est. 4e
Montreal, PQ H3L 3T1, Canada
E-mail: jbeaumont@mtq.gouv.qc.ca
Fax: 514-873-5391
Phone: 514-873-5890

Jeff Beckwith
Puget Sound Energy
8001 S. 212 Street
Kent, WA 98032, USA
E-mail: jbeckw@puget.com
Fax: (253) 395-7022
Phone: (253) 395-7058

Yves Bedard
Quebec Ministere des Transports
475 Boul. de l'Atrium, 4e etage
Charlesbourg, PQ G1H 7H9, Canada
E-mail: ybedard@mtq.gouv.qc.ca
Fax: 418-646-0003
Phone: 418-380-2003

Hans Bekker
Ministry of Transport
Public Works & Water Mgt
PO Box 5044
Delft, 2600 GA, The Netherlands
E-mail: g.j.bekker@dww.rws.minvan.nl
Fax: 31-015-251-8555
Phone: 31-015-251-8470

Francis Belisle
Hydro Quebec Production-Manicouagan
135, boul. Comeau
Baie-Comeau, PQ G4Z 3B1, Canada

Peter Bell
ENSR Corp
27755 Diehl Road
Warrenville, IL 60555, USA
E-mail: pbell@ensr.com
Fax: 630-836-1711
Phone: 630-836-1700

Mary Beth Benedict
Nova Scotia Power
PO Box 910
25 Lakeside Park Drive
Halifax, NS B3J 2W5, Canada
E-mail: mb.benedict@nspower.ca
Fax: 902-428-7564
Phone: 902-428-7503

Ilona Berbekar
Trans Canada Pipelines
801-7th Avenue SW
Calgary, AB T2P 3P7, Canada
E-mail: Ilona_Berbekar@Transcanada.com
Fax: 403-290-7227
Phone: 403-290-8001

Franck Berry
White Pine Environmental Inc.
564 Windermere Street
Vancouver, BC V5K 4J2, Canada
E-mail: fcberry@telus.net
Fax: 604-253-7116
Phone: 604-253-7715

Ken Berry
Land Matters Ltd.
4004 Violet Street
North Vancouver, BC V7G 1E3, Canada
E-mail: kberry@bcgas.com
Fax: 250-490-2606
Phone: 250-490-2606

Walter BidLake
New Brunswick Power
515 King Street
PO Box 2000 F
Fredericton, NB E3B 4X1, Canada
E-mail: WBidLake@nbpower.com
Fax: 506-458-3572
Phone: 506-458-3464

Brian Bietz
AB Energy & Utilities Board
640-5th Ave S.W.
Calgary, AB T2P 3G4, Canada
E-mail: brian.bietz@eub.gov.ab.ca
Fax: (403) 297-8398
Phone: (403) 297-4303

Tiffanie Billey
AXYS Environmental Consulting Ltd.
600-555 4th Ave S.W.
Calgary, AB T2P 3E7, Canada
E-mail: tbilley@axy.net
Fax: 403-269-5245
Phone: 403-750-7673

Mark Bisett
Williams-Gas Pipelines, Transco
2800 Post Oak Blvd
Houston, TX 77056, USA
E-mail: mark.g.bisett@williams.com
Fax: 713-215-4551
Phone: 713-215-2781

Michelle Bissonnette
HDR Engineering
6190 Golden Hills Drive
Minneapolis, MN 55416, USA
E-mail: mbissonn@hdrinc.com
Fax: 763-591-5413
Phone: 760-278-5910

Karen Black
Trans Canada Pipelines
801-7th Avenue SW (28th Floor)
Calgary, AB T2P 2P7, Canada
E-mail: karen_black@transcanada.com
Fax: 403-290-7227
Phone: 403-290-6035

James Bloemker
Williams-Gas Pipelines, Transco
2800 Post Oak Blvd
Houston, TX 77056, USA
E-mail: james.d.bloemker@williams.com
Fax: 713-215-4551
Phone: 713-215-2656

Keith Boras
Lacombe County
5432-56th Avenue
Lacombe, AB T4L 1E9, Canada
E-mail: kboras_lacombecounty@rttinc.com
Fax: 403-782-3820
Phone: 403-782-6601

Andre Bouchard
Universite de Montreal, IRBV
4101 est, Rue Sherbrooke
Montreal, PQ H1X 2B2, Canada
E-mail: andre.bernard.bouchrd@umontreal.ca
Fax: 514-872-9406
Phone: 514-872-2216

Peter Boucher
Halloran & Sage LLP
225 Asylum Street, One Goodwin Square
Hartford, CT 06103, USA
E-mail: boucher@halloran-sage.com
Fax: 860-548-0006
Phone: 860-297-4650

John Bowen
Ontario Hydro Services Co.
114 Culloden Road
Ingersoll, ON N5C 3R1, Canada
E-mail: john.bowen@ohsc.com
Fax: 416-345-5401
Phone: 416-345-5401

Renee Bowler
Ontario Ministry of Environment
40 St. Clair Ave. W, 7th Floor
Toronto, ON M4V 1M2, Canada
E-mail: bowlerre@ene.gov.on.ca
Fax: 416-327-2936
Phone: 416-327-5510

James Boyle
Boyle Associates
27 Gorham Road, Suite 12
Scarborough, ME 20902, USA
E-mail: JPBoyle@aol.com
Fax: 207-883-6039
Phone: 207-883-6040

Michael Boyle
Federal Energy Regulatory Comm.
888 First Street, N.E., 62-47
Washington, DC 20426, USA
E-mail: michael.boyle@ferc.fed.us
Fax: 202-208-0353
Phone: 202-208-0839

John Bridges
Western Area Power Admin
PO Box 281213
Lakewood, CO 80228-8213, USA
E-mail: bridges@wapa.gov
Fax: 720-962-7263
Phone: 720-962-7255

Grete Bridgewater
Canadian Pacific Railway
Suite 2000, 401-9th Avenue, S.W.
Calgary, AB T2P 4Z4, Canada
E-mail: grete_bridgewater@cpr.ca

Jacques Brisson
Universite de Montreal
Institut de Recherche en Biologie Veg
4101 est, Rue Sherbrooke
Montreal, PQ H1X 2B2, Canada
E-mail: brisson@magellan.umontreal.ca
Fax: 514-872-9406
Phone: 514-872-1437

Mark Brobbel
Dillon Consulting Ltd.
1405,101-6th Ave S.W.
Calgary, AB T2P 3P4, Canada
E-mail: mbrobbel@dillon.ca
Fax: 403-215-8889
Phone: 403-215-8880

Anne Brown
Levenson Brown Consulting
1835 South Bragaw St, MS-568
Anchorage, AK 99512, USA
E-mail: browna@alyeska-pipeline.com
Fax: 907-787-8322
Phone: 907-787-8094

Christine Brown
EUB, Surveillance Branch
640 5th Avenue SW
Calgary, AB T2P 3G4, Canada
E-mail: christine.brown@gov.ab.ca
Fax: 403-297-7168
Phone: 403-297-2228

Neil Brown
Arbor Consulting Ltd.
3736 66 Street
Camrose, AB T4V 3N4, Canada
E-mail: arbor@telusplanet.net
Fax: 780-672-8667
Phone: 780-679-8200

Paul Brown
Kinder Morgan, Inc.
370 Van Gordon Street
Littleton, CO 80123, USA
E-mail: paul_brown@kindermorgan.com
Fax: 303-984-3190
Phone: 303-914-7853

Robert Brown
Alberta Infrastructure
Peace Region, Room 301
Provincial Building 9621-96 Ave
Peace River, AB T8S 1T4, Canada
E-mail: Robert.P.Brown@gov.ab.ca
Fax: 780-624-2440
Phone: 780-624-6280

Juliet Browne
Verrill & Dana, LLP
One portland Square
Portland, ME, USA
E-mail: jbrowne@verrilldana.com
Fax: 207-774-7499
Phone: 207-774-4000

Charles Burdick
Central Hudson Gas & Electric Corp
284 South Avenue
Poughkeepsie, NY 12601, USA
E-mail: cburdick@cenhud.com
Fax: 914-486-5894
Phone: 914-486-5740

Andre Burroughs
Hydro Quebec
855 rue Sainte-Catherine est 9e etage
Montreal, PQ H2L 4P5, Canada
E-mail: Burroughs.Andre@hydro.qc.ca
Fax: 514-840-3933
Phone: 514-840-3000-4439

Mario Buszynski
SENES Consultants Limited
121 Granton Drive, Unit 12
Richmond Hill, ON L4B 3N4, Canada
E-mail: mbuszynski@senes.on.ca
Fax: 905-764-9386
Phone: 905-764-9380

Kim Butler
Municipal District of RockyView #44
911-32nd Ave N.E.
Calgary, AB T2M 4L6, Canada
E-mail: asb@gov.mdrockyview.ab.ca
Fax: 403-277-5977
Phone: 403-230-1401

Nancy Cain
Cain Vegetation Inc.
5 Kingham Road
Acton, ON L7J 1S3, Canada
E-mail: cainvegetation@sympatico.ca
Fax: 519-853-1359
Phone: 519-853-3081

Lauren Caldwell
BC Hydro
6911 Southpoint Drive
Floor EO5
Burnaby, BC V3N 4X8, Canada
E-mail: lauren.caldwell@bchydro.ca
Fax: 604-528-2940
Phone: 604-528-2103

David Cameron
ENSR Corp
35 Nagog Park
Acton, MA 01720, USA
E-mail: dcameron@ensr.com
Fax: 978-635-9180
Phone: 978-635-9180

William Candler
Georgia Power Company
5131 Maner Road
Smyrna, GA 30080-7321, USA
E-mail: wjcandle@southernco.com
Fax: 404-799-2141
Phone: 404-799-2151

Kenneth Carothers
SWCA Inc, Enviro Consultants
114 North San Francisco St., Suite 100
Flagstaff, AZ 86001, USA
E-mail: kcarothers@swca.com
Fax: 520-779-2709
Phone: 520-774-550

Sheila Castellano
El Paso Energy
PO Box 1492
El Paso, TX 79978, USA
E-mail: castellanos@epenergy.com
Fax: 915-496-2475
Phone: 915-496-3034

Darrell Chambers
Dow AgroSciences Canada
1144 29th Ave N.E.
Calgary, AB T2E 7P1, Canada
E-mail: dbchambers@dowagro.com
Fax: 403-735-8841
Phone: 403-735-8864

Nancy Champayne
University du Quebec
C.P. 500
Trois-Rivieres, PQ G9A 5H7, Canada
E-mail: nancy-champayne@vgtr.uquebec.ca
Fax: 819-376-5084
Phone: 819-376-5053

Alan Chan-McLeod
BC Hydro
6911 Southpoint Drive
Burnaby, BC V3N 4X8, Canada
E-mail: alan.chan-mcleod@bchydro.com
Fax: 604-528-8290
Phone: 604-528-1723

Anthony Clevenger
University of Calgary
625 Fourth Street
Canmore, AB T1W 2G7, Canada
E-mail: tony_clevenger@pch.gc.ca
Fax: 403-760-1371
Phone: 403-762-3240

Ken Colosimo
National Energy Board
444 7th Avenue S.W.
Calgary, AB T2P 0X8, Canada
E-mail: kcolosimo@neb.gc.ca
Fax: 403-292-5875
Phone: 403-292-4926

Edward Colson
Colson & Associates
9 Corwin Drive
Alamo, CA 94507, USA
E-mail: edcolson@aol.com
Fax: 925-837-0818
Phone: 925-837-6309

Stephen Compton
Northern Ecological Assoc, Inc.
33 Park Street
Canton, NY 13617, USA
E-mail: scompton@neanewyork.com
Fax: 315-379-0355
Phone: 315-386-3704

John Confer
Ithaca College
953 Danby Road
Ithaca, NY 14850, USA
E-mail: confer@ithaca.edu
Fax: 607-274-1131
Phone: 607-274-3978

Dusty Cooper
D.J. Silviculture ENT. Ltd
14025 Moberly Road
Winfield, BC V4V 1A6, Canada
E-mail: djcooper@silk.net
Fax: 250-766-2677
Phone: 250-766-2677

Patricia Cooper
Golder Associates Ltd.
10th Floor, 940 6th Ave SW
Calgary, AB T2P 3T1, Canada
E-mail: pcooper@Goldler.com
Fax: 403-299-5606
Phone: 403-276-8916

Henri Coumoul
Autoroutes du Sud de la France
Quartier St Anne-Vedene
Vedene, Le Pontet 84967, France
E-mail: aline.vinel.@asf.fr
Fax: 04-90-32-7330
Phone: 04-90-32-9005

Jean-Maurice Coutu
Environment Canada
17th Floor, Place Vincent Massey
351 Joseph Blvd.
Hull, PQ K1A 0H3, Canada
E-mail: jean-maurice.coutu2@ec.gc.ca
Fax: 819-953-4093
Phone: 819-953-0554

Tracey Cove
Alberta Environment
Box 70028 Bowness Postal Outlet
Calgary, AB T3B 5K3, Canada
E-mail: tracey.cove@gov.ab.ca
Fax: 403-297-8803

Allen Crabtree
Navigant Consulting Inc.
703 Bridgton
Sebago, ME 04029, USA
E-mail: allen_crabtree@rminc.com
Phone: 207-787-2531

Steve Craycroft
Essex Environmental
637 Main Street
Half Moon Bay, CA 94019, USA
E-mail: scraycroft@essexenv.com
Fax: 650-712-1190
Phone: 650-726-8320

Andrew Cressman
Environmental Resources Management Inc.
2666 Riva Road, Suite 200
Annapolis, MD, USA
E-mail: andrew_cressman@erm.com
Fax: 410-266-8912
Phone: 410-266-0006

Jim Crinklaw
ATCO Electric
PO Box 2426
10035-105th Street
Edmonton, AB T5J 2V6, Canada
E-mail: jim.crinklaw@atcoelectric.com
Fax: 403-420-5410
Phone: 403-420-7183

Michael Crowder
The Barker Ranch Ltd.
85305 Snively Road
West Richland, WA 99353, USA
E-mail: gdbarker@gte.net
Phone: 509-967-3023

Ted Currie
Dept of Fisheries & Oceans
PO Box 5030, 343 Archibald Street
Moncton, NB E1C 9B6, Canada
E-mail: CurrieT@mar.dfo-mpo.gc.ca
Fax: 506-851-6579
Phone: 506-851-3650

Lynette Curthoys
Essex Environmental
637 Main Street
Half Moon Bay, CA 94019, USA
E-mail: lcurthoys@essexenv.com
Fax: 650-712-1190
Phone: 650-726-8320

Angelo Dalcin
Canadian Pacific Railway
Suite 2000, Gulf Canada Square
401 9th Avenue SW
Calgary, AB T2P 4Z4, Canada
E-mail: angelo_dalcin@cpr.ca
Fax: 403-319-3883
Phone: 403-319-6145

Kevin Dalgarno
BC Hydro
1401 Kal Lake Rd
Vernon, BC V1T 8S4, Canada
E-mail: kevin.dalgarno@bchydro.com
Fax: 250-549-8667
Phone: 250-549-8549

William Danchuk
Dominion Resources
CNG Tower
625 Liberty Avenue
Pittsburgh, PA 15222-3199, USA
E-mail: William_A_Danchuk@dom.com
Fax: 412-690-7633
Phone: 412-690-1362

Sylvie de Blois
Universite de Montreal
4101 est, Rue Sherbrooke
Montreal, PQ H1X 2B2, Canada
E-mail: deBloiss@magellan.umontreal.ca
Fax: 514-872-9406
Phone: 514-872-8488

Paul de la Bastide
UNI VIC/Science Stores
Petch Building, Suite 116
Victoria, BC V8P 5C5, Canada
E-mail: pdelabas@uvic.ca
Phone: 250-721-6319

Susana De La Zerda
Avifauna Ltda, ISA
AA 3751
Bogota, Columbia
E-mail: guberekz@unete.com
Fax: 571-285-4550
Phone: 571-232-9838

Amy Dierolf
Florida Power Corporation
PO Box 14042
Mail Code - BB1A
St. Petersburg, FL 33733-4042, USA
E-mail: amy.dierolf@fpc.com
Fax: 737-826-4216
Phone: 727-826-4327

Darren Dillenbeck
Dow AgroSciences Canada
71 Essex Lane
Sault Ste. Marie, ON, Canada
E-mail: dsdillenbeck@dowagro.com
Fax: 705-941-9696
Phone: 705-254-9586

Kendall Dilling
TransCanada Transmission
801-7th Avenue
Calgary, AB T2P 3P7, Canada
E-mail: kendall_dilling@transcanada.cam
Fax: 403-290-7227
Phone: 403-290-6281

Elizabeth Dolezal
Natural Resource Group Inc.
1800 International Centre
900 2nd Ave S.
Minneapolis, MN 55402, USA
E-mail: endolezal@nrginc.com
Fax: 612-347-6780
Phone: 612-347-7866

Jean Domingue
Naturam Environment Inc
31 Marquette
Baie Comeau, PQ G4Z 1K4, Canada
E-mail: jean.domingue@naturam.ca
Fax: 418-2889
Phone: 418-296-8911

David Dominie
E/Pro Engineering & Enviro Consulting
41 Anthony Avenue
Augusta, MA 04330, USA
E-mail: ddominie@eproconsulting.com
Fax: 207-621-7001
Phone: 207-621-7084

Jean Doucet
Transenergie
800 Maisonneuve E.
21st Floor
Montreal, PQ H2L 4M8, Canada
E-mail: doucet.jean.2@hydro.qc.ca
Fax: 514-840-3137
Phone: 514-840-3000

Larry Duchesne
Alberta Infrastructure
Land Planning & Documentation
3rd Floor, 6950-113 St
Edmonton, AB T6H 5V7, Canada
E-mail: Larry.Duchesne@gov.ab.ca
Fax: 780-422-5419
Phone: 780-422-7492

Brett Dumas
Idaho Power Company
PO Box 70
Boise, ID, USA
E-mail: bdumas@idahopower.com
Fax: 208-388-6902
Phone: 208-388-2330

Shawn Duncan
Maritimes & Northeast Pipeline
Suite 1600, 1801 Hollis Street
Halifax, NS B3J 3N4, Canada
E-mail: sduncan@mnpp.com
Fax: 902-490-2222
Phone: 902-490-2213

Gordon Dunn
Tera Environmental Consultants
Suite 205, 925-7th Avenue S.W.
Calgary, AB T2P 1A5, Canada
E-mail: gdunn@teraenv.com
Phone: 403-265-2885

James Durand
BSC Group
33 Waldo Street
Worcester, MA 01608, USA
E-mail: jdurand@bscgroup.com
Fax: 508-792-4509
Phone: 508-792-4500

Roderick Dushnicky
Alberta Infrastructure
3rd Floor
6950-113 Street
Edmonton, AB T6H 5V7, Canada
E-mail: rod.dushnicky@gov.ab.ca
Fax: (780) 422-2661
Phone: (780) 422-1135

Mark Ealey
Golder Associates Ltd.
209, 2121 Airport Drive
Saskatoon, SK S7L 6W5, Canada
E-mail: Mark_ealey@golder.com
Fax: 306-664-9733
Phone: 306-665-7989

Dan Eddy
Midland Vegetation Mgt Inc.
8459-23rd Ave NE
Calgary, AB T1Y 7G9, Canada
E-mail: d.eddy@midlandvegetation.ca
Fax: 403-285-9205
Phone: 403-285-9111

Don Elsenheimer
HDR Engineering
6190 Golden Hills Drive
Minneapolis, MN 55416, USA
E-mail: delsenhe@hdrinc.com
Fax: 763-591-5413
Phone: 763-278-5909

Carol Engstrom
707 8th Ave S.W.
Calgary, AB T2P 3G7, Canada
E-mail: carol.engstrom@husky-oil.com
Fax: 403-298-6227
Phone: 403-298-6175

Henry Epp
Digital Environmental Management
301, 1114 22nd St West
Saskatoon, SK S7M 0S5, Canada
Fax: 306-934-2572
Phone: 306-975-3867

Robert Erickson
Earth Tech
300 Baker Avenue
Concord, MA 1742, USA

William Erickson
Bonneville Power Admin.
1520 Kelly Place
Walla Walla, WA 99362, USA
E-mail: wterickson@hpa.gov
Fax: 509-527-6314
Phone: 509-527-6249

Bret Estep
Georgia Transmission Corp.
2100 E. Exchange Place
Tucker, Georgia 30085, USA
E-mail: bret.estep@gatrans.com
Fax: 770-270-7872
Phone: 770-270-7358

Daniel Eusebi
ESG International
361 Southgate Dr.
Guelph, ON N1G 3M5, Canada
E-mail: deusebi@esg.net
Fax: 519-836-2493
Phone: 519-836-6050

Paul Evanoff
SmithGroup JJR
110 Miller
Ann Arbor, MI 48104, USA
E-mail: pevanoff@aa.smithgroup.com

James Evans
615 West Maude Avenue
Arlington Heights, IL 60004, USA
E-mail: JamesMEvans@lightfirst.com
Phone: 847-577-5778

Marcus Eyre
National Energy Board
444 7th Avenue S.W.
Calgary, AB T2P 0X8, Canada
E-mail: meyre@neb.gc.ca
Phone: 403-299-3906

Sheryl Faminow
Ghostpine Environmental Services Ltd.
608 Willacy Drive SE
Calgary, AB T2J 2C9, Canada
E-mail: ghostpine@cadvision.com
Fax: 403-271-6778
Phone: 403-271-6822

Kathleen Farley
State of AK, DNR, State Pipeline
411 W Fourth Ave, Suite 2-C
Anchorage, AK 99501-2343, USA
Fax: 907-272-0690
Phone: 907-271-4476

Alison Farrand
National Energy Board
444 7th Avenue S.W.
Calgary, AB T2P 0X8, Canada
E-mail: afarrand@neb.gc.ca
Fax: 403-292-5875
Phone: 403-299-2761

Kenneth Farrish
Steven F. Austin State University
Arthur Temple College of Forestry
PO Box 6109 SFA Station
Nacogdoches, TX 75962-6109, USA
E-mail: kfarrish@sfasu.edu
Fax: 409-468-2489
Phone: 409-468-2475

Al Fedkenheuer
ALCLA Native Plant Restoration Inc.
3208 Bearspaw Dr. NW
Calgary, AB T2L 1T2, Canada
E-mail: fedkenhp@cadvision.com
Fax: 403-282-7090
Phone: 403-282-6516

Randall Fee
Pacific Gas and Electric Co.
1050 High St., 3rd Floor
Auburn, CA 95603, USA
E-mail: rgf7@pge.com
Fax: 530-889-3780
Phone: 530-889-3825

Thomas Field
ANR Pipeline Company
500 Renaissance Center
Detroit, MI 48243, USA
E-mail: thomas.field@coastalcorp.com
Fax: (313) 496-2143
Phone: (313) 496-5621

Kenneth Finch
205 Villiard Road
Parish, NY 13131, USA
Phone: 315-963-8964

Chris Finley
National Energy Board
444 7th Avenue S.W.
Calgary, AB T2P 0X8, Canada
E-mail: cfinley@neb-one.gc.ca
Fax: 403-299-3110
Phone: 403-299-3117

Warren Fleming
University of Alberta
7-51 General Sciences Building
Edmonton, AB T6G 2H1, Canada
E-mail: wdf@ualberta.ca
Fax: 790-436-4158
Phone: 780-492-9084

Carol Forrest
URS
1615 Murray Canyon Road
Suite 1000
San Diego, CA 92108, USA
E-mail: carol_forrest@urscorp.com
Fax: 619-293-7920
Phone: 619-294-9400

Christian Fortin
Foramec Inc.
70. rue Saint-Paul
Quebec, PQ G1K 3V9, Canada
E-mail: cfortin@foramec.gc.ca
Fax: 418-392-5826
Phone: 418-692-4828

Piers Fothergill
Tera Environmental Consultants
Suite 205, 925-7th Avenue S.W.
Calgary, AB T2P 1A5, Canada
E-mail: pfothergill@teraenv.com
Fax: 403-266-6471
Phone: 403-265-2885

David Frazier
URS Corp.
282 Delaware Ave
Buffalo, NY 14202, USA
E-mail: dave_frazier@urscorp.com
Fax: 716-856-2545
Phone: 716-856-5636

Gina Fryer
Tera Environmental Consultants
205, 925-7th Avenue., S.W.
Calgary, AB T2P 1A5, Canada
E-mail: gfryer@teraenv.com
Fax: 403-266-6471
Phone: 403-265-2885

Roberto Fuertes-Thillet
Puerto Rico Electric Power Auth.
PO Box 363928
San Juan 00936-3928, Puerto Rico
Fax: 787-289-4660
Phone: 787-753-6449

Tony Gale
Ecology and Environment, Inc
1999 Brtyan Street, Suite 2000
Dallas, TX 75201, USA
E-mail: tgale@ene.com
Fax: 214-245-1001
Phone: 214-245-1060

Donald Gartman
722 Chappell Road
Charleston, WV 25304, USA
E-mail: dongartman@aol.com

Paul Gayer
Kinder Morgan, Inc.
PO Box 281304
Lakewood, CO 80228-8213, USA
E-mail: paul_gayer.kindermorgan.com
Fax: 303-914-7700
Phone: 303-914-7804

Scott Gedak
National Energy Board
444 7th Avenue S.W.
Calgary, AB T2P 0X8, Canada
E-mail: egedak@neb.gc.ca
Fax: 403-292-5503
Phone: 403-299-3674

Jose Gerin-Lajoie
University du Quebec
590 Principalle
Grodines, PQ G0A 1W0, Canada
E-mail: flone@globetrotter.gc.ca
Phone: 418-268-3062

Diana Ghikas
National Energy Board
444 7th Avenue S.W.
Calgary, AB T2P 0X8, Canada
E-mail: dghikas@neb.gc.ca
Fax: 403-299-3110
Phone: 403-299-2797

Regan Giese
Geo-Marine, Inc
150 A N. Festival Drive
Las Cruces, NM 88011, USA
E-mail: rgiese@geo-marine.com
Fax: 915-858-2153
Phone: 915-585-0168

Karl Gilmore
Tera Environmental Consultants
67 Sandringham Way NW
Calgary, AB T3K 2V6, Canada
E-mail: kgilmore@teraenv.com
Fax: 403-266-6471
Phone: 403-365-2885

Neil Gilson
Prairie Farm Rehabilitation Administration
Room 600, 138-4th Avenue SE
Calgary, AB T2G 42G, Canada
E-mail: gilsonn@em.agr.ca
Fax: 403-292-5659
Phone: 403-292-5723

Phil Gizzi
New York Power Authority
Valenti Road,
PO Box 200
Gilboa, NY 12076, USA
E-mail: gizzi.p@nypa.gov
Phone: 607-588-6061

Randal Glaholt
Tera Environmental Consultants
Suite 205, 925-7th Avenue S.W.
Calgary, AB T2P 1A5, Canada
Fax: 403-266-6471
Phone: 403-265-2885

Catherine Godden
Ecos Consulting (Aust) Pty Ltd.
1136 Ord Street
West Perth, Western Australia 6005
Australia
E-mail: cathygodden@ecos.con.au
Fax: 61-94815006
Phone: 61-94815456

Colleen Goertz
Trans Canada Pipelines
801-7th Avenue SW (28th Floor)
Calgary, AB T2P 2P7, Canada
E-mail: colleen-goertz@transcanada.com
Fax: 403-290-7227
Phone: 403-290-6064

Edward Gonzales
Duke Energy
675 Western Ave #4
Manchester, ME 04351, USA
E-mail: EdGonzales@Duke-Energy.Com
Fax: 207-621-8229
Phone: 888-876-4080

John W. Goodrich-Mahoney
Electric Power Research Institute
Suite 805, 2000 L Street N.W., Suite 805
Washington, DC 20036, USA
E-mail: jmahoney@epri.com
Fax: 202-293-2697
Phone: 202-293-7516

Arthur Gover
Pennsylvania State University
L.M.R.C. Orchard Road
University Park, PA 16802, USA
E-mail: aeg2@psu.edu
Fax: 814-863-1184
Phone: 814-863-1184

Joyce Greenfield
Prairie Farm Rehabilitation Administration
Room 600, 138-4th Avenue SE
Calgary, AB T2G 42G, Canada
E-mail: greefieldj@em.agr.ca
Fax: 403-292-5659
Phone: 403-292-5723

Rodney Gregory
Williams Gas Pipeline
22909 N.E. Redmond-Fall City Road
Redmond, WA 98053, USA
E-mail: rod.p.gregory@williams.com
Fax: (425) 868-4915
Phone: (425) 868-1010 x2052

Scott Grindal
AXYS Environmental Consulting Ltd.
600-555 4th Ave S.W.
Calgary, AB T2P 3E7, Canada
E-mail: sgrindal@axys.net
Fax: 403-269-5245
Phone: 403-750-7669

Don Grossbevndt
BP Amoco Plc
240 4th Ave SW
Calgary, AB T2P 2H8, Canada
E-mail: grossbdr@bp.com
Fax: 403-233-1195
Phone: 403-223-1677

Colin Guild
TransCanada Transmission
PO Box 670
Vegreville, AB T9C 1R, Canada
E-mail: colinguild@transcanada.com

Steve Gundry
Veco Canada Ltd
1200, 240 4th Avenue SW
Calgary, AB T2P 4H4, Canada
E-mail: steve.gundry@veco.com
Fax: 403-231-6049
Phone: 403-231-6027

John Hair
J.D. Hair and Associates, Inc.
2121 South Columbia Avenue, Suite 101
Tulsa, OK 74114, USA
Fax: 918-742-7480
Phone: 918-747-9945

Osmo Haltia
Ministry of Trade & Industry
PL 37
Helsinki 00131, Finland
E-mail: osmo.haltia@ktm.vn.fi
Fax: 358-9-1602656
Phone: 358-9-1604785

Kerry Hanley
Trans Gas
1945 Hamilton Street
Regina, SK S4P 2C7, Canada
E-mail: khanley@saskenergy.sk.ca
Fax: 306-525-3422
Phone: 306-777-9647

Tom Hanthorn
Maritimes & Northeast Pipeline
Suite 1600, 1801 Hollis Street
Halifax, NS B3J 3N4, Canada
E-mail: thanthorn@mnpp.com
Fax: 902-490-2222
Phone: 902-490-2211

Wayne Harper
Portland Natural Gas Trans System
18 Commons Ave
Windham, ME 04062, USA
E-mail: wharper@pngts.com
Fax: 207-892-4786
Phone: 207-892-0281

Joe Harrietha
International Boundary Commission
Natural Resources
573-615 Booth Street
Ottawa, PQ K1A 0E9, Canada
E-mail: jharriet@Nrcan.gc.ca
Phone: 613-992-1414

Jill Harriman
BC Hydro
6167 Cranbrook Hill Road
Prince George, BC V2M 7C7, Canada
E-mail: jill_harriman@hotmail.com
Phone: 250-561-4887

James Hartman
Western Area Power Admin
U.S. Dept of Energy
PO Box 3700
Loveland, CO 80539-3003, USA
E-mail: hartman@wapa.gov
Fax: 970-461-7213
Phone: 970-461-7450

John Hawkins
Hydro One Networks Inc.
483 Bay Street
Toronto, ON M5G 2P5, Canada
E-mail: jd.hawkins@hydroone.com
Fax: 416-345-5677
Phone: 416-345-5219

Thomas Hayes
East Ky Power
PO Box 707
Winchester, KY 40391, USA
E-mail: tom@ekpc.com
Fax: 606-744-6008
Phone: 606-744-4812

Timothy Hayes
Cinergy Corp.
1000 E. Main Street
Plainfield, IN 46168 1765, USA
E-mail: thayes@cinergy.com
Fax: 317-838-2490
Phone: 317-838-1725

Howard Heffler
Alliance Pipeline Inc.
1200, 605 5th Avenue S.W.
Calgary, AB T2P 3H5, Canada
E-mail: hefflerh@alliance-pipeline.com
Fax: 403-266-1604
Phone: 403-517-6301

George Hegmann
AXYS Environmental Consulting Ltd.
600-555 4th Ave S.W.
Calgary, AB T2P 3E7, Canada
E-mail: ghegmann@axys.net
Fax: 403-269-5245
Phone: 403-750-7668

Dana Heil
Georgia Transmission Corp.
2100 E. Exchange Place
Tucker, Georgia 30085, USA
E-mail: dana.heil@gatrans.com
Fax: 770-270-7775
Phone: 770-270-7983

Steve Henderson
Westcoast Energy Inc.
3985 22 Ave
Prince George, BC V2N 1B7, Canada
E-mail: shenderson@wei.org
Fax: 250-960-2080
Phone: 250-960-2036

Rose Herman
EPCOR Utilities Inc.
7 Floor, 10065 Jasper Avenue
Edmonton, AB T5J 3B1, Canada
E-mail: rherman@epcor-group.com
Fax: 780-412-3479
Phone: 780-412-3252

Raymond Hinkle
URS Corp.
201 Willowbrook Blvd.
Wayne, NJ 07470, USA
E-mail: ray_hinkle@urscorp.com
Fax: 973-785-0023
Phone: 473-812-6886

William Hintz
Mycologic Inc.
C/O University of Victoria
Bio Dept, PO Box 3020
Victoria, BC V8N 2Y2, Canada
E-mail: whintz@uvic.ca
Fax: 250-721-7102
Phone: 250-721-7104

Jeff Hohman
East Ky Power
PO Box 707
Winchester, KY 40391, USA
E-mail: hohman@ekpc.com
Fax: 606-744-6008
Phone: 606-744-4812

Bruce Hollen
2311 NE 96th Court
Vancouver, WA 98669, USA
E-mail: Hackjspot@earthlink.net
Fax: 360-896-8363
Phone: 360-896-8363

Debbie Hollen
Bonneville Power Admin.
5411 NE Hwy 99
TF-DOB-1
Vancouver, WA, USA
E-mail: dahollen@bpa.gov
Fax: 360-418-2449
Phone: 360-418-2216

Harvey Holt
Purdue University
Dept of Forestry & Natural Resources
1159 Forestry Building
W. Lafayette, IN 47907-1159, USA
E-mail: hholt@fnr.purdue.edu
Fax: 765-496-2422
Phone: 765-494-3585

Robert Honig
ENTRIX
5252 Westchester, Suite 250
Houston, TX 77005, USA
E-mail: rhonig@entrix.com
Fax: 713-666-5227
Phone: 713-662-1937

Richard Hoos
EBA Engineering Consultants
Sun Life Plaza, Suite 5850
1100 Melville St.
Vancouver, BC V6E 4A6, Canada
E-mail: Rhoos@eba.ca
Fax: (604) 684-6241
Phone: (604) 685-0275

Mike Houser
Ensight Environmental Enterprises
PO Box 59, Site 272, RR 2
St Albert, AB T8N 1M9, Canada
E-mail: ensight@telusplanet.net
Fax: 780-973-5528
Phone: 780-973-5578

Daniel Hushion
Alliance Pipeline Inc.
400, 605 5th Avenue S.W.
Calgary, AB T2P 3H5, Canada
E-mail: dhushion@alliance-pipeline.com
Fax: 403-266-1604
Phone: 403-517-6305

Garth Imeson
Trans Mountain Pipe Line Co Ltd.
Box 3198
Sherwook Park, AB, Canada
E-mail: garthi@tmpl.ca
Fax: 780-449-5901
Phone: 780-449-5918

Sheila Innes
BP Amoco
PO Box 200, Station M
Calgary, AB T3E 3N3, Canada
E-mail: innesse@bp.com
Fax: 403-233-6318
Phone: 403-233-1908

James Irving
R.R. #1, Box 27
Lumsden, SK S0G 3C0, Canada
E-mail: irving2j@vregina.ca
Phone: 306-345-2528

Linda Irving
R.R. #1, Box 27
Lumsden, SK S0G 3C0, Canada

Bjorn Iuell
Norwegian Public Road Admin.
PO Box 8142 Dep.
Oslo 0033, Norway
E-mail: bjorn.iuell@vegvesen.no
Fax: 47-22-07-36-79
Phone: 47-22-07-30-10

Catharinus Jaarsma
Wageningen University
Land Use Planning Group
Gen. Foulkesweg 13
Wageningen 6703 BJ, Netherlands
E-mail: rinus.jaarsma@users.rpv.wau.nl
Fax: 31-317-482166
Phone: 31-317-482050

Michael John Jaeger
Public Serv Commission Wisconsin
PO Box 7854
Madison, WI 53707-7854, USA
E-mail: jaegem@psc.state.wi.us
Fax: 608-266-3957
Phone: 608-267-2546

Ray Jakubczak
BP Exploration (Alaska) Inc.
PO Box 196612
Anchorage, AK 99519-6612, USA
E-mail: jakubcrs@bp.com
Fax: 907-564-4754
Phone: 907-564-4664

Andrea Jalbert
Trans Canada Pipelines
801-7th Avenue SW (28th Floor)
Calgary, AB T2P 2P7, Canada
E-mail: andrea_jalbert@transcanada.com
Fax: 403-290-7227
Phone: 403-290-6804

Don James
Don James & Associates Ltd.
320-3rd Street NE
Calgary, AB T2E 7W5, Canada
E-mail: donjames@netcom.ca
Fax: 403-264-7057
Phone: 403-260-6726

Tom Jansson
Sudkraft Elnat Syd AB
205 09 Malmo
Sweden
E-mail: tom.jansson@sydkraft.se
Fax: 46-40244210
Phone: 46-4025 5969

David Jenkins
Foster Wheeler Enviro.
133 Federal Street, 6th Floor
Boston, MA 02110, USA
E-mail: djenkins@fwenc.com
Fax: 617-457-8498
Phone: 617-457-8230

Carey Johannesson
Enbridge Inc
2900 421 7th Avenue SW
Calgary, AB T2P 4K9, Canada
E-mail: carey.hohannesson@corp.enbridge.com
Fax: 403-231-7390
Phone: 4930231-5984

Byron Johnson
Great River Energy
17845 U.S. Hwy 10
Elk River, MN 55330, USA
E-mail: bjohnson@grenergy.com
Fax: 612-241-6226
Phone: 763-241-2426

Jon Johnson
Pennsylvania State University
L.M.R.C. Orchard Road
University Park, PA 16802, USA
E-mail: jmj500psu.edu
Fax: 814-863-1184
Phone: 814-863-1184

Michael Johnson
Bonneville Power Admin.
5411 NE Hwy 99-TF DOBI
Vancouver, WA, USA
E-mail: mdjohnson@bpa.gov
Fax: 360-418-2261
Phone: 360-418-2161

Richard Johnstone
VMES
912 Baylor Drive
Newark, DE, USA
E-mail: richard.johnstone@conectur.com
Fax: 302-283-5828
Phone: 302-454-4841

Ian Jones
Geo-Engineering Ltd.
217, 3016-19 Street NE
Calgary, AB T2E 6Y9, Canada
E-mail: ijones@geo-engineering.net
Fax: 403-291-0186
Phone: 403-250-8850

Jeanne Jones
Mississippi State University
Box 9690
Miss State, MS 39762, USA
E-mail: jjones@cfr.msstate.edu
Fax: 662-325-8726
Phone: 662-325-2219

Rodney Jones
Western Area Power Admin
U.S. Dept of Energy
PO Box 3700
Loveland, CO 80539-3003, USA
E-mail: rjones@wapa.gov
Fax: 970-461-7213
Phone: 970-461-7371

Rob Kalichuk
Manitoba Hydro
1140 Waverley Street, PO Box 815
Winnipeg, MB R3C 2P4, Canada
E-mail: rkalichuk@hydro.mb.ca
Fax: 204-474-4683
Phone: 204-474-4241

Daniel Kearney
Wintergreen-Daniel Resources Inc.
Box 8 Site 7, RR #1
Sundre, AB T0M 1X0, Canada
E-mail: kearneyd@telusplanet.net

Jon Keener
American Transmission Company
1302 South Broadway
DePere, WI, USA
E-mail: jkeener@atcllc.com
Phone: 920-338-6551

Geoffrey Kempter
Asplundh Tree Expert Co.
708 Blair Mill Road
Willow Grove, PA 19090-1701, USA
E-mail: gkemp@asplundh.com
Fax: 215-784-1366
Phone: 215-784-1364

Alan Kennedy
Imperial Oil Resources
237-4 Ave S.W.
Calgary, AB T2P 3M9, Canada
E-mail: alan.j.kennedy@esso.com
Fax: 403-232-5861
Phone: 403-237-3485

Keith Kennedy
Trans Canada
10 Boundary Road
Redcliff, AB T0J 2P0, Canada
Fax: 403-548-8323
Phone: 403-548-8319

Sandra Kerkhof
Tera Environmental Consultants
Suite 205, 925-7th Avenue S.W.
Calgary, AB T2P 1A5, Canada
E-mail: Skerkhof@teraenv.com
Fax: (403) 266-6471
Phone: (403) 265-2885

John Kerkhoven
Petro Canada Oil & Gas
PO Box 2844
Calgary, AB T2P 3E3, Canada
E-mail: jkerkhov@petro-canada.ca
Fax: 403-296-3032
Phone: 403-296-6345

David Kerr
Golder Associates Ltd.
Suite 1000, 940 6th Ave SW
Calgary, AB T2P 3T1, Canada
E-mail: dkerr@golder.com
Fax: 403-299-5606
Phone: 403-299-5610

Lana Khitrik
URS Corp.
282 Delaware Ave
Buffalo, NY 14202, USA
E-mail: lana_khitrik@urscorp.com
Fax: 716-856-2545
Phone: 716-856-5636

Robert Kinash
Manitoba Hydro
Property Department
PO Box 815
Winnipeg, MB R3C 2P4, Canada
E-mail: bkinash@hydro.mb.ca
Fax: 204-453-6236
Phone: 204-474-4073

Brandon Kish
Columbia Gas Transmission Corp.
1700 MacCorkle Ave
Charleston, WV 25304, USA
E-mail: bkish@ceg.com
Fax: 304-357-2438
Phone: 304-357-2687

Heidi Klein
Mackenzie Valley Environmental
PO Box 938
Yellowknife, NT X1A 2P9, Canada
E-mail: exec@mveirb.nt.ca
Fax: 867-920-4761
Phone: 867-873-9029

John Knapp
Columbia Gas Transmission
950 Manifold Road
Washington, PA 15301, USA
E-mail: John Knapp/TCD/ColumbiaGas@
ColumbiaGas
Fax: 724-223-2579
Phone: 724-223-2788

John Kobasa
CMS Gas Transmission & Storage
330 Town Center Dr.
Dearborn, MI, USA
Phone: 313-982-8815

Linda Kokemuller
Maine Dept of Environ Protection
312 Canco Road
Portland, ME 04103, USA
E-mail: linda.k.kokemuller@state.me.us
Fax: 207-822-6303
Phone: 207-822-6329

Nicole Kokinos
BSC Group
33 Waldo Street
Worcester, MA 01608, USA
E-mail: nkokinos@bscgroup.com
Fax: 508-792-4509
Phone: 508-792-4509

Joe Kolb
1311 Piney Woods
Friendswood, TX 77546, USA
E-mail: sskolb@neosoft.com
Phone: 281-992-5317

Paul Kolenick
SaskPower
2025 Victoria Ave.
Regina, SK S4P 0S1, Canada
E-mail: pkolenick@saskpower.com
Fax: 306-566-3428
Phone: 306-566-2903

Mark Korn
Allegheny Power
800 Cabin Hill Drive
Greensburg, PA, USA
E-mail: mkorn@alleghenypower.com
Fax: 724-830-5020
Phone: 724-838-6722

Patrick Kraft
Osmase, Inc
980 Ellicott Street
Buffalo, NY 14209, USA
E-mail: pkraft@osmose.com
Fax: 716-882-7822
Phone: 716-882-5905

George Kroupa
Terraform Environmental Consultants
244 Neil Avenue
Winnipeg, MB, Canada
E-mail: george@terra-form.net
Fax: 204-663-4359
Phone: 204-663-4359

Carl Kuhnke
Terra Remote Sensing Inc
1962 Mills Road
Sidney, BC V8L 5Y3, Canada
E-mail: carlk@terraremote.com
Fax: 250-656-4604
Phone: 250-656-0951

Ernest Ladkani
Ensource Inc.
21807 Maple Bluff Drive
Houston, TX 77449, USA

Pamela Ladyman
Canadian Pacific Railway
760-2755 Lougheed Highway
Port Coquitlam, BC V5X 1B2, Canada
E-mail: pamela_ladyman@cpr.ca
Fax: 604-944-5130
Phone: 604-944-5160

Douglas Lake
Natural Resource Group Inc.
1800 International Centre
900 2nd Ave S.
Minneapolis, MN 55402, USA
E-mail: djlake@nrginc.com
Fax: 612-347-6780
Phone: 612-347-7875

Jane Lancaster
Kestrel Research Inc.
Box 42, Site 4, RR 1
Cochrane, AB T0L 0W0, Canada
E-mail: janelanc@telusplanet.net
Phone: 403-932-2269

Drew Lanham
Clemson University
261 Lehotsky Hall
Clemson, SC 29634-0331, USA
E-mail: lanhamj@clemson.edu
Fax: 864-656-3304
Phone: 864-656-7294

Sandra Lare
Northern Ecological Assoc, Inc.
451 Presumpscot St.
Portland, ME 04103, USA
E-mail: slare@neamaine.com
Fax: 207-879-9481
Phone: 207-879-9496

Christean Larouche
GEO-3D
3981 Mont Royal
St. Hubert, PQ J4R 2H4, Canada
E-mail: clarouche@geo.3d.com
Fax: 450-926-3050
Phone: 450-926-1020

Richard Lauzon
AXYS Environmental Consulting Ltd.
600-555 4th Ave S.W.
Calgary, AB T2P 3E7, Canada
E-mail: rlauzon@axys.net
Fax: 403-269-5245
Phone: 403-750-7658

Richard Law
Ace Vegetation Control Service Ltd.
2001-8th Street
Nisku, AB T9E 7Z1, Canada
E-mail: rlaw@acevegetation.com
Fax: 780-955-9426
Phone: 780-955-8980

Calvin Layton
NSTAR Services Co.
151 University Ave
Westwood, MA 02090, USA
E-mail: calvin_layton@nstaronline.com
Phone: 781-441-8213

James Leadbetter
Fisheries & Oceans Canada
Habitate Management Div
B505 5th Floor, Bay 1006
Dartmouth, NS B2Y HA2, Canada
E-mail: leadbetterj@mar.dfo-mpo.gc.ca
Fax: 902-456-1489
Phone: 902-426-6027

Bruce Leeson
Parks Canada
Room 552-220 4th Ave S.E.
Calgary, AB T2G 4X3, Canada
E-mail: bruce_leeson@pch.gc.ca
Fax: 403-292-4404
Phone: 403-292-4438

Robert LeMay
National Energy Board
444 7th Avenue S.W.
Calgary, AB T2P 0X8, Canada
E-mail: rlemay@neb.gc.ca
Fax: 403-299-2781
Phone: 403-299-3187

Victoria Lenney
Potomac Electric Power Company
701 9th Street, NW
6th Floor
Washington, DC 20068, USA
E-mail: vllenney@pepco.com
Fax: 202-872-3472
Phone: 202-331-6543

Normand Lesieur
Hydro Quebec
800, de Maisonneuve est
21st Floor
Montreal, PQ H2L 4M8, Canada
E-mail: lesieur.normand@hydro.qc.ca
Fax: 514-840-3137
Phone: 514-840-3000

Vic Lewynsky
BC Hydro
1401 Kalamalka Lake Road
Vernon, BC V1T 8S4, Canada
E-mail: Vic.Lewynsky@BCHydro.com
Fax: 250-558-5875
Phone: 250-549-8657

David Lind
Land & Forest Service AB Gov't
Box 450
Lac La Biche, AB T0A 2C0, Canada
E-mail: dave.lind@gov.ab.ca
Fax: 780-623-2126
Phone: 780-623-4133

Ron Link
Alberta Infrastructure
23rd Floor, 6950-113 Street
Edmonton, AB T6H 5V7, Canada
E-mail: ron.link@gov.ab.ca
Fax: 780-422-5419
Phone: 780-422-1987

Wayne Lloyd
Westcoast Energy Inc.
1333 W. Georgia Street
Vancouver, BC V6E 8K9, Canada
E-mail: wlloyd@wei.org
Fax: 604-691-5877
Phone: 604-691-5877

Chipper Loggie
Exxon Mobil
1835 South Bragaw St, MS-568
Anchorage, AK 99512, USA
E-mail: loggiec@alyeska-pipeline.com
Fax: 907-787-8322
Phone: 907-787-8089

Scott Lounsbury
Enbridge
21 West Superior Street
Duluth, MN 55802, USA
E-mail: scott.lounsbury@uspl.enbridge.com
Fax: 218-725-0139
Phone: 218-725-0145

Fran Lowell
Natural Resource Group Inc.
1800 International Centre
900 2nd Ave S.
Minneapolis, MN 55402, USA
E-mail: flowell@nrginc.com
Fax: 612-347-6789
Phone: 612-347-7871

Stuart Lunn
PanCanadian Petroleum Ltd.
150 9th Ave S.W.
Calgary, AB T2P 2S5, Canada
E-mail: stuart_lunn@pcp.ca
Fax: 403-268-7808
Phone: 403-268-7868

Michael Lychwala
TRC
Boot Mills Soth, Foot of John Street
Lowell, MA 1852, USA
E-mail: mlychwala@trcsolutions.com
Fax: 978-453-1995
Phone: 978-656-3638

John MacDonald
University of Calgary
#221, 2451 Dieppe Ave SW
Calgary, AB T3E 7K1, Canada
E-mail: macdonald.greystone@home.com
Fax: 403-271-7162
Phone: 403-271-7110

Erven MacKintosh
ESG International
361 Southgate Dr.
Guelph, ON N1G 3M5, Canada
E-mail: emackintosh@esg.net
Fax: 519-836-2493
Phone: 519-836-6050

Terry MacNeill
Applied Geoprocessing Inc.
10302 121 Street
Edmonton, AB T5W 1K8, Canada
E-mail: tmacneill@geooprocessing.ca
Fax: 780-447-4762
Phone: 780-453-2292

Remo Maddalozzo
Asplundh Canada Inc.
26050 315 Ave
Aldergrove, BC V4W 2Z6, Canada
E-mail: asplundh-BC@telus.net
Fax: 604-856-8899
Phone: 604-856-2222

David Maehr
University of Kentucky
Forestry, 205 Cooper Bld
Lexington, KY 40546-0073, USA
E-mail: dmaehr@pop.uky.edu
Fax: 606-323-1031
Phone: 606-257-4807

Bill Magdych
URS
1615 Murray Canyon Road
Suite 1000
San Diego, CA 92108, USA
E-mail: bill_magdych@urscorp.com
Phone: 619-293-7920

Wayne Mancroni
Central Hudson Gas & Electric Corp
284 South Avenue
Poughkeepsie, NY 12601, USA
E-mail: wmancroni@cenhud.com
Fax: 914-486-5764
Phone: 914-486-5734

Robert Mann
Manitoba Hydro
1140 Waverley Street, PO Box 815
Winnipeg, MB R3C 2P4, Canada
E-mail: jrmann@hydro.mb.ca
Fax: 204-475-0273
Phone: 204-474-4267

Sandy Marlin
El Paso Energy
1001 Louisiana Street
Houston, TX 77009, USA
E-mail: marlins@epenergy.com
Fax: 713-420-6229
Phone: 713-420-2227

James Marshall
Ohio State University
Dept. Evolution, Ecology, and Organismal Biology
1735 Neil Avenue
Columbus, OH 43210, USA
E-mail: marshall.298@osu.edu
Phone: 614-523-0210

Wayne Marshall
National Energy Board
444 7th Avenue S.W.
Calgary, AB T2P 0X8, Canada
E-mail: wmarshall@neb.gc.ca

Angella Martell
5400 Westheimer Court
Houston, TX 77056, USA
E-mail: asmartell@duke-energy.com
Fax: 713-627-5975
Phone: 713-627-5488

Doug Martin
BC Environment
205 Industrial Road E
Cranbrook, BC V1C 6H3, Canada
E-mail: doug.martin@gems7.vob.bc.ca
Fax: 250-489-8506
Phone: 250-489-8548

Paul Martin
TRC
Boot Mills Soth, Foot of John Street
Lowell, MA 01852, USA
E-mail: pmartin@trcsolutions.com
Phone: 978-656-3631

Sandra Martindale
National Energy Board
444 7th Avenue S.W.
Calgary, AB T2P 0X8, Canada
E-mail: smartindale@neb.gc.ca
Fax: 403-292-5875
Phone: 403-299-3374

Todd Mattson
Natural Resource Group Inc.
1800 International Centre
900 2nd Ave S.
Minneapolis, MN 55402, USA
E-mail: tamattson@nrginc.com
Fax: 612-347-6780
Phone: 612-347-3367

Donald McCabe
Alberta Environment
2938-11 St. NE
Calgary, AB T2E 7L7, Canada
E-mail: Don.McCabe@env.gov.ab.ca
Fax: (403) 297-5944
Phone: (403) 297-5671

Robert McCallum
Indian Oil & Gas Canada
Suite 100, 9911 Chula Blvd
TsuuTina/Sarcee, AB T2W 6H6, Canada
E-mail: mccallumr@inac.gc.ca
Fax: 403-292-5618
Phone: 403-292-5176

William McCarthy
Natural Resource Group Inc.
1800 International Centre
900 2nd Ave S.
Minneapolis, MN 55402, USA
E-mail: wfmccarthy@nrginc.com
Fax: 612-347-6780
Phone: 612-347-7870

Brian McConaghy
TransCanada Tower, Floor 21
405-1st. St., SW
Calgary, AB T2P 5H1, Canada
E-mail: brain_mcconaghy@transcanada.com
Fax: 403-920-2330
Phone: 403-920-7783

Rachel McCormick
University of Calgary
2500 University Drive
Faculty of Environmental Design, PF 2105
Calgary, AB T2N 1N4, Canada
E-mail: rkmccormick@home.com

Ian McDonald
Ace Vegetation Control Service Ltd.
2001-8th Street
Nisku, AB T9E 7Z1, Canada
E-mail: imcdonald@acevegetation.com
Fax: 780-955-9426
Phone: 780-955-8980

Jack McGee
Idaho Power Company
PO Box 70
Boise, ID, USA
E-mail: jmcgee@idahopower.com
Phone: 208-388-2759

Terry McGuire
Parks Canada
Room 552-220 4th Ave S.E.
Calgary, AB T2G 4X3, Canada
E-mail: Terry-McGuire@pch.gc.ca
Fax: 403-292-4886
Phone: 403-292-4707

Rita McKenzie
Purdue University
Forestry & Natural Resources
1159 Forestry Building
W. Lafayette, IN 47907-1159, USA
E-mail: ritam@fnr.purdue.edu
Fax: 765-496-2422
Phone: 765-494-3625

George McLachlan
Duke Energy
675 Western Ave #4
Manchester, ME 04351, USA
E-mail: gamclachlan@duke-energy.com
Fax: 207-621-8229
Phone: 888-876-4080

Kevin McLoughlin
New York Power Authority
PO Box 200
Gilboa, NY 12076, USA
E-mail: kevin.mcloughlin@nypa.gov
Fax: 607-588-9826
Phone: 607-588-6061

Blair McMahon
Tetres Consultants Inc.
603-386 Broadway
Winnipeg, MB R3C 3R6, Canada
E-mail: bmcmahon@tetres.ca
Fax: 204-942-2548
Phone: 204-942-2505

Joseph McMullen
Terrestrial Environmental Specialists, Inc.
23 County Route 6, Suite A
Phoenix, NY 13135, USA
E-mail: tes@dreamscape.com
Fax: 315-695-3277
Phone: 315-695-7228

Troy Meinke
Alliance Pipeline Inc.
6385 Old Shady Oak Road, Suite 150
Eden Prairie, MN , USA
E-mail: troy.meinke@alliance-pipeline.com
Fax: 952-944-9166
Phone: 952-983-1009

Denis Mercier
GEO-3D
3981 Mont Royal
St. Hubert, PQ J4R 2H4, Canada
E-mail: dmercier@geo-3d.com
Fax: 450-926-3050
Phone: 450-926-1020

Dennis Mitchell
Alberta Infrastructure
Infrastructure Building, 3rd Floor
6950-113 Street
Edmonton, AB T6H 5V7, Canada
E-mail: dennis.mitchell@gov.ab.ca
Fax: (780) 422-8949
Phone: (780) 427-3900

Jonah Mitchell
Parks Canada, Wood Buffalo National Park
PO Box 750
Fort Smith, NT X0E 0P0, Canada
Fax: 867-872-3910
Phone: 867-872-7900

Rich Mogensen
Marsh Resources Inc.
236 Transco Road
Mooresville, NC 28115, USA
E-mail: Rich.K.Mogensen@williams.com
Fax: 704-655-9707
Phone: 704-892-7761

Eric Mohun
AXYS Environmental Consulting Ltd.
600-555 4th Ave S.W.
Calgary, AB T2P 3E7, Canada
E-mail: emohun@axys.net
Fax: 403-269-5245
Phone: 403-750-7670

John Moir
Asplundh Canada Inc.
9205 37 Avenue
Edmonton, AB T6G 5K9, Canada
E-mail: moir@asplundh.com
Fax: 780-461-7883
Phone: 780-462-5806

Nelsen Money
Pacific Gas and Electric Co.
12081 Lodestar Drive
Grass Valley, CA, USA
E-mail: nrm2@pge.com
Fax: 530-889-3389
Phone: 530-889-3330

Pamela Money
Pacific Gas and Electric Co.
12081 Lodestar Drive
Grass Valley, CA, USA
E-mail: PRR5@PGE.WM
Fax: 530-889-3833
Phone: 530-889-3811

Clyde Moore
International Boundary Commission
1250 23rd Street NW, Suite 100
Washington, DC 20037, USA
Fax: 202-736-9015
Phone: 202-736-9102

Sonia Morales
University of Calgary
2500 University Drive
Faculty of Environmental Design, PF 2105
Calgary, AB T2N 1N4, Canada

Stephen Morawaski
Tennessee Gas Pipeline Co.
8 Anngina Drive
Enfield, CT 01071, USA
E-mail: morawskis@epenergy.com

David Morrell
NY State Dept of Public Service
Agency Building 3
Albany, NY 12054, USA
E-mail: dsm@dps.state.ny.us
Fax: 518-474-5026
Phone: 518-486-7322

Todd Moss
Moss Environmental Services Inc.
136 Schooner Close NW
Calgary, AB T3L 1Z1, Canada
E-mail: mosst@ibm.net
Phone: 403-804-6219

Javed Mubashar
University of the Punjab
Main Brother's Lab (PVT) Ltd.
112/10 Township
Punjab, Lahore, Pakistan
E-mail: khizerinayat@hotmail.com
Phone: 5111167-841786

John Muehlhausen
Natural Resource Group Inc.
1800 International Centre
900 2nd Ave S.
Minneapolis, MN 55402, USA
E-mail: jwmuehlhausen@nrginc.com
Fax: 612-347-6780
Phone: 612-347-6783

Sepp Muhlberger
ARC Inc.
7535 Flint Road SE
Calgary, AB T2H 1G3, Canada
E-mail: muhlbergerj@arcinc.ab.ca
Fax: 403-543-1944
Phone: 403-543-1940, ext 7

Wade Munro
Manitoba Hydro
1140 Waverley Street, PO Box 815
Winnipeg, MB R3C 2P4, Canada
E-mail: wmunro@hydro.mb.ca
Fax: 204-474-4974
Phone: 204-474-4710

Dean Mutrie
Tera Environmental Consultants
Suite 205, 925-7th Avenue S.W.
Calgary, AB T2P 1A5, Canada
E-mail: dmutrie@teraenv.com
Fax: 403-266-6471
Phone: 403-265-2885

Julie Myhre
Natural Resource Group Inc.
1800 International Centre
900 2nd Ave S.
Minneapolis, MN 55402, USA
E-mail: jamyhre@nrginc.com
Fax: 612-347-6780
Phone: 612-347-6784

Ted Nelson
Nelson Const
600 Reilly Ave
Farmington, NM 87401, USA
Fax: 505-327-6332
Phone: 505-327-6331

Edward Neuhauser
R & A, Niagara Mohawk Power Corp.
300 Erie Blvd W.
Syracuse, NY 13202, USA
E-mail: Neuhausere@NiagaraMohawk.com
Fax: 315-428-6503
Phone: 315-428-3355

Brian Nolan
ATCO Electric
10035-105th Street
Edmonton, AB T5J 2V6, Canada
E-mail: brian.nolan@atcoelectric.com
Fax: 780-420-5410
Phone: 780-420-7843

Logan Norris
Environmental Consultants, Inc.
4045 NW Dale Place
Corvallis, OR 97330, USA
E-mail: Logan.Norris@orst.edu
Fax: 541-737-5814
Phone: 541-737-6557

Christopher Nowak
SUNY-ESF
220 Marshall Hall
1 Forestry Drive
Syracuse, NY 13210, USA
E-mail: canowak@esf.edu
Fax: 315-470-6956
Phone: 315-470-6575

Craig Nyrose
ATCO Electric
1006-15 Ave
Nisku, AB T9E 7S5, Canada
Fax: 780-955-6234

Carey Oakley
Law Gibb Group
2100 Rivershase Center, Suite 450
Birmingham, AL 35202, USA
E-mail: cboakley@lawco.com
Fax: 205-686-9508
Phone: 205-733-7600

Paula Oberg
PO Box 7485
Drayton Valley, AB T7A 1S6, Canada
E-mail: poberg@ualberta.ca
Phone: 780-5427133

Kevin Ogilvie
Ontario Ministry of Transportation
355 Counter Street
Postal Bag 4000
Kingston, ON K7L 5A3, Canada
E-mail: ogilvie@mto.gov.on.ca
Fax: 613-540-5106
Phone: 613-384-1307

Charles Olenik
GPU Energy
2800 Pottsville Pike
Reading, PA, USA
Fax: 610-921-6736
Phone: 610-921-6843

Carrie Oloriz
Conor Pacific
807 Manning Road NE
Calgary, AB T2E 7M8, Canada
Phone: 204-9316

Stuart Olsen
Midland Vegetation Mgt Inc.
8459-23rd Ave NE
Calgary, AB T19 7G9, Canada
E-mail: s.olsen@midlandvegetation.ca
Fax: 403-285-9205
Phone: 403-285-9111

James Orr
Asplundh Tree Expert Co.
708 Blair Mill Road
Willow Grove, PA 19090-1701, USA
E-mail: jimorr@asplundh.com
Fax: 215-284-1366
Phone: 215-784-4244

Wayne Ortiz
Manitoba Hydro
12-1146 Waverley Street, PO Box 815
Winnipeg, MB R3C 2P4, Canada
E-mail: wortiz@hydro.mb.ca
Fax: 204-475-0273
Phone: 204-477-4059

Mark Ostendorp
EPRIsolutions
100 Research Drive
Haslet, TX 76052, USA
E-mail: mostendo@eprisolutions.com
Phone: 817-234-8213

Kevin Owen
Iroquois Gas Transmission
One Corporate Drive Suite 600
Shelton, CT 06484, USA
E-mail: kevin_owen@iroquois.com
Fax: 203-925-7213
Phone: 203-944-7035

Kevin Pape
Gray & Pape, Inc
1318 Main Street
Cincinnati, OH 45210, USA
E-mail: wkpape@graypape.com
Fax: 513-287-7703
Phone: 513-287-7700

Gil Paquette
Duke Engineering and Services
500 Washington Ave
Portland, ME 04103, USA
E-mail: gapaquet@dukeengineering.com
Phone: 207-775-4495

Sylvain Paquette
C.P. 6128 Succ.
Centre-ville
Montreal, PQ H3C 3J7, Canada
Phone: 514-343-7500

Scott Paradise
Canadian Pacific Railway
501 Marquette Ave
Room 804, PO Box 530
Minneapolis, MN 55440, USA
E-mail: scott_paradise@cpr.ca
Fax: 612-347-8170
Phone: 612-347-8257

Erkki Partanen
Fingrid OYJ
PL 530
Helsinki 00131, Finland
E-mail: erkki.partanen@fingrid.fi
Fax: 358-303-955213
Phone: 358-303-955156

Susan Patey
University of Calgary
2500 University Drive
Faculty of Environmental Design, PF 2105
Calgary, AB T2N 1N4, Canada

Sandra Patty
Maryland Dept of Natural Res.
580 Taylor Avenue
Tawes Bld. B-3
Annapolis, MD 21401, USA
E-mail: spatty@dnr.state.md.us
Fax: 410-260-8670
Phone: 410-260-8660

Lionel Peel
Telus Communications Inc.
5E 411-1st S.E.
Calgary, AB T2G 4Y5, Canada
E-mail: lionel.peel@telus.com
Fax: 403-530-5876
Phone: 403-530-5876

Howard Pelkey
N B Dept of Environment
PO Box 6000
Fredericton, NB E3B 5H1, Canada
E-mail: Howard.Pelkey@gnb.co
Fax: 506-453-2390
Phone: 506-444-5045

Wally Peters
Land & Forest Service AB Gov't
Box 450
Lac La Biche, AB T0A 2C0, Canada
E-mail: wally.peters@gov.ab
Fax: 780-623-2126
Phone: 780-623-4137

Douglas Pickard
West Kootenay Power
Box 130
Trail, BC B1R 4L4, Canada
E-mail: dpickard@wkpower.com
Phone: 250-368-0514

Lois Pittaway
Tera Environmental Consultants
Suite 205, 925-7th Avenue S.W.
Calgary, AB T2P 1A5, Canada
E-mail: lpittaway@teraenv.com
Fax: 403-266-6471
Phone: 403-265-2885

Melissa Pockar
Alliance Pipeline Inc.
400, 605 5th Avenue S.W.
Calgary, AB T2P 3H5, Canada
E-mail: melissa.pockar@alliance-pipeline.com
Fax: 403-266-1604
Phone: 403-517-6347

David Polster
Polster Environmental Services
5953 Deuchars Drive
Duncan, BC V9L 1L5, Canada
E-mail: gsingleton@seaside.net
Fax: 250-746-5307
Phone: 250-746-8052

Phil Potak
New York Power Authority
Valenti Road, PO Box 200
Gilboa, NY 12076, USA
E-mail: phil.potak@nypa.gov
Fax: 607-588-9826
Phone: 607-588-6061

Artasith Pothiapinyanvisuth
Petroleum Authority of Thailand
555 Vibhavadee Rangsit Rd
Banglehaen
Bangkok 10900, Thailand

James Potts
Potomac Electric Power Company
701 9th Street, NW
Washington, DC 20068, USA
E-mail: jspotts@pepco.com
Fax: (202) 872-3472
Phone: (202) 872-2274

Philippe Poullaouec-Gonidec
Universite de Montreal
PO Box 6128 Succ. Centre-Ville
Montreal, PQ H3C 3J7, Canada

Peter Prier
ESG International, Inc
361 Southgate Drive
Guelph, ON N1G 3M5, Canada
E-mail: pprier@esg.net
Fax: 519-836-2493
Phone: 519-836-6050

Jay Pruett
American Electric Power Company
1616 Woodall Rodgers Freeway
Dallas, TX 75202, USA
E-mail: japruett@aep.com
Fax: (214) 777-1380
Phone: (214) 777-1175

David Purcell
SWCA Inc, Enviro Consultants
114 North San Francisco St., Suite 100
Flagstaff, AZ 86001, USA
E-mail: dpurcell@swca.com
Fax: 520-779-2709
Phone: 520-774-5500

Cynthia Pye
Sorel Environmental Services Ltd
1338R-36Ave NE
Calgary, AB T2S 2E9, Canada
E-mail: cpyc@sorel.ca
Phone: 403-219-1262

Elizabeth Quarshire
National Energy Board
444 7th Avenue S.W.
Calgary, AB T2P 0X8, Canada
E-mail: equarshie@neb.gc.ca
Fax: 403-299-3602
Phone: 403-299-2734

Martin Rajotte
Hydro Quebec
Environment Distribution
1000 Boul. Michel-BOHEC
Blainville, PQ J7C 5L6, Canada
E-mail: rajotte.martin@hydro.qc.ca
Fax: 450-433-6116
Phone: 800-361-4119

Ian Ramsay
ICR Environmental
PO Box 29 Stn. PBC
Kelowna, BC V1Y 7N3, Canada
E-mail: icramsay@home.com
Fax: 250-763-0835
Phone: 250-763-0850

Jeff Randolph
East Kentucky Power
PO Box 707
Winchester, KY 40391, USA
E-mail: jeffr@ekpc.com
Phone: 859-744-4812

Pamela Rassmussen
Xcelenergy
1414 West Hamilton Ave, PO Box 8
Eau Claire, WI 54702, USA
E-mail: pamela.jo.rasmussen@xcelenergy.com
Fax: 715-839-2480

James Rawlins
East Ky Power, PO Box 707
Winchester, KY 40391, USA
Fax: 859-744-6008
Phone: 859-744-4812

William Rees
Baltimore Gas and Electric Company
PO Box 1475 Dept 36
Room 301 Front St
Baltimore, MD 21203-1475, USA
E-mail: William.T.Rees@BGE.com
Fax: 410-291-3677
Phone: 410-291-3479

William Regan
Natural Resource Group Inc.
1800 International Centre
900 2nd Ave S.
Minneapolis, MN 55402, USA
E-mail: wjregan@nrginc.com
Fax: 612-347-6780
Phone: 612-347-6797

Scott Reid
Golder Associates Ltd.
2180 Meadowvale Boulevard
Mississauga, OH L5N5S3, Canada
E-mail: sreid@golder.com
Phone: 905-567-4444

Carl Reimer
Westcoast Energy Inc.
Bag Service 6180
Fort St. John, BC V1J 4H7, Canada
E-mail: creimer@wei.org
Fax: 250-262-3410
Phone: 250-262-3456

Richard Revel
University of Calgary
2500 University Drive
Faculty of Environmental Design, PF 2105
Calgary, AB T2N 1N4, Canada
E-mail: revel@ucalgary.ca
Fax: 403-284-4399
Phone: 403-220-3622

Kirt Rhoads
Williams Gas Pipeline
295 Chipeta Way
Salt Lake City, UT 84108, USA
Phone: 801-584-6763

Howard Richards
Newfoundland and Labrador Hydro
PO Box 2002
Bishop's Falls, NF A0H 1C0, Canada
E-mail: howard_richards/nlhydro@nlh.nf.ca
Fax: 709-258-2346
Phone: 709-258-2358

Paul Richards
National Grid USA
55 Bearfoot Road
Northborough, MA 01532, USA
E-mail: paul.richards@us.ngrid.com
Fax: 508-890-4706
Phone: 508-421-7549

Joel Rinebold
Connecticut Siting Council
Ten Franklin Square
New Britian, CT 06051, USA
E-mail: siting.council@po.state.ct.us
Fax: 860-827-2950
Phone: 860-827-2935

Debbie Ristig
Reliant Energy Pipeline Services
525 Milam Street
Shreveport, LA 71101, USA
E-mail: dristig@reliantenergy.com
Fax: 318-429-3927
Phone: 318-965-5047

Bart Robinson
Yellowstone to Yukon Conserv. Initiative
710-9th Street
Studio B
Canmore, AB T1W 2V7, Canada

Jorge Roig Soles
Red Electrica de Espana
PO Del Conde De Los Gaitanes, 177
LA Moraleja Alcobendas
Madrid 28109, Spain
E-mail: jroig@ree.es
Fax: 34-916504542
Phone: 34-916508500

Chad Roper
Triangle Laboratories, Inc.
801 Capitola Dr.
Durham, NC 27713, USA
E-mail: Chad_oper@compuserve.com
Fax: 919-544-5491
Phone: 919-544-5729

Loreta Rosselli
ISA-ABO
Dg. 109 No 26-10 (8)
Bogota, Columbia
E-mail: lrosselli@yahoo.com

Diane Ross-Leech
Pacific Gas and Electric Co.
Mail code B24A
PO Box 7640
San Fransisco, CA 94120, USA
E-mail: dpr5@pge.com
Fax: 415-973-9201
Phone: 415-973-5696

Rob Rowland
ESG International
361 Southgate Dr.
Guelph, ON N1G 3M5, Canada
E-mail: rrowland@esg.net
Fax: 519-836-2493
Phone: 519-836-6050

Keith Sanftleben
Midland Vegetation Mgt Inc.
8459-23rd Ave NE
Calgary, AB T19 7G9, Canada
Phone: 780-487-0112

Gerry Sarich
BC Gas Utility Ltd.
16705 Fraser Highway
Surrey, BC V3S 2X7, Canada
E-mail: gsarich@bcgas.com
Fax: 604-576-7105
Phone: 604-576-7084

Mike Sawyer
Citizens' Oil and Gas Council
5678 Brenner Crescent N.W.
Calgary, AB T2L 1Z4, Canada

Chuck Scarborough
Georgia Transmission Corp.
2100 E. Exchange Place
Tucker, Georgia 30085, USA
E-mail: chuck.scarbourgh@gatrans.com
Fax: 770-270-7775
Phone: 770-270-7953

Greg Scarborough
BC Hydro
6911 Southpoint Drive
Pod EO5
Burnaby, BC V3N 4X8, Canada
E-mail: greg.scarborough@BCHydro.bc.ca
Fax: 604-528-2940
Phone: 604-528-1721

Paul Schaap
Dillon Consulting Ltd.
#130-10691 Shellbridge Way
Richmond, BC V6X 2W8, Canada
E-mail: pschaap@dillon.ca
Fax: 604-278-7894
Phone: 604-278-7847

Valentin Schaefer
Douglas College
PO Box 2503
New Westminster, BC V3L 5B2, Canada
E-mail: valschaefer@shaw.ca

Ron Schafer
BC Gas Utility Ltd.
16705 Fraser Highway
Surrey, BC V3S 2X7, Canada
E-mail: rschfer@bcgas.com
Fax: 604-576-7105
Phone: 604-868-4560

Tony Schlenker
Lorrnel Consultants
400 6th Street SW
Calgary, AB T2P 1X2, Canada
Fax: 403-265-3874
Phone: 403-233-0900

Mike Schmaltz
Trans Canada Pipelines
801-7th Avenue SW
Calgary, AB T2P 2P7, Canada
E-mail: michael_schmaltz@transcanada.com
Fax: 403-290-7227
Phone: 403-290-8048

Fiona Schmiegelow
University of Alberta
Dept of Renewable Resources
751 GSB
Edmonton, AB T6G 2H1, Canada
E-mail: fiona.schmiegelow@ualberta.ca
Fax: 780-492-4323
Phone: 780-492-0552

Jacki Schneider
Trans Mountain Pipe Line Co Ltd.
7815 Shellmont Street
Burnaby, BC V5A 4S9, Canada
E-mail: jackis@tmpl.co
Phone: 604-268-3008

Paul Schorn
Dow AgroSciences Canada
201-1144 29th Ave N.E.
Calgary, AB T2E 7P1, Canada
E-mail: pschorn@dowagro.com
Fax: 403-735-8819
Phone: 403-735-8824

Paul Schouten
Ecomark Ltd.
110, 1525-170 St
Edmonton, AB T5P 4W2, Canada
E-mail: schouten@telusplanet.net
Fax: 780-481-2431
Phone: 780-444-0706

Ian Scott
Canadian Assoc Petroleum Producers
2100, 350 7th Ave S.W.
Calgary, AB T2P 3N9, Canada
E-mail: scott@capp.ca
Fax: 403-366-3261
Phone: 403-267-1132

William Scott
65 Shaver Avenue North
Etobicoke, ON M9B 4N5, Canada

Gary Searing
LGL Limited
Environmental Research Associates
9768 Second Street
Sidney, BC V8L 3Y8, Canada
E-mail: gfs@lgl.com
Fax: 250-655-9761
Phone: 250-656-0127

Nalwanga Faridah Sendagire
Makerara University
PO Box 28530
Kampala, Uganda
E-mail: uicbplsc@imul.com
Fax: 256-41-254-829
Phone: 343-941

Jack Shaw
Northern Ecological Associates
451 Presumpscot St.
Portland, ME 04103, USA
E-mail: rtrettel@neamaine.com
Phone: 207-879-9481

Philip Sheridan
Old Dominion University
Meadowview Biological Research St.
8390 Fredericksborg Tnpk
Woodford, VA 22580, USA
E-mail: meadowview@pitcherplant.org
Phone: 804-633-4336

Gwen Shrimpton
BC Hydro
8475 128 Street
Surrey, BC V3W 0G1, Canada
E-mail: gwen.shrimpton@bchydro.bc.ca
Fax: 604-543-1540
Phone: 604-543-4155

Scott Shupe
Niagara Mohawk Power Corp.
300 Erie Boulevard, West
EAD, A-2
Syracuse, NY 13202, USA
E-mail: shupes@niagaramohawk.com
Fax: 315-428-3549
Phone: 315-428-6616

Ajay Pal Singh
U.P. State Irrigation Dept.
SDO Ganga Canal, IV/50
Peerbaba Officers Colony
Rorkee
District-Haridwar, Uttranchal, India
E-mail: apsingh1957@yahoo.com
Phone: 91-1332-78743

Glen Singleton
BC Hydro
6911 Southpoint Drive
Burnaby, BC V3N 4X8, Canada
E-mail: glen.singleton@bchydro.bc.ca

Rajendra Prasad Sitoula
Sulabh International Nepal
Bishalnegar, Kathmandu-5
Post Box 5083
Kathmandu, Nepal
E-mail: atharai@wlink.com
Fax: 977 1-432243
Phone: 977 1-432243

Richard Skarie
Natural Resource Group Inc.
1800 International Centre
900 2nd Ave S
Minneapolis, MN 55402, USA
E-mail: rlskarie@nrginc.com
Fax: 612-347-6780
Phone: 612-347-6786

Stephen Slack
5307 58 Ave
Barhead, AB T7N 1N1, Canada
E-mail: slack@ualberta.ca

Holly Smith
Fisheries & Oceans Canada
1278 Dalhousie Drie
Kamloops, BC V2C 6G3, Canada
E-mail: smithho@pac.dfo-moo.gc.ca
Fax: 250-851-4951
Phone: 250-851-4879

Ian Smith
IDS Consulting Services
PO Box 245
Berwick, Victoria 3806, Australia
E-mail: ian@idconsulting.com.au
Fax: 61-3-9796-2968
Phone: 61-3-9707-5358

Mary Smith
Central Maine Power
83 Edison Drive
Augusta, MA 04330-6009, USA
Fax: 207-621-3887
Phone: 207-626-9547

Don Snider
Alberta Infrastructure
2nd Floor 4999-98 Ave
Edmonton, AB T6B 2X3, Canada
E-mail: don.snider@gov.ab.ca
Fax: 427-0353
Phone: 780-415-1387

Kenneth Sott
Santee Cooper
One Riverwood Drive
Moncks Corner, SC 29461, USA
E-mail: knsott@santeecooper.com
Fax: 843-761-4105
Phone: 843-761-8000

Mark Southerland
Versar
9200 Rumsey Road
Columbia, MD, USA
E-mail: southerlandmar@versar.com
Fax: 410-964-5156
Phone: 410-740-6074

Linville Spangler
East Ky Power
PO Box 707
Winchester, KY 40391, USA
E-mail: linville@ekpc.com
Fax: 859-744-6008
Phone: 859-744-4812

David Speer
Progress Land Services Ltd.
14815 119 Ave
Edmonton, AB T5L 2N9, Canada
E-mail: daves@progressland.com
Fax: 780-454-6172
Phone: 780-454-4717

John Steenberg
Enron Gas Pipeline Group
PO Box 1188
3AC-3140
Houston, TX 77251-1188, USA
E-mail: john.steenberg@enron.com
Fax: 713-646-7867
Phone: (713) 646-7317

Janet Stephenson
Murphy Bros. Inc.
3150 5th Ave
East Moline, IL 61264, USA
E-mail: jstephenson@murphybrosinc.com
Fax: 309-752-7015
Phone: 309-756-1030

Dianna Stoopnikoff
Trans Mountain Pipe Line Co Ltd.
2355 Trans Canada Hwy West
Kamloops, BC, Canada
E-mail: diannas@tmpl.ca
Fax: 250-371-4001
Phone: 250-371-4017

John Strub
NY State Dept of Public Service
Agency Building 3
Albany, NY 12223, USA
E-mail: jms@dps.state.ny.us
Fax: 518-474-5026
Phone: 518-473-2937

Thomas Sullivan
National Grid USA
25 Research Drive
Westboro, MA 01532, USA
E-mail: thomas.sullivan@us.ngrid.com
Fax: 508-389-2725
Phone: 508-389-9086

Marie Swanson
Seattle City Light
700 5th Ave Suite 3300
Seattle, WA 98104, USA
E-mail: marie.swanson@ci.seattle.wa.us
Fax: 206-386-1630
Phone: 206-233-3929

Reginald Sweeney
Dept of Fisheries & Oceans
PO Box 1006
Dartmouth, NS B2Y 4A2, Canada
E-mail: sweeneyr@mar.dfo.mpo.gc.ca
Fax: 902-426-1489
Phone: 902-426-2253

Bonnie Swift
Stantec Consulting Ltd.
1122 4th Street SW
Calgary, AB T2R 1M1, Canada
E-mail: pswift@stantec.com
Fax: 403-716-8037
Phone: 403-716-7128

Carl Tammi
ENSR Corp
35 Nagog Park
Acton, MA 01720, USA
E-mail: ctammi@ensr.com
Fax: 978-635-9180
Phone: 978-635-9500

Songkiert Tansamrit
Petroleum Authority of Thailand
555 Vibhavadee Rangsit Rd
Banglehaen
Bangkok 10900, Thailand
E-mail: 240299@ptt.or.th
Fax: 5372182
Phone: 5372150-1

Ken Taylor
TransCanada International
801-7th Avenue SW
PO box 2535, Station M
Calgary, AB T2P 3P7, Canada
E-mail: ken-taylor@transcanada.com
Fax: 403-261-5262
Phone: 403-261-5385

Prem Bahadur Thapa Magar
Sulabh International Nepal
Bishalnegar, Kathmandu-5
Post Box 5083
Kathmandu, Nepal
E-mail: atharai@wlink.com
Fax: 977 1-432243
Phone: 977 1-432243

Marie-France Therrien
Canadian Environmental Assessment Agency
200 Boulevard Sacre-Coeur
Hull, PQ K1A 0H3, Canada
E-mail: Marie.France.Therrian@ceaa.gc.ca
Fax: 819-997-4931
Phone: 819-953-2537

David Thomas
ENSR Consulting
6060 McDonough Dr Ste O
Norcross, GA 30093, USA
E-mail: dthomas@ensr.com
Fax: 770-209-9880
Phone: 770-209-7167

Don Thompson
Petro Canada Oil & Gas
PO Box 2844
Calgary, AB T2P 3E3, Canada
E-mail: dthompso@petro-canada.ca
Fax: 403-296-3740
Phone: 403-296-6799

Elizabeth Thomson
Fisheries & Oceans Canada
501 University Cresent
Winnipeg, MB R3T 2N6, Canada
E-mail: ThomsonB@dfo-mpo.gc.ca
Fax: 204-983-2402
Phone: 204-983-2380

Bo Thorngren
Vattentall AB
Bygdevagen 18
Lentuna 1919750, Sweden
E-mail: bo.thorngren@network.vattenfall.se
Fax: 46-623-2701
Phone: 46-623-2700

Susan Tikalsky
Resource Strategies, Inc.
22 North Carroll Street, Suite 300
Maidson, WI 53703, USA
E-mail: tikalsky@rs-inc.com
Fax: 608-251-5941
Phone: 608-251-5904

Robert Tillman
G.Tillman & Associates
1971 Beach
Rock Stream, NY 14878, USA
E-mail: gus@onlineimage.com

Michael Timpson
Peterson Environmental Consulting Inc.
1355 Mendota Heights Road, Suite 100
Mendota Heights, MN, USA
E-mail: mtimpson@petersonenv.com
Fax: 651-686-0369
Phone: 651-686-0151

Peter Tischbein
E/Pro Engineering & Enviro Consulting
41 Anthony Avenue
Augusta, MA 04330, USA
E-mail: ptischbein@eproconsulting.com
Fax: 207-621-7001
Phone: 207-621-7094

Russel Travis
Westcoast Energy Inc.
Bag Service 6180
Fort St. John, BC V1J 4H7, Canada
E-mail: rtravis@wei.org
Fax: 250-262-3638
Phone: 250-262-3471

Roger Trettel
Northern Ecological Associates
451 Presumpscot St.
Portland, ME 4103, USA
E-mail: rtrettel@neamaine.com
Fax: 207-879-9481
Phone: 207-879-9496

Kathryn Trudell
Electric Power Research Institute
321 Seth Circle
Madison, WI 53716, USA
E-mail: ktrudell@epri.com
Phone: 608-221-4975

Suphon Tubtimcharoon
Petroleum Authority of Thailand
555 Vibhavadee Rangsit Rd
Banglehaen
Bangkok 10900, Thailand
E-mail: 230073@ptt.or.th
Phone: 5373013

Darin Tucker
Trans Canada Pipelines
801-7th Avenue SW (28th Floor)
Calgary, AB T2P 2P7, Canada

Michael Tyrrell
Earth Tech
300 Baker Avenue
Concord, MA 01742, USA
E-mail: mtyrrell@earthtech.com
Fax: 978-371-7889
Phone: 978-371-4240

Sarintip Vaewhongs
Petroleum Authority of Thailand
555 Vibhavadee Rangsit Rd
Banglehaen
Bangkok 10900, Thailand
E-mail: 250401
Fax: 5373060
Phone: 5373074

Laura Van Ham
National Energy Board
444 7th Avenue, SW
Calgary, AB T2P 0X8, Canada
Fax: 403-292-5876
Phone: 403-299-2769

Teri Vierima
Resource Strategies Inc.
22 N Carroll St. Suite, 300
Madison, WI 53703, USA
E-mail: tvierima@rs-inc.com
Fax: 608-251-5941
Phone: 608-251-8767

Ronald Volverde
Institut Costarricense de Electricidad
Dpto de Geologia, ICE
Apdo 10032-1000
San Jose, Costa Rica
E-mail: rovalv@icelec.ice.go
Fax: 506-220-8212

George Walsh
Ecology and Environment, Inc
368 Pleasant View Drive
Lancaster, NY 14086, USA
E-mail: gwelsh@ene.com
Fax: 716-684-0844
Phone: 716-684-8060

John Ward
John Ward & Associates Ltd.
PO Box 75070 Cambrian
Calgary, AB T2K 6J8, Canada
E-mail: jward@cadvision.com
Fax: 403-282-6764
Phone: 403-282-6764

Walter Watt
Trans-Northern Pipelines Inc.
45 Vogell Road, Suite 310
Richmond Hill, ON L4B 3P6, Canada
Phone: 905-770-3353

Carol Weed
Gray & Pape, Inc
1318 Main Street
Cincinnati, OH 35210, USA
E-mail: cweed@graypape.com
Fax: 513-287-7703
Phone: 513-287-7700

Tom Wells
BC Hydro
Vegetation Maintenance
8475-128th St (LMS Admin)
Surrey, BC V3W 0G1, Canada
E-mail: thomas.wells@bchydro.com
Fax: 604-543-1540
Phone: 604-543-4151

Chief Roy Whitney
c/o Diane Meguinis Tsuu T'ina Nation
9911 Chaiila Boulevard
Tsuu T'ina (Sarcee), AB T2W 6H6, Canada

Monique Wilkinson
Utilicorp Networks Canada
1202 Centre Street South
Calgary, AB, Canada
E-mail: monique_wilkinson@transalta.com
Fax: 403-267-3997

Randy Williams
5 Single Pine Lane
Madisonville, LA 70447, USA
E-mail: randyandliz@charter.net
Fax: 985-845-9053
Phone: 985-845-8128

Karl Willrich
University of Saskatchewan
611 University Drive, 402
Saskatoon, SK S7N 3Z1, Canada
E-mail: kjw846@mail.usask.ca
Fax: 306-525-3422
Phone: 306-777-9401

Marianne Windell
Vattentall AB
Bygdevagen 18
Sollentuna 1919750, Sweden
E-mail: marianne.windell@network.vattenfall
Fax: 46-623-2701
Phone: 46-623-2700

John Wingfield
New York Power Authority
Valenti Road
PO Box 200
Gilboa, NY 12076, USA
E-mail: wingfield.j@nypa.gov
Fax: 607-588-9826
Phone: 607-588-6061

Don Wishart
TransCanada International
801-7th Avenue SW
PO Box 2535, Station M
Calgary, AB T2P 3P7, Canada

Thomas Wojtalik
Tennessee Valley Authority
1101 Market Street
Chattanooga, TN 37402-2801, USA
E-mail: tawojtalik@tva.gov
Fax: 423-751-4760
Phone: 423-74-3130

Mark Wolfe
Tennessee Valley Authority
129 Pine Road
Norris, TN 37828, USA
E-mail: mhwolfe@tva.gov
Fax: 865-632-1493
Phone: 865-632-1467

Terry Wolverton
Tuscarora Gas Transmission Co.
PO Box 30057
Reno, NV 89520, USA
E-mail: twolverton@tuscararagas.com
Fax: 775-834-3886
Phone: 775-834-4667

Michael Wood
EBA Engineering Consultants
270, 200 Rivercrest Drive SE
Calgary, AB T2C 2X5, Canada
E-mail: mwood@eba.ca
Fax: 403-203-3301
Phone: 403-203-3355

Terrence Yakich
American Transmission Company
N19 W23993 Ridgeview Parkway W.,
PO Box 47
Waukesha, WI 53187-0047, USA
E-mail: tyakich@atcllc.com
Fax: 262-506-6704
Phone: 262-506-6865

Josh Young
East Kentucky Power
PO Box 47
Winchester, KY 40391, USA
E-mail: joshyoun@ekpc.com

Kevin Young
The Louis Berger Group Inc.
75 Second Ave, Suite 700
Needham, MA 02494, USA
E-mail: kyoung@louisberger.com
Fax: 781-444-0099
Phone: 781-444-3330

Robert Young
Nova Scotia Power
PO Box 910
25 Lakeside Park Drive
Halifax, NS B3J 2W5, Canada
E-mail: robert.young@nspower.ca
Fax: 902-456-1820
Phone: 902-428-7560

Darrel Zell
Parks Canada
Box 900
Banff, AB T0L 0C0, Canada
E-mail: darrel-zell@pch.gc.ca
Fax: 403-762-3240
Phone: 403-762-1421

Brian Zelt
E2 Environmental Alliance Inc
Suite B24, 6020 2nd Street SE
Calgary, AB T2H 2L8, Canada
E-mail: bzelt@e2canada.com
Fax: 403-212-4013
Phone: 403-212-4065

John Zimmer
Coler & Colantonio, Inc
101 Accord Park Drive
Norwell, MA 02061, USA
E-mail: jzimmer@col-col.com
Fax: 701-982-5490
Phone: 781-982-5473

Roberta Zwier
ENSR
2005 Cabot Blvc West
Langhorne, PA 19047, USA
E-mail: rzwier@ensr.com
Fax: 215-757-3904
Phone: 215-757-4900

Author index

Abrahamson, L.P., 47
Albrecht, S., 509
Alkiewicz, E., 527
Allen, Jr., H.A., 73
Amodeo, J., 807
Anderson, P., 171, 279, 891
Anderson, P.G., 735
Anderson, T.R., 389
Antoniuk, T., 209, 279, 861
Arévalo-Camacho, J., 111, 797
Arner, D.H., 57
Arranz Cuesta, R., 797

Ballard, B.D., 47, 83
Barnes, J.T., 907
Barnett, B.D., 495
Battaglia, B.M., 127, 591
Battey, J., 255
Bédard, Y., 147
Bélanger, L., 147
Bélisle, F., 309
Bender, M., 697
Bermejo Bermejo, E., 111
Berry, F., 825
Bissonnette, M., 517
Bloemker, J.D., 293
Bossenberry, T., 201
Bouchard, A., 103
Bourassa, J.-P., 147
Bridges, J.M., 389
Brindley, A., 537
Brisson, J., 103
Brown, C.M., 705
Burke, J.D., 927
Buszynski, M., 875

Cain, N.P., 179
Caldwell, L., 825
Cameron, D., 599, 609
Champagne, N., 147
Choate, K.D., 89
Clark, D., 201
Clevenger,, A.P., 267
Compton, S.A., 583, 743
Confer, J.L., 373
Crabtree III, A.F., 11
Craycroft, S., 883
Cressman, A., 843
Crowder, M.R., 403
Curthoys, L., 819

Dalgarno, K.D., 63

de Blois, S., 103
de la Bastide, P.Y., 665
De La Zerda, S., 363, 395
Dolezal, E., 861, 891
Domon, G., 155
Donaldson, J.M., 233
Dost, F., 649, 673
Doucet, G.J., 309, 383
Dunn, G., 171

Ealey, M., 165
Eccles, R., 245
Engstrom, C.J., 919
Etherington, K., 201
Eusebi, D.S., 263
Evans, J., 509, 599, 609, 717

Fedkenheuer, A.W., 927
Fellion, P.G., 583
Finch, K.E., 47
Finley, C.G., 219
Fleming, W., 431
Frazier, D., 527
Fryer, G., 171

Galicia Herbada, D., 111
Garant, Y., 309
Gérin-Lajoie, J., 147
Glaholt, R.G., 765
Glover, E.J., 97
Gómez Manzaneque, F., 111
González Cantalapiedra, L., 111, 797
Goodman, J., 689
Goodrich-Mahoney, J.W., 287, 791
Goulet, G.M., 919
Grindal, S.D., 439
Guild, C., 3

Haggie, M.R., 73
Hair, J., 609
Harper, H.W., 753
Heffler, H.R., 833, 853
Hegmann, G., 245
Hiebert, C., 825
Hinkle, R., 509
Hintz, W.E., 665
Hornbeck, G.E., 439
Huffman, T., 717

Jaarsma, C.F., 553
Jalbert, A., 201, 697
Jenkins, D.F., 195

Jenkins, J., 673
Johnstone, R.A., 73
Jones, J.C., 57, 621

Kennedy, A.J., 411
Khitrik, L., 527
Kingston, L.A., 179
Kohler, M.F., 233
Kokemuller, L., 869
Kott, F.J., 901, 911
Kowalczyk, D.L., 843

Lacroix, G., 147
Lake, D.J., 853, 861
Lanham, J.D., 327, 337
Lare, S.J., 127
Lauzon, R.D., 439
Leskiw, L.A., 927
Lévesque, E., 147
Lounsbury, S., 345
Lowell, F., 345
Lychwala, M., 421

Mackintosh, E.E., 629
MacNeill, T., 547
Magdych, B., 573
Marshall, J.S., 355
Martin, P.D., 725
Martínez García, F., 111
Mattson, T.A., 911
Mays, P.A., 89
McGuire, T.M., 447
McKague, K., 179
McLachlan, G., 421, 883
McLoughlin, K., 29, 319
McMullen, J.M., 471
Metikosh, S., 697, 717
Mills, M., 807
Montpetit, C., 155
Morla Juaristi, C., 111
Morrall, J.F., 447
Mozuraitis, E.J., 629
Muehlhausen, J.W., 901
Mutrie, D., 3
Myhre, J., 891

Nathanson, E., 509
Neuhauser, E.F., 47, 355
Nicholas, N.S., 89
Nichols, M.J., 337
Nixon, J., 201
Norris, L.A., 649, 673
Nowak, C.A., 47, 83

Nunas, M., 765
Nyrose, C., 547

Oberg, P., 455
O'Neill, E., 83
Ong, S., 765
Ostendorp, M., 563
Owen, K.C., 907

Paquette, S., 155
Paradise, S., 517
Patty, S.S., 537, 843
Penick, N., 185
Perot, Jr., A.M., 537
Pettapiece, W.W., 927
Pfaender, F., 689
Pockar, M., 279, 891
Poirier, B., 825
Polster, D.F., 121
Post, J.R., 705
Poullaouec-Gonidec, P., 155
Prier, P.G., 263

Read, R., 63
Reid, S., 697, 717, 735
Revel, R.D., 135, 219, 705
Rhodes, Jr., O.E., 403
Richards, F.P., 807

Rinebold, J.M., 233
Robertson, T., 777
Rohner, C., 455
Roig-Solés, J., 111, 797
Roper, C., 689
Rose, A.K., 89
Rosselli, L., 363, 395
Rowland, R.C., 629

Santillo, D.J., 583, 743
Satheesan, S.M., 483
Scarborough, G.C., 777
Schaefer, V., 303
Schmidt, J., 599, 609
Schmiegelow, F.K.A., 431, 455
Shamoun, S.F., 665
Sheridan, P.M., 185
Shrimpton, G., 665
Shupe, S.D., 355, 471, 637
Simmons III, J.E., 327
Singh, A.P., 483
Smith, F.S., 807
Southerland, M.T., 537
Steel, E., 599, 609
Stoklosar, S., 717
Strebel, D.E., 537
Strom, K., 245
Struger, S., 179

Tammi, C., 599, 609
Thomas, D.P., 465
Thompson, E.R., 383
Tikalsky, S.M., 287
Trettel, J.R., 127, 591, 743, 753
Trottier, D., 147
Tyrrell, M., 421, 725, 883

VanBossuyt, Jr., R., 649, 673
VanDruff, L.W., 355
Van Ham, L.A., 135
Vierima, T.L., 791
Virgl, J., 165

Waltho, N., 267
Wells, T.C., 63
Wesenger, D.P., 263
Wierzchowski, J., 267
Willems, G.P.A., 553
Wingfield, J., 527
Wojtalik, T.A., 89
Wolfe, M.H., 89

Young, R.F., 97

Zhu, H., 665

Keyword index

accidental deaths, 483
aerial patrol, 563
aesthetic, 155
agronomic species, 165
alliance, 819
alpine, 135
anurans, 309
approval, 901
aquatic effects, 717
assessment, 563
audit, 875
autecology, 83
avian diversity, 373

balancing resources, 63
Banff National Park, 267
basal herbicide, 47
basidiomycete, 665
benthic ecolosystem, 765
bentonite, 599, 609
best management plan, 517
best management practices (BMPs), 753
bibliography, 287
biocontrol agent, 665
biodiversity, 185, 303, 309, 319, 537, 765
biological assessments, 911
biological control, 103
bird flight diverters, 395
birds, 309, 355, 389, 403
bogs, 185
boreal mixedwood forest, 431
British Columbia, 825
brook trout, 705
brown trout, 705
brush control, 179
buffer zones, 309
burning, 57
business communications, 797
butterflies, 337
butterfly, 345

cables, 807
Canada, 833
canal, 483
carbohydrate, 689
channel, 483
clear-cut (CC), 73
Clemson Island prehistoric culture, 293
co-location, 195

co-location of telecommunications facilities, 233
collision rates, 395
collisions, 389, 403
commitment tracking, 279
common corridors, 11
communications, 263, 791
compatible vegetation, 97
competition, 89
compliance, 853, 883, 891
compositional analysis, 455
condition, 563
confrontation among animals, 483
connectivity, 303
conservation, 363, 537
conservation biology, 411
constructability, 201, 883
construction, 717, 725, 819
corridor, 465
cost, 255, 609
cover, 591
cover crop, 103
creative mitigation, 293
crop yield, 629
cumulative effects, 209, 245
cumulative effects assessment, 245
cumulative environmental effects, 219, 843

dam and pump, 735
database, 287, 697, 861, 891
decay, 689
deer browse, 383
defect, 563
Delaware, 73
designing, 483
differences, 263
digital images, 563
digital orthophotographic base maps, 527
digital video, 563
directional drill, 919
disking, 57
disruption or destruction of fish habitat (HADD), 705
disturbance, 135
diversity, 591
documentation, 263
drill fluid, 599
drill method, 609
due diligence, 279, 891
dungeness crab, 765

ecological integrity, 165
ecological restoration, 621
ecology, 553
edge effect, 363
edge effects, 431
electric transmission, 233
electric transmission lines, 83
electrocutions, 389
emergency, 825
emissions, 553
endangered species, 319, 345, 411, 517, 537
Endangered Species Act, 911
engineering limitations, 609
environment, 279, 287, 447
environmental, 861, 869
environmental assessment, 201, 833
environmental compliance, 255
environmental inspection, 891
environmental management, 825
environmental management programs, 255
environmental management systems, 263, 875
environmental monitoring, 825
environmental stewardship, 537
erosion, 869
estuarine, 725
evaluation tool, 927

Federal Energy Regulatory Commission, 833
FERC, 869
fish, 743
fish cover, 705
fish habitat, 705, 735
fish habitat augmentation, 777
fisheries, 725
Fisheries Act, 705
flumed crossings, 717
flurprimidol, 673
forest fragmentation, 363
forest management, 111
forest songbirds, 431
forest wetlands, 89
forests, 483
fosamine ammonium, 649
fragmentation, 303
framework, 219
functions, 573

Geographic Information Systems (GIS), 179, 537, 547, 563

glyphosate, 649
gopher tortoise, 465
GPS, 179, 563
greenway, 303
greenways, 537
ground wire marking, 395
ground wires, 403
groundline, 689

habitat compensation, 777
habitat fragmentation, 509, 843
habitat management, 373
habitat preference, 373
habitat(s), 509
habitat-suitability index models, 327
Harmful Alteration, 705
hart's-tongue fern, 911
HDD, 725
herbicide, 47, 57
herbicide application, 373
herbicides, 29, 89
high tension lines, 395
highway rights-of-way, 517
highways, 447, 483
hine's emerald dragonfly, 911
historical, 629
horizontal directional drill, 735
human health risk, 673

ice storm, 383
imazapyr, 649
impact assessment, 209
impact mitigation, 825
impacts, 389, 599
inadvertent returns, 599, 609
infography, 797
inhibition potential, 103
innovative technology, 843
inspection, 255, 563, 861, 883
inspector, 853
inspectors, 869
integrated pest management, IPM, 29
integrated vegetation management (IVM), 29, 73, 83, 179, 665
inventories, 63
inventory, 563
joint use, 195

Kananaskis Country, 919

land conservation, 843
land use, 537
landscape, 147
landscape indices, 209
landscape monitoring, 155
large woody debris, 777
Latin America, 495
legal, 233
legume, 57
life history, 83
linear, 219
linear construction, 279
linear development, 431

linear developments, 483
linear facilities, 263
linear landscape features, 455
linear projects, 509
lupine, 345

maintenance, 179, 791
man–elephant conflicts, 483
management, 147
management system, 201
marine pipelines, 765
maritimes, 819, 883
metsulfuron methyl, 649
Minnesota, 517
minor rural roads, 553
mitigation, 127, 171, 267, 345, 389, 421, 853
mitigations, 447
mitigative measures, 219
mixing zone, 753
modeling, 553
monitor, 853
monitoring, 383, 421, 907
monitoring plan, 127
mycoherbicide, 665

National Energy Board, 833
national park, 447
natural gas pipeline, 465, 583
natural resources, 869
natural revegetation, 135
neotropics, 363, 395
nesting, 389
New York Power Authority, 527
noise, 553
notification, 901
Nova Scotia Power Inc., 97

O&M, 901
observations, 403
open cut, 725
open-cut crossings, 717
orangeville reinforcement pipeline, 875
outages, 389
overseeding, 57

paclobutrazol, 673
park, 807
partridge pea, 57
perch, 389
performance evaluation, 267
performance standards, 573
permits, 907
permitting, 421, 573, 833
pesticides, 29
petroleum industry, 135
picloram, 649
pipeline, 599, 725, 819, 919
pipeline construction, 471, 697
pipeline construction, impacts, 439
pipeline crossing, 705
pipeline impacts, 629

pipeline protection, 637
pipeline routing, 495
pipeline(s), 509
pipelines, 245, 833
pitcher plants, 185
planning, 267, 697, 843
plant succession, 121
planting, 89
power lines, 111, 403
power plants, 537
powerline corridor, 47
prescriptive maintenance, 63
procedures, 907
protected areas, 483
protected species, 465
public, 791
public acceptance, 797
public consultation, 919
public participation, 807
pyrite, 621

Québec, 155
quadrat, 591

railroads, 483
rangifer tarandus caribou, 455
rare plant populations, 127
rare plants, 171, 411
reclamation, 135, 621
reclamation criteria, 927
reclamation evaluation, 927
reclamation standards, 927
reclamation success, 927
reconstruction, 383
regulation, 233
regulations, 853
regulatory, 255, 861, 907
regulatory compliance, 825
relative dominance index (RDI), 73
releve', 591
replanting, 127
representative areas, 209
reseed, 345
resource development, 455
restoration, 103
revegetation, 165, 573, 583
Richardson's ground squirrel, 439
rights-of-way (ROW), 29, 57, 63, 89, 111, 135, 147, 179, 287, 319, 327, 337, 355, 383, 471, 509, 527, 537, 621, 705
right-of-way maintenance, 637
right-of-way management, 83, 431
riparian, 89
riparian habitat, 777
riparian zone, 665
risk, 875
roadside vegetation, 155
ruderal habitat, 465

scope, 901
sea cucumber, 765
Section 106 compliance, 293
sediment, 717, 735

sediment control, 637
sediment grain size distribution, 753
sediment transport modeling, 753
sedimentation, 725
seeding, 103
select-cut (SC), 73
selective herbicide, 355
selective maintenance, 179
selective treatment, 73
sensitive species, 363
shared rights-of-way, 11
shrub dynamics, 47
shrubland guild, 373
shrubs, 89, 355
significant plant communities, 171
siting, 233, 791, 807
skippers, 337
small mammals, 309
software, 861
soil acidity, 621
soil assessment, 927
soil bioengineering, 121
soil erosion, 121
soil segregation, 583
soils handling, 201
sour gas, 919
Southeastern US, 337
species diversity, 165
species richness, 165
speckled alder, 97
spermophilus richardsoni, 439
stable community, 97
stakeholder, 201
stakeholders, 263
steep slopes, 121
stem-foliar herbicide, 47
stewardship, 287

strategy, 791
stream, 743
stream crossings, 777
stream disturbance, 753
stream dynamics, 637
stream restoration, 637
streams rivers sediment, 697
study area, 209
succession, 165
suitable habitat, 127
superflume, 735
survey methodology, 171
survivorship, 89
suspended sediment, 743

telecommunications, 233
threatened species, 319
threshold, 201
thresholds, 209
toxicity, 649
transcolorado, 883
transmission, 63, 807
transmission corridors, 777
transmission lines, 537
transportation corridors, 11
triclopyr, 649
triggers, 245
tropical forest, 495
TSS, 753
turbidity, 743, 753
turnover, 901

undesirable and desirable vegetation, 47
United States, 833
unstable slopes, 121

upland, 73
urban, 303
user's perception, 155
utility corridors, 11

variance, 853
VDOT, 185
vector, 819
vegetation, 111, 147, 421
vegetation assessment, 171
vegetation inventories, 527
vegetation management, 29, 103, 165, 319, 517, 649
vehicular traffic, 483
view shed, 797
visual impact, 797
visual simulation, 797

water, 743
water quality, 753
watercourse crossing, 705
weed control, 179
wetland, 573
wetland impacts, 471
wetland monitoring, 591
wetland restoration, 471
wetlands, 583
wildlife, 327, 421
wildlife crossing structure, 267
wildlife telemetry, 455
wildlife use index (WUI), 73
wireless, 233
wood, 689
woody debris, 471
woody decay, 471
woody stems, 89